# The Irish Industrial Exhibition Of 1853: A Detailed Catalogue Of Its Contents ...

John Sproule

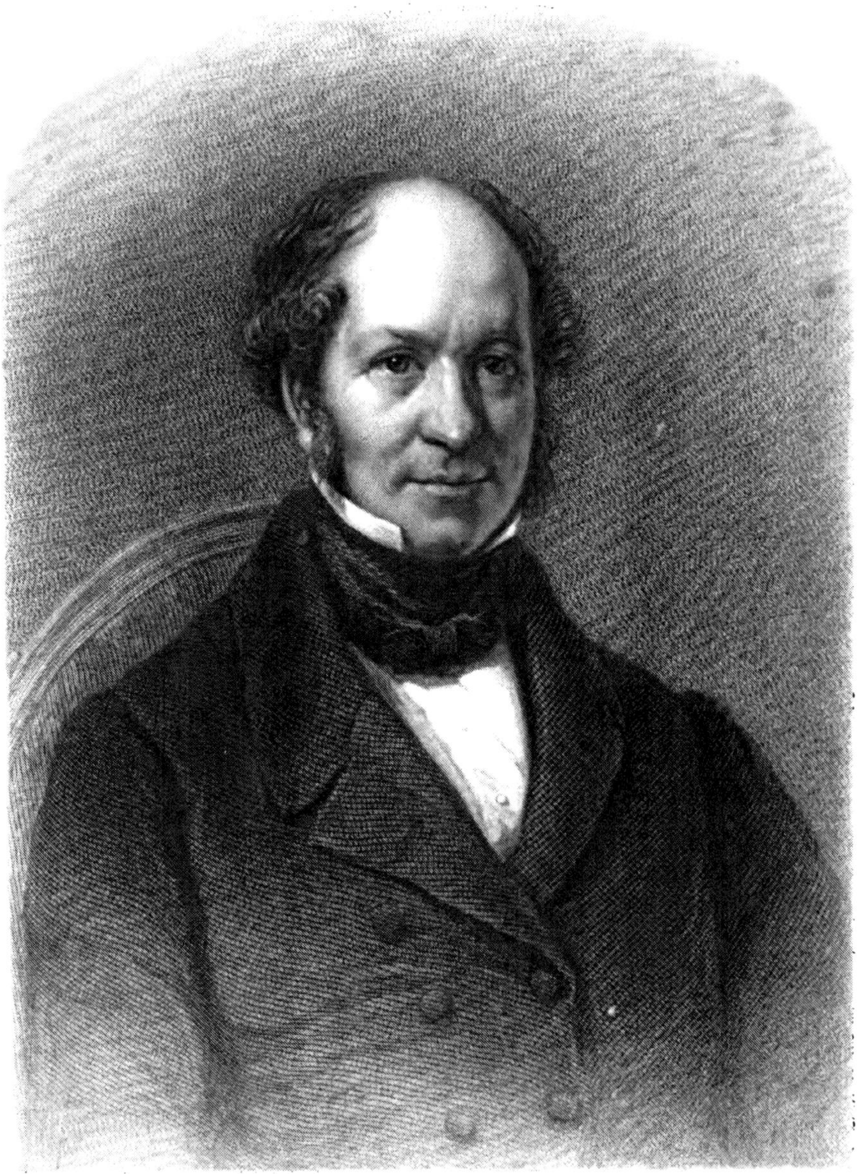

Wm Dargan

0

THE

# IRISH INDUSTRIAL EXHIBITION

OF

# 1853:

## A DETAILED CATALOGUE OF ITS CONTENTS,

WITH

Critical Dissertations, Statistical Information,

AND

ACCOUNTS OF MANUFACTURING PROCESSES IN THE DIFFERENT DEPARTMENTS:

ALSO

A PORTRAIT OF MR. DARGAN, ENGRAVED ON STEEL, ACCOMPANIED BY A MEMOIR;

A LITHO-CHROMOTYPE VIEW OF THE CENTRE HALL OF THE EXHIBITION;

AND

NUMEROUS ILLUSTRATIONS ON WOOD.

EDITED BY

JOHN SPROULE,

ASSISTED BY EMINENT LITERARY AND SCIENTIFIC MEN.

DUBLIN:

JAMES McGLASHAN, 50 UPPER SACKVILLE-STREET.

LONDON: WILLIAM S. ORR AND CO.

1854.

DUBLIN:
Printed at the University Press,
BY M. H. GILL.

# IRISH INDUSTRIAL EXHIBITION, 1853.

## Executive Committee.

GEORGE ROE, ESQ., Chairman.
MAJOR FAIRFIELD, Deputy Chairman.

THE RIGHT HON. THE LORD MAYOR.
THE LORD TALBOT DE MALAHIDE.
THE HON. GEORGE HANDCOCK.
THE HON. JOHN P. VEREKER.
SIR JOHN KINGSTON JAMES, BART.
SIR ROBERT KANE.
SIR EDWARD M'DONNELL.
THOMAS BALL, ESQ.
WILLIAM BARKER, ESQ., M. D.
JOHN BARLOW, ESQ.
JOHN BARTON, ESQ.
JOHN D'ARCY, ESQ.
WILLIAM DARGAN, ESQ.
LUNDY E. FOOT, ESQ.
ROBERT HARRISON, ESQ., M. D.
NATHANIEL HONE, ESQ.
WILLIAM DIGGES LA TOUCHE, ESQ.
JOHN LENTAIGNE, ESQ.
J. W. MURLAND, ESQ.
JOHN PENNEFATHER, ESQ.
WILLIAM HENRY PORTER, ESQ.
JAMES STIRLING, ESQ.
WALTER SWEETMAN, ESQ.

SIR CUSAC P. RONEY, Secretary.
JOHN C. DEANE, ESQ., Assistant Secretary.

The following arrangement of Sub-Committees for the different Departments was made immediately after the formation of the Executive Committee:

## Finance Committee.

HON. GEORGE HANDCOCK, Chairman.

SIR EDWARD M'DONNELL.
MAJOR FAIRFIELD.
L. E. FOOT, ESQ.
GEORGE ROE, ESQ.
WALTER SWEETMAN, ESQ.

## Building Committee.

SIR EDWARD M'DONNELL, Chairman.

SIR ROBERT KANE.
WILLIAM BARKER, ESQ., M. D.
WILLIAM DARGAN, ESQ.
W. D. LA TOUCHE, ESQ.
J. W. MURLAND, ESQ.
JAMES STIRLING, ESQ.

## Fine Arts Committee.

LORD TALBOT DE MALAHIDE, Chairman.

SIR JOHN KINGSTON JAMES, BART.
JOHN BARTON, ESQ.
ROBERT HARRISON, ESQ., M. D.
JOHN LENTAIGNE, ESQ.

## Manufactures Committee.

WALTER SWEETMAN, ESQ., Chairman.

HON. J. P. VEREKER.
L. E. FOOT, ESQ.
W. H. PORTER, ESQ.
JAMES STIRLING, ESQ.

## Agricultural Committee.

LORD TALBOT DE MALAHIDE.
THOMAS BALL, ESQ.
JOHN BARLOW, ESQ.
JOHN D'ARCY, ESQ.
NATHANIEL HONE, ESQ.

## Officers.

| | |
|---|---|
| General Superintendent, | MR. R. A. THOMPSON. |
| Chief Financial Officer, | MR. T. D. JONES. |
| Inspector of Accounts, | MR. H. BROWN. |
| Secretary to the Committee, | MR. ROBERT HERON. |
| Assistant General Superintendents, | MR.* J. O'HAGAN.<br>MR. FREDERICK G. HEATLY. |
| Superintendents of Districts, | District 1.—MR. C. C. ADLEY, C. E.<br>District 2.—MR. W. CARR.<br>District 3.—MR. C. H. BINGHAM.<br>District 4.—MR. A. CORRIGAN. |
| Deputy-Superintendents of Districts, | District 1.—MR. J. KENNEDY.<br>District 2.—MR. J. P. BYRNE.<br>District 3.—MR. W. H. PHIBBS.<br>District 4.—MR. S. J. POMMORET. |
| Superintendent of the Foreign Department, | MR. F. M. HARMAN. |
| Deputy-Superintendent of Foreign Department, | MR. A. A. JACOB. |
| Superintendent of the Catalogue Department, | MR. WILLIAM M'DERMOTT. |

## Office Department.

| | |
|---|---|
| Sale of Season Tickets, | MR. NICKSON. |
| Correspondence, | MR. KILLINGLEY.<br>MR. CURRY. |
| Registry of Letters, etc., | MR. A. FERGUSON.<br>MR. A. FERGUSON, JUN. |
| Charge of Postage and Delivery of Letters, | MR. BYRNE.<br>MR. REA. |
| House Steward, | MR. BRESLIN. |
| Custom House Agents, | W. B. & C. PALGRAVE and CO. |

*** The Arrangement of the Sculpture was intrusted to John E. Jones, Esq.; and the Hanging of the Pictures to John Gernon, Esq.

# PREFACE.

THERE are few persons, who had the opportunity of visiting the Irish Industrial Exhibition of 1853, who will not regard as a desideratum the publication of some fitting record of it; which, while presenting a detailed Catalogue of its contents, would contain an adequate account of the Building, which formed so important a feature of the Exhibition, and would also take advantage of the opportunity thereby afforded to enforce some of those lessons which that great demonstration was so well calculated to teach. Even as a souvenir of the Exhibition such a work could not fail to prove acceptable. The occasion, moreover, afforded the means of combining instruction with amusement,—of blending information on a variety of subjects with a record which would be regarded with interest by the most distant posterity. It was with a view of supplying such a desideratum that the present volume has been published.

The great number of publications to which the Exhibition of 1851 gave birth shows the feeling entertained on this subject; and it is not going too far to state, that the influence of these works, in promoting the object for which it was founded, was little, if at all, inferior to that of the Exhibition itself. It was not expected that the cosmopolitan display in Hyde Park would do much in the way of bringing new discoveries to light; it was intended rather as a means of improving the public taste generally, and as a stimulant to increased exertion on the part of the contributors to it. A desire was created for further information than the mere inspection of the specimens of the products of the different departments of industry furnished; and a new literature, as it were, may be said to have in consequence sprung up, to which many of the most eminent men of the day contributed. But, as in the history of Expositions of Industry, we find that each succeeding demonstration added to the difficulty of insuring the success of that which was to follow, and for which increased attractions must of course be provided, so in a corresponding degree would the responsibility of subsequent chroniclers be increased by the success of those who preceded them. In looking over the array of names of the contributors to what may be called the literature of the Exhibition of 1851, the most adventurous might well be deterred from becoming the chronicler of any subsequent Exposition. Still, the Irish Industrial Exhibition had so many features peculiar to itself, that it would be matter of regret if no attempt were made to place before the public some lasting record of it. In the manner in which it was got up, through the munificence of a single individual; in the peculiar position of the country at the time, just recovering from the effects of a degree of prostration almost unparalleled in history; in the circumstance of its being one of a series of Exhibitions which had been held triennially on the same premises for a length of time past; and in the fact of its being the last display of the kind in these countries, at least during the present generation,—all these circumstances conspire to make the publication of some fitting record of it a necessary complement of the Exhibition of 1853; while the difficulties that stood in the way could not fail to insure an increased measure of indulgence, on the part of the public, for any shortcomings by which it might be characterized.

There is a further circumstance which also adds to the value of some permanent record of the Great Irish Industrial Exhibition—arising out of the fact of its being the last demonstration of the kind in these countries, at least during the present generation. The Industrial Exhibitions may be said to have commenced and ended, so far as Great Britain and Ireland are concerned, with the series held on the premises of the Royal Dublin Society, in this city. The magnitude of the Exhibitions of 1851 and 1853 would have caused a long interval to elapse before any future attempt could be successfully made; but such attempts the almost faery creation of the Crystal Palace Company at Sydenham have rendered unnecessary. The progress of manufacturing industry will be there at all times indicated. There the highest point of excellence attained will be seen. There every new invention will be displayed, the place being regarded as the great arena for bringing such matters under the notice of the people of all countries; and with hosts of other auxiliaries more or less remotely bearing upon such Exhibitions generally, but all combining to enhance the attractions of the collection at Sydenham, Industrial Expositions will come to be regarded as among the things of the past, for which, as it were, the necessity no longer exists. Hence a further reason why the Exhibition of 1853 should not be permitted to pass away without some enduring memento of it.

Influenced by these considerations, and finding that no other attempt was likely to be made to supply so obvious a desideratum, I determined to turn some materials, which had been collected under my auspices, for a somewhat kindred purpose, to account. With a view of contributing their quota to the Exhibition, Messrs. Gunn and Cameron, the proprietors of the "General Advertiser," published in the Building a weekly sheet, entitled the "Exhibition Expositor," devoted to the illustration of its contents, the management of which was placed in my hands; and although the form of many of the papers written for that publication was not adapted for their appearance in a permanent shape, still the mass of information which they contained was available as an important contribution to any permanent work on the Exhibition that might be got up; and accordingly, the materials which had been collected for the "Expositor" have formed the groundwork of the present volume. My connexion with the Exhibition, through the "Expositor," while it impressed me strongly with the necessity of some permanent record of it being published, also familiarized me with the requirements of such a work, and encouraged me to undertake the responsibility of bringing it out,—a responsibility for encountering which I might otherwise be very fairly obnoxious to the charge of presumption.

In the preparation of the materials for this work the leading consideration has been, to take advantage of the opportunity to place before the public useful information on industrial subjects,—to, in fact, carry out, as far as possible, the intention of the Founder of the Exhibition, by making it ancillary to progress. The arrangement was founded upon that adopted by the Royal Commissioners of the Exhibition of 1851, to carry out which an entire reconstruction of the Official Catalogue became necessary. In the treatment of the several subjects the peculiar branches of industry which they involve have been discussed, without devoting much space to individual contributions; and especial prominence has been given to matters of local interest or importance. Thus, commencing with the department of Raw Materials, the reader will find in the present volume such an amount of information on our Industrial Resources as is not to be found in any other work extant; the papers in this department being chiefly written by Mr. W. K. Sullivan, the person of all others, perhaps, most competent for the task. It is, indeed, to the varied attainments of Mr. Sullivan, in connexion with matters of an industrial character, that this work owes its chief value; and to the readiness with which his valuable co-operation was afforded I am glad to have an opportunity of bearing testimony. In reference to our great staple branch of industry, the Linen Manufacture, I was also fortunate in obtaining the co-operation of Mr. Macadam, the very efficient Secretary of the Royal Society for the Promotion and Improvement of the Growth of Flax in Ireland,—the most competent authority on the subject. To several of the articles to be found throughout the work I might refer with some confidence, as containing information either presented in a peculiar and interesting point of view, or which has not hitherto been before the public in a popular form. Not pretending to have any considerable amount of special technical knowledge, I feel that my own contributions are, perhaps, those to which the least value is to be attached; and on looking over the whole, when now completed, I also feel that, in the general arrangement, several improvements might have been introduced. The materials, however, were only prepared as the printing of the work proceeded; and the time which I was able to spare from my ordinary duties, as the Editor of one of the local journals, scarcely admitted of that attention being paid to some of the minor details that would have been desirable.

In apportioning the space to be devoted to the several Classes, the extent to which useful information was available was more kept in view than that to which they were represented. Thus, while the Class of Mining and Mineral Products was but in some respects imperfectly represented, it is treated of at greater length than any other, as being, strictly speaking, the basis whence the products in all the other classes are derived. Towards the end of the volume, however, several subjects are treated much more briefly than was originally contemplated, from the circumstance of the work having considerably exceeded the intended limits. This is particularly the case with the section devoted to the Fine Arts, the department which formed the most prominent feature of the Exhibition; and it was with a feeling of very great regret I found myself unable to devote a larger space to the very accomplished writer having charge of that department, more especially as in his hands it would have been turned to good account. I should also observe, that the original intention was to illustrate copiously with wood engravings; but it was found that this could not be done without unduly extending the size of the work, and in some degree interfering with its utilitarian character. Wherever engravings have been introduced it has been with a view of illustrating the subject discussed, disregarding altogether any attempt at mere pictorial display.

A correct list of exhibiters, and of the articles which they respectively contributed, is obviously important as a matter of record; while it is also due to the enterprise and public spirit which induced so many parties to come forward at, in many cases, a great immediate pecuniary sacrifice. However elegant may be the Building, and however excellent the arrangements otherwise, it is obviously upon the manner in which the exhibiters discharge their duty that the success of any great Exposition must be dependent; and while in the exhibition of certain classes of goods an adequate return in the shape of increased business may be calculated on—and in fact has been realized —there are other departments in which no such hope could be entertained. It is, in short, only by becoming acquainted with the expenditure incurred by some of the exhibiters that the value of the services which they have rendered can be properly estimated; and it is simply due to these parties to place the position which they held upon record in any enduring memorial of the Exhibition. To insure accuracy, as far as possible, in this department, circulars have been forwarded to nearly the whole of the exhibiters, with a view of being enabled to correct any errors that might have escaped detection in the Official Catalogue, and the corrections obtained in this way, both in addresses and in the enumeration of articles exhibited, have been made available in the present volume,—a distinguishing feature of which is, its being a Detailed Catalogue of the Irish Industrial Exhibition.

The introduction of the Portrait of the Founder of the Exhibition will not be considered out of place as the frontispiece of this volume,—a work which has been specially engraved with a view to its appearance here. The high estimation in which Mr. Dargan is so deservedly held by all classes will make his portrait an acceptable addition to the Catalogue of the Exhibition; and in the brief Memoir which appears in a succeeding page, I have to regret that a more ample measure of justice could not be done to his character than such a mere outline affords, without offending that sensitiveness which he has invariably manifested in reference to anything in the shape of public display. Quietly and unobtrusively pursuing his career of usefulness, it would, however, be unjustifiable to further interfere with that privacy which he has at all times been desirous to maintain.

To the illustration of the Exhibition Building considerable attention has been devoted on account of its temporary character. Ere long the verdant sward on Leinster Lawn will not show a trace of the Irish Temple of Industry, which in its day formed so great an object of attraction as to bring visitors to it from almost all parts of the civilized world, and which reflected no less credit on the genius of its architect than on the liberality and patriotism of its founder; but this circumstance only rendered it the more necessary that such details, pictorial and otherwise, should be introduced as would convey an adequate idea of it. For this purpose, in addition to the series of illustrations on wood, the litho-chromotype engraving representing a view of the Centre Hall has been introduced—a work which, while it has added very materially to the expense of each copy of the book, has at the same time contributed much to its value. A further feature in connexion with this work is deserving of notice here—the fact of its being produced in this city,—Mr. Forster, of Crow-street, being the engraver.

I may also be excused for referring to the mechanical execution of this volume as a specimen of Irish industry. Not only has it been printed here, but this has been done from types cast at the Irish Letter Foundry of Marr, Thom, and Co., of this city; and it has been bound by Mr. Pilkington, of Abbey-street. Such a reference as this can scarcely be regarded as inappropriate in a book on the Irish Industrial Exhibition. The high character of the work executed by Mr. Gill at the University Press is well known; but I am glad to be able to refer to this Catalogue as a specimen of Irish workmanship generally, being the result of native enterprise in every department.

It only remains to be added, that although the extent to which abstract opinions are introduced is very limited, still it may be necessary to observe that individual contributors are responsible only for the sentiments expressed in their own communications. The writers include gentlemen holding diverse views on political and social questions, but amongst whom there was a thorough unity of opinion as to the necessity of some such work as the present being produced, and also as to the propriety of the general plan which has been adopted. With some two or three exceptions, the names or initials of the writers are appended to the several articles, and these are again repeated in the Table of Contents.

J. S.

Dublin, *July*, 1854.

# MEMOIR OF WILLIAM DARGAN.

THERE are few more interesting branches of study than the extent to which particular individuals stamp the impress of their own character on that of the community to which they belong. In every age, of which we have any record, and in every country with whose political and social history we are acquainted, we find men who, in virtue of some distinguishing characteristic, stand out in relief from their fellows, and become, as it were, beacons to be followed by others. The examples of this class, which will occur to the mind of every reader, must be numerous,—and that, too, in every walk of life in which men can obtain celebrity. Again and again we find instances in which surprising revolutions have been effected, even in one generation, through the agency of a single individual. And we do not here speak of the effects of mere inventions, some of the most important of which have been the result of accident, and, therefore, have no necessary relation to any peculiar characteristic of those with whom they originated. We refer rather to those peculiar traits, the persistent exhibition of which has so often shed a halo around particular individuals, obtaining for them distinguished places in the history of the human race, and causing their names to be remembered to the most distant posterity as benefactors of their species. Of such persons our appreciation will naturally be influenced by the extent to which the popular applause of the day has been courted or disregarded, by the degree in which the arts of the demagogue have been resorted to or despised, and by the general effect which has been produced. Thanks to the improved spirit of the age, we can now accord honours to a Howard or a Wilberforce which in other times would have been reserved for the heroes of war. We have now come to learn that there are triumphs of more lasting value than those won on the battle field,—those of benevolence over sordid selfishness, of enlightenment over ignorance, and of industry over idleness,—and the leaders in the achievement of which have claims on our regard not less strong than those of the most victorious generals. Crusades which result in such triumphs as these form important epochs in the history of our race; and in according a due measure of homage to their leaders we are simply discharging an imperative duty, as we thereby not only enforce important lessons, but also direct attention to examples for imitation. The pioneers of social progress are, in fine, the true heroes of a utilitarian age; and among those of this class, whose names will be treasured not less by a distant posterity than by their contemporaries, every Irishman, whatever be his class or creed, will assign a distinguished place to the subject of this Memoir.

But in proportion as the great social reformers claim our regard, we find their career destitute of those thrilling incidents which the historian and the painter can so well turn to account. Their triumphs have been the result of continuous action, in which, perhaps, an isolated brilliant incident is not to be found. Hence the contrast which they present to the politician and the warrior. In the one case we can merely look to results, comparing the end with the means available for its attainment; in the other, every step forms, as it were, a resting-place from which to take a retrospective survey, and, perhaps, expatiate upon character. Hence, also, the reason why such a Memoir as this must be necessarily brief,—referring chiefly to the circumstances of the country at the time Mr. Dargan appeared upon the public stage, and the peculiar manner in which he adapted his policy to these circumstances with, as it has turned out, such happy results. And here we must observe, that those acquainted only with the Ireland of to-day can scarcely form an idea of what it was even so late as some twenty years ago. Self-reliance and persistent application in carrying out an object were then but little known. The cry of the press and of the people was for aid from external sources to enable them to do what they only could accomplish of themselves; and the enterprise which did not hold out a hope of an immediate reward was too often abandoned without a fair trial. "Encouragement" was wanted for everything, on some further ground than its own merits. A trader not unfrequently recommended his goods on the ground of the alleged great number of hands which he employed, and not on the quality of the articles which he offered for sale; and one's "patriotism" was ever and anon appealed to in this manner by way of "encouraging" native industry. The consumer was, in fact, importuned to buy certain things because they were Irish, and not simply because they were good. A combination of spurious patriotism and benevolence was thus mixed up with trading operations, which presented for the time an effectual bar to progress; and, in addition to the want of perseverance which usually characterized efforts of industrial enterprise, business of any kind was considered to be unbecoming in any one claiming the position of a gentleman. Work designed merely to afford "employment" was not supposed to be beneath the attention of the highest in the land; but a pseudo-gentility forbade its being undertaken with a view to realize a profit upon it. At that period the line of demarcation was regarded as clear between individual and general interests, the two being supposed to be but very sparingly identical. It would be foreign to our present purpose to inquire into the origin of such a state of things, or the causes from which it arose; but, without entering upon this point, it is plain that, until a sweeping change was brought about, true progress was impossible.

Such was the condition of Ireland at the period when the subject of this Memoir first came before the public. A great ordeal has since been gone through. Important changes have been effected throughout our entire social system. Many of the delusions under which we then laboured have since disappeared, and there is a promise of a bright future before us. To assert that this was the work of a single individual would be simply absurd; but, at the same time, we do not hesitate to maintain that the position which Mr. Dargan occupied as a pioneer in the new movement was more important than may appear at first sight, no less to his own credit than to the advantage of his country.

The epoch to which we have referred was characterised by the commencement of the Railway System—by the introduction of those iron highways of civilization now considered so essential to the development of the resources of a country—whose prosperity has, in fact, come to be measured by the extent to which railways have been constructed. It was a period at once critical and important in our social history. The injurious effects of false steps then, it might require generations to remove. The construction of the various lines of railway with which the country was so soon to be intersected involved a series of works on a scale of magnitude so far beyond anything previously undertaken, as to be without any of those advantages derivable from experience. It required a surpassing degree of enterprize—the quality then so much at a discount;—and the apprehension of difficulties to be encountered might reasonably have been increased by the fact of having to go to work with untrained and wayward workmen, whose general rate of wages was miserably low, and who, as a matter of course, had not been subjected to that practical training which efficient and well paid-for service demands. The data on which calculations could be made were scanty; the drawbacks were sufficiently apparent to discourage the most adventurous; while imperfect execution in the early stage of these great works would have struck such a blow at the extension of the railway system here, as to be productive of incalculable mischief. The feeling which then prevailed in the sister country, with reference to the unsettled condition of Ireland, was such as to deter persons there from thinking of embarking in any work in Ireland involving the management of hundreds of the peasantry. We were, in fine, left to our own resources; and the Occasion brought forth the Man. The contractor for the first line of railway was William Dargan, then comparatively unknown beyond the private circle of friends whom he had inspired with a high estimate of those qualities which have since stood out in such bold relief. It is unnecessary to add that the confidence then reposed in the embryo great Contractor was not misplaced. The promises with which that work was commenced were fulfilled to the letter; and the same may be said of every one of those works which he has since executed. Wherever his operations extended a change was also soon manifest in the workmen. Prompt payments and liberal wages secured an ample supply of hands, and prevented any resistance to the salutary control and supervision required. The tempting rates of wages paid to the persons in his employment brought workmen from all parts of the country to offer their services; yet it is a gratifying circumstance that he has never had a formidable "strike" to contend with. Although frequently aware that for the time they could have seriously embarrassed their employer by preventing the execution of the contract at the stipulated period, yet of such a state of affairs advantage was never taken by those in his employment. A feeling of gratitude towards their common benefactor, and a consciousness that they would be dealt with *firmly* as well as *kindly*, at all times prevented the counsel of ringleaders of mischief from receiving much attention. While, therefore, the execution of large public works has usually a demoralizing tendency on the districts in which they are situated, this could never be said of Mr. Dargan's operations. He has really done more than has ever fallen to the lot of an individual to elevate the character of the labourers of his country. He has fulfilled to the letter every one of the numerous engagements into which he entered; the character of the Irish railways, as regards construction, stands second to that of none in the world; and while achieving these important results he has shown to us what may be effected by a single individual, by the exhibition of those qualities on which the greatness of every nation is founded. He has afforded an example of the identity of individual and general interests more powerful than all the lessons which political economists could teach—an example of great value at any time and under any circumstances, but which was especially so under the peculiar conditions to which we have above referred. Enlightened enterprise, persistent application, and high and honourable dealing have enabled Mr. Dargan to attain a position which the most exalted in the land might envy; while in his success we have a forcible illustration of the pseudo-patriotism which has hitherto prevailed amongst us.

One of the first occasions on which Mr. Dargan occupied a prominent position in connexion with those public works with which he has subsequently become so much identified, was in the construction of the great Holyhead road, designed by Telford, which was then regarded as the most important line of communication of the age. The experience which he obtained in making the Holyhead road, pointed him out as the person, of all others, best fitted to construct the then proposed line of road between this city and Howth; the one being justly regarded as the complement of the other. Some of our readers may recollect that this route was at one time considered as much a triumph of engineering skill, in facilitating the communication between London and Dublin, as the present one now is. The graceful suspension bridge across the Menai Straits not inaptly occupies a position close to that of Mr. Robert Stephenson's later great work—each forming, in its way, an illustration of the extent to which science and enterprize were laid under contribution in the age in which it was constructed. It was not, however, merely the stupendous suspension bridge and the respective harbours of Holyhead and Howth that then attracted attention. The roads on either side of the Channel were far in advance of anything which that period elsewhere exhibited. That from this city to Howth was long regarded as one of the sights in the vicinity of the metropolis, from the admirable surface it continued to present for a series of years. How times are changed! Locomotion by common roads, unless for short distances, will soon be ranged with the things of the past.

The line of railway from this city to Kingstown was the first, and for several years the only one in Ireland; and considering the locality through which it passes, its construction must then (now over twenty years ago) have been attended by considerable difficulties. In that day it was, moreover, a work of considerable magnitude. There was, however, no hesitation on the part of the directors in confiding the execution of it to Mr. Dargan; and taking into account the period at which it was constructed, this line forms to the present day a triumph of engineering and constructive ability.

After the completion of the Kingstown Railway, many years elapsed before much further progress was made towards the extension of the system in Ireland. Its advantages were but imperfectly understood, and little idea was entertained of the extent to which it was destined to revolutionize society. Canal conveyance was still in the ascendant, and a company was formed for opening up the line of communication between Lough Erne and Belfast. For the construction of the Ulster Canal, Mr. Dargan's tender was accepted; it was ready for traffic within the specified time, and the satisfactory manner in which that great undertaking was executed still further added to his reputation.

The formation of the Ulster, the Dublin and Drogheda, and the Great Southern and Western Railway Companies, followed in close succession, in all of which the services of Mr. Dargan were available in carrying out the extension of the system. The Great Southern and Western, and the Midland Great Western lines, are, however, his great works, and the admirable manner in which they have been constructed forms the subject of commendation with every one who passes along them. To enumerate the various works that he has either wholly or in part constructed would, in fact, be almost to give a complete list of the Irish railways; as he has had only some two or three competitors in the field, and these on a comparatively small scale.* On a rough calculation we find he has constructed over 600 miles of railway, chiefly within the past ten years. We further find that the contracts which he has at present in hands cover an extent of over 200 miles of railway, without taking into account several other large works. The magnitude of such a range of operations can scarcely be appreciated unless by those conversant with the execution of them; involving, as it does, one of the most extensive organizations ever formed by an individual.

One of the great elements of Mr. Dargan's success is to be found in that accurate discrimination of character which enables him to select in every instance properly qualified persons for positions of trust, having regard in every important appointment to the possession of the peculiar qualification required. This at all times insures his operations going forward with the regularity of clockwork, at the central establishment in this city as well as throughout the country. His mind is thereby free from anxiety, and relieved from the necessity of any attention to details. The excellent arrangements at head-quarters enable him to go about from place to place wherever his presence may be required; and the most cursory inspection of his operations in any particular district is sufficient to satisfy him as to how they are going on. When we consider that during the time the arrangements connected with the Exhibition occupied so much of his attention, he had in hands contracts the aggregate amount of which did not much fall short of £2,000,000, we cannot fail to admire the admirable machinery by which everything was carried forward without the slightest interruption. This is probably Mr. Dargan's great *forte*, as it, undoubtedly, has been the cardinal element of his pre-eminently successful career.

In connexion with the development of the railway system, Mr. Dargan has rendered much more important service than the mere formation of the principal lines. It will be recollected that a few years ago railway enterprise in Ireland was at a frightful discount; and for the construction of even some of the promising lines, funds were with difficulty made available. It was in vain that calls were made on the shareholders, as they were not responded to. And the tardy and limited aid afforded at the eleventh hour by the Government could not be calculated on, until a certain proportion of the capital had

* The only important lines with which Mr. Dargan has not been connected are, the Londonderry and Enniskillen and the Londonderry and Coleraine Railways. These have been constructed by Mr. William M'Cormick, another Irish contractor, who has attained a position of great eminence; but whose operations have been chiefly on the other side of the Channel.

been previously paid up. But even this condition was not at all times easily fulfilled. These were circumstances in which a man like Mr. Dargan could render incalculable service. An ordinary contractor could, or at all events would go to work only on the condition of being paid as he progressed; any failure as to punctuality of payment being manifestly a violation of the contract. Mr. Dargan, however, having once assured himself by careful inquiry of the ultimate success of the undertaking, was at any time prepared to disregard the usual considerations as to payment. The bonds or shares of the company he would take as cash; and we could enumerate a list of projects which were carried out through his instrumentality in this manner. When once he was known to be connected with an enterprize, it soon after obtained the confidence of the public, and was ere long crowned with success; and we believe that we are correct in stating that for some time past he has not only been the largest holder of Irish railway stock, but that he is the largest railway proprietor in the United Kingdom.

The high character which Mr. Dargan had attained in connexion with the great undertakings which he has for years carried out, and the estimation in which he is so deservedly held by all classes, contributed in no small degree to the success of the Exhibition. To an appeal from almost any other quarter no such response would have been made as that which ensured the demonstration of 1853 being a triumphant one. Seldom was the value of personal character better illustrated than on that occasion. So soon as the announcement was definitely made that he had undertaken to provide a suitable building for a great Irish Industrial Exhibition, a feeling of confidence was inspired in the public, generally, that it would be a successful one. Not merely in this country, but throughout the manufacturing districts of the sister countries, the most cordial response was made. Noblemen and gentlemen vied with each other in contributing to the Exhibition; and treasures of Art were freely forwarded to the Committee, which had never before been out of the possession of their owners. Among the earliest promises of support was one on the part of Her Majesty and of his Royal Highness Prince Albert; and in addition to valuable contributions, the Queen and the Prince honoured the Exhibition with a visit. In foreign countries the project of the Irish Industrial Exhibition was also favourably entertained. The fame of its founder was not unknown even at foreign Courts; and the strong sympathy which the object called forth was testified by the valuable contributions of the Emperor of the French, the King of the Belgians, the King of Holland, and the King of Prussia. The recognition as national of a demonstration founded by a private individual is, indeed, a circumstance without parallel; but all this was no more than the occasion demanded or than the effort deserved. While the antecedents of the founder of the Exhibition furnished an assurance that whatever undertaking he entered into would be fulfilled to the letter, the generous disinterestedness, and the total absence of any feeling of self which he displayed, were such as deserved to enlist the sympathy so freely accorded. In the then transition state of Ireland he felt assured of the great service that would be rendered by an Exhibition in the Irish capital; and having satisfied himself on this point, any risk of pecuniary loss which the project might entail did not weigh with him a moment in determining to carry it out. And of the good faith in which he fulfilled his part in connexion with that great undertaking the public do not now require to be told. Again, and again, were the Committee of gentlemen entrusted with carrying out the enterprize entreated to allow no pecuniary considerations to weigh in making every necessary arrangement to bring the affair to a successful issue. Nobly, then, did the founder of the Exhibition discharge the onerous duty which he undertook; and well did such an effort deserve the cordial, and we may add the enthusiastic, response which the occasion called forth.

Any doubts that might have been entertained as to the success of the Exhibition, or the service which it was destined to render in promoting that progress which had so auspiciously set in, were dispelled after the opening. Then, indeed, the value of the obligation under which Mr. Dargan had laid his countrymen was appreciated, and some anxiety was felt as to the most fitting method of recording it. A motion on the subject was brought forward in the Corporation of this city by Town Councillor Boyce, now Lord Mayor elect; but it was very properly decided by that body that any testimonial, whether in the form of a statue or other object, emanating merely from the Corporation, would not be an adequate national acknowledgment of the gratitude of the people of Ireland to one of the most distinguished of her sons; and accordingly a requisition was got up for holding a public meeting in this city to take the subject into consideration. Of that requisition it may be said that it was without precedent on account of the number and respectability of the names attached to it, and the fact of their comprising those of men of all parties. Headed by the Duke of Leinster, the requisitionists included forty peers, six prelates of the Established Church, fifteen Roman Catholic bishops, forty-nine Members of Parliament, a large proportion of the magistracy of the country, and a host of the professional, mercantile, and trading classes, the entire number amounting to over 2200. The meeting held in the Round Room of the Rotundo on the 14th July, 1853, pursuant to that requisition, was one of the most numerous, respectably attended, and enthusiastic, that has ever been held in the Irish metropolis, while the very mention of the name of the man whom they had met to honour called forth bursts of enthusiastic applause. The Lord Mayor occupied the chair, and the several resolutions were proposed and seconded by His Grace the Duke of Leinster, the Marquis of Westmeath, the Right Honourable Francis Blackburne, Sir William Rowan Hamilton, Sir Robert Kane, Sir Edward M'Donnell (Lord Mayor Elect), Sir Thomas Deane, John Barlow, Esq., governor of the Bank of Ireland, John Ennis, Esq., chairman of the Midland Great Western Railway Company, John Lentaigne, Esq., John F. Maguire, Esq., M.P., Mayor of Cork, and William Fry, Esq., T.C. The following resolutions were adopted by the meeting:—

"That, considering the great benefits conferred by Mr. Dargan on the industrial population of Ireland, not only in the vast amount of employment he has given, but also in the lesson he has so successfully taught, this meeting is of opinion that he is entitled to our warmest approbation and most grateful acknowledgments."

"That, while we rejoice in being able to congratulate Mr. Dargan upon the prosperity which, under Providence, has resulted to himself from the exercise of his unwearied industry and indefatigable perseverance, we are yet of opinion that a great and combined exertion should be made throughout the country, to perpetuate, in connexion with his name, the remembrance of the good he has effected; and that all classes of our countrymen be invited to co-operate actively in a measure which will not only be complimentary to the 'workman's friend,' but permanently useful in extending industrial education."

"That, with a view to carry out successfully the object contemplated in the foregoing resolution, a committee be now selected, to whom shall be entrusted the duty of collecting funds, which it is hoped will be commensurate with the great object proposed, such committee to consist of the following gentlemen, viz.:—the Peers of Ireland who have signed the requisition; the Representatives of Ireland who have signed the requisition; the mayors of all the corporate cities and towns of Ireland; the movers and seconders of the resolutions of this day; and the Right Honourable the Lord Mayor, John D. Atkin, John Barlow, Joseph Boyce, Alexander Boyle, Robert Callwell, Francis Codd, Thomas Crosthwaite, Joseph Cowper, John D'Arcy, Jeremiah Dunne, John Ennis, Fergus Farrell, William Fry, Thomas M. Gresham, Arthur Guinness, Sir George Hodson, George Hoyte, Thomas Hutton, Colonel La Touche, William Long, John M'Donnell, Sir Edward M'Donnell, James W. Murland, Denis Moylan, Sir Timothy O'Brien, Valentine O'Brien O'Connor, John O'Connell, Thomas O'Hagan, Sir Colman O'Loghlen, William Harvey Pim, James Perry, James Power, Patrick Read, John Reynolds, George Roe, Patrick Sweetman, and Thomas Wilson."

To the Committee thus nominated Sir Robert Kane and John Ennis, Esq., were appointed honorary secretaries. The consideration of the precise form which the proposed testimonial should assume was very properly postponed until some idea could be had of the funds available for the purpose; and after the most mature deliberation it was decided that the Dargan Testimonial Committee should co-operate with that of the Irish Institution (an association having its origin in the Exhibition), in founding a permanent institution with which the name and great public services of Mr. Dargan should be prominently connected. The idea of establishing a National Gallery of Art in Dublin was derived from the Exhibition, and the preliminary step towards the attainment of this object was the founding of the Irish Institution. Hence the propriety of the Testimonial Committee co-operating with this new association in carrying out a project so fraught with important advantages to the country at large.

The royal visit to Ireland during the past season was so especially complimentary to the subject of this Memoir, as to call for something beyond a mere passing notice here. The warm interest taken in the Exhibition by Her Majesty and His Royal Highness Prince Albert was manifest from the first announcement of the project. In addition to becoming exhibitors the Queen and the Prince intimated their intention of visiting the Irish Palace of Industry—a structure the very name of which was of hopeful augury; and of that visit the royal recognition of the services rendered by Mr. Dargan to his country formed the most significant incident, while the manner in which that recognition was conveyed was not less gratifying to the people of Ireland than it was complimentary to the object of it. The great Industrial Captain of the age was for the time the most honoured subject of the realm. Coming to Ireland to visit the Exhibition, and to express sympathy with the object of it, Her Majesty determined that this should be done in the most marked manner possible; and, accordingly, Mr. and Mrs. Dargan had the honour of receiving at their own residence a visit from the Sovereign—an event the announcement of which was received with the most intense satisfaction throughout the length and breadth of the land. Seldom, indeed, has a royal favour been more appropriate than that conferred by the visit so graciously paid by the Queen and the Prince Consort to Mr. Dargan; and seldom has such a compliment been so well deserved as in the case in question. But the signal marks of the royal favour to the founder of the Exhibition did not end here. Some time after the royal visit to Mount Anville, Mr. Dargan, in conversation with some of his friends, expressed his anxiety to obtain busts of the Queen and the Prince Consort. This circumstance was, in some way, brought to the knowledge of Her Majesty, whereupon a letter was transmitted to Mr. Dargan by Her Majesty's commands, stating, that in consequence of Her Majesty having learned that he had expressed a wish to possess busts of the Queen and Prince Albert, Her Majesty would have much pleasure in presenting him with them—an intimation which was accompanied by the further gratifying compliment, that the busts of the Queen and Prince should be executed by any Irish artist whom Mr. Dargan might select. The required sittings for these mementos of the royal visit were soon afterwards given to Mr. John E. Jones, who was nominated by Mr. Dargan for the purpose.

The allocation of the funds collected for the proposed National Testimonial to Mr. Dargan has already been indicated, but as the last sheet of this Work was issuing from the press, an event has occurred in connexion with this Testimonial of the most gratifying character,—that of an Act being passed by the Legislature for placing the Irish National Gallery on a proper basis, and for securing the necessary steps being taken for giving due effect to the wishes of the subscribers to the Testimonial fund. The inadequacy of the sum collected (about £6,000) to carry out by itself any great special object, and the uncertainty at all times attendant upon voluntary contributions, induced the Government to come forward and confer on the project that stability which it could not otherwise attain. The founding of a Gallery of the Fine Arts in the Irish metropolis is *per se* an object deserving of the attention of the Government; but we have also reason to believe that a desire to aid the Dargan Testimonial Committee had no small influence in the determination of the course which has been adopted. At the opening of the Exhibition a title waited Mr. Dargan's acceptance—an offer which he respectfully declined. Although declined, the offer was gratifying, as showing a desire in high places to co-operate with the Irish people in every possible way in paying honour to the man who had proved himself to be a true benefactor of his country; and, failing in the first instance, it is creditable to the Government that so much alacrity should have been shown on an occasion where the self-denial and retiring disposition of Mr. Dargan could not stand in the way of paying what was at once an individual and a national compliment. In no other way could the idea of the Testimonial be carried out so much in accordance with the views and wishes of him who is the object of it, as by making it in some way ancillary to progress; and the Irish Government has come forward in a very handsome manner to place the new Institution on a proper basis. A great National Institution has thus, as it were, grown out of the Exhibition, with which the name of the founder of the Exhibition must be for ever indissolubly connected: and that not merely by statue or inscription, but in the Statute-Book of the country,—the Act of Parliament here referred to making special provision for carrying out the objects of the Dargan Testimonial Committee.

The circumstances which we have here recorded, must, as a matter of course, be eminently gratifying to Mr. Dargan. But while we are far from supposing that he is insensible to the good opinion of his fellow-men, the honours so profusely and, at the same time, so justly accorded to him, do not induce him to deviate in the smallest degree from pursuing the even tenor of his way. He still exhibits the cordiality, unaffected manner, and straightforward character which secured for him hosts of friends in times past, and which, at the present day, obtain for him the respect of all classes of his countrymen,—we say, advisedly, of all classes. A personal enemy he could scarcely have, and, we know, that a political enemy he could not have at all; inasmuch as in a country distracted by political and party strife, he had at all times the good sense to avoid allying himself with any class of politicians, and has hence become a universal favourite. The intervals snatched from the extensive business in which he is still engaged are passed in retirement at his residence Mount Anville, near Dundrum. There he is surrounded by all those enjoyments and luxuries that wealth and a refined taste can command. From that retirement which he prizes so much we have not here presumed to attempt to withdraw the veil. In this brief Memoir we have dealt with Mr. Dargan simply as a public man; and in wishing him all the happiness that can result from a consciousness of a faithful discharge of duty, we feel assured that we but feebly give expression to the earnest aspirations of every Irishman.

# CONTENTS.

[The name or initials of the writer are usually appended to each article throughout this Work; but as the name has not always appeared in full, it has been considered advisable to indicate the authorship of the several contributions in the Table of Contents,—an arrangement which, it is hoped, will be satisfactory to the reader.]

# INTRODUCTION.

THE great peculiarity of the present age is its eminently practical character; a result of the extension of manufacturing and commercial industry. The intercourse between different nations is vastly on the increase. A sort of almost cosmopolitan competition has in consequence sprung up, that lends a stimulus to improvement. And it is with nations as with individuals; fertility of invention, mechanical skill, and indomitable perseverance, are required on the part of a community to enable them to attain a respectable position in the great commonwealth of industry and enterprise—a position the attainment of which is a work of time, and one which can only be enjoyed by unremitting exertion.

Exhibitions of different kinds have long been recognised, by the people of almost every civilized country, as amongst the most efficacious means of leading to the introduction and extension of improvements. Thus the various Associations for the Promotion of the Fine Arts hold annual exhibitions of painting and sculpture. The numerous Agricultural Societies that spread their ramifications throughout the length and breadth of the land, through the agency of public competition encourage the improvement of live stock and of husbandry generally. To Horticultural Exhibitions we are indebted for many of the wonderful improvements that have been introduced within the last half century in the different departments of gardening—for the gorgeous floral beauties which decorate our parterres and conservatories, and the delicious fruits that enrich our desserts. This principle has therefore been long recognised and acted upon, with the best results, not only in this but in other countries. So long ago as 1756 the Society of Arts in London offered prizes for specimens of manufactures of different kinds, and exhibited the works which were brought forward in competition for them. The Royal Dublin Society adopted the practice at a still earlier period, and has continued it until the present day, attention being, however, until lately, confined to special objects.

But to our French neighbours must be awarded the credit of having originated what may be properly termed Expositions of Industry. The Marquess D'Aveze, on his appointment as Commissioner of the Royal Manufactories of the Gobelins, of Sèvres, and of the Savonnerie, in 1797, determined on converting the chateau of St. Cloud, then uninhabited, into a bazaar for the exhibition and disposal of the productions of these several establishments; but, at the moment he was ready to carry out the design, he was obliged, by a decree of the new Directory, to quit the kingdom. On his return in the ensuing year, the Marquess planned an Exhibition of a still more imposing character, which comprised the richest furniture and marqueterie of the period; the finest clocks and watches; the superb china of Sèvres and Angoulême; the silks of Lyons; and a variety of other interesting and remarkable objects. This demonstration was held in 1798, and so great was its success that a second took place in 1801, a third in 1802, and a fourth in 1806. Notwithstanding the then unsettled state of affairs in France, on the last occasion there were no less than 1400 exhibitors, and the collection remained open for the inspection of the public for twenty-four days. After that period political and military manœuvres absorbed public attention, to the comparative exclusion of consideration for the peaceful pursuits of industry; and it was not until 1819 that the fifth Exposition was held in France. The sixth took place in 1823, and the seventh in 1827, when a great building was erected for the purpose in the Place de la Concorde. The eighth Exhibition was held in 1834, and the ninth in 1839, when upwards of 4000 competitors entered the field, thus indicating the great importance attached by the people to these demonstrations. In 1844 and 1849 the Expositions of Industry were repeated in the French capital, each occasion being attended by an increasing measure of success, as compared with that which preceded it; and it is beyond question that these Exhibitions contributed in no small degree to raise the manufactures of France to that pre-eminence for which they are so justly celebrated.

The influence of the Parisian Exhibitions soon extended to a greater or less extent throughout the Continent of Europe, in several capitals of which they were imitated with various degrees of success; and it is scarcely to be doubted, that to them, many branches of manufacture owe the excellence which they have attained. Governmental encouragement laid the foundation of that excellence: but it may be safely assumed that these periodic displays also did much in encouraging artists and manufacturers to increased exertion, besides diffusing a knowledge of what had been already accomplished. If the royal and imperial establishments could go to work regardless of cost, their produce was not brought into the market to compete with private enterprise; while a sort of standard was thereby attained which it became the province of private enterprise to imitate under the healthy influence of public competition—the general taste being meanwhile improved by the successive Exhibitions of what we now-a-days term Art-manufactures. But it will be observed that all these displays were due to the respective governments of the countries in which they were held. Freedom of action on the part of Continental communities, in a collective capacity, was then, as it is still for the most part, unknown; and under no other circumstances could national demonstrations of any kind take place than under the immediate direction of the Executive. This is a point which it is necessary to bear in mind, in any inquiry as to Expositions of Industry not having at an early stage occupied attention in the United Kingdom. With us such movements were not supposed to be legitimately within the province of the Government; and while adequate existing organizations were not in being to carry them out, the feeling in their favour was not sufficiently strong until lately to insure special machinery being devised for the purpose. As already observed, we have had during a considerable part of the last century Exhibitions in various departments of industry,—the Society of Arts in London, and the Royal Dublin Society here, being pioneers in this direction. It was not, however, until 1829, that the idea of a general Exhibition on the Parisian plan was seriously contemplated in these countries. In that year an effort was made by the Royal Dublin Society to originate periodic displays of this class, the holding of which should afterwards be a part of the Society's operations; but it was not till 1834 that the design was fully realized, the first General Exhibition of the products of Manufacturing Industry held in the United Kingdom having taken place on the premises of the Society in that year. A Committee of Manufactures was thereupon added to the executive body of the Society, and the holding of periodic Exhibitions became a regular part of its business, greatly to the increase of the Society's usefulness, and to the public advantage. As the movement progressed, each succeeding demonstration surpassed the preceding one in importance and the interest attached to it by the public, until they have been brought to a climax by the recent Great Exhibition, which may therefore be regarded as the continuation of the Triennial Exhibitions of the Royal Dublin Society.*

* The Triennial Exhibitions of the Royal Dublin Society have unquestionably exercised a very important influence on manufacturing progress in Ireland, while they have at the same time reflected great credit on the Society itself. The origination of these was brought about by Isaac Weld, Esq., who, for many years, was one of the Honorary Secretaries of the Society, and is now one of the Vice-Presidents. During the early part of the present century Mr. Weld was travelling on the Continent, and in Paris he became acquainted with the operation and results of the Expositions there. Subsequently, while at Naples, he happened to be able to visit an Exhibition on the Parisian plan; and after his return to this country he brought the subject under the notice of the Royal Dublin Society. In the Proceedings of the Society we find the following notice of motion, dated February 12, 1829:

*Notice of a Motion by* ISAAC WELD, ESQ., *Honorary Secretary.*

"That a Committee be appointed to take into consideration, and to report the practicability of establishing, under the auspices of the Society, an Annual Exhibition of Specimens of the Manufactures and Productions of Ireland, conformable to the plan which has long been adopted in Paris and in other capital cities of the Continent; and to suggest such measures as might facilitate the arrangement, together with the estimates of the probable expenses attendant thereon."

The proposition thus brought forward was received with acclamation. Richard Griffith, Esq. (now LL. D., and Chairman of the Board of Public Works), at once accompanied Mr. Weld in a round of visits to the principal manufacturers in the city and suburbs, who one and all highly approved of the scheme, and promised to become contributors in the event of an Exhibition being finally determined on. A series of resolutions was adopted by the Society in reference to the foundation of Exhibitions as part of the ordinary business, among which it was resolved that the inhabitants of every part of Ireland be invited to aid the movement. The description of manufactures admissible having been stated, it was further agreed upon that nothing should be received unless there be "clear and satisfactory proof" that it was the production of Ireland. To carry forward the proposed undertaking, the Vice-Presidents and Secretaries, with Edward Houghton, William Willans, John Patten, Hugh Hamill, Richard Griffith, Robert Hutton, R. B. Bryan, Esqrs., Dr. Wall and Dr. D'Olier, were appointed the first Committee of Manufactures.

As the period approached for carrying out the project it

The French Expositions have been all along of a strictly local character. In 1849 M. Buffet, the Minister of Agriculture and Commerce, with a view of ascertaining the sentiments of the manufacturers on the subject, sent circulars to the Chambers of Commerce throughout France, suggesting that contributions from foreign

became evident, notwithstanding the apparent enthusiasm with which it was received, that the necessary support from contributors could not be calculated on, to insure a successful commencement; and to the great disappointment of those gentlemen connected with the Society, who had taken so much trouble in the matter, it was found that the proposed demonstration must be postponed. Unavailing regrets were then expressed when it was too late to remedy the apathy of the past. In 1833, however, a Committee was again appointed, with a view of carrying out the object, of which the late Sir Edward Stanley was Chairman. Taking advantage of the interest which had been previously awakened, this Committee succeeded in holding an Exhibition of Manufacturers in May, 1834, which, for a first effort, was eminently successful. The adjudication of prizes formed an important feature of this and all succeeding Exhibitions of the Society: among the premiums then awarded were gold and silver medals in almost every branch of manufacture. The list of exhibitors on that occasion shows that they were chiefly from this city, and that the movement had so far failed to make any deep impression in the provincial towns.

The intention in connexion with these Exhibitions, in the first instance was, that they should take place annually; but this was soon found to be impracticable. In 1835 an Exhibition was held, in which there appeared to be a falling off from that of the previous year. In the succeeding year, 1836, a resolution was adopted by the Society, reconstituting the Committee of Manufactures; and the latter body, at one of their preliminary meetings, agreed to report that, in their opinion, it would not be expedient to have the Exhibition of Irish Manufactures more frequently than *Triennially*. They further recommended the postponement of the then approaching display, which recommendation was adopted by the Society.

In 1838 it may, therefore, be said that the first of the Triennial Exhibitions took place. Of that Exhibition the Proceedings of the Society contain much more ample details than of any of its predecessors; and from these we find that the visitors, during the short time the Exhibition was open, amounted to 20,000; that the goods were generally of a high character; that medals were distributed chiefly for superior broad-clothes, to the Messrs. Willans; for tabinets, to Mr. Atkinson and Mr. Reynolds; and for machinery, to the Messrs. Mallet. Among other plans taken to render the Exhibition useful and attractive was the delivery of a Course of Lectures by Dr. (now Sir Robert) Kane, on each day during the time the Exhibition was open, the topics being connected with Manufacture, or Art as applied to its assistance. This last-mentioned feature is one deserving of more than a passing notice, from its having been repeated without intermission up to the present period, and having also been adopted in connexion with the Exhibition of 1851. These early lectures, too, were regarded with much interest: and it may not be out of place to mention that they laid the foundation for the publication of the celebrated treatise on the "Industrial Resources of Ireland," by Sir Robert Kane, a volume which, while it established the reputation of the author, indirectly reflected no small degree of credit on the Society under whose auspices the materials for it had been collected.

The Exhibition of 1841 differed little from its predecessor. That of 1844 was, however, on a more extensive scale than any of the previous ones, and it at the same time bore evidence of the great service rendered by the Society in promoting manufacturing progress. In the Address of the Committee in the last-mentioned year it is stated that the object of such demonstrations is to discover "what Ireland is capable of affording from native production and native talent." The linen and woollen manufactures were largely represented on that occasion, and articles displaying artistic ornamentation received premiums in the adjudication which took place. It should also be observed, that many contributions were then sent from the provinces. The country at that period enjoyed a large measure of prosperity, and its effects were manifest in the Triennial Exhibition.

We now come to that of 1847. It may be observed, as a remarkable feature in the history of this particular Exhibition, that when the Committee of Manufactures seemed anxious to adjourn it to the following year, from the depressed state of the country, the manufacturers themselves met, and urged the matter with a promptitude which showed their appreciation of its importance. The Committee appointed to adjudge the Honorary Medals and Certificates on that occasion express in their Report the highest satisfaction with its results. Notwithstanding that it was undertaken at a period of unexampled depression, in consequence of the disastrous failure of the potato crop, when the business of the country was in almost every department more or less paralyzed, the specimens of native manufacture were superior to those exhibited at any previous Exhibition. Unrivalled as our tabinets had always been, they appeared then to have made still greater exertions towards excellence. In tabinets, cambrics, linens, damask, and lace, Messrs. Atkinson, Fry, Coulson of Lisburn, and James Forrest and Sons, were chiefly distinguished. The Messrs. Willans contributed largely in specimens of superior woollens; Hutton and Dawson in carriages; M'Cullagh, of Belfast, in pianofortes; and Cordner in fringes. The Ladies' Industrial Society received a warm encomium, both for the neatness of the goods exhibited by them, and the praiseworthy object sought to be attained, in elevating the industrial character of the female poor. Altogether the value of such assemblages in keeping up a lively and salutary competition in trade and manufactures, had at that period become strongly impressed upon the public mind.

The Exhibition of 1850 was still greater and more comprehensive in its design than any of its predecessors. On this occasion it had been decided to admit the produce of other countries, the effect of which was that many departments of the industry of England and Scotland were well represented. The Catalogue of articles occupies 104 pages, and contains, besides those manufactures for which Ireland is peculiarly remarkable, a vast number of miscellaneous articles of curious workmanship. This display had also a much more extensive representation of the country's home trade than had hitherto been seen in the Irish metropolis. It was visited by a deputation from the Commission appointed to carry out the Exhibition in Hyde Park in the ensuing year, and who were then engaged in perfecting the arrangements for that purpose. In their Report the Committee of Manufactures speak in the highest terms of their unexampled success, as indicative of an improved condition of the country, as well as the beneficial influence of such demonstrations. The liberality of opening its honours and prizes to the *rivalry of other nations*, is a peculiarity in the history of the Royal Dublin Society's latter Exhibition, which should not be overlooked. The last Triennial Exposition, properly so called, was not so much a native as a general collection—the fit precedent of that greater and grander gathering which, at the next period of the usual Exhibition, was destined to eclipse the glories of every previous effort.

The brief detail which we have now given of the Exhibitions of the Royal Dublin Society, which have this year been brought to an appropriate termination, appears to be necessary to remove the misconceptions entertained regarding the connexion between the Exhibition of 1853 and its predecessors held by the Society.

countries should be invited; but the replies were so unfavourable that the idea was abandoned. The state of France at the time was unpropitious for successfully carying out a great cosmopolitan Exhibition. Not only was the internal condition of the country unsettled, but the high protective duties levied on the importation of foreign goods would naturally prevent their manufacturers from taking them to a country in which, in any case, they had no chance of opening up a market, owing to the fiscal restrictions that prevailed. The more liberal commercial code of England, and the feeling of perfect security which existed in that country, conspired to make it the scene of the first Great Exposition of the Industry of all Nations. Accordingly, the suggestion of His Royal Highness Prince Albert was responded to with a heartiness worthy of a great cosmopolitan demonstration. The period had arrived when it could be appropriately made. Through the relaxation of the protective duties levied on the importation of foreign goods, the manufacturers of other nations naturally looked forward to an extension of their trade with the United Kingdom, and therefore eagerly availed themselves of the opportunity of thus displaying their wares before their new customers. The Government, though disclaiming any responsibility on account of the proposed Exhibition, was willing to afford every encouragement to the project; and, accordingly, our ministers at the various foreign courts were instructed to use their influence to procure contributions to it. Hence the foreign display in the Crystal Palace was all that could be desired, rendering the Exhibition itself a truly cosmopolitan one, in every sense of the word. The high personal character of the Prince Consort, and the estimation in which he is deservedly held by all classes of the people at home, insured its success so far as regarded its becoming an exposition of native industry, so soon as it became known that he had taken the project under his own immediate superintendence; and to the indefatigable perseverence of His Royal Highness, his courageous defiance of all risk of failure, and his sagacity even in matters of detail, much of the success of the Exhibition of 1851 was really due. Before any definite steps were taken on that occasion, a deputation was appointed to visit the principal towns of the United Kingdom, with a view of ascertaining how far the movement was likely to be responded to. This circumstance is worthy of note, from the contrast which it presents with the course which would have been adopted in any other country. Elsewhere not only the initiative but the entire responsibility would have been undertaken by Government; but with us any such action must be comparatively independent of the Government, the only facilities provided in that quarter being exemption from vexatious restrictions. And in connexion with the proceedings of this deputation, it is in no small degree creditable to the municipal authorities and leading men of this city, that it was in Dublin the proposal of His Royal Highness Prince Albert was first heartily responded to;—a circumstance no doubt due to the influence exercised by the Triennial Exhibitions of the Royal Dublin Society.

The Exhibition of 1851 was eminently successful. The result of that first effort to bring together the fruits of the industry of all nations showed the wisdom of the proposal. The various incidents connected with it have now become matter of history, being chronicled in parliamentary reports and other official documents, even to the minutest details. It is therefore unnecessary to refer to it at greater length in this place; and we shall dismiss this part of the subject by quoting an extract from the celebrated speech of its royal founder at a dinner given by the Lord Mayor of London to the chief municipal authorities of the United Kingdom:—"The Exhibition of 1851 would," he said, "afford a true test of the point of development at which the whole of mankind has arrived, and a new starting-point from which all nations would be able to direct their future exertions."

It will be recollected by those who visited the Hyde Park Exhibition, that while the position occupied by Ireland, as a whole, was eminently creditable, yet some districts were greatly wanting in responding to the call which had been made upon them. Thus, while the staple industry of Belfast was amply represented, while the tabinets of this city and the lace-work of Limerick were held in due estimation, it was observed that Cork had contributed little to the Crystal Palace. This circumstance was freely commented upon at the time, greatly to the disparagement of the people of "the beautiful city;" and they, apparently conscious of the great mistake which they had committed, and anxious to make amends, determined to have an Exhibition of their own; which accordingly came off in the summer of 1852, and, for a provincial demonstration, was a highly successful one. The result of the Hyde Park Exhibition afforded information for the guidance of others in a similar direction, and justified the people of Cork in making a considerable preliminary expenditure, on the faith of being reimbursed by the fees for admission, having besides raised a considerable sum by appealing to the public for subscriptions. In this respect they were not disappointed. The Exhibition remained open about four months, during which the daily number of visitors was often from 2000 to 3000. Further testimony was thereby borne to the success and beneficial effects of Expositions of Industry.

But it will be apparent that each successful effort threw increasing obstacles in the way of succeeding ones. That which a few years ago would have come off with *eclat* would now fail to attract attention. Thus, while for a series of years, the Triennial Exhibitions of the Royal Dublin Society had been regarded with increasing interest, each occasion adding vastly to the number of exhibitors which came forward as compared with the preceding one, the recent experience of the public threw obstacles in the way of future progress apparently insurmountable. The display which in 1850 was regarded as highly creditable would not pass muster in 1853. On previous occasions almost every apartment in the Society House was thrown open for the purpose, but the accommodation thus afforded would contain but a very small proportion of any collection likely to attract attention after the Exhibition of 1851. The difficulty lay in providing suitable accommodation—in fact, in making such arrangements as would insure the co-operation of the public. To accomplish this, the Society in its corporate capacity possessed no resources whatever; and hence it became matter for anxious consideration whether these Triennial Exhibitions, which had already conferred such signal advantages upon the country, were to be given up, without some effort being made to worthily consummate the series.

It was at this stage that Mr. Dargan made his now famous proposal to the Society; which was, as a matter of course, promptly accepted, and led to the recent Great Exhibition. Intimately identified with industrial pursuits, no person was better able to appreciate the beneficial effects of such Exhibitions than Mr. Dargan; and after witnessing the results of the Exhibition in London, and more recently that in Cork, he became still further impressed with the field that existed for a suitable demonstration in the Irish metropolis, as well as of the benefits that would ensue therefrom; and he determined to supply the funds when the occasion arose for carrying the project into effect. The circumstance of the past season being that for the usual Triennial Exhibition of the Royal Dublin Society seemed to present the fitting opportunity; and, as a member of that body, knowing the peculiar position in which the Society was placed, after a rough calculation of the sum required for the purpose, he made the following proposal:—

"Dublin, 24th *June*, 1852.

"Mr. Dargan, understanding that the year 1853 will be the year for holding the Triennial Exhibition of Manufactures of the Royal Dublin Society, and being desirous to give such Exhibition a character of more than usual prominence, and to render it available for the manufactures of the three kingdoms, proposes to place the sum of £20,000 in the hands of a Special Executive Committee, on the following conditions, viz.:—

"1st.—That a suitable Building shall be erected on the lawn of the Royal Dublin Society.

"2nd.—That the Opening of the Exhibition shall not be later than June, 1853.

"3rd.—That the Special Executive Committee shall be nominated by three gentlemen on the part of Mr. Dargan, to be named by him, and by three gentlemen to be selected by the Council of the Royal Dublin Society from that body.

"4th.—That Mr. Dargan shall have the nomination of the Chairman, Deputy-Chairman, and of the Secretary of the Special Executive Committee.

"5th.—That at the termination of the Exhibition, the Building shall be taken by Mr. Dargan, and shall become his property at a valuation by competent persons.

"6th.—That if, after payment of all expenses, the proceeds of the Exhibition do not amount to £20,000, with interest thereon at 5 per cent., Mr. Dargan shall receive the proceeds, less all expenses incurred.

"If the proceeds, after payment of all expenses, shall amount to £20,000, with interest thereon at 5 per cent., Mr. Dargan is to receive £20,000, with interest thereon at 5 per cent.

"If the proceeds, after payment of all expenses, exceed the sum of £20,000, with interest thereon at 5 per cent., the Executive Committee is to have the disposal of the surplus.

"The amount of the valuation of the Building to be considered as cash paid to Mr. Dargan.

"William Dargan."

From the terms of the above proposal it will be seen that, come what might, Mr. Dargan could gain nothing from the Exhibition in a pecuniary point of view, while he ran all the risk of loss. This point it is necessary to bear in mind, to be able duly to appreciate the disinterested patriotism which the proposal exhibits.

The foregoing communication was brought forward at the Meeting of the Royal Dublin Society held on Thursday, the 24th June, when it was unanimously resolved—

"That the Society had heard read with much gratification the public-spirited and highly important proposal of their esteemed member, Mr. Dargan, and feel called upon to co-operate with him in his praiseworthy desire to stimulate the manufacturing interests of Ireland, through the instrumentality of this Society's Exhibitions. They therefore cordially assent to the terms of Mr. Dargan's proposition; and it is hereby referred to the Council to take such steps, in conjunction with Mr. Dargan or his appointees, as may be necessary to give full effect to the same."

The acceptance of Mr. Dargan's proposal was no sooner conveyed to him than active measures were adopted to carry out the necessary arrangements for the proposed Exhibition, in a manner worthy of the object in view, of the patriotic and energetic founder of it, and of the noble Society upon whose premises and in connexion with which it was to take place. The site, though contracted so far as regards space, was unquestionably the best that could have been selected; and on an eligible site, every one knows, a great deal of the success of such a demonstration depends. The central situation contributed much to the comfort and convenience of the public, who visited the Exhibition there much oftener than if it had been situated at a greater distance. In this point of view alone, it will therefore be seen that the co-operation of the Royal Dublin Society was of great value.

The Executive Committee nominated on the part of Mr. Dargan and the Society held their first meeting on the 5th July, at which C. P. Roney, Esq., now Sir Cusac Roney, was appointed Secretary, and John C. Deane, Esq., Assistant Secretary. The energy which these gentlemen brought to the discharge of their duties, and the successful manner in which they advocated the claims of the Exhibition on every occasion, show that more judicious appointments could not have been made. Offices for the Committee were taken at No. 3, Upper Merrion-street; and it was resolved, even at that early period, that the Exhibition should be opened in the first week of May, 1853. The Committee, by public advertisement, invited architects and others to send in designs for a temporary building suitable for the purposes of the Exhibition, on or before the 31st day of July. The then estimated extent of the building was from 100,000 to 140,000 superficial feet, and the cost of construction was limited to £15,000.

On the 7th August, the Committee appointed a Jury of three* professional men to assist them in deciding on the designs sent in, and on the 12th of August, on their recommendation, the first prize was awarded to Mr. Benson, of Cork; the second, to Messrs. Thomas Deane and Woodward, also of Cork; and the third, to Mr. Richard Turner, of Dublin, who had already distinguished himself in the competition for the Crystal Palace in London. In one week afterwards (August 18th), possession of the ground was obtained; the main lines of the proposed building were at once staked out; and immediately workmen proceeded with the foundations and the preparation of the semicircular ribs of the roof; so that by the 10th of September no less than three of the ribs of the Southern Hall were completed, and several more were in progress. On the 18th September the first rib of the Main Hall was commenced. The work progressed so rapidly that the Committee were enabled to invite His Excellency the Earl of Eglinton, then Lord Lieutenant, to honour with his presence the raising and placing of the first iron column on the 25th of October. By this time the lawn of the Royal Dublin Society had assumed a singular appearance, resembling a huge timber-yard. Immense logs of wood were piled on each other in cargoes; stacks of deals rose in hills; sawyers were working wherever room for a pit could be found; the grass was covered by the platforms for constructing the ribs, which lay about in apparently endless confusion; carpenters plied their vocation in every direction:—the whole producing a din of occupation that chimed in well with the hopes of ultimate success, and the energy of those who were carrying out the undertaking.

Considering the comparatively short period available for the construction of the building, and the probability that various modifications and additions would become necessary during its progress, which could not be foreseen at the commencement of operations, it was determined that it should be carried on under the supervision of the Committee without the intervention of a contractor. Under Mr. Dargan's auspices this course was the best that could have been adopted, more especially as the accommodation subsequently provided was so much greater than was originally contemplated. The first point was to secure the services of the

* Charles Lanyon, Esq., Architect, C. E.; G. M. Miller, Esq., C. E.; and G. W. Hemans, Esq., C. E.

architect whose plan had been approved of, to personally superintend the erection of the building; and at great personal inconvenience Mr. Benson undertook this duty. In reference to the manner in which he discharged it, it is almost unnecessary to say a word. Every part of the building, even to the most minute details, afforded evidence of the consummate ability of the architect.

But it was not less necessary to provide an adequate building than to bring the claims of the Exhibition properly before the public, so that due provision would also be made for the character of its contents. After some deliberation, an arrangement founded upon that adopted for the Exhibition of 1851 was decided on; and an official document, of which the following is a copy, was extensively circulated by the Executive Committee:—

REGULATIONS OF THE COMMITTEE.

1. The Lawn of the Royal Dublin Society has been fixed upon as the Site for the Exhibition.

2. The Building will be provided for the Exhibitors free from rent.

3. The productions of all Nations will be admitted.

4. The general plan for the division of the Exhibition will be similar, as far as practicable, to that adopted at the suggestion of His Royal Highness Prince Albert for the Exhibition of 1851, viz.:—

| | |
|---|---|
| Raw Materials, | Manufactures, |
| Machinery, | Fine Arts. |

These four divisions were further classified as follows:—

Raw Materials.

I. Mining, Quarrying, Metallurgical Operations, and Mineral Products.
II. Chemical and Pharmaceutical Processes and Products generally.
III. Substances used as Food.
IV. Vegetable and Animal Substances, chiefly used in Manufactures as Implements, or for Ornament.

Machinery.

V. Railway and Naval Mechanism; Machines for direct use; Carriages.
VI. Manufacturing Machines and Tools.
VII. Civil Engineering; Architectural and Building Contrivances.
VIII. Naval Architecture, and Military Engineering; Ordnance, Armour, and Accoutrements.
IX. Agricultural and Horticultural Machines and Implements.
X. Philosophical Instruments, and Processes depending upon their use; Musical Instruments; Horological Instruments; Surgical Instruments.

Manufactures.

XI. Cotton.
XII. Woollen and Worsted.
XIII. Silk and Velvet.
XIV. Mixed Fabrics, including Shawls.
XV. Manufactures from Flax and Hemp.
XVI. Leather, including Saddlery and Harness, Skins, Fur, Feathers, and Hair.
XVII. Paper and Stationery; Printing and Bookbinding.
XVIII. Woven, Spun, Felted, and Laid Fabrics, when shown as Specimens of Printing or Dyeing.
XIX. Tapestry, including Carpets and Floor Cloths; Lace and Embroidery; Fancy and Industrial Works.
XX. Articles of Clothing for immediate, personal, or domestic use.
XXI. Cutlery and Edge Tools.
XXII. Iron and General Hardware.
XXIII. Working in Precious Metals, and in their Imitation. Jewellery, and all articles of Vertu and Luxury, not included in the other classes.
XXIV. Glass.
XXV. Ceramic Manufacture, China, Porcelain, Earthenware, &c.
XXVI. Decoration, Furniture, and Upholstery, including Paper Hangings, Papier Machie, and Japanned Goods.
XXVII. Manufactures in Mineral Substances, used for Building or Decoration, as in Marble, Slate, Porphyries, Cements, Artificial Stones, &c.

XXVIII. Manufactures from Animal and Vegetable Substances, not being Woven or Felted, or included in other Sections.

XXIX. Miscellaneous Manufactures and Small Tools.

Illustrations of Processes will form a portion of the Exhibition.

FINE ARTS.

XXX. Sculpture, Models, and Plastic Art; Oil and Water-colour Paintings (not Portraits), Enamels, Frescoes, Drawings, Engravings.

5. All goods and articles for Exhibition must be delivered at the Building, free of any charge to the Committee, and at the risk of the Exhibitor. The reception of goods and articles will commence on the 1st of March, and none can be received after the 31st of March, 1853.

6. Articles and Packages will be unloaded at the Building. Should Exhibitors, or their Agents, not be present, the articles will be unpacked by the officers of the Committee with the utmost possible care, but at the risk of the Exhibitors.

7. Tickets will be issued by the Superintendent to every Exhibitor, his Agent, or Servant, to enable him to pass into the Building until 1st May, between certain hours, to arrange the Articles for Exhibition, which ticket he will be called upon to produce on entrance, and give up when required.

8. Rough Counters and Wall Space will be provided.

9. The most effectual means will be taken, through the agency of the Police and otherwise, to guard against fire, and protect the property in the Exhibition; but the Committee cannot be responsible for losses that may be occasioned by Fire, Robbery, Accident, or Damage of any kind.

10. Exhibitors may employ (under the Regulations of the Committee) Assistants to preserve and keep in order the articles they exhibit, or to explain them to visitors.

11. Free Admission, within certain limits, will be given to Exhibitors or their Agents.

12. Exhibitors cannot remove their goods, or substitute others for them, during the period the Exhibition shall remain open.

13. The Prices of Articles exhibited may be affixed.

14. The Steam and Water Power required for the purposes of the Exhibition will be supplied gratuitously.

15. Shrubs and Flowers will be admitted into the Building for the purpose of ornament.

16. Highly inflammable articles will not be admitted.

17. Each Person or Firm intending to exhibit will be good enough to fill up the accompanying Form of Application for Space, and to transmit it to the Secretary. As it is the intention of the Committee to examine and decide upon these applications as soon as possible, exhibitors are requested to return the Form at their earliest convenience; and in no case can an application for space be received later than the 1st of December, 1852.

18. At the proper time the necessary Forms of Invoice, and other Documents, will be transmitted to parties to whom space shall have been allotted.

19. Suitable storage will be found for all Packing Cases, and the goods exhibited will be repacked with the utmost possible care, but at the risk of the Exhibitor.

20. Every Article sent separately, and every Package, must be legibly marked with the name of the Exhibitor or Exhibitors, and also with the Section and Class, whether Raw Materials, Machinery, Manufactures, or Fine Arts, in which it is proposed the Articles shall be exhibited.

21. The Railway and Steam Packet Companies have kindly consented that Articles exhibited, and not sold, shall be conveyed back by the same route as they were forwarded, free of charge.

22. The Committee propose at the earliest period to take the necessary steps for procuring an Act of Parliament to facilitate the Registration of Designs proposed for Exhibition, and to protect Exhibitors against piracy.

23. The general objections to Prizes have induced the Committee to determine that none shall be awarded.

By Order of the Committee,

C. P. ROBEY, *Secretary.*

The programme here given is interesting as a matter of record, and as showing the points on which the arrangements of the Executive Committee differed from those adopted in 1851. While good faith was maintained with the public so far as regarded the opening of the Exhibition on the day announced, it was found to be inexpedient to insist on a rigid compliance with the above rules on the part of Exhibitors, and goods therefore continued to be received up to the opening. The distribution of prizes as rewards of merit had hitherto been the rule on such occasions; but the inconvenience which was found to result from the system in 1851, the difficulty in carrying it out, and the great dissatisfaction at all times certain to be expressed by disappointed candidates, induced the Executive Committee to abandon the idea so far as regarded the Exhibition of 1853; in which respect the public concurred as to the wise policy of the course adopted in the latter case. Again, the propriety of permitting or refusing prices to be affixed to the goods came under discussion, when a decision was arrived at contrary to that come to by the Royal Commissioners in 1851. When so much trouble and expense was about to be incurred by Exhibitors it was deemed advisable that on this point they should be left to exercise their own discretion, without any conditions being imposed upon them: an arrangement which, we believe, met with universal approbation. In the only remaining point to which we deem it necessary to refer, the Committee did not succeed in realizing the conditional promise which they made to Inventors, as an inducement to come forward,—that of taking the necessary steps for procuring an Act of Parliament to facilitate the Registration of Designs proposed for Exhibition, and to protect Exhibitors from piracy. This, it will be recollected, was one of the features of the Exhibition of 1851, though the extent to which the privilege then accorded was taken advantage of was very much less than was anticipated; and this circumstance probably prevented the proposed arrangement from being carried out on the recent occasion. Be this as it may, however, the fact of no such privilege having been obtained we feel called upon to record here.

Meanwhile, Mr. Roney had been deputed by the Committee to proceed to the manufacturing towns, with a view of urging personally the claims of the Exhibition. His exertions there were attended by such eminent success that it was considered advisable that he should go to Paris for a similar purpose. He subsequently went to Brussels, the Hague, Berlin, and several other places on the Continent, and everywhere met with the most ready assurances of support,—kings and nobles, manufacturers and mechanics, combining to add to the attractiveness of the Dublin Exhibition, and at the same time to acquire for themselves and their country an honourable name among the artists and artisans of the world.

While Mr. Roney was advocating the cause of the Exhibition on the Continent, it was resolved that Mr. Deane should proceed to England and Scotland, with a view of furthering its objects. For this purpose he paid several visits to those cities and districts from which the largest amount of co-operation was to be expected. In Glasgow a meeting was convened by the Lord Provost, at which Mr. Deane attended; and after fully detailing the nature of the arrangements made and contemplated, promises of support were given, which have been amply realized; and the importance of the co-operation of the citizens of Glasgow was the more valuable as it combines within itself almost the whole of the manufactures of the sister countries. Mr. Deane visited in succession Edinburgh, Kirkaldy, Dundee, Stirling, Liverpool, Manchester, Birmingham, Sheffield, Leeds, and a number of other places, from all of which considerable contributions have been made to the Exhibition.

In securing contributions to the Fine Arts Hall Mr. Deane was also eminently successful. From the Continent liberal promises of support had been received; and in juxtaposition with the Continental works, he was anxious to have the modern English School well represented. With this object he set about trying to get from every Academician and Associate a specimen of their works, which was certainly a good idea. But to obtain this directly was found to be impossible, inasmuch as their current efforts were in preparation for their own Exhibition, to the success of which they were bound in the first place to contribute, and their earlier works had, of course, passed into other hands. The addresses of the chief purchasers Mr. Deane then obtained, with a view of appealing directly to them to further his object. Applications were accordingly made to the Duke of Devonshire, the Marquis of Londonderry, Lord Yarborough, Lord Northwich, Mr. Munroe, Mr. Barry, Mr. Young, and other noblemen and gentlemen known to have valuable collections of English pictures; and they were in most cases responded to in a manner which demanded the cordial acknowledgment of every one interested in the success of the Exhibition. Manchester, Liverpool, Preston, and other manufacturing towns are known to be rich in pictures of the highest class, from the great wealth of many of the inhabitants, which enables them to become liberal patrons of the Fine Arts; and the extent of their contributions on the occasion in question has shown that they are equally liberal in the use of the treasures which they possess, when any important object is to be attained thereby.

The Fine Arts Court and that devoted to Antiquities formed characteristic features of the Exhibition. Before the opening, however, much unfavourable criticism was indulged in on account of the alleged undue importance attached by the Committee to a class of objects, the propriety of the admission of which to an

Industrial Exhibition was said to be doubtful. But the result shows that in this respect a wise discretion was exercised. The Committee state, in the Introduction to this section of the Official Catalogue, "that it has not been without consideration that the claims of the Fine Arts—in their abstract character, and viewed apart from utilitarian industry (if, indeed, they can ever be justly so viewed), have been recognised. The difficulty of exclusion appeared at the least as great as of admission. It is not easy often to draw the line of demarcation between objects which come within the strict limits of the Fine Arts and those Arts which are purely utilitarian in their character. There are few of the latter which do not, to a greater or less extent, include or intimately ally themselves to the former; and, therefore, were the boundary to be defined with a scrupulous determination to exclude every article whose object is not solely utilitarian, the result would be to reject from the Exhibition much that now finds a place within it. When the mere necessities of life have been satisfied, civilization superadds to the useful the ornamental, and soon learns to recognise it as a necessity of life also; for the perception of the beautiful is innate to the mind of man, and when the useful has been achieved, the cravings for the beautiful will seek to be satisfied. Hence Sculpture, in the most extended acceptation of that term, enters into the composition of a vast proportion of the articles designed for utilitarian purposes. The same may be said of Painting. In truth it is difficult, when once we have emerged from the rudest and most elementary state of society, to deny that the Fine Arts are themselves utilitarian. The desires of the eye for that which is beautiful in form and colour, if not essential to mere existence, assuredly are so to the enjoyment of life; and hence Sculpture and Painting, in the abstract, may, it is presumed, be fitly exhibited without transgressing the strict limits which should be assigned to an Industrial Exhibition. Under this conviction the Committee have admitted works of Fine Art which are not utilitarian, in the ordinary sense of the word; and they have done so the rather that the study of Sculpture and Painting is essential to perfection in the ornamentation of almost everything in ordinary use. Nor let it be forgotten, as one of the *uses* of the Fine Arts unconnected with industrial objects, that the statuary and the painter contribute to the pages of history as well as the scribe or the printer. The former perpetuates and diffuses the forms and the character of historical persons and events, of natural history, scenery, and costume, as the latter cannot do."

The cheering promises of co-operation from all quarters, and the numerous applications for space, soon rendered it evident that the limits of the original building were too narrow to give due effect to the undertaking. On this becoming apparent Mr. Dargan interposed, by placing a further sum of £6000 at the disposal of the Executive Committee; this, too, was rapidly exhausted, and the demands for space kept still largely in excess of what the Committee had to dispose of. But again and again Mr. Dargan increased his advances, with the full determination that nothing should be wanting to insure the successful carrying out of this great national undertaking. Thus to the original building, comprising only the Centre Hall and the Northern and the Southern Halls, with the adjoining Corridors, were gradually added the Halls for the Fine Arts, Machinery in Motion, Naval and Railway Machinery, the Courts for Furniture, Agricultural Implements, Carriages and Antiquities: occupying in their aggregate a larger space than what was intended to be covered by the first design.

Considerable progress had been made in the execution of the works at the end of December, in spite of the weather, which for two months had been extremely and unusually wet and boisterous, and which fitly ushered in the terrible storms of Christmas Eve and the Monday morning following. They occasioned a considerable amount of damage to the building in its then incomplete state: a great portion of the roof-trusses having been blown down, as were also many parts of the Southern Hall and Galleries. The ground then exhibited a lamentable appearance of wreck, which seemed almost irretrievable; but in a short time the skill and energy of the parties employed had restored things to their former position. The delay caused by the storm was still further increased by the constant succession of foul weather, which continued, with only slight intermission, during the whole after-progress of the building; so that its completion at the period assigned for the opening is a strong proof of the excellence of the arrangements, and of the zeal with which they were carried out. The extraordinary rapidity with which the work was carried forward may be judged by the fact, that the first of the ribs of the Central Hall was raised to its place on the 2nd of March, and notwithstanding the extreme difficulty of the operation, from the weight and vast dimensions of the ribs, and the great height at which they stand from the ground—although on several days the frozen snow on the scaffolding rendered it too dangerous an operation to be proceeded with—all the framing of the roof was in its place in six weeks from that date.

By the 1st of March the Southern Hall was so far completed as to enable the space under the Gallery to be used as a temporary store for the reception of the goods which then began to be sent in by the Exhibitors. A portion of it was converted, for the time, into a sort of bonded warehouse, in which the contributions from foreign countries were deposited under the surveillance of custom-house officers, who took a note of the contents of every package, on the understanding that duty was to be paid on any article not re-packed at the close of the Exhibition. In this respect every facility was afforded to foreign Exhibitors by the authorities under the Board of Inland Revenue. During the period the Exhibition was open, the foreign department was practically a bonded warehouse; the payment of duty being only demanded on such articles as were disposed of here.

On the 21st of March the sale of season tickets commenced. By a reference to a return which will be found in a subsequent page, it will be seen that the revenue from this source was highly satisfactory; the number of season ticket-holders, in proportion to that of the ordinary visitors, being very much greater than in the case of the Exhibition of 1851. The Royal Commissioners fixed the price of season tickets at £3 3*s*., and £2 2*s*., for gentlemen and ladies, respectively; from which rates, however, our Executive Committee considered it advisable to make a reduction; and accordingly, the price of gentlemen's tickets here was £2 2*s*., and that of ladies' £1 1*s*., boys under twelve years of age being admitted at the same rate as ladies. The number of season tickets sold previous to the opening of the Exhibition was 10039, producing the sum of £14437 10*s*.

The day originally fixed for the opening of the Exhibition being Ascension Day, it was considered desirable to make a change in this respect, and accordingly the Executive Committee came to the determination to alter the time from Thursday, the 5th, to Thursday, the 12th of May. The exertions that were made on the part of those engaged in the construction of the Building, as well as that of the Exhibitors, to prepare for the opening, were truly praiseworthy. The urgent necessity which existed to push forward the work so as to have the Building ready in due time rendered it necessary that almost every hand should be employed that was presented; and it may therefore be readily supposed that amongst the hundreds thus provided with work there were many very inefficient persons in every department. Still, the good feeling which pervaded that immense multitude during the progress of the Building was deserving of high commendation; and to it the most cordial testimony was borne by Mr. Dargan at the civic banquet which took place on the day of the opening of the Exhibition, when he observed "that often as he visited the Building during the previous three months, very few agreed with him that it would be finished by the 12th of May; and there was not one of the 1000 to 1500 working men who did not know that he had it in his power to embarrass the operations, if he chose, either by irregularity or by combination, or some other impropriety of the kind, and so prevent the Exhibition from being opened on that day; yet, with that knowledge, they never did a single act of the kind—a circumstance which could scarcely have happened in any other country." But, notwithstanding the exertions that had been used, there was still much to do at the period of the opening to complete the arrangements. Immense packages from different parts of the United Kingdom, and from the Continent, remained unopened, and many had still to be delivered. Yet, on the whole, we believe that the arrangements for the opening ceremonial on that occasion were even further advanced than was the case at the opening of the Exhibition of 1851. Nothing, in fact, was wanting to give effect to the demonstration of the 12th of May. And what then remained to be completed was carried forward without at all interfering with the convenience of the visitors; for whom, from the very commencement, ample attractions were provided.

The opening ceremonial was arranged on a scale of great splendour and magnificence. The eminent adaptation of the building for a musical performance, the fact of one of the finest organs in the United Kingdom being available for the purpose, and, above all, the appropriateness of such a demonstration, induced the Committee to decide on a musical fete at the opening, on a scale which has seldom been surpassed. In the arrangements for this purpose, Dr. Stewart was to preside at the organ, and the orchestra was placed under the direction of Mr. Joseph Robinson, an arrangement which afforded a sufficient guarantee for the performance being everything that could be desired. In order to have a sufficiently powerful orchestra for the occasion, it was resolved that it should consist of the almost unprecedentedly large number of 1000 performers, including the principal vocalists and instrumentalists of this city and of the provinces.

With such preparations the musical entertainment of the opening was naturally looked forward to by the thousands of anxiously expectant ticket-holders as the great feature of the day.*

Invitations had previously been sent by the Committee to a large number of official and other distinguished personages, for the opening ceremonial, at which 10,039 ladies and gentlemen had also secured the privilege of being present, by the purchase of season-tickets. From all parts of the United Kingdom distinguished strangers arrived in town, to take part in the proceedings; and such was the interest manifested even in the great metropolis, that a special express train left London for Holyhead on the previous day, with visitors to the Exhibition; the journey then performed being the most expeditious on record between the two capitals. During the previous few days unusual bustle and activity were apparent throughout the city, and the 12th being a general holiday, not only at the various public establishments, but also among the merchants and traders generally, and the weather, moreover, having been highly propitious, the streets on that morning presented a scene of animation and gaiety, in character with the anticipations entertained of the approaching festival.

* The following Programme of the ceremonial was adopted by the Executive Committee:—

His Excellency the Lord Lieutenant, Grand Master of the Most Illustrious Order of St. Patrick, having signified his pleasure to attend the above in state, the following Programme has been approved:—

The carriages of the Knights and Officers of the Most Illustrious Order of St. Patrick will assemble in the Upper Castle-yard, at half-past eleven o'clock, and await the arrival of His Excellency from the Viceregal Lodge, Phœnix Park, on which the whole will proceed through the Lower Castle-gate, by Dame-street, College-green, Grafton-street, Nassau-street, Leinster-street, and Clare-street, to the grand entrance of the Exhibition in Merrion-square, in the following order:—

Carriages of the Knights and Officers
of the Most Illustrious Order
of St. Patrick.

His Excellency's Household.

HIS EXCELLENCY.

On arrival at the Exhibition, his Excellency will be received by a Guard of Honour. The carriages will set down and file off as directed by the Commissioners of Police.

His Excellency will be received at the entrance by the Executive Committee.

A procession will then form as follows:—

Members of the Committee,

two and two.

Officers of the Order of St. Patrick.

Knights of the Most Illustrious Order of St. Patrick,
two and two, according to their Stalls, wearing
the Collar of the Order.

His Excellency's State Household.

Aides-de-Camp. HIS EXCELLENCY THE LORD LIEUTENANT,
Grand Master of the Illustrious Order, wearing the
Collar of the Order, and the Brilliant
Diamond Badge, and Star of
Grand Master. Aides-de-Camp.

HER EXCELLENCY THE COUNTESS OF ST. GERMANS.

In this order they will proceed, conducted by the Executive Committee, two and two, to the throne prepared for His Excellency.

When the Procession moves up the middle avenue of the Centre Hall to the Dais, the Orchestra, which will consist of 1000 Performers, will play

The National Anthem.

Their Excellencies having taken their seats, the Orchestra will perform

The Hundreth Psalm.

Handel's Coronation Anthem.

"Queen of the Isle, Victoria, reigneth, the glory of all nations.
Let all the people rejoice and say, God save the Queen!
Allelujah! Amen, Amen, Allelujah!"

Then the Chairman, accompanied by the Members of the General Committee, and the principal Officials of the Exhibition, will present an Address to the Lord Lieutenant, at the conclusion of which he will introduce Mr. Dargan, and also Mr. Benson, the Architect, to his Excellency.

The Orchestra will then perform

Mozart's Motette.—"Oh God, when thou appearest."

After which the Right Honourable the Lord Mayor of Dublin, in his robes of office, accompanied by the Members of the Corporation, in their civic dresses, will present an Address from that body.

To which His Excellency will reply.

At its termination, the Orchestra will perform

The Hallelujah Chorus.—*Beethoven.*

This having been concluded, a Procession will be formed, and the Chairman, with the Members of the Committee and the principal officers, will conduct His Excellency and the Countess of St. Germans round the Building, during which the Orchestra will perform

March from Athalie.—*Mendelssohn.*

Their Excellencies having returned to their seats on the Dais, the Orchestra will perform

The Hymn of Praise.—*Mendelssohn.*

"All men, all things, all that has life and breath, sing to the Lord;
Praise the Lord with lute and harp; in joyful song extol the Lord.
And let all flesh magnify His might and His glory.
Praise thou the Lord, O my spirit, in my inmost soul."

Which being concluded, His Excellency will command the Ulster King of Arms to declare

THE EXHIBITION OPEN.

After which the Orchestra will perform

"The Heavens are telling."—*Haydn.*

The Orchestra will afterwards perform

The Hallelujah Chorus.—*Handel.*

Which being terminated, their Excellencies will leave the Building with the same ceremony as on their entrance, the Orchestra performing

The National Anthem.

The doors of the Exhibition were opened to those having the privilege of admission at ten o'clock; one of the side-entrances being specially reserved for members of the Royal Dublin Society, who were distinguished by wearing their badges. Numbers of anxious visitors at once thronged to Merrion-square to catch an early glimpse of the Building, the appearance of which soon became gorgeous in the extreme. The feelings produced on entering the Centre Hall were those of amazement and delight. The noble proportions of the Building, the apparently countless succession of arches presented on either side, the vistas between them, which conveyed an idea of almost unlimited extent, the array presented by an orchestra of over 1000 performers surrounding Telford's great organ, the cheerful and appropriate colouring of the decoration harmonizing so well with all around, the brilliant assemblage of rank and fashion assembled to do honour to the occasion: the *tout ensemble* thus presented has seldom being equalled, much less surpassed. The large number of official personages present was indicated by their peculiar costume, the gay colours of the military uniform contrasting curiously with the dresses of the judges and authorities of the University. On entering the door almost the first object that attracted the attention of the visitor was Marochetti's equestrian statue of the Queen, placed in the centre of the Hall; and ranged along either side were massive works of statuary, the colossal statue of Mr. Dargan, by Jones, occupying a prominent position on the right-hand side, near the upper end of the Hall. The general effect was also much heightened by a variety of evergreen shrubs being judiciously interspersed throughout the Building.

By previous arrangement the members of the Corporation, headed by the Lord Mayor, went in procession to the Castle to accompany the viceregal party in state to the Exhibition. The knights of St. Patrick there also joined the procession, in the uniform and wearing the insignia of the Order.

On the entrance of the Lord Lieutenant the orchestra struck up the National Anthem. After a short pause the Hundredth Psalm was given, and rarely have the words of the inspired Psalmist resounded with such soul-stirring effect. When over 1000 performers took up the words

> "With one consent let all the earth
> To God their cheerful voices raise,"

the sensation produced thereby was eminently calculated to rouse devotional feelings, even in the minds of the most thoughtless. The well-trained notes of the unprecedentedly large number of performers appeared as if proceeding from some single wondrous voice; and the instrumentation was equally creditable and effective. Handel's Coronation Anthem followed, with the introduction of the new words, "Queen of the Isles, Victoria reigneth," which was admirably rendered, the execution fully realizing the ideas of the great composer.

At this stage of the proceedings the Executive Committee presented an address to the Lord Lieutenant, of which the following is a copy. The address was read by the Chairman, George Roe, Esq.:

"MAY IT PLEASE YOUR EXCELLENCY,—Having reached this period of labours commenced under the auspices of your predecessor, and fostered by your own consent and zealous encouragement, a period which, whilst it inaugurates an epoch in the history of this country, terminates in a great degree our most important functions, we, the Executive Committee, feel proud to salute the representative of our most gracious Queen in this noble structure, raised by the enterprise of one of our countrymen, Mr. Dargan, and designed by the genius of another, Mr. Benson, as a Temple dedicated to Industry and the Arts, the history of which is, we trust, destined to fill one page in the annals of Ireland, unstained by an allusion which any class of our countrymen could desire to see erased.

"Your Excellency is too well aware how many difficulties beset any unselfish attempt at public good, and it must be gratifying to you to know that from almost every part of Europe the Committee has experienced the most ready and valuable assistance. Her Majesty and Prince Albert, in becoming contributors to this Exhibition, have not only sanctioned this undertaking by the authority of their names, but given a stimulus by their example, largely contributing to its success; and the other sovereigns and people of Europe have placed us under deep obligations, both by the contributions we see around us, and also by their prompt and generous co-operation from the commencement of our labours to the present time.

"We feel much pleasure in alluding to the Institution with which we are so closely connected, one which has been long and intimately associated with the industrial progress of this country, which first planted those seeds, the fruits of which we now witness, and to whose labours in the encouragement of Exhibitions of Industry and Art for upwards of a century, we owe, in a great degree, our present success; and we gladly acknowledge the unceasing and generous desire evinced by the Royal Dublin Society to promote the success of this undertaking from its commencement to the present time.

"In directing your Excellency's attention to the objects of Exhibition around us, we will not detain you by making any especial reference to the rich and varied illustrations of art and industry from Great Britain and foreign countries, we will only express our hope that Ireland may be found, in some specific branches of manufacture, to hold a position not only gratifying to our national pride, but also calculated to prove that there are sources of wealth in this portion of Her Majesty's dominions well worthy of further development, and likely to enable us to hold a position amongst those nations of the world devoted to Arts and Manufactures.

"In conclusion, we most fervently pray that it may please Almighty God to pour down his blessing upon us, and to make this great undertaking the commencement of a new era in the history of Ireland; and that from the 12th of May, 1853, annalists may date a period when industry and public order, with their inseparable companions, happiness and wealth, shed their abundant blessings over this portion of Her Majesty's dominions; and that when the traveller shall hereafter visit this neighbourhood to inspect the birth-place of our greatest general, he may also view this locality with interest, where by the increased enterprise and patriotism of one man was gained the peaceful, yet not inglorious triumph of industry and genius."

His Excellency returned the following reply:

"GENTLEMEN,—I congratulate you on the completion of the great work of which you have so ably and so satisfactorily directed the execution.

"I congratulate you also on the beauty of the Building, on its perfect adaptation to its purpose, and on the value as well as the variety of its contents.

"The liberal and patriotic conduct of Mr. Dargan, by whom alone you have been enabled to raise this noble structure, entitles him to the gratitude of his countrymen and the admiration of other nations.

"The skill and science displayed by Mr. Benson are, indeed, remarkable, and place him high among the architects of modern times.

"As the representative of our most Gracious Sovereign I receive with satisfaction your dutiful and grateful acknowledgments of Her Majesty's goodness, and that of Her Royal Consort, in becoming contributors to this Exhibition.

"It is gratifying to me to know that the Sovereigns of many foreign States have generously assisted you from the commencement of your labours to the present time.

"The Royal Dublin Society, in promoting the success of this enterprise, has only done that which was to be expected, from a body that has laboured unceasingly for more than a century to advance the progress of Art and Science in this country.

"I learn with pleasure, though without surprise, that all classes of the community have evinced a generous desire to aid in the performance of this ardous task.

"I concur with you in the hope that this Exhibition will show, that in some departments of Art, Irish productions are already excellent, and that Ireland possesses sources of wealth which are worthy of further development.

"That it may please Almighty God so to prosper this undertaking as to make it the means of diffusing throughout the land the love of peaceful and industrious pursuits is a prayer in which I cordially and fervently join."

The Chairman then formally introduced Mr. Dargan to His Excellency. This was the signal for one of the most cordial demonstrations on the part of the assembled thousands that has ever been witnessed. The position of Mr. Dargan at that moment was one that even a sovereign might envy; surrounded by the wealth and intelligence of his native land, in the Temple dedicated to Industry, erected solely at his expense; all joining in enthusiastic acclamations of respect, which were again and again repeated. This was, indeed, an occasion without parallel.

The presentation of Mr. Benson to the Lord Lieutenant, which next took place, was also cordially responded to, and followed by loud demonstrations of applause. No one could contemplate the triumph which he had achieved in the construction of the beautiful Building in which the ceremony then took place, without a feeling of respect and admiration for the talent of the architect by whom it was designed. His Excellency cordially congratulated Mr. Benson on the very successful result of his labours, and thereupon conferred the honour of knighthood upon him.

The orchestra, after this ceremonial was gone through, performed "Mozart's Grand Motette in C." An address was then presented to the Lord Lieutenant by the Corporation of Dublin. The address was read by the Lord Mayor, and ran as follows:

"MAY IT PLEASE YOUR EXCELLENCY,—We, the Corporation of Dublin, gladly avail ourselves of this opportunity of congratulating your Excellency and our fellow-citizens on the successful completion of this great undertaking, so creditable to its founder, Mr. Dargan, and to our country. Deeply interested, as we all are, in the prosperity of the city, we rejoice sincerely at an event which must confer the greatest advantages on all classes amongst us, by the promotion of self-reliance, the diffusion of industrial education, and the cultivation of a taste for the Fine Arts. In conclusion, we beg to expres our earnest hope that this Great Exhibition of the industry of many Nations may fully realize all the benefits to this country which are so dear to the heart of its generous and patriotic originator."

His Excellency returned the following reply:—

"My Lord Mayor and Gentlemen,—I fully participate in the sentiments which you have expressed. The Inauguration of the Great Industrial Exhibition of 1853 is indeed an event of no ordinary interest and importance. I concur with you in hoping that this Exhibition will fulfil the intention of him whom you justly designate as its generous and patriotic originator, by promoting the diffusion of industrial education, and the cultivation of the Fine Arts amongst all classes of the community."

Beethoven's Grand "Hallelujah Chorus" was next performed by the orchestra; after which the Viceregal party was conducted by the Chairman and members of the Executive Committee round the Building; the orchestra, in the meantime, performing Mendelssohn's "March from Athalie." The several distinguished visitors having returned to the dais, and resumed their places, "The Hymn of Praise," by the same great composer, was effectively given by the orchestra; and on this being concluded, Ulster King-at-Arms, by direction of His Excellency, declared the Exhibition to be open, invoking at the same time the blessing of Almighty God upon it.

The Grand Chorus by Hadyn, "The Heavens are Telling," was then performed; and Handel's "Hallelujah" terminated the performance. The Lord Lieutenant and suite shortly after retired, the orchestra, with the addition of five military bands, playing the National Anthem.

The scene presented by the opening of the Exhibition was such as to make an indelible impression on the minds of those who were present on the occasion. The admirable adaptation of the building for the intended purpose, its lofty proportions, and its grand architectural effect, were the themes of unqualified commendation; more especially when viewed in connexion with the short time in which it had been erected, the noble object for which it was designed, and the circumstance under which it was called into existence. Then, indeed, the feeling of admiration of the patriotism which called it forth pervaded every breast; and no second opinion was entertained that the promise to provide a building for a Great Industrial Exhibition had been well redeemed.

At an early stage of its progress plans of the building were forwarded through the Earl of Eglinton, then Lord Lieutenant, to the Queen, with a detail of the means that had been devised for carrying out the project; the result of which was, that Her Majesty and His Royal Highness Prince Albert at once signified their intention of becoming contributors to it. But the interest manifested by the Queen and the Prince Consort in the success of the Irish Exhibition was still further exemplified by the royal visit to it in the course of the summer, when Mr. Dargan had the satisfaction of receiving his Sovereign in the Great Temple of Industry erected by his own munificence. Shortly after the opening a semi-official announcement was made in reference to the contemplated royal visit; which, however, it was known, could not conveniently be made until the close of the Session of Parliament. This, at length, took place in the end of August; and it is not too much to say that the enthusiasm with which the Queen was received was considerably promoted by the circumstances under which Her Majesty appeared amongst us. In the honour conferred upon Mr. Dargan every one felt a compliment as it were paid to himself. In the private visit of Her Majesty to the founder of the Exhibition,—the first that has been paid by a British Sovereign to a Commoner in modern times,—the people saw a recognition of the dignity of Labour, an acknowledgment of the importance of well-applied persistent Industry, which could not fail to be attended by beneficial effects in a country in which it had been the fashion for a spurious and affected gentility to sneer at such pursuits. A great demonstration had been made calculated materially to improve the condition of the country; and it was especially gratifying on such an occasion to find the royal sympathies so thoroughly enlisted in its favour.

The first visit of Her Majesty and Prince Albert to the Exhibition took place on Tuesday, the 30th of August. On that day so great was the anxiety manifested to be present, that from eight o'clock in the morning crowds surrounded the doors waiting for admission. Shortly after ten o'clock the arrival of the royal party was announced at the principal entrance in Merrion-square, where they were received by the Executive Committee. Her Majesty and Prince Albert, accompanied by the ladies and gentlemen composing the royal suite, were conducted along the left-hand side of the Centre Hall to the dais, where arrangements had been made for their reception, and for the presentation of Addresses from the Executive Committee and from the Corporation of the City. The Chairman of the Committee having received from Mr. Deane, the Assistant Secretary, the Address from that body to Her Majesty, proceeded to read it; after which it was presented in due form. Her Majesty handed the Address to Lord Granville, from whom she received the reply thereto, which she read in a clear and distinct tone, and then handed the document to Mr. Roe. The Address to His Royal Highness Prince Albert was read and presented in a similar manner by the Chairman of the Executive Committee, to whom also the Prince handed his reply after reading it. This ceremony being over, the royal party proceeded down the right-hand side of the Central Hall to examine some of the more prominent objects; after which they again returned to the dais, where Addresses were presented by the Corporation to Her Majesty and to His Royal Highness Prince Albert. During this visit Mr. Dargan was formally presented to Her Majesty, by whom he was cordially received, and warmly congratulated, for the disinterested patriotism which he had exhibited, of which the brilliant scene then around them was one of the fruits. After remaining nearly two hours in the Building, the royal party quitted by the Grand Entrance.

The following is a copy of the Address presented by the Executive Committee to Her Majesty:—

"*To the Queen's Most Excellent Majesty.*

"May it please your Majesty,—We, the Executive Committee of the Great Industrial Exhibition of 1853, tendering a dutiful welcome to your Majesty on your arrival in this part of your dominions, desire to express our feelings of loyal and devoted attachment to your throne and person.

"Recollecting the deep gratification which your Majesty afforded to your Irish subjects by your gracious visit to this Metropolis on a former occasion, we cannot fail to attribute our being honoured by your august presence this day to your Majesty's special wish to foster and encourage an enterprise having for its object the industrial and intellectual improvement of your people.

"In this Building, raised at the cost of a high-minded and generous individual, whose name is honourably identified with projects of practical utility to his country, we present for your Majesty's inspection a collection of Arts and Manufactures from most of the Nations of Europe.

"To your Majesty and your Royal Consort we offer our grateful thanks for the early and gracious encouragement extended to this undertaking, by your promise of those contributions which now grace the Exhibition.

"Acknowledging with gratitude the hearty co-operation we have received from England and Scotland, as well as from foreign countries, in promoting that success which we have laboured to realize, we earnestly pray that your Majesty and your Royal Consort may long live to witness and enjoy the increased prosperity of your subjects, and their advance in all that can elevate a nation."

Subjoined is a copy of Her Majesty's reply:—

"I receive with sincere pleasure your Address, and I thank you for the expression of your loyal and devoted attachment.

"I willingly contributed to this collection of Arts and Manufactures from most of the countries of Europe, the object of which was to promote the industrial and intellectual improvement of my people; and it has added much to my gratification, in revisiting this portion of my dominions, to see the complete success of an enterprise which has been carried out in a spirit of energy and self-reliance, and with no pecuniary aid but that derived from the patriotic munificence of one of my loyal subjects."

The Address of the Executive Committee to His Royal Highness Prince Albert was in the following terms:—

"*To His Royal Highness Prince Albert, &c.*

"May it please your Royal Highness,—Impressed with feelings of the deepest respect for your Royal Highness's exalted position, and gratefully appreciating the advantages which the country has derived from your constant labours to promote its best interests, we offer you our cordial congratulations on your arrival in the metropolis of Ireland.

"As President of the Exhibition of all Nations of 1851, your Royal Highness will, doubtless, regard with pleasure a renewed effort to develop improvement in the arts and manufactures of the United Kingdom.

"In the rich and varied display of natural and artificial productions which our exertions have collected together, your Royal Highness will observe many indigenous to our Irish soil, and others the result of Irish hands and enterprise.

"Deeming it of paramount importance that this interesting portion of her Majesty's empire should keep pace with the industrial progress of the world, we have not hesitated to invite the competition of wealthier and more advanced communities to stimulate the dormant capabilities we possess, and to improve the knowledge and taste of our countrymen.

"The gracious patronage and presence of Her Majesty and your Royal Highness cannot fail to aid materially these important objects, and demand what we most respectfully tender—our grateful and dutiful acknowledgments. We are deeply sensible of the condescension which has induced Her Majesty and your Royal Highness to give so effective a proof of approbation to our humble efforts for the improvements of Ireland.

"We feel bound to attribute to an honoured and enterprising individual the merit of having enabled this Committee to co-operate with the Royal Dublin Society in giving a character of more than usual prominence to their Triennial Exhibition of Manufactures which was to be held this year, and of having erected this Temple of Industry which Her Majesty and your Royal Highness now grace by your presence.

"Of the practical value of Exhibitions it is unnecessary to dilate in the presence of your Royal Highness, who has so ably advocated their public utility; but we may be allowed to direct your attention to a distinguished peculiarity of the Exhibition of 1853, which extends the principle laid down by the Royal Commission of 1851, so as to include Painting, the highest order of the Arts, and also examples of the industrial and artistic products of bygone ages, whereby their progressive advance can be traced from the earliest times to the present.

"We fervently desire that Her Majesty and your Royal Highness may long and frequently enjoy such displays of peaceful industry as are now presented; and that each repeated royal visit may find Ireland improving in arts and manufactures, affording fresh sources of gratification to Her Majesty and your Royal Highness, and additional bonds of gratitude to Her Majesty's person and throne."

To the foregoing Address His Royal Highness replied as follows:—

"GENTLEMEN,—I thank you most sincerely for your very kind and gratifying Address.

"It is with more than ordinary satisfaction that I again find myself in this city at a time when the energy of the Irish people, aided by the noble liberality, which you so justly commend, of a single individual, has opened to the world an Exhibition, in which I rejoice to hear from you that articles of native produce, and of native art and industry, occupy so large a space.

"Most cordially do I respond to the prayer with which you conclude, that each succeeding visit of the Queen may find Ireland advanced in Art, in Agriculture, and, I would add, in the comfort, happiness, and prosperity of her people."

The Addresses of the Corporation are also deserving of a place here, from their connexion with the Exhibition, and having been presented in the Building. The following is a copy of that presented to the Queen:—

"MAY IT PLEASE YOUR MAJESTY,—We, the Lord Mayor, Aldermen, and Burgesses of the city of Dublin, approach your Majesty to tender our congratulations on your safe arrival in this country, and our assurances of devoted loyalty and attachment to your Majesty's throne and person.

"We recognise in your Majesty's gracious visit to this Temple of Industry and Art, dedicated by munificent patriotism to the service and instruction of Ireland, an additional proof of your Majesty's solicitude to promote the interest and prosperity of your Irish subjects.

"To encourage the industry, to foster the energies, to inspirit the enterprise of a people, are amongst the most exalted duties and the dearest prerogatives of a Constitutional Sovereign. History will record, as we are gratefully reminded to-day, that these had been the proud characteristics of your Majesty's peaceful and glorious reign.

"It is not, may it please your Majesty, to the evidences of triumphant genius by which you are surrounded that we desire especially to entreat your Majesty's attention; these are but the emblems of the new era which they are here to inaugurate, and of the new spirit which has happily been evoked in Ireland.

"It will be more grateful to your Majesty to be assured that our countrymen, of every class, at length appreciate the truth, that energy, perseverance, and self-reliance are the best foundations of individual and national prosperity; while with humble gratitude we rejoice to add, that the same All-wise Disposer of human events, who but a few years since visited this island with unprecedented calamity, now deigns to smile on the industrial struggles of our people, and that in every quarter of the land can be seen indications of steadily progressive improvement.

"That improvement, under the favour of Divine Providence, will but be promoted by the most extended communication between the two parts of the United Kingdom; and we venture to entreat your Majesty's patronage and support for every practical effort to achieve this great national object.

"Permit us, most Gracious Sovereign, to express an ardent hope that every increased facility of communication between the two islands will the better enable your Majesty to gratify the affections, and promote the material welfare of your Irish subjects, by frequent visits to our shores.

"Your Majesty may be assured that, throughout your wide dominions, there are none more dutiful, more loyal to their Sovereign, none more devotedly attached to your Majesty."

Her Majesty's reply to the foregoing Address was as under:—

"I accept, with sincere pleasure, your congratulations on my safe arrival in this country; and I receive with the greatest satisfaction your assurances of devoted loyalty and attachment.

"It is my anxious desire to encourage the industry of my Irish subjects, and to promote the full development of the great natural resources of Ireland; and I share with you in the confident belief that the striking display of beautiful productions of Art and of Industry by which I am surrounded is to be appreciated not only as evidence of successful genius, but as a happy manifestation of that persevering energy which, under the blessing of Divine Providence, is an unfailing source of national prosperity."

In the Address from the Corporation to His Royal Highness Prince Albert, a graceful compliment is paid to the position which he occupied in connexion with the Great Exhibition of 1851:—

"May it please your Royal Highness,—We, the Lord Mayor, Aldermen, and Burgesses of the City of Dublin, approach your Royal Highness on your arrival in this country to offer the assurances of our profound respect.

"We rejoice to be afforded the opportunity of testifying in this Hall those sentiments in which we participate with every class of our fellow-countrymen.

"Emanating directly from a patriotism unparalleled in the history of our country, this Great Exhibition is still the result of that wisdom and genius which have marked your Royal Highness's distinguished career.

"To you belongs the grand idea of arousing the intelligence of the world in a generous competition to promote the Arts of Industry and Peace, and we congratulate your Royal Highness on the glorious scene around you, which presents a practical proof that your teaching and example have not been in vain.

"We devoutly pray that your Royal Highness may long be spared to foster and support the new spirit which you have called into existence, and to promote the arts of civilization and peace amongst all classes of the people of these realms.

To the foregoing Address His Royal Highness replied in the following terms:—

"My Lord Mayor and Gentlemen,—Your cordial and flattering reception demands my warmest acknowledgments.

"It is with peculiar satisfaction that I have received the gratifying expressions of your kind feelings towards me, under the roof of a Building dedicated to the promotion of the arts of civilization and peace, amongst all classes of the people of these kingdoms and of the world; and I truly rejoice to think that in promoting such objects you take the surest method of advancing that which I, in common with yourselves, have deeply at heart—I mean the prosperity of Ireland."

The royal visit on this occasion was, for the most part, one of ceremony; but on the mornings of the three following days Her Majesty and His Royal Highness Prince Albert, accompanied by the Prince of Wales and Prince Alfred, visited the Exhibition, and minutely inspected its contents, going regularly through the several departments. These visits took place at an early hour, before the public were admitted, the Exhibiters being in attendance for the purpose of giving any required explanation.

In the further progress of the Exhibition there is little calling for special observation in this place. Towards the close, the rate of admission was reduced to 6*d*., particulars of which will be found in detail in a succeeding page. As in the case of the Hyde Park Exhibition, increasing numbers continued to visit it until the close, which for some weeks before had been announced to take place on Monday, the 31st of October. The attendance on the previous Saturday reached the large number of 23,116 persons. Within the last few days of the closing, a strong feeling was manifested in favour of keeping the Building open another week, for the accommodation of large numbers of persons, especially of the working class, who had not previously opportunities, or had neglected them, of visiting the Exhibition. An urgent appeal was made to this effect to the Executive Committee, but the public notification having taken place, and the arrangements for the closing ceremonial having been made, it was considered by the Committee that it would not be keeping with the public that good faith which had hitherto characterized all proceedings connected with the Exhibition, to accede to such an application. The fiat had gone forth, and could not be reversed.

The closing ceremonial on the 31st of October was witnessed by over 12,000 persons; some of whom were there for the first time, but many others were present to get a last look of the almost fairy scene, the contemplation of which had for months previous afforded so much gratification, and, it may be added, supplied so much useful information. Through the instrumentality of the Exhibition the season had been rendered one of unusual brilliancy and attraction in Dublin, and that which had been the occasion of all was about to pass away as a dream, without leaving even a vestige behind to indicate the peaceful triumph of industry which had been achieved. As the hour drew nigh for the closing ceremonial, four o'clock, P.M., the examination in detail of the numerous objects of attraction was abandoned, and last lingering looks were taken at the *coup d'œil* which surrounded the visitors. How different the feelings of that moment from those which crowded themselves upon the mind at the opening? Then, all was joyous anticipation. Faint glimpses of the rich intellectual banquet provided had been caught, which only increased the feeling of impatience to participate more largely of it. Now, all was about to pass away. The last act of the great drama of 1853—that which ever after must shed a lustre on Ireland, and which had already materially improved her position in the estimation of surrounding nations—was drawing to a close. The curtain was about to fall amid enthusiastic demonstrations of applause as to the character of the performance—clouded, no doubt, by the anticipation that in another moment all would be at an end. At that moment the full value of the obligation which the founder of the Exhibition had conferred upon his country came to be duly estimated. At the opening, all was, to some extent, a brilliant promise; at the close, the fruit had been enjoyed.

A musical performance was deemed the most fitting mode of bringing the Exhibition to a termination; the ceremonial on the occasion somewhat resembling that of the opening. The semicircular space beneath the great organ was converted into an orchestra, which accommodated upwards of 500 performers, under the direction of Mr. Joseph Robinson. A dais, covered with scarlet cloth, was erected in front of the orchestra, and thereon were placed two handsome chairs, for the Lord Lieutenant and the Countess of St. Germans. Surrounding the dais were large numbers of distinguished personages. On either side were several military bands, to assist in the orchestral performance. The following was the programme; and it is unnecessary to add, that the manner in which it was gone through left nothing to be desired by the most fastidious:—

| | |
|---|---|
| The Hundreth Psalm, as at the Inauguration—Organ and Orchestra, . . | Arranged by *J. Robinson.* |
| The Heavens are telling—Organ and Orchestra, . . . . . . . . . . | *Haydn.* |
| The Exhibition Grand March—Military Bands, . . . . . . . . . . | *R. P. Stewart,* Mus. D. |
| Grand Hallelujah Chorus—Organ and Orchestra, . . . . . . . . . . | *Handel.* |
| March from Athalie—Military Bands, . . . . . . . . . . . . . . | *Mendelssohn.* |

On the termination of the musical performance, Mr. Cusac P. Roney, the active and energetic Secretary of the Exhibition, was introduced to the Lord Lieutenant by the Chairman of the Executive Committee; and thereupon he received the honour of knighthood amidst the cordial greeting of those present, and the hearty congratulations of his friends.

The ceremonial was then concluded by His Excellency formally declaring the Exhibition to be closed; and in doing so he said:—"I cannot declare the Great Industrial Exhibition of 1853 to be closed, without expressing an earnest wish for the health, happiness, and prosperity of the man to whom we are all indebted for the instruction we have received from the many productions of Art and Nature which are contained within these walls. I also desire to acknowledge the liberality of the owners of those treasures, for permitting them to be exhibited. Let me also pay a tribute of praise to the Committee, the Secretaries, and the other Officers connected with it, for the zeal, the assiduity, and the intelligence with which they have discharged their many duties. Lastly, let me, in the name of this assembly, offer to Almighty God our heartfelt thanks for having blessed and prospered this undertaking."

Having now briefly traced the history of the Exhibition of 1853, it only remains to consider how far it fulfilled its functions, and to note some of the peculiar circumstances connected with it; referring the reader to the statistical statements herewith appended, for further information respecting the attendance of visitors, matters of finance, and several other particulars.

A distinguishing characteristic of the Irish Exhibition was, the manner in which it was got up; in which respect it was unique. Those interested in such matters will recollect, that in the preliminary arrangements for the London Exhibition, the chief difficulty was to obtain the necessary funds to insure the originators of it from pecuniary loss. This was attempted, in the first instance, through the agency of a private firm embarking in the undertaking as a commercial speculation; but it was soon ascertained that the arrangement then entered into was founded upon a very imperfect idea of the requirements of the enterprise; and after being completed, the agreement to that effect had to be abandoned. The next expedient was an appeal to the public, more especially to those likely to become Exhibiters, for subscriptions, to form the necessary preliminary fund to save the promoters harmless; in this way, a sum of £67,896 was actually paid in to the credit of the Royal Commissioners, and which nearly covered the building contract with Messrs. Fox and Henderson. Although, therefore, a large surplus was available at the close of the Exhibition of 1851, it will be seen, that as a starting-point, it was deemed necessary to obtain pecuniary aid from the public, to such an extent as would meet any possible deficiency that might arise. In like manner, when the Cork Exhibition of 1852 was determined on, a similar policy was pursued; the amount of subscriptions obtained going far to defray the expenses of the building department. Unlike, therefore, all previous efforts in the same direction, where a large expenditure was involved, it has already been seen that the Exhibition to which these pages are devoted owed its origin solely to the public spirit of a single individual; who, when he saw the opportunity for making a great movement for the improvement of the country, determined that the necessary funds should not be wanting, whatever might be the risk thereby involved. By its connexion with the Royal Dublin Society, and by vesting the management of it in an Executive Committee composed of men of high character and station, an appearance of nationality was, as it were, imparted to the Exhibition, while in reality it was a private undertaking, its founder being the only party responsible for any loss that might accrue; though nothing could possibly be gained thereby, as any surplus left, after defraying all necessary charges, was to be devoted to some work of public utility. This, then, is one of the peculiar features of the late Exhibition, and one, moreover, which smoothed many of those difficulties incidental to any undertaking of the kind, where so many persons are to be conciliated whose interests may be, in some degree, conflicting. If an Exhibiter felt that he had anything to complain of in the arrangements connected with his department, or if any regulation was made which seemed to bear hard on particular individuals—all was submitted to with a good grace, lest any apparent opposition might interfere with the success of the Exhibition, in which almost every one felt a sort of personal interest, in the hope that Mr. Dargan might be no loser thereby. This feeling of the Exhibiters towards the founder of the Exhibition was not less cordially testified during its progress, than by the banquet with which they celebrated its closing. Each and all appreciated the generous munificence to which they were indebted for the great cosmopolitan demonstration in which they had the opportunity of taking part; and which is likely to be the last of the kind in the United Kingdom during the present generation.

On looking over the financial statement, to be found in a succeeding page, it will be seen that in one respect the Exhibition has not been so successful as could have been wished, inasmuch as it has entailed on the founder of it a considerable pecuniary loss. For some time past, it has been generally supposed that such would be the case; still the official announcement of the fact will not be received with the less regret by the public. So far as regards Mr. Dargan himself, we believe this to be wholly an immaterial consideration. The manner in which he, from time to time, made one advance after another, until the £20,000, supposed in the first instance to be sufficient, was increased to four times that sum, showed that in his estimation, the pecuniary success of the Exhibition was a secondary affair—that, in short, any feeling of this kind should not be allowed to stand in the way of every necessary requirement being supplied. The attainment of the object in view was not to be measured by the loss of a few thousand pounds; and at the Exhibitors' Banquet the Chairman of the Executive Committee announced that Mr. Dargan was perfectly satisfied with the result of the Exhibition in a pecuniary point of view, though it was then well known that the accounts would show a considerable deficiency. But still the public will not the less regret that the balance is not the other way, or that the act which conferred so much honour on the country, and, it may be added, such signal advantages, should have been attended by any pecuniary sacrifice whatever.

Although unsuccessful in a department which by many persons may be regarded as of primary import, the Exhibition has otherwise gone far to realize the most sanguine anticipations that could have been formed regarding it. That it accelerated the progress of improvement which had previously set in, is beyond question. It has done much to make the people of other countries acquainted with the capabilities of Ireland, with the resources which she possesses, and the extent to which they are developed; and of the thousands of strangers whom it has brought to our shores, several have already become settlers amongst us. It has shown the departments of industry in which we excel, as well as those in which we are deficient—and that on evidence not to be questioned—in either case affording incentives to further exertion. So far as the great body of the Exhibiters are concerned, it has been eminently successful; as, through the absence of all severe restrictions on the part of the Committee, in the way of affixing prices or disposing of their goods, a large amount of business was transacted—indeed, through the Exhibition, we have reason to know that many persons have made what to them are fortunes. And further, the Exhibition has been of essential service, by the extent to which it enforced the value of persistent and well-directed industry and self-reliance—those qualities, the absence of which amongst us has hitherto been so much lamented. In the addresses presented to the Queen, Prince Albert, and the Lord Lieutenant, to be found in preceding pages, the extent to which this doctrine is referred to is worthy of note, and is in the highest degree significant; while gratifying testimony is borne to its now being generally recognised and acted upon. In this point of view, therefore, the lessons taught by the Exhibition will bring forth good fruit. Nor must we omit to mention, that amongst the more tangible immediate results of the Exhibition is the founding of a Gallery of the Fine Arts, which may be said to have sprung out of the magnificent collection in that department—an Institution which has already been open to the public; which in all time to come cannot fail to serve as a gratifying memento of the great demonstration out of which it originated; and which is destined to confer substantial advantages upon a people proverbial for their appreciation and love of Art.

That the arrangements of the Executive Committee were generally satisfactory to the Exhibiters may also be inferred from the enthusiasm with which the Exhibiters' Banquet to Mr. Dargan and the members of the Committee was got up. That great demonstration was among the gratifying incidents of the Exhibition; and so anxiously was the opportunity seized for paying such an appropriate compliment, that many parties came from distant parts of England and Scotland to attend on the occasion. We the more readily refer to this topic, on account of the clamour so needlessly raised by some discontented persons whose province seems to be for ever to find fault, and by others who have been disappointed in their expectations, and who, in consequence, are seldom at a loss to find parties to whom to attach all the blame. Now that the whole proceedings can be reviewed in connexion with the experience derived therefrom, it is easy to perceive where improvements might have been introduced; but this is manifestly an unfair way to come to a conclusion, as all past events are solely to be judged by the extent of information available at the time. However excellent may be the arrangements for any such demonstration as that which so recently took place on Leinster Lawn, Exhibiters are not thereby relieved of the responsibility of looking after their property; and if, through carelessness, they delegate this duty to other hands, they may calculate on some articles being missing, and on others getting injured. For this they have themselves to blame. The gentlemen comprising the Executive Committee devoted a large amount of time to working out the undertaking, for which they have by no means got the credit which they deserve. That the leading Officials also exerted themselves with diligence may be gathered from the testimony which is available on the subject. The Secretary was rewarded by having the honour of knighthood conferred upon him; the Assistant Secretary, Mr. Deane, on the close of the Exhibition, was offered an influential position at Sydenham as an acknowledgment of his persevering and successful exertions on behalf of our great Irish demonstration; and Mr. Jones, the chief Financial Officer, in addition to receiving a testimonial here, consisting of a handsome service of plate, was also rewarded by an appointment at Sydenham. In recording the history of the Exhibition these are circumstances which we would be scarcely justified in passing over without notice; and they afford a satisfactory answer to the carpings to which we have referred.

We now proceed to place some statistics connected with the Exhibition before the reader, commencing with an account of the sale of Season Tickets. The receipts in this Department were highly satisfactory; the number of season ticket-holders being as large as could reasonably have been expected. As compared with the returns of the Exhibition of 1851, the account contained in the following page presents some curious features. The prices in London were respectively £3 3*s.* and £2 2*s.* for gentlemen's and ladies' tickets, and here, £2 2*s.* and £1 1*s.*; boys under fifteen years of age paying in the latter case the same as ladies. The total number of season tickets sold in 1851 was 25,605, of which 13,494 were gentlemen's, and 12,111 ladies' tickets; while here the total number was 12,952, of which there were only 4418 gentlemen's tickets. In London it will be seen, that among the holders of these tickets the gentlemen had a considerable majority; but here the ladies had nearly two to one. This is certainly a singular circumstance. The Table will also show the rate at which the sale progressed. The increased sales from the 5th to the 9th of July were owing to the rumoured royal visit, which was supposed to take place about that time; and again when the intention of her Majesty to visit the Exhibition was officially announced, a demand arose for the season tickets, from an impression that the holders of these only would be admissible on certain days.

TABLE SHOWING THE SALE OF SEASON TICKETS DURING THE EXHIBITION.

| DATE. | LADIES. | GENTLEMEN. | BOYS. | RECEIPTS. £ | s. | d. |
|---|---|---|---|---|---|---|
| Previous to opening, | 6208 | 3711 | 120 | 14437 | 10 | 0 |
| May 13, . . | 118 | 135 | 9 | 416 | 17 | 0 |
| " 14, . . | 64 | 29 | 5 | 133 | 7 | 0 |
| " 16, . . | 41 | 16 | 7 | 84 | 0 | 0 |
| " 17, . . | 100 | 36 | 0 | 180 | 12 | 0 |
| " 18, . . | 61 | 15 | 6 | 101 | 17 | 0 |
| " 19, . . | 50 | 27 | 4 | 113 | 8 | 0 |
| " 20, . . | 71 | 22 | 4 | 124 | 19 | 0 |
| " 21, . . | 72 | 22 | 4 | 126 | 0 | 0 |
| " 23, . . | 63 | 17 | 2 | 103 | 19 | 0 |
| " 24, . . | 59 | 22 | 1 | 109 | 4 | 0 |
| " 25, . . | 49 | 10 | 2 | 74 | 11 | 0 |
| " 26, . . | 35 | 7 | 4 | 55 | 13 | 0 |
| " 27, . . | 29 | 17 | 0 | 66 | 3 | 0 |
| " 28, . . | 28 | 8 | 1 | 47 | 5 | 0 |
| " 30, . . | 39 | 9 | 0 | 59 | 17 | 0 |
| " 31, . . | 36 | 12 | 0 | 63 | 0 | 0 |
| June 1, . . | 38 | 11 | 4 | 67 | 4 | 0 |
| " 2, . . | 30 | 13 | 0 | 58 | 16 | 0 |
| " 3, . . | 30 | 7 | 2 | 48 | 6 | 0 |
| " 4, . . | 40 | 10 | 0 | 63 | 0 | 0 |
| " 6, . . | 16 | 5 | 1 | 28 | 7 | 0 |
| " 7, . . | 20 | 5 | 2 | 33 | 12 | 0 |
| " 8, . . | 9 | 2 | 1 | 14 | 14 | 0 |
| " 9, . . | 14 | 1 | 0 | 16 | 16 | 0 |
| " 10, . . | 16 | 1 | 0 | 18 | 18 | 0 |
| " 11, . . | 24 | 3 | 0 | 31 | 10 | 0 |
| " 13, . . | 13 | 6 | 0 | 26 | 5 | 0 |
| " 14, . . | 12 | 4 | 0 | 21 | 0 | 0 |
| " 15, . . | 19 | 3 | 0 | 26 | 5 | 0 |
| " 16, . . | 20 | 5 | 0 | 31 | 10 | 0 |
| " 17, . . | 17 | 7 | 0 | 32 | 11 | 0 |
| " 18, . . | 17 | 11 | 0 | 40 | 19 | 0 |
| " 20, . . | 8 | 6 | 0 | 21 | 0 | 0 |
| " 21, . . | 11 | 1 | 0 | 13 | 13 | 0 |
| " 22, . . | 16 | 2 | 1 | 22 | 1 | 0 |
| " 23, . . | 12 | 5 | 1 | 24 | 3 | 0 |
| " 24, . . | 15 | 1 | 0 | 17 | 17 | 0 |
| " 25, . . | 3 | 1 | 1 | 6 | 6 | 0 |
| " 27, . . | 2 | 0 | 1 | 3 | 3 | 0 |
| " 28, . . | 7 | 1 | 0 | 9 | 9 | 0 |
| " 29, . . | 4 | 2 | 0 | 8 | 8 | 0 |
| " 30, . . | 9 | 1 | 0 | 11 | 11 | 0 |
| July 1, . . | 6 | 2 | 0 | 10 | 10 | 0 |
| " 2, . . | 8 | 1 | 0 | 10 | 10 | 0 |
| " 4, . . | 6 | 0 | 0 | 6 | 6 | 0 |
| " 5, . . | 19 | 3 | 1 | 27 | 6 | 0 |
| " 6, . . | 25 | 6 | 0 | 38 | 17 | 0 |
| " 7, . . | 40 | 7 | 0 | 56 | 14 | 0 |
| " 8, . . | 19 | 2 | 0 | 24 | 3 | 0 |
| " 9, . . | 14 | 1 | 0 | 16 | 16 | 0 |
| " 11, . . | 9 | 2 | 1 | 14 | 14 | 0 |
| " 12, . . | 8 | 1 | 0 | 10 | 10 | 0 |
| " 13, . . | 4 | 0 | 0 | 4 | 4 | 0 |
| " 14, . . | 5 | 1 | 0 | 7 | 7 | 0 |
| " 15, . . | 7 | 2 | 0 | 11 | 11 | 0 |
| " 16, . . | 3 | 1 | 0 | 5 | 5 | 0 |
| " 18, . . | 5 | 1 | 0 | 7 | 7 | 0 |
| *Carried forward*, . . . | 7723 | 4259 | 185 | 17,247 | 6 | 0 |

| DATE. | LADIES. | GENTLEMEN. | BOYS. | RECEIPTS. £ | s. | d. |
|---|---|---|---|---|---|---|
| *Brought forward*, . . | 7723 | 4259 | 185 | 17,247 | 6 | 0 |
| July 19, . . | 4 | 2 | 0 | 8 | 8 | 0 |
| " 20, . . | 4 | 1 | 0 | 6 | 6 | 0 |
| " 21, . . | 2 | 1 | 0 | 4 | 4 | 0 |
| " 22, . . | 4 | 1 | 0 | 6 | 6 | 0 |
| " 23, . . | 9 | 2 | 0 | 13 | 13 | 0 |
| " 25, . . | 1 | 0 | 0 | 1 | 1 | 0 |
| " 26, . . | 4 | 1 | 0 | 6 | 6 | 0 |
| " 27, . . | 5 | 0 | 0 | 5 | 5 | 0 |
| " 28, . . | 2 | 1 | 0 | 4 | 4 | 0 |
| " 29, . . | 5 | 0 | 1 | 6 | 6 | 0 |
| " 30, . . | 5 | 2 | 0 | 9 | 9 | 0 |
| Aug. 1, . . | 6 | 1 | 0 | 8 | 8 | 0 |
| " 2, . . | 3 | 1 | 0 | 5 | 5 | 0 |
| " 3, . . | 5 | 0 | 0 | 5 | 5 | 0 |
| " 4, . . | 3 | 1 | 0 | 5 | 5 | 0 |
| " 5, . . | 9 | 1 | 0 | 11 | 11 | 0 |
| " 6, . . | 8 | 0 | 0 | 8 | 8 | 0 |
| " 8, . . | 9 | 0 | 1 | 10 | 10 | 0 |
| " 9, . . | 2 | 2 | 1 | 7 | 7 | 0 |
| " 10, . . | 2 | 0 | 0 | 2 | 2 | 0 |
| " 11, . . | 5 | 0 | 0 | 5 | 5 | 0 |
| " 12, . . | 4 | 0 | 0 | 4 | 4 | 0 |
| " 13, . . | 11 | 0 | 0 | 11 | 11 | 0 |
| " 15, . . | 5 | 2 | 0 | 9 | 9 | 0 |
| " 16, . . | 3 | 2 | 1 | 8 | 8 | 0 |
| " 17, . . | 10 | 5 | 0 | 21 | 0 | 0 |
| " 18, . . | 11 | 1 | 0 | 13 | 13 | 0 |
| " 19, . . | 8 | 1 | 0 | 10 | 10 | 0 |
| " 20, . . | 12 | 0 | 0 | 12 | 12 | 0 |
| " 22, . . | 14 | 2 | 0 | 18 | 18 | 0 |
| " 23, . . | 28 | 8 | 1 | 47 | 5 | 0 |
| " 24, . . | 23 | 6 | 0 | 36 | 15 | 0 |
| " 25, . . | 38 | 7 | 0 | 54 | 12 | 0 |
| " 26, . . | 63 | 12 | 1 | 92 | 8 | 0 |
| " 27, . . | 96 | 14 | 1 | 131 | 5 | 0 |
| " 29, . . | 148 | 50 | 2 | 262 | 10 | 0 |
| " 30, . . | 16 | 22 | 1 | 64 | 1 | 0 |
| " 31, . . | 1 | 1 | 0 | 3 | 3 | 0 |
| Sept. 1, . . | 1 | 0 | 0 | 1 | 1 | 0 |
| " 2, . . | 0 | 1 | 0 | 2 | 2 | 0 |
| " 3, . . | 0 | 1 | 0 | 2 | 2 | 0 |
| " 5, . . | 3 | 1 | 0 | 5 | 5 | 0 |
| " 7, . . | 0 | 1 | 0 | 2 | 2 | 0 |
| " 10, . . | 2 | 0 | 0 | 2 | 2 | 0 |
| " 12, . . | 10 | 0 | 0 | 10 | 10 | 0 |
| " 13, . . | 4 | 0 | 0 | 4 | 4 | 0 |
| " 17, . . | 0 | 1 | 0 | 2 | 2 | 0 |
| " 21, . . | 1 | 0 | 0 | 1 | 1 | 0 |
| " 22, . . | 1 | 0 | 0 | 1 | 1 | 0 |
| " 23, . . | 0 | 1 | 0 | 2 | 2 | 0 |
| " 26, . . | 1 | 0 | 0 | 1 | 1 | 0 |
| " 28, . . | 1 | 0 | 0 | 1 | 1 | 0 |
| " 29, . . | 1 | 0 | 0 | 1 | 1 | 0 |
| Oct. 3, . . | 1 | 0 | 0 | 1 | 1 | 0 |
| " 4, . . | 1 | 0 | 0 | 1 | 1 | 0 |
| " 10, . . | 0 | 1 | 0 | 2 | 2 | 0 |
| " 12, . . | 0 | 1 | 0 | 2 | 2 | 0 |
| " 31, . . | 1 | 1 | 0 | 3 | 3 | 0 |
| TOTAL, | 8339 | 4418 | 195 | 18,238 | 10 | 0 |

The Return commencing on the next page shows the rate of admission, the number of persons paying at the doors, the number of season ticket-holders, and the total number of persons of all classes admitted on each day, during the entire period the Exhibition remained open.

TABLE SHOWING RECEIPTS AND ATTENDANCE DAILY DURING THE EXHIBITION.

| DATE. | ENTRANCE FEE. | AMOUNT RECEIVED AT THE DOORS. | NUMBER OF PERSONS WHO VISITED THE BUILDING. | | | |
|---|---|---|---|---|---|---|
| | | | Paying at Doors. | With Season Tickets. | Total for Day, exclusive of Exhibitors. | Total for Day, including Exhibitors. |
| | s. d. | £ s. d. | | | | |
| May 12, Thursday, .... | .... | ........ | .... | 10138 | 10138 | 12000 |
| „ 13, Friday, ...... | 5 0 | 72 10 0 | 290 | 2833 | 3123 | The number of Exhibitors and Attendants admitted during this period was not reckoned at the Exhibitors' door; but, estimating the admissions at 1000 per day, the total number would be 28,000. |
| „ 14, Saturday, .... | 5 0 | 57 15 0 | 231 | 3209 | 3440 | |
| „ 16, Monday, ...... | 5 0 | 58 0 0 | 232 | 4882 | 5114 | |
| „ 17, Tuesday, ...... | 5 0 | 79 15 0 | 319 | 5385 | 5704 | |
| „ 18, Wednesday, ... | 5 0 | 70 10 0 | 282 | 4066 | 4348 | |
| „ 19, Thursday, .... | 5 0 | 61 0 0 | 244 | 3484 | 3728 | |
| „ 20, Friday, ...... | 5 0 | 83 0 0 | 332 | 4449 | 4781 | |
| „ 21, Saturday, .... | 5 0 | 73 15 0 | 295 | 4553 | 4848 | |
| „ 23, Monday, ...... | 2 6 | 91 15 0 | 734 | 4262 | 4996 | |
| „ 24, Tuesday, ...... | 2 6 | 105 7 6 | 843 | 3329 | 4172 | |
| „ 25, Wednesday, ... | 2 6 | 116 7 6 | 931 | 3824 | 4755 | |
| „ 26, Thursday, .... | 2 6 | 106 5 0 | 850 | 3355 | 4205 | |
| „ 27, Friday, ...... | 2 6 | 119 2 6 | 953 | 3829 | 4782 | |
| „ 28, Saturday, .... | 2 6 | 107 10 0 | 860 | 3602 | 4462 | |
| „ 30, Monday, ...... | 2 6 | 114 15 0 | 918 | 3953 | 4871 | |
| „ 31, Tuesday, ...... | 2 6 | 146 10 0 | 1172 | 3638 | 4810 | |
| June 1, Wednesday, ... | 2 6 | 156 17 6 | 1255 | 4214 | 5469 | |
| „ 2, Thursday, .... | 2 6 | 117 17 6 | 943 | 2956 | 3899 | |
| „ 3, Friday, ...... | 2 6 | 121 10 0 | 972 | 3150 | 4122 | |
| „ 4, Saturday, .... | 2 6 | 141 12 6 | 1133 | 4529 | 5662 | |
| „ 6, Monday, ...... | 1 0 | 156 16 0 | 3136 | 2640 | 5776 | |
| „ 7, Tuesday, ...... | 1 0 | 193 8 0 | 3868 | 2915 | 6783 | |
| „ 8, Wednesday, ... | 2 6 | 108 15 0 | 870 | 2348 | 3218 | |
| „ 9, Thursday, .... | 1 0 | 193 12 0 | 3872 | 2052 | 5924 | |
| „ 10, Friday, ...... | 1 0 | 183 15 0 | 3675 | 3126 | 6801 | |
| „ 11, Saturday, .... | 2 6 | 119 0 0 | 952 | 4754 | 5706 | |
| „ 13, Monday, ...... | 1 0 | 244 11 0 | 4891 | 3720 | 8611 | 9872 |
| „ 14, Tuesday, ...... | 1 0 | 201 6 0 | 4026 | 2610 | 6636 | 7492 |
| „ 15, Wednesday, ... | 2 6 | 121 2 6 | 969 | 3934 | 4903 | 5406 |
| „ 16, Thursday, .... | 1 0 | 252 17 0 | 5057 | 2772 | 7829 | 8742 |
| „ 17, Friday, ...... | 1 0 | 255 2 0 | 5102 | 3040 | 8142 | 9432 |
| „ 18, Saturday, .... | 2 6 | 186 17 6 | 1495 | 3690 | 5185 | 6878 |
| „ 20, Monday, ...... | 1 0 | 251 11 0 | 5031 | 1834 | 6865 | 7847 |
| „ 21, Tuesday, ...... | 1 0 | 250 1 0 | 5001 | 2982 | 7983 | 7227 |
| „ 22, Wednesday, ... | 2 6 | 138 17 6 | 1111 | 3704 | 4815 | 6043 |
| „ 23, Thursday, .... | 1 0 | 275 7 0 | 5507 | 1815 | 7322 | 7892 |
| „ 24, Friday, ...... | 1 0 | 209 17 0 | 4197 | 2448 | 6645 | 7548 |
| „ 25, Saturday, .... | 2 6 | 110 12 6 | 885 | 3227 | 4112 | 5403 |
| „ 27, Monday, ...... | 1 0 | 249 2 0 | 4982 | 2190 | 7172 | 7809 |
| „ 28, Tuesday, ...... | 1 0 | 228 6 0 | 4566 | 2645 | 7211 | 7932 |
| „ 29, Wednesday, ... | 1 0 | 153 18 0 | 3078 | 3030 | 6108 | 7214 |
| „ 30, Thursday, .... | 1 0 | 207 10 0 | 4150 | 1770 | 5920 | 7156 |
| July 1, Friday, ...... | 1 0 | 214 19 0 | 4299 | 2267 | 6566 | 7547 |
| „ 2, Saturday, .... | 2 6 | 124 15 0 | 998 | 3441 | 4439 | 5698 |
| „ 4, Monday, ...... | 1 0 | 279 18 0 | 5598 | 2272 | 7870 | 8743 |
| „ 5, Tuesday, ...... | 1 0 | 231 3 0 | 4623 | 2593 | 7216 | 8193 |
| „ 6, Wednesday, ... | 1 0 | 196 2 0 | 3922 | 2469 | 6391 | 7442 |
| „ 7, Thursday, .... | 1 0 | 255 4 0 | 5104 | 3537 | 8641 | 9437 |
| „ 8, Friday, ...... | 1 0 | 230 14 0 | 4614 | 2409 | 7023 | 8006 |
| „ 9, Saturday, .... | 2 6 | 97 7 6 | 779 | 2712 | 3491 | 4329 |
| „ 11, Monday, ...... | 1 0 | 281 2 0 | 5622 | 2602 | 8224 | 9743 |
| „ 12, Tuesday, ...... | 1 0 | 248 19 0 | 4979 | 2014 | 6993 | 8556 |
| „ 13, Wednesday, ... | 1 0 | 251 0 0 | 5020 | 2546 | 7566 | 8207 |
| *Carried forward*, .... | ... | 8705 2 6 | 185,768 | 179,748 | 315,516 | 431,779 |

| Date. | Entrance Fee. | | Amount received at the Doors. | | | Number of Persons who visited the Building. | | | |
|---|---|---|---|---|---|---|---|---|---|
| | | | | | | Paying at Doors. | With Season Tickets. | Total for Day, exclusive of Exhibiters. | Total for Day, including Exhibiters. |
| | s. | d. | £ | s. | d. | | | | |
| *Brought forward,* . . . . | . . . | | 8705 | 2 | 6 | 135,768 | 179,748 | 315,516 | 431,779 |
| July 14, Thursday, . . . . | 1 | 0 | 262 | 12 | 0 | 5252 | 2705 | 7957 | 9116 |
| „ 15, Friday, . . . . . | 1 | 0 | 252 | 8 | 0 | 5043 | 2393 | 7436 | 8617 |
| „ 16, Saturday, . . . . | 2 | 6 | 128 | 10 | 0 | 1028 | 1548 | 2576 | 3302 |
| „ 18, Monday, . . . . . | 1 | 0 | 304 | 7 | 0 | 6087 | 2086 | 8173 | 9017 |
| „ 19, Tuesday, . . . . . | 1 | 0 | 254 | 11 | 0 | 5091 | 4589 | 9680 | 10079 |
| „ 20, Wednesday, . . . | 1 | 0 | 249 | 1 | 0 | 4981 | 2369 | 7350 | 8763 |
| „ 21, Thursday, . . . . | 1 | 0 | 263 | 14 | 0 | 5274 | 3099 | 8373 | 9489 |
| „ 22, Friday, . . . . . | 1 | 0 | 227 | 8 | 0 | 4548 | 2168 | 6716 | 7397 |
| „ 23, Saturday, . . . . | 2 | 6 | 97 | 5 | 0 | 778 | 2356 | 3134 | 3642 |
| „ 25, Monday, . . . . . | 1 | 0 | 301 | 15 | 0 | 6035 | 2085 | 8120 | 9134 |
| „ 26, Tuesday, . . . . . | 1 | 0 | 192 | 9 | 0 | 3849 | 1083 | 4932 | 6016 |
| „ 27, Wednesday, . . . | 1 | 0 | 222 | 13 | 0 | 4453 | 1360 | 5813 | 6714 |
| „ 28, Thursday, . . . . | 1 | 0 | 256 | 4 | 0 | 5124 | 2173 | 7297 | 8014 |
| „ 29, Friday, . . . . . | 1 | 0 | 241 | 17 | 0 | 4837 | 1922 | 6759 | 7942 |
| „ 30, Saturday, . . . . | 2 | 6 | 89 | 17 | 6 | 719 | 1788 | 2507 | 3322 |
| Aug. 1, Monday, . . . . . | 1 | 0 | 267 | 10 | 0 | 5350 | 2028 | 7378 | 8135 |
| „ 2, Tuesday, . . . . . | 1 | 0 | 243 | 2 | 0 | 4862 | 2111 | 6973 | 8043 |
| „ 3, Wednesday, . . . | 1 | 0 | 245 | 6 | 0 | 4906 | 2144 | 7050 | 8094 |
| „ 4, Thursday, . . . . | 1 | 0 | 247 | 1 | 0 | 4941 | 2016 | 6957 | 7463 |
| „ 5, Friday, . . . . . . | 1 | 0 | 254 | 1 | 0 | 5081 | 1848 | 6929 | 7717 |
| „ 6, Saturday, . . . . | 2 | 6 | 115 | 0 | 0 | 920 | 2424 | 3344 | 4104 |
| „ 8, Monday, . . . . . | 1 | 0 | 376 | 6 | 0 | 7526 | 2076 | 9602 | 10416 |
| „ 9, Tuesday, . . . . . | 1 | 0 | 281 | 18 | 0 | 5638 | 1884 | 7522 | 8207 |
| „ 10, Wednesday, . . . | 1 | 0 | 259 | 17 | 0 | 5197 | 1831 | 7028 | 7879 |
| „ 11, Thursday, . . . . | 1 | 0 | 284 | 16 | 0 | 4696 | 1843 | 6539 | 7383 |
| „ 12, Friday, . . . . . | 1 | 0 | 260 | 12 | 0 | 5212 | 1808 | 7020 | 7932 |
| „ 13, Saturday, . . . . | 2 | 6 | 121 | 17 | 6 | 975 | 2283 | 3258 | 3703 |
| „ 15, Monday, . . . . . | 1 | 0 | 742 | 18 | 0 | 14858 | 2041 | 16899 | 18103 |
| „ 16, Tuesday, . . . . . | 1 | 0 | 270 | 8 | 0 | 5408 | 733 | 6141 | 6858 |
| „ 17, Wednesday, . . . | 1 | 0 | 229 | 19 | 0 | 4599 | 897 | 5496 | 6914 |
| „ 18, Thursday, . . . . | 1 | 0 | 232 | 4 | 0 | 4644 | 1641 | 6285 | 8116 |
| „ 19, Friday, . . . . . . | 1 | 0 | 211 | 4 | 0 | 4224 | 1686 | 5910 | 6512 |
| „ 20, Saturday, . . . . | 2 | 6 | 121 | 7 | 6 | 971 | 2132 | 3103 | 3812 |
| „ 22, Monday, . . . . . | 1 | 0 | 328 | 6 | 0 | 6566 | 1610 | 8176 | 9416 |
| „ 23, Tuesday, . . . . . | 1 | 0 | 222 | 9 | 0 | 4449 | 1708 | 6157 | 7091 |
| „ 24, Wednesday, . . . | 1 | 0 | 280 | 5 | 0 | 5605 | 1851 | 7456 | 8487 |
| „ 25, Thursday, . . . . | 1 | 0 | 300 | 19 | 0 | 6019 | 1663 | 7682 | 8704 |
| „ 26, Friday, . . . . . | 1 | 0 | 349 | 10 | 0 | 6990 | 2029 | 9019 | 10004 |
| „ 27, Saturday, . . . . | 2 | 6 | 182 | 17 | 6 | 1463 | 2454 | 3917 | 4763 |
| „ 29, Monday, . . . . . | 1 | 0 | 452 | 0 | 0 | 9040 | 4864 | 13904 | 15416 |
| „ 30, Tuesday, . . . . . | 2 | 6 | 105 | 10 | 0 | 844 | 2867 | 3711 | 3207 |
| „ 31, Wednesday, . . . | 1 | 0 | 200 | 19 | 0 | 4019 | 1719 | 5738 | 6219 |
| Sept. 1, Thursday, . . . . | 1 | 0 | 351 | 4 | 0 | 7024 | 2223 | 9247 | 10314 |
| „ 2, Friday, . . . . . | 1 | 0 | 357 | 10 | 0 | 7150 | 4008 | 11158 | 12016 |
| „ 3, Saturday, . . . . | 1 | 0 | 80 | 0 | 0 | 1600 | 1866 | 3466 | 4008 |
| „ 5, Monday, . . . . . | 1 | 0 | 304 | 18 | 0 | 6098 | 2328 | 8426 | 9418 |
| „ 6, Tuesday, . . . . . | 1 | 0 | 206 | 13 | 0 | 4133 | 2221 | 6354 | 7108 |
| „ 7, Wednesday, . . . | 1 | 0 | 221 | 13 | 0 | 4433 | 1987 | 6420 | 7814 |
| „ 8, Thursday, . . . . | 1 | 0 | 213 | 2 | 0 | 4262 | 1430 | 5692 | 5816 |
| „ 9, Friday, . . . . . | 1 | 0 | 217 | 18 | 0 | 4358 | 1955 | 6313 | 7602 |
| „ 10, Saturday, . . . . | 1 | 0 | 130 | 6 | 0 | 2606 | 1973 | 4579 | 5219 |
| „ 12, Monday, . . . . . | 1 | 0 | 248 | 4 | 0 | 4964 | 1642 | 6606 | 7173 |
| „ 13, Tuesday, . . . . . | 1 | 0 | 223 | 16 | 0 | 4476 | 1570 | 6046 | 6917 |
| „ 14, Wednesday, . . . | 1 | 0 | 212 | 12 | 0 | 4252 | 1384 | 5646 | 6741 |
| „ 15, Thursday, . . . . | 1 | 0 | 197 | 19 | 0 | 3959 | 1685 | 5644 | 6214 |
| „ 16, Friday, . . . . . . | 1 | 0 | 186 | 6 | 0 | 3726 | 1603 | 5329 | 5847 |
| „ 17, Saturday, . . . . | 1 | 0 | 161 | 14 | 0 | 3234 | 2293 | 5527 | 6341 |
| *Carried forward,* . . . . | . . . | | 22,501 | 6 | 6 | 400,145 | 297,826 | 697,971 | 863,529 |

| Date. | Entrance Fee. | | Amount received at the Doors. | | | Number of Persons who visited the Building. | | | |
|---|---|---|---|---|---|---|---|---|---|
| | | | | | | Paying at Doors. | With Season Tickets. | Total for Day, exclusive of Exhibiters. | Total for Day, including Exhibiters. |
| | s. | d. | £ | s. | d. | | | | |
| *Brought forward*, . . . . | . . . | | 22,501 | 6 | 6 | 400,145 | 297,826 | 697,971 | 863,529 |
| Sept. 19, Monday, . . . . . | 1 | 0 | 217 | 19 | 0 | 4359 | 1382 | 5741 | 6414 |
| „ 20, Tuesday, . . . . . | 1 | 0 | 162 | 2 | 0 | 3242 | 1351 | 4593 | 5204 |
| „ 21, Wednesday. . . . | 1 | 0 | 205 | 8 | 0 | 4108 | 1994 | 6102 | 6816 |
| „ 22, Thursday, . . . . | 1 | 0 | 178 | 15 | 0 | 3575 | 942 | 4517 | 5403 |
| „ 23, Friday, . . . . . . | 1 | 0 | 150 | 13 | 0 | 3013 | 1282 | 4295 | 4714 |
| „ 24, Saturday, . . . . | 1 | 0 | 127 | 17 | 0 | 2557 | 2131 | 4688 | 4957 |
| „ 26, Monday, . . . . . | 1 | 0 | 190 | 12 | 0 | 3812 | 1246 | 5058 | 5495 |
| „ 27, Tuesday, . . . . . | 1 | 0 | 144 | 6 | 0 | 2886 | 1236 | 4122 | 4904 |
| „ 28, Wednesday, . . . | 1 | 0 | 157 | 0 | 0 | 3140 | 1621 | 4761 | 5116 |
| „ 29, Thursday, . . . . | 1 | 0 | 126 | 1 | 0 | 2521 | 730 | 3251 | 3704 |
| „ 30, Friday, . . . . . . | 1 | 0 | 109 | 13 | 0 | 2193 | 1447 | 3640 | 4257 |
| Oct. 1, Saturday, . . . . | 1 | 0 | 93 | 8 | 0 | 1868 | 1742 | 3610 | 4317 |
| „ 3, Monday, . . . . . | 1 | 0 | 169 | 13 | 0 | 3393 | 1450 | 4843 | 5591 |
| „ 4, Tuesday, . . . . . | 1 | 0 | 130 | 8 | 0 | 2608 | 1053 | 3661 | 4219 |
| „ 5, Wednesday, . . . | 1 | 0 | 134 | 7 | 0 | 2687 | 1163 | 3850 | 4694 |
| „ 6, Thursday, . . . . | 1 | 0 | 105 | 17 | 0 | 2117 | 1094 | 3211 | 3514 |
| „ 7, Friday, . . . . . . | 1 | 0 | 104 | 14 | 0 | 2094 | 807 | 2901 | 3619 |
| „ 8, Saturday, . . . . | 1 | 0 | 109 | 16 | 0 | 2196 | 2859 | 5055 | 5918 |
| „ 10, Monday, . . . . . | 0 | 6 | 135 | 1 | 0 | 5402 | 1240 | 6642 | 7690 |
| „ 11, Tuesday, . . . . . | 0 | 6 | 105 | 8 | 0 | 4216 | 1233 | 5449 | 6119 |
| „ 12, Wednesday, . . . | 0 | 6 | 132 | 0 | 0 | 5280 | 1836 | 7116 | 7714 |
| „ 13, Thursday, . . . . | 0 | 6 | 126 | 14 | 6 | 5069 | 1485 | 6554 | 7162 |
| „ 14, Friday, . . . . . . | 0 | 6 | 113 | 13 | 0 | 4546 | 2167 | 6713 | 7793 |
| „ 15, Saturday, . . . . | 0 | 6 | 115 | 16 | 0 | 4632 | 2646 | 7278 | 8275 |
| „ 17, Monday, . . . . . | 0 | 6 | 206 | 17 | 6 | 8275 | 1354 | 9629 | 10214 |
| „ 18, Tuesday, . . . . . | 0 | 6 | 156 | 9 | 0 | 6258 | 2732 | 8990 | 9816 |
| „ 19, Wednesday, . . . | 0 | 6 | 91 | 11 | 6 | 3663 | 705 | 4368 | 5104 |
| „ 20, Thursday, . . . . | 0 | 6 | 139 | 16 | 0 | 5592 | 1980 | 7572 | 8482 |
| „ 21, Friday, . . . . . . | 0 | 6 | 102 | 13 | 0 | 4106 | 1356 | 5462 | 6074 |
| „ 22, Saturday, . . . . | 0 | 6 | 148 | 2 | 6 | 5925 | 3441 | 9366 | 10416 |
| „ 24, Monday, . . . . . | 0 | 6 | 248 | 12 | 0 | 9944 | 1818 | 11762 | 12508 |
| „ 25, Tuesday, . . . . . | 0 | 6 | 128 | 1 | 0 | 5122 | 1355 | 6477 | 6917 |
| „ 26, Wednesday, . . . | 0 | 6 | 258 | 2 | 0 | 10324 | 2780 | 13104 | 14117 |
| „ 27, Thursday, . . . . | 0 | 6 | 325 | 14 | 6 | 13029 | 997 | 14026 | 15104 |
| „ 28, Friday, . . . . . . | 0 | 6 | 354 | 0 | 6 | 14161 | 2732 | 16893 | 17863 |
| „ 29, Saturday, . . . . | 0 | 6 | 422 | 16 | 6 | 16913 | 5053 | 21966 | 23116 |
| „ 31, Monday, . . . . . | 2 | 6 | 550 | 2 | 6 | 4401 | 6657 | 11058 | 12500 |
| Total, . . . . | . . . | | 28,981 | 6 | 6 | 589,372 | 366,923 | 956,295 | 1,149,369 |

We have now the two great items of receipts—the proceeds of the sale of season tickets and of the payments at the doors for admission. By arrangements made with the railway companies excursion tickets were admissible, and a few of the English visitors availed themselves thereof. Towards the close, the Irish railway companies conveyed passengers to and from Dublin at very low rates, the railway ticket also including admission to the Exhibition; but this movement was unfortunately delayed until too late a period of the season to realize the expectations which might very reasonably have been formed regarding it. The entire amount received by the Committee, as the result of these arrangements, was the comparatively trifling sum of £1414 6*s.* 7*d.* The persons admitted in this way have been included in the Tabular Statement with those coming under the head of Exhibiters. A further source of income arose from the sale of admission tickets in the Office, for the convenience of employers who might desire to send their work-people; and from an early period of the Exhibition these were available, admitting without reference to date, but obtainable only on ten shillings' worth of tickets being purchased at a time. The amount received from this source was £767 16*s.* 6*d.* The entire sum, therefore, received for admission to the Exhibition was £49,401 19*s.* 7*d.*

Owing to the continuous arrivals of goods for some time after the Exhibition opened, the Official Catalogue was not ready for delivery to the public until the 31st of May. The sales for three weeks were thereby lost, still the entire number sold was fully what could fairly have been reckoned on, taking as a guide the Exhibition of 1851. On that occasion the entire number of visitors was 6,039,195, and the number of copies of the shilling edition of the Catalogue sold, 285,854; here the visitors amounted to 1,149,369, and the Shilling Catalogues sold to 50,123.

The following Account shows the disbursements and receipts connected with the Exhibition:—

STATEMENT OF DISBURSEMENTS AND RECEIPTS.

| Dr. Outlay. | £ | s. | d. | Receipts. | £ | s. | d. | Cr. £ | s. | d. |
|---|---|---|---|---|---|---|---|---|---|---|
| Salaries and wages, | £8442 | 12 | 9 | Season tickets, | | | | £18,238 | 10 | 0 |
| Travelling expenses, transport of goods, and foreign expenses, | 4982 | 11 | 4 | Receipts at door, | | | | 28,981 | 6 | 6 |
| Printing and advertising, | 4357 | 5 | 10 | Railway, excursion, and day tickets,† | | | | 2,182 | 8 | 1 |
| Office expenses, | 1740 | 2 | 6 | Proceeds of Catalogues, | | | | 2,928 | 0 | 3 |
| Furnishing Exhibition Building and offices, | 3314 | 16 | 6 | Rent of refreshment rooms, | | | | 550 | 0 | 0 |
| Wages of Police in care of Building, &c. | 2889 | 14 | 7 | Received for keeping sticks and parasols, | | | | 265 | 2 | 0 |
| Corporation for flagway in Merrion-square, | 200 | 0 | 0 | Received for use of retiring rooms, | | | | 52 | 18 | 4 |
| Ditto, for pipe-water, | 326 | 11 | 11 | Profit on sale of ticket cases, | | | | 23 | 1 | 4 |
| Gas, | 303 | 3 | 0 | Ditto, returned by Mr. Woodhouse on sale of medals in the Exhibition, | | | | 11 | 12 | 0 |
| Music, | 1510 | 0 | 5 | | | | | £53,232 | 18 | 6 |
| Payment to families of sufferers by the accident in the Building, | 275 | 10 | 10 | Value of Building, | £12,000 | 0 | 0 | | | |
| | | | | " Machinery, | 2,500 | 0 | 0 | | | |
| | £28,342 | 9 | 8 | " Water-closets, | 700 | 0 | 0 | | | |
| | | | | " Sundries, | 800 | 0 | 0 | | | |
| | | | | | | | | 16,000 | 0 | 0 |
| Cost of Building,* | 59,871 | 2 | 1 | Balance, | | | | 18,980 | 13 | 3 |
| | £88,213 | 11 | 9 | | | | | £88,213 | 11 | 9 |

I certify that the above statement of Disbursements and Receipts is correct.

HENRY BROWN,
Auditor of Accounts to the Committee,
3, *Ashbrook Terrace*.

*April* 7, 1854.

From the foregoing Statement it will be seen, that the deficiency in the receipts, as compared with the expenditure, is £18,980 13*s.* 3*d.* We may observe, that the sum which appears in the account as the value of the Building is that at which it was estimated by Mr. Lanyon, Mr. G. W. Hemans, and Mr. G. M. Miller, these gentlemen having consented to value it at the request of the Executive Committee. The other items of assets are those actually realized by the sale of the several articles.—J. S.

* Of this sum, there was paid in wages, £17,212 16*s.* 6*d.* distributed as follows:—carpenters, £8738 12*s.* 7*d.*; labourers, £4120 15*s.* 5*d.*; smiths, £344 3*s.* 2*d.*; masons, £613 1*s.*; sawyers, £1729 10*s.* 1*d.*; sundry labour, £421 0*s.* 10*d.*; engine men, £54 1*s.* 10*d.*; staff, £1191 11*s.* 7*d.* For timber there was paid, £20,074 7*s.* 2*d.*; and for iron and iron-work, £4374 0*s.* 5*d.* including the following items:—iron, £329 8*s.* 7*d.*; ironmongery, £523 9*s.*; iron-work, £2150 17*s.* 8*d.*; nails, £949 13*s.* 2*d.*; screws, £420 12*s.* The charge for plumbing was £488 19*s.* 4*d.*; for felt for roof, £1335 14*s.* 5*d.*; for glass and glazing, £1836 4*s.* 7*d.*; for cast-iron pillars, £1705 18*s.* 6*d.*; for paint and painting, £3573 1*s.* 10½*d.*; for sundry materials, £1778 5*s.* 9*d.*; for stationary engine and gearing, £2944 2*s.* 8*d.*; for water-closets, £716 13*s.* 8*d.* This amount also includes, contingencies, £2080 13*s.* 2½*d.*; architect's fee, £1200; premiums for designs for building, £100; insurance of building, pictures, &c., £450 4*s.*

† The sum paid to the Finance Committee of the Exhibition by the several Irish railway companies for the issue of admission tickets was thus distributed:—Dublin and Kingstown, £541 18*s.*; Great Southern and Western, £517 4*s.* 6*d.*; Dublin and Drogheda, £167 17*s.* 6*d.*; Dublin and Belfast Junction, £42 8*s.* 6*d.*; and the Midland Great Western, £65 19*s.*; making, in all, £1884 17*s.* 6*d.* derived from this source.

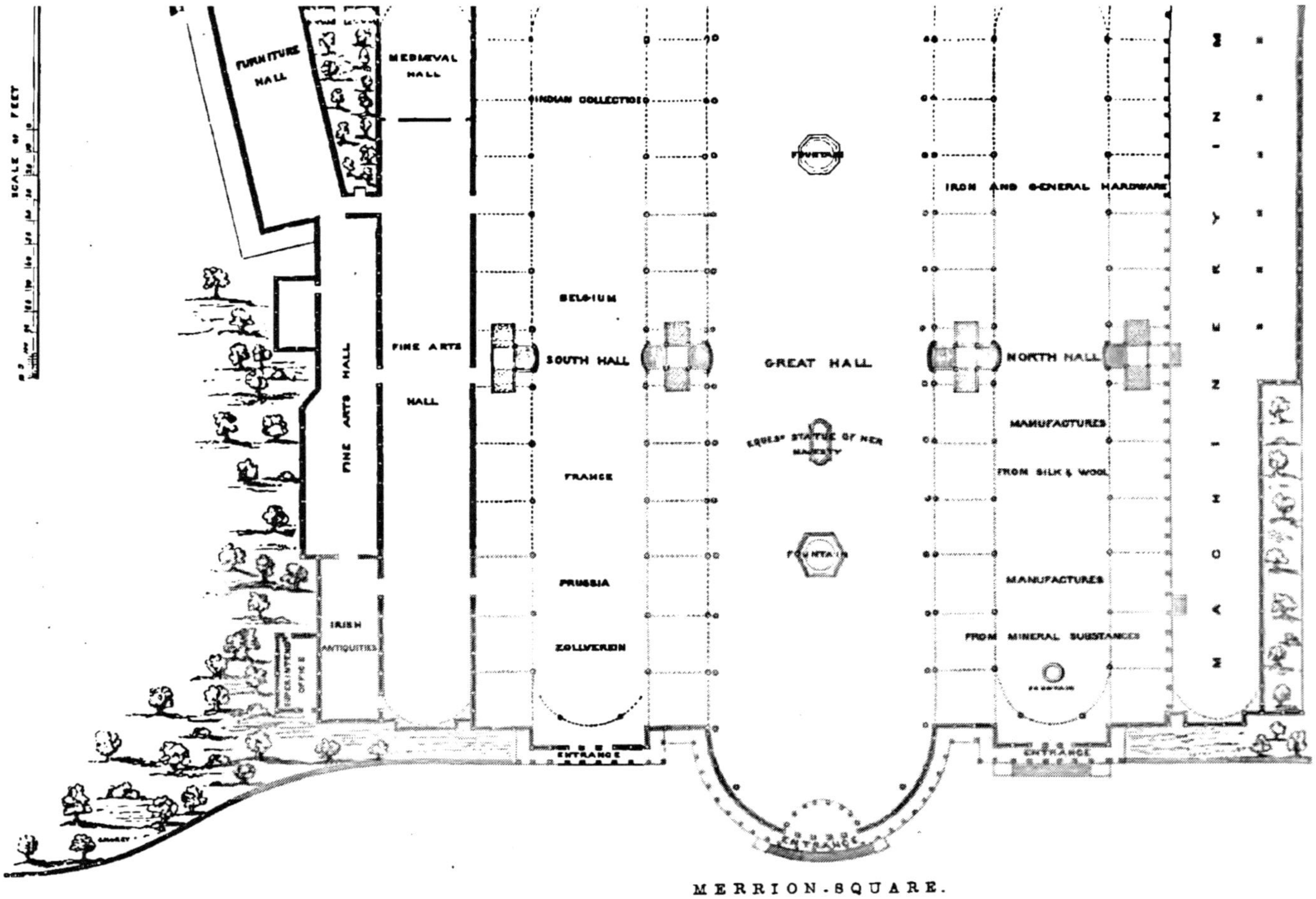
SCALE OF FEET
FURNITURE HALL
MEDIEVAL HALL
INDIAN COLLECTION
IRON AND GENERAL HARDWARE
FINE ARTS HALL
FINE ARTS HALL
BELGIUM
SOUTH HALL
GREAT HALL
NORTH HALL
FOUNTAIN
EQUESTN STATUE OF HER MAJESTY
FRANCE
PRUSSIA
ZOLLVEREIN
MANUFACTURES FROM SILK & WOOL
MANUFACTURES FROM MINERAL SUBSTANCES
IRISH ANTIQUITIES
SUPERINTENDS OFFICE
FOUNTAIN
M A C H I N E R Y I N M
ENTRANCE
ENTRANCE
ENTRANCE
MERRION-SQUARE.

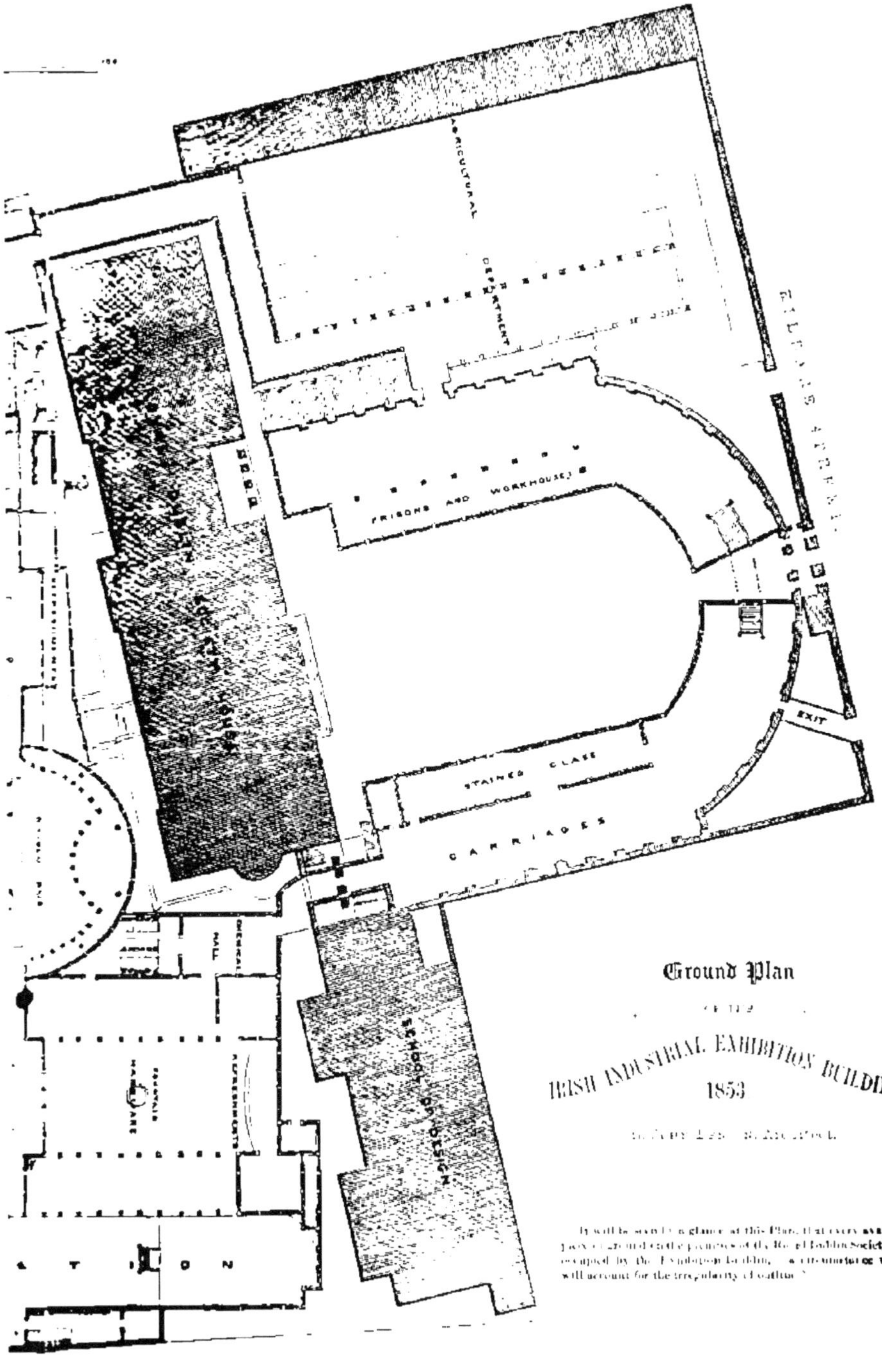


## Ground Plan

OF THE

## IRISH INDUSTRIAL EXHIBITION BUILDING, 1853

It will be seen by a glance at this Plan, that every available piece of ground on the premises of the Royal Dublin Society was occupied by the Exhibition building, — a circumstance which will account for the irregularity of outline.

# THE EXHIBITION BUILDING.

THE erection of Buildings of huge dimensions for temporary purposes may be said to have introduced a new order of architecture, whose development is pregnant with results which it is now difficult to estimate. The Exhibition Building in Hyde-Park impressed the spectator who saw it for the first time with a feeling of astonishment—the extent of the structure being so much greater than what could have been previously realized to the mind; and, as a *first* effort, it was undoubtedly entitled to much commendation. The combination of glass and iron, of which that Building mainly consisted, was then supposed to be the best that could be adopted, taking all the essential requisites into account—economy and facility of construction, combined with the smallest sacrifice in the value of the materials after being removed. But experience showed that notwithstanding the adaptation of these substances, so far as fulfilling some of the required conditions, the use of them was attended by great and serious drawbacks, which, perhaps, experience alone could have developed. It is, however, beyond question that the Crystal Palace showed that the materials of which it was composed could be effectively used to a much greater extent than they hitherto had been; and this has already been practically illustrated by what may truly be called the People's Palace at Sydenham, a structure which will long serve as a memorial of the enterprise and inventive powers of the age in which it was erected. But it was reserved for the architect of the Dublin Exhibition Building to show the adaptation of another material—wood—which, for any temporary purpose, is assuredly the best that could be employed—combining the required conditions to an extent possessed by no other. It can be used with facility; it is inexpensive; and afterwards it is of greater comparative value than any other substance. It further admits of any required degree of architectural effect being obtained, a desideratum which the use of glass can go a short way in securing. If, therefore, a triumph was achieved by Sir Joseph Paxton in the Exhibition Building of 1851, by indicating the extensive use to which a hitherto little employed material could be turned—a not less important triumph has been gained by Sir John Benson in the same direction. Taking a new path, and making use, also, of a hitherto little used material, our Irish architect has produced a building altogether unique; fulfilling in an extraordinary degree every desired condition; possessing a symmetry which could scarcely have been calculated on with such large dimensions; combining architectural expression and elegance; and indicating the path to be pursued on all future occasions in designing structures of a similar character.

The original design furnished by Sir John Benson consisted of the seven portions extending from the gallery adjoining the Fine Arts Hall, to that which runs along the Court for Machinery in Motion; all the other portions of it being subsequent additions. It will be seen on reference to the ground-plan that it required considerable ingenuity to procure the area required in so limited a site. A more imposing general effect would have been produced externally had it been possible to have presented the whole building in one general perspective; but this is the only subject of regret, and may well be disregarded, when the other great objects of the Exhibition were so fully attained.

Commencing with the Great Hall, it may be regarded as the finest apartment ever erected. Its dimensions are 425 feet long, 100 feet broad, and 105 feet high.* The roof is formed of semicircular main ribs 25 feet apart, resting on trusses (a portion of which forms the roof of the adjoining gallery), and connected by a

* The corresponding dimensions of the Transept of the Crystal Palace were—Length, 408 ft.; breadth, 72 ft; height, 107 ft.

F

trussed wall-plate, as we may term it, which also forms the support of the intermediate ribs. The portion of the first-mentioned truss immediately under the arched rib is supported by two cast-iron columns, five feet apart from centre to centre, which again fit, with turned bearings, into cast-iron bases secured to rubble blocks. By this arrangement it will be perceived that the roof of the gallery adjoining is constructed so as to act as a buttress, and transmit any tendency to an alteration of the figure of the main roof to the other portions of the building, and by their combined mass effectually to resist it.

The main ribs of this and the other arched roofs are strikingly novel in their construction. Some approximation had before been made to the use of circular arcs of timber in roof-construction, but only with success as long as they were merely auxiliary to ordinary trussing, as in the roof of the old Halle aux Blé at Paris, and that of a riding-school at Moscow; but we believe that on no former occasion had a roof been constructed whose strength consisted wholly of the inflexibility of timber arches in the direction of the radius, produced by the peculiar laminated structure adopted in this instance; the lamination being in planes parallel to the base (supposing each semicircle to be a portion of a cylinder), and not in concentric rings. This latter mode of construction is exceedingly liable to change of figure even under comparatively small amounts of pressure, and would, if adopted by Sir John Benson, have necessitated the use of numberless tie-bars, and other expedients to counteract that tendency; which would at once have seriously injured the harmony of general outline, and would have rendered the construction tedious, and barely possible, without very expensive scaffolding.

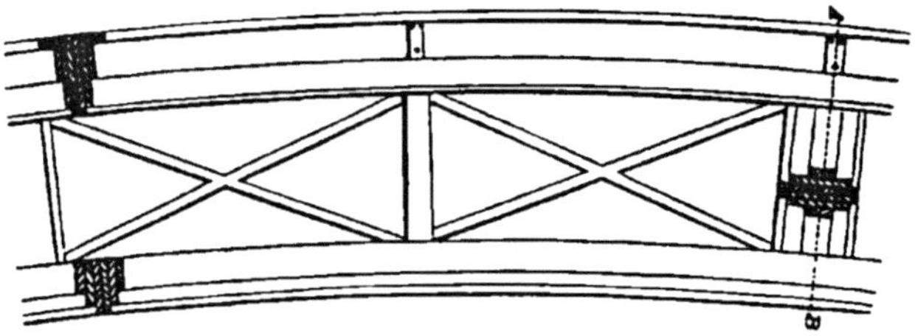


Portion of one of the Semicircular Ribs of Roof.

Above is an engraving of a portion of one of the ribs of the Great Hall, with sections represented by shading, to show the construction. It will be perceived that it consists of two concentric laminated ribs, bound together, and (what is equally essential) kept asunder by timber struts, assuming to some extent the lattice form—the lattice bars being also designed for effect, as well as being serviceable in the construction. The upper or outer rib consists of 10 laminæ, varying from 1½ inches to 2 inches in thickness, and from 4 inches to 18 inches in depth—the rule being observed of presenting the least quantity of material to resist compression, the greatest to resist extension. The breadth of the rib at top is 18 inches, and at bottom it is only 3 inches. The lower rib is formed of 1½ inch and 2 inch laminæ,—six in number,—and is 12 inches deep and 10 inches wide. The principal connecting struts, which occur at 25 feet apart (from centre to centre) are also laminated; each separated piece being connected by a splayed dove-tailed joint to the top and bottom ribs; and, to increase the stiffness of the connexion, a blade of boiler-plate iron, ¼ inch thick, is interposed in the centre. These peculiarities of construction will be more clearly seen by the accompanying illustration, which shows a section of the great rib taken through the principal strut, *A B*.

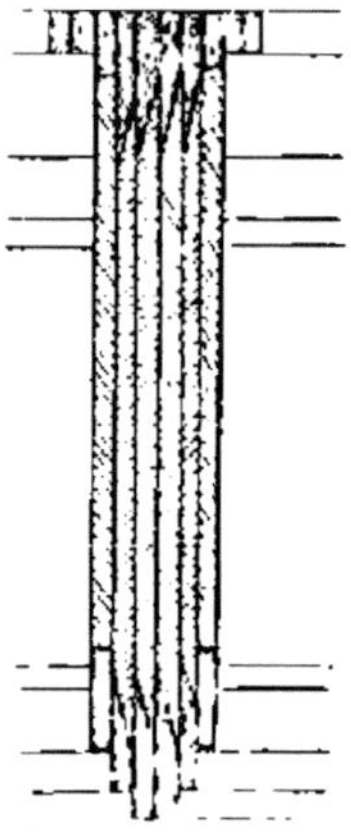

Section of one of the Great Ribs of the Roof

The process of preparing and putting together these monster ribs was exceedingly simple. Sufficiently large floors having been prepared, the outline of the full size was struck out on them. From it the necessary number of templets or gauges were prepared, and then the process was simply this:—The workmen brought the planks of the thicknesses required from the saw-pits; one set of carpenters marked on them the outlines of the templets; a second set sawed them out to the shape; a third set stitched the edges together (with nails,

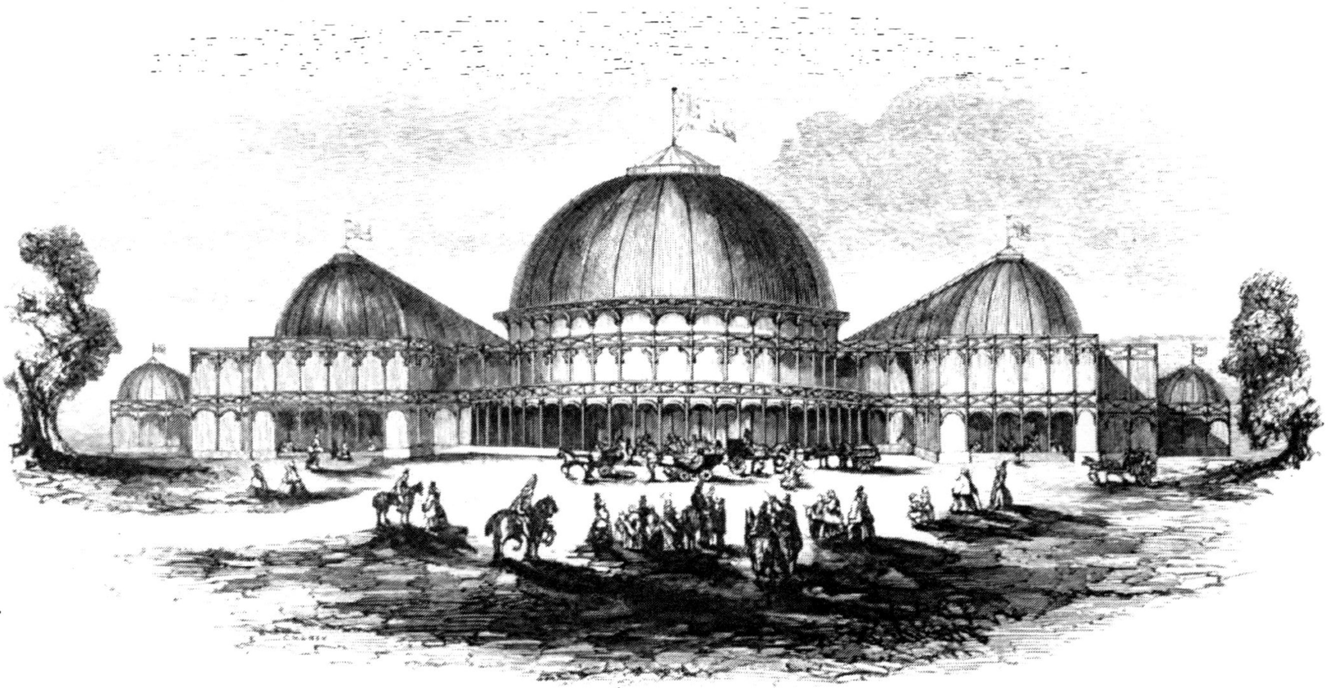

Front View of The Irish Industrial Exhibition Building.

not needles) to gain the requisite width, and planed them on the edges and exposed parts as required; a fourth set finished the adjustment on the prepared floor, and roughly secured them in their place with nails; while a fifth set bored the auger-holes, and screwed them firmly home. From each set of workmen being engaged in only one simple operation, the whole business was carried on with great accuracy and despatch. The final operation with the rib was fixing on the cast-iron sockets to receive the purlins. These sockets were screwed on the upper flange at 8 feet 3 inches apart from centre to centre. The rib was then ready for hoisting and fixing in its place; having occupied about 20 carpenters, sawyers, and labourers about four days; containing about 7 tons of timber, 1 cwt. of plate-iron, and about 1500 screws; and weighing, with the purlin sockets, nails, &c., nearly 9 tons.

The purlins, resting on the cast-iron sockets, are formed of a plank 12 inches deep, and 4 inches thick, with an additional piece, 4 inches square, applied on each side at the upper edge, making it T shaped. The ends were formed exactly to fit the iron sockets, and bored for the screw-bolts on the ground, leaving literally nothing to do to them, or with them, but to hoist them up, drop them into their places, and secure them by inserting an iron bolt, and screwing on its nut. Each purlin weighs about 6¼ cwt., is 25 feet long, and is intersected by minor ribs, which are laminated in eight thicknesses, corresponding with those of the main ribs. Having very little weight to bear, they are built hollow, but they are still important for affording nailing-room for the sheeting, and also for forming panels on the inner surface.

The construction of many of the circular portions of the Building involved some very nice problems of carpentry, the correct execution of which was of the very last importance, as the perspective effect of the several Halls depended on attention to these details. The slightest mistake or misfit would have remained a permanent eyesore. Among the most prominent portions were the purlins of the circular ends of the various Halls; for each series or tier of which a distinct and separate mould, representing a portion of the interior of the circular end of the roof, was required, and which, if inaccurate in the smallest degree, would have produced a painfully distorted effect. To the credit of the hands employed, these were all made and set in their places, fitting with the most perfect accuracy, without any opportunity of previously trying them.

Except the difference of dimensions, the various portions of the roofs of the minor Halls are precisely similar to those of the Centre Hall, and the mode of erecting and fitting the different parts in their places did not differ from that which has been already described.

The means employed to raise the first of the great ribs, which was the first whole rib at the western end of the Great Hall, were as follows:—It was first carried to and deposited in the immediate neighbourhood of its permanent position, the chord-line being somewhat diagonal to the building to allow room for lifting the arch, which was a little wider than the space between the Galleries. The operation of raising it to its place consisted of two branches: 1st, getting the arch on its legs; and, 2nd, elevating it to its position on the Building. Each of these had to be executed by the aid of special machinery, and was separate and distinct in itself, requiring its own precautions, and presenting its own risks and difficulties. For the first operation, —that of raising the arch from the horizontal to the vertical position, making it stand on its legs,—there was placed a pair of "sheer-legs" in the centre of the chord of the arch, from the top of which a rope was attached to the centre of the arch, which, being hauled, and the feet simultaneously kept in their position, the rib was gradually raised until it became upright. But this process, so rapidly described, occupied nearly a week for its consummation. With all the forethought that had been expended on the subject, one element, and, as far as this stage of the operation was concerned, a very important one, seems only to have been partially attended to. A peculiarity of all properly constructed beams is, that while each possesses the fullest required strength in the direction of the strains likely to occur to it in its ordinary functions, its strength in other directions is only accidental, and, generally speaking, is reduced to a minimum from the necessity of producing the greatest amount of effect with the least quantity of material. Thus, the power of resistance of an ordinary joist or rafter, whose dimensions are 6 inches by 2 inches, to a strain acting in the direction of the depth, or the greater dimension, would be represented by the number 72, while its power of resistance to a force acting in the direction of the breadth, the lesser dimension, would be represented by the number 24. Looking on these great ribs as simple beams, their relative strength to resist the two forces is about as 1 to 25; and, consequently, although designed with a superabundance of strength for the fulfilment of their function as part of a roof, on raising the first from the ground its strength in the opposite direction proved to be barely sufficient to keep the materials in their places during the operation. But even in this temporary and partial failure, the excellence of the principle of the construction was rendered very apparent by the great amount of change of figure in a lateral direction that took place, without any diminution of the strength of the arch. The forms assumed during the lifting of the first rib were certainly most extraordinary, and most discouraging. If the reader can imagine to himself a horse-shoe, 100 feet across and 50 feet high, and weighing 9 tons, bending and twisting about like a piece of brown paper or soft wax; or,—to illustrate the difficulty, let him lift a fishing rod by the small end,—he will then have some idea of the nature of the difficulty. Of its extent he can have none but from seeing the operation attempted. By the adoption of certain simple precautions all difficulty was, however, overcome. The first precaution was confining the ends of the arch by a chord-line; the second, hauling at many points at once in raising the rib; and the third, which was intended to correct any change from the true figure, which might happen in spite of the two former, was to bolt stout pieces of timber to each other in pairs on opposite sides of and enclosing the arches, and projecting some feet above and below them. By hauling on the top or bottom of these pieces a sufficient leverage was acquired to twist the arch-rib laterally, and remove any deflection that it might have acquired previously. On the adoption of these expedients, about twenty minutes sufficed to raise each rib from the horizontal to the vertical position.*

The second operation—that of raising the ribs from the ground, and putting them in their places—was easily accomplished. For this purpose, travelling cranes were erected on the roofs over the adjoining galleries, the tackle from which was adjusted a little over the point, where a line drawn horizontally through the centre of gravity of the beam would intersect it on each side. To prevent accident, guide-ropes from several portions of the beams were at the same time made fast to crab-winches on the ground, and slackened as it ascended. When the rib had been raised to a little over its permanent position, the travelling cranes were slowly moved until they arrived over the framework on which it was to rest, and it was lowered to its place, and secured there—the guide-ropes staying it in its proper position, while the same series of operations was performed with another. There was something really imposing in the appearance of the large mass travelling steadily through the air to its destined place; but, considered in reference to the great difficulties that had been overcome, and of which the operation was the successful result, the operation became one of intense interest. On the placing of each rib, the purlins connecting it with its predecessor were raised, dropped into their places, and the nuts securing them screwed home. The intermediate ribs were next hoisted and screwed, each part becoming the scaffold or ladder for fixing its successor. The nailing on of the timber-sheeting then commenced, after which the roof was ready for its final coating of paper and tarred-cloth outside, and paint inside.

The roof of the Great Hall consists of 14 semicircular, 8 quadrant, and 26 intermediate ribs; and 322 straight and 160 curved purlins.

The description of the construction of the roof of the Centre Hall applies to that of the roofs of all the Building. In every case the timber-sheeting was covered with canvass, steeped in coal-tar. A layer of brown paper was interposed to prevent the tar appearing on the under surface. It was then covered with boiled tar or mineral paint, and finally lime-washed. As much anxiety was expressed about the combustible nature of this covering material, from its being so easily affected by heat, it may be interesting to mention that (paradoxical as it may seem), it will not burn. The tar prevents all risk, for by melting around any spot that may have become ignited, it puts the flame in the condition of that of a candle which has been snuffed too low down, and it is extinguished by the excessive supply of what would ordinarily feed it. This statement is not a matter of mere theory, but is founded on the result of direct experiments at the Exhibition Building, where every means were exhausted to try and get a bit of the covering to continue burning, without success. The coating of lime, also, put an end to any probability of ignition by casual sparks.

The great ribs are supported on a timber framework, which is an extension of the roof of the side gallery adjoining; and they rest simply on it, being only secured by two iron bands, as shown in the annexed engraving, which will give a clear idea of the principal points of the construction of the roofs and galleries.

* The only scaffolding used in the construction of the Building beyond what the parts already put together afforded, was required for raising the quadrant ribs for the Great Hall, where the Building, presenting a mere timber wall—the "ποῦ στῶ" that puzzled Archimedes—rendered it necessary to erect a platform. This is a feature of the design which should not be overlooked.

It will readily be perceived that the truss of the gallery-roof has been designed to act as a buttress to the great roof, and distributes any tendency to horizontal motion it might exhibit over the adjoining space. Each of these trusses is carefully secured to lattice-trusses, running at right angles to them, and acting as wall-plates, connecting the roof and its supports in the direction of the length of the Main Hall. To render the structure secure against any amount of vibration, the cross-ties were inserted, where they could be placed without inconvenience at two places in the length of the Gallery, which rendered those parts of the building—huge, vertical, trussed girders—capable of resisting any motion of the roofs of the greater halls.

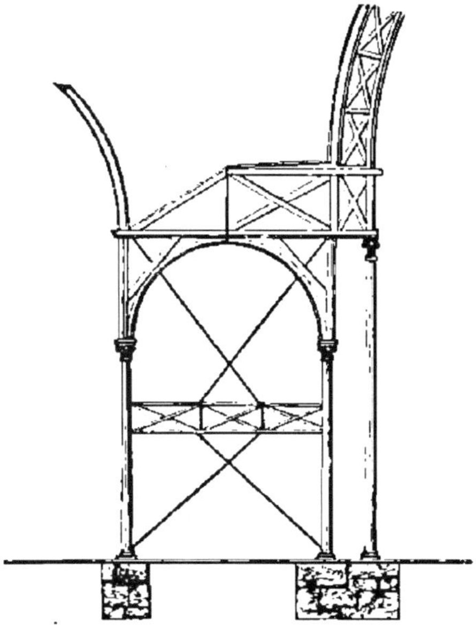

Section showing Construction of Roofs and Galleries.

It will be perceived that the roof of the Gallery is supported on three cast-iron columns, of which the one to the left bears the arches of the smaller hall, and the two on the right carry the weight of the great ribs. The column on the extreme right is 38 feet long, cast in one piece, except the base, and weighs over 3 tons. The other columns are each in two separate castings, the bases in all cases being detached. The mode of fixing the columns was to set the bases, the upper edge of which was planed true and smooth, on the blocks of masonry prepared to receive them. The lower part of the column was then simply dropped in its place, and secured by joining to it the wrought-iron girders intended to support the floor of the Galleries. A scaffold was thus gained for carrying on the Building a stage higher. All the junctions of the columns (which were cast by Messrs. Young, of Edinburgh) having been previously carefully prepared, they were built on each other, and the other parts secured to them with great rapidity and accuracy.

The four Galleries exhibit in their construction an excellent combination of strength and lightness. The system of the construction will be readily understood by regarding each Gallery as a line of squares—the angles being the cast-iron columns, and the sides wrought-iron girders—the columns standing 25 feet apart from centre to centre. By reference to the annexed engraving of a portion of one of the girders, it will be perceived that it consists of a top flange, formed of two pieces of L iron, 3½ inches by ½ an inch; having a piece of deal bolted on it, both for convenience in fixing the flooring boards, and as additional resistance to compression. The bottom flange is similar to that at the top, consisting also of two L pieces. The uprights consist of two pieces of T iron, 3 inches by ½ an inch, placed back to back. The cross-pieces are flat, 3 inches by ½ an inch. The weight of the whole is about 9 cwt. These girders were very carefully and severely tested before they were fixed, or were even brought on the ground; and with the most satisfactory results. The two girders first made were arranged a little above the ground: and a platform of timber having been placed on them to receive the weights, they were loaded gradually with ascertained weights of iron, and the deflections carefully observed, and noted, for each increase of weight. The girders deflected gradually to the extent of 5–16ths of an inch

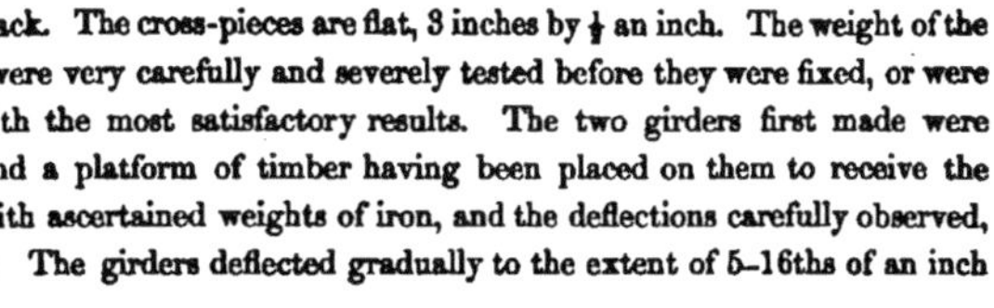


Portion of Girder of Gallery.

until the eighth ton, when there was no farther yielding until the fourteenth ton, when a gradual deflection of rather less than 1-16th of an inch per ton took place up to the twenty-second ton, when the experiment ceased. The beams were left for several days with the load on them, but without producing any perceptible increase of deflection. They were then unloaded, and were found to have retained a permanent deflection of 5-16ths of an inch, which may be attributed to the tightening of the various bolts, &c. They were then straightened and again operated on, with the intention of ascertaining their ultimate strength by breaking. The same ratio of deflection was observed as on the former trial, but the intention of breaking them was abandoned after the thirty-second ton had been put on, from the difficulty of piling more metal on them without danger to the men who were engaged in the operation. This latter experiment was carried on by Sir John Benson, in presence of Mr. Fairbairn of Manchester.

More recently, further experiments were conducted by Sir John Benson, again assisted by Mr. Fairbairn, on a finished square of the gallery itself, more as a satisfaction to the public than from any doubt as to its competency to bear any weight incidental to its position. This was, if possible, a severer test than what had previously been adopted. It consisted in packing the platform with men as closely as they could be made to stand, the living burden amounting to not far short of 20 tons; but whether this load was in violent motion or at rest, the amount of deflection was exceedingly trifling, and far within a safe limit.

The flooring of the halls is formed of three-inch deals, laid with a narrow space between them, for the disposal of the dust. The floor of the galleries is of two-inch deal, ploughed, and tongued with hoop-iron.

The staircases adjoining the Centre Hall have proved a puzzle to persons unacquainted with the principle of their construction; the landing half-way up appearing to have no support. They form a very nice piece of workmanship. It is also deserving of note that the steps leading to the dais at the extreme end of the Grand Hall were cut from a single plank 76 feet in length.

It will be observed that a striking difference exists between this Building and that erected in Hyde-Park for the Exhibition of 1851, not only in the general form and outline, but also, and more particularly, in its internal character and effect; and in no respect is this more markedly exhibited than in the quantity and quality of the light admitted into the Building. Up almost to the very completion of the Building the general opinion was that there would be a great deficiency of light; but for these fears we need scarcely observe that there was no foundation. The arrangement in this respect, in Sir John Benson's design, was excellent. In addition to a limitation of the quantity of light, its quality has been materially improved by the use of rolled and fluted glass, of a rough surface, and grayish-green colour. A cool, grayish tone prevailed, and there is an entire absence of direct rays of sunshine; so that the most delicate tints of pictures, and fabrics of various kinds, left the Building nearly as pure and fresh as when the articles were first deposited there. In the Fine Arts Courts, especially, it was felt by all that Sir J. Benson had, in the words of H. R. H. Prince Albert, "*solved the problem of lighting a Picture Gallery.*" There have been used in glazing the Building about 70,000 superficial feet of glass, and 17,500 lbs. of putty—there being in the Great Hall alone 26,864 feet of sash-bars of deal, 4½ inches by 1½ inches, requiring to produce them 560 deals, 12 feet long. The whole of the glass used was one-eighth of an inch in thickness.*

The exterior wall of the Building was formed of timber uprights, 12 inches square at the angles, and 12 inches broad by 6 inches deep for the intermediate posts. These are secured by a horizontal piece 12 inches by 4 inches, at the level of the floor; two others, 3 feet apart at the level of the gallery-floor, separated and strengthened by cross-pieces; and on the top a similar pair of ties have been introduced to form the wall-plate of the roof. The spaces left were filled in with timber-sheeting, inch thick. Round the bottom of the lights in the roofs, light galleries were carried, both for the facility of making repairs, and to afford ready access in case of fire.

The dimensions of the other principal portions of the Exhibition Building are as follows:—Each of the galleries is 325 feet long, and 25 feet broad, each story being 18 feet high. The Northern and Southern Halls are 375 feet long, 50 feet broad, and 38 feet high to the springing of the arches, making the total height about 65 feet. The Hall for the Fine Arts is 325 feet long, 40 feet broad, and 18 feet high to the springing of the arches, or 38 feet in all. The Hall for Machinery in Motion, which exhibits the same ex-

* The quantity of balk timber used in the construction of the Building was 2800 tons; of deals there were 42,000, of the standard of 12 feet by 9 inches by 3 inches; besides 400,000 superficial feet of inch-thick sheeting. Of the cast-iron columns there were 450 tons; and of hammered iron for girders supporting the galleries, there were 60 tons.

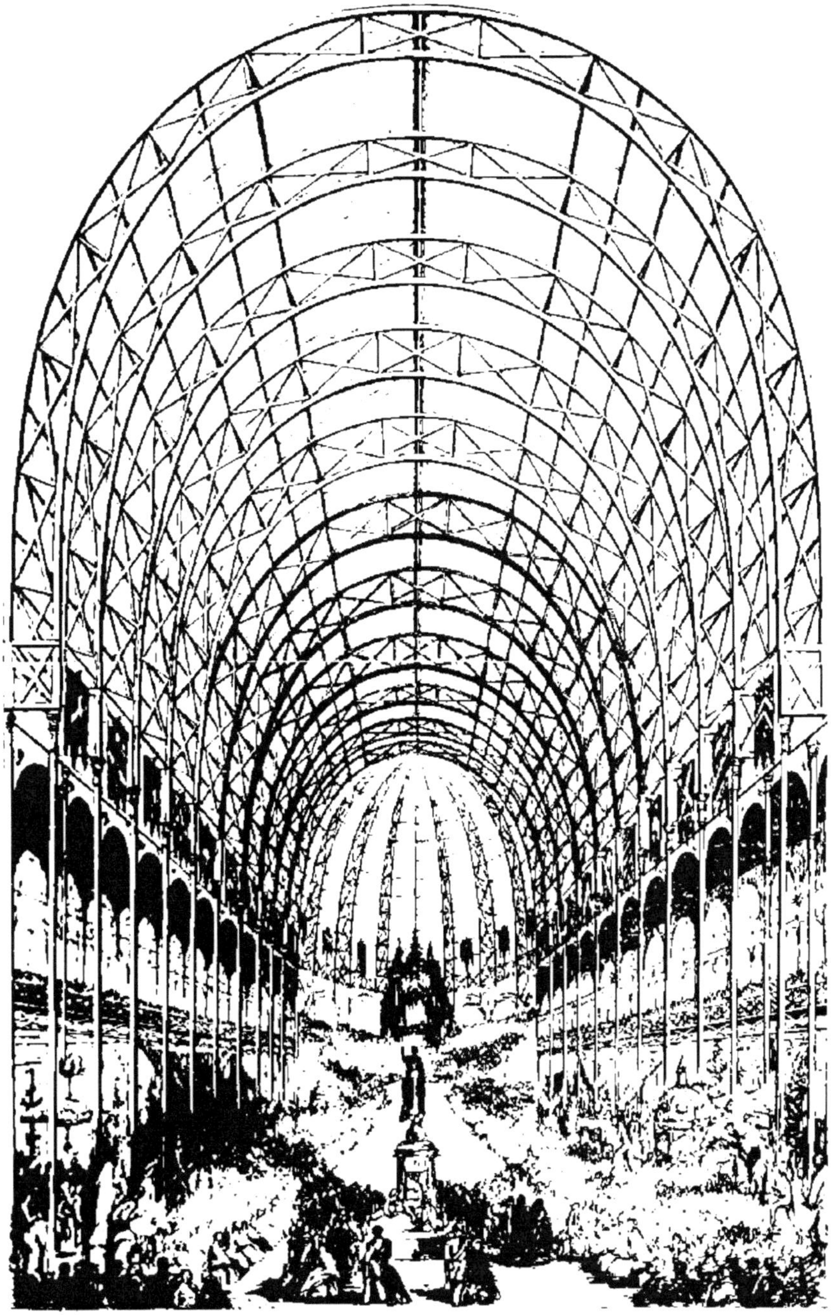

Centre Hall of The Irish Industrial Exhibition Building.

ternal appearance as that for the Fine Arts, is 450 feet long, 40 feet broad, and 46 feet high, forming a very beautiful perspective, from its endless succession of columns and arches. The remaining halls follow generally the proportions of that for the Fine Arts. The Building covered a space of about 265,000 superficial feet, over one-third of the area of the Crystal Palace, and nearly twice that of the Exhibition Building at New York. This will be shown more clearly by the annexed diagram, which presents the three Buildings,

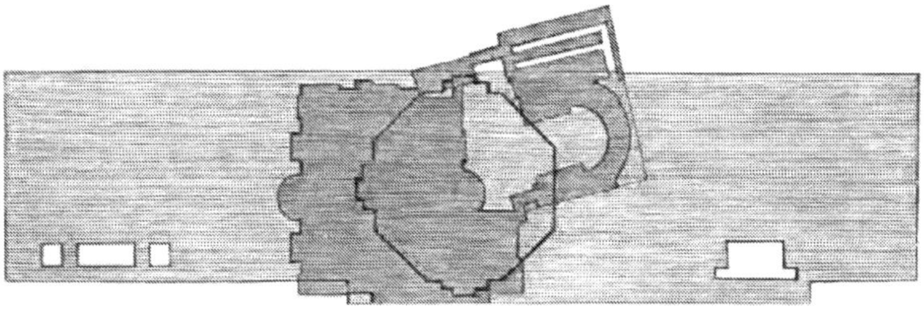

Diagram showing comparative Sizes of the Exhibition Buildings of London, Dublin, and New York.

projected on each other to the same scale;—the large parallelogram showing the Crystal Palace of 1851,—the irregular outline being that of the Dublin Building,—while the octagonal and smallest plan is that of the New York Building. It is worth observing, however, that in general there has been very great economy of space in the Dublin Building; the passages and vacant portions having been reduced to their smallest dimensions, to afford the space demanded by the contributors. The relative areas of the three may be represented as follows:

| | |
|---|---|
| London . . . . . . . . . . . | 17½ acres. |
| Dublin . . . . . . . . . . . | 6½ „ |
| New York . . . . . . . . . . | 3¾ „ |

By a comparison of the elevations of the three Buildings, the distinctive and peculiar features of the Dublin Exhibition may be seen to great advantage.* The appearance of the Crystal Palace is familiar to

* The ground floor of the New York Exhibition Building is a regular octagon, 365 feet in diameter. This measurement does not include the three Entrance Halls, each of which, projecting 27 feet, is 40 feet wide. On either side of these Entrances offices are attached, projecting 18 feet from the main building, and 27 feet in width.

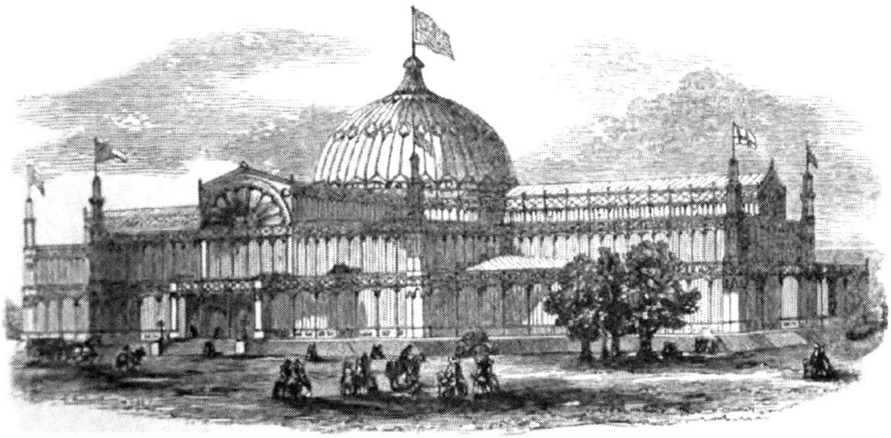

Elevation of New York Exhibition Building.

The interior consists of four great divisions, each having a main avenue, with side aisles, which are connected on the ground-floor by four triangular sections, covered by a sort of flat lean-to roof. These main avenues unite in the centre of the Building, and together form a Greek cross; this shape being also preserved in the Gallery-floor, access to

every one, as those who have not seen the original cannot fail to have met with numerous representations of it, and therefore it is unnecessary to reproduce a sketch of it here. Of our own Exhibition Building, a view will be found annexed. The New York Building seems to have derived its distinctive features from Sir Joseph Paxton's design; but there is an originality of conception about the Dublin Building, which distinguishes it from either of the others, and which imparts to it that architectural effect, in which they are so deficient. It has been said, and with truth, that the Hyde Park structure formed the commencement of a new era in the application of glass to purposes of more extended utility than it was hitherto supposed to be susceptible of; but we venture to predict that this remark in its widest signification is still more applicable to our Irish Exhibition Building, as having certain peculiar characteristics about it to a greater extent than has been hitherto attained.

As the Halls were covered in, it became necessary to decide on the mode of decoration, and the Executive Committee, at the request of Sir John Benson, invited Mr. Lanyon, of Belfast, to assist in deciding on this very important point. After some preliminary experiments, they determined on giving to the roofs a somewhat similar appearance to that which they presented before they had been covered over with the sheeting; when the various ribs, purlins, and other constructive portions appeared to form panels of blue sky, in frames of unpainted deal.

The general effect of the decorations has been much improved by the introduction of heraldic devices in the triangular-shaped spaces on each side of the arches along the front of the galleries. This was a happy idea; and Mr. R. F. Davis, whose knowledge of the subject peculiarly fitted him for the task, obligingly undertook to superintend the preparation of the arms of the various countries, corporations, and important personages, to be used for the purpose. The contrast which these exhibit to each other, and the effect of the gorgeous colouring which they occasionally presented on the sober tints around them, was very fine indeed. The following is a list of these decorations, as arranged in the different Halls:—

## LIST OF ARMORIAL BEARINGS.

### CENTRE HALL.

| | |
|---|---|
| 1. Ireland. | 2. England. |
| 3. Wales. | 4. Scotland. |
| 5. Isle of Man. | 6. Berwick-upon-Tweed. |
| 7. Prince Albert. | 8. Lord St. Germans. |
| 9. Lord Eglinton. | 10. William Dargan. |
| 11. Province of Leinster. | 12. Sir John Benson. |
| 13. Province of Connaught. | 14. Province of Munster. |
| 15. Archbishopric of Armagh. | 16. Archbishopric of Dublin. |
| 17. Lord Mayor of Dublin. | 18. Late Lord Mayor of Dublin. |
| 19. City of Dublin. | 20. City of Galway. |
| 21. Archbishopric of Tuam. | 22. Archbishopric of Cashel. |
| 23. University of Dublin. | 24. Queen's University. |
| 25. Royal Hospital, Kilmainham. | 26. Royal Hibernian Military School. |
| 27. City of Cork. | 28. Town of Belfast. |
| 29. Guild of Merchants. | 30. Guild of Glovers and Skinners. |
| 31. Guild of Barbers, Surgeons. | 32. Guild of Weavers. |
| 33. Guild of Carpenters, Millers, Masons, &c. | 34. Guild of Dyers. |
| 35. Guild of Cooks. | 36. Guild of Goldsmiths. |
| 37. Guild of Tailors. | 38. Guild of Coopers. |
| 39. Guild of Bakers. | 40. Guild of Feltmakers and Hatters. |
| 41. Guild of Shoemakers. | 42. Guild of Cutlers, Painters, Paperstainers. |
| 43. Guild of Tanners. | 44. Guild of Bricklayers and Plasterers. |
| 45. Guild of Smiths. | 46. Guild of Hosiers. |
| 47. Guild of Butchers. | 48. Guild of Curriers. |
| 49. Guild of Saddlers, Upholsterers, &c. | 50. Guild of Brewers and Maltsters. |
| 51. Guild of Tallow Chandlers. | 52. Guild of Joiners. |

which is got from the alternate sides of the central octagon. The materials employed are chiefly iron and glass.

The following are the principal dimensions:—Diameter of dome, 100 feet; height of dome from floor to skylight, 122 feet; height of main avenues in the clear, 67 feet; height of first story in the clear, 24 feet; height of second story in the clear, 21 feet; height of aisles, 45 feet; height of triangular sections, 24 feet; width of avenues, 41 feet 5 inches; width of galleries, 54 feet; width of each front, 149 feet 5 inches; diameter of each of the octagonal towers, 8 feet; height of towers above side-walk, 75 feet; area of principal floor, 111,200 square feet; area of entrances, halls, and offices, 6000 square feet; area of galleries, 62,000 square feet. There are on the ground floor 190 columns, 21 feet above the floor, 8 inches diameter, cast hollow, of different thicknesses, from half an inch to one inch thick. On the gallery-floor there are 122 columns.

The accompanying illustration, in conjunction with the particulars here given, will enable the reader to form a tolerably accurate idea of the New York Exhibition Building, which, it may be observed, was not opened for some six or eight weeks after the period first announced.

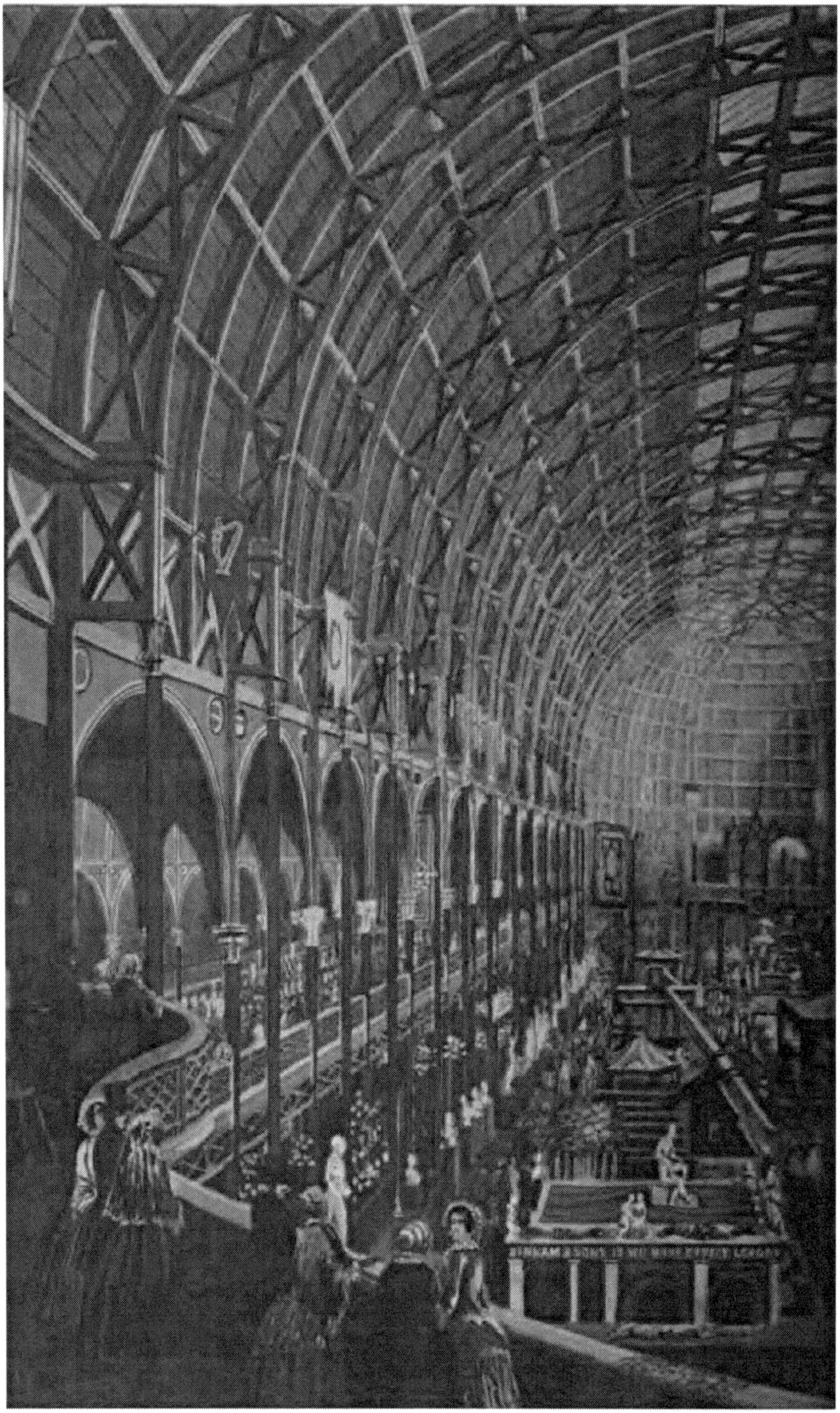

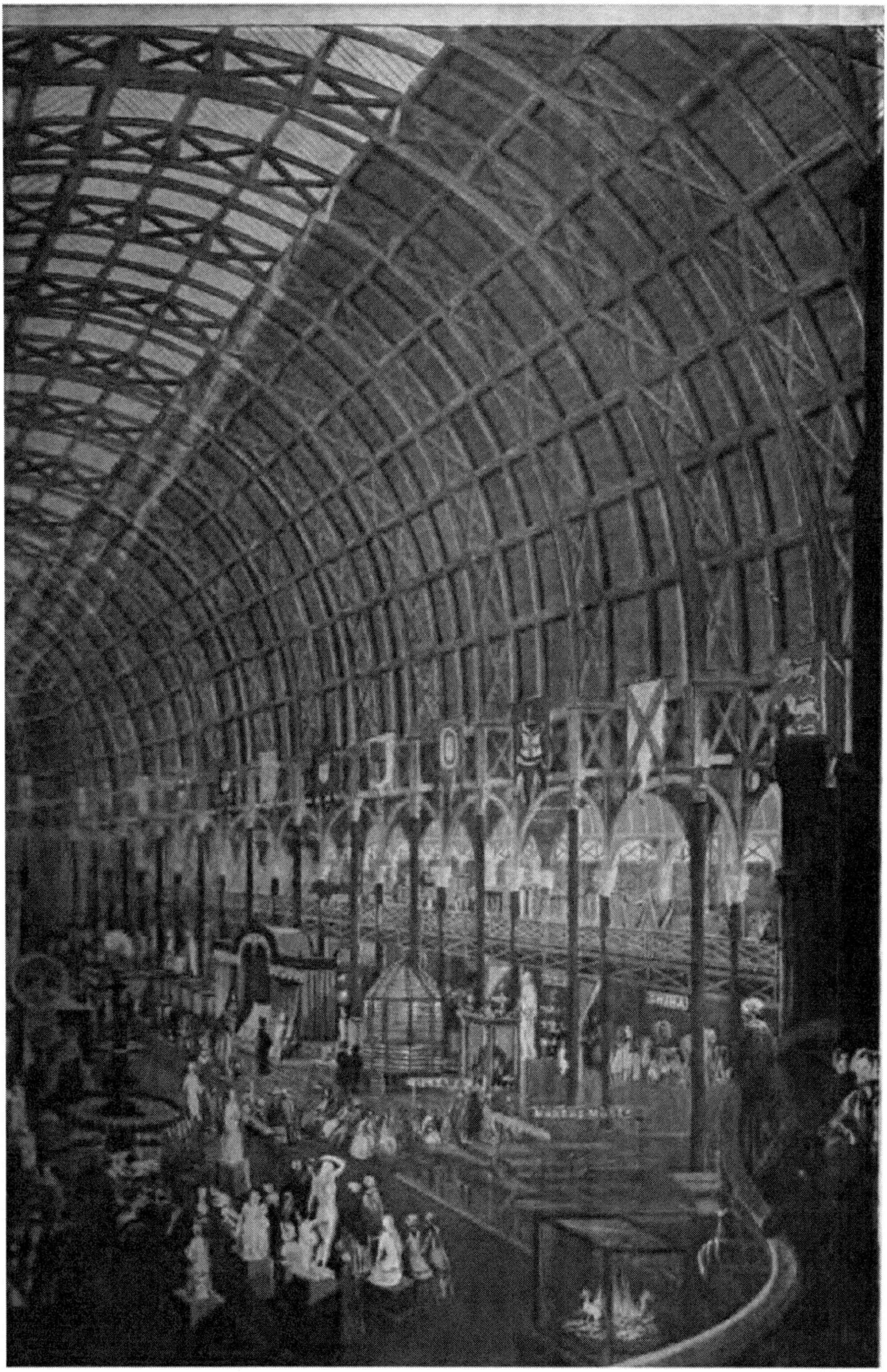

NORTHERN HALL.

53. Royal Dublin Society.
55. *Earl of Harrington.
57. *Charles Cobbe, Archbishop of Dublin.
59. Earl of Grandison.
61. Sir Arthur Gore, Bart.
63. *Robert Downes.
65. *William Maple.
67. Thomas Prior.
69. Town of Drogheda.
71. City of Waterford.
73. Bishopric of Waterford.
75. City of Limerick.
77. Bishopric of Limerick.
79. College of Physicians.
81. Bishopric of Derry.
83. University of Oxford.
85. Bishopric of Cloyne.
87. University of St. Andrews.
89. Bishopric of Clogher.
91. City of London.
93. Bishopric of Down.
95. City of Manchester.
97. Bishopric of Kildare.
99. City of Worcester.
101. Bishopric of Leighlin.
103. Town of Liverpool.
105. Bishopric of Meath.
107. Ballast Office.

54. Royal Irish Academy.
56. *George Stone, Archbishop of Armagh.
58. *Earl of Kildare.
60. *Viscount Lanesborough.
62. *Sir Thomas Taylor, Bart.
64. *Rev. John Wynne, D. D.
66. Lord Clarendon.
68. Province of Ulster.
70. Town of Enniskillen.
72. City of Kilkenny.
74. Bishopric of Ossory.
76. City of Londonderry.
78. Bishopric of Killala.
80. College of Surgeons.
82. Bishopric of Dromore.
84. University of Cambridge.
86. Bishopric of Cork.
88. College of St. Nicholas, Galway.
90. Bishopric of Clonfert.
92. City of Edinburgh.
94. Bishopric of Elphin.
96. City of Birmingham.
98. Bishopric of Killala.
100. City of Leeds.
102. Bishopric of Kilmore.
104. City of Glasgow.
106. Bishopric of Raphoe.
108. Ordnance.

Thus marked (*) were Founders of the Royal Dublin Society to whom the Charter was granted, A. D. 1731.

---

SOUTHERN HALL.

109. East India Company.
111. *Turkey.
113. Persia.
115. Mahrattas.
117. Siam.
119. China.
121. Egypt.
123. *Grand Turk.
125. Mogul.
127. Malta.
129. Heligoland.
131. Brabant.
133. *Belgium (Tricolor).
135. Ionian Islands.
137. *Austria (Merchant).
139. *Greece.
141. *Portugal.
143. *France (Eagle).
145. *France (Tricolor).
147. *Norway (Lion).
149. *Norway (Merchant).
151. Mecklenburg-Schwerin.
153. *Denmark.
155. *Bremen.
157. *Hanover.
159. *Russia.
161. *America.
163. *Prussia.

110. Japan.
112. China.
114. Batavia.
116. Java.
118. Tripoli.
120. Sandwich Islands.
122. *Brazil.
124. Buenos Ayres.
126. Hayti.
128. Duchy of Oldenburg.
130. *Netherlands.
132. *Belgium (Tricolor).
134. *Belgium (Lion).
136. Duchy of Hesse.
138. Switzerland.
140. *Sardinia.
142. *Spain.
144. *France (Tricolor).
146. *France (Eagle).
148. *Sweden (Merchant).
150. *Sweden.
152. Brunswick.
154. Grand Duchy of Baden.
156. *Lubeck.
158. *Hamburg.
160. Saxony.
162. *Bavaria.
164. *Austria.

This mark (*) indicates nations having Consuls in Dublin.

Besides the decoration by means of the heraldic devices placed on each side of the arches, the appearance of the Centre Hall was very much improved by the addition of banners suspended opposite the openings of the arches along the line of the galleries. These were well executed, and they still further contributed to the grand effect which this noble apartment was calculated to produce on the mind of the spectator.

The arrangements for supplying motive power for the machinery, and water to the Building, are deserving of note. For the purpose of generating steam, two large tubular boilers were placed in a detached yard on the premises of the Royal Dublin Society, at the north-west corner of the Lawn. From these steam was conveyed to two engines, each of twenty-five horse power, supplied by Mr. Fairbairn, as well as to some minor engines. By the large engines a shaft was put in motion, over 300 feet long; by which, in turn, motion was communicated, through the intervention of strapping, to the various machines in that department. The shafting was carried along the centre of the Machinery Court on the tops of cast-iron pillars, placed securely on stone foundations.

The principal ground water-tank was situated at the western end of the Machinery Court; it communicated with the pipes pervading the whole premises, and supplied, by means of a forcing-engine, water to large tanks adjoining the Society House, and placed at a height of 54 feet from the floor, for the use of the several fountains. The water was conveyed to the premises by a 6-inch main from Herbert-place. Besides surrounding the premises along the boundary, lateral branches were carried across the building from north to south, on which there were fourteen fire-plugs and four stand-cocks; so that in the event of any accident from fire, the most complete and ample facilities existed for at once extinguishing it. The admirable character of the arrangements in this respect prevented any of the water from going to waste; the overflow of the fountains being conveyed to the underground cistern, thence to be forced up to the elevated cisterns already alluded to. Connected with the Exhibition there were about two miles in length of water-pipes laid down.*

J. H. O.

* The description of the Irish Temple of Industry, to which the preceding pages have been devoted, affords more triumphant testimony to the genius of its architect than could be supplied by the most laboured encomium. It was destined to pass away after having fulfilled its function, and soon there will not be left even a trace of it behind; but the recollection of what it was will not fade from the minds of the present generation. Among the thousands who regarded that Building with an admiration approaching to enthusiasm, there was scarcely a single individual who did not express a hope, that on some future occasion the architect by whom it had been designed would be provided with an opportunity of furnishing in a permanent form an illustration of that genius which he so successfully exhibited on Leinster Lawn.

For the last eight years Sir John Benson has filled the situation of County Surveyor of the East Riding of Cork, to which he was appointed in April, 1846, on the retirement of Mr. Leahy. The duties of an officer of this class are more of an engineering than of an architectural character,—the formation and repair of roads, and the construction of bridges,—though, to a considerable extent, both qualifications are combined, and county buildings are not of less consequence than county bridges.

Sir John Benson is a native of Collooney, in the county of Sligo, where at an early age he distinguished himself by his knowledge of architecture. In the remodelling and improvement of Markree Castle, by Gwilt, he first appeared before the public in a professional capacity, and he then afforded evidence of that ability which he has since so strikingly displayed. So successfully did he execute the task which he then undertook, that he was at once intrusted with the furnishing of plans for several important buildings in the west of Ireland. Among them we may mention a number of large fire-proof mills; the beautiful little church of Knocknaree, designed in the pure mediæval style of architecture, the first of that character erected in the country; the Dominican Church and Convent in Sligo; and many others,—all affording evidence of the master mind by which they were designed.

As an engineer, the state of the public works in the East Riding of Cork shows that Sir John Benson ranks deservedly high in that profession. During the progress of the relief works carried on in the famine, we believe that he had charge of the largest district assigned to any single officer in Ireland; and while such an enormous mass of details was thereby to be got through, it is a circumstance deserving of note that a single useless work was not then undertaken in that district, and that, while the wants of the starving people were ministered to, the rate-payers had good value for their money from the manner in which it was expended. Since that period several hundred miles of new road have been constructed in the East Riding in the most creditable manner. For some three or four years past, Sir John has also acted as engineer to the Cork Harbour Commissioners, during which a long range of quays has been rebuilt, a steam-boat pier at Monkstown has been constructed, and a pier and harbour at Ring. Under his directions a powerful dredge-boat and river-barges have been constructed for the Commissioners, each capable of carrying 150 tons, with only four and a half feet in depth of water. In all these works, the most important and the most trifling, the same evidence of a master mind has been apparent. But the crowning triumph for so far has been the Exhibition Building, which was not less remarkable for its adaptation for the intended purpose than for the symmetry of its proportions, and the care which was bestowed in working out even the minutest details. In some of the minor arrangements of the Building the ability of the architect was strikingly exemplified. Seldom, indeed, has the honour of knighthood been more worthily bestowed than it was at the opening of the Exhibition.

The flood, which in the month of November last caused so much injury in the vicinity of Cork, especially in reference to the destruction of the bridges, enabled Sir John to show an illustration of the despatch with which works can be carried on, on a large scale, under proper arrangements. He had by that casualty to set about replacing no less than thirty-one county bridges carried off by the floods. Among those swept away, it will be recollected, was St. Patrick's Bridge, across the Lee, in the City of Cork,—a situation where the absence of the usual thoroughfare would be attended with vast inconvenience, and where, therefore, immediate steps were necessary to replace it. A temporary wooden bridge was accordingly constructed, 216 feet long, and 40 feet wide, which was completed in the short space of eighteen days.

Among the works now in progress, of an architectural character, under the charge of Sir John Benson, we may mention the Church of St. Vincent de Paul in Cork, and the Athenæum in that city, which latter may be said to be a restoration of the Fine Arts Hall of the Cork Exhibition Building, turned into a permanent Temple of Art.

Sir John married in September, 1849, Mary Clementina Pyne, daughter of the late John Smith, Esq., of the 56th Regiment. He is now in the prime of life, and we may yet expect that he will make many valuable contributions to the architecture of his country.

Few visitors to the Great Irish Exhibition but were struck with the richness and splendour of the Building more almost than by any of the objects which it contained. It was not only remarkable for the rapidity with which it was erected, for the sufficiency of its plans, and for the enormous mass of its carefully worked materials: it did not merely excite admiration for the convenience of the whole structure in the space which it afforded to so many countless objects of every size and substance, and the easy and abundant access to each unit of them, so ingeniously secured for the crowds of admiring spectators. The Exhibition Building, besides all these things, filled the mind by an imposing magnificence of general form, and by a truly architectural harmony of proportion in its interior, which made its splendid halls not mere bazaar-like receptacles of objects of manufacture and taste; but themselves, too, examples of and incentives to something higher and grander in design than had before been attained. The Building itself was perhaps the most successful novelty exhibited, both in Art and Manufacture, and Sir John Benson, at the same moment that he proved himself one of the ablest practical architects and engineers of his country, has made good his claim to the honours of genius itself.

In listening to the many criticisms of the crowd on the strikingly original design which the Exhibition Building presented, we have been strongly impressed by the observation that no one seemed to find fault with what he found there; and that the only desire expressed by those who did not choose to confess themselves entirely satisfied was for some additional feature which, it was thought, might have been adopted to add greater splendour to the details, or to crown the whole work with a greater air of architectural completeness. Such criticism, however, appears to be founded on a mistake with respect to the conditions imposed on the architect, and the special objects of the Building. If the problem had been to construct a great permanent public edifice, and to do this regardless of expense, so as, by fully realizing the aspiration of the artist, to lead back the new generation from the depraved taste of which we have recently had so many illustrations, to something worthy of the *chef-d'œvres* of the last century, then indeed we should be entitled to require a design showing the full development of the architect's genius; but then, too, he should have had the advantage of abundant leisure to compose and mature his plans, and sufficient time to put them into execution. The Exhibition Building, however, was, and in the nature of things it must have been, undertaken in a totally different manner. It was to be constructed in a few months; it was to consist of the least expensive materials; it was to be denied any accessories of mere ornament; it was, in fact, exclusively intended to supply convenient and suitable accommodation for an immense collection of goods of every kind, and to do this upon a site in which the space was but limited, and at the smallest expense possible under the circumstances. The principal design, therefore, of necessity, regarded merely the interior; and the external elevation was only to be as little unsightly, as little awkward as possible. We shall not then need to criticise the external plan, although to even that very much of praise is due for its mere beauty and grandeur; and within the limits it properly deserves, we shall hereafter take some notice of it. But our present purpose is to point out that which in the interior of the Building claims to be remembered after the structure shall have been removed, which was the chief object of the required design, and in which we believe the architect has attained success as complete as it has been hitherto unprecedented.

The general plan of the Building will be best understood by reference to the engravings and to the statistics of its size and proportions, which will be found in another place. The great feature of the whole was certainly the Grand Hall in the centre; so far as we are aware, the largest and most magnificent apartment that has yet been erected. Its effect was very much interfered with by the manner in which some of the articles were arranged in it, and which prevented its being seen from any good point of view. After the goods were placed in the Building a satisfactory view of this Hall could only be obtained from one of the organ galleries, the best point of view being in that over the entrance; but the spectator in a gallery was necessarily so greatly elevated that his eye lost much of the immense size of the room, and much, too, of the charm of its proportions. Had the Centre Hall been unincumbered by the larger objects crowded into it, the *coup d'œil* would long haunt the imagination of every educated visitor; and cleared, as it was, of these obstructions, while the building remained in existence as a temporary Winter Garden, it is not too much to expect that a permanent impression may have been made upon the public mind, in accustoming it to the enjoyment of architectural forms which, preserving the most extreme simplicity of structure and of material, united the superb magnificence of giant dimensions with harmony of general proportion, and the repose of quiet and unpretending details.

The dimensions of the Great Hall were, in round numbers, 400 feet by 100, with a height of 100 to the highest point of the semicircular arch of the roof. These figures represent a proportion of the parts which, in the case of an apartment of such enormous size, is, perhaps, as nearly perfect as could be desired. The very great length would, indeed, in a structure of smaller extent, and built with four parallel walls, destroy the harmony of the whole with its parts; but, in the interior of a vast edifice like that of the Exhibition, the eye cannot take in the idea of length so well, and measuring much more easily the breadth and height, and both these being so very great, the still greater length ceases to occupy the attention with undue emphasis. The circular termination of the Hall at both ends also greatly adds to this effect, and diminishes the consciousness of extreme length, by making the vaulted semi-domes, with their ribs converging to a common centre a good deal within the extreme points of the length of the roof, seem very much nearer to the spectator than they really are. The comparative length, breadth, and height (which were, of course, the subject of careful calculation in this regard), together with the form of the two ends of the Hall (there being no gable end as in the London Building) are the cause in Sir John Benson's design of that harmonious completeness of effect which elegant proportions can alone confer upon an architectural interior; and in this respect there can be no comparison at all between this beautiful Hall and the Glass Transept of Hyde Park, which might have been longer or shorter by a hundred feet or more, without in the least interfering with its merits. In this Hall the eye recognises a *whole*, capable of taking rank as a thing of substantive importance and meaning, and not merely a vast mass of building without a definite beginning or end, inspired by no independent *idea*, and of no significance save as a vast shed for the temporary protection of its useful contents. And, in almost all other points of comparison, the Crystal Palace suggests similar remarks in contrast to the Dublin Exhibition Building. The former was admirable in many ways as a useful erection for its intended purpose: the latter was all that too, but it was somewhat more. It possessed by itself a special beauty and elegance of its own, apart from and independent of its utilitarian attractions.

In the little of ornament admissible in this design, Sir John Benson adopted the best principle, that of making the very supports—the very skeleton itself—the decoration of the walls and roof. He distinguished supporting ribs from the mass of surface by a peculiar colour, and thus brought out the meaning of his plan by emphasizing the lines of support. Those lines themselves were simple in the extreme, and by their very simplicity assisted in adding to the impression of gigantic size; while terminating, as they all did, in the symmetrical curves of a semicircular roof, the eye was gratified by the gracefulness, as much as the mind by the practical significance, of their forms. The tall and slender shafts of the supporting pillars of deep blue, standing out in relief against the lighter colours of all the rest of the Building, supplied an expression of massiveness to the principal supports without impairing the lightness necessary to the whole. The roof itself, in its ribs, its slight cross-beams, and its colour of delicate blue, appeared so mere a web of light and airy canopy, poised upon the enduring strength of the dark supporting pillars, that its immense mass suggested no impression of weight or of closeness. One felt as in a solid building, not a mere garden glass-house; but one felt that there was room to breathe as in the open air.

The Side Halls (on the north and south of the centre), constructed on the same plan, but on a smaller scale of height and breadth, were equally successful. Their greater comparative length was not felt as a blemish, because they were intended to be divided by lofty partitions or screens into various compartments. The arrangement was such as by long side passages from end to end to convey the idea of each of these Halls as a whole; while the lateral divisions of the length, being of greater or less extent according to the space required for the accommodation of particular articles, or of the produce of particular factories or of separate nations, secured a constant variety, and prevented that overwhelming sense of sameness which fatigued the mind of the visitor in passing through the interminable repetitions of the London Exhibition. These Side Halls were separated from the great central apartment by a sufficient space of transverse passages, or divisions, to prevent their interference with the unity of the principal feature of the Building, on the one hand, and to protect their proportions from too close a comparison with its grander and more magnificent forms, on the other. But a sufficient number of these broad transverse passages were left open to the light to permit the eye to enjoy the splendid breadth of space, which the almost square shape of the ground plan of the entire suggested.

Another point of comparison between the Dublin and the London Building, in which the former attained complete success, was one, which, to many people may appear, at first view, somewhat strange. It is in the article of light. The Glass Palace at Hyde Park admitted light through the whole of its roof and part of its sides. The Exhibition there seemed to be designed to approach as nearly as possible in effect to one held absolutely under the canopy of sky and clouds. The Dublin Building, on the other hand, bore a semicircular roof, of which the greater part was closed, and the brightness of day was only admitted by a moderate skylight extending in the centre along the length of each domed Hall. In London, it was found in practice (paradoxical as it may appear in words), that there was too much light, to see the objects exhibited to advantage. A very large proportion of the manufactured goods, likely to form a part of any modern Exhibition, consists of linens, silks, cottons, and other woven fabrics; and it is found in practice, that to make a proper examination of these but a very moderate amount of light ought to be admitted. The same remark applies to ornamental furniture and to most of the smaller works of Art designed for domestic purposes. Accordingly, it was observed by those who know how much the knowledge of the principles of taste is cultivated on the Continent, that the French and the Austrian departments in the London Exhibition were so arranged as by a proper disposition of the hangings to exclude the excess of light, so that not only were the articles arranged in these departments seen individually to the best advantage, but they were made mutually to support each other in producing a general effect, full of harmony and good taste. In Sir John Benson's design, so accurately had he foreseen the necessity of closely limiting the amount of light to be admitted, that when his Halls were approaching completion, it was a common observation that the Exhibition would be left in the dark. When, however, it was at last thrown open in a fully finished state, it was found that every portion of the vast edifice was abundantly supplied with light,* and that even in the most cloudy weather. It was discovered that the absence of the glare of open air daylight secured to the linens and other textile fabrics an opportunity of being understood, a possibility of being compared and judged, of which these classes of manufacture were (except in the French department) notoriously deprived in London. Had the same skill been shown in the arrangement of the goods which characterized the labours of the architect, the Dublin Exhibition would indeed have seemed a fairy palace.

We shall not stop to particularize the convenient arrangement of the Galleries erected around the various Halls, because they will be perfectly understood by reference to the plan of the Building. The idea of enabling the visitor to traverse the whole of the Galleries without descending to the ground floor is especially deserving of commendation, and the manner in which it was carried out was particularly ingenious. The means of communication between the Galleries at either side of the Centre Hall formed at one end a magnificent balcony overlooking Merrion-square, and which, in fine weather, was a favourite place of resort for those who were fatigued by the examination of the objects within. The whole design was originally confined to the three great Halls, with their adjoining corridors or side aisles. As Mr. Dargan's plan of munificence was enlarged, so also grew the Building; and two smaller lateral Halls were added, to accommodate the Fine Arts on one side, and, provide a fit space for Machinery in Motion on the other. The external appearance of these additional Halls was the same; their form that of the principal one in the centre, their proportions only being different: but their interiors were entirely dissimilar, and each of them for its particular purpose was found to be so convenient as to leave nothing to be desired. The floor of the Machinery Hall (advantage being taken of the inequality of the site of the Building, which slopes considerably towards the north) was much lower than that of the adjoining Hall and passage, or gallery between them. The latter was open to the top, so that the Hall of Machinery was altogether open at one side, and afforded an admirable *coup d'œil* of its very varied contents, set in motion, as they were, by bands passing over a single vast axle which extended almost from end to end of the Hall, and was worked by Fairbairn's steam-engine at the upper end. The dizzy confusion of a close succession of rapid-moving, loud-sounding machines, so painful at first on entering a room full only of such objects, was thus altogether avoided. Looking down across the balustrades at the side of the adjoining Hall, the whole arrangement of so many machines could at once be understood, and any one of them could be singled out at leisure for special observation, to which the most convenient access was secured by broad flights of steps leading down into that Hall at certain distances throughout its length.

* The only exception was the passage between the Southern Hall and the Fine Arts Court, in which unfortunately some beautiful French castings and French leathers, as well as many finer articles (and among them some beautifully coloured wax-lights from Spain) were exhibited. But the Fine Arts Court was, in fact, an addition to the general design, and in adopting it the advantages of this intermediate passage or corridor were necessarily sacrificed.

At the opposite side of the Building a corresponding Hall was appropriated to the Fine Arts, which also was an addition to the original design. This Hall was, of course, entirely separated from the adjacent divisions of the Building, not only because the Fine Arts would have been degraded by making them serve as mere ornamental accidents and accessories in the midst of a bazaar of general manufactures, but also because the utmost amount of wall space was found necessary to contain the great number of valuable paintings contributed to this interesting portion of the Exhibition. The communications between the Fine Arts Hall and the rest of the Building was effected by two entrance doors; and once having passed the threshold of one of these, the visitor felt himself in a new atmosphere, quite apart, as it were, from that of the Great Industrial Exhibition itself.

The construction of a Picture Gallery of such great size, and of so simple a form, excited at the time a great deal of interest, and gave rise to no small amount of discussion. Experience has since shown that no part of the whole edifice was more satisfactory in its result than this; and artists as well as the public have borne testimony to the success of this Hall as a room designed for the exhibition of Paintings. It would be out of place here to enter into any considerations respecting the internal decorations of the Fine Arts Gallery, with respect to the colour of the walls and roof, and other such arrangements, not strictly forming part of the architect's design: upon them some remarks will be found in another part of this volume. But whatever criticism these arrangements may call forth, there is but one opinion as to the general form and proportions of the Fine Arts Hall. It has proved to be the very best room for the suitable exhibition of Paintings of all sizes, that has been yet erected; and its proportions of height and breadth, as well as the disposition and extent of the skylight, by which it was lit, deserve the attentive study of all those to whom at any future time may be committed the charge of constructing a gallery for such a purpose. The amount of light admitted was abundantly sufficient, without being over-excessive: the height of the glass portion of the semicircular roof from the ground and from the summit of the perpendicular walls, on which on each side the various Paintings were disposed, was such as to secure an equal distribution of that light, while the smallest cabinet pictures upon and below the line of vision were completely visible in all their parts: the great breadth of the room prevented the appearance of crowding, which even in the Louvre is felt somewhat painfully: and the largest works (with the exception, perhaps, of Etty's immense picture from the history of the Maid of Orleans, a picture coarsely painted, and drawn with so much ruggedness that its true effect is only produced at a very great distance comparatively with its size) were admirably seen from their proper points of view, no one work being sacrificed to its neighbour, or to the exigencies of a crowded Exhibition. In a permanent building we should have, perhaps, preferred to have had the great length of the Gallery broken (by projecting pillars, or even walls) into a number of compartments, preserving each of them, like separate rooms, a juster proportion of length to breadth and height; but if a long gallery is to be used, it could scarcely be better adapted for the purpose than that designed by Sir John Benson.

The smaller apartments, appropriated to the Gallery of Ancient Masters and to Irish Antiquities, were further additions to the whole plan, and consisted merely of the side offices and sheds constructed for refreshment-rooms, police-offices, &c., suddenly converted into a line of galleries at the moment the necessity for such accommodation arose. Neither these, nor the passages and galleries drawn round the Dublin Society House by the south, and again rejoining the Exhibition Building on the northern side, need here be commented on. The architect made admirable use of the space upon which he was obliged to erect such extensive additional buildings, but their shape and design in detail depended absolutely on the arbitrary conditions which the situation necessarily imposed upon him. The whole interior of the gigantic structure, its general design, and the architectural arrangements, both as to the substantial and the merely ornamental part, were altogether excellent; and, as regards every part of the Building, its convenience, simplicity, and good taste, were equally conspicuous.

To the exterior of the Exhibition Building, also, much of praise is due, but with certain qualifications. Here, in particular, the talent of the architect was necessarily allowed little scope. The objects of the edifice were fulfilled by any building, however rude and plain, on the outside, which afforded space and light within, for the convenient and appropriate disposition of the contents. In Paris itself no attempt was made to render architectural in form the exterior of the temporary wooden buildings, in which the great Quinquennial Expositions of France have been held. In London, also, there was no architectural effect. In Dublin the designer was placed under the same conditions, with regard to expense, as elsewhere; but here he did, within limits narrowly prescribed, make at least the nearest approach possible to the union of grand architectural effect, with cheapness of cost and simplicity of material. A comparison of the ground plan, with the front elevation of his work, will show how successfully he was able to secure variety of form, though adopting a plan of Building everywhere the same; and how he secured that variety not by the weak expedient of heaping together incongruous pettinesses, having no relation to the body of the edifice, but by arranging the bulk of the Building in a few grand masses, differing greatly in size, but keeping among themselves an exact and graceful proportion. The semicircular form of Sir John Benson's roofs afforded much facility to such an arrangement; and in front these roofs presented the appearance of enormous domes, so many of which naturally suggested the idea of a Turkish or Saracenic structure. Had the architect been allowed a larger expenditure upon the ornamental, or in strictness unnecessary, part of the Building, this idea might have been well carried out. Viewed at either side of the centre, the great length of the roofs, as they were, certainly gave the whole an over-heavy and cumbrous appearance. Had the Eastern mode of decoration, both in colour and form, been adopted, this effect would have given place to one of boundless brilliancy and splendour. Tall minarets of different heights, disposed between the vast masses of roof, chiefly along the front, would have broken the disagreeable consciousness of the immense height of the mere roof in proportion to that of the walls on which it rested; and the use of gay colours on the top as well as the front of the Building would have removed the impression of crushing weight, which the vast dark mass overspreading the light woodwork necessarily created. Such decorative accompaniments, too, would have marked a meaning upon the whole design, and one peculiarly appropriate to a gigantic bazaar, which, strictly speaking, our Exhibition properly was. But while thus suggesting what the Building might have been, it must not be forgotten that the plans of the architect were circumscribed by necessary conditions, which it was not in his power to modify. If, in the interior of the edifice due to his genius, everything over which Sir John Benson had direct control was in so high a degree tasteful and beautiful, as well as satisfactory for its purpose, we need not hesitate to declare our conviction that, having regard to the circumstances in which he was placed, his exterior elevation was not less successful. Suggesting, as the whole design does, so much of original ideas in a yet untried direction, we may fairly expect that the Exhibition Building itself will also produce wholesome fruit among us in future generations; and we cannot avoid expressing a hope that this effort of the architect, novel as it is, may lead him also at some future time to develop his complete power in the construction of an original work of a more permanent character, which may add new glory to a nation that had once, and may have again, a name in the world.

P.

# CLASS I.

---

## MINING AND MINERAL PRODUCTS.

A RAW MATERIAL may be considered, in its widest sense, as any substance of mineral, vegetable, or animal origin which, by the application of skilled labour, can be converted into some article useful to man. Thus, marble, ores, cotton, and wool are raw materials, which, by the application of labour, become chimney-pieces or statuary, metals, cloths, and calicoes. These examples represent the simplest kind of raw materials, —that is, natural products. But there are many other substances to which skilled labour has been applied, and which are consequently manufactured articles, and yet may, under certain circumstances, constitute the raw material of other manufactures. For example, cotton yarn, although an article manufactured from raw cotton, may be considered as the raw material of the weaver; and similarly rags constitute that of the paper-maker; the products of whose manufacture, in its turn, constitute that of the papier-maché manufacturer.

Independent of the natural classification of Raw Materials into mineral, vegetable, and animal, we may divide them into *chemical*, or such as are employed in chemical manufactures; and *mechanical*, or those used in such as are of a purely mechanical character. The great characteristic of chemical raw materials is their wonderful capability of undergoing transformations in *nature*, so that no trace of the original body is apparent to the eye; while the mechanical raw materials undergo, in general, but a change in *form*, the original material being still usually distinguishable in nearly all the applications made of it. The former classification is, however, the simpler form; it is the one which was adopted in the arrangement of the Exhibition, and which we shall use in the present Work. Taking them, therefore, in this order, we have first to consider the subject of

### MINERAL MATERIALS.

In former ages the destiny of a nation depended partly on its geographical position and physical characteristics, and partly on the accident of individual will. A new element has gradually developed itself, which would now appear to be the most powerful agent in swaying the social and intellectual tendencies of nations, namely, geological structure. To take an example,—Architecture, an art, which depends in a great degree upon the comparative abundance and quality of building materials. Where these are bad, or scarce, or expensive, architecture never progresses. Thus, in parts of Holland, stone is so difficult to be procured that every building is composed of brick. We would not, therefore, go to Holland to look for a general development of high art in building, although we may find a few isolated structures of great beauty. Why has Rome developed her architecture? Because it is situate upon the tertiary travertino. Why is there such a general tendency to ornamental architecture in the houses of Paris? Because the soft tertiary limestone of Montmartre is cheap and abundant. To build the palaces of Genoa in Ireland would require more wealth than would raise up half-a-dozen of the finest cities of Italy.

But it is when we turn to social life and industrial pursuits that we are struck with the remarkable influence of physical geography and geological structure. Thus, in countries formed of great plains, intersected by but few rivers, there is a natural tendency to assume an unsettled, nomadic life—whilst the prevalence of primary and crystalline slate rocks, which always abound in metalliferous deposits, naturally direct the attention of the population to mining pursuits.

If we look at the map of Europe, we shall find how perfectly geological is the distribution of the great manufactures of European nations. How strikingly this is illustrated in England we can learn, by looking at a geological map of that country, when we will find that every coal-field is the seat of one or several manufactures, and that the outlines of these deposits, and the other associated rocks, would also indicate where population is densest and property most valuable. Turning to the Continent, we find the industry of the Lower Rhine, and of the Meuse, is on great coal-fields, and to the combination of similar causes the development of industry in French Flanders, and in Silesia, is owing.

The existence of abundance of Mineral Raw Materials in a country, accordingly, constitutes one of the principal elements of its prosperity; provided always that its geographical position and physiognomy admit of the economic employment of such resources, by affording facilities of communication, either by means of the sea, or of canals, navigable rivers, or roads. The mere existence of mines does not, in itself, constitute an element of prosperity, a fact which is well illustrated by the case of Siberia. The mineral riches of that region are unbounded, its rivers are among the largest and deepest in the world, its soil is rich beyond example, but its climate makes it a desert, and its rivers end in a sea of ice.

A nation may also possess great resources, an excellent climate, and an admirable geographical position, such as Spain, and may yet take very little advantage of them. But, if we examine minutely into its circumstances, we shall find that some apparently insignificant circumstances connected with its position and climate, have retarded its progress, and produced an anomalous social and political condition of things. But will this state of things last? Certainly not,—such a nation has all its future before it; and the gradual development of its resources which must insensibly take place to meet its ordinary wants, or those new ones imposed upon it from without, by the progress of civilization in other nations, will one day dissipate the social and political anomalies which now exist.

Again, we may find a case where a nation comparatively poor in natural resources, or possessing Mineral Raw Materials of inferior qualities, may, by skill and perseverance, vie with the more favoured nations, where the very abundance, superiority, and consequent cheapness of raw materials, tend to lower the value of skilled labour, especially of an artistic kind, and do not necessitate that exercise of ingenuity and of taste which is developed in the less favoured country; or, in other words, where the natural conditions are most favourable, scientific skill and artistic taste will be more slowly developed than where the conditions are unfavourable, because more skill must be expended in the latter case in order to render the article of higher value, and thus compensate for the increased cost of the raw material. Matter is thus, as it were, conquered by Mind; and it is fortunate for human progress that where prosperity cannot result from purely natural causes, it may be attained by moral and intellectual development.

Such general considerations show, that the department of Mineral Raw Materials must not only be placed first in the Catalogue, but also, perhaps, first in order of importance. And yet to the generality of visitors to an Exhibition, the objects coming under this denomination afford little that is attractive, as in most cases they possess no beauty of form or colour, being usually mere shapeless masses. The same cause which renders them unattractive to the public has undoubtedly prevented a very large number of examples from having been exhibited. However much this is to be regretted, we cannot be surprised at it, for to collect the mineral raw materials of a district requires a considerable amount of knowledge, and that too of a kind which is very rare, and not very popular. Then, again, with regard to the usual metallic ores, their Exhibition could scarcely be of the slightest use in a mercantile point of view to the mine owner, whilst the collection of a proper series would be attended with considerable trouble. Indeed, we may consider the parties who sent illustrative specimens of ores to the Exhibition as among its most generous supporters.

It is an invidious task to be fault-finding, still we cannot help regretting, even now that the Exhibition itself has passed away, that greater exertion was not used to obtain an adequate representation of the mineral resources of the country. There is a general opinion prevalent, not alone in Ireland, but elsewhere, that this country abounds in mineral wealth of all kinds; and accordingly, every intelligent foreigner who visited the Exhibition inquired at once for the department where he would find specimens of the rich ore, fuel, porcelain clay, glass-sands, cements, &c., which he had so often read of. But such were not to be found; and the result has been that these men have gone away with the impression, either that the so much talked of wealth of Ireland was, to some extent, a myth, or that those engaged in its representation knew not in what consisted either the mineral wealth of a country, or the means of furthering its manufacturing industry.

In proceeding to summarize the contents of the department of Mineral Materials, we may observe, that to the great mass of our readers, a catalogue of names would convey but few definite *ideas*, and, we may add, that even an examination of the specimens which appeared in the Exhibition would scarcely be more useful. This opinion does not necessarily lead to the conclusion that the uneducated visitors to an Exhibition learn nothing by going there. An Exhibition cannot teach the nature of substances, or the transformations which they undergo in the workshop, in being manufactured into various articles; but it awakens the perceptive faculties, and leads men to think; and when it has done this, it has fulfilled a glorious mission. If, while the memory still retains the impressions of the objects seen in the Exhibition, we could pass them all in review, show the origin and nature of each raw material, and point out the manufactures of which it is the basis, and follow it in all its endless changes of form in the hands of the workman, until it is at length transformed into the object intended, we might be able to indelibly stamp upon the mind those vague and unconnected impressions which would otherwise soon fade away, and thus as it were create a mental motive power which would rapidly build up industry around us. It is with an intention somewhat of this kind that we are now about, as we enumerate each class of articles in the Exhibition, to attempt in a few words to present to our readers such a history of each material, and each manufactured article, as will enable them to understand the nature of the materials and the processes through which they pass; and, above all, the intimate relations which exist between different branches of industry, and the importance of a study of the laws of nature—that is, of science in its widest acceptation—to all who wish to be successful Industrials. With this view we shall endeavour to show, the natural conditions under which the several materials occur, their geographical distribution, especially in our own country, and the nature of the preparation which they receive to fit them for commerce. Similarly, when we come to the discussion of the article manufactured from these materials, we shall, wherever deemed necessary, tell the history of the manufacture, and the causes, if any, which retarded its progress; describe the various stages of manufacture; and finally, point out how far the particular manufacture would be suitable to our circumstances in case it has not been already developed amongst us.

Such is our object and such our plan. It will be for our readers to decide how far we shall fulfil the one and complete the other. The task is not an easy one, and we hope, therefore, that the importance of the object and the hearty desire to contribute to the best of our ability to the industrial improvement of the country, will induce our readers to pass lightly over the many faults of commission as well as of omission, of which we have no doubt we shall be guilty during the execution of our task. If we succeed in producing in the public mind, even in only a few cases, the idea that the prosecution of industry is a noble occupation which in our days, and in countries like Ireland, requires, perhaps, a greater combination of skill and knowledge, than the so-called learned professions; and, finally, that an unbounded field lies open to persevering skill and industry in Ireland; we shall consider our objects fully attained, and our labours more than rewarded.

### METALLIC ORES, AND THEIR DISTRIBUTION.

If there is nothing that is very attractive in the appearance of great masses of ore to invite attention, or appeal to the senses, there is much to satisfy the mind. Those rock-like masses contained within them the secret of man's power, the very basis of all else within the Exhibition; and the discovery of that secret in the early ages of human history constitutes the first starting-point of civilization. So strongly has mankind felt this, that all early peoples have placed among their divinities those who first separated metals from their ores. Without the discovery of metals we would have been condemned to the unredeemable bondage of barbarism.

Every step of progress in mining and metallurgic arts has always been accompanied by a corresponding gain of power. Thus, in ancient times, the possessor of bronze weapons subdued the warriors armed with bone and flint, whilst the former in turn yielded to the superior force of iron. Even in our times that nation which produces most metals wins the peaceful victories of commerce. It is a metal which forms the motive-power of states, and too often the sole guiding principle of human actions.

This word *Metal*, in its common acceptation, is well understood. Few persons will be at a loss to understand what are the properties which characterize metals when we speak of copper and iron; but science has given a wide meaning to the word, and has shown us that there are many other substances, which, although agreeing in many respects with copper, iron, and gold, differ in a considerable degree in others. We cannot here enter at length into this subject, but we may just state, that all the bodies thus brought into one group under the name of metals by chemists, can be conveniently classified for our purpose into three divisions, depending upon their relation to the air, or rather to one of its elements—oxygen—which has a remarkable tendency to unite with most bodies. The first division comprises what are called *noble metals*—gold, silver, &c.; these, when exposed to the air, do not rust or oxidize—that is, do not combine with oxygen. The second class, comprising copper, lead, iron, &c., rust: but the process takes place so slowly, unless under peculiar circumstances, that their utility is not much diminished by this slow oxidation; and the third comprises a number of little-known metals, such as potassium, which rust so rapidly, in contact with air and water, that in some cases they produce a vivid combustion when placed in water, and which consequently are of scarcely any utility in their metallic condition.

The ancients knew but few metals, but these few comprised the greater number of those which are useful in the metallic state. Gold and silver appear to have been among the earliest known, probably because both are principally found in Nature in the condition in which we employ them—that is, in the metallic state—in small masses, or disseminated through rocks or gravel. The other metals—of the second and third divisions above specified—exist in Nature in a state of chemical combination with certain substances. Now, one of the results of the chemical combination of two bodies is to produce a new one totally different from those of which it is formed; hence, the combinations of the metals which exist in Nature—and which, when they exist in sufficient abundance to be of practical value, are denominated *Ores*—have little or no resemblance to the metals which they contain. Look, for instance, at those blackish, earthy-looking masses exhibited as *clay-ironstone*. What a striking contrast they presented to those beautifully polished pieces of machinery in motion in the neighbouring hall! And yet they contain the iron of which these machines are made. What is the difference between those yellow masses called copper ore and the material of our copper coinage? Simply, that it is combined in the former with sulphur. The substances with which metals are thus combined in ores are not numerous. In general it is oxygen, one of the constituents of air and water; carbonic acid, another substance existing in the atmosphere, and which is familiarly known to all as the gas which effervesces from champagne or soda water; sulphur; and silica, one of the many forms of which is flint.

Looking at a piece of Ore gives but little information, and presents but little interest, unless we know how it occurs in nature, the preparation which it undergoes to fit it for the operation of extracting the metal which it contains, and the nature of the process employed. This sort of information we shall endeavour to supply as briefly as possible; but as the subject is extensive we shall have to divide it—and, for the present, we purpose showing how Metallic Ores occur in the earth, and the countries where they are chiefly found. In performing this task, we shall endeavour to do more than satisfy mere curiosity. We shall, as far as our space permits, allude to the economic conditions which are required to render the existence of rich ores in a country of practical value, and point out their relations to the social condition of a people.

Many of the Metals of the third class constitute important elements in the composition of rocks, such as limestone, which contains a beautiful metal of a silvery lustre. But the greater part of the metals of the other two classes—that is to say, those which are commonly known as metals—do not, if we except iron, constitute any of the elements of ordinary rocks, and are only found in certain localities, and under peculiar conditions. Thus we rarely find metalliferous deposits in flat countries, while, on the other hand, we find few mountainous districts without them.

The most casual observer in the neighbourhood of Dublin must have noticed that there is a remarkable difference between the arrangement of masses of rock in a granite quarry and in a limestone one. In the latter he will observe a regular series of beds placed one over another, sometimes horizontally, like the courses of masonry in a wall, and sometimes inclined at an angle. In a granite quarry, on the other hand, although a number of joints or cracks will be seen, there is a total absence of this bedding or stratification, as it is called. Rocks deposited like limestone are called sedimentary or *stratified*, and are supposed to have been produced by deposition from water; those like granite are called *unstratified* or *igneous* rocks, because supposed to have been formed by the action of heat. The stratified rocks being placed one over the other like bricks in a wall, it is quite clear that the under ones were deposited first. For example, slate rocks are usually found below limestone, and are therefore older, while chalk occurs above, and is therefore more recent. The igneous rocks are of various ages, even where they occur under sedimentary rocks. Granite, however, in relation to most other rocks, may be considered a very old one.

Now it would appear that the age of the rock has something to do with the metal which is found associated with it. Thus tin is ranked as one of the oldest metals, because only found in the oldest rocks known. Then comes bismuth; copper, lead, and zinc occur in rocks of various ages; gold, silver, and cobalt are considered comparatively new, while iron is of all ages. The mineral wealth of a country is, therefore, to some extent, indicated by its physical geography and geology.

When a metal is found associated with a rock, it does not at all follow that it is of the same age as that rock, although it may not be found in any more recent one. This brings us to consider the peculiar conditions under which metals occur, and these we shall class under two denominations, neglecting all minuter subdivision, which neither our space nor object would permit us to dwell upon. Ores then occur either in Banks, which are probably contemporaneous in formation with the associated rocks, or Veins, which are considered to be posterior to them.

A *Bank* may be considered as a bed of mineral matter similar to an ordinary bed of rock, and varying in thickness from a few inches to many yards. They are, in fact, only distinguishable from the adjoining rock by their composition. It is necessary to remember, however, that the whole mass of such banks is not metalliferous. The metallic portion is usually scattered through a stony matrix, or interleaved with it, or it forms thin layers or small veins crossing it in every direction, or disposed in nets, or in scattered nodules. A good example of the latter was presented by clay ironstone, of which some specimens in the Exhibition, from Castlecomer, showed the form of the nodules. The term *Ore* is, however, in most cases, applied to the whole mass of the bank when it is worked for the metallic portion.

Besides the clay ironstones of the coal fields many other ores occur in this way. The celebrated mines of iron in Sweden and Norway, for instance, are of this character, and even copper and lead frequently occur in the same way. Sometimes these banks are of enormous thickness, and of considerable dimensions, and even constitute entire mountains, as the Taberg in Sweden, which is a hill of about 500 feet in height, entirely composed of magnetic oxide of iron. At Gellivara, in Lapland, and in Styria, similar iron mountains occur.

A *Vein* may be considered as a rent or fissure in a rock, which has become subsequently filled up by substances differing more or less from the surrounding rock, only a variable portion of which consists of metallic compounds, the rest being of a stony character, and called *gangue*, or vein-stone, examples of which were presented by nearly all the specimens in the Exhibition. The substances which usually form the veinstone are quartz, carbonate of lime or calc spar, fluor or Derbyshire spar, barytes, &c. Sometimes all these together exist as vein-stone, and but very rarely does it consist of only one; nevertheless some one of these predominates in certain parts of the vein, and very frequently characterizes entire mining districts. In the same way the metallic contents of a vein are very rarely confined to one metal. For example, tin is usually accompanied by tungsten and arsenic; lead, by silver and zinc; copper, by silver, zinc, arsenic, &c.; and iron pyrites or sulphur-stone is found in nearly all veins.

The metallic portions are variously distributed in the vein. Sometimes they form a single band throughout the centre of it; sometimes a number distributed in a sort of parallel series. These bands are occasionally continued for a great distance, at other times they break off at certain intervals and again recommence. Sometimes irregular metallic masses occur, called by the miners *bunches of ore*. The most certain veins are those containing bands of metallic matter, and the least profitable and uncertain are those where irregular masses are found, because in those cases the working of the mine is conducted as a mere hazard. The distribution of metallic matter in a vein has thus sometimes as great an influence upon its economical value as its comparative richness; a poor vein, but of uniform composition for a great length, being in general more advantageously worked than rich veins where the ore is irregularly distributed. The greater number of the veins, or lodes as they are called in Cornwall, are of the former character; and hence although the dressed ore, that is the ore as it is prepared for sale, does not yield on an average more than 8 per cent. of copper, the Cornish mines are always profitable.

Veins pass in a direction from the surface downwards. They scarcely ever descend in a perpendicular direction, but in many cases do not differ very much from it. Occasionally they are very much inclined; this inclination gives them a certain direction in relation to the horizon, which enables us to divide veins into classes. It is very singular that the great majority of rich mineral veins run in a direction differing little from east and west, and are hence supposed to be connected with the magnetism of the earth. The veins which run in a more or less north or south direction are in general poor, and in numerous instances even contain only clay and quartz. Miners call the first *right-running veins*, and the latter *cross-courses*.

Some veins run five, ten, or even more miles through a country, when very much inclined. In general, the richer the vein the greater will be its length; thus the celebrated silver vein called the *Veta Madre*, or Old Mother, at Guanaxuato in Mexico, is worked along an extent of eight miles. Although some few cases are supposed to have been observed of the termination of a vein or lode at a considerable depth, still the greater number continue beyond the limits of the deepest mine. The thickness of a vein may vary from a few inches to 150 feet, which is about the thickness of the silver lode just mentioned. Even the same vein may vary in the space of two or three fathoms, from a few inches to eight or ten feet; from three to four feet may, however, be considered as an average size of good veins.

There are some curious circumstances connected with veins as we descend into the earth. For example, in Cornwall tin is only found to a certain depth, after which copper becomes abundant. Again, certain ores of silver in Peru and Mexico are only valuable near the surface, while the veins of silver in Germany, on the other hand, are only productive at a certain depth, the upper portion containing only iron. Connected with the latter point, it is necessary to observe that an opinion prevails among geologists that veins are somehow connected with igneous action, that is to say, that most metallic veins are either in igneous rocks, such as granite, or immediately connected with them. This is so far true that the principal rich mining districts of all countries are so situate. But there are many mines where no trace of igneous rocks has been observed, such as the celebrated quicksilver mines of Idria, the mines of Poggau in the valley of the Mur, and many others in England, such as the great lead district of Derbyshire. The existence of such mines unconnected with igneous rocks has hence led to the modified view that rich metallic veins, although more abundant in granite and other igneous rocks, are less connected with the nature of the rock than with the existence of great cracks or dislocations in the strata. Such dislocations are found in all mining districts, no matter what the including rocks may be. We have specially mentioned this peculiarity of veins, because it is sometimes stated that some of our richest mines, such as Knockmahon and Berehaven, which are in slate, and apparently totally unconnected with igneous rocks, must on that account be soon exhausted. There exist, however, no facts to support such an opinion, and the oldest mines of England and the Continent worked in similar rocks appear to be as inexhaustible as those situate in granite or in the immediate neighbourhood of it.

Mineral districts, we may further observe, are in most cases circumscribed within certain narrow limits. For example, the celebrated mining district of Freiburg, in Saxony, is only about ten miles long and five miles broad, and yet there are at least eight different systems of veins, for the most part containing different metals, within this small tract; and to come nearer home, we may draw two lines almost parallel through the counties of Dublin and Wicklow, and separated by only a few miles, and find that one would pass through nearly every district where lead has been found, and the other through the places abounding in copper.

We have already mentioned that the metals when found in nature are in a state of combination with other substances; some of them combinations of no importance in an industrial point of view, and others, although largely used in other countries in their manufacture, are not found in sufficient quantity in Ireland to be economically employed. In briefly noticing the ores of the different metals, we shall consequently confine ourselves to those of common occurrence with us, commencing with iron, the most valuable and abundant of the metals.

*Ores of Iron.*—The important ores of iron are four in number: 1. The *magnetic oxide of iron*; 2. The *red oxide* or hematite, including bog-iron ore; 3. *Spathose iron*, which is almost a pure carbonate of iron; and, 4. *Clay-ironstone*.

The first, or magnetic oxide, is the richest ore of iron; but although it occurs, as in Sweden, in immense deposits, it is the least widely distributed. It occurs in many parts of Ireland; among others, in a bed of great boulder-like masses, several miles long on the Aughrim river. It yields the finest iron perhaps of any of the ores of that metal.

The second class of iron ores are also compounds of iron with oxygen, but containing more of the latter element, with the addition of a certain amount of water. The ores of this class are of various degrees of purity, according to the proportion of foreign substances mixed up with the ore. For example, bog-iron ore, which may be considered as a hematite, and which consists of a sort of clinkery mass, which forms in most bogs,—very frequently from the accumulation of the ferruginous skeleton of a microscopic animalcule, the *gaillonella ferruginea*,—is so impure from the presence of a number of other substances, that the iron made from it is hard, and so brittle that it can only be employed in casting ornaments. Many examples of this kind of iron were in the Exhibition, among which we may especially mention the beautiful casting of the Last Supper, after Leonardo da Vinci, from Berlin, and the delicate ornaments for the person, such as buckles, bracelets, &c., from the same place. Hematite is the most diffused ore of iron. In England it is, with one or two exceptions, merely employed to enrich the poor ores of the coal districts, although in many places it occurs under such circumstances as would enable it to be worked alone on a great scale. In France hematite is very abundant, and is largely worked; when pure it yields admirable iron, some of the finest specimens of the Berry-iron being made from it. In other countries, also, it is extensively worked. We possess in Ireland several deposits of this class of ore, which are extremely rich, many of them giving sixty per cent. of iron; this is especially the case in Tyrone, where it is associated with the coal and fire-clay of that county, and is there popularly known as *eagle-stone*.

Spathose iron, when pure, is of a white colour, and resembles in appearance the white veins of calc-spar, which occur in many limestone quarries. Its surface rapidly becomes red, however, on exposure to the air. Immense deposits of this ore occur in Styria, from which, in great measure, the celebrated iron and steel of Austria are made. It also occurs abundantly in Catalonia, where considerable quantities of iron are made from it, the quality of which is quite as celebrated as that of Styria or Sweden. Some deposits of this ore occur in Ireland, among which we may mention one on the property of the Marquess of Downshire, in the county of Down.

Clay-ironstone is also chiefly a carbonate of iron, but a very impure one, being, in fact, a carbonate mixed with a variable quantity of indurated clay mud. It occurs in beds and nodules, imbedded in slaty clay, associated with beds of coal in all countries. Though, with few exceptions, it is the most impure and poorest ore of iron, not yielding in its raw state more than from 20 to 35 per cent. of metal; it is nevertheless at present the most important ore of iron, and the one from which the greater part of the supply of that metal is obtained. This arises from the happy combination in the districts where it occurs, of all the economical conditions necessary for the successful manufacture of iron.

Iron being the most widely diffused metal in nature, we may naturally expect to find it abundant in Ireland. It is one thing, however, to find an ore of iron, and another to obtain it in such quantity and under such conditions as would permit of its being worked with profit. In coal districts clay-ironstone occurs abundantly, and thus we have the two chief raw materials at a cheap rate. The fire-clay for building the furnaces, and the limestone for fluxing are also, in general, found on the spot. It is to this curious combination we have above alluded in speaking of clay-ironstone. At Arigna and other districts in the neighbourhood of Lough Allen, situate upon the Leitrim coal basin, such favourable conditions coexist; and accordingly some years ago, a considerable manufacture of iron was carried on there, which did not, however, long survive the swindling of stock-jobbing,—the bane of Irish industrial enterprises. Within the present year the manufacture has again commenced at Creevelea, not far distant from the original scene of operations, under, we hope, more favourable auspices. Ironstone occurs also, associated with coal in immense quantities, in Kilkenny, but hitherto no attempt has been made to utilize it, notwithstanding that in America, and in Wales, considerable quantities of iron are now made with anthracite coal. The same remark applies to the ironstone of the Munster coal-field. In the County Tyrone the coal is bituminous, and yields good coke; and in addition to the ironstone, which is abundant, a very rich hematite, as we have already remarked, is also found, so that the circumstances of that coal-field are, so far as we can judge, very favourable to the establishment of the iron manufacture.

The other ores of iron are also very abundant, but as they are not associated with coal, they can never form the basis of a manufacture. Many of them are, however, so pure and rich, that, when easily worked, and where situated advantageously for transport, they might be profitably employed to raise the quality of the poor ores of other districts. Among these we may mention the magnetic iron of the valley of the Aughrim River in Wicklow, and some deposits of spathose iron in the county of Down. In former times a considerable quantity of iron was made from such ores with charcoal, and to that circumstance, among many others, we owe the unfortunate destitution of wood which prevails in this country.

The illustration of iron ores in the Exhibition was very small; the only important series exhibited being the highly interesting collection of ironstones and associated grits, coals, and sandstones, contributed by Mr. William Murray on the part of the Monkland Iron and Steel Company, Glasgow. This series represented in a very complete manner the coals, ironstones, limestones, and sandstones of the coal-fields of Lanarkshire. This coal district contains from twenty to thirty seams of coal, of which from five to six are usually worked in a colliery, having an aggregate thickness of about twenty feet. The whole area of coal in the county is about 150 square miles. Considerable quantities of iron are made in this district, of which the series here mentioned contain a very complete illustration. A few samples of the celebrated black-band ironstones of Argyleshire, both raw and calcined, were also exhibited by the Eglinton Iron Company of that county. The only Irish ores of iron exhibited were the clay-ironstones of Castlecomer in Kilkenny, sent by the Honourable C. Wandesforde; some small pieces of spathose iron from the new red sandstone in the county of Down, contributed by the Marquess of Downshire; and two small specimens of micaceous iron ore from Limerick and Clare. The ironstones of the Lough Allen district were totally unrepresented in the Exhibition.*

*Copper Ores.*—Copper, although less abundant than iron, is found under quite as various conditions, for example, copper pyrites, sulphuret of copper, grey copper, and malachite; but there are very few of the ores of any practical importance. Only the two former possess any interest for us, as being the ores found in workable quantities in Ireland.

Copper pyrites is of a deep brass colour, and consists of about thirty-five per cent. of sulphur, thirty of iron, and thirty-four of copper. As the ore is seldom found pure, the usual commercial ore contains much iron. Nearly all the Cornish ores consist of this mineral, as well as the greater part of those shipped from this country to England. The sulphuret of copper is of an iron-grey colour, sometimes purplish and iridescent.

When nearly pure, it would contain about twenty-one per cent. of sulphur, and seventy-seven per cent. of copper, but it is always more or less contaminated with pyrites. In general, the copper pyrites ore, when prepared for sale, does not, in Cornwall, yield more than an average of eight per cent. of copper, and the Irish about ten per cent. This is owing to the large quantity of veinstone or gangue mixed up with it, and which would cost too much to wash out, it being found cheaper to smelt it, in consequence of the low price of fuel in Wales, where the greater part of the copper ores of England and Ireland are smelted.

As copper ores have always been of more importance in Ireland than those of iron, so they were much better illustrated in the Exhibition, but the specimens were exclusively Irish. The chief mining districts represented were the copper pyrites of the Vale of Avoca (Ballymurtagh and Connary); Knockmahon, in the county of Waterford; Berehaven, county of Cork; Dhurode mine, in the same county: argentiferous sulphuret of copper, Shallee and Gurtnadyne mines, county of Tipperary: and argentiferous purple copper from Clontoo mines, near Kenmare.

Copper is almost exclusively found in the slate rocks in Ireland, and hence the supposition already noticed, that they will soon be worked out. It is principally developed in five districts:—1. Wicklow; 2. Waterford; 3. South-west of Ireland, comprising parts of Cork and Kerry; 4. Tipperary, and parts of Limerick; and 5. The west of Ireland, comprising parts of Galway and Mayo; of which the first four only were properly represented in the Exhibition.

*Lead Ores.*—Galena, or sulphuret of lead, a compound of lead and sulphur, of a colour and appearance remarkably resembling lead itself, is the only workable ore of that metal. It occurs in veins and irregular bunches or nests in rocks of various ages—granite, slates, limestone, &c. Galena usually contains more or less silver, which, when in sufficient quantity, is extracted. In the average of Irish ores the silver does not exceed from seven ounces to ten ounces in each ton of lead, but some of the ore from Kilbreckan, in the county of Clare, is stated to have contained 120 ounces per ton. The collection of lead ores in the Exhibition was also exclusively Irish, and was much more extensive than that of copper; nevertheless, it by no means adequately represented the resources of the country in this respect. Among the specimens most worthy of notice in this collection we would certainly place, in the first rank, the complete series from Luganure and other mines of the Mining Company of Ireland. Fine specimens were also exhibited of the argentiferous lead ores of Silvermines, in the county of Tipperary, the property of the General Mining Company of Ireland; some fine crystallized specimens, showing the veinstone from Glengola mines, county of Galway; specimens from Lansdowne mines, Kenmare; argentiferous lead from Clogher and Castlemaine mines, in Kerry; Kiloinogue, near Bantry, county of Cork; and with antimony, from Kilbreckan, county of Clare. Some specimens were also exhibited from Newtownards, in the county of Down, which, with the exception of one or two

* In the Official Catalogue, Dr. Moore, of Saville-row, London, was mentioned as the exhibitor of a collection from this district, but it was not to be found in the Exhibition.

contributions by the Marquess of Downshire, were the sole representatives of the mineral wealth of the North of Ireland.

*Zinc Ores.*—There are only two ores of zinc of any commercial importance:—1. The sulphuret of zinc or blende, which is a compound of sulphur and zinc, and usually accompanying other metallic sulphurets, especially that of lead or galena, being called by the miners of that mineral *jack;* it occurs principally in veins in all rocks below the chalk: and, 2. The Carbonate of zinc or calamine, which is either an earthy-looking, reddish-grey mineral, or a hard, yellowish-grey mass, resembling in a very striking manner magnesian limestone in its external appearance. It is usually found associated with calcareous beds of the chalk group. There are two kinds of blende, one denominated black blende, and the other yellow blende. They are found in greater or less quantity in all lead mines; specimens have, however, been exhibited only from two—Luganure, in the county of Wicklow, and Glengola, in the county of Galway; the latter beautifully crystallized. Calamine has not yet been found in any quantity in Ireland. Several specimens of this ore were exhibited by the *Vieille Montagne* Zinc Company, from their celebrated mines in Belgium. Calamine may yet be found in the chalk districts of the North of Ireland, especially in Antrim, if properly sought for.

We have now noticed all the important Ores exhibited, and we may dismiss the others in a few words. There were a few specimens of manganese, but with one exception they were very trivial. This metal, although not employed in the metallic form, is of great importance in the manufacture of chlorine, bleaching powder, &c. It has been found in several parts of Ireland, but the only deposit hitherto discovered of sufficient importance to be worked continuously is that at Glandore, in the county of Cork. The Mining Company of Ireland exhibited samples of sulphuret of antimony from the mines of Clontibret, in the county of Armagh. The veins which have been discovered there are, however, very unimportant, and were, therefore, relinquished by the Company after an unsuccessful attempt to work them. Some beautiful specimens of native sulphuret of antimony, together with the fused commercial sulphuret and the regulus, as sold for mixing with lead for making printers' types, from near Luxemburg, were exhibited in the Belgian department.

Summing up, then, all the examples of Irish ores shown in the Exhibition, we have the following as the extent to which this department of industry was represented: *Iron* was exhibited from five districts in five counties; *Copper* from nine districts, spread over eight counties; *Lead* from twenty districts, in ten counties; *Zinc* from two districts, in two counties; *Antimony* from two districts, in two counties; and *Manganese* from three districts, in three counties.

## EXTENT OF IRISH MINERAL WEALTH AND MINING INDUSTRY IN IRELAND.

It must be obvious to all that the previous summary possesses value only when we are in a position to compare it with the actual condition of Mining Industry in this country. Unfortunately, the data necessary to do so are very difficult to be obtained. The owners of mines seem unwilling to give accurate statistical information, at least such as would be of a character to indicate the true condition of mining industry. There exists no record office in this country whence accurate information of the progress of commerce, manufactures, and mining industry, would be communicated from time to time to the public. All such statistics are amalgamated with those of England and Scotland, and hence we have to wade through an immense mass of documents to glean a few simple numerical facts. And how often does this labour lead to no result, so completely Imperialized are the numbers. We have endeavoured, as well as we could, to separate a few of the most important facts relating to Irish mining, which we shall give in the following summary.

*Iron* has been found in sufficient quantity to form a probable source of manufacturing industry in twenty-two districts, distributed over sixteen counties—that is, provided the other necessary economical conditions coexist. In six of those districts the iron occurs as clay-ironstone. It has been worked to a greater or less extent at various times in ten localities, in three of which the ore was clay-ironstone. With the exception, however, of those carried on in the Arigna district, those workings were on a small scale.

*Copper* has been discovered in 100 districts in twenty-one counties; there have been workings carried on at various times in fifty-one districts in twelve counties.

*Lead* has been found in 128 districts in twenty-three counties; in twenty-seven districts the lead is known to be sufficiently argentiferous to allow of the profitable extraction of the silver; fourteen in which blende or sulphuret of zinc is associated with the lead ore; and three in which antimony occurs. Lead has been worked to a greater or less extent in sixty-eight districts, in twenty counties.

Of the other metals, *Cobalt* has been found in two counties; *Tin* in two counties; *Antimony* in four counties, in one of which it occurs unassociated with other metals; *native Silver* in eight localities in six counties; *Gold* in four counties; *Manganese* in five counties. By the term *district* we sometimes mean a group of mines; for example, the Berehaven mines, the Knockmahon mines, &c., are really a number of distinct lodes in the same district, and sometimes also worked under the same management. In the summary just given, every such group would only count as one district.

The veins in many of the localities herein enumerated may not contain ore enough to pay for its extraction, or even, perhaps, to be worthy of a search; nevertheless, there can be no doubt that there is a wide field for profitable investment in Irish mines. We must, however, warn our readers from falling into the usual error of some of our sanguine countrymen, who are always talking of our alleged boundless mineral resources. Our mines, if judiciously and spiritedly worked, would confer, doubtless, a great benefit upon the country; but it is time to lay aside imaginative pictures, and content ourselves with the reality, which is simply this,—that our mineral resources are comparatively small. Cornwall alone produces about ten to twelve times as much copper as the whole of Ireland; and one district of Derbyshire more lead. It is beyond doubt, that our mining industry is not yet fully developed; but in this, as in many other branches of industry, our progress has been greatly retarded by bubble speculations blown in London for stock-jobbing purposes. We have abundance of money in Ireland to develop a prosperous trade, but we are deficient in enterprise Would that Irishmen learned a little more of the spirit of self-reliance, and thought less of that bugbear, "English capital," which has too often tended to bring every good project for introducing manufactures into this country into discredit.

It is gratifying also to know that, with one or two honourable exceptions, all the really *bonâ fide* speculations, and those which have been well and perseveringly managed, have been got up in Ireland, and with Irish capital, and that the bubbles are chiefly of foreign manufacture. Without wishing to draw any invidious comparisons, we cannot help alluding here to the services which the pioneer of Irish mining industry—the Mining Company of Ireland, has rendered to this country since its establishment in 1824. With a subscribed capital of £140,000 alone, it has paid in wages the sum of £1,400,000. At present it employs about 2000 people in its mines and collieries, and pays in weekly wages £900. We only regret that its operations are not more extended, and that there are not a dozen such companies at work.

There is no branch of industry subject to greater fluctuations than that of Mining, not only from the variation in the productions of the mines themselves, and of the market value of ores, but also from the jobbing connected with shares in these countries. Nevertheless, the following Tables show that a considerable amount of real progress must have taken place in mining industry in Ireland within the last few years. From other considerations we are also convinced that Irish Mining Industry is, at present, in as healthy a condition as it has been for many years past.

Formerly all Irish copper ores were sent to Swansea to be smelted, where accurate statistics of the quantity sold were kept. During this period, therefore, the Swansea Tables represented the actual condition of Irish copper mining. Lately, however, considerable quantities are sent to other places, and the Swansea returns consequently no longer indicate any definite results. The following Table shows the quantity sold at that port for the five years ending 1852:—

| | Tons. |
|---|---|
| 1848, . . . . . . . . . . . . . . . . . . . . | 12,586 |
| 1849, . . . . . . . . . . . . . . . . . . . . | 9,772 |
| 1850, . . . . . . . . . . . . . . . . . . . . | 10,191 |
| 1851, . . . . . . . . . . . . . . . . . . . . | 10,998 |
| 1852, . . . . . . . . . . . . . . . . . . . . | 9,995 |

In order to show how far these numbers are from indicating the true quantity of copper ore raised in Ireland, we give the following Table, representing the quantity raised at Ballymurtagh, in the county of Wicklow, for the eight years ending 1851, and the quantity sold at Swansea:*

| Year. | Total Copper Ores raised. | Sold at Swansea. | Sold at other Ports. | Year. | Total Copper Ores raised. | Sold at Swansea. | Sold at other Ports. |
|---|---|---|---|---|---|---|---|
| 1844. | 7130 tons. | 3635 tons. | 3495 tons. | 1848. | 7621 tons. | 1317 tons. | 6304 tons. |
| 1845. | 6816 " | 2836 " | 3980 " | 1849. | 7783 " | 1233 " | 6550 " |
| 1846. | 7318 " | 2564 " | 4754 " | 1850. | 6754 " | 339 " | 6415 " |
| 1847. | 6012 " | 964 " | 5048 " | 1851. | 6026 " | 102 " | 5924 " |

The following Table represents the results of the workings of the chief Copper Mines in Ireland for the five years ending 1852, so far as our information goes:

| Year. | | Berehaven, Co. Cork. | Knockmahon, Co. Waterford. | Ballymurtagh, Co. Wicklow. | Lackamore, Co. Tipperary. | Holyford, Co. Tipperary. | Ballina, Co. Mayo. | Gurtnadyne, Co. Tipperary. |
|---|---|---|---|---|---|---|---|---|
| | | tons. cwts. qrs. lbs | tons. cwts. qrs. lbs | tons. cwts. qrs. lbs | tons. cwts. qrs. lbs | tons. cwts. qrs. lbs | tons. cwts. qrs. lbs | tons. cwts. qrs. lbs |
| 1848 | Quantity of ore raised .... | 5872 0 0 0 | 4674 0 0 0 | 7621 0 0 0 | 152 0 0 0 | 302 0 0 0 | | |
| | Produce of copper ........ | 583 8 1 10 | 383 16 1 25 | ............ | 17 13 1 8 | 73 18 1 9 | | |
| | Per centage of copper in ore | 9 7-8th 1-16th | 8 1-4th | 5 | 11 5-8th | 24½ | | |
| 1849 | Quantity of ore raised .... | 5812 0 0 0 | 2787 0 0 0 | 7783 0 0 0 | 114 0 0 0 | | | |
| | Produce of copper ........ | 607 2 3 30 | 247 1 0 25 | ............ | 10 8 2 7 | | | |
| | Per centage of copper in ore | 10 3-8th 1-16th | 8 7-8th | ............ | 9 5-8th | | | |
| 1850 | Quantity of ore raised .... | 6137 0 0 0 | 3314 0 0 0 | 6754 0 0 0 | 101 0 0 0 | ............ | 59 0 0 0 | 154 0 0 0 |
| | Produce of copper ........ | 639 6 0 12 | 264 14 0 5 | ............ | 11 6 3 7 | ............ | 6 7 3 18 | 16 9 1 23 |
| | Per centage of copper in ore | 10 3-8th 1-16th | 8 | ............ | 11 1-4th 1-16th | ............ | 11 5-8th 1-16th | 10 5-8th 1-16th |
| 1851 | Quantity of ore raised .... | 6969 0 0 0 | 3624 0 0 0 | 6026 0 0 0 | 204 0 0 0 | | | |
| | Produce of copper ........ | 710 5 3 27 | 290 11 1 18 | ............ | 16 8 2 4 | | | |
| | Per centage of copper in ore | 10 1-8th 1-16th | 8 | ............ | 7 7-8th 1-16th | | | |
| 1852 | Quantity of ore raised .... | 5692 0 0 0 | 3471 0 0 0 | ............ | 140 0 0 0 | 89 0 0 0 | | |
| | Produce of copper ........ | 591 0 3 10 | 315 11 1 0 | ............ | 8 14 0 14 | 16 18 1 19 | | |
| | Per centage of copper in ore | 10 3-8th | 9 1-16th | ............ | 6 1-8th 1-16th | 19 | | |
| | | £ s. d. | £ s. d. | £ s. d. | £ s. d. | £ s. d. | £ s. d. | £ s. d. |
| 1848 | Value of ore ............ | 36818 4 6 | 24470 0 6 | 15022 0 0 | 1164 12 6 | 5465 2 6 | | |
| 1849 | Ditto ............ | 45868 16 0 | 18046 3 0 | 15342 0 0 | 745 12 6 | | | |
| 1850 | Ditto ............ | 47687 15 0 | 19708 6 6 | 13818 0 0 | 863 0 0 | ............ | 590 13 6 | 1339 9 6 |
| 1851 | Ditto ............ | 53810 0 6 | 21573 7 6 | 11878 0 0 | 1218 8 6 | | | |
| 1852 | Ditto ............ | 54687 19 6 | 29285 14 0 | ............ | 794 8 0 | 1802 5 0 | | |
| 1851 | Number of persons employed ............ | 1200 | 600 | 950 | 50 | | | |
| 1852 | Ditto ...................... | 1200 | 800 | ............ | 50 | | | |

* Under the term copper ores, all iron pyrites containing 2 or 3 per cent. of copper, are included; the latter are sold at Liverpool at a higher price than the ordinary pyrites, while the rich or true copper ores are sent to Swansea to be smelted. The copper pyrites are first employed for making oil of vitriol, and the copper is then extracted from the residual clinker; but the rich ores are directly smelted.

The preceding Table does not contain the results of the workings of Cronebane, Tirgoney, Connory, and Ballygahan, as none of the returns which we have seen exhibit the slightest agreement with one another. For example, the quantity of ore raised in 1851 at Ballymurtagh was estimated by the Company at 6026 tons; but, according to the Custom House authorities of Dublin, the total quantity of copper ore exported from Arklow and Wicklow, or, in other words, the whole produce of all the Ovoca mines, Ballymurtagh, Cronebane, &c., was only 2064 tons. If we except those just mentioned, the copper mines not included in the preceding Table were only a few scattered workings, partaking more of the character of trials than of permanent mining operations. If we estimate the production of all the Wicklow copper mines at 9000 tons of ore, the total copper ore raised in Ireland in 1852 may be estimated at about 18,000 tons; one-half of which would yield about 4 per cent., and the other about 9 per cent. of copper; or about 1170 tons, or one-tenth of the copper produced by Cornwall alone in that year. The total number of persons engaged in copper and sulphur mining may be estimated at about 4200, of whom 2000 are employed in the Vale of Ovoca in Wicklow. Irish copper mining appears to have fully maintained its position in 1853, or rather, perhaps, it improved. The only returns of produce which we have as yet seen are those of Knockmahon, which mines yielded 3106 tons of ore, valued at £31,254, or about £10 per ton of ore. The high price of copper has contributed very much to the prosperity of copper mining generally during the past year.

PRODUCE OF IRISH LEAD MINES IN OPERATION IN 1851–52.

| COUNTIES. | NAMES OF MINES. | 1851. | | 1852. | | | |
|---|---|---|---|---|---|---|---|
| | | Quantity of Ore raised. | Quantity of Lead produced. | Quantity of Ore raised. | Quantity of Lead produced. | Quantity of Silver extracted. | No. of Persons employed. |
| | | Tons. cwts. | Tons. cwts. | Tons. cwts. | Tons. cwts. | Ounces. | |
| CLARE, . . . | Kilbrickan, . . . . . . . . | . . . . . | . . . . . | 72 0 | 40 0 | 4000 | 30 |
| „ | Annaghlough, . . . . . . | . . . . . | . . . . . | 400 0 | 310 0 | . . . . | 100 |
| DOWN, . . . . | Newtownards, . . . . . . | 1643 11 | 894 13 | 1795 0 | 1420 0 | . . . . | 400 |
| „ | Conlig, . . . . . . . . . . | 191 0 | . . . . . | 49 4 | 40 0 | . . . . | 50 |
| CORK, . . . . | Bantry. . . . . . . . . . | . . . . . | . . . . . | 18 0 | 10 0 | 70 | 20 |
| GALWAY, . . | Glengola, . . . . . . . . | 60 0 | 42 0 | 50 0 | 39 5 | 140 | 30 |
| „ | Galway Mines, . . . . . . | . . . . . | . . . . . | 8 0 | 1 19 | | |
| LOUTH. . . . | Dundalk, . . . . . . . . . | . . . . . | . . . . . | 52 10 | 38 15 | . . . . | 10 |
| TIPPERARY, . | Shallee, . . . . . . . . . | 465 5 | 279 4 | 287 0 | 172 4 } | 12000 | 300 |
| „ | East and West Shallee, . . | . . . . . | . . . . . | 438 0 | 295 0 } | | |
| „ | Gorteenadiha, . . . . . . | . . . . . | . . . . . | 76 0 | 50 10 | 300 | |
| WICKLOW, . . | Glenmalure, . . . . . . . | 105 0 | 65 10 | 201 0 | 144 5 | 950 | 40 |
| „ | Luganure, . . . . . . . . | 740 0 | 584 0 | 1057 0 | 661 0 | 4822 | 400 |
| „ | Arklow, . . . . . . . . . | 18 0 | 14 0 | . . . . . | . . . . . | . . . . | 20 |
| LIMERICK, . . | Gurtnadyne, . . . . . . | . . . . . | . . . . . | 76 0 | 57 0 | | |
| | Total, . . . . . | 3222 16 | 1829 7 | 4569 14 | 3279 18 | 22282 | 1400 |

The total number of persons engaged in lead mining in Ireland in the year 1852 may be estimated at about 1450,* being an increase of about 15 per cent. over 1851. In 1853 the lead mining industry fully maintained its position, and, perhaps, even improved, as there was considerable activity in making searches, and in re-opening old workings. We have not been able as yet to collect any statistics for 1853, with the exception of Luganure, which produced 932 tons of ore, value £11,742, or an average of about £12 10s. per ton: and Newtownards, which in the first six months of the year produced 851 tons of ore,—the whole produce of the year being expected to reach 1800 tons, or about the same as in 1852. In order to enable our readers to form some notion of the proportion which Irish lead ores bear to those obtained in Great Britain, we shall add a Table of the production of lead in Great Britain and Ireland for the five years ending 1852:—

| | 1848. | | 1849. | | 1850. | | 1851. | | 1852. | |
|---|---|---|---|---|---|---|---|---|---|---|
| | Lead Ore. | Lead. | Lead Ore. | Lead. | Lead Ore. | Lead. | Lead Ore. | Lead. | Lead Ore. | Lead. |
| | Tons. | Tons. | Tons. | Tons. | Tons. | Tons. | Tons. | Tons. | Tons. | Tons. |
| England, . . . | 54,538 | 39,142 | 60,124 | 41,168 | 63,565 | 44,462 | 64,102 | 45,103 | 62,411 | 43,813 |
| Wales, . . . . . | 16,305 | 11,122 | 19,711 | 13,889 | 21,098 | 14,876 | 19,814 | 14,813 | 18,379 | 13,708 |
| Ireland, . . . . | 1,912 | 1,188 | 2,789 | 1,058 | 2,895 | 1,746 | 3,222 | 1,829 | 4,493 | 3,222 |
| Scotland, . . . | 2,588 | 1,736 | 1,421 | 957 | 3,117 | 2,124 | 3,113 | 2,140 | 3,499 | 2,381 |
| Isle of Man, . . | 2,521 | 1,665 | 2,826 | 1,585 | 2,175 | 1,218 | 2,560 | 1,402 | 2,415 | 1,835 |
| Total, . . . | 77,864 | 54,853 | 86,821 | 58,702 | 92,845 | 64,426 | 92,311 | 65,287 | 91,197 | 64,959 |

The whole of the lead, therefore, manufactured in Ireland in the year 1852 formed only one-nineteenth of that produced in Great Britain.

* The preceding Table includes all the Irish lead mines of any importance worked in 1852; but as many trials were made during that year, there is an apparent discrepancy between the total number of men employed, as just given, and that in the Table; the former including those engaged in making trials as well as in actual, permanent mining operations.

The persons employed at lead and copper mines may be divided into two classes, those who work under ground, and those employed on the surface. The proportion which these two classes bear to each other is, of course, variable. Taking Newtownards as an example—of the 400 persons employed there, about 220 work under ground, and 180 are surface workers. These two classes are paid very differently; the surface workers are usually employed by the week, and can be had at Newtownards for about 7*s.* each per week. The underground workers are paid by contracts, or "bargains," which are put up to auction once a month; their average earnings may be estimated at about 15*s.* per week. These numbers would also represent the condition of Luganure lead mines, and, perhaps, that of most Irish mines. In some mines, however, a considerable tax is levied upon the workmen, and one which is very unjust, and of a very questionable benefit to the proprietors. The miners purchase their tools and other requisites from the captain of the mines, at the rates fixed upon by the proprietors. Now, we know instances in which a profit of *one hundred per cent.* has been charged upon these things! It is reasonable to charge the expenses attendant upon the purchase and conveyance of stores to the mines, because it is absolutely necessary that a stock of them should be always kept on hand, and even a small profit may be added, but certainly not more than what an ordinary trader would be satisfied with.

Miners are very much exposed to accidents. We must, however, add, that the majority of those which do occur arise from intemperance; in too many instances they are improvident, and, consequently, when illness comes upon them they fall into the most abject misery. In Belgium, and many other countries, there is an admirable organization for relieving such distress, the principle of which is in operation in many cases in Great Britain, namely, by deducting a small per centage from the wages. This is not the place for going into details upon the subject; but surely rich companies, like the Mining Company of Ireland, ought to initiate such a system; which, without taking one penny from their pockets, would be of great benefit to themselves indirectly. The excessive profit above alluded to might be well applied to such a philanthropic object.

## MINING OPERATIONS.

Our subject would be incomplete if we did not detail how ores are extracted from the earth, and the various processes through which they pass in the extraction of the metal. To render such an account intelligible and interesting to the general reader is at all times difficult, but it becomes more so when but little space can be devoted to it, and when, in addition, it is without the aid of illustrative diagrams.

The first operation of mining consists, undoubtedly, in discovering the lode or vein, which is as frequently the result of chance as of skill. Still, even chance may be materially assisted by the observance of a little system. Water is the chief agent in such searches, for when a vein comes to the surface, and happens to cross the bed of a stream, portions of the metallic matter will be gradually washed down into some hollow. An examination of the beds of ravines, or of railway or new road cuttings, will also often lead to good results. Independent, however, of all these accidental methods, lodes are discovered by an operation, termed in Cornwall, from whence we have borrowed in Ireland nearly all our mining terms, *shoading* or *costeaning*. In a district where no mineral veins are worked, and where consequently the direction in which they would be likely to run would not be known, two series of pits are sunk through the surface deposit or soil, to the depth of two or three feet into the rock. The pits of each series are sunk at regular intervals in a straight line, the direction of one series being at right angles to the other so as to form a kind of cross. The pits are subsequently joined by galleries, so that, no matter in what direction a vein may run, part of it will be laid bare where it is cut by the line of the shode pits and connecting galleries. Where other lodes have been discovered previously in the neighbourhood, and consequently the general direction of veins in the locality ascertained, one line of shode pits sunk at right angles to that direction will suffice.

We shall suppose a vein has been discovered, and that it looks sufficiently promising to warrant some attempt at working being made; the next operation is to drive a long gallery from the side of the neighbouring valley, if the vein has been discovered in a hill, in the direction of the lode. This gallery is called an *adit level*, and serves to drain off the water from the upper part of the lode. This done, and the lode still promising favourably, a shaft is sunk perpendicularly, somewhat like an ordinary pump well, until it strikes the lode, through which it is carried and continued at the other side to a certain depth. From this shaft, which is seldom less than thirty-two inches in diameter, a number of horizontal passages or galleries, or, as they are usually termed, *levels*, are cut to meet the lode. These levels are usually three or four feet wide, and about six feet high, but are sometimes larger, and sometimes, unfortunately, smaller, and are of various lengths, some existing which are four or five miles long. These levels, which run from the shaft towards the lode, are called *cross-cuts*, and are usually provided with tram-ways for the transport in waggons of the ore and rubbish to the shaft, up which it is lifted by means of two buckets called *kibbles*, alternately ascending and descending. When operations are first commenced, the kibbles are lifted by a simple windlass or *tackle*. This is afterwards replaced by a machine called a *gin* or *whim*, worked by horses or water; or steam power is employed where the operations are sufficiently extensive, and facilities exist for their application.

When the levels are cut through a solid rock, nothing further is required; but where the rock is soft, the roof must be supported, and in many cases all the sides, with wood,—an operation termed *timbering*. Very often, however, as in railway tunnels, bricks and stones are employed instead of wood. When the lode is reached, a number of cross-cuts are run from the shafts to the surface of the lode; the extraction of ore properly commences by running a series of levels in the mass of the lode itself, and following its direction. As these galleries are, however, excavated at different depths, sixty feet often intervening, all the ore lying between the galleries, that is to say, the greater part of it, would be left untouched, for the portions excavated in making the galleries would bear but a very small proportion to the whole mass. To extract the sheet of ore therefore, which lies between the levels, it is necessary either to excavate from an upper to a lower level, which is called *stoping*, or working up from a lower to a higher one, which is technically termed *rising*. The cavities thus left are subsequently filled up with rubbish.

When the workings are carried below the range of the *adit level*, and in all cases where the circumstances of the locality do not permit of the construction of such a level in the first instance, the water which is continually flowing in from the surrounding rocks as it would into a well, when sunk, is pumped up the shaft. When a mine is worked for some time, several new shafts are sunk, in the deepest of which the pumps are usually worked, the other serving for the descent of the miners, and the extraction of the ore. It frequently happens, however, that all the shafts are used for both purposes. These additional shafts are serviceable in another way also, because, by their means a current of air can be established through the various workings, the draught going down one shaft and up another. The same power is used for pumping the water as for extracting the ore; but, in general, water is preferred where practicable. And hence, from this fact, as well as the great importance of water for all subsequent operations in the dressing of the ores, the economizing of water is carried in mining districts to an extent unknown elsewhere. The miners descend the shaft to the level, in which they work by means of perpendicular ladders in one of the shafts, giving themselves light with small oil lamps hooked on the finger; or, as is almost universally the case here, with tallow candles, which they stick with a piece of plastic clay to the front of hemispherical felt hats, made so stiff as to withstand a strong blow, and thus protect them from a piece of the roof falling, or from hurting their heads in low passages. The appearance of a number of miners thus accoutred is very singular,—they look like so many spectres moving about in the thick atmosphere. The effect is still more striking when seen in the neighbourhood of a steam-engine working away several hundred feet under ground, as is sometimes the case, and in a darkness broken only by the lights thus stuck in the miners' hats.

It is unnecessary to describe the manner in which a miner works, or the tools which he employs, as any person who has seen a quarryman at work can realize the mode in which it is done. The miner uses gunpowder for blasting rocks exactly as is done in an open quarry; but some rocks are so hard that even blasting will not effect the miner's object, and he has to adopt other means, which consist in piling up fuel against the part which he wishes to act upon, and, setting fire to it, the rock becomes intensely heated, and splits in various directions, and may then be removed in the ordinary way,—this method is now only practised in one or two mines on the Continent.

*Preparation and Concentration of the Ores to fit them for Smelting.*—By the operations of the miner the ore, constituting the lode, is broken into fragments of various sizes, so that when it comes to the surface it looks like a mass of rubbish out of a quarry, and to the inexperienced eye very unlike what most people in their imagination picture ore to be. To obtain the metal from this mass it must be subjected to two different series of operations, the one mechanical, the other chemical. The mechanical operations are of three kinds, crushing, sifting, and concentration by washing. The object of the first process is to bring the whole of the ore to a convenient state of comminution; that of the sifting to classify the sizes of grains; and the washing to remove as much as possible of the gangue from the ore. The crushing is either effected between rollers, or by great pestles of wood shod with iron. The sifting is effected in the ordinary way, or by machines. The principles upon which the washing, or concentration is effected, are simply that the relative rapidity with which bodies fall in water, or other liquids, depends upon three circumstances:—1. The specific gravity; 2. the size; and 3. The form,—this being the order of their importance. If we suppose a quantity of stuff, such as the mixture of ore and rubbish from a mine to be thrown into water, under the action of density alone, we should find that the ore would first reach the bottom; if size alone influence the fall, the larger pieces would first reach the bottom; and, lastly, if form alone acted, the spherical would fall quicker than the cylindrical, and the latter quicker than flat discs. It is quite clear, therefore, that we could not effect the separation of ore from gangue by throwing it into water as long as the mass contained pieces of different sizes and shapes; hence the necessity of crushing, and stamping, and sifting, in order to bring the grains to as great an uniformity of size and form as possible. In proportion to the perfection to which this uniformity is brought, will be the effectual separation of the gangue and consequent concentration of the ore.

The importance of paying the greatest attention to this branch of mining may be judged of from the fact, that with the same raw copper ore, the same expenditure of time, labour, power, and expense, we obtain very different qualities of marketable ore, according to the manner in which the crushing and sifting was effected. To give an example,—we have known a case where one part of a parcel of ore-stuff produced an ore yielding 7 per cent. of copper; whilst the other part, by a slight and apparently unimportant modification of the process, was so concentrated as to yield 10 per cent.

The series of operations by which ores are washed varies with each metal, with the country, and even the locality. To convey an idea of them we shall select one example,—the metal being lead, and the series of operations that usually adopted in Ireland.

The first operation to which the *ore-stuff* as it comes from under ground is subjected is that of *grating*, which consists in sorting the ore by means of sieves made like the common sieves used for screening gravel for mortar. The large pieces are then washed in a stream of water, which flows into a pool in which the fine mud washed off is caught, after which they are *spalled*, that is, broken into pieces about the size of the fist, or even smaller. The ore thus broken is then *cobbed*, that is, broken with a hammer in such a way as to separate the dead part from the metallic portions. The ores in this operation are sorted into three lots: the first consisting of veinstone or gangue, and containing no ore, or only so small a quantity that it would not pay for its extraction, which is accordingly thrown away as waste; the second, called *halvans*, the poor ore, which consists of so intimate a mixture of veinstone and ore that the latter cannot be separated without a series of mechanical processes; the third, the *sorted mine or fat ore*, consisting of the pieces of pure ore, or that which contains very little gangue. The fine portion, which had passed through the sieves in the operation of grating, and termed by the miners *smalls*, is then subjected to an operation termed *jigging*, which consists in putting the ore into a sort of square box with a sieve bottom; this box is then placed in a tub of water, and jerked up and down in the water by means of a lever or swing. During this operation the water enters by the bottom of the box, and lifts for an instant the particles of ore and gangue, which in falling again sink in the order of their specific gravity, so that the metallic parts being the heavier sink to the bottom, while the gangue comes to the top, and is removed from time to time by the workman with a shovel, and unless it is worth jigging again, is rejected. By this means the ore is obtained in the bottom, separated from a large part of the gangue. The upper portion, being much poorer than the lower, is separated, and considered also as *halvans*, a term which is applied to all poor ores. We have now the three classes of ores:—1. *The fat ore*; 2. *Halvans*; and 3. *Jigged smalls*; which are treated separately by another series of operations to be afterwards described. The fat ore is subjected to the operation of the stamping machine, which consists of a number of huge pestles of wood, armed at their lower ends with masses of iron, and supported vertically in a framework of wood so as to be movable up and down. The motion is effected by means of a horizontal axis, turned by a water-wheel, and having a number of wipers projecting from it, which in their revolution catch a projecting shoulder of the pestles and toss them up, and then allow them to fall into a long cavity, the bottom of which is covered with iron. Into this cavity the ore is put, and is crushed by the falling of the pestles, the stamped ore being carried away by a current of water flowing underneath the pestles, and deposited in its course according to its relative richness, thus effecting a first washing. Instead of these, stamp-crushing cylinders may be employed, and with much greater effect, except where the gangue is too hard, in which case the stamps are best adapted for crushing the ore into fine powder. A very pretty working model of such a series of stamps was exhibited by Mr. P. J. Klassen, intended to represent a quartz crushing-machine, but equally well adapted for ores generally.

The crushed stuff obtained by either of these methods is next *trunked*, an operation which is performed in what is called a *trunk buddle*, which consists of a box into which a stream of water flows, and of a large cistern with a flat bottom. The crushed ore from stampers or cylinders is placed in the box, and is continually agitated by a workman with a shovel; the stream of water carrying away the finer particles into the cistern, where it is deposited, forming what is called *slime* or *slich*, whilst the coarser particles remain in the box, and are removed from time to time. In the case of rich ores, the coarse ore is now sufficiently pure for smelting, and is laid aside in heaps, or, as the miners say, sent to pile, under the name of *crop ore*, otherwise it is jigged in the manner already described when very coarse; or simply *tossed* or *tozed*, when only like coarse sand. This latter operation consists in violently agitating the ores in water, and then allowing them to subside, a result which is sometimes accelerated by what is called *packing*, that is, beating the keeve in which the ore is tossed with a hammer; after which the ore, if not sufficiently cleansed, is washed upon what is called *a flat buddle*, which differs very little from the trunk buddle. The skimmings from the operation of jigging the crop ore are again subjected to the stampers and washed, and the clean ore sent to pile. The slime which flowed into the cistern in the operation of trunking is now washed in what is called *a nicking buddle*, which consists of a slightly inclined table, called the nicking-board, along the top of which runs a spout having a plug in its centre. At the lower end of the nicking-board is a flat board, and below that is a tank, sometimes called the *sleeping table*. The ore is spread upon the inclined table, and a thin sheet of water is made to flow over it, which forms a series of rills in the ore, and gradually washes the mud into the tank, over the bottom of which the ore is strewn according to its purity, that which is deposited closest to the nicking-board being the richest. The clean slime obtained in this way is then sent to pile. We have now got three kinds of clean ore:—1. The *crop ore*, jigged and washed; 2. The clean slime from the nicking-buddles, which was separated from the crop ore; and 3. The slime from skimmings of the crop ore, crushed and washed. The halvans and smalls are treated in exactly the same way; it is, however, usual to mix them both together when crushed. In this way there are from five to six different qualities of ore produced at the mine, the difference between them consisting merely in the amount of gangue which they contain.

In jigging the smalls, and in the other various operations, a certain quantity of fine matter, technically called sludge,* is carried away by the water, which is, however, not allowed to go waste, but is made to pass through a series of pits called *buddle holes* or *slime pits*, where it deposits, and after a time is collected and washed, forming another quality of slime ore. The series of operations, which we have just described, is as nearly as possible that followed at the Luganure Mines, near the Seven Churches, in the county of Wicklow; and the Mining Company of Ireland, who work those mines, exhibited a case containing a nearly complete series of specimens illustrative of the process. The General Mining Company of Ireland also exhibited some samples of dressed ore, but, not having a complete series illustrative of the stages of the preparation, we are unable to say whether the process which we have described is the same as that followed at their mines.

The object of all these operations is to remove as much of the gangue or veinstone from the pure ore as possible; the more perfect the system of washing the purer will be the ore, and the better fitted will it be for the operations of the smelter. In Great Britain, where fuel is so cheap, the washing is not in general so perfect as it is on the Continent, where scarcely one-half per cent. of ore is left in the waste. But as fuel is not so cheap in Ireland, it might be worth our while to adopt the Continental system, which has grown up under circumstances more similar to our own than to those of England.

### THE SMELTING OF LEAD ORES.

After undergoing the mechanical operations which have been already described, the ore is fit for the chemical operation of extracting the metal by smelting. The general principles of this process are the same, no matter what the metal may be. The washed ore consists of a mixture of some metal in combination with oxygen and sulphur, mixed with more or less foreign matter derived from the veinstone, and consisting usually of quartz, but sometimes also of sulphate of barytes, fluor spar, and other substances; all of which it is desirable to remove, and thereby obtain the metal in a free state. This object is effected by employing some substance which, when heated with the ore, combines with the foreign matter, and sets the metal free. As illustrations of this process we shall select one or two examples, the first of which shall be

* This term is also applied to all fine metallic matter in suspension in water.

lead, because we have described in detail the operations of its mechanical preparation, and also, because the manufacture of lead was the best illustrated of any of the metals in the Exhibition.

The ordinary lead ore, as it is sent to the smelting-house, consists of galena, which is a compound of lead and sulphur, with a variable portion of gangue. The object of the smelter is to get rid of this sulphur and gangue; to effect which the ore is first roasted—that is, exposed to the action of air at a high temperature, by which both the metal and the sulphur take in oxygen, and form sulphate of lead; which is again decomposed the moment of its formation, a great part of the sulphurous acid going off and leaving oxide of lead, producing sulphate of lead and metallic lead. Some of this separates, while another part combines with some of the undecomposed ore. At this stage the smelting process commences; and consists in stopping the supply of oxygen, and providing substances rich in carbon to take away the oxygen from the lead—and lime to take the sulphuric acid which has been formed; and convert the gangue into a species of glass, and thus prevent it from combining with the lead. The roasting is conducted in some places in one furnace, and the smelting in another; but at Ballycorus, the only lead-smelting works in Ireland, one furnace serves for both operations. This furnace is what is called a reverberatory one, and consists essentially of two parts: first, the hearth upon which the ores are spread, and which is dish-shaped, and domed over with brickwork; and second, the fire-place, which is an ordinary furnace-grate, the flame of which passes into the hearth, and is made to sweep over its surface by the form of the roof; after which the smoke and gaseous matter pass into a long horizontal flue, which is sometimes 100 yards long, and which terminates in an upright chimney, from 100 to 120 feet high. Supposing the furnace to be in full action, and that an operation is just finished, a quantity of ore, which for each charge is usually about one ton, is introduced into the furnace through a hopper, and is spread over the hearth; here it is roasted at a very moderate heat, produced by the effect of the previous operation. During the roasting the ore is occasionally turned over with rakes, and at the end of two hours the operation is completely finished. The doors are then shut and a strong fire made, which produces a vivid red heat in the interior of the furnace, which is maintained from two and a half to three hours—the mass being from time to time stirred. A little lime is added occasionally in the last two hours, by the action of which and of the gaseous matter of the coal, the lead is reduced, and collects in the basin-like cavity of the hearth, from which at the proper time it is run off into a cistern, and thence ladled into moulds of iron, the quantity contained in each mould being called a *pig of lead*; examples of which were exhibited by the Mining Company of Ireland, and by J. Byers, of Stockton upon Tees.

The gangue and part of the sulphur form with the lime a slag or clinker, which is raked out of the furnace, and, as it still contains a portion of lead, is laid aside. A quantity of the ore is also carried off by the draught of air which sweeps through the furnace, and is deposited in the long horizontal flue. It is thence removed from time to time, and subjected along with the ore slags to a second operation, similar in every respect to that to which the ore is subjected in the first instance; and in this way an additional quantity of lead is obtained—which is, however, in general inferior in quality to the lead obtained directly from the ore.

Before proceeding to describe the processes employed in the smelting of other metals, it will be convenient to complete our observations upon the subject of lead. With this view we shall briefly state the mode in which silver is extracted from lead, the manufacture of pipe and sheet lead, and shot.

### SEPARATION OF SILVER FROM LEAD.

Many ores of lead contain a small quantity of silver, the presence of which renders the lead obtained from them hard and unfit for many purposes to which that metal is usually applied. Formerly, when the quantity of silver was large, it was extracted by an operation called *cupellation*, which consisted in melting the lead in a large dish-like crucible made of the powder of burnt bones, or more generally of white marl, placed in a sort of reverberatory furnace, and causing a blast of air to pass over its surface. The melted lead combines with the oxygen and forms litharge, which, assisted by the force of the blast, flows out of the furnace, leaving the silver behind in combination with a small portion of the lead. The charge for such a cupel is usually about 5 cwts.; but during the operation, which lasts from fifteen to eighteen hours, further portions are added until from 80 to 90 cwts. have been added. If a ton of the lead contained originally 15 ozs., and 80 cwts. or 4 tons were thus operated on, there would be in the cupel 60 ozs. of silver in combination with about 1 cwt. of lead. Such a mass is called *rich lead*, and is laid aside until a sufficient quantity of it is obtained to yield from 1000 to 2000 ounces of silver; it is then submitted to the action of a blast of air, until the whole of the lead is oxidized into litharge, which is raked off, leaving a mass of silver behind, silver not being capable under such circumstances of being oxidized. The litharge thus obtained, together with the cupel broken up, which is found to absorb a quantity of the litharge, is reduced in a furnace with coke, and the lead cast into pigs as before. The lead thus produced is known as *refined lead*—that produced directly from the ore being called *common* or smelter's lead—is exceedingly pure and soft, and may be applied to the manufacture of sheet lead. By this process a good deal of lead was lost—at least seven per cent.—and there was a great consumption of fuel. It could not, therefore, be profitably adopted with any lead that did not contain from fifteen to twenty ounces of silver per ton. But such leads are very rare, and the usual process was to mix such rich with poor lead, so as to form a mixture which would contain enough of silver to pay for the cost of cupellation.

Some years ago Mr. Pattison, of Newcastle, made a very happy invention, by which the silver, even when existing in the proportion of only three ounces to the ton, might be profitably extracted. This ingenious and important process is founded upon the property that when lead containing a little silver is melted, and then gradually allowed to cool, a portion of the lead will crystallize out, as salt does out of brine, leaving the silver in the fused portion. If we remove the lead crystals by a sort of drainer, and repeat the process, we will be gradually able to remove the greater part of the lead; leaving an alloy of silver of gradually increasing richness behind. In this way we may produce from lead containing only three ounces per ton, an alloy containing thirty ounces, while, with lead containing ten ounces, which many of our Irish leads do, we can obtain a rich lead containing 100 ounces. The operation is performed in simple iron pots, capable of holding about three tons of lead each, set in brick-work, and heated by a fire. The crystallized lead, as fast as it is removed by the drainer, is remelted, and cast into pigs, and is sent into commerce without any more preparation; and although not absolutely free from silver, the quantity present does not exert much influence upon its quality. When the silver-lead remaining in the pot is sufficiently rich, it is cupelled in the way already described. The saving by this process must be evident, for instead of having to cupel 100 tons of lead, 90 are now merely crystallized, and only 10 are to be cupelled. The importance of this invention may be judged of by the fact mentioned by Sir Robert Kane, that formerly Irish lead was so hard that it was considered of inferior quality, and was obliged to be exported to England or to Holland, where it was mixed with richer leads and refined, and was frequently re-imported into Ireland. Several years since the Mining Company of Ireland introduced this process into their smelting works at Ballycorus, where it is still carried on with success. It was at these works that the fine cake of silver, weighing 1604 ounces, and worth about £450, which was in the Exhibition, was obtained in the way just described from lead produced by smelting the ore of Luganure. Mr. Byers also exhibited a small cake of silver and a pig of refined lead; and the General Mining Company of Ireland exhibited a small button of silver and several samples of litharge, obtained from the cupellation of their ores, from Silvermines in Tipperary.

The litharge produced in this process may be reconverted into lead by heating it with coke in a particular form of furnace. A good deal of it, however, finds a direct market for boiling with linseed oil, to render it drying. It is also used in the preparation of some kinds of varnish, and in the manufacture of flint-glass, enamels for watch dials, red lead, and some other mattters.

## MANUFACTURE OF SHEET LEAD AND LEAD PIPE.

The chief applications of lead, in its metallic form, are for the manufacture of sheet lead for roofing houses, lining cisterns, making chambers for the manufacture of oil of vitriol, for the manufacture of white lead, and of lead pipe. The process by which the sheet is formed is simple. It consists in casting a large plate of lead, about seven inches thick, and weighing several tons, and passing it between two polished steel rollers until it is rolled out to the required thickness; a point which is regulated with screws by which the rollers can be brought to any distance required. Lead pipe is formed in two ways, one by drawing, and the other by pressure. The former process may be considered as a species of wire-drawing. A cylindrical bar of lead is cast in the first instance with an iron core or rod of a certain diameter; when cold this core is removed, and a long rod of the same thickness is inserted in its place; and the whole is then arranged in a kind of mechanism which travels along a table, and forces the cylinder through a series of rings of steel, of gradually decreasing diameter, successively presented to it. By this means the cylinder is continually lengthening and diminishing in diameter, but as the iron core undergoes no change, a pipe of uniform bore is at length produced. It is scarcely necessary to remark, that the softer the lead the more adapted it will be for making lead pipe, by drawing in the way just described; in fact it is only refined lead that can be advantageously employed for that purpose. The great disadvantage of this process is, that the pipe, although in other respects perfect, cannot be made in lengths exceeding twenty or thirty feet. But by what is called the pressure process not only can a pipe of any length be produced, but any kind of lead, hard or soft, may be used. If we suppose a cylindrical iron chamber, with a bottom which moves up and down, air tight, in it, a kind of piston in fact; and that on its top is placed another cylinder of much smaller diameter, into the upper orifice of which can be fitted a series of rings of different diameters, and in the axis of which and of the smaller cylinders can be placed a sort of core or iron rod of any desired thickness; and if the lower cylinder be filled with melted lead, very little hotter than its fusing point, and that we now force the piston in its bottom upwards,—the melted metal will be forced into the upper cylinder, where it will become so far cooled that it will become pasty; and on the pressure of the piston from below being continued, will be driven in a solid form through the ring forming the open orifice of the smaller cylinder, and will issue out in the shape of a long rod of the same size as the ring. In passing through the small cylinder and ring, however, the semifluid metal will surround the iron core or rod which is placed in the axis of the cylinder, and the rod in passing out will be hollow; will be a lead pipe in fact. In practice the lead pipe thus made is carried up to about ten or twelve feet to allow it to cool sufficiently, and is passed over a wooden pulley or drum, and then wound into a coil on a kind of windlass. The piston which forces up the lead in the large cylinder is attached to the ram of a hydraulic press, worked by water or steam. The cylinder in which the melted lead is put usually contains about 3 cwt. of metal; and in order to keep so large a mass sufficiently fluid it is surrounded with a jacket of sheet iron, in which a small fire is made. The length of pipe which can be made in one operation is determined by the quantity of lead which the large cylinder or reservoir can hold.

Several samples of sheet lead were exhibited from the works at Ballycorus, and by M'Garry and Sons from the Palmerstown mills. Davidson and Armstrong of Manchester exhibited some of the thin sheet lead used for packing tea in China and for exporting snuff in these countries, and also a sheet of lead plated on both sides with tin during the operation of rolling, the tin being subsequently polished. The object of this plating, which is very ingenious, was to enable the lead to be applied for making water cisterns, and for other domestic purposes, without subjecting those using it to the danger of being poisoned. Samples of the pipe made at Ballycorus by the drawing process were also shown by the Mining Company. The pressure process was illustrated by samples from Palmerstown Mills, and by some fine coils of gas pipe made by T. Hodges of this city. The latter indeed illustrated in a remarkable manner the great lengths of pipe which could be made by this process,—one coil being 2400 feet long, and another, of inch pipe, 1100 feet, and weighing one ton! Messrs. Davidson and Armstrong also exhibited some pipe which, like their sheet lead, possessed the peculiarity of being plated inside and outside with tin. The gas pipe made in this way is stiffer than that made of pure lead; it is also very durable, and, from the tin retaining its brightness, it is much better adapted for glass gaseliers than the ordinary composition gas pipe, which is an alloy of lead and tin.

### MANUFACTURE OF SHOT.

There is a natural tendency in all fluids to assume a globular condition, under certain conditions; even water will do so, as we can see in the case of dew, and when sprinkled on a dusty floor. It is on this property that the manufacture of shot is founded. Pure lead is, however, ill adapted for the manufacture of shot, as the grains are usually hollowed or flattened and form tails; to remedy which a certain quantity of arsenic must be added, the usual proportions being 3 parts for each 1000 parts of pure lead, or 8 parts for the same quantity of hard lead, which, as being cheaper, is the kind usually employed. The alloy thus formed is called by the workmen *poisoned metal*. The present process of manufacturing shot, such as that exhibited by the Mining Company of Ireland, and made at their shot tower at Ballycorus, is very simple and interesting. At the top of a large tower, with a series of floors having trap-doors in the centre, and which when open afford an uninterrupted fall of at least 150 feet, is a large iron pot with a fire-place; and in this pot two or three tons of the poisoned metal are melted. This melted metal is then poured into hemispherical cullenders, the bottoms of which are pierced with holes of the diameter of the shot to be made, and are kept at a proper temperature by being placed in a kind of chafing dish with burning charcoal. These cullenders are placed over the openings in the floors, and the metal falls in a shower of metallic drops through the traps into tubs of water placed at the bottom. The smaller the shot, the less the height required through which it is to fall, because the sooner it cools; for example, the smaller size shot may be produced by a fall of 100 feet, while the larger size, such as swan drop, requires at least 150 feet. All the holes in the cullender are of the same size, still the grains of shot will not be all equal; hence the different sizes must be separated by means of sieves with holes of the proper sizes; after which the shot must be subjected to another sorting in order to separate all the grains which are ill formed. For this purpose a handful of the shot is spread upon a board which is slightly inclined, and in this position gets a gentle horizontal motion, by which all the perfectly spherical shot roll off the board into a chest made to receive them, whilst the irregular ones are caught by very slight ledges on the sides of the board, and are reserved for a remelting. The perfect grains are now ready to undergo the last operation or polishing, which consists in introducing the grains into a small octagonal barrel with a little black lead; the barrel is then made to revolve, and thus causes the grains to polish each other.

Large quantities of shot are made at Ballycorus, near Dublin, of which samples, representing the whole series of sizes, were exhibited by the Mining Company of Ireland.

### SMELTING OF ZINC ORES.

Although the ores of zinc are not as yet found in sufficient quantity in Ireland to form the basis of a manufacture, we cannot avoid giving some details of the processes connected with the preparation of that metal, because it affords an example of a smelting process quite different from that of lead or iron; besides the applications of zinc have now become so numerous, and so important, that some knowledge of the history of the metal must be interesting, and there was scarcely one of these applications which was not illustrated in the Exhibition.

The separation of zinc from its ores is simple, especially in the case of calamine. As comparatively little zinc is now made in Great Britain, from the superiority and cheapness of Belgian and German zinc, we shall describe the process followed at the works of the Vieille Montagne Company, near Liege in Belgium, whose contributions formed so important a feature of the Exhibition. The ores found in that district are calamine, or carbonate of zinc, silicate of zinc, which is scarcely at all employed in the manufacture, and some oxide,—a complete series of samples of which were exhibited. At the smelting-houses these ores are simply divided into white ore and red, a classification which corresponds with their chemical composition, the white being the richer ore, usually containing 46 per cent. of oxide of zinc, whilst the red, which derives its colour from a large quantity of iron, contains about 33 per cent.

The veinstone of these ores at Vieille Montagne is always clay; so that, unlike lead or copper, the gangue is readily separated by a good washing, after which it is roasted in a sort of furnace, exactly like an ordinary limekiln. The roasted ore is then ground under edge runners, somewhat like those employed in oil mills, and mixed with half its weight of bituminous coal, similarly ground. The mixture is afterwards passed through a very fine sieve, when it is ready for reduction. An ordinary zinc smelting-house consists of four distinct furnaces, built together so as to form a kind of square block of masonry, with a common chimney, divided into four compartments, in the centre. Each furnace consists of an arched recess, into which are built forty-six earthen retorts, arranged in seven rows of six each, and one of four, much in the same way that gas retorts are placed. Each retort is three feet eight inches long, and is fitted with an adapter of cast iron, which acts as a condenser, to which is fitted a cone of wrought iron, the narrow end of which is only about one inch in diameter. We will suppose the retorts at a bright red heat at six o'clock in the morning, the hour at which the charging usually commences. The mixture is introduced into them by means of a semi-cylindrical shovel, in the same manner as the coal into gas retorts. The cast-iron adapters are then fitted on and the heat raised; in a short time a quantity of carbonic oxide issues from the mouths, and burns with a pale blue flame. Gradually the flame becomes brighter, assuming at the same time a greenish white, fringed with red tint, and white fumes are given off. These appearances indicate that the metallic zinc has begun to come over. The conical hood of sheet iron is now luted on, and the greatest care taken to keep the temperature of every part of the furnace as equable as possible. After the lapse of two hours the workman takes off the cone, and removes the oxide of zinc which has collected in it, and which was formerly mixed with fresh ore, but part of which now finds direct employment as a paint. This done, a ladle is held under the beak of the retort, whilst the foreman rakes out the liquid zinc which had collected in the shoulder formed by the earthen retort and the cast-iron condenser. The zinc in the ladles is then poured into moulds, having raised letters on the bottom, representing the words *Vieille Montagne*. These moulds give the zinc the form of rectangular cakes or ingots, weighing about 75 lbs., in which form it comes into commerce. One of those ingots was exhibited among the Company's collection. When the whole of the zinc is thus withdrawn, the cone is again luted, and the firing continued for two hours longer; when the same operation is repeated, and so on until five o'clock, when the operation is finished. The residue is then withdrawn from the retort, and the same series of operations recommenced.

Two charges are thus operated upon in twenty-four hours; the whole quantity of ore required for each furnace being about 500 kilogrammes, or 1102 lbs., to which is added half that quantity of coal. The total product during that period may be taken at about 620 lbs. of metallic zinc, which, with dross capable of being reduced very readily, makes the total produce of zinc about 660 lbs., or 30 per cent. of the ore. The furnaces are usually worked continuously for two months, when they must be allowed to cool down, to be repaired.

The greater part of the zinc made is employed as sheet, for which purpose it requires to be exceedingly pure, and is therefore remelted in a reverberatory furnace. The rolling of zinc into sheets differs from that of lead only in the metal being passed through the rollers while at a temperature equal to about that of boiling water.

In 1851 the Vieille Montagne Co. had five establishments, employing 2640 workmen, and produced 11,675,851 kilogrammes of zinc (11,593 tons), or 78 per cent. of the zinc of Belgium, and 23 per cent. of the zinc of Europe. Of this quantity, 6000 tons were rolled into sheets; the remainder, together with 2500 tons purchased by the Company from other sources, especially from Silesia, were sent to their factories in France. They employ forty-two furnaces, each having forty-six crucibles in constant activity. A premium is allowed to the workmen upon all economy of raw materials, which amounts in a year to about 800 francs (£40) per furnace, the half of which is paid at once, and the remainder at the end of the season; 2½ per cent. is deducted from all wages and premiums, 1 per cent. of which forms an annuity fund for aged widows and orphans, and 1½ per cent. for a sick fund. In consequence of these admirable arrangements the Vieille Montagne Company have one of the most intelligent, moral, and laborious bodies of workmen in Europe.

A mere enumeration of the articles comprising the collection of the Vieille Montagne Company, in the French Department of the Exhibition, and in the Irish and British one, would be perhaps the best possible summary of the uses to which zinc could be put in the arts. Besides constituting one of the elements of that extremely important alloy, brass, zinc is now employed for the production of cast architectural ornaments; as a substitute for bronze in the production of works of art, of which so large a number were exhibited; of forms for sugar refiners,—an application which is said to have this advantage over the wrought-iron ones now in use, that, when injured, the old material will still possess half the original value; nails of all sizes; wire cordage; bars for making bolts; plates for galvanic batteries, and for protecting iron from rust; and galvanized iron for roofing, &c. But it is in the rolled condition that it is chiefly used; as for example, in the making of baths, water tanks, buckets, spouts, pipes, roofs, &c.; for plates for engraving music; for anastatic printing; for sheathing vessels (a vessel has lately been constructed almost altogether of zinc in France); stamped mouldings, and other ornaments for furniture and architectural decoration, an application of which we shall speak in another place.

Zinc has also been used as a material in the manufacture of glass, especially for optical purposes; and lastly, an important use is now made of it in the production of white paint, which is not liable to become black by the action of sulphuretted hydrogen. Four varieties of the paint are made: the first is called *snow-white*, and may be applied in all cases where Paris white (blanc d'argent) was formerly used; it covers equally well, and remains white, which the other does not. The second is *zinc-white*, which is fully equal to the finest white lead, covers quite as well, is as durable, and remains white. The third is *stone-gray*, the quality of which is the same as the last, its only difference being in the shade; it is well adapted as a ground colour, and as a paint for iron-work, or for the interior of houses, being more durable under the influence of air and weather than white lead. The fourth variety, or *gray oxide*, is particularly adapted for ship-painting, external wood-work of out-offices, or as a ground for more expensive colours on stone or cement. At first, the oxide was formed by burning the metal in a current of air; but it is now generally produced directly from the ores. The introduction of this oxide as a substitute for white lead originated in France, and certainly constitutes one of the most remarkable gifts which chemical science has recently bestowed upon the industrial arts.

The Vieille Montagne Company exhibited samples of the four varieties just mentioned, and also a number of shades of yellow, green, blue, &c., of which zinc-white formed the base or diluting element. Several samples were also exhibited by Langston, Scott, and White, of Lombard-street, London.

### SMELTING OF IRON, AND MANUFACTURE OF WROUGHT-IRON AND STEEL.

From the mode and abundance in which iron ores usually occur, there is not the same necessity for subjecting them to the complex series of mechanical operations by which other ores are prepared, and which have been already described in the case of lead. The only treatment they undergo previous to introducing them into the smelting furnace is to pick them, and break them into small pieces.

The furnace employed in iron smelting, and usually called a *high-furnace*, consists of—1. *The hearth*; 2. *The boshes*; and 3. *The cone* or *body*. This hearth is a sort of quadrangular box, slightly smaller at the bottom than at the top, being in ordinary sized furnaces about 2 feet 8 inches at bottom, 3 feet at top, and about 6 feet deep. It is made of the most refractory sandstone, the joinings being cemented with fire-clay. One side of this box does not reach fully to the bottom, so that a hole equal to the whole width of the hearth, and about half its height, is left. The block, which lies above this opening, and forms the upper half of the same side of the quadrangular hearth, is called *the tymp*. This hole is not, however, left completely open, for a sort of prismatic or wedge-shaped piece, called the *dam-stone*, fits into it, leaving, however, an open space of about five to six inches between it and the tymp. The inner edge of this wedge is bevelled off; and as its base is turned in so as to form part of the wall of the hearth, a sort of inclined plane is formed by the dam-stone from the ground around the furnace to the vacant space between it and the tymp. The part of the hearth below the tymp, and corresponding in depth to the height of the dam stone, is called *the crucible*. The boshes consists of a truncated cone, about 8 feet high, the base or wider part being turned upwards, so that the narrow end fits on the box constituting the hearth. Above the boshes comes the cone or body, which consists of another truncated cone, about 36 feet in height, with its base fitting upon the boshes. As the point of junction would produce a sharp angle, it is usually rounded off so as to form a narrow cylindrical zone, called *the belly*. The narrow opening at top of the body is called *the throat* or *tunnel head*, and over it is built a chimney, about 12 feet high, the whole height being thus about 62 feet. The external masonry of the boshes and body is formed of common brick, and for such a furnace 180,000 to 190,000 bricks would be required. The inner surface is composed of the most refractory fire-bricks, and the furnace described would take from 50,000 to 60,000 of these fire-bricks. The inner coating of fire-brick of the body is termed *the shirt*, and is usually separated from the external masonry of common brick by an interposed coating of broken clinker and sand, for the purpose of preventing the furnace from cooling. The other three sides of the hearth are pierced with holes, into which are fitted conical iron pipes, called *tuyeres*, through which the blast is introduced into the furnace. These tuyeres enter the hearth a little above the level of the tymp, that is, above the part called the crucible, and each has a different inclination so as to prevent the blast passing through each from meeting in the furnace. As the tuyeres are exposed to a very intense heat, they are surrounded by a case through which circulates a current of cold water. The blast is produced by a blowing-machine, usually consisting of a cast iron cylinder, in which works a solid piston, and by means of a set of valves alternately opening, a quantity of air is drawn into the piston at each stroke, and forced into a lateral chamber, whence it passes by a main tube with three branches to each of the tuyeres. The force required to work the blowing-machine of a furnace may be taken at from 26 to 30 horse-power; and some idea may be formed of the extent of the smelting works in Wales and other celebrated iron districts of Great Britain, when it is stated that some of the blowing-machines now employed require 350 horse-power to work them, each machine thus serving for twelve furnaces. The quantity of air required by each furnace when in full blast is about 3600 cubic feet per minute, the usual pressure of the blast being about 2½ lbs. on the square inch.

Where practicable, iron furnaces are built at the foot of a declivity, and it is also usual to construct several of them in one block of masonry. In such cases a tramway is carried from the elevated ground to the top of the furnaces, on which there is constructed a platform. The ore, flux, and coal or coke, are brought in trucks along this tramway, and thrown directly into the throat of the furnace.

Previous to smelting it is necessary to roast the ore, which is effected by interstratifying layers of it with small coal, and setting fire to the heap; occasionally it is roasted in a furnace constructed like a common lime-kiln. By this roasting, clay-ironstone, the smelting of which as the most important ore of iron in those countries we shall describe, loses its carbonic acid, as carbonate of lime or limestone does under similar circumstances. In setting the blast furnace to work it is first carefully dried, then filled up with the fuel, and the blast allowed to play into it with gradually increasing force, until the full power is acquired; by this time the fuel will have sunk in the body of the furnace, and a quantity of ore and flux is now introduced, and upon this is laid a layer of coke. This operation is repeated as often as the mass sinks in the furnace, but with gradually increasing charges of ore, until, in the course of a few days, the proper proportions of fuel and ore are attained, after which the furnace is considered to be in full working order.

In the top of the furnace the temperature is not very high, but it increases until it attains its maximum in the hearth a little above the tuyeres. As the ore, flux, and fuel pass through these gradations of temperature as they sink in the furnace, various chemical changes take place; but it is when the ore reaches the lower part of the boshes that the perfect reduction is effected. Here the carbon of the fuel takes the oxygen from the iron, whilst the flux or lime unites with the gangue, consisting of clay or silica, and also with a portion of the iron, forming a compound resembling in composition black bottle-glass. The mass having undergone this change, and become semi-fused, sinks into the hearth, where the intense heat at once fully liquefies the iron and the combination of the lime and gangue, both of which fall in a shower into the crucible below the tuyeres. Here the two fluids arrange themselves according to their relative densities, the iron sinking to the bottom, and the glassy scoriæ floating on the surface, and thus protecting the former from the oxidizing action of the blast entering just above it. According as the process proceeds, both accumulate until the crucible is full, and the slag gradually overflows the edge of the dam, through the opening between the latter and the tymp, and runs down the inclined plane. Formerly this slag was raked off the inclined plane, but in many furnaces, at present, the dam-stone is not formed with an inclined plane; and cast-iron waggons may, in consequence, be brought up to the tymp, and the slag allowed to flow into them, and, when full, carried off by means of a tramroad. In this way the slag is obtained in the form of rectangular blocks, which may be employed for a great many purposes where an indestructible material would be required, or in the manufacture of bottle-glass, &c. When we recollect that the quantity of slag is five or six times the volume of iron, we may estimate the weight of the former, annually produced, at from 4,000,000 to 5,000,000 tons. This would, no doubt, form a beautiful material for making slabs of glass for roofing public buildings, for the floors of water-closets, water-pipes, cisterns, and a thousand other purposes.

After some time the crucible would become full of melted iron, but before that takes place it is drawn off through a hole in the side of the furnace, which is kept plugged with fire-clay. Previous to performing this operation, which is technically called *tapping*, a number of parallel trenches are formed in sand on a flat surface near the furnace; each series of these trenches is crossed by a main trench, which is again connected with a channel which goes to the *tapping-hole*. When all is ready the blast is shut off, and the plug of clay is withdrawn; the melted iron rushes out, and flows along the main channels into the parallel trenches, which mould it into semi-cylindrical bars; and these, when cold, are broken off from the bar moulded in the main channel, and which is called a *sow*, while the former are termed *pigs*: hence the term *pig-iron*. These operations are performed once or twice in the twenty-four hours, according to the construction of the furnace.

Most iron ores contain small quantities of phosphoric acid and sulphur, and so do the fuel and flux employed; these substances are reduced by the blast as well as the iron, and with some others, such as potassium and iodine, from the potash and soda in both, and silicium, derived from the silica of the gangue, enter in minute proportions into combination with the iron, and materially affect its quality. The nature of the ore and fuel has consequently considerable influence upon the character of the iron; even the form of the furnace and the pressure of the blast appear to act similarly. When the ore is pure, such as fine spathose iron, &c., and wood-charcoal the fuel, the iron has a pretty uniform quality; but with clay-ironstone and coke, or anthracite, there is great variation; even two successive tappings will often be found to yield iron of different qualities. The different kinds of pig-iron produced in this way may be classed under three heads:—1. *Gray-iron*, which is the best in quality; as its name imports, the colour of its fracture is an uniform gray, and is highly crystalline. It is very soft, and well adapted for making bar-iron, and, when remelted, makes the best material for castings for machinery. Even without examining the fracture of a bar, the smelter is able to distinguish whether he has gray iron by the colour of the scintillations which it throws out, which are blue for gray iron, and brilliant white when the iron is what is called white iron. 2. *Mottled iron*, which, when broken, exhibits a peculiar mottled appearance, is of a lighter colour, and less crystalline than gray iron, and does not flow so freely. When the gray tint predominates it makes good castings, which may be turned, filed, and polished with facility. 3. *White iron* is the worst description of iron, and is only used for coarse castings. It is usually so hard as not to be cut with tempered steel, and is easily recognised by the white colour and lamellar structure of its fracture, and also by the colour of its spark, and the pastiness which it exhibits as it flows from the tapping-hole. When made with good ore and pure fuel, it is readily converted into bar-iron.

The quantity of coal consumed in making iron is enormous, a good deal of which must be wasted in heating the air of the blast after it enters the furnace. To avoid this loss, Mr. Neilson, of Glasgow, patented, in the year 1829, the application of the hot-air blast. For this purpose he passed the air before entering the tuyeres through iron pipes heated by a furnace. It is not too much to say that this process has completely revolutionized the iron trade by diminishing the amount of coal consumed, and increasing the amount of work which can be done in a given time. Formerly, and in many cases still, a separate furnace was used to heat the air for the blast, but the waste gases from the mouth of the blast furnace are now economically employed for that purpose. The usual plan is to place the contorted iron pipe, now used for the purpose of heating the blast, on the platform of the furnace, and to tap the latter near the throat, and make a portion of the hot gases pass over the pipe, and heat the air passing through it. Where anthracite coal is used, a quantity of steam must be mixed with the air of the blast, for the production of which the waste gases are also employed. Every furnace of this kind is therefore surmounted by a steam boiler and a hot-air apparatus, the gases for which are tapped from both sides of the throat. As the gases escaping from a furnace are at a very high temperature, perhaps as high as 1700° to 1800° Fahrenheit, and as the air of the blast need not exceed 600° Fahrenheit, a very small portion of the waste gases suffices to heat the blast, and even to produce sufficient steam to work the blowing-machines, &c. In some of the large iron works in Wales and Scotland one-sixth of the whole gas given off from the tunnel-head is considered capable of heating the blast, and from two-fifths to one-half to heat the blast and work the blowing-machines, &c. Great economy of fuel is effected in this way. In South Wales to produce one ton of pig iron three to three and a half tons of coal were formerly required, but by economizing the blast, from 1½ ton to 1 ton 18 cwts. are now sufficient to produce the same quantity. In Scotland 2 tons 5 cwts. are allowed to the ton of pig-iron.

Experiment has shown that the whole of the mixed gases issuing from the tunnel-head are combustible, even after they are cooled down to the ordinary temperature of the atmosphere. According to the experiments of Bunsen and Playfair, the composition of this gaseous mixture, eight feet below the top, taken from a furnace at Alfreton, in Derbyshire, was as follows:—

| | |
|---|---|
| Nitrogen, | 54·77 |
| Carbonic Acid, | 9·42 |
| Carbonic Oxide, | 20·97 |
| Light Carburetted Hydrogen, | 8·23 |
| Hydrogen, | 6·49 |
| Olefiant Gas, | 0·85 |
| Cyanogen, | 0·00 |
| | 100·000 |

When we consider that a mixture such as that represented by the preceding Table, and which contains so many of the combustible products of the coal, escapes at a temperature of 1800° Fahrenheit, it must be evident that an immense amount of fuel is wasted in the manufacture of iron, even where a part of the hot gases is employed for heating the blast. Indeed, Bunsen and Playfair considered that 81·54 per cent of the heat produced at the furnace of Alfreton, during the making of the experiments, the results of one of which we have quoted above,—was totally lost; and we may safely say that full 60 per cent. of it is lost in every furnace in Great Britain,—in other words, more than three millions of tons of coal are actually converted into smoke and gas, annually, without any corresponding benefit. On the Continent, and in Sweden, where fuel is expensive, not only is the heat of the waste gases economized, as in England, but the gases themselves, by their burning, form fuel for calcining the ore previous to smelting it, producing steam to work hammers, squeezers, and other machinery employed in the manufacture of bar-iron, and what is of still more importance, in the refining and puddling processes. So great is the economy and so perfect the means now adopted in some of the Swedish iron furnaces, that one ton of *merchant's bar-iron* is produced by a quantity of fuel equivalent to

2 tons 5 cwts., or 2 tons 10 cwts. of coal, whilst in Great Britain 4 tons 5 cwts. to 4½ tons are required to effect the same thing in the best regulated works, and there are districts where six and seven tons are still used to make one ton of commercial bar-iron.

When Sir Robert Kane wrote the "Industrial Resources" he estimated the cost of producing one ton of pig-iron at Arigna as follows:—

| | | | |
|---|---|---|---|
| 4 tons of coal, at 4*s*. 9*d*., | £0 | 19 | 0 |
| 3 tons of ironstone, at 5*s*., | 0 | 15 | 0 |
| 15 cwts. of limestone, at 2*s*. per ton, | 0 | 1 | 6 |
| Labour and general expenses, | 1 | 2 | 6 |
| | £2 | 18 | 0 |

which was about the average cost in well-conducted works in Great Britain. Since that period improvements have been so great that in 1851 the expense of production had fallen nearly 30 per cent., as the following statement of the cost of making one ton of pig iron in Scotland in 1851 will show:*—

| | | | |
|---|---|---|---|
| 32 cwts. of calcined ironstone (black or clay-bed), and containing 62.5 per cent. of iron, at 12*s*. per ton, | £0 | 19 | 2 |
| 45 cwts. of coal, at 4*s*. per ton, | 0 | 9 | 0 |
| 16 cwts of "cinder," at 1*s*. 6*d*. per ton, | 0 | 1 | 3 |
| 7 cwts. of limestone, at 3*s*. 6*d*. per ton, | 0 | 1 | 3 |
| Labour, | 0 | 3 | 3 |
| Sundries, inclusive of horses, | 0 | 2 | 0 |
| Interest on capital, &c. (£20,000), | 0 | 3 | 4 |
| Cost of production of one ton of pig-iron, | £1 | 19 | 3 |

The cost of making iron during the past year was, however, much more than this, as the price of coals was much higher, and wages had also increased considerably. At page 154 of the "Industrial Resources" Sir Robert says:—"But I am far from believing that it would be prudent in any person now to enter upon this branch of manufacture. We are not yet ready for it, nor is the time fitting. The iron trade of England and Scotland has been for some years in an exceedingly depressed state. The prices of pig-iron are from £2 15*s*. for Clyde iron to £3 15*s*. for No. 1 Welsh iron, on which it may be at once calculated, from the estimates already given, there can be but little profit." In the commencement of 1853 Clyde iron fetched £3 11*s*. 6*d*. per ton, which rose to £3 16*s*., but very soon fell to £2 8*s*. 6*d*., being the lowest figure it reached during the year, after which it rose to £3 8*s*., and finally, in the beginning of this year, it had reached £3 18*s*. to £3 19*s*. If it required the elaborate calculations in the "Industrial Resources" to prove the possibility of making iron with profit eight or ten years ago in Ireland, it does not seem probable, at first sight, that it could be done now, especially when we recollect that during a considerable part of the year the prices were as low as when Sir Robert Kane wrote, while the cost of making the iron had fallen very considerably: and yet, strange to say, it is just at this period a successful effort is being made to revive the iron trade of Lough Allen. And how is this? Improvements in manufacture are the cause. This important fact ought to be impressed on the minds of all, that in proportion as the processes of a manufacture are improved, the value of the possession of cheap raw materials diminishes. While the processes are rude, the more favoured countries have a monopoly of the trade; as they become perfect, the less favoured nations, if they make up by intelligence what they want in natural advantages, are enabled to take a fair share. If the Swedish processes of utilizing the gases to the full extent, and the machine of Bérard for washing coal, were introduced into Ireland, we have no doubt that a considerable iron manufacture would soon spring up in this country.

*Manufacture of wrought-iron.*—Pig-iron is employed in two ways, either for castings, or for the manufacture of wrought-iron. When the iron is of good quality, it is sometimes run directly from the tapping-hole into moulds for making castings, but it is more usual to remelt the pigs in a particular kind of furnace, called a *cupola*, and then cast it.

It has been already remarked that during the reduction of iron from its ores in the furnace, a certain quantity of carbon, silicium, and other substances, enter into combination with it. The process of making wrought-iron consists simply in getting rid, as completely as possible, of these substances, the presence of which renders the iron brittle. The English process of effecting this object consists of two consecutive series of operations, the one termed *refining*, the other *puddling*. The former is effected by melting the pig-iron with coke, in a rectangular hearth, under a strong blast of air from six tuyeres, three at each side. Under the action of this blast a part of the carbon is burnt out, and nearly the whole of the silicium converted into silicic acid, which unites with a portion of the iron, and forms a rich slag. The operation being finished, the metal is run into flat moulds; when cold it is hard and brittle, and is covered with blisters somewhat like ordinary blister steel. In this condition it is called *fine metal*. The usual charge for an ordinary English refining furnace varies from 1 to 1½ tons, and about 10 tons may be refined in twenty-four hours; 4 to 5 cwts. of coke being necessary for each ton of metal refined; the loss sustained by the pig iron during the operation varying from 13 to 17 per cent. The second class of operations now commence; the fine metal is broken up into convenient sized pieces, and piled on both sides of the hearth of a reverberatory furnace, somewhat similar to that already described in the smelting of lead. Here it fuses, and being exposed to the action of the air, its surface oxidizes, and part of the oxide of iron thus formed reacts upon the carbon, which it converts into oxide of carbon, which burns at the surface into carbonic acid, whilst another portion unites

* Mining Journal, No. 821, p. 237, for 1851.

with the remainder of the silicium, converted into silicic acid by the oxygen of the air, forms a basic slag, which again reacts upon another portion of the carbon. During this part of the operation the workman or puddler keeps constantly stirring the melted mass with an iron tool called the *paddle*, in order to expose fresh surfaces to the air. Gradually the metal becomes granular, or, as the workmen say, dry; when this occurs the fire is increased until the mass cements, and a part of the scoriæ is run off. The *balling* process now commences, and consists in collecting the agglutinated mass into a number of separate balls, which have the appearance of a coarse sponge. These balls are then removed from the furnace, and the slag pressed out either by subjecting them to the blows of a heavy hammer, weighing about 3½ to 4 tons, and making nearly 100 blows in a minute, or by means of machines called *squeezers*. The balls of iron, thus compressed and purged from slag, are next passed between grooved rollers, the grooves varying in size according to the pattern of the bar, by which they assume the form of bars, termed *puddled bars*.

Puddled bar-iron is extremely hard and brittle, and has many flaws and cracks. The ball, after coming from the hammer, is at once subjected to rollers, which, instead of having rectangular grooves, give the bars the rough shape of a rail. When the iron is wanted for ordinary wrought-iron, and must therefore be malleable, the puddled bars are cut into lengths by means of a powerful shears; these pieces are then piled in a peculiar kind of reverberatory furnace, termed the *mill furnace*, where they are heated to the welding point, and then passed between a series of rollers, termed *finishing rollers*, which, being more accurately made than the roughing rollers, by which the puddled bars are formed, give a greater uniformity and finish to the bars, which are known as *mill bars*. The operation of puddling lasts about two and a half hours, the charge for each furnace being about 3½ to 5 cwts.; about ten charges may thus be made in the twenty-four hours. The consumption of fuel is greater in the operation of puddling than in that of refining, every ton of puddled iron taking one ton of coal. The loss upon the refined iron is estimated at from 8 to 10 per cent. Owing to the smallness of the charge which can be worked in a puddling-furnace, one refining furnace will produce fine metal for five puddling ones.

*Sheet-iron.*—In many districts of the Continent, as for example in Styria and Catalonia, the bars are formed by simple hammering, and in the same way it is made into sheets; but in Great Britain and the chief iron districts of Belgium and France, sheet-iron is made by rolling between cylinders, as in the case of lead and zinc. Two sets of rollers are employed, one for roughing, and the other for finishing. The iron is first made into flat bars, then cut into lengths, equal to the required width of the sheets to be made, heated to redness in a reverberatory furnace, and passed through the first set of rollers two or three times. These rudely formed plates are again heated in another furnace, and passed between the finishing rollers, after which each sheet is beaten with a wooden mallet to remove the scales which attach to the surface. For most purposes, the surface of the sheet is now sufficiently even; but for the manufacture of tin plate, the plates must be again heated to dull redness, and piled upon a perfectly flat and even metal surface, and compressed together by a powerful hydraulic press. So perfect are the processes now in use for rolling iron, that sheets as thin as ordinary paper can be made; the material known as "iron paper," used for making covered buttons, and manufactured in Bohemia, is of this description. The iron for making tin plate must be of the best quality, and must have been produced and worked in all its stages with wood charcoal (in certain parts of the manufacture peat charcoal could be substituted).

*Manufacture of Steel.*—Steel is simply iron combined with about one-half per cent., or even less, of carbon, and differs, therefore, but little from cast-iron, except that the latter contains much more carbon and several other impurities. This fact will explain the process followed in many countries for making steel directly from cast-iron. In Styria, large quantities of iron are obtained from very pure spathose iron, charcoal being the fuel employed. The process consists in melting bars of cast-iron in a kind of refining furnace, and oxidizing out a considerable part of the charcoal, until the iron becomes granular, and passes into the condition of wrought-iron. Another bar is added, which again melts the pasty mass, but the action of the blast soon renders it pasty again; when this has taken place, another bar is so arranged in the furnace that when it melts it will fall only on the centre of the previous mass, now become spongy, and it will melt,—an operation which is repeated a number of times. The whole mass, which has somewhat the form of a circular cake, is removed from the fire, and cut up into wedge-shaped pieces. As the centre of the cake contains most carbon, from the continued addition of fresh cast-iron, the narrow end of each wedge will be more perfect steel than the thick end, where so much of the carbon has been burnt out that it assumes the character of malleable iron. These wedge-shaped pieces are drawn into bars, one end of which is highly carbonized steel, and passing gradually from that end to the other into steeled iron—no two parts of a bar are, therefore, of the same quality, in which state they would be very unfitted for use. The more carbon, however, which steel contains, the more brittle it is; and this fact presents a mode of separating the different qualities. Each bar having been hardened as much as possible, by heating it red-hot, and then plunging it into water, is allowed to fall upon an anvil, by which the very brittle parts break off; the remainder then receives a series of blows, by which further successive pieces are broken off. The broken pieces are classified according to the appearance of the fracture, and then welded in such a way that a nearly uniform mass is produced. This kind of steel, which is denominated *natural steel*, is of the best quality, but is very expensive.

In Great Britain steel is made by a process, termed *cementation*, from malleable bar-iron. Very little British iron is used for this purpose, being too impure; the best adapted for the purpose being that variety of Swedish iron known in commerce as "hoop L." The process of cementation consists in heating a number of bars of iron, interstratified with fine charcoal powder, in a kind of chest for a considerable time. The usual furnace for this purpose consists of two rectangular chests, about 7 or 8 feet long, and 2 to 3 feet wide and deep, made of fire-tiles, or firestone grits. Sometimes the chests are made double the length just stated, but the steel made in the small ones is preferred. These chests are set in brick-work and domed over, and are heated by a fire. The temperature must be carefully regulated so as to soften the iron, but not to melt it. The longer the operation lasts the harder will be the steel; chisels, and other cutlery tools, require about nine to eleven days; steel for knives and scissors, known as shear steel, take from six to eight days; and spring steel, and that used for saws, &c., four to five days. When the iron is fully converted into steel the furnace is allowed to cool down, and the bars are removed; when taken out the surface of the bars is found to be covered with small blisters, produced from the escape of gaseous matter from the softened metal during the process; hence the term *blistered steel.*

As in the case of natural steel, the bars of blistered steel are not of uniform density, and are, therefore, cut up into short lengths, and welded together, and then drawn into bars. In this way their quality is improved, and the mass rendered homogeneous and fit for the manufacture of cutlery. The term *shear steel* is applied to the metal after having undergone this operation, perhaps from the fact of wool-shears, and similar cutting instruments, being made from it.

To make perfectly homogeneous steel, in either of the ways just described, is expensive; and, as it is very often necessary to have such an article at a cheap rate for cutting tools, such as plane irons, chisels, &c., it is melted, and a kind of steel termed *cast steel* is obtained. In the process of producing cast steel, about 30 lbs. of blistered steel are placed in a crucible of refractory fire-clay, and heated for three or four hours in a peculiar furnace until it melts, whereupon the crucible is withdrawn and its contents poured into moulds. Cast steel is difficult to work from its brittleness, and cannot be brought to a welding heat with safety; but by sprinkling the surfaces to be welded with borax or yellow prussiate of potash, the operation of welding may be effected at a much lower temperature than could otherwise be done. It is sometimes useful to combine the hardness of cast steel with the tenacity of malleable iron, which is effected by uniting a plate of steel, and a plate of iron face to face; an operation founded upon the remarkable property which steel has in a melted state of uniting itself with a finely polished surface of iron. The compound bar thus made may be rolled and hammered in the ordinary way; and in forming the cutting edge the soft iron is ground bevel and the steel alone forms the edge. The same object can also be effected by an operation termed *case-hardening*, which consists in converting the external portions of a wrought-iron object into steel, leaving the internal portions still in the condition of malleable iron. For this purpose it is only necessary to subject the objects to the process of cementation, as in making blistered steel, but arresting the process when the transformation of the iron into steel has proceeded far enough into the mass of the iron.

Before concluding our notice of iron it may be well to mention, that an operation is sometimes performed the very reverse of the conversion of iron into steel by cementation. If fine cast-iron be heated in a chest with peroxide of manganese, or oxide of iron (hammer-scales), the oxygen of the oxide employed gradually converts the carbon of the cast-iron into carbonic oxide, and the iron itself into malleable iron. In this way stirrup buckles, bits, and an immense number of similar articles, are first cast, and then converted into wrought-iron by this species of cementation.

The processes which we have described in the preceding observations were more or less perfectly represented in the Exhibition. The Monkland Iron Company, to whose fine series of specimens, representing the geological structure of the Lanarkshire coal-field, we have already referred, exhibited a very complete and highly instructive series of specimens illustrative of the manufacture of iron in that district. This series consisted of six varieties of ironstone, both in their raw and calcined state:—1. Black band; 2. Clay band; 3. Ironstone balls; 4. Calder-Braes soft clay band; 5. Calder-Braes black band; and 6. Muscle band; five varieties of pig-iron with the corresponding "cinder" or slag; splint, and other coals, and limestone or flux employed; fine metal broken into pieces for the puddling furnaces, and showing the peculiar cells produced by the escape of the carbonic acid gas; calcined cinder, technically called *bulldog*, produced in the refining furnace, and also used in the puddling process; part of a puddled ball showing the nature of the granular spongy mass; specimens of a puddled bar showing the fracture; specimen of mill bar showing the fracture; and various specimens of rails, angle iron, &c. The Coalbrookdale Company exhibited samples of their gray, mottled, and white pig-iron, and of puddled and finished bars. The Coalbrookdale works is one of the most important in the kingdom, both from their extent and antiquity. The first foundry erected in the valley was about 200 years ago, and has been in the family of the present proprietors about 150 years. The total number of persons in the employment of the Company at mining operations, smelting and founding, is between 3000 and 4000. Shropshire was one of the first important iron-producing districts in England; but, being limited in extent, the production is not likely to increase beyond that which it has attained at present, which is about 120,000 tons. In 1852 there were twenty-seven furnaces in blast and thirteen out of blast; there are about seventeen seams of coal, averaging from 2 feet to 5½ feet in thickness, but there is a seam of sulphur coal about 7 feet in thickness. There are about 32 square miles of workable coal, but the field is much broken up by faults, the dislocations being sometimes as much as from 600 to 700 feet. The quality of the iron is considered to be good, and at Coalbrookdale works castings have been brought to great perfection.

Hird, Dawson, and Hardy, exhibited a series of specimens of Low Moor iron, but we did not observe any of the raw materials. Low Moor iron is perhaps the best in Great Britain for making wrought-iron of great tenacity, such as that for boiler plate and railway axles, for which purpose it is in great request. Some of the specimens exhibited were very remarkable, especially a railway axle twisted into a kind of knot, showing its extraordinary tenacity and softness; many of the other specimens were twisted into regular loop knots. The other iron works in the same district are also celebrated for the quality of their produce. In 1850 there were sixteen furnaces, ten in blast, and six out of blast, in the northern district of Yorkshire; the annual produce of which may be estimated for that year at about 25,000 tons. The beds of coal in this district are thin; the only seam used for iron making being that called "the better bed coal" which is only two feet thick.

Allaway and Sons, of Sydney, exhibited some samples of tin plates, and of the iron from which they were made. These plates were worked with wood charcoal from the Cinderford iron, the chief works in the forest of Dean, in Gloucestershire. The iron of this district is made from the hematite, and is chiefly employed for the manufacture of tin plates. About 30,000 tons are annually made; but large quantities of the ores are now sent to South Wales to enrich the poor ores of that district.

A good series of Sheffield steel was exhibited by Johnson, Cammel, and Co. Sheffield is the great centre of British steel manufacture; the annual production being about 18,000 tons, the number of cementing furnaces about 120, and cast steel melting furnaces about 100. Not more than one-eighth of the iron converted into steel in Sheffield is British, the remainder being chiefly Swedish. The only specimens of commercial Irish-made steel were the samples of blister steel exhibited by Classon and Courtney of this city, which appeared to have been well made, and of rather uniform quality. Some samples of steel and of edge instruments made with it were exhibited by Professor Davy; this steel was manufactured with turf, which therefore rendered these objects of great interest, not for the novelty of the fact, as many tons are annually produced on the Continent with similar fuel, but as directing attention to an exceedingly important application which might be made of peat charcoal. Some specimens of the natural steel of Styria were also exhibited in the department of the Zolverein, to which we shall have occasion to again allude when describing that section of the Exhibition.

In concluding our remarks on the subject of Ores and Metals, it may be interesting to give a few statistics of the iron trade. In 1851 the production of iron in Great Britain was two and a half millions of tons, one-third of which was employed in castings, and two-thirds in the manufacture of wrought-iron. To produce this quantity 700 million of tons of ore, 2,700,000 tons of limestone, and 13,000,000 of tons of coal were consumed; and 650,000 to 700,000 persons directly or indirectly employed. The following Table represents the condition of the iron manufacture in 1852:—

| | High Furnaces. In Blast. | High Furnaces. Out of Blast. | Total. | Tons of Iron produced. |
|---|---|---|---|---|
| Scotland, | 113 | 31 | 144 | 775,000 |
| South Wales, | 135 | 27 | 162 | 635,000 |
| Ditto, Anthracite, | 12 | 23 | 35 | 31,000 |
| South Staffordshire, | 127 | 32 | 159 | 725,000 |
| North Staffordshire, | 17 | 4 | 21 | 90,000 |
| North Wales, | 6 | 7 | 13 | 30,000 |
| Shropshire, | 27 | 13 | 40 | 120,000 |
| Durham, | 18 | 8 | 26 | 110,000 |
| Northumberland, | 7 | 6 | 13 | 35,000 |
| Yorkshire and Derbyshire, | 35 | 7 | 42 | 150,000 |
| | 497 | 158 | 655 | 2,701,000 |

The following Summary shows the relative position of the different countries as to their production of iron:

| | | Tons. |
|---|---|---|
| Great Britain in | 1836 | 1,000,000 |
| Ditto in | 1840 | 1,396,000 |
| Ditto in | 1852 | 2,701,000 |
| France in | 1840 | 348,000 |
| Ditto in | 1846 | 522,000 |
| Prussia in | 1851 | 348,000 |
| Russia in | 1838 | 189,000 |
| Belgium in | 1849 | 146,000 |
| Sweden in | 1850 | 97,394 |
| Spain in | 1849 | 65,000 |

We have been unable to obtain late statistics of France and Russia, but there can be no doubt that the production of the former is now little short of 1,000,000 tons; and that of the latter has also considerably increased.

It would occupy too much space to give the statistics of the other metals. We shall give in the following Table the chief manufacturing countries of Europe, in the order of their production of the four most important metals after iron:—

| Lead. | Copper. | Zinc. | Tin. |
|---|---|---|---|
| Spain. | Great Britain. | Prussia. | Great Britain. |
| Great Britain. | Russia. | Belgium. | Saxony. |
| Austria. | Austria. | Spain. | Austria. |
| German States | Sweden and Norway. | Austria. | |
| Russia. | Prussia. | Russia. | |
| Prussia. | | | |

### IRON PYRITES OR SULPHUR ORE.

There is a very important ore of iron which we omitted from our list of iron ores, because it is very rarely employed as a source of the metal, namely, iron pyrites. This substance is a compound of sulphur and iron, in the proportion of 54·26 of the former to 45·74 of the latter. It is one of the most universally diffused metallic minerals in Nature, being found in rocks of all ages, sometimes diffused through their mass, frequently in distinct cubical or pentagonal dodecahedral crystals, and often in deposits and veins of considerable extent. In its pure state it has a pale golden-yellow colour, and is often mistaken by the peasants and by many who should know better, for gold. When it occurs in great masses, however, it is rarely pure, and consequently its colour is rather of a yellowish-gray, and in this state does not yield more than from 30 to 40 per cent. of sulphur.

The great importance of pyrites, at present, is as a source of sulphur and of sulphuric acid. Previous to 1841 the whole of the oil of vitriol, or commercial sulphuric acid used in manufactures, was obtained from native sulphur, which is found in great abundance in a district in Sicily between Cattolica and Girgenti, and also near Naples, and in the Solfaterra in Tuscany, as a product of volcanic action. In that year some difficulties arose between the Governments of Great Britain and Naples relative to the sulphur trade, so that for some time the usual supply was cut off. Pyrites, hitherto neglected as a source of sulphur, or indeed for any purposes in these countries, came to attract attention, and in a few months it was employed to an enormous extent in the production of sulphuric acid.

The first idea of employing pyrites for this purpose originated with M. Dartigues, who employed it in France in 1793,—a year memorable in the history of industrial arts by the number of discoveries made, all depending upon the same cause—the impossibility of obtaining supplies from foreign countries. To this struggle we are indebted for the process of making artificial soda, artificial indigo, and many others of equal importance. It is difficult to imagine why Dartigues' idea should have been so little thought of previous to 1841; and its use in that year was a sort of re-discovery. The history of industry is full of incidents of this kind, all showing how much of industrial progress depends upon fortuitous circumstances, and how little really upon the supposed genius of a people. A history of manufacture and commerce from this point of view would not only be interesting, but also highly instructive.

Without going the whole length which Liebig does, of saying that the amount of oil of vitriol consumed by a people may be taken as the index of their material civilization, there can be no doubt that it forms one of the greatest elements of modern manufactures. More than this we need not say to point out the immense importance of iron pyrites, which is now one of the chief if not the principal raw material for the production of sulphuric acid. But as many of our readers may not be conversant with the relations of manufactures with one another, we shall give a short summary of the manufactures of which pyrites may form one of the raw materials, either directly or indirectly, as oil of vitriol or sulphur. We are the more inclined to do so because such a summary forms one of the most perfect examples of the endless and wonderful transformations which an apparently worthless material is capable of undergoing, and of the numerous uses which it is thus made to subserve.

From iron pyrites we may obtain sulphur, which in turn serves to make gunpowder; and enters into the composition of most fire-works, and into that of several kinds of lucifer matches, and for the preparation of sulphuret of carbon, for vulcanizing India rubber and gutta percha, and causing silver to deposit bright in electro-plating. Mixed with soda, pipe-clay, and other substances, we convert it into that most beautiful of colours, artificial ultramarine, so much used as a brilliant dye for ladies' dresses. In the form of sulphurous acid we may employ it to bleach woollen and silk goods, straw bonnets, horse-hair for crinoline bonnets and lawyers' wigs, for purifying and whitening strings for musical instruments, guts for sausages, gold-beaters' skin, isinglass, and for whitening damaged wheat. If we roast it in the air we get copperas, and by strongly igniting this copperas with gypsum or alabaster we have Venetian red. The copperas itself forms the basis of ink, and with colouring matters it dyes blacks, buffs, and lilacs. Distilled at a high temperature, this copperas gives a peculiar kind of oil of vitriol employed for dissolving indigo, to make damp blue or indigo lake; whilst the residue of the distillation forms cutlers' crocus, employed for polishing steel. Copperas also serves as an admirable disinfectant for absorbing noxious gases, such as sulphureted hydrogen, and fixing ammonia evolved by putrescent matter.

When pyrites is disseminated through particular kinds of slate, it assists in the formation of alum, which in its turn forms the basis of lake colours, and is used in the dyeing of reds and pinks, the manufacture of tawed or alum leather, the sizing of papers, and the satining of room-papers. Again, when burned in a particular way, the sulphur of pyrites is converted into oil of vitriol or sulphuric acid, a substance employed in the preparation of a whole host of other acids, among others, margaric, oleic, and stearic acids, and in the purification of certain fats and oils, especially tallow for the manufacture of mould candles; phosphoric, citric, and tartaric acids, for the use of the calico printer; nitric and muriatic acids, which are largely employed in dyeing and many other operations. Sulphuric acid, when mixed with chalk, produces the carbonic acid which, by the impregnation of water with it, forms soda and other artificial mineral waters. It is also employed in the electro-plating of metals, in pickling, or cleaning brass and copper-plates previous to polishing them for pressing paper, and iron-plates previous to tinning them; whitening plates of silver before stamping them in the mint; in the refining of gold and silver; in the preparation of a great number of drugs, such as ether, sulphate of mercury, sulphate of quinine, &c.; in staining woods; in carbonizing the ends of piles to prevent them from decaying; in the preparation of garancine, the pure colouring matter of madder used for dyeing Turkey reds, pinks, and lilacs; in the manufacture of blacking; in the raising of hides previous to tanning; in the coagulation of blood for manure; in the separation of ammonia from gas liquor, and in the dissolution of bones for the same purpose; in the preparation of gun-cotton and of collodion for photography; in the preparation of glucose or syrup of starch, and of solid starch sugar; and, finally, it is employed in the great manufactures of soda and bleaching-powder—the former being used in making glass, soap, &c., and both in the bleaching of linen and cotton goods. Such are a few among the almost endless applications which can and are now made of this comparatively unattractive substance, iron pyrites, which most persons would pass by without observation.

Directly, however, iron pyrites can only be said to have three applications:—1. The manufacture of oil of vitriol; 2. The manufacture of copperas or sulphate of iron; and, 3. The manufacture of sulphur. When heated in a current of air, nearly the whole of the sulphur is gradually burnt out; the sulphur, combining with some of the oxygen of the air, forms sulphurous acid, the gas which is formed by the burning of sulphur under similar circumstances. If this gas be passed into leaden chambers it may be converted into oil of vitriol in the usual way. If, however, the mineral be heated in close vessels, it gives off only one-third of its sulphur, in a free condition, or about 17 per cent. By employing a strong heat as much as 27 per cent. may be obtained, but as the pyritic mass would be partially fused, the difficulties involved in the process would more than counterbalance the increase of production of sulphur. When the heat would not be sufficient to slag the pyrites, the residue after the separation of the sulphur has a dark-gray colour, and is composed in 100 parts—of iron, 56·76; sulphur, 43·24 parts. A similar compound is found in Nature, and is known by the name of magnetic pyrites.

The residual mass just mentioned, when exposed to the air and moistened, rapidly decomposes, absorbing oxygen from the air, and forming sulphuric acid and oxide of iron, which combine and produce copperas, and by lixiviating the mass this salt may be obtained in a crystalline state. In many coal-fields,—such, for example, as at Coal Island, near Kanturk in the county of Cork, &c.,—beds of slaty coal are found so impregnated with pyrites, that the coal obtained from them, when exposed to a moist atmosphere, gradually undergoes a species of slow combustion with the production of sulphate of iron. In Germany most of those beds are utilized, and large quantities of copperas and alum are produced in this way, the former being employed for making fuming or Nordhausen acid. A good deal of sulphur is also distilled from pyrites; but in these countries it is rarely used for any purpose but that of making oil of vitriol. Some years ago a Mr. Lees patented a very ingenious process for obtaining sulphur from pyrites, the profitable application of which depended on the pyrites containing some copper, which it very often does. By this process he was enabled to make from 100 tons of pyrites, containing 2 per cent. of copper, 30 tons of sulphur, and 2 tons of fine copper.

Where coal would not cost more than 10 to 14 shillings per ton, and where the facilities of transporting an article of so small a value as pyrites would not be good, it would, undoubtedly, be very profitable to extract from it, on the spot where it is found, the greater part of the sulphur and copper; and thus, instead of having to send to great distances 100 tons of a substance worth about 13*s*. or 14*s*. per ton, two articles would be obtained, one of which would be worth £5 to £6, and the other £80 or £90.

Most pyrites are auriferous and argentiferous, and a new branch of trade has sprung up, founded upon the extraction of the excessively small quantities of the precious metals which exist in the residual slag, which is raked out of the pyrites furnaces after burning out the sulphur. Gold is also stated to exist in the *gossan* (a ferruginous substance forming part of mineral lodes) of the Wicklow mines, and from which it is said it can be extracted for a very small sum per ounce, so as to produce fabulous profits.

There were three exhibitors of pyrites. The chief and almost sole seat of pyrites mining, not alone in Ireland, but perhaps in the world, is the county of Wicklow. The following Table, which gives the number of tons of that mineral exported from that county since the year 1840, will be interesting to our readers:—

| Year. | Tons of Iron Pyrites, each Ton 21 cwts. | Year. | Tons of Iron Pyrites, each Ton 21 cwts. |
|---|---|---|---|
| 1840, | 40,176 | *Brought forward*, | 307,246 |
| 1841, | 77,388 | 1847, | 40,508 |
| 1842, | 40,457 | 1848, | 41,239 |
| 1843, | 39,186 | 1849, | 45,627 |
| 1844, | 34,961 | 1850, | 74,044 |
| 1845, | 39,018 | 1851, | 102,438 |
| 1846, | 36,060 | 1852, | 97,988 |
| *Carried forward*, | 307,246 | Total in 13 years, | 709,090 |

## FUEL.

Although we have treated of Ores first, it is not that we believe them of more importance than Fuel, but simply because they formed the most prominent feature in the Raw Materials of the Exhibition. A country may be rich in ores, and yet not afford the means of extracting the metals from them; and, indeed, in Ireland, we are compelled to send the greater part of ours to England, not because we are in want of fuel, but because it can be had cheaper in Wales. On the other hand, a country without a single mine of iron, lead, or copper, but with abundance of cheap fuel, may be able to develop a great many metallic manufactures. Fuel is the great element of modern industry; it is then of the utmost importance to know how we stand with regard to this first element.

The substances used for fuel are wood, turf, and coal. In early times wood was the sole article of fuel, as it is still of a large part of the world. The use of the two latter is of comparatively modern date, and it is difficult to say which was soonest taken advantage of. When we recollect that in Sweden, a country abounding in turf-moors, the people are almost utterly ignorant of the use of peat as a fuel, it would seem as if that substance was the last source of heat brought into use. In Ireland wood is completely out of the question as a fuel, for we have not enough to supply our wants for building purposes. And here we may remark, that it is strange that more efforts are not made to plant our mountains, and thus supply one of the first elements of civilization to the peasant—the means of making comfortable houses. There remain, then, but turf and coal as sources of fuel in Ireland. As turf is found on the surface, and, therefore, geologically speaking, is the more recent of the two, we shall speak first of it.

*Peat.*—Highly as we estimate a cheap supply of fuel, we are far from agreeing with some of our sanguine countrymen, who consider our peat bogs as a true California, and a special blessing from Providence. We look upon them as nuisances which cool the surrounding country, prevent its proper drainage, breed disease, and demoralize the population on their borders. We might gladly forego all the advantages which they could give us as fuel if we could get rid of them at once and for ever. As this cannot be done, it behoves us to see what way we can utilize them. That the present system of working our bogs to obtain peat does so but very imperfectly is evident enough, and is well illustrated by the fact, that even in Galway, which is, as it were, an island in the midst of turf-moors, and where coal is dearer than on the east of Ireland, peat not only costs more than coal, but the supply is even precarious.

Lime can be perfectly burned by means of turf; in Holland nearly the whole of the enormous quantities of bricks and tiles made in that country are burned with turf. Bread can be baked, beer can be manufactured, mills set in motion, and in fact all the common manufactures of a country which require fuel can be carried on with turf; and yet we know districts, situated in the immediate vicinity of large bogs, to which coal is drawn by horses a distance of thirty miles, to burn lime for agricultural purposes. The only reason we can see for such a state of things is simply that, with the present system of obtaining turf, the coal is the cheaper in the end. One ton of coal is usually considered equal to about three tons of ordinary turf; the former costs in the central parts of Ireland, situated along the line of canals, from 15*s*. to 16*s*. per ton, and may cost even as much as 20*s*. where no facilities of carriage by water exist. Where coal is preferred in such districts, the turf must cost from 5*s*. 4*d*. to 6*s*. 8*d*. per ton; and yet, by a proper system of cutting and drying, a ton of turf, dried and stacked, may be produced for about 1*s*. 8*d*. to 2*s*. From this it would appear that the equivalent of a ton of coal could be produced in the turf districts of Ireland, under ordinary conditions, for about 9*s*.; and when the turf would be used close to a bog, worked on a large scale, for, perhaps, 6*s*. In Liverpool, the St. Helen's coal costs per contract, for very large regular supplies, from 8*s*. to 9*s*. per ton (not including exceptional years like the present); in Manchester the average cost of coal to the manufacturers is fully as much; whilst in London it is, perhaps, 14*s*. to 15*s*. per ton for the cheapest kinds of coal; the average price for the whole of England being 5*s*. 7*d*. per ton. Were a good system of working our bogs adopted, and proper furnaces for burning the turf constructed, there can therefore be no doubt that it could be had at a cost sufficiently low to enable a manufacturer to compete with the average of the English ones, so far as fuel is concerned.

Although as early as the year 1630 a patent was granted "for manufacturing iron, lead, tin, and salt, as also the burning of bricks, tiles, lime, &c., with the fuel of peat and turf reduced to a coal," and that a host of others have been since taken out "for improvements in the preparation, &c., of peat," but little change has taken place in the old, wasteful, and inefficient system of cutting and drying turf. We have had within the last few years at least a dozen companies, who were to have altered the whole face of the country by some wonderful plan for utilizing peat, the only trace of which may perhaps be some old brass door-plates telling of their existence. Would that some of them had left a good system of cutting and drying turf after them; for then, at least, their existence would not have been in vain. In Germany and France, where fuel is still dearer than in Ireland, the mode of working the bogs is much more effective and economical than with us; a good deal of it being artificially dried in a kind of oven, which might be advantageously introduced into this country. A modification of one of these ovens was proposed for that purpose by Mr. Robert Mallet; and so far as we can judge from his drawings and descriptions, the plan appeared to be well calculated to effect its object; but no person appears to have attempted to test it practically, although thousands are ready to grasp at other schemes, at once chimerical and expensive.

In the Fichtelgebirge in Bavaria, where turf is abundant, the cost of producing one ton of artificially dried fibrous turf may be taken at about 2*s*. 5*d*., and of the dense black turf about 1*s*. 3*d*. to 1*s*. 4*d*., the mean of both being considerably under 2*s*.; and yet the men earn 1*s*. 1*d*. a day, and the women and children on an average from 4½*d*. to 5½*d*. In France wages are higher, especially in the south, and consequently turf cannot be so economically produced; nevertheless, out of about 2800 turbaries in the whole country, 2400 are fully worked, giving employment to about 53,000 persons during part of the summer.

Besides supplying domestic uses, lime-kilns, breweries, and bake-houses, turf, in its raw state, is used in Germany in a number of manufactories, such as the vitriol-works of Kamnig and Smelzdorf, in Silesia; in numerous salt-works and other chemical factories, and has lately been substituted, to the extent of one-half, for wood-charcoal in the manufacture of iron, without, it is said, affecting the quality of the metal produced. Another important application of turf is the manufacture of charcoal, which, if it could be made at a cheap rate, would find many applications. In France very large quantities are made at Pont St. Maxence, about eighteen leagues from Paris, and at Crouy sur Ourcq, near Meaux, for the Paris markets, where it is employed in stoves and kitchens as a substitute for wood charcoal. It is also largely employed by smiths, especially in the Vosges. At Oberndorf, in Wurtemberg, a good deal of iron is refined with turf charcoal for the manufacture of arms, which are forged with the same fuel, as also at Albruck, in the Schwarzwald, and many other parts of Germany. Indeed, for refining and puddling iron, and manufacturing steel, either by the continental method or by cementation, it is not necessary to char the turf at all, for, so long ago as the year 1800, iron was refined at a small establishment at Neustadt an der Dosse with considerable success; and, since 1837, the puddling furnaces of the Royal Iron Works at Weierhammer, in Bavaria, have been exclusively worked with turf.

Turf charcoal is usually made in Germany in heaps, which appears to be the only economical process for obtaining it. Each heap is made 50 feet long, 5 to 6 feet wide, and about 4 feet high; a fire channel goes the whole length of the heap, which is hollowed out, in the centre of its length, into a sort of small basin, from which passes a small gutter to carry off the liquid. The fire channel is sloped from both sides towards this basin, which is made of bricks, with the interstices filled with clay, and also the whole channel, so as to prevent the liquid sinking into the earth. At every ten feet distance a fire hole is left, into which the fire is to be introduced, and which is to be stopped up, as well as the ones at the end of the fire channels, except those on the side opposite to that from which the wind blows. Between each two opposite holes a small chimney is left in the roof. The ground is levelled before making the heap, and is covered over with sand. When the heap of turf is built up, a covering is laid on, composed of clay, sand, and chopped straw, the latter being added to prevent the covering from cracking, a portion being also kept to stop any cracks which may form in the covering during the operation of firing.

When everything is ready the firing commences, for which two workmen are necessary, in order that the whole may be ignited simultaneously. In the commencement of the operation a thick black smoke is evolved from the chimneys; this gradually thins and assumes a grayish-white colour, which in its turn thins in proportion as the moisture of the turf evaporates. This can be observed best by placing the hand from time to time over the chimney, which will remain dry when all the moisture is gone. As soon as this occurs the fire must be gradually choked. Turf charcoal thus prepared is largely employed in the metallurgic operations carried on in Saxony and in Bavaria; the cost in the latter country being usually about 13*s*. 8*d*. per ton weight of charcoal from turf of medium density, delivered a distance of about 3½ miles. If it could be produced at that rate in this country, and we have no doubt that it could be done at 11*s*. to 12*s*. per ton, there is nothing to prevent a number of small Sheffields springing up around our bogs.

If ever our bogs are utilized on a large scale, it appears that it will be in this way. There seems to be little hope of economically making charcoal in iron furnaces of any description. A great deal is made in that way both in France and Germany, but here it would not successfully compete with coal as a fuel unless it could be made at a cheap rate. Although it is not probable that iron can be economically smelted with raw turf, and certainly not with turf charcoal, which would fall to powder from the weight of the ore if used alone; and even if it did, it usually contains too much sulphate of lime and phosphoric acid to yield good iron; yet there can be no doubt that it would answer for puddling and refining iron, for which purpose it is scarcely inferior to wood charcoal, and vastly superior to the coke of coal. It would also be well adapted for forging small hardware of a superior quality, such as harness furniture, cutlery, tin plates, &c.

Turf charcoal, although not used for manufacturing purposes in Ireland, has become an article of commerce in consequence of a novel application which has been made of it for deodorizing. All porous bodies absorb liquid and gaseous substances, a property which peat charcoal possesses in a very high degree, and hence when fetid water or other putrescent matter is placed in contact with it, the smell immediately disappears. This is an application which will, no doubt, very considerably extend itself, and become one of the most agreeable luxuries in crowded cities, at the same time that it will conduce very much to the public health and comfort. Here, however, our eulogiums must cease, for although we cannot deny that peat charcoal has some manuring properties, we consider its application as a substitute for guano or other manure as simply absurd, and not worthy of further consideration.

Considerable quantities of turf charcoal were made some time ago by the Irish Amelioration Society, near Robertstown, in the county of Kildare, but by a process which, however ingenious, was so expensive that it could not be produced at less than from 20*s.* to 25*s.* per ton. There was, notwithstanding the large field which is opened, but one exhibitor of turf charcoal, Mr. T. Sadlier, of Tullamore, who also exhibited a very ingenious portable water-closet, if we may apply the term, for turf charcoal in powder was employed instead of water. Mr. Sadlier's object, in turning his attention to this subject, has been chiefly with a view of affording employment to those around him; but it would seem that he has only to attend to economy of production to be able to carry on an extensive trade in the article of turf charcoal.

The great bulk of turf, which renders its transport expensive, as well as the difficulty of drying it, which confines the season for cutting it to a few months in summer, have led to a number of projects for compressing it by mechanical means, and thus getting rid of both difficulties at the same time. About two years ago a patent was taken out for separating the water from the turf by the use of a centrifugal machine of a peculiar structure, assisted by the action of steam, which it was supposed would burst the half-decomposed cells of the plants forming the peat. The dried mass thus obtained was then to be subjected to a temperature sufficient to induce an incipient distillation of tar, after which it was to be passed, while still in a heated and softened state, between two compressing rollers. The material produced in this way is certainly of remarkable density, and possesses the essential requisites of a first-class article of fuel to as great an extent as any other artificial fuel with which we are acquainted. For the manufacture of wrought iron, and for locomotive steam-engines, it would appear to be peculiarly adapted. Its commercial value, in relation to other kinds of fuel, is a point on which we cannot venture an opinion, as this must depend on the price at which the compressed peat can be supplied. That the quality is excellent there can be no doubt, and that the demand would be all but unlimited is equally certain—the only element in reference to which further information is required being the cost of production on a large scale.

Specimens of the compressed turf above alluded to, made in Kerry, were exhibited. These were produced at the works of a Company formed to carry out the project, and, so far as regarded the quality of the article, they left little to be desired. It was also intended to make charcoal, but instead of allowing the liquid and solid portions, which are volatilized during the charring, to escape, they were to be collected, and the ammonia and acetic acid separated from the liquid, in the form of sulphate of ammonia, and the latter as acetate of lime. The salt of ammonia would find a market as a manure, and the acetate for calico-printing, &c., whilst the semi-solid tar was proposed to be employed in making gas, or in preserving wood, on Bethel's principle, now so well known.

There is another Company engaged in carrying out some other applications of turf, which are exceedingly novel. They introduce a quantity of turf into a blast furnace, similar to an ordinary high furnace, by which the whole of it is resolved into gaseous matter and ash; this gaseous matter, on being conducted through a refrigerator, deposits a quantity of water containing ammonia, pyroxylic spirit or wood naphtha, and acetic acid, which are separated by peculiar processes, and about 3 or 4 per cent. of tar, which yields several oils, and a solid fat-like body, resembling spermaceti in appearance, called paraffine, which has been applied to make candles. The chief feature in this process is that no charcoal is sought to be made, and that the cooled gases, after depositing the water and tar held in suspension, are combustible, and serve as the fuel by which all the subsequent operations are carried on. As no specimens of this branch of industry have been exhibited, and as, moreover, the experiment which is now about to be made on a large scale near Athy will finally decide the question of its practicability as a commercial speculation, we need not allude to the subject further here.

*Coal.*—By the most superficial examination of peat we are enabled to ascertain its origin, for, with the exception of the very dense kinds obtained from the bottom of the bogs, the plants which have contributed to its formation are still distinguishable. For the most part these plants belong to the families of mosses among the cryptogamic plants and Cyperaceæ, and Juncaceæ among flowering plants; the two latter including the different varieties of sedge and rushes. The roots of many other flowering plants, such as heath, &c., also form a small proportion of peat, especially of that found on the tops and declivities of mountains. To some extent we can thus form an idea of the mode of its formation; for all vegetable matter, under the action of air and water, slowly decays with the evolution of carbonic acid, or, in other words, undergoes a species of slow combustion. Where the action of the air has full play, and but little water is present, the decomposition is very rapid, and the greater part of the mass is converted into gaseous compounds, little remaining but the inorganic elements of the plants, and some vegetable matter having acid properties, and to which the general term *humus* is applied. Where the dead plants are, however, completely immersed in water, and where their mass is considerable, and the climate of the country rather cold, the air can only act very slowly; and although the same changes, with some modifications, will take place as in the other case, immense periods of time may elapse before they are completely decomposed. Most bogs being saturated with water, peat may therefore be considered to be produced in this way. This brief explanation will show the chemical changes connected with the formation of peat bogs, but it does not account for the circumstances under which their formation first commenced. Many historical proofs are in existence of the recent formation of such bogs, by the sudden destruction of forests; but, assuredly, the greater number of ours do not owe their origin to any modern causes with which we are acquainted. Some people have supposed that our great central bogs have been shallow lakes; which, being so far drained as to allow of plants growing in them, the gradual accumulation of the remains of these plants, owing to the slowness of their decomposition in consequence of being immersed in water, as already stated, gave rise to the production of peat. However plausible this explanation may appear at first sight, it is far from satisfactory, and does not at all account for the masses of peat found on our mountains, and which are, at this moment, gradually disappearing. We are therefore constrained to consider the origin of peat as yet unsettled, and its formation to belong to some period long antecedent to our present era.

If it be so difficult to arrive at a solution of the problem as to the origin of peat, how much more difficult is it in the case of coal? It is not even settled yet what coal is? Geologists have, at various times, brought to light the remains of many plants, now no longer existing as part of the Flora of the earth; some being gigantic reeds and club mosses, and others being curious representatives of our coniferous plants, such as the pine; but all apparently of a kind which could only grow in warm tropical regions. Coal was supposed to have been the altered remains of these plants, as we find impressions of their stems, leaves, and fruit, in the greatest abundance in the beds of shale or soft slate, associated with those of coal; and even entire stems converted into coal. This view, it now seems, is denied, and from an examination of specimens of coal with the microscope, it is asserted that coal is the product, not of such plants, but of wood. The presence of trunks of trees in peat bogs, and even whole masses of turf composed of decayed wood, has also given rise to the opinion that peat was produced mainly from timber trees; and, in Ireland, the existence of peat bogs on the tops of mountains is even considered as a perfect proof of their having been formerly thickly wooded. But a careful examination of these mountains will show that, although the valleys and declivities of most of them may have been wooded, very few of the more elevated ones, and perhaps none of those covered with peat, have had trees growing upon them in historic times, with the exception, perhaps, of a few isolated ones upon the sheltered watersheds of a chain; and in scarcely any instance can the peat upon them be traced to the decay of timber trees. Perhaps the new view of the origin of coal may depend upon the same error,—the generalizing of a few isolated cases.

Whatever doubt may exist as to the particular kind of vegetation from which coal has been produced, there seems to be now none whatever that it has been formed from some kind of plants, and, perhaps, in some instances even from animals. Referring to our former observations, when speaking of Mineral Veins, we stated that, in consequence of the regular superposition of one rock upon another, the lowermost in the series must have been produced before those above it; and that hence, knowing the position of any rock in the general series, we may fix upon its relative age to all others, no matter where we may find it. The number of rocks of distinct ages thus ascertained is considerable; but they naturally group themselves into a series of divisions, distinguished by certain characteristics, especially by the nature of the remains of animals and plants found imbedded in them. It is unnecessary to remind our readers that we are here speaking of those rocks which are known to have been deposited from water, such as slate and limestone; granite, and other rocks supposed to have been produced by the action of heat, do not come under the same law; and as they have no relation to coal, our present observations have reference solely to water-formed rocks. The lowest, that is the oldest, of these divisions have received empiric names derived from some localities where they are largely developed, and have been first well studied, as for example, the Cambrian and Silurian rocks, the former being derived from the ancient name of Wales, and the latter from one of the mythological deities of that country. These rocks contain but very few remains of plants or animals; and as coal has been formed from such remains, we need scarcely expect to find any deposits of it associated with Cambrian or Silurian rocks. Above these, and therefore formed at a more recent period, come a great group of rocks, which, from their extraordinary richness in the remains of vegetables, have been termed the *carboniferous* formation. One of the subdivisions of this group is called the *coal measures*, and consists of numerous alternations of beds of coal, grits, slaty clay, &c. In most cases these beds have been deposited in shallow basins or hollows, somewhat as our turf moors have been, and hence the term *coal basin* applied to such deposits. Some of these coal measures contain twenty and even fifty distinct beds or seams of coal; the entire thickness of the series of rocks in one locality being, perhaps, not more than 100 feet, whilst in others it may reach 2000. The thickness of the beds of coal also varies considerably, from a few inches to 20 or 30 feet; for example, at Wolverhampton, in South Staffordshire, there are nine seams of coals in a thickness of 115 yards from the surface, having the following thicknesses:—

| Name of Seam. | Thickness in feet and inches. F. | I. | Name of Seam. | Thickness in feet and inches. F. | I. |
|---|---|---|---|---|---|
| No. 1. Great Seam, | 30 | 0 | *Brought forward,* | 48 | 11 |
| 2. Heathen Coal, | 2 | 8 | No. 6. Fire-clay Coal, | 9 | 0 |
| 3. Rubble Coal, | 2 | 4 | 7. Little Coal, | 2 | 0 |
| 4. Stinking Coal, | 8 | 0 | 8. Bolton Coal, | 9 | 0 |
| 5. New Mine Coal, | 6 | 4 | 9. Singing Coal, | 3 | 6 |
| *Carried forward,* | 48 | 11 | Total, | 67 | 5 |

Subsequent to the deposition of the beds of coal, and the interstratified beds of clay-ironstone, grits, &c., they have been in many cases disturbed by the intrusion of dykes of igneous rocks, or by the occurrence of great cracks, and the upheaving of one part of the basin or *field*, as it is sometimes also denominated, or the depression of part of it. Some of the dislocations thus produced are on a great scale,—one part of a seam of coal being known to have separated from the rest and sunk to the extent of more than 600 feet. Another kind of disturbance has also happened in some fields: instead of one or two great dislocations being produced, the whole of the beds are contorted and broken as if the whole mass had been liquid, and had become solidified just as it was agitated by a great wave. The effect of this kind of disturbance, upon what was originally a coal-field of great area, is to produce a number, as it were, of small, distinct basins, precisely as we find in the Munster coal-field, which extends over parts of the adjoining counties of Cork, Kerry, and Limerick. These dislocations, or *faults*, increase very much the difficulty and expense of coal mining; it may often happen that, in working a seam of coal, it may suddenly terminate by a fault, so that the miner has to sink a shaft, perhaps 100 or more feet, to find the other part which had sunk down.

Above the coal measures come a number of other groups of rocks, all more or less rich in organic remains; but, strange to say, no deposits of coal, such as we have just described, have as yet been found. In some of the higher, that is, more recent numbers of the series, thin beds of a peculiar kind of coal have been discovered; but these are so unimportant that we are entitled to state that coal belongs almost exclusively to one group of rocks, and was only formed in quantity during one period of geological time.

Peat is the product only of certain limited portions of the earth; but during the period of the formation of coal, the conditions under which it was formed appeared to exist on every part of the surface of the globe. We find it at Melville Island, within the polar circle, all through the north temperate zone, in America, in Europe, and in Asia; in several inter-tropical regions, in South America, in Africa, the Indian Archipelago, and Australia. At present about 320 principal coal-fields are known; but every day adds to the number. It is only within two or three years that the discovery of coal in Port Natal in Africa was fully established. And even so late as 1851, the best works connected with the subject of coal considered its existence in the South American Continent as doubtful, and yet, in 1852, from 150 to 170 tons per day were raised at Coronel, at a short distance from the harbour of Talcahuano, and not far from Conception in Chili. Many of the Spanish writers of the beginning of the eighteenth century mention the existence of coal in several parts along the coast of the Pacific, and at the opposite side of the Cordilleras, especially in Brazil and Uruguay; indeed, it has been worked to some small extent in the province of Santa Catherina in the former country. There can be no doubt that when the great central regions of South America become as well known as those of North America, immense coal-fields will be discovered there.

There is nothing in the whole range of human industry which to our mind is more calculated to create a feeling of wonder and admiration of the arrangement which pervades all the laws of Nature than the stores of fuel now disentombed from the earth, at convenient distances from the shores of every ocean and sea, to supply the machinery of human intercourse. It is probable that the elements of these immense masses of coal at one time existed as carbonic acid in the atmosphere, and were gradually abstracted from it by the leaves of these truly primeval forests which covered the earth in ages so long passed that the history of mankind affords no unit by which to measure them. These plants, instead of decaying and returning their elements to the atmosphere, were entombed in the earth, and must have therefore considerably affected the constitution of the former. We are now rapidly restoring that carbonic acid to the atmosphere; and if we continue for a few centuries more the combustion of coal at our present rate, we shall be gradually approaching a condition of the atmosphere similar to that which existed at the first development of organized life on the globe.

Leaving those subjects of speculation, and returning to the more practical part of our subject, coal may now be considered as the basis of all the great industries of the world. The amount of coal, therefore, existing in a country may, to a certain extent, be considered an index of its manufacturing capabilities. The following Table will serve to give an idea of the resources in this respect of the chief nations which at present occupy themselves with industry, or are likely soon to do so:—

| | Area of Coal in Square Miles. | Proportion of Coal Area to that of the whole Country. | Annual Production. |
|---|---|---|---|
| Great Britain, | 8,139 | 1 : 11 | 36,000,000 |
| Ireland, | 850 | 1 : 48 | 220,000 |
| France, | 1,788 | 1 : 100 | 5,000,000 |
| Belgium, | 517 | 1 : 20 | 6,250,000 |
| Spain, | 3,408 | 1 : 52 | 1,000,000 |
| Prussia, | 1,200 | 1 : 90 | 5,000,000 |
| Bohemia,* | 1,000 | 1 : 20 | 380,000 |
| United States, | 133,569 | 1 : 20 | 4,500,000† |
| New Brunswick and other British maritime Provinces of North America, | 18,000 | 2 : 9 | |

This Table does not, however, represent the true relative proportions of coal in each country; as a small field may have a greater number of workable seams, and consequently a much greater thickness of coal than a large field. For example, in Coalbrookdale, to which we have already alluded, there are 17 seams,

* The whole production of Austria in 1848 was 810,165 tons. Coal is very abundant in the several provinces of Austria. Moravia and Silesia stand next, in point of production, to Bohemia; the Duchies of Austria come next; and in the fourth rank come Illyria and the coast of the Adriatic.

† This only includes the anthracite: the bituminous coals are scarcely at all worked as yet.

giving about 40 feet thick of coal, while in the Lancashire coal-field there are 75 seams, making a total thickness of 150 feet; and in the South Welsh coal-field 30 seams, giving 100 feet thick of coal. Judged in this way, the coal-fields of Spain are among the richest known, especially those in the Asturias, which have about 100 seams, averaging from 3 to 12 feet in thickness. There are 50 seams in the largest of the Belgian coal-fields, but they are thin: 103 in the basin of the Saare, on the frontiers of France and Germany, averaging from 1½ to 15 feet; and 18 in that of St. Etienne, in the north of France.

The coal-fields of the United States are as yet but imperfectly examined. So far as has been ascertained, the number of seams is not large, but they are of good thickness. Their prodigious area, however, throws the coal-fields of Europe completely into the shade. They may be classed in three great groups:—1. The Apalachian or Alleghany group; 2. That of the Missouri; and 3. The Illinois. The Alleghany coal-fields occupy a tract of country about 750 miles long, and 85 to 90 miles of mean breadth, forming part of eight States,—among others, of Kentucky, Michigan, Virginia, Georgia, Maryland, Ohio, Pennsylvania, &c. Their entire area may therefore be estimated at more than 70,000 square miles, or about 44,800,000 acres, having an average thickness of at least 20 feet of excellent coal, partly anthracite, but chiefly bituminous, abounding in seams of cannel coal. In Western Virginia one seam is 9½ feet thick, so that in one-third of the whole area the total thickness is fully 40 feet. The Illinois group of coal-fields is situated in the great basin of the Mississippi, and spreads over an area of about 56,000 square miles, or 35,840,000 acres, the greater part being bituminous, some being quite equal to ordinary cannel coal. The third, or Missouri coal district, is but very little known, the area as yet ascertained not exceeding, perhaps, 10,000 square miles; but there is reason to believe that when better known it will be found equal in extent to the Mississippi group of coal-fields. The following Table will give an approximative idea of the distribution of coal area in the chief states:—

| | Square Miles. | Acres. |
|---|---|---|
| Michigan, | 5,000 | 3,200,000 |
| Kentucky, | 13,500 | 8,640,000 |
| Ohio, | 11,900 | 7,616,000 |
| Virginia, | 21,195 | 13,564,800 |
| Georgia, | 150 | 96,000 |
| Maryland, | 550 | 352,000 |
| Pennsylvania, | 15,437 | 9,879,000 |
| Illinois, | 44,000 (?) | 28,160,000 |
| Indiana, | 7,700 | 4,928,000 |
| Tennessee, | 4,300 | 2,752,000 |
| Alabama, | 3,400 | 2,176,000 |
| Missouri, | 6,000 | 3,840,000 |

Taking the produce of an acre of coal, one foot thick, to be only 1418 tons,* the coal-fields of the Apalachian group alone, at an average thickness of 20 feet, would supply the present consumption of the whole world, estimated at 60 millions of tons per annum, for 21,175 years. What a glorious destiny lies before those countries, and how curious that colonization and freedom should have taken such a rapid and extended development in those very regions where the elements of future greatness lie buried in such profuse abundance in the soil. The Newcastle coal-field in England still contains coal enough for 1000 years at the present rate of working, and the South Wales one is capable of supplying the consumption of Great Britain for 2000 years to come, long before which period, it is to be hoped, the necessity of using coal as a fuel will have ceased, and electricity, perhaps, take its place.

Peat, as it is well known, varies very considerably in its structure from the surface to the bottom of the bog; in the same manner coal appears to vary according to its relative age. Thus, a kind of coal is found among the newer rocks, especially those belonging to the group termed tertiary, of a deep brown colour, and retaining very often the perfect structure of wood, between which and true coal it is intermediate; hence the name *lignite* applied to it. Immense deposits of this substance, though of comparatively small area, are found in Silesia, Styria, Hesse-Darmstadt, Nassau, and other parts of Germany bordering the Rhine, where it is now used as fuel for domestic and manufacturing purposes. It burns with a considerable flame, but it contains a large amount of ash, and is, therefore, unfitted for the manufacture of iron, although in many districts where it is found rich deposits of spathose iron occur. The charcoal made from lignite, independent of its great quantity of ash, is very bad, and withstands with difficulty the blast of a forge bellows. Beds of lignite are also found in England and Scotland, of which the best known in the former is that at Bovey-Tracy, in Devonshire. In Ireland there is a very important development of this fuel on the northern and eastern shores of Lough Neagh. Three beds are known in that locality, in a depth of 76 feet, one 20 feet, one 25 feet, and one 15 feet thick, making a total of 60 feet. It has been but very partially worked, the chief locality being at a few miles from the road between Ballymena and Ballymoney. Three tons of good lignite are considered in Germany to be equal to two tons of ordinary coal. No examples of this fuel were exhibited.

Of the true coal there is an almost endless variety, but all may be classed under three heads:—1. Bituminous; 2. Steam coal; and 3. Anthracite. The first is too well known to need description, as it constitutes the kind of coal used for domestic purposes, and for a great many manufactures. It burns readily, cakes together, and flames. When distilled, it yields a large amount of gas and tar, hence the name *bituminous*. There is a particular variety of bituminous coal, termed *cannel* coal, which, when distilled, gives off, as volatile products, gas, tar, &c., as much as from 40 to 60 per cent. From containing this large quantity of volatile matter, it readily takes fire, and burns like a candle; and is hence much used for drawing-room

* This estimate is founded on the old wasteful system still to a great extent practised. As, however, some allowance must be made for unworkable seams, &c., it is better to take the lower estimate.

fires. It not only yields the largest quantity of gas of any other coal, but also the richest in quality, and is consequently used to a very large extent in making gas. It does not often constitute an entire bed, but occurs in bands in seams of ordinary bituminous coal. In some coal-fields, however, many entire seams pass insensibly into cannel coal. When compact, it is often manufactured into ornaments in imitation of jet; but it is brittle, and much heavier than that substance, which is not found associated with true coal, but in rocks of much more recent date than those constituting the coal measures. That at Whitby in Yorkshire, for instance, which is much employed in making necklaces and other ornaments, occurs in what is called the lias formation. True jet is found in Languedoc, in the Asturias in Spain, in many parts of the Alps; in Gallicia, and in Massachusets in America. Considerable quantities of cannel coal occur in Scotland, where the inferior kinds are called *parrot;* and *splint coal*, in the Newcastle coal-field, and to some extent in those of Yorkshire and Derbyshire. The most important locality of cannel coal for us in Ireland, however, is Lancashire, or rather that part of the coal-field of that country in the neighbourhood of Wigan, whence we get the chief supply for our gas-works. The richest of the Wigan cannels is, perhaps, that known as *Orrell Wigan.*

Bituminous coals are the best adapted for making coke, in consequence of the sort of semi-fusion which the coal undergoes; and immense quantities are employed for this purpose in Great Britain for locomotives and iron making. The usual process now adopted to make coke is to burn the coal, with a very slight access of air, in peculiar furnaces, built in long ranges. Each oven holds a charge of from two to four tons of coal. After the first charge has been burned, and the coke withdrawn, the dome still retaining a considerable amount of heat, a fresh charge is then introduced, and ignited at the top by means of wood or straw, favoured by the heat thus retained, the doors and vents, or small chimneys on top, being left open. As soon as the combustion has fully set in, the draught is carefully regulated, and the coking proceeds from the top downwards, the gas produced being in this way effectually burned.

The kinds of coal termed *steam coal* contains but very little volatile matter, but, on the other hand, they are rich in carbon; they are hence unfitted for making gas, but well adapted for producing steam, and for making iron. As the same weight of this kind of coal is capable of yielding a greater amount of heat than bituminous coal, it is peculiarly adapted for steam navigation in long voyages, and is, indeed, the only kind now employed for that purpose. The greater part of the coals of Wales is of this class, and is of excellent quality, burns well, and with a certain amount of flame, and in general with but little ash. While the bituminous coals, without including the cannel, contain about 30 per cent., and often even 37 to 38 per cent. of volatile matter, and would yield by close distillation about 62 to 70 per cent. of coke,—steam coal contains not more than from 10 to 15 per cent of volatile matter, and would, therefore, yield from 80 to 85 per cent. of coke. In practice, so large a per centage of real coke could not, however, be obtained, as part of it would be consumed during the process of carbonization.

The third kind of coal, *anthracite*, contains scarcely any volatile matter, and consists of carbon and a little ash; it ignites with difficulty, and gives scarcely any flame, but with a strong draught it produces a most intense heat. It is heavier than bituminous or semi-bituminous (steam) coals. Anthracite has always been a favourite fuel for drying malt and corn generally, and for burning lime; but, until within a very few years, it was deemed unfit for making iron, or producing steam, or, indeed, for any other purpose than those just mentioned. By improvements, however, in the form of furnaces, and especially by allowing a jet of steam to mix with the air entering the furnace, it may now be employed wherever ordinary coal can be used. No less than 30,000 tons of iron are now made with anthracite in Wales; and in the United States it is also extensively used for the same purpose, for oceanic steam navigation in many of the river steamers, and even for locomotives. A short time since, a peculiar form of furnace for using it in making glass was patented by the Messrs. Chance of Birmingham. Anthracite coal exists in great abundance in the western part of south Wales, in Scotland, and in many parts of the Continent.

Coal, therefore, exhibits a complete series of gradations in composition, from wood to pure carbon, the latter being represented by anthracite, which may be considered as the natural coke of coal. This view would necessarily suppose, that there was going on in the earth a gradual slow distillation of the coal beds, and that the greater the antiquity of the coal, the more of its volatile matter will it have lost, and the nearer will it have approached to the condition of anthracite, after which scarcely any further change could take place. If this be true, carbonic acid must be given off in great abundance from deposits of brown coal or lignite, and compounds of hydrogen and carbon, as well as carbonic acid from bituminous coals; such being the substances which should be formed during the transformation of which we have spoken. This view was put forward by Liebig, and is singularly in coincidence with the facts observed in coal mines. In lignite mines large quantities of carbonic acid, called by miners *choke-damp*, are evolved, whilst in bituminous coal mines the dangerous *fire-damp* of the miner, or carbureted hydrogen, makes its appearance; and as the coal approaches the condition of anthracite, the fire-damp diminishes, and is again replaced by the choke-damp. According to this hypothesis, brown coal or lignite would in time yield bituminous coal, and all the beds of the latter must have at one time passed through the intermediate state of lignite. Of this, however, there are no proofs.

The mode of extracting coal from the earth differs essentially, as may be supposed, from that followed in lead and copper mining. In the one case the substance to be extracted usually exists as a *vein*, running in a certain direction; coal, on the other hand, always occurs as a *bed* more or less inclined, and extending over acres, and, it may be, square miles. There is, however, no general system of coal mining, local circumstances giving rise to peculiarities of working. In these countries there are two methods employed, one called the *pillar and stall working*, and the other the *long wall.* The former consists in cutting a number of levels or galleries through the mass of the coal at right angles to each other, thus leaving a number of square pillars to support the roof. In collieries where the seam worked is at a comparatively small depth, the pillar and stall (also called board or wicket in some collieries) are of the same size; but in working deep-seated beds, where the weight of the roof is great, the pillar left standing may sometimes be as much as three or four times the size of the stall, or, in other words, only from one-fourth to one-fifth of the coal would in such cases be removed. In general, however, *it is intended to remove* those pillars subsequently, but there are actually collieries in England worked upon the principle of losing them! Even where this is not the case, the pillars, in the course of a few years, become weakened, and the roof softened, by the infiltration of water, the result of which is, that the roof sinks in, and even frequently the surface of the ground, destroying buildings, &c. This result, which is attended with a loss of the coal existing as pillars, is called by the miners *a creep*. Sometimes, where the pillars are left so weak as to be unable to bear the pressure of the roof, they give way at once and are crushed to powder, a fracture of the roof being produced at the same time. This accident, which is called a *thurst*, is often attended with great loss of life. When the pillars are to be removed, it is usual to prop up the roof close to the pillar of coal with props of wood; this support, termed a *jud*, is in its turn removed, when the roof falls, or sinks in and forms a gradually increasing mass of ruins, termed the *goaf*. This mass of ruins affords great facilities for the accumulation of fire-damp; and it is generally upon its edge, during this *robbing* of the pillars *and drawing of the juds*, as these operations are termed, that all those frightful explosions, of which we read, but too often occur.

In certain districts, especially in Yorkshire, where facilities exist, such as freedom from water in the roof, the absence of buildings, and especially of rivers upon the surface, &c., the long wall working is adopted. In this method the whole of the coal is at once removed, the workings being carried on from the extremity of the bed towards some point as a centre where the shaft is situate. In this case also the roof falls in and forms a mass of ruins termed the *gob*. So extensive have been the workings in some collieries, that these masses of ruins, termed goafs and gobs, are often ten to fifteen acres, and even more, in extent. In Staffordshire, where the beds of coal are very thick, an essentially different system of working is adopted: levels are driven from the shafts to the extremity of the coal, and when the limit is reached, the colliers commence at one or both sides of this level, a sort of level at right angles to it of about twenty yards wide, leaving, however, here and there a number of pillars of coal about six to eight yards square to support the roof. When this cross level or *side lane* has been excavated, another is commenced parallel to it; but, in order to render the roof secure, a partition or wall of coal, nearly as thick as the side lane itself, is left standing between them, termed the *fire rib*. A colliery worked in this way consists, therefore, of a long level or street, with a number of side lanes at right angles to it, separated from each other by great walls of coal. When each side lane is worked out, the entrance is generally built up to keep in the gas as much as possible.

The pillars left in these lanes bear but a small proportion to the enormous weight of the roof, and a great many accidents are consequently occurring in those mines. During the working of the *whole coal* there are, however, but few accidents comparatively speaking; but when the pillars left standing are removed, and the props also successively taken away, so as to allow the roof to fall, the greatest caution is required to avoid loss of life. Where the roof consists of loose shale, it tumbles at once; but where it is formed of sandstone, a very large area, sometimes as much as 400 square yards, will remain standing after the removal of the props, so as to form an immense cavern. As its size is being continually added to, it will finally reach a point beyond which it can no longer resist; when this is attained, the superincumbent strata becomes greatly agitated for a day or two, and will finally fall with a tremendous crash, producing a gush of air through every part of the mines, and but too often an explosion of fire-damp.

These accumulations of fire and choke-damp in coal mines necessitate a system of ventilation. In many collieries this is effected by means of great fires, which are kept continually burning at the bottom of a shaft; which acts as a chimney, and thus produces a strong draught which draws the air from the mine, fresh air being introduced by another shaft. As it is of the greatest consequence that this current of air should circulate through every part of the workings, doors are placed in various parts of the levels so as to prevent the current taking the shortest way to the upcast shaft. Recently a number of ventilating machines have been introduced instead of this wasteful and clumsy method; and anemometers are employed to indicate and register the rapidity of the currents of air, and thus show where the ventilation is imperfect. One of those instruments was exhibited by Mr. M. Dunn.

As fire-damp, which differs but little from common gas, produces explosive mixtures with common air, candles, or other open lights, cannot be used in mines where this gas is evolved, without risking the danger of explosions. Previous to 1815 the miner obtained the necessary light for his work by means of a contrivance called the steel mill, consisting of a small disc of steel, which was made to revolve with great rapidity by means of a ratchet-wheel worked with a handle. This wheel in its revolution rubbed against a piece of flint, and produced a succession of bright scintillations. This defective source of light had the additional disadvantage of requiring a boy to work it. In 1813, Dr. Reid Clanny invented a safety lamp, consisting of an insulated light, to which the air necessary to maintain the combustion was provided by means of a pair of bellows. In 1815 Sir Humphrey Davy invented his celebrated safety lamp; the principle of which is, that wire-gauze cools any flame placed in contact with it, below the point of incandescence, and hence it cannot pass through the gauze. The "Davy," as the lamp is now universally called, consists of a common oil-lamp, surrounded by a cylinder of gauze. When this lamp is introduced into an explosive mixture of fire-damp and air, the gas may burn within the cylinder of wire-gauze, but, from the cooling action of the latter, cannot pass and communicate the flame to the surrounding mixture. This simple and ingenious contrivance has undergone very many modifications since Davy's time, the most important being that made by M. Muesseler, which consists of an ordinary oil-lamp, surrounded by a cylinder of fine glass, half an inch thick, and three inches high, surmounted by a cylinder of wire-gauze. A second cylinder is inclosed in this, which reaches to very nearly the flame of the lamp, and acts as a chimney, up which the hot air passes, while a corresponding current of cold air flows down from the top between the two cylinders. The use of the glass is to prevent the action of the currents of air which are always flowing through collieries, upon the wick. The improved lamp of Dr. Clanny is almost identical with that of Muesseler.

The introduction of the "Davy" has been of immense importance to coal mining; numbers of collieries previously relinquished were again worked, and millions of tons of coal thus preserved. But in the hands of careless and ignorant workmen it is far from being an absolute safeguard against explosions, as sad experience has but too often proved. A very interesting collection of seven safety lamps, showing the chief modifications which the original simple Davy has undergone down to the present day, was exhibited by Mr. Mathias Dunn, of Newcastle-upon-Tyne, who also exhibited that curious relic of coal mining, a steel mill.

Although coal is now a necessary of life, the foundation of all the industry of Great Britain, and indeed of most parts of Europe, it is singular that its use should have commenced so recently. We are not aware of any mention of coal as a distinct article of trade earlier than the charter granted by Henry III. in the year 1239 "to the goode men of Newcastle to dig coals outside the walls thereof." From this date, however, the consumption rapidly increased, and already, in 1246, there was an export of coals, which from that fact received the name of *sea coal*. In 1306 it must have been very extensively used in London, for a notion got abroad that its smoke was productive of the plague and many other destructive diseases; and the Parliament accordingly petitioned King Edward I. to prohibit the burning of coals as dangerous to the health of the people. The King accordingly issued his proclamation, "That not only in the city of London, but all havens, towns, and many places within the land, the inhabitants, in general, are constrained to make their fires of sea coal or pit coal, even the chambers of honourable personages, and of necessity, have devised the making of iron, glass, bricks, &c., with the said sea coal." This proclamation appears to have had but little effect, and accordingly a commission of oyer and terminer was issued for the purpose of punishing by fines all who burned sea coal within the city or its immediate neighbourhood; and when guilty of a second offence, in addition to the fine, to demolish their furnaces, and providing for the strict obedience of the commands to the proclamation for the future. Notwithstanding these stringent measures, ten shillings' worth of coal was used at the coronation of Edward III. From this time its use appears to have steadily increased; but still, even as late as the reign of Elizabeth, it had not become general, for Harrison, in his Description of England, published in 1577, states:—"Of coal mines we have such plenty in the north and western parts of our island as may suffice for all the realme of England; and so must they doe hereafter indeed if wood be not better cherished than it is at this present. I dare affirm that if woods do go so fast to decay in the next hundred years as they have done, and are like to do in this, it is to be feared that broom, turf, brakes, whins, ling, hassock, rush, &c., and sea coal, will be good merchandise even in the city of London, whereunto some of them have already gotten ready passage, and taken up their innes in the greatest merchants' parlors." In 1627 the first recorded patent for the smelting of iron with coal alone was granted; and during the reign of Charles I. it came to be used in London exclusively as a fuel.

With the gradual increase in the consumption of coal, great improvements were made in the mode of extracting it, but much yet remains to be done, not alone in the engineering of collieries, and especially in the registrations of plans, but in abolishing the odious system of contracting for mines by that ignorant, griping set of men termed *butty-colliers*, with whom the public is familiar from the graphic pictures of D'Israeli in his "Sybil." Under this system, and the absence of education and rational amusement, the people employed in the collieries of Great Britain have sunk to a state of degradation perhaps unparalleled in the history of the human race.

Hitherto we have not spoken of the coal-fields of Ireland, but we shall now say a few words upon that subject. Before doing so, however, we must observe, that since Mr. Griffith's survey of them many years ago, nothing further of a definite character has been done, or at least published, in that direction; there is therefore, nothing new to be added to Sir Robert Kane's admirable chapter on Coal in the "Industrial Resources of Ireland." Our remarks on the subject will be very brief, and for fuller details we must refer our readers to that work.

There are seven coal-fields in Ireland, of which three are situate in Ulster, one in Leinster, two in Munster, and one in Connaught. It is a remarkable feature of those coal-fields, that while all the northern ones are bituminous, those in the south are anthracite, and the Connaught field, which stands geographically between both, is also intermediate in quality, being, indeed, but little more bituminous than the kind of coals we have described as steam coal. The following Table contains the chief facts of importance connected with those deposits:—

| COAL-FIELD. | County in which situated. | Number of Seams of Coal. | Total thickness of Coal Measures examined | Total thickness of Coal. | Thickness of thickest Seam. | Total estimated Area. | Number of which have been worked. |
|---|---|---|---|---|---|---|---|
| | | | F. I. | | F. I. | ACRES. | |
| 1. Ballycastle, . . . | Antrim, . . . | 6 | . . . . . | About 14 feet. | 2 6 | . . . . . | Nearly all worked out. |
| 2. Monaghan, . . . | Monaghan, . | . . . | . . . . . | 1 foot to 14 inches. | 8 0 | | |
| 3. { Coal Island, . . . | } Tyrone, . . { | 6 | 720 0 | 22 to 32 feet. | 10 0 | 7000 | 3 (?) |
| { Anahone, . . . . | | 3 | 171 (?) | 14 feet. | 9 0 | 320 (?) | Only the 9 foot seam. |
| 4. Lough Allen, . . . | Leitrim, . . . | 3 (4?) | 204 (?) | 6 ft. 9 in. | 8 feet. | 20,000 (?) | 2 |
| 5. { Castlecomer, . . . | Kilkenny, } | 8 | 984 0 | 22 feet (of real coal). | 10 feet, containing about 4 feet of good coal. | 8100 (?) | 3 (nearly worked out). |
| { Modubogh, . . . . | Carlow, } | | | | | | |
| { Rushes, . . . . . | Queen's. } | | | | | | |
| 6. Slieveardagh, &c., . | Tipperary, . . | 3 (?) | . . . . . | 4 ft. 9 in. | 2 0 | | |
| 7. Munster, . . . . . | Cork, Kerry, and Limerick. | 6 (?) | . . . . . | . . . . . . . | 2 to 3 ft. | | |

An examination of this Table will show how little really definite information we have as yet obtained with reference to the Irish coal-fields. Thus, for example, we know almost nothing of the Munster coal-field, which is spread over by far the largest area of any of the others; indeed, it is one of the largest coal areas in these countries. And yet that coal-field is situated in precisely those parts of Ireland farthest removed from a supply of English and Scotch coals, and where fuel must consequently be most expensive. Of the amount of ignorance which prevails upon the subject of Irish coal in the absence of some reliable statistics and surveys, we have only to refer to an article on the subject of coal in the Illustrated Catalogue of the London Exhibition of 1851, and the statistics of which are based upon a work which constitutes the chief authority upon the subject of coal in Great Britain and America, in which it is stated that Ireland contains 1,850,000 acres, or 2890 square miles of coal area,—that is, more than France and Belgium put together! No more useful, and, we would add, necessary work could be undertaken, than an accurate survey of the whole of the Irish coal-fields. This is, however, not to be hoped for with the present limited funds of the Geological Survey of Ireland, which cannot afford to have a special mining geologist, and can only consequently obtain the casual assistance of the English one, whose time is already more than fully occupied.

Imperfect as is our information upon the extent and value of our coal-fields, that relative to the quantity now annually raised is still more so. The published statistics of recent date refer only to three collieries,—Slievardagh in the Tipperary field, Ballylehane in the Carlow part of the Leinster coal-field, and a small one called Lisnacon in Cork. The former, worked by the Mining Company of Ireland, yielded, in 1853, 6842 tons of coal, and 30,087 barrels, of 24 cwts., of culm, giving a total of 42,946 tons. During the same year Lisnacon Colliery yielded 2203 tons of coal and culm (small coal). In 1852 Ballylehane Colliery yielded about 6000 tons, which, perhaps, also represents the produce of 1853. We regret being unable to give the quantities raised at Castlecomer, in the county of Limerick, in Tyrone, and especially in Leitrim. Sir Robert Kane estimated the production of the Castlecomer Collieries in 1845 at 120,000 tons per annum, the coal being sold at 11*s.* 6*d.*, and the culm at 4*s.* per ton; and, so far as we are aware, it has not since diminished. The total quantity at present raised in Ireland may therefore, perhaps, be estimated at about 220,000 tons, of which about 170,000 tons are anthracite, and 50,000 bituminous coal.

Up to a very recent period the Irish coal mines were worked in a very imperfect manner. To give an example, no less than 1200 shafts have been sunk in the one district of Castlecomer since the first working of that field, about the beginning of the last century; many of them not being more than 100 yards apart! Even at present the management of most of them is not all that could be desired; and many improvements of great importance, which have been made in other countries, especially in the utilization of waste, pyritic shale, &c., and in the sifting and purifying of coals, are here unknown. We may instance one made several years ago by M. Berard, and now used extensively on the Continent, and even in England, for separating pyrites and shale from coal. The machine used for this purpose is cheap and simple; it costs but £400, and is capable of cleaning from 120 to 140 tons of coal in a day at an expense of one penny per ton! The importance of this machine in Ireland cannot be overrated, inasmuch as many of our best beds of coal are highly pyritic; and most of them being thin, a large part of the coal obtained from them is in the condition of small coal, especially the anthracite, which is very brittle, and is always largely mixed with fragments of shale and slaty coal. That this is the case, we have only to refer to the returns from Slieveardagh, already quoted, by which the culm raised is seen to be more than five times the quantity of large coal. Our coals are also rich in ash; but by Berard's machine experience has shown that coals, containing as much as 26 per cent. of ash, may be so perfectly washed as to yield only 2½ per cent. Need we say more to point out its utility?

This is not the place to enter into the question of the improvements which might be advantageously introduced into our collieries, even if our limited space permitted us to do so. But there can be no doubt that in this branch of industry, perhaps more than any other, we stand in need of education.

There were ten exhibitors of coal, from ten localities, representing eight distinct coal-fields, of which one-half were anthracite, and the other bituminous. Of these, five exhibitors showed Irish coal from six localities, representing four coal-fields, three being anthracitic, and one bituminous. There were three English exhibitors, representing two bituminous coal-fields; one Scotch, representing one bituminous; and two Welsh, representing the anthracite and cannel coal of Wales. Of these, three series of specimens deserve special mention: namely, that of the Monkland Iron Company, who exhibited a block of six inches cube of each bed of coal, worked in the great Lanarkshire coal-field in Scotland, being part of the fine series of sandstone, ironstone, &c., already alluded to, as sent by that Company (this was unquestionably the most important and intelligently selected series in the Exhibition): the sections of the entire seams now worked by the Mining Company of Ireland at their collieries of Slievardagh in the county of Tipperary, and Lisnacon in the county of Cork; and the sections of the seam now worked at Castlecomer, in the Kilkenny part of the Leinster coal-field, contributed by the Hon. C. Wandesforde. No examples of the coal of the northern coal-fields were exhibited; indeed Ulster contributed scarcely any examples of her mineral products of any kind. There were two exhibitors of coke, one specimen of which, made from Marley Hill coal, Newcastle-upon-Tyne, shown by J. Shield, Son, and Co. of Ringsend, was a good example of the peculiar structure of the coke produced from that class of coal.

## SALT.

We now come to the examination of a mineral product which is amongst the most widely diffused in Nature, and which is of immense importance in the animal and vegetable economy. Every one is acquainted with that substance which, as it were to mark its universal occurrence and usage, we call *common salt*. But very few persons are fully aware of the sources from which it is obtained, or the manifold uses to which it is applied. A century ago its employment was confined to the preservation of animal and vegetable substances, and as a condiment. At the present day it assists, as the source of nearly all our soda and chlorine, to bleach our textile fabrics and our paper; to make our soap; and even one of the principal elements of our glass has existed as salt. This compound enters very largely into the composition of many rocks, such as certain varieties of granite, and traces of it occur everywhere in the soil, and in the water of rivers.

When rocks are exposed to the action of water, they become in time altered. Certain substances capable of dissolving in it are washed out, and gradually carried by the streams and rivers to the ocean. Sometimes the rock undergoes complete decay, and crumbles away, giving rise to masses of clay, sand, and gravel, constituting soils; the two former, when sufficiently pure, forming materials for the manufacture of glass and porcelain. One of the principal of these dissolved substances is soda, which, as before remarked, is found in exceedingly minute quantities in all river waters; for it is unnecessary to remark that the decay of rocks is a slow process, requiring periods of time of which our historic epochs would be merely years. The ocean would thus appear to be a great reservoir of the soluble elements of rocks, and accordingly we find considerable quantities of soda dissolved in sea-water. This soda, although not all existing in the form of salt in rocks, finds itself, in great part, transformed into that substance during its passage from the hills to the ocean.

The quantity of these soluble substances which exist in sea-water may be estimated to form about 3½ per cent. of its weight, the salt alone forming a little more than two-thirds of that quantity, or about 2½ per cent. Owing, however, to the unequal evaporation from the surface of the sea in different regions of the globe, these proportions are subject to considerable variation. In some of the inland lakes of Asia the quantity of salt is enormous. Thus, in the water of the Dead Sea, salt forms one-fourth of its weight: and whole regions of the flat steppes of the Kirghis, lying between the Aral and Caspian Seas, consist of a barren wilderness covered with an efflorescence of salt.

Salt is also found in masses interstratified with other rocks; and hence the name of rock-salt when derived from this source. It is principally found in a group of rocks which lie above those in which coal is usually found, and hence the group is sometimes called the *saliferous formation*. The most characteristic rocks usually associated with the salt consist of red and variegated sandstones, called by geologists the new red sandstone, gypsum, and marls. The former are admirably adapted for building purposes. Some of the finest old Gothic churches on the Continent, as those of Strasburg, Spires, Munster, are built of this stone; and in England it has been also employed, as, for instance, in Chester Cathedral. This rock occurs near Belfast, and many of the new buildings erected in that town are constructed of it. Deposits of salt of this kind are found in almost every country in the world; and many of them are remarkable for their extent, such as the mountain of salt, 600 feet high, and 1200 feet wide at its base, which occurs at Cordona, in Catalonia; and at Wieliczka, in Gallicia, the deposit is 500 miles long, 20 miles wide, and 1200 feet deep, and the extent of the operations, and the size of the galleries cut in the salt, have given rise to the most extravagant tales of whole villages of miners who never come above ground. Although such stories are fabulous, still the appearance of these enormous crystal galleries, when lit with torches, presents one of the most singular subterraneous spectacles in the world.

Rock-salt scarcely, if ever, exists of sufficient purity to be used directly; although near Liverpool it is found colourless, and as clear as glass. In general it is of a reddish colour, from the presence of ferruginous clay intermixed with it, from which it can be readily purified by mere solution in water, when the earthy matter will subside to the bottom of the vessel.

The preparation of salt presents us with one of the most beautiful adaptations of the laws of Nature to a certain end, which we know of. Salt and many similar substances are capable of dissolving in water, and when this water is removed by evaporation they separate again in certain regular geometrical shapes—that is, they are said to crystallize. In this way salt always assumes the shape of a cube. As a general rule, most of these bodies are more soluble in hot water than in cold; and we also find that many of them do not immediately crystallize in hot solutions after a certain portion of the water in which they were dissolved is evaporated, but remain dissolved until after the liquid has somewhat cooled down. Common salt offers a singular exception to this law; for it is nearly equally soluble in cold as in boiling water, and separates readily in small crystals from its boiling solution. Were it not for this almost exceptional property the purification of salt from the substances which are usually found in Nature with it, would be at once difficult, tedious, and expensive.

Nearly all the salt consumed in Ireland is obtained by evaporation; and in many places, especially in Cork, the process is effected by the waste heat from the operation of lime-burning, the evaporating pans being placed over kilns which are in continuous action. In England a large part, and in Germany and other parts of Europe the greater part, of the salt is obtained from springs of water which in passing over beds of salt dissolve large quantities of it. Many of those springs contain but very little salt; sometimes not much more than exists in sea water, but sometimes by boring to great depths, as is done for Artesian wells, these springs are brought directly from the salt beds; and thus in many cases saturated solutions are at once obtained, as at Droitwitch in Worcestershire, where an iron pipe is sunk directly into the salt to the depth of 173 feet, allowing a saturated brine containing 42 parts in 100 of salt to come to the surface. At Wimpfen, near Heilbronn, on the Neckar, a boring has been effected to the depth of about 370 feet, and extending about 23 feet into the salt. An iron pipe is let down this bore into the salt, and through this pipe the brine is pumped up, whilst fresh water flows down the sides of the bore and thus replaces the brine. In this way great caverns are gradually dissolved out of the salt; these caverns act as natural tanks for dissolving the salt and allowing the sediment to deposit, and thus save all the expenses of mining. At Prussian Minden the deepest boring of this kind yet effected is carried on, but has not as yet reached the salt. In 1843 it had reached the enormous depth of 2515 feet under the surface, and 2105 feet under the sea-level. This process of boring appears to have been practised from the most ancient times in China, for at Kia-ting-fu, in a district 50 miles long, and from 20 to 25 miles broad, there are at least 20,000 such borings, averaging from 5 to 6 inches in diameter, and from 1500 to 1800 feet deep. It sometimes happens that coal lies under the salt, and that the inflammable fire-damp given off by the former escapes through the borings, as is the case in Cheshire, but it does not appear that it has ever been put to any use there; in China it appears to have been used as a fuel for the evaporation of the brine in the district just alluded to.

Where fuel is abundant and the brine strong, it is evaporated directly; but the brine of the great majority of the springs upon the Continent is too weak to pay for the quantity of fuel which would be necessary, and hence other means are employed to effect this object. Previous to the sixteenth century the evaporation of brine was effected by making it fall on a quantity of rope of enormous length, stretched backward and forward, the effect of which was to divide it into spray, and thus expose a large surface to the influence of the atmosphere. At Moutier, in France, this process is even still followed, and so perfectly is it conducted, that by passing the hot brine ten or twelve times over these ropes salt is obtained without any evaporation by artificial heat. Towards the middle of the sixteenth century a contrivance known as the *thorn-wall* was introduced into Germany and parts of France from Lombardy, where it appears to have been for some time in use on the Adriatic coast. This process is called *graduation;* a name, however, which applies equally to the rope process, and consists in pumping up the brine into a large shallow cistern supported on a framework of wood, and of considerable height. Under this cistern, and within the framework, is built up a sort of wall composed of brushwood, but chiefly of faggots of black-thorn—hence the name of thorn-wall. The brine is let fall through these faggots by means of a series of perforated tubes, by which an immense surface is exposed; and the thorn-wall being placed in an exposed place, a current of air passes through the brushwood while the brine is trickling down, and thus effects an exceedingly rapid evaporation. After passing two or three times through the thorn-wall so much water is evaporated that it will pay to have the brine boiled down with fuel. The brine in most of these springs is much more impure than when made directly by the dissolution of rock-salt. After the separation of the salt, the residual liquor, or, as it is called, the *mother liquor*, contains a number of other saline substances, such as sulphate of potash, salts of magnesia, &c. Sometimes these are employed in the manufacture of sal-ammoniac, or they might be employed with great advantage in the preparation of artificial manures. Occasionally such brine springs contain iodine and bromine, which give to the mother liquors medicinal properties, as those of Salzhausen and Kreuznach.

Some notion may be formed of the quantity of water evaporated by means of these thorn-walls when it is stated that, at the salt works of Schönebeck, near Magdeburg, which produce about 30,000 tons of salt annually from a brine which contains only 12 per cent. of salt, or nearly five times as much as sea-water, the quantity of water evaporated from the whole thorn surface on a warm summer's day amounts to sometimes 1,443,000 cubic feet, or 8,989,890 gallons!

When the salt is extracted directly in the solid form, the mode of mining does not differ much from that employed in working coal mines. The salt is blasted, and large pillars are left standing, so that a ground-plan of the whole would represent in some degree the appearance of a chess-board. Subsequently these pillars, as in coal mines, are also removed.

As we have before remarked, the sea is a source of salt. This is especially the case on the coasts of warm maritime countries, but it is by no means confined to them; for even in Siberia the inhabitants are enabled to obtain sufficient salt for their use by taking advantage of the circumstance that when salt water freezes, the ice contains no salt, and so by repeatedly freezing a quantity of sea-water an exceedingly strong brine is at last obtained.

In Portugal, Spain, and the south of France, great quantities of excellent salt are produced by the evaporation effected by the sun in large ponds called *salt-gardens*, which are cultivated from March to the end of September. These gardens are simply a number of shallow ponds, laid out on a stiff clay soil, on the coast, and protected from the action of the tides. The principle upon which they are constructed is, to expose the largest possible surface to the action of the sun. The first pond, which is usually about five feet deep, has a sluice, by means of which it can be filled from the sea. Here the water is allowed to deposit its mud and become clear. From this pond it passes by means of a pipe into a second pool, much smaller and shallower, and divided into compartments by narrow dykes, so arranged as to cause the brine from the settling pond, entering at one angle, to describe a circuitous course through every part of the pond before it escapes at the opposite angle into the third pond, which is still shallower than the second, but is subdivided like it. From the third pool it passes into the fourth, where it begins to crystallize. The salt, as fast as it forms, is collected with rakes into small heaps on the narrow dykes which separate the ponds. The mother liquor, after the first crop of salt, is run into another series of smaller and shallower ponds, where a second and third crystallization of salt takes place, but of an inferior quality to the first. When no more salt separates, the residual liquor is run into the sea. The salt as it is first raked out of the ponds and made into heaps is very impure, the principal foreign substances being chloride of magnesium, a compound analogous to salt, the soda of the latter being replaced by magnesia. This substance is very deliquescent, that is, it imbibes water from the atmosphere and becomes liquid. It is this impurity which causes salt to become damp in winter. To get rid of this and other foreign matters, the salt, after it has sufficiently drained from the mother liquors on the dykes, is piled into great heaps, and thatched with dried grass, and is thus protected from the rain; but the moisture of the atmosphere gradually liquefies the chloride of magnesia, which, in draining away, washes the greater part of the other impurities with it.

It has been found that if we mix solutions of Epsom salt and common salt together, and expose the mixture to a low temperature, about that of the freezing point, they will decompose one another, and we will obtain glauber salts. Upon this fact,—and upon the curious law that a mixture of two salts differing in the nature of their acids and base, augment each other's solubility in water, but that, on the other hand, a mixture of two salts resembling each other by their base or acid diminish each other's solubility; thus, chloride of sodium and sulphate of magnesia, which are different in acid and base, augment each other's solubility when present in a liquid; while chloride of sodium and sulphate of soda, having the same base, diminish each other's solubility,—upon these facts is founded the improved mode of cultivating salt gardens, by which the mother liquors remaining after the salt are economized. This process, which promises to found a great branch of industry, we owe to the laborious and beautiful researches of M. Balard. To understand the process, it is necessary to give the composition of sea-water in detail, such as it is found at Cette, in the Mediterranean, where this industry is now carried on:—

COMPOSITION OF SEA WATER IN 10,000 PARTS:

| | |
|---|---|
| Chloride of Sodium, . . . . . . . . . . . . . . . . | 294·24 |
| Chloride of Magnesium, . . . . . . . . . . . . . | 32·19 |
| Chloride of Potassium, . . . . . . . . . . . . . | 5·05 |
| Sulphate of Lime, . . . . . . . . . . . . . . . . | 13·57 |
| Sulphate of Magnesia, . . . . . . . . . . . . . | 24·77 |
| Carbonate of Lime, . . . . . . . . . . . . . . . | 1·14 |
| Oxide of Iron, . . . . . . . . . . . . . . . . . . | 0·03 |
| Bromide and Iodide of Sodium, . . . . . . . . . | 5·56 |
| Total, . . . . . . . . . | 376·55 or 3·765 per cent. |

The great mass of the salt (chloride of sodium) is first removed in the way just described, and the mother liquors, still containing a good deal of salt, and all the other substances enumerated, are set aside in special ponds, where, after some time, they furnish one or two crystallizations of Epsom salt (sulphate of magnesia). The liquid is then passed into another pond, where it yields a crystallization of sulphate of potash, or of the double sulphate of potash and magnesia—a portion of the Epsom salt and a part of the chloride of potassium decomposing one another as the liquid becomes concentrated, forming chloride of magnesium and sulphate of potash. The mother liquor resting on these crystals is again run into another pond, where it yields a crystallization of double chloride of potassium and magnesium. Finally, the mother liquor resting on these salts may be applied as manure, or employed for the manufacture of bromine or iodine, in the former of which it is very rich. These operations constitute the summer work. For the winter work three ponds are set aside. Into the first the whole of the impure sulphate of magnesia, dissolved in fresh water, is put, unless it be more profitable to sell part of it purified as crystallized Epsom salt; into the second is run a quantity of concentrated brine, set apart for this purpose before any salt had crystallized out; and into the third is put the heaps of impure salt obtained from the last crystallizations of the brine, and which still contains sufficient impurities to render it unfit for domestic purposes. As soon as the season appears propitious—that is, as soon as it is cool enough—these three liquids are mixed together in certain proportions, the salt being in excess. In one or two cold nights the whole of the Epsom salt will be decomposed by the common salt, glauber salt or sulphate of soda crystallizing out, owing to the low temperature and the presence of excess of salt, which, having the same base (soda) as the glauber salt, will, as before remarked, render it more insoluble. The mother liquor is run off the crystals before the warm part of the day commences, and they are removed and dried.

The sulphate of soda serves for the manufacture of soda ash; and thus does away with the necessity of employing the large quantity of oil of vitriol usually employed to convert common salt into sulphate of soda. The salts of potash find ready employment in the manufacture of alum, and the chloride of potassium may be employed in the manufacture of nitrate of potash or saltpetre. The bromine and iodine are employed in medicine and photography, and the latter also in the dyeing of silk.

The following are the results of the annual working of a salt garden at Baynas, which covers 370 acres:—

| | |
|---|---|
| 10,000 | tons of Common Salt. |
| 550 | „ of Crystallized Epsom Salt. |
| 450 | „ of Double Salts of Potash, Soda, and Magnesia. |
| 1,000 | „ of Sulphate of Soda, or Glauber Salt. |

If the whole of the Epsom salt were employed for the preparation of sulphate of soda, the total product of the latter would, in this case, be 1325 tons.

It is very difficult to estimate the quantity of salt consumed for domestic purposes in Europe; for that produced affords no indication of it, in consequence of large quantities being employed in the salting of hides, the glazing of stone-ware, the manufacture of hard soaps, soda, and many other chemical manufactures. Towards the end of the last century, Necker calculated that in those parts of France where the population had purchased exemption from the *gabelle* or salt tax, the annual consumption was about 19¼ lbs. per head; and M'Culloch estimates it for Great Britain at 22 lbs. per head. These numbers do not evidently represent the quantity directly and indirectly consumed as food, as they include the salt employed for other purposes. Including these, however, M'Culloch's estimate would be pretty nearly correct if applied to the whole of Europe; as the following statement of the present statistics of salt, perhaps the most complete ever published, will show:—

| | Tons. | | Sources whence obtained. |
|---|---|---|---|
| Great Britain, . . . | 726,000 | . . . | Brine springs and rock-salt. |
| France, . . . . . . | 860,000 | . . . | 300,000 tons from the sea, the remainder from brine springs and rock-salt. |
| Spain, . . . . . . . | 300,000 | . . . | Principally from the sea. |
| Portugal, . . . . . | 250,000 | . . . | Sea-water. |
| Norway, . . . . . . | 3,000 | . . . | Sea-water. |
| Germany, . . . . . | 350,000 | . . . | Brine springs. |
| Switzerland, . . . . | 11,500 | . . . | Brine springs. |
| Italy, . . . . . . . | 234,000 | . . . | Springs, 12,000; rock-salt, 2000; sea water, 220,000. |
| Hungary, Transylvania, Gallicia, . . . . . . | 272,000 | . . . | Two-thirds from rock-salt. |
| Wallachia, . . . . | 20,000 | . . . | Rock-salt. |
| Greece, . . . . . . | 20,000 | . . . | Sea-water. |
| Russia, . . . . . . | 350,000 | . . . | More than half from the sea, and one-third from springs. |

These quantities make a total of 2,896,000 tons, which, at an average cost of 15*s.* per ton, represent a sum of £2,172,000. Of this about

| | | |
|---|---|---|
| 1,277,000 tons were obtained | | from sea-water. |
| 1,223,000 | " " | from brine springs. |
| 396,000 | " " | as rock-salt. |

There are several countries in Europe which contain no salt, such as Holland and Belgium; but they have a considerable trade in refining English rock-salt.

Enormous quantities of salt are exported from England; thus the quantity of salt exported in the year 1851 was 456,642 tons. Nearly the whole of the rock-salt raised is exported, with the exception of small quantities used to strengthen the brine of some springs; so that out of the larger quantity of salt produced in England, not more than from 150 to 170,000 tons is obtained as rock-salt. The rock-salt is principally found at Norwich, in Cheshire, the number of salt beds in the district being five, varying from 6 inches to 40 feet in thickness, the depth at which they are worked being from 50 to 150 yards below the surface. The production of salt in the district is not confined to rock-salt. Immense quantities of white salt are also made from springs; indeed more than two-thirds of all the salt produced in Great Britain is made there, the whole of which is sent down the river Weaver to Liverpool. The quantity thus sent down in 1844 was

| | | |
|---|---|---|
| White salt, . . . . . . | 461,419 | Total, 553,112 tons. |
| Rock-salt, . . . . . . . | 91,693 | |

The brine springs of Droitwich, in Worcestershire, yield about 70,000 tons annually, of which about 30,000 tons are exported from London, Gloucester, and Bristol. The salt obtained from the Staffordshire springs goes chiefly to Hull.

The enormous increase which has taken place in the consumption of salt as a condiment and for the preservation of articles of food, since the sixteenth century, bears no proportion to the increase of population. And when we consider how indispensable the use of salt is to the animal economy, we cannot help thinking that in ancient times, and during the middle ages, the scarcity of salt, especially in inland countries, must have been injurious to the health of the people, and productive of many diseases; more especially as the use of culinary vegetables containing salt was but little practised. If our space permitted, we could bring together a series of curious facts connected with the manufacture and commerce of salt which would illustrate the foregoing supposition. It is curious, too, that salt should at all times have been an object of monopoly, and subject to the most preposterous taxes; and is even so still in some countries. As an instance of the extent to which this was carried previous to the fifteenth century, we may refer to the trade which the Venetians carried on in this article, the manufacture of which they brought to a high degree of perfection; indeed the *thorn-wall*, already alluded to, appears to have been first invented by them. Venice owed the commencement of her prosperity, it may be said her very existence, to the preparation of salt in the surrounding Lagunes, and which her situation at the mouths of the Po, the Brenta, and the Adige, enabled her to supply to Milan, Ferrara, and the whole of North Italy. In process of time the Venetians seized upon the salt-works of their neighbours. Thus the works of Cervia belonged to the city of Bologna; but by a treaty the whole of the salt made there was monopolized by the Venetians, who regulated the quantity to be produced, and even had officers for that purpose upon the spot. In the thirteenth and fourteenth centuries they either possessed or farmed all the salt-works on both sides of the Adriatic, at Trapana in Sicily, in the Ionian Islands, Greece, the Levant, and the coasts of Africa, and were the sole importers of the salt of the Black Sea, and of the Caspian, and even of that collected in the Asiatic steppes. They also succeeded in obtaining the privilege of carrying all the rock-salt raised in South Germany, Croatia, Styria, &c.; and once forced a King of Hungary to shut up his salt mines. The maritime and fluviatile populations of the Adriatic were deprived of the right to export their salt, and those of the north of Italy to use any other; in a word, five-sixths of all the trade in salt of the southern half of Europe was in the hands of the Venetians, whilst that of Northern Europe was monopolized by princes and feudal barons, who charged the most exorbitant price for it—an objection which did not certainly apply to the Venetians, who sold excellent salt at a very moderate price. The sale of foreign salt by any subject of the Republic was punished as a crime against the State; his house was razed, and himself condemned to perpetual banishment. But the Venetian salt monopoly did not end there, for the commerce was carried on by companies, each of which had the privilege of supplying a particular country or district, and none other. We believe it may be asserted with truth, that, for fourteen centuries, one half of the wealth which flowed into that remarkable city was derived from salt.

Previous to the year 1852 no salt had been found in Ireland; our consumption being supplied by refining English rock-salt, and partially by the importation of sea-salt from Portugal, called in commerce *bay-salt*. In that year, however, abundance of rock-salt was discovered near Belfast. As we have already remarked, the rocks with which salt is associated lie above the coal formation, and hence in England coal is found in some districts beneath the new red sandstone. This rock being considerably developed in the neighbourhood of Belfast, the Marquess of Downshire commenced a series of borings through it, for the purpose of ascertaining if coal occurred there. These operations were carried on at Duncrue, about eight miles from Belfast. After boring a depth of 230 yards, a dark-coloured bed of rock-salt, 46 feet in thickness, was discovered. The boring was carried through that bed, and, at some distance below, another bed, scarcely inferior in thickness to the first, was cut through, the latter being much purer than the upper bed, and would probably yield 96 per cent. of pure salt. We are not aware whether the boring is still continued, or whether any rock of an older date than the coal-measures has yet been reached.

Borings are also being carried on at Carrickfergus, and some thin beds have been cut through already, although the two shafts sunk have as yet only reached the respective depths of 112 and 108 feet. This gives hope that thick beds, like those of Duncrue, will be found at a greater depth. It was also announced, about a year ago, that a bed of salt, 16 feet thick, had been found, 70 feet below the surface, at Red Hall, the seat of David S. Ker, Esq., M. P., but we are without further particulars regarding it.

A fine block of the Duncrue upper bed, weighing about 30 cwts., was exhibited by the Marquess of Downshire, and certainly formed one of the most interesting specimens in the Exhibition. J. Hill, of Great Brunswick-street, in this city, exhibited specimens of both beds, and a series of specimens of excellent salt prepared from them. These samples were remarkable for their quality, and were well got up.

## SUBSTANCES USED FOR BUILDING AND ARCHITECTURAL ORNAMENTATION.

### MARBLE.

Lime, which is a compound of a metal called calcium with oxygen, one of the elements of the air, is a very abundant substance in Nature, entering more or less into the composition of a great number of rocks. When combined with carbonic acid, the gas of soda-water, it forms carbonate of lime, which is the most abundant compound of it: for under the name of limestone, chalk, travertino, &c., it constitutes immense deposits of rock in almost every part of the globe. It may appear strange to most persons that the beautiful marble of numerous groups and busts which adorned the Exhibition is the same material, chemically speaking, as chalk. The difference is one of *form*, and not of *nature*.

If we examine a piece of ordinary chalk, we shall find that it is composed of an impalpable powder, agglutinated together into a more or less hard mass. No traces of geometrical form can, in general, be distinguished in the minute particles of which it is composed; it is *amorphous*, or without form. Often, indeed, the microscope shows that this apparently impalpable powder consists in great part of the inorganic remains of infusorial animalculæ, of which thousands of millions would scarcely form one cubic inch of chalk. An examination of a piece of white marble, on the other hand, shows that it consists of an agglomeration of minute crystals, like a piece of lump sugar, cemented together. Taking white marble as one end of a series, and chalk as the other, it is possible to find rocks, constituted of carbonate of lime, to correspond to all intermediate degrees. As we approach the marble end of the series, the crystalline grains predominate over the cementing matter, which is amorphous; and as we approach the chalk end, the amorphous element predominates, and the crystals finally disappear. When a rock, composed of carbonate of lime, is distinctly crystalline, and sufficiently hard to retain a polish, it is called *marble*.

Rocks composed of carbonate of lime are of all geological ages; but when found associated with the lowest or oldest of all the groups of stratified rocks, they are distinguished by the name of *primitive limestone*. In general, these old rocks have been more or less altered by the action of heat, which has given to many a highly crystallized character, especially to the beds of limestone; and where the carbonate of lime was originally pure, the colour of such limestones is white. Sometimes they are gray or dove-coloured, as the much admired *bardiglio*, or dove-coloured Italian marbles.

Primitive limestone is largely developed in several mountain chains, as in the Alps and Appenines. When very hard, uniformly crystalline, and of a perfectly pure white colour, it constitutes statuary marble. Of this kind are the celebrated marbles of Carrara and of Paros. It was from quarries situated in the latter island, which is one of that numerous group of small paradises dotted over the Ægean Sea, that the marble of those master-pieces of Grecian art—the Venus de Medici, the Apollo of Belvidere, and the Antinous, was obtained. Paros was not the only one of the Grecian islands which was celebrated in ancient times for statuary marble. Scio, Lesbos, and Samos, were also in high repute for their marbles, and the latter still more so for a temple of Samian marble, dedicated to Juno. This temple, among other treasures of art, contained statues from the same marble of Jupiter, Minerva, and Hercules, by Myron, one of the greatest sculptors of Greece. Another locality famed for its marble was Pentilicus, from which the materials for building the Parthenon, at Athens, were obtained. All these quarries are no longer worked, at least not for the purposes of art, those of Paros being in the same condition in which they were left 2000 years ago; and they exhibit, in a remarkable manner, the skill with which they were worked.

The Romans obtained a good deal of their statuary marble in Italy, especially from the quarries situated near the small town of Carrara, in the duchy of Massa di Carrara, which forms part of the territory of the Duke of Modena. These quarries are worked at present on a great scale, and supply seven-eighths of the statuary marble of the world. In all probability the beautiful faultless marbles in some of Hogan's works in the Exhibition were from this locality. Carrara marble is of a perfectly pure white, and possesses a certain kind of transparency; while Parian marble, although equally, if not more transparent, has a beautiful, delicate, yellowish, flesh-like tint. It is necessary to remark, that the same quarries which yield the first quality Carrara marble here alluded to contain a far greater quantity of what is called second marble, and of the dove-coloured or bardiglio marbles above mentioned. The second quality Carrara statuary marble has a cold, bluish tint, and is not free from streaks. The statue of Davis is of this material, as were the Drummer of David d'Anger, and the Christ of Dieudonné. For many subjects it is, perhaps, preferable to the first quality. In consequence of the heavy duties levied upon the exportation of Carrara marble, quarries have been opened at Serravezza and other parts of Italy. A good deal of marble is also obtained from Sicily, which, although inferior to Carrara in whiteness and transparency, is more easily worked.

Marble has been found in other countries, such as Spain, the United States, &c. At Sheffield, in Massachussets, in the latter country, a variety of white marble is found remarkable for the size of the blocks which can be obtained, 50 feet in length having been frequently extracted. The beautiful colonnade of Corinthian columns which surrounds the Girard University, at Philadelphia, is built of this marble.

Statuary marble is also found in Ireland, in the county of Donegal, and in Connemara in Galway. To be suited for statuary purposes, marble should be uniform in tint, and free from seams and fissures. Blocks of this kind, free from cloudings, are rare even in Carrara, where they are satisfied if one block in ten is fit for the chisel of the sculptor. Good statuary marble is also very fine-grained. The Donegal marble possesses none of these qualities. All that we have seen of it as yet abounds more or less in small cracks, and is stained from the infiltration of water from the surface along the lines of these cracks, besides, the grain is coarse. Some specimens of the Connemara white marble are very pure, but we have not seen any very large blocks. Like that from Donegal, it is also a good deal cracked, and too coarse-grained for the finer specimens of art; but we have no doubt that, *if properly worked*, good blocks would be found well fitted for chimney-pieces and other architectural decorations. The specimens usually exhibited, being generally quarried from parts of the rock near the surface, are more calculated to show its defects than to encourage its employment.

In most countries there are found immense beds of limestone of various geological ages, some from below the coal, that is older than it, and others newer than it. To the former belong all our limestones in Ireland, while the Portland stone which forms the columns of the Bank, and which is also the material of Farrell's colossal figures of the Madonna and Child, is an example of the latter. The former are usually very hard, compact, and sometimes nearly as crystalline as primitive limestone; they break generally with a peculiar smooth surface; and, from the resemblance of the broken surface to some forms of shells, are said to have a *conchoidal* or shelly fracture. This peculiar hardness and evenness of texture render them capable of assuming a high polish, and many of them are consequently employed as marble. These rocks are usually coloured, sometimes uniformly as the black ones, but more usually unequally, so as to produce a variegated effect, which is often very beautiful. The colouring matter of the various shades of black and gray is *charcoal*, derived from the remains of animals, and probably also of vegetables. White is the natural colour of carbonate of lime, while the various shades of red, yellow, purple, &c., are principally produced by compounds of iron. It must not be inferred from what is here stated that it is only the old limestones which are sufficiently hard to serve as marbles. Many varieties of marble have also been obtained from beds of the same age as Portland stone; they are not, however, so general, and there is a much less variety of colour among such marbles than among those derived from beds of the age of our limestone rocks. They are usually of a grayish tint, and are occasionally sprinkled with rounded dots, which look like the roe or eggs of a fish, hence the name *oolitic* is sometimes applied to such marbles. Other shades also occasionally occur. Even the most recent deposits of carbonate of lime may have the characters of marble, the most essential of which is being crystalline, as is shown by the marble-like casts of medallions, &c., which are at present manufactured at the baths of San Fillippo in Tuscany. Here a number of warm springs issue, so loaded with carbonate of lime held in solution by carbonic acid, and with gypsum, that the water has been known to deposit a solid mass of rock 30 feet thick in twenty years; this water is conveyed by a pipe to the top of a chamber, whence it is allowed to fall as a kind of dense rain from a height of about 12 feet to 14 feet; a number of twigs being interposed to break its fall and scatter it about in spray, which, falling upon the moulds that are intended to be copied, and which are previously washed with a little solution of soap, coats them with a marble-like deposit.

In a country where such deposits are even now forming, one may expect to find a great variety of marbles of various ages; and accordingly, Italy has been celebrated for its coloured marbles from the remotest antiquity, and even still supplies Europe with a large part of the marbles employed in decoration. The Italians have a complete marble nomenclature, and many of these names are well known in other countries. Among the most celebrated are the ancient marbles so admired in antique vases, mosaics, &c., such as the *nero antico* or black antique, which is a beautiful intense black marble; the *rosso antico* or red antique, which is a deep blood-red marble, sprinkled with minute white dots; the *giallo antico* or yellow antique marble has a deep yellow colour with black rings, and sometimes rings of another shade of yellow; and the *verde antico* or green antique, which is of a clouded green colour, consisting of a mixture of a mineral called serpentine and limestone. The *oriental verde antico* was not marble, but a porphyry. The precise localities from which these marbles were obtained is not now known, the quarries being, in all probability, concealed by rubbish; but they appear to have been found in abundance in Greece and Asia Minor, as well as in Italy. Lately an announcement was made in some journals, that the quarries of the *verde antico*, and *nero antico*, had been discovered in Greece, but we are unable to say what amount of credence is to be given to the statement. Many modern marbles resemble them so completely that they may be considered identical; for example, the verde antico, or *verde antique*, as it is called by the French, is found at Genoa, and in Tuscany, and is one of the most prized marbles of Italy. There is a variety of it termed *polzivera di Genova* and *vert d'Egypte* by the French. At Bergamo is found a beautiful black marble called *paragone*, which is scarcely inferior to the *nero antico*.

Among the other celebrated Italian marbles we may mention the *panno di morte*, or death-shroud, which is a black marble with a few white shells scattered through it; the *brocatello di Siena*, or brocade of Sienna, which has a yellow ground, with irregular veinings of bluish red, or purple. The *portor* is a beautiful marble from the *Porto Venese*, hence the name, which was so much employed in the decoration of the palace of Versailles, under Louis XIV. The ground is of a beautiful black with veinings of yellow, which have a charming effect. The *mandolato* is a light red marble, with yellowish white spots like almonds, whence the name from the Italian *mandola*, an almond; it comes from Lugezzana. At Verona are found some beautiful marbles; one, a red inclining to yellow, and another with a paste composed of striæ of red and green, with large, pure, white, foliated spots. One of the most remarkable marbles is the *lumachelle*, or fire marble, which is a dark brown shell marble, having a curious effect upon light, emitting a number of *chatoyant* or fire-like reflections.

The marbles of the rest of Europe are very little known, although lately a number have been economically applied in Belgium, France, and Germany. It is said that Spain and Portugal abound with beautiful marbles; some from the latter country were exhibited at the London Exhibition of 1851. In England marble is found in several localities; but, with the exception of those of Derbyshire, they are not remarkable for quality of stone, or beauty of colouring. The principal marbles worked in Derbyshire are:—1. The black, large slabs of which, free from small veinings of calcareous spar, are rare, although in other respects it is handsome; 2. The encrinital marble, which is the most abundant; its colour is chiefly various shades of gray; as its name indicates, it is full of fossils of the stems of encrinites; 3. The *rosewood* marble, which has markings somewhat like those of rosewood, is rather pretty, and very hard, bearing a good polish; but the beautiful part of the rock is only six inches thick; 4. The *russet*, or *bird's eye*, is of various shades of gray, from light to brownish, having numerous minute fossils scattered through it,—whence the name. A very extensive trade has sprung up in Derbyshire in those marbles, many of the slabs being exported to St. Petersburg, and even to the Mediterranean, and a great amount of employment is afforded on the spot in the manufacture of ornaments, and of chimney-pieces, which are too often very bad copies of tasteless originals.

From the great development of limestone in Ireland we may naturally expect to find a great number of varieties of coloured marbles in this country. This rock occupies the great central plain of the island, the most striking feature in its physical geography; its total area being about 15,000 square miles, or fully one-half of the entire country. In this space there are known at least 150 localities, where the limestone is sufficiently hard and crystalline to bear a high polish, and sufficiently varied and effective in colour to be ornamental. Our space prevents us from giving a list of these localities, which, indeed, without some more accurate information than has yet been collected with reference to them, would possess but little value. We shall, however, indicate a few of the more important localities, classifying them according to the colour of the marble found in each.

*Black Marble.*—The chief localities of this marble are Kilkenny, particularly at Millmount; the neighbourhood of the town of Galway, about Oranmore; Listowel and Tralee, in the county of Kerry; Doneraile, Churchtown, and Mitchelstown (black and white), in the county of Cork; Lyons and Ballysimon, in the county of Limerick; Inch, two miles west of Ennis, in the county of Clare; Castlebiggs, in the county of Tipperary; Milford, in the county of Carlow; and Craigleath, in the county of Down. Of these the Galway marble is probably the purest and intensest black, many specimens of it being in this respect little, if at all, inferior to the much-prized *paragone* of Italy. The Kilkenny marble, when freshly cut and polished, is often of an intense black, but in course of time large white fossil-markings make their appearance, which much impair its beauty. The marbles of all the localities which we have just mentioned would, however, be well adapted for decorative purposes. In some quarries of black marble masses of rock are found composed in great part of the remains of corals, especially of the Madrepore, which, when cut across the bundles of tubes forming the coral, and the surface polished, yield exceedingly beautiful slabs of black marble, thickly studded, like Mosaic work, with oval spots, sometimes having a perfectly stellated appearance of pure white. Such masses are, however, rare, and no constant supply could be reckoned upon.

*Gray Marble.*—Marbles of this colour, as may be anticipated, are the commonest; there is scarcely a county in Ireland, in which limestone occurs, where good gray marbles may not be found. This is especially the case in the county of Cork, particularly in the neighbourhood of the city of Cork, and at both sides of its harbour; for example, at Ballinlough, close to the city, a very good gray is found; at Carrigaline and Monkstown, on the western side of the harbour, and at Cloyne and Middleton, on the eastern side; the varieties found at Cloyne and Carrigaline are dove-coloured, and similar to some of the marbles called *bardiglio* in Italy; a good gray is also found at Kilcreagh, about ten miles west of the city. The other localities, where well-marked varieties are found, are:—At Powerscourt, near Clonmel, in Tipperary; at Fenit and Listowel, in Kerry; at Clonmacnoise, in the King's County; in the county of Clare; at Clogrennan, and several other localities, in Carlow; near Galway; and in the part of that county bordering the Shannon, opposite Clonony; in the county of Longford; close to the town of Drogheda, where it is partially employed in the construction of the Boyne Viaduct. Many of these are highly fossiliferous, such as the *crinoidal* or *encrinital* marbles of Clonmacnoise, the fossils of which are chiefly encrinites, resembling thin discs; and the *Madrepore marble*, in which the fossils are the same as those already alluded to in speaking of the corresponding black fossil marble. These varieties constitute the *pietra stellaria* of the Italians. The cloudings in some varieties of gray marble pass insensibly into yellow, reddish-yellow, or red; as, for instance, in that found at Clonony, in King's County, the ground being gray, and the cloudings and mottlings various shades of yellowish-red, sometimes passing into yellow, and resembling many of the commoner Sienna marbles.

*Red Marble.*—The principal counties in which red marbles are found are Cork, Kerry, Limerick, and Armagh. The common mottled-red of Churchtown, in the county of Cork, is very good, but the mottles are sometimes too large, and the colour too high. There are, however, some varieties which are very beautiful—for example, we have seen a specimen composed of a blood-red paste, with foliated white masses, and slightly bluish purple veinings, and others in which the red shaded off insensibly into purple, the white portions assuming a weak yellow tint. The variety of tints which the Armagh marbles assume is also very remarkable: pure red is rare, the tints inclining rather to brown or to yellow, and sometimes passing into decided shades of these colours. Occasionally the red passes into purple, and even into bluish purple, producing a very fine variety. The Armagh marble very often contains fossils, but they are not always well marked, and the points of contact with the paste in which they are set are sometimes very soft, so that it does not polish uniformly. There are few marbles, however, in Ireland, which would find a larger market if the quarries were vigorously worked. A beautiful variegated marble is found near Killarney, which, although, properly speaking, a red one, may be mentioned here. The paste appears to be gray, and is mottled with yellow, brown, and pure white, the latter in part tinged with cloudings of red. Another fine marble occurs also in Kerry at Dunkerrin, in which the predominating colours are yellow and white, passing into bluish purple, and mottled with dark-brownish red, grayish-black, gray, purplish-gray, and pure white cloudings. The Limerick red marbles are chiefly found at Pallaskenry and Ballinamona. They consist usually of a slightly developed gray or dove-coloured paste, mottled with red, occasionally passing into yellow; they are often so fossiliferous as to form true encrinital marbles, some varieties of which are of great beauty.

*Green Marbles.*—The green marbles of Ireland, like the *verde antico* of Italy and Greece, are not carbonate of lime, but serpentine, or rather a mixture of the two; serpentine itself being a combination of silicia, one of the commonest forms of which we have in flint, and magnesia. Its usual colour is green, but it is sometimes found of a beautiful rich, dark-reddish brown, sometimes mottled with red, or with cloudings of red and green. When serpentine is of a rich oil-green colour, and translucent, it forms the noble serpentine. The green are probably the finest of all our marbles, and many specimens are not inferior to the verde antico; they are confined to the county of Galway, the two best known localities being Ballinahinch and Clifden. The colours vary from a light oil-green to dark olive-green, and nothing can exceed the beauty of the veinings, of which there is an extraordinary variety.

Irish marbles have been but very little worked; nor has there been any extended application of such as have been worked. With few exceptions, chimney-pieces are the only articles manufactured from them. It is surprising that the filthy wooden blocks and benches of our butchers have not long since been universally replaced by marble slabs; indeed, it would be desirable if the greater part of the fittings of all shops where provisions are sold were formed of marble. A vast number of applications of marble might be made in the furniture of houses, especially in kitchen tables, shelves for pantries, toilet tables, &c. Perhaps one of the causes which have prevented such an extension of their use, is the great expense of working the material. There can be no doubt that wood will always be cheaper than marble; but we believe that it would be possible to reduce the cost of the commoner kinds of marble slabs, &c., to one-third their present price, by the application of machinery. At a time when steam or water has nearly superseded animal power of all kinds, it does seem absurd to see a man slowly sawing a block of stone with an ill-contrived and clumsy instrument, such as would have been used 3000 years ago; and this too, notwithstanding the numerous contrivances which have been invented for effecting the operation. There are several machines for sawing, planing, moulding, carving, and rough polishing stone in use in Great Britain, America, and elsewhere. If these machines could be introduced into Ireland, and an improved system of quarrying adopted, we have no doubt that the working of marbles would become, in the course of a few years, an extensive, useful, and lucrative branch of trade; which it never can become by hand manipulation.

The first extensive collection of specimens of Irish marbles made, was that in the Hall and Galleries of the Museum of Irish Industry; the great utility of which led the Royal Dublin Society to make a similar collection for the Exhibition. This latter series, although without any varieties which were not already well known, was very good. Besides the collection of the Royal Dublin Society there were several other specimens contributed by marble manufacturers or private individuals.

There were in all thirty-eight slabs exhibited from twenty-four localities; of these the Royal Dublin Society procured directly, or subsequently purchased from parties who had sent them to the Exhibition, thirty-four. There were twelve bust pedestals from ten localities; of these the Royal Dublin Society either purchased, or had directly prepared, eight. There were seven chimney-pieces of Irish marbles, from seven localities, contributed by six exhibitors. There were, besides, seven tables and table tops, from six localities, and belonging to five exhibitors; one baptismal font, of Kilkenny black marble, and one door-case of mottled red marble, from Churchtown, in the county of Cork, belonging to the Royal Dublin Society. We have also to add three blocks of marble, in the rough, from two localities. There were several exhibitors of articles manufactured from foreign marbles, of some of which particular mention will be made subsequently. A small case, exhibited by Mr. J. Penny, of the Museum of Irish Industry, contained a very large and pretty collection of small squares of Irish marbles from about fifty localities; this series was well adapted for illustrating the variety of colours which we possess, and their adaptation to making inlaid work.

### INLAID WORK IN MARBLE AND PIETRA DURA.

In ancient buildings marble was extensively used, and as, even in Italy, the finer kinds are rare, and, consequently, expensive, it was usual to cut the fine blocks into thin plates or veneers, and coat the inferior kinds with them. The halls of the public buildings and palaces were also floored with different kinds of marble cut into dice, or lozenge-shaped pieces, and arranged in geometrical patterns, to which the name *tesseræ* was applied by the Romans. This kind of work constituted originally the *opus musivum*, or mosaic, of the ancients; but gradually, instead of merely incrusting the walls with marble of one colour, or making simple geometrical figures of two or more differently coloured marbles, figures of trees, birds, and other animals, were cut out of them, and inlaid in a slab of some other variety of marble. This kind of mosaic was brought to great perfection by the Italians during the fourteenth, fifteenth, and sixteenth centuries, especially at Florence. The Florentines, however, only used marble as the matrix; the substance inlaid being jasper, cornelian, different varieties of agates, chalcedony, amethyst, the halb-opal, noble serpentine, and other pseudo gems, and even Labrador felspar (which, as is well known, has a *chatoyant* lustre), lapis-lazuli, malachite (native carbonate of copper), &c. To produce work of this kind a well-polished slab of marble of the required form and size, and from an eighth to three-sixteenths of an inch thick, was prepared. Upon this the pattern was drawn and then cut out; the stones to be inlaid were then cut by the lapidaries' wheel, as in ordinary gem setting, to the size of the pattern, and cemented into their places fully polished; for, if finished when inlaid, great inequalities would be produced by the unequal wearing of the different stones, in consequence of having different degrees of hardness, especially where malachite and lapis-lazuli are employed. The slab thus made was veneered upon another and thicker slab of marble or wood, according to the object intended to be made. Instead of inlaying marble, ivory is sometimes inlaid in this way. The kind of work just described is known as *pietra dura*, or true *Florentine mosaic*, imitations of which are now commonly made in different parts of Europe; but, instead of pseudo gems, different coloured marbles, glass, malachite, &c., are employed. Besides a number of objects inlaid with regular patterns, a great many tables are inlaid with tesseræ, arranged in geometrical figures, or as chess-boards. Sometimes table tops are made of a number of pieces of determinate figure, but all more or less different, and sometimes of unequal size. These are known as *scrap tables*, and are about the most tasteless and absurd productions upon which money and time can be squandered. Another class of this latter species, of peculiarly "British" manufacture, consists of cementing a number of irregularly formed pieces of marble together, and then polishing the compound, which is veneered upon a slab of slate or marble. This species of work is not, properly speaking, mosaic, but rather a sort of artificial pudding stone or brecciated marble; it is difficult to say which is the most tasteless. There is a further kind of mosaic of a most remarkable character, made of glass, and known as Roman mosaic, to which we shall refer more at length when we come to speak of glass.

Although there were few specimens of mineral inlaid work in the Exhibition, still nearly every variety was illustrated. There were two admirable specimens of pietra dura, one in marble, and the other in ivory. The first consisted of a circular table of black marble, beautifully inlaid with a border of fruit, flowers, birds, &c., composed of chalcedony, agate, milk quartz, halb-opal, lapis-lazuli, malachite, &c. This beautiful specimen of Florentine mosaic was contributed by the Marquess of Drogheda. The other specimen consisted of an exquisite ivory cabinet said to have been presented to a Duke of Mantua by one of the Medici family, and now in the possession of Mr. Cooper of Markree Castle. It is one of the choicest examples of this kind of work which we have ever seen.* Mrs. White, of Killikee, exhibited a table of geometrical Mosaic composed chiefly of marbles with malachite and lapis-lazuli, and in which the harmony of colours was well observed. This table was a good example of the modern imitations of this class of work. Of the magnificent specimen of Roman mosaic, exhibited by the same lady, we shall speak in another place. Mr. Bernal, of Limerick, exhibited an inlaid chess table. There were two examples of the *scrap table*, and one of the artificial brecciated marble, in the Exhibition.

## BUILDING STONES.

There were very few building stones exhibited, notwithstanding the abundance which exists in Ireland. Besides the marbles, the greater number of which are used for building purposes, the specimens exhibited belonged to three classes of rocks—granites, sandstones, and slates. Granite is an igneous rock, composed of three minerals, quartz, felspar, and mica, and is of various colours, according to the nature of its constituents. Some varieties of felspar are white, others are pink, and some are even red; there are three different coloured micas—white, green, and black. The combination of these colours, then, gives rise to a great number of shades. There are certain rocks resembling granite, in which the whole or a great part of the mica is replaced by a dark green mineral called hornblende. This kind of rock is called syenite, and forms, in many cases, a very ornamental stone, especially when the felspar has a rose tint. A great many of the ancient monuments of Egypt are formed of a rock of this character.

Closely allied with granite and syenite is another rock termed porphyry, or rather several rocks, for the word has now a generic meaning. True porphyry consists almost entirely of felspar, but existing in two different forms, one forming a compact mass or paste, in which are disseminated crystals of the same mineral. These crystals are of various sizes, sometimes being exceedingly small, and occasionally as much as a half or three-quarters of inch long. The colour of the paste is rarely the same as that of the crystals, the latter being of a much paler tint than the former, and very often white; the usual colours of the paste are red, brownish-red, or green, but sometimes masses are found of a gray or even black colour. Porphyry is capable of receiving a very fine polish, and has been used for a great variety of purposes, such as pillars, door-cases, vases, &c. The red porphyry of Egypt has long been celebrated for its beauty and durability; the paste is of a brownish-red colour, and is sprinkled over with small spots of felspar crystals, of a nearly pure white.

All granites and porphyries are not equally durable; indeed some decay with an amazing rapidity. The cause of this decay is not yet well understood; but it appears to depend as much upon chemical constitution as upon mechanical aggregation. Some felspars contain potash, and others contain soda; experience and theory show that soda granites decompose more readily than those containing potash. The coarser the texture of granite the less durable it is; hence, when that stone is selected for the erection of public buildings, it should be fine, and uniform in texture. It should also be free from small crystals of iron pyrites disseminated through it, or any ore of iron, as these, on exposure to the weather, will rust, and thus destroy or deface the stone. The obscurity in which this question is involved can be judged by the fact that often, in the same quarry, a portion of the rock, appearing to differ in no respect from the rest, will totally decompose in a few years. There are four principal localities where granite is found in Ireland:—1. The range of mountains stretching from near Dublin through the county of Wicklow, and parts of the counties of Wexford and Carlow. 2. The Mourne Mountains, in the county of Down. 3. The mountains of Connemara. 4. A part of the county of Donegal. The granites of Newry and Wicklow do not differ much in external appearance; in both, the felspar is white and the mica black or white, or a mixture of both. When fine-grained, they make excellent building stone; but that obtained from some parts of Wicklow, and from near Dublin, are very decomposable, as may be seen by some of the public buildings in Dublin, the stone of which has crumbled away in some parts in the course of a half century. The granite of Connemara is very often coarse-grained, and in many cases of a reddish tint. Some good red granite is found in the Donegal granite range, especially at the celebrated gap of Barnesmore, and would form a highly ornamental building stone, and one, too, we believe, of great durability. The Wicklow granite, with white mica, was represented in the Exhibition by a bust-pedestal, from Kingstown, a model of Killiney Obelisk, and another, together with a

* This cabinet was purchased at Florence in 1838, and was stated to have been sold by a Duke of Mantua, who had received it from one of the Medici family. Frederick (II.) de Gonzaga was the first Duke of Mantua, by creation of the Emperor Charles in the year 1530. Subsequently, on the decease of one of his successors, Francis IV., without issue, the Duchy devolved upon Cardinal Ferdinand de Gonzaga, who resigned his Cardinal's hat, and married twice. His second wife was Catherine de Medici. Upon his death, without issue, in 1627, the Duchy was claimed by Charles de Gonzaga, Duke of Nevers. This claim was resisted by the Emperor Ferdinand II., and Mantua was taken by the Austrians in 1630 and pillaged. Duke Charles had, however, previously sold large portions of the Gonzaga collections. The cabinet is evidently of ancient manufacture, and it is conjectured that its epoch was the fourteenth or fifteenth century. The work bears a strong resemblance to that in the Certosa of Pavia, commenced at the end of the fourteenth century. It is not improbable that it was sent to Mantua in the times of Catherine de Medici, and it is probable that it was one of the articles sold by Duke Charles de Gonzaga. This cabinet was certainly one of the gems of the Exhibition.

baptismal font, from Blessington. The Donegal red granite was represented by a bust-pedestal. None of the other granites were represented. One specimen of a very fine green porphyry, from Lambay Island, was exhibited by Lord Talbot de Malahide. A few specimens of a peculiar brecciated porphyry, worked into tazzas, &c., were among the pretty collection of serpentine works from Penzance.

*Sandstones* consist of small grains, chiefly silica, aggregated into a compact rock, the grains being cemented together by various substances. Sometimes it is carbonate of lime, sometimes silica or iron, and sometimes clay. The nature of the cementing mass has considerable influence upon the character of the rock; iron is, however, the most usual, and the one which forms the most typical sandstone. There is a great variety of colour, from white, through gray, yellow, red, and brown, to black. Sandstones are of all geological ages, from the lowest sedimentary rocks to the most recent. The older rocks are usually the most compact, and in general contain some felspar grains, and frequently a large quantity of clay, which gives them more or less of an argillaceous character. When sandstones are very hard, and their fracture harsh, and contain small siliceous pebbles, they are usually called *grit*. If the rock consist not of grains of sand, but of a number of pebbles cemented together, it is designated a *conglomerate*; which is further subdivided into *pudding-stones*, when the pebbles are rounded, and *breccia* when they are angular. And as these pebbles may consist of any kind of rock, there exists a considerable variety of these compound rocks, which are distinguished by the nature of the pebbles of which they consist. Sandstones are generally excellent materials for buildings; but for this purpose they should be firm, and uniform in texture, and free from iron pyrites or iron sand, which would, by their rusting, not only spoil their appearance, but render them liable to peel off on exposure. Many sandstones, especially those from the thick beds of what is called the new red sandstone, or from the variety of colours from white to dark brown which it exhibits, the variegated sandstone (and which as we have already remarked, lies above the coal measures) are exceedingly soft when first quarried, but gradually become hard when exposed to the atmosphere. Others again, especially those rich in clay, although compact and hard when freshly quarried, crumble away rapidly on exposure. The durability of this class of stones depends, however, very much upon the nature of the climate; and that of Ireland severely tests building stone. Any sandstone which will bear exposure for some weeks, after being saturated with a solution of glauber salt, may be considered fit for use.

Sandstones are found abundantly in Ireland; those, however, associated with the older rocks, although compact and firm, are in general very shaly, and the beds are so full of cracks and joints that large masses cannot be readily had. There are many exceptions, however, one of which deserves special mention, namely, the beautiful white quartzose sandstone found near the village of Rosenalis, in Queen's County, and we believe, in many parts of the principal chain of hills, as well as in the sub-chains, bordering the eastern side of the Shannon in that and the neighbouring counties, and, perhaps, also in Clare. This sandstone works beautifully, and is exceedingly durable; masses of it exposed for centuries appearing to have undergone no change. A great number of the ancient monumental crosses, quoin-stones, and mullions of the ecclesiastical buildings in the central part, and even in the east and west of Ireland, appear to have been made from this rock, or from very similar ones. The early date at which it was worked may be judged from the fact, that one of the singular dish-shaped stones found in the Rath of Newgrange, on the Boyne, is made from this stone. Two door-pillars, with capitals and bases, of this stone were exhibited by Mr. R. Cassidy, of Monasterevan, and although many years exposed to the weather, appeared unaltered. The Marquess of Ely exhibited two blocks of sandstone, or, as this kind of rock is sometimes called, *freestone*, from near Enniskillen, which had much the same character as the Rosenalis stone. This stone is admirably adapted for building, and is even capable of an ornamental application. We have no hesitation in saying that both this and the Rosenalis stone would form an excellent substitute for the much more expensive Caen-stone so much employed in ecclesiastical edifices, as the fine polish of the surface of one of the blocks showed. None of the new red sandstone from Belfast or Dungannon was exhibited. Some of the grits and sandstones in the collection of the Monkland Iron Company are admirably adapted for building purposes. Many sandstones, especially of the coal-measures, contain such a large amount of clay that they appear as if rudely laminated, and may be split into flags. Of this kind are the Carlow calcareous flags, which are so much used in Dublin; and those of the county of Clare, a specimen of which was exhibited.

*Slate* is the generic term applied to all fine-grained argillaceous or clayey rocks breaking into thin laminæ. When the laminated character is but imperfectly developed, the term *shale* is used; when it is so perfect that the rock readily splits into thin even plates, it is called *roofing-slate*. The colour of slate rocks is as various as the degree of lamination; the chief colours are, however, gray, greenish-gray, green, purplish, and dark blue. Roofing slate is almost always of the latter colour. Slate rocks insensibly pass into grits according as the argillaceous constituent diminishes, and that of sand increases; the property of laminability diminishing in the same degree; the finer and more argillaceous the slate, therefore, the better adapted it is for yielding roofing-slate. When slate rocks are in contact with large masses of igneous rocks, especially with granite, they undergo a remarkable change, being, as it were, baked into what is called mica slate, which sometimes passes almost completely into mica, one of the constituents of granite. Where the rock thus altered had been originally a fine-grained slate, and the baking not proceeded very far, it may still be used for roofing-slate, being more durable than the unaltered rock, although the slates are not so even.

Good roofing-slate should be of an uniform fine grain, should split easily into even plates, which may be easily pierced with holes by a sudden blow of a sharp-pointed instrument without being fractured; its colour should not be very dark, as that indicates a large quantity of carbonaceous matter, the presence of which assists in the decomposition of the slate; it should also be free from pyrites; and finally, it should not absorb much water either by its surface or edges, a point which is readily ascertained by weighing a piece of the dry slate, plunging it in water, and then weighing it again after the surface had partially dried.

Although the less perfectly laminated slate-rocks are sometimes used as a building material, they are not well adapted for that purpose. The finer kinds of roofing-slate, when large-sized slabs can be obtained, are adapted for many useful purposes, besides the roofing of buildings; such as the construction of cisterns, acid condensers, ridge-tiles, and water-tables of Gothic buildings, rustic-tables, billiard-tables, benches for laboratories, baths, &c.

The slates which come into commerce for roofing purposes are of nine different sizes, and there is a very curious nomenclature employed to denote them. Thus, the smallest, which are 16 inches by 8, are called *ladies*, then come the *countesses*, of which there are three sizes; then *duchesses*, of which there are two sizes, the largest being 24 inches by 12 inches. These six sizes are sold by the thousand, consisting of 1200 slates; a thousand of the ladies weighing about 25 cwts.; and the duchesses, of the size just mentioned, about 3 tons. The sizes above the latter are respectively *queens*, *rags*, and *imperials*, and are sold by weight.

Roofing-slate occurs abundantly in Ireland; especially in Wicklow, the south of the county of Cork, Kerry, at Killaloe, in the county of Clare, and in Donegal; but the only localities where it is worked extensively are Glanmore, in the county of Wicklow, Killaloe, and Valentia, in Kerry; all of which were represented in the Exhibition. The slates of Killaloe and of Valentia are remarkable for their durability, and we believe also those of Glanmore. Large slabs are obtained at all three places; and are made into tables and other objects, examples of most of which were in the Exhibition, but, with the exception of Valentia, not to any extent. The slabs which can be obtained at the latter quarries are of remarkable size, as was well illustrated by the specimens placed in front of the Exhibition Building. The cisterns from these quarries exhibited were well deserving of attention, and remarkably cheap, the price for one of about 1200 gallons being not more than from £8 to £10. A number of articles, such as baths, &c., made from the celebrated Penrhyn Slate Quarries (Bangor), were also exhibited. These quarries are of immense extent, and of great importance, and employ about 2000 workmen.

#### GYPSUM, ALABASTER, PLASTER OF PARIS, SCAGLIOLA, AND PLASTIC IVORY OR PROTEAN STONE.

*Gypsum.*—When lime combines with sulphuric acid, it forms sulphate of lime. This substance, in combination with water, constitutes the kind of rock known as gypsum, and is the material from which plaster of Paris is made. It rarely occurs associated with the older rocks, but abundantly in those above the new red sandstone, but more especially among what are called tertiary rocks, such as those upon which Paris and London are situated, and which are among the newest with which we are acquainted. Gypsum occurs in several forms in Nature; when crystallized it is transparent, and from its lamellar structure may be split into thin plates, which were formerly used as a substitute for window glass, especially in Germany, where it was known under the names of *Marienglass* and *Franeneis* (Mary's glass and woman's ice). This form of gypsum is now chiefly used in the manufacture of sealing wax, in paper-staining, and in making an exceedingly fine kind of plaster of Paris for the preparation of the so-called *plastic ivory*. When gypsum consists of an aggregation of minute crystalline grains, constituting a semi-transparent or rather translucent mass, it is *alabaster;* when, on the other hand, it consists of a dense mass, without any apparent crystalline structure, and perfectly opaque, it is the ordinary dense gypsum used for making plaster, and as one of the modern elements of *cheapness* (?) in the manufacture of mustard, pepper, and many other substances; and also as a manure.

Gypsum consists of 79·07 of sulphate of lime, and 20·93 of water; when heated to a temperature of about 272° Fahrenheit, or about that of a baker's oven, it loses almost the whole of its water, but is capable of again combining with it on being moistened. If the gypsum be powdered after being baked, and then moistened, it will solidify; upon this property is founded its use as plaster of Paris. To prepare this substance the gypsum is placed in a sort of oven, where it is heated until it loses nearly the whole of its water, after which it is ground in a mill usually similar to that employed for making wheaten flour, but sometimes by stamps, cylinders, or edge stones, when it is ready for use. The chief point in the preparation of plaster of Paris is the burning, or rather baking. If only half the water be driven off it will not set; if it be heated above the temperature just mentioned, it will become what the workmen term "dead-burned," and will no longer combine with water, while if three-fourths only be driven off, its maximum point of setting appears to be reached. The common kilns used for baking it, like the ordinary baker's oven, are heated directly by the flame of the fire, and even in some cases the fire is actually made in the kiln itself; which, when the latter is sufficiently heated, is raked out, and the gypsum introduced, the baking being thus effected by the heat retained by the oven. The result of this system is that the gases of the flame sometimes come in contact with small portions of the gypsum at a high heat, and convert it into a substance called sulphuret of calcium: which, being placed in contact with water, evolves the stinking gas, sulphureted hydrogen, and in other respects injures the quality of the plaster. All these difficulties may be obviated by using hot air, the temperature of which could be regulated, and which, where large quantities of the gypsum would be operated upon, would be more economical than the present system.

It would be out of place, even if our space admitted of it, to describe here the mode of making plaster casts; but we shall say a few words upon the application of plaster of Paris as stucco. In this kind of work a ground is first laid on of inferior plaster of Paris, simply mixed with water; upon this is then laid a coating of a finer kind, mixed with size or glue. The addition of the size enables the surface to be rubbed smooth with pumice-stone; after which it is washed over with a milk made with fine plaster, and a much stronger solution of glue; when dry the surface may be polished with tripoli or rotten-stone, any desired colour being given by mixing the proper pigment with this milk. Where it is desirable to produce a hard surface capable of receiving a marble-like polish, it is impregnated with linseed oil, and polished with linen rubbers. From some cause or other the ceilings, walls, &c., coated with plaster of Paris in Dublin, and elsewhere in Ireland, invariably crack after some time, a result which is almost unknown in Paris, where the art of stuccoing is carried to great perfection. Perhaps one of the causes of this defect is to be traced to the bad quality of the gypsum, and the imperfect mode of baking it, on the one hand, and to the addition of large doses of lime, on the other. The modern style of building mere shells also adds to it, by the great extent of settling which such slight masses of brickwork are subject to, and the considerable deflection which takes place in the floors when the weight of a few persons comes upon them.

Plaster of Paris may be hardened so as to bear a more perfect polish than ordinary stucco-work, and not be very readily scratched. This is effected by the addition of certain saline substances, such as alum, borax, silicate of potash, or soluble glass. If an object in plaster, such as a bust, be soaked for a month in a solution of alum in twelve to thirteen parts of water, and then wiped and allowed to dry fully in the air, it will become so hard that it can no longer be scratched with the nail, and will lose much of the brittleness of ordinary plaster casts. Casts treated in this way become stained, and are always liable to attract moisture from the atmosphere. If baked gypsum be moistened with a solution of alum, or raw-powdered gypsum be well mixed up with a similar solution, and exposed to a red heat, a mass will be obtained of a dull milk-white, or more usually a slight cream colour, which may be readily pulverized, and will set quite as well as ordinary gypsum, especially if a weak solution of alum be employed in making the paste. Casts prepared of the compound thus formed, although taking a longer time to dry, are unusually hard. They may be exposed to the weather for some time, and may be washed with a sponge without injury, and even immersed in boiling water, without diminishing their hardness. Those prepared by steeping in a solution of alum, on the contrary, will become quite soft; so much so indeed as to receive the impression of the fingers if soaked for a few hours in cold water. The substance known as Keene's cement, and now largely employed, is nothing more than plaster prepared in this way. If carbonate of potash or pearl-ash be mixed with the alum, so as to form a basic alum, we have Martin's cement; and if for the alum we substitute borax, we have Parian cement.

*Scagliola* is another material of the same kind, now much employed in decoration. It is simply a stucco made in imitation of coloured marbles, pieces of real marble, and other stones, such as granite, felspathic, and micaceous sand, &c., being often added; a compound of alum and gypsum being mixed with the glue instead of common plaster of Paris. The successful imitation of coloured or brecciated marble in scagliola may be considered as a kind of fresco-painting, and depends entirely upon the skill and taste of the workman. Every shade of colour intended to be imitated must be produced separately by mixing the pigment with a portion of the aluminized gypsum, and working them into a paste with size dissolved in a solution of alum. These paints, as it were, are then laid on upon the object to be coated, according to the kind of marble or other stone to be imitated, the fine veinings being produced by working a number of the coloured mixtures together in a sufficiently pasty condition to admit of their complete union without producing a fusion of the colours. When the surface has dried and become hard, it is rubbed even with pumice-stone, washed with a sponge, and then roughly polished with rotten-stone and charcoal, the final polish being given with tripoli or rotten-stone and oil, and finally with oil alone. By this means a very fine polish, nearly equal to marble, may be given to it; and, when executed with skill and taste, it is scarcely inferior in beauty to many variegated kinds of that material. The usual specimens are, however, sadly deficient in taste, the manufacturer's object apparently being to produce combination, sinning against all the laws of colour, and resembling nothing ever found as a rock.

Common plaster of Paris casts resemble, in many respects, the dense gypsum, from which a good deal of the plaster of commerce is made; and as this differs from alabaster only in its molecular structure, many persons have imagined that it might be possible to convert plaster into a material resembling that beautiful substance. The nearest approach which has yet been made to the solution of this important problem is Cheverton's invention of the so-called *proteus stone* or *plastic ivory*. This substance, which is well adapted for carvings in imitation of ivory, and the manufacture of various ornaments, is made by exposing the plaster cast, or block of the same substance, to a temperature varying from 250° to 350° Fahrenheit during twenty-four hours, by which the whole of the water combined with the sulphate of lime is driven off, and the material reduced to the condition of plaster of Paris. After undergoing this operation it still retains its form, but is exceedingly friable. Sometimes dry pulverulent plaster is pressed into the moulds, instead of casting it in the moist state; but in this case, also, it is subjected to the drying process, although the plaster had been previously baked. If it is intended that the object should have a certain translucency like alabaster, it is then soaked in some transparent hard varnish, purified olive oil, or melted stearine. If, on the other hand, it is intended that it should be quite opaque, this operation is omitted. The objects are hardened by immersing them for a moment in water at a temperature of from 64° to 67° Fahrenheit. This operation is repeated every ten or fifteen minutes, until the sulphate of lime is completely saturated; by which means the mass becomes crystalline, and harder than alabaster. The important part of the process is the stage-wise combination of the water with the sulphate of lime, and unless great care is bestowed upon it the mass crumbles to powder. By mixing various pigments with the water, any desired colour may be given to the plaster.

If sand be fused with about three or four times its weight of pearl-ash, a silicate of potash or glass is formed, which is quite soluble, and has been occasionally employed to impregnate wood, which it renders incombustible. If plaster casts be worked with this substance, the sulphate of lime and silicate of potash mutually decompose each other, and form a new compound, which is exceedingly hard, bears a good polish, and may be washed with soap and water.

Gypsum is found in immense quantities in the neighbourhood of Paris, hence the term *plaster of Paris*. In England it exists in greatest abundance in Derbyshire, Nottinghamshire, and Cumberland. That brought from France is considered the best, probably because it is so very hard and crystalline, for the harder the natural gypsum, the better is the plaster; the superiority of the Paris gypsum may also be owing to the presence of a small quantity of clay which exists in it. The form of gypsum known as alabaster occurs abundantly in Italy, especially in Tuscany, where it is largely employed in the manufacture of ornaments. Gypsum occurs in several parts of Ireland, but the most important, and indeed hitherto the only, localities where it has been discovered in workable quantities are at Carrickmacross, in the county of Monaghan, and near Lough Allen, in the country of Leitrim. That found at the former is of excellent quality, and would, no doubt, be admirably adapted for making plaster, and might be largely introduced into Dublin for that purpose, as the freight, with the present facilities of transport, would, we believe, be less than that paid for the English gypsum now exclusively used here. The Leitrim gypsum is of very peculiar quality, consisting of a dense white mass, filled with blackish crystals, about a quarter of an inch wide, and from a quarter to half an inch long, of a form of sulphate of lime known as celestine. Considerable quantities of gypsum may yet be discovered in the neighbourhood of Belfast. A large block of the Carrickmacross gypsum, from the Shirley estate, in the barony of Farney, and a sample of the plaster made from it, were sent to the Exhibition towards its close; a small piece of the peculiar gypsum of the county of Leitrim was also exhibited. Mr. Davis, of this city, exhibited samples of raw English gypsum, and several cast slabs of plaster, of various qualities, which appear to have been well baked. We believe the only exhibitors of scagliola were the Messrs. M'Anaspie, of Great Brunswick-street, and the specimens shown by them were too small to judge of the artistic execution of their work, which, it is needless to observe, is the chief point in scagliola. The material appeared to be good, and to be capable of a high polish. The only specimens of plastic ivory which we recollect having seen in the Exhibition were a few small statuettes, of great taste, and boxes ornamented with alto-relievos, in the German Department; the statuettes were not cast, but were original designs, carved out of a block of the prepared substance, which appeared to be a beautiful material for the purpose, but softer than what is used in England. The substance used to give them translucency was stearic acid. There were no specimens of alabaster in its natural state, but there were several vases and flower-baskets of Tuscan alabaster; one of the former was exhibited by a gentleman of Dublin, the others were placed in the German Department, although the work of and exhibited by an Italian,—somewhat on the same principle, we suppose, that no distinction was made between the productions of Ireland and those of Great Britain.

### ROMAN AND PORTLAND CEMENTS, ASPHALTE FLAGGING, ETC.

Cement, in its widest sense, means any liquid or plastic substance capable of solidifying, by which bodies may be firmly bound together. In this sense many of the materials which we have described are cements; but it is, perhaps, better to restrict the term to those of mineral origin, in which the lime is employed in the condition of carbonate of lime, or caustic lime; and to include those described in the last section, in which the lime is employed as sulphate or gypsum, under the term *plasters*. If we burn a piece of limestone or chalk, we deprive it of its carbonic acid, and reduce it to the condition of caustic lime; which, on being moistened with water, will combine and solidify a portion of it, and become slaked or hydrated lime. If this compound be exposed to the atmosphere it will gradually absorb the carbonic acid, which is always present in minute quantities in the atmosphere, and become the same substance, chemically speaking, that it was previous to having undergone the operation of burning. Its form will, however, be completely altered; instead of being a hard compact mass it will be quite pulverulent. If, however, it be mixed with a large quantity of sand, and placed as mortar between stones, it will, in course of time, become quite hard and bind them together. The cause of this cementation is not well understood; but, so far as we can judge, it is attributable to:—1. The action of the lime upon the sand, by which part of it is converted into silicate of lime, which is insoluble; 2. The crystallization of part of the caustic lime;* and 3. The peculiar force which causes certain substances to abstract from a solution a portion of the solid matter which it may hold dissolved without combining with it, and which even acts to some extent between one solid and another made into a paste with water. This is the same force which causes dye-stuffs, &c., to adhere to tissues. That these forces may produce their full effect, the mortar must gradually dry, and hence, in the presence of water, scarcely any binding action could take place. There are some limestones, however, which, when properly burned, will actually become hard even under water,—and on this account they are called *hydraulic limes*, from their capability of being employed in hydraulic structures. It is quite evident that the cause of the settling of such limes is to a great extent different from that of common mortar. In this case the cause is apparently altogether chemical, for we find, on analyzing these limestones, that they do not consist of pure carbonate of lime, but contain a variable proportion of a material consisting chiefly of silicates of alumina, with some potash and soda. When such limestones are burnt, the carbonate of lime which they contain is converted into caustic lime; this reacts upon the silica compounds and forms a combination which solidifies in water. The more, therefore, of this clay-like substance which exists in a limestone, up to a certain point, the more rapidly and perfectly will the resulting lime solidify under water. This kind of impure limestone is found in most countries, and must exist abundantly in Ireland if properly sought for. A very good variety, which has stood the test of experience, is found on the shores of Lough Ree, a few miles above Athlone, and was employed in the construction of the locks and other works on the Shannon. One of the best in Great Britain is that which occurs at Aberthaw in the Island of Anglesea. This limestone belongs to what is called the lias formation; and, as the limestones of this group are thinner than those of the older limestones from which we get our marbles, they are usually more impure, and hence there can be no doubt that the patches of it which occur in the north of Ireland, in the counties of Londonderry and Antrim, must contain beds capable of yielding hydraulic lime.

As the earthy components of natural hydraulic limestones are not chemically combined with the lime before burning, we may naturally expect that if we add clay or other silicates to pure powdered limestones, and then burn them, we shall obtain an artificial hydraulic lime. This is not only true, but further there are certain natural substances which, without previous burning, are capable of forming similar compounds. This fact was well known to the Romans, who employed for that purpose a soft porous rock, consisting of a kind of volcanic ashes, containing pumice-stone, and somewhat similar in composition to it. This substance occurs in great abundance on the shores of the beautiful and classic bay of Baia, near Naples, and on that of Naples itself, being, in both cases, the result of volcanic action. This rock was reduced to powder, and brought to Rome in considerable quantity under the name of *Pulvis Puteolanus*, where it was used and mixed with an equal quantity of lime, in the construction of aqueducts and public buildings. The ancient Puteoli having since Italianized its name into Puzzuoli, the *Pulvis Puteolanus* is now known as *Puzzolana*. A similar

* Fresh mortar consists of burned lime and lime-water, or lime held in solution. According as the water evaporates from the mortar, the lime held in solution precipitates in the form of minute crystals, which tend to bind the lime, gradually converted into carbonate, together; which in time becomes an indurated mass.

substance is found in the volcanic district of the Rhine, near Bonn, and in many parts of France, &c. Beyond using the natural puzzolana wherever it could be found, no attempt was made to substitute other substances until towards the end of the last century. One of the earliest, and now best known, because very successful attempts, was that of Parker and Wyatt, for which a patent was granted in London, in the year 1796, under the name of "Roman cement," and now sometimes called *Parker's cement*. This cement is made from earthy calcareous nodules, abounding in the London clay and other beds belonging to the tertiary formation, found at Sheppy, the Isle of Wight, on the coasts of Kent, in Essex, and in Yorkshire. These nodules are frequently washed out of the clay beds by the action of the tidal curents along the coasts, and are then dredged up, especially at Sheppy. The chief source, at present, is Harwich, on the Essex coast, the quantity manufactured from the material obtained there being, at least, 2,000,000 bushels, annually. Similar nodules, or as they are called, septaria, from the Latin word *septum*, an enclosure, in consequence of being found enclosed in the clay, are found in Hampshire, from which a lighter-coloured cement, known as *medina cement*, is made. Some of the clayey limestone beds of the lias formation are also used for cement, generally with the addition of some clayey substance. Of this kind is the article known as Atkinson's or Mulgrave cement. The most perfectly artificial of all the cements made is, however, that known as *Portland cement*, which is composed of a mixture, in certain proportions, of ordinary limestone, and the clay or fine alluvial deposits of certain rivers, especially of those which have flowed over extensive beds of clay, and soft limestone, or chalk; this mixture, after being dried, is burnt. The name Portland is not derived from the materials, but simply from the colour of the cement being like that well-known building stone. This cement is very strong; indeed, from some experiments made in London, in 1851, it would appear that Portland cement is nearly four times as strong as the best natural cements; an important property which renders it well adapted for making concrete. When ten to twelve parts of gravel, or fragments of rock, are mixed with one part of Portland cement, an extremely powerful substance of this kind is formed, which is often capable of bearing greater weight than similar solid masses of the rocks to which the pebbles forming the concrete belong. Certain qualities of iron slags or "cinder," when reduced to powder, are well adapted for making good cements, on being baked with clay and lime. A few years since a Mr. Ransome patented a kind of artificial stone, with which he proposed to produce architectural ornaments. His process consists in dissolving flints in a solution of caustic soda, under a pressure of from 50 to 80 lbs. on the square inch, by which he obtains a silicate of soda. This compound is then mixed with pipe-clay and ground flints, and worked into a paste, which is moulded into the desired forms. Inferior clays, such as clay marls and fine sand, may be used instead of the pipe-clay and flints for coarse articles; in either case the moulded article is baked so as to form a hard semi-vitrefied mass, which is said to be durable.

There were only two exhibitors of cement in the Exhibition: namely, Mr. Davis, of this city, who exhibited a series of slabs formed of Roman and Portland cements, of different qualities (the septaria, from the London clay, and the prepared cement); and the Messrs. M'Anaspie, also of Dublin, who exhibited Portland cements and castings made with it. None of these cements appear to have been prepared with Irish materials, although no place can now be said to be deficient in the means of making cements, and in Ireland they exist in great abundance, though not exactly of the same kind as those used in England. Indeed, we believe that no artificial cement is now made in Ireland.

There only remains to notice one more cement,—and that which was, perhaps, first invented,—namely, *asphalt*. This peculiar substance occurs under various conditions in several parts of the world. In the island of Trinidad it is found forming a sort of lake, almost in a state of purity; it also occurs on the shores of the Dead Sea, and at Avlona in Albania, in a more or less pure form. In general, however, it is found impregnating beds of limestone, as in Dalmatia, Carinthia, the Tyrol, the States of the Church, and in various parts of France, England, Scotland, and in America, &c. The bituminous or asphalte stone thus formed rarely contains more than from 10 to 20 per cent. of bitumen; for example, the celebrated Seyssel asphalte stone which occurs at Seyssel, in the department of Ain in Burgundy, contains only 8 per cent. of bitumen, and 92 of carbonate of lime; and that of the Val de Travers, in Switzerland, 12 per cent. If this asphalte rock be subjected to distillation, a thick oil, containing about 50 per cent. of the unaltered asphalte, passes over; and on subjecting the oil to re-distillation, a quantity of a volatile oil is separated, which is known under the name of petroleum or rock oil, leaving the asphalte behind. The separation of the petroleum is also carried on by Nature, for wherever we find deposits of asphalte we are also generally sure to find more or less oil in the springs. Asphalte may be considered as the natural tar resulting from the distillation of coal, or from vegetable matter generally; and where, as at Aussig, in Bohemia, a mass of melted basalt is found to have come in contact with a bed of brown coal or lignite, the latter is converted into charcoal, and in the immediate neighbourhood occurs the tar or asphalte, the volatile oils of which are constantly passing off as petroleum in the springs. The natural petroleum has not the disagreeable smell of coal-tar naphtha, and that collected from springs is often aromatic. At Rangoon, in Burmah, there are, it is said, 500 such springs, which yield 412,000 hogsheads of oil per annum, which is used for burning in lamps. Near Amiano, in the Duchy of Parma, there is a very abundant spring, which is used for lighting the city of Genoa. Considerable quantities of impure petroleum are also obtained in the States of Ohio, Kentucky, and New York, and is known in commerce under the name of Genesee or Seneca oil, from its having been formerly collected by the Seneca Indians. Petroleum, or rock oil and asphalte, were both well known to the ancients, the former having been much used by the Egyptians in the process of embalming bodies; it was also used in lamps, as at Agrigentum, in Sicily, hence the name of Sicilian oil given to it by the Romans. The use of asphalte as a cement or mortar is of very old date, as its name which is Greek, and which is derived from a root which signifies to make firm or stable, sufficiently indicates. In Nineveh, Babylon, and other ancient cities, it seems to have been almost exclusively used for cementing bricks; and in Egypt, water-conduits, cisterns, and cellars were coated with it. With the fall of ancient civilization asphalte fell into disuse, and, as far as we are aware, was scarcely if at all employed until the discovery and working of the asphalte stone of the Val de Travers, by D'Erynys, about the year 1712.

The process of making a pavement with it is very simple. The bituminous stone is reduced to powder, and mixed with from 3 to 7 or 8 per cent. of pure asphalte in a melted state, by which a mastic is formed, which serves admirably to cement gravel or sand into a compact mass, well suited to form floors of kitchens, footways, sewers, and water conduits. The fine footways of the Boulevards and of the Champs Elysée, in Paris, are made with asphalte, as are also many of the promenades of Vienna. Several portions of footway were also laid down in London, but its use has not extended as much as it deserves. It is very durable, exceedingly smooth, and quite impervious to water, and would be admirably adapted to form the floors of kitchens, especially in cities, where, as in Dublin, the absurd practice exists of making subterraneous kitchens.

A kind of asphalt may also be obtained by distilling coal tar, which resolves itself into liquid oils known under the name of coal-naphtha, and used for various purposes, and a solid black pitchy substance which remains behind. If this substance be mixed with some powdered limestone, it will form a kind of artificial asphalte; or a concrete may be made with gravel by means of it. These artificial compounds are almost as durable, when well made, as the natural asphalte, and might be very largely employed for flooring and coating the walls of cellars. Where not subject to a wearing action it is very imperishable, and is at the same time completely impervious to water. The introduction of this substance, as a flooring material for kitchens and other parts of the basements of houses, would be very beneficial in a hygienic point of view. Damp earthen floors are, as every one knows, exceedingly injurious to health, and must tend to retard in a great degree the proper development of children. One of their most common effects is to produce diarrhœa, especially when combined with the want of sufficient wholesome food. Now a floor of artificial asphalte is nearly as warm as one of boards; asphalte being a great non-conductor of heat, and being absolutely impervious to water, effectually prevents the absorption of water containing vegetable or animal matter, which in earthen floors is continually giving off unwholesome exhalations. What better material, therefore, could be found for forming the floors of cottages for the working classes?

We regret that no examples showing such an application were exhibited, and we still more regret that the whole class of articles suited for the general consumption of the poorer classes have been, as it were by general consent, forgotten; and yet we have all kinds of tents and furniture for Australia. Why the wants of millions should be neglected, and those of a few thousands carefully attended to, appears to us inexplicable, and certainly does not speak well for the solicitude of the public for the progress of social improvement. Indeed, it would appear that a visitation of cholera, or some other epidemic, is required to remind people of their duties in this respect.

There is another application of coal-tar pitch, and of the heavy oil obtained in the distillation of the tar, which is of great importance, and which, although coming partially under another section, we shall mention here; namely, the manufacture of roofing felt. This consists of refuse tow and scutching waste, and waste cow-hair from tan-yards impregnated with coal-tar, or with the semi-solid mass left after the distillation of the light naphtha, the whole being pressed into a sort of cloth. Specimens of this roofing felt were exhibited by Messrs. Ritchie and Sons. It is very light, 100 square feet of it weighing not more than 42 or 43 lbs. When stretched on a roof and nailed on with copper nails (or iron nails dipped in melted tar, and coated over with a mixture of tar and lime), it is very durable; it will last a number of years with an occasional coating, say every three or four years, of the tar and lime mixture. Such a felt would be preferable to the filthy mass of decaying straw with which the majority of cabins and out-offices throughout the country are covered, and which is such a fertile source of fever and other diseases. We have all the materials, too, to make it: thousands of gallons of tar can be had in almost every town in Ireland; our tan-yards supply the hair, and there is a rapidly increasing supply of coarse scutching waste becoming available in every part of the country. Here is one of the numerous fields for enterprise which the country presents.

The only exhibitors of asphalte flagging were F. Ritchie and Sons of Belfast, who showed samples of the tar, the raw asphalte obtained from it, a large square of flagging, and a piece of concrete. They also exhibited samples of three qualities of roofing felt. The Messrs. Ritchie deserve great credit for the energy and success with which they have contrived to utilize so many waste products of manufactories.

### BRICK, ROOFING-TILES, TERRA-COTTA ORNAMENTS, MOSAIC, AND ENCAUSTIC TILES, &c.

All rocks, irrespective of their age or geological position, may be classified under three groups, depending upon composition:—1st. Those which are principally composed of lime, such as limestone and chalk, and termed calcareous rocks; 2nd. Those composed of grains of sand, cemented together, such as sandstone or grit, the term arenaceous being applied to the whole group; and 3rd. Rocks in which a large quantity of a substance called alumina exists, such as slate-rocks, and which are included under the general name of argillaceous rocks. There are some rocks, such as granite, which may be said to combine the qualities of the two latter classes just mentioned,—the arenaceous and the argillaceous. Granite consists, as already remarked, essentially of two minerals, quartz and felspar, with which are intermingled shining plates of another mineral called mica. When the rock is completely disintegrated, the quartz, which is almost pure silica, is found in the form of small grains constituting sand, while the felspar is rich in alumina.

In process of time these rocks undergo decay from the action of water and air, and yield up their soluble constituents to the water which bears them away, whilst a more or less decomposed detritus is left behind. In the case of arenaceous rocks, the mass thus left consists of sand and pebbles; but in the case of slaty and granitic rocks, it consists, besides, of a peculiar soft, adhesive substance termed *clay*, of which most soils are good examples. If such a mass happen to be in the course of a stream of water, this substance, from its fine state of division, will be washed out, and held in suspension by the water, will be carried to some lower place where a calm pool or lake is found, and will be there deposited, and form a bed. Great deposits, evidently formed in a somewhat similar way, are found in every part of the world; their qualities depend, of course, upon the rocks from which they were derived. It is necessary to remark here that, geologically speaking, beds of clay are also considered as rocks; but in the previous observations we have, for convenience' sake, used the word rock in its common signification of a mass of hard-stone.

When clays are formed from granite rocks, they are usually white or yellowish-white, and are very adhesive or plastic; when resulting from the decomposition of slaty rocks, they are more or less coloured and sandy; and when limestone mud gets intermingled, their plasticity is greatly diminished. The plastic element consists of some combination of silica (quartz or flint in a peculiar condition) and alumina (one of the constituents of alum), with more or less water; but a perfectly pure combination of this kind rarely occurs in Nature, there being always present various quantities of sand, iron, lime, magnesia, potash, &c. The less of these substances present, the richer or *fatter* the clay, whilst clay containing a great deal is called *poor*. These substances not only exert an influence upon the plasticity of a clay, but also upon its relation to fire; the nearer a clay is in composition to a pure silicate of alumina, and the more silica it contains, the more infusible it is; but an admixture of iron or lime will give it the character possessed by a mixture for making bottle-glass; for when subjected to a heat depending upon the amount of these foreign substances, it will melt.

The finer clays, or such as are infusible and white, are very rare, while those which contain lime, such as ordinary clay marls, and those rich in iron, such as brick clays, are common. A clay may contain so very little foreign substances as to be infusible, and yet have sufficient iron to give it a colour; for we may remark here, that the colour which a clay assumes on being burned depends upon the iron which it contains.

The fine white clays (*kaolin*) are used in the manufacture of porcelain, and are found usually in granitic countries; the inferior white clays (*pipe-clay*) are usually found in coal districts, and are used in the manufacture of earthenware and pipes; these we shall have to mention again in speaking of those manufactures: at present we shall confine ourselves to the coloured clays. These we may conveniently divide into the infusible, or fire-clays, which burn either of a buff or of a dark colour; and the fusible, or ordinary brick clays, which burn of various colours, especially of a pale yellow and bright red. The fire-clays are chiefly obtained from beds associated with coal, very frequently forming the underlying stratum, and hence called *coal-seat*, though they are also found under many other circumstances, and even on the surface. They are generally of a bluish-black colour, and of a hard slaty texture; a good example of which is afforded by the well-known Stourbridge clay. The fusible clays are derived from various sources, but are very often superficial deposits, constituting the subsoils of large tracts of country. They usually contain a certain amount of carbonate of lime; and in some cases so much as to be true marls. They also frequently contain some sand and pebbles; when, however, the proportion of sand amounts to one-fourth of the entire mass, it is not considered as clay in the strict sense of the word, although that substance may be separated from it by washing. Indeed, there are few loose superficial deposits, such as soils and subsoils, that could not be thus made to yield clay.

The economical uses of the fire-clays are chiefly for the manufacture of brick destined to withstand great heat, the construction of furnaces of various kinds, pots for fusing glass, retorts, &c. The fusible, or common clays, constitute the materials from which our usual building bricks, roofing and flooring tiles, draining pipes, garden pots, common pottery, are made. Both kinds are employed in the production of figures and ornaments in what is called *terra cotta*, or baked earth. As our present object has reference solely to the use of clay for Building and Ornamentation, we shall confine our observations to the articles coming within that category.

*Bricks.*—The most important point connected with the manufacture of bricks is the selection of the clay. In the case of common bricks they must be hard, and capable of bearing pressure, without, at the same time, being heavy. One class of bricks may, taken singly, be capable of bearing a much greater pressure or weight than another; but, being much heavier, this advantage may be lost by the counterbalancing drawback. They must not fall to powder, or crack on exposure to wet or frost, and must be quite free from foreign matter, such as iron pyrites, nodules of limestone, roots of plants, or pebbles. If iron pyrites exist in the clay it will burn in the kiln into oxide of iron when the heat employed is high, and will thus leave a kind of cavity in the brick; with a moderate heat a kind of basic sulphate of iron will be formed, which will rapidly decompose under the influence of air and water, and tend to disintegrate the brick. Nodules of limestones will be burned into caustic lime, and by subsequent moisture becoming slaked, their expansion will injure the brick, and assist in its decay. The presence of vegetable matter will leave cavities in the bricks when burnt, and will cause large numbers to fly in the firing.

The more plastic a clay is, or, in other words, the purer it is, the more will it contract in the firing. This fact has a double importance to the brick-maker. In the first place, a very *fat clay*, as rich plastic clays are called, will yield exceedingly dense bricks, and are not, therefore, the best adapted for forming the most serviceable bricks. And, in the second, very few clays are homogeneous, the upper part of a bed being, in many cases, fatter than the lower, a fact easily accounted for,—as a mixture of sand and clay, suspended in water, and allowed to settle, will deposit a large portion of the sand first, and the finest clay last. If, therefore, the clay employed in brick-making be not uniformly mixed, one part may be fatter than another, and the brick in firing will contract unequally. The chemical composition of a clay is also of great importance in judging of its quality. The presence of lime, up to a certain point, is not injurious, provided it does not exist as pebbles, and that it is uniformly distributed through the mass; indeed an addition of lime to fat clays is an advantage. A clay, which alone might not be well adapted for brick-making, may be improved by the addition of certain substances, such as lime-sand, or by admixture with other clays of different qualities. Indeed it rarely happens that any clay possesses naturally all the necessary qualities for making good brick, and a skilful manufacturer will always know what materials, and in what proportions, must be added to render his clay suitable. Thus, in the neighbourhood of London, the very fat clays are mixed with coal ashes, or with sand. And in Paris refuse slaty coal is used, as the slaty parts of the anthracite beds are in America.

Freshly dug clay does not make good bricks, even when it possesses all the necessary qualities to which we have alluded; it requires to be aged, that is, exposed for a considerable time to the action of the air, which appears to produce some chemical change in the mass. This agency is very much hastened by the action of frost, exposure to frost for a few days being more efficacious than a year's exposure to ordinary weather.

In the manufacture of very inferior brick the previous exposure of the clay is omitted, and it is simply thrown into a pit and covered with water until it is perfectly softened. For the superior kinds of brick the moist clay, instead of being slightly worked up and then moulded, is subjected to an operation termed *treading*, which consists in working it up with the naked feet upon a board into an uniformly plastic mass. This inartificial method has been, to some extent, superseded by other processes in which machinery is employed. For example, in England the clay, after sufficient exposure to the atmosphere, is agitated with water and passed through sieves which separate the coarser particles, whilst the finer portions are run into pits or tanks, where they are allowed to deposit, and the excess of water being withdrawn, the sediment is worked up into a plastic mass. A machine is sometimes used on the Continent for effecting the same object; consisting of a horizontal axis, carrying a number of flat spokes which are made to revolve in a kind of trough, where the clay is beaten up into a thin mass, the whole of the stones being separated. It is then passed through a series of sieves into the mixing pit, where the additions of lime, sand, coal-ashes, or other material deemed necessary, are made. Where very superior qualities of brick are required, or where the clay is used for making terra cotta, this *slip*, as the clay-mud used for moulding objects is called, is ground in a pug-mill, or under edge stones.

Bricks are fashioned either by the hand in moulds, or by machinery. The former, or primitive method, is still the one chiefly employed, in consequence, strange as it may seem, of its economy. The number which a brick-maker is able to mould in a day is extraordinary, varying, according to the strength and ability of the workman, the size of the bricks, and the quality of the clay, from 2,000 to 10,000, or even 16,000. Each moulder requires the service of a carrier and two boys. The machines invented for making bricks may be classified into five divisions:—1. Those consisting of a single mould, nearly the same as the hand mould worked by machinery. One of the earliest of this kind was invented in the year 1813, but many improvements have since been effected, the most important being rendering the working continuous. 2. This class differs from the first, in principle only, in several moulds being worked at the same time. The first of this kind was employed in America in 1819, the motion in it being backwards and forwards. This motion was replaced by a rotatory one in 1826; and the latter has been adopted in several recent patents, as, for instance, in those of Leahy and of Nash. 3. The machines of this class are simply a species of dies which cut the bricks out of a cake of clay prepared separately. This principle does not appear to have been adopted in any recent machine. 4. This class of machines produces a continuous band of clay, corresponding in thickness and width to the dimensions of the bricks intended to be made. This band of clay is forced by pressure through an orifice, exactly as in the ordinary draining-tile machine, the difference being that the orifice is rectangular instead of being round, and has no core or mandril, as the bricks must be solid. This long band of clay is delivered upon a flat table, where it is cut of the proper lengths by means of wires moved up and down at certain intervals. The earliest machine upon this principle was that of Hostemberg, first employed in St. Petersburgh in 1807; and, perhaps, the most perfect is that of Terrasson-Fougères, which is capable of cutting from ten to forty bricks at one operation. One of these machines, costing from £30 to £38, is capable of forming about 25,000 bricks in a day. 5. For the fifth class of machines the clay is used in its dry state. One of the most perfect of this kind is that recently patented by Nasmyth and Minton. The chief feature consists of a series of moulds into which the powdered material is introduced, and subjected at first to a gentle pressure, which gradually increases until the whole of the air enclosed in the powder is forced out, and then to a rapid and strong pressure of about 150 tons, which finishes them. The motion is continuous, and the machine feeds and discharges itself.

There is an American machine, of very simple construction, belonging to this class, invented by Mr. Stephen Ustick, of Philadelphia, which produces bricks directly from the untempered clay, and thus saves almost all previous operations.

Made bricks may be much improved, for certain purposes, by subjecting them to pressure before firing. One of the most recent machines for effecting this object is that of Houget, which is a modification of the American anti-friction press of Dick. Its action is very slow, and the expense of pressing must, therefore, be very great.

The observations which we have made on the subject of clay apply equally well, whether it is intended to make bricks, roofing, flooring, or draining tiles, garden pots, or other coarse pottery. With regard to the roofing and flooring tiles, and which are moulded exactly like bricks, it is evident that, with a slight modification, any of the machines above alluded to may be made to produce them. All these articles, however, must be made with a much fatter clay than that employed for bricks; and, in the case of roofing tiles and coarse pottery, greater care must be observed in the preparation of the clay.

The bricks after being moulded are allowed to dry either in the open air or by artificial means, the latter being always adopted with the finer kinds. When fully dried they are burned either in kilns or in clamps, that is, in great heaps covered over with clay: the latter is the cheaper method, because large quantities may be burnt at once, and no expense is entailed for buildings; but the finer kinds cannot be thus burned, and they are only adapted for coal as a fuel. The process of burning in clamps is also very slow, varying from twenty to fifty days, according to the size of the heap. The kilns used in brick-making are of two kinds, close or open; the former has the advantage of consuming much less fuel than the latter. Indeed, the economy may sometimes amount to from one-half to two-thirds of the entire quantity used. The close kiln is a true oven, where the bricks are piled and heated by the flame of fire, while the open kiln is not unlike a lime-kiln. The greater part of the bricks made in Holland, where such enormous quantities are employed, is burned in open kilns, as many as three millions being burned in one operation, and the chief fuel being turf. In all cases where the latter fuel is employed, kilns are preferable to clamps.

The method of manufacturing fire-bricks and tiles differs in many respects from that adopted for common brick. Thus at Stourbridge, near Birmingham, the most celebrated English locality for such articles, the lumps of clay as they are dug up are laid in heaps until they are fully dried, when they are ground in a kind of pug-mill. A portion of this clay is then moistened with water and worked into a plastic mass, and made into cubical bricks of about seven inches, which are sharply fired, and subsequently ground into a coarse powder, and sifted to separate dust and the coarser lumps. In this state the burnt clay has a pale, flesh-red colour. The brick mixture consists of the finely powdered raw clay, with a certain portion of this brick powder, and is worked up in the ordinary way, and moulded by the hand in iron moulds, or, where larger objects are to be made, in wooden ones. The firing is effected in close ovens of a cylindrical form for six feet, covered with a dome fourteen feet high; upon this dome is built another (somewhat lower) cylindrical chamber, which ends in an arched copula. Eight or ten fire-places, heated with coal, open into the lower chamber, the flame of which passes through numerous openings in the dome into the second chamber, in the arched roof of which are a number of round holes for the escape of the smoke.

The colour of bricks, as we have already had occasion to observe, depends chiefly upon the amount of iron which the clay contains; but it is also very much influenced by the manner of burning. If the clay does not contain much iron, and that the firing is effected in close kilns, the colour is grayish or yellowish-white. If, however, it contains a large quantity of the red oxide of iron, they will be red, but where this kind of bricks are exposed to the reducing action of a smoky flame, they assume a blackish-brown colour, especially when fired at a high heat. Fire-clay usually contains a certain quantity of organic matter, and, when not rich in iron, will generally burn of a pale buff colour in closed kilns; but if a mixture of burnt clay of a red colour and bluish slaty clay be burned together, the resulting colour will be brownish-black from the formation of the black oxide of iron by the partial reduction of red oxide in the burnt clay by the organic matter in the raw material. Hence the reason why the Stourbridge bricks are of that colour.

*Terra cotta.*—The strict meaning of this term is baked clay, and in this sense it includes bricks, and any other article made of clay and then burnt. In its common acceptation it applies only to vases, figures, and other ornaments made of baked clay. This application of the material appears to be of an antiquity little inferior to that of bricks, as we possess specimens from the Assyrian cities, and from Egypt, at least 3000 or 4000 years old. Besides tombs, lachrymal and cinereal urns, we find that vases, ornamented in different ways, formed part of the prizes at the games, and that statues of considerable size, such as the statue of Jupiter by Turianus, mentioned by Pliny as adorning the Capitol,—and another nearly 6½ feet high, of great beauty, still preserved in the Museum of Naples,—were made by the Greeks and Romans. After the fall of the Roman Empire the art fell into disuse, but towards the end of the fourteenth century, Nicolo d'Arezzo revived it in Italy, from whence it passed into France and Spain, but it does not appear to have been in much favour. Of late years, however, it has assumed new life on the Continent, and many houses are ornamented with terra cotta in Toulouse, Vienna, Berlin, and other continental cities. The art has also been lately revived in England, but has not yet been much applied to architectural ornamentation.

Ornaments in terra cotta may be made either of common clay or of fire-clay; in both cases, however, the material requires to be carefully prepared, and to be reduced to the finest state of division. In the manufacture of figures and ornaments in terra cotta we have three things to consider:—1. Sharpness of outline and perfect uniformity of contraction; 2. Durability; 3. Colour. From what we have already said, with reference to the great contraction which fat clays undergo in firing, it must be evident that pure plastic clay would not be adapted for the production of fine draperies, or, in fact, for making figures or sharp ornaments at all. The addition of exceedingly fine sand and lime to a fat clay diminishes its contractibility, but the addition of the latter ingredient prevents the articles from being baked at a high temperature, as otherwise the finer lines, such as the folds of drapery, or the face of figures, would undergo a semi-fusion, and lose all their sharpness, while, on the other hand, the durability of terra cotta depends to a great extent upon the temperature at which it is fired. The most imperishable of materials is, perhaps, semi-fused clay; hence the higher the heat employed, the better adapted will be the articles to withstand the weather. Clay baked at a low temperature, and containing much lime, is very perishable; the lime is gradually dissolved out by the rain falling upon it, and the frost disintegrates it by the freezing of the water which it absorbs.

Fire-clays consequently yield the most durable articles of this kind, but also the least perfect as to sharpness. By burning a large portion of the clay, and thus destroying its property of contraction, and mixing it with a portion of fresh clay, and by the addition of substances which assist in the cementation of so imperfectly plastic a mass, such as lime, and certain clays containing a large amount of silica in a state capable of being dissolved by caustic potash and soda, a mass may be made which will be capable of representing the sharpest lines of a figure or ornament.

As terra cotta figures and ornaments are always baked in close kilns, and are sometimes even placed in separate cases in the kilns, only two principal colours can be obtained, brick-red and buff. The colour cannot be so easily altered as in the case of the other qualities, and consequently little choice is left.

Terra cotta is a beautiful material for adorning the façades of public buildings and large houses. Experience has also shown that, when properly made, it is of remarkable durability. Even the marly clays of Toulouse, Paris, and Berlin, are made to yield articles capable of lasting for centuries; and certainly the climate of the latter is a sufficient test of the durability of the article. One of the great objections to the use of terra cotta in buildings is its expense. It is certainly much dearer than Portland or Roman cement, with which in other respects there is no comparison; while, on the other hand, it is much cheaper than stone, and, with one or two exceptions, much more beautiful. From the facility with which the most beautiful figures or elaborate ornaments may be cast in ordinary plaster moulds, and vases and other round objects thrown upon the potter's wheel, the most varied and artistic style of ornamentation may be adopted in the fronts of houses and public buildings. That it is *very much* cheaper than stone there can be no doubt, for it is used in Paris, where one of the best and easiest worked stones in Europe exists; and if found advantageous there, how much more so would it be here, where stone for working ornaments and figures is very expensive, and has to be imported? In Berlin also, Corinthian columns, and other ornaments made of vitrified terra cotta, which would resist the weather for centuries, may be had for much less than one-third of those carved in stone.

One of the great drawbacks under which Dublin and many other cities in these countries, labour, is the dull monotony of the unvaried walls of brick; with rectangular apertures for windows, and doors which seem to have been all made from the same design. The introduction of terra cotta ornaments into the decoration of houses would banish this monotony, and help to communicate life and picturesqueness to our cities. And as the character of the architecture of a city has considerable influence upon that of its inhabitants, we have no doubt the change would also be very beneficial in this respect.

We possess abundance of materials in Ireland for the manufacture of the finer kinds of bricks, tiles, &c., and of terra cotta. We would merely mention a few localities in which they are now to some extent utilized; namely, the fine red class, associated with the marl beds, so abundant in the counties of Wicklow and Wexford, especially at Dunganstown and Wicklow in the former county, and Courtown Harbour in the latter; the great deposit of clay-burning of a pale red at Youghal, in the county of Cork; the fine red clay of Florence Court, near Enniskillen; and that of Larne, in the county of Antrim. And, lastly, the fire-clays forming the coal-seat of all the beds of coal mentioned in the section on coal in the preceding pages, are adapted for this manufacture. There is scarcely a county in Ireland in which superior clay for brick, draining pipe, and tile making, may not be found. Notwithstanding this abundance of the raw material, and, we may add, of fuel in the neighbourhood of bogs, it is singular to find so many miserable and incommodious houses (we do not allude to the mud cabins of the peasants, for which there is a distinct cause), built of stone at a cost which would have constructed excellent brick buildings. Due attention is not paid in Ireland to the preparation of the clay used for bricks, and especially to the separation of limestone pebbles, whence most of our bricks are of inferior quality. Although red clays are very abundant, we are almost altogether dependent upon England for our supply of that coloured brick. Some very superior specimens of a very fine red brick are now, however, being made at Courtown Harbour. There were two defects in the first made there, which we hope have been since corrected; namely, they were too dense, the clay being too fat, and requiring an addition of lime or marl, and was not apparently weathered enough; and the size was very inconvenient for some kinds of brick-work. The first defect was excusable enough, as it is only in old works that a good stock of well-weathered clay can be had; and, besides, it requires some experience to learn the proportion for mixing the other ingredients with the clay. But the second defect ought to have been avoided, because all common bricks should have such a proportion between length, breadth, and thickness, that they will always fit in any kind of bond. Irish manufacturers should remember that it is not enough to simply produce an article; they must produce it of a quality equal to the best of the kind to be found elsewhere, else their efforts will be unsuccessful. But above all, they should attend with great care to the minute details, such as those to which we have alluded, as inattention to them frequently does more injury than real inferiority.

There were but few clays suitable for the manufacture of bricks, tiles, or terra cotta ornaments, exhibited. With the exception indeed of a series of specimens collected by the Dublin Society, there were only two exhibitors whose contributions deserve especial mention; namely, those of the Hon. C. Wandesforde, who exhibited some of the fire-clay from the coal-measures of Kilkenny, and of Mr. J. K. Fahie, from the corresponding series in Tipperary, who also had a good specimen of alluvial red clay. With the exception of a small specimen contributed by the Limerick Local Committee, the fire-clays of the great Munster coal-field were unrepresented; while no specimens whatever of the Leitrim and Tyrone coal-fields were exhibited.

There were only eight exhibitors of bricks, of whom two were exclusively British, and five Irish. Five exhibitors contributed common bricks, four being Irish, and one Scotch; and six contributed fire-bricks, of whom four were exclusively Irish, and two British. All the Irish bricks exhibited were of excellent quality, and presented striking evidence, so far as they went, not only of the rapidly increasing tendency to utilize our mineral resources, but of considerable improvement in the style of manufacture. So far as we could judge from the arrangement of the raw material department of the Exhibition, there were only two exhibitors of roofing tiles, one Irish, and one English. The former were from Courtown Harbour, and were of excellent material, the fat clay of that locality being admirably adapted for tiles. We must not forget to mention, that among the bricks exhibited by Mr. Fahie, of Tipperary, were some of the hollow ones now so much recommended for building cottages, and for division walls of houses. These bricks are made upon the same principles as draining pipes, and are readily formed by the machine of Terrasson-Fougères, by a slight modification of the apertures, in which a number of mandrils are arranged.

The contributions of ornamental terra cotta were much more numerous than those of bricks or tiles, the total number being fourteen; of whom only one was Irish, seven Scotch, three English, one Irish exhibitor of Scotch articles, and two German. The articles exhibited were also very numerous and varied, and may be classified into:—1. Figures; 2. Vases and fountains; and 3. Purely architectural ornaments. There were only four exhibitors of figures, of whom three deserve mention,—two being German, and one English. In excellence of execution, and quality of material, the first place belongs to M. March, of Charlottenburg, near Berlin. His specimens were of two very distinct materials, one a beautifully fine red clay, evidently calcareous, and not very highly fired. One of the figures of this material, representing Polyhymnia, was admirably executed, and showed in a remarkable manner the adaptation of the material to produce true works of art: the drapery was especially deserving of commendation. The other material employed by M. March belonged to the class of difficultly fusible clay, and was highly fired, and would, no doubt, withstand the action of the weather for ages, being exceedingly dense, and not absorbent of moisture. The colour was also peculiar, being of a grayish-yellow, with a distinct olive shade, which looked well in the small statuettes. In the same department were exhibited four allegorical figures of Winter and Summer, being part of a series of eight, representing the Four Seasons, each season being indicated by a male and female figure. These figures were after the original designs by Professor Leib of Munich. The colour was very good, being a yellowish-gray, and would harmonize well with many kinds of building stone in use. The material appeared to be very good and durable, though not highly fired, having a sort of cement-like character. The next exhibitor, whose figures deserve especial mention, is Mr. Blashfield of London. The clay employed by him is obtained from the tertiary beds of the London basin, and appears to have been prepared with great care, and to be very durable. It is much whiter than any of the others exhibited, and does not differ much, indeed, from some Portland stone, with which it would harmonize very well.

The number of vases exhibited was very great; but, with the exception of those of Mr. Blashfield, and of the Messrs. Bell of Glasgow, and some small vases of semi-vitrified clay from Berlin, they were all rather coarse, and of very poor design. The clay used by the Messrs. Bell appears to be the usual fire-clay of the coal-measures of Lanarkshire, some of which was in the collection of the Monkland Iron Company. The other vases exhibited were made of similar materials from the coal-measures of different districts, and were of good quality, and would yield very durable ornaments; it is, therefore, to be regretted that so little attention is paid to design by the manufacturers of terra cotta. Several fountains were exhibited, among which we may mention a very pretty one designed for a *parterre*, made of the red Berlin clay, already mentioned, and the large one which was erected in the Central Hall of the building, exhibited by Ferguson, Miller, and Co. of Glasgow. Of purely architectural ornaments there were few exhibitors; those deserving special mention, being M. March of Berlin, who exhibited some admirably executed Corinthian capitals, and a few other things, in semi-vitrified fire-clay, which we should consider imperishable, and certainly far cheaper than stone; those of the Farnley Iron Company, who contributed some ornamental trusses, mouldings, and balusters, which were well executed, and of excellent materials, and were worthy of attention; and those of the Messrs. Bell of Glasgow, whose balustrade, in a fine grayish-white material, was admirable. Under this head we may also include chimney-tops, of which there were no less than eight exhibitors. This appears to be one of the most general applications of terra cotta, as it is also a useful one, doing away with several feet of heavy brick-work on the tops of chimneys, and of those very rude and ineffective contrivances called slate-pots. Terra cotta pots have a great advantage over the cast-iron ones sometimes used, in being very much lighter for the same

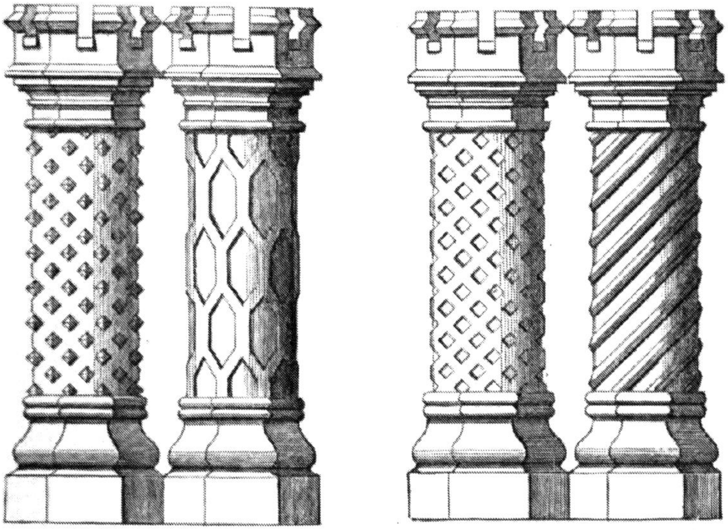

Chimney Tops in Terra Cotta, exhibited by the Farnley Iron Company.

size, while, when well made, they are, perhaps, as durable. The Farnley Iron Company exhibited a great variety of these articles, suitable for different styles of houses, the designs of a few of which are represented

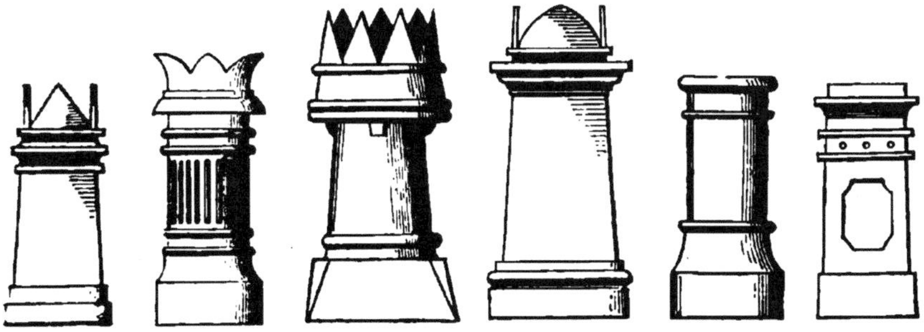

Chimney Tops in Terra Cotta, exhibited by the Farnley Iron Company.

by the annexed engravings, and which will also show the general character of the examples exhibited by the other contributors.

There is a very appropriate application of terra cotta which we must not omit to mention before concluding this part of our subject, namely, for flower-boxes for mignionette, &c., and for pendant or bracket flower vases. Examples of these were contributed by the Farnley Iron Company, by J. Doulton, Jun., of Liverpool, and by M. March of Berlin. The pendant and bracket vases in red terra cotta of the latter were exceedingly tasteful.

The only examples of Irish ornamental terra cotta exhibited were two small vases after the antique, and very well executed, contributed by Beresford and Kelly, of Florence Court, near Enniskillen. We hope to see this branch of manufacture gradually develop itself amongst us.

*Venetian and Encaustic Tiles.*—The art of forming tesseræ from baked clay, and constructing mosaics similar to the geometrical ones in marble already mentioned, is of very old date. At first the tesseræ were plain, or were simply stained or covered with a glaze made by covering the surface with galena, the common ore of lead, mixed with a little clay, and then firing them again; but afterwards indented patterns were formed in them by forming the tessaræ in moulds having the patterns in relief. These indentations were sometimes filled up with various pigments, often fused into a glass. Pavements formed of simple tessaræ, of one or more colours, and arranged so as to produce geometrical patterns, were called Venetian mosaics, from having been much used in that city in the middle ages; whilst those with indented or relievo patterns, consisting of monograms or other symbolic devices, or arabesques, were called *encaustic*. The latter were much used in ecclesiastical architecture, and also by the Moors of Spain, who generally filled the indentations with coloured enamel glasses. The celebrated Moorish palace of the Alhambra, at Grenada, was richly decorated in this way. Sometimes the tesseræ of geometrical mosaics were covered with similar enamel glasses, of beautiful shades of green, white, &c. With the decline of ecclesiastical architecture this art fell into complete disuse, and has only been very lately revived. The persons who have done the most for this revival have undoubtedly been the Messrs. Minton, Hollins, and Co., of Stoke-upon-Trent, not only by the beauty of the articles produced by them, but still more by the great improvements which they have been the means of effecting in the processes of manufacture. Mr. Singer, of Vauxhall, also contributed materially to this revival by his process, patented in 1839, of cutting out tesseræ from thin bands of clay by machinery, and when baked of joining them together so as to form large slabs, by means of cement.

Messrs. Minton and Hollin's collection of tiles were among the most interesting contributions to the Exhibition, no expense apparently having been spared by them in getting it up. The whole of the varieties exhibited may be referred to six types:—1. Buff and coloured indented diaper tiles; 2. Venetian and other varieties of mosaics; 3. Encaustic or inlaid tiles, from two Greek words, signifying to burn in; 4. Imitations of the Alhambra tiles with enamels; 5. Majolica tiles, or imitations of the glaze and colouring of the celebrated majolica ware of the sixteenth century; and 6. Dutch or glazed tiles. The buff indented diaper tiles are made from the fire-clay associated with the Staffordshire coal. The clay is ground in a kind of mill to the state of very fine powder; and in this state is introduced into square, oblong, or other form of moulds, and subjected to a pressure of about 150 to 250 tons in a hydraulic or other press. On being taken from the mould the clay is found to be compressed into a very small space, and to adhere together into a solid mass. Perfectly dry clay would not adhere in this way sufficiently, and it is, therefore, necessary that a certain amount of moisture should remain in it previous to the operation of moulding. When removed from the mould their surfaces are polished with a piece of bent tin-plate, and they are then packed in cases of refractory fire-clay called seggars, a great number of which are piled in a kiln similar to that employed in the burning of earthenware, where they are fired at about the temperature required for the latter. Many of these diaper pattern tiles are subsequently ornamented with narrow borderings of various colours, especially of red and gold, or blue and gold; and the surface is often covered before firing with a wash of fine white clay, to which is sometimes added a little enamel glass, which, in the firing, gives a sort of semi-fused glaze. The coloured tiles are only used for decorating walls, and when employed under suitable conditions are extremely beautiful. The mosaic tiles are made of finer clays than the last. The material is prepared in the same way as for ordinary terra cotta, and, being capable of vitrifying to some extent in firing, it may be stained throughout its mass of any desired colour. Being coloured with the proper pigment, it is then brought to a highly plastic condition, and is passed between rollers which laminate it into thin sheets or ribbons. These ribbons are cut into large squares; and their surfaces being slightly oiled to prevent adhesion, fifteen or twenty of them are laid on each other, and the pile laid on a kind of table, over which is placed a frame in a horizontal position, and sliding up and down in upright grooves. This frame has a number of fine wires placed crossways, somewhat like a sieve, the meshes, if we can so call them, being square, or oblong, or triangular, hexagonal, or octagonal, or segments of circles, according to the form desired to be given. When this frame is made to descend, the wires pass through the pile of clay sheets and divide them into a number of pieces of the given form, which are dried and burnt in the usual way. With the tesseræ thus made and coloured, black, blue, red, buff, cane green, white, and an almost endless variety of patterns, may be produced. The mode of laying them down as a pavement is very simple: the tesseræ are arranged into a mosaic of the desired pattern, with faces down upon an exceedingly flat surface; a shallow frame is then arranged around them, and a layer of cement poured over them, and upon this cement, before it fully hardens, is laid a layer of ordinary tiles, over which is poured another layer of cement, and sometimes even a second layer of tiles. In this way slabs of a very large size may be produced, and laid down as flags for flooring.

Encaustic or inlaid tiles consist of three distinct parts,—the body, the inlaid pattern, and the back. The body is composed of ordinary fire-clay similar to that used for the diaper tiles, and is worked up into a plastic mass, which is moulded in iron moulds under a screw press. These moulds have raised patterns, which produce an indented or *intaglio* pattern upon the surface of the tile. The tiles thus formed are allowed to become dry, and the indented pattern is filled up by pouring over the surface of the tile a thick milk or slip composed of the white clays of Dorset and Devon, so much used in making earthenware, to which is added some pigment if coloured patterns are to be produced. Sometimes, where polychromic patterns are desired, different coloured slips are used, and poured into the parts of the pattern intended for each. When partially dry the surface is scraped even, until the face of the original tile or buff-coloured clay makes its appearance, when the indented pattern alone will be filled with the finer stained clays. If the tile thus prepared were fired, the body would contract more than the pattern, and the tile would be bent, and, perhaps, the latter fractured; it is hence necessary to apply a coating of the same fire-clay used for the pattern to the back, to counteract this difference of contractibility; and as this clay, when hard burned, would not adhere well to the cement employed in laying them down, the back is pierced by a number of holes by means of projections in the mould, into which the soft cement is able to penetrate and form a solid bond. The Alhambra tiles are formed upon the same principle as the ordinary encaustic tiles, with this difference, that in the former fusible pigments are used instead of coloured clay slips. This is the technical difference; but it must be confessed that there is a beauty of design and a harmony of colour in the true Alhambra tiles, which is still more characteristic of them, and which it is extremely difficult to equal. The majolica tiles are not so much distinguished by form as by the coloured glazes with which they are covered; thus we may have indented or plain tesseræ covered with a monochromic glaze, or large tiles with foliated or arabesque indented patterns glazed, but not filled up, with different coloured enamels. The great peculiarity of majolica colours is their softness and depth, which is the result of the soft enamel pigments employed. The Dutch tiles are true earthenware, and we must, therefore, defer any further description of them until we come to speak of that substance, when we shall also have an opportunity of making some further remarks upon the fused pigments and enamel colours employed in the manufacture of Alhambra and majolica tiles.

A great variety of all these different kinds were exhibited in the department allotted to the Raw Materials, and a still more beautiful and varied collection in the Mediæval Court, showing the mode of setting them, and their application to floors and to lining walls. Among the examples of the encaustic tiles in the latter department were several large slabs, representing Scripture and other subjects, monograms, &c., wrought in white, deep blue, cane and red-coloured clays, which were very beautiful. Some coats of arms, made in similar materials and style, were also admirably executed; but, perhaps, the best thing in the whole collection of encaustic tiles was a small circular tile, upon which was represented a head apparently of Ceres, surrounded with ears of corn. Such designs, although by no means adapted for floors, show the perfection to which the manufacture of these tiles has been brought by Messrs. Minton and Hollins.

Mr. Fahie, of Tipperary, exhibited a few specimens of his first attempt to produce tesselated pavements, and, although very rude and imperfect, both in design and execution, they deserve to be mentioned specially as proof of the growing industrial energy of the country, which only requires facilities for acquiring information to progress and prosper.

## MANUFACTURES FROM CLAY NOT EMPLOYED FOR BUILDING AND DECORATION.

The clays and other materials used in the manufacture of porcelain and earthenware, although belonging to the class of Mineral Raw Materials, and included under that section in the present Catalogue, will be more fully noticed under the head Porcelain and Earthenware. It will also be better to defer our observations upon a peculiar class of manufactures in clay, namely, glazed sewerage pipes, until we come to that section; as the nature and properties of the materials, and the processes employed, will be better understood when studied in connexion with the whole subject of porcelain, &c. The observations which we made in the present section upon the qualities and preparation of clays apply equally well to all the other manufactures in that material. And here we may remark, that it is difficult to classify manufactures of this kind, so as to refer each article to the class to which it really belongs. Thus, all articles made in clay, properly speaking, belong to the fictile manufactures; and yet there is so great a distinction technically between the simple manufactures of terra cotta of all kinds and that of earthenware, that it is preferable for all purposes of illustration to include under the present section those articles made of clay alone without glaze or varnish, and to group all those covered with a glaze under the head Earthenware and Porcelain.

*Draining Pipes.*—Every clay which will make good roofing tiles, and we may even add bricks, will answer for making draining pipes; and, as in the case of the roofing tiles, fat clays, which would yield too dense bricks, will make excellent pipes. The formation of the pipe, too, is so perfectly analogous to that of some machine-made bricks, that an ordinary brick machine on the principle of Terrasson-Fougères, differs but very little from a pipe or tile machine, of which there were examples in the Exhibition, which will be noticed under the section devoted to agricultural machines. The manufacture of draining pipes, being now a necessary appendage to all good farming operations upon a large scale, mostly appertains to the domain of agriculture; but the introduction of the system of pipe-draining will, undoubtedly, render great service to the country in a manufacturing point of view. A few years ago, with very few exceptions, even the coarsest articles of common pottery were imported from England; but the great expense attending the importation of draining pipes, and the still more expensive carriage of them into the interior of the country, gradually led to their production on the spot. The manufacture of bricks soon followed in many instances; and the transition from these to that of coarse pottery was easy. We have no doubt that in a few years the commoner kinds of earthenware will also be produced; already efforts in this direction have been very successful. This is but one of the many examples, showing that the importance of the introduction of a manufacture into a country cannot be always judged by the amount of employment it gives, or the value of the products yielded; but that the number of others which in course of time it inevitably brings along with it must also be taken into account.

There were six exhibitors of draining pipes, all of whom were Irish; and they were all well made and of durable materials. Those from the Florence Court Works, Courtown Harbour, and Kinlough Tilery, county of Leitrim, were deserving of high commendation from the excellence of their form and the great variety of sizes exhibited. The material employed by Mr. Fahie partook of the character of a fire-clay, and must be very durable; his pipes were also very well formed.

*Common Pottery.*—The only difference between the articles coming under this designation and those already described is *form* alone; most of the one being moulded or formed by pressure, whilst the other are moulded upon the potter's wheel. We may therefore dispense with any further observations than to notice the contributions of the different exhibitors. So far as we have been able to ascertain, there were only four exhibitors of common pottery, of whom three were Irish, and one English. Among these the Messrs. Beresford and Kelly, of Florence Court, near Enniskillen, deserve the first place. Too much credit cannot, indeed, be given to these gentlemen for the perfection to which they have brought this branch of trade. The garden pots and other articles manufactured at their works are quite equal to the very best made in any part of England. Those produced at the Courtown Harbour Works, belonging to Mr. James, were scarcely inferior to those just mentioned. The Local Committee of the county of Kerry exhibited some common pots for domestic purposes, which, although leaving much room for improvement, were not below the average of similar articles sold; such a contribution evinced considerable discrimination of the wants of the country, and therefore deserves commendation. The examples of common pottery contributed from England were evidently exhibited alone on account of the *glaze*, for the *form* was very rude. The glaze was of a pale yellow, and very transparent, and appeared to be very hard and much less liable to crack and scale than the ordinary lead glaze employed for this kind of ware.

*Crucibles and Clay Retorts.*—The pots or crucibles in which brass, silver, steel, and other metals are melted, require to be of an extremely refractory character. Pure silicate of alumina, that is, a combination of silica with one of the constituents of alum, is one of the most infusible compounds known; the nearer, therefore, a clay approaches to that substance in composition, the better adapted it will be to form crucibles and other articles required to withstand a great heat. Silica, in a nearly pure form, as it is in many white sands, is also very infusible, provided nothing is melted with it which has a tendency to form glass, such as soda, lead, &c. Hence, the quality of a crucible depends, in a great measure, upon the uses to which it is put; thus steel may be melted in a pot composed of a mixture of clay and sand, whilst lead or soda or compounds containing them would rapidly attack it, and perhaps run through it. For melting such substances, crucibles composed of a clay consisting chiefly of silicate of alumina (and free, as far as possible, from bases such as iron, soda, potash, or lime, or siliceous sand) are required. The celebrated Hessian crucibles from Gross Almerode, in Germany, consist of a mixture of equal parts of clay, free from bases, and fine siliceous sand. They are hence very infusible, and stand the fire without cracking, the sand diminishing the contractibility, but at the same time rendering the crucibles unfit for melting glass, lead, &c., which would readily attack the free silica. The pots used in most of the glass factories in these countries are made from Stourbridge clay, without the addition of sand. This clay is chiefly silicate of alumina, containing a little iron; articles made of it are, however, liable to contract to a great extent at a high temperature, and therefore to crack. A substitute for the sand is employed to diminish this effect, consisting of powdered *sherds*, that is, portions of the clay previously burnt and reduced to powder, as we noticed in speaking of fire-brick. If, however, too much sherds be employed, the crucibles or pots become so porous as to allow any very fusible substance to strain through them. Another substance which has the same effect as the sherds is hard coke (powdered), natural graphite, or black lead, or the artificial graphite which forms as a thick crust on the inside of gas retorts. All these substances have much the same composition, consisting chiefly of carbon in a very incombustible form. The crucibles formed with a mixture of graphite or black lead are very much used, especially in melting silver, gold, &c., as the smooth and dense surface which the graphite gives to the pot allows the whole of the metal to flow out, and does not absorb any minute globules,—a matter of great importance in the melting of gold and other valuable metals.

The *debris* of decomposed granite, especially that left after washing out the fine clay used in the manufacture of china, is largely used in the manufacture of cheap crucibles for various purposes. Considerable quantities of them are made near Redruth and Truro, in Cornwall, and are known in commerce as Cornish pots. Good crucibles are also sometimes made from the clays of the tertiary formation, such as those found near London. In Holland similar clays are used, and even the alluvial clays of rivers; some of the crucibles known as Dutch pots are made from such materials, and are of very good quality. The same necessity does not exist for strongly firing crucibles before being used as in the case of fire-bricks, which it is of importance should have suffered their full amount of contraction before being built into the masonry. Some crucibles are accordingly sent into commerce merely dried, and not burned, whilst others, like the Hessian and Cornish, are previously fired at about the temperature employed for stoneware.

A very useful application of fire-clay has been made within the last few years, namely, to the production of gas retorts, which are now found, we believe, to be far more durable than those from iron, and much more economical. The preparation of the clay for this purpose is exactly the same as that described in noticing fire-bricks. But as it is of the greatest consequence that the burnt material should have sufficient porosity to allow for contractions and expansions consequent upon changes of temperature, about one-fourth of the weight of the clay of sawdust, powdered coke, or anthracite, is added, which is completely burnt out in the firing. Clay retorts are usually three inches thick, and are made both D-shaped and oval, either by moulding, or rather building up with the hand, or by pressure in a kind of mould. They must be dried and fired with the greatest care, the latter operation lasting fourteen days, as upon the mode in which these operations are performed, as much as upon the quality of the clay, will depend the durability of the retorts.

There were four exhibitors of melting-pots, three Irish and one English. The Messrs. Morgan and Rees, of London, contributed a very complete and excellent series of crucibles of different kinds and forms. Amongst them were examples of Hessian, Cornish, and London pots; English and German black lead pots for melting brass, and a fine class of the latter for gold and silver refiners' use, most probably made at Passau, in Germany. One of these was shown which had been used sixty times, which is extraordinary. There were also some pots made from the celebrated clay of Beaufois, in the department of the Ardennes, and very largely employed by the French refiners. The Irish pots, exhibited by Beresford and Kelly, were apparently of good quality, but this is a point which could only be judged of by an analysis of the clay, and by experience.

The fact, however, of having exhibited crucibles is already a great advance, and as there is scarcely a single article of clay so easily made, we hope, before long, to see a large trade in these things. There is, certainly, no lack of fire-clay in Ireland, and that of very excellent quality.

There was but one exhibitor of clay retorts, the Garnkirk Coal Company, whose productions appeared to be excellent, being of a very pale colour, smooth, and completely free from cracks. The price of such retorts is about £2 8*s*., and if they last two years, as is asserted, there can be no doubt that there would be considerable economy in their use. Here is a still more important application of our fire-clays than the last, and one, too, for which they are well adapted, if some persons with a little energy and skill would take the matter up.

*Tobacco-pipes.*—Various materials were used by the aboriginal inhabitants of America for the manufacture of pipes, but the best known and most typical of these was a kind of indurated clay rock, termed pipe-stone. Its colour was generally red, as that found at Coteau de Prairies on the Missouri, and which has been called Catlinite, in honour of Mr. Catlin, the delineator of the Indian tribes. It is also found of a dark-grayish colour, as, for example, that used by the Indians of Oregon and other parts of the N. W. coast of America. It is a true clay, and is actually in process of formation in several places, among others at Nepigon, on the northern shore of Lake Superior. The pipes cut from this material are remarkably porous, and absorb the empyreumatic oil produced by the destructive distillation of the tobacco with great avidity, becoming deeply coloured. When tobacco was introduced into Europe, various substitutes for the American pipe-stone were brought into use, but the most successful were those made of baked clay. The present style of clay pipe appears to have been first adopted at Cologne and other parts of the Lower Rhine; at all events that city became famous for its pipes about two centuries ago. The clays usually employed at present for pipe-making are the plastic clays of the tertiary formation, especially the lower beds. That used in these countries is found in Dorsetshire, especially in the small peninsula called the Island of Purbeck. In its natural state it is of a bluish-white colour, and burns of a perfect white, forming a very porous and absorbent mass. It is largely employed as an ingredient in the manufacture of earthenware, but in that of pipes it is used unmixed with any other substance. To produce good pipes from this or any other clay, it appears to be necessary to keep it in a moist state for a considerable time, otherwise the pipes will be deficient in porosity. The process of pipe-making is exceedingly simple, and need not be described here. The method of burning is, however, of great importance, both as to the quality of the pipe, and especially to its form. In some places the pipes, when sufficiently dry to be fired, are arranged in a number of seggars, or pots, like an ordinary brass-founder's melting-pot, the vacant spaces between the pipes being filled with sherds, consisting of broken seggars or tobacco-pipes reduced to powder. Each seggar is covered with a conical hood, and the whole are then arranged in a kind of kiln. In London, where very superior pipes are made, a large close kiln, of a cylindrical shape, surmounted with a dome, and around which the flames play, is employed. On the inside of the kiln a number of very narrow shelves or projections are formed, and in the centre is an upright pillar, upon which are a number of projecting rings. The pipes are arranged in an inclined position in such a kiln by placing the bowls upon the shelves with their stems all directed towards the centre, where their ends rest upon the projecting rings. The advantage of this system, independent of the complete exclusion of the flame, which sometimes discolours the pipes in the common kiln in use, is, that the pipes support very little weight during the firing, the several layers being supported independent of each other, and hence the stems maintain the form originally given to them. In Ireland the pipe-kilns are usually small, and the whole charge of pipes is arranged without any seggars or supports, so that the lower layers are usually deformed from the weight of the upper ones resting upon them. When the kiln is filled with the pipes, some sheets of paper are laid upon them, and then a cover of moist clay formed upon the paper, which is burned off in the commencement of the firing; leaving a solid clay cover, which protects the pipes from the direct action of the flames.

The only exhibitor of clay tobacco-pipes was James M'Loughlin, of Francis-street, in this city, who contributed a case containing a great variety of sizes and forms of common and fancy clay pipes, among which were some imitations of Dutch pipes. They were well formed and well burned, and apparently of excellent material. Most of the pipe-works in Ireland are on a very small scale; and, unfortunately, their proprietors have rarely capital enough to build improved kilns, or to keep a sufficient stock of clay on hands to insure an uniform and well-aged material. We believe that, with one or two exceptions, among whom we can reckon Mr. M'Loughlin, the Irish pipe-makers import their moulds from England and Scotland, notwithstanding the facilities with which such simple instruments might be made by any good smith. It is to be regretted that the great deposit of fine white plastic clay, supposed to be nearly seventy feet in thickness, which exists in the county of Tipperary, between Cahir and Clonmel, is not brought into use for the manufacture of pipes; the samples of this clay which have been tried were chiefly from the upper parts of the bed, and were not sufficiently aged, and could not, therefore, be brought into just competition with the Dorsetshire clay.

### GRINDSTONES, HONES, AND ROTTEN-STONE.

The stones used for grinding cutlery, &c., are sandstones of various qualities. Having already described that class of rocks, we need only make a few remarks in this place upon the peculiar properties which are required to constitute a grindstone. The quality of a sandstone suited for this purpose depends upon three circumstances:—1. The hardness of the stone as a mass, or, in other words, the nature of the cementing material; 2. The size and uniformity of the grains of sand; and 3. The nature of those grains as to whether they are highly crystalline or amorphous quartz. The common revolving grindstones are generally obtained from the new red sandstone, while the finer kinds used in polishing steel, iron, and copper work, and setting the points of gravers, &c., are chiefly obtained from the fine hard grits and argillaceous sandstones of the older rocks. The fine arenaceous varieties of mica slate constitute another class known as rag-stones, sometimes employed as scythe-stones. No rule can, however, be laid down with regard to the class of rocks which yield stones for any particular purpose, as the same quality of stone may be found among rocks of various ages. Thus a large number of the scythe-stones coming into commerce in these countries are obtained from hard siliceous concretions, about from six to eighteen inches in diameter, which form a bed about four feet thick, and known by the local name of greensand, in the lower beds of the cretaceous or chalk series of rocks, in the Blackdown Hills, Devonshire.

Polishing stones, on the other hand, are more or less altered siliceous slates, as distinguished from arenaceous slates, in which the grains of silica would be more or less visible. This kind of stone, called by the different names of novaculite, hone-slate, &c., is found more abundantly of a good quality, than the finer kinds of grindstones. It may be said to belong exclusively to the older slate rocks, and is of various colours, sometimes of a light grayish or buff, sometimes green, and sometimes dark blue. There were four exhibitors of grindstones and hones, none of which represented Irish collections. The chief collection was contributed by C. Meinig of London, and it was certainly a very remarkable one. In it were to be found specimens from Turkey, Persia, Bohemia, Spain, France, Italy, England, Wales, Scotland, Ireland, Arkansas and Niagara in the United States, Peru, &c., in slips, hones, pencils, circular stones, &c., mounted and unmounted. Among the other contributions was a collection of green oil-stones from Snowdon in Wales. We possess analogous rocks in abundance in this country; the hones of Kerry and Donegal are of very superior quality, and we may add those of Wicklow, but unfortunately they were unrepresented.

Rotten-stone and tripoli are nothing more than silica in an extremely fine state of division, and are either composed of the siliceous remains of animalculæ or of minute crystalline grains. When the mass is earthy in character, although composed of nearly pure silica, owing to the fineness of the grain, it is called tripoli; when, on the other hand, it forms a very light friable mass, harsh to the feel, and not unlike a rotten brick, it is called rotten-stone. In general, however, any finely divided siliceous matter which can be used for polishing silver, Britannia metal, brass, may be called tripoli.

There was but one exhibitor of rotten-stone, and the specimen exhibited could scarcely be admitted to come within that definition. Some of the fine siliceous matter exhibited by Mr. Deering, of Cork, under the name of silex, would form an excellent tripoli; and indeed occurs under somewhat similar circumstances to the rotten-stone of Bakewell in Derbyshire.

### FULLER'S EARTH.

This substance is a peculiar hydrated silicate of alumina; that is, a combination of water, silica, and alumina, generally containing a small quantity of silicate of iron, which communicates a greenish tinge to it. It has very remarkable properties, which enable it to be readily distinguished from other earthy substances, one of which is that *it is apparently almost totally soluble in water.* Its use in the arts depends upon its forming a kind of soap, with oil or grease, which it effectually removes from cloth in the process of fulling. There were samples of supposed fuller's earth exhibited, which, although resembling externally in some degree that substance, were little more than a friable clay rich in peaty matter. These mistakes are natural enough in this country, where so few opportunities have hitherto existed for learning the nature and uses of our raw materials; but we hope that the lessons taught by the Exhibition, and the many other facilities now afforded of acquiring more accurate information upon such subjects, will soon put an end to all such mistakes, and at the same time bring to light the mineral resources of Ireland.—W. K. SULLIVAN.

---

The Geological Maps, Sections, and Specimens, exhibited by Richard Griffith, Esq., LL.D., though they may have been passed by by the mere loiterer in search of amusement, yet were highly interesting and instructive to every one in search of information. They had still another point of interest: they are the record of a long life, great part of which has been passed in earnest labour in the pursuit of a favourite science. Dr. Griffith is the father of Irish geology; single-handed he has grappled with the structure of a great and complicated country like Ireland, and has in his last improved edition produced one of the best general geological maps now published of any country in the world.

No one who has not attempted it knows how much labour is required to construct the first geological map of any large district,—how great an amount of knowledge of details must be acquired, and how much patience and perseverance in harmonizing the general results must be exercised, before the boundary lines, and the little patches of colour, can be so placed as to tell the truth, and to tell it in an intelligible and striking manner. Although, to our great regret, and that of all scientific men, the many other important avocations of Dr. Griffith's life have prevented his publishing the results of his labours otherwise than by putting them on his map, yet by that map he must continue to be known as long as the science of geology has a life or a history in Ireland, or in the world. The sections exhibited were calculated to give the spectator some idea of the labours on which were grounded the results depicted on the map. It is not merely a surface map of the boundaries of different kinds of rock; those several masses of earthy matter have been so observed that their position when covered by others, deep in the bowels of the earth, becomes a matter of easy and direct inference. Materials have, in fact, been accumulated for constructing a model as well as a map, which would show the internal structure of Ireland to a depth often far below the level of the sea. The sections exhibited might be looked on as the representation of slices cut out of such a model.

The series of fossils, again, might be looked at in several lights, all equally interesting. First of all, they are the remains of many curious and interesting forms of animal and vegetable life that had never been seen living by the eye of man. They are thus interesting to the naturalist as coming in to complete the series of organic existences, and to fill up the gaps and lacunæ which are to be found in the gradations of organic beings now living on the globe. Secondly, they are interesting to the philosopher, and indeed to mankind generally, as not merely forming a portion of the great mass of organic existences, but as unfolding a history of events; as having an order of succession among themselves, proving that their several sets did not live promiscuously on the globe, but formed successive races of animals and plants; each race coming into existence, increasing and multiplying, occupying the length and breadth of the earth, and then gradually dying out to make room for their successors. They thus become records and documents of a history otherwise concealed in the depths of a remote eternity; and have well been likened to the medals of a race and a dynasty of which no other remnants have been preserved. Thirdly, and lastly, they, in consequence of this succession, become of vast interest and importance to the practical geologist and miner; for as each particular set of rocks in a country is apt to be characterized by peculiar mineral substances useful to man, so we are enabled to recognise any particular group of rocks by the kinds of fossils it contains. The mere variety in the nature of the rock is not sufficient to tell us what group it belongs to, for limestones and sandstones, shales and clays, occur over and over again in every group of rocks, and are often undistinguishable one from another. One little shell, or even fragment of a shell, the leaf of a plant, or the scale of a fish, is, therefore, often of far more value to the practical man than tons of rock specimens.

In the search after coal, for instance, the rocks occurring at the surface in any particular portion of the country might be part of the group in which the coal is found, or they might belong to the group below, or the group above the coal-bearing strata. In order to discover their exact position, and therefore to be assured of the chance of reaching coal below that part of the surface of the ground, within a reasonable depth, the mere examination of the nature of the rock is often insufficient. The most practised geologist might be deceived by trusting to such indications alone, but if he finds in the rocks one of their characteristic fossils, he is then on sure ground, and feels as absolutely certain of the relative position of the rocks as he would of the age of a coin bearing a legible impress and inscription.

In the collection of the fossils exhibited by Dr. Griffith, therefore, the intelligent spectator might read the original documents on which his work was founded, while in the sections and maps he saw depicted the results at which he, together with other men of science, had arrived,—the general history in the compilation of which those documents had been used.—J. B. J.

---

1. ABBOT, H., Mullingar, Co. Westmeath, Proprietor.—Block of Galway marble.

2. ALLAWAY & SON, Sydney, Gloucestershire.—Charcoal tin plates made of Cinderford iron; specimens of the iron from which the plates are made.

3. ANSTED, D. T., Manchester, St. London, Proprietor.—Specimens of native gold, and ingot of gold, from Virginia and North Carolina; garnet rock, associated with the auriferous rock in Virginia; auriferous quartz and crystalline native gold from California.

4. ARMSTRONG, W., New Hall, Ennis, Proprietor.—Silver, lead, and antimony ores, from Kilbreckan Mines; sand-stone flags from the Kildeema Quarry; slate flags from the Kilkee quarry, Co. Clare.

5. BALLANTINE, ALEXANDER, Upper Dorset-street, Dublin, Manufacturer.—Chimney-piece of Galway black marble; baptismal font of Caen stones; bust pedestal of marble, from Skerries, Co. Dublin.

6. BARNES, W. H., Tamworth, Staffordshire, Manufacturer.—Original designs for pipe bowls, modelled in fine clay, from Glascote Clay Works, near Tamworth; modelled designs in clay for glasses for inkstands, and various other purposes; set of draughtsmen in same material; design for a terra top.

7. BELL, J., & Co., Glasgow Pottery, Glasgow, Manufacturers.—Balustrade and large vases in terra cotta.

8. BERESFORD & KELLY, Florence Court, Enniskillen, Manufacturers.—Earthenware, crucibles, bricks, tiles, &c., all produced at the Florence Court Tile Works.

9. BLACKBURN, B., Valentia, Co. Kerry, Producer.—Articles in slate from the quarries in the Island of Valentia, Co. Kerry, viz.:—Round tables for the Refreshment Room, flooring slabs, roofing slates, cisterns to contain 1200 and 500 gallons, billiard table slabs, garden seats, orange tree box, table of slate polished.

10. BLACKER, ST. J. T., Ballylongford, Co. Kerry, Proprietor.—Hollow bricks for building, drainage tiles, pipes, and collars.

11. BLASHFIELD, J. M., Mill Wall, Poplar, London, Manufacturer.—Figures in terra cotta of Diana, from the antique, and of Flora, from model by Bayley; flower pots of various designs; copy of Warwick vase; copy of antique vase; copy of antique tazza; bust of her Majesty the Queen, from a bronze by H. Weigall; bust of the late Duke of Wellington, from a model by H. Weigall; antique bust of Bacchus; copy of antique group of the Niobe; copy of Roubillac's Cupid Sleeping; bowls and vases; consoles; basket flower pot; flower tray; group of virgin and child; terra cotta copy of antique bust of Ariadne; pedestals (various patterns).

12. BLOOD, W., Wicklow, Proprietor.—Specimens of Wicklow pebbles, with cabinet, neatly arranged.

13. BROWNE, MARKHAM, Connoree Mine, Rathdrum, Proprietor.—Samples of copper ore and sulphur stone or iron pyrites; dressed copper ore as sent to market; raw copper, copper slags, and other products of the smelting of copper ore.

14. BROWN, R., Surbiton-hill, Surrey, Inventor and Manufacturer.—Improved Italian tiles, grooved ridge tiles, ornamental plain tiles and valley tiles, plain Gothic ridge tiles.

15. BROWN, R., Ferguslie Fire Clay Works, Paisley, Manufacturer.—Vases, chimney tops, glazed pipes with socket joints, cattle trough, all made of fire-clay.

16. BUTLER, J., Liverpool, Proprietor.—King and Pemberton coal, cannel coal, and coke, from the mines of the Moss Hall Company, Ince, near Wigan.

17. BYERS, J., Stockton-on-Tees, Producer and Manufacturer.—Specimen of lead ore, from Willy Hole Mine, Teesdale; specimen of silver and litharge from lead; one pig each of refined, common, and slag lead; sheet and pipe lead.

18. CASH, J., Dhurode Mine Company's Office, Throgmorton-street, London.—Copper ores from the Dhurode Mine, in West Carberry, Co. Cork, on the estate of Lionel J. Fleming, Esq.

19. CASSIDY, ROBERT, Monasterevan.—Two pillars of siliceous sandstone, beautifully worked, from the quarry of Rosenalis, Queen's Co.

20. COALBROOKDALE COMPANY, Coalbrookdale, near Wellington, Shropshire, Producers.—Samples of pig-iron, bar-iron, and plates, gray pig-iron for light and heavy castings, strong gray forge pig-iron, mottled pig-iron, white pig-iron, samples of forge and of finished bars, chequered plates of various designs for floors.

21. CLASSON & COURTNEY, Bridgefoot-street, Dublin.—Specimens of blister steel.

22. COOPER, E. J., Markree, Co. Sligo.—Inlaid cabinet.

23. CORCORAN, BRYAN, & Co., 36, Mark-lane, London, Manufacturers.—A four-feet diameter millstone for grinding wheat.

24. D'ALTON, J., Summer-hill, Dublin.—Specimens of bog-iron ore and of coal from Clonmore, in the Co. Mayo.

25. DAVIDSON & ARMSTRONG, Piccadilly, Manchester. —A roll of laminated lead, manufactured for the Chinese market, and used by them for lining tea chests, also by our merchants, for packing snuff for export, &c., &c.; roll of pure lead, plated with block tin on both sides, and polished, used for making cisterns for containing water for drinking and culinary purposes; roll of quarter-patent gas pipe, plated with pure tin,—the plating preserves the lead, stiffens the pipe, and renders it suitable for ornamental glass, chandeliers, &c.; length of 5-inch lead pipe, plated inside and outside with block tin.

26. DAVIS, S., Dublin, Manufacturer.—Roman cement and plaster of Paris, Roman cement stone, Portland cement.

27. DEANE, A., York-terrace, Cork.—Chimney-piece and table tops manufactured from marble, raised on the estate of exhibitor, in the Co. Cork.

28. DEERING, J., & Co., Middleton, Co. Cork.—Samples of silex and clay, of a beautiful white colour, found associated with the limestone at Rostellan, Cork Harbour, and well adapted for the manufacture of earthenware, and as tripoli, &c.

29. DENNY, Sir EDWARD, & W. T. CROSBIE, Proprietors. —Pipe drain tiles, manufactured at Gurrane Tilery, near Tralee.

30. DOULTON, J. Jun., Liverpool Pottery, St. Helen's, Lancashire (exhibiting in connexion with H. Doulton & Co., Lambeth, London), Manufacturer.—Terra cotta vases, of various styles and forms, with pedestals; pendant vases; mignionette boxes; laburnum pedestal; ornamental brackets, trusses, and chimney-tops; fern cases and ornamental garden pots; all in terra cotta.

31. DOVE, D., Glasgow, Producer.—Grindstones, from quarries near Glasgow; stones, from Burnfield Quarry.

32. DOWNSHIRE, Marquess of, Hillsboro', Proprietor.—Block of rock-salt, weighing about 30 cwts., from Duncrue, in the Co. Antrim (from beds 860 feet below the surface); copper pyrites, galena, manganese, spathose iron, fullers' earth, and emery-stone, from the Co. Down; granite baptismal font, from Blessington, Co. Wicklow; granite *debris*, commonly called "freestone," from the same county; specimens of galena in veinstone of calc spar, from Blundell Mines, Edenderry; flag of pyritic or alum shale, covered with a crystalline mass of iron pyrites, from Ballybunnion, Co. Kerry.

33. DROGHEDA, The Marquess of, Moore Abbey, Monasterevan.—An inlaid table.

34. DUNN, M., Newcastle-on-Tyne, Inventor and Proprietor.—Anemometer to show the velocity of air-currents in mines; steel mill used for giving light in mines before invention of the safety lamp in 1815; section of Jarrow Colliery; seven safety lamps by different makers; specimens of coal and ironstone, from the Newcastle coal-field

35. EDMONDSON, J. & Co., Dame-street, Dublin.—Terra cotta vases and fern cases.

36. ELY, Marquess of, Ely Lodge, Enniskillen.—A pedestal of polished freestone, a block of rough freestone.

37. EVANS, S., Newtownards Mining Company.—Specimens of lead ore, from the Newtownards Mines, Co. Down.

38. FAHIE, J. K., Tipperary, Manufacturer and Producer.—Filter, vases, &c., of stoneware; drainage pipes; fire-bricks; hollow bricks; tesselated tiles; white, black, and red clays, from Co. Tipperary.

39. FARNLEY IRON COMPANY, Wortley, near Leeds, Manufacturers.—Vases and pedestals, baptismal fonts, urns, flower-boxes, balusters, chimney-tops, and shafts; ornamental trusses, architectural mouldings, sanitary tubes, closet pans, &c., all in terra cotta, and in various styles.

40. FAWCETT, J., Douglas, Isle of Man, Proprietor.—Coal and gypsum, from Leitrim.

41. FERGUSON, MILLER, & Co., Heathfield, Glasgow, Manufacturers.—Fire-bricks, ornamental terra cotta, glazed sewerage pipes, set of three Gothic chimney-tops, ornamental wind-guard ditto, vases in variety, terra cotta fountain 24 feet high.

42. FIELD, H. C., M. D., Blackrock, Dublin.—Crystal of quartz, weighing 87 lbs., found on the property of Exhibitor, in the Co. Londonderry.

43. FLAVELLE, J., 4, D'Olier-street, Dublin, Importer and Proprietor.—Specimens of gold as found in the matrix, and washed gold from the districts of "Ophir," the "Turon River," "Braidwood," the "Hanging Rock," or Peel River diggings, Port Philip, &c., &c.

44. FLOOD, HENRY, Viewmount, Whitehall, Kilkenny, Proprietor.—Flags suited for street flagging and flooring generally; a chimney-piece, made from flags, suited for cottages or second class bed-room.

45. GAILLARD, fils aîné, La Ferté, sous Jouarre, France (agent, G. Dornbusch, London), Manufacturer.—French mill-stones.

46. GARNKIRK COAL CO., Garnkirk, near Glasgow.—Vases, flower-pots, chimney-pots, and gas retorts, manufactured from fire-clay.

47. GENERAL MINING CO. FOR IRELAND, Burgh-quay, Dublin.—Specimens of silver lead ores, argentiferous copper ores, iron pyrites, from Gurtnadyne and Shallee, near Silvermines, Co. Tipperary.

48. GODFREY, Sir W. D., Bart., Kilcoleman Abbey, Co. Kerry.—Lead ore containing 82 per cent. of lead, and 40 oz. 16 dwts. of fine silver per ton, as per assay, raised at the east Annagh Mines on the Godfrey estate, Castlemaine, in the Co. Kerry.

49. GRAVES, REV. JAMES, A. B.; LALOR, JOSEPH, M. D.; CARTER, SAMPSON, JUN., C. E., on the part of the Literary and Scientific Institution.—Geological model map of the county of Kilkenny, showing specimens of the rocks and clays in their relative positions; a collection of minerals and fossils from the same locality.

50. GREAT PEAT WORKING COMPANY OF IRELAND.—Specimens of compressed peat made by Gwynne and Hayes' patent.

51. GREEN, J. B., Lower Baggot-street, Dublin.—Specimens of purple sulphuret of copper, from Horse Island, Co. Cork.

52. GRIFFITH, RICHARD, LL.D., Chairman of the Board of Public Works.—Geological map of Ireland (improved and corrected from former maps published); a reduction of ditto; series of geological sections and views representing the relations of the different rocks, and the chief physical facts connected therewith, in some of the most important geological districts of Ireland. Cabinet of the fossils of the carboniferous series of rocks of Ireland, collected by exhibitor, and systematically arranged in eighty drawers, according to the subdivisions of those rocks shown on his geological map. Cabinet of the fossils of the Irish rocks belonging to the Silurian formation, collected by Exhibitor, and systematically arranged in sixteen drawers, as specified on his geological map.

53. HALL, W., Castlecomer, Co. Kilkenny, Inventor and Proprietor.—A working model of a winding machine for mining operations, by which motion is instantaneously stopped or reversed while the steam-engine or water-wheel is at full speed.

54. HEADECH, W. Killaloe, Manufacturer.—Roofing-slates, slate flags.

55. HENDERSON, J., Townsend-street, Dublin.—Bridgewater, Welsh, and Irish bricks; Welsh slates; chimney-tops, wind guards (registered); vases and pedestals; Grecian chimney-piece; pipes, &c., made of fire-clay.

56. HILL, J., Great Brunswick-street, Dublin, Manufacturer.—Specimens of salt, manufactured from the rock-salt of the new mines of Duncrue, Carrickfergus, on the Mar-

quess of Downshire's estate; viz., stoved salt for table use, Irish fine or butter salt, Irish coarse or provision salt, crystallized salt for bakers' use, pink table salt, bittern, with a sample of the rock-salt.

57. HIRD, DAWSON, & HARDY, Low Moor Iron Works, near Bradford, Yorkshire.—Specimens illustrative of the manufacture of iron, &c.

58. HORAN, MICHAEL, Beresford-place, Dublin, Manufacturer.—Scrap tables of Irish marbles and petrifactions.

59. HODGES, T., Middle Abbey-street, Dublin, Manufacturer.—Coil of composition gas-pipe, on roller, containing 2400 feet in one length, weight, 8 cwts.; coil of inch lead pipe, on roller, containing 1100 feet in one length, weight, 20 cwts.; made from Irish lead.

60. HOEY, R., City-quay, Dublin, Producer.—Geological model of a colliery, Wigan, Lancashire (Earl of Crawford and Balcarras Proprietor), coal therefrom; cannel and anthracite from South Wales.

61. HUTCHINS, S., Fortlands, Charleville, Cork, Proprietor.—Copper ore from Berehaven, Co. Cork.

62. HUXHAMS & BROWN, Exeter.—Millstones of French burrs.

63. JACOB, Dr., Ely-place, Dublin.—Drawing of a horse and cart, made from the coloured sands of the Isle of Wight.

64. JAMES, C. H., Cavendish-row, Dublin.—Pig-iron; clay band ironstone, raw and calcined; black band ironstone, raw and calcined, from Eglinton Iron Company, Ayrshire.

65. JAMES, J., Courtown Harbour, Co. Wexford, Manufacturer.—Draining pipes, tiles, bricks, and pots.

66. JOHNSON, CAMMEL, & Co., Cyclop Steel Works, Sheffield, Manufacturers.—Specimens of steel, in great variety, for the use of engineers, machinists, ship-builders, and other purposes.

67. JOHNSTON, W., Kinlough House, Ballyshannon.—Specimen of tiles for drainage purposes.

68. KAY & HILTON, Fleet-street, Liverpool.—French burr runner millstones.

69. KENNETH, A., & Co., Kilwinning, Ayrshire, Manufacturers.—Fountain, sun-dial pillar, chimney-cans, and glazed pipes, made of fire-clay.

70. KENNY, COURTNEY, Ballinrobe, Co. Mayo.—Black and white Irish marble tables; pyramids in marble; specimens of double refracting spar, from the Co. Mayo; specimen of amethyst, from Achill; specimen of rock crystal, from Blasket Island, Co. Kerry.

71. KERR, W. H., & Co., Worcester, Manufacturers.—Samples of felspar, clays, and other materials used in producing earthenware.

72. KERRY, LOCAL COMMITTEE OF THE COUNTY OF.—Chimney-piece of Kerry marble; marble slab; bust pillar marble; draining tiles, and pottery made in Co. Kerry; specimens of lead and copper ores, from the Kenmare mines at Cloontoo and Shanagurry.

73. KLASEN, P. J., Ferbane, King's County.—Working model of a quartz crushing and cleaning machine (scale, one inch to the foot).

74. KYLE, S. M., Archdeacon of Cork, Dyke House, Cork.—Specimen of amethyst, from Co. Cork.

75. LAWRIE, W., Downham Market, Designer and Producer.—Alms-box and pedestal for a church, in Caen stone, carved (style, early English).

76. LEE, J., Dale End, Birmingham, Inventor.—"Combination" gold-digging tool, available for use as a shovel, scrape, pick-axe, granite breaker, and crow-bar; a patent oval tubular crow-bar.

77. LIMERICK LOCAL COMMITTEE, D. W. RAIMBACH and W. FITZGERALD, Secretaries.—Samples of copper pyrites, iron pyrites, galena, hematite, micaceous iron ore, carbonate of barytes, glass-sand, fire and pottery clays, anthracite culm, naturally compressed peat, from the counties bordering the Shannon; building stone, from the city of Limerick; and red marble, from Ballysimon.

78. LITTLE, P., Dorrington-street, Hulme, Manchester, Designer and Manufacturer.—Table slab of Galway marble, inlaid with Egyptian and Italian marbles.

79. LONDON & PENZANCE SERPENTINE CO., Mr. JOHN ORGAN, Manager, Penzance, Cornwall, Producer.—Ladies' inlaid work-tables, octagon vases, Albert vase, pedestal and vase, chimney-piece, pair of Luxor obelisks, scrap inlaid zodiac vase, pair of Hebe ewers, pair of King's needles, large ink-stands, pair of Hebe jugs, and centre piece, pair of large bell vases, large tazza, Wellington tablets, pair of fluted vases, miniature table, crosses, polished slab.

80. MARSHALL, S., Letterkenny, Proprietor.—Potters' clay, peat, lead ore, and other minerals, from Co. Donegal.

81. M'ANASPIE, P. & T., Great Brunswick-street, Dublin.—Portland and granite stone cements, castings, &c.; imitation of ornamental marbles in scagliola.

82. M'CULLAGH, D., Armagh, Manufacturer.—Chimney-piece of Armagh marble.

83. M'GARRY, MICHAEL, & SONS, Cook-street, Dublin.—Samples of sheet and pipe lead made by the pressure process.

84. M'LOUGHLIN, JAMES, Francis-street, Dublin.—Clay tobacco-pipes.

85. MEINIG, C., Leadenhall-street, London.—Hones, oil-stones, and grindstones, mounted and unmounted, from various parts of the world.

86. MILLAR, JOHN, Edinburgh.—Statue of Her Majesty the Queen and His Royal Highness Prince Albert, in hard fire-clay, capable of resisting the weather; eagle vase and pedestal, richly carved in stone, from Malta; wine-cooler and cover, from Staffordshire.

87. MINING COMPANY OF IRELAND, R. P. ALLEN, Secretary, Lower Ormond-quay, Dublin, Producers and Manufacturers.—Specimens of copper ore, showing the various stages of the mechanical preparation of the ores to fit them for smelting; native copper and argentiferous lead from Knockmahon Mines, county of Waterford; samples of lead ore, and a complete series of specimens illustrative of the system of crushing and concentrating them, from Luganure Mines, county of Wicklow; argentiferous lead ore and native silver, from Ballycorus mine, county of Dublin; pig lead, samples of sheet and lead pipe; samples of different sized shot; cake of silver, weighing 1600 oz., made by Pattinson's process, from lead obtained from Luganure ore, and litharge obtained in the cupellation of the rich lead at the Ballycorus Lead Smelting Works; samples of native sulphuret of antimony, from Clontibret Mines, in the county of Armagh; anthracite coal and culm (small coal) from the Slieveardagh collieries in the county of Tipperary, and Lisnacor, in the county of Cork.

88. MINTON, HOLLINS, & Co., Stoke-upon-Trent, Staffordshire, Manufacturers.—Specimens of indented diaper tiles, plain and coloured and gilded; encaustic tiles of various patterns; Venetian and mosaic tiles; imitations of Alhambra and Majolica tiles; Dutch tiles, plain and printed.

89. MOLLOY, J., Tullamore, King's Co., Manufacturer.—Marble table and dish; fish carved from marble, the produce of Ballyduff Quarries, near Tullamore.

90. MONKLAND IRON AND STEEL COMPANY, W. MURRAY, West George-street, Glasgow, Producers.—A series of specimens, 6-inch cubes, illustrative of the various rocks composing the Lanarkshire coal measures; specimens of the various ironstones in the raw and calcined state; coal and limestone, &c., used by the Company in the manufacture of iron; a complete series showing all the stages of the manufacture of pig and wrought-iron; samples of railway angle and other iron, &c.

91. MOORE, REV. OGLE, Blessington, Co. Wicklow.—Black oxide of manganese.

92. MORGAN & SONS, Llanelly, Carmarthenshire, Producers.—Anthracite, or stone coal, for drying malt, hops, and corn; fuel for ocean steamers, steam boilers, for Arnott's stoves and cooking purposes.

93. MORGAN, R. W., Lower Gloucester-street, Dublin, Importer.—Green oil-stone hones from Snowdon, North Wales.

94. MORGAN & REES, Jewin Crescent, London, Importers and Proprietors.—Plumbago melting-pots for refiners, one of which has been used sixty times at Brown & Wingrove's, London; German and English black-lead melting-pots, Hessian crucibles for goldsmiths and assayers, Cornish and London crucibles for chemists, creosote employed by French refiners, skittle-pots used by silversmiths, &c.

95. NIXEY, W. G., Moor-street, Soho, London.—Small block of fine plumbago, artificially prepared for the manufacture of pencils, by the compression of plumbago powder.

96. NICHOL, W. & P., Dalkey.—Obelisk of Dalkey granite; model of a monument.

97. O'FLAHERTIE, G. F., Lemonfield, Oughterard, Proprietor.—Galena, barytes, fluor spar, carbonate of lime, sulphuret of zinc, iron pyrites, from county of Galway.

98. OLIVER, Northumberland, Proprietor.—Two drawings of Walbottle colliery.

99. PADGETT, WM. & Co., Tipperary.—Fire-bricks.

100. PENNY, J. (Museum of Irish Industry), Stephen's-green, Dublin.—Specimens of Irish marbles.

101. POWER, JAMES, Harcourt-street, Dublin.—A marble vase.

102. QUILLIAM & CREER, Castletown, Isle of Man, Manufacturers.—Cruciform monument in Manx marble.

103. RITCHIE, F., & SONS, Belfast.—Asphalte flagging.

104. ROAKE, J. W., Newbury, Berkshire.—Peat from Newbury, Berkshire.

105. ROBINSON, J., Belfast, Designer and Manufacturer.—Stone flower vase; Sienna marble chimney-piece.

106. ROYAL DUBLIN SOCIETY, Proprietors.—A collection of the marbles of Ireland; door-case; bust pedestals; granite columns. Samples of steel made from bar-iron, by a new process, in the Society's laboratory. A collection of 245 specimens, representing the natural rocks, minerals, soils, &c. &c., of the county of Dublin, presented to the Society by Henry O'Hara, Esq., C. E. A collection of forty specimens of plastic clays, adapted for the manufacture of bricks, draining pipes, and common pottery.

107. ROYAL HIBERNIAN MINING COMPANY, Gracechurch-street, London.—Specimens of silver lead ore from Clogher and Castlemaine Mines, in the county of Kerry.

108. RUSSELL, Mrs., Dunfanaghy.—Specimens of Dunlewey marbles, West Donegal, the source of employment in Mrs. Russell's Missionary Industrial Schools.

109. RUTHERFORD, J., Castle-street, Belfast, Manufacturer.—Stucco and alabaster pedestals, painted in imitation of marble.

110. SADLIER, THOS., Mulla, Tullamore, King's Co., Manufacturer.—Uncharred peat; peat charcoal, in sods, and granulated; apparatus for household use of peat charcoal.

111. SHIELDS, J., SON, & Co., Ringsend Docks, Dublin, and Ballymacarrett, Belfast, Manufacturers.—Railway and foundry coke made from Marley Hill coal; coal from Marley Hill Colliery, Newcastle-on-Tyne.

112. SKELLERN, R. H., Great Castle-street, Regent-street, London.—Coloured sands from Alum Bay, Isle of Wight.

113. STEPHENS, —, Melbourne, Australia.—The "Prince Albert" nugget of gold, weighing nearly six pounds.

114. SYNGE, F., Glanmore, Ashford, Co. Wicklow, Producer.—Specimens of slate flags manufactured from the Glanmore Slate and Flag Quarry.

115. TALBOT DE MALAHIDE, Lord.—Minerals; Green porphyry and red conglomerate, from the island of Lambay; lias limestone, from Marston, Somersetshire.

116. THOMAS, W., Producer.—Silver lead ore, containing 41oz. of silver to the ton, from Killinogue Mines, county of Cork.

117. VIEILLE MONTAGNE ZINC MINING COMPANY, per H. F. SCHMOLL, Agent General to the Company, 12, Manchester Buildings, Westminster, Producers.—Specimens of calamine, silicate of zinc, and other ores, from Vieille Montagne, Belgium; slab of raw zinc or spelter; specimen of distilled zinc, illustrative of the old process of distillation; rolled zinc, of different thicknesses.

118. WALKER, J., Corran, Larne, Co. Antrim.—Fire and common bricks and crucibles; clay suited for fire-proof, cane, and Rockingham wares; various samples of other useful clays; flint, raw and prepared, for potters' use; limestone and other materials employed by the potter.

119. WANDESFORDE, HON. C. B. C., Castlecomer, Proprietor.—Anthracite, ironstone, fire-clay, slate-clay, for red pottery, and alum shale for the manufacture of alum.

120. WARNER, P., Ardrie, by Saltcoats, Ayrshire, Proprietor.—Smoke nuisance and wind guard chimney cans; fire and common bricks.

121. WATSON, H., Newcastle-upon-Tyne, Manufacturers.—Sir H. Davy's, The George Stephenson, and The Clanny safety lamps, used in the coal mines of Northumberland and Durham.

122. WHITE, Mrs., Kilikee, Co. Dublin.—Two tables in Florentine mosaic.

123. WICKLOW COPPER MINE COMPANY, per E. BARNES, Resident Director, Producers.—Specimens of ores, &c., from Ballymurtagh Mine, county of Wicklow.

124. WILLANS, OBADIAH, Island-bridge, Dublin, Proprietor.—Ores of iron, lead, manganese; decomposed granite, yellow ochre, sulphate of barytes, and rotten-stone, from Donegal and Leitrim.

125. WILLIAMS, D., Bangor, North Wales, Manufacturer.—Billiard tables, baths, cisterns, grave-stones, and other articles made of slate.

126. WOODWARD, BROTHERS, Rhos-y-Medre Quarries, near Ruabon, Denbighshire, Manufacturers.—Welsh grindstones in variety.

# CLASS II.

---

## CHEMICAL AND PHARMACEUTICAL PREPARATIONS AND PROCESSES.

ALTHOUGH it would be difficult to point out a single manufacture in which chemical forces do not play a part, yet there are some in which these predominate so much, that we may call them Chemical Manufactures. To this category belong those of porcelain, of dyed and printed fabrics, leather, the production of artificial soda, &c. In some of these manufactures a certain substance is made to undergo changes in composition, or in colour, by the addition of chemical agents, but without undergoing any considerable change in form. In others, again, a number of natural or artificial substances are mingled together, and fashioned into various articles by mechanical means, which are directly available as utensils, and for other purposes. And, finally, there is a third class, which consist in the preparation of a number of chemical compounds, such as acids, alkalies, pigments, from mineral, vegetable, and animal substances, which constitute in part the raw materials of the chemical processes employed in the two first classes of chemical manufactures.

It is only with the manufactures forming the last-named division that we have now to deal. Under this head would come all the non-metallic elementary substances, such as sulphur, phosphorus; salts, such as alum; organic compounds produced by various chemical processes, such as tartaric acid, wood spirit, varnishes, and mineral, vegetable, and animal pigments, such as white lead, indigo, carmine, &c. To this class also belong all those rare substances which exist in minerals, plants, and animals,—those isolated by the chemist, and those produced artificially by him. And, finally, we may also include in this class the different preparations employed in medicine.

Class II. was but very imperfectly represented in the Exhibition, although examples of nearly all the groups of substances which we have enumerated were to be found there. Some of the chief chemical manufacturers in Ireland contributed nothing, and the same remark will equally apply to the far more extensive ones of Great Britain. Most of the specimens were small, and there was a total absence of those great crystallized masses which formed so remarkable a feature in the Exhibition of 1851.

We shall notice in the following pages such of those substances exhibited as present any special interest from an Irish point of view; such as are interesting from their origin or uses; and, finally, those of the rarer substances which possess peculiar scientific interest.

### IODINE AND SALTS OF POTASH CONTAINED IN SEA-WEED.

From time immemorial a peculiar industry has existed on the maritime shores of the south of Europe, which consists in burning a number of plants belonging chiefly to the same family as the common mangel wurzel and beet, and collecting the ashes which, made principally from one plant, is called in Spain *barilla*; whilst made from another plant, it is called at Narbonne, in France, *salicor*. These ashes contain a number of soluble salts, which may be washed out of them, and which consist, for the most part, of soda in combination with certain acids. For example, it contains soda in combination with muriatic acid or spirits of salt, constituting common salt; with sulphuric acid, constituting glauber salt or sulphate of soda; and with carbonic acid, the peculiar gas which communicates effervescing properties to soda-water, champagne, &c., constituting the common carbonate of soda of commerce, which is familiarly known as washing-soda. The ashes of these plants contain also small quantities of potash, chiefly in combination with the same acids as the soda, which it resembles in a very remarkable way. The ashes of many trees, and indeed of most land vegetables, although resembling, in a striking degree, the ashes forming barilla, differ from the latter in this way, that whilst the barilla is characterized by a predominance of carbonate of soda, the ash of trees consists chiefly of potash. In countries where large forests exist, such as North America, Russia, Sweden, Hungary, Illyria, &c., the ashes of wood, consumed as fuel for domestic or manufacturing purposes, or of the stumps and branches of timber trees cut down for supplying the timber used in commerce, is lixiviated with water, which dissolves the soluble matter; this liquor is then evaporated in a pot until a solid saline mass, of a brown colour, is obtained, which is hence called in commerce *pot-ashes*, or when calcined so as to burn out all traces of organic matter, and assume a pure white or slightly bluish white colour, *pearl-ash*. The potash in this mass, like the soda in barilla, exists in combination with many acids, but a large proportion is always present as carbonate. If we burn sea-weeds we shall obtain another ash, called *kelp* in Ireland and Scotland, which contains both alkalies, although from the rude and imperfect process usually followed, a good deal of what naturally exists in the sea-weed is lost. All these substances were formerly used in the manufacture of soap and glass, and in bleaching; their value depending almost entirely upon the quantity of carbonate of potash or of soda which they contained. Since the beautiful discovery of Le Blanc, by which carbonate of soda can be obtained from common salt, the trade in barilla has nearly ceased, as did that from kelp, until a curious discovery again rendered it important. This was the discovery of the substance called *iodine*. An ingenious manufacturer, of the name of Courtois, contrived a process by which the potash salts existing in kelp, and which had hitherto been of little use, might be utilized in the manufacture of nitrate of potash or saltpetre, which, in consequence of the protracted wars then waging in Europe, was in great demand for the manufacture of gunpowder. In endeavouring, in 1812, to decompose whatever salts remained in the mother liquors of his kelp leys by sulphuric acid, he discovered iodine, the true nature and properties of which were made known by Gay-Lussac, to whom Courtois submitted the new substance. In 1826, M. Balard, during his researches, already alluded to in our article on salt, discovered another substance analogous to iodine, to which the name of *bromine* has been given.

At first neither of these substances had any practical value; and they were mere chemical curiosities, but Coindet having shown that the action of burnt sponge, and certain mineral waters,—employed in the cure of *goitre*, a peculiar disease, to which many persons are subject in the mountainous districts of Europe, especially in the Alps,—depended upon the iodine which they contained, large quantities were soon employed in medicine. There was one exhibitor of iodine in the Exhibition, who, we believe, is a very large manufacturer, Mr. John Ward, of Ramelton, in the county of Donegal. The samples which we have seen of his products were remarkable for their purity as commercial articles; and now that this manufacture, especially the production of potash salts, is becoming every day more important, we are glad to find that it is become a permanent Irish manufacture. A small specimen of iodine, among the contributions of the Dublin Chemical Society, deserves also to be noticed, as evidencing a good deal of progress by the members of that body, who have associated themselves for the worthy object of mutual improvement.

A large quantity of iodine is employed in combination with potash, under the name of iodide of potassium, of which considerable quantities are manufactured in Dublin and exported. The preparation of this substance is very simple, the great point to be attended to being, that there be no excess of potash on the one hand, or the resulting salt would attract moisture from the atmosphere, or of iodine on the other, which would give an orange tint to the product. The salt prepared in Dublin is free from both these faults, and is in every way creditable to the manufacturers; as the beautiful samples, probably the finest made in Great Britain, exhibited by the Apothecaries' Hall, by Boileau Brothers, and by Boyd and Goodwin, fully prove.

As the sea seems destined in future to be the great source of potash, the applications of which are continually extending, the manufacture of the salts of kelp, and of sea water itself, must gradually become developed into a great and lucrative branch of industry; and as Ireland has undoubted advantages for engaging in it, we will say a few words upon the process by which the different salts are separated, in order to direct attention to the subject. As we are not acquainted with the process adopted by Mr. Ward, we shall describe that followed by MM. Cournerie, of Cherbourg in the north-east of France, who, after M. Courtois, the discoverer, are the oldest manufacturers of iodine in Europe, and to a great extent the inventors of this branch of industry. From the imperfect mode in which kelp is prepared by the peasantry, a good deal of the alkalies is dissipated, and the carbonates especially are decomposed, so that kelp rarely contains more than 2 to 3 per cent. of carbonate of soda out of the 33 to 56 parts of soluble salts which it contains; a quantity which is too unimportant to be extracted separately, and is usually neutralized by some sulphuric acid, in order to convert it into sulphate in the commencement of the operation. The kelp purchased from the peasantry is reduced to a coarse powder, and is then placed in rectangular filters having a false bottom of sheet-iron, pierced with holes, two-thirds of the filter being filled. These filters are arranged in pairs, so that while one is being filled the other is working, the water being let in upon the kelp by means of a cock, until it has risen several inches above it. After resting for some short time upon it, a cock in the bottom is opened, and the liquor filters through, carrying with it, in solution, the greater part of the chlorides of sodium (common salt) and of potassium, which are much more soluble than the sulphate of potash, the greater part of which remains undissolved behind. The liquid, after passing through the first filter, is pumped up upon the second, by which means a very strong saline ley or solution is obtained, which is now boiled down in a battery of three pans, the cold liquor coming first into the pan farthest from the fire, and the final concentration being effected in the pan placed directly over it. At a certain degree of concentration the common salt begins to crystallize out, and is removed, as fast as the crystals form, by a ladle pierced with holes. The fire is then stopped off, and after a repose of about five minutes, to allow the whole of the salt to subside, the liquor is drawn off into a wooden crystallizer lined with lead, where the sulphate of potash separates and adheres to the sides of the vessel as a hard crust; whilst chloride of potassium, being more soluble, does not crystallize for some time, when it separates in much larger crystals; these are easily separated on drawing off the liquor, which is again evaporated as before. The residue of kelp left in the filter is now washed with boiling water, which dissolves out the sulphate of potash, with some chloride of potassium and sodium. These are separated by evaporation and crystallization, as in the former case; the process being, however, conducted in another set of pans and crystallizing vessels. The salts thus separated are further purified by re-crystallization, the mother liquors of all being put together for the extraction of the iodine and bromine, which is done as soon as all the salts which can be separated by the process just described have been obtained.

The mother liquors resulting from the working up of large quantities of kelp, and which have been so far evaporated for the separation of the other salts, consist of nearly concentrated solutions of iodide and bromide of potassium or of sodium. Chlorine, the peculiar gas obtained from common salt, and employed in bleaching, is passed into the mother liquors with the object of taking away the potash from the iodine, and setting it free; chloride of potassium being at the same time formed. On allowing the whole to rest, the iodine precipitates to the bottom of the vessel; the liquid is decanted off, and the iodine washed with a little water and put to drain in a clay pot with a pierced false bottom, after which it is dried by placing it upon paper resting upon a layer of dry wood ashes or plaster of Paris; when this has taken place, it is distilled in vessels of clay of a peculiar form. The liquor decanted from the iodine is now evaporated to dryness, and distilled in vessels of lead with a mixture of black oxide of manganese, and oil of vitriol or sulphuric acid, upon which the bromine passes over, and is collected in vessels containing concentrated sulphuric acid, in which it sinks, and is thus preserved from fuming and injuring the health of the persons employed. Iodine is a solid substance in crystalline scales of a grayish-black colour; when heated, it readily volatilizes, forming a vapour of an exceedingly beautiful violet colour. Hence the name *iodine*, from a Greek word signifying *violet*. Bromine, on the other hand, is a liquid of an intensely deep red colour, and a density nearly three times that of water, and producing, even at an ordinary temperature, a highly irritating and insupportable vapour. Hence, the name *bromine*, from a Greek word, signifying *fetid smell*. No specimens of this substance were exhibited, and we do not know whether Mr. Ward prepares any from his mother liquors. The substances obtained from kelp are, therefore, sulphate of potash, chloride of potassium, common salt, iodine, and bromine, which would be produced in the following approximate proportions: for each 100 lbs. of sulphate of potash there would be obtained 113 lbs. of chloride of potassium, 150 lbs. of common salt, 1 lb. 2½ oz. of iodine, and from 1 to 1½ oz. of bromine.

To such of our readers as may be unacquainted with the uses to which potash is applied in the arts, it may be interesting to mention a few of the manufactures in which it is employed. We shall, at the same time, mention a few of the chief uses of the very similar substance, soda; and also those in which one of those bodies may be substituted for the other.

### APPLICATIONS OF POTASH AND SODA.

#### OF POTASH.

- Bohemian glass.
- The finer kinds of flint glass.
- Saltpetre, for gunpowder.
- Potash alum, for dyeing, and the preparation of lakes.
- Chlorate of potash for detonating gun caps.
- Prussiate of potash.
- Soft soaps.
- Manufacture of chamois leather.
- Preparation of strings for musical instruments.
- And a great variety of salts used by chemists, and in medicine, such as cream-of-tartar.

#### OF SODA.

- As salt for culinary purposes.
- Bicarbonate of soda for effervescing draughts, and as a substitute for yeast in making bread.
- As borax (a compound of soda with a peculiar acid called boracic) for making artificial gems, for glazing china and earthenware, and for soldering gold, platinum, and other metals.
- As carbonate of soda, for washing for domestic purposes, bleaching, manufacture of lakes, hard soap, resin soaps, window glass, and some kinds of flint glass, plate glass, bottle glass, &c.
- As phosphate of soda in calico printing, &c.
- And in various compounds used in medicine, &c.

#### USES COMMON TO BOTH.

- In various kinds of glass, in which both alkalies are employed.
- In bleaching vegetable tissues.
- In making lawn finer, and making artificial lawn and muslin from coarse cotton fabrics.
- In cleansing wool and woollen fabrics.
- And in the preparation of various compounds of chlorine for disinfecting purposes, and as bleaching agents by the laundress, &c.

## ALUM.

We have frequently alluded in the preceding pages to the composition of clay, which was stated to be chiefly a combination of silica and alumina. The former we know in many forms, as flint, rock, crystal, &c.; the latter very rarely occurs in an uncombined state; the beautiful gem, known as the sapphire, may be considered as almost pure crystallized alumina. Alumina is the oxide of a metal, which, having lately been obtained in considerable quantity, appears to be possessed of very remarkable properties; among which we may enumerate that, while it is lighter than glass, it is of a brilliant silver white, and does not tarnish, and bears a high polish like silver, and like it may be drawn into wire, cast, and rolled into plaster. It is, however, with its combination with oxygen, that we have to deal at present; that compound of alumina is a base, and will combine with an acid and form a salt. Thus, with sulphuric acid or oil of vitriol, it forms sulphate of alumina; with vinegar, acetate of alumina; both of which are used in dyeing, the latter being commonly known as *red liquor*. The sulphate of potash, obtained from kelp, if mixed with a solution of sulphate of alumina, will form what is called a double salt, which will crystallize in octahedrons or eight-sided figures. Alum is a good example of a curious law of chemistry, which we cannot do more than allude to here. It is this:—that some substances resemble one another so completely in certain of their chemical characters, that one may be substituted for the other in a compound, *without* altering the shape in which the substance would crystallize. In the case of alum, for instance, we could take out the potash and put ammonia or spirit of hartshorn in its place without producing any perceptible change to the eye in the nature of the alum; or we could take out the alumina and replace it with the red oxide of iron—which is the peculiar substance that gives the red colour to soils—and the form of the alum would be unchanged, but not its colour. Finally, we might take out the iron and put another peculiar substance in its place called oxide of chromium, but we could not put chrome or iron in place of the potash. If we suppose a wall built of flat tiles and of bricks, and that the tiles represent potash and the bricks alumina, we may take out a tile and replace it by a piece of anything else having the same shape, but not by a brick; and in like manner we could replace the brick by something in the same form. In this way we get different kinds of alum—thus we have potash alum, and soda alum, and ammonia alum, &c.; but it is only those alums having alumina in them that are used in commerce, as their action in general depends upon this substance.

Alums occur naturally formed in many volcanic districts, such as Mont d'Or, in France, but especially in Italy, as at the Grotta di Alume on Cape Miseno. The greater part employed in commerce is, however, produced artificially, from two sources—one the *alum-stone*, and the other the *alum-slate* and *alum earth*. The former is a kind of alum already formed, but having more alumina than is required to form true alum, and is a volcanic product. Although it occurs in many districts, it is, nevertheless, a comparatively rare substance, the principal locality in Europe being at Tolfa, near Civita Vecchia, in the States of the Church. A considerable quantity of alum is there produced by burning the stone in heaps, or in peculiar furnaces, after which it is moistened with water, and allowed to crumble for four or five months; it is thus converted into a soft mud, out of which the alum is washed, and is obtained in crystals, covered with a ferruginous rose-red powder. It may be distinguished by this tint from English alum, to which it is superior in purity from iron, and is hence principally employed in dyeing the finer shades of pinks, &c. Roman alum is sometimes called cubic alum, in consequence of some of the crystals occasionally occurring in the form of cubes, and was first made by Jean de Castro, in the year 1460 or 1465. Previous to that period, all the alum consumed in Europe came from Rocca, the modern Edessa, in Syria, hence the name of rocc-alum.

In the alum-stone we have seen that the alum exists ready formed to a great extent. This is not the case with alum-slate and alum-earth, which merely contain the materials for making the sulphate of alumina; it being necessary to add nearly the whole of the potash. Alum-slate is the principal material used in these countries for the manufacture of alum; it consists of a decomposing slate, of a black colour, from the presence of bituminous matter. The alumina of the alum is derived from the slate, the sulphuric acid being produced from iron pyrites, a compound of sulphur and iron, which is disseminated both in small crystals, of a golden yellow colour, and chiefly in a minute state of division as a black powder. By the action of the air upon the surface of these rocks, a species of combustion takes place; the pyrites absorb oxygen from the air, by which the sulphur is converted into sulphuric acid, which, in great part, leaves the iron, and combines with the alumina of the slate, forming sulphate of alumina, and this gradually effloresces to the surface, where it forms crystals. This is a very slow process, and for manufacturing purposes it is often necessary to hasten it, by quarrying a quantity of the rock, and building up great pyramidal ridges, the ore being mixed with more or less coal, according as may be necessary to keep up a slow combustion or roasting for some time. The heap, when thus prepared, is set fire to, and burns for about 60 to 70 hours, the bituminous matter of the slate also acting as a fuel. By this roasting the slate loses about 25 to 30 per cent., and sometimes even one-half, of its bulk. When sufficiently decomposed, the roasted ore is lixiviated, that is, washed with water in a series of cisterns, arranged one higher than another, so that the liquid from one may pass readily into the next. This liquid, which consists of sulphate of alumina, sulphate of iron, or copperas, sulphate of magnesia, and some other salts, formed in the roasted ore, is then evaporated in a long cistern, formed of brick and cement, and arched over so as to form part of a flue, through which, and consequently over the surface of the liquid, the flame from a furnace is made to pass; the liquid is thus made to boil at the surface, while the vapour is carried off by the draft. When sufficiently evaporated, it is run into leaden or copper cisterns, heated at the bottom, in which the evaporation is finished; and it is then passed into the settling cisterns, where any sediment deposits. Sulphate of potash, or of ammonia, or chloride of potassium (the former being best adapted), is next added, when a double salt will be formed, which will be precipitated in the form of a fine powder, termed *alum-flour*. This powder has a brownish colour, from the mixture of compounds of iron; to free it from this colour it is washed with a little water, then dissolved in boiling water, so as to form a concentrated solution, which is allowed to settle, and is then run into vessels called *roaching or growing casks*. These casks are about 5 feet high, and about 3 feet in diameter, and formed of a number of staves, nicely fitted together, and bound with hoops, which can be readily taken off. Here crystals begin to form, which hang down from the top, and shoot out from the sides, whilst a layer is deposited on the whole of the inside of the cask In ten days or a fortnight, according to the kind of weather, the hoops are taken off, and the staves removed, when a perfectly formed cask of alum is exposed. A hole is then bored in the side of it, near the bottom, through which the liquid remaining after the separation of the crystals, and called *mother liquor*, is run off.

To make one ton of alum about 130 tons of roasted shale, and about 410 lbs. of sulphate of potash, are required. The mother liquor from the *alum flour*, when acid, is placed in contact with pieces of old iron, some of which will be dissolved; and a quantity of copperas may be got from the solution, after which a quantity of crude Epsom salts may be obtained, which by crystallization will be obtained pure.

The chief uses of alum are,—for dyeing tissues of a pink and other shades of red; for forming the basis of lake and other colours; for satining room papers; for sizing paper; for making scagliola, Keene's, Martin's, and other cements; for the manufacture of glove and other tawed leathers; for making sulphate and phosphate of alumina; for the clarification of syrups, &c.

No alum is made in Ireland, and yet we possess the materials in abundance; along the coast of Kerry, especially at Ballybunnion, near the mouth of the Shannon, alum-slate occurs in immense masses. Associated with the beds of coal in the Coal Island coal-field, in the county of Tyrone, are considerable quantities of bituminous shale, highly impregnated with iron pyrites, and well adapted for the manufacture of alum. At Castlecomer, and other parts of the Kilkenny coal-field, a similar rock occurs, a specimen of which was exhibited by the Hon. C. B. C. Wandesforde. In most of these localities facilities exist for the economical manufacture of alum; and it is to be hoped that this source of industry will soon be taken advantage of, as well as those founded on the manufacture of kelp and sea-water, pointed out in speaking of iodine.

There was but one exhibitor of alum, W. Moberly, of Landsend, near Whitby, who contributed a half cask, showing the mode of crystallization, and other peculiarities. The Whitby Alum Works are the chief works of this kind in Great Britain; the quantity annually made there averaging from 3000 to 4000 tons.

## SUBSTANCES USED FOR DYEING, OR AS PAINTS.

### PRUSSIATE OF POTASH.

In most large cities there is a class of poor persons who make their livelihood by collecting the offal of the houses, and disposing of it for the purposes of different manufactures. Nowhere is this class so developed as in Paris, where the *chiffonier* forms a peculiar type, almost unknown elsewhere. It is more than probable that not a single one of our readers ever thought of what becomes of the various objects which such persons are seen collecting. Year after year we buy clothes of wool or cotton, we wear them out to a certain point, they then pass into other hands,—what becomes of them after? They are not annihilated, they may change form, but, nevertheless, the elements of which they are composed do not cease to exist. Let us examine the ragman's basket,—what do we turn up first? We have pieces of cotton and linen rags,—the raw material of the paper-maker, who transforms these unsightly objects, probably, into the most delicately-scented note-paper. Here, again, we have pieces of paper of all kinds,—what can they be for? They form materials for making pasteboard, dolls' heads, and occasionally *papier mache*. What a singular history we have here; the ball dress of a lady drops into the rag-basket, reappears as a *billet doux;* disappears again, to reappear once more in the drawing-room, or the nursery, as a work-box or a doll. Returning to the basket, we find pieces of woollen cloths of different colours,—what use can we put them to, as they do not make paper? The bits of scarlet cloth which are dyed with cochineal are boiled with soda, to extract the colouring matter, which is used in dyeing chessmen, billiard-balls, &c.; or we may sort the different coloured cloths, and prepare from them materials for making flock papers for rooms, or we might make roofing felt of them. From the bones rejected from our dinner-tables are made knife-handles, buttons, and a thousand other articles of a similar kind; or we may obtain oil from them, on the one hand, from which soap is made; and, on the other, glue, or the most transparent gelatine, from which ornaments, or visiting cards, may be made,—the residue being burned to make ivory-black for the manufacture of blacking, or phosphorus for the manufacture of lucifer matches; or we may use it for manure; or as an element in the manufacture of earthenware; and, finally, we may distil the entire bone and get an ivory-black fit for making sugar white, whilst another substance is at the same time obtained, from which smelling salts are made. Thus the bones thrown to the dogs, in this utilitarian age, may come back to us again on our dinner-table, as a part of our dress, as the medium of our politeness, as a means of washing our hands, lighting our fires, and blacking our boots; and, finally, as the contents of that all-important article, a lady's smelling bottle! Could our readers have supposed that a ragman's basket supplied the raw materials for so many manufactures? And yet so it is; modern chemistry has taught us how, out of the most vile and apparently the most worthless rubbish, the most useful and frequently the most beautiful articles may be elaborated. The Exhibition was full of examples of such transformations; let us select one. We will suppose we have a quantity of old woollen rags too bad to be used for any of the purposes before mentioned, and animal offal, such as comb-makers' shavings, pigs' toes, dried blood, &c.; if we calcine these substances for a considerable time with pearl ash, or carbonate of potash (which is the principal ingredient in the ash left by trees when burned), and some iron filings, in an egg-shaped iron pot, stirring it from time to time,—we shall obtain a mass which, when boiled with water, the insoluble impurities removed, and the liquid evaporated, will yield beautiful yellow crystals of a substance known as *prussiate of potash.*

But what is the use of these yellow crystals? We shall recount a little of their future history. Distilled with oil of vitriol, the salt is decomposed, and prussic acid formed, the most violent of all poisons—prussic acid made from woollen rags, blood, and pigs' toes! What more striking example of the wonderful transformations effected by chemistry! This acid, in a peculiar state of combination with iron, forms what is called ferro-prussic or ferro-cyanic acid, which, combined with potash, forms the yellow salt of which we are speaking: and which, although it may be said to contain prussic acid, is nevertheless quite innocuous. If instead of distilling it with sulphuric acid, we fuse it at a bright red heat, the iron separates, and we get a white salt containing prussic acid in combination with potash, and which is to a great extent poisonous. Thus a little iron alone is sufficient to alter all the properties of this curious substance. The white salt made in this way is largely employed in preparing solutions of gold and silver for electro-plating; and the greater part of the silver and gold with which the various electro-plated articles in common use have been coated, has existed at one period in combination with this white substance. Another use of this yellow salt is to produce prussian blue, which is formed by adding to a solution of it in water some sulphate of iron or green copperas, when the ferro-prussic acid will part company with the potash; the latter will unite with the sulphuric acid of the copperas, leaving the iron of the latter to unite with the ferro-prussic acid to form the prussian blue. This powder has various uses; it is used as a paint, and to make thumb and button blue for the laundress: it is used to colour confectionery, and by the Chinese, whom the Europeans have learned to imitate, to make green tea. But its principal use is in calico printing. When used for the latter purpose, however, the prussian blue is usually made in the cloth itself. If we thicken a solution of green copperas with gum or with flour, and print a particular pattern upon a piece of white cotton, and then pass it through a bath of the yellow salt dissolved in water, we shall obtain the pattern in prussian blue so much admired by ladies. In general, the beautiful dark blue dresses, with white patterns, are made by covering the whole of the calico with prussian blue, printing the pattern upon it with caustic soda, or potash thickened with pipe-clay; the caustic substance decomposes the prussian blue, leaving the iron in the cloth as a buff pattern; but by washing in a bath of oxalic acid the iron is removed, and the pattern remains of a beautiful white. Thus may worthless woollen rags and similar vile things come back again to us; at one time in our tea, while they may have assisted to make the spoon with which it is stirred; at another, as a brilliant-coloured flower upon our room papers; or finally, as the colouring material of a lady's dress.

Prussian blue was discovered in Berlin, hence the name, and was first made in Great Britain, about eighty years ago. It was then sold at two guineas the pound; but at present the average price, wholesale, is not more than 1*s.* 9*d.*, the finest sorts costing 3*s.* 6*d.* to 4*s.* per pound.

Prussiate of potash was not known in commerce, in a crystallized state, until about the year 1825, when it was sold at 5*s.* per pound, but at present it only costs 1*s.* 3*d.*; whilst the quantity made increased from 10 tons in 1825, to 1040 tons in 1850. There are, we believe, twelve factories where it is at present made, which could produce about twenty tons per week, but the demand is very fluctuating, a matter not to be wondered at, if we recollect that its principal application depends entirely on the ever-varying taste of the ladies. We may estimate the annual value of all the prussiate of potash manufactured in Great Britain at about £150,000.

A new application of this salt has just arisen; and an exceedingly curious one it is. Various attempts have been made to apply the light produced by the passage of a current of electricity between the poles of a voltaic battery to illuminating purposes, but from various causes it has not been very successful. One of these is, that, after a time, the action of the battery diminishes, from the quantity of zinc dissolved by the acid forming a solution which prevents the further action of the acid. Dr. Watson states that he has solved this as well as the other difficulties of the case. The mode in which he proposes to effect this is, simply to add some yellow prussiate of potash to the zinc cells of his batteries, which precipitates the zinc, as fast as dissolved, in the form of a beautiful pigment, nearly equal to ultramarine. Where the Callan or iron battery is employed, the iron is precipitated, as fast as dissolved, in the form of ordinary prussian blue; thus converting what was a difficulty into a source of profit, and adding another to the already innumerable instances of what chemistry can do for the progress of industrial art, and consequently of humanity itself.

The chief contributor of prussiate of potash was W. Dawson, of Leith, who exhibited a large crystallized mass of it, along with a large collection of pigments.

## ULTRAMARINE.

In many parts of the world, but especially in Siberia, is found a beautiful mineral of a bluish colour, called *lapis lazuli*, from which is prepared the pigment known as ultramarine, so prized by artists. As every part of the stone is not blue, it must be subjected to a series of operations to free it from the uncoloured parts; for this purpose it is broken into pieces the size of a hazel-nut, and is then heated red-hot, and thrown into cold water acidulated with vinegar, an operation which is repeated seven or eight times, until the stone is capable of being reduced easily to a fine powder. This done, the powder is ground upon a stone, with a mixture of honey and a resinous substance used for staining mahogany, called dragon's blood. When sufficiently ground it is dried; after which it is worked up with a mixture of Venice turpentine, rosin, pitch, bees' wax, and linseed oil, placed in a cloth and kneaded in pure water; the ultramarine thereby is separated, the sand and other impurities remaining in the waxy mass. This operation is sometimes repeated where it is desirable to obtain the pigment of very superior quality. The price of true ultramarine varies with its quality from about £3 to £8, or even £10 per ounce. This extremely high price naturally led persons to attempt to produce it artificially, especially after Clement and Desormes had shown that its composition was very simple; being, in fact, principally composed of silica, alumina, soda, and sulphur—substances which would be represented by pipe-clay, common carbonate of soda, and flowers of sulphur. This was effected in 1824 by M. Guimet, of Paris, who has always kept his process secret, and still prepares the best artificial ultramarine made. Others have, however, also solved the problem, among whom we may mention Robiquet and Professor Gmelin, of Tübingen. The process of the former consisted in heating, in a closed vessel, a mixture of two parts of china clay, three of sulphur, and three of dried carbonate of soda: the resulting spongy mass, when cold, was of a grayish-green colour, and was reduced to powder and washed with water, under the influence of which, and of the air, it becomes gradually of an azure blue. When sufficiently washed, it is again ignited, to drive off any excess of sulphur. A great many other processes have been proposed and a number of factories established in different parts of Europe, where immense quantities of it are manufactured, the price falling in proportion. When first made, M. Guimet charged £1 per ounce for it, but at present a pound weight of it may be obtained for a much less sum.

Ultramarine is applied to many purposes besides oil and water-colour painting, consequent upon the great fall in its price; such as paper-staining, giving a delicate blue to writing-paper, and for the manufacture of thumb and button blue for the laundress, for which it is beautifully adapted. But probably the most important application which has been made of artificial ultramarine is to calico-printing. When worked up with albumen or white of egg, and printed on cotton cloth, and then exposed to the action of steam, the albumen is coagulated, and the colour is found to be firmly fixed upon the tissue. Patterns printed in this way are very beautiful, and are now much worn by ladies, but the material and process being much more expensive than in the case of prussian blue, from which it is very easily distinguished, its use is proportionably restricted. The great disadvantage attending the use of artificial ultramarine is its liability to have the colour discharged by the slightest trace of acid. In the case of tinging paper, to remove the disagreeable effect of too great whiteness, this objection would have been fatal, as the alum used in sizing the paper, so as to enable it to bear the ink, is more or less acid; but science has always its remedy, and in this case it simply proposed adding to the size a little basic acetate of lead, which neutralized the acid of the alum, at the same time that it improved the size.

## ORCHIL, CUDBEAR, LITMUS, ETC.

When the surface of a rock has undergone a certain amount of decay, under the influence of the carbonic acid of the atmosphere, spots or stains, sometimes white, sometimes black or grayish-green, make their appearance upon it. These spots are owing to a kind of plants termed lichens, which stand among the lowest in the scale of organized creation. Some consist of a white, or some other coloured, earthy-looking, and friable substance, often dotted with brilliant little cup or button-like points of a brilliant yellow or red, and sometimes of a brown, black, or white. Many varieties, however, produce large fronds or stems, and have thus a greater resemblance to the more perfect plants. Their growth is not confined to the surface of rocks alone, many varieties grow upon the bark of trees, and upon decaying wood. Like sea-weed, the lichen has been made subservient to the use of man; one variety, the common Iceland moss, being employed as food and in medicine. The chief use, however, of lichens is for the production of colours.

If we take a quantity of these lichens, and grind them into a paste under a vertical millstone, with some water, and then mix the pulpy mass with urine and ammonia (spirit of hartshorn), or the latter only, in a wooden trough, and allow the mass to undergo a peculiar fermentation for the space of about fourteen days, a peculiar change will take place; the grayish, dirty-looking paste will be converted into a beautiful rich violet mass, to which the name *orchil*, or in French, *orseilles*, is given. If the operation be continued for about a month, and the red mass which is formed dried and powdered, we shall have *cudbear*; and finally, if we use a little potash and slaked lime along with the ammonia, in the first instance, and press the fermented mass so as to obtain the whole of the colour in the liquid, and then thicken it by the addition of some chalk or plaster of Paris, so as to form a stiff paste, which is then formed into squares, we shall have *litmus*, or *turnsole*. The latter is of a peculiar blue, and is rendered of a bright red by the slightest trace of acid, for the detection of which it is used by chemists. Orchil is usually a thick liquid mass, of a most beautiful violet colour, but both it and cudbear may be obtained of various shades of red, blue, violet, and chocolate. These colours are formed by the action of the ammonia upon a number of curious substances which exist naturally in the lichens, some of which yield beautiful crystalline compounds. The lichens chiefly employed are the *Roccella tinctoria* and *corallina*, the *Lecanora tartarea* and *parella*, the *Variolaria lactea* and *dealbata*, several species of the genera *Parmelia*, *Umbilicaria*, &c., large quantities of which are annually imported from various parts of the world.

A colouring substance, prepared from lichens, appears to have been known to the ancient Greeks, but was lost in the middle ages. In the fourteenth century it was either rediscovered or introduced into Florence, from the Levant, by the descendant of a German, named Ferro, or Frederigo, who had settled there about a century previously, and from whom is descended one of the oldest and principal families of Florence, called at first Oricelarii, and in modern times, Rucellai, a name which is unmistakably derived from *oricello*, the Italian for orchil. The ordinary red violet powder, cudbear, was first introduced into commerce by Dr. Cuthbert Gordon, who called it after his mother's name.

Orchil and cudbear are employed in the dying of silk and woollen tissues. The colour produced by these substances is very beautiful, but very evanescent, and is hence rarely employed alone; their chief use being to give lustre and bloom to other colours, and even to white silks. Unfortunately, manufacturers are seldom contented to *use* it, for in England it is *abused* to an enormous extent in giving a false and an alluring bloom to goods; indeed the inferior quality of many of the English dyed fabrics may be attributed, in some degree, to the unrestricted employment of this cheap material. Many a lady has had cause to regret the effect of a promenade in the sun upon her pretty silk dress or ribbons, the short-lived bloom of which has been called forth by a little orchil.

Many of the fine violet, lilac, mallow, and rosemary flower tints of artificial flowers are produced by orchil: and thus does the barren and flowerless lichen, the first form of vegetation which springs into existence upon the bare rock, serve to produce some of the most delicate tints which imitate Nature in their beauty as well as in their evanescence.

There were two exhibitors of orchil and cudbear; the contributions of one of which were specially worthy of attention. The case exhibited by Wood and Bedford, of Leeds, contained specimens of the *Roccella tinctria*, from Angola, Madeira, and Valparaiso; *Roccella fuciformis*, from Lima, Mauritius, and the East Indies; another variety of *Roccella*, from Mogadore; *Parmelia perlata*, from the Canary Islands; *Lecanora tartarea*, *Umbilicaria pustulata*, and *Gyrophora murmia*, from Sweden. The collection of manufactured products exhibited by them was equally complete, containing specimens of Nos. 1, 2, and 3, cudbear; red, blue, violet, and chocolate liquid, and paste orchil, a sample of the ammonia employed in the preparation, with specimens of silk and woollen threads dyed with cudbear and orchil, and a specimen of white marble stained with the latter. Burton and Garraway, of London, contributed several specimens of lichens and prepared cudbear, woollen and silk thread, morocco skin, and patent gelatine, dyed with it, and several samples of silk, printed in various shades of red, violet, purple, &c., with similar preparations.

### VARNISHES AND LACQUERS.

Any liquid which, when spread over a substance, leaves on evaporation a thin coating of a solid hard substance, having a sort of vitreous lustre, as if the surface was composed of glass, may be considered as a *varnish*. Varnishes must, consequently, consist of two distinct classes of substances—liquids, which readily evaporate when exposed to the air; and solids, which are capable of being dissolved in those liquids, and which remain behind as a hard vitreous-like coating. The solid substances employed in the manufacture of varnishes are all of vegetable origin, and belong to that class of substances which, like tannin, are principally found in the bark of trees. These are usually considered under three heads—gums, resins, and gum-resins. Gums are exudations from the bark of trees, which dissolve, or at least soften, in water, so as to form mucilages, but are insoluble in spirits of wine. Resins are similar exudations, which are capable of being melted by heat, dissolve in spirit of wine, but not in water; and gum-resins are substances of like origin, containing, as the name imports, mixtures of gums and resins. Although, properly speaking, a solution of gum in water, such as is used to stiffen and give lustre to silk and other textile fabrics, must be considered, according to our general definition, as a varnish, that word in commerce is confined to solutions of the true resins. But as these substances are not soluble in water, that liquid cannot form an ingredient of ordinary varnishes—the liquids which are usually employed being spirit of wine or analogous fluids, essential oils, and drying fixed oils. These latter do not fulfil one of the conditions which we laid down above as constituting a varnish—namely, that the liquid should evaporate readily; but, in fact, drying oils are themselves varnishes, inasmuch as they become resins from the action of the air. Every resin is not equally well adapted for making varnishes; some will never harden perfectly, others, again, have peculiar colouring matters in them which limit their applications; hence it is very rare to find a varnish composed of only one resin; the usual custom being to mix several so as to obtain a compound having properties suited to the object for which the varnish is intended. Before giving the composition of a few such mixtures, we shall enumerate the chief ingredients at present employed in varnish-making, and say a few words about their origin.

RESINS CONSTITUTING THE VARNISH.

Copal, amber, lac, mastic, sandarach, elemi, benzoin, common resin, olibanum (gum-resin), anime, Venice or other turpentine, bitumen, and common pitch.

SUBSTANCES USED TO DISSOLVE THEM.

*Alcohol series.*—Alcohol or spirit of wine, of various degrees of strength; wood spirit or methylic alcohol; ether.
*Volatile or Essential Oil series.*—Oil of turpentine; oil of rosemary, and other essential oils.
*Drying Oil series.*—Linseed oil (boiled); poppy ditto.
*Naphtha series.*—Coal tar naptha; oils from distillation of wood and turf tar; petroleum.

All these substances, if we except the bitumen and pitch, yield colourless or more or less brown transparent varnishes; but as it is desirable sometimes to have varnishes of other colours, various substances are employed for that purpose—the most common are the gamboge and dragon's blood, common aloes, saffron, lampblack, &c.

*Copal.*—Several kinds of this gum come into commerce, apparently the product of different trees, natives of Africa, America, the East Indies, and New Zealand. That which comes into commerce under the name of Levant copal is the best; and is usually met with in the form of moderate-sized round masses, either colourless or of a slight lemon yellow colour, and very transparent and hard. It is very difficult to dissolve copal in anything. When exposed to the vapour of alcohol or oil of turpentine, however, it gradually softens and finally dissolves. This process being tedious, and by the ordinary mode of manufacture attended with the loss of a considerable quantity of alcohol, a number of devices have been proposed to effect its rapid dissolution. One of these is singular: it consists in powdering the copal very finely, and leaving it exposed to the air for about twelve months, at the end of which time it is found to dissolve readily in spirit of wine. By either of these processes, a beautiful varnish may be obtained, which dries readily, and is exceedingly hard, and nearly colourless. The usual way employed, however, is to take advantage of the property which certain essential oils have of softening the copal, and thus rendering it more easily soluble. A quantity of the copal, in pieces, is taken and moistened with oil of rosemary or with oil of lavender; after some time certain pieces begin to soften, while others remain unacted upon; the former are selected for making a spirit varnish, whilst the latter are set aside to be employed in making varnishes with fixed oils. Those selected for the spirit are reduced to powder, which is then moistened with oil of rosemary or lavender, and in some time is reduced to a pasty mass, to which spirit of wine or turpentine is gradually added to bring it to a proper consistence. A little camphor, dissolved in spirit, or in oil of turpentine, also dissolves copal; but unfortunately the varnish prepared in this way, or even by the means of oil of rosemary, is always somewhat soft, and has never the beauty or durability of those prepared by the first processes. If copal be placed in a funnel heated by some charcoal in a peculiar form of furnace, it melts, and will then be found to dissolve readily in alcohol. But here also we are met by a difficulty. The copal, after this treatment, becomes darker in colour, and the varnish formed is softer than by the other processes. Fat oils dissolve copal; but the varnish made in this way, in addition to both the objections just noticed, is attended by a third—that its use is limited. Ether and petroleum or rock oil are good solvents, but are too dear, and the former evaporates too quickly, while coal tar naphtha has a bad smell. We have been thus particular in our notice of copal, because it makes one of the finest varnishes known, and because it enables us to show that a good deal of skill and care are required to prepare good varnishes, and that a knowledge of chemistry is almost indispensable to those who would attempt to improve their processes.

*Amber* is a fossil resin of a yellow or brown colour, found in greatest abundance in the beds of clay on the Baltic shores of Prussia. Small pieces have also been found accompanying the beds of lignite or brown coal on the shores of Lough Neagh. When of a light colour, and transparent, the large pieces are employed for making necklaces, and other ornaments, and also as mouth-pieces for expensive tobacco-pipes. Some of the large pieces often contain enclosed in them the remains of insects, especially of a species of dragon fly, in the most beautiful state of preservation. The small pieces, not fit for making ornaments, are employed for making varnishes. Like copal, it is very difficult to dissolve it, and is all but insoluble in alcohol; although, by melting in the same way as we have described in speaking of copal, such a solution may be obtained; but it, too, loses by this process its transparency, brilliancy, and hardness. When dissolved in oil of turpentine it yields fine brilliant varnishes of great hardness, which are much prized for certain uses, as are also those made with the fixed oils.

*Lac.*—There is found on the banyan or religious tree of the Hindoos, and several allied plants (*Ficus Indica, Ficus religiosa, Croton lacciferum*), indigenous to the East Indies, a small insect (*Coccus ficus*), the female of which pricks the small juicy twigs in the month of January; from the wound thus made a quantity of fluid flows and covers the insect, and when hard forms a sort of nest composed of cells. Here the insect swells out into an egg-shaped, almost motionless, sack, filled with a beautiful red fluid, in which, in the month of October, about twenty to thirty elliptical eggs, or rather maggot-like bodies, appear, and swim about in the red fluid, upon which they live. When the whole of the fluid is consumed they bore through the sack and escape; but long before this, in fact even before the appearance of the maggots, the twigs are collected and dried in the sun, and form what we call *stick-lac*, which serves the double purpose of dyeing, for which it is employed in Bengal, and also in Europe, and of making varnishes and sealing-wax: the dyestuff is derived from the animal, the resin from the vegetable. Lac is brought to Europe in various other forms; for instance, we have seed-lac, lump-lac, and shell-lac, the former of which consists simply of the grains of lac separated from the twigs, and the latter of the seed lac melted, and then made into different forms by the natives of India, the colour being in general removed by boiling in water. The watery solution is then boiled down to a paste, which, on being dried in the sun, and cut into squares, forms *lac dye*, a substance employed to dye woollen goods of a beautiful scarlet. Shell-lac is the best known of these, and consists, when of superior quality, of thin plates of a very brittle and hard resinous substance, of a light brown colour, passing into orange, and sometimes of a deep ruby red,—hence the names orange and ruby shell-lac; the inferior qualities are much less transparent, darker in colour, not unlike glue in appearance, and occur in thicker plates. Shell-lac may be bleached by exposing it spread into thin plates to the sun, or by chlorine water, or by passing muriatic acid gas through it, suspended as a fine powder in water. In its unbleached state it is admirably adapted for making varnishes, but when bleached it loses a good deal of its properties, and is then principally employed in the manufacture of sealing-wax, which consists of shell-lac, coloured by the addition of some colouring material, and of a little Venice turpentine, &c. It is very difficult to dissolve raw lac completely in alcohol, although portions of it are readily soluble; and the same objections which we have mentioned in the case of copal exist against the employment of other dissolving liquids, such as fixed oils,—which are, nevertheless, the principal ones employed in the manufacture of lac varnishes. By powdering lac, and exposing it to the action of the air for a long time, it will become soluble in spirit of wine, as in the case of copal, the varnish retaining all the qualities of the lac uninjured.

*Mastic.*—This resin is the product of a tree called the *Pistacia lentiscus*, or mastic pistacia, and several other species, which are found in Persia, Egypt, and in the Mediterranean countries, especially on the Greek island of Scio, and also in Candia. These plants belong to the family of the *Anacardiaceæ*, or cashew-nut tribe, a family rich in resin. Our supply chiefly comes from Smyrna and Constantinople, in two forms:—first, as round, or somewhat flat, oval grains, from the size of a grain of barley to that of a bean of a pale yellow colour, and semi-transparent; and, secondly, of much larger-sized grains, much less transparent, occasionally mixed with foreign substances of a darker and less uniform colour. The first, called *mastic in tears*, is collected on the trunk of the trees, from which it exudes naturally, or from incisions made on purpose; and the second is collected on the ground around the tree, and is called *common mastic*. This resin has an agreeable odour, a slight aromatic flavour somewhat bitter, readily softens between the teeth, and hence has been used to sweeten the breath; and on this account has received the name of mastic, from the same root as our word masticate. It dissolves readily in oil of turpentine, but does not dissolve completely in ordinary spirit of wine; the portion left undissolved, if left exposed for some time to the air, becomes soluble. Mastic makes an excellent varnish, soft, but elastic, and when mixed with amber, copal, and lac varnishes, prevents them from drying too fast, rendering them at the same time more durable, and less liable to crack than they would otherwise be.

*Sandrac, or Sandarach* is the product of a North African tree, probably the *Calitris quadrivalvis*, closely allied to the common juniper, and resembles mastic in a great many respects; it is distinguished from the latter by being less transparent and whiter, and by not softening between the teeth. It forms an important part of most spirit varnishes, except those made with lac, and renders them brilliant and dry. As it very rarely occurs pure, it is usually boiled before use with caustic soda or potash.

*Anime* is the product of the locust tree, which is found in Brazil, Martinique, and Virginia. In external appearance it is not unlike copal. It dissolves in alcohol, but a small part requires to be boiled, and is then liable to crystallize out. It is an exceedingly bad material for varnish-making, because it makes the varnish difficult to dry, and leaves it always more or less soft.

*Benzoin* is obtained by incision from the *Styrax benzoin*, a native of Siam and Sumatra, and occurs in commerce in the form of brittle masses, composed of grains of red, brown, and white colours; the grains of the latter colour looking like almonds set in a dark paste. In varnish-making it has nearly the properties of mastic, but is too much coloured to be employed for transparent varnishes.

*Elemi* appears to be derived from two sources,—one a shrub which grows in Ceylon, Ethiopia, and in the East Indies; and the other from another shrub of the same genus, which is indigenous to South America. Both belong to the order of plants called *Amyrideæ*, which is allied to the family of plants to which the orange belongs. It is usually of a yellowish, or whitish-yellow colour, and is very soluble in alcohol and ether. It is a valuable ingredient in varnish-making, rendering the harder varnishes less brittle.

*Olibanum, or Incense*, of which there are two kinds, is but little used for varnishes, its principal use being the manufacture of pastilles, &c. The kind which comes into commerce in these countries is the product of a tree found in the East Indies, and belonging to the same family as that which produce the gum elemi just mentioned, and is probably superior to the better known incense of the East, which is a product of Arabia and Abyssinia.

Our space forbids us from going further into this part of the subject; in fact it would take a volume to describe properly the properties of the resins which come into commerce; and we could fill pages with the mere names of new resins which the progress of science and of commerce is daily making known, and which are being gradually introduced into the arts.

As before remarked, few of these substances are employed alone, mixtures being made according to the liquid used as a solvent, and to the objects intended to be varnished. For convenience sake, varnishes may be divided into three classes:—1. Those made with spirit of wine, or wood spirit. 2. Those made with oil of turpentine, or other volatile oils. Under this head we would include those made with tar naphtha, &c. 3. Linseed and other fat oil varnishes.

Spirit varnishes are the most brilliant, transparent, and colourless of all, but they are also, as a general rule, the least durable, and the most liable to crack. They are usually employed for furniture, picture-gilding, musical instruments, &c. Turpentine varnishes resemble in many respects spirit varnishes; but they are more elastic, and less liable to crack than the latter, and are at the same time somewhat less brilliant. Oil varnishes are the strongest and most durable of all, but they are also the least transparent and brilliant. Occasionally turpentine and oil varnishes are mixed, by which a mixture is obtained partaking of the character of the two. Oil varnishes are chiefly employed for coaches, tea-trays, and other hardware, and common papier mache goods, &c.

In order to afford our readers an idea of the variation in the composition of varnishes for different purposes, we shall give a few illustrations. But it must not be understood that the composition which we give is the very one employed (in fact each manufacturer has his own); or that those which we give are necessarily the best. As, however, the variations in the composition of different varnishes, for the same purpose, takes place within certain limits, those which we shall give will be sufficient for the purpose in view; namely, to teach the nature of varnishes, and the general principles which guide the manufacturers in adapting them for various purposes:—

FURNITURE SPIRIT VARNISH.

| | | | |
|---|---|---|---|
| Copal, | 3 oz. | Venetian turpentine, | 2½ oz. |
| Sandarach, | 6 „ | Powdered glass, | 4 „ |
| Mastic in tears, | 3 „ | Alcohol, | 2 lbs. |

SPIRIT VARNISH FOR VIOLINS, GUITARS, ETC.

| | | | |
|---|---|---|---|
| Sandarach, | 4 oz. | Venetian turpentine, | 2 oz. |
| Seed or shell-lac, | 2 „ | Powdered glass, | 3 „ |
| Mastic, | 1 „ | Alcohol, | 2 lbs. |
| Benzoin or elemi, | 1 „ | | |

The varnish for musical instruments is usually coloured by the addition of half an ounce of dragon's blood, and a little annotto or saffron. Furniture is sometimes lacquered of various colours, such as white, black, &c.; the colour is usually mixed with the varnish and used as a paint, over which is laid, when dry, a fine transparent varnish, composed of three ounces of sandarach, one ounce of mastic, half an ounce of Venetian turpentine, and 1 lb. of spirit of wine.

ESSENCE VARNISH FOR PICTURES.

| | | | |
|---|---|---|---|
| Mastic, | 120 parts. | Powdered glass, | 50 parts. |
| Finest turpentine, | 15 „ | Oil of turpentine, | 360 „ |
| Camphor, | 5 „ | | |

AMBER VARNISH FOR PAPIER MACHE.

| | | | |
|---|---|---|---|
| Amber, | 3 parts. | Shell-lac, | 5 parts. |
| Sandarach, | 5 „ | Asphalt, | 4 „ |
| Mastic, | 5 „ | Lampblack, | 4 „ |
| Common resin, | 5 „ | Oil of turpentine, | 12 „ |

VARNISHES FOR GOLD WARES.

| | | | |
|---|---|---|---|
| Mastic, | 30 parts. | Saffron, | (A little.) |
| Sandarach, | 30 „ | Turpentine, | 8 parts. |
| Gamboge, | 15 „ | Oil of turpentine, | 180 „ |

To which is to be added 100 parts of fine boiled linseed oil.

BRUNSWICK BLACK FOR IRON WORK.

45 lbs. of asphalt, boiled for six hours.

6 gals. of boiled linseed oil, and 6 lbs. of litharge, boiled together until they become strong, and then mixed with the asphalt. The whole boiled until it can be rolled into pills, and then reduced to the consistence of varnish, with 25 gals. of turpentine.

Tea-trays, and other articles of hardware, are japanned of various colours, by mixing the colouring material—which for white is, white lead; for yellow, chrome or Naples yellow, &c.—with a copal varnish, made with copal and linseed oil, or a mixture of copal and shell-lac with linseed oil, the proper consistence being given by turpentine. When this varnish or paint has dried, it is polished with a little powdered pumice-stone and water; the figures or ornaments, or gold bordering, &c., are laid on this, and a layer of the same copal varnish (without colour) laid on over the whole. In japanning iron, zinc, or tin vessels in this way, they must be heated in a kind of stove, so as to make the varnish flow freely over them. The varnish for the bodies of coaches is made with copal and a mixture of oil and turpentine; in order to render them more drying, anime resin is usually employed, and a quantity of sugar of lead, litharge, and copperas, added.

Before concluding our remarks on this subject, it will not be uninteresting to our readers to learn the nature of the materials and the mode of applying them in the East, whence we have derived the idea, and still obtain the finest examples, of lacquered wares. Indeed, any notices of varnishes in the present Catalogue would necessarily be incomplete, unless it included such an account, when it is recollected how important a feature the lacquered wares of Japan and China formed in the Exhibition, and the little information generally possessed upon this subject.

The word *lac*, from which we derive our word lacquering, is probably of Persian origin, and signifies a shining red colouring substance. Persia and Arabia are remarkable for the quantity of resins and odoriferous oils and balsams which they produce, and it is probable that the art of covering objects with a varnish of them is of very ancient date, and was, doubtless, introduced into Egypt from them; for it appears certain that the ancient Egyptians were acquainted with this art. They must have used the liquid resins as they flow from the trees, as they do still in many eastern countries, for they could not have been acquainted with our solvents. The Japanese, who prepare probably the finest varnish in the world (from which fact comes our word *japanned ware*), do it in this way. The tree from which the resinous substances flows is stated to be a variety of the shumac, and to be found in Carolina and Virginia, in America; but any statements of this kind must be received with great doubt. Whatever the nature of the tree is, the process of extraction is simply incising the bark and collecting the liquid which flows, and which is at first but lightly coloured, but becomes black by the action of the air. The juice is then filtered through the finest paper, mixed with a small quantity, perhaps not more than the hundredth part, of an oil obtained from the *Bignonia tomentosa*

This natural varnish is preserved for use in well-closed jars of porcelain; and is frequently coloured with vermillion and other strong colours, a deeper black when required being communicated by the addition of fine lamp-black. It was with this varnish that the different lacquered objects in the Japanese collection were varnished, an examination of which would show us that we are very far from having as yet produced a varnish equal to the Japanese. Our best varnishes crack in a few years, and are either too brittle when sufficiently hard, or too soft when sufficiently flexible; the Japanese lacquer, on the other hand, may be put upon straw and on cloth with the most perfect success, and will last for centuries. In the Exhibition there were two baskets of straw lacquered inside, and a straw lacquered cabinet. The production of red lacquer, by means of vermillion, was also illustrated in the Dutch collection by two tables and a tea-tray. There was a beautiful set of fourteen cups of papier mache in part coloured with vermillion, as also one of the lacquered straw baskets just mentioned. Another exceedingly pretty example of the same kind of red lacquer consisted of a small table with plates of lacquered wood to hold confectionery. This superiority of the Japanese varnishes over the European is not to be attributed to their greater skill; but simply that they employ the natural varnishes, whilst we are obliged to produce them by artificial means.

Next in point of quality to the Japanese lacquered wares, stand the Chinese, of which there were many specimens in the Exhibition well worth examining, especially a beautiful table-top and some trays in the Gough collection, and a small cabinet in Hewett's Chinese collection. The Chinese lacquer is a native varnish, the product of a tree called Tsi-chou, or the lac tree, indigenous to several of the southern provinces of China, and is frequently cultivated. There are three principal kinds of varnish, prepared directly from trees, in China, the names of which are derived from the three cities where they are prepared, and are, in all probability, produced from three different plants. The Nien-tsi is the best, giving to the articles varnished with it a beautiful brilliant black, but it is the least abundant. The Si-tsi resembles the first-named, but is less brilliant, and not so dark-coloured; the two are usually mixed together. The third kind, named Kouang-tsi, is of a yellow colour, and is the most abundant and commonly employed. Previous to use, the varnishes, preserved as before mentioned in closed pots in cellars, are evaporated to the proper consistency, by exposure in shallow trays to the sun; and then mixed with a certain quantity of Tong-yeou or tea oil, obtained from a plant of the same genus as that from which tea is produced. This oil, which in many respects resembles oil of turpentine, is usually prepared by boiling with a little white arsenic, which acts like litharge in giving it drying properties. Another process is to mix it with the dried matter of ox-gall and a little green vitriol or copperas. The Chinese make an imitation of the Japanese varnishes, which they call Yang-tsi, which signifies a varnish which comes from beyond the sea, thus showing its origin. This varnish consists of the third variety above mentioned, the Kouang-tsi, mixed with a finely-powdered charcoal of deer-horns and a little of the tea oil. There are also other varieties of varnish made chiefly with the Kouang-tsi: as for example, the Tchao-tsi, which is transparent, and of a yellow colour, and consists of equal portions of varnish and tea oil laid on a ground covered with gold dust, mosaic gold, or powdered copper-leaf, usually known as Dutch metal, so as to imitate aventurine. The same effect is produced even still more beautifully, by covering the objects with Kin-tsi, and then dusting this varnish over with gold dust, mosaic gold, &c., over which is laid, when dry, a coating of Tchao-tsi, so that the gold appears between two layers of varnish. Arabesque ornaments and figures in gold leaf are frequently laid on in this way between two layers of varnish. In the Japanese Collection were several examples of this style of decoration, especially the magnificent lacquered Buddha altar-piece, the panels of the doors of which were executed in this way. An imitation of this kind of work is sometimes made on English papier mache, but it appears not to be so perfectly executed as the Oriental. The very usual gold ground, which has a flame-like appearance, with tints varying from brass-yellow to reddish orange, seen on a great variety of japanned ware in Europe, is made in a different way, by colouring the under varnish with annotto, dragon's blood, and saffron.

There was but one exhibitor of the raw material of varnishes, Boyd and Goodwin, of this city, who contributed a very good series of small specimens of the resins and gum-resins most usually employed. Among these were some of Levant copal, of very remarkable purity; and a larger lump of fine Brazilian copal, which deserves especial mention. There were four exhibitors of varnishes, one Irish, one English, one French, and one Belgian. The Irish exhibitor was Samuel Boyd of this city, who contributed a collection of the varnishes in common use, both in oil, turpentine, and spirit, which appeared to be good, and to support the character already acquired by his house for that article. P. F. Reusens, of Antwerp, exhibited a series of fine oil copal varnishes, chiefly intended for coachmakers' use, among which were some nearly colourless, a quality rarely possessed by varnishes of this class. The largest collection of varnishes was that exhibited by Soehne, Freres, Paris, whose contributions consisted of twenty-three samples of spirit varnishes, adapted for wood, metal, ormolu, water-colour, crayon, or pastel, and lithographic drawings, photographs, gun-barrels, artificial flowers, leather, plaster casts, gilded frames, and re-varnishing old oil paintings.

When describing the examples of japanned ware and papier mache, allusion will be made to the examples of varnished and lacquered ware which appeared in the Exhibition.

### THE RARER CHEMICAL SUBSTANCES.

*Alcohols and compound Ethers.*—No better or more striking proof of the value of abstract science can be pointed out than the large number of practical applications which have been recently made of substances formed by the chemist in his researches, and which, at first sight, appeared to be mere curiosities, devoid of all practical interest. Among these we may mention chloroform, collodion, sulphuret of carbon, and nitrobenzol. Every one is acquainted with the uses of the first for preventing the sensation of pain in surgical operations; the second is now become equally well known from its employment in photography; sulphuret of carbon has many uses, one of the most curious being that dependent upon the property which it has of causing silver to deposit bright in electro-plating. The history of nitrobenzol is still more interesting; it was discovered in 1834, by Mitscherlich, and is prepared by distilling benzoic acid with lime, and acting upon the aromatic oil produced, and known as benzol, by nitric acid. The substance thus obtained was a heavy oil, of a highly aromatic odour. Even had a practical application of this oil suggested itself at the time, the great cost of its production would have effectually prevented its use. Hofmann, however, in 1845, proved the existence of benzol in the oil obtained in the distillation of coal-tar; and Mansfield, in 1849, invented a process for its separation. An immediate use was made of these discoveries to produce sweet nitro-benzol, which, from the remarkable analogy of its smell to that of oil of bitter almonds, is sold under that name, sometimes with the addition of the word artificial, but very often without it. It is also used in perfumery, under the name of *essence de mirbane*. When pure, it may be employed with perfect safety in confectionery, because, unlike ordinary oil of bitter almonds, it is quite free from prussic acid.

We have been led to the preceding observations by the examination of a case of rare chemicals, contributed by P. Squire, of London, containing a series of alcohols and ethers, which possess some peculiar interest. Common spirit of wine consists of a mixture of water with a peculiar substance termed alcohol, which is a compound of ether and water; the latter existing in the alcohol in the same state as in slaked lime, and, therefore, not to be confounded with the water merely mixed with it. If we separate the combined water, we obtain the well-known substance, ether, which, in its turn, is capable of combining with a number of acids to form a series of substances termed compound ethers. All substances having an analogous chemical composition are termed alcohols, and from them a similar series of compound ethers may be produced. Thus, there is obtained in the distillation of wood and of turf a peculiar kind of spirit, commonly called pyroxylic spirit; and in the rectification of whisky a peculiar oily fluid, to which that liquid owes its flavour, termed fusel oil, having an insupportable smell. Both these substances are alcohols, the former being called methylic alcohol (derived from wood), and the latter amylic alcohol (derived from starch, from which whisky is produced), the ordinary alcohol being called ethylic alcohol (derived from the word ether). A few years since Cahours proved that the essential oil of an American plant, called the *Gaultheria procumbens*,—which is much used in perfumery,—consists of a peculiar acid in combination with the ether of wood spirit, that it was the salicylate of oxide of methyl, and accordingly he produced it artificially. This fact, coupled with that of the extraordinary resemblance between the smell of several compound ethers and the more aromatic fruits, has led to a singular application of the former.

There is obtained by the distillation of butter a peculiar oily acid called butyric acid; if this be combined with ether so as to form a compound ether, termed by chemists butyrate of oxide of ethyl, we shall obtain a fluid having the odour of pine-apples when diluted with spirits. This substance is much employed in Ireland to produce "old whisky," especially that variety known as "old pine-apple," and in England to flavour an acidulated drink called pine-apple ale. Pure butyric ether is, however, rarely employed for this purpose; the usual method employed being to make a soap with butter, and distilling this with whisky and oil of vitriol. Several other ethers are produced at the same time, but the mixture answers very well as a substitute for the pure article. Considerable quantities of this preparation are made in Dublin, and are largely employed by the makers of "old" malt whisky.

When fusel oil or amylic alcohol is heated with potash, it is converted into a peculiar acid found ready formed in Nature, in the plant called the *Valeriana officinalis*. It is also produced in the rotting of animal substances, and is one of the causes of the smell of old cheese. It likewise exists in several fish oils, such as that of the dolphin. If a salt of this acid be distilled with some fusel oil and oil of vitriol, a compound ether is produced, the valerianate of oxide of amyl, which has exactly the odour of apples when diluted with alcohol. Or the same agreeable odour may be produced by mixing bichromate of potash, fusel oil, and oil of vitriol, together, and distilling the mixture. If acetate of potash, that is, a combination of potash and the acid of vinegar, be distilled with fusel oil and oil of vitriol, another compound ether, the acetate of oxide of ethyl, is produced, which, when added in very small quantity to alcohol, produces the delicate odour of the jargonelle pear. Considerable quantities of both are now manufactured in London, especially of the latter, which is used for flavouring barley-sugar, under the name of pear drops. Several other compounds of the same kind are also made and used by perfumers, confectioners, and liqueure-makers, such as cognac and grape oils, &c. used for making "British brandy."

It is certainly a singular fact to find the most delicate odours produced by a union of two exceedingly disagreeable ones, and one of which is to some extent the cause of many disgusting putrid smells; nor is it less singular to find that the acid of rancid butter, united with the substance, to diminish the quantity of which in whisky it requires to be stored for several years, should be employed for the very purpose of giving to new whiskey the flavour acquired by age. Some exceedingly pure samples of these compound ethers were in the case of Mr. Squire, above alluded to, and among them was a sample of the salicylate of methyl or artificial oil of the *Gaultheria procumbens* of Cahours. A few samples of some of those compound ethers were also exhibited under the name of artificial essences, by W. H. Galbraith, of London.

*Vegetable Alkaloids, and Neutral Organic Substances existing in Plants.*—Among the most curious facts elicited by modern chemical investigation, there are few more interesting than the discovery that the peculiar properties which distinguish many plants, especially those which are employed in medicine, are owing to the presence of small quantities of certain substances, the greater number of which are crystalline; and, when separated from the plant, still exhibit those peculiar effects on the animal economy for which the plants themselves are distinguished. Thus from fever-bark is obtained quinine and several other crystalline substances; from opium, morphine and narcotine; and from tobacco, a peculiar narcotic oily substance; whilst from tea may be obtained a substance called *theine*, which recent investigations have shown to be identical with *caffeine*, the peculiar principle of the coffee.

In the whole history of human drinks no more striking and inexplicable fact is presented to us than this, that two plants differing in external form should have been selected as materials to form drinks in two different parts of the world—the one in Ethiopia, in Africa, the native home of the coffee; and the other in China, in the eastern extremity of Asia, which science should subsequently show depended for their action on the human body upon identically the same substance! The singularity of the matter does not end here, however, for the Brazilians prepare with the seeds of the *Paulinia sorbilis* a kind of pasty mass, which they call *guarana*, and which they employ to make an infusion or drink for the cure of dysentery and other similar diseases; and the Indians of Paraguay from the most ancient times prepared a drink from the dried leaves of a plant called the *Ilex Paraguayensis*, small quantities of which have from time to time come to Europe under the name of *Paraguay tea*. It is a curious circumstance that both these substances should contain caffeine. Finally, the seeds of the cacao tree or *Theobroma cacao*, from which cocoa and chocolate are prepared, contain a substance called *theobromine*—from the name of the plant, which is derived from Greek words, signifying "food of the gods"—so analogous to caffeine that it is probable that further investigations will show them to be derived from the same body. We thus see that not only in the Old World, but also among the ancient inhabitants of the New, drinks were sought out, having a special action upon the nervous system. We may remark here that chocolate also is an Indian drink, our word being derived from the Mexican or Aztec word *chocolatl*. And now, strange to say, the chemist comes and shows that their active principles—that to which they all owe that soothing effect upon the body which has recommended their use to all the peoples of the earth, and which has helped so much to civilize the world by doing away to a considerable extent with the necessity of exciting fermented drinks—is the same substance!

Theine may be very simply prepared from tea, by adding to an infusion of it basic acetate of lead (which is a compound of vinegar with lead), and ammonia (spirit of hartshorn), by which a number of substances are thrown down as a precipitate, leaving the theine in solution, with a slight excess of lead, which is then removed by means of sulphureted hydrogen, a peculiarly fetid gas. The solution thus freed from the other substances existing in the tea, and from the excess of lead, is then concentrated; that is, the greater part of the water is evaporated at a very gentle temperature,—and on cooling, the theine, nearly pure, will crystallize out, and may be further purified by dissolving in water and filtering through charcoal prepared by burning blood. In the same way we could prepare it from the other substances which we have mentioned as containing it. Gunpowder tea contains in every 100 lbs. about from 2 lbs. 3 oz. to 4 lbs. 1½ oz. of theine, and ordinary tea from 2¼ lbs. to even 5 lbs.; whilst the same quantity of Paraguay tea does not contain more than from 1½ oz. to 2 oz. West Indian coffee is said to contain more than the Mocha coffee, but both contain less than tea.

Caffeine or theine, as we may indifferently call it, when heated, volatilizes and condenses in a crystalline form, and when its solution is heated nearly to boiling, a portion will always pass off with the vapour of the water—a fact which is of importance to ladies, for if they heat their tea too long or too highly, they injure it, as the caffeine will go off, and nothing will be gained in return but a quantity of bitter astringent matter. Theine has a slightly bitter taste, and, as may be easily imagined from what we have above stated relative to the proportion of it present in tea and coffee, a very small quantity of it would act upon the nervous system. A magnificent specimen of caffeine, beautifully crystallized and of remarkable purity, was exhibited by T. and H. Smith, of Edinburgh, who also contributed a fine specimen of another of those neutral bodies named *aloin*, obtained from aloes. Caffeine is called a neutral body, because it does not enter into combination with acids. *Quinine*, *narcotine*, &c., on the other hand, form salts, many of which crystallize, and are hence termed organic bases, or *vegetable alkaloids*, from resembling in this respect the alkalies. Several of these bases, of which there are now a great number, were exhibited in the collection of pharmaceutical preparations of the Apothecaries' Hall of Ireland. It is unnecessary to describe here their mode of preparation, as in principle it is the same as that just described for caffeine.

Within the last few years a number of organic bases have been obtained from gas-tar and other artificial products, some of which are remarkable. This fact has led to the hope that perhaps it may be possible to produce those naturally contained in plants by artificial means. Such a discovery would be of immense benefit to the poor, who are now unable to use such specifics as quinine, in consequence of its high price.—W. K. SULLIVAN.

---

1 APOTHECARIES' HALL OF IRELAND, THE GOVERNOR & CO. OF, Mary-street, Dublin.—Chemical and pharmaceutical preparations, manufactured in the laboratory of the Apothecaries' Hall; specimens of drugs as imported and prepared.

2. BOILEAU, BROTHERS, Bride-street, Dublin, Importers and Manufacturers.—Chemicals in great variety.

3. BOILEAU, JOHN GEORGE, & Co., Mary's-abbey, Dublin, Importers and Manufacturers.—Specimens of chemical preparations.

4. BOYD & GOODWIN, Merrion-row, Dublin, Importers and Manufacturers.—Pharmaceutical and chemical specimens; specimens of resins and gum-resins used in varnish-making.

5. BOYD, SAMUEL, Mary-street, Dublin.—Specimens of varnishes.

6. BROTHERTON, WILLIAM, North-street, Wandsworth, Surrey.—Rape seed oil; olive oil.

7. BURTON & GARRAWAY, Bethnal-green, London.—Lichens used in the manufacture of orchil and cudbear; orchil; cudbear; indigo in the raw state; extract of indigo.

8. COONEY, C., Back-lane, Dublin.—Indigo and other blues, prepared as button, thumb, and fig blues, for making up white linen and cotton fabrics.

9. CORRY & Co., Belfast, Manufacturers.—Ornamental stand of aërated waters, manufactured by patent improved machinery.

10. COUPLAND, HENRY, Liverpool.—Raspberry vinegar, acid, and syrup of lemon.

11. DAWSON, W., Leith.—Colours, and specimens of prussiate of potash.

12. DUBLIN CHEMICAL SOCIETY, Capel-street, Dublin.—Preparations by the members, consisting of prussian blue; oxide and sulphate of iron, from Irish ore, with specimen; carbonate, oxide, and sulphate of zinc; acetic acid; oxalates of iron, ammonia, and potash; sulphates of magnesia and potash; benzoic acid; oxide, carbonate, and sulphate of iron and zinc; prussian blue; acetic acid (all from Irish ores); iodide of potassium; acetate of zinc; ammoniocitrate of iron; oxide of mercury; oxide, acetate, carbonate, chloride, nitrate, and sulphate of lead, from Irish ore, with specimen; nitric acid (pure); phosphate of silver; muriate and sulphate of ammonia; iodine, from Dublin Bay sea-weed; carbonate, bicarbonate, and sulphate of

soda; tartar emetic; arseniate of potash; valerianates of iron and zinc; muriatic acid (pure); boracic acid; phosphate of ammonia, bicarbonate of potash; arsenite, nitrate, and sulphate of copper, from Irish ore; chromate and iodide of lead, iodoform, gun cotton, collodion.

13. DYAS & HARMAN, Cork.—Dawson's rat poison.

14. ELLAM, JONES, & Co., Markeaton Mills, Derby, Manufacturers.—Specimens of the emery of commerce, or rhombohedral corundrum stone, from Naxos, in the Grecian Archipelago, in its native and manufactured state, used for grinding and polishing steel, iron, glass, &c., and by lapidaries; mineral, chemical, and vegetable colours, raw and manufactured, for oil paints and paper staining.

15. JENNINGS, T., Brown-street, Cork, Manufacturer.—Specimens of pure calcined magnesia, carbonate of magnesia, and strong solution of carbonate of magnesia, pure carbonate of magnesia in blocks.

16. LANGSTON, SCOTT, & WHITE, Grand Surrey Canal Dock, Rotherhithe, and Lombard-street, City, London, Manufacturers.—White oxide of zinc, an innoxious substitute for white lead, of various shades and qualities, used for paint, and in numerous manufactures, also for chemical purposes; zinc driers, without litharge or lead base.

17. MAXTON, R., Chemical Works, Saltcoats.—Specimens of magnesia.

18. MOBERLY, W., Landsend, near Whitby, Manufacturer.—Half cask of alum, sample of refined Epsom salts.

19. MOFFAT, G. D., Dundas-street, Edinburgh.—Pure medicinal cod-liver oil, characterized by its freedom from taste and smell.

20. MURPHY, W., M. D., Arthur-place, Belfast, Manufacturer.—Aërated waters, carbonic acid gas in solution, effervescent tonics.

21. MURRAY, Sir J., M. D., Temple-street, Dublin.—Specimens of magnesia and camphor in chemical union in a fluid form; a bottle of fluid magnesia and camphor, from which the carbonic acid having been expelled by heat, the magnesia and camphor held in solution by that gas become again insoluble, the magnesia falling to the bottom, and the camphor floating on the top of the liquid after being boiled.

22. PENNEY, HENRY, York-place, Baker-street, London.—Samples of varnishes.

23. SMITH, T. & H., Duke-street, Edinburgh, Manufacturer.—Caffeine, the crystalline and characteristic principle of coffee; aloin (discovered by the exhibitors, 1850), the cathartic principle of the aloes; two samples exhibited, made from the Socotrine aloes.

24. SQUIRE, P., Oxford-street, London.—Specimens of the principal alcohols, and corresponding acids; compound ethers; specimens illustrating the indigo series; tartaric and paratartaric acids; specimens of crystals; pharmaceutical preparations.

25. STEPHENS, H., Stamford-street, Blackfriars-road, London, Manufacturer.—Specimens of liquid colours for staining woods, and of woods stained therewith; liquid colours for writing purposes; and a specimen of blood preserved more than four years by the oil of tar, showing its strong antiseptic qualities.

26. TUSTIAN, J., & USHER, R., Milcombe, near Banbury, Oxon, Producers and Manufacturers.—English rhubarb powder; English rhubarb, trimmed and untrimmed.

27. VIEILLE MONTAGNE ZINC COMPANY.—Specimens of oxide of zinc as substitutes for white lead in painting.

28. WARD, JOHN, Ramelton, Co. Donegal.—Muriate of potash, sulphate of potash, and iodine, manufactured from sea-weed.

29. WOOD & BEDFORD, Leeds, Manufacturers.—The varieties of lichens employed in the manufacture of lichen dyes; specimens of orchil and cudbear of different kinds and qualities; illustrations of the use of these colouring matters in the arts of dyeing and printing.

# CLASS III.

## SUBSTANCES USED AS FOOD.

UNDER the denomination of Substances used as Food a great variety of articles are included, most of which are so well known to the public as scarcely to require any special notice. Some of these are of a character which, at first sight, might seem to prevent them from being included in this category; but in any such arrangement as we are obliged to adopt, it is often a matter of no small difficulty to guard against such anomalies as the grouping together of the substances in this class presents. The class of Miscellaneous Articles it is desirable to abridge as much as possible; but this can only be done by the occasional introduction into the other classes of articles, having only a remote connexion with the substances which impart to it its character. Tobacco, for example, seems to have little relation to substances used as food; but in placing it here we merely adopt the arrangement carried out in the Exhibition of 1851. Some of the articles coming under this head may also belong to the succeeding one, as being used in manufactures,—such as starch, dextrine, and some others; but, instead of too rigidly adhering to any mere formal arrangement, discussing a portion of the subject in one place and concluding it in the other, we have, to preserve the continuity of the descriptions, usually disposed entirely of it at one time; making reference to that description on other occasions when it appeared to be necessary to do so.

The articles comprising this class are not attractive in appearance to the casual observer, and hence much less attention is devoted to them than they deserve; a circumstance which may account for the comparatively small space which they occupied in the Exhibition. Yet what can be more important than the determination of the quality of substances used as food in connexion with the manner in which they may have been produced, and the countries whence they may have been derived? Collections of the same article, belonging to the vegetable kingdom, may supply information as to climatic influences upon its growth, more especially in reference to the quality of the samples; and excellence in both quantity and quality is more frequently combined than is commonly supposed. The quality of the class of articles to which we now more especially allude may also be guessed with tolerable accuracy by the eye alone; while in the case of animal substances further criteria are necessary than can be thus supplied.

In the sections which follow, the subjects have been treated at a length commensurate with their importance in an Irish point of view, and the necessity which exists for placing before the public reliable information upon them. Thus, the production of root crops, and the manufacture of beet sugar, have been discussed in detail,—from their being, as it were, Irish questions, and being, moreover, in some degree connected with each other. It does not admit of doubt that, for the production of roots, the soil and climate of this country are peculiarly adapted; a circumstance which also warrants the conclusion, that in Ireland the beet sugar industry will one day be extensively carried on. In reference to the growth of roots, however, very vague, and, as we believe, incorrect notions prevail; and hence the necessity of the subject being fairly discussed in a work designed to facilitate the progress of Irish industry.

### I.—THE VEGETABLE KINGDOM.

The character of the representation of this class has been already indicated, as being much more limited than could have been desired. The chief deficiencies were in this division; there being of some important articles no specimens in the Exhibition. This was the case with tea and some other substances; and we now more particularly refer to the circumstance by way of accounting for the omission of all notice of such articles in the general remarks which follow.

#### THE COMMON CEREALIA, GRASSES, FODDER PLANTS, ETC.

The commonly cultivated cerealia—wheat, oats, and barley—was tolerably well represented, through the enterprise and good taste of one of the leading seed houses of this city, Messrs. W. Drummond and Sons of Dawson-street, and of Stirling, who exhibited 150 specimens of these grains, showing, in many cases, the full length of straw, so as to afford an idea of the character of the variety. It is also due to the Messrs. Drummond to state, that the idea of first establishing Agricultural Museums in Great Britain originated with them; or, at all events, they were the first to act upon it, by the formation of an Agricultural Museum at Stirling some twenty years ago. There can be no doubt of the great value to the science of farming of well-selected exhibitions of its produce, and the extent to which the principle is now carried out shows the value attached to it. Reverting, however, to the cerealia in the Exhibition, we may observe, that specimens of agricultural produce become really valuable, in the way of affording information, when details are furnished of the circumstances under which they have been produced. It is a distinguishing feature of agriculture, as compared with any other branch of industry, that its operations are dependent on circumstances, and that practical rules taken in the abstract are of little value, as they must be modified by a variety of considerations, with which only the practised eye can deal. Hence the value of the details of agricultural practice. When we hear of abnormal accounts of produce, or see extraordinary specimens of the products of farming, we can only turn the information to account by a knowledge of the conditions under which they were obtained.

Oats and barley are produced of good quality in Ireland, and in general yield a fair return; but the growth of wheat is not so satisfactory, owing chiefly to the humidity of the climate during the summer. The extent of land devoted to wheat has accordingly been on the decrease of late; and there can be little doubt that experience will show the propriety of carrying out this policy still further, and of paying increased attention to those other crops for which the soil and climate are found to be specially adapted.

Important contributions to this department were made by the Messrs. Drummond, Alderman Farrell, and Messrs. Toole and Mackey, consisting of collections of different varieties of dried grasses, and other herbage and forage plants; many of which had the roots attached to them, thus showing the habits of the variety to which they belonged. The great attention which is now devoted to the judicious selection of this class of plants is one of the most remarkable features of modern farming. The period is not distant when the land intended to be laid down from tillage to grass was left to Nature to supply the plants for the purpose. The consequence was, that on all the inferior class of soils the grass was almost worthless for two or three years; while, even in the best situations, the return of the first season was miserable. But by the use of red clover and some of the grasses, especially the Italian rye grass, an amount of forage is now obtained from the first year's grass which ranks it amongst the most valuable crops of the rotation. The seeds of this class of plants were exhibited in great variety.

When on the subject of agricultural grasses, it will not be out of place to point out the great neglect manifested by many of our farmers in the selection of the proper kinds; and to economize in the outlay for these seeds, the sweepings of the hay-loft are often used, than which nothing can be more absurd. With the class of farmers who adopt such a practice the hay is seldom of good quality; and, besides, the seed thus obtained contains many of the seeds of the most pernicious weeds, which, when thus introduced, require years to get them eradicated.

*Malt.*—Of malt there were only two collections of samples, that of Messrs. J. and W. Taylor, of Bishops, Stortford, comprising the varieties commonly used; and that of James Asprey, of Sandleford, containing samples of pale and brown malt. The process of malting is one of extreme simplicity; still it is one of those which require to be performed with so much care that the slightest inattention may be destructive to the batch: on this account, therefore, it would have been desirable that specimens produced in this country should have been exhibited; more especially as some of the fermented beverages made in Ireland have obtained an almost cosmopolitan reputation.

Malt may be obtained from any of the cerealia, but barley is almost exclusively used for the purpose, for which it is peculiarly adapted. In the process of malting, a portion of the starch contained in the grain is converted into sugar and dextrin by an artificially excited germination, which is suddenly checked by the application of heat at that stage, when the desired object is best attained. Either a deficiency or excess of germination tells upon both quality and quantity of the malt; the former being also effected by the drying, which requires a carefully regulated temperature according to the object in view. The quality of the barley also affects that of the malt so much that only certain kinds are considered to be suited for the purpose. The barley must not only have been well ripened, but it must also have been well preserved, as after the slightest change in chemical composition it becomes totally unfitted for malting.

In the process of malting the grain has to be thoroughly soaked in cold water, which is done in large cisterns or tanks. The barley will thereby absorb about half its own weight of water, which is attended by a considerable increase of bulk. At this stage it is removed to be spread in the floor of the malt-house, from twelve to sixteen inches in depth. Germination now sets in, during which considerable heat is evolved. The mass requires to be repeatedly turned to preserve in it a uniformity of temperature, which should range from 55° to about 62°. Germination will have progressed sufficiently when the young shoot has reached about the length of the grain whence it proceeds, and the rudiment of the young stem begins to make its appearance. The growth is then stopped by removing the grain to the malt-kiln, where it is placed on frames of wire gauze, and dried at first at a temperature of 90°, which is gradually increased to about 140°. As has already been remarked, on the attention devoted to these processes will depend the quality of the produce.

The varieties of malt usually employed by the brewer are:—1. Pale, or amber malt, which furnishes the chief ingredient in the manufacture of ale, beer, and porter; 2. Brown malt, which is used to impart flavour; and 3. Roasted or black malt, used as a brown colouring matter for porter. These varieties are obtained by using a higher or lower temperature in the kiln in which the malt is dried.

The subject of the application of malt for feeding cattle was much agitated a few years ago, in conjunction with efforts made to obtain a repeal of the malt tax. The change which takes place in the grain in the process of malting was supposed to be favourable to the development of flesh and fat, when used for feeding purposes. This led to a series of experiments being undertaken by Dr. Thompson, of Glasgow, by the direction of the Government, the result of which was to show that the prevailing opinion as to barley being better in the state of malt than in its original condition was without any adequate foundation.

By a recent Parliamentary Return we find that the annual consumption of malt in Ireland is about 1,300,000 bushels.

### PULSE.

The illustrations of this important class of plants were confined to samples of beans contributed by Messrs. Drummond, of this city, and Mr. Fordham, from Berkshire; of peas, by Mr. Asprey, from the same county; and pea-flour, exhibited by Mr. Styles, of London. There was certainly a grievous want of appreciation of the real objects of the Exhibition on the part of the agricultural interest, otherwise the whole illustration of the products of agriculture would not have been confined to the enterprise of one of our leading houses in the seed trade, and some three or four amateurs. Beans and peas are little grown in Ireland; but that is the very reason why the illustration of what is doing would have been important, as we have undoubtedly many successful growers of both crops. In point of nutritive qualities they stand above all others; and the pea, in many forms, is an article of food much prized, but the bean is unpalatable, and difficult of digestion as human food. Both, however, form excellent food for the domestic animals. For horses, bruised beans have long been in high repute, and when ground they are admirably adapted for the fattening of pigs. From the difficulty of harvesting the crop in this humid climate, and the very early period at which the seed must be sown, beans have hitherto found little favour in Ireland, even with our best farmers, who regard the bean as a hazardous crop.

The cultivation of the pea is not subject to the same drawbacks as that of the bean, in point of early seed-time or difficulty of harvesting; the pea is ripe at a comparatively early period of the season, and its entire cultivation and management are attended with little difficulty. It only succeeds well on the lighter class of soils, while the bean, on the other hand, is most successfully grown on the heavy clays. The pea is, however, grown to a still smaller extent in this country than the bean, though in some of the light gravelly soils which are occasionally met with, there can be little doubt that it would yield a profitable return. As an article of human food, pease, in different forms, are held in deservedly high estimation. White pease are grown to a considerable extent in England, for being converted into what is termed split pease, which are used for pea-soup. The great peculiarity of this variety is its dissolving readily into a sort of semi-fluid mass, and when they do so they are termed boilers, and command a high price. The non-boilers, as the other varieties are termed, are also largely employed for domestic use, the difficulty of boiling them soft being removed by the addition of a small quantity of carbonate of soda to the water used for the purpose. A species of pease-meal is much used by invalids in Scotland, in the form of porridge, from its combining the properties of being light and easily digested, and at the same time of being highly nutritious. A competent authority on this subject states, that much of the so-called Revalenta Arabica, sold at an enormous price in our shops, is the common pease-meal, to be usually had at about 2*d.* per pound.

## AGRICULTURAL ROOTS.

Towards the close of the Exhibition the contribution of a great variety of roots formed a feature in this department suggestive of some remarks on the circumstances under which this class of farm produce can be most advantageously grown. We have seen that for the growth of wheat our climate is by no means so favourable as that of many other countries; and that, however remunerative it may have been under a system of artificial prices, yet, under the influence of unrestricted competition, a portion of the extent of ground hitherto usually devoted to it must give place to some of the other cultivated crops. But the circumstances which render the climate of Ireland unfavourable to the production of wheat of fine quality favour the growth of root crops of all kinds. Of this the specimens to which we have referred afforded abundant evidence; and the collections of Irish roots annually displayed in the Agricultural Museum of the Royal Dublin Society, and also at the Shows of the Smithfield Club, in London, have further illustrated the fact, that for the production of root crops of all kinds the soil and climate of Ireland are admirably adapted.

Bearing in mind the utilitarian objects of the Exhibition, and that they will only be attained in as far as they stimulate the progress of improvement; and regarding the tillage of the soil as the great staple industry of Ireland, a brief review of the considerations involved in the successful growth of root crops will not here be out of place. We must premise, however, that the reader must not expect to find in these pages essays on any branch of husbandry, or details of agricultural operations. We merely purpose to consider the circumstances under which the best crops of roots can be produced; and we do so more in the hope of stimulating inquiry than with a view of speaking dogmatically on the subject.

It is generally conceded that in point of gross produce, under favourable circumstances, the average returns of turnips, beet, and other crops, obtained in Ireland, exceed those of any other country. Individual roots of these crops, ranging from fifteen to twenty pounds weight, have, in fact, ceased to be a novelty. With a well pulverized soil, high manuring, and careful management, crops are grown in this country which astonish the English and Scotch farmers. The circumstance of premiums being offered for large roots stimulated exertion in this direction; and for some time past the intervals between the rows have gone on increasing, as well as the distances between the plants in the rows, in order still further to develop the property so much desired. So far, in short, had this system of growing monster roots been carried, that the inquiry was suggested as to whether this was really the way in which the largest amount of nutritious produce was to be obtained off the land. In the prosecution of this inquiry we have to consider, first—the effect of wide intervals and large roots, as contrasted with closer intervals and medium-sized roots, on the gross produce from a given surface; and second, the relative value of large and small roots in point of nutritive properties. In other words, we have to determine whether as large a gross produce might not be obtained by the growth of roots ranging from three to five or six pounds weight each, as by the production of those varying from seven or eight up to twenty pounds; and further, what is the relative value of a given weight of roots of each class. The *primâ facie* case is in favour of medium-sized over large roots in point of nutritive properties, and if, on further investigation, it should turn out that ten tons of the one are worth twelve or thirteen tons of the other (which is the case), then, indeed, the fancied superiority of these large roots would be only a delusion. This is obviously one of the most important problems in rural economy, and one on which it behoves the farmer to see that he is well informed.

Another circumstance affecting the quality of roots, whether of large or small size, is the direct application of manure, which is injurious in the case of any of the cultivated crops, whatever be their character. Moderate-sized roots are, of course, obtained by growing them close together; but the evil here alluded to can only be remedied by the application of the manure before the final preparation of the land for the seed, by which means it becomes intimately distributed throughout the soil, instead of being, in larger quantity, in contact with the plants.

The contemplated introduction of the beet sugar industry some time ago first gave form to the above inquiry, as it was important to determine the constitution of Irish roots, as compared with those of other countries. With this view an extensive series of experiments was conducted in the winter of 1851–52 in the Museum of Irish Industry, to determine the value of Irish-grown roots so far as the sugar manufacture was concerned. In the process of that inquiry a great variation in the quality of different specimens was found to exist, and, on further examination as to the causes on which such variation was dependent, it was found that the quantity of sugar and the nutritive qualities generally of roots increased or diminished with their size. The specimens then examined (over 100) were so numerous as to guard against the error so often committed of drawing a general conclusion from a small number of observations, and the result left no room for doubt that the law was of general application so far as this class of produce was concerned. In the succeeding season the inquiry was followed up at the Museum with a still more extended range of experiments, when similar results were obtained. A summary of these results we propose to place before the reader; but before doing so it will not be uninteresting to consider some of the circumstances on which successful root tillage is dependent.

The conditions which are necessary to insure the fertility of the soil are eminently deserving of consideration, in this or in any other branch of husbandry. Experience has shown that the liberal application of farm-yard manure is conducive to fertility, which is also known to be promoted by deep and minute pulverization. But in what manner do these agents operate? Is the effect of the manure owing to its directly supplying the food of plants, or to its action upon the soil, or to the influence of both combined? Again, how does the deep and fine tillage prove ancillary to luxuriant vegetation? Hitherto these inquiries have received little attention from the practical farmer; though it is apparent that, until a certain approximation is made towards their satisfactory solution, he is, to a great extent, working in the dark. Experience teaches him that by the adoption of a prescribed course of action a certain effect is produced; but until he becomes acquainted with the *modus operandi* of his business, he cannot tell whether the same effect might not be produced by other and less expensive means. The teachings of experience are not to be neglected, especially in the management of practical operations; but in the present age of active inquiry and general progress, it is anything but consolatory to find that the great bulk of those engaged in the most important branch of human industry are satisfied with a blind adherence to routine practice, with but little inquiry to ascertain how far that practice is in accordance with the results of scientific investigation. Science unaided by practice will do little for the farmer; but we may fairly question the propriety of that practice which is not sustained by science. The merest routine agriculturist, with the aid of certain appliances, can confidently calculate on producing a given result; but the important consideration remains to be determined as to whether or not such result has been obtained in the most economical manner. We have long since ceased to give much credit to the mere production of large crops of any kind, or to even morbid obesity in live stock, without reference to the means and appliances available for the purpose. We are beginning to look more to the economy of means than hitherto; but it is obvious that in this respect our reliance shall be on little less than guess-work, until we make some progress in becoming acquainted with the nature of the action of the means which we employ. It is by such information that we shall be able to determine whether or not there is an undue expenditure for the object to be attained. It is only after having definitely ascertained the character of the conditions to be fulfilled, that we can come to a satisfactory conclusion as to the most economical agency for the purpose.

A finely comminuted state of the soil is a constant and essential condition for the production of luxuriant crops. When we come to consider the extent to which this should be carried out, economical considerations will be involved, depending upon the proportion which the expense incurred thereby will bear to the increased value of the crops. The productiveness of garden tillage, as compared with that of the field, is mainly owing to the great depth to which the soil is finely pulverized in the former case. Where other circumstances have been equal, the most casual observer cannot fail to detect the difference which there is between the crop on that portion much carted upon in applying the manure, as compared with the rest of the field. If this cartage has taken place while the soil is damp, it becomes absolutely ruinous; and in this way much of that fine tilth has often been destroyed, which had been attained at the expense of great previous labour. Some recent investigations have shown, that under favourable circumstances the roots of our commonly cultivated crops penetrate much deeper into the soil than is usually supposed; and some of the specimens in the Exhibition illustrated this property in a remarkable manner. The beet, flax, and some other plants, have been known to extend their roots over three feet in depth, and there is little doubt that, under such circumstances, any obstacle which would have impeded their progress would, in a corresponding degree, have interfered with their growth. Every shower of rain that falls upon the land is fraught with fertilizing matters, which become distributed through the soil, where ready ingress and egress is provided for the moisture that falls upon it. Rain water is charged with ammonia, which it absorbs from the atmosphere; it also contains a considerable quantity of carbonic acid gas. In this way, there is little doubt, that plants derive at all events the greater part of the azote which they contain, and a portion of their carbon. During the alternations of drought and moisture the atmosphere also pervades the soil to a considerable depth, fulfilling thereby an important function in the economy of vegetation. In the case of highly cultivated land, every shower becomes a great storehouse of nutriment, as well as acting the part of a solvent, through the intervention of which the inorganic constituents of the soil are presented in an acceptable form to the rootlets so profusely distributed through it. In the absence of this high pulverization moisture slowly penetrates the soil, and as slowly passes away from it. Becoming stagnant, it is without any of those fertilizing ingredients which it in the first instance contained, and a fresh supply of which becomes impossible. In wet weather the crops upon it suffer from excess of moisture, and at other times from drought. It is an apparent anomaly that the soil which suffers most at one season from an excess of water is most liable to be effected by a deficiency of it at another; yet such is the case. A highly pulverized soil rarely sustains injury from drought unless it be greatly deficient in organic matter; while that which is compressed becomes filled with cracks and fissures in dry weather, thereby presenting an undue amount of evaporating surface, to the great injury of the crop. In maintaining that deep and minute pulverization is a fundamental condition of good tillage, we are not, therefore, trenching upon debateable ground. But when we come to consider the depth to which this pulverization should be carried, the question of expense comes to be taken in account with the effect to be produced. The tendency of late has, however, been in favour of much deeper tillage than was some time ago considered necessary. The depth of an ordinary furrow slice was formerly the extent to which the soil was stirred up; but now the subsoil plough is made to penetrate from fourteen to eighteen inches; and the increased fertility of the land thereby obtained has been found to amply repay the expense incurred.

Keeping in view the great value of this highly pulverized state of the soil, the practice of the farmer should be regulated so as not only to insure its being produced, but also to maintain it as far as practicable. Treading upon or working the soil in damp weather is, therefore, to be avoided as much as possible, as well as cartage of any kind upon the land after being prepared for the crop. Yet, among the many inconsistencies which appear in farm management, there is none greater than that much labour should be expended in finely pulverizing the soil, and that directly after the carts should be made to pass over it repeatedly, in applying a large dressing of heavy manure; the application of which, at that particular time, is not only injurious to the land, but is distressing to the horses from the difficulty of the cartage. It is clear, therefore, that it is only by the application of the manure before the first ploughing is given, that this primary condition of good husbandry can be fully attained. This will, of course, only apply to the manure made in summer and autumn; but the winter manure may be used before the first cross-ploughing in preparing the land for green crops; in which case it will be thoroughly combined with the soil by the subsequent ploughings and harrowings, and all cartage will be avoided when it is ready for the seed. The extraordinary exertion required at that season of the year on the farm is chiefly owing to the great labour imposed by the application of the manure; and hence, by the improved practice, the work would be more equally distributed throughout the year than is at present, which in itself would be no inconsiderable advantage.

The great value justly attributed to farm-yard manure is owing as much to its mechanical effect upon the soil, as to its directly supplying substances to be taken up by the growing crops; and that this effect may be produced to the greatest extent, it is plain that the manure should be intimately combined with the soil, which it can only be, by being applied previous to the preparation of the land for the seed. While the unctuous rich appearance, resulting from the liberal use of that manure, is so favourable to a high degree of fertility, its direct application to any of the growing crops materially interferes with their quality. The effect of culture upon the potato has been well ascertained from its being an article of human food; and it is known that in the case of that tuber, high manuring produces a sample scarcely fit for use. We have reason to believe that the same holds good with all other crops. We attain by a direct application of manure an increase of bulk at the expense of quality; and as we come to regard the latter consideration as it deserves, we shall see the necessity of so modifying our practice as to insure the combination of quality with quantity. The astounding difference produced in the quality of the sugar beet by the direct application of manure has been forcibly exhibited by the experiments on the subject, conducted at the Museum of Irish Industry, already referred to. The gardener well knows that forced productions of any sort are of very inferior quality, and the same holds good in the field; yet attention is so apt to be attracted by anything out of the common course, that the production of monstrous roots has been for some time past the rage, without the slightest consideration as to their quality.

With the land properly drained, and the manure applied previous to the last workings, raised drills become no longer necessary in the culture of green crops, which may then be planted in rows on the flat surface. In this case a material difference may take place in the distances apart at which the plants are grown. There has been ample experience to show that on the flat surface all sorts of root crops may be conveniently and successfully grown at intervals of from sixteen to twenty inches between the rows, and horse-hoes in abundance may be found for cleaning crops at such distances. There is no room for speculation as to whether or not this practice can be carried out, as it has been already adopted with the best results. The previous due preparation of the land will leave no root weeds to be contended with during the growth of the crop, and the annual weeds may be kept down without difficulty. Besides, it must be borne in mind that the production of weeds is largely increased by the manure being deposited in the ordinary manner; and hence the weeding will be less difficult when the manure is distributed throughout the soil.

Among the objections which are urged against this practice, it is stated that with deep tillage, and the manure being distributed through such a large mass of soil, its influence would be little felt—that the fertilizing matters which it contained would be washed away by the rains, from their being soluble—and that however apparently specious the theory may be of deep and minute pulverization combined with winter manuring, in practice it would be wasteful, the effect of the high tillage being to permit of the fertilizing matters being carried away with a rapidity of which we can now form no conception. It is also urged that economy of manure is best promoted by the prevailing practice; that while the stock is deficient it behoves the farmer to apply it as directly as possible to his crops; and that, in fine, it is only after a high degree of fertility has been obtained that the proposed change can be safely adopted.

Now, in all discussions on these subjects, it is incumbent upon us to keep a high standard of excellence in view. We make a great mistake by continuing to found our calculations upon mediocrity. The cultivation of an acre of land in a high state of fertility is not more expensive than under opposite circumstances; on the contrary, generally speaking, it will be less, while the produce will be greater. If the farmer, then, is obliged to work with deficient means, it will clearly be his interest to concentrate his energies on a diminished space, so as to bring it up to the highest point of production, in preference to encountering the expense of tillage of a larger extent, yielding little over half produce. Under high tillage, the bare saving of seed is no inconsiderable item, amounting in the case of wheat to a large proportion of the whole rent of the land. The objection that any proposed course of management is only suited to the circumstances under which a high degree of fertility has been obtained goes therefore for nothing; as it is manifestly the interest of the farmer that this condition should in any case be secured.

Referring to the economy of manure, it is demonstrable that true economy will be studied by enriching the whole mass of the soil, and thus securing a uniform degree of fertility. In this way that porous character will be imparted, to which reference was before made, as presenting the requisite facilities for the roots of the growing crops extending themselves in all directions, so as to be able to take advantage of the fertilizing matters derived from the rain and atmosphere; and which are more important for the progress of healthy and vigorous vegetation than all the manures that could be directly applied.

An opinion is entertained to the effect that pulverization may be carried too far, especially when in combination with thorough drainage, and that the action of heavy rains on the soluble matters of the soil may run no small risk of carrying them off,—in short, that the discharge of the drains in such cases might be a sort of diluted liquid manure, which derived its value at the expense of the soil. In this case the propriety of the distribution of the manure through the land would be doubtful; moreover, if the soluble matters of the manure were liable to be carried off in this manner, winter manuring would be a wasteful practice, as the fertilizing matters applied at that period would run some risk of being altogether carried off before seed-time, so that beyond some mechanical effect upon the soil the manure would exercise no influence upon the crop. This is a highly plausible speculation; but it is nothing more; though it has been again and again brought forward in opposition to that highly pulverized state of the soil which is now known to be favourable to vegetation, and it affords an apposite illustration of the ingenuity exercised by the opponents of innovations on established practice. The investigation of this subject has, however, done much for the progress of scientific agriculture, while it has demonstrated that the apprehensions now adverted to are totally groundless. It is too much the habit even of the intelligent practical farmer of the present day to decry the labours of scientific men in connexion with the business of husbandry. But sneers of this kind have contributed no little to impede the progress of improvement, which requires science and practice to go hand in hand, the one elucidating the other. Even in these inquiries the value of scientific investigation is seen to be by no means inconsiderable, as we shall see more clearly in the sequel.

Other things being equal, it will be at once perceived that on the absorptive powers of the soil much of its fertility will depend; that is, the extent to which it imbibes and retains the fertilizing matters, so that they may be available for the growing crops. Accordingly, it is found that, however highly the soil may be pulverized, or however perfectly drained, the particles of earthy matter possess the property of retaining alkaline substances of all kinds which may be supplied by manure. In sandy soils this takes place only to a very limited extent, and hence these are technically called "hungry soils" from their so readily parting with fertilizing matters. To the farmer it has long been known that certain soils require the application of manure much more frequently than others; but the circumstance to which this was owing does not seem to have, until lately, attracted that attention to which it is entitled. The subject has recently been very fully investigated by Professor Way, the substance of whose researches we now propose to briefly notice.

In the preliminary stage of the inquiry it was found that all soils capable of profitable cultivation retained any alkaline substances applied to them in solution; and when salts, with alkaline bases, were used, the alkali alone was absorbed, the acid being set free. The action, moreover, was instantaneous, leaving no room for supposing that the result could be varied by any excess of moisture, such as would occur in heavy rains. If sulphate of ammonia, potash, or soda, were applied to the soil, the filtered liquor proceeding from it would contain sulphate of lime; and where muriates or nitrates of these alkalies were used, muriate or nitrate of lime would result. Professor Way found that the organic matters of the soil had nothing to do with this action; that the addition of carbonate of lime did not increase the absorptive power for the alkaline salts; and even that a soil in which carbonate of lime did not occur might still possess, in a high degree, the power of removing ammonia or potash from solution. The stiffest and most tenacious clays, taken from considerable depths, which had never, since their deposition, been exposed to atmospheric influences, and which were free from organic matter or carbonate of lime, were found to possess the absorptive property to the fullest extent.

An examination of the soils in which this property of absorption existed showed that a considerable proportion of clay was invariably present. In fine sands it does not exist at all. The inquiry of the manner in which the action takes place, as well as the precise changes which occur in the soil during the process, are evidently points of great practical importance, as well as interesting objects of scientific research. In an early stage of the inquiry, Professor Way states that he felt convinced the absorptive property was due to a small quantity of some definite chemical compound,—a circumstance which imparted additional interest to the investigation. A salt of lime was, in all cases, found in the resulting solution from the soil, where this absorptive property was proved to exist, after being acted upon by liquid manure; and since many of the soils examined did not yield to pure water any considerable quantity of lime, and therefore did not contain any soluble salt of that base; further, when treated with acids, they did not give any indication of the presence of carbonate of lime; the compound could not be any of the ordinary salts of lime. What, then, was the nature of this salt? The large quantity of silica present in certain soils, some of which is known to exist in the form of silicate of lime and other alkaline silicates, seemed to Professor Way to point to salts of this acid as most probably the true cause of the absorptive property. The silicate of lime is very slightly soluble, and, not being capable of absorbing ammonia, it became evident it was not to this salt the property was due. The compound silicates were therefore examined for the purpose, as being derived from the granite rocks to which clay owes its origin, and as being therefore present to a considerable extent in clayey soils. But the different natural silicates, when digested in a solution of sal-ammoniac, did not appear to possess the power of combining with the ammonia—a circumstance which showed that it was not to the undecomposed remains of the granitic rocks in the clay that the property is owing. Double silicates formed artificially were very naturally supposed to exhibit chemical action more readily than after, as in the case of the granite rocks, undergoing the agency of heat; and, accordingly, salts were produced without the aid of heat, of the same composition as felspar and albite. When the resulting compound was digested in a solution of muriate of ammonia, the excess of the latter salt being washed away by distilled water, the precipitate was found to contain ammonia in considerable quantity. Professor Way, therefore, considers that with these double silicates of ammonia and other bases, the greater part, if not the whole, of the phenomena of absorption of manures are connected; and he entertains a hope that these compounds, which have a very important relation to the growth of plants, may yet be manufactured at a sufficiently low cost to make them available as manure. Hence, one of the very important objects which may be attained by this inquiry.

In the investigation of the properties of the silicates, it was observed that there is a regular order of decomposition between the silicates of each base and the ordinary salts of other bases. Thus, that of soda is decomposed by salts of lime, potash, or ammonia; the potash silicate is again decomposed by lime or ammonia; and that of lime by the silicate of ammonia. From a silicate of alumina, and any of the other bases, for example, the base will be dislodged in the order mentioned. Nitrate of potash will decompose silicate of soda, and a potash silicate will be formed, whilst ammonia will replace any of the other bases. The silicates, therefore, without exception, are capable of absorbing ammonia, which is known to be one of the most important agents in vegetation; and the discovery of this fact is instructive, as it exhibits so very certain a provision for the retention of ammonia in the soil. It matters not, whether any one or more of these compounds is present; so that one of them is there, the ammonia supplied by the manure, or obtained from the atmosphere, will be equally retained to be available for the use of the growing crops. And the order in which the decompositions take place is not a little remarkable. Thus, for the retention of ammonia, four other bases are made responsible. Next comes potash. And then soda, which is the alkali of least importance in the economy of vegetation. Lime is less securely provided for than any of the others; but the precaution in this case is the less necessary from the great abundance in which lime exists. In reference, however, to the decompositions, the rule only applies to the action of the *salts* of different bases upon the silicates. Sulphate of lime cannot displace the ammonia from its silicate, but the action of the caustic alkali itself would be very different; for not only would silicate of ammonia be decomposed by lime, but the silicates of potash and alumina would also be decomposed by it. This is a point of some importance, as it may lead, among other things, to the discovery of the true cause of the evils of over-liming land, which may be mainly owing to the ammonia of the soil being driven off: and what may only be a useful application of lime to one soil may be destructive to another; as from the smaller proportion of other silicates for the lime to act upon, it may attack the ammoniacal compounds, and, by driving off the ammonia, impoverish the land.

In the inquiries instituted by Professor Way, it has, therefore, been shown that a power of absorption is possessed by soils not referable to either the organic matter, the sand, or the lime which they contain; and further, that pure clays, free from any of the ordinary salts of lime or soda, possess the property in a high degree. But the activity of clay can only be due to some compounds of silica, from which their further investigation becomes a matter of great importance. The ammonia, potash, and other alkaline ingredients of manure, being under the influence of the soil converted into double silicates, the question may be asked, how are they ultimately made available for the use of plants? If the compounds so produced are insoluble in water, how is the ammonia or potash liberated for the purposes of vegetation? But these salts are *not altogether* insoluble in water. The double silicate of alumina and ammonia, when treated with distilled water, gives to it ammonia, though in small quantity; but carbonic acid water dissolves the ammonia from the double silicate rather freely; and as water naturally contains carbonic acid gas, it follows that the solubility of the ammoniacal silicate will be very considerable. But it is still more soluble in a solution of common salt. In these various ways Professor Way contends that an abundant supply will be available for the purposes of vegetation. The value of an application of common salt may be chiefly owing to these phenomena.

The bearings, in a practical point of view, of the inquiry here adverted to cannot be mistaken; and it further shows the great service which science is calculated to render in the business of husbandry. We thus see, to some extent, the reason why deep pulverization is so essential to the maintenance of a high degree of fertility in the soil. Atmospheric action contributes to these changes taking place. And moreover, if the alkaline solutions cannot freely penetrate the soil to the utmost extent to which the roots of plants are likely to extend, the absorptive power can be but sparingly called into action; and the fertilizing matters, being retained in their original state, are liable to be washed away by every shower that falls.

The conclusions to which we are irresistibly led by a full investigation of the subject appear, therefore, to be—that the maintenance of a highly pulverized state of the soil, to the greatest practicable depth, is essential to the development of its fertility; that the fertilizing matters which may be applied, if intimately incorporated with the soil, are in little danger of being washed out by any rains that may fall upon it, which removes the only feasible objection that could be urged to winter manuring; that the direct application of bulky manure, to root crops of any kind, imposes the necessity of growing these crops with wider intervals between the rows than would otherwise be necessary, while the fact is indisputable, that in all cases it exercises an injurious action upon the quality of the produce; and that by growing this class of crops at closer intervals than have hitherto been adopted, applying the manure at least before the final preparation of the land for the crop, there is good reason to believe that while the quality of the produce will be greatly improved, the gross quantity may not be seriously, if at all, diminished. Nor is there the slightest reason to doubt that, by the adoption of the practice here indicated, the conditions necessary for insuring a high degree of fertility in the soil will be better fulfilled than under the present practice; which also has the further drawback of adding, in an enormous degree, to the amount of labour to be performed at the busiest season of the year.

Reverting again to the composition of our root crops, it is obviously important that the quantity of solid matter which they contain should be as great as possible; as in any case the quantity of water in them is large, varying from four-fifths to nine-tenths of their whole weight. In the tabulated results obtained at the Museum of Irish Industry in 1851–52, we find that some of the roots of the sugar beet, grown by Messrs. Dickson, of Belturbet, contained over 93 per cent. of water, while others, of the same variety, grown by James Sinclair, Jun., Esq., of Holyhill, near Strabane, contained less than 78 per cent. of water. In the one case, 100 tons of roots would yield only 7 tons of solid matter, and in the other, 22 tons. The produce of Mr. Dickson's roots is stated to have been 46 tons per Irish acre, which was, no doubt, regarded as highly satisfactory; and so it was, in the absence of any question being raised about quality; but the quantity of solid food afforded to the acre would be little over three tons, which, again, is miserably small. Mr. Sinclair's roots produced 28 tons to the Cunningham acre,—which happens to be the measure employed in that district,—or about 35 tons to the Irish acre, yielding 7¾ tons of solid food. The casual observer would here award the palm to the larger produce, though it requires no argument to show that, in an economical point of view, a very great mistake would be made by so doing. The acreage produce in the latter case is perhaps rather under the average of what good farming would afford; though, when we come to learn the quality of the crop, the yield is seen to be highly satisfactory.*

* The confessedly great importance of the subject will justify our inserting at length a Report on the subject of the second investigation at the Museum, which is pregnant with instruction to the agriculturist:—

"*On the comparative value of large and small roots, with some considerations on the culture of Root Crops in general, by* WM. K. SULLIVAN, *Chemist to the Museum of Irish Industry, and* ALPHONSE GAGES, *Assistant Chemist.*

"In the Parliamentary Report on the composition of the Sugar Beet, containing the results of experiments made during the year 1851 and 1852 in the Museum of Irish Industry, we drew attention to a fact already well known to the sugar manufacturers on the Continent, that very large roots contained less sugar than those of a medium size. Now this fact is of very great importance, indeed, we may say, of vital importance to the manufacturer of beet sugar; to him the first consideration is the per-centage of sugar in the roots, whilst to the farmer the gross weight of the crop has hitherto been the great object—the former looks to *quality*, the latter to *quantity*. But our experiments, as well as those of preceding chemists, have fully demonstrated that the solid matter of the beet scarcely varies in composition, or at least only varies within very narrow limits; that it is the water alone which increases and diminishes in relation to the other constituents; and that hence, if the per-centage of sugar be smaller in one root than in another, the total amount of solid matter available for food or other purposes will also be smaller.

"In nearly all previous analyses, the comparative weight of the roots examined was but little attended to, and where a comparison was instituted, it was between roots grown in different localities. A perusal of the Report already alluded to will show, however, that owing to the influence of soil, manures, &c., large roots grown in one field may be better than small roots grown in another. Hence the doubt which has existed upon the subject. Again, roots taken from one locality alone, no matter how many may be submitted to examination, could lead to no definite result, because the seed usually sold is not always of uniform quality, some of the grains being unripe, others crossed by a different variety, and many other causes which it is unnecessary to notice; and as it may so happen that the small roots may be derived from the imperfect seeds, they would naturally be of inferior quality. It was, therefore, necessary to examine a great number of roots from different localities; and instead of taking only one or two roots from each field to select three or more of the smallest roots, and three or more of the largest, grown as nearly as possible under similar conditions.

"The total number of roots examined is about 430, which give between seventy and eighty examples obtained from nine different counties; a number which we are sure will be considered sufficient to warrant us in drawing a conclusion. We have extended our examination to nearly all root crops without distinction.

"We shall now confine ourselves to the total amount of solid matter which these different roots contained; that is, to the amount of matter which remains after the removal of all the water, leaving the consideration of a number of important questions to a subsequent period. It is unnecessary for us to remark, that the first elements in the comparison between root crops is the relative amount of solid matter which they contain; it is indeed at the present moment the only definite one. When we compare two different crops of the same plant, it is quite clear that we are justified to a great extent in pronouncing that crop the best which contains the largest amount of solid matter, because, as we remarked already, the composition of that solid matter is pretty constant, even in different varieties of the same plant. But when we compare roots belonging to different genera of plants, we must make allowance for difference of composition; these are points, however, which we shall return to on another occasion.

"An objection to this mode of comparison is sometimes made, and but for the fact of its being held by many intelligent agriculturists, we would not consider worthy of notice. They consider that the water contained in vegetables is of considerable importance in the nutrition of animals. No doubt it is; but does it not strike such reasoners that these vegetables which contain most solid matter already contain far more water than is necessary for the animal economy, and that it is not very profitable to be paying for an additional quantity, by purchasing roots consisting of an innutritious sponge filled with water, which is very frequently the character of the large roots. They also believe that in drying roots, some valuable element goes off with the water, and thus escapes the chemist's balance. We shall only say, that the age of *auras* is past, and that such a mode of explaining physical facts is simply absurd.

"If large roots contain less solid matter than small roots, we ought naturally to expect that roots of from fifteen to twenty pounds should give a minimum result. We have not as yet had an opportunity of examining roots of this size. Indeed many of the large roots sent to us, as such, were in some instances under three pounds. Hence our results are founded upon the examination of very ordinary-sized roots, and are, therefore, the more valuable, as they refer not alone to the few crops of 'monster roots' grown by wealthy agriculturists, but to the plants as they are usually cultivated.

"Out of upwards of seventy samples of roots, making altogether, as we have already remarked, 430 different specimens, we have found only three exceptions to the rule that small roots are superior to large. The first case occurred with six roots of long red mangels, grown by Mr. J. Macdonnell at the Model Farm of Larne, in the county of Antrim. The mean per-centage of solid matter in the large roots was 14,936, and in the small 14,721, that is practically the same. Now the cause of this exception was, that the seed was not uniform; the heaviest root, which weighed 6 lb. 10¼ oz., was a different variety from all the small; it had white flesh and a rose-red skin, while the three small ones were remarkable for the amount of colouring matter which they contained. As a general rule, all varieties of the beet having white flesh are superior to those having alternating red rings, and the latter to those coloured red throughout their mass. It is, however, very often difficult to decide upon a point of this kind, as nearly all the roots which we have examined were grown from seed which appeared to have been more or less crossed by other varieties, and hence, many of the roots thus partially altered had a great tendency to throw out their flower stalk during the first year, by which, of course, all increase in solidity in the bulb is arrested. Perfectly developed seed from a fully formed variety, produced under proper conditions, does not run to seed the first year, except where it is placed in contact with fresh manure, rich in nitrogen, and in a moist soil.

"The second exception occurred with six roots grown by Lord Clancarty. The average of the large roots, the heaviest of which was only 4 lb. 8 oz., was 14,701 per cent. of solid matter, and of the small ones 14,287 per cent., or a very

In the production of root crops there can, in fact, be no doubt that high manuring is inimical to the growth of roots of good quality. It has hitherto, however, been generally supposed that in the application of manures to root crops too large a quantity could scarcely be used. It is well known that in the culture of grain this does not hold good; that over-manuring produces an excess, in fact a bulky crop of straw, but that it will be little less. In this case also, the cause of the exception can be explained. The two small roots which contained the least per-centage of solid matter were unripe, and had grown in a great measure out of the soil, by which the quality was deteriorated. Our own results have before led us to the conclusion, that in cultivating beet, the bulb should be covered up so as not to have it projecting out of the soil; an opinion which is opposed to that of most practical men, who urge as a proof against it, that if you cover up turnips you cause them to finger. Now what does this prove? That the soil is not sufficiently broken up, and that if you surround a young bulb with a mass of mud clay, it cannot expand equally, but will send out branches along the lines of least resistance. In practice the farmer may find that a theoretical opinion does not apply, but he rarely perceives that the reason why it does not is simply that the proper conditions are not fulfilled.

"If we cut a beet root at right angles to its longer axis, we find that it is composed of a series of alternate rings of vascular and cellular tissue, and if we examine the vascular tissue, and the cellular tissue in immediate contact with it, we shall find that it contains far more sugar, and, consequently, solid matter, than the remaining cellular tissue; very frequently double the amount. This observation was first made by Payen, and we have fully confirmed his opinion in our report of last year. But not only does the composition of the beet vary from without inwards, but it also varies in an equal, and indeed, in a still greater degree, if we examine it from above downwards. If we divide a beet root into five parts by sections at right angles to the longer axis; the first forming the crown, and terminating at the limit of the insertion of the leaf's stalks; second, a segment immediately below the crown, varying from a half-inch to one inch in thickness; third, the body of the root; fourth, the point of the root about one inch in thickness, and from one to two inches long; and fifth, the bifurcation of the root, and the small roots,—we shall find that the sugar, and, consequently, the solid matter contained in each of those parts, varies very considerably. Mr. A. Rehring, of Edderitz, obtained the following results from an examination at successive periods of these different parts.

| Date of Experiment. | Per-centage of Sugar. | | | | |
|---|---|---|---|---|---|
| | Crown. | Segment of Root below the Crown. | Body of the Root. | Point of the Root. | Bifurcations and smaller Roots. |
| 28th October, . . . . | 2·01 | 8·74 | 12·07 | 10·47 | 5·41 |
| 15th November, . . | 2·00 | 8·94 | 12·31 | 10·89 | 7·34 |
| 20th December, . . | 1·23 | 8·61 | 12·08 | 10·64 | 7·20 |
| 12th February, . . . | 0·32 | 7·34 | 11·72 | 10·49 | 6·5 |
| 1st March, . . . . . | 0·02 | 5·02 | 11·45 | 10·32 | 5·94 |

"From these experiments, it results that the segment below the crown contains only about two-thirds of the sugar contained in the body of the root, and as the thickness of this segment is increased by allowing the root to protrude out of the soil, it will easily be understood that such a practice must be erroneous. We have a great many interesting results upon this point, but as they are not immediately connected with our present object, we shall reserve them.

| | Name of Grower. | Weight of Large Roots. | Weight of Small Roots. | Per-centage of Solid Matter in Large Roots. | Per-centage of Solid Matter in Small Roots. | Number of Tons of Large Roots equivalent in Value to 100 Tons of Small. |
|---|---|---|---|---|---|---|
| | | lb. oz. lb. oz. | lb. oz. lb. oz. | | | Tons. |
| Sugar Beet. | Ninian Niven, Drumcondra, . . . . . . . . | 3 11¼ to 4 2 | 1 3¼ to 1 11¾ | 10·408 | 17·427 | 167·43 |
| | P. O'Hagan, Market-Hill, . . . . . . . . | 3 2¼ ,, 4 9 | 1 3¼ ,, 1 7¾ | 15·782 | 19·785 | 125·36 |
| | Lord Talbot de Malahide, Malahide, . . | 3 3¾ ,, 7 10½ | 1 10¼ ,, 2 12¼ | 13·461 | 15·756 | 117·06 |
| | Rev. W. R. Townsend, Aghada, . . . . . | 3 9¾ ,, 4 8¾ | 0 7¾ ,, 1 4¾ | 12·949 | 15·321 | 118·38 |
| | Lord Clancarty, Garbally, . . . . . . . | 2 9 ,, 2 15¼ | 0 14¼ ,, 0 14¾ | 14·671 | 17·152 | 116·91 |
| | William Kelly, Portrane, . . . . . . . . | 4 13 ,, 5 14 | 0 8 ,, 1 4¾ | 14·863 | 15·892 | 106·92 |
| | Robert Hawkins, Enniscorthy, . . . . . . | 5 13½ ,, 13 4 | 1 12 ,, 3 0¾ | 8·731 | 11·194 | 128·20 |
| | Daniel Humphries, Middleton, . . . . . . | 3 11½ ,, 3 15¼ | 1 4 ,, 1 14 | 14·104 | 16·285 | 115·46 |
| Long Red Mangel Wurzel. | Dr. Kirkpatrick, Glasnevin, . . . . . . . | 6 4¾ ,, 8 6¾ | 1 0¾ ,, 1 9¾ | 12·284 | 14·683 | 119·53 |
| | Lord Talbot de Malahide, . . . . . . . . | 6 15¾ ,, 9 13¼ | 3 8¾ ,, 4 3¾ | 10·588 | 12·244 | 115·64 |
| | Rev. W. R. Townsend, Aghada, . . . . . | 6 15¾ ,, 7 6½ | 0 10 ,, 1 5 | 10·788 | 15·911 | 147·48 |
| | R. Boyle, Ballymoney, . . . . . . . . . . | 4 9 ,, 6 10 | 1 8¾ ,, 1 12¾ | 11·835 | 13·462 | 113·74 |
| | J. Macdonnell, Larne, . . . . . . . . . . | 4 8¾ ,, 6 10½ | 2 8¾ ,, 2 12¾ | 14·936 | 14·721 | exception. |
| | J. Andrews, Comber, . . . . . . . . . . | 4 8¾ ,, 4 8¾ | 1 2 ,, 1 3¾ | 13·697 | 17·810 | 130·02 |
| | Lord Clancarty, . . . . . . . . . . . . . | 3 4¾ ,, 4 8 | 1 1¾ ,, 1 4¾ | 14·701 | 14·287 | exception. |
| | Andrew Templeton, Clandeboye, . . . . | 3 12¾ ,, 4 0½ | 0 12 ,, 1 2 | 14·265 | 16·033 | 109·62 |
| | William Kelly, Portrane, . . . . . . . . | 6 14¾ ,, 9 3 | 0 6½ ,, 0 7¾ | 10·986 | 15·624 | 142·18 |
| | Robert Hawkins, Enniscorthy, . . . . . | 8 6¾ ,, 10 2 | 1 13¼ ,, 2 4¾ | 9·413 | 14·088 | 149·66 |
| Orange Globe Mangel Wurzel. | Ninian Niven, Drumcondra, . . . . . . . | 9 0 ,, 9 15¾ | 2 0¾ ,, 2 10¾ | 11·884 | 12·583 | 106·88 |
| | Dr. Kirkpatrick, Glasnevin, . . . . . . . | 6 15½ ,, 8 14 | 0 14¾ ,, 1 12 | 11·115 | 13·775 | 123·93 |
| | David Moore, Glasnevin, . . . . . . . . | 3 13 ,, 4 5 | 0 10½ ,, 0 12 | 10·690 | 15·194 | 142·13 |
| | Rev. W. R. Townsend, Aghada, . . . . . | 6 11 ,, 7 5 | 1 1¾ ,, 1 6½ | 11·665 | 16·125 | 137·60 |
| | Andrew Templeton, Clandeboye, . . . . | 2 9¾ ,, 8 2 | 1 1¼ ,, 1 4¾ | 14·321 | 14·097 | exception. |
| | William Kelly, Portrane, . . . . . . . . | 5 15¾ ,, 7 5 | 0 8 ,, 0 14¾ | 11·941 | 13·366 | 111·93 |
| | Robert Hawkins, Enniscorthy, . . . . . | 8 5¾ ,, 10 2 | 1 12¼ ,, 1 15¼ | 8·567 | 11·722 | 136·82 |
| | Rev. W. R. Townsend, Aghada, . . . . . | 6 4 ,, 7 4½ | 1 0¾ ,, 2 0¾ | 11·347 | 13·806 | 121·67 |
| | William Kelly, Portrane, . . . . . . . . | 5 14 ,, 9 2 | 0 14¾ ,, 1 6 | 11·949 | 13·769 | 115·23 |
| | Robert Hawkins, Enniscorthy, . . . . . | 8 11 ,, 9 13 | 1 7¾ ,, 2 2½ | 7·050 | 9·208 | 130·60 |
| Swedish Turnips. | Lord Talbot de Malahide, . . . . . . . . | 6 12¾ ,, 9 0¾ | 2 2¼ ,, 3 5¼ | 11·206 | 12·930 | 115·38 |
| | Ditto, . . . . . . . . . . | 7 12¾ ,, 9 13¼ | 2 1¾ ,, 3 8¾ | 10·948 | 11·470 | 104·81 |
| | Rev. W. R. Townsend, Aghada, . . . . . | 4 14 ,, 5 10½ | 0 14½ ,, 1 9 | 11·684 | 12·770 | 109·30 |
| | R. Boyle, Ballymoney, . . . . . . . . . . | 6 5¼ ,, 6 12 | 1 2 ,, 1 5¼ | 13·781 | 16·254 | 118·37 |
| | J. Macdonnell, Larne, . . . . . . . . . . | 6 14¾ ,, 7 8¼ | 2 3½ ,, 2 5¾ | 12·068 | 12·798 | 106·00 |
| | Robert Cassidy, Monasterevan, . . . . . | 11 6¾ ,, 12 0 | 0 15 ,, 1 2¾ | 10·104 | 11·983 | 118·60 |
| | Ditto, Ditto, . . . . . . | 6 6 ,, 9 8½ | 0 12 ,, 1 0 | 10·083 | 12·348 | 122·41 |
| | J. Andrews, Comber, . . . . . . . . . . | 6 8½ ,, 7 3¾ | 0 13¼ ,, 0 14¾ | 11·080 | 12·627 | 113·96 |
| | Lord Clancarty, . . . . . . . . . . . . . | 5 10 ,, 6 12¾ | 0 13¾ ,, 1 4½ | 11·187 | 12·300 | 109·94 |
| | Andrew Templeton, Clandeboye, . . . . | 6 5½ ,, 8 12¾ | 1 4½ ,, 1 14 | 10·937 | 12·133 | 110·93 |

"The third exception to the rule was in the case of roots of orange globe mangel, grown by Mr. Andrew Templeton, of Clandeboye, in the county of Down. We cannot account for this case; but we may remark that the large roots

very deficient in value; and, singular enough, the same principle appears to hold good in farming generally. Although in the growth of roots the injurious effects of over-manuring are not so apparent, they are not the less certain. As in the case of grain husbandry, we may have an increased gross weight, but this may be actually a disadvantage. When alluding to high manuring in this sense, we allude chiefly to farm-yard ma-

were under 4 lbs., and the small roots between 1 and 2 lbs., so that they might not have reached their natural limit of development.

"As it would evidently be impossible to go into the details of all the analyses, we shall confine ourselves to a *resumé* of the results, as given in the preceding page. And as the value of a small difference in the per-centage of solid matter may not strike persons unaccustomed to scientific calculations, we shall express such differences in tons of raw roots. Thus, if the average per-centage of solid matter in roots of a certain size was 13·461, and in small roots, 15·756, the difference may be considered trifling, but when it is seen that 100 tons of such small roots would be equal to 117 tons of the large ones, it will at once be perceived how important, in a practical point of view, such a difference becomes.

"From these results we are justified in concluding that the larger the root the smaller will be the per-centage of solid matter it will contain. If we could select a number of seeds of a bulbous plant exactly alike in ripeness, size, and endowed with the same degree of vitality, and plant them in the same soil and under exactly the same conditions, there can be no doubt that after the bulbs would have been formed, the per-centage of solid matter would be at a maximum, and that as they increased in size it would diminish. But as it is nearly impossible to find roots grown under such conditions, we need not be surprised that this diminution is not very regular. Thus, we often find roots of 3 lbs. contain more than roots of 1 lb.; these exceptions are not, however, of very frequent occurrence, as will be seen by consulting the Tables containing the detailed results. If, however, we group the roots grown upon a field according to size, and leave considerable differences between the weights of the roots of each group, we shall find by taking a sufficient number of roots that this gradual diminution in the solidity of roots as they increase in size becomes very evident in the mean results. Thus, in the seventeen roots of white Silesian beet examined from the crop grown on the Island of Lambay, by Lord Talbot de Malahide, there were:—

4 roots of from 6 to 8 lbs. weight, which gave as a mean per cent. of solid matter, . . . . . . . . 12·541
5 roots between 3 and 5 lbs., . . . . . . . . . . . 14·197
8 roots under 3 lbs., . . . . . . . . . . . . . . . . 15·756

Or, in other words, 100 tons of roots under 3 lbs. would be equal to 125·56 tons of 6 to 8 lb. roots; and to 110·98 tons of 3 to 5 lb. roots whilst 100 tons of the latter would be equal to 113·14 tons of the 6 to 8 lb. roots. Here we have a very regular mean diminution of solid matter.

"That the diminution of the per-centage of solid matter commences very soon after the perfect formation of the bulb is remarkably borne out by the analyses of red carrots grown by Mr. Robert Boyle, at the Workhouse Farm of Ballymoney, in the county of Antrim, the average of the large roots being 12·131 per cent., the heaviest root being only 1 lb. 14½ oz., whilst the small roots gave an average of 17·818 per cent. of solid matter, the smallest root being only 2¼ oz., and contained 19·724 per cent.

"By comparing a great number of roots our average results are free from the influence of exceptional cases. It was with this object in view that we made such a number of analyses. Hence, on comparing all sorts of the same kind, we find that the rule of small roots being superior to large is not only true when grown in the same field, but also when the roots grown over a whole district of country are compared. Of course, a considerable difference between the weights of each group of roots compared must be allowed. The following Table contains the results of our examination, with the exception of those varieties of which we have had too few examples:—

| SIZE OF ROOTS. | White Silesian or Sugar Beet. | Long Red Mangel Wurzel. | Orange Globe Mangel. | Red Globe Mangel. | Swede Turnips. | Red Carrots. | White Belgian Carrots. |
|---|---|---|---|---|---|---|---|
| Average of Roots above 7 lbs., . . . . . . . . | 10·204 | 10·017 | 10·785 | 8·704 | 10·755 | . . | . . |
| " " 5 " . . . . . . . . | 11·653 | 11·476 | 11·028 | 10·115 | 10·257 | . . | . . |
| " " from 3 to 5 lbs., . . . . . . . . | 15·708 | 14·934 | 13·974 | 12·060 | 12·810 | . . | . . |
| Average of all Roots, . . . . . . . . | 14·532 | 13·635 | 12·645 | 11·188 | 12·081 | 13·370 | 12·980 |

"With reference to this Table we have to remark, that the number of roots of the red globe mangel and red carrots was too small to afford a fair average. It is probable that if we had an opportunity of examining a larger number, we should find a higher average for the former, and a lower average for the latter; inasmuch as one sample of roots of the red globe mangel was far inferior in quality to the other samples, whilst the opposite case occurred with the red carrots.

"This Table presents some curious results, and of considerable practical importance. Besides showing in the clearest manner the influence of size, it also leads to the remarkable conclusion, that the white Silesian or sugar beet affords the largest return of solid matter of any root-crop usually cultivated. Another result not less important is, that carrots are very little superior to Swede turnips, and inferior to nearly all the varieties of the beet. When we direct attention to the fact, that carrots are sold at from £2 to £2 10*s*. per ton, we need not dwell further upon the necessity of farmers looking a little more closely to the quality as well as to the quantity of the crops they cultivate.

"Should the view which we have taken be found by further investigation to be universal, of which we believe there can be no doubt, the present system of giving prizes for the largest roots must be reversed, and the premium awarded to him who produces the largest amount of solid food from a given space of ground; in other words, the whole system of root-cropping must be amended.

"We regret to have to state that these results lead directly to the conclusion, that nearly all the analyses hitherto published on the composition of root crops, on the influence of manure on their composition, and, above all, on the influence of manure upon the gross weight of the crop, as utterly useless. This is a startling proposition, but one which is nevertheless perfectly true. At present we shall not enter into the subject of the general composition of roots, as we shall have occasion to go into it fully hereafter; but with regard to the influence of manure upon the gross weight and composition of a crop, we will point out in a few words how completely valueless previous results are, because the influence of size was not considered.

"We will suppose an experiment to have been made with mangel wurzel or Swede turnips, by sowing them on two or more plots of ground manured with different manures. When fully grown, a few roots from each plot are sent to a chemist to examine; if he happens to take a 2 lb. root from one plot, and a 4 lb. root from another, it is quite clear that the former will in all probability contain a larger per-centage of solid matter than the latter, and hence, the manure with which the small root was grown will be pronounced to have a decided superiority over that with which the larger was grown, whilst the reverse might be the truth. And if a

nure, though purely inorganic manures may also be in excess. Thus, the nitrates applied in large quantity to corn crops lead to an undue production of straw, which is seldom accompanied by a fair yield of grain; and the investigation carried on at the Museum shows that injurious effects on the quality of roots may be produced by the presence of certain saline ingredients. Wherever organic matter prevails largely in the soil, as in boggy land, or where over-manuring takes place, we have therefore reason to believe that the quality of the roots will be inferior. And as regards manuring, the inference, from what has been stated, clearly points out the propriety of the application before winter, that it may be thoroughly worked up with the soil when the land is ready for the crop. At the period of sowing, some of the portable manures may be put in with the seed, so as rapidly to push on the young plants in their early stage, when they are peculiarly susceptible of injury. In this way the most perfect tillage may be secured, as well as the best quality of produce; and to those who are accustomed to carry on extensive spring operations, in which the cartage and application of the manures form the heaviest item, the advantage will be appreciated of having all this, or the greater part of it, gone through in the end of autumn and during the winter. How often has a fine tilth, which there has been great labour to obtain, been totally destroyed by spring cartage, to the great detriment of the succeeding crop? But as our farmers come to look more to the quality of their crops, and less to mere quantity, the practice here indicated will come to be adopted—farm-yard manure will be generally applied before the land gets the first ploughing, and at seed-time such hand manures will be used as the peculiar circumstances of the case may render expedient.

The considerations which have here been adverted to cannot fail to suggest the expediency of a considerable modification of the practice of growing root-crops generally. It is well known, for instance, that it is the application of bulky manure in the spring which imposes the necessity of the present wide intervals between the rows of our drill crops; but by autumn or winter manuring this is obviated; and hence the measure of distance may be that sufficient to admit of horse-labour between the drills, which may be 18, instead of, as at present, 26 to 30 inches. With rows 18 inches apart, and spaces of from 5 to 6 inches between the plants, roots averaging from 2 lbs. to 4 lbs. each may be produced with facility. Supposing the entire crop to average roots of 1 lb. each, at 5 inches apart in the rows, there would be 69,696 plants to the acre, weighing over 31½ tons; and at 6 inches between the rows, 58,080 plants, weighing, in round numbers, 26 tons. Grown in this way, it will be seen that a crop of comparatively small roots will yield a very satisfactory produce: nay, even more than those monstrous overgrown roots at wider intervals; while one ton in the former case may be worth two in the latter, for any purpose to which the crop may be applied. The intervals here mentioned are small as compared with those usually left between root crops; but it will be recollected that the size of roots calculated on is also small, only a fraction of what some of our farmers boast that they obtain. These calculations are also chiefly designed to give an idea of the comparative produce by the two methods of tillage; as that strict accuracy which implies a given distance between the plants throughout a field is not to be expected in practice.

## HOPS.

The hop plant, so important in the manufacture of fermented beverages, was represented by excellent samples from three exhibitors, the illustration of which must have been interesting to the people of this country, few of whom have opportunities of becoming acquainted with it. This plant presents many peculiarities; its growth in these countries is confined to comparatively small districts in the south-eastern part of England, where, however, it receives great attention; and its culture involves a larger outlay than perhaps any of our other crops, varying from £35 to £60 per acre. The returns from it are exceedingly variable, from the extreme liability of the plant to suffer from disease, ranging from a little over 1 cwt. to 10 cwt. per acre; and, unlike other crops known to our farmers, the duration of a plantation is almost indefinite, usually lasting, according to the situation and kind of treatment, from ten to twenty years, while some of the hop gardens at Farnham have not been changed for a new stock of plants since the introduction of hop culture into England, more than 300 years ago. The hop also presents the further peculiarity that it is the only plant grown in the United Kingdom under the surveillance of the Commissioners of Inland Revenue; the crop being subject to the payment of excise duty, the aggregate amount of which has varied of late years from £34,000 to £250,000 per annum; a rate of variation which shows the extremely uncertain nature of the crop, the quantity of land devoted to it being tolerably constant, being about 50,000 acres. The great value of the hop, under favourable circumstances, illustrates more forcibly the value of what is termed high-farming than any other of our cultivated crops; and although its entire tillage and management are exceptional, yet from the examination of hop culture, as practised in some parts of the south of England, the agriculturist may derive many suggestive hints worthy of being acted upon in his ordinary operations. The outlay there in tillage, in manures, and in saving the crop, is so large as almost to appear fabulous to those

number of roots are sent from different parts of the country, and consequently liable to be grown at different intervals, the chances of error will be still greater.

- Nothing can be more fallacious than the present system of studying the influence of manures upon the gross weight of a crop. In the first place it is evident from the preceding results, that from the extraordinary variation which may take place in the relation between the water and solid matter in the same variety of root, the gross weight tells us nothing; for we are to suppose that the object of the farmer is to grow food, and not woody fibre and water. And in the next place some manures, such, for instance, as nitrate of soda, cause plants to grow rapidly, and in the case of root crops to produce large bulbs, which give a large gross weight, but no corresponding proportion of food.

"We are not practical agriculturists, and consequently are not disposed to hazard any positive opinion as to the way in which the largest amount of solid matter per acre can be produced. Still we would suggest the propriety of growing the plants closer than is customary at present in Ireland, by which the roots will be prevented from attaining a size, while an equal gross weight of produce to what is now obtained may be produced, and that of a very superior quality."

unacquainted with the details of management; but the enterprising and successful hop-grower is aware that it is only by this liberal outlay (of course judiciously made) that he can calculate on an adequate return.

The chief application of the hop is for the purpose of preserving and imparting a peculiar flavour to fermented liquors, known as ale, beer, and porter. To some extent the hop is used medicinally, and in the process of dyeing, but the application to these purposes is inconsiderable. The stalk or bine yields a strong fibre, capable of being manufactured into a coarse kind of cloth, which, however, is not to any extent carried out in practice. It is therefore for the brewer that the crop is cultivated. The only parts of the hop flower entering into the composition of these fermented drinks are probably the seeds, and the yellow glutinous adhesive matter around the outer integument of the seeds, situated at the bottom of the petals. The taste of the seed itself is oily, somewhat resembling that of the cocoa-nut, but the surrounding substance has an exceedingly bitter taste, while it emits a strong but very peculiar aromatic flavour. This aroma, which is very agreeable, is extremely volatile; and hence the necessity for closely packing the hops, as is done in practice, when they are to be preserved. Under any circumstances, however, much of the aroma of the hops will be lost by keeping; a circumstance rendering it indispensable that they should be used as fresh as possible, especially in the manufacture of superior descriptions of ale and beer.

The first mention of the hop in our Statute-books dates so far back as 1552 (5 Edw. VI. c. 5), when certain immunities and privileges were granted to hop-grounds. In 1603 several Statutes and regulations were made for the curing of hops, which were to be carried out under the inspection of the officers of excise. In 1710 a duty of *3d.* per pound was imposed on all hops imported into England; and in 1734 a duty of *1d.* per pound was imposed on all grown in the country, which in 1805 was fixed at *2d.* per pound, subject to a drawback of 10 per cent. in favour of the grower. In 1840 a further duty of 5 per cent. was imposed upon the whole of the previous charge; the actual duty being thereby raised to *17s. 7½d.* per cwt. On imported hops the duty is now £2 5s. per cwt.; previous to 1846 it was £4 *5s.*, and until the passing of the tariff of 1842 it was £8 *8s.* per cwt.—a rate of duty which amounted to a virtual prohibition on importation.*

The cultivation of the hop in England is at present confined to the counties of Kent, Sussex, Surrey, Hampshire, Worcestershire, and Hereford; the quantity grown in the two counties last mentioned is inconsiderable. Great variation in quality characterizes the produce of these districts, dependent upon climate and geological peculiarity. The Excise regulations, to some extent, trammel the culture, depriving the farmer of that freedom of action which he enjoys in other departments of his business; while the returns, hazardous at all times, are rendered still more so by a tax being placed upon them. It may fairly be presumed that, in the event of the abolition of the duty, the culture of the hop would not be so exclusively confined to certain districts as it is at present, though there seems to be no room to doubt that these are the localities best suited for the purpose.—J. S.

## PEARL BARLEY.

Barley has naturally two husks, one a coarse siliceous outer one, and the other a delicate, thin, dark-coloured one, corresponding to the husk of wheat. The husk of the latter is thick, and in the manufacture of flour, when properly conducted, is generally separated in the discs, and may be removed almost completely in the process of bolting. If barley be ground in the same way as wheat, its internal husk is so thin and soft, that it is readily reduced to so fine a powder that no amount of subsequent bolting can separate it; and hence common barley meal cannot be applied to make bread, gruel, &c., in consequence of the dark disagreeable colour which this husk in powder gives to the prepared articles. Pearl barley is nothing more than common barley deprived of both these skins. This object is effected by kiln-drying the barley, and then introducing it into a sort of case in which a millstone revolves with great rapidity, so as to produce a kind of triturating action between the grains of barley without crushing them, the effect of which is to rough-shell them. The barley is then laid on a floor and damped, and allowed to lie for about forty-eight hours, when it is again passed through the mill, which removes the softened inner husk. Only good plump and solid barley is fitted for this operation.

Pearl barley is an excellent article of food, and cannot be too highly recommended. Considerable quantities have been always consumed in Scotland, whence also our supply has usually been derived; hence the term Scotch barley, sometimes applied to a particular kind of it. French barley differs but little from that just noticed, and is so called from its being very largely prepared there, and formerly exported in considerable quantity.

There were three exhibitors of these different kinds of prepared barley; two Irish and one English. Up to within a few years no pearl barley was made in Ireland; but Mr. George Waters, of Cork, then connected with the firm of James Daly and Co., perceiving the advantage which would attend its manufacture, for which there was abundant material, while the process was exceedingly simple, had a machine set up in a mill near Cork, where it is still manufactured, and samples of which were exhibited by the present firm of James Daly and Co., and also by Mr. Waters himself, who is now manufacturing it on his own account. The other exhibitor was Mr. Styles, of London, who contributed a case containing a series of samples of ground pearl barley, and other preparations from grain. This pearl barley flour, or meal prepared in a particular way, but not differing in principle from that just described, is in great repute under the name of Ashby's patent barley, as a food for children, and is sold at a high price. We hope to see this branch of manufacture extended, and the use of the prepared barley become general.

* The last annual return respecting hops shows that in 1853 there were 49,867 acres of land in England under the cultivation of hops, and the amount of duty on the growth of the year was £277,824, the quantity charged with duty being 31,751,698 lbs. The return for Scotland is "*nil*," and for Ireland, "that the duty on hops does not extend to that country." 22,647 cwt. of foreign hops were charged with duty, for home consumption, in the United Kingdom and there were exported 802,103 lbs. of English hops, the greater portion of which went to Australia.

### COFFEE.

Coffee consists of the seeds of the *Coffea Arabica*, a tropical shrub, indigenous to Ethiopia, and thence transplanted into the province of Yemen, in Arabia, in the end of the fifteenth century. The first notice which appeared in Europe is, perhaps, that of a German physician, of the name of Leonhard Rauwolf, whose work was printed in 1573. Some twenty years subsequently a much more accurate description was published by another physician, of the name of Prosper Albini, who was connected with the Venetian Consulship of Alexandria, in Egypt. The first public coffee-house was opened in London in 1652, in Newman's-court, Cornhill, the site of the present Virginia coffee-house; the first opened in France was at Marseilles, in the year 1671, although the use of it was known to a few as early as 1640. The first *cafe* in the neighbourhood of Paris was opened, in 1672, at St. Germain; but its use was well known in Paris since 1669, having been rendered fashionable by Solyman Aga, the Turkish Ambassador to the court of Louis XIV.

The seeds, or coffee beans, are contained in a berry-like fruit, somewhat like a cherry, each berry having two seeds. The flesh in which the seeds are enveloped being very tough, the berries are generally obliged to be fermented in order to obtain the seed. The composition of the seed is very peculiar, its chief features being the presence of caffeine (which we have already noticed), a quantity of fat, and of a nitrogenous or animalized substance similar to that found in beans and other leguminous plants, and analogous in many respects to the curd of milk; and, finally, a peculiar acid having very astringent properties. In their natural state the berries of coffee are bitter, and have no aroma, at least not very perceptibly so, and are exceedingly tough, and, therefore, difficult to be ground. They are, therefore, roasted in a closed globular or cylindrical vessel, which turns on an axis over a fire at a temperature of about 380° Fahr. Some peculiar changes take place during this operation which as yet are imperfectly understood; we know, however, that an aroma is produced, that a certain portion of the caffeine, which is in part in combination with the peculiar acid above alluded to (the caffeic acid) is volatilized; and, finally, that the acid itself is transformed into another. It is to this loss of caffeine that we must attribute the fact, that unroasted coffee has more effect on the nerves than roasted coffee. A good deal of the flavour depends upon the roasting, and to this cause is, perhaps, to be attributed the superiority of French prepared coffee. The coffee seeds are always washed in France previous to roasting, and each kind of coffee is roasted separately, and during periods of time differing for each; thus Mocha is roasted until it has assumed a delicate reddish yellow, by which it loses about 14 to 15 per cent.; whilst West India coffee, which, in France, is obtained from Martinique, is roasted until it has lost 20 per cent. of its weight, and become of a decided chestnut brown. In these countries the roasting or preparation of coffee is not at all understood; coffees, no matter whence they come, or how grown, are all roasted for the same time, and to the same shade of colour.

Coffee is now grown in a great many countries; the Dutch introduced it into Java about the year 1680, and from thence to Surinam, in South America, whence it spread into the West India Islands, &c. The best coffee is that of Mocha, which is the product of a dry climate; as a general rule, a dry climate, and a light soil, are more conducive to excellence of quality and delicacy of flavour or odour in all plants, than a rich, rank soil, and a humid climate. After the Mocha comes, perhaps, the Jamaica, the Ceylon, Costa Rica, Demerara, &c.

There were but two exhibitors of coffee, the samples exhibited being from Brazil and Guiana. Since the lowering of the duty upon coffee its consumption has considerably increased; the quantity entered for home consumption in 1851 was 32,564,194 lbs., and in 1852,—35,044,376 lbs.

### CHOCOLATE.

The *Theobroma cacao*, or tree which yields the chocolate, is a remarkable plant, belonging to a family allied to the Malva, and, like all the plants of that tribe, distinguished by the beauty of its deep green-coloured foliage. It is a native of the South American tropical regions and of Mexico, where it flourishes in the hot and humid valleys, heat and moisture being necessary for its development. Previous to the time of the ill-fated Mexican Emperor Montezuma the culture of the cacao was very considerable in Mexico; and a peculiar drink, termed chocolate, was prepared from it, with the addition of a little maize flour, the root of a certain plant, and the pods of the fragrant vanilla, a plant of the family of the Orchidæ. The Spaniards soon appreciated the value of the tree, and accordingly introduced it into the Canaries and the Philippines. It is now, however, but little cultivated in Mexico, and, with the exception of a few plantations in the province of Tobasco, the whole of the cacao used in making chocolate in that country, is imported from Guatimala, Maracaybo, Caraccas, and Guayaquil. But even in Caraccas, which has always been famous for the quality of its cacao, the plantations now thrive less luxuriantly, as cultivation has rendered the climate less humid than formerly; whilst its culture is rapidly extending in the eastern provinces of New Barcelona and Cumana, especially in the hot, humid, woody regions between Cariaco and the Golfo Triste.

The flowers of the theobroma break out from the bark of the stems and from the roots, and produce a cucumber-like fruit, about ten inches long, consisting of a reddish-white pulp, in which are imbedded from twenty-five to fifty kernels or cacao seeds, covered with a kind of skin. When the fruit is ripe it is opened, and the seeds removed and heaped up in pits, in which they are loosely covered, and there they are allowed to undergo a kind of fermentation during several days, the heap being carefully examined from time to time. By this process they become darker in colour, and lose much of the peculiar bitterness which they possess in the fresh state. Very little has been done to elucidate the chemical composition of the cacao kernels; the chief peculiarities are, however, the presence of a peculiar mild fat, of the consistence of butter, to the extent of from 43 to 53 per cent.; a peculiar nitrogenous body to which we have already alluded in speaking of caffeine, termed theobromine, and which is, perhaps, the substance richest in nitrogen which is now known; and lastly, some substance which develops by roasting the fine aroma of well-prepared chocolate. The usual mode

T

of preparing chocolate is to roast the beans, in exactly the same way as the berries of the coffee are prepared, by which they become aromatic, less bitter, and very brittle. They are then broken under a wooden roller, and winnowed to separate the husks, which, under the name of shell, are sold to the poorer people, who, by long boiling, obtain a kind of decoction which is considered wholesome, and is even used by many wealthy invalids. It is, no doubt, harmless, and by the aid of the imagination may, perhaps, be wholesome. The seeds, thus freed from their husks, are ground by machinery, at a sufficient temperature to melt the fat, which thus yields, with the rest of the kernel, a kind of paste that solidifies on cooling, and may be moulded into squares,—a method of preparation well known to the Mexicans before the Conquest. Sometimes a quantity of sugar is worked up with the paste.

A great many qualities of cacao seeds come into commerce, of which that from Urituco, near San Sebastian, in the province of Caraccas; Capiriqual, in the district of New Barcelona, already mentioned; and Esmeralda, at the junction of the Orinoco and the Guapo, and in the richest part of the region of primeval forests, are the most celebrated; whilst that from the West Indies is the worst. The produce of the former districts, as well as of the coasts of Guatimala, are exported to Mexico, France, Spain, and Italy, which accounts for the superiority of the chocolate prepared in those countries over that produced in Great Britain, whose supplies of seeds are derived from the West Indies. It is possible, also, that cultivation may have produced varieties of the theobroma, as in the case of the apple and the pear; and certainly at the time of the expedition of Cortes four varieties were indicated by the Mexicans. The Spanish Americans do not use the vanilla in making their chocolate, as the Mexicans did; they believe it to be unwholesome, especially for those of an excitable temperament. Nearly the whole of this delightful spice now collected is sent to Europe, and although it grows luxuriantly in Tropical America, its price is very high, and is hence not so much employed as it otherwise might be.

Cacao berries formerly, and, we believe, still to some extent, perform the same office in parts of Mexico as the small shell-fish, the *Cypræa moneta*, does on the coast of Africa, namely, serves as money; 15 kernels being equivalent to about one farthing. This is not the only case of an article of food being used for this purpose, for the tea, made into bricks, and used to such a large extent in central Asia, is employed in the same manner. Indeed, at Kjachta and Maimatschin, the frontier towns of the Russian and Chinese empires, brick-tea is the chief circulating medium between the merchants of both nations.

There were two exhibitors of chocolate, Fry and Sons, of Bristol, and L. A. Monteiro, of London. The Messrs. Fry contributed a very interesting and complete series, consisting of specimens of the pod, dried and preserved in spirit of wine; specimens of the leaves, flowers, wood, &c., of the *Theobroma cacao;* views of a *caca hual*, or cacao plantation, and other scenes in the Island of Trinidad; specimens of nibs and shells; varieties of seeds, among others the pale, gray, and dark Trinidad in the raw state, and the latter in the roasted, also, Domenic a Nicaragua, Grenada, bright and dark, Caracoa, Caraccas, &c. Amongst the manufactured articles were specimens of granulated, flaked, soluble, and homœopathic cocoa (a kind of inferior chocolate), chocolate de voyage, &c. Mr. Monteiro exhibited some Caraccas and British West Indian seeds, and three varieties of chocolate, the first quality made of Caraccas seeds alone, the second of a mixture of the latter and West Indian seed, and the third of West Indian alone.

Chocolate is not much employed in these countries, the total imports being 6,773,960 lbs. in 1851, and 6,268,525 lbs. in 1852, of which only 3,024,338 lbs. were entered for home consumption in 1851, and 3,382,944 lbs. in 1852. Perhaps the chief cause of this is to be found in the bad quality of the cacao seeds imported into Great Britain, and the still worse quality of the articles manufactured therefrom. The greater part of the articles sold under the name of cocoa and chocolate, &c., in these countries, consist of sago or potato fecula, mixed with cocoa-nut butter from the cocoa-nut palm, and not to be confounded with the theobroma, and a little real ground cocoa-nibs, the whole cocoa being coloured with some extract of a dye-wood. If the characteristic of the Messrs. Fry's homœopathic cocoa be that of all the medicines bearing that name, namely, the presence of only minute traces of the essential substance, in this case of the cacao, we believe we might safely recommend seven-eighths of every kind of cocoa and chocolate sold, to the followers of the doctrine of Hahnemann as containing only infinitesimal doses of the cacao. Nowhere, except, perhaps, in Mexico, is chocolate to be obtained equal to that made in France; the appreciation in which that agreeable, wholesome, and highly nutritious beverage is held there, can be best estimated by the great variety of ways in which it is prepared, and the number of machines which have been constructed for its preparation.

### TOBACCO.

Man has certainly some very curious habits, for some of which, such as smoking tobacco and using snuff, it is very difficult to account. We have already drawn attention to the striking coincidence of the use of drinks containing the same or analogous nitrogenous substances by the inhabitants of different countries. The smoking of another class of substances, also containing peculiar nitrogenous bodies, such as opium, the *Canabis sativa* or Indian hemp, and the tobacco, is not less remarkable; and would seem to point to a strong feeling which exists amongst mankind for the use, under certain circumstances, of some exciting or narcotic substances, as a substitute for physical exertion and the unfettered use of the animal powers.

Under the name of tobacco is included the leaves of a number of plants belonging to the genus Nicotiana and family of the Solanæ, which also includes the potato. Some species of this genus appear to have been originally indigenous to China and Hindostan, as well as to America, whence the knowledge of tobacco first came to Europe. It was observed in Hayti by Columbus, where it was called by the aborigines *cohoba*, or *cohobba*, and the sort of forked tube used for smoking it, *tabacco*. The first account of this custom was brought to Europe in 1496, by a priest named Romano Pano, who accompanied Columbus on his second voyage. It was used as snuff, as well as smoked, both in Mexico and Peru, and was called in the former *yetl*, and in the latter *sayri*. According to Humboldt, tobacco, rolled into cigars, was in common use amongst the chiefs of the court of Montezuma, not only to aid their after-dinner siesta, but also to assist in producing sleep after breakfast. Styrax balsam and other odoriferous substances were often mixed with the tobacco, in order to perfume the air. It appears that the use of tobacco was confined to the higher classes among the Aztecs, as it was among all the tribes of Indians, the *calumet* or pipe of peace being smoked by the chiefs in council.

Besides its use for smoking, tobacco was esteemed by the Aztecs and Peruvians a specific for tooth-ache, colic, scurvy, and many other diseases; and it appears that it first became known in Europe for these properties, as we learn from a curious treatise, originally written in Latin, upon the subject, by Jean Neander, a physician of Leyden. According to this authority, the first special notice of the plant made in Europe was by Jean Nicot, a native of Nismes, and Ambassador for Francis I. at the court of Lisbon. He was presented by a Flemish gentleman, then Keeper of the Royal Records, with a strange plant lately brought from Florida. He willingly accepted the plant, and, in consequence of its rarity, carefully cultivated it in his garden. He also confirmed, by many trials, its medicinal qualities for the cure of colic; and the success of these cures was so great that the tobacco began to be cultivated in several parts of Portugal, under the name of the Ambassador's herb. On his return to France some time after, he presented a quantity of the seeds of this plant to the Queen-Mother, Catherine de Medicis, who, on learning that it was a valuable specific, wished to give it her own name, and hence it was called *l'herbe à la Reyne Catherinaire et Médicée;* or herb of the Queen, Catherine and Medici, and thus came into vogue. It is from this Jean Nicot that the botanical name of the genus of plants, to which tobacco belongs, was called by botanists Nicotiana, and the peculiar principle of that plant, Nicotine. About this time also it was introduced into North Italy by Nicolas Tornabon, an ecclesiastic who was then on an embassy in France, and who sent some plants to his uncle, Alphonse Tournabon, another ecclesiastic; hence the name *Tournabone*, by which it was known. At Rome it was called Sainte Croix herb, because it was introduced there by the Cardinal Sainte Croix, Apostolic Nuncio to Portugal. It was also called the *sacred herb;* but it would occupy pages to merely enumerate the names given to it during the first years after its introduction, most of which have reference to its medicinal properties.*

The practice of smoking tobacco gradually followed in the track of its use as a medicinal plant, and in a short time was common over the greater part of Europe; it having been introduced into Germany and the whole of middle Europe by Charles V. It is difficult to say whether the introduction of smoking into England be due to Admiral Drake or to Sir Walter Raleigh; in either case the period of its introduction was somewhere about the year 1586. When smoking first began to be practised it met with the most desperate opposition. That most absurd and pedantic of kings, James I. of England, laid a duty of six shillings per pound upon all tobacco imported into England. In Switzerland, smokers of tobacco, or inn-keepers who permitted its use in their houses, were punished by the magistrates. In Russia, even so late as the year 1634, the smoking of tobacco was punishable with death; and even long subsequent, with the loss of the nose. Dozens of treatises were written to prove its wonderful qualities, and an equal number to prove that it was poisonous and filthy. The most celebrated of the latter is the *Counterblaste to Tobacco*, by James I., which describes smoking to be "a custome loathsome to the eye, hatefull to the nose, harmefull to the braine, dangerous to the lungs, and in the blacke stinking fume thereof neerest resembling the horrible Stigian smoake of the pit that is bottomlesse." The gallants of that day smoked tobacco; indeed it appeared to be then the particular fashionable hobby, and, if we are to believe King James, quite as expensive as racing or any of the specialities of the genus of this day. "Now how you are by this custome disabled in your goods let the gentry of this land beare witnesse; some of them bestowing three, some foure hundred pounds a yeere upon this precious stinke, which I am sure might be bestowed upon many farre better uses. I read, indeed, of a knavish courtier, who, for abusing the favour of the Emperor Alexander Severus, his master, by taking bribes to intercede for sundry persons in his master's eare (for who he never once opened his mouth), was justly choked with smoke, with this doome: *Fumo pereat qui fumum vendidit:* but of so many smoke-buyers as are at this present in this kingdome, I never read nor heard." The fine gentlemen, on their side, did not fail to laud the plant in much the same style that its opponents depreciated it. Thus Ben Jonson, in *Every Man in his Humour*, makes Captain Bobadil say—"Sir, believe me (upon my relation) for what I tell you the world shall not reprove, I have been in the Indies (where this herb grows), where neither myself nor a dozen gentlemen more, of my knowledge, have received the taste of any other nutriment in the world for the space of one and twenty weeks but the fume of this simple only. Therefore it cannot be, but 'tis most divine. Further, take it in the nature, in the true kind, so, it makes an antidote that, had you taken the most deadly poisonous plant in all Italy, it should expel it, and clarify you, with as much ease as I speak. And for your green wound, your balsamum and your St. John's wort, are all mere gulleries and trash to it, especially your Trinidado; your nicotian is good too. I could say what I know of the virtue of it, for the expulsion of rheums, raw humours, crudities, obstructions, with a thousand of this kind; but I profess myself no quacksalver. Only thus much—by Hercules, I do hold it, and will affirm it (before any prince in Europe) to be the most sovereign and precious weed that ever the earth tendered to the use of man." The exaggeration of this eulogium is, however, as nothing to that of the following denunciation of Cob, the water-bearer, in the same play:—"By Gods me, I marle what pleasure or felicity they have in taking this roguish tobacco! It's good for nothing but to choke a man, and fill him full of smoke and embers; there were four died out of one house last week with taking of it, and two more the bell went for yesternight; one of them (they say) will ne'er 'scape it; he voided a bushel of soot yesterday, upward and downward. By the stocks, an' there were no wiser men than I, I'd have it present whipping, man or woman, that should but deal with a tobacco pipe: why, it will stifle them all in the end, as many as use it; it's little better than ratsbane or rosaker." That the idea of the bushel of soot is not a mere joke of "old Ben," but a common prejudice of the time, we have the following statement upon royal authority:—"Surely, smoke becomes a kitchin farre better than

* Nicot thus describes tobacco in his dictionary: "Nicotiane est une espece d'herbe de virtu admirable pour guerir toutes navrures playes ulceres, chancres, dartes et autres tels accidents au corps humain."

a dining chamber, and yet it makes a kitchin also, oftentimes, in the inward parts of men, soyling and infecting them with an unctuous and oily kind of soote, as hath bene found in some great *tobacco* takers, that after their death were opened."

Neither the restrictions nor pamphlet of King James, however, produced very much effect upon the public mind any more than the law of his predecessor, Elizabeth, denouncing indigo as an invention of the devil, and forbidding its use under severe penalties. For in the course of the succeeding century it was deemed fashionable at most European courts to use snuff to such an excess, that the lace then much used in the front part of the shirts of the nobility was always variegated with the brown powder, as the hair was with powdered starch. This extravagant use of snuff was carried to such an extent that Pope Innocent XII. had to publish a special Bull to prevent its use in the church of St. Peter.

Tobacco requires a rich soil and a warm climate, and although it will grow even in Ireland, and is cultivated to a considerable extent in Europe, it may be considered as a tropical or sub-tropical plant. The growth of plants depends upon so many circumstances that we may naturally expect to find considerable variations in their composition according as the conditions of growth varies. This is more especially the case with the leaves where the changes constituting the process of growth take place. Accordingly, we find that tobacco varies in composition to a great extent. The finest tobacco is that produced in the province of Varinas, near Caraccas, and in Cuba. Next to these come the tobaccos of the Philippines and of Trinidad, although but little is now grown in the latter, and its fame is much fallen from the days when a "pipe of Trinadado" was considered as the greatest luxury to be purchased. The chief part of the tobacco now consumed in Europe comes, however, from the United States, especially from Virginia, Maryland, and Carolina, that from the first named being considered the richest. Considerable quantities are also grown in Europe, but with the exception of that produced along the valley of the Danube, and its tributaries in Hungary, and in Turkey, it is of very inferior quality. It has been grown along the Upper Rhine since 1697, and in the neighbourhood of Magdeburg and other parts of North Germany ever since 1676. It is also largely cultivated in France, in the departments of the Pas-de-Calais, the Bas Rhin, Nord, Lot, Lot-et-Garonne, Ille-et-Vilaine, Var, and Bouches-du-Rhone. The seed is, however, obliged to be freshly imported from time to time, as after five years the tobacco becomes abominable, especially where rich nitrogenous manures are employed, which is almost always the case, as otherwise the crop would not pay. Tobacco was formerly attempted to be grown in Ireland, but happily for those who indulge in smoking, the production of a rank and fetid substitute for real tobacco has been prevented.*

It has not yet been decided what is the true cause of the pleasure experienced in smoking; but it is usually attributed to a peculiar colourless, oily liquid, which, like quinine and morphia, acts as a base, forming salts with acids. This liquid has a slight smell of tobacco, but when mixed with ammonia or spirit of hartshorn, or when gently heated, it becomes nauseous, and pungent to a very high degree. It irritates the eyes and nose, and in small doses of a few drops it is poisonous; in lesser doses it produces vomiting. The quantity of this substance present in tobacco is very variable according to the locality whence obtained; the statements published with respect to this point are not, however, very definite. As in the case of the theine in tea, the results of the first experimenters were too low. According to the latest analyses, the dried tobaccos from—

| | | | |
|---|---|---|---|
| Department of Lot | contained | 7·96 | per cent. of Nicotine. |
| " Nord, | " | 6·58 | " |
| Virginia | " | 6·87 | " |
| Maryland | " | 2·29 | " |
| Havannah less than | | 2 | " |

Besides nicotine, tobacco appears to contain other substances rich in nitrogen, one of them resembling in many

* With some inconsiderate persons the prohibition of the growth of tobacco in this country is one of the Irish grievances. We are gravely told that the Irish farmer should be allowed to devote his land to the production of any crop he pleases, without any interference on the part of the Government. Nothing can be more plausible than this; and if a fair field and no favour were only demanded, such a claim would be irresistible. Large sums were undoubtedly made by the growth of tobacco in Ireland previous to the prohibition; but it must be recollected that such profits were realized under a system of protection, by which an import duty was levied on the foreign article at least ten times the value of the tobacco itself; while it cost *5d.* to *6d.* per pound, the duty was *5s.* It must be obvious that if the plant was grown to any extent in this country the revenue must suffer for the especial advantage of the tobacco growers. The only course open to the Government was, therefore, either to place the native and foreign grower on equal terms, or altogether prohibit the home production. The fact of the usual price of Irish tobacco being *1s. 6d.* per pound, while that of the imported article ranged from *5s.* to *8s.* per pound (duty included), showed that the indigenous could not compete with the foreign article, on equal terms. Even were there no difference in quality, it is not pretended that tobacco could be produced in this country at *6d.* per pound, which should be the case if no special advantage was extended to it; but as the relative value of the two articles to each other is about in the proportion of 1 to 4, the price of the native tobacco should be *1½d.* when that of the foreign tobacco is *6d.* Had the revenue from tobacco been inconsiderable there could have been little objection to throw the trade entirely open; and the experience of a single season would have dispelled the delusion as to the supposed advantages derivable from tobacco culture in the United Kingdom; but inasmuch as some five millions sterling per annum were derivable from that source,—a sum which could not be trifled with,—the only course open to the Government was to prohibit tobacco culture altogether. Those who complain of this being done simply contend that the community should be heavily taxed for their especial benefit. When tobacco of good quality cannot be grown, under any circumstances, in this climate, it is plain that the production of the article could only take place under a system of protection. The position here contended for is so obvious that it almost savours of puerility to occupy space in illustrating it. It is, however, notorious that the prohibition is made a grievance of; and the fact of this being so only shows how little the mass of the people think for themselves on questions of this character.—ED.

respects morphia, one of the most active substances present in opium; the other is a peculiar basic substance also, about which we know but little. The remaining substances contained in tobacco differ apparently in nothing from those contained in other dried leaves, except, perhaps, in being, like all plants containing peculiar nitrogenous substances, rich in gluten-like bodies.

The tobacco of commerce has, in many cases, undergone a peculiar fermentation, induced by laying the partially dried leaves in heaps for a week or two. The effect of this process is to decompose part of the gluten-like bodies just mentioned, and which would give the odour of burnt horn or glue to the smoke, and also to volatilize a portion of the nicotine. Sometimes, however, the leaves are merely dried before being sent into market. The manufacture of tobaccos in these countries is very simple: the small bundles in which the leaves are tied up by their stems are opened out, and laid upon a floor, generally of flags, and sprinkled with water so as to thoroughly damp them, and afterwards allowed to soak for about twenty-four hours, during which they undergo a slight fermentation. Tobacco which has not been previously fermented requires to be laid for a longer time; and in order to induce the fermentation, a dilute solution of treacle or liquorice or decoction of figs, technically called *sauce*, is used whenever it can be done with impunity, for the Excise regulations forbid the use of anything but water. Where the tobacco has been previously very highly fermented, a *sauce* is made with salt which always assists in keeping the tobacco damp; the salt retards the fermentation, and prevents the tobacco becoming too much heated. A good deal of the flavour of the tobacco depends upon the management of this fermentation, for it would appear that its peculiar aroma is the result, in a great measure, of that process. After the fermentation the leaves may be opened out and sorted, and the different kinds mixed which are necessary for the kind required; for it is proper to remark here that tobacconists almost invariably mix a number of different tobaccos, as, for example, Virginia and Maryland, in order to produce certain qualities of the manufactured article.

The various qualities of tobacco sold here,—such as *shag-returns*, *bird's-eye*, *twist* or *roll*, *pigtail*, *cavendish*,—only differ in the quality of the tobacco employed, the removal or not of the mid-rib or vein, and the form given to it. In Ireland, twist or roll is the usual kind made; and is simply a small rope spun from the finest leaf,—rolled into a coil, and subsequently subjected to considerable pressure. Bird's-eye and shag are the usual forms in England; these latter require to have the mid-rib removed or torn away. The leaves, after undergoing this operation, if necessary, are laid upon one another, until a sufficient pile is formed, which is then pressed into a cake about two or three inches thick. It is then cut by a peculiar kind of machine into thin shreds; after which it is opened out and dried upon hot plates. Some tobaccos, like that of Varinas, come into the market in a twisted form, differing from our twist only in being much lighter-coloured, almost perfectly dry, and twisted rather into rope than into a cord. This kind of tobacco constitutes the knaster or canaster of the Germans,—a name which is derived from the Spanish word *canasta*, a basket, the varinas rolls being usually packed in baskets. This kind of tobacco requires no preparation except cutting up. In France the well-known *caporal* is usually made of a mixture of the tobaccos of Maryland, Kentucky, and home-grown, moistened with salt water, fermented to a slight degree, and then cut up. The machines for effecting this object are both ingenious and simple; they consist of two endless cloths moving in opposite directions, the movement of which brings it between rollers (by which it is pressed together) and then under an oblique knife which moves up and down with great rapidity. The shreds of cut tobacco are next passed over long tables formed by a series of cylinders of cast-iron, placed in juxtaposition, and heated by steam. This operation gives a crisped appearance to the tobacco, which it retains in commerce; and, in addition, favours the evaporation of a portion of the nicotine and of the essential oil which would otherwise give a disagreeable flavour. It is then picked, and placed on trays to dry, and afterwards left in a mass for about one month.

*Cigars* consist simply of a little bundle of loosely rolled leaf, around which is coiled spirally a thin leaf, and then another termed the *robe*, which is previously trimmed; one end of the cigar is cut even with a knife, whilst the end of the robe is wound round the other so as to form a cone, the extremity being pasted with a paste browned with chicory. They are then dried and sorted according to the colour of the robe. The names usually printed upon cigar-boxes, when they do not refer to the maker, express the degree of this colour, such as *maduro*, *colorado*, *colorado claro*, and *amaryllo*, which express the order of intensity. When cigars are made in Europe, great care is bestowed upon the selection of the leaf for the robe, which is generally obtained from Guayaquil or Trinidad, and on the Continent from Hungary; the good leaves of Virginia are, however, often used for the inferior kinds. Formerly the tobacco used for making cigars in Europe was not fermented, being merely moistened, but the cigars thus made being exceedingly acrid, it is now usual in Paris to ferment the leaves for some days in double barrels covered with felt, so as to retain the heat produced, during which a large quantity of ammonia is disengaged. It is also usual to wash and press the leaves intended to form the robes, by which a gummy matter is removed which would otherwise blacken and puff up, when burned. Cigars are made by hand. Some time ago a Mr. Maddy invented a machine for making them. The tobacco intended for the interior is inserted into a groove, and the robe is placed under a rolling cloth which carries it along, at the same time that it rolls it round the cigarette which is to constitute the centre. The cigar comes out well formed, but it has to be trimmed, which complicates the affair. Each machine requires nine persons, all of whom must be very intelligent, attentive, and habituated to its use; and it produced about 3500 cigars in a day; but the same number of work-people would make an equal quantity by hand.

*Snuff.*—In the manufacture of superior snuff great care is bestowed upon the selection of the leaves employed, which are usually the rankest, or those which have been cultivated upon highly manured land, and which are, therefore, rich in nicotine, and the other nitrogenous substances that give rise to the production of ammonia by fermentation. There are two very distinct classes of snuff in use: one, a dark-brown damp powder, in coarse grains; and the other, a brownish-yellow, dry, and comparatively fine powder. The former is the kind chiefly used on the Continent, and, to some extent, in England; the latter constitutes the *high toast*, and other varieties almost exclusively used in Ireland. The best damp snuff, or, as it is sometimes incorrectly called, *rappee*, is, perhaps, that made at the great manufactory in Paris. The following is its mode of preparation:—A quantity of the leaves of Virginian, Kentucky, and indigenous tobacco from certain districts, and the *debris* of the leaves from all sources, are mixed, and laid in troughs or compartments having a bottom of flags, and then moistened with salt water. Two reasons have led to this use of the salt: the first is, that the great quantity of gluten or animal-like matter which the tobacco contains renders it liable to undergo a rapid putrefaction; the second is, that the salt being hygroscopic keeps the leaves sufficiently moist for the process of manufacture, and for their subsequent use as snuff, as we have already noticed in the case of tobacco for smoking. The leaves thus moistened are allowed to repose for two or three days, in order to equalize the humidity of the mass. The moisture contained at this stage may be estimated at 20 per cent. of the mixture. It is then cut up by a machine, and stacked up into heaps about nine feet high, where it is allowed to ferment during about four and a half months, during which the temperature rises to about 70°; in this way the mass gets an uniform colour and an ammoniacal odour. The management of this process requires considerable skill and attention; if the fermentation be carried on too long, or the temperature allowed to rise too high, the chopped leaves carbonize and become a mass of mould. The fermented tobacco is now *rappee'd*, that is, reduced to powder in a sort of conical mill, or rather mortar, in which revolves a vertical roller or pestle having its surface, as well as that of the mortar, cut like a coffee mill into knife edges; the rappee'd tobacco is then sifted. The grinding was formerly performed with hand-mills, and was an exceedingly unhealthy occupation, as the work-people were in an atmosphere of tobacco. At present seven men are sufficient where 700 were formerly required. The powdered tobacco is next placed in cases for two months, moistened again, and turned from one vessel into another. During these operations the temperature again rises, and the mass gradually arrives at the condition in which it is sold. The whole operations, from the entrance of the tobacco until it passes into consumption, occupies about twenty-two months. Dry snuff, or high toast, is quite a different article, and takes a much shorter time in its preparation. The chief feature in its manufacture is the stoving or toasting of the tobacco leaves, which are then simply ground to form the snuff. A good deal of the stalks and ribs of the leaves, which must be removed in the manufacture of cigars and other prepared tobaccos, are employed for this kind of snuff; and they are sometimes exclusively employed for that purpose. In the manufacture of snuffs, the sauce used for fermenting the leaves is sometimes very complex; in most cases some sugar, honey, or decoction of figs, is added, and some salts, such as carbonate of ammonia, pearl-ash, nitre, and, occasionally, some odoriferous materials to produce an agreeable perfume. With the exception of alkaline salts, all these things are, however, forbidden in the United Kingdom by the Excise laws at present in force.

In some countries the relaxation of the laws against smoking has been succeeded by the equally unjust system of making the trade in tobacco a monopoly. This is the case in France, Austria, &c., where the manufacture is in the hands of the Government, and in the former country even the sale. A different system is adopted in these countries, which is scarcely better in principle, and is much worse so far as the article produced is concerned. The consumers of tobacco are forbidden, by a most unheard-of protective duty, from the enjoyment of the superior tobaccos manufactured on the Continent and America, in order to foster the production of a most filthy and unwholesome article made at home; whilst our manufacturers are absolutely forbidden to make the slightest improvement. Some notion may be formed of the system of protection now in force, in this much vaunted free-trade age, when it is stated, that common twist tobacco is protected against cavendish by a differential duty of nearly 300 per cent., or 1800 per cent. of the original price of the cavendish.

It is only within the last century, or century and a half, that the inhabitants of civilized nations have begun to use extensively as drinks, or for smoking, or chewing, substances acting as narcotics, or excitants of the nervous system. The question naturally arises, what will be the effect of these substances upon the human race? As yet we have no data to form even the most hypothetical speculations as to its influence on our physical or intellectual powers; but it is impossible to avoid thinking that the 500 to 600 millions of pounds of tea, and the, perhaps, still greater quantity of tobacco, and which, according to Schleiden, produces annually about 1000 millions of pounds of carbonic acid, not to reckon the chocolate, coffee, Paraguay tea, and opium, now consumed in the world, must, in the course of time, produce some action upon mankind. We leave the speculation on this point to some Anti-Excitation Society to follow out.

There were three exhibitors of tobaccos and of snuff; and, so far as the varieties made in Ireland go, the contribution of all three were very complete, fully illustrating this branch of trade. Of the quality of tobacco there is but one way of judging, and we are, therefore, unable to speak practically of the samples exhibited; but the well-merited reputation of the contributors is a guarantee that it was excellent.

The following Table gives the number of pounds of tobacco consumed in Great Britain and Ireland for the first year of each decennial period of the present century, and for the year 1852:—

| | |
|---|---|
| 1801, | 16,904,752 lbs. |
| 1811, | 21,876,267 „ |
| 1821, | 15,598,152 „ |
| 1831, | 19,533,841 „ |
| 1841, | 22,309,360 „ |
| 1851, | 28,062,841 „ |
| 1852, | 28,558,939 „ |

Considering the great increase of population, this Table would seem to indicate that, relatively, there was a diminution in the quantity of tobacco consumed during the last half century; and that, generally speaking, the increase in the growth of tobacco has not kept pace with the increase of population, appears evident from the following Table, representing the exportation of tobacco from the United States, the chief source of tobacco in the world, since 1800:—

TABLE *showing the Total Exports of Tobacco from the United States from the Year* 1801 *to* 1851.

| Year. | TOBACCO IN LEAVES. | | Mean Price per Pound in Cents. | Manufactured Tobacco. | Tobacco in Powder (Snuff). | Value in Dollars of the Manufactured Tobacco, inclusive of Snuff. |
|---|---|---|---|---|---|---|
| | Quantity in Hogsheads. | Value in Dollars. | | | | |
| | | | | lbs. | lbs. | |
| 1801 | 103,758 | Not fixed. | Not fixed. | 472,282 | Included under the head Manufactured Tobacco. | Not fixed. |
| 1802 | 77,721 | 6,220,000 | 6⅝ | 233,591 | | |
| 1803 | 86,291 | 6,230,000 | 6 | 152,415 | | |
| 1804 | 83,341 | 6,000,000 | 5⅞ | 298,139 | | |
| 1805 | 71,251 | 6,341,000 | 7⅝ | 428,460 | | |
| 1806 | 83,186 | 6,572,000 | 6¼ | 381,738 | | |
| 1807* | 62,236 | 5,476,000 | 7½ | 274,952 | | |
| 1808† | 9,576 | 838,000 | 7½ | 86,332 | | |
| 1809 | 53,921 | 3,774,000 | 5⅞ | 350,835 | | |
| 1810‡ | 84,134 | 5,048,000 | 5 | 529,285 | | |
| 1811 | 35,828 | 2,150,000 | 5 | 752,553 | | |
| 1812§ | 26,094 | 1,514,000 | 3 | 588,618 | | |
| 1813 | 5,314 | 319,000 | 5 | 283,512 | | |
| 1814 | 3,125 | 232,000 | 6½ | 79,377 | | |
| 1815 | 85,337 | 8,235,000 | 8 | 1,034,045 | | |
| 1816 | 69,241 | 12,809,000 | 15½ | 576,246 | | |
| 1817 | 62,365 | 9,320,000 | 12½ | 1,115,874 | 5,080 | 281,509 |
| 1818 | 84,337 | 10,241,341 | 10 | 1,486,240 | 5,513 | 373,875 |
| 1819 | 69,427 | 8,874,167 | 10½ | 926,833 | 13,710 | 237,192 |
| 1820 | 83,940 | 8,188,188 | 8 | 593,358 | 4,996 | 149,589 |
| 1821 | 66,858 | 5,798,045 | 7½ | 1,332,949 | 44,552 | 149,083 |
| 1822 | 83,169 | 6,880,020 | 6½ | 1,414,424 | 44,602 | 157,182 |
| 1823 | 99,009 | 6,437,627 | 5⅜ | 1,987,507 | 36,684 | 154,955 |
| 1824 | 77,883 | 5,059,355 | 5½ | 2,447,990 | 45,174 | 203,789 |
| 1825‖ | 75,984 | 5,287,976 | 6⅞ | 1,871,368 | 53,920 | 172,353 |
| 1826 | 64,098 | 5,347,208 | 6⅞ | 2,179,774 | 61,801 | 210,134 |
| 1827 | 100,025 | 6,816,146 | 5¾ | 2,730,255 | 45,812 | 239,024 |
| 1828 | 96,278 | 5,480,707 | 4¾ | 2,637,411 | 35,655 | 210,747 |
| 1829 | 77,131 | 5,185,370 | 5⅝ | 2,619,399 | 19,509 | 202,396 |
| 1830 | 83,810 | 5,833,112 | 5½ | 3,199,151 | 29,425 | 246,747 |
| 1831 | 86,718 | 4,892,388 | 4¾ | 3,639,856 | 27,967 | 292,475 |
| 1832 | 106,806 | 5,999,769 | 4¾ | 3,456,071 | 31,175 | 295,771 |
| 1833 | 83,153 | 5,755,968 | 5¾ | 3,790,310 | 13,453 | 288,973 |
| 1834 | 87,979 | 6,595,305 | 6½ | 3,956,579 | 57,826 | 328,409 |
| 1835 | 94,353 | 8,250,577 | 7½ | 3,817,854 | 36,471 | 357,611 |
| 1836 | 109,442 | 10,058,640 | 7⅝ | 3,246,675 | 56,018 | 435,464 |
| 1837 | 100,232 | 5,765,647 | 4⅛ | 3,615,591 | 40,883 | 427,836 |
| 1838 | 100,593 | 7,392,029 | 6⅛ | 5,008,147 | 75,083 | 577,420 |
| 1839 | 78,995 | 9,832,943 | 10⅜ | 4,214,943 | 42,467 | 616,212 |
| 1840 | 119,484 | 9,883,657 | 6¾ | 6,787,165 | 37,132 | 813,671 |
| 1841 | 147,828 | 12,576,703 | 7 | 7,503,644 | 68,553 | 873,877 |
| 1842 | 158,710 | 9,540,755 | 4⅛ | 4,434,214 | 42,668 | 525,490 |
| 1843 | 94,454 | 4,650,979 | 4⅛ | 3,404,252 | 20,455 | 278,819 |
| 1844 | 163,042 | 8,397,255 | 4⅜ | 6,046,878 | 28,668 | 536,600 |
| 1845 | 147,168 | 7,469,819 | 4½ | 5,312,971 | 44,399 | 538,498 |
| 1846 | 147,998 | 8,478,270 | 4¾ | 6,854,856 | 52,458 | 695,914 |
| 1847 | 135,762 | 7,242,086 | 4⅛ | 7,844,592 | 37,051 | 558,950 |
| 1848 | 130,665 | 7,551,122 | 4¾ | 6,698,507 | 36,122 | 568,435 |
| 1849 | 101,521 | 5,804,207 | 4⅛ | 7,159,397 | 49,888 | 613,044 |
| 1850 | 145,729 | 9,951,023 | 5⅝ | 5,918,583 | 44,690 | 648,832 |
| 1851 | 95,945 | 9,219,251 | 8 | 7,235,858 | 37,422 | 1,143,547 |

## STARCHES AND SUGARS.

One of the most beautiful results of modern chemistry, and one which must be eminently suggestive to every inquiring mind, is, that all the various forms of organic nature, from the parched lichen on the rock to man himself—the most delicate coloured flower as well as the wonderfully constructed eye and brain by which it is appreciated—are composed, in great part, of four substances, which, in our present state of knowledge, are considered elements, namely, oxygen and hydrogen, carbon and nitrogen. The atmosphere consists of two, oxygen and nitrogen; and water of two, oxygen and hydrogen; carbon also exists in the atmosphere, in combination with oxygen, forming carbonic acid—a gas which we constantly breathe into the atmosphere, and which forms the food of plants. Thus, in water and air we have the chief materials of

* Decrees of Berlin and Milan.
† Embargo laid on Continental ports.
‡ Establishment of the Government monopoly in France.
§ War between Great Britain and the United States.
‖ Reduction of the duty in Great Britain.

the vegetable and animal worlds—the infinite variety which exists in both being the result of the different proportions in which they combine. As a house is composed of various materials, such as stone, brick, wood, &c., which are in their turns compounds of various elements, so plants are composed of various substances, built up of the elements just mentioned. We may divide these substances into two groups; those which contain only three elements, the constituents of water and carbon, and those which are formed of the whole four. If we take a whole plant, we shall find that its framework consists of woody matter, the chief part of which is made up of a substance called *cellulose*, an example of which we have in a more or less pure state in fine cotton or linen. This woody matter consists either of a series of cells, such as is presented by the pith of the elder tree; or it forms tubes such as the fibres just mentioned. All the other substances existing in plants are found either in a solid form or dissolved in water in those cells; they are very numerous in some plants, and in others comparatively few; but the greater number exist in such small quantity that they may be left out of consideration altogether in examining the general question of vegetation. The really important substances are about seven or eight in number, which we shall divide, according to the number of elements which enter into their composition, into two series. In the series composed of three elements we have cellulose (the subtance already mentioned as constituting the frame-work), starch, gum, or dextrine, sugar and oils; and in the series composed of four elements we have gluten, albumen, and one or two other similar substances. The latter exist in very small proportion compared with the mass of the plant, and are very intimately related to one another, and it is curious to find them most abundant in the seed; but probably the most curious point connected with them is, that a series of bodies, either identical with them, or at least closely related to them, constitutes the great mass of animals. In other words, plants consist in great measure of substances containing three elements, and animals of substances with four elements; hence the cause why the seeds of plants constitute the most nutritious food for animals, because they are rich in the constituents of the animal body.

Cellulose, starch, gum, and sugar, are very intimately connected together, but are not so to the oil series, although the latter contains the same elements; and as we have nothing to do with it at present, we shall leave it out of consideration, and confine ourselves to the former. In these four substances the oxygen and hydrogen are in the same proportion as in water; we may, therefore, consider them as composed of carbon and water, and to differ only by the amount of water which they contain, or rather, we should say, some only differ, for starch and cellulose do not differ in their composition, but only in their form—in the way in which their ultimate particles are arranged—hence the facility with which these substances pass into one another. Cellulose is the material of the formed cell; dextrine and sugar is the soluble substance from which the cellulose is made, and starch is the stock of material, laid by, as it were, from which the sugar and dextrine can be formed as required; gum being the intermediate stage of that transformation. During the growth of the plant these substances are continually transformed into one another by the action of substances containing four elements; in fact, the life of a plant is nothing more than a series of such transformations; and hence the substances like gluten play an important part in Nature, by producing all those singular changes.

Though these substances, chemically speaking, are so nearly related, how different are their applications in the arts! Who that sees the fibre of linen could imagine that it was, except in form, identically the same body as the starch with which it is stiffened by the laundress, and that both differed from sugar only by the latter containing a little more of the elements of water? With these few remarks, which are necessary in order to properly understand the relations of the various substances which we are about to treat of, we shall now take up the practical part of our subject.

## STARCH.

Starch is found in almost every vegetable; indeed, it is probable that at some period of its existence every vegetable contains starch; but it does not occur in all vegetables in precisely the same form; for example, the starch of wheat and other cereal grains differs very considerably from that of potatoes in the degree of cohesion between its particles, and in the size and form which their granules assume. All the bodies which can be properly reckoned as starches may be divided into three classes—common starch, lichen starch, and inuline. Common starch is the first link between cellulose and dextrine, or gum; lichen starch is intermediate between common starch and dextrine; and inuline is the link between common starch and sugar. Lichen starch forms the great mass of the mucilaginous substance which is obtained by boiling Iceland and Carrigeen moss; inuline is a kind of starch which is soluble in boiling water, and which is found in the roots of the dahlia and of the dandelion. Neither of these starches have as yet been applied to any use, if we except that which the Chinese have made of the *Gigartina tenax*, a species of sea-weed which, on being boiled, yields a kind of vegetable glue, consisting, in great measure, of lichen starch, which is largely employed in the manufacture of transparent lanterns, for which the Chinese are so celebrated. The mode in which these lanterns are made is very simple. A sort of netting is first formed, which is then impregnated with the glue, somewhat in the same way that buckram is stiffened with starch; in the former case, however, the meshes of the cloth are completely filled with the glue, forming a transparent sheet, to which the threads passing through it give considerable strength. In Hewett's Chinese Collection in the Exhibition were several lanterns formed in this way. They also use it for windows, the material so employed being somewhat similar to the thin sheets of gelatine prepared in France, and occasionally used here for printing address cards, examples of which were in the Exhibition.

Common starch being, therefore, the only kind at present employed for industrial purposes in Europe, we shall leave the other kinds entirely out of consideration.

Common starch is usually divided into two varieties—*amylum*, or starch of wheat, and other cereal grasses, the seeds of plants belonging to the leguminous family of plants, such as peas and beans, and the seed of the beet, &c.; and *fecula*, under which name we may include the starch of potatoes, arrow-root, sago, &c. These two varieties differ only in their form; in nearly all their other properties they are identical, with one or two remarkable distinctions, such as that presented by the action of caustic potash. If the starch of wheat be moistened with water, containing about 2 per cent. of potash, it will undergo very little change, whilst the globules of fecula swell into thin, transparent plates. Such a change, however, can only be observed with a microscope; but a more apparent difference is this, that the granules of wheaten starch, owing to their peculiar flattened figures, have a certain adherence, and when a mass is allowed to dry, it splits up into prisms, while the starch of potatoes falls into a gritty powder.

*Wheaten Starch.*—The composition of all plants varies considerably according to the climate of the country; the amount of sunshine during the year; the soil; the manure; the period of ripening of the plant; and, finally, in the case of those plants which present several varieties, by the variety employed. For example, the wheats of rich warm countries contain more gluten and less starch than those of cold countries, under the same conditions of culture; by means of manure, wheat as rich in gluten as that of Sicily and of Venezuela, may be produced in these countries, although it must be observed that, nevertheless, it will not yield as good flour, or keep as long, and will be more subject to disease. The average of northern wheats may be taken at about 68 to 70 per cent. of starch, and 17 to 15 of gluten; the richer the wheat is in gluten the more nutritious it is, and the better will be the bread which is made from it, other conditions being equal; but the less gluten, on the other hand, the more starch will be obtained. Some wheats, for example, contain as much as 75 to 76 per cent. of starch, and only 10 to 11 of gluten, and wheat has even been grown which contained no gluten whatever; such cases are, however, rare.

Formerly wheaten starch was extracted in a most imperfect manner. The bruised grain or meal was mixed with four or five times its volume of water, and was then left to undergo fermentation for the space of fifteen to twenty-eight, or thirty days, according to the temperature of the atmosphere; some sour water from a previous operation, having been first added to assist in commencing the fermentation. During this operation, the object of which was to separate the gluten, by partially decomposing it and rendering it to some extent soluble, a most abominable stench was produced, and the business was altogether of the most unhealthy kind. By this process nothing but starch was obtained, the whole of the gluten being destroyed. The gluten, however, is now obtained perfectly pure by an exceedingly simple process, the whole of the disagreeable smell of the old method being at the same time avoided.

The new process consists of mixing the flour with about half its weight of water, and rapidly working it into a dough with the hand or by mechanical means, and then leaving it to absorb the water, for about twenty minutes to half an hour in summer, and about one hour in winter; after which the starch is washed out in a kind of semi-cylindrical trough, the sides of which are formed of wire gauze. In this trough a cylindrical-fluted roller, of the same length as the trough, is made to move backwards and forwards, and work the dough against the sides, while a fine jet of water washes out the starch, which filters through the wire gauze; the gluten remaining behind, and, gradually becoming more adhesive, finally forms a tough elastic mass. The water which carries off the starch, and which amounts usually to about five times the weight of the mass of dough, passes from the cylinder into a cistern, where it reposes for a space of twenty-four hours; during this time the starch deposits, and the water which contains the dextrine, sugar, and soluble salts, is decanted off. The starch is not yet pure, however, portions of gluten still adhering to it which give it a gray appearance; to get rid of this difficulty M. Martin, of Vervins, the inventor of the process, places it in a vat, with about three times its bulk of water, and causes it to ferment by the addition of about 5 per cent. of sour water from a previous operation, at a temperature of 77° Fahr. This operation, which takes place in a closed room, and which lasts six to eight days, gives scarcely any smell; it is in fact nothing more than a kind of vinegar fermentation, the acids produced partially dissolving the gluten without injuring the starch, which is then washed twice with water; a period of twenty-four hours being allowed each time for repose. It is now strained through fine silk, after which it is allowed to deposit. When this has taken place, the surface of the deposit is still usually of a grayish tint, and is scraped off and washed apart, forming starch of the second quality. The portion under the layer, scraped off, forms the first quality, and is placed upon trays, having their bottoms pierced with holes, and then covered with a loosely fitting plate of sheet-iron; these trays are arranged upon a floor covered with thick plates of plaster of Paris, which rapidly absorb the water that drains through the holes in the tray. The cakes after this operation have a certain degree of consistence, and are divided into four parts, and placed in a drying room at the ordinary temperature, during from twenty-four to thirty-six hours; after which they are placed in a stove, heated in a peculiar way, which we shall notice presently where they split into the needle-shaped masses of prisms which are so well known as characteristic of wheaten starch.

The principal use of wheaten starch is for stiffening linen for domestic purposes.

We are not aware that gluten has been put to any use in Ireland; but in France, where the advantage of soups, as a part of the dietary of the people, is fully appreciated, it is extensively employed in the manufacture of vermicelli, maccaroni, and granulated gluten. These substances, which are so favourite an article of food in Italy and in other parts of the south of Europe, can only be made from the finest Sicilian wheat, which is exceedingly rich in gluten. By the addition of freshly prepared gluten, however, to our ordinary wheaten flours, articles of this kind, quite equal, in every respect, to the best Neapolitan maccaroni or vermicelli, may be prepared. This manufacture is very well worthy of the attention of our starch-makers.

*Potato Fecula.*—The composition of potatoes is still more variable than that of the cereal grains. All bulbous and tuberous roots contain a very large proportion of water, which is subject to very considerable variation, and hence the quantity of solid matter which potatoes may contain is very variable. For example, the common lumpers of our peasantry are very prolific, and are hence cultivated largely; but one ton of them does not contain in general the same amount of food as 15 cwts. of the smaller but superior varieties. Under these circumstances we need scarcely remark, that the amount of starch which a manufacturer can obtain from a given weight of potatoes varies very considerably. From the small quantity of water which grain contains, it may be preserved with very little change for several years, but it is different with potatoes; unless preserved with the utmost care they begin to change very soon after their removal from the ground; and the first constituent which is altered is the starch, which gradually passes into other substances, so that by the end of spring scarcely any starch can be obtained. For example, potatoes which yield in October,

November, and December, 17 to 18 per cent. of starch, give no more than 15 in January, 13 in March and April, and, perhaps, not more than 7 to 8 in the end of the latter month. Hence, whilst the manufacture of wheaten starch may be carried on throughout the whole season, that of potatoes is confined to the period of the year commencing in October and ending in February. When we come to speak of beet sugar we shall have occasion to notice the same phenomena connected with that manufacture.

The process by which potato starch is now made is very perfect; at least it is so on the Continent, where a considerable amount of ingenious mechanism, a good deal of which has been imitated from the manufacture of beet sugar, has been introduced into it. We shall accordingly describe the most perfect mode, even although it may not be the one in use at home, as it would evidently be a waste of time to describe processes which had better be discarded at once from practice, and placed amongst the archives of the history of the manufacture. The first operation is that of *soaking*, which consists merely in placing the potatoes in a tub with water for eight or ten hours, in order that the clay attached to them may soften. They are then *washed* in a common cylindrical washing machine. The washed roots are next *rasped* by a rasping machine. The pulp as it passes from the rasp is received on a sheet of fine wire gauze, of which there are six or seven placed at short distances over one another. Over these sheets a double endless chain, joined by transverse bars or scrapers of iron the width of the wire cloth, passes by means of a series of pulleys and guide rollers; owing to the onward motion of this chain, the pulp is carried from the lower sheet of gauze to the second by means of the scrapers of iron which roll it along: thence to the third, and so on until it reaches the top, and is discharged into a reservoir. During this ascent of the pulp, a dense rain is made to fall on the upper sheet of gauze, through which it passes, carrying the last traces of starch from the exhausted pulp on to the second, and thence to the third, and so on to the last, where it comes upon fresh pulp. By thus presenting successive layers of pulp to the descending water a much smaller quantity of the latter is required, whilst the starch is effectually washed out, and at the same time strained by means of the wire gauze. The water loaded with starch passes from the last wire gauze into a slightly conical cylinder or drum, the periphery of which is formed of the finest wire gauze or silk, where it is still further strained, and thence passes into a cistern or reservoir, whence it is carried to the purifying vats by a lifting wheel. Here it is freed from sand and other impurities by being agitated and syphoned off before the starch deposits into other vats, where it is allowed to deposit the water decanted off. The grey coat, or *starch grease* as it is called, is scraped off and washed apart for No. 2 fecula, and the fine white starch drained on trays as already described for wheaten starch, and when of sufficient consistence turned out upon plates of plaster, where it is allowed to dry during six to twelve hours. Each cake is afterwards broken into eight or twelve pieces, which are placed in a drying closet upon shelves of wood, well protected from dust, and dried at the ordinary temperature of the air, after which they are stoved in a current of hot air. A very nice form of stove has been contrived for this purpose; it consists of a chamber heated by an arrangement of hot pipes, and having a series of endless bands of cloth passing over rollers at each side of the building, placed over one another. The wet starch is spread upon the upper cloth, where, being sufficiently dried, the cloth is made to revolve, by which the starch is precipitated upon the sheet below, and thence upon the next, and so on, until it arrives at the bottom; having in this way passed from the lowest to the highest temperature, by which it is gradually dried. It is afterwards passed between brass rollers and bolted through a machine similar to that employed for flour; and is then fit for sale as *dry starch*, although it still contains 18 per cent. of water. If this starch were placed in a damp atmosphere it would rapidly absorb water, so that at last it would reach 35 per cent. of its weight; in this state the grains adhere together, and are still capable of taking in more water, constituting *green starch*, as the starch obtained in that stage of its manufacture, when it has been drained on plaster of Paris, is called.

Fecula of potatoes is at present employed for a number of purposes; as, for example, in sizing of very fine papers, for the manufacture of starch sugar, imitations of tapioca and sago, in the manufacture of comfits and other light confectionary, as an addition in the manufacture of vermicelli and semola, for the manufacture of white dextrine, and of leiokom or roasted starch, or, as it is sometimes called, British gum. When used in articles intended as food it must be treated, during the process of washing in its manufacture, with about 1 per cent. of its weight of carbonate of soda dissolved in about fifty parts of water, which removes a peculiar nauseous oil that would render it highly disagreeable if used in confectionary. In order to imitate tapioca or sago it is only necessary to take potato starch in its green state, that is, after being drained on plaster of Paris, and sprinkle it upon plates heated to about 302° Fahrenheit, by which the granules swell suddenly and cement together, forming a sort of horny starch very much resembling sago. The pulp remaining after the extraction of the starch is used for feeding pigs on the Continent, and to some extent in Ireland; although we have heard of a case where a manufacturer was compelled to pay for its removal, the farmers of this country not being sufficiently accustomed, as yet, to manufactures, to appreciate the value of factory residues.

*Sago and Cassava.*—In most tropical countries the natives prepare several varieties of starch, many of which come into commerce in these countries under the names of arrow-root, tapioca, sago, &c. The fine collection of the products of British Guiana contained a number of samples of arrow-root and tapioca: and some arrow-root, tapioca, and sago were also contributed from Brazil. Tapioca is obtained from the yucca,—a plant familiar to those who visit our botanic gardens. It is from this plant that the Indians prepare a kind of meal abounding in the starch just named, and called cassava, a number of samples of which, and of the cakes made from it, were in the Guiana collection. Sago is the starch obtained from several varieties of palms and other allied plants by a process somewhat similar to the old process of starch-making. Considerable quantities of this starch are purified in these countries, and used for the same purpose as potato fecula. We believe the starch of the cassava could be advantageously used for the same purpose, and might form a considerable article of commerce from Guiana.

*Dextrine.*—One of the most important applications of potato and sago fecula is in the manufacture of British gum or torrified starch. If fecula be exposed in trays to a temperature of 410° Fahrenheit, it loses its water, and undergoes a peculiar change by which it becomes soluble in water, and in many respects resembles gum Arabic, which it replaces in the arts to a considerable extent. This substance is called *dextrine*, from a peculiar property which it has of bending a ray of polarized light towards the right hand when it has passed through a solution of it. Several specimens of this leiokom, or torrified starch, were exhibited by C. Cooney, of this city, made by the old process of roasting, just mentioned. But as this process gives the product a yellowish or buff colour which unfits it for getting up lace and lawn and replacing the finer kinds of starch called *amidon-lis*, used for that purpose, other processes have been invented on the Continent by which a dextrine can be obtained as perfectly white as the finest starch. The simplest of these processes, invented by the distinguished chemist, Payen, consists in mixing 1 ton of dry fecula with about 4½ lbs. of pure nitric acid of a specific gravity of 1·36 to 1·40, diluted with about 67 to 68 gallons of water, and spreading the mixture upon trays, which are then placed in a drying room at the ordinary temperature of the atmosphere until the starch is sufficiently dried to fall into powder spontaneously; it is then reduced to powder, and spread in layers about one inch in thickness upon trays of brass, which are placed in a stove heated by steam to a temperature of 212° Fahrenheit, for some hours; or, by heating it somewhat higher, the change is effected much sooner, but great care should be taken lest the temperature should be raised so high as to colour it. Dextrine may also be obtained as a syrup, by the action of an infusion of malt; but in this case it will always contain a certain quantity of starch sugar, which will render it more or less hygroscopic or attractive of moisture. If starch be boiled for a considerable time under a pressure of six atmospheres, it will also yield a syrup of starch gum. We would strongly recommend a study of these various processes to our manufacturers; especially as the manufacture of starch is carried on to some extent in Ireland, at the same time that dextrine has scarcely been applied to a tithe of the purposes for which it is admirably adapted. We shall give here a few of the applications of dextrine; but we must, however, observe, that we do not pretend to give one-half of those which have been made on the Continent, and might be introduced here with advantage.

APPLICATIONS OF DEXTRINE.

For stiffening and making up tulles, laces, gauzes, &c., and, in fact, all kinds of cotton and linen tissues.
Sizing, or preparation of linen or cotton warps for weaving, especially of the finer articles.
For thickening the mordants used in printing on silk, woollen, and cotton.
In calico printing, for thickening both mordants and colours, when the latter are employed in what is called padding.
Liquid gum for fixing on labels (for this purpose dextrine syrup is used).
For thickening colours for printing room-papers.
As mucilaginous baths for block printing on silk.
For the preparation of adhesive bandages for reducing fractures of the bones, which is one of the most ingenious applications which has been made, and many others which our space forbids us mentioning.

Nearly all the dextrine prepared in these countries is employed in calico printing, and stiffening cotton goods.

By the action of sulphuric acid, or of diastase (the active principle of malted grain), a kind of sugar can be made from starch; but as no specimen of it was exhibited, we shall not further allude to it.

There were nine exhibitors of starch; seven of whom contributed samples of wheaten starch, five being Irish, and two Belgian; three of potato fecula; three of sago, and one of leiokom or torrified starch.

SUGARS.

To most persons the word *sugar* has but one meaning, referring to the substance in common use, which, from its principal source, is denominated *cane sugar*. The chemist, however, applies the name to several substances having very different properties. For example, in grapes and most fruits there exists a kind of sugar which, like cane sugar, has the property of crystallizing, and which is called *grape sugar*. These two kinds of sugar are intimately related to each other, and only differ in their constitution by the grape sugar containing a little more of the elements of water than that of the cane. Their properties are, however, very different. Sulphuric acid, when poured upon cane sugar will blacken and finally char it, while it has scarcely any action upon grape sugar unless strongly heated with it. Cane sugar boiled with caustic alkalies, such as potash, undergoes no alteration of colour, while grape sugar, treated in the same way will be instantly decomposed. In their sweetening properties there is also a great difference, for it is found that three parts of cane sugar are equal in this respect to five of grape sugar.

When cane sugar is boiled with vegetable acids, such as lemon juice, it takes up the elements of water and passes into grape sugar, and even in the cold a similar transformation is slowly produced. When heated with certain substances containing nitrogen, which exist probably in all plants, it decomposes into another kind of sugar, differing very materially from grape sugar, and into an acid identical with the acid of sour milk. This sugar is found in nature, forming the principal part of the substance used in medicine under the name of *mannite*, and which is obtained from some trees indigenous to the shores of the Mediterranean.

If we compare the chemical composition of the cane and grape sugars with starch, we shall find that they only differ by the one containing somewhat less of the elements of water than the other; and experiment has shown that if starch be boiled with dilute sulphuric acid it will be converted into a sugar similar to, if not identical with, grape sugar. This important fact points out the source whence a good deal of sugar is obtained in plants.

From what we have already stated in speaking of starch, it will be seen that sugar must be universally present in all plants. It fills, to some extent, the office to plants of the blood in animals, by providing them with the material for forming their cells. It will, of course, be understood when we say sugar is universally present, that we allude to some of the many forms of that substance, and not to cane sugar alone. There are, however, many plants which contain only cane sugar, such as the sugar cane, the beet, the sugar maple, the melon, the seeds of the chesnut, &c.; but from what we have already remarked in reference to the action of acids upon cane sugar, none of it can exist in acid fruits. We may, therefore, divide plants into two classes with reference to the sugar which they contain: first, those with neutral saps containing cane sugar or some modification of it; and second, those with acid saps and grape sugar.

The mere fact of a plant containing cane sugar or some of its modifications does not prove that it can be economically employed for obtaining sugar on a great scale; for, independently of the fact that it should contain a sufficient per-centage of it to render its extraction profitable, it should exist in a form capable of crystallizing—it should be *crystallizable cane sugar*.

At present our supply of sugar is obtained almost entirely from the beet and the sugar cane, in both of which there is only found crystallizable cane sugar; although, during the process of manufacture, a considerable but variable portion of it is converted into an uncrystallizable sugar, known under the name of molasses. It is to the production of this substance that we must attribute the origin of the mistake, that uncrystallizable sugar existed ready formed in the cane and beet.

*Sugar from the Cane.*—The use of the beet as a source of sugar is of recent date; but it is impossible to say when it was first made from the cane. It appears to have been known and largely employed in China and India for several thousand years, and even to have been known to the Greeks and Romans at the commencement of the Christian era. The first positive historical account which we have of the manufacture of sugar from the cane dates from the time of the first Crusade, when the Christian army discovered fields of cane growing near Tripolis, in Syria, from which sugar was made. The Venetians had, however, imported the sugar itself into Europe as early as the year 996; and in 1319 imported into London a cargo of 100,000 lbs. of sugar, and 10,000 lbs. of candy. The Mahometans, in their course to the westward, successively introduced the sugar cane into Egypt, Cyprus, Candia, Malta, Sicily, and finally into the south of Spain, where it was largely cultivated. It is supposed, however, that the cane was cultivated in Andalusia before the invasion of the Arabs, who merely introduced the process of boiling the juice. In 1148 there were many plantations of it in Sicily, and sugar formed a considerable article of trade. In 1420 the celebrated Prince Henry of Portugal introduced it into Madeira, and thence it found its way into the Canary Isles and St. Thomas's. These islands supplied Europe with sugar until the introduction of the sugar cane into America. In the middle of the sixteenth century the Portuguese introduced it into Brazil, and not long after discovered the advantage of cultivating it by negroes. In 1506 Pedro de Arença introduced it into Hayti, where, in 1518, there were no less than twenty-eight sugar factories. From this period the manufacture gradually spread over the greater part of tropical America; but its development was greatest in Brazil, which, in the end of the sixteenth and beginning of the seventeenth century, supplied Europe with sugar. Since the middle of the seventeenth century, however, the West Indies have been formidable rivals of Brazil, and at present send from four to five times as much sugar into Europe as the latter. The first export of sugar from Barbadoes took place in 1640; but it was not for several years after that Jamaica became a great sugar country. When the English took it from the Spaniards, in 1656, there were only three sugar plantations in the island.

The cultivation of the sugar cane in the Mediterranean countries, whence it was introduced into America, has almost gradually died out. In Sicily, however, at Melilli and Avola, which were among the earliest parts of Europe where the sugar cane was first cultivated, there are still some sugar plantations. And its cultivation has been re-introduced into Spain within the last few years, the first factory having been put up at Torre del Mar, near Malaga, in 1846; Mehemet Ali also introduced it into Egypt; and in 1830 some plantations were established at Grusien, and in 1833 at Taglysch, in the Russo-Caucasian provinces. It is singular that after the lapse of more than 200 years the sugar cane should be again brought back from America to those very districts whence it was originally taken to that continent.

The sugar cane belongs to the same family as the different varieties of grass, wheat, barley, and oats, and which is known to botanists as the *Gramineæ* or grasses. There are several varieties of it cultivated, but the greater part of the sugar which comes to Europe is obtained from three:—1. The common or Creole cane, being the variety first introduced into America from Europe; 2. The Batavian or striped cane, which is the one grown in Java; and 3. The Otaheite or O'Tahiti cane, which grows most luxuriantly, and yields the largest amount of sugar. The latter was brought, as its name indicates, from the islands of the South Sea, where it grows luxuriantly; and its juice is employed by some of the inhabitants (for example, those of Easter Island) as a drink to counteract the effects of salt water, which for want of fresh they are obliged to drink,—an object which it appears to effect in a most remarkable manner.

The sugar cane is a marsh plant, and requires a very warm climate, and a good, deep, rich soil. It grows to the height of from eight to ten feet; and under very favourable circumstances even to a height of twenty feet, with a diameter from one inch to one inch and a half. The stem, which when mature has a hard rind, is composed of a number of joints from three to four inches long, which send forth leaves. The leaves are about three to four feet long, and from one to two inches wide, and resemble those of many grasses in a remarkable manner. The cane is usually propagated by cuttings, called *cane tops*, which are pieces of from fifteen to twenty inches long, containing some buds and cut from near the top of the cane. These are planted in rows three or four feet asunder, the plants being placed at intervals of two feet; the best period for planting being from August to November. In the eleventh or twelfth month of their growth they begin to *arrow*, that is, they throw out a great flower stalk seven or eight feet in height, and about half an inch in thickness, a specimen of which, with a long dried cane, was exhibited in the admirable and truly interesting collection of the products of British Guiana, sent from that colony. Sometimes this does not take place until the thirteenth or fourteenth month; when it does, the plant has arrived at its period of maturity for the manufacture of sugar. The stem is then heavy, smooth, very brittle, and has somewhat of a pale straw colour with a tinge of violet.

When the canes are considered ripe, they are cut close to the ground, and then sometimes reduced into lengths of three or four feet for convenience of grinding in the mill. The roots or stoles left behind send out shoots like plantations of osier, which are called *rattoons*, being a corruption of the French word *rejettons*.

The rattoons are usually ripe in about twelve months; and when they are cut down another crop of rattoons shoots up. In some countries this process is repeated for ten or twelve years; the heaviest crops being obtained in the first year, after the planting of the canes, which, to distinguish them from the rattoons, are called *plant canes*. An acre of land yields on an average about twenty tons of canes, although an acre of plant canes sometimes gives as much as thirty tons, whilst the fourth or fifth rattoon may only give ten tons, or even less.

The cut canes are conveyed to a mill, consisting of a number of grooved rollers, between which the canes are passed, and the juice squeezed out; the motive power being water, wind, or steam, and even in some cases cattle. The pressed cane is tied up in bundles, dried in the sun, and under various names, such as *trash*, *mogass*, *bagasse*, &c., is employed as fuel in boiling the sugar. The cane generally contains in 100 parts, 90 of juice, which is very nearly a pure solution of sugar, amounting to from 14 to 22 per cent. of the juice; the amount being greatest just when the cane is ripe, but gradually diminishing as the season advances; and as the cutting season extends over a period of four to five months, the variation is very great. Independent of this, the effect of soil, manure, moisture, temperature, &c., is considerable; so that it is probable that the amount of sugar contained in the cane as it goes to the mill, for a whole season, is not more than 14 per cent. in the favourable countries; but it is much less in India, and some other places where sugar is produced.

Of the 90 per cent. of juice in the cane, not more than half is pressed out, the rest remaining in the bagasse, and employed as fuel. Even in many places this quantity is not obtained; but where improved machinery is employed, from 75 to 80 per cent. can be expressed, which is probably the general amount which can be economically obtained.

There is present in the juice small portions of the nitrogenous substances already alluded to; which, aided by the high temperature of the air in the tropics, would soon produce fermentation. It is, therefore, necessary to get rid of these substances. This is effected by heating the juice in large copper vessels called clarifiers, and adding about from 1 to 3 lbs. of lime, or technically *temper*, per 100 gallons of juice. The lime combines with the foreign substances, which are in consequence thrown up in the form of a scum, leaving the liquor clear. The juice is then drawn off into the largest of a series of five copper vessels, the last and smallest being called a *teache*, because it is in it the juice is boiled to the consistence necessary to enable it to crystallize; the proper point of concentration being judged by *touch*, that is by drawing out a bit of the thick syrup between the thumb and fore-finger. All these vessels are heated by the same fire, the smallest or teache being placed directly over it. The juice is first boiled in the large copper, and some more feculencies or scum which come to the surface removed; and having lost a certain amount of water it is passed into the next, and so on until it arrives at the teache, where the full degree of concentration is attained, when it is run off into a large cylindrical vessel called a *cooler*. Each finished charge of the teache run into the cooler is called a *skipping*.

From the cooler, the juice, now a thick syrup, is transferred into rectangular wooden boxes, of which there are usually six, each being about five or six feet wide, seven feet long, and about one foot deep. When the cooler above mentioned is not employed, the syrup is transferred directly from the teache to these crystallizers, which are hence sometimes called coolers; here grain is gradually formed, that is, the sugar crystallizes. When this has fully taken place, the sugar is *potted*, that is, transferred into a number of sugar hogsheads, having their bottoms pierced with some nine or ten holes; through each of these holes the stalk of a plaintain leaf is stuck, which rises above the cask, and protrudes below the bottom. These hogsheads are placed upon a framework of wood, in a large building called the *curing-house*, the floor of which is formed into a sort of reservoir or cistern, by wood, lead, or cement. The sugar, or rather granulated syrup, is allowed to remain here from three to six weeks, according to quality, during which time the portion of the syrup which has not crystallized drains off, leaving the crystallized portion more or less dry. This liquid, known as West Indian molasses, consists of sugar in two states; one in which it is uncrystallizable, and the other in which it is crystallizable, the latter forming from 60 to 65 per cent. of the whole. When the sugar is sufficiently drained, it is put into hogsheads and exported. Sometimes the molasses is also exported to Europe, where it is employed for various purposes; among others it is reboiled, and a large quantity of sugar made from it. Large quantities of it are, however, retained in the sugar countries; and with the waste canes, and washings of the sugar house, it is diluted with water and fermented, when it yields the well-known alcoholic liquor *rum*; some seven or eight excellent specimens of which were exhibited in the Guiana collection.

As the sugar obtained by the process just described is more or less of a dark colour, in consequence of the charring of a portion of it in the teache, a process is employed in many sugar-producing countries for whitening it, termed *claying*. This process consists simply in placing the granulated mass formed in the coolers in a number of pots of clay or iron, of exactly the shape of a loaf of sugar, and having small holes in their ends; and then placing a mass of pure moist clay on the top of the sugar, the water from which, percolating through the sugar mass, washes out the liquid, leaving a network of crystals of sugar behind. By renewing the clay several times the sugar may be produced of great whiteness. The produce thus obtained is termed *clayed sugar*, of which there were samples in the Brazilian collection, such as the white sugar from Maro, Pamam, Bahia, and also from Berbice, in the Guiana collection; Brazil, Cuba, and the East Indies, being the countries where it is mostly produced.

The process which we have just described is very imperfect, in proof of which it is only necessary to say, that not more than from 6 to 7 per cent. of sugar is obtained out of the 14 which exists in the cane. Within the last few years great improvements have been effected; but as these improvements have arisen in great measure from the manufacture of sugar from beet root, we shall have an opportunity of speaking of them when referring to that manufacture. We may remark, however, that the process just described is still the one by which a large part of the sugar of commerce is made, the beet root machinery being only employed as yet by the most enterprising manufacturers. Indeed, it appears that its employment, although enabling the planter to make more sugar from the same quantity of canes, and of a very superior quality, does not enable him to make it cheaper, which, after all, is the final object of all improvement. In the Guiana collection were some fine samples of Demerara sugar, prepared by these improved processes, and which it was interesting to be able to compare with the samples of Irish beet sugar exhibited. We may here observe that British Guiana in this respect is by far the most advanced of the British Colonies.

Imperfect as the process just described is, that pursued in India is far more so. The land in India is cultivated by miserable peasants called *Ryots*, ground down by the Zemindars, who in turn are not much better off. The Ryots grow the cane in small patches, express the juice, boil it down with all its impurities into an inspissated mass termed *rhab*, or, as it called by the Europeans, *rob*. Occasionally they remove the scum formed during the boiling down of the juice, and by some attention in other matters prepare a better kind of sugar, which, according to the locality where it is made, has received various names, but which is usually called *goor* or *kheur*; the term *jaggery* is applied by Europeans to a variety commonly used in making sugar. Another class of persons, called *Goldars*, purchase the goor, reboil it, and make the sugar which comes to England as Benares and Burdwhan sugars. The mill employed in grinding the canes is one of the most miserable construction possible; it consists of the stump of a tamarind tree fastened into the ground, leaving about two feet projecting, in which is cut a hollow so as to form a kind of mortar: the pestle is a tree about eighteen feet long, and about ten to twelve inches in diameter, having one end rounded so as to rub against the bottom. This pestle is worked by cattle attached to a bamboo framework of the rudest kind; the juice squeezed out of the cane, which for this operation is obliged to be cut up in small pieces, flows out of a hole in the side of the mortar into an earthen pot, whence it is removed from time to time, to be boiled at first in earthern pots and then in those of iron, to be further prepared for the market.

*Sugar from Beet Root.*—The cultivation of the beet appears to have been first practised in the south of France; Olivier de Serres, a celebrated agriculturist in the time of Henry IV., of France, recommended it as food for cattle. In Germany, also, its cultivation is of an old date. The variety at first cultivated in both countries appears to have been the *disette* of the French and the *mangel wurzel* of the Germans, the meaning of which is *famine root*, a term which sufficiently indicates the high appreciation in which it was held. In the middle of the last century several varieties appear to have been commonly cultivated in Germany, when Marggraf published in 1747 the results of an investigation which he had undertaken as to the presence of sugar in indigenous plants. At this period sugar had become a considerable article of commerce, and, owing to the continued wars in which Europe was then plunged, the price of sugar rose enormously. The idea struck Marggraf that some plant might be found suited to the climate from which a sufficient quantity of sugar could be obtained, instead of the honey which was then largely employed as a substitute for foreign sugar. Finding by his experiments that the different varieties of the beet contained more sugar than other plants, he proposed to manufacture it from the white beet, since called the Silesian beet, which contained the largest quantity. Olivier de Serres, already mentioned, suspected that the beet contained and might be employed for sugar manufacture; but to Marggraf belongs the honour of first determining its quantity. Marggraf's idea was not then acted upon in consequence of peace having been re-established soon after; but in 1796, that is fifty years afterwards, Achard, an apothecary of Berlin, led by the high price of sugar, took up the idea of Marggraf, and established a small factory at Cunern, in Silesia, where he produced a very inferior brown sugar. An account of his experiment was published in the "Annales de Chimie," in Brumaire of Year VII. of the French Republic, in the form of a letter to Van Mons. In this letter he states that he could manufacture sugar at a little less than 2¾*d*. per pound, and he also pointed out the great value of the pulp, molasses, and leaves of the beet for various purposes, especially for feeding cattle. This letter produced a great sensation in France, having been reprinted in every newspaper. By some the idea was taken up with enthusiasm, as a means of freeing the country from the monopoly which Great Britain then enjoyed in colonial produce; by others it was ridiculed as an absurdity. The Institute of France then numbering some of the first men of science in the world among its members, did not, however, partake of the latter opinion, and accordingly they appointed one of their members, Deyeux, to proceed to Germany, and make a report upon Achard's process; which report was published in the following year. Consequent upon this report two small factories were established in the neighbourhood of Paris; one at St. Omer, and the other in the old Abbey of Challes. These factories did not fulfil the promises of Achard, and they were given up, amidst the ridicule of those who had been always adverse to the manufacture, and who filled the print-shops with the most grotesque caricatures. The whole affair would have doubtless ended there, but for the celebrated Berlin and Milan decrees of the Emperor Napoleon, establishing what was called the "Continental System," the object of which was to shut out England from the trade of the Continent. Enormous duties were placed upon all colonial articles, especially upon sugar, so that its price was at once quadrupled; and the result was to cause inquiry to be made by chemists as to some indigenous source of sugar. Their attention was first directed to the juice of the grape, before its fermentation into wine, in the belief that by improving the process a sugar equal to colonial sugar could be obtained—a belief which it is unnecessary to say was erroneous, as the two sugars are quite different in nature. The juice of the grape contains 20 to 23 per cent. of sugar, whilst that of the beet yields only 10 to 14 per cent., the latter having besides a most disagreeable taste; for some time, consequently, no attention was paid to beet root as a source of sugar, whilst every housewife in the south of France made her supply of grape sugar in her kitchen, according to the directions published by the celebrated Parmentier. At length the beet sugar question was again agitated, in consequence of some reports which had been circulated relative to the success of a small factory established at Krayn, in Silesia, by Baron Koppy, as well as of the original one of Achard's, at Cunern. It was asserted that in these factories from 4 to 6 per cent. of sugar was produced; which was rather startling when contrasted with the results obtained by the Commission of the Institute, in the Year VIII. of the Republic, which was only 1 per cent. Hermbstadt, a Prussian chemist, published a small tract in 1809, detailing several improvements which he had effected in the original processes, and according to which he stated that he obtained 3 per cent. of fine sugar. Deyeux, who was at this time pharmacien-in-chief to Napoleon, again took up the subject, but without better results than before. Derosne, another apothecary, by following the process of Hermbstadt, obtained 2 per cent. of inferior sugar; from this he made a loaf, which he presented to Napoleon, who placed it under a glass-case on his chimney-piece, as the first loaf of beet sugar ever made. In the year 1811 we find two experiments recorded; one by Barruel and Isnard, the former of whom was a well-known chemist, in which only 1½ per cent. of sugar was produced, and the other by M. Drappiez, of Lille, who obtained 3 per cent. of sugar. It was probably the result in the latter case which caused Napoleon to give directions to Deyeux to publish a small treatise upon the subject, and to encourage the erection of a number of factories; among which we may mention those erected by the celebrated chemist Chaptal, and by the geometer Monge. In one of these model factories erected by the Government, the first loaf of refined sugar made in the regular way was produced and presented to the Emperor. The cost of this loaf was said to have been £1600! and was the cause of a flood of caricatures, some of which were exceedingly grotesque; for example, one represented George III. taking his coffee, and supplying his sugar from an immense West Indian hogshead, whilst Napoleon, on the other side, might be seen straining every nerve to squeeze sugar out of a beet-root which he holds over his coffee-cup. In 1812 M. Bonmatin effected some improvement in the mode of manufacture, an account of which was published in the Moniteur, by order of Napoleon. But neither the favour of the Government, the model factories, the able men who devoted themselves to the subject, nor the high price of sugar, could make the industry progress, although Achard was known to have been making a fortune. People were not, however, to be so easily discouraged, for when the results of Achard's improved processes became known, the number of small factories that sprung up in France was amazing; 150 having, it is said, been erected in half a year. Fortune favoured these bold efforts. Several improvements were effected in the processes, one of which placed the manufacture for ever out of danger.

In the year 1812, the Chief Surgeon of the Military Hospital at Montpelier asked a friend of his, M. Figuier, an apothecary of that town, to prepare for him a bottle of liquid blacking; which was at that period made from honey, ivory, black or burnt bones, and vinegar. The surgeon sent his friend a bottle of red wine vinegar sufficient to make the bottle of blacking, and into this Figuier put the honey and the bone-black, and sent it to the hospital, where it was placed upon the table in the surgeon's room. On coming in, and finding that the whole of the solid matter had subsided to the bottom of the vessel, and that the supernatant liquid was colourless, the surgeon imagined that it could not be his vinegar, and that consequently some mistake must have occurred; he accordingly returned it to the apothecary, who soon discovered the cause. He communicated his discovery to Derosne of Paris, who was then engaged in sugar refining. The latter at once applied the bone-black to decolorize syrups, and found its action remarkable. This was the great turning-point in the history of the beet sugar manufacture.

We have dwelt at this length upon the early history of this curious manufacture, for the purpose of contrasting the difficulties of its early infancy with that which it has had to encounter in the attempts to naturalize it in Ireland; and we cannot help coming to the conclusion, that if it has made so little progress in this country with so few real obstacles, it would have assuredly died had the discovery been made here.

In order to give the reader an idea of the first processes employed to make sugar from the beet, and enable him to judge of the progress it has since made, we shall describe the process recommended by Deyeux, and published by order of Napoleon. The beet roots were washed in a tub, then grated by the hand with an instrument exactly like a kitchen grater, and squeezed in a wooden screw-press, by which from 30 to 35 per cent. of juice was obtained out of the 95 which the beet contains. The juice was then boiled into a syrup, some persons adding a little chalk or lime to it, to separate feculencies. When it had attained a certain degree of concentration it was boiled with ox blood, strained, boiled down once more, and then put into a warm room upon flat trays; where, if the process was well conducted, a portion of it crystallized out in the course of about twenty days, otherwise the whole was destroyed. The syrup was after that drained off, and the crystals were put upon linen cloths to drain. Sometimes a little water was poured upon them, and the mass pressed. We can scarcely form an idea of the kind of sugar which was made in this way; it was a brown or blackish mass, having little the appearance of sugar. Such was the beet sugar manufacture in the year 1812!

If we consider that at this period beet sugar enjoyed protection to an extent almost approaching a monopoly, it will not appear surprising that, as soon as the Continental System was abolished, and peace established in 1815,—which led to the reduction in the price of sugar to one-half,—the manufacture should receive a shock. So great, indeed, was the effect of these events, that in the course of a few months three-fourths of the trade was extinguished. The rapid succession of inventions and improvements which had occurred in the interval, between 1812 and 1815, had, however, communicated so much vitality to it, that it was not only saved from utter extinction, but even soon rallied; and in 1819 no less than 100 factories, much larger than those erected before the Peace, were in full activity. Since then it has gone on with varying fortune, but, nevertheless, gradually improving, and extending itself. Up to 1840 it enjoyed considerable protection in France, but in consequence of the high price of sugar, and the clamour of the colonial interest, the Government proposed to levy a duty of 45 francs the 100 kilogrammes, or about 18*s.* the cwt., and to indemnify any manufacturer who would relinquish the trade. The Chamber of Deputies did not accept the project, but imposed a duty of 25 francs the 100 kilogrammes, or about 10*s.* the cwt., by which they left the indigenous sugar a protection of 20 francs the 100 kilogrammes, or nearly 8*s.* per cwt. This, however, did not satisfy the colonial interest, especially as the manufacture of beet sugar, checked for a while in 1840 by the uncertainty as to how the Legislature would act, began to increase rapidly. Accordingly the Government proposed, in 1843, the compulsory closing of all the factories; at the same time awarding them an equitable indemnity. The Chamber of Deputies again refused to ratify the Government measure of annihilation; but, giving way to the complaints of those interested in colonial sugar, they added 5 francs per 100 kilogrammes to the duty on beet sugar, and a like sum additional for each succeeding year, until the duties upon the French colonial and beet sugars would be equalized; which was effected in 1847. The effect of the hostility of the Government, in 1843, was most disastrous to the manufacture; fully one-half of the factories having been closed up, and the proprietors of the others very much discouraged. Nevertheless, in the face of the increasing duty, it again prospered. Then came the Revolution of 1848, which re-emancipated the negroes, upon whom slavery had been again imposed under the tyrannical government of Napoleon, after it had been solemnly abolished in 1793. The immediate effect of this measure was a considerable diminution in the production of French colonial sugar, and an increase in the cost of production. This state of things increased the clamours of the colonial interest, and of all those who saw in the continued increase of the indigenous sugar manufacture a probable source of injury to the mercantile marine of France; the trade in sugar occupying a tonnage of from 80 to 100,000. The result was that, after protracted debates, a new tariff was promulgated in June, 1851, which increased the duty on beet sugar to the extent of 5 francs the 100 kilogrammes, or about 2*s*. the cwt.; thus giving the French colonial sugar a protection to that extent. The beet sugar in its turn was protected against foreign tropical sugar by a differential duty of about 4*s*. 9*d*. the cwt. This protection would, under any circumstances, be merely nominal, and does not seriously affect the manufacture one way or other. Protection means monopoly to a certain extent; but it is clear that such monopoly can only exist where the article protected is not sufficient to supply the wants of the community; the deficit must consequently be introduced from abroad, and pay the protecting premium, the result of which will be, that the price of all the sugar consumed in the country will be increased to that extent. The usual consumption of sugar in France varies from 110,000 to 130,000 tons annually. Now if the French colonies and the beet sugar factories cannot together produce this quantity, it is quite clear that foreign sugar must be imported, paying the highest duty, which would of course raise the price of all sugar. The reverse is, however, the case, for the colonial sugar imported into France, and the beet sugar produced there, are more than sufficient to supply the consumption. Taking the ten years ending 1851, there was a very considerable excess in eight years of that period; whilst in only two was the production and consumption balanced. In one year the excess over consumption actually amounted to 30,000 tons, which was obliged to be exported to other countries, in which it had to compete with Cuban and Brazilian sugar, at the same time that the price at home was lowered to very nearly the same standard. Judging by the common opinion, we might imagine that such a competition would soon destroy the beet sugar manufacture. Nevertheless, in the face of that very tariff, the production of indigenous sugar in France rose from 70,461 tons, in 1851, to 82,409 tons in 1852, or very nearly 17 per cent. in one year; and the increase during the past season is supposed to be in about the same proportion.*

So much for the history of the beet sugar industry; we shall now proceed to detail briefly how the manufacture is carried on. The juice of the sugar cane being nearly a pure solution of sugar, the manufacture of sugar from it is practicable with the rudest apparatus; but the case is different with the beet, the juice of which is exceedingly rich in foreign matters which tend to decompose the sugar. Hence much more effective apparatus and more skilful processes are required for making beet sugar than sugar from the cane. With the exception, however, of the operation of extracting the juice from the beet, the principles upon which the processes of manufacture are founded are the same in both cases; and the beet sugar machinery, with the exception alluded to, can be employed for making sugar from the cane. But while this perfect and complicated system is necessary to enable the beet sugar to compete with the produce of the tropics, its use in the manufacture of the latter appears to confer no economical advantage, merely enabling a better sugar to be made.

The first operation through which the beet roots pass in the manufacture of sugar is the removal of the crown and of the small rootlets; an operation performed by the farmer, who delivers the roots pretty nearly in the condition required, and employs the portions cut off for feeding pigs or for manure. A certain quantity of earth still adheres to them, which must be removed by washing; this is performed by introducing them into a long cylinder, called from its inventor Champonnois's Washing Drum, formed of laths separated by intervals of about two inches, the cylinder being made to revolve in a trough containing water in which it is nearly half immersed. The roots are put in at one end by means of a hopper, and are caught up and ejected at the other end, having been thoroughly scoured during their passage through the drum.

The beet is composed of a number of cells in which the juice, containing the whole of the sugar dissolved in it, is imprisoned. To get it out, therefore, we must, if possible, burst them asunder, and the more effectually this is done the greater will be the amount of juice obtained. This is partially attained by means of a rasping machine, consisting of a drum turning on an axis, and having a number of saws so inserted into it parallel with that axis, as to leave only the teeth projecting. The usual length of these saws is about thirteen inches, and there are generally about 150 inserted into each drum, which is made to revolve at the rate of from 500 to 700 revolutions per minute, so that each tooth has a velocity of about 800 to 1000 feet per second.

The effect of the rasp is to convert the beet into a fine pulpy mass, which, as fast as it is produced, is subjected to pressure in order to separate the juice. For this purpose an adaptation of the ordinary hydraulic press is employed. The pulp is introduced into knitted bags of woollen yarn and laid in a pile upon the table of the press; the bags being separated from each other by plates of sheet-iron or discs of wicker-work. The presses employed are capable of exerting a pressure of about 300 lbs. upon the square inch. About 70 to 75 per cent. of the juice is expressed in this way; after which the bags are dipped in water, or a small stream is allowed to fall on the pulp by opening the sack, or they are exposed to steam as long as it is condensed; in this way a considerable quantity of water is absorbed by the mass, which acts like a sponge, and it is again pressed. By this second pressure the total per-centage of juice is raised to 85, but by again moistening them,

* One of the commonest of the many ill-founded objections which have been urged against the manufacture of beet sugar is, that the price of sugar in France is usually a penny per pound higher than it is with us. This is perfectly true; but the duty upon sugar in France is double what it is now in the United Kingdom: the amount of that excess of duty being a little more than one penny per pound, which thus accounts for the difference. A comparison between the short prices of sugar at Rouen, Nantes, and Dublin, during the past year will show that it was from 6*d*. to 1*s*. per cwt. cheaper at the Continental ports than it was here.

and pressing a third time, as much as 95 per cent. of juice has been obtained; that is, practically, the whole. In such cases it is usual to use the expressed liquor of the third pressing for moistening the bags after the first pressure, and to add a small quantity of tannin to the water, which preserves the juice from alteration.

The juice is also extracted by maceration; that is, by repeatedly washing the pulp with successive portions of water until it is quite exhausted; but this process is not now much used. By combining it, however, with pressure by the ordinary means, good results have lately been obtained. The pulp is first pressed, and the partially exhausted cakes are introduced into buckets, arranged in ten rows or series upon an endless chain passing vertically over two pulleys, somewhat in the manner of the buckets in a dredging vessel. The bottoms of the buckets are formed of wire gauze, so as to allow the water which is let in from above to percolate through the pulp in the first series of buckets, and then through the second, and so on. The water as it passes out of the tenth series of buckets will be nearly as rich as juice, because as it passes from one series to another it takes up more and more sugar. The upper series of buckets, when their pulp is exhausted, descend on the same chain on the opposite side, and discharge their moist pulp, which is mixed with fresh pulp from the presses to which it furnishes water, and, by the action of *endosmosis* and *exosmosis*,* causes it to cede part of its saccharine matter. The mixed pulps are then subjected to pressure in other hydraulic presses, and yield a juice which marks only one degree less than the normal juice.

The juice obtained by any of these methods contains a great many other constituents of the beet, such as substances containing nitrogen, which must be first removed. The juice, as it comes from the press, is accordingly introduced into the defecating pan, which is a copper vessel provided with a double hemispherical bottom, capable of being heated by steam. The juice is first heated from 140° to 158° Fahrenheit, when the albumen is coagulated, and separates in gray flocks, which, when they come to the surface, are skimmed off. The other nitrogenous substances do not coagulate by heat, nor does the albumen when the beet has undergone alteration from growth or other causes. To remove these substances, as well as organic acids, milk of lime is stirred in, as soon as the albumen has coagulated; and this addition at once precipitates the malic and other acids present, as insoluble lime-salts, and also the greater part of the nitrogenous substances not coagulated. During the first month of the season about 3 lbs. of lime (unslaked) are employed for every 100 gallons of juice. As the season advances, however, this quantity is increased to 6 lbs., and sometimes even to 10 lbs. The temperature at which the lime is added varies from 140° to 178° Fahrenheit. Steam is then turned on until the liquid just commences to boil, when the whole of the albumen and other impurities separate and come to the surface, where they form a thick clot. When the operation has been successfully performed, the impurities form a connected mass like the curd of milk, which soon detaches itself from the sides of the pan, and allows a light straw-coloured liquid, free from all suspended matter, to come to the surface. The clear liquid is then drawn off, and passed through granulated animal charcoal. The juice retained by the impurities is afterwards obtained by a screw-press. A great many processes have been proposed to effect the defecation of beet-juice, instead of that just described; but our space forbids us from noticing more than one, which will probably come into general use. The defect in the ordinary process is the great difficulty of regulating the quantity of lime to be added; if too much be employed, it will injure the sugar in the subsequent boiling of the syrup; if too little, the whole of the impurities will not be removed, and the juice will become sour. M. Rousseau obviates these difficulties by adding a large excess of lime, which precipitates almost everything, the lime itself being subsequently removed by a stream of carbonic acid gas, produced by forcing a quantity of air through a stove containing ignited coke. The oxygen of the air is completely burned into carbonic acid gas, which is purified by being made to pass through water.

We may also mention here that the whole process of rasping, pressing, and, in some factories, the defecation also, may be superseded by using dried roots. This plan is the invention of Schützenbach, and consists in cutting up the beet by a machine into thin slices, which are dried at a gentle temperature, not exceeding 140°, by which they lose four-fifths of their weight in water; and in this condition may be stored away like corn, even for a period of years. To extract the sugar, the dried roots are introduced into closed vessels, where they are treated with successive portions of boiling water until the whole of the sugar is extracted, the vessels being so arranged that the fresh-water comes in upon nearly exhausted slices, and finally passes over fresh ones, by which means a very strong syrup is directly obtained. In some factories a small quantity of lime-water is employed, so that the syrup when obtained is already defecated; but the residue could only be used as manure, and not for feeding cattle; lately, however, the syrup has been first separated, and then defecated, by which the residue retains its value as food for cattle. The great merit of this process is, that the beet may be grown in the most advantageous places, sliced and dried, and sent to the factory, which may be placed in the most desirable position as regards fuel and labour; and a factory may work the whole year instead of from 120 to 150 days, as it can only do when operating altogether upon green roots.

In whatever way the juice be defecated, it will always be more or less coloured; and when defecated with lime, a quantity of foreign matter will remain unprecipitated by that substance, whilst some of the lime will combine with the sugar. All these impurities are removed by filtration through charcoal.

The first filters employed in the manufacture of sugar consisted of willow baskets, lined with woollen cloth; these exerted no decolorizing agency. In the end of the last century Lowitz discovered the decolorizing action of wood charcoal, and in 1798 Kels applied it to the manufacture of sugar; but since the dis-

* If two fluids, such as water and a solution of sugar in water, be separated by a porous diaphragm, as a piece of bladder, there will be a tendency of the water (which will more readily wet the membrane than the syrup) to pass into the syrup: this tendency is called endosmosis, or passing in. This is always accompanied by a tendency of the syrup to pass into the water, and thus establish a balance; which tendency is called exosmosis or passing out. It is one of the most universal phenomena of nature, and is continually taking place wherever two fluids of different densities are separated by porous bodies, such as the tissues of plants; and hence plays an important part in the economy of vegetation.

covery of the extraordinary power of burnt bones in decolorizing organic solutions, and especially since its general application by Payen and Pluvinet, it has been used for decolorizing and purifying syrups. At first the charcoal, in the state of fine powder, was added during the boiling of the syrup, which was afterwards filtered through an arrangement of long bags, known as Taylor's filter, which is a modification of that employed by Payen. In 1828 Dumont made the important modification which is now in use; he found that, by granulating the charcoal to about the size of the coarsest gunpowder, and removing all dust, a larger decolorizing surface could be exposed to the juice, and that the filtration would take place more rapidly. This simple operation formed an epoch in the history of the sugar manufacture.

The filters now in use are cylindrical sheet-iron vessels, varying from 10 to 20 feet high, and from 1½ to 3 feet in diameter. Each filter is provided with a false bottom, pierced with holes; this is covered with canvass, upon which the charcoal is placed until it reaches about 12 to 18 inches of the top; another piece of canvass is laid upon it, and over this a metallic plate pierced with holes, through which the juice to be acted upon is admitted to the filters. The filters are always kept full, so as to keep the liquid in perfect contact with the whole of the charcoal.

The juice, as it passes from the filter, is evaporated to about 25° of Beaumé,* or to the consistence of a thin syrup, when it is again passed through the charcoal. In making fine sugar, in one direct series of operations, the syrup is passed three times through the charcoal, at 25°, 12°, and at 5° to 6° of Beaumé.

The syrup is now ready for boiling. The object of this operation is to get rid of as much water as is necessary to allow crystals of sugar to form. Sometimes the juice is boiled in a simple open pan placed over the fire, or in various forms of pans heated by the passage of steam through a coil of pipe; the former method is now entirely abandoned in beet sugar works, although it is almost universally employed in boiling the juice of the sugar-cane in the colonies. The temperature at which the syrup boils, after passing the second time through the charcoal, is very high, being 220° Fahrenheit, and gradually increases until it has finished boiling, when it reaches 266°. Such a temperature is, however, injurious to the syrup. The temperature at which a liquid boils is influenced by the pressure of the atmosphere; thus, what we call the temperature of boiling water is only the temperature of water boiling in open vessels when the pressure of the atmosphere on a square inch of surface is equal to that of a column of mercury 30 inches high and 1 square inch at the base. If we reduce the pressure the temperature will fall; and if we substitute for water syrup of ordinary density, we shall find that if we reduce the pressure to 1 inch of mercury it will boil at 125°, and even with an imperfect vacuum, indicated by a pressure of four inches of mercury, the boiling point will only be 175°. It is clear, therefore, that if we could boil our syrups in a vacuum, the injurious action of a high temperature would be completely obviated. This was effected by Howard, in 1812, by the Vacuum-Pan.

The vacuum-pan now in use consists of a hemispherical copper pan, provided with a worm of the same material, through which steam is passed for heating the syrup. This pan is surrounded by a cast-iron jacket, between which and the pan a space is left for the circulation of steam, and which thus assists the coil in evaporating the syrup. A copper hemispherical dome is fastened over the pan by means of flanges; and to the top of this dome is attached a kind of chamber with a man-hole, by which the pan can be cleaned. A pipe connects this chamber with an overflow vessel which catches any syrup that may accidentally boil over, and which is, in its turn, connected with an air-pump, by which the apparatus is exhausted. A vessel of known capacity, but generally containing about 35 gallons, is also attached to the pan, by which any given quantity of syrup can be introduced into the pan as it is required. There is inserted into the dome a barometer for indicating the pressure, a thermometer for ascertaining the temperature, and an apparatus, called a proof-stick, by which small quantities of the syrup may be examined, from time to time; and, finally, a peep-glass to enable the sugar-boiler to see into the interior, and thus examine the condition of the contents. In the bottom is placed a cock by which the syrup, when boiled to the proper degree, may be drawn off.

The vacuum is maintained by means of the air-pump, and by various contrivances for condensing the steam. It is quite clear that if some means were not adopted for rapidly carrying off the steam formed from the evaporation of the syrup, an atmosphere of steam, of gradually increasing tension, would be formed, which would at once cause the temperature of the syrup to rise. The vapour is, therefore, conducted into a condenser, the form of which varies very considerably in different pans. In a modification of the apparatus invented by M. Roth no air-pump is used, the vacuum being produced from the commencement by a current of steam which drives the air before it. The vacuum, in this case, is maintained by the condensation of the vapour produced from the evaporation of the syrup, in a separate apparatus, into which a current of cold water is allowed to pass as a dense rain. This arrangement is very effective; the boiling of the usual charge of a pan 80 inches in diameter, which is about thirty loaves of sugar, is usually completed in a quarter of an hour. The quantity of water consumed by this form of pan is enormous, as much as from 104,000 to 105,000 gallons being required in twenty-four hours. Sometimes a condenser or long worm is employed instead of a shower of water, and the condensation has even been effected by cold juice instead of by the latter, the condensed water itself being used to feed the boiler, so that no waste of heat takes place. There have been various other contrivances for effecting the same object as the vacuum-pan; but as few of them have fulfilled the object of their inventors, and as none have come into use, we need not notice them further here.

The proper point of concentration by boiling is judged of by a series of tests which are purely empirical. They consist in the examination of a small quantity of the syrup, and by the appearance presented when a portion is drawn out between the thumb and forefinger, or when it is thrown into water.

When the syrup is boiled in an open pan, or in any vessel where the temperature passes that of boiling water, no crystals are formed in the vessel; but in the vacuum-pan, where the temperature is low, crystals are readily formed. The usual temperature of the syrup up to this point is 180° to 190°, but as soon as the grain begins to form, the temperature is lowered to 160°: and, finally, when the process is nearly completed,

* This is an instrument similar to what is used to ascertain the quality of milk, and is employed to indicate the density of the syrups; it is called, after the constructor of the scale employed upon it, Beaumé's Saccharometer.

it is allowed to fall to 145°. As soon as the sugar-boiler ascertains that the crystals are in a sufficiently advanced state, he admits another measure of syrup, and repeats this until the whole charge is disposed of. Grain, as the crystals are termed, is formed generally in about twelve to sixteen minutes, and a full charge, technically called *a skip*, is finished in from one and a half to two and a half hours, according to the quality of the syrup.

The syrup, when boiled, is run into a vessel, called *a cooler*, when the sugar is boiled in an open pan; where it is allowed, under continual agitation, to cool down to about 180°. It is called *a heater*, when boiled in a vacuum pan; for the syrup issues at a temperature of about 145°, and is then suddenly heated up to 180°. From this vessel it is ladled into large open chests, where the crystallization is completed. Formerly the syrup from the heater was ladled directly into forms or moulds, at one time made of porous clay, and now made of sheet-iron, of the exact shape of a loaf of sugar, the ends of which had small holes in them which were plugged with pieces of linen cloth. In from twenty-four to thirty-six hours the crystallization is completed; the plugs are then withdrawn, and the uncrystallized syrup allowed to drain out. In whatever way the separation of the syrup from the crystallized sugar is effected, the former is again boiled, and a second crop of crystallized sugar, known as sugar of the second jet, is obtained; and when good, a third time yielding sugar of the third jet. The syrups obtained from this third operation are allowed to rest in cisterns for some four to six months, when a large quantity of an inferior sugar, called the fourth jet, is produced.

A beautiful process was proposed by Schützenbach for separating the molasses from the sugar. When the syrup has attained a certain density, it is run off, and a number of charges are mingled together in the heater, the temperature is elevated to about 170°, and the mass thoroughly agitated and allowed to rest for eighteen or twenty-four hours, when it becomes nearly solid. This mass is then transferred to trays or boxes about eighteen inches square and six inches deep, and having a bottom of wire-gauze. The boxes are so arranged that a current of steam is made to pass through the space which they occupy, so as to keep it saturated with moisture at a temperature of 88°, and thus prevent the syrup from drying upon the crystals. In some factories these boxes are made six feet long, three feet wide, and three feet deep. The drainage takes place with great rapidity, and by a process known as *claying* or *liquoring*, perfectly white sugar can be obtained.

For some time the agency of centrifugal force has been employed to effect this object. The machine for this purpose consists of a drum formed of a framework of iron and a periphery of wire-gauze. This drum is made to revolve by an upright axis at a speed of from 1000 to 1800 revolutions per minute, and is surrounded by a case, the bottom of which is arranged like a gutter, and having a draw-off cock. The mixture of sugar and syrup is introduced into the revolving drum, where by the action of the centrifugal force it is strained, the dry crystalline sugar coating the interior of the drum, and the syrup passing through the gauze. These machines are usually 4½ feet in diameter, and contain a charge of about 2 cwts. which is completely drained in from five to eight minutes. To employ the centrifugal machine with economy the sugar must be crystallized in large grains, as otherwise a portion of it would pass through the fine gauze. The sugar produced by the first crystallization from the juice is readily obtained of this character; but that from the third boiling, especially from inferior juice, is never so well crystallized, as the syrup becomes smeary; hence at this stage, Schützenbach's process would be more economical. Although the centrifugal machine is still very much employed, and will, no doubt, always continue to be so, the sanguine expectations at first entertained of it have not been fulfilled, and it has been given up in more than one factory on account of the inferior yield of sugar obtained by it.

By the process above described we could only make what is called *raw sugar*,—that is, sugar in which a certain quantity of impurities still remain behind; if we would obtain perfectly pure sugar, we must submit this raw sugar to a series of processes called refining. The impurities consist of saline matter which always exists in the juice of plants, uncrystallizable sugar and some other substances, the nature of which is not well understood. As these impurities exist in raw tropical sugar as well as in that from the beet, the process of refining is the same, no matter whence the sugar is obtained. In the manufacture of beet sugar, however, owing to the perfect nature of the apparatus, there is no necessity to make raw sugar; as the purest white sugar may be produced directly from the roots by one series of operations. But as raw sugar is still made from the beet, and as a considerable trade in refining the low tropical sugars is carried on in these countries, we shall briefly describe the series of operations adopted for this purpose.

The first process is technically called *blowing up*; and consists in passing steam through a solution of raw sugar, to which lime-water, blood beaten with switches to separate the fibrine, and a little animal charcoal powder, are added, until it boils. The albumen of the blood is coagulated by the heat, and forms a clot, which, as it were, strains the liquid as it comes to the surface. Milk or white of egg, is now to a great extent substituted for blood.

The second process consists in passing the mixture through linen or cotton filters, by which a clear solution is obtained.

The third process consists in passing the clear solution through charcoal, as already described. In this operation the solution is rendered colourless, and a further quantity of impurities is separated.

The other operations consist of boiling, filling in the forms or moulds of sheet-iron, and draining the molasses, which are exactly similar to the corresponding operations that we have before described.

When the drainage is completed, the operation of *liquoring* is to be performed. It consists of washing out the impure syrup imprisoned between the network of crystals in the mould, with a solution of pure sugar: an operation which is repeated several times, and each time with a purer sugar than the preceding one. When the sugar in the moulds is sufficiently drained from the last syrup in the *clairçage*, as the washing operation is termed, the moulds are turned on their base and struck gently to separate the sugar from their sides: again inverted, and allowed to rest for twenty-four hours, when they are ready for stoving.

For the operation of *stoving*, the loaves of sugar are removed from the forms and arranged in a stove from eighteen to twenty-six feet long, and from twelve to sixteen feet wide; heated either by steam or hot air. Each stove usually contains from 2000 to 4000 loaves, which are exposed at first to a temperature of 77°, gradually raised to 122°. When perfectly dried the loaves are removed from the stove, the tops and bases cut off, and a new tip formed, and then papered up. The reason for cutting off these parts is, that the sugar at the tip of the form is always contaminated with the last traces of the impure syrup; and is, therefore, of a darker colour than the mass of the loaf.

The first syrup which flows from the moulds before the liquoring is technically called *green syrup*, while that obtained during the claying or liquoring is called *clayed syrup*. The former is employed for the manufacture of inferior white sugar, and the latter for a sugar intermediate between the first quality and the inferior kinds. The clayed syrup obtained during the third operation of the *clairçage* is, however, generally used again for the first or second stage of the operation.

There is, therefore, obtained in the process of refining several qualities of sugar, which are distinguished by the size of the moulds employed. Thus the first product is put into moulds of a small size, and is usually superior in quality, and gets three or more liquorings, and is hence known under the name of *double refined*. When the liquoring is not pushed so far, or when the syrups of the second or third operations of *clairçages* are employed, larger forms are used, and the loaves are called *single refined*. The loaves which are obtained in working up the green syrups of double refined sugar, and the clayed syrups of inferior sugars, and the *tips* of inferior qualities, give what are called *lumps*. *Bastard loaves* are obtained from materials somewhat inferior to those employed for lumps, and are made in the largest-sized moulds. Lumps and bastards scarcely differ from one another except in the quality of the materials; the former get, however, usually one liquoring more than the latter.

The green syrups, and syrups of the first *clairçage* derived from the bastards and lumps, yield bastard muscovado sugar, the drainage from which forms the last product of the process, known as *refiner's treacle*.

The term *clayed*, employed in the preceding observations, refers to the old process of placing a layer of wet clay on the top of the mould, the water of which, as we described in speaking of cane-sugar, washes out the impurities in the sugar under it. Although this process is now rarely followed, a solution of sugar being almost universally substituted, the word *claying* is still employed to designate the operation of washing the sugar, whether performed by clay or syrup.

*Residues of the Beet-Sugar Manufacture.*—There is perhaps no manufacture more in accordance with the spirit of modern manufacturing industry, which inculcates that there be no waste—that everything be utilized—than that of beet-sugar. It is, in fact, a perfect analysis of the plant, each constituent of which is applied to some useful purpose.

In the first place, the pulp or solid matter of the beet after the extraction of the juice, and which usually forms about 20 per cent. of the beet employed (that is, five tons of raw beet give one of pulp), forms an excellent food for cattle and pigs; and is accordingly much prized on the Continent, where it is readily purchased at a high price, chiefly in consequence of the facility with which it can be preserved; so that it is available in the end of spring and commencement of summer, when the supply of roots is exhausted.

A considerable quantity of the nitrogenous elements of the beet is pressed out in the juice, and is removed, as already described, in the operation of defecation, by means of lime; the scum thus separated, together with the offal of the roots, &c., forms a very rich manure.

The dust, which is continually being produced by the reburning of the animal charcoal in this manufacture, is usually sold to make blacking.

There is no residue, however, which has been more thoroughly utilized than the uncrystallizable sugar or treacle. No matter how perfectly each operation may be performed, the whole of the sugar cannot as yet be extracted in a crystallizable form. A portion of it is always undergoing a peculiar change by which it loses the property of crystallizing; this substance, with the soluble salts, which accompany the sugar, and other impurities, constitute what is called molasses or treacle. The molasses derived from cane-sugar, and which comes into commerce from the West Indies, still contains a large quantity of sugar, owing to the imperfect process of manufacture followed in the colonies; and having an aromatic odour, is employed by confectioners, or is reboiled to extract sugar from it, and the treacle left after the separation of the sugar, under the name of *refiners' treacle*, is used in distilleries, or in making ginger-beer, ale, &c. Beet treacle, on the other hand, has usually a very beety, disagreeable flavour, which forbids its use in many cases where cane-sugar treacle can be employed; and hence special applications of it have been made, the three principal of which we shall enumerate. It is well known that sugar is capable of combining with certain basic substances, such as lime, lead, &c., and forming compounds, some of which are soluble and others insoluble. One of the most singular of these is the compound with barytes, discovered by Peligot. If a solution of caustic barytes be added to a solution of sugar, no effect will be produced, but if the mixture be heated to the boiling point, the whole of the sugar separates as an insoluble saccharate of barytes, and may be repeatedly washed with cold water without any sensible loss. Three or four years ago Dubrunfaut discovered by this means that the whole of the sugar contained in beet molasses could be separated—that it, in fact, was all *crystallizable sugar*. The process, as carried on by him and Le Play, at La Villette, near Paris, is very simple. A boiling solution of caustic barytes is poured into the molasses, which instantly solidifies to a porous crystalline mass, insoluble in water. This mass is then well washed with water until all impurities are removed, when it forms a thick magma of a pure white colour. The mass is then introduced into large wooden tanks, of from 1760 to 2200 gallons capacity, into which is forced, by means of pumps worked by steam, a constant stream of carbonic acid, produced by burning lime. By the action of the carbonic acid the thick magma gradually becomes fluid, and after some time it will be found converted into a perfectly clear solution of sugar, in which carbonate of barytes is suspended. To remove the latter it is filtered through cotton bags, and when these have drained they are slightly pressed in a screw-press, and then in a powerful hydraulic press, in order to remove the whole of the syrup. The syrup thus obtained marks from 18° to 22° of Beaumé's areometer; it still contains traces of carbonate and bicarbonate of barytes in solution, which may be removed either by gypsum or sulphate of alumina; after which it is clarified with blood or white of egg, skimmed, filtered, and boiled, and crystallized in forms, by which refined sugar of the best quality is directly obtained. The carbonate of baryta may be reconverted into caustic barytes any number of times by mixing it with a little wood charcoal powder and igniting it. The loss of barytes sustained by each operation is replaced by sulphuret of barium, which is easily made from sulphate of barytes.

According to the statements which have been published regarding the results obtained on a great scale, it would appear that 50 per cent., or fully one-half of the whole weight of beet molasses can be thus recovered as sugar. And as nearly 40,000 tons of molasses are annually produced in France, if the whole were worked up by Dubrunfaut's and Le Play's process, 20,000 tons of *refined sugar* would be thus recovered, or fully one-fourth of the whole present production of beet sugar in that country. The importance of this process may best be judged by comparing the money values of the original molasses and of the refined sugar produced from it. The highest price realized by beet molasses is about £5 per ton, so that the value of the entire beet molasses of France may be taken at £200,000; whilst, if the sugar were extracted and sold at only £30 per ton short price, the sum realized would be £600,000.

It is singular that the process is not equally applicable to molasses from the sugar-cane. For while it has been perfectly established, by the practical results obtained in several factories, that there is *no uncrystallizable sugar in the beet molasses*, it appears that fully one-half of that contained in the molasses of tropical sugar, and which usually contains from 60 to 70 per cent. of saccharine matter, is uncrystallizable sugar which cannot be recovered by the baryta process.

The second application of beet molasses is to the manufacture of spirit. This process is also the invention of Dubrunfaut, and is, if possible, still more ingenious than the last mentioned. The treacle is diluted with sufficient water to enable it to be fermented; the residuent wash remaining in the still is then employed to dilute another portion of the treacle to be similarly dealt with. This process is repeated until the saline matter and impurities increase to such a degree, that the fermentation cannot be further carried on. The liquid is then introduced into a thick iron boiler, where it is used for generating steam for effecting the distillation of another portion of the fermented liquor, until it becomes so saturated that it begins to thicken. In this way the whole of the sugar contained in the treacle is converted into alcohol, while the whole of the soluble salts contained in the beet juice, and which would not pay for their extraction by the evaporation in the ordinary way, can be economically obtained. The thick mass just mentioned is now dried and incinerated at a gentle temperature, dissolved in water, and the different salts separated by a crystallization. The salts thus obtained consist of carbonate and sulphate of potash, chloride of potassium, and carbonate of soda. Although the whole quantity of soluble saline matter contained in the beet frequently does not amount to one-half per cent., and rarely to one per cent., yet when immense quantities of treacle, which contain the whole of the soluble salts of the beet, are converted into alcohol, the quantity of these salts thus cheaply obtained is very large. For instance, the total weight of mixed salts produced at the single factory of Waghäusel, in Germany, is said to amount to 150 tons per annum.

Instead of producing alcohol, the treacle may be converted into vinegar, which may be employed in the manufacture of white lead, or in the production of acetate of soda, or of alumina, &c.

Having thus given a history of the different stages of the manufacture of beet-sugar, so far as our space would permit, it only remains to indicate what is the present yield of sugar from the beet, and how far this branch of industry is adapted to the circumstances—physical and economical—of Ireland.

From the very nature of the beet, and the variations in its composition produced by conditions of growth, as well as from the property which sugar has of not crystallizing when mingled with certain substances, such as salts, &c., it is not to be expected that the yield of sugar should be constant, or that the whole could in practice be extracted. Improvements are, however, being rapidly made; and the contrast afforded by the results obtained forty years ago, and those of the present day, lead to the conclusion that before long the whole of the sugar contained in the beet will be extracted economically. Although the usual average produce is not more than 6½ per cent., many manufacturers who attend to the growth of their beet obtain 7 and 7½ per cent., and in certain cases, even 9 per cent. has been reached. Some idea may be formed of the rapidity with which the manufacture has improved, by the fact that in 1841, 27 tons of beet were required in some factories in Prussia, to produce one ton of marketable sugar; in 1842, 22½; in 1843, 19¾; in 1844, only 19, whilst at present, it is said, one ton of sugar is produced by less than 15 tons of roots. As a general average the present produce may be taken at from 3 to 4 per cent. of superior sugar; 2 to 3 of second quality; and 1 to 2 of inferior sugar; 2 per cent. of molasses being the usual produce at present. Of course it will be observed that when the maximum per centage of first quality is obtained, the quantity of the inferior kinds diminishes: so that where 4 per cent. of superior sugar would be produced, there would, perhaps, be only 2 per cent. of second, and 1 per cent. of inferior sugar, or in all, 7 per cent. The proportion of the different qualities depends equally upon the process of manufacture, and upon the quality of the roots.

It may be considered almost superfluous to discuss the question of the adaptation of the beet sugar manufacture to this country; for no one, we feel assured, will doubt that the climate and soil of Ireland are eminently suited for the growth of root crops. As it is, however, dependent altogether upon only two conditions, we shall say a few words upon the subject. 1st. Do roots grown in Ireland contain as much sugar as those grown in France and Germany under similar conditions? 2nd. And if so, can that sugar be extracted as cheaply here as there? The first question has been fully answered in the affirmative, by a long series of experiments, and by the practical experience of working on a large scale. The subject of the growth of roots having been already discussed very fully, we need not enter into this part of the subject further here. We may, however, remark, that the observation above made with regard to the practical results now obtained on the great scale by Dubrunfaut and Le Play, and on a more limited scale in Ireland, afford the best answer to those who have asserted that the beet root, especially that of Ireland, contained uncrystallizable sugar. The second condition may be still more briefly noticed. In the manufacture of sugar there are three economical elements—the cost of labour, the cost of the raw material, and the cost of fuel; the first is as cheap here as in any part of Europe; with regard to the second, we are confident that roots could be grown here as cheaply as in most parts of France; whilst the cost of fuel is very much lower here than in that country. These two conditions being answered in the affirmative, and it having been already shown, in the clearest manner, that beet sugar does compete successfully with tropical sugar in France, there can be no doubt that this branch of manufacture would prove eminently successful in Ireland if conducted with SKILL and ENTERPRISE.

The beet sugar industry has of late years had the misfortune to be considered as a hot-house plant requiring care and protection,—like a delicate child between "two doctors," one of whom pronounces it cannot live a day, and the other that, alas! although it may reach its manhood, it will certainly be carried off, owing to its weak constitution, by some epidemic in the shape of tropical sugar, the manufacture of which is to be so improved at some indefinite period that it will completely swamp the beet sugar. Granting for the moment that such may be the case, an assertion which we, however, deny, notwithstanding the eminent "opinion" in favour of this view,—should that deter us from enjoying its present benefits? What manufacture is there which is not subject to the same casualty—that is not liable to be influenced, or even altogether superseded, by the gradual changes in the habits and tastes of society, or by some new processes, which are in turn superseded by others? And yet capital is invested in these new improvements.

The character of the resources of Ireland is very different from that of England. Our mines are in general poorer, our coal inferior, and that fortunate association of the various raw materials which is required in some of the most important manufactures that give to England her chief power as a great manufacturing nation, is much rarer in Ireland. We must therefore make, by skill and artistic taste, what we lack in geological wealth. To us, a manufacture that has grown up under peculiar difficulties, in countries that, like our own, are poor in those resources which form the real basis of England's prosperity, that require skill and perseverance to carry it out, and that can only succeed by a system of economy unequalled perhaps in any other branch of industry, ought to be particularly welcome. Where the beet sugar manufacture has grown up, a new and rational system of agriculture has been created, which enriched the districts immediately concerned; the land has in some places quadrupled in value; the number of cattle has been more than doubled; the produce of grain and of other crops has increased in an equal proportion; and it has created an intelligent class of workmen in the midst of the most backward rural districts. To it France is almost entirely indebted for the gradual growth of a manufacture of machinery; for no manufacture has ever enlisted a greater amount of ingenuity and skill in its service, or given rise to a greater number of inventions, many of which have found application in other branches of trade, than that of beet sugar. The amount of skill, both chemical and mechanical, that is required to successfully carry on the beet sugar manufacture, and the totally new ideas of the economy of manufactures and of agriculture that it gives rise to, have wonderfully developed the whole industrial energy of those districts where it is now in activity:—a result which is also to be expected from its spread in Ireland.

The manufacture of beet sugar was well represented in the Exhibition. Mr. William Hirsch, on the part of the Irish Beet Sugar Company, contributed a very complete collection of specimens illustrative of the manufacture, from the raw root to the sugar. There were also a number of loaves made by one series of operations from the beet without the usual refining process. An interesting feature of this collection consisted in a series of views of the interior of the factory at Mountmellick,—the first complete one erected in Ireland. The small collection from the Museum of Irish Industry was chiefly interesting in consequence of being composed of specimens obtained during the progress of the researches carried on in that Institution to determine the comparative value of Irish-grown roots. It was an exceedingly complete collection, showing the different qualities of sugar, raw and refined, the beet sliced and dried, the scum used as a manure, the dried pulp, the molasses, and the three series of products which can be made from the latter:—1. The saccharate of baryta, prepared by precipitating the sugar in the molasses by caustic baryta and the refined sugar prepared from it; 2. Acetic acid or distilled vinegar and acetate of soda prepared from beet treacle; 3. Alcohol made from beet treacle and carbonate of potash, bicarbonate of soda, chloride of potassium, and sulphate of potash prepared from the residue after the distillation of the alcohol. Some samples of refined beet sugar of remarkable purity were exhibited by the Messrs. Claus and Carron, of Ghent. The colourless transparent candy, exhibited by the same firm, could not be surpassed for purity or regularity of crystalization.

We will here glance at the present sources of our supply of sugar, and the quantities at present manufactured, of which the following Table may be considered to give a close approximation:—

| | | | | |
|---|---|---|---|---|
| British Possessions in the West Indies | | (1851), | 154,880 | tons. |
| Mauritius, | | „ | 50,000 | „ |
| British East Indies, | | „ | 78,286 | „ |
| Siam, | | „ | 10,000 | „ |
| French Colonies, | | „ | 90,000 | „ |
| Dutch, | Java, | „ | 82,000 | „ |
| | Guiana, | „ | 15,000 | „ |
| | Phillipine Islands, &c., | „ | 28,000 | „ |
| Spanish, | Cuba, | „ | 240,000 | „ |
| | Porto Rico, | „ | 40,000 | „ |
| Louisiana, | | „ | 100,000 | „ |
| Brazil, | | „ | 100,000 | „ |
| Danish and Swedish Colonies, | | „ | 12,000 | „ |
| Beet Sugar, | | (1852) | 180,000 | „ |
| Total, | | | 1,175,166 | tons. |

Nearly the whole of this enormous quantity is consumed in Europe and the United States of America; and if we estimate its cost at £22 per ton, its total value will be represented by £25,853,652, to which we must add 50 per cent. for duty, making a total of £38,780,478, or nearly *thirty-nine millions sterling*, paid for sugar by the people of Europe and America. Immense quantities of sugar are also consumed in the sugar-growing countries themselves, and this is especially the case in India and China, so that it is probable that the total quantity of sugar made throughout the world at present amounts to at least 3,000,000 of tons, which, exclusive of duty, would be worth at least sixty millions sterling! Among sugar-consuming countries it is probable that Great Britain stands first, the quantity retained for home consumption in 1852 being 306,330 tons, whilst the quantity imported direct into Ireland the same year amounted to only 23,385 tons, making a total of 329,715 tons. It is probable that the consumption of sugar in Ireland amounts at present to more than 40,000 tons, as we get a good deal from London, Liverpool, Bristol, and Glasgow, which is not included in the numbers above given. Taking, therefore, the consumption of sugar in Great Britain at 300,000 tons, and the population at 20,793,000, the average consumption per head in Great Britain is about 31 lbs., and for Ireland, 13¾ lbs., and for France about 10 lbs., which is very nearly the mean of the whole of Europe and the United States. Some notion may be formed of the great social change which has taken place in England within the last century, as indicated by the change of food which must have occurred to require such an enormous quantity of sugar, when we state that the total quantity of sugar consumed in England in the year 1700 was only 10,000 tons.

## II.—ANIMAL KINGDOM.

### PRESERVED MEATS, MILK, ETC.

Vegetable substances in their natural state contain a large quantity of water; leaves and other succulent parts often containing as much as 95 per cent. This water fills the cells, and holds dissolved in it sugar, dextrine, and substances containing nitrogen; these matters gradually alter the sugar, and convert it into other substances, the nature of which will depend upon certain conditions, such as temperature. Thus, the sugar may be converted into alcohol and carbonic acid, into acetic acid or into lactic acid (the acid of sour milk), and a kind of gum. These changes are usually termed fermentation, but being essentially different, that word is more usually applied to the case when alcohol is produced. If vegetable matter be exposed to the air, the production of acid just mentioned may be considered as only one of the first links in a great chain of changes and transformations, the final result of which will be the total resolution of the substances into water, carbonic acid, ammonia, and earthy matter. Where large masses of vegetable matter are thus exposed, these changes take place with great rapidity, and fetid smells are produced, and the substances are said to putrefy. If we expose animal matter under similar circumstances, there can be no fermentation like that produced where starch or sugar is present; and putrefaction accordingly sets in at once.

Vegetable and animal substances may, however, be prevented from undergoing any of these changes even for centuries; a fact which is of great practical importance—for it is often useful to preserve fruits and vegetables, which arrive at maturity at one season, to be used at another; whilst it is an absolute necessity to preserve meat for a considerable time for the use of sailors during long voyages. This object may be effected in different ways, among which we may include:—by cold, drying, salting, placing in spirit of wine, boiling with sugar, absolute exclusion of air, and, finally, by antiseptic agents.

The method of preserving by cold is evidently of little practical importance, as it can only be carried out in certain regions. Animal or vegetable matter inclosed in ice is imperishable, as has been fully proved by Palas's discovery of the remains of the extinct mammoth in Siberia; and it is well known that frozen meat, milk, &c., may be preserved throughout the winter in the northern parts of Europe. The preservation of potatoes and root-crops in pits and cellars comes under this category, but in this case it is rather a postponement of decay aided by the vitality still existing, although dormant, in the root, than a perfect preservative, which could only be effected by a temperature below the freezing point, and which in the case of roots would be liable to destroy the germinating power.

One of the most effectual, as it is also the simplest and most usual mode of preservation, is by drying; for no putrefaction can take place unless moisture be present. It is in this way that grapes, currants, and other fruits, corn, &c., are preserved by drying in the sun or in stoves. Meat and fish may also be preserved by drying them. In Mexico it is quite usual to cut up the flesh of a cow into thin ribbons, and hang them on posts near the houses exposed to the heat of the sun until they become perfectly dry, after which they are tightly tied in bundles until required. Salting is nothing more than a species of drying, and depends for its action upon the phenomenon of *endosmosis* and *exosmosis*. If we separate two fluids of unequal density by an animal membrane, such as a bladder, it will be found that the tendency of the fluids to pass through the bladder and mix will be very different, and will depend upon the nature of the fluids and upon their relative density. If a piece of fresh meat be placed in strong brine, we shall have an exactly analogous case, the water contained in the animal tissues and containing certain substances in solution, having a lower density than the brine, will pass out and mix with the brine, while but very little of the latter will penetrate the meat. If a quantity of dry salt be laid upon fresh meat, a portion of it will be dissolved by the surface moisture; the solution thus formed upon the surface of the meat will induce an exosmosis of the juice of the meat with a slight endosmosis of the brine, and this will go on until from one-third to one-half is drawn out. Meat thus perfectly dried will not undergo decay, because the whole of the moisture remaining is so loaded with salt that the fibre of the meat is scarcely moist enough to admit of putrefaction commencing. Independent of this purely mechanical action, the salt also exerts an antiseptic influence. Curing meat by salting, although one of the most usual methods, and, as far as the arresting of putrefaction goes, one of the most effective, is very injurious to the nutritive qualities of the meat. If the salt merely removed water, the meat would suffer no loss in quality; but the fluid which is drawn out and mixes with the brine consists of the juice of the flesh, and abounds with phosphoric acid, potash, creatine, albumen, and many other substances—with, in fact, all those substances which form the constituents of soups or the extract of meat. This brine is thrown away, and hence the more perfectly the process of salting has been effected the more completely the meat is exhausted of its most valuable elements. It is perhaps to the absence of these essential ingredients of nutrition in salt meat that we must attribute the evil consequence of its exclusive use on board ships.

The action of alcohol in preserving animal and vegetable substances resembles very much that of a strong brine. Alcohol cannot wet an animal tissue, hence it cannot penetrate it; and if, accordingly, a piece of fresh meat be immersed in strong alcohol, it will be gradually dried by the exosmosis of the juice into it, as in the case of brine above mentioned. Except for the preservation of anatomical preparations, and natural history objects, spirit of wine can never have any practical application. The preservation of fruits, &c. by boiling with sugar and steeping in vinegar, is also dependent upon the same law.

Air appears to be quite as indispensable as moisture during the process of putrefaction, and hence, if we could completely shut it out, we would be enabled to preserve meat or other animal and vegetable matter for an indefinite period. This process would have the additional advantage that the substance preserved would retain all its nutritive qualities unimpaired, whilst its natural flavour would be unaltered. In Italy and the south of France, and in Spain, fowls partially boiled are preserved by immersing them in melted goose-grease, which, on cooling, solidifies and effectually prevents all contact of air. Similarly, eggs are greased or immersed for a moment in milk of lime, so as to stop up the pores, and thus keep them fresh by preventing all contact of air. Large quantities of provisions are now also preserved by simple exclusion of air. The vegetables or meats are introduced into tin boxes, and packed as closely as possible and boiled, after which the lid is soldered on, and the boxes again immersed in boiling water for some time. Sometimes the first boiling is effected before the introduction of the meat into the canisters. A small hole is left in the lid for the escape of the air which is driven out by the steam, after which it is then soldered up, and the boiling continued for some time longer, until the oxygen of any traces of air left in the box has been converted into carbonic acid, which has no action whatsoever upon the viands. Some of the meats, soups, and vegetables, preserved in this way by Mr. John H. Gamble of Cork, and left on the beach in Prince Regent's Inlet after the wreck of the "Fury" in 1825, were found in 1833 by Sir John Ross in the most perfect preservation, although annually exposed to a variation of 172° of temperature, namely, from 92° below zero to 80° Fahr. above it! And some boxes of the vegetables and soups were found there after nearly a quarter of a century, in perfect preservation, by Sir James Ross. These preserved meats would be a great boon to the sailor; but unfortunately frauds are easily, and, we regret to say, very frequently committed; and in consequence of the disastrous results which might follow were a ship's crew to be entirely dependent upon them, their use has hitherto been very restricted. No attempt can be made to test the quality of such substances without exposing them to the atmosphere, when decomposition would at once set in.

The only other means by which animal and vegetable food may be preserved, which we need mention, is by the agency of antiseptic substances. There are many bodies, such as corrosive sublimate, and to some extent arsenic, &c., which possess the property of preventing the putrefaction of animal substances; but the most remarkable of these is creasote, a peculiar oily liquid which is obtained from wood-tar, and which has derived its name from its preservative qualities (κρεας, flesh; and σωζω, I preserve). Meat exposed to the vapours of this substance, or dipped into a solution of it, will gradually dry up and have the appearance of being smoked, and will not putrefy even if exposed to the heat of the summer's sun. From time immemorial, meat has been dried in the smoke of wood fires, by which it acquired a peculiar flavour, and a brown colour, and lost its susceptibility of putrefying. After the discovery of creasote in tar, it was found that it also existed in smoke, and it is almost certain that the preservative action of the latter is owing to the presence of creasote. Vinegar obtained by the distillation of wood contains creasote, and hence its preservative action upon meat immersed in it.

In the preservation of meat by smoke, it is usual to give it a preliminary salting, so as to get rid of a certain portion of water contained in the fresh meat. The quality of the cured meat, especially of bacon, depends to a certain extent upon the amount of this salting, and the mode in which it is effected. In every case salting is injurious to the quality of the meat, by depriving it of its nutritious juices; the less the meat is salted, therefore the better will be the bacon, but the more difficult will be the process of smoke-curing. The nature of the fuel which produces the smoke seems also to exert a considerable influence upon the quality of the meat; the young green wood of the beach, for instance, is said to yield the most delicate hams. It is proper, however, to remark that the breed of the pig, but above all its food, are also among the most important causes influencing the quality of smoked meat. Pigs fed upon acorns, as in Westphalia, and upon acorns, chestnuts, and other nuts, as in the neighbourhood of Bayonne, and allowed the full freedom of the forests, and as they use but little salt, and cure entirely with wood, the choicest hams in the world are produced there. As a general rule, dry nutritious food, such as refuse corn, bran, &c., yields a much better quality of bacon than watery food; in the latter case, too, the lard is not so firm, and is much more liable to become rancid, and the meat loses more in the salting, and the cured bacon is not at all juicy. A good deal of judgment appears, therefore, to be required in the selection of the pigs and curing of the bacon in these countries: and that a good deal of the success depends upon the skill is proved by the reputation which Limerick, and more recently, Belfast and Cork, have acquired in the production of superior bacon, and which is entirely due to a few individuals.

Considering the great importance of the provision trade, and the peculiar relation of Ireland to it, it was but very imperfectly represented in the Exhibition. Mr. Farrell, of Dublin, exhibited some casks of mess pork and beef, the appearance of which could be readily judged of in consequence of one of the heads of each cask having been formed of a plate of glass. At the close of the Exhibition it was in prime condition, and appeared to have been cured in the most skilful manner. Mr. Mac Vey, of Dublin, exhibited a number of hams, middles, &c. of bacon, which were particularly deserving of commendation, as he appears to have understood that salt and smoke are only means for preserving the meat, and not simply for flavouring it; and that, consistently with that object, the less of either they receive the better.

Mr. Fadeuilhe, of London, exhibited a number of samples of his preserved milk, which is simply that fluid deprived of its water, and seasoned with sugar. Such a preparation would be a great boon to persons going on long voyages in this tea-drinking age; but hitherto all attempts to produce an article which would yield a sweet-flavoured milk on dissolution in water have been very unsuccessful. The product exhibited by Mr. Fadeuilhe laboured under the disadvantage of absorbing moisture from the atmosphere and becoming damp, and, in this state, of getting a cheesey or rancid flavour.

The meat biscuits of Mr. Warriner, of Birmingham, deserve special mention in consequence of the singular nature of the preparation. In many countries, especially in South America and Australia, large numbers of cattle and sheep are boiled down for their fat alone. After the removal of the layer of fat from the surface of the broth, and the separation of the fragments of bone and the fibrine of the meat, a rich soup may be obtained, containing the juices of a large quantity of the meat and a certain portion of the solid part of the meat itself rendered soluble by the continued boiling. By the evaporation of this liquid an extract can be obtained, one pound of which contains the rich and nutritive juices of perhaps 30 to 40 lbs. of the fresh meat. Mr. Warriner uses such an extract prepared in Australia as one of the ingredients of his biscuits; and we have no doubt that the articles prepared by him are exceedingly nutritive, and would, unquestionably, be of incalculable service on ship-board, because they supply all those important constituents which salt meat has lost, and thus perhaps would check, to a great extent, scurvy.*

### HONEY.

Although no honey was exhibited as such, a few observations upon the nature of that substance may not be out of place in connexion with the various forms of hives exhibited, especially as some of these contained swarms of bees engaged in the production of the article.†

* The preservation of meat and vegetables first attracted public attention in the very laudable inquiries as to how the wants of navigators to distant regions could be best ministered to, when without access to fresh supplies. The measures adopted for the discovery of a north-west passage gave a practical value to what had hitherto been regarded as little more than matters of curiosity, and the Admiralty, accordingly, stimulated the manufacturers to great perfection in the art. But the value of this process was soon found to be of much greater extent than that it should be confined to the crews of vessels on distant voyages. In new countries, so little is the flesh of sheep and cattle sometimes in demand, that they have not been unfrequently destroyed for the skin and fat, allowing the flesh to go to waste from inability to preserve it; and in such cases large curing establishments would add greatly to the produce. In our own country, too, at the various fishing stations, it becomes an object to be able to preserve a portion of the stock of fish taken, for which there may not be an adequate immediate demand.

The regulations of the Exhibition of 1851, so far as regarded the awards of prizes for meritorious articles, enabled an opinion to be pronounced on their quality, for which there was no opportunity at our Exhibition; and the Report of the Jurors of that department was highly complimentary to the character of the goods brought under their notice. From that Report we learn that "several hundred canisters of meat were exhibited from various countries, and some of these by many different persons. Their merits were tested by a selection from each; the cases were opened in the presence of the Jury and tasted by themselves; and when advisable, by associates. The majority were of English manufacture, especially the more substantial viands; France and Germany exhibiting chiefly made dishes, game and delicacies of meat, fish, soups, and vegetables." And the reporter of the department further observed that although "the contents of all the cases of whatever kind have lost much of the freshness, taste, and flavour peculiar to newly killed meat—they are soft, and as it were, overdone—yet the nutritious principles are perfectly preserved. As nutriment, they are unexceptionable: they are wholesome and agreeable, and often pleasantly flavoured. Vouchers were given for some of the samples tasted by the Jurors having been preserved for twenty-five years and upwards: these were in a perfectly sound state, and did not perceptibly differ from the contents of canisters only a few months old. So long as the sealing remains sound, the viands appear to undergo no change. Any difference between the contents of the properly preserved cases was to be attributed to the state of the food before preparation, or to the cooking, and not to the method employed for preserving, which is simple, and universally applicable." In reference to the preserved vegetables exhibited on the same occasion, we find from the authority just quoted, that vegetables preserved in a similar manner have been considered by the Jury with the animal food. Generally speaking, their flavour was fresher than that of the meats, especially in the case of those abounding in the saccharine principle, as beet, carrots, parsnips, salsafy, which preserve to advantage. The more farinaceous do not preserve so well, such as green peas, &c., whilst those abounding in volatile oils are hardly worth preservation at all (especially cabbages, turnips, and celery), except as antiscorbutics.—ED.

† There are few more interesting subjects of inquiry or objects of regard than the study of the economy and management of bees; affording at once a source of recreation, especially to the young, in being acquainted with the habits of these curious creatures, and adding to the comforts of the bee-keeper's household without involving almost any corresponding outlay. The attention which has been received in a utilitarian point of view has enabled much to be learned of their peculiarities, information on which is now readily available in a great variety of publications—in fact there is almost no work on rural economy without something on what is termed bee culture. A swarm of bees may be had for 15*s.* or 20*s.*, and with this as a parent stock a large colony may soon be had if placed under circumstances favourable to their operations.

To enter at length into the details of bee culture would be out of place here. Almost any warm corner with a southern aspect will do for the apiary; as a general rule richly cultivated agricultural districts are the best suited for bees; and they thrive but in the vicinity of extensive gardens, or woody or heathy countries abounding in natural flowers. We may observe, however, that the climate of this country is in general too wet for the successful management of these creatures; some seasons, indeed, are so unfavourable that the entire stock is destroyed. In such cases the bees are unable to collect their wonted supplies of honey during the summer, and hence deficiency of winter food follows. Feeding bees is an important department of their management; but when the natural food is not to be had it becomes difficult to maintain the stock in health.

The glass hive, or we should rather say, the small glass case containing a swarm of bees, which was exhibited by J. Edmundson & Co., of this city, formed one of the most attractive objects in this department. Several kinds of beehive were exhibited, but the experience of the most successful apiarians is in favour of the common cottage hive, which is both inexpensive and effective.—ED.

A honeycomb consists of three distinct substances—the membranous tissues forming the cells, composed of cellulose, the substance which forms the walls of the cells of plants; a coating of wax with which the membrane is lined, and which gives solidity to the cells; and the thick saccharine liquid known as honey. If a piece of fresh honeycomb with its cells full of honey be inverted on a dish, the pure honey will flow out, constituting *virgin honey*. If this be allowed to rest for some time, it will divide itself into two parts, the one consisting of a number of sphericles of a pale yellowish or almost whitish colour, and formed of a number of crystals radiating from the centre; and the other a thick syrup. The crystalline sphericles are a true sugar, and in every sense identical with grape or fruit sugar; whilst the syrup contains the same sugar with a certain portion of wax, and very often and perhaps, indeed, always, a quantity of a sugar having the same composition as cane sugar, but in an uncrystallizable form. Gum and mannite, or manna sugar, have also been obtained, especially in the turpentine-like honey; but it is probable that they are products of decomposition, for they are not present in good fresh honey; and moreover, we know that under certain circumstances cane sugar is decomposed into mannite, gum, and lactic acid (the acid of sour milk), which is also usually present in honey whenever mannite has been noticed in it. The tendency of some honeys to a turpentine consistence, that is, to decompose, and give rise to the production of mannite, lactic acid, and gum, appears to be intimately connected with the system of management of the bees, with the plants upon which they feed, and upon many other little understood causes. When we also recollect that there is very considerable differences in the composition of the wax of one season compared with that of another, it will be seen that there is much room for investigation in this branch of rural economy.

It is not yet known whether bees are capable of elaborating sugar from their ordinary food; for the parts of plants such as the nectaries, the anthers, &c., upon which bees settle and collect food, abound in ready-formed sugar. They are, however, undoubtedly capable of transforming cane sugar into grape sugar; for, independent of the fact that the pollen of some plants and the entire sap of others contain only cane-sugar, bees fed on the common sugar produce abundance of honey. Bees appear to possess the power also of transforming sugar into wax, a change which the chemist has never yet been able to effect artificially, but which the progress of science may yet place within our power. Although the conversion of sugar into wax is a far more difficult chemical problem than the transformation of sugar into cellulose, with which it is so intimately related, as may be gathered from our observations upon starch, and which, indeed, has been already to a great extent effected artificially, it will, we have no doubt, appear much more strange to our readers to find that bees possess the power of elaborating woody matter. Yet such is the case, for there can be no doubt that the material of their cell walls is secreted by the bees in the same manner as the honey and wax. The singularity of this fact does not end here, for recent researches show that many cells exist in animals composed of true cellulose, or, in other words, of true vegetable matter! This curious discovery, which was first established with reference to the mantle of the oyster, has been since much extended, and it is now fully proved that it exists in the bee, and in many other insects, and even in the brains of some of the higher animals—being perhaps formed from sugar, which we now know to exist almost as universally in the animal organism as in that of the vegetable.—W. K. S.

---

1. ALLMAN & Co., Bandon, Co. Cork, Manufacturers.—Specimen of whisky.

2. ANDREWS, W., Brazilian Consul, Castle-street, Dublin.—Specimens of Brazilian produce, comprising coffee and coffee plants; sugar canes, sugar.

3. ASPREY, JAMES, Sandleford, near Newbury, Berks, Producer.—Specimens of malt and pease.

4. BLACKNEY, Hugh, Bally Ellen, Goresbridge—Bee-hives, of various constructions.

5. BROWN & POLSON, Paisley.—Granulated starch, made from wheat; powder starch, from sago flour; pulverized farina, from diseased potatoes; gluten, from wheat.

6. BURGESS, E., Pill-lane, Dublin, Manufacturer.—Snuff, made solely from pure Virginia tobacco-stalks; roll tobacco, made of pure Virginia leaf.

7. COONEY, C., Back-lane, Dublin, Manufacturer.—Starch, manufactured from wheat; sago flour, and potato flour.

8. DALY, J. & Co., Cork, Manufacturers.—Whisky, in wooden and glass casks; specimens of Irish manufactured pearl barleys.

9. DRUMMOND, W., & SON, Dawson-street, Dublin, and Stirling, N. B.—290 dried specimens of grains, grasses, and other plants used in agriculture; samples of the seeds of the grains and grasses, &c., generally cultivated in Ireland; coloured drawings, in full size, of 40 varieties of garden and farm vegetables and roots.

10. FADEUILHE, V. B., Newington Crescent, London, Inventor and Manufacturer.—Patent solidified milk, and the grated substance of solidified milk.

11. FARRELL, F., Capel-street, Dublin.—Specimens of hay, clover, and other seeds; a selected assortment of agricultural grasses, suited for the improvement of pasture and meadow lands.

12. FARRELL, J., Leinster-market, Dublin.—Specimens of mess beef and pork, in casks.

13. FOOT, LUNDY, & Co., Essex-bridge, Dublin, Manufacturers.—Lundy Foot's snuff of three kinds, viz.:—Hightoast, Scotch, and stalk, made solely from the leaf and stalks of Virginia tobacco; Virginia leaf tobacco and stalks; same fermented previous to roasting; same roasted ready for grinding; cavendish, nailrod, negrohead, pigtail, roll tobacco, and various cut tobaccos.

14. FORDHAM, T., Snelsmore-hill, East Newbury, Berks, Producer.—Samples of agricultural produce, viz., wheat, Fordham's improved white, red lammas, and Australian white; Fordham's prolific white-eye, and haricot and horse beans; chevalier, black and skinless barley; ears of maize; a few dried pods; dried specimen of [maize] Indian corn, with three ears, grown in Berkshire, in 1852, from acclimatized seed.

15. FRY & SONS, Bristol, Importers and Manufacturers.—Specimens of pods, leaves, flowers, wood, &c., of the theobroma cacao tree; cocoa-nuts as imported; manufactured chocolate, and cocoa; paintings of views in Trinidad, &c.

16. GOODBODY, R., Tullamore, King's Co., Manufacturer.—Snuffs and tobaccos.

17. IRISH BEET SUGAR COMPANY, per W. HIRSCH, Mountmellick, Queen's Co., Manufacturers.—Specimens illustrating the beet-root sugar manufacture; beet-root seed, beet-roots, beet-root pulp; juice of beet-root defecated and

concentrated; syrup of the beet-root crystallized; samples of soft sugar from first, second, and third crystallizations; treacle from first and second crystallizations; the same, boiled; molasses; soft sugar-loaves and lumps; pressed scum from defecating-pans; animal charcoal for filtering; five views of the different processes carried on in the factory at Mountmellick.

18. JENNINGS, T., Brown-street, Cork, Manufacturer.—Wheaten starch; crystal white wine and brown vinegar.

19. KIBBLE, T., Grentree, Hadlow, Kent, Producer.—Hops.

20. LEA & PERRIN, Broad-street, Worcester.—Worcestershire sauce.

21. LUGTON, G., Leinster-street, Dublin, Manufacturer.—Rounds of spiced beef.

22. LYTLE, —, Belfast.—Specimens of wheaten starch.

23. M'ARTHUR, J., Capel-street, Dublin.—Roots, in various stages of growth, showing the effect of deep tillage on vegetation.

24. M'CANN, J., Drogheda, Manufacturer.—Samples of oatmeal, coarse and fine, as used for stirabout, gruel, and bread.

25. M'GARRY & SONS, Palmerstown and Ashtown Mills, Dublin, Manufacturers.—Irish mustard and oil-cake.

26. M'VEY, E., James's-street, Dublin, Manufacturer.—A whole preserved pig; hams, middles, and joles of bacon; mess pork; refined lard, in kegs, rings, and bladders; mutton hams, and ox-tongues, dried and smoked.

27. MONTEIRO, L. A., Phillimore-place, Kensington, London, Manufacturer.—Specimens of chocolate, sweetened without any admixture of colouring matter whatever, made of Curacao cocoa, Curacao and British West India cocoas combined, and of British West India cocoa; and chocolate lozenges, of pure Curacao cocoa; all roasted by the new process.

28. NEIGHBOUR, G., & SONS, High Holborn, London.—Neighbour's unicomb glass bee-hive, stocked with living bees; the ladies' observatory glass bee-hive, stocked with living bees; improved cottage hive, with thermometer, 3 bell glasses, &c.; single box hive; Nutt's collateral bee-hive; Taylor's amateur 8-box hive; 8-bar straw hive, protected from the weather by a case of the same material, with zinc roof; Neighbour's cottage hive; improved bee-feeder; implements for removing honey from the boxes; bee glasses, of various patterns and sizes.

29. OXLEY, W. & Co., Manchester.—Improved cottage bee-hive.

30. PIM, THOMAS & SAMUEL, Mountmellick, Queen's Co., Manufacturers.—Specimens of starch.

31. REILLY & SONS, Westmoreland-street, Dublin, Manufacturers.—Pickled and smoked ox-tongues; potted meats; vin au lait, or milk-punch; restoration jelly; bottled fruits; fancy jars of pickles; and various sauces, preserves, &c.

32. ROE, WILLIAM, Mountrath Mills, Queen's County.—Flour, bran, wheaten-meal, &c.

33. RUSSELL, G., Wilmington, Kent, Producer.—Hops.

34. SMITH, J., Rye, Sussex, Producer.—Hops.

35. SMITH, M., Copper-alley, Dublin, Manufacturer.—Model of a pig, cast in rendered lard, with other ornamental devices of same material.

36. STYLES, T., Upper Thames-street, London, Manufacturer.—Samples of and illustrations of the mode of packing Ashby's prepared groats, barley, and pea-flour, for the production of gruel, &c., in a few minutes.

37. SULLIVAN, WILLIAM K., Stephen's-green, Dublin.—Series of specimens illustrative of the manufacture of beet sugar, obtained in carrying out the experiments for the Government Report at the Museum of Irish Industry in Stephen's-green.

38. TAYLOR, J. & W., Bishops Stortford, Hertfordshire.—Specimens of malt,—white, for making pale ale; coloured, for beer and porter; amber, for giving colour and flavour; and brown or blown, used for making porter.

39. TOOLE & MACKEY, Westmoreland-street, Dublin.—Collection of agricultural seeds.

40. TUCKER, E., Belfast.—Specimens of wheaten starch and crown glue.

41. WARRINER, GEORGE, Snow-street, Birmingham.—Biscuits made of essence of meat.

42. WATERS, G. & Co., Green Distillery, Cork, Manufacturers.—Specimens of whisky, of different ages, in two glass barrels, and one of polished oak, with brass hoops and glass heads, exhibited as a beautiful specimen of coopering; samples of Scotch and pearl barley, manufactured at the Green Distillery Mills.

43. WEEKES, T., Great Britain-street, Dublin, Manufacturer.—Roll of manufactured tobacco.

44. WOTHERSPOON, R., Glenfield Starch Works, Paisley, Manufacturer.—Specimens of starch, made of East India sago, by a peculiar process, and solely by manual labour.

# CLASS IV.

---

## VEGETABLE AND ANIMAL SUBSTANCES USED IN MANUFACTURES.

THE substances comprehended in this class conclude the department of Raw Materials; and the list now remaining to be disposed of in this section of the Exhibition is far from being an extensive one. As a whole, this department was by no means so amply represented as might have been expected, or could have been desired, particularly in a country whose raw materials constitute the chief source of her wealth, and whose manufacturing industry, in many branches, may be said to be only in embryo. But so little have industrial pursuits been attended to in times past, and so small is the amount of special knowledge generally available on such matters, that the importance of an adequate illustration of the resources of the country in this respect was not duly appreciated. We have already seen in the foregoing pages that the extent of the raw materials available as the basis of successful manufacturing industry is much smaller than has been commonly supposed, and that the boasted treasures of Ireland in this department were simple exaggerations, inconsiderately indulged in by those who did not know better; but this only formed an additional reason why the materials that are unquestionably available should have been carefully represented. We may also remark, that many of the deficiencies which the Exhibition presented arose from an imperfect acquaintance with the real objects of such a display. Many parties who could have effectively contributed were deterred from doing so, under the impression that they should not come forward unless with articles entirely out of the common course, either as specimens of extraordinary natural objects, or gems of manufacturing skill; forgetting that the Exhibition was designed to show the existing condition of manufacturing industry, and the character and, as far as possible, the extent of raw materials available for it, more particularly with reference to Ireland. For the same reason there was little trouble taken by the producers of the common articles of every-day life to enter the lists of competition unless with extraordinary things; overlooking the circumstance that excellence in common things, taking quality and price together, is of much greater national importance than the display of surpassing skill in producing articles of luxury, the demand for which must ever be limited and capricious.

Of many of the substances belonging to this class there were no illustrations in the Exhibition; and by the arrangement which has been adopted in treating of the two preceding classes, several matters have already been disposed of which might come in for some consideration here. Cotton, flax, silk, wool, and oils and fats, are, therefore, the matters to which we still find it necessary to refer: arranging these as products of the vegetable and animal kingdom, oils and fats being common to both.

### I.—THE VEGETABLE KINGDOM.

#### COTTON.

Although there were but few samples of cotton exhibited, the very great importance of the manufactures founded upon that material demands a few brief observations upon its nature and the sources whence it is obtained.

The vascular tissue of all plants consists of a number of tubes composed of cellulose, upon which is deposited a sort of incrustation of another woody substance. Where these vessels are arranged so as to form a stem, and the incrusting matter is deposited in considerable quantity, wood is formed. In other cases, the vascular tissue, although arranged in parallel bundles, so as to constitute a stem, is intermingled with a considerable quantity of cellular matter, and is, comparatively speaking, but little crusted over. This is the case in the flax plant, the hemp, the nettle, and in most herbaceous plants; and hence, by getting rid of the cellular tissue, we are enabled to isolate the vascular tissue, which is obtained in the condition of a number of long threads or fibres, as is familiar to most persons in the case of the flax and hemp. In some plants we are presented with analogous fibrous matter in an isolated state, as a sort of appendage to the seed, apparently for the purpose of enabling them to be borne through the air. Thus the seeds of the common dandelion have a number of hair-like appendages, formed of a kind of fibrous tissue; but it is in the seeds of the willow and of the cotton grass, or *Eriophorum vaginatum*, the silk plant, *Asclepias Syriaca*, &c., that this fibrous appendage becomes so developed as to resemble the fibre of flax. Various attempts have been made to utilize these fibrous matters, but hitherto unsuccessfully, in consequence of their shortness, comparative coarseness, and the difficulty of procuring a supply. Amongst the curiosities of the Exhibition was, however, a piece of cloth contributed by Mrs. Veevers, composed of a mixture of cotton and the down of the *Eriophorum*. In most tropical and sub-tropical regions several allied genera of plants are found, the seeds of which are enclosed in capsules filled with a fine downy fibrous matter, which, unlike the plants just mentioned, consist of fibres sufficiently long to admit of being spun into thread, and can be obtained in large quantities with great facility. The chief of these genera of plants is the *Gossypium*, of the family of the *Malvaceæ*, which is the one now almost exclusively cultivated, and which includes several species, some herbaceous and some shrubby. That which is principally grown in Europe (Macedonia, Malta, Sicily, Calabria, the Levant) and in the East Indies, is the *Gossypium herbaceum*, which is a herbaceous plant, about two to three feet high, and which may be considered as an annual, although it is sometimes biennial. Its fruit consists of round three-lobed capsules, of about the size of a small walnut, with seeds of the size of small peas. The *Gossypium herbaceum* produces yellow flowers from the month of August to the month of October, which, like those of several other plants, only open fully during a few hours; at this time their functions of fecundation are effected, and they then wither and die. Immediately after this the seed capsules begin to swell out, and are at first of a green colour, which, as they approach the period of their maturity, passes into brown. When fully ripe, the capsule bursts, and the fibrous down, with its attached seeds, protrudes, and is immediately collected, in order that it may not fall upon the ground or be carried away by the wind. The species of cotton plant indigenous to North America, and chiefly cultivated in Carolina and Georgia, is the shaggy *Gossypium hirsutum*, which is also an annual plant, though sometimes lasting two years. It grows frequently to the height of a man, and produces a four-lobed seed capsule of about the size of a moderate-sized apple. It would appear that this species is merely a variety of the *Gossypium barbadense*; at least Dr. Forbes Royle, who has very recently investigated the subject, considers that the sea-island, New Orleans, and upland Georgian, are obtained from a variety of that species. Among the shrub species of the cotton plant with true woody stems may be specially mentioned the *Gossypium arboreum*, which sometimes grows to the height of eight to twelve feet in the East Indies, in Egypt, and some districts of Spain; the *Gossypium religiosum* of India and China, which produces a yellow cotton employed to make some kinds of nankin; the *Gossypium barbadense*, which is indigenous to the West Indies and South America. Dr. Royle considers the Pernambuco, Peruvian, Maranham, and Brazilian cottons to be produced from a species quite distinct from any of those named the *Gossypium Peruvian* or *acuminatam*, which is distinguished by black seeds which adhere together firmly. But it is now difficult to say to which species any particular cotton coming into the market belongs, as the species peculiar to each country have been introduced into the others: for example, the Brazilian species just named has long since been introduced into India. The ordinary cotton tree, met with both in America and in the East Indies, and which one reads of in descriptions of squatter-life in America, is not a Gossypium; it is the *Bombax pentandrum*; it sometimes reaches a height of twenty feet, and attains a considerable thickness.

The use of cotton, as a material for the manufacture of clothing, appears to have been one of the earliest inventions of mankind; for Herodotus tells us that there were trees growing wild in India which produced a kind of wool superior to that of the sheep, which the natives manufactured into cloth, and clothed themselves with. The name cotton seems to establish the great antiquity of its application to the manufacture. This word appears to be derived from the Arabic *kutun*, which is evidently derived from the same root as the Hebrew word *cotnot*, the term applied to the first clothing of man. In China the use of cotton is quite as ancient as in India. Two kinds are produced there, the white, or *mie wha*, obtained from the *Gossypium herbaceum*; and the *tze mie wha*, or yellow cotton, employed to produce the much-admired nankin cloth. According to some, as we have remarked above, this kind of cotton is obtained from the *Gossypium religiosum*, whilst according to Mr. Fortune it is the product of a mere variety of the *Gos. herbaceum*; but Meyen, who is perhaps the best authority upon this subject, is of opinion that the true nankin belongs to a distinct species, to which he gives the name *Gossypium nankin*. Cotton cloth was also known at some remote period to the Mexicans; at all events it was in common use among them on the first arrival of the Spaniards. The Mediterranean countries appear to have known the use of cotton through the Moors from the seventh or eighth century. Whilst the intercourse between Russia and Central Asia made the Russians acquainted with it as early as the ninth century, according to the Russian historian Karamsin; and already in the middle of the thirteenth century, according to the same authority, cotton cloth formed a common material of dress in Russia. But notwithstanding this early introduction of cotton cloths into Europe, and its cultivation and extensive manufacture in Spain by the Moors, the first cotton cloth arrived in England only in the year 1590; and it was only about the same period that the Dutch introduced the manufacture of cotton fabrics into Holland. Religious persecution introduced it, as it has done many other branches of manufacture, into England in the reign of Elizabeth, from Holland, then almost in its infancy in the latter country.

The Oriental origin of the whole cotton manufacture of Europe is fully shown from the names by which most of our cotton fabrics are even still distinguished, and which are in almost all cases derived from the names of places where the particular article was manufactured, such as calico, muslin, jaconets, mullmuls, tarlatans, bukes, betalles, tanjeebs, terridams, chintzes, dorcas, &c. The great seat of the muslin manufacture in India was Dacca, and the beauty of the fabrics once manufactured there may be judged by the fact, when first introduced into Europe, Dacca muslin fetched ten to twelve guineas per yard. It has been stated that muslin has been produced in India of which 30 ells weighed only 4 oz.; and in the collections of the East India Company, in London, are specimens made from yarn of which 20 yards weigh only one grain! The cheap, but much less durable and far less beautiful imitations of Indian fabrics, by European machinery, have now nearly extinguished the cotton trade of the East; and instead of a considerable export of cotton fabrics from India, that country is now flooded with the cheap goods of Manchester.

The raw cottons from different countries differ very considerably in their qualities, not only because they are often, as we have before remarked, produced by different plants, but also because the growth of cotton, like that of all other vegetable substances, is influenced by the climate, soil, and system of cultivation. The colour is usually white, or yellowish, but sometimes even brownish or reddish. But it is in the length and fineness of the fibres that the greatest difference is observed. In this respect cotton may be divided into two classes, the *short-stapled* and *long-stapled* cottons, the longest fibres of the former being scarcely an inch long, and those of the latter about two inches. The different cottons used in Europe are produced in eight different districts; and the products of the different countries included in each district very often present certain analogies of character and quality.

The first district is that of North America, which includes the cottons of Georgia, Louisiana, New Orleans, Carolina, and Tennessee. Georgia produces both the long- and short-stapled cottons; the former being considered the best grown in any part of the world. This kind of cotton has a somewhat yellowish colour, a soft and delicate fibre, and can be employed in the manufacture of the finest fabrics; it grows chiefly upon the low sandy islands which dot the shores of Lower Carolina and Georgia,—hence the name *sea-island cotton*, by which this kind is known. It is considered that the spray of the sea exercises a peculiar influence upon the cotton, rendering its filaments longer and more silky; for when transplanted beyond the influence of the salt water it deteriorates. The upland or short staple cotton of Georgia is known by the name of *bowed cotton*, an appellation which was given to it on account of the process formerly made use of to separate the seeds from the filaments. This operation was performed by striking a mass of the pods with bows to which strings were attached—threshing it in fact—in order to loosen them previous to separating the seeds with the hand. These two varieties are further distinguished by the seeds of the long-stapled cotton being black, and that of the short green. Bowed Georgia cotton rarely admits of being spun to No. 40 yarns, and very frequently yields only from 10 to 20. It is usually spun with an equal quantity of Egyptian cotton, and can then be employed for much higher numbers. The Louisiana cotton has a sort of bluish-white colour, and is superior to the bowed Georgia, but inferior to the Brazilian and to many West Indian kinds. Yarns up to No. 50 may be spun with it. The Carolina is also considered superior to the bowed Georgia; but the Tennessee and New Orleans are inferior. These varieties usually consist of weak filaments; parcels of the latter sometimes, however, yield yarns as high as 100.

The West Indian cottons may be considered as long-stapled, and to belong, in general, to the better class of cottons, coming in that respect after the sea-island, Bourbon, the best Spanish, and the Brazilian kinds. That produced in Porto Rico is usually considered the best; then follow, in about the order of their quality, Curaçao, Haïti, Martinique, Guadaloupe, Barbadoes, Jamaica, St. Christopher, St. Lucia, St. Thomas, Grenada, St. Vincent, Dominica, Tortola, Montserat, the Bahamas, Cuba, Antigua, &c. The latter is of about the same quality as the best sorts from the Levant.

South America yields cottons of excellent quality, and among them the Brazilian may be considered the best, especially that of Maranhao, or Maragnan, Bahia, and Pernambuco, from which yarns up to No. 250 may be spun. These three varieties come next after the sea-island and Bourbon in quality. The cottons of Minas-Geraes, Para, and Ceara are, however, very much inferior, and frequently yield only No. 60 yarns. But the worst of all the Brazilian cottons is that of Rio Janeiro, which is only considered to rank with the lowest of the West Indian cottons. Of the other South American cottons, that of Cayenne, which is very long, white, and shining, is the most prized, and is considered to rank immediately after the Brazilian; then follows that of Surinam, with long yellow filaments, which often spin up to No. 200. The cotton of Demerara, Essequibo, and Berbice (many samples of which are brownish, coarse, and impure), are much shorter, and may almost be classed among the short-stapled. Next, in order of succession, come Lima, the Caraccas, and Cumana, both the latter being slightly yellowish, and often dirty; and finally, the Carthaginian, still more impure and coarse than the last-mentioned.

The East Indian cottons are, in general, of less value than the American, and even than the better kinds of the Levant, and are also much less used than either. The best known is that from Surat, which is dirty yellowish, and although fine, is of an exceedingly short staple. Then come those of Madras, Siam, and Bengal: the latter is white and silky, and yields yarns to No. 50. The yellow Nankin cotton comes also under this head.

Under the term Levant cottons may be understood all those sorts produced in European or Asiatic Turkey. To this category belong the Macedonian, the Smyrnian, and that of the Levant, properly so called, all of which are distinguished by a great degree of whiteness, but a very short staple, and cannot be spun of a higher number than 60.

Africa contains three cotton districts: the first is the island of Bourbon, which yields one of the best sorts of cotton, almost equal to the best sea-island, although it gives a great deal of waste in working. It is very uniform, pure, fine, and silky, and almost equals in whiteness the Levant sorts, and may be spun to very high numbers. The second is the Senegal, the cotton of which is usually of about the same quality as the low West Indian, or the good Levant. The chief peculiarity of this cotton is the facility with which the seeds may be separated from the filaments. And the third is Egypt, the cotton of which, known under the name of Maco, or Maho, has a fine easily spun filament, and is well adapted for mixing with other sorts of cotton; it is, however, generally ill cleaned, and mixed with unripe portions.

The Italian cottons are the produce of Malta, Sicily, and Naples. The best is the Sicilian, and that from the neighbourhood of Naples (Castellamare and Della Torre), and more usually considered to rank with those of Louisiana, or with the medium sorts of West Indian. The Malta cotton ranks with the low West Indian.

The finest of the Spanish sorts is the Motril from the province of Panada; this cotton ranks with the best Brazilian, and, owing to the fineness of its filaments, admits of being spun of very high numbers.

In comparing the cotton grown in one district with that grown in another it must be remembered that, apart from the general character of the cotton of a locality, many different qualities will be obtained, and accordingly for commercial purposes cotton is divided into three qualities—"good," "medium," and "low."

The operation of separating the seeds from the filaments of cotton is simple in the case of the long-stapled varieties. For this purpose a machine called a gin is used, consisting of two rollers of wood placed close to one another, and turned by means of a pinion and handle. The cotton is passed between the rollers, which, being too close to admit the seeds, the latter are separated. Such a contrivance is, however, of very little use for cleaning the short-stapled cotton, although it has been and is still used in some countries; and to do so by hand, except perhaps in India, would be far too expensive. Indeed, so great were the difficulties of cleaning the short-stapled cotton felt to be in the United States of America, that fifty years ago the cultivation of cotton in that country was almost entirely confined to that of the sea-island along the coast, notwithstanding the adaptation of so large a portion of the Southern States to the cultivation of the upland cotton. So little importance was attached to the cultivation of cotton of any kind at that period in the States, that Mr. Jay, when negotiating a commercial treaty with the English Government, allowed a clause to be introduced which prevented them from exporting from the United States in American ships any articles which had been formerly supplied by the West Indies, among which was included cotton! In 1793, Eli Whitney invented his gin, by which the upland cotton may be perfectly cleaned, and thus rendered its cultivation an object of importance to the American States; the result of which was, that the British cotton manufacture received an impulse, perhaps as great as that given by the invention of Arkwright. This machine consisted of a cylinder whose surface was covered with teeth, formed of iron wire; and they were inserted into the wood at about three-fourths of an inch apart, thus presenting a serrated appearance. During the revolutions of this cylinder the teeth catch the cotton wool and draw it from a hopper in which it is placed, through openings in a number of iron straps placed in contact with them. These openings are made too narrow to permit the seeds to pass through, and they are brushed from the plates into a receiver below. The revolving cylinder with the cotton attached meets with a second cylinder moving in an opposite direction, supplied with brushes, which remove the cotton from the teeth of the first cylinder. A Mr. Holmes substituted combs, formed by cutting a number of teeth in plates of iron, which he then fastened on the cylinders, and with some other trivial modifications the machine has proved most effective. A gin worked by oxen is capable of cleaning from 600 to 900 lbs. of cotton in a day, a quantity which would require from twelve to eighteen of the most active labourers to clean by hand. The importance of Whitney's invention may be appreciated from the following Table, which shows the condition of the cultivation of cotton in America before and since the introduction of the gin. It further appears, that while the export of sea-island cotton has been stationary, that of upland cotton has been rapidly increasing every year.

| Year. | Cotton of the whole world consumed in Europe. | Cotton produced in the United States. | Capital invested in its production in the United States. |
|---|---|---|---|
| 1790 . . . | 490 millions of lbs. . . . | 2 millions of lbs. . . . | 3,500,000 dollars. |
| 1800 . . . | 520 " . . . | 48 " . . . | 30,000,000 " |
| 1810 . . . | 555 " . . . | 80 " . . . | 134,000,000 " |
| 1820 . . . | 630 " . . . | 180 " . . . | 300,000,000 " |
| 1830 . . . | 820 " . . . | 385 " . . . | 650,000,000 " |
| 1840 . . . | — " . . . | 790 " . . . | 1287,000,000 " |

Wonderful as has been the growth of the cotton manufactures, not alone of Great Britain, but of all European countries, and of the United States itself, it does not seem to have yet reached its limit, and each year adds a new increment to its amount. This is not the place, however, to enter into the consideration of the cotton trade, which will be further noticed in a subsequent part of these pages.

The following Table shows the quantities and sources of our supply of cotton wool for the last five years, extracted from recent returns of the Board of Trade:—

| | 1849. | 1850. | 1851. | 1852. | 1853. |
|---|---|---|---|---|---|
| | lbs. | lbs. | lbs. | lbs. | lbs. |
| United States, . . . . . . . . . . . . | 634,504,050 | 493,153,112 | 596,638,962 | 765,630,544 | 658,451,796 |
| Brazil, . . . . . . . . . . . . . . . | 30,738,133 | 30,499,982 | 19,339,104 | 26,506,144 | 24,190,628 |
| Mediterranean, . . . . . . . . . . . . | 17,369,848 | 18,931,414 | 16,950,525 | 48,058,640 | 28,353,574 |
| British Possessions in East Indies, . . . | 70,838,515 | 18,872,742 | 122,626,976 | 84,922,432 | 181,848,160 |
| British West Indies and British Guiana, . | 944,307 | 228,913 | 446,529 | 703,690 | 344,060 |
| Other countries, . . . . . . . . . . . | 1,074,164 | 2,090,698 | 1,377,658 | 3,960,992 | 2,078,562 |
| Total, . . . . . . . . . . . . . . | 755,469,012 | 663,576,861 | 757,379,749 | 929,782,448 | 895,266,780 |

The district from which samples of cotton were exhibited as raw materials was the South American. In the collection of Brazilian produce were several samples of superior long-stapled cotton, chiefly from Bahia and Maranhao; and in the collection from Guiana were a number of samples of well-grown and carefully cleaned cottons, the product of the province of Demerara. Specimens of raw cotton were exhibited by Jonas Brook and Brothers, of Meltham, in connexion with illustrations of the process of cotton-spinning. In the collection of the East India Company was a model of a kind of roller gin used in the East for cleaning cotton. In the Machinery Court was also a small roller gin, exhibited at work, invented by Colonel Grant, and destined for long-stapled cotton.—W. K. S.

### FLAX.

The Dublin Exhibition, whether it be taken as a national or a universal display of raw products and manufactured articles, would be incomplete did it not contain specimens of flax, as the material—and of linen fabrics, as the productions—of a branch of industry which forms one of the four great textile manufactures of the globe, and which, in Ireland, stands out in bold relief from all other departments of skilled labour, both from the high point of excellence which it has attained, and from its magnitude as a source of employment, and as an important item in the exports of the United Kingdom. Great attention has been for some years past devoted to the improvement of flax cultivation by the Government of all countries where the plant is grown. In Ireland it was for upwards of a century committed to the charge of a Board of Trustees, appointed by Parliament, whose functions ceased in 1828; while, thirteen years afterwards, a voluntary association, the Royal Society for the Promotion and Improvement of the Growth of Flax, was organized at Belfast, and has since continued energetically to prosecute its labours.

It is difficult to say whether the animal or the vegetable kingdom was the first to supply a woven fabric for the use of man; certainly flax and wool were spun and woven long before cotton or silk. The use of hemp is almost of as great antiquity as that of flax. Commerce has lately made us acquainted with other textiles which have been made subservient to useful purposes by human ingenuity. Among these are jute—the fibre of *Corchorus capsularis*, of which we had a specimen in the case of samples exhibited by the Royal Flax Society, as illustrative of the foreign fibres used in the Irish linen manufacture; China grass, *Urtica nivea*, which has been experimentally tried of late; New Zealand flax, *Phormium tenax*; Sunn hemp, *Crotolaria juncea*; cocoa-nut fibre, *Cocos nucifera*; and Manilla hemp, *Musa textilis*. With the single exception of cotton, flax is employed to a greater extent than any other vegetable fibre, not only in the British Islands, but throughout the entire of Europe.

The frequent mention in the Old Testament of the use of flax furnishes conclusive proof that at a very early period of the world's history the nations of the East were familiar with it. The Hebrew word *Pishtah* is supposed to indicate the flax plant, and the earliest mention of it is in the time of Joseph, 1700 years B. C., when Pharaoh is stated in the book of Genesis to have arrayed himself in vestures of fine linen. Two centuries later, in the time of Moses (Exod. ix. 31) the plague of hail is represented as destroying the Egyptian flax crop—"And the flax and the barley were smitten; for the barley was in the ear and the flax was bolled." Many other allusions in the sacred writings go to prove that 3500 years ago linen was the national manufacture of Egypt; and the antiquities, which at the present day so strangely attest the civilization of the ancient Egyptians, abundantly establish this fact. On the walls of Egyptian tombs are representations of spinning distaffs and looms; and that these were employed for the manufacture of flax alone is evident from the fact that all the mummy wrappers are made of linen. This point, which had long been a subject of disputation among the learned, was set at rest by the microscope, which clearly distinguishes the fibres to be those of flax. It is very strange that some of these mummy cloths are of a texture rivalling the finest cambric made now-a-days; although the spinning and weaving were most rudely performed, and the quality of the material by no means adapted to fine purposes, unless the plant has degenerated on the valley of the Nile since the days of the Pharaohs. We may assume that Egypt, if not the only habitat of the plant, was, at least, the earliest country in which it was industrially employed. In the book of Joshua, the spies who went to examine Jericho are described as hidden among the flax. From Egypt and Syria the Phœnicians or the Greek colonists probably transported the culture of flax to Europe; and it rapidly spread over countries congenial to its growth. Homer alludes to its manufacture in Greece, and the Athenian and Roman marbles chronicle the mode of conducting the processes. The early traditions of Germany and Gaul make frequent mention of flax, and there is reason to believe that in no part of the European continent was its culture unknown.

But with the progress of knowledge, and the better understanding of the capabilities of climates and soils, this culture naturally diminished in unsuitable localities, and became chiefly concentrated in others, possessing all the requisites for its successful prosecution. Between the forty-fourth and sixtieth parallels of latitude the great development has taken place. North of these the climate is unfavourable; where flax is grown further south, it is the seed and not the fibre which is economized.

The temperate zone is the true flax region; for within its limits the fibre attains the greatest length and the finest quality. Northern latitudes at the extreme verge of this belt, or beyond it, are unfavourable to the maturing of fine fibre, from the shortness and great heat of their summers. To perfect a soft, yet strong and lustrous fibre, easily divisible into minute filaments, slow and regular growth is requisite. A powerful sun draws the plant too rapidly to maturity, and tends to a habit of branching and bearing a large quantity of seed, and the fibre is then found to be coarse and harsh. A mild, humid climate promotes regularity of growth, the plant is tall and straight, the stems fine and branchless, and the fibre in perfection for the purposes of manufacture.

If we study the map of Europe in relation to the distribution of flax culture, we shall find that the portions whose geographical position insures the climate in which it has been stated that the flax plant flourishes best, are precisely those which are most celebrated for the quantity and the quality of their production. The margin of the ocean, from the southern extremity of the Iberian peninsula, to a high northern latitude in that of Scandinavia, and the shores of the Baltic Sea, exactly indicate the *locale* of the great mass of flax husbandry; for there the soft western breezes, loaded with moisture from the sea, furnish that atmosphere in which the plant luxuriates. In Portugal and the Biscayan provinces of Spain, a considerable breadth is grown, while in the centre and south of the latter country very little is to be found. Passing the Pyrenees, French flax culture would appear to be almost confined to a belt accurately defining the littoral of the Atlantic, and rarely penetrating far inland. Gascony, Anjou, Vendée, Brittany, and Normandy, are its chief seats. On the shores of the English Channel, the Belgian provinces of East and West Flanders and Antwerp comprise by far the greater proportion of that flax culture which has attained such celebrity; and following the coast line of Holland, the provinces of Zealand and Friesland are again the chief districts of supply. On the German Ocean and North Sea, Denmark and its Duchies and the Scandinavian coast still maintain the principle; and diverging into the Baltic, Hanover and Prussia, and the maritime governments of Russia,—Courland, Riga, Revel, Pskoff, and Petersburg, on the one side, and the Swedish and Finnish shores on the other,—provide vast quantities of fibre for export; while the last fields of the plant wave on the shores of the White Sea, and during the short midsummer give life and activity to the commerce of Archangel, hermetically sealed during the rest of the year. As outliers of this flaxen zone are the British Isles, of which Ireland chiefly sustains the character; while in the sister island, the culture which had dwindled into insignificance appears again about to take an important position. The United Kingdom, from its insular position, and its consequent large share of the watery tribute of the Atlantic, is peculiarly adapted for flax culture.

The extreme west of Europe is, therefore, the great flax region, as the tropical and extra-tropical portions of America are the great cotton region. From localities so widely apart, and so differently characterised, the spindles and the looms of the Old World, and more especially of the British Isles, derive their supply of two vegetable substances which are converted by the ingenuity and industry of man into a wide range of useful articles, adapted to the clothing of the persons, the furnishing of the dwellings, and the fitting out of the ships of civilized nations; whose products are carried by commerce to the farthest ends of the earth, for the comfort and use of man, from the barbarism of Africa to the high development of North America.

Next to climate, soil is the most important topic in treating of the production of flax; and the plant is to be found on a wide range of soils. In the artificially enriched sands of Belgium, the polders of Holland, the vegetable mould of the Bocages, or, to come nearer home, in the peat of Connaught, the limestone of central Ireland, and the clay-slate of Ulster—in each and all of these excellent flax can be grown. But the best soil of all others is furnished by the alluvial deposit of rivers. Holland and Belgium, composed of the alluvium brought down by the Rhine, the Scheldt, and the Meuse; the rich lands on the banks of our Irish rivers; the valley of the Nile, with its yearly overflow; the shores of the Oder, the Vistula, the Niemen, and the Dwina,—all furnish examples of the alluvial deposits so peculiarly suited to the growth of this very important plant.

We may next glance at the relative quantities of this valuable fibre which each country furnishes to commerce, and the following statement will show an approximation to the average yearly produce of the chief flax-growing states:—

| | | |
|---|---|---|
| Russia, | 150,000 | tons. |
| Austria, | 65,000 | " |
| The Zollverein States, | 60,000 | " |
| France, | 55,000 | " |
| Belgium, | 30,000 | " |
| Holland, | 16,000 | " |
| Great Britain and Ireland, | 40,000 | " |
| Scandinavia, | 10,000 | " |
| Spain and Portugal, | 4,000 | " |
| Italian States, | 12,000 | " |
| Turkey, | 5,000 | " |
| North America, | 2,000 | " |
| Egypt, | 3,000 | " |
| | 452,000 | " |

This quantity would occupy a breadth of about 1,800,000 acres, and at £50 per ton, would be worth £22,600,000 in the state of fibre. As it is calculated that the fibre enters to the extent of one-third into the value of the fabric, on this estimate the total annual value of the linen fabrics manufactured and consumed throughout the world would appear to be nearly £70,000,000 sterling. Indeed, this figure, large as it appears, is probably considerably under the actual amount.

The smaller of the two cases contributed by the Royal Flax Society contained specimens, both in the scutched and the hackled state, of those foreign flaxes which are ordinarily consumed in the Irish linen manufacture,—Russian, Dutch, Flemish, Courtrai, and Egyptian. The first and the last of these are only employed for the coarser fabrics, and the common sorts of Irish are also used for the same purpose; the other three are made into all the finer kinds of linen, cambric, lawn, and damask; and our native flax furnishes, with the Dutch, the chief material for medium qualities, a certain and increasing proportion of it being suited for the finest kinds, although as yet the great bulk of the latter is made from Flemish and Courtrai fibre.

The vast quantity of flax produced by Russia is of a quality similar to these samples. Its strength fits it for coarse fabrics, but its harshness and dryness, and the impossibility of dividing it into minute filaments, render it unsuitable for finer purposes. Hence it is largely used in Scotland, where the manufacture of the heavier and coarser goods, such as sail-cloth and bagging, is chiefly carried on. But as the bulk required for this branch of the trade is great, we find that out of the 80,000 or 90,000 tons of flax annually imported into the United Kingdom from foreign countries, Russia furnishes 50,000 to 70,000, or about 75 per cent. of the whole. The Egyptian fibre is of similar quality, or even coarser, and less suitable for medium fabrics. The inferiority in the quality of Russian and Egyptian flax is owing to the very short summer of Russia, and the heat of the sun, on the one hand, and the hotness and aridity of the climate of Egypt on the other; the growth of the plant being too rapidly hurried forward. Russian flax is worth at present from £35 to £50 per ton, and Egyptian, £30 to £45.

In Egypt, latterly, a good deal of scutching machinery has been introduced, and a Belfast engineering firm has furnished the entire supply. Mehemet Ali and his successors wisely concluded that the marketable value of the Egyptian fibre would be increased by the introduction of proper machinery in place of the very rude appliances formerly employed for cleaning it. Persons from Ulster were engaged to superintend the working of the mills, and also to instruct the Fellahs in an improved method of culture.*

* A graphic trait of Mehemet Ali's character for energy and punctuality is related by the Belfast mechanic who erected the first Egyptian scutch-mill. When the machinery was nearly complete, an officer of the Pacha arrived one day and told the mechanic that his Highness was desirous of seeing the mill at work, inquiring the exact time that it would be ready. The mechanic fixed a day, and was warned by the officer that the Pacha would be highly displeased if the machine should not then be ready. A very early morning-hour was named by the millwright, in the expectation that the Egyptian ruler would not appear until late in the day, and that time would thus be given for the machinery being properly trained before his arrival. The appointed day came, and a few minutes before the hour the engine was set on, and some hands were put into the stands to scutch. Scarcely had they begun when a cloud of dust was observed

In Russia, where it is so largely grown, flax is uniformly scutched by hand, by the peasants on the immense estates of the nobles. It is sorted into qualities, at the ports of shipment, by officers appointed for this purpose by the Government.

In the Royal Flax Society's smaller case were specimens of Flemish and Courtrai flax, both scutched and hackled. Messrs. Collings, Fréres, and Maingi, of Courtrai, exhibited a series, including three samples from Lokeren, in the Pays de Waes, all of beautiful quality, some white and blae Bruges, and three fine specimens from Courtrai. Baptiste Van Weil, of Grembergen, near Termonde, showed some fibre and straw, neither of fine quality. P. J. Verbeck, East Flanders, had also some flax, as well as hemp, the quality fair. These afforded a good idea of the Belgian flaxes, and the extreme fineness, softness, and lustre, with the neatness of handling, must have been apparent to the most casual observer. Indeed, Belgium has long been considered almost unapproachable in the quality of her flax fibre, and its export to Great Britain and Ireland, France, Spain, and Italy, is a very important source of wealth to that industrious little state, reaching an average annual value of £800,000. Few sorts bring under £70 per ton; and up to £150 or £160 is paid for the finer kinds, while the latter have been occasionally sold at upwards of £200 per ton. But even this high price is greatly outdone by the fibre from which the Mechlin and Brussels lace is made, as it has been known to sell for £4 per pound weight when hackled, or nearly £9000 per ton! Yet even in this extreme case, so little does the value of the material enter into that of the exquisitely fine and tasteful product, that a lace handkerchief, weighing about two ounces, has been sold for 2500 francs, or £100! There were two kinds of Belgian flax in the Society's case, one, marked "Flemish," and the other, "Courtrai." These were equally fine, but differed much in colour, the former being of a slaty-gray, and the latter of a yellowish-white. This difference was caused by the mode of treating the flax. The former is pulled when the stems are green, and after the seed-capsules have been removed by drawing the stalks through a "rippling-comb." The flax is steeped in pools of water until fermentation has decomposed the gum or gluten which connects the fibre with the wood; and after drying on the grass, it is bruised, and the fibre cleaned out by the scutching operation. The Courtrai flax is treated differently; it is produced not merely from the plant grown about Courtrai, but from what is carted to that place from other districts of Belgium, many of them thirty or forty miles distant. The reason of this is, that the River Lys, which, rising on the other side of the French frontier, flows by Courtrai, and falls into the Escaut at Ghent, possesses peculiar properties for the fermentation of flax, such as no other river is yet known to afford. It is found that flax straw, steeped in this famous stream, yields a fibre of a very superior quality to what is steeped anywhere else; and as Courtrai is the chief seat of operations, all the flax steeped in the Lys is termed Courtrai flax, whatever may be the locality of its growth. When it is intended to steep flax in the Lys, the straw after pulling is dried in the field, then stacked, and, after the seed is threshed out, is sold to factors, who purchase from the growers, and steep for their own profit. From May to September the river all about Courtrai is filled with wooden crates, containing flax straw, and anchored in the stream. Those who are familiar with the disagreeable odour exhaled from pools in which flax is being steeped might naturally suppose that about Courtrai the nuisance would be intolerable, not to say dangerous, to public health. It is not, however, complained of by the people of the district, probably because they derive so much profit and employment from the trade of steeping; and what is very strange, in 1832, when the cholera raged in Belgium, the districts along the River Lys were totally free from it, nor has it ever been stated that any disease, epidemic or endemic, is more prevalent in the steeping localities than in others.

The sums received by the Belgian farmers for their flax crop are such as to appear almost fabulous; £40 to £60 per acre being quite a common return, and for the very finest kinds sometimes £80 to £100 per acre. The manufacturers of Leeds and Belfast are the best customers for this fine fibre, and the higher numbers of yarn, those from 160 leas (fifteen hanks to the pound), and upwards, are almost exclusively spun from Belgian flax. Some of the Belfast spinners send their buyers regularly to the Belgian districts to select the flax on the spot. To produce the sort of fibre for the lace manufacture great care and attention are requisite. The richest and most thoroughly pulverized soil is chosen; the seed is sown about double the usual thickness; and every weed carefully eradicated from time to time. Branches and stakes are fixed in the ground, with lines intersecting like the meshes of a net, in order that the wonderfully fine stems of the flax, as they grow up, may have support, as otherwise they would be prostrated with the first high wind or heavy shower. The stems are pulled green and steeped, and the utmost pains are taken to pick out coarse stalks. When scutched the fibre is again most carefully examined, and every filament which shows any defect is removed. The yield of this lace flax is, of course, not large, and great expense is incurred in the details of management and preparation; but the profits are nevertheless extraordinary.

The case of flax samples above referred to also contained a specimen of fibre grown in the county of Cork, by Mr. Cummins of Anne Mount. This is a very favourable result of a trial of the Courtrai system of drying flax straw, and steeping it in rivers. Hitherto experiments of this nature have been unsuccessful in Ulster, as it has been almost invariably found that the fibre of dried straw, if steeped in pools or streams, turns out of inferior quality, being harsh, dry, and coarse. It would appear, however, from this specimen, which was very similar in rich yellow colour to Courtrai flax, and equal in quality and fineness to the lower marks of that description, that the water in which it has been steeped possesses some properties analogous to the Lys,

in the distance, heralding the approach of the punctual old Pacha. Alighting from his horse, he entered the scutch-mill, and without uttering a word, squatted down right opposite the scutchers, was handed his pipe, and sat tranquilly smoking, and fixedly gazing at the whirling blades of the mill, for two whole hours—the shoves and tow thickly showering on his venerable beard. He then arose, briefly expressed his satisfaction by a "Mashallah!—well done!" and ordering a purse to be handed to the millwright, in acknowledgment of the satisfaction with which he had witnessed the operation, departed as rapidly as he had come. Since then many scutch-mills have been put up in Egypt, and the fibre has consequently appeared in our markets much better cleaned than formerly.

and it is not improbable that in other parts of Ireland water may be found which will insure fibre of fair quality from dried flax straw. The advantage of the Courtrai method is, that the seed obtained by drying the plant is much superior to that which has been separated from the green stems as pulled.

Notwithstanding the greatly increased area of Irish flax cultivation, the increase of the manufacture has been continually outstripping it. For the range of purposes to which Irish flax is applied, no other kind is better suited; and there is consequently a very considerable export from Belfast and Derry, which further necessitates the import of foreign flax as a balance. The finer sorts of the latter are absolutely required, as little Irish flax is equal to them in quality; while for coarse yarns it is often more profitable to employ Russian than Irish flax. The latter, indeed, occupies the middle place between the Belgian and the Russian, but owing to the description of fabrics chiefly made in Ireland, it is employed to a much greater extent than both those sorts combined. Taking the average of the last three years, we find the annual import of foreign flax into Ireland to be as follows:—

| | | |
|---|---|---|
| From Russia, | 4325 | tons. |
| " Egypt, | 105 | " |
| " Holland, direct, | 90 | " |
| " France, direct, | 12 | " |
| " Belgium, Holland, and France, &c., *via* English and Scotch ports, | 3480 | " |
| Total, | 8012 | |

Taking the relative proportions of each, the average value of all may be assumed at £60 per ton; so that Ireland would thus appear to pay nearly half a million sterling annually to foreigners, for the proportion obtained from them of the raw material of her linen manufacture.

It is to be observed, in explanation of the last item in the above abstract, that, owing to the great facilities of steam communication with the sister island, and the equally great development of traffic between the latter and the chief continental states, our spinners find it more advantageous to obtain their supplies of several kinds of foreign flax by way of Great Britain, than to bring them direct into Belfast. It will be seen, in a future portion of our subject, that these causes operate to a great extent in the direction of our imports and exports; and the difference between the known and the apparent extent of our transactions with foreign countries has led to much confusion among persons not thoroughly conversant with the features of the case.

In concluding this notice of the foreign flaxes shown in the Exhibition, we shall pass by some French and Prussian samples, to recur to them again, as they illustrate some of the patent methods of steeping, of which we have yet to treat, and only now allude to a series from Holland. Messrs. Collings and Maingy's specimens included some blae Dutch of middling quality, some Zealand or white Dutch, coarse white North Holland and coarse Friesland. These were a fair average of the sorts supplied by Holland, and possessed many points of resemblance to Irish flax.

The flax plant is grown in Holland in immense flats, offering a curious contrast to the small plots of the Belgian *petite culture*. The aspect of many hundred acres of the rich green stems, with their delicate blue flowers waving in the breeze, is a beautiful sight in the month of June, and leads the reflective mind to pass in review the various transformations which the graceful plant must assume before it is spread as a snowy and tasteful fabric on the tables of the rich; as gauzy cambric, grasped by fair hands, wafting rich perfume through the crowded ball-room; as a coarse but serviceable garment, enveloping the sturdy boor; or as heavy canvass swelling its bosom to the embrace of the boisterous winds, and carrying the gallant bark and her precious freight to distant shores. Before it can assume these various forms, it will be torn from its natal soil; drowned in the ditches of a marshy hollow, it will undergo partial decomposition; then, freed from its grosser elements, it will repose on the verdant sward until the last traces of the muddy and unsavoury pool are washed away by the rain and dew, and evaporated by the sun. Bruised by heavy stones, and then beaten by hard blades of wood, it will next appear in long and lustrous filaments. Imprisoned in bales, it will be carried to the quays of Rotterdam; steam on the water, and steam on the land, will alternately transport it across an arm of the sea, an island, and another watery channel, and it will again see the light in the midst of a great Ulster factory, whose whirring wheels and clanking engines suggest the tortures it has yet to suffer. Seized by a strong hand, it will be torn through a horrid row of close-set iron pins; or, severed into lengths, between the jaws of a devouring monster of steel, it will be squeezed into clasps, to be pushed into another implement of torture, where it will be raised and lowered, torn and scraped, and, losing a third of its substance, be carried on to another room. There, finding itself among the gentler sex, it might hope for more tender treatment, but this hope will soon be extinguished. Either by itself, or joined with companions in misfortune,—kindred fibres from the steppes of Russia, or the green vales of Ireland,—it will be softly laid on a leathern couch. But this Procrustean bed carries it between two ruthless cylinders, which begin a series of pressing and squeezing, of drawing and jagging tortures, which continue until sadly attenuated; but withal firmer, softer, and straighter, it is carried to another machine, where it is partly twisted, to enure it to the next operation. For here it is forced to pass through heated water, and dripping and swollen, it is caught by a whirling spindle, whose grasp tightens, until our exhausted fibre becomes a miserable shadow of its former self, but yet so hardened by misfortune as to be fitted for taking a useful place in the world. After some drying, and winding, and boiling in caustic ley, and drying again, and smearing with paste, our fibre finds itself in a machine, at which is seated a man, who, by quick and regular movements of foot and hand, makes it take an extraordinary flight from one end to another, up and down, across and along, and at last it finds itself bound up, with many companions, in a close embrace. Although it has yet to undergo certain trials, its fate in life is fixed and constituted. The associated fibres, now inseparable in weal and woe, are boiled in ley, dipped first in one strange chemical liquid, and then in another, and afterwards once more see the light of the sun, and once more repose on the soft grass. This is a moment of peace, and its effect is evidenced by the beauty then assumed. All grosser matter has departed, unable to bear the hard ordeal undergone, and the purity of what remains is evidenced by a dazzling whiteness, which covers the green meadow like a wreath of snow. But this repose is soon interrupted, for the fabric is carried away to a building where it is again soaped, and rubbed, and scoured, and washed, until it absolutely pains the eye with whiteness. Then it is dried, and its heaviest trial, though it is the concluding one, is being beaten, or beetled, with heavy wooden beams, the rapid succession of whose unremitting blows re-echoes from the sides of the glen. Men and machines take it afterwards, and put it through a variety of manœuvres, until at last, folded and flattened, white and shining, it is clothed with gaudy trappings of gold and tinsel, of purple and crimson; and in a few weeks it is riding on mule-back at the foot of the Andes, or carried by snorting river-monsters up the mighty Mississippi, or lying in the caravanserai of the Moslem, or spread out before the gaze of the devout citizens of Rome.

Such, if a fanciful, is yet a faithful tracing of the various processes required to bring the flax plant to the state of finish, in a bleached fabric, fitted for the numerous uses to which it is applied. It is a curious study to consider the variety of agencies through which these are severally accomplished. The farmer and the labourer, the merchant and the mariner, the engineer and the mechanic, the factory girl and the weaver, the bleacher and the designer,—men, women, and children, are all supplied with work. Coal is dug out of the bowels of the earth, iron is smelted in furnaces, wood is turned in lathes, leather is tanned and cut into belts, rags are made into paper, all to aid in the conversion of a vegetable material to the use of the human race; and what moments of inventive inspiration, what years of intelligent trial, what varied researches into the secrets of nature, have been necessary in order that the world might be supplied at easy cost with an article of comfort and utility! We may be truly proud that on Irish ground, and by Irish hands, this textile manufacture has reached a point of excellence which is unequalled elsewhere.

Reverting to the flax industry as more immediately connected with Ireland, it is probable that this country was indebted to the Phœnicians for this valuable plant, as it is known that after reaching the Straits of Gibraltar, with their colonial and trading establishments dotted along the coast of Africa, that enterprising people pushed out boldly into the ocean and visited the British isles, where they carried on a considerable commerce. From whatever source our island derived the flax plant, it speedily adopted its culture and manufacture; and at the time of the English Invasion the inhabitants were partly clothed in linen garments of a yellow colour and of preposterous width. Whether the yellow dye was obtained from saffron, with which the intercourse of Ireland with Spain must have made the people acquainted, or whether, as is highly probable, the flax fibre was not used in the steeped state, but simply as removed mechanically from the stems and retaining the greenish-yellow tint of the gum, we cannot say. The latter idea is not improbable, as in the Cork gaol, where the prisoners are employed in separating unsteeped fibre from the straw, and in spinning and weaving it, the fabrics made have exactly the colour indicated by the historians of the English Conquest. Under English rule, several efforts were made to foster and improve the culture and manufacture of flax. In the reign of Charles II. the Earl of Strafford, then Lord Lieutenant, imported Dutch seed, Flemish looms and workmen, and sent a cargo of Irish linens to Spain, at his own risk. In Queen Anne's reign, 1699, the Board of Trustees of the Linen and Hempen Manufacture was constituted by Act of Parliament, but it did not enter on its functions until 1711, from which date it continued to exist until 1828. In 1757 Ireland consumed all the flax she produced, and imported from foreign countries to the value of £138,144. In 1783 this import had decreased to £11,982, and in 1816 it had not only ceased, but was replaced by an export to the value of £72,500. It would be very difficult to estimate the quantity of flax annually grown in Ireland during the seventeenth and eighteenth centuries. The culture was then distributed over the whole island, and the fibre was employed for the cottage manufacture which then exclusively prevailed. No exact means of estimating the breadth of cultivation was available, and the Linen Board could only guess at it from the known importation of sowing seed, a basis which, when recently collated with the Government statistics, has been found to be very untrustworthy. We may, however, feel pretty certain, that at no period did the breadth of flax attain a figure at all approximating to the extent of late years. Confining ourselves to the certain data afforded by the Government statistics, the following Table will show the progress since 1847:—

| | |
|---|---|
| 1847, | 58,312 acres. |
| 1848, | 53,863 „ |
| 1849, | 60,314 „ |
| 1850, | 91,040 „ |
| 1851, | 138,619 „ |
| 1852, | 137,009 „ |
| 1853, | 175,008 „ |

It will be seen that, although there may be fluctuations arising from indifferent crops or occasional low prices for flax while grain was at unusually high prices, as in 1848, yet the growth has not only steadily advanced, but has increased in a surprising ratio, evidently proving that farmers find it a lucrative branch of agriculture. The value of the fibre of the Irish flax crop will give an idea of its importance. Assuming the average yield to be 5 cwt. per statute acre, we should have this year a product of 44,000 tons, which at £52 per ton, the present average price, would give nearly £2,300,000. This is entirely exclusive of the value of the seed. And what makes the crop peculiarly valuable to the farmer is the fact that more labour is employed from the first preparation of the soil until the fibre is brought to market, than is required in the case of any other kind of crop. The labour of every description on the 175,000 acres may be estimated at £1,200,000.

Markets for the sale of flax are very numerous in Ulster, and have lately been established in some of the chief towns of the other provinces. It is not unusual for from £10,000 to £12,000 to be paid away in a northern market town in a few hours, when the flax season is at its height, by the spinners' buyers, who attend to purchase from the farmers. The specimens of flax in the Exhibition, contributed by Messrs. J. Preston and Co., of Belfast, showed the manner in which it is ordinarily made up for sale, in bundles weighing 16¼ lbs. each, which is called a *stone*.

The Irish flax crop is not altogether consumed in the Irish linen manufacture, although the latter works up an amount of raw material about equal to the annual home production. Certain qualities of foreign flax are imported, as we have before shown, to the extent of about 8000 tons yearly. On the other hand, a quantity of Irish flax, varying in amount, is exported to England, Scotland, France, and the United States of America. Last year it reached 8189 tons, being distributed as follows:—

| | |
|---|---|
| To England, | 3076 tons. |
| „ Scotland, | 4137 „ |
| „ France, | 971 „ |
| „ United States, | 5 „ |
| | 8189 „ |

The value of this export was £409,410, and the value of the foreign flax imported was £461,820, so that the two nearly balance. England and Scotland have always been buyers of our flax to an extent proportionate to our capability of supplying them; and France has lately become an important customer, while a few years ago we exported scarcely any beyond Great Britain. The growth of this export trade, closely following the expansion of the home culture, will be seen in the following Table, taking Belfast, the chief port of shipment, as a criterion:—

IRISH FLAX EXPORTED FROM BELFAST.

| | 1850. | 1851. | 1852. |
|---|---|---|---|
| To England, | 666 tons. | 1269 tons. | 2276 tons. |
| „ Scotland, | 684 „ | 2286 „ | 3006 „ |
| „ France, | 107 „ | 436 „ | 971 „ |
| „ United States, | — „ | 10 „ | 5 „ |
| | 1457 „ | 4001 „ | 6258 „ |

This is a feature of great importance as regards the future prospects of Irish flax-growers; since it clearly shows that, in so far as the home culture increases, will the sister island and foreign linen manufacturing states seek in our markets a large proportion of the common and medium qualities which they have hitherto procured from Russia and other countries. When it is remembered that fully 90,000 tons of foreign flax are yearly imported into the United Kingdom, 19,000 into France, and 6000 into Belgium, it will be seen that there is a large opening for our flax, especially as the bulk of the import into all these countries is of descriptions of fibre with which our flax can most favourably compete, both as to quality and price. It is no unusual thing to see at the quays of Belfast, a British schooner loading flax for Havre or Landerneau, alongside a French lugger discharging Indian corn from Bayonne, or wheat from Nantes. There are some who would lament the importation of foreign grain, and others who would object to flax as not being a food crop. To such persons, the lesson to be learnt on the Belfast quays is an instructive one: it shows Ireland exchanging a produce which she is eminently fitted by nature to furnish, for French grain, which the climate of that country is better suited to produce. And in every £100 worth of flax with which the former pays the latter for her grain, upwards of £50 represent the element of labour, while in £100 worth of grain, labour will only appear to the extent of £10 or £15. If Ireland were shut out from all extraneous sources of supply in the articles of food, and if her soil were incapable of furnishing the amount of aliment required for her population, flax, as not edible, might be objected to, though even in this case the value of the seed, as beef-making material, should be considered. But as Bishop Berkeley's "brazen wall" is not likely to be realized, we cannot but rejoice in the rapid spread of a crop which supplies our great staple textile with its raw material, is a source of much profit to the farmer, of great employment to the labourer, and the surplus of which can be exchanged for cheap food with other nations.

*Modes of preparing the Fibre.*—The Exhibition supplied examples of the various modes which have been of late years adopted with a view to shorten the process of steeping, to render it more regular, and to substitute for the uncertainty arising from variations of temperature, and the unequal amount of care and skill among flax-growers, the method and system of establishments making a special business of this important department of flax management.

From time to time different plans have been tried, both at home and abroad, for shortening the steeping process, and for securing more certain results. It has been repeatedly observed, that so critical an operation as the steeping of flax should not be left to the grower of the plant, as it is found that in proportion to the amount of knowledge and experience which he possesses, the result will be satisfactory or the reverse. In other branches of agriculture, simple and expeditious means are available for the preparation of the produce for market; but in the case of flax, the plant, after harvesting, has to be submitted to a long series of processes before the fibre can be obtained in a marketable state. The flax-grower, in fact, was required to conduct operations which involved chemical changes and semi-manufacturing operations, and the great principle of division of labour was neglected in the routine ordinarily pursued in flax-growing countries. It was further evident, that the cultivation of the plant would become much more general if the grower could at once find a market for his crop when at maturity, and not be obliged to undertake the critical processes of steeping, drying, &c. In certain districts of the north of Ireland the grower of the crop is sufficiently acquainted with the details involved in its preparation for market to carry them out successfully, but in other parts of the country the absence of this knowledge forms the great drawback to the extension of flax culture. It is not here necessary to go into a detail of the different inventions brought before the public, having for their object the solution of this question; it will be sufficient to notice those which have already been attended with a certain degree of success, which are in actual operation in Ireland and elsewhere, and which were exemplified in the Exhibition itself. All of these set out with the principle, that the flax crop at its maturity should be pulled and dried in the field, and that it should be sold by the grower to persons whose business it should be, for their own profit, to convert it into a marketable commodity. And the first and most immediately recognisable advantage suggests itself in the economizing of the seed—a product shamefully neglected in Ireland, though most carefully utilized elsewhere.

The most simple mode of treating the dried straw was first suggested about three-quarters of a century ago to the Irish Linen Board, and has subsequently been revived in France; but in both these cases it had to be abandoned, from the application of the fibre to unsuitable purposes. The mode in question consists in the separation of the fibre, by chemical means, from the stems of the plant, without any previous steeping or maceration of the latter. In order to understand this, and, indeed, the entire *rationale* of the steeping process, it is necessary to explain that the stem of the flax plant, after the seed has been removed, consists of a woody centre, in some cases hollow, and in others solid, which is covered, just as a tree is with its bark, by longitudinal fibres, constituting the flax of commerce, but cemented together with a gummy or resinous substance, which must be got rid of before the fibre is suited for the manufacture of linen. This gum-resin is acted upon by moisture and by variations of temperature, and is very destructible in acids and alkalies; and as, in the processes of manufacture, all these agents are brought into play, it is necessary, in order to obtain an even and solid bleached fabric, that the gum should be cleared away before the fibre is spun, woven, or bleached. When the *dry system*, as it is termed, of separating the fibre, was first brought out, this destructibility of the gum was not sufficiently considered, and, as a natural consequence, the bleached fabrics made from such flax were of very uneven quality, being, indeed, quite unsaleable. The dry process has recently been revived, and the use of the fibre so prepared has been properly restricted to purposes where the yarns are dry-spun, and the fabrics not bleached, and, indeed, in many cases, further secured against deteriorating agencies, by being coated with oil, pitch, or paint, as in the case of tarpaulins, railway truck-covers, rick-covers, &c. For a considerable range of purposes this dry fibre is now coming into use, and as it can be furnished at a low price, it is actually being substituted for hemp, jute, and similar textile materials. An equal weight of flax straw will give a much larger yield of this dry fibre than of steeped fibre, as the former contains the additional weight of the gum. It is obvious also, that the expense of steeping and drying being saved, its preparation must be much more economical. It brings in the English market £25 to £35 per ton. As yet its preparation is confined to a few localities, the chief person engaged in it being Mr. Roche, M. P. for the county of Cork. In the Royal Flax Society's smaller case was to be seen a specimen of this article. At the Cork County Gaol, as before mentioned, the prisoners are employed in this process, and also in making coarse fabrics for their own use. As a general rule, it may be stated, that although much trouble and expense may be saved by this dry system, and inferior qualities of flax straw be more properly treated by it than by steeping, yet it would be highly injudicious so to prepare good qualities, since the difference between £30 per ton for the dry fibre, and £80 to £110 for the best kinds of steeped fibre, would be too great a sacrifice. The limited range of purposes to which it is at present believed to be applicable must also curtail its extension, unless it be able to compete permanently with Russian hemp, when the latter is at its ordinary price. Of hemp the United Kingdom imports about 45,000 tons annually, chiefly from Russia, valued at £1,700,000. If, with the inferior flaxes of Ireland, we could replace even a portion of this large sum, it would be an important consideration.

The interesting series of specimens exhibited by Messrs. J. Leadbetter and Co., of Belfast, furnished an example illustrative of *Watts' system* of retting, or the *steaming process*, recently introduced. This method consists in placing the dried flax and straw, after the seed has been separated, in iron chambers, having a ledge on the roof, so as to render the latter capable of containing cold water. When the straw has been placed in the chamber on a perforated false bottom, the door is closed by screws, and steam is driven in by a pipe round the chamber and between the bottoms. The steam penetrates the mass of flax, and softens it, the operation being further facilitated by the condensation of the steam on the cold roof, which produces a continuous shower of water, and a decoction of the extractive matters of the straw is thus obtained. In eight to twelve hours the straw is taken out of the chamber, and is passed through metal rollers, heavily weighted, which press out the greater part of the water, splitting and flattening the straw longitudinally. The latter is then easily dried, and in a few hours is ready for scutching. The water, which is in fact a vegetable extract, is employed in the patentee's concerns for feeding pigs, joined with other feeding-stuffs. It differs from the steep-water produced in the ordinary methods in not being offensive to the smell. This arises from its being simply an infusion of the flax stems, in place of holding in suspension the products of the decomposed gum, &c. The system thus briefly described has been in operation last autumn in three concerns established by Messrs. Leadbetter in Ulster. As yet its real merits can scarcely be estimated, in so far as the quality of the fibre thus created for manufacturing purposes is concerned.

The Exhibition contained several examples of another system, which has now been some years introduced and which is carried on, with various degrees of success, in Great Britain and Ireland, and in France and Germany. This is generally known as *Schenck's system*, or the *hot-water steep*. It was introduced into Europe in 1847, when the inventor, Mr. Schenck, of New York, who had already applied the process in the treatment of hemp, came over to Belfast and laid his plans before the Royal Flax Society. The Committee of that body, after a careful scrutiny, and repeated experiments extending over a period of two years, made a Report recommending the general adoption of the system, especially in districts where flax culture was being introduced, and where it was peculiarly desirable that the grower should have an immediate market for his raw produce, without being obliged to undertake the operation of steeping and scutching, with which he was totally unacquainted, and for which he did not possess the necessary facilities. In the last annual Report of the Royal Flax Society, it was stated that eighteen establishments on Schenck's system were at work in Ireland, capable of consuming the produce of about 7000 acres of flax annually. In England there are five, and in Scotland two, three in Germany, and one in France. The quality of the flax produced in these different concerns has been very variable, according to the manner in which the straw is saved by the growers, the skill and care bestowed on the details of working, and the various modifications of the process which have been introduced. As a general rule, the fibre retted in the Irish concerns has been of indifferent quality, while in the English, Scotch, and foreign, it has been very superior. The specimens contained in the Exhibition included series from two Irish retteries, those of Messrs. Hughes, of Clonmel, and Hay, of Dunleer; of two English, Messrs. Neilson and Co., of Selby, and Aitken, of Spalding; of two foreign, Messrs. Scrive Freres, of Lille, and Wellman and Weber, of Bernstadt, Silesia. All of these were of excellent quality, and it would be difficult to say where the palm of superior merit should be awarded. A recent improvement in treating the flax straw after the hot-water steep, which has been borrowed from Watts' system, viz., the rolling of the wet straw, was well exemplified in the case contributed to the Exhibition by Messrs. Hay. The fibre is thus totally freed from the impurities so much objected to by spinners in hot-water steeped flax, which arose from the deposit of the decomposed gum on the fibres; and the simple process of rolling has already, though only lately introduced, told upon the value of the flax brought to market from the retteries, and consequently upon the success of the entire system. It is worthy of remark, that the samples of English and foreign straw exhibited were generally very much better saved than the Irish, from more care being paid to the drying after pulling.—J. M.

## SILK.

The production of silk is really one of the most curious branches of human industry; and when we reflect on the large quantity of that beautiful material which is annually consumed throughout the world, and that the whole of this is the secretion of the larvæ of a species of moth, we are lost in admiration of the brilliant and important effects realized, through comparatively simple and apparently insignificant agencies. If we examine a cocoon of silk, the production of one of those creatures, see how small the quantity which it contains, only a few grains in weight; and consider that from that material millions of human beings are richly arrayed; that our furniture is covered with it; our hangings formed of it; and our carriages lined with it; and that, moreover, it possesses a degree of tenacity almost unexampled in any organic substance:—when we reflect upon all this, we may see what could be done by human agency if well directed, or even by individual efforts when continuously applied. The silk in a single cocoon weighs only between two and three grains; and yet the quantity of silk annually consumed in the manufacture may be estimated by thousands of tons weight!

The art of making the filamentous substance emitted by the silk-worm available for the use of man is said to have originated in China, and is of very remote antiquity. The ancient records of that country describe the queen as surrounded by her female attendants all engaged in the silk manufacture; the art being practised, according to them, over 2000 years before the Christian era. The cultivation of the silk-worm appears to have been confined to that country until the time of the Emperor Justinian, the raw material being purchased by the people of Persia and India, by whom it was manufactured. In the reign of that monarch the trade is alleged to have been brought into Europe by two Persian monks who had travelled in China; and who succeeded in bringing a quantity of the eggs, secured in a hollow cane, to Constantinople, where they were hatched, and the larvæ fed and reared on the leaves of the white mulberry. For six centuries the breeding of silk-worms in Europe was confined to the Greeks of the Lower Empire; but in 1147, Roger, King of Sicily, in his conquest of Greece, took many of the people engaged in this species of industry, whom he compelled to prosecute their avocations at Palermo. A knowledge of the management of silk thus spread through Italy, and eventually to Spain and France. In the reign of James I. many efforts were made to introduce the culture of the mulberry tree and the rearing of silk-worms into England; but it is almost needless to add that they signally failed, as did all succeeding attempts, so far as regarded making the results commercially profitable. From the present consumption of the silk of the United Kingdom, which is accordingly all imported, it is estimated that nearly 20,000,000,000 of these creatures must annually live and die.

The silk-worm is the *Bombyx mori* of entomologists, so called from its favourite food. Like all the creatures of the class to which it belongs, it undergoes, during its career, several transformations. The eggs are deposited during the summer by the female, then existing in the form of a moth. They are about the size of grains of mustard seed, and of a yellowish colour, which soon changes to a brownish cast. They are covered with a liquid which causes them to adhere to the cloth or paper on which the moth is made to deposit them, but from which they are easily freed by immersion in cold water; and being afterwards dried and kept at a proper temperature, they may be preserved with perfect safety during the winter and spring, until the food for them is available. The temperature at which they should be kept is about 55° of Fahrenheit. The method of hatching these eggs is curious. In France they are tied round the girdles of the women during the day, and placed under their pillows at night; but when agency of this kind is not available to the desired extent, the eggs are placed in a room in which a temperature of about 80° is maintained, and in the course of eight or ten days they are hatched. Sheets of paper on which mulberry leaves have been spread are then placed over the worms, the paper being pierced with holes, through which they come to the leaves; and by proper ventilation, the maintenance of the necessary temperature, and a due supply of their favourite food, they grow apace. When first hatched they are of a black colour, and about quarter of an inch in length. When about a week old the head of the worm becomes considerably enlarged, and it gets into a state of lethargy, in which it remains about three days. This condition is apparently caused by the tightness of the skin, the growth of which did not keep pace with the development of the worm; but on casting the skin active vitality becomes again apparent, and the creature greedily consumes its food. An examination of the cast-off skin will show that the covering has been thrown off the animal entirely, even to the jaws and teeth. In about five days more another moulting takes place, the worm meantime increasing in growth; and so on until the fourth and last skin is got rid of, when the animal will have increased to two inches in length. The voracity of the creature is extraordinary, unless when moulting.

The chrysalis remains dormant in the covering thus provided, for a shorter or longer time, according to the temperature of the climate. In Eastern countries the usual period is about eleven days; in the most southern parts of Europe, eighteen; in France, twenty-one days; and in these countries, about a month, unless the cocoons be placed under the influence of artificial heat. When the period arrives for obtaining its liberty a lubricating liquor is exuded, calculated to facilitate the process; and by some time continuously knocking its head against the cocoon, it emerges from it in the form of a butterfly. The business of reproduction soon takes place, the female depositing her eggs in a place previously prepared for them, after which the butterflies terminate their existence. It is, however, only those cocoons intended for seed that are allowed to develope the chrysalis within them; for which purpose the finest specimens are selected, taking care that there are an equal number of males and females, the former being distinguished by being sharper and more pointed at the ends than the latter. The chrysales are destroyed in the cocoons of which the silk is to be preserved; as, if allowed to come to maturity and obtain their liberty, the silk would thereby be broken, and rendered valueless.

The number of eggs produced by the female moth varies from 200 to 500, and it is estimated that about 200 cocoons will yield an ounce of seed, that is of these eggs. Under favourable circumstances one ounce of seed will produce 80 lbs. of cocoons, or even more. The silk of a cocoon weighs about two and a half grains, and affords a length of thread varying from 750 to 1150 feet.

For the amateur who may desire to witness the economy of these interesting creatures the lettuce may suffice as food for them, as the quality or quantity of the material produced in such a case is not of much consideration. The cocoons with the worms alive in them, called seed cocoons, are easily obtained. By attention to the brief outline which we have here given, a new stock may be produced; and without much trouble the entire phenomena connected with the production of silk may be illustrated.

We may observe, that attempts have been made to obtain a substitute for silk from other animals, as the spider and the pinna, but they have not been successful. Other kinds of food, too, have been tried with the silkworm, besides the mulberry leaves, as those of lettuce and other vegetables, but any results obtained in this way have not been satisfactory. There is, therefore, little prospect of the production of silk being successfully carried on in the United Kingdom.

In addition to the illustrations of the products of silk and the processes of manufacture in the Exhibition, cocoons were contributed by Messrs. W. Fry and Co.; in these the material could be seen in its primary state, and in connexion with them the foregoing outline of how they are produced will not be uninteresting to the general reader.

The silk-worm, on attaining its full size, begins to discharge a viscid secretion in the form of pulpy twin filaments, proceeding from the twin orifices in the nose of the insects through which they are projected. These threads are laid parallel to each other, and are glued together by a kind of glossy varnish in which they are enveloped. The cocoon which the insect instinctively winds about itself serves as a defence against living enemies, and to modify the influence of changes of temperature. The specific gravity of the fibre thus formed is 1·3, water being 1: and it is by far the most tenacious or strongest of the textile fibres, a thread of it being three times as strong as one of flax of equal diameter. Some varieties of the silk fibre are pure white, but the usual colour is that of a golden-yellow.*

On the silk trade some further remarks will be found in the section of the work where the article is regarded as a branch of manufacture, and to these we would direct the attention of the reader. Under absurd fiscal regulations it languished for years, though these were framed with a view of promoting its extension. Of late, however, it has been annually growing in importance, as may be seen by a reference to the subjoined figures, which show the imports from 1840 to the present time.

IMPORTS OF SILK FROM 1840 TO 1853, INCLUSIVE:

| Years. | Raw. | Thrown. | Total. |
|---|---|---|---|
| 1840, . . . . . | 3,759,016 lbs. . . . . | 289,294 lbs. . . . . | 4,048,310 lbs. |
| 1841, . . . . . | 3,365,785 „ . . . . | 231,343 „ . . . . | 3,597,128 „ |
| 1842, . . . . . | 3,951,773 „ . . . . | 397,407 „ . . . . | 4,349,180 „ |
| 1843, . . . . . | 3,476,313 „ . . . . | 383,573 „ . . . . | 3,859,886 „ |
| 1844, . . . . . | 4,149,932 „ . . . . | 400,986 „ . . . . | 4,550,918 „ |
| 1845, . . . . . | 4,354,696 „ . . . . | 511,832 „ . . . . | 4,866,528 „ |
| 1846, . . . . . | 4,407,264 „ . . . . | 432,453 „ . . . . | 4,839,717 „ |
| 1847, . . . . . | 4,133,302 „ . . . . | 312,651 „ . . . . | 4,445,953 „ |
| 1848, . . . . . | 4,471,735 „ . . . . | 1,070,989 „ . . . . | 5,542,724 „ |
| 1849, . . . . . | 4,991,472 „ . . . . | 614,770 „ . . . . | 5,606,242 „ |
| 1850, . . . . . | 4,942,407 „ . . . . | 469,527 „ . . . . | 5,411,934 „ |
| 1851, . . . . . | 4,608,336 „ . . . . | 412,636 „ . . . . | 5,020,972 „ |
| 1852, . . . . . | 5,832,551 „ . . . . | 426,463 „ . . . . | 6,258,014 „ |
| 1853, . . . . . | 6,480,724 „ . . . . | 828,493 „ . . . . | 7,309,217 „ |

* The silk husbandry, as it may be called, is completed in France within six weeks from the end of April; and thus affords the most rapid agricultural return, requiring merely the advance of a little capital for the purchase of the leaf. In buying up cocoons, and in the filature, indeed, capital may be often laid out to great advantage. The most hazardous period in the process of breeding the worms is at the third and fourth moulting; for upon the sixth day of the third age and the seventh of the fourth, they in general eat nothing at all. On the first day of the fourth age, the worms proceeding from one ounce of eggs will, according to Bonafous, consume upon an average 23 lbs. of mulberry leaves. On the first of the fifth age they will consume 42 lbs.; and on the sixth day of the same age they acquire their maximum voracity, devouring no less than 228 lbs. of leaves. From this date their appetite continually decreases, till on the tenth day of this age they consume only 56 lbs. In general the more food they consume the more silk will they produce.

A mulberry tree is valued in Provence at from six-pence to ten-pence; it is planted out of the nursery at four years of age; it is begun to be stripped in the fifth year, and affords an increasing crop of leaves to the twentieth. It yields from 1 cwt. to 30 cwt. of leaves, according to its magnitude and mode of cultivation. One ounce of silkworm eggs requires for its due development into cocoons about 15 cwt. of mulberry leaves. One ounce of eggs is calculated to produce 80 or 100 lbs. of cocoons; and about 8 lbs. of reeled raw silk are produced from 100 lbs. of cocoons.—URE.

## WOOL.

The bodies of mammalian animals are covered with peculiar substances to which the names of hair and wool are given. These consist of a number of more or less fine fibre-like bodies, which take their root in numerous minute vascular bulbs, lying immediately beneath, or we might almost say embedded in the skin. Hair and wool have certain common characteristics. Hair consists of two parts, the external cortical matter, or hair tissue, and the medullary matter or core, which is sometimes wanting, for it does not in all cases extend through the whole length of the hair. The hair tissue consists of numerous parallel bundles of fibres, a fact which is sufficiently evident in decaying hair, which splits up at the end. Wool resembles hair in many of its peculiarities, the chief point of difference being, that while the surface of the latter is smooth, that of the former is serrated, a quality upon which the *felting* power of wool depends. This difference is not, however, perceptible to the naked eye or touch; indeed, it would be very difficult to point out any perceptible qualities distinctive of the two substances. The bristles of the hog and the fine wool of the lamb can no doubt be readily distinguished from one another, for these are the extreme examples of the two substances; but in many cases they pass so completely into each other, that it is often impossible to mark the line of demarcation; and hair and wool have the same chemical composition.

The common impression is, that wool is confined to the sheep, but experience shows that a great variety of other animals produce it also, and that under the long hair of the goat, for example, there will generally be found a certain amount of true wool; and we might go even further, and consider that with very few exceptions the external covering of all mammalian animals is a variable mixture of hair and wool.

If we examine some sheep's wool in its natural condition we shall find it more or less covered with a peculiar substance termed *the yolk*, composed chiefly of a true potash soap. This substance is soluble in water, and so abundant is it that in many cases a fleece loses half its weight by simple washing. The yolk is a natural secretion, the proper production of which is intimately connected with the growth of the wool and with the health of the animal. In the latter respect by matting the wool together it preserves the animal from wet and cold; while as regards the quality of the wool it is thin, harsh, and wiry where the yolk is deficient. This is not only true as regards the whole fleece, but also relatively as regards the wool of different parts of the body; for example, the best wool is found on the breast and shoulders of the sheep, and there, too, the yolk is most abundant. In many northern countries, and especially in Scotland, where the yolk is found to be deficient, so important is a due quantity of it deemed, that a substitute for it is sought by smearing the sheep over with a mixture of tar and butter.

The quality of wool varies in the first place according to the race of the sheep, to confine ourselves to the chief wool-bearing animal, and in the second to the part of the animal from which it is taken. Upon the first depends the old and more obviously simple system of classification into *long* or *combing wool*, and into *short* or *clothing wool*. The former may be further classified into two divisions,—one, having a staple of about eight inches, or perhaps shorter, and best adapted for the manufacture of worsted goods of the finest quality, is now, properly speaking, the *long wool*; and the other, termed *middle wool*, having an average staple of about five inches, and is used for making friezes, flannels, army and navy cloths, blankets, baizes, carpets, druggets, bockings, cassinets, &c. The finest long wool is produced by the Leicester breed of sheep, the middle wool being produced by a cross between the Leicester and several other breeds, as for instance, the South Downs—it is in fact the wool of nearly all the half-breeds in the country. The short staple wool is typified by the wool of the merino sheep, little of which is produced in these countries, and which was formerly imported in great measure from Spain, the original country of this variety; but it is now obtained from Germany, the Cape of Good Hope, and Australia. This kind of wool is chiefly used in the production of fine cloths. The classification of the wool-stapler, who purchases from the farmer, and then sells to the manufacturer, is to a certain extent founded upon the second source of difference of quality—the parts of the body whence it was obtained; for example, that on the sides of the neck and shoulders, the ribs, and back, is the finest part of the fleece; and next to this comes that which covers the thighs. But difference of race has also to do with the wool stapler's classification, for the wool on the breast of one sheep may be equal to that on the back of another; hence it is often not so much the object to separate the wools of the different parts of the body as to put all the wool which may be adapted for one particular purpose by itself. In these countries the chief divisions are termed, according to their order of quality, *the picklock*, *the prime*, *the choice*, *the super*, *the head*, *the downrights*, *the seconds*, *the abb*, *the livery*, and *the short coarse or breech wool*. A good fleece would generally come under the first four, although portions might even belong to the sixth or seventh.

The qualities by which wool is judged are fineness, trueness, soundness, softness, elasticity, colour, felting property, and curling. The most important of these qualities in wool-sorting is fineness, and accordingly the picklock or super electa is the finest, and the breech wool the coarsest. There is an instrument by which the degrees of fineness may be accurately measured, called Dollond's Wool Micrometer, each degree of which is equal to 0·0001 or $\frac{1}{10000}$ of an inch. The finest wool, such as that of the Nigretti Merino, would measure about 4 such degrees, or the $\frac{1}{2500}$ of an inch, and the thickest about 30 degrees, or about $\frac{1}{333}$ of an inch; the longer the wool, in general, the thicker it will be. The fineness of wool is very much influenced by the temperature of the country, the nature of the soil, the pasture, and many other circumstances upon the knowledge of which the growth of good wool-bearing sheep materially depends. Trueness is that quality which indicates that, there are no coarse hairs standing up through the wool, and no irregular shaggy patches, but rather a uniformity of growth over the whole body, and a freedom from what are called *breaches*, or withered portions in the fibres themselves, the result of starvation. Soundness means the strength of fibre, and is intimately connected with the quality of trueness, especially with the absence of breaches; this quality is of especial importance in long wool which is to be combed. Softness is a most important quality of wool, not merely as regards the general taste of the public, which demands articles with a fine soft pile, but also because harsh, wiry wool, is more brittle and suffers more injury than soft wool in the various operations. Elasticity is an extremely important quality of wool, especially in the coarser kinds, for upon it depend the production of a rich nap upon blankets and other thick woollen fabrics, and the various fanciful naps. Connected with it is the power of extension which the fibres are capable of undergoing before they break; this is less in the merino and other fine wools than in the long-stapled; for example, a fibre of merino will bear to be stretched to the extent of from 32 to 40 per cent. of its length, whilst the wool of the common coarse-woolled sheep is capable of being stretched from 40 to 50 per cent. The colour is comparatively of minor importance, although a pure white and semi-translucent fibre yields the finest dyed cloths. The felting property, on the other hand, is of the greatest importance in estimating the qualities of wool, but especially when intended for clothing purposes. This property depending upon the serrated structure of the wool fibres, we have a measure of it in the number of serrations in a given space, for the greater the number of these, the greater will be the tendency of the fibres to catch one another. For example, the fine Saxony merino wool contains about 2800 serrations in an inch, the South Down, or middle wool, about 2000, and the long Leicester wool about 1800. The best quality upon which the comparative value of wool depends is its curled form, which is one of the most characteristic distinctive properties between wool and hair. Like the felting property just noticed, this is of the greatest importance in clothing wools, for the fineness of the thread which can be spun, and consequently the fineness of the cloth which can be made, depends upon the minuteness and number of the corkscrew-like ringlets which the wool assumes. If these be large, the greater number of them are broken by the carder, and the fibres cannot entangle sufficiently to form a strong thread. The thicker the fibres the less of these spiral curls in a given space; thus, wool from $\frac{1}{500}$ to $\frac{1}{600}$ of an inch in thickness has from twelve to fifteen curls in an inch, whilst that which only measures from $\frac{1}{1500}$ to $\frac{1}{2000}$ of an inch has from twenty-eight to thirty-two. Hence, it is, that the Saxony wool, which is the finest, is best adapted for making cloths, whilst the long wools, which are thicker, are the worst.

The breeding of sheep for their wool has not received that development in Ireland of which it seems capable. The old mountain short-woolled sheep is now nearly extinct. For several years past immense numbers of South Downs and Leicesters have been imported, and the breeds generally considerably ameliorated, but whether from sufficient care not being bestowed upon them, or from other causes, we have repeatedly heard that in a short time the wool of English imported sheep deteriorates and becomes wiry, harsh, and coarse. Perhaps this may be accounted for by the deficiency and character of the yolk, a sufficient quantity of which is more necessary in this damp climate than elsewhere. The samples of Irish wool at the Exhibition were of excellent quality, but as we are not aware whether the sheep which yielded them were imported recently, or were fully acclimated animals, we cannot say how far they may be taken as samples of the quality of the wools which we can grow.

There can be no doubt that much still remains to be done in improving the quality of our wools, and especially in determining the influence which our climate has upon the different kinds. A few well-conducted experiments would effect this object; but as the improvement of quantity, and not of quality, seems to be the kind of agricultural progress most favoured in Ireland, some time may elapse before this important and desirable object is effected. The success which has attended the production of wool in England, where the long-stapled is, perhaps the best in the world, ought to be an encouragement to efforts of this kind.

## OILS AND FATS.

There is a class of bodies, very widely diffused both in animals and vegetables, to which we apply the term *fatty substances*. They are lighter than water, are insoluble in it, and are sparingly so in anything else. Some of them are solid, but melt at a very gentle heat, and others are liquid. We have an example of the former class in tallow, and of the latter in olive oil, while an intermediate class is formed by hog's lard, butter, &c. In the animal body fats are usually found in the brain, coating the intestines, and in the cellular tissues. Although there is no part of plants without some traces, the greater amount exists in the seeds. The common walnut, for example, is found to contain from 40 to 70 per cent. of its weight, the hazel-nut or filbert 60 per cent., the cabbage seed 30 to 39 per cent. of oil.

If we subject tallow to considerable pressure we obtain a solid residue and a liquid oil; and even the most fluid oils contain a certain portion of solid fats. This fact accounts very simply for the varied consistence of fats. When the liquid constituent predominates we have liquid oils; where the solid is in excess we have solid fats; while in lard of pigs and in butter the proportions are nearly balanced.

When the entire of the solid constituents of an oil are removed, there remains a liquid fat, which in most cases is a peculiar substance termed *oleine*, so called from its close resemblance to oils. The solid constituents of fat consist, on the other hand, of one or more analogous solid substances, the chief of which are called *margarine*, from the Greek word for pearl, from the pearly lustre of some of its compounds; *stearine*, from the Greek word for solid, because it is the most solid of all the common fats; and *palmatine*, so called from its being the chief constituent of a peculiar solid fat procured from a species of palm. If either of these substances be heated with potash, soda, or any other similar bodies, called by chemists *bases*, they are decomposed into a peculiar acid substance which unites with the base employed, forming a compound which is called a soap, the process being termed saponification; whilst another substance is separated, which, chemically speaking, is analogous to alcohol or spirit. In fully nine-tenths of the known fats this body is an oily or syrupy substance, having a sweetish taste, soluble in water, and known by the name of *glycerine* or fat-sugar. In wax, and also in spermaceti, the analogous substance is solid. Until very recently glycerine was not applied to any use; but it is now employed medicinally in cutaneous diseases, and extensively in perfumery. We could also separate the glycerine from the fat acids, by heating the original fatty matters with sulphuric acid. Thus we obtain margaric acid from margarine, stearic acid from stearine, palmitic acid from palmatine, and oleic acid from oleine,—the three former being solid, the latter liquid.

The solid acids, in whatever way obtained, may be distilled under certain conditions without injury, and may thus be procured as beautifully white crystalline masses. The liquid oleic acid cannot, however, be distilled in the same way without decomposition. In some fats, as for example, butter, there are found some other liquid or oily fats besides the oleine, which may be readily distilled at a moderate temperature, and which are hence called volatile oily acids. The compounds of these acids with glycerine are very unstable, and hence fats containing them are liable to decomposition; and as when free these oily acids have a peculiar and distinct odour, this decomposition is termed rancidity. These acids, as well as several others, having analogous chemical properties, may also be obtained from fats containing only oleic, margaric, and stearic acids, by oxidations with nitric acid or some other oxidizing agent, and even by the slow action of the air. These *volatile oils* should not be confounded with what are called *essential oils*, which, although, no doubt, intimately connected with ordinary fats, are totally distinct substances; they are obtained in the distillation of the leaves, flowers, bark, and other parts of plants, and find their chief employment in perfumery.

Although oleic acid has been spoken of as one acid, but it is probable there are several. At all events we can divide the different forms of oleine into two distinct classes, depending upon their behaviour to the oxygen of the air. There are certain oils of which the type is linseed oil, which, when spread out in thin coats, absorb oxygen, and are rapidly or slowly, according to the particular oil subjected to the process, transformed into a yellowish resinous mass, which dries into an effective and permanent varnish. Such oils are technically called *drying oils*, and are the vehicles used for preparing the colours for oil-painting, which art entirely depends upon the property just noticed. They also enter into the composition of certain varnishes. The oils which do not possess this property, or *non-drying oils*, such as the rape and olive oils, could not, as will be easily understood, be employed in oil-painting; but from the fact of their not absorbing oxygen they do not thicken on keeping, and are therefore peculiarly adapted for burning in lamps, for dressing wool, and for lubricating machinery, for which purposes the drying oils are quite unsuited.

The number of solid fats and oils which are found in animals and plants is very great, and each year adds considerably to the number of the latter. As it would be impossible in our space even to enumerate all, we shall confine our observations to those kinds of most importance to the manufacturer.

*Tallow.*—We shall commence with the solid fats, the most important of which is *tallow*, including under this term the fat not only of the cow but of the sheep, horse, goat, &c., the common article coming into commerce being, in fact, a mixture of all these. The term *suet*, which is a corruption of the French word *suif*, is applied only to the fat of the sheep, which is the most solid, the whitest, and the most prized material for the manufacture of candles. The fat of beef contains about 70 to 75 parts of stearine, and 25 to 30 parts of oleine in 100 parts, while the fat of mutton usually contains 70 of stearine and 30 of oleine, and the fat of pork or lard only 38 parts of stearine and 62 parts of oleine. These proportions are very variable; but the causes of the variation, although forming a curious instance of the effect of physical agents upon animal life, have not been studied. The fat of oxen has less consistence than that of bulls, and that of cows less than that of oxen. In young animals the fat is whiter than in old ones, it gradually deepening in colour as the age of the animal increases; nevertheless, the finest and most prized fat is obtained from animals at full maturity. The fat of precocious animals has never the consistence of those less so. The difference in this respect, in the case of the new breeds of animals, some of which rapidly arrive at maturity, is remarkable. The influence of climate is also very marked. Thus it has been found in practice that the fat of animals reared in warm countries is firmer, and contains more stearine than of those in cold countries; for example, the tallow of Cuba and tropical America will yield sometimes over 10 per cent. more stearine than that obtained from Northern Russia, and the same rule applies to the animals of plains and mountains. But this is the more interesting when we find an analogous phenomenon in plants. The vegetable oils of temperate and cold regions are in nearly every case liquid, while the major part of those which come to us from the tropics are solid. We have here one of the most beautiful provisions of nature, without which the functions of animal life would not go on so perfectly; for if the fat of animals in northern countries, or the vegetable oils of plants, contained as much stearine or other solid fats as those of warm tropical countries, it might in many cases solidify from the cold in the fine vessels and cellular tissue at the surface. In the warm-blooded mammalia the fat is more or less solid, and in the cold-blooded fishes and reptiles it always consists of liquid oil; and, furthermore, the fat in the tissues surrounding the heart, and in general in the interior of the body, is richer in stearine than that lying immediately beneath the skin. But of all the influencing causes there can be no doubt that food is that which produces the most marked effect. In general watery food will produce a fat in cattle of less consistence, and containing less stearine, than in those fed on dry food; a fact which is well illustrated by the Russian tallow, which, notwithstanding the nature of the climate of Russia, is more prized by candle-makers than our own tallow.

It is impossible to form any accurate estimate of the quantity of tallow employed in Great Britain annually, much less the quantity used in making candles. But the quantity imported in the year ending the 5th of January, 1852, was 61,179 tons, of which Russia alone supplied a little over 30,000 tons.

*Palm oil*, or, more properly, palm butter, stands next in importance to tallow, no less than 30,427 tons having been imported in 1851, and the imports are increasing every year. This fat, which may be said to represent tallow in the vegetable kingdom, is solid, of an orange red colour, and a peculiar aromatic odour, and of the consistence of firm butter, is obtained by boiling the kernels of the fruit of a species of palm called *Elais Guianensis*, or, according to others, that of several species of palm. Palm oil, when fresh, contains about 30 per cent. of solid fat, and 70 of liquid; but as it comes to Europe it is rancid, and contains a part of its acid free, which makes it more solid.

*Illipa oil.*—This oil, which is also called Bassia oil, resembles palm oil in many respects. It, however, contains stearine instead of palmatine, and is of a light greenish-yellow colour, and of the consistence of butter at ordinary temperature, but melts into a yellow fluid at the very moderate temperature of 82½° Fahr. It is obtained from the olive-shaped fruit of the *Bassia latifolia*, or makwah tree, which grows in the sterile hilly regions on the Coromandel coast and Bengal, and especially in China. Another variety of *Bassia*, indigenous to the interior of Africa, produces a fat called *galam butter*, which is like palm oil.

*Cocoa-nut butter* is a solid fat of a white colour, and the consistence of hog's lard; it is obtained from the kernels of the cocoa-palm, which are called in commerce *copperah*, and contain about 60 per cent. of oil. The native countries of the cocoa-palm are Ceylon, the Maldive Islands, Siam, Malabar, and parts of Bengal, and also, it is said, Brazil. The total quantity imported in 1851 into Great Britain was 2799 tons.

The other important oils, of which we make mention here, are *olive oil*, obtained from the fruit of the *Olea Europæa*, a tree belonging to the same family of plants as the jasmine, and which is the sweet oil of commerce,—and, besides its use as a condiment, is employed in immense quantities in the preparation of wool; and *rape, colza, and cabbage oils*, obtained from the seeds of different species of the genus *Brassica*. Messrs. M'Garry and Son, of this city, were the only Irish exhibitors of rape oil, which they manufacture on a large scale. The chief use of these oils is for lighting purposes. *Poppy oil*, obtained from the seeds of the common poppy, is also a useful oil, resembling in many respects olive oil, for which it is often fraudulently substituted. The seeds of many other plants are also capable of yielding excellent oils, and are sometimes cultivated for that purpose, such as the mustard, the gold of pleasure, &c. The seed oils here spoken of are all, more or less, non-drying. Among the drying oils the most important is, undoubtedly, the oil of linseed, which is now being manufactured very largely in every part of the country.

Among the animal oils of greatest importance after tallow we may mention sperm oil, which is found mixed with the solid fatty substance known as spermaceti in the head of several kinds of whale, but especially in that of the *Physeter macrocephalus*. Messrs. Rathborne, of this city, who are among the oldest purifiers of sperm in these countries, exhibited an excellent series illustrative of the process of purification; among them was a magnificent pyramid of crystalized spermaceti, which formed one of the ornaments of the Centre Hall. Several other fish oils come into commerce and are used for a great many purposes,—such as seal oil, cod liver oil, and herring oil, which was formerly made in large quantities. A good deal might be done in this direction on our coasts if our fisheries were in an advanced condition.—W. K. S.

---

1. AITKEN, A. & M. L., Pinchbeck, near Spalding, Lincolnshire.—Flax, dressed in the raw state.

2. BROOK, JONAS, & BROTHERS, Meltham Mills, Huddersfield.—Specimens of raw cotton of different qualities.

3. CODY, P., Windsor Terrace, Portobello, Dublin.—Specimens of shells of various kinds employed in the manufacture of buttons.

4. DARGAN, WILLIAM, Mount Anville, Co. Dublin.—Three fleeces of wool of this year's clip, from sheep bred by exhibiter.

5. DAVIS, W. H. Newbury, Berkshire.—Specimens of South Down wool.

6. DAVY, EDWARD, Crediton, Devon, Flax-spinner and Manufacturer.—Specimens of flax and tow, prepared under a patent recently granted to exhibiter.

7. FRY, WILLIAM & Co., Westmoreland-street, Dublin.—Specimens of raw and thrown silk.

8. HUGHES, THOMAS & JAMES, Clonmel.—Samples of prepared flax.

9. KYLE, WILLIAM COTTER, Clare-street, Dublin.—Horns, skulls, &c., of wild animals from Cape of Good Hope.

10. LAWSON, THOMAS.—Specimens of Cheviot wool.

11. LEADBETTER, J., & Co., Belfast, Manufacturer.—Specimens illustrative of Watt's process for the preparation of flax; flax straw as from the field; flax straw with seed and capsules taken off and made ready for steam chambers; flax seed; flax seed capsules or husks; flax straws steamed in chambers; flax straw with epidermis removed by wet rolling; fibre after scutching.

12. MAHONY, M., & BROTHERS, Camden-place, Cork.—Irish wool in the fleece, and sorted; wool in the several stages of the spinning processes.

13. MARSH & EDENBOROUGH, Salvador House, Bishopsgate-street, London.—Colonial wools.

14. MILLNER, H., Blue Bell, Dublin.—Irish long and short wools for clothing and combing purposes.

15. MOSS, S. S., Kilternan Cotton Mill, Golden Ball, Co. Dublin.—Specimens of raw cotton.

16. M'GARRY & SON, Palmerstown Mills, near Dublin.—Specimens of rape oil produced by Exhibiters.

17. NELSON, J., & Co., Selby, Yorkshire.—Flax prepared on a new process, and dressed by improved machinery.

18. OGLEBY, CHARLES, & Co., Lambeth, London.—Refined spermaceti in block.

19. PRESTON, J., & Co., Belfast.—Samples of flax in the undressed state, grown in the counties of Down, Antrim, Monaghan, and Armagh.

20. PRICE'S PATENT CANDLE COMPANY, Belmont, Vauxhall, Surrey.—Specimens illustrating the Company's patent processes for making palm oil and other fatty substances into pure white candles by distillation, &c.; specimens of the palm oil fruit, and of vegetable tallows, butters, and waxes.

21. RATHBORNE, J. & J., Essex-street, Dublin.—Crude oil from the spermaceti whale, and specimens showing the different stages of manufacture; bees' wax; a block of refined spermaceti, illustrative of its crystallization.

22. ROYAL SOCIETY FOR THE PROMOTION AND IMPROVEMENT OF THE GROWTH OF FLAX IN IRELAND, Belfast, per JAMES MACADAM, Junior, Secretary.—Series of specimens illustrating the preparation of the flax plant for manufacturing purposes:—1. Flax straw, dried with the seed on. 2. Flax straw, after steeping; samples of seed; sample of seed capsules. 3. Flax straw, steeped and rolled for scutching; sample of scutching-tow. 4. Scutched flax fibre of various qualities. 5. Hackled flax fibre of various qualities. 6. Hackle tow of various qualities. 7. Line and tow *sliver*. Series of samples of foreign flax, used in the Irish linen manufacture, and of Irish and English flax, treated by peculiar processes, viz.:—Samples of Russian, Dutch, Belgian (Courtrai and Flemish), and Egyptian flax, in the scutched and hackled state; samples of English and Irish flax, prepared by the patent processes of Schenck (hot water), and of Watt (steaming), and of Irish flax, dried and steeped on the "Courtrai" system. Specimens of flax and flax cotton sent in 1774 to the Society of Arts by Lady Moira, of Montalto, Ballinahinch.

23. TUCKER, FRANCIS, & Co., Kensington, Middlesex.—Specimens of spermaceti, stearine, and margarine.

24. WHELAN & O'BRIEN, Dublin.—Samples of Irish grown hogget and wedder fleece wool, Wicklow mountain's wool; Australian wool; alpaca wools, white and brown.

# CLASS V.

## MACHINES FOR DIRECT USE, INCLUDING CARRIAGES, AND RAILWAY MECHANISM.

IN preceding pages we have discussed at length the department of Raw Materials as forming the great basis whence the others are primarily derived, and we now come to treat of the agents by which they are fashioned into the necessaries and luxuries of life; commencing with the class of objects which develop the application of a source or sources of power, either supplied from simple combinations of elementary agents, or obtained from applications of dynamical laws. The different kinds of articles coming under the general denominations of Machinery now claim our attention.

There were few parts of the Exhibition more attractive to the student or the merely curious observer than that devoted to machinery; and no part more interesting to the people of this country, as we saw there what makes man the ruler of insensate matter—not the exercise of the tyrant force of demoralizing warfare, but the power of increased intelligence and enterprise, and that agency which, in proportion to its extension amongst us, will not only increase our national wealth and capital, but will also bring moral blessings in its train. We need here hardly refer to the economic advantages of machinery, or point out the fallacies contained in the objection to its introduction or use amongst a people; as there are few who do not willingly, in the present day, admit them. He who contemplates, even superficially, the progress of mankind, must see that every step is supported by the aid of machinery. When Tubal-Cain first worked in metals he must have had recourse to simple machines to fashion his cunning workmanship. The Homeric age used machinery, and the war-chariot of Hector and the shield of Achilles required machinery to fashion them. In the loom of Penelope was contained an element as purely mechanical as that of Jacquard, the principle being gradually developed with advancing knowledge. The spade and the plough, the first implements of the warfare of man against stubborn nature, were as essentially machines as the winnowing, threshing, or reaping machines, of our own day; and we might as well expect to return to the times when men fought for acorns or dug roots with their hands from the earth, as to expect that machines should not be contrived, not alone to supplant, but to aid and further human labour. Temporary evils have, no doubt, frequently followed the use of machinery; but how small the evil compared with the amount of good. The first introduction of power-looms, threshing machines, stocking frames, and other machines, by substituting machine power for human agency, effected a temporary loss upon a class; but when we consider the enormously productive power at small cost, the diminution of human toil, the certainty of effect, the comfort and happiness distributed, we must feel strongly the blessings conferred upon mankind by these applications of human knowledge; and when we consider what machinery has done—and which could not be done without it—the working of mines, the propulsion of ships against wind and tide, the powers of locomotion it affords us on land, the methods of measuring time, and many other things which machinery alone can effect; we feel that if the curse of labour was inflicted on man as a punishment, the accompanying blessing was the intellectual power which enabled him to invent machinery to mitigate the infliction.

The effect of an examination of this department was also able to show us what we so much need—the cause of England's advance and our deficiency, and to teach us that it is only by competition in improvement we can hope to equal or excel other nations. The artisan who deplores the loss of work by the substitution of a machine for human labour could not fail to see, by a glance at the operation of many of the machines exhibited at work, the hopelessness of a contest between the two. If he inspected a crushing mill, he must have seen that it is in vain to hope to contend with machinery in the economic working of mining produce. If he saw a power loom or slubbing machine in operation, he might well despair of supplanting them by his own or fellow's labour. Hence, his mind would be at once set, not upon a competition hopeless and absurd, but to endeavour to apply machinery already invented, or improve what is defective in it. This has frequently been the effect on the minds of the more intelligent of our artisans; and we know cases in which great improvements were made in the machinery of poplin weaving and other manufactures by workmen studying machinery, guided by this spirit.

In considering the subject of machinery, there are different points of view in which it may be regarded. We may consider a machine as anything which alters the direction of a force; as when we alter a direct motion or force, such as that of gravity, the wind, or steam, into a circular one; or which apparently increases a power by making it act through a longer time or space. No machine actually increases or creates power. The force of the wind on the sails of a windmill, or of steam urging the piston of an engine, cannot be increased by any mechanical contrivance. It must be diminished; but the intervention of machinery, by altering the *direction* of the force, and converting a direct into a circular motion, applies the force, as we require it, to grind our corn or twist our thread, and in this way proves serviceable; or by the intervention of levers, by making a small power act through a great space, we produce effects otherwise unattainable.

## I.—STEAM-ENGINES, ETC.

The steam-engine, as the great source of motive power, must claim a large share of attention in the consideration of machinery generally. It may, in fact, be regarded as the prime agent of modern progress. The expansive power of steam and its applicability as a motive power were no sooner established than invention was on the rack to discover the most effective and economical means of turning it to account; and the improvements which have been introduced in the construction of the steam-engine during the present century have been fully commensurate with its great importance. Considerable modifications have been rendered necessary by the peculiar kind of the service required; and hence, few things can be more unlike than the engines which propel our vessels on the ocean and those through whose instrumentality conveyance upon our great iron highways is carried on. Yet the various forms of the steam-engine may be included in the two classes of condensing and non-condensing engines; or, as they are called, high and low pressure engines, from the circumstance of the steam in the one case, after having performed its functions, being discharged into the atmosphere, while, in the other, it passes into another vessel, where it is condensed, to form a vacuum.

To enter into a detailed account of the construction of the several modifications of the steam-engine would far exceed our present limits. With the exception of marine engines, the varieties in common use were represented in the Exhibition; while several specimens were entitled to high commendation for the ingenuity and excellence of workmanship which they displayed. The high pressure engine furnished by Messrs. Fairbairn and Co., and which supplied the motive power to the Machinery Court, was an excellent example of the class to which it belonged. Of the smaller sized engines there were also several good specimens; and to the satisfactory illustration of these we are disposed to attach considerable importance from the growing tendency which is now manifested in favour of the extended use of steam power. Even for farming purposes the steam-engine has become a desideratum from the great saving of labour which it effects, and the economy which it admits of being carried out. Wherever farming operations are extensively carried on, the use of the steam-engine has, in fact, become indispensable. And here, as well as in other cases, modifications have been introduced in accordance with the object sought to be attained. Of late, a useful kind of non-condensing engine has been brought to great perfection for such purposes. It somewhat resembles a railway locomotive engine; the difference being, that instead of motion being conveyed from the engine to a driving wheel, the wheels in this case merely serve for the transference of the engine from one place to another by extraneous power, and for its support when at work. An engine of this class was exhibited by Messrs. Barret, Exall, and Andrews, and was placed in the Agricultural Department. These engines are now supplied by most of the English manufacturers, the advantages which they are supposed to possess in admitting to be removed from place to place securing a considerable demand for them. It is, no doubt, very convenient to be able to take the threshing or other machinery to where the material to be operated on is situated rather than bring the material to the machine; and it might frequently be found desirable that several persons should join together in procuring such machinery in situations where the size of individual farms would not permit of the outlay being made for any one farm. On the relative advantages of fixed and movable engines for farming purposes there seems, however, to be no little difference of opinion; and on a review of the question this is only what might be expected from the great number of considerations involved. The movable engine is, in the first place, very expensive, and any work requiring to be done by machinery can rarely be so well executed in any other place as in the farm-yard.

## II.—APPLICATIONS OF CENTRIFUGAL FORCE.

We have next to direct attention to a class of machines possessing, from the wondrous effects they seem to produce from very slight causes, considerable interest, and which have lately come much into use for various familiar purposes—we mean the class of *Centrifugal Machines*, which comprise Pumps, Drying Machines, Blowers, Machines for refining Sugar—all of which were to be seen in operation in the Machinery Court, and were well calculated to excite astonishment in the mind of the spectator.

Before we notice one of the important applications of the principle used in this class of machinery, we may briefly explain the principle itself, which is a simple corollary from well-known mechanical laws.

When a particle or mass of matter is set in motion by any force in a given direction, its inertia will carry it forward in the direction of such force; and no change of direction or diminution of velocity can take place unless a new force or forces be applied. Hence it follows, that no particle of matter can revolve in a circle round a centre except under the action of two forces; one tending to move it in a tangential direction from the circle, the other to move it to the centre. When these forces balance each other exactly, the body moves in the circle; when the latter prevails, the mass or particle falls to the centre; when the former, it flies from the centre, and is hence said to be influenced by Centrifugal Force. Of these forces in a state of balance or equilibrium we have in nature examples in the planetary motions; the moon and other satellites, and the planets revolving round their centres of motion, under the action of these two forces. When we swing a ball attached to a string held in the hand, it is under the action of the force applied to set it swinging; which, were it unrestrained, would cause it to move only in a straight line, but the force of the string compels it to move in a direction intermediate between the direction of the two forces, and it revolves in a circle. If we cause it to revolve with great rapidity, and the string be let go or break, the ball will then move in the direction of one force, and will fly off in a straight line from the circle in which it previously revolved, and with a velocity and force corresponding to the speed at which it was moving. From the same cause, a servant's mop throws off from the cloth the particles of water adhering to it; the centrifugal force, when it is made revolve with rapidity, overcoming the cohesive attraction of the water and cloth.

Now, it will be evident from this explanation that the Centrifugal Force will be proportioned to the velocity of the system in motion, and that when air, water, or solid matter revolves round a centre, its tendency to leave that centre and fly off in a tangential direction will be in proportion to its velocity, and that in fact we can increase the force almost without limit by increasing the speed or velocity of motion. It would also appear, when a mass of matter in the form of a circular disc revolves, the force exerted on the particles of the mass increases as we pass from the centre towards the circumference; for this simple reason, that these move with a greater velocity or through a larger space than the particles nearer the centre, the velocity of each particle increasing directly as its distance from the centre of motion. In practice it is also found that the tendency of bodies to which motion is thus communicated is to fly from the centre around which they revolve with a force equal to the square of their velocity.

### THE CENTRIFUGAL PUMP.

It has just been stated that bodies in a state of rotation have a tendency to fly from their centre of motion with a force equal to the square of their velocity; and in employing this law for the elevation of water, it is manifest that a machine so constructed as to avoid leakage and friction, with a minimum degree of resistance, will accomplish all that can be effected by mechanical ingenuity.

In attempting to construct a centrifugal pump, a very large number of inventors have exhausted their skill in making arrangements of spiral or curved arms on an axle, or in endeavours to find the supposed angle or curve with the diameter, which the fluid would make in passing off, being apparently in ignorance of the fact that, in obedience to the law of centrifugal force, the escaping fluid takes the shortest line to reach the circumference; or, in other words, that each particle of matter in a state of rotation, when free to escape, moves directly in the line of the radius until it reaches the circumference, and thence follows the tangential line until influenced by gravity, or some other disturbing force.

In Gwynne's Pump the difficulties of previous attempts would appear to have been obviated. The centrifugal pump in the Exhibition was quick in action, small in size, compact in structure, capable of being placed in any situation, and of being applied to every description of work. Differing from the household pump, its power may be indefinitely increased, its volume of water made ample, and its flow continuous. Superior to the forcing pump, it has scarcely any appreciable friction; is not restricted in action by the intervention of an air chamber; and it has no parts which can easily get out of order, no useless reduplications of apparatus, and none which can in any degree impede the flow of water. It has a rotatory action, by which a centrifugal movement is given to the enclosed water, which it discharges in radial lines coincident with the direction of the centrifugal force, into a flattened spheroidal chamber, constituting the body of the pump; and this chamber has but one exit pipe, placed at a tangent with its circumference. The water, as it is thrown off from the open periphery of the revolving piston, is forced up the discharge pipe in quantities, and at a rate proportioned to the size of the pump and the speed at which the piston is driven.

In the construction of this pump the piston is formed of two concave discs, placed parallel, with their concave surfaces towards each other. Two saucers, placed in corresponding positions, would give a popular idea of the arrangement. Between these discs is a single arm or impeller, radiating from a boss or hollow axis, mounted on a shaft which works horizontally, vertically, or at any intermediate angle. The impeller, which regulates the distance between the discs of the piston, varies in breadth. Its narrowest part is at the outer edge of the piston, and it becomes gradually broader until its edge intersects the inner surface of the opening in the suction side of the piston, from which line to its extremity, at the boss, its edges continue parallel to each other, and at right angles to the axis of the shaft.' The discs, or inner surfaces of the piston, do not meet at their outer edges, but leave an annular opening around the whole circumference. This annular opening may be closed by a band of metal (or the whole piston may be cast in two halves); and in this band is cast a series of tangential openings. The form of piston may be varied, and the number of impellers and tangential openings increased, according to the diameter of the piston, and the nature of the substance required to be acted upon.

The piston is enclosed in a case of circular form, placed parallel and concentrically with the discs, and this case, which acts as a receiver, is bolted to any convenient stand or frame. From the circumference of the case or receiver rises, at a tangent with it, the perpendicular discharge pipe. The area of this receiver should exceed both those of the discharge pipe and of the annular openings on the circumference of the piston, in order that an uninterrupted flow of the water may be maintained; and to prevent the water from rotating in the case, and to give it a direction upwards to the discharge pipe, a stop or plate is placed on one side of the base of the discharge pipe, reaching from thence to the edge of the piston, and sometimes extending on both sides of the piston to the joint between the piston and the outer case, and generally in the line of direction of the radius of the piston. A space is also left between the side of the piston and that of the case, at least equal in size to that of the annular openings in the sides of the piston.

Around the opening in the sides of the piston is a collar or projection, extending outwards half way to the case. In the case is a circular hole, somewhat larger than the one in the piston, and through this hole is passed the suction pipe, which pipe is riveted or bolted to the outer case. The inner end of this pipe has cast on it a collar or projection corresponding in shape, and concentric with, the collar on the piston, and on its outer end is a flange or screw, to which any ordinary suction pipe may be attached. The joint between the suction pipe and piston being carefully made, and so situated that no sand, gravel, or other gritty matter can lodge on or near it, the wear is so reduced as to become imperceptible. The suction pipe may be curved at its outer end if desired, and its internal diameter may be made larger than the opening into the piston, so as to compensate for the bearings cast in it, and which carry the inner journal of the shaft. These bearings are made three or more times the length of their diameter, and the water lubricates them effectually, so that very little wear takes place. The joints between the pipe and piston may be made round, or at any desired angle. The bearings in the suction pipe form a small hollow cylinder inside the pipe and on the same axis with it, and it is supported by two or more arms extending from its exterior surfaces to the interior surface of the suction pipe. The whole pipe, with the bearing, cylinder, and its supports, are cast in one piece.

An important feature of this pump is its not being liable to go out of repair for years of continuous action. Nor will its efficacy be interfered with by sand or earthy matters in the water—a great advantage over the common pump, which is rendered useless when such obstructions are to be encountered. The quantity of water operated upon is also much greater than a given extent of power can propel with any other pump; while its simple construction enables it to be supplied at a comparatively moderate expense.

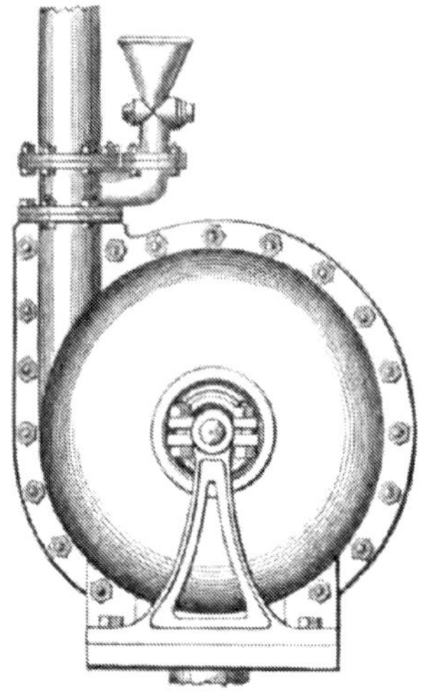

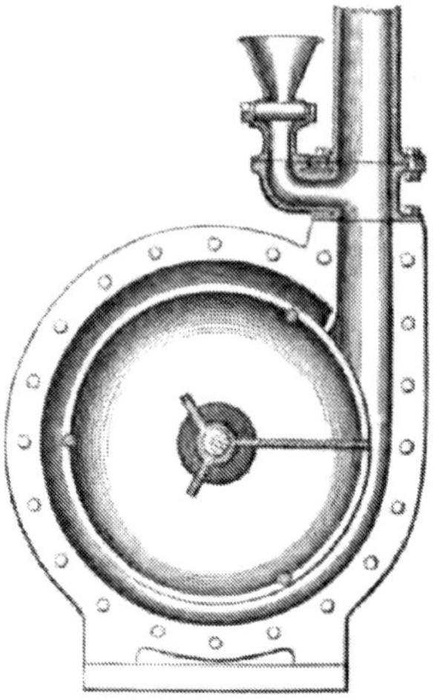

Fig. 2.

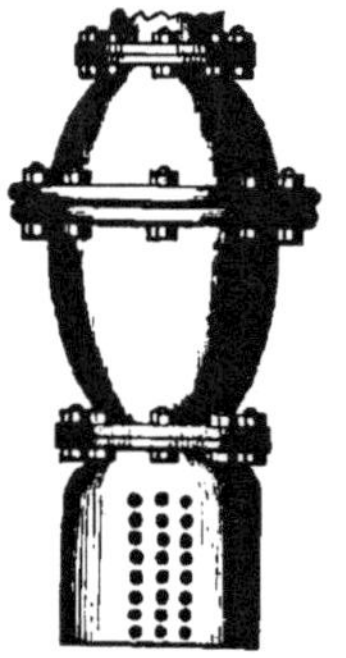

Fig. 1.

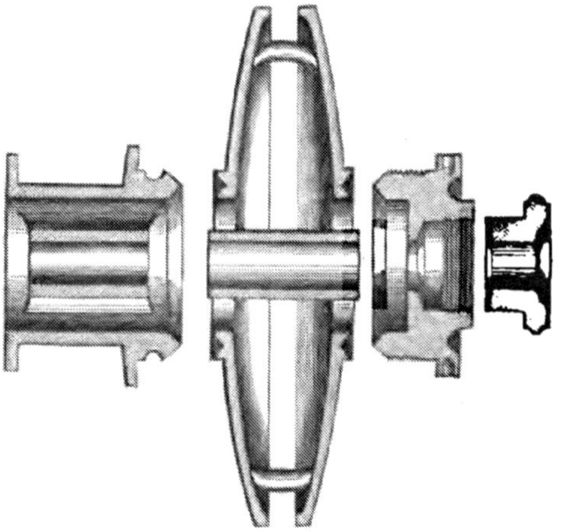

Fig. 3.

Illustrations of Gwynne's Centrifugal Pump.

The description here given will be readily understood by a reference to the accompanying engravings. An external view of the pump, with the valve to be attached, is shown in Fig. 1. Figures 2 and 3 are sections which so clearly illustrate the internal construction of the pump as not to require any further detailed reference to them.

The *Drying Machines* for cloth, sugar, &c., act on the same principle, only the motion is horizontal instead of vertical. For drying machines, a vessel of the form of a common washing tub, the sides made of perforated metal, is made to revolve within another vessel, on a vertical axis, with great velocity. The cloth to be dried is placed in the interior vessel, and the centrifugal force causes the water to rush out with great rapidity; and by means of a current of warm air passed in at the centre of the machine, complete drying of the cloth may be effected. Sugar also may be dried, and is to a large extent in practice—its liquid impurities being removed by a similar application of these simple principles. The operation of the Centrifugal Machine in separating molasses from sugar is one of great interest, from its effectiveness, and the despatch with which it is accomplished. A mass of crystallised sugar, when in the molasses, is unforbidding in appearance; and those unacquainted with the manufacture might well be at a loss to know how the one was to be separated from the other. But on this semi-fluid substance being placed in the centrifugal machine, it has only to be a few minutes in rapid motion, when the sugar will be found forming a coating in the inside of the machine something like the porcelain lining of saucepans, the whole of the molasses being driven through the perforated sides of the cylinder. This class of machines was represented by those contributed by Messrs. Manlove, Alliott, and Co., of Nottingham.

## III.—RAILWAY MACHINERY AND PERMANENT WAY.

The construction and maintenance of railways have now become great branches of industry, affording scope for the display of talent of the highest order, as well as giving employment to thousands of our population. The value of the experience which has been derived from the working of the railway system may be estimated from the great difference which appears between present and past estimates for construction and maintenance. For years after the opening of the Liverpool and Manchester Railway, the great item of expenditure was in the introduction of improvements; as no sooner was some new modification made than it was superseded by something else. Of late, great and satisfactory progress has been made, more especially in the construction of what is called the rolling stock. But in the formation of the permanent way the prevailing practice of using wood as the sleepers for the iron rails seems opposed to the spirit of the age, which is so much in favour of the extended use of iron wherever practicable. The perishable nature of wood under such circumstances is a great drawback. Hence the adaptation of any use of iron for this purpose which would seem to fulfil the desired requirements is of great value. The growing conviction of engineers that iron may be substituted for wood as a railway sleeper—even where wood is most favourably circumstanced as to ballast, drainage, and climate; and that the employment of iron becomes an imperative necessity where the sleeper is exposed to a burning sun, a destroying insect, to rapid or extreme changes of temperature,—leaves little to be desired by those interested in the employment of iron for that purpose.

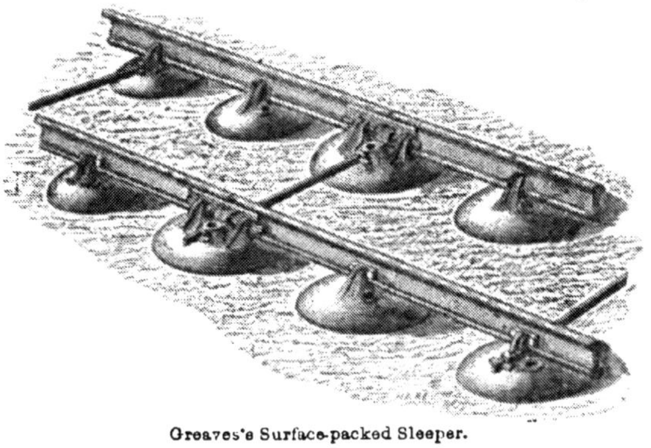

Greaves's Surface-packed Sleeper.

The accompanying illustrations represent one of the most valuable inventions that have yet been brought before the public for substituting iron for wood in the construction of railways,—the surface-packed sleeper of Mr. Greaves, with the fish-joint chair, patented by Mr. Douglas. The general arrangement is shown in the first engraving; by which the way in which the rails are supported and joined together is indicated. The distances between the ties and supports may be easily regulated according to the general construction of the line and character of the traffic; the tie bars being so placed as to preserve the working angle or tilt, and the perfect gauge of the rails.

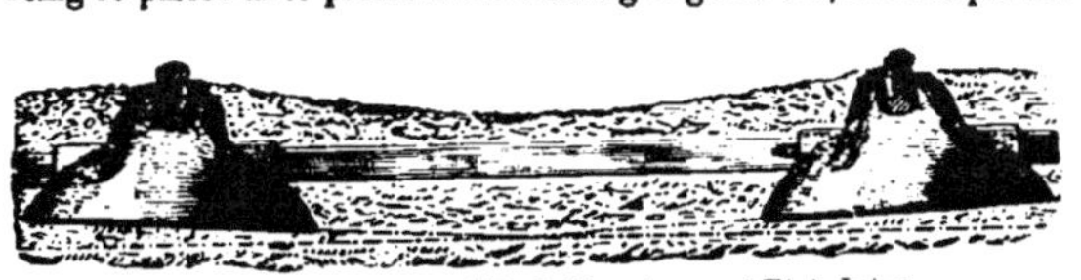

Section of Sleeper, and End Elevations of Fish-Joint.

The form of the sleeper and end elevation of the fish joint are seen in the annexed engraving. The conical form of the sleeper admits of a given strength being secured with the smallest amount of metal, while the elasticity derivable from the use of wood is thereby secured. The ballast supporting the sleeper being always dry, it yields to the pressure of the train when passing over, which is hence distributed over a large area. The position of the sleeper and connecting rods, in relation to the ballasting of the line, is also shown in the figure, the rails only appearing above the surface. The construction of the fish-joint is further illustrated by the sketch of the side elevation in the margin. One obvious advantage of this joint is the facility with which it permits the removal of a defective or worn out rail without disturbing the sleeper or ballast.

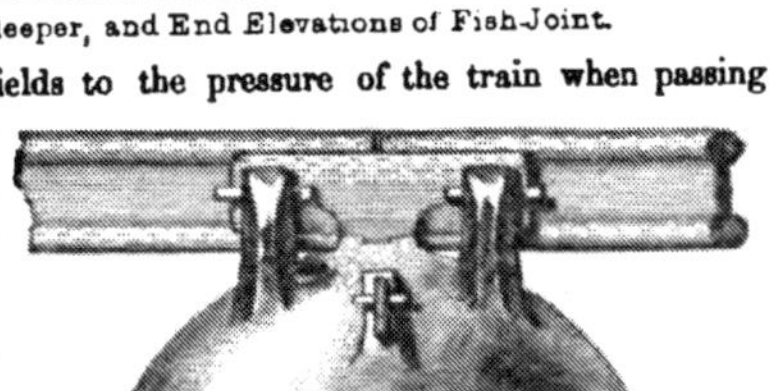

Side Elevation of Fish-Joint.

The leading consideration which will occur to every one in reference to the use of the cast iron sleeper is its great durability; and it appears that the prime cost of laying down a line of rails in this way is not greater than with wood. By many of the leading engineers it has been adopted, and with uniform success, the experience of the three or four years during which it has been in use leading to its gradual extension.

## IV.—CARRIAGES.

The Carriage Department of the Exhibition was a highly satisfactory one; presenting as it did a variety of carriages from the best manufacturers both in this country and in England. Comparing the illustration of the Department here with that of 1851, we find that in Hyde Park there were altogether 100 exhibiters, of whom 69 belonged to the United Kingdom, the remaining 31 exhibiters being distributed over eleven foreign countries. The total number of carriages, not including Bath chairs, velocipedes, sleighs, and some of those other articles not much in use, was only 107, of which 79 belonged to exhibiters in the United Kingdom. And now coming to our own Exhibition we find that there were 32 exhibiters in it, who contributed over 60 carriages of different kinds. Of these 18 were Irish and 14 belong to different parts of Great Britain. In the Belgian department there were two handsome carriages contributed by Jones, Brothers, of Brussells, the only specimens of foreign workmanship in this department in the Exhibition.

Carriage building is a department of industry in which there is a greater degree of equality between the character of the work of the metropolis, and that of the provincial towns, than, perhaps, in any other. The finest specimens of workmanship find their way almost to all parts of the country, and the local coach-maker is thereby furnished with a sort of standard for imitation. The vehicles turned out by Hutton and Sons, Magill, and Quan, of this city, and Bathurst of Belfast, were in every way creditable specimens of workmanship. In the carriages exhibited there was little of novelty, with one or two exceptions. Some improvements, however, were manifest in the form of the smaller class of carriages, in which a main object is to combine economy and convenience. When alluding to form we may observe, "that the coach builders of the present day have had no easy task to perform in meeting the new demands of the age, which require them to construct vehicles to convey the greatest number of persons. It can hardly be expected that in carriages of such a description they can preserve those outlines which have been esteemed elegant and graceful."* In reference to price, the authority from which we here quote remarks that "it is obviously very difficult to determine the exact intrinsic value of an article like a carriage, and to judge positively whether the affixed price is excessive or not. The cost is often much increased by ornament, finish, or contrivance, that might advantageously be dispensed with, and thus a carriage, otherwise extravagant in price, be reduced to a standard of reasonable cheapness. Extravagant prices may fairly diminish their claim for approval; but at the same time we are convinced that what may be deemed high prices are not always exorbitant prices, but that, with carriages as with household furniture, the lowest priced may often prove to be the dearest purchase."

There is one circumstance in connexion with this department which we cannot pass without a remark, and that is the very indefinite notions which the names used by carriage builders, as applied to their goods, convey. Any one who took the trouble to compare the several articles with the descriptions given by the exhibiters must have found certain names applied to carriages which have undoubtedly but few features in common; while in other cases vehicles, apparently identical in construction, differing merely in upholstery and decoration, are distinguished by very different names. Even those specially acquainted with carriage building are not less put about than the general public by this absurd nomenclature. It has its origin, no doubt, in the folly of the public in hunting after novelty; as a manufacturer has only to give some fancy name to a new carriage, introducing at the same time some slight modification in the construction of it, to secure the patronage of unthinking customers.

Among the vehicles in the Carriage Court, which challenged more than ordinary attention from the visitor, was one of the Bianconi cars, so familiar to travellers in the South and West of Ireland. There is little in this vehicle to attract special notice, further than it is one of the numerous "long cars" which occupy many of the leading lines of road in twenty-one counties of Ireland; the establishment presenting one of the most extraordinary instances to be found of a great conveyance organization by a single individual.† The career of Mr. Bianconi supplies a striking illustration of what may be effected by prudent enterprise and well-directed industry. A stranger to the country, with little capital, and without any fortuitous advantages, he commenced his career in Ireland in a very humble way; and got on step by step, adding to his savings, gradually acquiring capital, and extending in proportion his field of operations, until he has at length acquired an ample fortune, besides being greatly instrumental in promoting the improvement of the country of his adoption. Commencing with running a car for the conveyance of passengers from Clonmel to Cahir, one after another was added to the establishment until the whole of the South and West was traversed by these vehicles. The extension of railway communication caused the long cars to be taken off many of their original lines, but it was only to extend them in other directions. The Bianconi cars now go as far north as Strabane; the north-eastern division of the island being in fact the only part of it through which they do not run. Up to the present time the establishment has gone on steadily increasing; and there are now not less than 2000 persons employed in it. The consummate tact and judgment exhibited in the management of this immense organization are not less to be admired than the enterprise which planned it. Kindness to and consideration for the employees have secured willing and faithful services. Mr. Bianconi's coaching establishment may in truth be regarded as amongst the most remarkable of the social institutions of the age.

* Jurors' Report of the Exhibition of 1851.

† At the meeting of the British Association, held in Cork in 1843, a paper was read by Mr. Bianconi in the Statistical Section, and attracted great attention at the time from the curious facts which it disclosed. The matter being one of permanent interest, an outline of that paper will not be out of place in these pages:—

"Up to the year 1815, the public accommodation for the convenience of passengers in Ireland was confined to a few mail and day coaches on the great line of road.

"From my peculiar position in the country, I had ample opportunities of reflecting on many things, and nothing struck me more forcibly than the great vacuum that existed in travelling accommodation between the different orders of society.

"The inconvenience felt for the want of more extended means of intercourse, particularly from the interior of the country to the different market towns, gave great advantage to the few, at the expense of the many; and above all, great loss of time. For instance, a farmer living twenty or thirty

Among the novelties of this department of the Exhibition the most remarkable was a jaunting car exhibited by Mr. Killinger of Westland-row, an article which, as our readers are aware, is peculiarly Irish. We annex an engraving of this car, from which it will be seen that, by an exceedingly simple modification, the

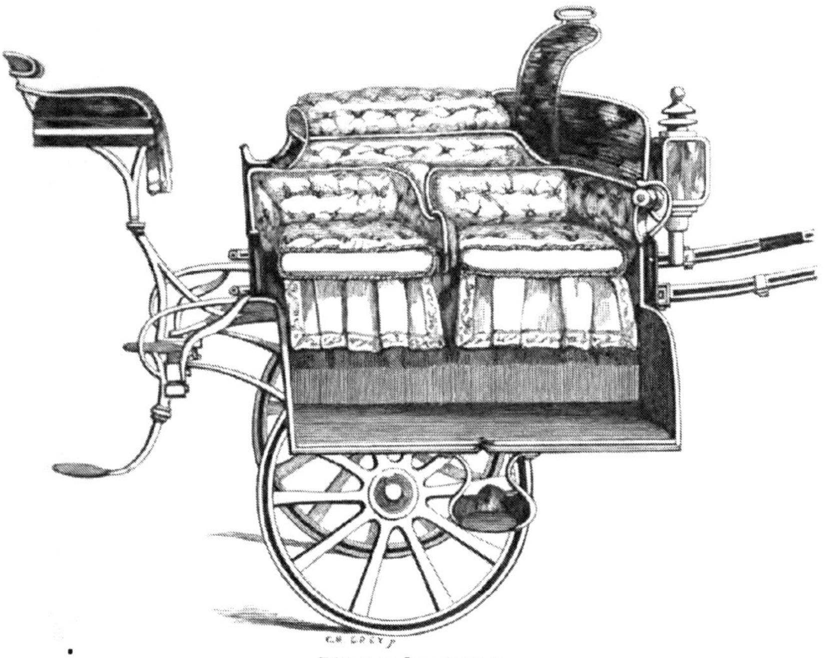

Killinger's Jaunting Car.

driver's seat is transferred from the front to the rere of the car; somewhat after the arrangement adopted in Hansom's cabs, which have been so long in use in London, and some of which may occasionally be seen in

miles from his market town, spent the day in riding to it, a second day doing his business, and a third day returning.

"In July, 1815, I started a car for the convenience of passengers, from Clonmel to Cahir, which I subsequently extended to Tipperary and Limerick; at the end of the same year, I started similar cars from Clonmel to Cashel and Thurles, and from Clonmel to Carrick and Waterford; and I have since extended this establishment, including the most insulated localities, namely, from Longford to Ballina and Belmullet, which is 201 miles north-west of Dublin; from Athlone to Galway and Clifden, 183 miles due west of Dublin; from Limerick to Tralee and Cahirciveen, 233 miles south-west of Dublin; and numbering 100 vehicles, including mail coaches and different-sized cars, capable of carrying from four to twenty passengers each, and travelling eight or nine miles an hour, at an average fare of 1¼d. per mile for each passenger, and performing daily 3800 miles, passing through over 140 stations for the change of horses, consuming 3000 to 4000 tons of hay, and from 30,000 to 40,000 barrels of oats annually, all of which are purchased in their respective localities.

"This establishment does not travel on Sundays, unless such portions of it as are in connexion with the Post Office or canals, for the following reasons:—First, the Irish, being a religious people, will not travel on business on Sundays; and secondly, experience teaches me that I can work a horse eight miles per day, six days in the week, much better than I can six miles for seven days.

"The advantages derived by the country from this establishment are almost incalculable; for instance—the farmer, who formerly rode, and spent three days in making his market, can now do so in one, for a few shillings; thereby saving two clear days, and the expense and use of his horse.

"The example of this institution has been generally followed, and cars innumerable leave the interior for the principal towns in the south of Ireland, which bring parties to and from markets at an enormous saving of time; and in many instances cheaper than they could walk it.

"This establishment is now in existence twenty-eight years, travelling with its mails at all hours of the day and night, and never met any interruption in the performance of its arduous duties. Much surprise has often been expressed at the high order of men connected with it, and at its popularity; but parties thus expressing themselves forget to look at Irish society with sufficient grasp. For my part I cannot better compare it than to a man merging to convalescence from a serious attack of malignant fever, and requiring generous and nutritive, in place of medical treatment. Thus I act with my drivers, who are taken from the lowest grade of the establishment, and who are progressively advanced according to their respective merits, as opportunity offers, and who know that nothing can deprive them of this reward, and a superannuated allowance of their full wages in old age, and under accident, unless their wilful and improper conduct; and as to its popularity, I never yet attempted to do an act of generosity or common justice, publicly or privately, that I was not met by reciprocity."

this city. The desired command is at once had over the horse. The driver, moreover, has everything completely within view, by which he is not only enabled to guard against any obstacle in the way, but to attend to the wishes of the occupants of the car in a much more effectual manner than under the ordinary arrangements; and his own position in relation to those whom he is driving is not in any degree obnoxious to the charge of being offensive to good taste, which is not the case with the common jaunting car. Nor can there be any objection to this arrangement on the ground of alleged undue interference with the draught of the car or weight on the back, as this is easily regulated by the position of the axle.

A. Menzies, of Glasgow, has rendered no small service to this department of the Exhibition by placing in it one of the omnibuses in use in that city; as it, in many respects, is a great improvement on the vehicles of the same class to be met elsewhere. Those who are familiar with the London omnibuses will recollect the great variety of forms of that useful carriage which has occasionally come before the public; but among the whole of these we certainly recollect none which combines so many of the requirements of such a vehicle as that to which we now refer, which, in height, width, and arrangements for ventilation, is almost everything that could be desired. It is drawn by three horses abreast, an arrangement of the horse-power not practised in either London or this city.—J. S.

---

1. BARRETT, EXALL, & ANDREWS, Reading, Manufacturers.—Portable steam-engine for agricultural purposes.

2. BELFAST IRON COMPANY, per T. M. GLADSTONE, C. E., Belfast, Manufacturers.—Patent double T wrought-iron for beams and joists of fire-proof warehouses, &c., instead of cast-iron.

3. BOAKE & REILY, Dublin, Inventors and Manufacturers.—Railway signal post, constructed of iron framework, with acrometric lamp.

4. BOYD, W., Jun., Walworth, Grand Canal, Dublin, Proprietor.—Model steam-engine, exhibited for superior workmanship.

5. CARRETT, MARSHALL, & CO., Sun Foundry, Leeds.—"Patent steam-pump," or "water lift," size, No. 3 A; can raise 22,000 gallons 50 feet high in ten hours, producing a continuous stream; applicable also for supplying steam-boilers with water.

6. DILLON, J., Upper Buckingham-street, Dublin, Inventor.—Improved railway break.

7. DRAKE, THOMAS, & SON, Aston's-quay, Dublin, Inventors & Manufacturers.—Portable fire-engine for ships' use, in wetting sails, pumping water out of tanks in hold, &c., with suction, hose, hand-pipe, and leather bucket; double barrel full waterway pumping-engine, with frame, fly wheel, crank, and pinion motion, and valves attached to movable doors for repairing without disturbing any of the works; Kirkwood's improved tubular water-closet, on cast-iron frame.

8. DUNN, HATTERSLEY, & CO., Windsor Bridge Iron Works, Manchester.—Models and drawings of patent turn-tables and traversers, for removing engine from one line of rail to another.

9. EASTWOOD & FROST, Railway Iron Works, Derby, Manufacturers.—Kirtley's patent rolled spoke solid wrought-iron railway wheels.

10. ELLIOTT, J., Division-street, Sheffield.—Quadrant weighing machine, adapted to both English and French weights.

11. FAIRBAIRN, WILLIAM, & CO., Manchester.—A 50 horse high-pressure engine (ordered by the Committee of the Great Industrial Exhibition for driving the machinery in motion); a wrought-iron tubular crane.

12. FARRELL, I., Fleet-street, Dublin, Inventor.—Model of improved railway break.

13. FIRE ANNIHILATOR CO., The Leadenhall-street, London, Exhibiters.—Phillip's patent fire annihilator.

14. GILSON, O., Dublin.—Model of self-acting break for railway passenger trains.

15. GOMPERTZ, LEWIS, The Oval, Kennington, near London, Inventor.—Prints of mechanical inventions on land and water locomotion, railway transit tooth machinery, and other objects.

16. GREAVES, H., Palatine Buildings, Manchester, Inventor and Proprietor.—Patent cast-iron surface packed sleepers, with various forms of joint sleepers and joint fastenings.

17. GREGORY, REV. Dr. T., Paget Priory, Kilcock.—Drawing and section of an improved locomotive passenger engine, by Val. Tighe Gregory, Esq., Superintendent of the locomotive department, St. Petersburgh and Moscow Railway.

18. GRENDON, T., & CO., Drogheda, Manufacturers.—Direct acting pumping engine: diameter of steam cylinder, 10 inches; of pump, 5 inches; length of stroke, 10 inches. Portable double cylinder, high-pressure, and condensing engine, 45 horse-power, on M'Naught's patent principle: diameter of condensing cylinder, 28 inches; length of stroke, 4 feet 6 inches; diameter of high-pressure cylinder, 25 inches. Improved upright tubular boiler for 45 horse engine. Agricultural steam engine, 4 horse-power.

19. GUY, R., Rutland Mills, Rutland Avenue, Dolphin's Barn Bridge, Dublin, Manufacturer.—Improved oiling-axles for Broughams, outside cars, &c.; improved mail patent axles.

20. GWYNNE, SON, & CO., Essex Wharf, Strand, London, Proprietors and Manufacturers.—Gwynne's patent centrifugal pump, with fittings, &c. This pump has a rotary movement, and works without valves.

21. HEWITT, T., Cork, Inventor and Proprietor.—Model of a mashing ton; the steam is applied whilst the machinery is in motion.

22. HUXHAMS & BROWN, Exeter, Inventors and Manufacturers.—Neck-winch, with two wooden rollers and ends.

23. IRISH ENGINEERING COMPANY, Seville Iron Works, Seville-place, Dublin, Manufacturers.—A vertical, direct acting, portable, high-pressure steam-engine and boiler, complete, on one bed-plate.

24. LAWRENCE, CHARLES, North Cumberland-street, Dublin, Manufacturer.—Small high-pressure steam-engine.

25. LEES, T., & SONS, Mottram-street, Stockport, Inventors and Manufacturers.—Compressed air alarm whistle.

26. MALLET, R., Engineer, Dublin, Inventor and Manufacturer.—Patent wrought-iron buckled plate for fire-proof and other floors; specification enrolled April, 1853.

27. MILLER, G. M., Engineer, Great Southern and Western Railway.—Portable high-pressure engine and boiler, with pumps, as used on the Great Southern and Western Railway.

28. PALMER, E. O., 8, Lower Dominick-street, Dublin, and Tralee, Inventor.—Model of self-acting break for railway carriages.

29. PEILE, J. J., Whitehaven, Inventor and Manufacturer.—Improved ships' screws for stowing ships' cargoes, &c.; turnip-cutters, with oil-cake crusher; straw or chaff cutter.

29. POLLEN, H., 10, Serpentine-avenue, near Dublin, Inventor and Proprietor.—Improved double railway signal lamp for night, and arms for day.

30. POOLEY, H., Albion Foundry, Liverpool, Manufacturer.—Patent dormant platform weighing machine; portable weighing machines on wheels, &c.; computer balance, dispensing with loose weights; indicator of large weighbridges for road or railway waggons; counter scales and weights; bankers' weighing machines, to weigh from 1 to 1000 sovereigns.

31. ROCK, J., JUN., Hastings, Sussex, Inventor and Proprietor.—Drawings of a patent railway carriage; model of patent railway buffers; goods' trucks, with patent tarpaulin roller; the simultaneous carriage step; a patent spring.

32. ROSS & MURRAY, Abbey-street, Dublin, Manufacturers.—Double-acting pump.

33. ROURKE, E., Dublin.—Small hydraulic ram.

34. SAMUELSON, M., & Co., Hull, Engineers.—Hydraulic press for extracting oil from seed, and making oil-cake; double kettle, for heating the seed; and small table steam-engine to work the press.

35. SAUNDERS, J. M., Dublin, Inventor.—A new railway guard alarm signal, for communicating between railway guard and engine-driver.

36. SEWARD, N., Cahirconlish, Pallasgreen, Co. Limerick, Inventor.—Model railway, forty-eight feet long and one foot wide, with reservoir carriages and small engine.

37. SHAND & MASON, Blackfriar's-road, London, Inventors and Manufacturers.—Patent ship fire-engine.

38. SHEKELTON, J., Dundalk, Manufacturer.—18 horse-power portable high-pressure steam-engine; 4 horse-power horizontal high-pressure steam-engine; upright tubular steam boiler.

39. SHERIDAN, THOMAS, Dublin.—Portable two-horse high-pressure steam-engine.

40. SHULDHAM, M., Portished, Bristol, Inventor.—Models of apparatus for an improvement in the mechanic power of the wheel and axle, and for transmitting power by ropes.

41. SIMPSON & SHIPTON, Manchester, Inventor.—8 horse-power reciprocating steam-engine; an excentric revolves in its own diameter, this being the most direct method of obtaining circular motion from the rectilinear. The chief features of this invention are economy in space, first cost, and consumption of fuel.

42. SLOAN & LEGGETT, T. J., Empire Iron Works, New York, Manufacturers.—Patent hydrostat for preventing steam-boiler explosions, invented by T. J. Sloan, 28, St. George's Road, New Kent-road, London.

43. THORNTON, J., and SONS, Birmingham, Manufacturers.—Hydraulic lifting jacks; improved railway screw and other jacks; railway signal and other lamps; miners' safety lamp; railway carriage wrench; Thornton and M'Connell's patent waggon couplins, &c.; exhibiters of Stirling's patent gun-metal for bearings; toughened cast-iron; hardened rails; tin zinc; leaded zinc; and Britannia metal; also Wright's patent ropes, &c.; Griffith's and Co.'s patent painted trays in oil; and tea service, made of patent tin zinc.

44. TURNER, R., Nassau-street, Dublin, Manufacturer.—A pendulous oscillating double cylinder high-pressure steam-engine, 1 horse-power.

45. TYLOR, J., & SON, Warwick-lane, London, Manufacturers.—Soda water machine, and bottling apparatus; diving machine and dresses; ships' fire-engines.

46. WARNER, J., & SONS, Jewin Crescent, London, Manufacturers and Proprietors.—Cast-iron frames, with wheel and pinion, and pumps for raising water to any height; overshot copper water-wheel, with three force-pumps; Warner's improved ship force-pump, or fire-engine; patent lift and force-pumps; church bells; London fire brigade engine; water-closets; water, gas, and steam-cocks, gauges, valves, unions, &c.; screw-down high-pressure cocks; garden syringes; gun-metal imperial standard measures and weights; plumber's cocks; steam and gas cocks.

47. WATT, F., and Co., London-street, London, and Birmingham, Manufacturers.—Working model of a locomotive engine, made by M'Murdoch, of Soho, in 1785, showing the application of steam to locomotion, as patented by Mr. Watt, in 1784; model of an oscillating engine, made in 1785, to illustrate Mr. Watt's patent of 1784 for making the cylinder work on an axis; machine invented by Mr. Watt about 1790, for registering continuously the successive but varying lengths of stroke in mining pumps.

## CARRIAGES.

1. ANDREWS, P., Gt. Brunswick-street, Dublin, Manufacturer.—A coach-car; an outside car; a family car; a velocipede.

2. ANNESLEY, R., Grafton-street, Dublin, Manufacturer.—Bath and Albert chairs, with hoods, aprons, and other fittings, &c.

3. BATES, E., Gorey, Co. Wexford, Manufacturer.—Self-balancing tax-cart.

4. BATHURST, W., Belfast, Manufacturer—A light step-piece-shaped park barouche, mounted on full C and under springs, with hind standard; a full-sized Basterna landau, with coach-box and hind seat, mounted on platform springs behind, elliptic do. in front, and self-acting steps to the body; a light Victoria-shaped pony phaeton, with hind rumble and large side splash-guards.

5. BIANCONI, C., Longfield, Co. Tipperary, Proprietor.—A fly mail car, used by Mr. Bianconi for the conveyance of mails and passengers, in 19 counties of the north, south, and west of Ireland.

6. BRUBIE, J., East Lothian Coach Works, Haddington, Inventor and Manufacturer.—Patent dog-cart, with shifting apparatus enabling the driver to regulate the weight on the horse's back without leaving his seat; the wheels and springs of an improved construction.

7. BROWNE, W., Gt. Brunswick-street, Dublin, Manufacturer.—A Basterna pilentum, forming a close or an open carriage; a Malvern cart, to carry four persons with luggage or dogs; a pony phaeton, with movable driving seat; an outside jaunting-car, built on the same principle as the one for which exhibiter was awarded the prize medal at the Exhibition of 1851.

8. BUCHANAN, J. & Co., Glasgow, Manufacturer.—An Australian dog-cart.

9. COATES, BLIZARD, & Co., Park-lane, Piccadilly, London, Designers and Manufacturers.—The Royal Maude Barouche, a new style of open carriage.

10. DAWSON, J. S., & SONS, Sackville-place, Dublin, Manufacturers.—A Clarence Brougham, with circular front; park phaeton; outside jaunting-car; a cab.

11. DILLON, J., Grafton-street, Dublin, Manufacturer and Proprietor.—A "Hansom" safety cab, the first built in Ireland; an outside jaunting-car.

12. DORAN, THOS., Upper Ormond-quay, Dublin, Manufacturer.—A light driving phaeton (Queen's pattern); a family outside car, with well, movable driver's seat, &c.

13. GORDON, J. F., Strangford, Co. Down, Inventor.—A four-wheeled carriage, with a new kind of fore axle, called "*The Caster Axle.*"

14. GRADY, R. E., Dawson-street, Dublin, Manufacturer.—An emempton, forming a close or open carriage at pleasure; a light driving phaeton; an outside car, with grass-hopper springs, &c.

15. HALLMARKE, ALDEBERT, & HALLMARKE, Long-acre, London, Manufacturers.—A circular-fronted Brougham; a park phaeton.

16. HOOPER, W., Haymarket, London, Designer and Manufacturer.—Working model of an elliptic spring Brougham.

17. HUTTON, J., & SONS, Summer Hill, Dublin, Manufacturers.—A dress coach, fully appointed for town use, built for Her Majesty; a chariot; a barouche, on C and under springs; an outside car with lancewood and whalebone shafts.

18. JOHNSON, JOHN, Leinster-street, Dublin, Manufacturer.—A town chariot.

19. KILLINGER, C., Westland-row, Dublin, Designer and Manufacturer.—Killinger's Irish jaunting car (registered); park phaeton.

20. LONGBOTTOM, R. I., Mortimer-street, London, Inventor and Manufacturer.—Noiseless carriage-wheel, with engine-turned iron tire, and vulcanized India-rubber band (Thomson's patent): truck wheels; model showing the method of fixing the India-rubber tire; piece of tire in use for above two years on a street cab in London, having travelled about 15,000 miles.

21. MAGILL, G., Redmond's Hill, Dublin, Manufacturer.—A Clarence; Brougham, with segmental front and back; a pony phaeton; outside car, with slides and screw by which the balance can be adjusted for or without a driver.

22. MAGILL, J., Mercer-street, Dublin, Inventor and Manufacturer.—Brougham, with semicircular glass front, affording an additional seat: sporting phaeton: a car on a new principle, adapted to carry seven persons.

23. MASON, W. H., Clapton, and Kingsland-road, London, Manufacturer.—A light mail phaeton.

24. MENZIES, A., Glasgow.—Omnibus and harness, capable of carrying seventeen inside and eighteen outside passengers.

25. MOLLOY, B., Kildare-street, Dublin, Proprietor.—A pedomotive, made in Bristol.

26. NEWENHAM, B., Broad-street, Bath, Designer and Manufacturer. — Three-wheeled bath invalid wheel chair, with patent ventilated head, &c.; a reclining spinal bed wheel chair.

27. NUTMAN, I., Lower Dorset-street, Dublin, Designer and Manufacturer.—Models of pedestrian carriages; an accelerator; and an improved pedomotive.

28. OFFORD, R., Wells-street, Oxford-street, London.—Crystal barouche; Clarence carriage.

29. PETERS, T., & SONS, London, Designers and Manufacturers.—A double Brougham, for one or a pair of horses; a single Brougham, for one or a pair of horses; a mail driving phaeton.

30. QUAN & SONS, Talbot-street, Dublin, Manufacturers.—Mail phaeton; a segmental-fronted Brougham, with improved lock; pony phaetons; outside cars (one similar to that ordered by His Royal Highness Prince Albert); pilentum phaeton; light phaeton for a pony.

31. ROCK & SON, Hastings, Sussex, Manufacturers.—Improved pony carriage with patent spring, invented by James Rock, Jun.; drawings of the patent diorpha carriage.

32. THOMSON, G., Stirling, Designer and Manufacturer.—Phaeton for one or two horses; lever balancing dog-cart, for regulating the weight upon the horse.

33. THORN, W. & F., John-street, Oxford-street, London, Inventors and Manufacturers.—An improved Brougham, with patent æquimotive springs and new carriage ventilator.

# CLASS VI.

## MANUFACTURING MACHINES AND TOOLS.

HAVING in the preceding Class, which illustrates the development of manufacturing power, considered the influence and general bearing of machinery upon social progress, any further remarks on this topic are unnecessary in this place; and from the limited space available for the present class it would be a hopeless task to attempt to convey an idea of the action of many of the machines included in this department.

It will be observed that by the division of Machinery into two classes it was designed to separate those agents which may be said to develop power to be further applied, from the machines which perform certain specific operations, such as carding, spinning, weaving, and the like. The peculiar characteristic of those belonging to the present class is, that they effect what was previously accomplished by human labour; and not only has the means of production been thereby almost indefinitely extended, but the cost has been at the same time diminished, and a certainty of operation has, in many cases, been established, rivalling, if not exceeding, anything depending upon human skill. The applications of machinery are increasing every day, and that to purposes which a short time ago it would have been regarded as simply impossible to effect by such means. The sewing machine is among the latest triumphs in this direction, the satisfactory working of which was illustrated in the Exhibition; and an examination of the simple and regular manner in which it performed its work could not fail to suggest the almost unlimited extension of such agency.

The representation of this department of the Exhibition was satisfactory; a great variety of machinery being in operation a portion of every day. In those for textile fabrics the different processes were illustrated, from the preparation of the raw material through the spinning and weaving, until the finished article was produced. Cotton, linen, and silk goods were produced in variety. Of looms there were several at work; some weaving the coarsest articles, and others ribbons and poplins. Printing presses of all kinds were in operation; and the publication of the "Expositor" weekly, during the whole period the Exhibition remained open, conveyed to thousands of visitors an accurate idea of printing machinery. The space at our disposal will not, however, admit of noticing the contents of this department in detail, to do which indeed would occupy a volume; and, following the course adopted with the previous class, we must rest satisfied with noticing a few of the articles, the whole of which, however, will be found enumerated in the Catalogue.

### FLAX-DRESSING MACHINES.

Up to a comparatively recent period the practice of the flax industry has been purely empirical, and mechanical science did little to economize the cost of production. Hence the great difficulty which attended its extension to districts where the growth of the crop was hitherto little known. By long habit the small farmers of some parts of Ulster attained a considerable degree of perfection in this branch of rural economy, though entirely ignorant of the principles involved in their management, and performing the whole work by manual labour. As consumption increased, and competition on the part of other countries extended, it became obvious that economy of production must be attended to, otherwise this branch of industry would fail to be remunerative to the farmer, and in time the chief supplies would be imported. So far as the mere growth of the crop is concerned, no great peculiarity is involved to distinguish it from general farm management: but when carried on on a large scale, the preparation of the crop for the spinner involves grave difficulties, to obviate which becomes a great desideratum. Commencing with the steeping or preliminary process necessary to separate the fibre from the woody stem, considerable progress has been made to systematize it, while the mechanical arrangements for dealing with it afterwards have also claimed much attention. The hand-scutching is laborious, and is, besides, inapplicable on a large scale; and although the scutch mill has been long in use, its operation has not been satisfactory, still leaving the invention of some suitable flax-dressing machinery a matter of national importance.

The stems of the plant, or, as it is termed, the flax straw, are first to be bruised, to break the woody core, and to some extent detach the fibre from it; and of the broken portions of the stem it has to be completely divested by what is termed scutching and hackling. The first process it is sought to effect by the machine exhibited by Samuel Lawson and Sons; which is one of great promise, from the satisfactory manner in which the dressing is performed, while as a specimen of mechanical ingenuity it is entitled to high commendation. In separating the flax from the straw by the hand, as when examining its quality, we take hold of a single stem between the points of the thumbs and fore-fingers, these being close, and opposite to each other. Then, beginning at one end of the stem, we with a gentle rubbing action work to the opposite end, loosening the flax from the straw as we proceed, and breaking the latter. When this is done, we next, holding the broken stem between the points of the thumb and fore-finger of the left hand, gently strip it downwards, between the nails of the thumb and fore-finger of the right hand, removing the broken straw from the flax, which concludes the operation. And such is the *modus operandi* of Lawson's machine. The flax, in passing between revolving rollers, is broken; and, in being drawn out again, the straw is stripped with gentleness, leaving the fibre at the full length it grew, and free from any waste, so that the operations of breaking and scutching are performed by one machine at one and the same time, which is the peculiar characteristic of this invention. The accompanying engravings represent a side and end view of the machine; which, we may observe, is composed almost wholly of iron, and may be characterized as a double machine comprised within a single framework. In each part or machine are a pair of rollers, a vertical alternate-moving framed beam, and a set of six or more flax-holders made of wood. Each roller is divided into four lengths, each piece being differently fluted—finest at the finishing end, and coarsest at the commencing end. The rollers are fed from

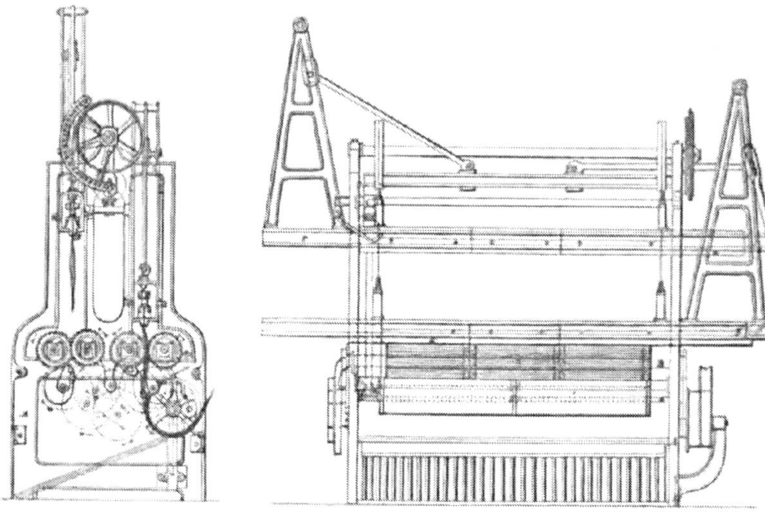

Lawson and Sons' Flax-dressing Machine.

above, so that they move inwards, and at the rate of 150 revolutions per minute. The two alternate-moving beams are framed or hollow, oscillate above the rollers, one perpendicularly between each pair, and are open at the bottom. Each flax-holder is composed of two pieces of wood, between which a handful of flax is held firm. It slides lengthways in the interior of the beam, each beam holding six of such flax-holders, four above the rollers, and one at each end, for the feeding and discharging. The rollers break the flax as it passes in between them, and scutch it as it is drawn up against their motion by the beam in its ascent. The beams hold the flax-holders, directing them, as they descend perpendicularly to the rollers, and drawing them up again when they ascend; and the flax-holders hold the flax by one end, the part operated upon by the rollers being suspended below, so that when they descend close to them, the whole is dressed to a given length, passing down and up between each of the divisions of the rollers before it is finished, when it is then reversed in the holder.

It is difficult to form an idea of the manner in which the operations thus described are performed without actually seeing the machine at work. The attendance immediately required is a person at one end to supply the handfuls of flax, and another at the other end to remove them when finished, thus economizing labour to the utmost extent, while the fibre does not appear to be subjected to any harsh treatment that would produce unnecessary waste. Six or eight handfuls per minute are dressed in this manner, a single machine worked by one-horse power being capable of turning out twenty-five stones of prepared flax per day. This invention, in short, cannot fail to perform an important part in revolutionizing this branch of industry. Great as has been the progress in it for some time past, and much as the production of the article has extended, it is only necessary to witness the action of such a machine as that to which attention is now directed to perceive that still further progress is yet to be made, of the extent of which it is difficult to form a conception. To the brilliant future of the linen manufacture, this, however, is but a step; the Messrs. Lawson being now engaged in carrying out further improvements. The effect of all these bids fair to place the linen trade on a par with the cotton manufacture.

The other flax-dressing machine in the Exhibition was that of James Combe and Co., of Belfast, designed to give the fibre the final dressing to prepare it for the spinner. This machine has two circles thirty inches diameter, with six gradations of hackles, and is suited for dressing flax about thirteen inches long, to spin to about 140 leas per pound, of which it will dress four to five cwt. per day, with four boys attending it; but the principle is equally adapted for, and has been successfully applied to, the finest as well as the coarser numbers of yarn. Both sides of the flax are hackled on each gradation or fineness of hackles before it passes to the next, by reversing the direction of the rotation of the circles of hackles, which is effected in a very simple manner by the action of the machine itself changing the position of a strap from one pulley to another: the circles are so light, and run so easily, that the reversing is accomplished without any appreciable loss of time, and is rather an advantage than otherwise, by causing the hackles to act gently when they first begin to cut into the flax. The machine is self-acting in all its movements, the attendants having merely to place the holders, filled with flax, in a slide, at one end of each circle, after which they are carried through the machine, and the flax is acted upon gradually, by hackles of each degree of fineness in succession. The hackle pins are arranged in lines, at intervals, varying from about a quarter of an inch to three or four times that distance apart, according to the fineness of the work for which the machine is intended. By this arrangement, a large number of hackles act simultaneously, and are passed through the flax, which enables the machine to do fine work with open hackles; and the flax lies so lightly on the points of the pins, that a great yield of dressed flax is obtained.

### MACHINES FOR WORKING IN WOOD.

While in one end of the Court appropriated to the objects included in this class the machines for working in iron might be seen in operation performing their allotted task with a degree of regularity which machinery only can do, close by there were machines for working in wood which were scarcely possessed of less interest. The cost of the raw material of carpentry often forms but a small proportion of that of the manufactured article; and this enhancement of its value will at once show the importance of any machinery which can diminish the cost of labour, or enable the country producing timber to send it to market in even a partially manufactured state. Now, this cannot be done in those thinly peopled districts where timber is grown, without the aid of machinery, whilst the cost of carriage precludes in many districts the possibility of profitable transport. The machinery exhibited by Mr. Furness, of Liverpool, showed what has been done in this direction. The ordinary sawing machine has been long known; but with it the use of machinery commonly ended. We all know the difficulty of the coarse planing of sawn wood, and the tediousness and difficulty of the operation. By the machinery to which we now refer the carpenter receives his planks coarse planed, ready for the highest exercise of his art and skill; this is effected by a spindle, which carries on it curved knives or plane irons, revolving with great velocity, and coming into contact with the wood as they revolve, so as to take off a minute shaving at each revolution. The wood, by the action of grooved rollers, is moved forward so as to bring successive portions under the action of the planing knives, and in this way a surface is smoothed in an incredibly short space of time. A similar machine is used for cutting mouldings, the revolving knives being shaped to the form of the moulding required, and six or seven feet of moulding can be turned out by this machine (only requiring a slight dressing or finishing to be fitted for doors, window frames, &c.), in the course of a few seconds. In fact, there is no form produced by the plane that cannot be given by this machine.

The morticing, tennoning, and boring machines of the same exhibiter show still further ingenuity. In the former of these a mortice chisel, of peculiar form, is made, by means of an excentric wheel, to move vertically with a precision surpassing that of the best workman. The work is set under it, and by the motion of the foot, or any other motive power, the chisel enters into action, cutting a mortice of the required depth almost instantaneously, so rapid does its motion appear. In the tennoning machine that portion of carpentry received by the mortice is cut; and, in fact, the laborious part of the work executed with a degree of accuracy, as well as rapidity, which is amazing. The tenon machine acts very simply. In it the action of the saw and planing machine are combined. By the former the cross cut of the tenon is made of the required depth by the saw, and then the action of the planing machine cuts off the wood at each side of the tenon. By such machinery the business of the carpenter will be reduced to fitting together the work prepared to his hand.

### WESTRUP'S CONICAL FLOUR MILL.

The conical flour mill comprises a combination of two pairs of mill-stones working together, the one pair placed above the other, so that the upper pair commence the grinding process, which is completed by the lower ones. There is a space between the two pair of mill-stones of about 27 to 30 inches in height; and the greater portion of this space is used as a vertical dressing mill, the spindle which drives the stones being filled with brushes, and the space enclosed with a cylindrical screen of fine wire-cloth mounted on a frame in the usual way. The upper stones in both cases are fixed, and the lower ones revolve. The former consist each of two parts, or semicircles, bolted together for convenience of fixing and displacing when needful; and they are capable of adjustment by means of fixed wedges or inclined planes on which they rest, so that by the action of a screw they are raised or lowered, and the grinding space adjusted with the utmost facility. The lower stones which revolve are convex, and the upper stones are concave and annular. The diameter is about 2 feet 6 inches, and the grinding surface on each side of this ring of stone 8 or 9 inches broad; the bevil of the cone in that width being about four inches. The small size of the stones necessarily requires great rapidity of action, the speed being about 250 revolutions per minute.

In the operation of this mill the flour is brushed through the wire-work of the vertical cylinder, and received in a casing of wood. The portions imperfectly ground pass into the lower pair of stones, and are reduced into meal ready for dressing in the ordinary way. The arrangement for supplying the grain is different from that ordinarily adopted. As it cannot be delivered in the centre of the upper mill-stones, a hopper or chamber is placed on one side, with a sliding-tube or feed-pipe in the top of it, and an upright spindle which, carrying a dish and revolving quickly, evenly distributes the corn.

The dimensions here given will be seen to vary very much from those of the parts of the ordinary flour mill. In the construction of the latter, there is a lower fixed circular stone, and an upper revolving one, the diameter of each being usually about 4 feet 6 inches. The average weight of these stones is about 14 cwt., and it is ordinarily found that the grinding surface presented is so extended as to render the delivery of the flour extremely slow and uncertain; and the evil arising from this is that the flour, finding only a partial escape, is triturated and retriturated, to its great injury. A single pair of such stones is calculated to require the power of a four-horse engine to maintain the needful speed. In the conical mill the weight of the running stone is reduced from 14 cwt. to 1½ cwt.; and by placing it beneath instead of above the fixed stone, a much more delicate adjustment of the running surfaces may be effected than is practicable under the old system. By a judicious modification of the ordinary mode of dressing, or rather by a combination of mill with the dressing machine, a perfect separation of the flour from the bran takes place at the moment they escape from the stones. The bran still remains in the mill, and falls by its own gravity to the second pair of stones, where it is further operated on; and thus nothing is left unconverted into flour. The corn is so short a time in passing through the mill that the bran is delivered in flakes, many of them nearly the entire skin of the wheat; and the grinding being so quickly done the flour comes away comparatively cold.

The construction of this mill will be easily understood by a reference to the accompanying engraving, which represents a section of it, to which also a scale of feet is appended. A, B, and C, indicate, respectively, the feed-pipe, chamber containing the feed-regulator, and the arrangement for acting upon it; D is the chamber over the eye of the stones, which receives the grain for the regulator; E and G are the fixed stones of the upper and lower course, and F and H the runners; I is the spindle upon which the runners work, being driven by the bevil wheel and driving shaft K; L is the iron frame sustaining the whole machine; M is the upright wire cylinder, and N the brushes acting upon it; and O and P are the regulators for adjusting the upper and lower stones.

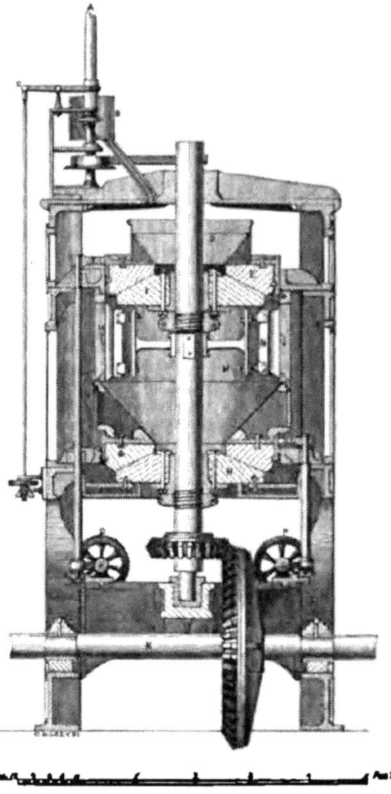

Westrup's Conical Flour Mill.

### THE SEWING MACHINE.

Of the various contrivances which the Exhibition presented for cheapening production, and for substituting the use of machinery for human labour, there was, perhaps, none so suggestive, certainly none more important in one sense, than the sewing machine, which was to be seen daily at work at the east end of one of the northern galleries. When we consider the enormous number of those who now ply the needle—the instrument of all others of most extensive use—and the wonderful powers of the machine which seems to be destined, to some extent at least, to take their place, we shall find that there were few objects in the Exhibition more deserving of attention. There can be no room to doubt that ere long all the coarser kinds of work will be performed by the sewing machine; the finer kinds of sewing, including all kinds of fancy work, being reserved for the seamstress. Who shall speculate on the changes which it must eventually introduce?

The sewing machine may be effectively used for all ordinary needle-work. It will make up an entire garment, with the exception of sewing on the buttons and working the button holes. It will get through the work with equal facility whether the material be light or heavy; hence we may conclude that its application, in the first instance, will be to the coarser description of work, which is at all times difficult to execute by hand labour. Stitching of corsets, making up sacks and carpets, sewing vamps of boots and shoes, may, for example, be done by the machine quite as well as by the hand. The stitches, moreover, will be of a uniform length, and the tension of the thread on each part constant, which is not always the case in sewing by hand.

The sewing machine was first introduced into these countries in 1846, when a patent was obtained for the invention, which we derive from the other side of the Atlantic; but this first attempt was found to be too complicated for ordinary use. Several modifications were subsequently made, until in 1851 the Lancashire Sewing Machine Company was formed; and short as is the time since the first patent was taken out, we are informed that so rapidly have subsequent improvements been made that the Company just named has thirteen patents, the machine in the Exhibition being founded on several of these patents.

In using the sewing machine, the cloth to be sewn is cut and basted as if for ordinary hand-sewing. It is then placed in a movable clamp under the needle, and is moved forward as the seam progresses. The direction of the seam is entirely at the command of the attendant, which in fact is the only matter to be looked to. The needle is fixed in a portion of the machine which moves up and down to make the stitches; and it is provided with a groove on each side which the thread occupies, the eye being removed but a small distance from the point. The grooves secure the thread from being chafed or worn, as is the case with ordinary hand-sewing. The portion of the thread passed through the cloth is only sufficient to make the stitch. There is a small shuttle working horizontally below the cloth, in connexion with the upright needle and thread; and after the needle passes through the cloth it rises sufficiently to allow the shuttle to pass through the loop thus formed, and made above the eye, after which the needle is withdrawn, catching the thread from the shuttle and drawing it into the cloth. The two threads stand in the relation to each other of the links of a chain, in the centre of the cloth, while both sides present a similar appearance, the seam being like that of a saddler or shoemaker. By a simple contrivance the amount of tension may be regulated at pleasure; that is, the threads may be pulled firmly or slightly as desired. That irregularity in sewing, proceeding from the stitches not being placed in the same right line, and which is so objectionable both as regards the strength and appearance of the seam when stretched, is entirely avoided by machine-sewing. The machine may be worked by the hand (a handle being turned round), or a band may be used wherever there is machinery in motion. It requires a space of a little over two square feet to stand on, and it may easily be carried about by one hand. The amount of work performed will depend on the speed at which it is driven; and may vary from 500 to 1000 stitches per minute, from which data the powers of the machine may be easily estimated.

The construction here described is that of the machine exhibited by Mr. Spackman, of Belfast, who is entitled to the credit of being the first to introduce it into Ireland. Various other modifications of it have been made, depending somewhat on the kind of work to be done; and a glance at any of them at work cannot fail to convince the most sceptical that the problem of sewing by machinery has been solved. The comparatively high price at which the machines are sold, and the formidable opposition which their use is sure to encounter from the workmen, will prevent their extension so rapidly as they deserve. They will, however, gradually make way despite of all opposition; and ere long we may expect to find all the ordinary sewing executed by machinery.

The sewing machine is, in fact, one of the triumphs of the age; and the excellence of its work is not more to be admired than its extreme simplicity when examined. It is, consequently, but little liable to go out of order. In one or two days an intelligent attendant can be taught to work it, and when set at work, the only attention required, as before observed, is to look after the direction of the seam.—J. S.

---

1. ATKINSON, R., & Co., Dublin, Proprietors.—Mahogany and brass-mounted Irish poplin loom, with Jacquard machine, and new brocading apparatus, at work.

2. BANK OF IRELAND, The, per W. GRAVES, Secretary, Dublin, Proprietor.—Grubb's numbering machine; Cotton's patent automaton weighing machine.

3. BENNETT, J., Manchester, Designer.—Plan of a radial drilling and boring machine, with self-acting down motion without change of gear; the table may be set to any angle for boring ships' knees.

4. COATES & YOUNG, Lagan Foundry, Belfast, Manufacturers.—A set of side pipes, with steam chests, and self-regulating conical valves of a new construction, calculated for a steam-engine of thirty horse-power.

5. CODY, P., Windsor Terrace, Portobello, Dublin.—Machine in operation, cutting, boring, and polishing shells, in the manufacture of buttons.

6. COMBE, J., & Co., Belfast, Inventors and Manufacturers.—Patent reversing cylinder hackling machine for dressing flax.

7. COURTNEY & STEPHENS, Blackhall-place, Dublin, Manufacturers.—Double acting patent platten printing machine; improved Columbian printing press.

8. CROSSKILL, A., Beverley, Yorkshire, Manufacturer.—Barnett's patent flour mill; Crosskill's patent excentric mill for grinding farm produce, &c.; Crosskill's patent excentric mill for grinding bones, minerals, &c.

9. DAWSON, JOHN, Greenpark, Linlithgow, Inventor and Proprietor.—Distillers' recording close safe, for the better securing the revenue arising from British spirits made in distilleries in the kingdom, and likewise for the protection of distillers, during the process of distillation, from thefts committed by their operatives at the worm ends.

10. DE BERGUE & Co., London, and Strangeway Mill, Manchester, Manufacturers.—Patent vulcanized Indian rubber buffers, draw-springs, and bearing-springs for railway carriages; model of a railway chair, recently invented—one of cast and one of wrought iron.

11. DE LA RUE & Co., Bunhill Row, London, Manufacturers.—Envelope folding and gumming machine (invented by E. Hill and W. De La Rue) folding and gumming sixty envelopes per minute.

12. EUSTACE, R. & J., Weavers'-square, Dublin, Manufacturers.—An improved girth web loom at work.

13. FURNESS, W., Liverpool, Manufacturer.—Machines for working in wood.

14. GARDNER, R., J., & W., Liverpool and Flint, Manufacturers and Importers.—Boxwood bobbins and bosses, lancewood creel pegs, for flax, cotton, and worsted spinners and weavers; boxwood gimlet heads, button moulds, squares for bobbin bushes, and scales or rules; lignum vitæ beam and rub-boards, for curriers and bleachers; boxwood blocks for wood engravers.

15. GIBSON, W., & Co., Glasgow.—Power and hand-loom shuttles for cotton, linen, and woollen weaving.

16. GLENNY, CHARLES, Lombard-street, London, and Balbriggan.—A frame at work making Balbriggan cotton hosiery.

17. GONNE, H., Clare-street, Dublin, Producer.—Printing, engraving, and lithography exhibited in operation.

18. GRAHAM LEMON & Co., Lower Sackville-street, Dublin, Manufacturers and Proprietors.—Steam confection pan at work, showing how comfits are made, and wrought by their workmen.

19. GREENWOOD, J., Water-lane, Leeds.—Circle used in combing wool; hand-hackles; gills for preparing flax and wool.

20. GUNN & CAMERON, Fleet-street, Dublin, Proprietors.—Double cylinder newspaper printing machine at work, printing the "Exhibition Expositor."

21. HALL, W., Castlecomer, Co. Kilkenny, Inventor and Proprietor.—Working model of an apparatus for converting dried peat into charcoal.

22. INGRAM, H., Strand, London, Proprietor.—Printing machine.

23. JONES, EDWARD, College-green, Dublin.—A velvet loom at work.

24. KEELY & LEECH, Grafton-street, Dublin, Proprietors.—A Jacquard loom at work weaving poplin.

25. KENNAN, T., & SON, Fishamble-street, Dublin, Inventors and Manufacturers.—Amateur turning lathes of different sizes and constructions, with many original contrivances for ornamental turning, &c.; slide rests, with Kennan's universal cutter, or excentric and fly cutters;

grinding-stones, on iron frames, with improved tool holders; portable vice stand, or filing bench; improved joiners' benches; circular sawing machines, to be worked by foot or power; machine for planing metals; right-line dividing-engine, capable of drawing a thousand lines per inch; letter copying and embossing presses; jointed ladder; apparatus for blasting roots of trees, &c.; improved apparatus for straining wire for fences; surface plates, or planoscopes; with various other mechanical tools and contrivances.

26. KERR, W. H., & Co., Royal Porcelain Works, Worcester.—Processes illustrating the manufacture of China and porcelain in its various stages, by workmen from the manufactory of exhibiters.

27. LAWSON, S., & SONS, Leeds and Belfast, Inventors and Manufacturers.—Patent double flax scutching machine; portable drilling machine; small slide lathe; a case showing the different stages of flax, from the seed to the linen cloth, in its finished state.

28. LEWIS, F., & SONS, Manchester, Manufacturers.—Sliding and screw cutting lathe; planing machines; portable drilling and boring machines; models of MacLardy and Lewis' patent spindles, for slubbing, roving, and doubling frames.

29. LONG, T., Paul's Works, Edinburgh, Manufacturer.—Improved Columbian printing press.

30. LYON, A., Windmill-street, Finsbury, London, Inventor and Manufacturer.—Noiseless sausage-making machines; seamless leather rollers for lithographic printing.

31. MANLOVE, ALLIOTT, & SEYRIG, Bloomsgrove Works, near Nottingham, Manufacturers and Proprietors.—Centrifugal sugar purifying machine and drying machine, with engine to work same; centrifugal drying machine, to be worked by hand; circular looms for making hosiery and woven fabrics; circular stocking frames; patent colour-extracting apparatus, invented by Aimé Boura.

32. MARLOW, BROTHERS, Merchants'-quay, Dublin.—Lithographic press and ink table; lithographic stones, with drawings thereon, to be printed in the Exhibition.

33. MASON, J., Rochdale, Inventor and Manufacturer.—Patent slubbing frame for cotton, flax, and other fibrous substances, with Mason's patent long collars or bearings to the spindles, separating plates, and other improvements; patent roving frame for cotton, flax, &c., with the patent collars and other improvements.

34. MIRFIN & SELBY, Leicester, Manufacturers and Proprietors.—Patent circular knitting machine, for making seamless elastic petticoats; specimen of yarn.

35. MORRALL, A., Studley, Redditch, Gresham-street, City, London, and Gravel-lane, Salford, Manchester, Inventor and Manufacturer.—Machines and apparatus for stamping, eyeing, filing, and polishing needles; model, showing the process of scouring needles; samples of needles made by hand, and the tools used, previous to the introduction of machinery, by exhibiter.

36. M'BRIDE, J., Glasgow, Inventor and Patentee.—Power-loom for working ginghams, &c., with patent shifting shuttle box apparatus to work two to five shuttles; patent combination of loose reed, with shifting shuttle boxes.

37. O'TOOLE, J. M., Hawkins'-street, Dublin, Proprietor.—Columbian printing press and improved metal inking table, with cases and type; plain and ornamental printing in operation.

38. OXLEY, W., & Co., Manchester, Manufacturers.—Working model of a patent steam-heating apparatus, suitable for flax-spinners, bleachers, &c., also, for ventilation; patent self-acting regulator, for working dampers of steam boilers; patent steam indicators, showing the pressure in steam boilers, and the vacuum in engines; Lee's and Haley's safety signals, for steam boilers; patent self-acting oil lubricators, for shafting; tin roving or sliver cans, for spinning mills, with various oil cans; store oil cistern, to hold 325 gallons; safety reflector, and large ornamental gas lamps.

39. PARKER, C. E., & C., Dundee, Inventors and Manufacturers.—Parker's patent power looms, and other power looms; Parker's self-acting, parallel, and step winding machines.

40. PEMBERTON, G., Dublin.—A model of steam-engine.

41. PIM, BROTHERS, & Co., George's-street, Dublin, Manufacturers.—Loom for the manufacture of velvets; Jacquard loom, with brocading machine, of the newest description, at work upon a pattern designed at the Dublin School of Design.

42. PRESTON, F., Manchester, Manufacturer.—Various spindles and flyers used in machinery for preparing, spinning, and doubling cotton, silk, wool, and flax.

43. PURKIS & NELSON, Joy's Entry, and Union-street, Donegal-street, Belfast, Manufacturers.—Hand and machine flax hackles and gills, made of Child's improved pointed and tempered steel hackle pins.

44. RYDER, W., Bolton, Lancashire, Inventor and Manufacturer.—Patent forging machine, to be worked by steam power; specimens of iron and steel forged, drawn down and swaged by same.

45. SERVICE, W., Rutland-terrace, Hornsey-road, Holloway, London, Inventor and Manufacturer.—Machine with new stop motion, for making elastic braid.

46. SMYTH & Co., Lower Abbey-street, Dublin, and Balbriggan.—A lace stocking-loom at work.

47. SPACKMAN, W., Belfast, Proprietor.—Sewing machine at work.

48. STRAKER, S., Bishopsgate-street Within, London, Manufacturer and Inventor.—Improved side lever lithographic presses, with and without registering machine, and of various sizes; lithographic inking table; French seamed printing rollers, and German stones.

49. SULLIVAN, T., Foots Cray, Kent, Inventor and Manufacturer.—Registered dandy rollers, for producing water-marks in machine-made paper.

50. TODD, BURNS, & Co., Mary-street, Dublin, Manufacturers and Proprietors.—Jacquard machine at work, manufacturing an original design in Irish poplins, brocaded in three colours; Jacquard machine turned by steam power, and at work, manufacturing original patterns in silk figured ribbons, in ten different pieces of various colours (made by SHARP, ODELL, & JURY, Coventry).

51. WAITHMAN, & Co., Bentham Mills, near Lancaster, Patentees and Manufacturers.—Two double-blow power looms, for weaving linen, &c., by giving the weft a double blow by only one turn of the crank.

52. WALLER, J., Suffolk-street, Dublin, Proprietor.—Copperplate printing machine; specimens of stamping note paper and envelopes in colours; armorial engraving; commercial and fancy engraving.

53. WALMSLEY, HENRY, Failsworth, near Manchester, Manufacturer and Proprietor.—Jacquard loom complete.

54. WARD & HODGKINSON, Belfast.—Hand hackles, machine hackles; gills used in the preparation of flax.

55. WATKINS, W. & T., Bridge-street, Bradford, Yorkshire, Proprietors.—Porcelain guides, steps, shuttle eyes, washers, &c., used in the weaving and spinning of cotton, worsted, flax, silk, &c.

56. WATSON, H., Newcastle-on-Tyne, Manufacturer and Proprietor.—Improved pulp strainer for the paper manufacture; Sir Humphrey Davy's, the George Stephenson's, and the Clanny safety lamps, used in the coal mines of Northumberland and Durham.

57. WESTRUP, H., London, Inventor.—Model of Patent conical flour mill.

58. WILSON & ARMSTRONG, Nassau-street, Dublin, Proprietors.—A stocking-frame at work.

59. WOODHOUSE, W., Molesworth-street, Dublin, Manufacturer.—Large press, with fly-wheel for striking medals; and lathes for skinning and edging medals, at work.

# CLASS VII.

---

## CIVIL ENGINEERING; ARCHITECTURAL AND BUILDING CONTRIVANCES.

THIS is a department which it is difficult to adequately represent in a public exhibition, as the plans or models afford but little idea of the adaptation of the works which they represent for the intended purpose. This remark applies especially to the business of the civil engineer, whose designs can seldom be judged without reference to the situation in which they are to be placed. When we admire beautiful models, it is the labour of the assistant that attracts our attention; as the professional engineer or architect could not spare time to be expended on such matters.

The practice of the civil engineer has only become really important within the past twenty or thirty years. It is remarkable that during that period more and greater public works have been executed in Europe than had previously been done since the earliest period of which we have any records. The railway, which has now become such an important agent in modern civilization, may be said to be a thing of yesterday; and so little attention was devoted in times past to facilitating communication between distant localities, that the oldest canal in England has not been constructed a hundred years.

The iron highways which are now spread over the country like a network, constitute the great triumph of modern engineering, compared with which the most remarkable of the works of ancient times fall into the shade. The viaducts by which we are able to cross valleys and rivers, and even arms of the sea, and the tunnels by which the locomotive passes under hills, when they stand in the way, will serve as enduring monuments of the engineering skill of the times in which they were constructed, and of the enterprise of the people, without which the plans of the engineer could not have been carried into effect. The first great engineering works were the canals, the formation of which at one period engaged so much attention as the medium of the conveyance of heavy goods of all kinds; and in the central districts of England a comparatively perfect system of communication was thereby organized. Its great drawback is the length of time occupied in the transit of goods, while to certain localities it could scarcely be extended at all. The formation of the celebrated Bridgewater Canal was followed by that of many others in England; in Scotland, the capitals of the east and west were connected; and even to this country the mania extended, no less than two lines being almost simultaneously formed from the Irish metropolis, extending in a westerly direction, for many miles running parallel and close together, thereby securing the failure of both as profitable commercial speculations. A series of years at the close of the last and the commencement of the present century may be appropriately called the Age of Canals, which was followed by that of Railroads; the one, moreover, bidding fair to upset the other. On the first introduction of railways they were regarded with alarm by the canal proprietors, and not unreasonably so. Further experience, however, showed these apprehensions to be to a great extent groundless. No considerable extension of canal communication has since taken place in any part of the United Kingdom; but so rapid has been the development of the industry of many districts through these facilities of intercourse, that the trade on canals has progressed apace, even where running in the same direction as lines of railway.*

* Great as has been the lottery which many persons have found railway shares, yet the fluctuations in that kind of property have not been nearly so great as in canals. We subjoin a statement of the sum paid per share in the principal canals on the other side of the Channel, and the present selling price, with the object of showing the extent to which the views of the promoters have been realized. How far the value has been affected by railways in any particular case we are unable to say. For this information we are indebted to the List of Messrs. Crosley, Brothers, 30, Cornhill, London, which is a perfect *vade mecum* on all matters connected with shares and stocks of every kind; while it is also interesting as showing the expense and trouble incurred by some of the London brokers in catering for the information of their customers. The List here referred to is published on the 1st and 15th of every month.

| Name of Canal. | Amount paid per Share. £ | s. | d. | Present Value. £ | s. | d. |
|---|---|---|---|---|---|---|
| Barnsley, | 160 | 0 | 0 | 48 | 0 | 0 |
| Basingstoke, | 100 | 0 | 0 | 4 | 0 | 0 |
| Brecknock and Abergavenny, | 150 | 0 | 0 | 60 | 0 | 0 |
| Bridgewater and Taunton, | 100 | 0 | 0 | 60 | 0 | 0 |
| Chesterfield, | 100 | 0 | 0 | 170 | 0 | 0 |
| Coventry, | 100 | 0 | 0 | 210 | 0 | 0 |
| Edinburgh and Glasgow, | 98 | 0 | 0 | 40 | 0 | 0 |
| Ellesmere and Chester, | 69 | 18 | 4 | 30 | 0 | 0 |
| Erewash, | 100 | 0 | 0 | 480 | 0 | 0 |

| Name of Canal. | Amount paid per Share. £ | s. | d. | Present Value. £ | s. | d. |
|---|---|---|---|---|---|---|
| Gloucester and Berkeley, | 100 | 0 | 0 | 15 | 0 | 0 |
| Grand Junction, | 224 | 10 | 0 | 65 | 0 | 0 |
| Grand Surrey, | 100 | 0 | 0 | 45 | 0 | 0 |
| Grand Union, | 100 | 0 | 0 | 22 | 0 | 0 |
| Huddersfield, | 100 | 0 | 0 | 30 | 0 | 0 |
| Kennet and Avon, | 39 | 18 | 10 | 7 | 10 | 0 |
| Lancaster, | 47 | 6 | 8 | 35 | 0 | 0 |
| Leeds and Liverpool, | 100 | 0 | 0 | 530 | 0 | 0 |
| Leicester and Northampton, | 83 | 10 | 0 | 28 | 0 | 0 |
| Loughborough, | 142 | 17 | 0 | 550 | 0 | 0 |
| Macclesfield, | 100 | 0 | 0 | 53 | 0 | 0 |

| Name of Canal. | Amount paid per Share. £ | s. | d. | Present Value. £ | s. | d. |
|---|---|---|---|---|---|---|
| Montgomeryshire, | 100 | 0 | 0 | 110 | 0 | 0 |
| Neath, | 107 | 10 | 0 | 195 | 0 | 0 |
| Nottingham, | 150 | 0 | 0 | 190 | 0 | 0 |
| Oxford, | 100 | 0 | 0 | 100 | 0 | 0 |
| Rochdale, | 85 | 0 | 0 | 66 | 0 | 0 |
| Stafford and Worcester, | 140 | 0 | 0 | 406 | 0 | 0 |
| Stratford-on-Avon, | 79 | 9 | 8 | 28 | 0 | 0 |
| Warwick and Birmingham, | 100 | 0 | 0 | 30 | 0 | 0 |
| Wilts and Berks, | 110 | 0 | 0 | 7 | 0 | 0 |
| Worcester and Birmingham, | 78 | 0 | 0 | 30 | 0 | 0 |

The first Act for the construction of a canal in the United Kingdom was that passed in 1755, under the authority of which the Sankey-brook Canal was executed, commencing in the river Mersey, and extending alongside, in a northerly direction, to Gerrard's Bridge; and only four years afterwards the Duke of Bridgewater obtained his first Act of Parliament empowering him to construct those stupendous works for which that nobleman and his self-taught assistant, Brindley, will occupy a prominent place in the page of industrial progress.

In the history of railway enterprise, the starting-point may fairly be regarded as the passing of the first Act in 1801; and, contrary to the commonly received opinion, which regards the Liverpool and Manchester line as the commencement of the system, there were no less than 1100 Acts of Parliament passed to authorize the construction of railways between 1801 and 1827. The first attempt to carry out this plan of locomotion was by the use of timber rails, the operation of which may be readily imagined as not very successful. So long ago as 1767 an attempt was made on a small scale to substitute iron for wood. Up to the beginning of the present century the rail or tram-ways were exclusively private undertakings, each being confined to the establishment—usually a colliery—with which it was connected. With a tolerably extended knowledge of the use of railways in the manufacturing districts, it is singular that no attempt was made to convey passengers in this way until the opening of the Liverpool and Manchester line; and hence the popular belief that it was the commencement of the system. In the prospectus of that work it was asserted by its promoters that at least one-half of the persons then travelling by coach between Liverpool and Manchester would most probably avail themselves of the railway, in consideration of the lower rate of charge for which they would be conveyed: the chief inducement held out to the public to take shares in the undertaking being the prospective profits from the transit of goods, as raw cotton, cattle, and coals—a circumstance which shows the small extent to which these works were then appreciated. Instead of only taking away one-half of the passengers from the mail and stage-coaches, these were soon put off the road altogether; and in subsequent calculations as to the probable returns from railways, it has been estimated, and with safety, that through the intervention of a railway the amount of passenger traffic would soon thereby be quadrupled, as compared to that previously conveyed by coaches. Goods traffic, which had up to that period formed the sole element of calculation in the construction of railways, soon came to be regarded as entirely a secondary consideration, the main source of revenue being that derivable from passengers.

It would be out of place here to go at length into the history of railway progress, for which, moreover, the models in the Exhibition connected with engineering do not afford the opportunity. One feature of the system in the United Kingdom, as distinguished from the practice of other nations, is deserving of note:—that whereas elsewhere the railways have been either constructed by or under the direct surveillance of the Government, here the *laissez faire* system has been the rule—leaving the formation of these great public undertakings to private enterprise. Both modes of proceeding have their drawbacks; and among those attendant upon the latter were the enormous law costs expended in obtaining acts of incorporation, and the absence of any regard for the requirements of the country generally in devising particular lines, the getting up of which was, in most cases, the work of a few private individuals.

The architectural designs, like the illustrations of civil engineering, were not numerous in the Exhibition. Here, however, adaptation of means to an end is more apparent and better understood by an inspection of the model or plan than in the case of works of engineering; and hence this section might have been enriched to a greater extent than it was with drawings and models.

We may here appropriately notice the extended application of glass for building purposes which has been made of late, some examples of which were in the Exhibition. The Crystal Palace, in Hyde Park, gave a great impetus to the use of this beautiful material for such purposes, the obstacles to which had been removed some years previously by the repeal of the duty on its manufacture; and the comparatively cheap rate at which glass can now be procured cannot fail to render the greenhouse and stove a necessary appendage to every comfortable residence, though in times past they were only thought of by the man of fortune. For a small sum a greenhouse can now be constructed; and it is unnecessary to dilate on the amount of amusement and instruction which it may be made the agent of communicating—the interesting employment which it may afford to the female members of the family—while to the rising generation the contents of a conservatory, however small, cannot fail to impart a taste for the culture of plants and flowers, and to supply the rudiments of a knowledge of the vegetable economy, which may be profitably turned to account in after life. In this point of view, therefore, we regarded with much interest the small conservatories in the Exhibition.

The portable houses designed for emigrants were also objects of attraction, at a time when so many are proceeding to the colonies. The Australian house, contributed by Mr. G. Kane, showed the large amount of accommodation which may be had in a small space and at a comparatively trifling expense, the whole admitting of being taken asunder and put up in little more than an ordinary packing-case. But although objects of this kind may be admired, as we do a rustic cottage, for a casual place of resort, yet when we look at them as places of constant residence, and compare the conveniences which they can supply with those of an ordinary dwelling, our enthusiasm for a cottage will be no little chilled. For such a country as Australia, a portable structure of this kind has its advantages. It supplies a temporary residence for the owner in the first place, until a permanent habitation can be provided; and it may afterwards be turned to account in a variety of ways, of which we can in this country form little conception. The idea of a portable house is so foreign to our ordinary notions of a human habitation that the novelty of the thing had much to do with the interest which the Australian cottages in the Exhibition excited.

In the several departments of this class, the catalogue subjoined will show the extent to which it was illustrated, so far as regards the number of Exhibitors and kind of articles. To the information thus supplied any general remarks would add but little. We shall, therefore, dismiss the subject with a brief notice of some of the considerations involved in the construction of farm buildings.

## FARM BUILDINGS.

The model of the farm-steading at Bellegrove, in the Queen's County, contributed by Mr. John G. Adair, was not alone deserving of an attentive examination, but it was eminently suggestive in reference to the comparatively small progress which has as yet been made in Ireland in the construction of suitable farm buildings. The requirements in this respect of an improved system of husbandry have been hitherto but little understood or appreciated; and the cases were few indeed in which the person preparing plans for such buildings possessed anything beyond a mere general knowledge of the operations and processes which he had to provide for. The most casual observer, in passing through a modern manufacturing establishment, cannot fail to be struck with the adaptation of means to an end. Everything that human ingenuity can devise for economizing labour is sedulously attended to; but this consideration is very imperfectly regarded in every branch of farming, and nowhere more so than in the arrangement of the buildings. Under improved farm management there are two departments of business, each requiring special and particular attention; the one consists in the tillage and improvement of the soil so as to make it yield the largest amount of produce; and the other of the economical conversion of a large proportion of that produce into meat for the butcher, and into milk, butter, and other articles. It is obvious that it is equally important to attend to the latter as to the former consideration. Good tillage will not avail unless the necessary arrangements are made for the disposal of the produce; and this can only be done by suitable buildings to admit of these arrangements being economically carried out.

The first consideration in buildings of any class is fitness for the intended purpose. To secure this it is obvious that a knowledge of the desired requirements must precede any successful effort to realize them. And not only should the plan of any intended farm-steading be adapted to the most improved system of management, but it should be specially designed for the farm, and even for the situation, in which it is to be placed. Some special knowledge of the details of agricultural practice is evidently required to attain this end,—a kind of knowledge in which the ordinary architect is wholly deficient. From the great number of comparatively small farms into which this country is divided, systematic farm-steadings, on a large scale, are but little required. Still there are some large farms to be met with, and, in many cases, extensive tracts of land are cultivated in connexion with the demesnes of the nobility and gentry; but even in such cases where any large expenditure is made, the most fantastic and unmeaning buildings are often produced, exhibiting an utter ignorance of the purposes for which they were required; and to attain some fancied symmetry every other consideration has been made subservient. Large sums have been occasionally expended on farm buildings by enterprising proprietors; but, with a tolerably extended knowledge of the country, we can point to few which could fairly be regarded as models deserving of imitation, or in which the cardinal rules to be followed in the preparation of plans for such buildings have not been completely ignored. On buildings of any pretension the outlay, in most cases, has been ridiculously extravagant. When the interest on this sum becomes a tax on the farmer's profits, any unnecessary expenditure becomes wholly unjustifiable; and every such case, instead of providing a model to follow, only serves as a beacon to others to guard against falling into similar mistakes.

Suitable farm buildings have now become a necessity of improved husbandry, without which it cannot be carried on. Hence the great importance of correct notions on the subject gaining ground in a country whose industry mainly consists in the tillage of her soil. The agricultural architect should be aware of the conditions under which the objects of the farmer can best be attained. He has to consider, for example, under what sort of treatment animals most readily take on flesh; for without such knowledge how can he provide the requirements? The proximity of certain classes of buildings is to be secured, the reason of which will be obvious. It is not, therefore, to be wondered that, in the effort to attain such objects on the part of the ordinary architect, sad blunders have been committed.

The force of these considerations will be readily admitted by every one acquainted with this country. While, therefore, we hear so much of reform in various departments, we believe that it is nowhere more urgently required than in the construction of farmeries. Every successful effort in this direction is of importance in a national point of view. The agriculturists of Ireland cannot attain a high position in their business until they are provided with the requirements of their peculiar trade.

The foregoing remarks have been suggested by the model of the farm-steading of Bellegrove, which, in its way, was one of the most important contributions to the Exhibition. From the model the character of the steading could be readily conceived, and the details could even be seen from the circumstance of each range of building having the roof detached, thereby admitting of its being lifted off to show the interior. Our appreciation of the design has also been enhanced, from having had the opportunity of inspecting the original; and we now more especially refer to it from the model being still available for the inspection of the public, having been deposited by Mr. Adair in the Agricultural Museum of the Royal Dublin Society.

The farm of Bellegrove contains 1100 statute acres of arable land, resting, throughout, on a limestone subsoil, and being peculiarly adapted for the growth of green crops. The four-course rotation of cropping has been adopted. Under the present system of management it is intended to bring 400 acres adjoining the steading to the highest point of production, which it is calculated will supply food to the cattle both in summer and winter. The remaining 700 acres are to be devoted to sheep-feeding,—on Swedish turnips on the land in winter, and on grass in summer.

The accommodation provided by the steading is for 200 head of cattle, in stalls; 100 store cattle, in yards, with open sheds; 16 horses, and 8 plough bullocks. In the arrangement of the buildings, the straw-house occupies the centre, straw being the article of all others in the greatest demand; and around it are disposed the houses to accommodate the stock, in proximity as they require more or less straw. At one end is the corn-barn and chaff-house, outside of which is the stack-yard, so elevated that the unthreshed corn is carried into the upper story of the barn where the threshing-machine is fixed. From the threshing-machine, which is worked by an 8 horse-power steam-engine, the straw is carried by rakes into the straw-house, the grain being winnowed at the same time, and by elevators transferred to the granary. A line of shafting from the steam-engine enables a straw-cutter, oat-bruiser, and saw-mill to be worked by it The engine not being at work more than one day in the week, no attempt has been made to economize the waste steam, which, were it more constantly available, could be used for cooking. Four yards, with shelter sheds, surround the straw-house, where the store cattle are kept. They are slightly excavated, and receive all the manure made on the premises, the liquid flowing into tanks in the centre of each, from which it is occasionally pumped over the heaps. The stable is fitted up with mangers only, no uncut fodder being given to the horses. The loft over the horses is formed of planks, two inches thick, tongued together with hoop-iron, and supported in the centre by the row of stall-posts and a bressemer, joists being dispensed with; and at the end of the stable are two loose boxes for sick horses. The fattening cattle-houses are fitted up with stalls, and a feeding passage at the head of each row. The feeding-troughs are of flags, as is also the gutter behind. The steading includes a cart shed, steward's office, cooking-house, piggeries, and forge; and we should observe that the doors of the several houses slide along the walls inside instead of turning round on hinges. Limestone is the building material used throughout, with the exception of the arches, which are formed of bricks. The timbering of the roofs is unusually light, though amply sufficient, and the whole is covered by best Bangor slates.

But the great feature about the farm-yard at Bellegrove is the extent to which economy has been carried out in its construction. Everything in the shape of unnecessary ornament has been dispensed with, and the scantlings have, in all cases, been carefully regulated according to the office which they are to fill, so as to guard against the slightest waste of material. The whole is, however, substantial. It, in fact, is admirably designed to show the largest amount of accommodation which can be secured by a given expenditure; and this is exactly the converse of the rule usually adopted in the farm-steadings of proprietors. The entire outlay for this large extent of accommodation has been only £2000.

---

1. ADAIR, JOHN G., Bellegrove, Ballybrittas, Queen's Co.—Model of farm-steading adapted for 1100 acres of land, having accommodation for 20 horses and 300 head of cattle; the machinery driven by an 8-horse steam-engine; erected on exhibitor's farm in 1852; made and modelled by Joshua Anderson, North Brunswick-street, Dublin.

2. BARKER, J. & E., Upper Abbey-street, Dublin.—Roof intended for the small tower of Lisnaskea new Church, Co. Fermanagh; with weather vane and lightning conductor on a new plan.

3. BEADON, W., Otterhead, Honiton, Devon, Manufacturer.—Patent imperishable roof gutter tiles; gable bricks, combining barge board and capping; wall gutter copings; tiles to keep walls dry by carrying off the drip; smooth roof tiles, forming a cheap, close, and impervious covering; especially adapted to barns, granaries, and other agricultural sheds; these inventions avoid all woodwork on external roofing.

4. BENSON, SIR JOHN, C. E.—Design for new town hall, Cork.

5. BLAND, JAMES F., Derriquin, Kenmare.—Model of Staigue fort.

6. COGHLAN, J., M. D., Wexford.—Models in card-board of a tower and an exchange; made by the owner, G. W. Hart, C. E., Australia.

7. BRUCE, J., Coleraine, Inventor.—Economic hay-rack, acted on by weight or spring; hollow tube, a fixture in a stable for tying horses; a model of stall with the fittings.

8. CORPORATION OF DUBLIN, THE, per Parke Neville, C. E.—Ordnance map of the city of Dublin, on the scale of 88 feet to one inch, with the lines of the sewerage laid down thereon; also showing the plan proposed by Mr. Neville for extending and improving the sewerage.

9. CULLEN, WILLIAM, Irishtown, Co. Dublin.—Model of a bathing stage for the sea coast.

10. CUTHBERT, C. D., North Frederick-street, Dublin, Designer.—Model of a design for a Mechanics' Institute, scale 8 feet to an inch, showing internal arrangement.

11. DEANE, SIR T., Dundanion, Blackrock, Co. Cork.—Architectural drawings.

12. DENCH, E., King's-road, Chelsea, London, Inventor and Manufacturer.—Two hot houses, 12 feet wide by 16 feet 6 inches long, each; two small conservatories.

13. DILLON, J., Upper Buckingham-street, Dublin, Inventor and Designer.—Design for a railway terminus; a specimen of a map reduced and drawn in different colours, with an improved pentagraph, by one operation.

14. DILLON, THOMAS A., Upper Buckingham-street, Dublin, Inventor.—Pontoon bridge; blasting apparatus by an endless cord and cork.

15. DOYLE, J., Donnybrook, near Dublin, Designer and Manufacturer.—Model of the testimonial erected in Limerick to Lord Monteagle; model of one-half of a double swivel bridge, proposed to be built at the Grand Canal Docks, Ringsend.

16. EYRE, S. R., Lord-street, Liverpool.—Model of St. Alban's Catholic Church, Liscard, Cheshire; model of the great Central Horse and Carriage Repository, Southwark; model of an Italian mansion, Prince's Park, Liverpool.

17. FARRELL, L., Fleet-street, Dublin, Inventor.—The Albert window, a model of an improved French window.

18. FULTON, H., M. D., Stillorgan, Co. Dublin.—Models; a temple, in a proposed new order of architecture; a gate-house, or labourer's cottage, exterior and interior, with a plan for effective ventilation; a railway bridge for crossing a river subject to occasional floods.

19. GEOGHEGAN, C., Westland-row, Dublin.—Design for a national monument to the late Thomas Moore.

20. GRANT, C. W., Lieut.-Colonel, Bombay Engineers, Brunswick House, Great Malvern, Somersetshire, Designer.—Model of a wrought-iron bridge, adapted for railways in India.

21. GRAVES, REV. JAMES, & LALOR, J., M. D., Kilkenny, on behalf of the Literary and Scientific Institution of Kilkenny.—Models of a new French window-sash.

22. HEALY, OLIVER, Ellen-street, Limerick.—Architectural drawings of a town hall, and farm-house and office.

23. HEMANS, G. W., Rutland-square, Dublin, Designer.—Manuscript map of part of Ireland (14 feet by 17 feet 6 in.), to illustrate a system of railways recommended for the province of Connaught.

24. KANE, G., 4, Dame-street, Dublin.—Portable Australian house.

25. KENNEDY, T. Kilmarnock, Inventor.—Water meter to uphold pressure (patented).

26. KENT, A., Chichester, Inventor and Manufacturer.—Green-houses glazed with Kent's patent weather-proof glazing, without putty or other adhesive composition.

27. KLASEN, P. J., Ferbane, King's Co.—Model of a girder, and truss timber, and iron viaduct, in two spans of 240 feet each (scale ½ in. to the foot).

28. LAVERTY, ALEXANDER, Giant's Causeway.—Model of the Giant's Causeway and Headlands.

29. LINEHAN, J., Nurney, Kildare, Designer.—Model, plan, and sections of a mode of house drainage, and for applying the liquid manure to the irrigation of land; plans and sections of works of arterial and thorough drainage, with tiles, as executed by exhibitor.

30. LYONS, J., D'Olier-street, Dublin.—Architectural designs for a Grecian Villa; Presbyterian College, Belfast; mansion-house recently erected at Abbeyfeale, Co. Limerick; and convent and schools, Ballinrobe.

31. MALONE, F., Maynooth, Co. Kildare, Designer.—Model of a double truss girder, on a new plan.

32. MANN, F., Dublin.—Model of a castle on one of the islands in Lough Erne.

33. M'SHERRY, M., James'-street, Limerick, Inventor and Proprietor.—Model of a boiler plate iron stove for heating conservatories, &c., by circulation of pure warm air, moist or dry, as required.

34. NIXON, T., Kettering, Northamptonshire, Inventor and Manufacturer.—Small greenhouse, glazed without putty, with improved ventilators, &c.; improved garden hand-frames of metal; shade of zinc and glass to preserve peas from frost; specimen of fret-work or lead light glazing.

35. OATES, W., Mirfield, Yorkshire, Inventor.—Model of a self-acting water sluice.

36. O'KEEFE, M. T., C. E., Patrick-street, Cork, Designer.—Model of Cork Harbour, with the adjacent towns and villages (scale, a foot to a mile); model of an iron spring distension girder foot-bridge (scale, one-half inch to a foot).

37. O'KELLY, Miss, Rochestown House, Dalkey.—Model of Claddagh Castle, in the Co. Galway, and of Gowran Abbey, in the County Kilkenny.

38. O'KELLY, M. J., Ussher's-quay, Dublin.—Model of intended monument to the memory of Daniel O'Connell, designed by George Petrie, Esq., LL. D.

39. PEAT, DAVID, Thirsk, Yorkshire.—Model of Thirsk Church.

40. POWELL, JOHN H., Westmoreland-street, Dublin.—Model of the fortress of Almeida, in Portugal, including ancient ruins, the River Coa, and the "Long and Narrow Bridge," defended on the 24th of July, 1810, against the French, by the 43rd and 95th Regiments.

41. RAYMOND, R., Moore Abbey, Monasterevan, Co. Kildare, Producer.—Model of Moore Abbey, the seat of the Marquess of Drogheda.

42. RITCHIE, F., & SONS, Belfast, Manufacturers.—Asphalte roofing felt; inodorous felt for lining damp walls, &c.; boiler felt; asphalte flagging.

43. SLOANE, JOHN S., Great Britain-street, Dublin.—Designs for a new bridge on site of present Carlisle Bridge, Dublin; markets, model lodging houses, baths and wash-houses, shops, &c., proposed to be erected on site of Cole's-lane Market, &c.; cast-iron lighthouse.

44. ROYAL DUBLIN SOCIETY.—Model of the Boyne Viaduct.

45. STOKES, HENRY, C. E., Tralee.—Model of an ancient hermitage, built of dry stone-work, situated in the townland of Galleross, in the Co. Kerry.

46. STOWELL, F., Castletown, Isle of Man, Designer.—Model of a geometrical staircase to reading desk and pulpit, all supported by one pillar,—presented to the Museum of Industry, Dublin.

47. ST. PATRICK'S, THE DEAN OF, Deanery House, Dublin.—Coloured drawings; interior of St. Patrick's Cathedral as proposed to be restored; elevations of north and south fronts; western and eastern elevation; and St. Patrick's Cathedral as it stood in 1843.

48. SYMES, S., Lower Dominick-street, Dublin, Producer.—Model of Killiney Hill, Co. Dublin.

49. TOWNSEND, WM. UNIACKE, Spa Hill, Kilfinane, Co. Limerick.—Model of Lansdowne suspension bridge across the Kenmare River, Co. Kerry.

50. VAUGHAN, E., Rutland-square, Dublin.—Map of Kilruddey Demesne.

51. WHITE, J. D., Cashel.—Model of the buildings upon the Rock of Cashel.

52. WILMOT, E., Hulme, Wakefield, Congleton, Cheshire, Designer.—Model and plans, with estimate, of a set of farm buildings for 300 acres, the roofs being made with bricks instead of timber and slates.

53. WHITEHEAD, —, St. Andrew-street, Dublin.—Portable Australian house.

# CLASS VIII.

## NAVAL ARCHITECTURE AND MILITARY ENGINEERING; ORDNANCE, ARMOUR, AND ACCOUTREMENTS.

THE illustrations of this class in the Exhibition were possessed of much interest. The first section of it was well represented by a variety of models. Of military engineering and pieces of ordnance there were, however, few illustrations. Of small arms the collection was very good, as might have been inferred from the extent to which this branch of manufacture is carried on amongst ourselves.

### NAVAL ARCHITECTURE.

The contributions of the Lords of the Admiralty to this department formed its distinguishing feature; embracing as it did models, with transverse sections, showing the construction of several of the finest vessels in the Royal Navy; and, besides, illustrating the progress of naval architecture from the time of Henry VIII. In no branch of industry has greater progress been made of late years than in the construction of our naval and mercantile marine. The growing commercial intercourse between these and other countries gave an impetus to the introduction of improvements in ship-building, the crowning triumph of which was the application of steam as a propeller, thereby rendering the voyager comparatively independent of wind and tide. The period is not distant when days, and even weeks in some cases, were spent in going across the Irish Channel, owing to the prevalence of adverse winds; but now the passage is performed in a few hours, and almost with unfailing regularity; and the efforts which are at present being made towards the improvement of trans-channel navigation, by the use of vessels of large tonnage and great steam power, will serve to convey some idea of what may yet be accomplished in this direction. To the commercial enterprise of the age the country is indebted for a mercantile navy of unparalleled magnitude and efficiency; and in this department successive Governments for some time past appear to have followed close in the wake of private enterprise. Many of our ships of war are now propelled by steam, by which the efficiency of this branch of the service has been materially increased. The Wooden Walls of England were, in short, never so invulnerable as at the present moment.

The rapid progress of naval architecture of late years may be estimated from the fact of the use of steam-ships extending only some thirty years back. The first successful attempt to traverse the ocean by steam was made in 1818, by an American captain. Subsequent to this, steam came to be extensively employed for the purpose of locomotion both by sea and land. With the use of this new propelling agent a modification of form became desirable. The bulk of the prow and stern was reduced, while an increase was made to the length. The paddle-wheel was the first medium of propulsion, and for some time the only one used; but some years ago the screw-propeller was applied in steam navigation, and with the best results. The "Rattler," of 888 tons, was the first ship in the navy to which the screw-propeller was applied, and with engines of 200 horse-power, a speed of ten knots an hour was obtained. The success in this case was so complete that the "Alecto," "Blenheim," "La Hogue," and others, were fitted up in the same manner in quick succession; and while further experience showed that the speed greatly exceeded anything calculated on, the efficiency of this class of vessels for general service became so confirmed that several first-class ships were soon after fitted up with this agency of locomotion.*

* The honour of having first imagined a vessel to be propelled by steam would seem to belong to Blasco de Garay, a Spaniard; and his plan was tried as early as the year 1543, by order of the Emperor Charles V., at Barcelona, on a vessel of 200 tons, which was propelled at the rate of three miles an hour. This experiment would appear to have fallen into oblivion. In 1736, Jonathan Hulls, in England, patented a plan for propelling with paddle-wheels; in 1789, Symington propelled a vessel on the Forth and Clyde Canal at the rate of nearly seven miles an hour; and again, in 1802, satisfactorily worked a steam-tug on the same canal; but it is to the undaunted perseverance of Robert Fulton, an American, that the honour is due of having carried the measure into practical execution; and in 1807 he made his first voyage, from New York to Albany, in the "Clermont," of 20 horse-power, at an average speed of five miles per hour. In April, 1812, Henry Bell, of Helensburgh, established a steam-vessel in the Clyde, and steamed between that place and Glasgow, also at the rate of five miles an hour. In 1818 a steam-ship crossed the Atlantic from Savanah to Liverpool; in 1838, just twenty years later, the "Sirius" and "Great Western" made their first voyage to New York; and now, as is well known, steam-ships, of 2000 tons burthen, and 500 horse-power, are navigating the Pacific and Indian Oceans.

The most successful effort at producing fast sea-going paddle-wheel steamers has resulted from the free competition permitted for the four mail steamers between Holyhead and Kingstown, a distance of 56 nautical, or 64½ statute miles, which was accomplished by the "Banshee" in 3 hours 26 minutes, or at the rate of 16·32 knots, or 18·8 statute miles an hour; the average time of passage being 4 hours

Of the numerous improvements which have recently been effected in the construction of ships, the space at our disposal would scarcely admit of a mere enumeration; and this applies not only to the vessels themselves, but to the means and appliances for working them. In the larger class of vessels, more solidity has been attained than was formerly available, by increased precision in joining together the several parts of the ship. The working of the timbers, as it is termed, is greatly prevented in a heavy sea, by such means. By an improved form in ships of war, much of the ballast previously necessary has been dispensed with; the chief modification for this purpose being an increase of breadth, greater stability, more space below for storage; and a larger field for exercise on deck, was also among the advantages secured by this improvement. By an examination of the forms of waves, produced by drawing vessels through a canal at different velocities, the form of vessels was gradually changed, so as to diminish the resistance at high rates of speed. The use of chain cables for those of hemp marked a further step in the path of progress, the latter being unsafe and being wanting in durability. The application of metallic conductors enabled the disastrous effects of the electric fluid to be guarded against; the great triumph in the attainment of this object being due to the invention of Sir W. Harris, who conceived the idea of making capacious metallic conductors an integral part of the masts and hull of the vessel, in order to bring the general fabric into a perfect non-resisting state. This idea has been realized by incorporating with the masts and hull a series of copper plates so arranged as to meet all the varying conditions of the spars, and so tied together that an electrical discharge striking upon any part of the vessel cannot enter upon any circuit of which the conductors do not form a part; and thus the ship is preserved from the effects of lightning at all times and under all circumstances. The substitution of iron for wood in the construction of vessels marked another step in the path of improvement. The use of such a material is peculiarly appropriate in the United Kingdom, where iron is so abundant and cheap. Exposed to great changes of temperature, wooden vessels soon give way, the number of agencies at work for their destruction being almost innumerable. Contrary to the common opinion, iron vessels can be made lighter than those of the same bulk of wood. They also escape better than wooden vessels when coming in contact with a sand-bank or with rocks; the security being still further increased by the vessels being divided into compartments, so that in the event of one part of the ship being stoved in, the entire destruction of the vessel does not necessarily follow.

When alluding to the precautions provided against shipwreck, we may notice the increasing attention which has of late been paid to the construction of life-boats. An ingenious modification of this useful article, in the form of a collapsible life-boat, appeared in the Exhibition, the invention of the Rev. Edward Berthon. The model represented a boat thirty feet by ten, calculated for the accommodation of sixty persons; and among its peculiarities is that it fills itself with air in eight separate and distinct compartments in a moment of time. Of necessity it is lowered on an even keel, if required it disengages itself from the tackles, it requires no ballast, it cannot be sunk, when collapsed it is but twenty-seven inches from the ship's side, it is ready to be lowered in an instant, and in using it no plugs or caulking are required.

The business of ship-building was at one time carried to a considerable extent in this city, as it still is in Cork, Belfast, and some other of our leading towns. Combination among the shipwrights was, however, carried to such an extent that it actually succeeded in driving this branch of business from the Irish metropolis. At present there is nothing done here beyond the most trifling repairs. Some time ago the British and Irish Steam Packet Company kept up an establishment designed mainly for the repairs of their own vessels; but it, too, has for some time past been given up, though it possessed the means of executing all kinds of work. The want of enterprise and perseverance on the part of those engaged in the trade here has had as much to do with its decline as the combination among the shipwrights; the latter it only required a determined and persevering effort to overcome. In the progress of the various inquiries which we have felt it necessary to institute in collecting the materials for the present volume we had frequently occasion to perceive the wonderful results brought about by the energy and well-directed efforts of a few individuals. Such efforts have often been the means of localizing trades which subsequently extended to be of colossal magnitude. But in no other branch of business has this been more the case than in that of ship-building. It is necessarily confined to a comparatively small number of capitalists. In the Irish metropolis ship-building languished from a variety of causes; but with its decline here it sprung into life and vigour in the capitals of the northern and southern provinces—Cork and Belfast having turned out some of the finest vessels in the mercantile navy of the United Kingdom.

8 minutes, equal to 18·84 knots, or 16 miles an hour for summer and winter.

The immense advantage of a submerged screw-propeller over the paddle-wheel, as an auxiliary to sailing vessels, in point of economy, in protection from shot, and as leaving the broadside of a ship of war free for guns, renders any sacrifice to accomplish the object, in the best manner, worthy of the nation. Passing over the early application of the screw, we come to the patent taken out by Mr. Francis Smith, in May, 1836, and that by Captain Ericsson, in July following. The former made his first trial in the "Archimedes," on the 20th September, 1837, which established the practicability of this propeller. In 1845 a trial of the relative merits of the paddle-wheel and screw took place between similar vessels, the "Rattler" and "Alecto," of 888 tons burden, and 200 horse-power, when, with the two vessels lashed stern to stern, the "Rattler" screw-propeller towed the "Alecto" astern, at the rate of 2½ knots an hour, in spite of all her efforts to the contrary. These experiments appear to have established a superiority for the screw of 17 per cent. With respect to economy, it appears that the original cost of paddle-wheel steamers, when fit for the sea, is about £5 9*s*. per ton greater than that of screw steamers, and that their current expenses for the year are about £8 per ton more than those of screw vessels. At the same time, the average measure of cargo for screw steamers is three-fourths of a ton for each ton of builder's measure, whilst for paddle-wheel steamers it is less than half a ton, or 83 per cent. less than the former.—*The Progress of Naval Architecture, by Captain Washington, R. N.—Lectures on Exhibition of* 1851.

## SMALL ARMS.

The manufacture of fire-arms was illustrated in the Exhibition by specimens from England, Ireland, France, Belgium, and Austria; but the largest and by far the most important portion of these was produced in the workshops of this city. The highly finished and varied assortment of sporting weapons exhibited in the South Gallery by three Dublin firms, Messrs. William and John Rigby, Messrs. Trulock and Sons, and Messrs. William and James Kavanagh, showed the high state of perfection to which this branch of manufacture has attained amongst us.

In examining the cases of fire-arms exhibited in the Southern Gallery, the attention of the visitor was attracted by parts of the gun in preparatory stages; and to render these more intelligible to our readers, we propose to sketch the progress of the work from the earliest to the most advanced stage, according to the methods employed in the best factories where the division of labour is systematically carried out. In pursuance of this object it will be found convenient to consider the gun as divided into four parts, viz., the barrel, the lock, the stock, and the mounting.

*Gun-barrels.*—The barrel naturally occupies our first attention, constituting as it does the projecting machine, to which the other parts are only auxiliary. We have accounts of cannons being used in Europe about the year 1340, yet there is no mention of hand-guns, that is, guns which had stocks, and were fired from the shoulder, until 1471. At that early period the small mechanical resources of the age were sorely taxed to produce a tube of the requisite strength and dimensions. The first cannons were made of bars of iron, so disposed side by side as to form a cylinder, and bound together by hoops; and these were often further strengthened by ropes coiled tightly round them. It is worthy of remark, that a brass gun exhibited in the Chinese Department by the Army and Navy Museum, and which was expressly manufactured for use against the English, is fortified along its entire length in this manner, thus affording a modern illustration of a practice which prevailed in Europe four hundred years ago. At a somewhat later period brass ordnance came into use, and their manufacture was brought to great perfection. Brass barrels were used for hand-guns also, particularly for blunderbusses, until a very recent date; but the superiority of wrought-iron, as the material for a tube required to combine strength with lightness, must have become evident to those engaged in the manufacture of small arms; and, accordingly, we perceive in some of the very oldest guns wrought-iron barrels, whose workmanship often displays considerable skill.

There are two processes by which a bar of iron is converted into a tube for the purposes of the gunsmith. First the simple though imperfect method of employing a flat bar, equal in length to the required barrel, and in width somewhat exceeding its circumference, and rolling it up until the edges overlap, to be finally welded along its entire length. Of late years an improvement has been effected in this method by the introduction of steam-power. A short bar is turned up and welded at one heat, and is then drawn out to the required length by passing it through successive rollers. Such barrels are only used for the plainest work, and are much inferior to those produced by the second method. In this more perfect process the bar of iron, now called a *strand*, is coiled round an iron rod or mandril of the same size as the required bore; and the spiral so formed having been brought to a welding heat, and struck on the end to join the edges, becomes a continuous tube in which the grain of the material runs round the barrel, thereby insuring the greatest amount of resistance to the expansive force of the charge. The advantages of the latter method are numerous. The fibres of the iron, instead of being torn asunder by bending the bar parallel to its length, are rather condensed and closed together; and, accordingly, the better description of barrels have been manufactured in this manner for a long period. Among these are included the varieties called stub-twist, plaited-twist, laminated steel, Damascus, &c., which all partake so far of the common character that they are forged according to this process, but differ in the preparation of the *strand*. Thus, in stub-twist, a bar of iron is made as follows:—A quantity of stubs, i. e., small pieces of iron or steel, are raised to a welding heat, and consolidated by a few blows, and then drawn down between rollers to the required size. The excellence of the material depends on the quality of the stubs employed; that being in most repute formerly which was manufactured from horse-nail stubs, or old horse-shoe nails collected by the farriers. Of late years these have deteriorated in quality, and it became necessary to apply, in the preparation of the strands, other processes which have for their object the purification of the iron, by twisting and hammering, and the introduction of carbon by a partial admixture of steel. The first of these—that of making plaited twist—is conducted as follows:—Two square bars of stub iron are separately twisted at a red heat until the whole rod has the appearance of a four-threaded screw, the threads being formed by what were the angles of the bar in its untwisted state; and one having a right-hand turn, the other a left. These rods, so prepared, are welded side by side to form the strand, and the grain of the iron presents, when finished, that feathered or plaited appearance whence it derives its name.

Steel barrels are made in a manner somewhat similar to the process just described, the material, instead of stub iron, being prepared from soft steel, which is decarbonized in the course of manufacture.

The process of making Damascus barrels is more complicated, as involving a greater number of stages. The strand in this case is composed of three or four twisted rods instead of two, and they are generally all twisted in one direction; but it is in the manufacture of the rods themselves that the essential difference consists. These are no longer stub iron or decarbonized steel, but are formed of from twenty to four-and-twenty alternate layers of iron and steel welded together. The effect of this arrangement is, that when the barrel is finished, and an acid applied to the surface, the iron layers are rapidly eaten away, while the steel remains comparatively intact; and the whole presents that beautiful pattern, celebrated (long before the method of production was understood) as some secret process known only to Eastern armourers, and supposed to have originated in Damascus. The credit of rediscovering it in these countries is due to a Dublin house, the Messrs. Rigby, of Suffolk-street, whose experiments were brought to a successful result in the year 1817.

Of late years the ingenuity of the gunsmiths has been expended in multiplying the number of methods of combining rods of iron and steel, to produce corresponding varieties in the pattern displayed by the grain of the iron in the finished work; and the French forgers have been very successful in this pursuit, as might be seen on an examination of the barrels exhibited in the French department. These specimens were very beautiful, and much finer in the twist than any produced in this country; but this is owing to the fact that the Damascene iron, instead of forming the material of the barrel, is merely an exterior plating used for ornamental purposes. This is also the case with the barrels of some of the matchlocks in Lord Gough's collection, in which the rods run lengthways from breech to muzzle, instead of transversely.

The barrel after welding is subjected to another process before boring, which consists in removing, by means of a large file worked by two men, the external surface which has been deteriorated by exposure to the fire at a welding heat. It is then hammered for some time, for the purpose of closing the pores of the iron and rendering it hard and elastic; the forging is then complete.

The rough tube is next passed into the boring shop, and screwed firmly into a slide in the rough boring bench. The point of a taper square steel bit, which is driven by steam-power at a very high velocity, is introduced into the hole left by the forger, and the barrel is pressed forward by means of a lever, while a stream of cold water plays on it from a flexible tube overhead; the hole is rapidly enlarged and straightened by successive bits, and when brought sufficiently near to the required size, the barrel is transferred to the fine-boring bench, to undergo a much slower and more particular process. The boring bit now to be used is no longer taper, but perfectly parallel, and a thin slip of wood is interposed between one side of it and the barrel. Two of the four edges are thus prevented from touching, and the elasticity of its resistance causes the others to cut finer and more regularly. The motion is slow, and abundant oil is supplied. When the bit has passed through the barrel a slip of paper is introduced between it and the wood, and the same process repeated until the required bore is attained. At intervals the work is removed from the slide, and struck with a hammer, to straighten it; and a skilful workman can at once detect the least inaccuracy by looking through the tube while he allows a ray of light to glance along its interior surface. When the fine-boring is completed, the barrel is mounted in a lathe and turned at both extremities to the required size, as a guide for the grinder, who then proceeds to reduce the exterior on an immense grindstone. These stones average six feet in diameter by twenty inches in width, and are driven at the rate of about 300 revolutions in a minute. The workman sits on a wooden block or horse, and laying the barrel across the surface allows it to revolve slowly in his hands. A stream of sparks flies from the whirring stone, strangely joined by a shower of spray from the water, which is constantly supplied; and in a short time the rough exterior of the forging is removed, and the barrel appears as round and perfect as if turned in a lathe. It now passes into the hands of the barrel-joiner, who screws it for the breeching; but before proceeding further inserts a temporary breech, and sends it to be proved. The next stage is to put on the ribs, which in double barrels includes, of course, the process of joining two tubes together. In Dublin this is effected by soldering. In London they are partly brazed and partly soldered, and on the Continent they are brazed along their entire length. This latter method is considered injurious to the temper of the barrels, as brazing requires a red heat, which softens them, and counteracts the good effect of the cold hammering before given.

After joining, the breeches are screwed in, and the *break off* or cover, the part which is screwed into the stock to receive the breeches, is fitted. We have now brought the barrels into that state in which they are ready for the stocks, and must turn our attention to the locks and mounting.

The gun in its infancy consisted, as we have before remarked, of a simple tube closed at one end, supported on a fixed platform, and was used only for the defence of fortified places; the transition was easy to less ponderous pieces carried by the soldiers, and set up in batteries when required. The use of waggons in transporting them would immediately suggest wheeled carriages, from which they could be fired, and so far cannon rapidly advanced; but at this stage, with modifications introduced by improvements in the manufacture, although with little difference of construction, they remain to the present day. They are now loaded and discharged as formerly; and while small arms have undergone a series of revolutions in the construction of the lock and the mode of ignition, great guns, if we except some recent instances in the navy, remain in all their primitive simplicity, uninfluenced by the tide of modern inventions. The Exhibition strikingly exemplified this fact; we look upon the matchlocks of the Sikhs, and see types of a weapon which has vanished from civilized Europe centuries ago. We expect to find in their cannon a similar retrospection, and, to our astonishment, behold field-pieces which, for proportion, manufacture, and perfection in detail, vie with our most modern efforts.

*The Lock.*—It is the construction of the lock, and the method of ignition, which constitute the most striking difference between ancient and modern guns. In the Gough collection, we observed a carbine with no further provision than a pan to contain the priming, and must have been discharged by applying a match with the hand. This is evidently the most primitive idea; and its many inconveniences must have soon suggested the matchlock, which has been, perhaps, more extensively used than any other, and is still common among eastern nations. Of this also we had numerous excellent specimens in the Exhibition, taken from the Sikhs. Their construction is simple and efficacious; a lever, one end of which is cleft to receive the match, works on a centre in such a position, that when the trigger is pulled, its cleft end describes an arc, and brings the fire into contact with the priming. The defects of such a plan are manifold; the match must be kept always lighting (no easy matter in a moist climate), and the instances are not a few in which the matchlock-man has blown himself up by letting the fire come in accidental contact with his cartridges.

The next notable change in the locks of European guns was to the wheel locks, in which sparks elicited by friction from pieces of pyrites, were employed to cause the ignition of the charge. They derived their name from a large steel wheel which formed the main feature of the lock; it was serrated on the edge, and connected by means of a chain to a powerful spring, the position of this wheel was under the priming, so that some of the powder rested on its edge, and it required to be wound up with a key before each discharge. An arm, carrying a piece of pyrites, was then shut down, so as to bring the mineral in contact with it, the point of contact being surrounded by the priming; and the lock was then ready for use upon drawing the trigger. The wheel, released from the catch hitherto confining it, spun round and caused sufficient friction with the pyrites to throw off a stream of sparks. These cumbrous machines were introduced about the time of Henry VIII., and continued in use until the invention of flint locks, which, in the reign of Charles II., began to supersede all former inventions. On the improvement of the latter, an immense amount of ingenuity was expended, particularly at the close of the last and beginning of the present century, with a view to insuring certainty of fire; but the end was never perfectly attained, and the introduction of percussion powder as an explosive agent consigned these complicated contrivances to oblivion. This discovery, destined to produce a complete revolution in gun locks, languished at first, through the defective plans adopted by the patentee, Mr. Forsyth; but the expiration of his patent was immediately followed by the invention of the copper cap and tube. The cap soon got the preference, and tube guns are becoming more scarce daily, while the former seem to fulfil every reasonable requirement. The lock, which actuates the hammer, is a most important part of every gun, and lock-fitting is a distinct branch of the general gun manufacture; it requires great skill in filing, turning, and fitting, and particularly in tempering steel.

*The Stock.*—The wood used almost universally for gun-stocks is walnut; and great care is required in the selection and seasoning for the best work. The trees are not cut down, but felled with the root, as the most valuable stocks are usually cut out of this part. They are then sawn into planks about two and a half inches thick; and after seasoning for some time, they are cut up into rough stocks, which are finally sorted and placed in proper store-rooms to dry. It is customary in some places to steam them, for the purpose of rapidly removing the sap and expediting the drying, but this practice destroys the toughness of the wood and lessens its durability. Maple, ash, and some other woods, are occasionally, though rarely used.

*The Mounting.*—The heel-plate, trigger, trigger-plate, and guard, with the tail-pipe, constitute what gunmakers call the mounting of a double gun; the first of these serves the purpose of protecting the butt from accidental injury, and improving the balance of the weapon. It is usually slightly hollowed, so that the gun may be raised rapidly to the shoulder, and steadied there by one movement. The triggers are the levers by which the lock is discharged, and fit in grooves in the trigger-plate; while the part of them which might be exposed to an accidental blow or pressure is protected by the guard. The tail-pipe serves as a finish and protection to the end of the stock, and receives the end of the ramrod to guide it into the groove of the stock.

We have now brought the different parts of the gun into that state in which they are in a condition to be joined together, and to form a complete and perfect whole; we will proceed to examine the subsequent stages, and discuss the principal improvements which have been, at different times, effected in the construction of fire-arms.

Having traced the progress of the manufacture of fire-arms through its various preparatory stages, we next make the acquaintance of the stocker. His tools consist of those used for wood only, and it is necessary that his chisels, gouges, &c., some of which are of very complex shape, should be of the best temper and exquisitely sharpened, otherwise it would be impossible for him either to work quickly or to display in the cutting of the wood that squareness and smooth surface which are the test of excellence. The barrels and cover, the locks and the rough stock, are handed over to him, and his business is to "let in" both of the former into the latter—that is, insert these into the wood, in the position they ought to occupy in the finished gun. The requisites for perfection in this branch are—1st. That no more wood should be removed than is absolutely necessary to let the iron work in, so that the two being in close contact around the edges of the lock-plate, &c., may exclude damp. 2nd. That the locks should come out and in without force. And 3rd. That the cutting should be square, clean, and finished from the chisel.

The rough-stocked gun and the mounting are next placed in the hands of another workman, called a "screwer together," who proceeds to let in the mounting, and confirm all by the various screws and bolts, which are requisite to keep everything in its place.

The next process is called "percussioning," and involves the use of various tools for iron, such as grinders, chippers, floats, files, &c.; and consists in making excavations in the rough breeches to receive the pillars on which the percussion caps are placed, and in filing and fitting the cocks or hammers, which, acted upon by the lock, explode them. In forming the curved surfaces which the excavations present, and in the lines of the cock, much taste, as well as skill, is required. The pillars must be perfectly parallel, and similarly placed in the two breeches, and, accordingly a guide, which is clamped to the barrels, is used in drilling the holes to receive them. The same workman puts in the platina bushings, which close the chamber of the breech, and which are pierced with a small hole to allow the air to escape when charging. When these processes have been completed, the gun assumes its proper form, and can, for the first time, be loaded and discharged; but the stock is still clumsy and rough, therefore it must go into other hands to be "made off," i. e., reduced to its final shape. Here again, taste, and an appreciation of beauty of form (which, strange as it may sound, can exist even in a gun-stock), are required; and the model for a clipper yacht is not more carefully curved and shaped than the wood-work of a first-rate gun. It must fit the cheek in one place, the hand in another, the shoulder in another, and yet preserve its symmetry. Every age is marked by a different method of "making-off" its stocks; and so distinct are these, that the antiquity of fire-arms can be nearly determined by their shape. Having acquired the proper form, the stock is next polished by successive processes, and the handle and other parts are carved, in order to make the grasp more firm. For this purpose, a simple chequer is used in this country, while on the Continent, in some cases, the wood-carver's art is exhausted in embellishing those parts capable of receiving ornament.

Before proceeding further, the workman should examine by trial the shooting of his gun, and make any alteration which his experience may suggest as likely to improve it in this particular. That being done, it is ready for the finishers, whose first business is to varnish or dry polish the wood, then polish the iron-work, and having sent the requisite portion to be engraved, complete the inside work of the locks and other unengraved parts. The best guns are polished by hand, with pieces of wood, of various forms, applied like a file, and fed with oil and emery of successive degrees of fineness; but for the common trade guns revolving wheels are used, which remove the inequalities of surface much more rapidly, but, at the same time, deteriorate from the squareness and correct fitting of the different limbs.

We will now follow the portion which has been cemented on the engraver's block, and see how he plies his art. He first marks a faint design upon the polished surface, and then, with graver in one hand, and hammer in the other, plunges boldly *in medias res*. Soon a complete outline reveals the pattern, and then, with other gravers, the shading is laboriously filled in. The English gun-engravers rarely use the hammer; their cutting is light and fine; but in Dublin a deeper ground and more relieved scroll-work is preferred, as it bears better the effect of time and ill usage. After engraving, the parts are returned to the finisher, who proceeds to case-harden or blue them. The former process consists in enclosing them in a metal box filled with ivory dust, and raising the whole to a red heat, at which they are retained for some time. This has the effect of carbonizing or converting into steel the outer skin of the iron; and, accordingly, when the pieces are thrown still red into cold water, they become perfectly hard on the surface. For the rest, those parts which, from lightness and shape, would not bear the sudden transition without bending or twisting, are coloured by another process called blueing, i. e., they are heated in a pan of glowing charcoal dust to the temperature at which the effect of oxidization turns them from straw-colour to a deep blue.

Our attention is now to be directed to the finishing processes which are applied to the barrel, and these in general consist in polishing, as before, and staining a brown colour, with certain acid preparations, which, acting with different degrees of intensity on the hard or soft part in the iron, produce differences in colour that display the grain of the iron, and, consequently, the manner in which the barrel was forged. Thus a twist barrel appears streaked with parallel bands running spirally round it, and a plaited twist presents a feathered or plaited pattern. The acid is applied at intervals of several hours, generally twice a day, by means of a small piece of sponge, and the coat of oxide which results is removed by the use of a brush made of fine steel wire.

Damascus barrels may be finished in the same manner, but it is considered preferable either to pickle or smoke-stain them. To effect the former they are dipped in a bath of strong acid solution, which eats away the iron and leaves the steel projecting, thus forming a regular raised pattern over the surface. Smoke-staining may be applied either to smooth barrels or to those roughened by the last process. It is produced by the chemical action of smoke, with which they are coated by passing them to and fro through a clear blaze from a pure description of coal, the successive coats being removed in the same manner as in acid stains. The result is a rich black colour, which resists damp better than any other. The separate portions of the gun may now be considered finished, and it only remains to be all put together, but here great care is required. Minor inaccuracies, which are unavoidable where so many different hands are employed, have to be corrected, and every part carefully examined and adjusted before the perfected whole can be transferred from the manufactory to the wareroom.

From the details which have now been given, it will be seen that the manufacture of a first-rate double gun is no simple matter; that it embraces a variety of processes, and requires a combination of art so widely different that a lifetime would scarcely suffice for any one man to become proficient in them all; but when, in addition to these, we refer to rifles, and notice the manifold new conditions which they introduce, we may safely conclude that an accomplished gunsmith must be considered, in the mechanical arts at least, a well-educated man.

*The Rifle.*—A perfect double rifle may be considered the *ne plus ultra* of gun-making. The reason of this will appear when we explain the conditions required. Since the time of Galileo, who was the first to investigate the laws which govern the flight of projectiles, the attention of scientific men has been constantly directed to the attainment of accuracy in ball practice. His theory, which admitted as insignificant the resistance of the air, was only true for bodies moving slowly, but when applied to artillery practice was totally erroneous. Nevertheless, the sanction of his name caused it to pass current for more than a century, until George Robins published his celebrated "New Principles of Gunnery." The experiments there detailed were accurate and decisive, and his conclusions just and true. He may be considered not merely to have commenced but to have entirely developed the present theory of projectiles. He demonstrated that the resistance of the air was not only appreciable, but so great that it presents an insuperable barrier to the increase of the velocity of shot beyond certain limits; and he also explained the source of accuracy in rifles, and suggested many improvements which the present age has seen perfected.

The object to be attained by rifling is to give a rotatory motion to the ball round an axis coincident with the axis of the bore, which is effected by cutting spiral grooves along the whole length of the interior surface of the barrel; for this purpose it is fixed in a frame, while a steel rod, bearing on its end a cutter of the proper form, is passed backward and forward through it by the agency of machinery. This cutter is guided into a spiral course by the rod upon which it is mounted being twisted and made to slide through a collar, or by some analogous contrivance. After one cut is made, the rod is turned round a portion of the circle by means of a dividing plate, and the same process repeated. In this manner two, three, four, or as many equidistant grooves as necessary, may be made. And finally, the bore is polished and equalized with a leaden plug cast in it, and fed with emery and oil. The inside being thus prepared, the next step is to fit it with a suitable bullet, and here again we enter on a wide field of inquiry. Suffice it to say, that a truly spherical bullet is more accurate at moderate distances than any other yet discovered; while elongated and conical ones have a decided superiority at long ranges, more penetration in every instance, and possess, besides, a facility, lately discovered, of being rendered expansive; which is of inestimable advantage in quick loading, as the balls slip down the barrel without the exercise of any force, but upon the explosion of the charge are so much enlarged that all the windage is destroyed, and the spiral motion effectually communicated. Before quitting the subject of rifling we wish to draw attention to a modification which, having been lately brought forward by some artists, particularly in America, has been received as an improvement by a considerable portion of the public. We allude to what is called an accelerated spiral; i. e., a spiral which, commencing at the breech with a very slight inclination, regularly increases in pitch, and reaches its maximum at the muzzle. The object proposed is to communicate the rotatory motion to the bullet in the most gradual manner; but it is by no means evident that this is effected by such an arrangement. The degree of pressure against the grooves, and the consequent strain on the projections of the bullet which fills them, depend as well upon the velocity with which it is moving as upon the pitch of those grooves. If this velocity were the same in every part of the bore, the theory of accelerated spirals is true; but if, as is actually the case, the ball, commencing from a state of rest, increases in speed until it leaves the barrel, then it is evident that a plan which defers the greatest degree of inclination in the grooves until it has reached its greatest velocity, rather increases than diminishes the evil it is intended to cure. In fact, this evil is more imaginary than real. In a well-made rifle, if the barrel be not corroded or foul inside, the ball cannot be made to trip the grooves by any increase of charge, and the simple practical method of proving this is to examine the marks of the rifling on balls which have been fired into some soft substance.

In whatever way the barrels are rifled, and however correctly each of them might shoot separately, the chief difficulty of making a double rifle is quite independent of these considerations; and arises from the fact that the barrels, if joined parallel, would not throw the balls in the same direction, but, owing to the influence of the recoil, would discharge them in considerably divergent courses; for the resistance supplied by the shoulder acts in a line between the two barrels, and, consequently, the recoil of the right sways the whole gun in that direction, and of the left in the contrary. To remedy this, a certain allowance is made in joining, and the tubes thereby converge towards the muzzle; but the extent of this convergence varies with the weight, bore, charge, and weight of ball of each particular gun, and cannot, consequently, be determined by rule. It is, therefore, necessary to resort to approximation, and, after the utmost care has been taken in joining, to try, by actual practice in the field, if the amount is sufficient. But if, as is usually the case, some alteration is required, the barrels must be taken asunder, and re-joined at the corrected angle; and the correction and trial have sometimes to be repeated half a dozen times before perfect accuracy is attained. The manner in which this correction is applied constitutes the chief difference between good and bad double rifles, as it generally happens, that the latter are turned out without any trial, or at best with an imperfect one.

We come now to speak of a subject, the importance of which cannot be overrated,—the accidents which are of so frequent occurrence in the use of fire-arms, their cause, and the contrivances proposed to prevent them. Every year the journals record cases in which the loss of life, of a hand, or of some other casualty, is the penalty of some trifling carelessness; but still the source of danger is unexplored, and preventive measures neglected; and this arises from the fact, that the remedies hitherto proposed have been either inconvenient in their use, or of such limited application, as to afford but very partial protection. Two of them only deserve notice, and these we allude to for the purpose of suggesting a method which we think would be more effective than either: they are the *stop-guard*, which had for many years a very general use, but which, instead of gaining strength with time, is now slowly disappearing; and the *safety-bent*, invented by the Messrs. Rigby more than twenty years ago, and generally found in their guns and those of other Irish makers, but which does not appear to have found its way across the Channel.

*The Stop-guard* is a contrivance which locks the triggers, and prevents them from acting on the lock until the gun is grasped by the hand in the firing position. This effectually prevents any accidental pressure on the trigger from charging the gun *when it is at full cock;* but it is no safety in any other case. The general objection urged is, that in the excitement of shooting, the stock is not always held in the manner which is required to disengage the bolt, and a disappointment is the consequence. Moreover, it requires to be kept clean and free from rust, which, from its position, is not always practicable without the assistance of a gunmaker; and, withal, accidents have happened even with guns which had this provision.

*The Safety-bent* is a much more simple affair, being merely a third bent in the lock, which acts almost immediately after the cock is raised off the pillar, and is perfectly calculated to prevent the casualties which frequently occur from the dangerous practice of carrying the gun with the cock down on the cap; for, in this position, if any impediment catches the finger-piece, the cock is slightly raised, but immediately becoming disengaged, owing to the circle it describes, it falls on the cap and explodes the charge. This generally happens when the person is drawing the gun towards him, and the consequences are often fatal.

Accidents, resulting in the loss of the right hand, which are frightfully frequent, arise from the sportsman, when hurried, incautiously reloading the right barrel with the left lock at full cock, when the slightest shock sometimes causes an explosion; and although the safety-bent may arrest the fall of the cock in this case, yet it appears to us as if something more were required. We, therefore, would suggest to practical men to construct a bolt which would interpose to prevent the cock from falling on the pillar, and be only withdrawn by a mechanism similar to the stop-guards, already described, when the gun is required to be discharged. This would combine the advantages of that contrivance and the safety-bent, and, if sufficiently simple in construction, fulfil every requirement. We cannot say so much for the plan exhibited by M. Brunel, of St. Etienne, which is a trigger-bolt, thrown in and out of gear by a small lever under the guard. To use it would require an amount of premeditation, which, if it were possible, would itself be sufficient to prevent any accident. Indeed, it may be taken as a general rule, that no contrivance of this kind which demands forethought in its use is of the least value; besides, it is to the lock, and not the trigger, to which the bolt ought to be applied. We hope that these observations may have the effect of awakening the attention of some one to this important subject, who may perfect a plan calculated to put a termination to those calamities whose recurrence we have annually to deplore.

We will now conclude with a brief notice of some of the more remarkable specimens in the Exhibition. First in the order of the Catalogue is a case of guns by Mr. Henry Allport, of Cork, which are very creditable to him as a manufacturer, and display in their finish, and the method of exhibition, considerable taste.

We next come to a variety of repeating pistols, by Colonel Colt, of Spring-gardens, London. The merits and demerits of these weapons have been so frequently discussed that it is superfluous to enter into the controversy. Some of the present collection are more highly finished than any before exhibited.

The guns, pistols, and rifles exhibited by Messrs. W. and J. Kavanagh, of Dame-street, are of excellent quality and high finish, and are good specimens of the work of that firm.

Messrs. William and John Rigby, of Suffolk-street, exhibited a large assortment of guns and pistols, the workmanship of which cannot be surpassed. In the centre was a frame supporting barrels in various stages, so placed that the interior could be examined, thus affording illustrations of the processes we have above described. Among the guns we particularly remarked a double rifle of unusual lightness; this was constructed by reducing the bore and using elongated balls, the latter being of an improved description, calculated to supersede the "Minie." We noticed among the improvements the continuous working, which adds great strength to the weakest part of the gun, the removable trigger, solid slides, and the single hair trigger for double rifles; also a very ingenious mould for casting "Minie" bullets. The Damascus barrels in the case of these exhibitors were smoke-stained as well as pickled, a novel finish, which is a great improvement over the bright barrels. Among the pistols were revolvers capable of firing eighteen shots in half a minute.

M. Westly Richards, of Birmingham, contributed a case containing double guns and rifles. His name is a sufficient guarantee of their quality.

A large assortment of guns, rifles, and pistols, was exhibited by Messrs. E. Trulock and Son, of Dawson-street. These specimens well sustained the character of the house.

In the French Department were several cases of barrels; there was also one gun in its case, with some two or three peculiarities of construction, which M. Brunel, of St. Etienne, claims as improvements. Among these was the trigger-bolt mentioned above, and the method of fastening the barrels in the stock, but we fear none of them promise to be of permanent value.

M. Bruer, of Liege, exhibited guns, pistols, &c.; and several other continental manufacturers contributed specimens of exquisite workmanship in this department, the extent of which will be indicated when noticing the productions of the respective countries to which they belong.—J. R.

---

1. ADMIRALTY, THE LORDS COMMISSIONERS OF THE, Whitehall, London.—Models of ships, viz.: the Great Harry (rigged), built in the reign of Henry VIII., in glass; the Royal George, 100 guns, sunk at Spithead, 1782; the Royal Sovereign, built at Woolwich, by Peter Pelt, in the reign of Charles I., 1687; the Queen, 116 guns, built at Portsmouth, 1840; the Vanguard, 80; the Cumberland, 70; the Vernon, 50; the Pique, 40; transverse sections of the Queen, 116 guns, and the Vanguard; half model of the Collingwood, 80, showing the interior (scale ½ in.); a series of nine boats for a first-rate ship; admiralty models of the Victoria and Albert, and the Fairy Royal Yachts (made by Daniel Harvest, ½ scale).

2. AICKIN, T., M. D., Merrion-square, South, Dublin, Inventor.—A life-boat, twenty feet long, eight feet beam, with air-cases, &c.

3. ALLEN, A. P., Hon. E. I. Co.'s Service, Ballystraw, County of Wexford.—Model of a corvette ship of 20 guns; scale, three-tenths of an inch to a foot.

4. ALLPORT, H., Cork, Manufacturer.—Double fowling-pieces; Minie rifles; small breech-loading rifle, for rook and rabbit shooting; pistols.

5. ARMSTRONG, R., Newbridge Barracks.—Wooden model of improved battery gun, also of a field gun, and balls for same.

6. BARRY, J. & W. M'G., South Bridge, Cork, Designers.—Models of a 50-gun frigate; a merchant screw steamer, 1100 tons (length over nine and a half times the beam); a paddle steamer; clipper yacht, 50 tons; clipper schooners of 200 and 150 tons; model of a screw vessel.

7. BERTHON, REV. E. L., Fareham, Hants, Inventor.—Patent perpetual logs, an hydrostatic instrument for indicating the speed of ships; clinometers and other instruments for showing the trim and list of ships; working model of a collapsible life-boat.

8. BURTON, E. H., 11, Wentworth-place, Dublin, Designer.—Model of a schooner yacht.

9. CANNING, J., Rockville, Malin, Donegal, Inventor.—A smooth-bored gun barrel, throwing conical bullets with the force and precision of a rifle.

10. CAREY, A. L., Smith's Buildings, Dublin, Proprietor.—A Java crisse, with Damascus blade, curiously wrought, and poisoned, the sheath of gold, enamelled and studded with diamonds—wrested from the Sultan of D'Jocjocarta, at the storming of his palace in the Crattan.

11. CLARKE, J. A., Birkenhead, Designer.—Model of a first-class merchant steamer, about 900 tons, fitted with patent paddle-wheels, and every other recent and patent improvement.

12. COCKBURNE, J., Sallymount, Ranelagh, Dublin, Designer.—Model of a brig.

13. CONLAN, W. J., Kingstown, Designer.—Fore and aft schooner model yacht for sailing.

14. COLT, Colonel S., Spring Gardens, Cockspur-street, London, Inventor and Patentee.—Patent repeating fire-arms or revolvers of different sizes and styles of finish; skeleton pistol, showing the working of the various parts; holster or cavalry, six shots; navy or belt, 7½ inch barrel, six shots; four, five, and six inch barrel for belt or pocket, five shots, all rifle barrels; repeating carbines, six shots.

15. COOPER, W., Corrig-terrace, Kingstown, Designer.—Half models of cutter yacht "Irish Lily," 80 tons, O. M.; American clipper pilot boats "Moses H. Grinnell," 117 tons, O. M., and "Mary Taylor," 94 tons, O. M.; a plan of a schooner yacht, proposed to cheat both "Old" and "Royal Mersey Yacht Club" measurement, with centre board astern.

16. COTTER, J. B., Monkstown, Co. Cork, Inventor.—Models of life-boats (scale, one inch to a foot); model of a truck for conveying life-boats from point to point; improved portable anchor for life-boats; samples of strong waterproof canvass for covering life-boats, and for ships and railway purposes (patented).

17. DICK, M., High-street, Irvine, Ayrshire.—An articulated metal tube, or protective covering for submarine or land telegraph wires and other purposes, being a continuous series of ball and socket joints, or form of spine or vertebral column. Model exhibiting an entirely new method (by means of vulcanized India rubber bags), of raising sunk vessels and other materials from deep water; model of a vessel, with variety of screw propellers, made and experimented with in the year 1828, invented by William M'Cririck, gunsmith, Irvine; two lances used at the grand Tournament at Eglinton Castle, in a tilting match between the Earl of Eglinton and the Marquess of Waterford.

18. DILLON, A. G., Upper Buckingham-street, Dublin, Inventor.—An improved lanthorn for telegraphing orders to the helmsman in steam-vessels.

19. DILLON, THOMAS A., Upper Buckingham-street, Dublin, Inventor.—Life-boat formed of three or more longitudinal pieces of timber, covered with hide or canvass, interlined with air-tubes; double conical expanding rifle bullet.

20. DWYER, M., Commander R. N., Samuel-street, Woolwich, Inventor and Proprietor.—Model and sections of a life-boat with expanding sides, which cannot be upset; model of a gun-brig, showing a new plan of coppering ships' bottoms; section of steam-ship, with improved method of hoisting and lowering the paddle-box boats; model of horizontal propeller; a bow section with relieving bitts; after body section; new plan of hanging rudder, and of steering, should the rudder-head be carried away; model of anchor for a 40-gun frigate; model of a boat with a safety-plug always ready.

21. FARRON, G., Boat Builder, South Shields.—Model of a boat.

22. GRANTHAM, JOHN, Liverpool, Designer.—Model of the screw steamer "Eagle," built for Mr. Dargan, from designs by exhibitor, to ply between Newry and Liverpool.

23. GRISDALE, J. E., Bloomsbury-street, Holborn, London, Inventor.—Model of a screw boat, with new form of rudder (called a "balance rudder"), having nearly equal resisting surface on each side of its axis or centre of motion; boat sterns, showing another application of the balance rudder.

24. HEALY, W., Harcourt-street, Dublin, Proprietor.—Model of a steam-boat, showing by a simple contrivance of machinery a manner by which the oar of the paddle-wheel can be made to feather, obviating the evil effects of back water, and also by the turning of a screw one paddle-wheel can be made to reverse its paddle, causing the boat to turn on its own centre.

25. HODSMAN, Banna Villa, Mountpleasant-avenue, Dublin, Manufacturer.—Models of self-igniting signal light, for the rescue of shipwrecked seamen, and the self-protector pocket light.

26. JUDSON, VINCENT, Barrow-street, Dublin, Designer.—Working model of a steamer with an improved screw propeller; model of an American schooner yacht.

27. KAVANAGH, W. & J., Dame-street, Dublin, Manufacturer.—Guns, pistols, and rifles.

28. KING, HARMAN, Hon. L., Newcastle, Ballymahon, Co. Longford, Inventor.—Model of an improved method of lowering boats from vessels in cases of wreck, fire, &c.

29. LAIRD, JOHN, Birkenhead.—Models of screw and paddle steam-ships of various sizes.

30. MANCHESTER, THE DUKE OF, Tanderagee.—Model of "the America," by Steers, of New York, the builder of the vessel; model of a famous Baltimore schooner, showing the different style of building.

31. MILLERS & THOMPSON, Liverpool.—Model of the clipper ship, "Star of the East."

32. MOXAM, P., Granard, Co. Longford, Inventor.—Model of steam-boat paddle-wheel.

33. NORTON, CAPTAIN, Cork, Inventor.—Models of projectiles for military operations, &c.

34. REDMOND, J., Donnybrook-road, Dublin.—Model of a boat.

35. RICHARDS, WESTLEY, Birmingham, and New Bond-street, London, Manufacturer.—Double-barrelled guns and rifle; large single rifle for shooting wild animals; patent five shot revolving pistol, with one barrel; duelling pistols.

36. RIGBY, W. & J., Suffolk-street, Dublin, Manufacturer.—Staunchion gun, with improved plan of ignition, &c.; case of twin double guns, with extra rifle, the locks, barrels, and triggers fitting either gun; single and double-barrelled guns, rifles, and pistols, with various improvements; revolvers, for six, twelve, or more shots, &c.; specimens of gun-barrels, rifled and otherwise; various parts of the gun, to illustrate the several stages of the manufacture; gun and pistol-cases.

37. ROBINSON, G. & Co., Cork, Manufacturers.—Models of a ship of 1000 tons, barque of 804 tons (now building), schooner of 150 tons.

38. ROCK, J., Hastings, Sussex, Proprietor and Exhibitor.—Model of a Hastings fishing lugger.

39. ROYAL HUMANE SOCIETY, Trafalgar-square, London, per J. CHARLIER, Secretary.—Models of pole and rope drags; ice-boat of wicker-work, covered with raw hide, on wooden rockers (made at Hamburgh), and breaker ladder used for extricating persons who have broken through the ice; print descriptive of the same.

40. SHEARER & BARR, Ardrossan, Ayrshire, Proprietors.—Five models of ships.

41. SMITH, H., Rotherhithe, London, Designer and Proprietor.—Model of a steam-vessel, intended for river navigation (scale, ½ inch to a foot).

42. SPARKS, W. S., New Bond-street, London, Manufacturer.—India rubber portable fishing and life-boat, inflated with air, with sculls, bellows for inflation, &c., to carry three persons, but capable of supporting more than twenty when used as a life-buoy.

43. TEAL, H., Ringsend, Dublin, Inventor and Designer.—Models of yacht, life-boat, and ship.

44. TRULOCK, E., & SON, Dawson-street, Dublin, Manufacturers.—Double and single-barrelled guns, rifles, and pistols, of various patterns and designs; large boat-gun for shore-shooting; centripetal double-barrelled gun; air-gun; gun and rifle-barrels in the stages of manufacture; gun and pistol-cases, &c.

45. WALKER, S. & Co., 12, Legge-street, Birmingham, Manufacturers.—Percussion caps, for military and sporting use; patent metallic gun wadding, &c.; metal lined caps.

46. WHITE, ARTHUR, Boot-lane, Dublin.—Guns, pistols, percussion caps, wadding, shot-belts, pouches, &c.

47. YARBOROUGH, THE EARL OF, Arlington-street, London.—Models of the bows and sterns of ships in her Majesty's service, designed by Captain Symonds, R.N., and presented by him to the late Earl of Yarborough.

# CLASS IX.

---

## AGRICULTURAL IMPLEMENTS AND MACHINERY.

THE application of mechanical science to agriculture possesses an interest which is not by any means confined to the tillers of the soil. Even to those having no special knowledge of agricultural pursuits, the inquiry as to how far the husbandman has taken advantage of the march of improvement, elsewhere so apparent, is well deserving of attention. A slight examination of the objects sought to be attained by the different classes of implements and machines will assist in the formation of an opinion as to their adaptation for the intended purpose. We shall thereby be enabled to estimate the character of the difficulties to be surmounted, the efficiency of the agency already employed; and, we would further hope, to ascertain the direction in which additional improvements are to be sought. In the application of mechanical science to the business of husbandry, the great drawback is in the manufacturer so imperfectly appreciating the nature of the work to be done; and hence, year after year, the same implements and machines continue to be produced without much modification. Occasionally a manufacturer is to be found who, by superior intelligence and enterprise, does not confine his efforts to the beaten track; and although they may may not always be successful, it is to such persons that we are indebted for the improvements hitherto effected. Farmers, as a body, are not only little fitted to suggest improvements, but when made by others they are even little disposed to adopt them. In the business of husbandry, capital and intelligence are not combined to the same extent as in any other branch of industry; and hence, although the most ancient art, it is the most backward. While a few years serve to effect a complete revolution in other trades and manufactures, the farmer is, for the most part, satisfied to tread in the footsteps of his fathers, not merely regarding with indifference those "new-fangled" notions which the spirit of the age irresistibly forces upon his attention, but often treating them with absolute ridicule.

The peculiar position of the agricultural interest led to efforts being made for its advancement at a much earlier period than associated co-operation was extended to any other object. Exhibitions of various kinds connected with agriculture have accordingly been held, to a greater or less extent, for nearly a century; and although the measure of success attained has not always come up to the expectations of the more sanguine supporters of such movements, still it is beyond question that much good was effected thereby. In the department to which our attention is on the present occasion more especially invited, a marked improvement has taken place through the various periodical Exhibitions that have been held in various parts of the country. In this way the Highland and Agricultural Society of Scotland has done much for the agriculture of that country; and during the past fifteen years the English Agricultural Society may be said to have effected a complete revolution in the implements and machinery of England, which previously stood so much in need of improvement. In this country less has been done than in any of the other divisions of the United Kingdom. Our exhibitions of agricultural implements and machinery have not been characterized by that novelty and variety which could have been desired; and many of the improvements introduced on the other side of the channel have been but slowly adopted in Ireland.

Hitherto, the case of Ireland has been exceptional in many respects, and perhaps in no other more than in the extent to which machinery was rendered available for agricultural purposes. The generally small extent of the holdings interposed a formidable obstacle in this direction. The occupants of such holdings can seldom duly appreciate the value of improved machinery and implements as tending to cheapen the cost of production; and, besides, they seldomer still possess the means of procuring them. Under such circumstances, active progress is out of the question. But a change is now gradually taking place in the condition of the agricultural interest in Ireland: the consolidation of farms, and the increased activity and skill which are now apparent as compared with the state of affairs even a few years ago, are of hopeful augury; the social revolution which has been in operation for some years has indirectly given an impetus to agricultural improvement. The indolent and unskilful farmer has been obliged to make way for others prepared to turn the circumstances in which they are placed to better account; and in the change thus going forward the influence of the Exhibition has been potent for good. While special knowledge was gained by the agricultural visitor in going through his own department, the general knowledge derived by an inspection of the operations going forward in the Machinery Court was scarcely of less avail. The application of machinery to other purposes cannot fail to have impressed the visitor here referred to with the small extent to which the practice was carried in husbandry, as well as the great field which presented itself in this direction for further improvement. The accuracy with which the most complex operations were there performed could not fail to be suggestive of what may be done for the farmer, provided the machinist and he who is to work it will only go hand in hand, which they must do to attain any good result.

The class of articles now under consideration may be appropriately separated into several subdivisions, from the similarity of the functions which they are required to perform, and the order in which the operations take place:—

Implements of tillage; as ploughs, digging machines, harrows, rollers and clod-crushers, cultivators, &c.
Drilling, hoeing, and sowing machines.
Harvesting machines; as reaping machines, rakes, and tedding machines, &c.
Barn and yard machinery; as threshing, winnowing, and other machines.
Drainage implements, and machinery.
Dairy utensils and apparatus; and miscellaneous articles.

Of each of these classes, we propose to notice the leading features; pointing out the more important improvements which have recently been effected, and suggesting the direction in which further improvements are to be sought in the more extended application of mechanical science to the business of husbandry.

## I.—IMPLEMENTS OF TILLAGE.

In duly estimating the comparative merits of different implements of tillage, and the special adaptation of each, we must first have correct notions of what is desired to be attained, and then consider the most efficient agencies for the purpose. An approximation to garden tillage is now recognised as the primary object of all good husbandry. The advantages of deep and minute pulverization are now thoroughly understood; and it is the question of expense which comes in to determine the extent to which this condition of the soil should be carried out. The general adoption of thorough drainage in lands naturally suffering from excess of moisture has removed the great obstacle to deep pulverization; and it is a significant fact that the depth of drains as well as that of tillage has been on the increase for years past. When the late Mr. Smith, of Deanston, first agitated the subject of thorough drainage, little over twenty years ago, a depth of two and a half feet was regarded as sufficient, under ordinary circumstances, for drains; and by the use of the subsoil plough, then also introduced, the soil was stirred some ten to twelve inches deep, which at the time was considered to be a great achievement. A few years, however, only elapsed until the necessity of deeper drainage than that here contemplated became manifest; and a depth of four feet for drainage became general. This, in turn, was followed by deeper tillage than had hitherto been considered practicable or necessary; and the ingenuity of machinists was soon set to work to ascertain how this object could be best attained. Some modification of the plough is still the best instrument for deeply penetrating the soil; and this will probably continue to be the case so long as animal labour forms the motive power employed. For securing a high degree of pulverization, once the soil has been stirred up, other agencies are advantageously used—such as scarifiers or grubbers. The action of these latter is only supplemental to that of the plough; but after a ploughing has been given, the combined action of the grubber and clod-crusher secures what is technically termed a fine tilth much more economically than it could be otherwise effected.

The necessity of deep tillage as a primary agent in securing luxuriant and vigorous vegetation was so fully discussed when considering the conditions involved in the growth of root-crops, in Class III., that it need not be further dwelt upon in this place. We may, however, observe that it leads to the introduction of machinery for sowing the various agricultural seeds, the use of which would otherwise have been inadmissible,—and to improved systems of general management, as, for example, the use of drill husbandry, even for corn crops. Thus, insensibly, as it were, a complete revolution comes to be effected in farm management, having as its basis and harbinger that deep and minute pulverization of the soil which is now recognised as an indispensable adjunct of good husbandry.

### THE PLOUGH.

The plough may be regarded as the primary implement of this class, and it is, indeed, symbolic of agriculture generally. Some apparatus intended to perform a function analogous to the operation of the plough was the first application of brute labour to the tillage of the soil. With some slight modifications it has come down to us from the remotest period of which we have any records; and the extent of these modifications was very small, indeed, until within the present century, when an almost endless diversity of form has been given to it to adapt it to the different circumstances in which it may be employed. With the impetus which Scottish agriculture received in the latter part of the last century great improvements were introduced in the construction of this implement; from the plough manufactured by Small until Wilkie of Uddingston so modified it that his form of the plough is, with slight variations, extensively used at the present day. We refer here to the Scotch ploughs, as they have been almost exclusively those introduced into this country.

In Scotland and Ireland the *swing plough* is almost universally employed; a term given to it to distinguish the plough without wheels from that to which one or more wheels are appended. Wheel ploughs are, however, in general use in England, the number of wheels varying from one to four. The addition of the wheels to a considerable extent dispenses with skill on the part of the ploughman, as the width and depth of the furrow slice are thereby determined with considerable precision; the duty of the ploughman with them being chiefly to attend to the implement at the headlands of the fields, to bring it round and replace it in its proper position. This alleged advantage the Scottish ploughman laughs at. He possesses the requisite skill to cut furrow slices with a degree of uniformity approaching what could be effected by the most exact machinery, and he, therefore, looks upon the wheel ploughs of the southern part of the island as clumsy excuses for the stupidity of the workmen. But the great objection to the use of the wheel plough in Scotland, as well as in this country, arises from the belief that it is of more severe draught than the swing plough; the exemption of skill on the part of the workman being attended by the imposition of additional work on the horses.

Those versant with the literature of agriculture will recollect that the controversy carried on for years as to the respective merits of the two classes of implements resembled the more recent "Battle of the Gauges;" but it is passing strange that the disputants on each side were satisfied to refer to the *opinions* of practical men on either side of the question, who were, of course, each equally positive as to the superior merits of their respective implements. It is obvious that nothing but a *trial* of different varieties of the respective kinds of ploughs, under similar circumstances, could settle the question; still this mode of deciding one of the most important points which could engage the attention of the agriculturist was not thought of; and until within a comparatively recent period no attempt was made on any rational grounds to determine the comparative merits of the wheel and swing ploughs, as regarded the execution of their work and the force required to propel them.

The circumstance to which we have now directed attention is one of more than ordinary significance, as showing how little agricultural matters are guided by rule, and the small extent to which definite calculations are made by the farmer. The different ploughing matches which were held in Scotland, as well as in this country, led to the exercise of a great degree of skill in the use of the swing plough; the regularity of the work executed by which appears quite marvellous to those who are not familiar with it; and in proportion as this dexterity was acquired, was there a growing contempt for the alleged lumbering English article, usually drawn by three or four horses, while the swing plough is almost invariably worked with two. The increase in the number of horses being seldom followed by any corresponding increase in either the depth or the quantity of work executed, still further tended to confirm the impression of the advocates of the swing plough as to its superiority, so far as regarded lightness of draught. But still definite information was wanted, on which to come to any satisfactory conclusion on the subject.

We have already mentioned, that the exhibitions of the Royal Agricultural Society of Engand have done much for the improvement of the implements and machinery of husbandry during the past ten or twelve years, and in no other branch more than in determining the comparative value of different kinds of ploughs. Until these meetings the wheel and spring ploughs were never brought together in actual competition. The influence of the Scotch agricultural shows extended but little beyond the border, especially so far as implements were concerned; and the strong prejudice prevailing north of the Tweed against the use of English implements prevented them from being brought to Scotland for competition. But shortly after the formation of the English Society, the shows of implements became one of its most attractive features. Practical trials of the several articles soon came to be arranged, and prizes were awarded according to the performance. These prizes came, as a matter of course, to be regarded by the farmer as badges of merit, leading to an enormous increase of business with those manufacturers that were fortunate enough to obtain them. Among other results which these trials afforded, there were some very startling ones connected with the lightness of draught of different kinds of ploughs, as indicated by the dynamometer; an instrument of essential service in all such inquiries, but which is little used for the purpose. Hitherto, there had been nothing brought forward on either side beyond mere matter of opinion, but at the trials in question a test was applied of unerring accuracy.

In an inquiry on the subject of draught in ploughing, we have to determine:—1. The absolute resistance when at work, *in different soils*. 2. The relative draught of the various forms of the implement when at *the same work*. 3. The relative resistance to the motion of the plough made by *the different sources* of its draught. 4. The absolute influence of the weight upon its draught. 5. The influence of velocity on draught. 6. That of inclination of surface of the ground. 7. The influence of depth. The variations are indicated, as already stated, by the dynamometer, which consists of an elliptic or spiral spring, whose length or width varies with, and thus indicates the strain upon it, the variations being denoted by an index, whose position shows the strain which is at any moment applied. The amount of draught is, of course, indicated by the weight which would be required to produce the same degree of tension, supposing it to be applied in a vertical position.

It would be out of place here to enter at length into the details of the investigations to which we have alluded, some of the results of which we can only give. The ploughs enumerated below were employed to open a furrow five inches deep and nine inches wide, in a variety of soils, with the following results, the weights being indicated in stones:—

| DESCRIPTION OF PLOUGH. | Sandy Loam. | Blue Clay. | Loamy Sand. | Strong Loam. | Moory Soil. | Average. |
|---|---|---|---|---|---|---|
| | st. | st. | st. | st. | st. | st. |
| Ferguson's Scotch Swing, . . . . . . | 19 | 50 | 19 | 35 | 23 | 29 |
| Clarke's do. do., . . . . . . | 20 | 52 | 17 | 38 | 23 | 29 |
| Berkshire One-wheel, . . . . . . . | 14 | 43 | 12 | 28 | 16 | 21 |
| Ransome's Two-wheel, . . . . . . . | 14 | 43 | 13 | 16 | 14 | 23 |
| Do. Swing, . . . . . . . . . | 18 | 44 | 16 | 14 | 21 | 26 |
| Do. Rutland Two-wheels, . . | 17 | 50 | 16 | 21 | 21 | 28 |
| Old Berkshire Wheel, . . . . . . . | 23 | 52 | 21 | 25 | 25 | 31 |

The differences indicated in this Table are very remarkable, and point to the necessity of taking further elements into account in the determination of the circumstances on which these differences depend. The weight of the plough, for example, has so much influence on the draught, that it should obviously be as light as is consistent with adequate strength. This will be seen more clearly by considering the large force required to move the plough even without a furrow-slice. The following are the results of some of Mr. Pusey's trials on the subject, the first column indicating the gross draught with a furrow five inches by nine; the second, the surface-draught, to be deducted from the former; and the third, the weight of the ploughs employed* :—

| Description of Plough. | Gross Draught. | Surface Draught. | Weight. |
|---|---|---|---|
| Ferguson's, | 19 stones. | 12 stones. | 15 stones. |
| Clark's, | 17 " | 12 " | 15 " |
| Berkshire Wheel, | 12 " | 8 " | 12 " |
| Ransome's Two-wheel, | 18 " | 8 " | 13 " |
| Do. Swing, | 16 " | 8 " | 10 " |
| Do. Rutland, | 21 " | 8 " | 15 " |
| Old Berkshire, | 16 " | 10 " | 10 " |

In the progress of the inquiry it was observed that, contrary to the prevailing impression, the draught did not increase in proportion to the depth of the furrow, a circumstance of the last importance when it is considered that deep tillage is one of the requisites of successful husbandry. By using Ferguson's Scotch swing plough upon a poor, moory soil, and taking a given width of furrow-slice, only varying the depth, the following were among the results obtained :—

| Depth of Furrow. | Draught in Stones. | Depth of Furrow. | Draught in Stones. |
|---|---|---|---|
| 5, | 28 | 9, | 31 |
| 6, | 28 | 10, | 40 |
| 7, | 25 | 11, | 50 |
| 8, | 30 | 12, | 50 |

The only other point to which we can here direct attention is the influence of the velocity upon draught in ploughing; or, in other words, the degree in which the resistance varies by the rate at which the animals progress. Here, again, the result is very different from what would at first sight be expected, showing that friction has much less to do with velocity than is ordinarily supposed. This comparative independence of the draught of agricultural implements on the rate at which they are drawn through the ground is a matter of considerable moment. It indicates the value of only employing animals which walk at a good pace, as they get through a great additional quantity of work without a corresponding effort. Paradoxical as it may appear, there is little more labour expended, so far as the implement is concerned, in ploughing an acre in six or eight hours than in doing half the work in the same time. The increased pace would of itself demand an additional effort, irrespective altogether of the work to be done; but experience shows that the draught of the plough, as indicated by the dynamometer, is but little affected by an increase of velocity, a fact which the farmer should seek to turn to practical account. The following Table, extracted from Mr. Pusey's Report, fully bears out these statements :—

| Rate of going per hour. | Time to plough an acre. H. M. | Variation in draught. |
|---|---|---|
| 1½ miles, | 7 20 | 23 stones. |
| 1¾ " | 6 30 | 23 " |
| 2¼ " | 4 0 | 22 " |
| 3½ " | 3 3 | 24 " |

The absence or presence of wheels is only one of the many points deserving of consideration in the adaptation of the plough for the intended purpose; and the results which we have given above will serve to show the extended field which presents itself for investigation, even as regards the apparently simple consideration of the best kind of plough for the farmer to employ. They also serve to show what might be effected by the application of energy, capital, and skill, to the business of husbandry; which owes its backward position to the absence of their combination.

Of wheel and swing ploughs there were numerous illustrations in the Exhibition; and it was especially interesting to the Irish farmers to see such specimens of the wheel ploughs as those exhibited by Ransomes and Sims, and J. and F. Howard. Few persons in this country have seen ploughs of this class; and whatever may be the respective merits of these instruments, it could not fail to be most interesting to inspect the mechanical arrangements for regulating the depth and width of the furrow-slice, so that the operation shall be as little as possible dependent upon the skill of the workman, a circumstance to which, as before observed, those who use the swing plough attach little value. But without adopting the wheel plough in its present form, it remains to be seen whether we could not make use of some of the ingenious contrivances which it exhibits.

The collection of swing ploughs was not so extensive as might have been expected from their being in almost universal use in this country; and of those in the Exhibition there were few which call for any special remark. Our agricultural readers will be acquainted with the high value attached by many persons to Barrowman's ploughs, which, however, are sold at a high price as compared with most of the ordinary ploughs. A tolerably good imitation of Barrowman's mould-board may be found in a plough, the manufacture of Millar, of Dunleer, exhibited by T. Eeles, of this city, and which was, besides, a creditable specimen of workmanship, contrasting favourably in the latter respect with many of the articles in this department, the construction of which seemed to be as rude as the purpose for which they are designed.

Into the peculiarities of swing ploughs it is unnecessary that we should enter at any length. The form of the mould-board is the point in which the great variation takes place; the efforts of the manufacturers

* The results of these trials have been reported by Philip Pusey, Esq., in the Journal of the Royal Agricultural Society of England; a periodical whose deservedly high character is in no small degree owing to the editorial labours of that gentleman, who has had charge of it from its commencement.

being directed to modify the mould-board according to the character of the soil in which it is to be worked, as well as the purpose for which it is intended. The ploughs in the collection exhibited by Ransomes and Sims admitted of being used either as swing or wheel ploughs, as may be desired; the beam being so formed as to allow the wheels being appended and removed at pleasure. In the engraving, an implement of this

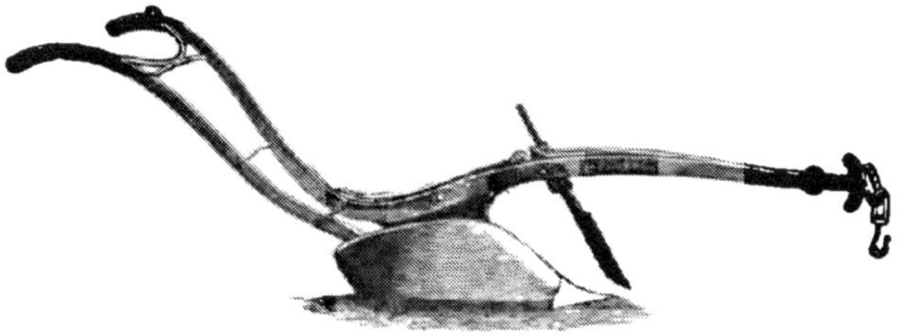

kind is figured. One wheel may be used, in which case it is made to pass over the unploughed land; or a second wheel may be appended, as in the annexed illustrations. Where extensive operations are carried on, an experienced ploughman may not at all times be available, and hence the value of being able to use the wheels. The depth is regulated with accuracy by the wheels; the one passing on the surface of the ground, and the other in the furrow.

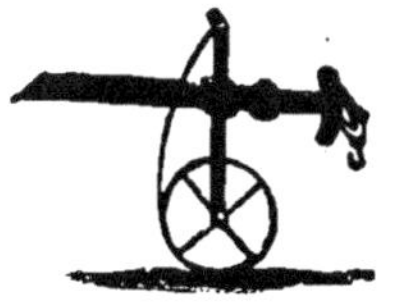

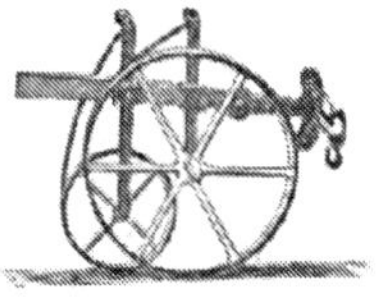

Of wheel ploughs we annex a further illustration, that here figured being also manufactured by Ransomes and Sims. For general purposes it has been proved to be an excellent implement, prizes having been awarded for it at various agricultural meetings held in England since 1844.

It is simple in construction, and light of draught; and the coulter-fittings are on a plan which affords facilities for placing the coulter in any required position. For this plough there is stated to be upwards of

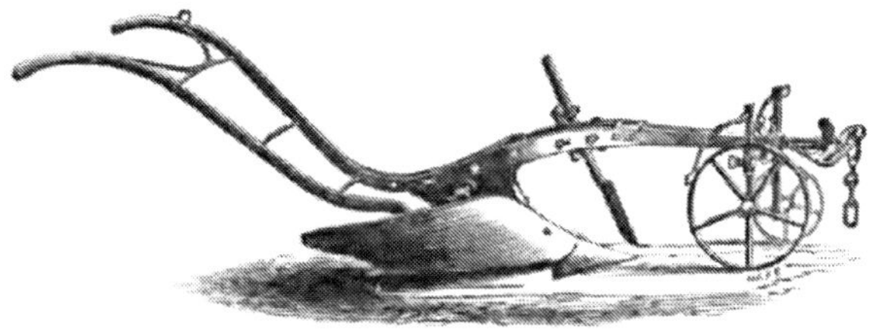

twenty varieties of mould-boards, according to the soil and purpose for which it is required. One peculiarity of such mould-boards is, however, the absence of that depth which characterizes those of what are called the Scotch ploughs.

In the purchase of such an implement as the plough there is a false economy exercised by many of our farmers, in seeking out cheap implements, almost without reference to any other consideration. An iron plough will last a life-time, and hence the best article should be procured almost irrespective of cost; for the difference in the manner in which the work of the farm is executed by one plough over another, in a single season, not to speak of the great difference which there is in point of lightness of draught, may far more than amount to the value of several ploughs. Yet, year after year, our farmers may be found looking after the cheapest implements, without thinking of any other points of difference between the implements of different manufacturers.

In addition to the common plough, used for purposes of ordinary tillage, a stronger kind of implements, known as subsoil and trench ploughs, have attracted attention for some years past, and deservedly so from the increasing importance of deep tillage in modern husbandry. It is now ascertained that, once in four or five years, the soil should get a stirring to a much greater depth than the ordinary working of it extends; and hence a fourth or fifth of the farm should be gone over in this manner every year. In the construction of these a greater degree of strength is required than in the common plough, on account of the increased strain upon them; and inasmuch as the soil is to be stirred up, and not turned over, the mould-board is dispensed with. Indeed, the common swing plough without a mould-board is sometimes used for the purpose.

In a previous part of this volume it has been seen that, so far as the Executive Committee was concerned, no attempt would be made to adjudicate upon the respective merits of the articles exhibited. To this rule the Agricultural Department formed an exception. Here the Committee were desirous of co-operating with the Council of the Royal Agricultural Improvement Society of Ireland; and with that view, so far as exhibitors were desirous of testing the merits of their goods, permission was given for their temporary removal for the trials, which were conducted under the auspices of the Agricultural Society. The annual Show of the Society having been held in a remote corner of the island, Killarney, it was considered advisable to hold a preliminary trial of implements in the neighbourhood of this city, the results of which would, in some degree, guide the Council in their subsequent arrangements. Accordingly, two days of the week before that in which the Killarney Show was held were devoted to experimental trials in the vicinity of Malahide, the investigations being concluded in the county of Kerry. As the final result of these trials, the first-class medal was awarded by the judges to William Graham, of Smithfield, for his swing plough. The wheel ploughs of William Ball, of Northampton, and Ransome and Sims, of Ipswich, were highly commended. A second-class medal was awarded to Robert Gray, of Belfast, for a trench plough. The subsoil plough of Robert Gray and Son, of Uddingston, obtained the prize medal, as being in the estimation of the judges the best implement of its class; and James M'Connell, of Dunleer, obtained a medal for his double mould-board plough. While on the subject of ploughs, we may direct attention to the subsoil plough exhibited by Ritchie and Sons, of Ardee, which was a very efficient instrument; and the double mould-board plough exhibited by the same firm was also a superior implement.

### DIGGING MACHINES.

Among the implements of tillage a digging machine naturally occupies a prominent place, provided it at all fulfils the function for which it is designed. The extent to which mechanical science has been applied to the cultivation of the soil, within the past quarter of a century, is quite marvellous, when compared with all that had previously been accomplished; and when we examine the course of that progress, the difficulties by which it has been beset, and the degree to which they have been surmounted, we are forced to the conclusion that very much still remains to be done in the same direction.

In any comprehensive scheme for economizing the tillage of the soil, there are two objects to be kept in view; one, the best and cheapest motive-power; and the other, how this power can be most effectively applied. The latter consideration only has received much attention, from our not being accustomed to look upon any other motive-power in tillage operations than that of horses and oxen. Hence, our implements have been especially adapted for the power which is to work them; and so little did the connexion between the two points attract attention, that when from time to time it was sought to apply steam-power, the trials were with the usual implements. Hence, also, the idea of ploughing by steam, on which so much labour and anxiety have been wasted, in the hope of being able to carry it out successfully. But those who were engaged in these investigations did not appear to consider, that although the plough may be, and no doubt is, the best form of instrument that can be used for turning up the ground when worked by animal power, yet it does not follow, that it may at all be adapted for steam-power, the successful use of which would be so great a desideratum. Nor is there much chance of the desideratum in question being attained, so long as such a line of investigation is pursued. It is not necessary that we should detail the different methods that have been from time to time adopted to carry out ploughing by steam. Suffice it to say, that they have one and all been unsuccessful; and such must continue to be the case until our mechanical engineers set about the object with a more correct appreciation of how it is really to be attained, than is involved in any such efforts as those already referred to.

The operation of such a machine as that invented by Mr. Samuelson, and which the inventor calls a digging machine, is suggestive in this respect. Here is an instrument designed for turning over and stirring up the soil on a great scale; but the circumstances must be peculiar under which it can be worked by animal power. The necessary extent of such power is also so great, that it may become a matter of doubtful economy to use it, even though it perfectly succeeded in performing the work. That such a machine as that under notice will yet be extensively employed in tillage operations is highly probable, but for this purpose horse power seems to be wholly inadequate.

This is not the place to discuss how steam is most likely to be effectively applied to the purposes of husbandry; but in the examination of such a machine as that of Mr. Samuelson, it is necessary that the principles which regulate its application should be taken into account. We have declared our total want of confidence in the success of what is termed steam-ploughing, because an obvious consideration has been overlooked in endeavouring to connect the steam-engine and the plough. If steam is ever destined to be applied to the cultivation of land, it must be through the agency of such machinery as this digging machine,— a consideration which our agricultural machinists should keep in view.

The operation of the digging machine is simple enough. By the aid of cranks, a number of flattened teeth are alternately elevated and depressed, as the machine is propelled, the digging apparatus being put in motion by the wheels of the machine. This instrument was tried at Malahide, with other agricultural implements; but we are bound to state, that that trial was scarcely satisfactory. The available horse-power was inadequate, and the whole arrangements for working the machine were defective, so that such a trial could scarcely be regarded as conclusive. Where the soil was partially loosened before, the digging machine acted fairly; but where it was compressed and hard on the surface, the machine passed along without producing almost any effect. An obvious remedy here would be to add to the weight, which would force the teeth into the ground. The strength would at the same time be added to; but in the same proportion we should be adding to the difficulty of working it, at least by animal power.*

* At the meeting of the British Association at Hull, last season, Mr. B. Samuelson read a paper on "Recent Improvements in Machines for tilling Land," which, as explaining the views of the inventor of the machine here noticed, we place *in extenso* before our readers.

"The mechanical disintegration of the particles of the soil, for the purpose of increasing its productiveness, has been practised more or less skilfully from time immemorial: until within the last hundred years or so, however, rather as a matter of routine, than in consequence of any apprehension

In addition to the digging machine invented by Mr. Samuelson, of Banbury, there is another, the invention of Mr. Henry Bleasdale, of Chipping, Lancashire, whose machine, we regret to find, was not in the present Exhibition, as it would have been interesting to judge of the respective machines by comparison. Both are alike in their digging, or rather forking parts, but very different in their cleaning apparatus. In Samuelson's machine there is a peculiar sort of scrapers, worked between each series of revolving spikes; while in Bleasdale's, instead of scrapers, there is a series of revolving forks that rotate in the opposite direction to that of the digging forks. There is, however, another arrangement of the digging apparatus which we regard as deserving of consideration, though, without seeing it put to the test, we are disposed to avoid

of the causes of its efficacy. It is true that the tendency of a plant to increase above ground in proportion to the extension of its roots below the surface may have been admitted, and the necessity of loosening the soil consequently enforced; still no serious attempt was made before the time of Jethro Tull, to ascertain the functions of the root in the vegetable economy.

"Omitting any reference in detail to the experiments of that pioneer of modern cultivation, it may be stated of him with truth, that his discoveries stand in the same relation to those of the great organic chemists of our day, that the solar systems of his predecessors stood to that of Copernicus—i. e. they afford a sufficient formula for the elucidation of some of the leading phenomena of the nourishment of plants, yet stop short of the laws which govern them. From the moment, however, when it was demonstrated that the inorganic constituents of vegetables are furnished by the decomposition of the soil itself, and of the earthy matters contained in the manures which are supplied to it, its mechanical subdivision ceased to be an empirical practice, for it became evident at once that, by presenting the greatest possible number of points to the action of air and water, the agriculturist facilitated such decomposition, in the same manner as the chemist assists his reactions, by reducing to powder the substances on which he operates.

"Hence, increased importance has of late been attached to the drainage of the subsoil, and the pulverization and deepening of the seed bed; and it is to some of the more recent mechanical contrivances for effecting the latter objects that I wish to draw your attention.

"The plough, which has so long been the principal, and will probably remain, for a long time to come, a most valuable implement of husbandry, has (among others) this inconvenience, that whilst it loosens and reverses the top soil, it compresses the bottom of the furrow in its progress. A partial remedy was applied to this evil at a considerable expense by the use of the subsoil plough, which bursts the ground immediately below the furrow.

"Meanwhile it has been sought to avoid the use of the plough entirely, in those cases where the complete inversion is not needed, and hence the introduction of various pulverizers, grubbers, &c., which have, of late, been used, no longer as auxiliaries, but as principals in cultivation. For the same reason digging with the spade or fork, hitherto confined to the operations of the gardener, has been practised recently with great success by many farmers, amongst whom I need hardly mention Mr. Mechi on the larger, and the Rev. S. Smyth, of Lois Weedon, on a more experimental scale. Horse and hand-hoeing are becoming more general every year, not merely for the purpose of destroying weeds, but also of exposing fresh particles of soil to decomposition; thus constantly increasing and renewing the supply of food at the disposal of the growing crop. Not content with these amplifications of the use of the accustomed farming tools, other more expeditious and more complete machines of cultivation have been sought after and invented. Omitting the various clod-crushers and harrows, these may be conveniently divided into:—1. Ploughing machines drawn by stationary steam-engines. 2. Locomotive steam-ploughs; and 3. Machines, chiefly rotary, for pulverizing by means of forks, spades, or claws.

"Amongst the first class, the most remarkable are the ploughing frames of Lord Willoughby d'Eresby and of the Marquess of Tweeddale, differing in their details, yet both attended, more or less, with some of the inconveniences of the horse plough; but successful, inasmuch as they substitute a more expeditious and powerful agent for animal traction. The Marquis of Tweeddale's ploughing machine consists of a frame, containing two double ploughs, resembling the common turnwrist plough, one-half of each being in the air whilst the other half is in the ground. The frame is drawn across the field by wire ropes attached to steam-engines, stationed at opposite headlands; both ploughs being reversed at each turn, so that the slices are always laid in the same direction. The work of each plough is 15 inches deep and 13 inches wide, equal to 26 inches in the frame, and the execution is faultless. By means of a beam about 18 feet long, projecting from each engine at right angles to the ploughing frame, and a simple apparatus attached to it, the ploughs are lifted at each turn and deposited two furrows, or 26 inches, in advance of their previous position. Thus the frequent removal of the engines is avoided. They are, however, locomotive, and run upon wooden trains laid for the purpose. The machine ploughs three acres per day, and requires four men to work it, besides a man and horse to bring water. The depth ploughed (15 inches) is, I believe, unprecedented except by the horse ploughing of the Marquess himself, who, I am informed, by the aid of the latter, so improved the fertility of two entire farms as to have raised their annual value in five years from 7*s*. 6*d*. to £3 per acre.

"A more decided advance in steam ploughing has been made by Mr. Usher, of Edinburgh, who boldly abandoned the old mode of traction altogether, and caused his steam-engine to cross the land on a broad roller, attaching to it a cylindrical framework of plough-points and mould-boards, which, whilst being lowered into the ground to the required depth, is made to rotate, disintegrating the soil more completely than the ordinary plough, without compressing the bottom of the furrow, the thrusts of the mould-boards, at the same time, aiding the forward motion of the engine, and enabling it to mount inclinations which it could not cope with by the mere adhesion of the roller. As at present constructed, the power is about 10 horses, and when worked to a depth of 7 or 8 inches, it will plough about six acres per day. Its great weight, about six tons, is a serious drawback, but I am inclined to think that it may be considerably reduced, and I know of no other rotatory machine, that so successfully inverts the soil, though it is still excelled in that respect by the ordinary traction ploughs. Usher's steam plough has been repeatedly worked in the Lothians, and I am not aware that its use was attended with any difficulties beyond those which must be expected in all new inventions.

"With reference to machines for digging by means of spades, I am not aware of any that have been put into actual operation. The machine exhibited by Thompson in the Agricultural Department of the Crystal Palace of 1851 will have been noticed by many of my auditors. It consisted of two series of spades at right angles to each other, the second series covering the spaces left by the first, and both being forced into the ground by a cranked shaft, borne in a rectangular frame.

"The last, and apparently the most promising division, is that of the rotary forking or clawing implements.

"A light machine of this kind was constructed so long as thirty years back by Morton, of Leith; but it comes rather under the class of revolving harrows than of cultivators properly so called. Foremost amongst the latter in point of date is that of Lady Vavasour, exhibited at the Show of the Royal Agricultural Society at Bristol, which, though unsuccessful, may be regarded as the precursor of the more practical rotatory forking and subsoiling machines that have since been constructed. Lady Vavasour's implement consisted of a cylinder, studded with prongs, set spirally around it, which penetrated the ground by the weight of the cylin-

speaking positively about it. We allude to that involved in the hay-shaking machine, in which a different kind of motion is conveyed to the parts in action from that employed in the digging machine. If the former were constructed of the necessary degree of strength to resist the strain upon them, we apprehend that the soil would be turned over with the same facility that the grass or hay is tedded by the hay-shaking machine, the operation of which is amongst the most successful applications of mechanical science to the business of the farmer. These remarks, however, are intended to be suggestive, indicating the path to be pursued and the conditions involved therein, rather than propounding any positive opinion, for which further information is yet clearly required.

der and framing, and broke it or tore it up as the latter was drawn forward.

"It was succeeded, after an interval of some years, by the cultivators of the Hon. Mr. Clive and of Josiah Parks. One of the latter has been used in subsoiling the estate of Mr. Marshall, at Patrington, near this town. Here the cylinder of Lady Vavasour, which had the inconvenience of forming, as it were, a taking-up roller, round which the earth wound itself until it formed a solid mass, in which the prongs entirely disappeared, is replaced by a number of discs, revolving independently of each other; the prongs also being made so long that the earth cannot easily reach their roots. Another step was the addition of cleaning or doffing-bars, for stripping the soil from the prongs. Of these, Roberts' machine affords an example. Its chief peculiarity, however, consists in the prongs being made to feather, somewhat like the floats of Morgan's paddle-wheel, the motion communicated to them resembling that of the fork in the hands of a man.

"I must not omit to mention the labours of Hoskyns, the talented author of the 'Chronicles of a Clay Farm,' which, with their humorous illustrations by Cruikshank, have contributed so greatly to popularize the subject of tillage.

"Though it will be evident at once to the mechanic that the writer is anything but familiar with the practical difficulties which would attend the use of locomotive steam-engines on such surfaces as those with which the agriculturist has to deal (difficulties, by the way, to which the rotary plough of Usher is subject in a far less degree), and though he assumes for his steam-cultivator a power of inverting the soil, which the means he employs would fail to insure, his description of the thing to be accomplished is so vivid, and his sketch of the engine, which, according to his view, is to effect it, is so neat a specimen of mechanical drawing by words alone, that I must claim your indulgence for quoting them here:—

"'I say that the plough has sentence of death written upon it, because it is essentially imperfect; what it does is little towards the work of cultivation, but that little is tainted by a radical imperfection—damage to the subsoil, which is pressed and hardened by the share, in an exact ratio with the weight of the soil lifted, plus that of the force required to effect the clearage and the weight of the instrument itself. Were there no other reason for saying it than this, this alone would entitle the philosophic machinist to say, and see, that the plough was never meant to be immortal.

"'Why, then, should we struggle for its survival under the new dynasty of steam? The true object is not to perpetuate, but as soon as possible to get rid of it. Why poke an instrument seven or eight inches under the clod to tear it up in the mass by main force, for other instruments to act upon, toiling and treading it down again, in ponderous attempts at cultivation wholesale, when, by simple abrasion of the surface, by a revolving toothed instrument, with a space as broad as the hay-tedding machine, or Crosskill's clod-crusher, you can perfect the complete work of communication in the most light, compendious, and perfect detail?

"'Imagine such an instrument (not rolling on the ground), but performing independent revolutions behind its locomotive, cutting its way down by surface abrasion into a semi-circular trench, about a foot and a half wide, throwing back the pulverized soil (as it flies back from the feet of a dog scratching at a rabbit hole); then imagine the locomotive moving forward on the hard ground, with a slow and equable mechanical motion, the revolver behind, with its cutting points (case-hardened) playing on the edge or land side of the trench, as it advances, and capable of any adjustment to coarse or fine cutting, moving always forward, and leaving behind, granulated and inverted by its revolving action, a seed-bed, seven or eight inches deep, never to be gone over again by any implement except the drill, which had much better follow at once, attached behind with a light bush-harrow to cover the seed.'

"Besides a modification, proposed by Usher, of his steam-plough, in which he substitutes rotary prongs for his points and mould-boards, involving, however, the difficulty, that he loses the aid to progression which the latter afford him—two other steam-cultivators have been projected, both of which possess, in common with that of Clott, the distinctive feature that the rotation of the cultivating tools is not derived from the progress of the carriage. The first is that of Stephen Brown, who has two series of rotary cutters, the second set working at intervals left by the first, and both driven through cross shafts from a small locomotive steam-engine, forming part of the implement, and which may either work its way across the field by its own adhesion, or be drawn by horses. The second is the Canadian machine, spoken of by Mr. Mechi in a recent letter to the 'Times.' It does not differ greatly from the preceding in its mode of operation, its novelty consisting in the arrangement of the parts, and in the adoption of a very light and compact form of engine. I have been requested by the inventor not to publish the details, as he has not yet secured his right to them in some foreign states.

"I will now describe the most recent rotary cultivators that have been put practically to work, viz., Bleasdale's and my own. The former somewhat resembles Parker's subsoilers, but, being calculated only to pulverize the surface soil, its weight is only about one-half that of Parker's, and that weight (one ton), instead of resting on two discs only, is distributed over seven. The chief novelty in it is the cleaning apparatus, consisting of an additional cylinder, suspended at an angle of about forty-five degrees above, and driven from the shaft of the primary or digging cylinder, and, therefore, revolving in the opposite direction to it. Its prongs act as a rotary comb in stripping the earth from those of the former. This machine was exhibited at the Gloucester Meeting of the Royal Agricultural Society, and on land previously broken by the plough, acted admirably as a pulveriser and weed extractor.

"Whilst engaged in some experiments with a machine somewhat resembling that of Parker's, my attention was directed to the steel digging forks which have lately been substituted with so much advantage for the old trenching fork; and it occurred to me that, by substituting light steel prongs for the wrought or cast-metal ones hitherto used in rotary implements, an efficient cultivating machine for horse-power, strong, yet comparatively light, could be made. In following out this idea, I have constructed my digging, or, more properly, forking machine, not altogether unsuccessfully, as may be inferred from the number of them which are already in use, notwithstanding the recent date of its introduction.

"The forks of my digging machine are made of the best cast-steel that I can procure, of a square section, slightly tapered, bent on the angle, and in pairs, at a cherry heat, and allowed to cool gradually. They are curved, so as to enter the ground easily, but to lift the soil as they come out.

"The upper portion of six such pairs being laid between two half discs of cast iron, grooved to receive them, the half discs being afterwards united by bolts, form a digging wheel of which the discs represent the boss, and the points of the forks the spokes; there is no hoop or tire. A number of these

## HARROWS.

Of the common harrow there were few illustrations in the Exhibition, we presume because it admits of less diversity of form than most other of the implements of tillage. The object of the harrow is to pulverize the soil, with which is frequently combined the further intention of covering different kinds of seeds. In this implement important improvements have recently been made. As formerly constructed, several of the teeth frequently followed in the same track when dragged along, in which case it was imperfectly performing its work; but in the more modern angular harrows this is effectually guarded against. The weight of the harrow and the size of the teeth are regulated by the character of the work to be performed; and so far as this implement is concerned, there is little to be desired.

digging wheels (seven in a full-sized machine) are hung on a bar, around which they rotate freely. Between each pair of wheels, and on the same bar, is hung a ring, which keeps them apart, and cleans the sides of the bosses. The frame containing the bar with the digging wheel also holds a number of cleaners, the ends of which scrape the soil from the circumference of the bosses, and force it from the prongs. This frame, to which the shafts and draught links for the horses are also attached, is itself hung in front on another bar, connecting two segmental frames, one on each side of the digging frame. These contain the wheels on which the implement rests when it is not in action, and which also serve to regulate the depth to which the forks of the digging frame are allowed to penetrate the ground. The segments at the back of the travelling wheel frames being toothed, two pinions gear into them, the place of which on the segments determines the height at which the digging frame is sustained; a winch attached to the latter works the pinions.

"When the horses move forward, the attendant throws out of gear a pawl, which holds the pinions at any given point; the digging frame runs down by its own weight, the prongs enter the ground, and the depth of their penetration is increased or diminished by turning the winch in opposite directions, thereby causing more or less weight to rest on the travelling and digging wheels respectively. Meanwhile, the resistance offered by the earth in front of the prongs causes the latter to revolve, and portions of the soil to be detached, which are thrown back after having been lifted and broken by contact with the cleaning bars.

"A full-sized machine weighs a ton, and breaks up (to a depth not exceeding ten inches) a breadth of three feet at a time, equal to that of four ploughs, and equivalent to about five acres in seven hours.

"The draught required varies with the nature and state of the soil, from four to seven horses. A smaller implement is made for occupiers of land whose horse-power is limited, capable of working about three acres in the same time with three or four horses.

"About thirty digging machines, corresponding with the description which I have given, are at work in various parts of this country; one of them in this immediate neighbourhood, on the estate of Mr. Robert Harrison.

"Whilst speaking of my digging machine, I think it right to state that it possesses, in common with all other rotary implements hitherto made or proposed, this disadvantage, as compared with the plough, that it does not completely invert the soil. I believe, however, that the occasions for such inversion are much more rare when we work with an instrument which leaves the ground broken, hollow, and mixed, like the digging machine, than with one which, like the plough, cleaves off a slice, and exposes its superficies only to the air; there being, in fact, this essential distinction between the two machines,—that one allows the air and water to descend, whereas, in the other, fresh soil must be brought up if it is to be acted upon by the elements. Hence also, an inconvenience is avoided by the forking, which often accompanies the attempts to deepen the mould, by means of the plough in plastic soils, namely, that the fresh soil so brought up forms a compact coating, and is, consequently, for several seasons, injurious instead of beneficial to vegetation.

"I need hardly point out that even were as many horses required for a given acreage with the digging machine as with the plough, there would still be a great gain both of horse and manual labour by the use of the former, since it effects, at one operation, the work of several ploughings and harrowings, or scufflings; but I am in a position to add, that it succeeded, during the dry weather in June, in preparing the ground for a crop on the strong clays in the vicinity of London, where a combination of the best implements previously in use could make no impression upon it.

"The forks tend to pull out and leave the weeds on the surface, and it is therefore useful in eradicating the couch-grass, the vegetation of which the action of the plough or scuffle, by cutting the tendrils, is calculated to promote.

"Besides the agricultural use of rotary forking machines, there are two others—one of them so obvious that I need hardly name it, viz., breaking up the ground, more especially on the clays and marls, for works of road and railway formation, to which purposes one of our most eminent contractors is about to apply it; the other, to prevent the silting up of the mouths of rivers or estuaries, by loosening the deposit at proper times, and allowing it to be carried away by the current or tide; and though the limits which I have assigned to myself in this paper, and indeed I may add, the absence of a thorough examination of this branch of the subject, prevent me from entering into any details as to the best mode of application, I cannot help stating my belief, that a very simple modification of the forking machine, dragged behind the Austrian Lloyd's steamers, which pass the Sulina bar of the Danube, would, without any dredging, have prevented the stoppage of the navigation, which had had such disastrous effects upon the shipping interests of Europe; and that an apparatus of very simple construction might be contrived even now, which would remove it at less cost, and with the application of less skill, than by the dredging machine.

"Whilst these improvements have been in progression, the spirit of invention has not slumbered, even at the antipodes; and we shall shortly see exhibited in this country an Australian forking-machine, not differing very greatly from some of those which I have brought under your notice. Mr. Wilson, the inventor, appears to have taken his hint from noticing in a track of a waggon-wheel on soft ground, that the side of the tire tends to abrade and throw back the earth. He prolongs the spokes of his wheels beyond the tire, in the form of spuds, which are segments of an epicycloidal curve, with a view to their encountering the least resistance in front or behind, as they enter the ground.

"Whatever may be the success of all or any of the cultivating machines which I have brought under your notice, enough has certainly been done to demonstrate that we have entered upon a new epoch in the mechanics of tillage, and that how long soever the dominion of the plough may be destined to last, it is not henceforth to reign alone. Meanwhile I was anxious to direct the attention of our machinists to a branch of their profession, than which none stands more in need of cultivation, and none will more amply repay it.

"We are dealing with a department of industry, which, until lately, was oppressed with an excess of human labour, whilst the whole of its produce was liable to be depreciated far more than any other in value, by a comparatively trifling increase in its amount. But now the tables are turned; the supply of agricultural labour diminishes daily, whilst consumption is extending beyond all precedent, and the cultivator of the soil looks eagerly to the mechanic to cheapen its operations, and jointly with the chemist, to aid him in making grow two blades where one only grew before."

The harrow is made indifferently of wood and iron; but the wooden harrow, when constructed of well-seasoned and good material, and kept painted, lasts many years, and is, therefore, generally preferred. Like all articles constructed of wood, it should not be longer exposed to the weather than necessary, and when done with for the time should be placed in the shed designed for the larger implements and machinery. The common rhomboidal harrow is one of the most approved forms of the implement, the lines made by the teeth in passing along showing that their action is evenly distributed over the surface. The angle of inclination is made to suit this object, which is the main point to be attended to in the construction of the harrow.

The early substitute for the harrow was a device as rude as could well be conceived. Many persons still alive can recollect thorn bushes being used for the purpose in different parts of Ireland, these being dragged by horses, and loaded with stones or other heavy substances, so as to insure the surface of the ground over which they were drawn being acted upon. The harrow is essentially a surface machine; but it is not intended to be confined to mere scratching of the surface. In certain cases it is to penetrate several inches into the soil, which the rude expedient to which we have just referred could not effect. When a great depth of fine tilth is required, some of the numerous cultivators should be employed, as they may be made to go as deep as the ploughing which preceded their use. The common harrow, drawn by two horses, will cover a width of about seven feet, so that a single turn could be given to an acre of land in about one hour. The length of the teeth varies from between two and three inches to nine and ten inches; and in placing these a constant rule is, that one of the angular portions of the teeth shall be made to go first, so as to diminish the resistance. Among the modifications of form deserving of attention, we may mention Mr. Coleman's expanding harrow, which is so constructed that the bars crossing each other are attached by a loose pin, on which they work freely. Thus, the width can be expanded or diminished at pleasure. This construction of the harrow is cumbrous-looking, but it is found effective in practice.

Two forms of the harrow have been devised by the late Mr. Smith, of Deanston, to whom the agriculturists of the United Kingdom are so much indebted for the numerous improvements which he introduced. One of those is called a web harrow, constructed of strong wire, with small rollers, either plain or serrated at the junction of the wires, and intended for covering the small kinds of seeds, as those of the grasses and clover. This harrow is now very much used, and specimens of it were contributed by several Exhibitors. The other is designed for loosening the surface of drills in which potatoes have been planted, and is at once a simple and effective instrument. It is made in two parts, each being convex, and connected by a bar across them, which admits of their separation to a greater or smaller distance, according to the width of the drills.

William P. Stanley, of Peterborough, obtained the prize at the trial of implements, for the best seed harrow.

### ROLLERS AND CLOD-CRUSHERS.

Although the functions of these implements are not in all cases identical, yet they so nearly resemble each other that they may fairly be classed together. The roller preceded the clod-crusher; but even the former is of comparatively modern use in husbandry. Until within a very recent date the roller has been of a rude description, being formed of a piece of a tree, into the ends of which pegs were driven; and to these the traces of the horses were fastened. Stone came next to be employed, as possessing the necessary weight in which the wooden roller was deficient: and this material, in turn, gave place to cast-iron cylinders, which, so far as regards the mere roller, leave nothing to be desired. The improved roller of this material is divided into two parts; which facilitates turning round at the end of the field, each moving freely on a common axle.

The use of the roller is sometimes to compress the surface of the land to protect it from drought; and occasionally with the further intention of finely pulverizing it, either during the early stage of the growth of corn crops, or when the ground is being prepared for green crops. For this implement the use of the clod-crusher has of late been substituted to a great extent; and it too has been made of various forms. Among these perhaps the most popular is that manufactured by W. Crosskill, of Beverley, which has again and again obtained prizes at the annual meetings of the National Agricultural Societies in each of the three divisions of the United Kingdom. It is one of the most important inventions for many purposes. For crushing or breaking lumps of earth, the common roller is of comparatively little value, as it merely presses them down; but this instrument, by means of its jagged iron teeth, crushes the most obdurate clods. It has also been found invaluable for pressing young wheat in March or April, when the soil has been swollen after the frosts of winter, and there is danger of the young plants being thrown out of the ground. Its action also tends to arrest the ravages of the wire-worm, which are so destructive in certain localities. In this class of implements no prize was awarded on the recent occasion.

### GRUBBERS OR CULTIVATORS.

This section of the implements of tillage includes a great diversity, both as regards construction and mode of application. The primary object to be attained in the cultivation of the soil is deep and minute pulverization; and, other things being equal, on the extent to which this condition is fulfilled by the farmer will depend his success. For this purpose the class of implements now under consideration come in aid of the plough and the harrow, and materially economize labour. Wherever boulders or stones of any kind are to be met with in the soil, the use of the grubber is, of course, inadmissible. It may be made to go as deep as the plough; and while it will pulverize the soil more effectually than could be done by the plough, a turn of the grubber will not cost one-fourth of what a ploughing would do, from the great space covered by the former implement.

This class of implements probably originated in a modification of the harrow, the teeth of which though well adapted for surface operations, or for covering seed, do not possess a form enabling them to penetrate the furrow slice with facility. By obliquely curving the teeth forward this object would be promoted; and if to this we add a framework capable of being elevated when the implement is being turned round at the ends of the field, we shall have the original form whence all the various modifications of the grubber have been derived.

The form and strength of the instrument will vary with the kind of work which it is designed to perform. Thus cultivators are sometimes employed with their broad edges in paring stubbles, and with their narrow teeth in stirring the land after being thus cleaned; and in stirring ploughed land in the spring to the depth of the last furrow slice, with the double purpose of pulverizing it and bringing root-weeds to the surface, which the slanting position of the teeth enables them to do. We may observe that with five teeth the grubber will afford good work for two strong horses, and with a framework to hold seven teeth four horses will be required. Among the earliest of the implements of this class was Finlayson's grubber, a modification of which still continues to maintain its position as one of the most valuable. To enter at length into the specialties of the different grubbers or cultivators would far exceed the limits of such a notice as the present. When the object to be attained is thoroughly understood, there will not be much difficulty experienced in selecting the implement best adapted for the purpose under any given circumstances; the latter consideration being at all times to be taken into account.

With regard to the economy of labour effected by the use of the grubber, it has been estimated that it will save just one-half of the horse labour which would otherwise be required by the plough, harrow, and roller, in pulverizing the land. Some exceptions to the use of cultivators will, of course, occur; but the substitution of these for the plough has been long successfully practised, though it has been by no means carried out to the full extent of which it is susceptible.

The collection of grubbers in the Exhibition comprised almost every form of this kind of instruments that has been produced. The two-horse grubber, exhibited by T. Eeles and Company, of this city, was the prize implement in this class.

### BENTALL'S BROADSHARE.

Among the important implements capable of being applied to different purposes there are few more valuable than Bentall's broadshare plough, which serves as a two-horse scarifier and subsoiler. On moderate-sized farms, where it becomes desirable to exercise economy in the purchase of implements, and where the extent of operations does not prevent the same article being used in different operations, the broadshare will be found eminently deserving of attention. The great saving which results to the farmer from the combination of three implements in one will be apparent. As a horse-hoe it may be used to pulverize the intervals between the rows of drill crops. When divested of its arms and tires it becomes an excellent sub-pulverizer; its employment being similar to that of other subsoil ploughs, in being made to follow in the track of a common plough. For this purpose the nuts on each side, by which the projecting arms are attached to the beam, are to be simply unscrewed, when the side apparatus may be removed, and the transverse cutters inserted into the slots cast in the frame, and wedged in. An eight-inch share must be applied to the hind part of the frame; but the arrangement of the parts will vary with the circumstances under which the implement is to be used. The depth to which it may be made to penetrate will also be variable, from six to sixteen inches.

An important application of the broadshare is as a substitute for the plough in the preparation of land for green crops. In a letter addressed some time ago, by Mr. Hannam, of High Deighton, near Wetherby, Yorkshire, to the Secretary of the Royal Agricultural Improvement Society of Ireland, he states that with Bentall's broadshare he was able to underwork six acres (statute measure) per day with three horses. The depth of the scarifying there given was three inches, but the implement could, of course, be made to go six inches deep, though with an increase of power and diminished extent of surface gone over. Mr. Hannam further stated that "every inch of ground is cut over; the light grubber and long-toothed harrow follow, and every vestige of couch and other weeds is thereby removed." No more competent testimony could be adduced than that of the writer of this letter as to the utility of the very valuable implement in question.

## II.—MACHINES AND IMPLEMENTS OF DRILL HUSBANDRY.

In this department of husbandry great changes have of late been effected: not only has the practice of drill culture greatly increased, but it has also been considerably modified in accordance with the results of the investigations of science; and corresponding changes have of course been required in the mechanical arrangements necessary to carry such a state of things into effect. The improvements which have been from time to time introduced into this country have been chiefly derived from Scottish agriculture; and although according to it, beans and root crops of all kinds have long been grown in rows, in the drill husbandry of Scotland there has been little modification for years past from the standard of raised drills from twenty-six to thirty inches apart, in which farm-yard manure has been plentifully deposited before sowing the seed. To grain crops drill culture has been hitherto but little applied either in Scotland or Ireland; yet, singular enough, such crops have been long drilled in England, where, until lately, root crops were sown broadcast. Up to the present period fields of turnips grown in this way may be seen in Suffolk, even on the same farm where grain is grown in rows. As agriculture has progressed, the tendency has undoubtedly been to grow all crops in rows except the herbage and forage plants, and in their case the cause of exemption will be obvious. Under a defective system of tillage this plan of culture becomes difficult to carry out, and the returns are insufficient to meet the extra expense incurred. Hence the appreciation of drill husbandry is invariably in direct proportion to the extent to which good general tillage is practised. For it deep and minute pulverization is essential, as well as that the soil should be thoroughly cleared of root weeds of every kind; and when these conditions are not secured, the cultivation of what are called drill-crops will be expensive and unremunerative.

In judging of the value of agricultural implements or machinery of any kind, a primary consideration is to become thoroughly acquainted with the functions which they are to fulfil, and the precise circumstances by which their action is to be regulated. Hence the necessity of our here noticing some of the peculiarities of drill husbandry. The requirements of the Scottish farmer in this respect are few, from that uniformity of practice to which we have already adverted. By the common swing plough, or with the double-mouldboard plough, the drills are formed, and reversed again on the manure being deposited. The sowing machines required are those for turnip seed, of a size to be worked either by hand or by horse labour. A horse-hoe and drill harrow combined, in which hoes and cutters can be substituted in the wings for teeth, and *vice versâ*, is the only other implement in general use, the entire culture between the rows being effected by it. But as the practice has become more extended, and carried on under a greater diversity of conditions and circumstances, and for other purposes, drills of various kinds came into use, both for depositing the seed and working the crop during its growth. The most important of these are the machines for sowing grain in rows, and the drills for general purposes, to be afterwards noticed.

DRILLING AND HOEING IMPLEMENTS.

Implements of drill husbandry must be modified according to the circumstances under which they are to be applied. Where the farms are not large, economy in the stock of implements becomes an important consideration; and one article is made to perform the functions of several, after having undergone the necessary modifications for the purpose. Thus, the drill plough, by the removal of the mould-boards, and substituting for them wings with teeth, is transformed into a drill harrow; and this again becomes a harrow or grubber according to the teeth which may be used. Of this class of implements a good illustration was exhibited in the collection of Ransomes and Sims, represented in the accompanying engraving. The first of these shows

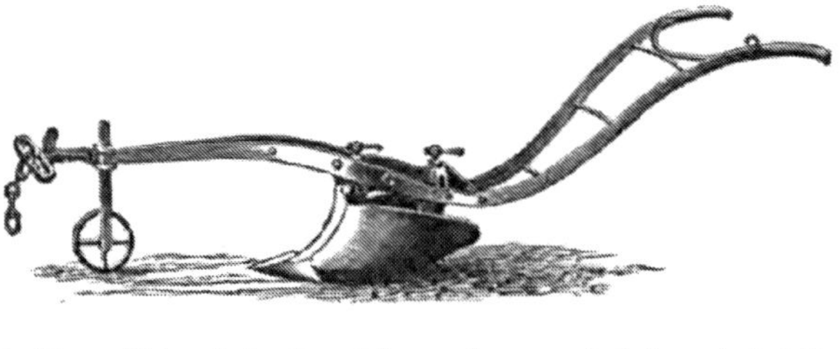

the common double mould-board plough used for opening up and closing raised drills, the wheel in front being removable altogether if desired. By means of the screw seen near the joining of the handle, the mould-boards may be contracted or expanded at pleasure.

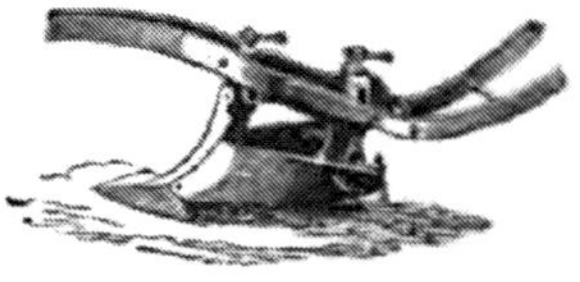

The second engraving represents another modification of mould-board, which admits of being used among growing crops, where the double plough would be productive of injury from the destruction of the foliage by the high mould-board. The farmer often finds it to be advisable to slightly earth up the roots, if it were merely to promote the tillage of the soil in the intervals between the rows; but he is obliged to forego it from the injury which the foliage would thereby sustain,—a drawback entirely removed by the use of the small mould-board figured in the margin.

The third engraving shows a horse-hoe or cleaning plough formed from the same implement by the removal altogether of the mould-boards and the introduction of two cutters behind; the share pulverizing the centre, while the hoes shave the sides of the raised drills. Flat hoes or teeth may be used here instead of the cutters, according to the state of the soil and the condition of the crop.

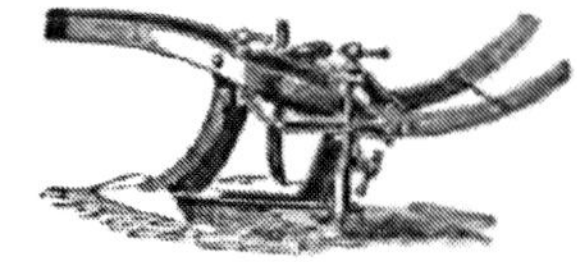

A further modification of this useful implement may yet be made by simply removing the mould-boards and changing the share, according to the nature of the work required to be done. A broadshare plough may thus be had, the character of which has been indicated in the preceding section. Among the entire range of our agricultural implements there is scarcely a more ingenious or useful modification than this; combining, as it does, economy and efficiency in a high degree; and on all the smaller class of farms it appears to be eminently deserving of attention.

There can be no doubt that loosening the soil, not only in its preparation for the crop, but also in the early stage of its growth, is of immense importance to insure the due development of the fertility of the land; and hence the great value of this class of implements. Repeated workings between the drills are also necessary to keep down weeds, which, if they once get ahead, destroy the crop.

In noticing the implements of drill husbandry we should not omit referring to the drill cultivation of grain which is extensively carried on on the other side of the Channel, the rows being from nine to fourteen inches apart, for which special adaptations of the horse-hoe are required. In the growth of green crops, too, there is reason to believe that as improved tillage advances, and the land is brought to a finer tilth, much narrower intervals will be used than are now employed. Instead of growing turnips and mangel wurzel at distances of from twenty-six to thirty inches apart in the rows, the period is probably not distant when eighteen to twenty inch intervals will be generally adopted. It admits of demonstration that by adopting the closer intervals, the increased number of plants would insure as large, if not a larger gross produce than is at present obtained; and such being the case, it has been ascertained that moderately-sized roots, weight for weight, are much more valuable than those of larger size. In considering the most effectual implements of drill husbandry, such considerations as those here adverted to are not to be overlooked. If we modify our practice, we must, in the same proportion, modify the means by which it is carried out.

SOWING MACHINES.

The arrangement of the machinery for sowing turnip seed is so well known that it scarcely requires any special description; and the apparatus for the purpose is made to sow one or two drills, according as it is to be worked by a horse or by hand. A roller is made to go before the coulters by which the seed is deposited, and another to follow after, which covers the seed, and completes the operation. This is the usual turnip-sowing machine, of which there were several illustrations in the Exhibition, the prize being awarded to that in the collection of T. Eeles and Co., of this city.

In connexion with the sowing machines, an apparatus is occasionally used for the distribution of the portable manures, the use of which has been growing in importance, and which, it may be fairly assumed, will be universal when the farm-yard manure ceases to be directly applied in the rows, as in the latter case the stimulant of the portable manure is required to push forward the young plants. The subject of the application of manures, and their effect on the quality of the crop, have been discussed at length in Class III., to which the reader is referred for further information. We are here concerned with the mechanical arrangements for the application of manure. The machine for this purpose may be adapted for the distribution of manure alone, without being designed for any other purpose; or it may also combine the arrangements for sowing the different kinds of seeds with those for depositing the manure; either being removable according as the two operations are to go forward at the same time, or the contrary. In the latter class of machines the prize was awarded to that exhibited by James Smyth and Son, of Peasenhall, Suffolk, the arrangement adapted in which is both ingenious and effective.

The corn drills are amongst the most valuable of the recent contributions of mechanical science to the business of husbandry. Their importance has not, however, been as yet sufficiently appreciated, simply because the great body of our farmers are not sufficiently alive to the gain to be derived from growing their corn crops in rows. While it cannot be doubted that excellent crops are obtained by broadcast tillage, it is equally certain that this system involves certain drawbacks, the removal of which is deserving of consideration. Thus, for example, the quantity of seed required for a given extent of land when sown broadcast is at least double what is necessary if sown in drills; and hence there is a saving of from 5*s.* to 10*s.* per acre in the outlay for seed, depending on the price of the seed and the usual quantity employed; which, on a large extent of land, would soon repay the entire outlay on the sowing machine. Sown in rows, there is also a degree of uniformity secured in the growth of grain crops scarcely attainable otherwise; and should any tillage be regarded necessary during their growth, facilities are provided for it.

Many experiments have been made with a view of eliciting information on this point, and the result has been uniformly in favour of drilling wherever the necessary conditions were fulfilled. This latter is an essential consideration, without which the practice cannot have a fair trial, and any results otherwise attained afford no reliable information. When drilling is systematically carried out by a proper and seasonable use of the horse and hand-hoe, the land is easily kept clean, and, consequently, yields its increase more uniformly and more independently of the seasons, than by the broadcast method of sowing, in regard to which the control of the cultivator over the land all but ceases as soon as he has scattered the seed and harrowed it in. The tillage between the rows of corn crops during their growth not only frees the soil of weeds, but in the case of autumn-sown seed, it breaks up the crust on the surface formed by the action of the weather; and by exposing new particles of earth to the atmosphere, causes many matters to be decomposed, thereby adding to the available supply of nutriment for the young plants. There is, besides, a uniformity of sample unattainable by broadcast culture, a consideration of no small importance when the produce comes to be brought to market. The Suffolk drill of R. Garrett and Son, one of the most valuable of its class, obtained the prize at the competition to which we have before referred. In the construction of this machine various improvements have from time to time been made, with a view of simplifying the arrangements, and rendering the different parts better adapted for the intended purpose. The coulters may be readily altered to deposit the seed at any distances that may be desired; and the delivery is regulated by cog-wheels of different speed, so as to drill from three to twenty pecks of grain per acre, and from one to six pounds of turnip seed, the machine being applicable for sowing the latter by merely changing the delivery barrel. The arrangements are contrived to insure an equally regular delivery when going up or down hill, as on level ground; by having two cog-wheels of different speeds, one placed on each end of the delivery barrel, either of which may readily be put in or out of gear as required to work the barrel from alternate ends, the small wheel when going up hill, and the large one when going down. By means of a fore-carriage steerage the utmost regularity may be secured on land ploughed flat; as by keeping the small fore-wheel in the track of the former large one, the parallelism of the lines is obtained. The arrangements of these drills for the attainment of the desired end are highly instructive, as well as suggestive of what mechanical science may yet do for agriculture.

We should observe, that the details here given equally apply to the machines exhibited by James Smyth and Son, of Peasenhall, which are also admirably adapted for the attainment of the object in view. The Messrs. Smyth have obtained a deservedly wide-spread reputation for their sowing machines.

Another machine deserving of a notice here is the general purposes drill, manufactured by R. Garrett and Son, which may be used to sow all kinds of seed, to distribute the portable manures, and as a horse-hoe;

thereby providing an admirable article for those moderate-sized farms on which it might scarcely be desirable to employ separate machines for each of these purposes.

This class of articles we regard with great interest, not less on account of their efficiency than because they are only suited to the practice of an improved system of husbandry. Wherever we see the corn drill employed, we may rest assured that the hand of progress has been actively at work.

## III.—HARVESTING MACHINES.

### REAPING MACHINES.

If there is one implement more than another whose appearance in the Exhibition was calculated to excite attention, it was the reaping machine contributed by Mr. Crosskill, of Beverley, the use of which has been regarded as forming a new era in agricultural improvement, and for a knowledge of which we are mainly indebted to the Exhibition of 1851. The appearance, on that occasion, of the American reaping machines created quite a sensation; and the excitement was sustained by the operation of M'Cormick's machine, at Tiptree Hall, where Mr. Mechi afforded an opportunity to the leading agriculturists of the country to see it at work. The statements made relative to the economy resulting from its use, as compared with the ordinary method of cutting down our grain crops, induced a very general belief that it was calculated to create as great a revolution in agricultural affairs as was effected by the power-loom in the manufacture of textile fabrics; and Brother Jonathan was extravagant in his boastings as to the obligation conferred on the people of Europe by the importation of this new invention from the United States.

Several efforts at the construction of machinery for cutting grain were made in England and Scotland soon after the beginning of the present century. At the commencement of it a person, named Boyce, obtained a patent for a reaping machine, which, however, never turned to be of any practical value. A London implement maker, of the name of Plunket, made another unsuccessful attempt about the same time. In 1806, Gladstone, a millwright, of Castle Douglass, in Kirkcudbrightshire, constructed a machine which excited great attention, but, although possessing much ingenuity, it, too, passed into oblivion. Mr. Salmon, of Woburn, and Mr. Scott, of Ormiston, were the next adventurers in the field. In 1812, the celebrated Mr. Smith, of Deanston, came before the public as an inventor in this department, and with very considerable promise of success. The Dalkeith Farming Society awarded a piece of plate of the value of fifty pounds for the invention, and the Highland Society made a similar recognition of their appreciation of its value. With the perseverance with which the late Mr. Smith was so remarkably gifted, the reaping machine was brought forward from time to time, from 1812 to 1835, sundry modifications and improvements being made in the interval. In the latter year it was brought out with remarkable eclat at the meeting of the Highland and Agricultural Society at Ayr. The trial then made seemed to impress those present with the idea that the problem had been solved of the application of machinery to the cutting of corn crops; but, notwithstanding all this, it made no further progress, the machine having never been employed on any extended scale. The next attempt was by Mr. Mann, of Raby, in Cumberland, who, in 1820, first brought before the public his idea. It was not, however, until 1832 that he fairly succeeded in practice in realizing the design, the execution of his machine at the meeting of the Highland Society at Kelso that year having been very satisfactory. Notwithstanding the numerous efforts made and the ingenuity displayed by several of the parties to whom we have above referred, none of their machines ever worked an entire harvest; and having brought them to the highest state of perfection of which they were capable, the inventors, one by one, were obliged to consign their bantlings to oblivion. The first really successful effort was made by the Rev. Patrick Bell, in 1826, for whose machine a sum of £50 was awarded by the Highland Society. In 1834 several of these machines were at work in Forfarshire; and it is also known that four of them were sent to America, and hence the origin of those brought to the Exhibition of 1851. The curious part of the affair is the little attention which for years it continued to attract from the proverbially shrewd Scottish farmers.

In the Exhibition in Hyde Park there were two claimants for attention in the introduction of the reaping machine—Mr. M'Cormick and Mr. Hussey,—and several trials were made during the harvest of 1851 to test their comparative merits. In certain cases the machine claimed to be the invention of one of these parties would not work at all, while in others a directly opposite result was attained. But, as before stated, the belief was that through the intervention of the Hyde Park Exhibition two important additions to our agricultural implements were made by the United States. Rival manufacturers lost no time in making arrangements with the respective parties for the requisite exclusive authority to make those machines in England, where a large trade was expected to be done in them; and so great was the sensation which they created that for the ensuing harvest (that of 1852) several hundred reaping machines were prepared. At the various agricultural meetings the use of the reaping machine was the prevailing topic; and one would have supposed that a new light had dawned on the agricultural public, who were for the time to come apparently prepared to make amends for the jog-trot pace at which they proceeded in the race of improvement in times past.

But while so great a sensation had been created by the use of the two imported machines, it appeared that the one invented by Mr. Bell, which was superior to either, and the original one from which the idea was taken, had been at work, in by no means a secluded corner of Great Britain, for upwards of twenty years, without exciting any considerable degree of attention, or scarcely being used beyond the farm of the inventor. What a commentary was this on the character of the farmers of the United Kingdom, so far as regards the adoption of improvements of any kind! The sensation which the two American machines created but ill accorded with the state of affairs which this discovery revealed. The machine invented by the Rev. Mr. Bell, of Carmylie, in Forfarshire, had been constantly used by the brother of the inventor from 1829 up to the present period. And when, in the autumn of 1852, the controversy waxed so strong as to the comparative merits of the imported articles, one of Bell's machines was brought under notice, and started in the race of competition; and, to the astonishment of every one, it left both of the others far behind. The trial was repeated again and again with like results. The machine invented by Mr. Bell, which the agriculturists had regarded with indifference for nearly a quarter of a century, turned out to be superior to the imported articles, the appearance of which created so great a sensation. The exhibiter of the Bell reaper in the present Exhibition manufactured Hussey's machines in 1852, in which we believe he did a large business; but so satisfied was he of the great superiority of the old but hitherto neglected article, that he at once gave up making the American machine, and now supplies his customers with that invented by Mr. Bell.

Strange, indeed, that such an implement as this should have been in use for such a long period in Scotland without attracting the attention of the proverbially shrewd people of that country. It would be regarded almost as a libel upon the people of Scotland to suppose that such a thing could be possible, had we not satisfactory evidence of the fact. Little blame can be attached to persons at a distance, inasmuch as they could have scarcely heard anything of the matter, beyond the simple record in the proceedings of the Scottish Agricultural Society of the award of the prize in 1829. Such indifference on the part of intelligent people to improvements under their own eyes is truly marvellous.

It may afford matter of speculation as to the cause of the reaping machine attracting so much attention in the United States, while it was neglected in the United Kingdom; but the difference in the circumstances of the two countries will, we think, explain this anomaly. In the former country labour is dearer than with us, while the value of grain is usually less. In these countries the entire cost of reaping a corn crop is only a few shillings per acre; and hence any considerable amount of waste on the part of the machine would more than counterbalance any economy from its use. In the United States the saving of labour would be more important than here, while the value of any given extent of waste of the crop would be less than with us. The reaping machine, or in fact any species of machinery for economizing human labour, is likely to be of more consequence to Brother Jonathan than it would be in the United Kingdom—a circumstance which will account at once for the superior attention which the machine in question received on the other side of the Atlantic.

But, as if to make amends for the indifference of the past, the use of the reaping machine has certainly extended very rapidly during the past two years; and if we were asked to point out an illustration of the benefits likely to result from these Great Exhibitions, we might triumphantly appeal to the case in question. Although Bell's machine did not appear in the collection in Hyde Park, yet the sensation caused by those that were there soon brought the original article from its obscurity, and it has, in its turn, already to a great extent supplanted them. Considerable disappointment was felt amongst the agricultural public in this country at not having the opportunity of seeing the reaping machines at work at the recent trial of implements; but it appears that the orders previously in the hands of the manufacturer were so numerous, that he was indifferent about exhibiting here during the past season.

As to the comparative expense of reaping by machinery and by hand, we find that a pair of horses will cut down fifteen statute acres per day, for which we find the following estimate in the Jurors' Report of the Exhibition of 1851:—

| | £ | s. | d. | £ | s. | d. |
|---|---|---|---|---|---|---|
| Cost of reaping 15 acres by hand, at 9*s*. per acre, . . . . . | | | | 6 | 15 | 0 |
| Horses and men for reapers, . . . . . . . . . . | 0 | 10 | 0 | | | |
| Binding and stooking 15 acres, at 2*s*. 6*d*. per acre, | 1 | 17 | 6 | | | |
| | | | | 2 | 7 | 6 |
| Saving per acre, 5*s*. 10*d*., or on 15 acres, . . . | | | | £4 | 7 | 6 |

Where the extent of land under grain crops is considerable, the saving here indicated would be important; and, what is of more consequence, the work is expeditiously performed, so that fine weather can be taken advantage of to an extent otherwise unattainable. The data, on which any one can found a calculation for himself, are that a pair of horses will get over fifteen acres in a day, and that a man and boy will be required to attend to them. The money value to be attached to the items will vary with the district in which the work is to be performed. Of the advantages likely to result from the use of the machine to the Scottish farmers, we have the following evidence from a highly competent authority, Mr. Hope, of Fenton Barns, in an address to the Haddington Farmers' Club:—"When the grain is fit for the sickle there is frequently some, nay, considerable difficulty in obtaining hands in sufficient numbers to cut it quickly down, and in this uncertain climate everybody knows that not a moment should be lost in having it in the sheaf, secure from wind, and as speedily as possible safe in the stack-yards from damaging rains. But even when reapers can be obtained, in foul weather as well as fair they must be fed, and it has oftener than once happened in my experience that I have had to feed large numbers for a week, while they did not work half the time. The expense this incurs is not the only mischief. I have been equally vexed for the poor people hanging about in wet weather, in uncomfortable lodgings, and not knowing what to do with themselves. At all times the introduction into the farm premises of forty or fifty, or, it may be, one hundred strangers, is a very serious matter. Little control can be exerted over them, and I never heard of their disposition or morals being inquired into. In fact, if they possess the requisite skill, and bone and muscle, we are generally glad to get them. The way that harvest matters are managed is the only thing in farming that I dislike. It gives me, indeed, positive pain to reflect upon it; there must be something wrong which renders such bands of reapers necessary, or rather makes it possible to obtain them as we have hitherto done in the Lothians—lodging them in barns, byres, and stables, sexes and ages mingled together, without the possibility of such a separation as common decency requires. It is a shocking moral evil, which every exertion should be made to abate. No wonder, then, that great excitement has been experienced in anticipating the practicability of reaping by machinery."

In Bell's reaping machine, which is represented at work in the annexed engraving, an endless web of cloth receives the corn after being cut, and lays it regularly aside as it passes along. The front of the machine is armed with a long series of shears extending the whole width, and so combined as to form a continuous series of open jaws, opening on one side of the blades, whilst they are closing on the other; for they cut on both sides, and alternately combine, right and left, with the upper blades respectively. The machine is pushed forward by two horses yoked to a pole behind, which passes between them, and to its

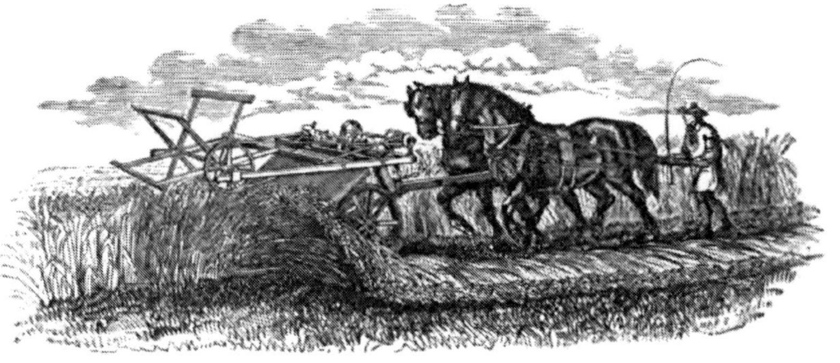

Bell's Reaping Machine.

hinder end they are attached in the usual way. The wheels are put out of gear when the machine is being removed from one place to another; and when at work they put the cutting and web portion of the apparatus in motion, by which the corn is cut and arranged for the binder to pick up. The cost at which this machine is supplied is forty guineas.

While on the subject of reaping machines, and more especially as having expressed a very decided opinion as to the superiority of that invented by the late Mr. Bell, we may direct attention to the result of the recent trials of the comparative merits of the several modifications of the machine, held under the auspices of the Royal Agricultural Society of England. At the Gloucester meeting of the Society no less than twelve of these machines were tested; and of five of these a further trial took place afterwards at Mr. Pusey's farm, in Berkshire; consisting of Bell's, manufactured by Crosskill; M'Cormick's, by Burgess and Key; Hussey's, by Dray and Co.; Hussey's improved, by O. Hussey; and M'Cormick's improved, by Samuelson. The various machines were attended by the manufacturers, and the report states that the trials were on the whole satisfactory. All the machines were seen to best advantage on the wheat and oat crop, more especially on the latter. There appeared, however, to be but one opinion—that, for cleanliness, evenness, and excellence of work, Bell's reaper surpassed all the others. The feature in this machine which called for the most unqualified approbation was the manner in which the crop was delivered to the binders, without requiring any one to rake it off or attend it, being left in swathes in a continuous line, and at such a distance from the standing crop that the machine could proceed with its work whether the cut corn was bound up or not. This is obviously a great advantage; for when the binding has to be carried forward to make way for the cutting of the next swathe, any slight derangement or delay in the operation of the machine sets the whole of the attendants idle. The judges were unanimous in awarding the prize to Bell's machine.*

* We take the following account of the trial at Pusey, which came off on the 13th and 16th of August, 1853, from the Mark Lane Express, the writer of which enters at some length into the mode of operation of the respective machines:—

"The first principle to be considered is the power that insures the action of the working parts of the machine. This power lies in the weight upon the driving wheel or wheels, which we will first notice. Bell's machine weighs about 16 cwt.; M'Cormick's, inclusive of the two men riding upon it, about 13 cwt.; Dray's Hussey, inclusive of one man riding, about 12 cwt.; and Mr. Hussey's, inclusive of two men riding, about 12½ cwt. But there is another element to be considered, namely the biting or holding power of the driving wheels. All these machines except Bell's had cogs or ribs crossing the rim of their wheels about six inches apart, and about an inch deep, to prevent the wheels from slipping. When at work these cogs or ribs, we observed, did great damage to the young clovers. When cutting the barley they also tended to clog when the land was wet. We, therefore, think that it would be better to do away with these cogs, and make the machines two or three hundred weight heavier, which we feel sure would be just as little draught for the horses as with the lighter machine and cog travelling-wheels. As far as this principle goes, it is in favour of Bell's machine, the weight being against him; therefore, taking these two principles into consideration, we think their driving power at par, but give the decided preference to Bell's mode of obtaining that power.

"The next thing that attracted our attention was the mode of attaching the horses, and the advantages accruing from each. Bell's is propelled by two horses, drawing from the end of a powerful pole which is fixed to the machine, and passes down between the horses and projecting out behind them, where a set of common swingletrees are fixed, and by which the horses draw. To the end of the said pole is fixed a cross bar with a pair of handles, by which the man guides or steers the machine, over which he has great power when the machine is at work—as we observed the gentleman who managed on this occasion steering the machine to cut within two or three inches of its full width. This part we liked much, because we feel confident that every good ploughman will be at home when called upon to work these machines.

"This system of propulsion gives the power of going into the field, and cutting the headland all round, then choosing which is the best direction to work, so as to accommodate the wind, the shape of the surface or the lay of the crop; then working back and forward, turning the swathes all one way, as a turnwrest plough does its furrows. This is an advantage of paramount importance in a hilly country, as well as on the plain, where the abundance of straw often causes the crops to be laid.

"All the other machines were drawn at the side, by the

### THE HORSE-RAKE.

Wherever hay-making is extensively carried on, the horse-rake is an indispensable instrument. From its efficiency, the economy of labour of which it admits, and the expedition which it secures in the event of rain being apprehended, it must, ere long, come into general use. Unless where great irregularities of surface occur, the grass or hay is collected by it as clean off the meadow as can be done by the hand-rake. But even for inequalities of surface, provision is made in some of the horse-rakes, by making the action of the teeth, each independent of the other, the several teeth working on separate handles. The regularity with which the hay can be collected in rows, to be made up into cocks, is a further advantage. Commencing at one side or end of the field, the horse goes forward clearing a space of eight, ten, or twelve feet in breadth; and when a quantity is collected, calculated to much impede the further working of the rake, it may be detached by the attendant in a moment from its burthen, to be either turned back to bring forward another row, or to proceed making several rows across the field. The horse-rake is now made by nearly the whole of our agricultural implement makers; several examples of it were in the Exhibition.

### THE HAY-MAKING MACHINE.

The hay-making or tedding machine is another important harvest requisite, combining, as in the case of the horse-rake, economy and expedition in a high degree. Rows of teeth are here placed on a skeleton cylinder, to which motion is communicated by the wheels as the machine moves forward; and when not intended to act, the teeth are turned down, so as to avoid contact with the ground. On first being used in the hay field, the hay-tedder is driven across the line of the swathe; and the manner in which it shakes up and distributes the grass over the surface far exceeds anything that could be done by hand. After this tedding, the motion of the machine may be reversed, and the grass is thrown behind, instead of being tossed up over it as before. Of this machine, several specimens were exhibited by different makers; and of its efficiency we cannot speak too highly.

## IV.—BARN AND YARD MACHINERY.

### THRESHING MACHINES.

The threshing machine has long been considered a necessity wherever agricultural operations are extensively carried on, the separation of the grain from the straw being precisely one of those processes on the farm to which the application of machinery is especially suited. The primitive method of performing this work

horses walking alongside of the standing crop. When these machines have their wheels well arranged, they have the advantage of Bell's for crossing ridge and furrow, but are badly suited for cutting along the ridges, on account of the great distance the wheels are apart; indeed, these machines are inferior to those propelled, except for crossing high ridges or deep furrows—a description of farming that we hope will soon be erased from amongst our fields, by the landlords progressing with the drainage of their wet estates with that spirit which is now pervading our country; thus enabling the tenant-farmer to call into his aid all the mechanical contrivances that the ingenuity of the age brings into use to enable us to compete in the market of the world, and at the same time 'live and let live.'

"The next point we observed was the principle of cutting used by each of these machines, which was of three sorts. First, the serrated cutter, working with a good draw cut, as in M'Cormick's: this is a first-rate simple cutter, taking rather less power than the clipping principle used by Bell; but it requires to be driven at greater velocity as compared with Bell's clipper, therefore causes more tear and wear; however, M'Cormick's cutter is very much cheaper than Bell's clippers, and easier managed. It was, therefore, our impression at first sight that, if that cutter was applied to Bell's machine it would be an improvement; but after we saw Bell's machine at work some time, we were convinced that there are very great difficulties in the way of carrying out that idea. In fact, when Bell's machine is cutting a six-foot swathe, there is above a foot thick of cut corn on the web at the delivery side, and which is all supported by the cutters, which are above a foot long: but if M'Cormick's cutter was used, the length of which is but one inch, there would be no support for the cut crop, which would therefore fall down before the cutters, and press the uncut crop to the ground, allowing the machine to pass over it. Then, it may be urged, that some space could be allowed between the cutters and the web to allow support to the cut corn; but when a very short grassy crop came to be operated upon, the cut corn would fall on the said space, out of the reach of the web, thereby frustrating the power of delivery. We are, therefore, satisfied that Bell's cutter and his delivery are members of a complete body, and, like bevil-wheels and pinions, cannot be parted, or used with any other differing in principle or make.

"The other description of cutter is that introduced by Hussey, which is on the chopping principle, therefore ill-adapted for cutting anything at all soft or elastic—which during last harvest did more evil to the rapid spread of reaping by machinery than will be got over for years. We heard that Crosskill was supplying his last year's customers with serrated cutters (the same he used at the York Show) at a low price: and we would advise those parties who are wedded to the chopper always to think of the serrated cutter when they are set fast with grass or damp.

"The next thing to be noticed was the means used to bring the uncut crop into a proper position for the cutters to operate most efficiently. This, in Bell's and M'Cormick's, was accomplished by a fan or reel, revolving over and a little in advance of the cutters, bending the crop back, insuring both the cutting and a good arrangement for delivery.

"In those machines on the Husseyan principle, the man bends back the crop with his rake; and it is certain that a hand, guided by an eye of intelligence, could, under awkward circumstances, combat difficulties better than the fan; but, inasmuch as labour-saving is the order of science, patriotism, and philanthropy, the fan or reel must be the best.

"The next thing to be considered is the mode of delivery, which was of three kinds. First, Bell's, with its self-delivery, in a beautifully arranged swathe, by an endless web. This takes a good deal of power, as it has to travel at a considerable speed above the progression of the machine. Mr. Croskill is deserving of great praise for the simplicity and neatness of the arrangements and details of machinery required to perform all the three actions, namely, the cutting, gathering, and delivery of the lightest or heaviest crop grown upon a farm. The mode of delivery adopted by M'Cormick is by a man raking off to the side, in parcels, for sheaves. This plan has the advantage of a farmer being able to cut

by the flail is tedious, expensive, and imperfect, unless in the most careful hands; and, even after the flail has done its duty, the best hand shaking will scarcely separate the whole of the loose grains from the straw, which, however, is effectually done by the shaker of the threshing machine. On small farms, machinery of any kind is inadmissible; and hence, the great drawbacks attendant upon a very limited extent of operations. By the aid of the threshing machine, a large quantity of corn can be prepared for market in a few days, if desirable, which is often a most important consideration, irrespective altogether of the manner in which the work is performed.

The principle involved in the construction of the threshing machine is exceedingly simple. The unthreshed corn is supplied through two feeding rollers, between which it is firmly held, while it is carried forward to be acted upon by a number of *beaters* fixed on the drum, which is merely a hollow cylinder. By the motion of the beaters the straw is carried forward to *shakers* in the other end of the machine, the bottom of the passage along which it is conveyed being formed of bars which admit the grain to pass through. Nor is there any considerable modification in these parts in any of the machinery in use, the threshing machine having undergone little change for the last quarter of a century. Indeed, there are few more striking instances of the extent to which really important matters connected with farming are neglected than the history of this machine presents. In its construction, the due execution of the work appears, for a length of time, to have formed almost the only consideration, without much reference to the economy of power applied. In practice, few opportunities occurred of testing the workmanship of one manufacturer against that of another; besides this being for the most part a fixture, it was conceived that no fair test of its capabilities could be had by placing it in any temporary situation for work. Year after year we accordingly find, that even the best manufacturers continued to turn out machines, the three-fourths of the power required to work which was necessary for merely putting them in motion. Thus, the four-horse power threshing machines actually required three horses to work them when empty, leaving to the fourth the whole labour of threshing the corn. The fact of such a large proportion of the power being required to overcome the mere resistance of the machinery was certainly a very startling one; and for the discovery of which we are indebted to the annual exhibitions of the Royal English Agricultural Society. The discovery dates no farther back than the Norwich meeting of 1849. On that occasion it occurred to Mr. Amos, the consulting engineer of the Society, to test the common threshing machine worked by horses when empty; and to the surprise of every one, such was the result then afforded. The duty performed was literally only 25 per cent. of the power employed; and if horses of less than average strength were put to the machines, they could not move them at all without being

without being obliged to move any of the cut crop, which is of considerable importance to those farmers who find it advantageous to leave their crop for some time untied up.

"The mode of delivery adopted by Dray was very good indeed, and easy work for the man, and simple of management; indeed we regretted to see so good a delivery impeded by a bad cutter; and if he had used a serrated cutter he would have run far closer, if not quite into the second place, at the Pusey trial.

"In Mr. O. Hussey's machine the delivery was the same as that in ordinary use upon his machines; but he has made a similar arrangement of his machinery to that made last autumn by Messrs. Garrett and Son, which is a great improvement where the land is wet and cloggy, preventing the dirt from getting amongst the machinery. He also had two wheels in front, to support the machine; and as they were hung upon a centre the horses guided them in their own track; therefore these wheels did away with the side-draught that was observable in all the other machines except Bell's.

"An immense number of noblemen, gentlemen, farmers, and others, gathered together to witness the trial of the lion machines of the day; more especially as our northern brethren had brought their Bell's machine, the champion of above five-and-twenty years, to contest for the laurels our American brethren had so well gained during the last two years. Many American friends were present, also a number of gentlemen from France, Germany, Prussia, and Russia, to see these trials carried out. They began about ten o'clock, on a beautiful standing crop of wheat, except a few laid pieces, where all the machines worked well; but after M'Cormick's machine had been beat in cutting along one end of his piece, and was observed by the judges to be passing on without cutting, they immediately went to Mr. Love, Mr Crosskill's manager on the occasion, and asked if he could cut laid wheat? when his reply was, that he wanted to see the crop Bell's machine could not cut. The judges took him at his word, and directed him to cut the before-said piece; when he charged the machine right into and across the middle of it, working back and forward, to the surprise and satisfaction of all parties present. We were pleased to notice that the weight of crop made scarcely any appreciable difference to its being cut. All the other machines had a trial on this piece of laid wheat, but did not work satisfactorily, except when meeting the lay of the crop. After this all the machines were taken to a piece of barley, laid all nearly as if it had been rolled, where, by the order of the judges, Bell's machine went down one side, and then right across the piece, and returned cutting and delivering in a satisfactory way. This machine, to get under the crop, was obliged to be placed so low that the cutter twice caught hold of stones, which brought the horses to a stand; but all that was done was to take out the stones and start off again. This was a severe test of the strength of the reaper, which it nobly overcame.

"All the other machines could make nothing of this crop, except Burgess and Key's. M'Cormick's having failed was lowered closer to the ground, when it cut tolerably well; but the delivery was bad. During the whole of these trials it rained heavily, which made awful havoc of the crop; but through the firm and good-humoured management of Mr. Fisher Hobbs, the steward, the crowd was kept from doing so much damage as, from the unfavourable state of the weather, might have been expected.

"All the machines were ordered to a field of winter beans, where the land was wet with rain but dry in nature. The crop was not heavy, with a good many broken-down stems. Bell's reaper again started first, and cut, gathered, and delivered beautifully, far excelling the scythe's work alongside. Burgess and Key's reaper was again the only competitor, but was still excelled by Bell's.

"Next a field of oats, a very heavy crop, just on the eve of being laid in several directions, in some places down. All the machines cut well here; but the cleanness, lowness of the stubble, and the beauty of the delivery by Bell's machine left the palm still in his favour; but the work altogether was very good, and the delivery satisfactory.

"The next, and last, was a good fair crop of barley, with a thick crop of clover amongst it. Here all the machines soon stopped cutting, except Messrs. Burgess and Key's and Bell's, both of which worked in excellent style; but the self-delivery in a beautiful swathe by Bell's reaper showed off to the greatest advantage; and the whole voice of the spectators was, that for cleanliness, even and lowness of cutting, and excellence of delivery, Bell's far surpassed its American competitors, even although much improved by British genius."

overworked. The discovery of such a very unexpected circumstance as this was not lost sight of by the very practical gentlemen having the management of that Society, to whose efforts in the cause of agricultural improvement the public are so much indebted. The facility of being put in motion, or, in other words, the amount of force necessary to overcome the resistance of the machinery, has, since that period, formed a main feature in judging of the comparative merits of machines brought forward for competition; and, as may readily be supposed, with the best results. The leading manufacturers have already benefited largely by the lesson. It will be obvious that this is the main field for inquiry. Great perfection has been attained in the manner in which the work is executed; and the points to which further attention is to be directed are, the lessening of the power required to a minimum, and the cheapening of the cost of construction so far as is consistent with efficiency and durability.

There has been a considerable tendency, of late, to produce portable threshing machines, originating in a belief as to their value from the facility of being removed from place to place; and also, because such machines are easily brought forward for competition at the usual agricultural exhibitions. There is no room for doubt as to the value under certain circumstances of the portable form of the threshing machine. Through its instrumentality the use of machinery may be available on many farms, which must otherwise be satisfied with the flail. In some two or three days, the contents of a small stack-yard may be got over, when the machine may be taken elsewhere to be similarly employed. To the circumstances of a large proportion of Ireland portable threshing machines are peculiarly applicable; and no small service would be rendered by proprietors in keeping them for the use of their tenantry. They might even be profitably turned to account by some enterprising farmer in every locality hiring out a machine to be superintended by his own servant, and worked, either by his own horses, or that of the farmer requiring the work done, as might be mutually arranged between the parties.

In the case of portable threshing machines, excellence of workmanship is a matter of paramount importance; as, being knocked about much, if loosely or imperfectly constructed, the machine will soon fall to pieces. In this respect, the machine exhibited by Ransomes and Sims, of Ipswich, was entitled to high commendation, as being, in every respect, a creditable specimen of workmanship; and we are not surprised that it should have carried off the prize at the various agricultural meetings. In this machine the beating drum has five arms or beaters, and revolves 310 times to each revolution of the horses; if the latter walk two miles per hour, the drum revolves between 900 and 1000 times per minute, threshing the corn quite clean without requiring the horses to proceed at a quick pace. The concave is serrated with studs of a diamond form, which are found of advantage in preventing the breakage of the straw or injury to the grain. The large wheel is cast with the ring separated from the arms, by which the probability of breaking, and the expense of repair in case of accident, are much decreased. The requisite speed of the drum is obtained by three pairs of wheels, an arrangement which has added considerably to the ease of working, and lessened the wear of the machine. To facilitate repairs at a distance from any regular factory, all the wheels except the large one are bored, and the shafts turned to gauges, so that any one may be replaced by a common mechanic; and the brasses may be supplied by new ones, sets of which may be obtained from the manufacturers. In the passage round, the horses have to step over the connecting rod; but in practice no difficulty is found to arise from this, as the animals soon learn to step over it without at all impeding their progress. By a proper adjustment of the screen or concave part against which the beaters act, barley may be threshed by this machine, and it may also be used for peas and beans. When required to be removed from one place to another, the machine is carried on two wheels, and is easily drawn by two horses. The manufacturers state, that by it five quarters of wheat may be threshed per hour, or about nine barrels of twenty stones each. At the trial of implements and machinery at the meeting of the Royal English Agricultural Society at Cambridge, sixty-one bushels and three pecks of wheat were threshed by one of these machines in an hour—certainly a very satisfactory rate of performance.

At the competition at Killarney, in connexion with the Exhibition, Richard Garrett and Son, of Leister Works, Saxmundham, obtained the prize for the best machine suitable for large farms; and Ransomes and Sims, of Ipswich, for that adapted for small farms.

### WINNOWING MACHINES.

Of the action of the winnowing machine it is unnecessary to enter into any detail, as it is now considered an indispensable requisite of every farm beyond those of the smallest size. The collection in the Exhibition contained those of the best makers, including almost all sizes and prices. The prize in this department was awarded to Richard Garrett and Son.

We need scarcely observe that all the large threshing machines have winnowing machines attached to them, the threshing and cleaning of the grain being performed at a single operation. The grain thus prepared is, however, scarcely sufficiently dressed for market, without the intervention of a further cleaning, so that the separate use of the winnowing machine in every case becomes requisite.

The several machines in this department presented no peculiarity worthy of special notice, though including most of those in common use.

### MACHINES FOR PREPARING FOOD FOR LIVE STOCK.

In no other department of farm management has the hand of improvement been more manifest than in the increased attention paid of late years to the preparation of food for live stock. Experience has amply confirmed the value of some preliminary preparation of either grain or roots; and it has also been ascertained that even straw and hay may be more economically used, after being cut up into a sort of chaff, than in its original state. However coarse the quality, provided it be wholesome, the addition of bruised oats and flax-seed jelly have only to be made to any hay or straw to cause it to be highly relished; and such compounds, we need scarcely observe, form highly nutritious as well as economical food. Here, also, the intervention of the steaming apparatus becomes necessary. Unless for horses of which active exercise is required, compounds of this kind have been found to comprise the best food that can be given to live stock of any description. In the eastern counties of England the practice has been rapidly gaining ground, having been introduced there by Mr. Warnes, of Trimmingham, in Norfolk, who commenced the growth of flax in that district, mainly with a view to the value of the seed for feeding purposes—the part of the crop which is so generally allowed to go to waste in Ireland. Such mixtures have the great advantage of admitting of the proportion of nutritive, ingredients being increased or diminished at pleasure, according to the kind of animals and the object in view. It is not, perhaps, going too far to say, that by the use of prepared food, one-fourth can be added to the number of live stock which any given extent of land can maintain.

In this department there were specimens from the principal manufacturers of agricultural implements: these articles coming now into general use. We subjoin engravings of the machines for cutting straw and bruising grain, exhibited by Ransomes and Sims, which were among the best of their class, in the Exhibition.

Of chaff cutters, the chief varieties are in the forms of the knifes, and the position in which they are placed. In that here figured the blades are well adapted for cutting; and it may be made to cut three different lengths

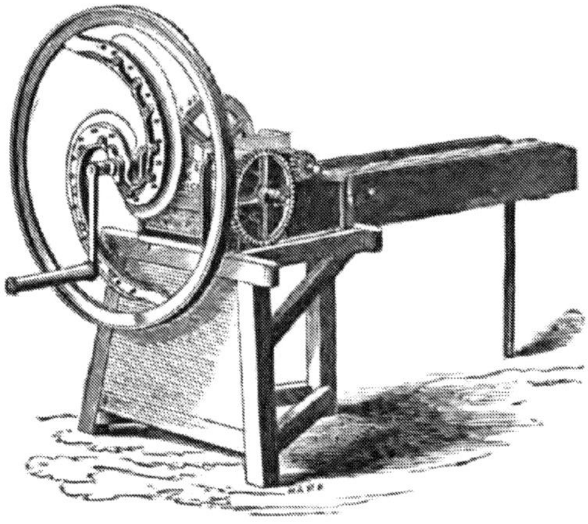

Ransomes and Sims' Straw and Hay Cutter.

of chaff—¼ in., ½ in., and ¾ in. It may be worked either by hand, horse, or steam-power. The mouth will admit of a feed ten inches wide by three inches thick, so that a large quantity of hay or straw could be cut by it in a few hours.

The machine, here figured, exhibited by the same firm, and known by the name of Biddell's Patent Universal Mill, presents the advantage of admitting of being changed to suit any kind of grain, from the largest bean to the smallest seed—an obviously important consideration on moderate-sized farms. For linseed, oats, or beans it is equally adapted; and worked by hand it will bruise from three to four bushels of oats per hour. Beans are little used in this country for horse food, and any arrangements for turning them to account are of less moment with us than in England; but the bruising of grain and flaxseed is of paramount importance on every farm. The latter substance is not used nearly to the extent which its feeding qualities would warrant. We expend thousands annually on the purchase of oil-cake, which is extensively adulterated, and often nearly worthless; while we neglect the genuine article, which cannot be so tampered with. The absence of proper means of preparing the flaxseed has hitherto formed a drawback to its use, which such machines as that here noticed are calculated to remove.

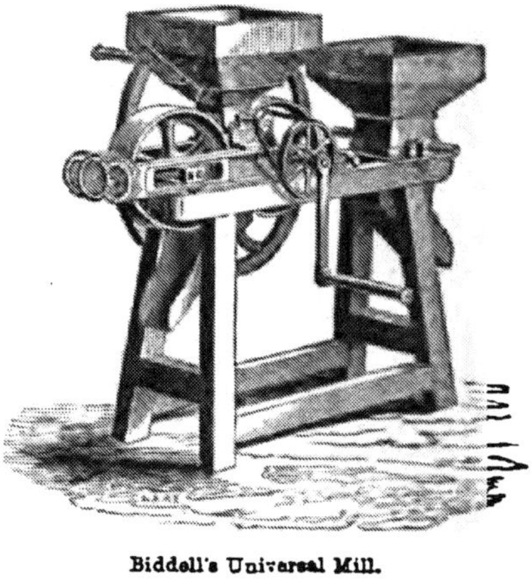

Biddell's Universal Mill.

A Steaming Apparatus has now become a necessity of every farm of more than a few acres in extent. To the manufacture of this class of articles great attention has recently been devoted, from the increasing demand for them. On a small scale a vessel is simply placed over a large boiler, the steam generated in which cooks the substance placed over it, the boiler being also occasionally used by itself, as in the case of the preparation of flaxseed jelly. On a larger scale the steam is generated in a boiler with a close top, and conveyed, by means of pipes, to vessels placed close by, containing the substances to be steamed; and the number of these vessels may be indefinitely extended with the capacity to generate steam. W. P. Stanley, of Peterborough, obtained the prize in this department.

## V.—DRAINAGE MACHINERY, AND IMPLEMENTS.

In this section the visitors had an opportunity, for a considerable part of the time during which the Exhibition was open, of seeing a machine at work making drainage tiles; it was exhibited by G. Ingram, of D'Olier-street. Tile drainage may be said to date only a few years back, the first great impetus given to it, after the advantages of thorough draining were established, being the prizes annually offered by the English Agricultural Society for improvements in the construction of tile machines. This brought hosts of candidates into the field, whose efforts were further stimulated by the great demand which arose for the machines. In the first attempts at tile draining, a cumbrous semicircular tile, made by hand, placed in the drain on a flat sole, was the only form available; the tiles costing 50*s*. and the soles 25*s*., per thousand—prices which may be said to amount almost to a prohibition of their use. In process of time, pipes came to be substituted, the cost of which ranged from 12*s*. to 18*s*. per thousand, according to size. We have thus for about 15*s*. what previously cost 75*s*., while the pipe is vastly superior to the semicircular tile and sole. At the meeting of the English Agricultural Society, at York, 1848, there were no less than thirty-four tile machines entered for competition. Such a circumstance certainly presented striking evidence of the extension of this branch of manufacture.

In the article of tiles the carriage forms a large item when the distance is considerable, yet, with clay in abundance for tile-making in this country, we continued, for a length of time, to import them; at the present time, however, there are tileries in different parts of the country where articles of good quality are produced.

Among the implements of drainage there are few calling for any special notice; more particularly as they are now so well known. In the Exhibition there were several good collections, among which may be mentioned that of J. Edmondson & Co., of this city, which obtained a prize.

While noticing this department, we may, not inappropriately, refer to the efforts now in progress for the adaptation of steam-power to drainage purposes; of which, however, we regret that we had no illustration in the Exhibition. In Hyde Park, in 1851, one of the most remarkable objects was the drainage plough exhibited by Messrs. Fowler & Fry, of Bristol, which did its work so admirably as to astonish every one. Horse-power was applied at the trial then undertaken in connexion with the English Agricultural Society; and not only did the plough, so propelled, make the opening at the proper depth in the soil, but it also deposited the pipes in their places with unfailing regularity. Steam has, however, it seems, been since successfully adapted to working this plough. The use of the implement is inadmissible where stones abound in the soil, as they would impede its action; but there are thousands of acres requiring drainage in which no such obstacles occur, and where the draining plough promises to be peculiarly valuable. There are few more remarkable triumphs of the application of mechanical science to agriculture than this invention presents; and there is certainly none more suggestive. On these grounds, then, we may be excused for referring to a trial which recently took place on the estate of P. W. S. Miles, Esq., at Kingsweyton, near Bristol, as reported in one of the local journals.

The steam-engine, although mounted on wheels, and capable of being transported from point to point, was, when employed, a stationary one, and worked by a horizontal cylinder. It had connected with it two drums, which were loose on the axles. Attached to the larger drum, which draws the plough forward, was a wire rope of beautiful manufacture, the breaking strain of which is 14 tons, the working strain being 5 tons. This drum was worked by two motions of the fly-wheel shaft, which gave a leverage of 22 to 1 on the plough, the drum making seven revolutions per minute. To the lesser drum, which was worked off the second shaft, was attached a rope, also of wire, but of smaller caliber, which drew the plough back when it had completed a furrow, to the side of the field from which it started and where it had to begin again. By an ingenious contrivance the drums were formed by the insides of two spur-wheels, so that practically the working was effected by ordinary spur gearing. The drums can be instantly thrown out of gear by clutches moving the pinions on a feather. The larger wire rope, on being wound on to the drum for the purpose of impelling the plough forward, worked round a sheave-wheel or pulley-block anchored to the field at such a point as to draw the plough at right angles to the engine, by which arrangement the necessity of shifting the engine was obviated to so great an extent that almost any field may be drained without once removing it from the position first taken up by it. To the front of the plough was attached a second sheave-wheel, round which the rope was doubled, thereby also doubling the power. The coulter of the plough is of iron, an inch in diameter at its widest point, so that the furrow made by it upon the surface of the land is scarcely perceptible, and generally disappears after the first shower of rain. It can be worked to a depth of four feet, and indeed deeper if necessary, and is so made that it can be raised or depressed by a hand-wheel under the control of the ploughman. The boring of the land is effected by means of a cast-iron mole or plug (the size of which is regulated by that of the tiles to be laid) keyed to the bottom of the coulter; and the most striking feature of the machine is, that as fast as it bores the land it lays in the tile piping, thus completing the drain as it goes, at the rate (when we saw it working) of 35 feet, and probably, under very favourable circumstances, 40 feet per minute. It should be stated, in order to the understanding of what follows, that as the engine wound the large rope on to the large drum, and drew the plough towards it, it at the same time unwound the small rope which was attached to the back of the plough from the small drum.

The mode of operation we will now endeavour to explain, assuming for our illustration a field of 1000 feet square, which has to be drained by drains ten yards apart from east to west. The engine would be fixed at the middle of the western edge; the plough would be placed on the eastern edge at ten yards from the southern edge of the ground, and an anchor and sheave-wheel would be rigged exactly opposite to it on the western edge. The large wire rope would be passed round the sheave-wheel, and thence on to the front of the plough, while the small wire rope would be connected from the back of the plough with another anchor, &c., rigged ten yards north of the plough—that is, at the point to which it would have to be drawn back, and from which it would have to commence again. The machinery thus arranged, the pipe tiles are strung on ropes of fifty yards long (the length being thus limited to economize time and labour in threading), but fitted with ingeniously contrived joints at either end, so that they can be readily and firmly joined together to any length required. These ropes are made of hemp for the sake of flexibility, while, as a matter of economy and durability, and to decrease friction as much as possible, they are coated with wire. The ropes being threaded and joined, one end is fixed immediately behind the mole, and the machine being set in motion by the steam-engine, the coulter cuts its narrow channel through the land, the mole bores and lifts the subsoil, and the pipes are drawn through the aperture, and closely and neatly put together, forming the drain. The sheave-wheels are then shifted, the plough drawn back by the small rope, and the second and succeeding drains are cut and piped in the same way. The ropes, after the tiles have been laid, are drawn out by horses, which is the only employment of horse-labour required. The plough is attended by a man, whose only duty seems to be to keep it upright where the land is not level.

The advantages to be derived from this invention are manifold. The first and most important is, of course, economy. One engine, with ten men and two horses, will do as much work as 120 men, and, under favourable circumstances, as much work as 150 men would do by the old system. A second advantage anticipated is the ability to drain in the summer season, when days are long and the weather favourable,—a desideratum not now obtainable on account of labour being at that period so fully occupied by other sources of employment. A third is, that drainage will be thereby better performed. The drains will be uniform in depth and straight, and the tiles will be closely and firmly laid; while the plough, by lifting the land, causes the water to percolate at once, and thus brings the drain into immediate action. No damage is done to the surface of the ground, which by the old process was always the case. With dry weather the machinery may be erected and a field drained one day, and on the next a casual observer would be unable to perceive that any change had taken place. With regard to its capabilities, Mr. Fowler, the inventor, calculates that with a single engine and plough he shall be able to drain about thirty acres per week.

## VI.—DAIRY UTENSILS AND APPARATUS.

The great varieties which have taken place in the forms of churns of late years, as well as the number of inventions that have been brought before the public from time to time, show the attention devoted to this department of rural economy; but, notwithstanding the high pretensions by which many of these so-called inventions were heralded, the number that stood the test of time and further experience are very few indeed. In the Exhibition there was no lack of churns, but there was less of novelty than might have been expected. The plunge churn, which was supposed to have been altogether superseded by the box churn, has again come forward to maintain its place in the race of competition, and with no inconsiderable chances of success.

The churn exhibited by C. and D. Young, of Edinburgh, and which was a modification of Drummond's, presented some peculiarities. In shape it is elliptic, and is separated by a division perforated at top and bottom into two compartments. A plunger or dash is provided for each of these chambers, so constructed as to insure a delivery of fresh air through the body of the cream at every stroke. A horizontal bracket stands above the churn, continued from the stand on which it is placed; and this bracket supports the driving or fly-wheel turned by the hand at one end, and an oscillating wheel in the centre. A connecting rod from the fly-wheel causes this centre wheel to oscillate from side to side, making at each time a part of a revolution, connected with the two shafts attached to it. Alternate up and down motion is thus communicated; as one falls the cream is forced through the apertures in the dash, and at the same time through those in the bottom of the central division; and as the other comes up the cream passes through the apertures at the top of the division. This, on the whole, was a very ingenious modification of the well-known construction on which it is based.

The churn of W. P. Stanly, of Peterburgh, obtained the prize in this department. In it there were two dashers fixed in the shaft, the form of the one being varied from that of the other. The shaft has two motions,—a revolving and a reciprocating, or up and down one. From the two movements a complete agitation is given to the cream, rendering the churn a highly effective one.

A cradle churn, invented by Dr. Farran, of Dungarvan, was also deserving of notice. The motion in this case is somewhat on the principle of the child's cot, the churn being suspended at some distance from the floor or bench on which it is to be worked. Two divisions are placed in the churn, through the apertures of which the milk is made to pass in moving backward and forward. Although simple, this arrangement is said to be effective. By it butter may be produced in from twenty-five to thirty minutes.

In determining the comparative value of churns, there are several particulars to be taken into account. The first is the quality and quantity of the butter produced, and the next the time and the facility with which the operation is carried on. Now, it so happens that these are seldom combined to the full extent. By some churns butter can be produced in less than three minutes; but the produce in such cases is rarely so good as when a longer time has been taken in the operation of churning. The form of the churn, too, must be such as admits of its being cleaned without difficulty,—a particular in which some of the varieties are sadly deficient. And, lastly, the construction should not involve any unnecessary expense. On the extent to which these characteristics are combined, giving due prominence to those of most importance, will depend the value of any particular modification of this instrument brought before the public.

Of the smaller dairy utensils there were few in the Exhibition, and these were confined to glass milk pans. Since the abolition of duty on glass, that substance has attracted much attention for dairy purposes, for which it is peculiarly appropriate. Porcelain is also an excellent material for holding milk, and is now coming into use for the purpose.

The subject of dairy management is one of great importance. In no other country do greater natural facilities exist for carrying it on than in Ireland; but any one who will take the trouble to examine the chief article of dairy produce in the market—butter—cannot fail to be impressed with the enormous waste which takes place from the very inferior quality of the butter, and the slovenly manner in which it is made up. The appearance of much of the butter in our markets is absolutely revolting, no inconsiderable quantity of it being totally unfit for human food.

In the preceding brief notice of the agricultural department of the Exhibition we have purposely avoided anything like a *resumé* of the articles which it included, as this would convey little information to the reader, and is besides rendered unnecessary by the detailed Catalogue appended herewith. We have also aimed at noting the peculiarities of a few of the implements and machines of agriculture, and pointing out their mode of action, rather than at giving any mere technical description of articles with which most of our readers will be, to some extent, familiar. In the limited space at our disposal we are desirous of exciting further inquiry, and suggesting the direction in which this is to be pursued, in preference to attempting to supply detailed information ourselves.

We have endeavoured to enforce the necessity of attention to the further application of mechanical science to the business of the farmer, so as to keep pace with the progress of improvement in that department of industry. One of the great features of the present age is the untiring ingenuity brought to bear upon efforts to cheapen the cost of production of every class of commodities; but the importance of attention to this the husbandman has not yet sufficiently learned. In every part of the United Kingdom there is much room for improvement in this respect, but more especially in Ireland, which is in many respects so far behind.

In discussing the improvements to be effected, and the economy to be carried out by the judicious selection of implements and machinery adapted to the circumstances in which they are to be used, we must not overlook the fact that their arrangement and the supply of the motive power to be employed are scarcely less deserving of consideration. On farms over 100 acres in extent, where a high standard of production is attained, steam-power will be found to be economical, from the facility with which it can be managed, and the ease with which it can be appropriated to a variety of purposes, as well as admitting of several operations being carried on at the same time. To enter at length upon this topic would be somewhat foreign to our present purpose. We may, however, mention that a good illustration, in many respects, of the economical arrangement and working of agricultural machinery may be seen at the Glasnevin Model Farm, in the vicinity of this city; a visit to which cannot fail to be highly suggestive of the future of agriculture, and the value of which, as a training establishment, cannot be over-estimated.—J. S.

---

1. BALL, W., Rothwell, Kettering, Northamptonshire, Inventor and Manufacturer.—The criterion prize plough; two-horse waggon.

2. BARRETT, EXALL, & ANDREWES, Katesgrove Iron Works, Reading, Berks, Inventors and Manufacturers.—Four horse-power patent steam-engine, with improvements for economizing heat; four horse-power threshing machine, with wooden frame, wrought-iron breasting, and wood and iron beaters; two horse-power patent threshing machine, with portable patent gear, and new arrangement for setting the breastwork; hand-power patent iron threshing machine, for two men; one horse-power patent gear; barley hummeller with iron framing; patent chain feed chaff-cutter, on a new principle; the paragon grain mill, with two rollers for crushing malt, oats, barley, and linseed, and a third, for splitting beans; oil cake mill; registered hay-making machine, with twofold motion for tedding or spreading the grass, and for lightly turning it; patent horse rake, with movable clearer; Reed's patent subsoil plough, or soil pulveriser.

3. BIGG, T., Great Dover-street, Southwark, Inventor and Manufacturer.—Sheep-dipping apparatus.

4. BOYD, J., Lower Thames-street, London, Inventor and Manufacturer.—Patent double action or self-adjusting scythes.

5. BURKE, R. H., Glencairn, Lismore, Co. Waterford.—The patent root-grater, for grating roots for cattle, pigs, poultry, &c., the joint invention of Exhibiter and Dr. Barter, of Blarney.

6. CLAYTON, SHUTTLEWORTH, & Co., Lincoln, Manufacturers.—Combined portable threshing, straw-shaking, riddling and winnowing machine, to be driven by steam-power.

7. COLEMAN, R., Chelmsford, Essex, Inventor and Manufacturer.—Patent drag harrows, cultivators, or scarifiers; patent expanding harrow; subsoil harrow or pulverizer.

8. CORCORAN, BRYAN, & Co., Mark-lane, London, Manufacturers.—A woven wire kiln plate.

9. CORPORATION OF DUBLIN, per Parke Neville, C. E.—Watering, scavenging, and gravel carts, manufactured by Mr. James Fitzsimons, Bridgefoot-street, under direction of the Borough Engineer.

10. CORRIGAN, ANDREW, Royal Dublin Society.—Model of a simple machine for irrigation purposes, invented by Dr. Spurgin, of the Polytechnic Institution, London.

11. COURTNEY & STEPHENS, Dublin.—A gorse machine and oat-bruiser, two-horse plough, harrows, and a double-acting pipe tile and brick-making machine.

12. CROSSKILL, W., Beverley, Yorkshire, Manufacturer.—Yorkshire wood plough; sets of Williams's patent iron seed harrows; patent serrated roller or clod-crusher, fitted with two travelling wheels; patent wheat roller and clod-crusher; two-row hand presser; Norwegian harrow; Ducie's drag harrow and scarifier, with extra steel paring shears; iron lever horse rake; double-action haymaker, with fore motion for making hay, and back motion for tedding it; iron horse hoe and harrow; broadcast portable manure distributer; turnip and manure drill, for peat charcoal, &c.; patent wheels and axle for farm carts; model farm cart; liquid manure cart; iron pump, with iron pipe; portable farm railway and railway truck; two-horse portable threshing machine; corn-dressing machine; potato washer; pig-troughs; Hussey's American reaper; Bell's original reaper, and other agricultural implements.

13. EDMONDSON, J., & Co., Dame-street, Dublin.—Winton's steel digging, hay, and dung forks, made from one piece of steel, without join or weld; spades, draining tools, &c.

14. EKLES, T. & Co., Mary-street, Dublin, Proprietors.—Hay and straw cutting machine; oat, bean, and flax-bruising machine; turnip slicer and cutter; single horse drill-grubbers; double drill turnip-sowing machine; improved cart axle with turned brushes; two-horse plough; Ferrabee's improved Budding's mowing machine; Hunter's registered hand-churn, &c.; farm, garden, and forest hand implements and tools; improved durable sheep-folding net; farm cart harness; Berwickshire farm cart.

15. FARRAN, C., Dungarvan, Manufacturer.—A cradle churn and a milk tub.

16. FERGUSON, J., Bridge of Allan, near Stirling, Designer and Manufacturer.—Model of draining plough; common iron plough.

17. FORBES, P., Shettleston, Glasgow, Designer and Manufacturer.—Common plough, with machinery for depositing seeds.

18. FORSHAM & Co., Cornwallis-street, Liverpool, Designer and Manufacturer.—Bean and oat-crusher; linseed and oat mill; hand mill and dressing machine for grinding and dressing flour.

19. FRASER, S., Mary-street, Dublin, Designer and Manufacturer.—Improved garden watering engines; cream-forcers for making butter and iced or whipped creams; potato steamers; imperial double-acting prize churns.

20. GARRETT, R., Leiston Works, Suffolk, Manufacturer.—Suffolk corn drill; small corn and seed drill; lever drill for vegetable seeds and manure; economical vegetable seed and manure drill; broadcast manure distributer; Garrett's patent horse hoe; horse and steam-power portable threshing machines on travelling wheels; winnowing machine; reaping machines and set of Norwegian harrows.

21. GRAY & Co., Uddingston, near Glasgow, Manufacturer.—One-horse Scotch farm cart; Scotch two-horse swing plough; parallel lever subsoil pulverizer; parallel hoe for drill crops; parallel expansion horse hoe; horse parallel five-tined drill grubber; horse equalizing draught bars; field grubber or cultivator; double drill turnip sowing machines, with improved seed distributers, concave iron rollers, &c.; improved chaff-cutting, and oat and bean-bruising machines; American churn.

22. GRENING, B., Church-gate, Manchester.—Field-gates, corn-rick stands, &c.

23. HILL, E., & Co., Brierly-hill Iron Works, near Dudley, Manufacturers.—Wrought-iron skim or paring plough; registered expanding horse hoe, for turnips, potatoes, &c.; iron sheep-rack, on four wheels, with roof and trough; wrought and cast-iron rick staddle or stand; iron fittings for a stable; samples of E. Hill and Co.'s continuous iron fences and hurdles; new sheep hurdle; materials for strained wire fences, consisting of wire, straining pillar, standards, and stays; specimens of game proof wire netting, painted and galvanized; iron garden seat, with foot stage; netting, plant guards; iron gates; guttering for roofs; iron barrow, with apparatus for heating tar.

24. HOWARD, J. & F., Bedford, Inventors and Manufacturers.—Patent iron plough, with wheels of various sizes and descriptions; patent iron swing plough; double breast or ridge plough; patent subsoil plough; sets of patent jointed iron harrows; patent three and four beam iron harrows; improved one-rowed horse hoe; trussed, equalizing, and steel-yard whippletrees; patent horse rake; improved corn-crusher and oil-cake breaker.

25. HUGHES, W., Valley Foundry, Holyhead, Anglesea, Inventors and Manufacturers.—Gorse or furze-cutting machines for hand and power; chaff-cutting machines, with an improved motion.

26. HUNTER, W. & J., Samuelston, Haddington, Inventors and Manufacturers.—Lever drilling machine; horse hoe for drilled grain.

27. INGRAM, G., D'Olier-street, Dublin, Proprietor.—Brick and tile machine at work.

28. KENNEDY, J., Aston's-quay, Dublin, Manufacturer.—Double and single drill turnip sowers; oat bruiser; turnip-cutters; hay and straw-cutter; drill grubber, and harrow; couch grass rake; steaming apparatus; winnowing machine; ploughs; six bull harrow of wrought iron; churn; family wheat mill.

29. KIRKWOOD, J., Tranent Foundry, East Lothian.—A horse hay rake; turnip cutter; two-horse plough; oil-cake mill; four-horse grubber; and set of harrows.

30. LA TOUCHE, Rev. THOMAS DIGGES, Upham, Killenaule.—Models of a harrow, drill dibbler and roller, drill scuffler or horse hoe, farm cart and grubber.

31. LE HUNTE, G., Artramont, Wexford, Proprietor.—Sheep netting, made by the Irish peasants.

32. LONGWORTH, DAMES F., Greenhill, Edenderry, Proprietor.—Net for confining sheep on pasture, &c., made of shreds of bog deal.

33. MASON, W., Navan, Co. Meath, Manufacturer.—Three-horse power threshing machine, corn-dressing or winnowing machine, worked by one man.

34. MILLOR, D., Dunleer.—Prize two-horse plough, drill grubber, cart axle with engine-turned ends.

35. MOLLOY, J., Rochestown Avenue, Co. Dublin, Inventor.—New churn, with cooler and stand; model of a horse-shoe for contracted foot.

36. MORROW, J., Banbridge, Co. Down.—Winnowing machine.

37. M'CONNELL, JAMES, Dunleer.—Iron ploughs.

38. O'CONNOR, H., Frederick-street, Limerick, Inventor.—Wheel and lever fourfold dash churn; model of horse-digging machine.

39. RANSOMES & SIMS, Ipswich, Manufacturers.—Patent iron ploughs, with one and with two wheels; patent trussed beam iron ploughs; set of patent trussed iron whippletrees; improved direct action horizontal steam-engine, of six-horse power; two-horse portable threshing machine; patent iron chaff engine, for hand or horse-power; small chaff engine; Gardener's double-action turnip cutter; Hurwood's patent metal mill for emigrants; patent double crushing mill; small bean mill; oil-cake breakers; grass-cutter; Tennant's registered grubber.

40. RICHMOND & CHANDLER, Manchester and Liverpool, Inventors and Manufacturers.—Hand chaff cutter; an improved chaff machine; corn crushers in variety.

41. RITCHIE, W. & J., Ardee, Co. Louth, Inventors and Manufacturers.—Farm cart with harvest frame and improved locker; six-drill corn-sowing machine, with self-acting coulters; improved two-horse swing plough; improved subsoil plough; drill plough, with improved mode of expanding and contracting mould-boards; new machine for ribbing wheat, oats, or barley.

42. SAMUELSON, B., Banbury (Agents in Dublin, Messrs. DRUMMOND & SONS), Manufacturers.—Samuelson's patent digging machine for thorough tillage of lands or breaking ground for railways; patent Gardner's turnip cutter with double action; Samuelson's registered Budding's lawn mower, with fore carriage; registered atmospheric churn.

43. SHERIDAN, H., & Co., Dublin, Manufacturers.—Draining, subsoiling, and other field implements and machines for horse and hand labour; machines and implements for the barn, haggard, farm-yard, dairy, and feeding shed; portable threshing machine; double-action vegetable-cutter, with grater attached.

44. SKELTON, S., Sheffield.—Farm and garden spades, and shovels of every description; draining tools; forge hammers, and other agricultural tools.

45. SMITH & ASHBY, Stamford, Lincolnshire, Manufacturers.—Smith and Ashby's new self-acting reaping machine; double-action hay-making machine, for spreading and turning hay, fitted with wrought-iron wheels; wrought iron horse-rake, for hay, corn, twitch, and stubble; lever hand-

rake, on iron frame, mounted on light wheels; chaff and litter cutting machines, for hand, horse, water, or steam-power; improved wrought-iron lever cultivator or scarifier; park and luggage cart mounted on springs; samples of Smith and Ashby's patent wrought-iron wheels and axles for carriages and for agricultural purposes.

46. SMITH, W., Kettering, Northamptonshire, Inventor and Manufacturer.—Steerage horse hoe with double bar.

47. SMITH, JAMES, & SONS, Peasenhall, Yoxford, Suffolk.—A six-rowed patent corn drill, upon the lever principle; an eight-rowed patent corn drill for corn and seeds; a ten-rowed patent corn and seed drill, with attachments of improved and patented inventions; a patent three-rowed turnip and mangold wurzel seeds and manure drill, adapted for three rows on the flat, and two on the ridge; a patent three-rowed turnip and mangold wurzel seed drill, for two on ridge or three on flat.

48. STANLEY, W. P., Peterborough, Northamptonshire, Manufacturer.—Registered roller mill for crushing linseed, oats, &c., for steam or hand-power; rape and linseed cake breaker; farmers' steaming and cooking apparatus; safety lever chaff engines; patent wrought-iron plough, with steel breast and two wheels; set of four-beam diagonal iron harrows; hand-labour machine, intended as a substitute for treadmills in gaols; improved churn; lever cheese press; machine for making pipes and drain tiles.

49. WEDLAKE, MARY, & Co., Fenchurch-street, London.—A manger feeding machine; convex chaff cutter; oat bruisers; Sinclair's drill; broadcast seed machine; turnip cutter; hay-making machine invented by the late Mr. Thomas Wedlake; sack-holder, filler, and truck combined.

50. WHITMEE & CHAPMAN, Fenchurch Buildings, Fenchurch-street, London, Inventors and Manufacturers.—Improved corn crusher, with steeled rollers.

51. WILKINSON, T., Oxford-street, London, Inventor and Manufacturer.—Patent box churn, on stand.

52. WILLISON, A., Dundonald, by Kilmarnock, Ayrshire, Inventor.—Patent threshing machine, with two flat beaters instead of the usual drum.

53. WINTON, H., Dove Mills, Birmingham.—A collection of digging forks, agricultural and horticultural spades, &c., which obtained several first prizes at the Royal English and Irish agricultural meetings.

54. YOUNG, CHARLES, D., & Co., Edinburgh, Glasgow, Liverpool, and London, Manufacturers.—Corn-rick stands; iron field-gates and posts; clod crusher; Drummond's patent churn.

# CLASS X.

---

## PHILOSOPHICAL, MUSICAL, SURGICAL, AND HOROLOGICAL INSTRUMENTS.

WE now come to a department of the Exhibition, the articles in which emphatically present illustrations of the triumphs of science in combination with manufacturing skill; the accuracy of the calculations on which their construction is founded being almost equalled by that of the handicraftman who in practice carries out the ideas of the philosopher. In each of the great divisions of this class triumphs of this kind may be pointed out. One does not know whether to admire most the simple though beautiful and sensitive arrangement of the balance which indicates less than the 1-100th part of a grain in weight; the singularly ingenious arrangement of the telescope which enables us to pursue our investigations in regions to which human fancy could not otherwise extend; the wonders of the telegraph, which is yet destined to enable us to hold, as it were, conversational communication with the people of the antipodes; the construction of those musical instruments, which, by comparatively simple means, can be made to give forth the most delicious melodies; the ingenuity displayed in arming the surgeon with the means of allaying human suffering; or the surpassing accuracy of the instruments for the measurement of time, whose variation for weeks together does not exceed a few seconds. Each and all of these may truly be regarded as amongst the triumphs of modern science. But than any of these the discovery of the daguerreotype and its kindred inventions is not less wonderful, as being destined to produce as great a revolution in pictorial illustration as any of the inventions already alluded to have done in their respective departments. Nor was there any other part of the Exhibition in which the progress attained was more clearly indicated than in that devoted to the objects included in this class. Of experimental philosophy it may be especially said that its position is truly indicated by the comparative perfection of the instruments which it employs, for here the perfection of the instrument is essential to the accuracy of any deductions drawn from its use. Chemistry, microscopical science, photography, and many other branches, are dependent for their progress on the accuracy and adaptation of the apparatus which they employ. The one, in fact, must keep pace with the other. Although, in many respects, the collection in the Exhibition was neither so complete nor extensive as might have been reasonably expected, still there were not wanting illustrations in every department, and some of these, moreover, among the best of their kind.

### I.—PHILOSOPHICAL INSTRUMENTS, AND PROCESSES DEPENDING ON THEIR USE.

In this department of the Exhibition we find, in a peculiar manner, evidence of mental progress allied to mechanical skill, which seems to be an attribute or characteristic of the present age. In former periods philosophical instruments were chiefly interesting as affording experimental illustrations of abstract laws; in the present age almost every department of physical science has given its aid in advancing man in the arts or the conveniences of life. Mechanical philosophy, which has done so much in every branch of industrial employment; optical science, which has handed to the artist its stereoscope and cameras, and laid down the scientific laws of colour and shade; electricity which has, by the electrotype, enabled us to recreate the finest efforts of the engraver, and convert into the most enduring material the perishable model of the sculptor:—all these, and many other boons, have been conferred upon the world by the philosopher, through the investigations carried on by his instruments of illustration and research.

A detailed enumeration of the articles exhibited in this department will be found in a succeeding page, and instead of attempting a *resumé* of them here, we prefer to notice at some length a few articles as types of their peculiar class. One of the most remarkable objects in this class, or indeed in the whole Exhibition, was Grubb's telescope, which our readers will recollect to have occupied a prominent place in the Centre Hall; and it demands something more than a passing notice at our hands. In like manner, the illustrations of the Telegraph suggest the necessity of some remarks on the progress of that wonderful invention; to these, also, we therefore propose referring at some length.

#### GRUBB'S TELESCOPE.

Amongst the philosophical instruments exhibited, there was probably none of greater interest or importance than the large telescope constructed by Mr. Grubb. Whether we consider it with reference to its scientific or practical value, or as a triumph of skill over many difficulties, this telescope afforded an object of great interest.

Of all the instruments which science has given to man, there are few which, for their immediate and remote advantages, have been attended with such results as the telescope. Let us for a moment consider what this instrument has done for us. By it we have discovered those laws of motion, or rather the verification of the laws, which have taught mankind the first truths of astronomy. By it we learn that there are systems like our own revolving round the sun, and yet themselves the centre of systems far transcending our finite minds from their vastness. By it we know the relative distances, sizes, and even weights of the heavenly bodies, and can search into space, and there discover amongst the faint lights that would appear only to augur embryo worlds, perfect systems of solar orbs, perhaps themselves the centres of systems vaster than our own. And these contemplations raise our minds to a due conception of that infinity on which

"Our souls ache to think,
Intoxicated with eternity."

We feel with what humbleness of heart we should approach their Author—to us invisibly or dimly seen in these His lowest works—and we feel with a force equal to a demonstration that these declare His "goodness without end, and power divine."

These moral uses of the telescope, however vast their importance may be to all well-cultivated minds, may not seem of that practical application which would be suited to an Industrial Exhibition; though we should regret to think that intelligent minds could separate the moral from the practical, the highest truth from its lowest application. But we know that there are many whose minds can only appreciate the value of science by its immediate results; and for them we shall note down some of the direct and practical results of this discovery.

Of all the benefits conferred by science upon the progress of mankind, few have been so great as those which have advanced the knowledge of navigation; and astronomy and other branches of physical science have mainly contributed to the progress of this all-important art. The compass guides the mariner across the trackless deep; but astronomy has given a certainty to his path, and traced it out by the beacon-lights set in the heavens, with accuracy so unfailing that the merest tyro in science feels he may sleep on his ocean voyage, under the guidance of the stars, with a much fuller assurance of safety than the ancient mariner felt in the patronage of his Pagan deities; and Castor and Pollux, the guiding stars of the Roman sailor, have become to the well-initiated navigator the guides of his path over the trackless waters, though he has discrowned them from their place on high Olympus, and given them their due position amongst the other creations of a supreme Hand. All this is mainly due to the results of astronomical science.

The true conception of the figure of the earth, and its position in a system revolving round a great centre, we owe to this science; and the revelations of the telescope have shown us that there are numerous systems similar to our own, obeying the same laws and subject to like influences. Astronomy has given us the means of determining our real position on the surface of the globe, by direct observation of the apparent places of the sun and stars; it enables the mariner to correct those errors of his course arising from the variation of the compass, and those currents which would otherwise lead him astray, so that at the end of months of wandering over the surface of the globe, he finds that he has followed as direct a track as though he had well-defined landmarks to guide him during his voyage. These practical applications of this science, which have depended so materially on the improvement of the telescope, have contributed to give it an interest and importance greater than it could have attained merely as an instrument for abstract scientific investigation.

From the time when Galileo, adapting the accidental discovery of the effect of compound lenses, converted the experiment of the children of Hansens into a means of making a complete revolution in astronomical science, the attention of the scientific world has been directed to the improvement of the telescope; and the names of Newton, Le Maire, Herschell, Lord Rosse, &c., at once occur to us as distinguished amongst a host who have spent years of labour in perfecting this instrument. Our readers are aware that two different forms or principles have been adopted in the telescope. In the first instrument constructed, the rays of light proceeding from the object were received on the surface of a convex glass, and (on optical principles) these converged to a point where an image was formed, possessing much greater brilliancy than when viewed by the eye, in the proportion of the area of the glass to the opening of the eye; and this image so formed was then viewed under a larger angle by the eye placed near it, assisted by a second lens—enabling the eye to view it under an increased angle, or magnified. Instruments of this construction were called *refractors*. In the instruments of Newton, Gregory, and Lord Rosse, the image of the object was formed by reflection of the rays from a concave reflector or speculum, being made to converge to a point where they formed a brilliant image of the object which was viewed by the observer, either directly, or through the medium of a convex lens. We shall not allude further to the latter class, but direct attention to the refracting telescope. Owing to two causes the improvement of this species of telescope was long deemed hopeless; and in all large instruments the principle of reflexion is only employed. These causes were, the difficulty of obtaining masses of glass of sufficient size and transparency to form large object-glasses, and the supposed impossibility of counteracting the dispersion of the rays of light, so as to obtain a colourless image of the object. This latter difficulty, however, was obviated by Dolland, who, by combination of two glasses of dissimilar materials, made their dispersive powers so different as to produce an image free from colour, or achromatic. But the difficulty of obtaining large masses of good glass remained; and it is only at present that this difficulty seems likely to be adequately overcome. With the modern improvements in glass manufacture, it is by no means impossible that we may have achromatic telescopes of great size and power, which will practically supersede even the monster reflectors of Herschell and Lord Rosse. We understand, that at present a glass is in progress of construction, the diameter of which will be thirty-nine inches, the largest ever constructed; and we can only express a hope, that the genius and enterprise of the firm (Chance & Co., of Birmingham), who have undertaken the wondrous enterprise, may be crowned with success, as there are few undertakings, of modern times, of greater difficulty than this, when we take into consideration the impediments to be overcome.

The obstacles to which we have alluded may be classed under two heads:—those arising from the extreme difficulty of obtaining glass fitted for the manufacturer, and the mechanical labour of grinding it with a good surface, and of the requisite curvature. Persons who are in the habit of seeing large plates of glass in mirrors, &c., of the purest transparency, and cut and polished without an apparent flaw, can scarcely believe in the extreme difficulty of obtaining a circular disc of glass, of a few inches' diameter, fit for optical purposes; and will hardly understand how, until within the last few years, the construction of large telescopes, on refracting principles, was considered impossible, owing to glass of the required purity not being attainable. This arose from the difficulty of obtaining a mass of glass of sufficient thickness and diameter free from those defects which would materially interfere with the passage of the rays of light through it. Streaks or striæ of different density from the other portions of the glass, specks, air-bubbles, inequality of colour—any of these causes would be destructive of the value of glass for optical purposes; and it is only within the last few years that these difficulties have been, in any great degree, overcome. The labours of Guinam, of Neufchatel, succeeded in producing a glass, having the requisite perfection, of six inches in diameter. A few years since, Bontemps obtained glasses in discs of 12 inches' diameter, some of which, when polished, were sold, we believe, for upwards of a thousand pounds. Latterly M. Bontemps has entered into partnership with the eminent firm of Chance & Co., and there is little doubt, that with the capital and skill conjointly brought to bear on this manufacture, we shall soon have the production of optical glasses brought to a still higher degree of perfection.

In the practical employment of large telescopes, either achromatic or reflecting, a great difficulty occurs, which, unless overcome, would completely interfere with their scientific application. This is the difficulty of giving them, at the same time, perfect facility of motion, and absolute steadiness and freedom from the slightest vibration. The difficulty of attaining this in large telescopes must be apparent, when we consider the length of the tube, from 30 to 50 feet, bearing either a mass of metal weighing, perhaps, tons in weight, or a mass of glass, 15 inches in diameter, and many inches thick; which, with its tube, might, as in the case of the Dorpat instrument, weigh 5000 lbs. This object Mr. Grubb has endeavoured to attain, and, we believe, with complete success.

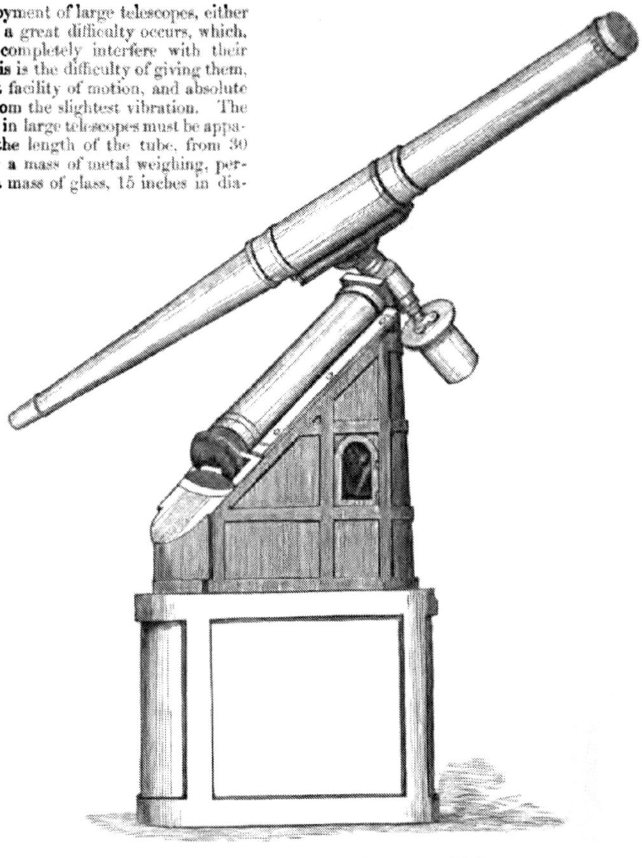

Grubb's Telescope, exhibited in Centre Hall.

To be scientifically of any value, a motionless stand and freedom from vibration are absolutely essential; of course, every vibration will be magnified by the instrument, and no correct admeasurement of an object could be made with the least perceptible oscillation of the tube or stand. Now, it may appear an easy matter to effect this, but in practice it is a matter of extreme difficulty, and various means are taken for the purpose. Some instruments, such as those meant only to observe stars passing the meridian, are either fixed between pillars of solid masonry, and allowed to move upwards and downwards, or attached to a solid wall—and in this way transit-instruments and mural circles are arranged, by which almost perfect steadiness is insured. Lord Rosse's great telescope, the tube of which is upwards of 50 feet long, and its weight 15 tons, is so arranged, that little or no lateral motion is given to the instrument, and it moves in the direction of the meridian principally, whereby the necessary mechanism required does not interfere with its perfect stability. But in instruments wanted to traverse considerable portions of the heavens at each side of the meridian line, it must be evident, that every complex motion must be provided for, and the difficulties of mounting are consequently greatly increased. In the instrument of Sir J. South, an achromatic of 12 or 14 inches' aperture, the arrangements for this purpose were so defective, that the observer was conscious of a persistent tremor of the instrument during observation, seriously interfering with scientific accuracy. But in the instrument of Mr. Cooper, of Markree (which was mounted by Mr. Grubb), and in the instrument in the Exhibition, so perfect are the mechanical adjustments, and so nicely balanced are all the parts, that whilst a child can direct it to the part of the heavens to be observed, the philosopher fails to detect in it the slightest motion interfering with correct observations.

We may now detail the principal points of importance in the instrument shown in the Exhibition. In it the tube was supported on a pedestal of masonry about eight feet high, the top of which was sloped in the direction of the earth's axis, and on the upper portion of which were placed the supports of the telescope, which allowed of its motion in different directions. These were connected with a system of clock-work contained in the upper or triangular portion of the masonry, which was intended to give motion to the telescope when mounted for use, so that on a star being brought into the field of view it would remain under observation, the motion of the telescope by means of the clock-work corresponding to the earth's motion. Without this arrangement an object would remain in the field of vision for too short a time for any lengthened observation.

The length of the tube of this telescope is upwards of twenty feet; the diameter at the centre is sixteen inches; at the end containing the object-glass, thirteen inches; at the other end, containing the eye-glass, eight inches; and the clear aperture of the object-glass is twelve inches. The tube itself is formed of strong tin plates, to which great stiffness and freedom from elastic tremor are given by means of a system of hollow diaphragms and longitudinal hollow ribs. The instrument is, at the same time, so light that, including object-glass and balance-weight, it weighs not more than than two and a half cwt. The entire weight which has to be set in motion is only twelve cwt.; and so perfect is the arrangement of counterpoises and reduction of friction that, notwithstanding the great diameters of the polar and declination axes (the former eleven and the latter ten inches), motion is produced by a force of three pounds applied at the end of the tube; and this great freedom of motion is attained without any sacrifice of steadiness, the slightest tremor not being perceptible during the motion of the tube.

We should mention, for the benefit of our non-scientific readers, that this instrument is the second largest achromatic telescope ever mounted; and we have reason to know that Mr. Grubb is prepared, not only to mount and adjust, but also to make in all their parts, telescopes on the same principle, two feet in diameter. We trust that ere long he will have the opportunity of exhibiting such a monster instrument.—W. B.

### PHOTOGRAPHY.

This is a strange age—the word impossibility is becoming almost obsolete—all the old landmarks of credulity are giving way, and the ghosts and spirits which used to frighten our ancestors have become antiquated, and a new set have come into fashion. A schoolboy may now, with a very moderate amount of pocket-money, possess himself of magic machinery such as Friar Bacon or Albertus Magnus never even dreamed of. The characteristic feature, however, of the new ghosts and the new magic is, that everybody may attempt to raise the one and perform the other; there are now no hidden mysteries—no freemasonry known only to the initiated—science is the property of all.

Of all the curiosities of natural magic, the most wonderful and the most suggestive is the art of producing pictures by the action of the sun's rays. What would our grandfathers have said, if some one told them, that by looking at a piece of glass or paper, their image would slowly appear on it? And yet, this is sober reality now. The statues and pictures in the Exhibition were exceedingly beautiful, and exhibited, in a wonderful manner, the creative power of man; the works in metal and in the textile fabrics showed to what an extent he has gained dominion over the powers of nature. All these things attracted crowds of admirers, and deservedly so; but there were some unpretending objects—small pictures and portraits—which in all probability excited no more attention than a few small prints in a window; and yet, these were specimens of the most wonderful art which has ever been discovered, and which is destined to effect wonderful changes in civilization. This art, of which there are many branches, is called by the general name of Photography, from two Greek words signifying *light-writing*.

The celebrated Leonardo da Vinci observed, that when a hole is cut in a shutter, in a dark room, the external objects will paint themselves on the opposite wall in all their proportions, true positions, and colours. It struck him, that if he made a small box, provided it with an aperture, and means of seeing into it, and placed it with its aperture directed towards external objects, he would have an opportunity of studying them at his leisure, as they should be represented upon a flat surface in a painting. This was the *camera obscura*, or dark chamber, which received its present form from a distinguished Neapolitan philosopher, named Porta, who placed a *convex lens*, or burning-glass, in the aperture, by which the light was concentrated, and the sharpness of the picture defined.

Long subsequent to the invention of the camera, the alchemists discovered in chloride of silver, a compound of silver with chlorine, the property of blackening when exposed to the sunlight.

We have now two points—an instrument by which external objects are represented in all their reality upon a flat surface, and a substance which is darkened in proportion to the amount of light which falls upon it. Could not a piece of paper, impregnated with such a substance, be employed as the flat surface, and we would have the picture copied in various shades, passing from white to black? Such was the idea which occurred to Wedgewood and Sir Humphrey Davy, in 1802, when they actually copied several objects by this means, but from the slowness with which the change took place, and the impossibility of preserving the image when made, the idea was fruitless.

In 1827, M. Niepce, of Chalon, a retired officer, who appears to have been engaged at the subject since 1814, presented a memoir to the Royal Society of London, detailing a process for fixing the pictures of the camera obscura, founded upon the property which the bitumen of Judea has, of being modified by the action of light to such a degree, as to become almost insoluble in oil of lavender. After dissolving the bitumen in the oil, he concentrated the mixture at a gentle heat, thus obtaining a sort of thick varnish, which he spread as a thin paint upon plates of silvered copper. The plate was next placed in the camera, after which it was immersed in a mixture of oil of lavender and petroleum, which rapidly dissolved off the resin from such parts of the plate as had not been altered by the action of the light, leaving the parts acted upon undissolved, and forming a complete picture of the object exposed to the camera; the shades being formed by the undissolved bitumen, and the lights by the surface of the metal. The lights and shades were, however, reversed—that is, the light in nature being represented by the darkest part of the picture. To this process he gave the name of *Heliography*, or sun-writing.

About a year before the reading of this paper, M. Daguerre, a very distinguished scene-painter of Paris, known by his invention of the diorama, and who had occupied himself for a considerable time with the same subject, learned from an optician in Paris, the friend of M. Niepce, that the latter knew how to fix the picture of the camera. He immediately placed himself in communication with the optician, and from that time their correspondence lasted till 1829, when M. Niepce proposed that they should associate themselves together for the purpose of improving the process of the latter, which they accordingly did.

Daguerre energetically entered upon the task; he replaced the bitumen by the resin which remains on distilling oil of lavender in its purification, and which has a remarkable sensibility to light. Instead of washing the plate, after its exposure in the camera, with oil of lavender, he exposed it to the action of its vapour produced by its spontaneous evaporation at the ordinary temperature. The vapour had no action upon the resin altered by the light, but it condensed upon the parts not thus acted upon, rendering them diaphanous; thus forming the shades, while the lights were formed of the whitened resin unacted upon by the vapour of the oil. This was a decided progress—especially the application of the vapour, as it contained the germ of the future discovery.

M. Niepce had long entertained the idea of strengthening the lights of his picture, by etching out the simple metallic surface laid bare, with some substance which would have little or no action upon the resin. For this purpose he tried iodine. One day it happened that a spoon was accidentally left on a plate of silver upon which he had been trying the iodine, and by the action of the diffused daylight of the room, its image was found upon the plate. This circumstance was not lost upon Daguerre; for the resin, he substituted the vapour of iodine; and for the essential oil of lavender, the vapour of mercury; and thus completed his discovery. Niepce died in 1833, and it was not until 1839 that Daguerre had so far perfected the process as to publish it.

*The Daguerreotype* consists simply in exposing a plate of silvered copper to the action of the vapours of iodine spontaneously evolved at the ordinary temperature. When the silvered surface has assumed a rich golden-yellow colour, it is placed in the focus of a camera, situated so as to allow the object which is to be delineated to form its image upon the plate. When after a short time it is taken out, no perceptible change will be found to have taken place; but if it be now submitted to the action of the vapours of mercury, the image is gradually rendered visible by the unequal condensation of the mercury upon the surface of the plate. Exactly as in the case of the resin, the part of the plate acted upon by the light alone condenses the mercury, the shadows remaining unaltered. After the image has been brought out by the mercury it is necessary to remove the iodine from those parts of the plate unaltered by the light, as otherwise the picture would be gradually destroyed on exposure to the air and light; this was easily effected by means of hyposulphite of soda. It will be seen that in this process the lights and shades are correct, simply owing to the superior brightness of the quicksilver; had any other less bright substance been used, we would have them reversed, as the change would be exactly similar to that which occurred in M. Niepce's bitumen pictures.

Beautiful as were the results obtained by Daguerre, the process was still very imperfect. The picture could only be seen at certain angles, in consequence of the mirror-like effect produced by the brilliant surface of the mercury; and at least fifteen minutes, and in many cases twenty-five minutes, were required to obtain an impression in strong sunlight. What a contrast between sitting in a glaring sunlight for nearly half an hour to obtain a portrait, and the almost instantaneous manner in which it is now obtained!

By improvements in the camera, considerable advance was made in the sharpness and finish of the portraits, which were almost exclusively the objects produced. These effects were considerably increased, and a greater harmony and depth of tone obtained by the accelerating process of M. Claudet, introduced in 1840, which consisted in exposing the iodized plate to the action of chloride of iodine,—while the time was reduced from minutes to seconds. The success which attended the first effort at improvement will be best judged of by the fact, that, immediately after its introduction, £60 was often received in one day by the two establishments opened in London.

In 1841, MM. Fizeau, Gaudin, and Leon Foucault, obtained images with still greater rapidity, by combining the employment of the vapour of bromine, or of its compounds, with that of iodine.

Still the image was to a certain extent evanescent and liable to injury by the action of the air, or of the slightest rubbing, until M. Fizeau succeeded in discovering a very simple and beautiful process for fixing the image. This effect was produced by covering the plate with a very dilute solution of chloride of gold—a combination of gold and chlorine, and obtained by dissolving gold in *aqua regia*—and adding to the chloride a small quantity of hyposulphite of soda, and then gently heating the plate, when a thin varnish of metallic gold is precipitated.

Many mechanical contrivances were after this introduced; such as those of M. Claudet, for polishing the plates, which very considerably assisted in the development of the art. Finally, Mr. Bingham invented the bromide of lime, which was soon replaced by the chloro-bromide of lime, by the Baron Gros—a compound of chlorine, bromine, and lime, which is the most constant and the most energetic of all the accelerating substances, and which gives exceedingly rich tones to the images.

But probably the most remarkable improvement that has been made is that by which daguerreotypes can be copied in the electrotype; or in other words, as has been well observed, we can have a picture "drawn by light" and "engraved by electricity."

Such is a brief history of the art of photography on plates of metal, to which the name of the daguerreotype has been given from its discoverer. It is not, however, the only process by which pictures may be produced by the action of sunlight.

*The Talbotype.*—It appears that as early as the year 1834, before Daguerre had succeeded with his process, Mr. Talbot had found a means of fixing the image produced in the camera, and that he was able to multiply this picture exactly as he could an engraving. It is curious that he did not publish the matter until M. Daguerre's success had attracted very considerable attention. The whole process of Mr. Talbot is quite different from that of Daguerre, as well as the material upon which the image is produced, which is simply paper.

It has been already remarked that the chloride of silver is blackened by the action of light. This is also the case with the iodide and other compounds of silver. The stronger the light, the deeper will be the colour produced. Now, if we place a piece of paper impregnated with either the iodide or the chloride of silver in the focus of the camera, we shall obtain a picture, but this picture will differ essentially from an artist's sketch. As the white parts of objects reflect more light than the coloured, and the light parts more than the shaded, the light parts of an object will be represented on the chloride of silver paper by the deepest shade, and the shaded parts by the light part of the paper. This is also the case with the daguerreotype, as already mentioned, but is obviated by the mercury. The reversed picture on the paper is called in the language of photography a *negative*, whilst a picture representing the true lights and shades is called a *positive* picture.

A picture produced upon paper cannot be fixed by mercury, therefore some other means had to be found to convert the negative picture into a positive one. Mr. Talbot effected this object by taking his negative picture and laying it on another sheet of paper prepared by iodide or chloride of silver, and pressing them together between two plates of glass, and exposing them to the action of sunlight. The light falling upon the negative picture passes through it and acts upon the prepared paper behind; but as the dark part of the negative will intercept a considerable portion of the light, while the uncoloured portion will allow it to pass freely through, we will thus have a second picture the reverse of the first—that is, one in which the lights and shades are natural—or, in other words, a positive picture.

But the chloride and iodide of silver are but slowly acted upon by light, and hence it would take a considerable time to produce a picture, unless we could find some accelerating substance, such as those already mentioned in the case of the daguerreotype; and this Mr. Talbot discovered in gallic acid, which acts upon paper covered with the iodide or chloride of silver in the same way as bromine on the iodized plate.

Mr. Talbot's process may be thus stated in a few words. He washed a piece of paper, by means of a small brush, with a pure solution of nitrate of silver, and then with a solution of iodide of potassium; the union of these two salts produces iodide of silver. When the paper had dried, it was washed with a solution of nitrate of silver, to which a certain quantity of gallic and acetic acids have been added. The paper was now ready for the camera, where it was exposed for from ten to fifteen minutes, after which it was washed with the same solution of gallo-nitrate of silver, under the influence of which the image appears as it does on the iodized plates of M. Daguerre under the influence of mercury; and as in the latter, the excess of iodine is removed by hyposulphite of soda, so in the former is the excess of the salt of silver by the same substance, or by bromide of potassium.

The negative image being thus complete, it was then necessary to recommence the whole process again, to obtain the positive picture. To this process he gave the name of the *Kalotype*, now usually called by the more appropriate name of the Talbotype, in honour of its discoverer.

This process attracted very little attention at the time of its publication—the beauty of the daguerreotypes being so manifest. Gradually, however, it began again to emerge from its temporary oblivion, by the researches of a number of scientific men, who occupied themselves with the question for a purely philosophical object; among whom must be especially mentioned the names of Sir John Herschel, Berard, Robert Hunt, Draper, &c. Thus we have the *chromatype* of Hunt, in which chromate of mercury, or of copper, is substituted for the iodide of silver; but it is not adapted for the camera, not being sensible enough. The *chrysotype* of Herschel, on the other hand, gives results quite equal to those of the talbotype. In this modification the paper is washed with a solution of ammonia, or citrate of iron; and the image is brought out by washing it with a solution of soda, or chloride of gold, or with nitrate of silver, and fixing it, in the first case, by washing it with iodide of potassium; and in the second, with hyposulphite of soda. Where the soda-chloride of gold is employed the image is formed of a thin varnish of gold, hence the name from χρυσος, the Greek for *gold*.

It would occupy too much space to notice all the ingenious improvements which have been effected in photography on paper, both in France and in England, since its revival in the former country in 1846. It appears that the improvements effected by M. Blanquart-Evrard, of Lille, are those to which the present condition of the art is mainly due. To him principally belongs the honour of having given it a commercial future.

The grand defects of the original process of Mr. Talbot were—first, that the solution being laid on with a brush, there was an unequal deposit of the iodide of silver; second, the coating was only superficial; and third, the mixture of gallic acid with nitrate of silver was very inconvenient, as the compound resulting from their mixture was very decomposable, and it was almost impossible to use it without producing spots, and destroying the images. The result was, that the pictures obtained were weak, the outlines not well marked, the half-tints scarcely developed: and hence there was a rigidity, lifelessness, and want of solidity about the whole, consequent upon the shadows not softening into one another. M. Blanquart obviated all these disadvantages by immersing the sheets of paper directly into a bath of iodide of potassium, and then into one of nitrate of silver; and instead of using gallo-nitrate of silver to bring out the image, he plunges it into a concentrated solution of gallic acid.

Hitherto the positive pictures were produced from the negative by the agency of light alone, which had the disadvantage of being, in all cases, a long operation, and of being very much dependent upon the weather; and, furthermore, even with the greatest care, the negative picture was only capable of yielding three or four positive pictures in a day.

M. Blanquart in taking his positive pictures proceeds just as when he makes a negative picture. He places the negative in contact with a sheet of prepared paper, and exposes them in a camera to the action of light from a half to one minute, and then dips the paper into the concentrated solution of gallic acid, or as Regnault has lately proposed, into one of pyro-gallic acid. Even where scarcely a trace of the positive picture can be detected upon the paper, and in many cases where the latter is perfectly white, the image is brought out by the gallic acid, and in this way one negative picture can give from 300 to 400 positive pictures in a day.

Photographic pictures are subject to the inconvenience of inequality of tint, but M. Blanquart has obviated this also, and he has shown that when a negative is too feeble it may be strengthened by dipping it into a bath of concentrated acetic acid, and subsequently into one of gallic acid, mixed with a few drops of nitrate of silver; when the shades, on the other hand, are too dark, he plunges the picture into water containing a few drops of bromide of iodine, and then into a slightly acid bath of hyposulphite of soda. These improvements are of great consequence, should photography become a branch of trade like engraving; which it appears to be destined to do.

Some charming effects may be produced by the addition of small quantities of certain substances to the bath of hyposulphite of soda, employed to remove the excess of iodide of silver. Thus, if we wish to develop the shadows, we have only to add a little nitrate of silver or a little glacial acetic acid. In the first case, the paper assumes a yellowish tint like China paper; while with the acetic acid it remains white; and with a few drops of ammonia it causes a reddish tint exactly like Roman sepia. These effects can be modified in a thousand ways, and thus every variety of tone may be produced.

The art of photography is not confined to metals and paper; sun pictures may be produced on plates of glass or ivory. We are indebted for this branch of the subject to M. Niepce de St. Victor, the nephew of the first discoverer. The process consists in spreading on a plate of glass a thin varnish of some substance which is capable of subsequently absorbing the sensitive preparation. For this purpose the white of egg was first used; then the white of egg dissolved in the whey of milk, or mixed with a little honey; and later still purified gelatine has been employed. The plate thus prepared is submitted to exactly the same series of operations as in the case of paper, and is capable of receiving every modification which can be applied to the latter. Lately *collodion*, that is gun-cotton dissolved in ether, has been used with remarkable success instead of the albumen or white of egg; and later still gutta percha mixed with the collodion. Both these modifications are due to Mr. Bingham.

A German, M. Pucher, has lately succeeded in obtaining pictures by coating glass with the vapour of sulphur, and rendering it sensitive by the vapour of iodine, the image being brought out by the vapour of bromine. As yet the results are not very good, but they possess one quality of importance which may give to photography a variety of applications—they are transparent.

Plates of glass, prepared in any of these ways, are admirably adapted for taking *negative* pictures, as they are not liable to be strained and distorted as those of paper are, and are not so liable to injury from other causes; they will hence be of immense utility when the preparation of positive photographs, as illustrations of books or other purposes, becomes a branch of general trade.

Within the last few months some very satisfactory results have been obtained by MM. Bareswil, Lerebrer, Lamercier and Halleux, in obtaining images directly upon lithographic stones, from which impressions may be printed. The process of the three first-named is founded upon the original one of M. Niepce; and that of Halleux upon the simple impregnation of the stone with a sensitive substance. The original idea of M. Niepce of engraving a sun picture has also been successfully effected by his nephew, M. Niepce de St. Victor, so that a daguerreotype may now be used directly to produce engravings.

*Scotography.*—Another branch of this varied and beautiful art remains to be mentioned; namely, the art of copying engravings, manuscripts, old documents, &c., by simple contact, and without the employment of a camera. To this process, for which we are indebted to M. Moser, the name of scotography has been given. In order to copy an engraving or the page of a book by this process, we have merely to take a silvered copper plate, of the size of the engraving, and having polished it and exposed it to the action of iodine and bromine in the same way as for the daguerreotype, we place it with its prepared face in contact with the engraved side of the print, the operation being performed with the light of a taper. A perfectly flat glass plate is then to be placed on the engraving so as to press it gently and evenly against the plate. This done, the whole kept tightly together is to be exposed from five to fifteen seconds to diffuse daylight, or from two to five seconds to the direct rays of the sun, according to the intensity of the light; the back of the print being turned towards the light, and consequently the sensitive side of the plate. They are then removed into a dark place, the glass and engraving carefully removed, and the image brought out with mercury, and fixed in the usual way.

It has occasionally occurred, that several objects have painted themselves on a daguerreotype plate in their natural colours; even the colours of a shawl and other parts of the dress of a lady, and the blue and other tints of the sky have been completely reproduced in this way. This has led to a hope that at no distant day this last but greatest improvement will be effected—obtaining photographic pictures with their natural colours. To understand the probability of our arriving at this result, it will be necessary to briefly notice some of the discoveries already effected in this direction, and, at the same time, to say a few words upon the peculiar power which acts in the production of photography.

It is well known that white light is compounded of several colours, and that by means of a triangular-shaped bar of glass, called a prism, a beam of white light may be decomposed, and a long, luminous, parti-coloured band produced on any white object placed behind the prism; the colours being arranged from above, downwards, in the following order—violet, indigo, blue, green, yellow, orange, and red. This image is called the *prismatic spectrum*. The rainbow, to a certain extent, presents the same phenomena. Towards the end of the last century, the celebrated Scheele discovered that the blackening effect of the solar rays upon salts of silver was confined principally to the violet rays. Subsequently Seebeck showed that chloride of silver exposed to the red rays did not blacken, but assumed a reddish tint; and that even when it had been blackened by exposure to daylight, it became much lighter by exposure to the red rays. Following out these experiments, he made the curious observation that chloride of silver becomes of a beautiful carmine red colour when exposed to the red rays produced by the union of the red and violet of two different spectra. Berard confirmed and extended these results; for he found that if the yellow, orange, and red rays were united by a burning glass, a brilliant focus would be produced, which does not blacken the salts of silver, even after an exposure of two hours, although in the much less brilliant focus produced by the union of the green, blue, indigo, and violet, the effect is produced in a few minutes.

Becquerel made the remarkable discovery, that if a piece of paper impregnated with bromide of silver be exposed for a moment to the action of the diffuse light of the day, or to the violet rays of the spectrum, until the first perceptible blackening commences, and then exposed to the red rays, the blackening will go on; thus showing that although the red rays alone would be incapable of commencing the change, they would have the power of continuing it when once begun. These curious actions are not, however, confined to the coloured rays of the spectrum. We can obtain equally curious results by employing light which has passed through coloured glass. Thus under violet glass chloride of silver is rapidly blackened, while under yellow it remains almost unaltered. But not only has the colour of the substance through which the light passes a remarkable action upon it in reference to its chemical action, but also its nature. Thus air, water, and steam, do not appear to diminish its power in this respect; or in other words, they are the most transparent to the rays having this blackening property; while the vapour of bromine, iodine, chlorine, and green bottle glass, &c., almost completely intercept them. A solution of yellow or neutral chromate of potash will prevent all blackening action by the light which passes through it, while red prussiate of potash will produce a brick red, and an ammoniacal solution of copper will produce a greenish brown.

But the influencing causes do not cease here. Thus, if we steep a piece of paper in nitrate of silver, and then wash it over with some particular chloride, we shall produce chloride of silver, which will render the paper sensitive. Now the nature of the chloride thus employed has remarkable influence upon the action of the light upon the chloride of silver. Thus if chloride of potassium be employed, and the paper be exposed to light transmitted through blue glass, it will be coloured light purple; through green glass, sky blue; through yellow glass, like violet; through red glass, red. Somewhat similar results are obtained if the paper be first blackened by exposure to white light, and then be exposed to light transmitted through different coloured glasses. And if to these beautiful results, the knowledge of which we owe principally to the researches of Hunt, Draper, and Malaguti, we add the important fact, that Seebeck, Herschel, and Becquerel, have succeeded in impressing an image of the prismatic spectrum, in all the vividness of its natural colours, upon prepared plates, we think we may consider, without being guilty of being over-sanguine, that the problem of producing photographs with their natural colours is soon destined to be solved.

It has been already remarked, that the greatest blackening or chemical action took place in the violet rays; but it is by no means confined to them, but even extends beyond the luminous part of the spectrum. And on further investigation it was found that the point in the spectrum where the maximum effect was produced depended upon the nature of the prism employed. Different kinds of glass when made into prisms have an effect on the width and position of the coloured spectrum; but the order in which the different kinds of glass range themselves according to this action have no relation with that which would correspond with chemical action. *The rays which produce chemical effects, therefore, although analogous in many respects to those which produce light, are quite distinct and are not luminous.* These rays are called by the very inappropriate name of *actinic*, from a Greek word signifying ray, and the property of blackening chloride of silver and producing other similar changes is termed *actinism*.

These rays play an important part in nature, as we have already seen. How rapidly the catalogue of substances susceptible of being changed by them is extending! But if we turn from the laboratory to nature, we find that it is through their agency the growth of plants takes place. The carbonic acid of the atmosphere, under the influence of sunlight, is decomposed; part of it serving in the plant to build up new cells, whilst a supply of fresh oxygen is poured into the atmosphere. By this action the green of the leaves, and the brilliant and varied tints of the flowers, are developed. Shall it, indeed, be in our power to copy these delicate colours by the very same agency under which they are produced? Their action must evidently go farther. Animal bodies must also fall within the sphere of their influence; there, however, we shall stop, for as yet we know nothing on this subject.

It will not be out of place to notice some of the applications of photography. Hitherto this beautiful art has been almost exclusively confined to the production of portraits; at least, commercially, it has not received any other extended application. Photography on metal plates is probably never destined to have any other application; but it is quite otherwise with photography on paper, which, since the improvement in the production of *positive* pictures, may be said to be in a fair way to compete with engraving.

To the artist it must be invaluable, in enabling him to seize upon those evanescent and ever-changing forms of clouds, that gorgeous play of light and shade which often accompanies the setting sun, and those magnificent atmospheric phenomena so often visible during a thunder-storm. It will also enable him to study the true *pictorial* difference which exists between the skies of different countries and the effects of certain atmospheric phenomena upon perspective, and upon the relations of light and shade.

Endless as are the forms of vegetable life, they may, as Humboldt has remarked, be all classed pictorially under one of eighteen or twenty characteristic forms which give the predominating character to the vegetation of different regions of the earth. What an invaluable aid would photography render to the landscape painter, by enabling him to delineate with all the truth of nature the peculiar types which vegetable life assumes in different parts of the world! And even in our own forest scenery many of the most charming contrasts are produced by variations in the forms of the leaves and the angles at which the boughs strike off from the trunk. The artist, in sketching this mixed foliage, often misses the characteristic feature, but the photograph, never. The assistance which it can give to the portrait and historical painter in his studies will be invaluable, in enabling him to seize upon those peculiar expressions of his subject which no effort can sustain sufficiently long to enable an artist to catch it and commit it to the canvass. In the study of draperies it will show, in the most beautiful way, the effect produced in certain lights by the materials employed to drape, such as those of silk, woollen, and cotton,—effects which it is often exceedingly difficult to appreciate fully, and hence artists are continually making serious mistakes from this cause alone.

We may here notice two recent applications of photography connected with the fine arts. M. Charles Blanc is publishing in Paris a number of photographs of the principal works of Rembrandt, and a beautiful application of the process of scotography above mentioned has been made also in France in the reproduction of the works of some of the old engravers. The first which have been published are the works of Mark Antonio Raymondi, the celebrated Bolognese engraver, by M. Benjamin Delessert.

To the antiquary it will be a boon, for by its means he may in a few moments obtain a faithful picture of any cherished relic of antiquity, from a coin to a cathedral. Inscriptions, brasses, manuscripts—in fact everything may be copied with a truthfulness that completely defies competition.

Looking at what it is likely to do for the delineation of the costumes, habitations, scenery, and productions of distant nations, when travellers will have become familiar with its employment, one can almost regret having lived too soon! At no very remote period most of our books of travel will be illustrated by photographs taken on the spot described. Already, indeed, a book of travels in India and Abyssinia has been issued in France illustrated in this way; and a series of photographs are being published of the buildings of Venice.

And last, though not least, its use to science must not be overlooked. It is already the best known means of measuring the relative amount of light given off by two luminous bodies. It is gradually being applied to render philosophical instruments self-registering, and the day is not far distant when the astronomer may repair to his bed, confident on finding in the morning that the revolving earth has carefully registered its journey through the heavens. Already, curious photographs of the moon have been produced, representing its surface in a most singularly beautiful manner. It has also been applied to copying specimens of insects, shells, and other objects of natural history; and at this moment MM. Donne and Foucalt are publishing some beautiful microscopic drawings, photographed by means of an arrangement of the solar microscope; and, more recently, MM. Deveria and Rousseau have presented to the French Institute some admirable photographs of the larger animals, and of skeletons. Some excellent photographs of pathological subjects have also been given in the London Microscopical Journal. Indeed, this process seems to be beautifully adapted for illustrating comparative osteology, both recent and fossil.

It is further applicable to the delineation of crystals in mineralogy, and of fossils and other similar objects. And how much more faithful would be a photograph of a rock escarpment, or other object which the geologist might desire to describe, than a mere pencil sketch? No doubt can be entertained that it would be possible to represent the contour of a country by this means, which would be a fact of immense importance, as it would enable the physical geography of a district to be properly studied.

Photography was well represented in the Exhibition, although there were no remarkable specimens illustrative of the recent improvements in the art. There were twelve exhibitors representing the daguerreotype, the calotype, and the collodion processes. Among the daguerreotypes, the large portraits of M. Claudet, of London, deserved especial mention, not alone from their excellence as portraits, but as proofs of the numerous difficulties which M. Claudet has succeeded in overcoming in the construction of his cameras. We have already mentioned the name of M. Claudet several times as connected with some of the earliest improvements in the art; but it is not merely in a technical point of view that his portraits are remarkable—they are equally so in the artistic grouping and disposition of the backgrounds, which in most photographic portraits is delineated in the same minute detail as the principal figure, and consequently diminishes very considerably the importance which the latter should hold in the picture. Another characteristic of M. Claudet's photographs is the absence of all violent contrast of light and shade, and that disagreeable undefinedness of outline produced by a strong glaring sunshine. Among his collection we noticed one of Heinrich Rose, the celebrated chemist of Berlin, which, technically and artistically, we consider to have been unrivalled. The portraits of Mr. Glukman, of Dublin, were equally worthy of commendation; and although all were of a small size, and hence were not so difficult of execution as those of M. Claudet, they possessed many of the qualities mentioned above Mr. Pinkney, of Dublin, also exhibited some good daguerreotypes, among which "A View of Upper Sackville-street" was exceedingly good. Mr. Mayall, who has been so eminently successful in the production of large daguerrotype views, exhibited some good ones of the interior of the "Great Exhibition of 1851."

There were several exhibitors of pictures produced by the talbotype process. Two portraits exhibited by Messrs. Moran & Quin, of London, and made by the Messrs. Henneman & Malone, who are, we believe, in immediate connexion with Mr. Fox Talbot, were very beautiful and truthful, and showed the immense progress which the kalotype process has recently made, and its superiority, even for portraits, over the usual daguerreotype, by its warmer tint, greater vitality, and the absence of all reflection at their non-insertion, a property not possessed by daguerreotypes, except by those made by Claudet, and, to a great extent, by those of Glukman also. Mr. E. K. Tenison, of Kilbonan Castle, exhibited a number of photographs of very large size, representing views in Spain. Although we have seen some French photographs, especially those of M. Martens, of Paris, far superior to those views, yet, when we take their great size into account, they were certainly remarkable examples, and showed what may be expected from this branch of art, when fully perfected. The finest and most effective specimen in the whole collection was a view of the city of Toledo; the view of the east end of Burgos Cathedral was also admirable; as were those of the Church of San Pablo, at Valladolid; and the Royal Palace of Madrid. There were two examples of the effects of treating the pictures with solutions of certain substances. One was a charming view of Cordova, of a peculiar and exceedingly agreeable warm yellow tint, produced by immersing the positive picture in extremely dilute muriatic acid. There was another example of this fine sunny, sepia-like tint, in a pretty view of the Gate of Cordova. The second example of the effect of certain solutions was a view of the Palio de los Reyes, or Escurial, which had a curious violet tint, produced by immersing the picture in a solution of chloride of gold in *aqua regia*. It was, in fact, to some extent, an example of the chrysotype of Herschel, above alluded to. Several of these photographs exhibited great inequality of tints, such as the Portal of Leon Cathedral, which was too black in the doorways; and the Congresso de los Deputados, or Chamber of Deputies, at Madrid, the foreground of which was absolutely black. It is probable, that had the negatives of these pictures been weakened by the process of Blanquart-Everard, they would have been excellent. This defect is most likely to occur in taking views of buildings where there is a great contrast of light and shade, and hence the process alluded to for weakening the negative is worthy of attention.

Mr. Robinson, of Grafton-street, exhibited a great number of French photographs, principally representing views in Paris, most of which were exquisite. One represented the façade of Notre Dame, and the place in front of it covered with an immense concourse of people, and with a procession, on the occasion of the marriage of the Emperor. This beautiful photograph, when seen through the stereoscope, was truly wonderful; the whole could not be more thoroughly realized by an actual spectator, than by looking at this little picture. We have, indeed, seen nothing which more forcibly impressed us with the extraordinary phenomenon of the action of light, or of the future value of photography, than this sketch. Mr. Robinson also exhibited some portraits and sketches taken by the collodion process, which he has helped very much to popularize in Dublin. Several very beautiful photographs taken by this process were exhibited by P. H. de la Motte, of London. The peculiarity of the photographs taken in this manner is their extraordinary delicacy, which is quite equal, if it does not exceed, that of daguerreotypes, and an agreeable softness of tint, whilst the harshness and mirror effect of the latter are perfectly obviated. Hitherto the kalotype process has made but little progress in these countries in consequence of being protected by a patent; the collodion process has, therefore, opened up a new field which, being free to all, is receiving the most rapid development.

But, perhaps, the most singular application of photography was that illustrated by the specimens exhibited by R. Smith of Blackford, in Perthshire, and which he calls "photochromatic printing." It is in fact a kind of calico printing in which the action of light replaces the printing machine. The woven fabric to be printed is prepared with some solution sensitive to light, and then exposed to the action of the sunlight, which passes through a glass plate upon which the pattern is formed by pasting pieces of black paper. A negative photograph picture made on glass with albumen or collodion, may also be employed so as to produce the most beautiful and varied designs. When it has been exposed for a sufficient length of time, which may vary from two to twenty-five minutes, the tissue is removed and the image fixed. For example, a white pattern may be produced upon a blue ground by employing citrate of iron and prussiate of potash, the cloth being subsequently washed in very dilute sulphuric acid. This would be in reality a kind of cyanotype. In the same way we may produce the chromotype with bichromate of potash; the chrysotype by dipping the cloth in ammonia, citrate of iron, and developing the picture with chloride of gold; the ferrotype by saturating it with succinic acid, chloride of sodium, a proto-salt of iron, and nitrate of silver, and developing the picture with sulphate of iron; and the fluorotype by dipping it into fluoride of sodium, and bromide of potassium, and then nitrate of silver, and developing the picture with sulphate of iron. As nearly all metallic salts are more or less acted upon by light, a pattern may be produced with any of them. The metallic oxides thus fixed in the cloth may be used as the mordant in calico printing, and by immersing the cloth, after the development of an image with oxide of iron, in a dye bath, say of madder, all shades, from black through violet, lilac, red, rose, amaranthus, &c., may be produced, and so on of every other colour. Mr. Smith uses a kind of machine by which the cloth, after exposure, is wound up, and a fresh portion exposed. It is exceedingly simple, and twenty of them may be attended by one person, in case the process should come to be commercially carried out. The specimens exhibited were very pretty, and showed what might be done in this way. A M. Wulff, of Paris, has lately succeeded in producing the most exquisite portraits, views of buildings, landscapes, and in a few seconds, upon any woven fabric; the precise effect being dependent chiefly upon the quality of the material employed. The probability is, therefore, that, sooner or later, ladies will be clothed in sun pictures.

There were several exhibitors of cameras, and other apparatus connected with photography. Mr. Robinson exhibited a number of cameras of French make, which, being very portable and cheap, and giving very satisfactory results, have had, we believe, an extensive sale among amateurs throughout various parts of Ireland: a fact of considerable importance, as experiments of this kind are sure to be fertile in creating a taste for experimental science. In most of those cameras a glass containing zinc, instead of lead, has, we believe, been used for the lenses; a great advantage which this glass possesses over the ordinary crystal or optical glass is, that while it has remarkable refractive powers, its dispersive powers are very small. This quality is of the greatest importance in photography. Messrs. Horne, Thornthwaite, & Co., of London, exhibited complete apparatus for the daguerreotype, kalotype, and collodion processes, which were finished in the first style of workmanship; but as the most important point in a camera is the quality of the lenses, and as of these we had no opportunity of judging, we offer no opinion upon them. The same remark will apply to the lenses and accelerators of Mr. R. Beaufort. Mr. T. A. Dillon exhibited a very simple and ingeniously contrived portable camera, which would, we think, be very convenient for excursions. Mr. Glukman exhibited a machine for polishing daguerreotypes, which appeared to possess some very considerable advantages over those which we have seen in common use. Our limited space, and the great length to which we have already extended the subject, forbid us from describing this, or any of the other photographic apparatus exhibited, at more length. Indeed, it would be of very little use to do so, unless we could establish points of comparison, by describing all the contrivances hitherto invented, which, it is almost needless to observe, would occupy many pages; and which would be in some degree foreign to the object contemplated in the preparation of the materials for the present volume.—W. K. S.

MEANS OF COMMUNICATION BY TELEGRAPH.

Among the inventions of the past half-century there have been few more important than this marvellous means of communication. Distance had been previously shortened by steam on land and water; and commerce, taking advantage of the facilities afforded by it, has largely increased the material comforts of the people. But the invention of the telegraph may be said to have inaugurated a new era in the history of human progress. We are only beginning to appreciate the value of this practical invention. Time by it is literally annihilated. the events of distant countries are known to us a few moments after their occurrence. Although the telegraph is yet imperfect, the Paris, Vienna, and Berlin news of the morning is printed and published in almost every part of these countries in the afternoon of the same day. That which, fifty years ago, could not be transmitted without a tedious and perilous journey of many weeks is now accomplished almost instantaneously; and no great length of time is likely to elapse until telegraphic communication has formed a sort of network, embracing within its meshes every civilized country on the face of the globe.

The discovery of the germ whence the present system of telegraphic communication has sprung may be traced to a very early period of human history. As early as six centuries before the Christian era, Thales of Miletus appears to have discovered the property of attraction in amber—the basis of future experiments in electrical science. Theophrastus and Pliny describe this peculiarity, and Strada (in one of his "Prolusiones Academicæ") makes observations respecting the power of magnets to move simultaneously when at liberty to vibrate freely. The principle, however, received no practical application from the ancients. Many interesting discoveries were made in modern times before Franklin's great experiments, but he is, notwithstanding, to be considered the father of the science. It was long known that electricity could be transmitted in its effects to a distance, for Dr. Watson, in 1747, sent an electric shock through a wire two miles in length, and subsequently the American philosopher, in his interesting researches, attained similar results. But previous to 1774 there is no mention to be found of an electric telegraph, or a transmission of intelligence by the agency of electricity. In that year a contrivance was made by Lesarge at Geneva, consisting of a transmitting wire for every letter of the alphabet, each being connected with a pith-ball electrometer at the end where the message was to be received. An electric current passing along the wire notified the intended letter by causing the pith-balls connected with it to diverge. The next advance of any value seems to have been made by Mr. Ronalds, of Hammersmith, in 1816. He operated through eight miles of wire, in a simpler manner, and with more striking results, than Lesarge. In his apparatus we find an approximation to those at present employed. At each end of his line Mr. Ronalds placed a dial-plate, furnished with the letters of the alphabet, in front of which he fixed a screen, with orifices so cut as to allow the appearance of each letter on the plate in succession as it revolved. The dial-plates revolved at equal rates by clock-work, and were arranged in such a manner as to present the same letter at the same time on each plate. Identical revolution of the plates being secured, the divergence of the pith-balls, caused by the electric influence, indicated the letter intended to be pointed out. Frictional electricity was used both by Lesarge and Ronalds; but, in 1844, Mr. Highton introduced a method of signalling by passing a spark through a sheet of paper, in which a hole was of course burned. These telegraphs were in turn superseded by the adaptation of the electrical discoveries of Galvani and Volta to the indicating of telegraphic signals.

Ampère, Faraday, and Arago added largely to electrical science, by showing that the passage of a magnetic current might be observed and recorded; and that in decomposing water galvanic electricity changed the colour. In Sœmmering's galvanic telegraph, made in 1809, a wire was appropriated to each of the twenty-four letters, as in Ronalds' contrivance, and these wires being led into separate jars of water, its decomposition indicated the letter intended. An explosion of gas was employed to excite the attention of the operator at the other termination of the line. Another step of improvement was the simplification of this plan by the reduction of the wires to two, by Schweiger.

In 1820 Ampère proposed to denote the passage of the current by the deflection of a magnetic needle, surrounded by a coil of wire, each letter of the alphabet having both a wire and a needle. Again, in 1832, this plan was much simplified by Schilling's telegraph, with five wires and five magnetic needles, the combined deflections of which formed signals for the alphabet. In this apparatus one of the needles gave warning by the ringing of a bell. One wire and one indicator were also proposed, and various other alterations suggested. In fact, no invention ever underwent so many changes before it became useful in practical application. For years it was a curiosity of science, and an interesting toy for the amateur, until the growing necessity for more rapid intercourse with persons and places at a distance converted it into one of the most important, as it is the most extraordinary, of modern appliances.

The telegraph consists of three parts:—1. The apparatus for the generation of the currents; 2. The means of their transmission from one station to another; and 3. The devices used for recording their passage.

1. For the purpose of generating the electrical currents the galvanic battery is employed, the frictional electricity used in the early telegraphs being entirely superseded.

2. There are two plans followed in laying the conducting wires. In some cases they are suspended in the air, the points of suspension being carefully insulated. The difficulty in this method is, that they are liable to be affected by electric storms, and to sustain more or less injury from various causes. Another course, now more in favour, and apparently proved by experience to be better, is to insulate the wires along their whole length in gutta percha tubing, and to place them underground. Neither atmospheric electricity, nor the influence of rain and fogs, can affect the buried wires. The chief, indeed the only, objection to this method is, the increased expense it renders necessary; but in most instances the telegraph companies have discovered that eventually the overground wires will prove the more expensive of the two, from the constant repairs which they necessitate, as well as the uncertainty of their action. Difficulties in working telegraphs, both above and beneath the ground, have been experienced from the defectiveness of the insulation; and, therefore, they have on many occasions failed. But this cause of disappointment has been to a great degree,

if not altogether, removed by a simple arrangement. The electric current passing along the wires, in acting upon needles or electro-magnets, produces a fresh battery circuit, and enables a succession of circuits to be carried on to an almost unlimited extent. The circuit being interrupted or completed, the needles placed within the influence of the currents vibrate; and if, instead of being those of the recording instrument, they are made to interrupt another circuit emanating from a fresh battery, the vibrations in the first circuit would be reproduced in the second, in the third, and so on. Thus the evil of defective insulation has been to a great degree remedied, and the length of a telegraphic line is really no practical obstruction to its successful working.

3. But to the observer of the operations the most curious and ingenious portion of the apparatus for communication by telegraph is, the arrangement for making the passage of the currents apparent, and for recording them. The instruments used for these purposes have been various. In one, an alphabet is constructed from the vibrations of the needle. The letters are separately signalled by the operator at the place of transmission, while as each is received it is written down. Although this method is apparently tedious, messages can thus be sent with remarkable rapidity, from the dexterity of the attendants acquired by practice, and the use of abbreviations. Where signs or cipher communications of any kind are transmitted, there is, however, increased liability to error. This form of telegraph is mostly employed in commercial intercourse, and works well where the messages are brief. In another arrangement the actual letter transmitted is exhibited at the distant end of the line, and separately signalled as in the previous case. But the objection to this method is, that the communications are made slowly. In a third form, the needle vibrations at the receiving stations are arranged so as to mark lines or dots constituting an alphabet by means of ink tubes attached. These lines are sometimes traced on a band of paper moved by machinery; but a chemically prepared paper has been used, on which the marks are made by the pressure of a point of wire forming them by the change of colour caused by the passage of the electric current. From seventy to a hundred letters have been transmitted per minute by this plan. In a fourth form of the telegraphic instrument, a fac-simile of the document to be transmitted is made at the receiving end. This copying telegraph has not yet succeeded in distancing its competitors in speed of operation, but it is expected to embody the principle of the great desideratum now required,—an electric telegraph capable of such rapidity and accuracy as to be useful to the mercantile public in confidential correspondence. In this instrument, the message being written by means of non-conducting ink on a conductive surface of metallic foil, the foil is made to encircle a cylinder. At the other end of the line a piece of paper, chemically prepared in the same manner, encircles a similar cylinder. Both cylinders revolving at the same rate, in connexion with a conducting point, turning round each in a similar spiral line, and an electric current being passed, a line is made, or a blank left, in the chemically prepared paper at the station of reception. This method has had little success hitherto, not more than twenty words in a minute having been transmitted, the great difficulty being to secure an equable revolution of the cylinders; but an American, Mr. Alexander Jones, has announced his invention of a copying telegraph capable of sending correctly 600 words per minute. It is not yet, however, in operation.

Before proceeding to notice the mode in which messages are conveyed by telegraph, something must be said respecting Dering's instrument, which appeared in the Exhibition. The ingenuity displayed in it was justly commended by the Jurors of the Exposition of 1851. Its peculiar characteristics are:—1. A new system of motion for the indicators, the object of which is to preserve them from oscillation. 2. Arrangements to secure greater readiness and certainty of action in the common indicators, whilst the battery power is reduced. 3. A plan for dispensing with the additional wires used for ringing the alarums. 4. A very ingenious contrivance for the conveyance of secret intelligence, by cutting off the communication with all the stations, except one or more, as selected by the operator, the excluded stations being brought into the circuit, when required, with the greatest facility. 5. An instrument for the purpose of protecting the apparatus from the effects of lightning, or other atmospheric influence. And sixthly, an effective mode of insulation for the wires.

In Mr. Dering's apparatus the indicating magnet (which is deflected) is suspended on either side by coil magnets, not by the simple action of the current (so as to have its centre of gravity below the points of suspension), by elastic magnets, or rigid magnets having flexible elastic supports; by the attraction of permanent magnets; or by the use of a pair of watch-springs, so adjusted as to give the indicating magnet a tendency to a vertical position when it is not under lateral influence. These peculiarities will be better understood by a reference to the accompanying engraving, which also illustrates to some extent the working of telegraphs generally.

In Fig. 1 the letters *a*, *b* represent a pair of elastic steel magnets attached by their upper ends to two brass studs, the lower ends being free to move, each in one direction, when acted on by an electric current passing through the coils of wire, *c*, *d*, *e*. If soft iron or other magnetic metal be employed, the ordinary well-known means of keeping them in a magnetic state will be resorted to. In the figure referred to, the indicators are represented as elastic and flexible from end to end; but they may be constructed partly rigid and partly elastic and flexible, or they may be rigid magnets from end to end, supported by any flexible elastic substance.

Figs. 2 and 3 show respectively a front and side view of a magnetic needle, brought to the vertical position solely by means of the weight *w*, placed immediately below the centre of motion *c*. Another mode of applying the same principle consists in suspending the magnetic needle, or other moving instrument, by its upper end. The whole, or nearly the whole, of the weight being thus immediately below the centre of motion, it becomes unnecessary to increase the weight at a lower point. The needles may be fixed in the usual manner upon an axis passed through the upper end, as near as possible to the very extremity; but it is preferred that one or both of the pivots on which the axis turns in this and all similar arrangements should rest in an angular aperture, and not in round holes, as is usually the case. This has the effect of diminishing the oscillations which the needle makes in returning to its position of rest.

Fig. 4 represents a magnetic needle, suspended by its upper extremity, and acted on by the coils of wire, *cc*. Fig. 5 is an enlarged view of the needle, showing the mode of suspension by an angular aperture from a hook of round wire. Another plan is to suspend the needle, entirely by attraction, from a fixed piece of soft iron, or from a permanent magnet, in which case the needle may be of soft iron, or other temporarily magnetic metal, and derive its magnetism by induction from the bar which supports it.

In applying electric currents to produce motion in needles and other magnetic bodies, the direct attractive or repulsive action exerted upon magnetic bodies is applied by coils of wire of circular or other convenient form on the passage of an electric current through them, in place of the deflective influence which has

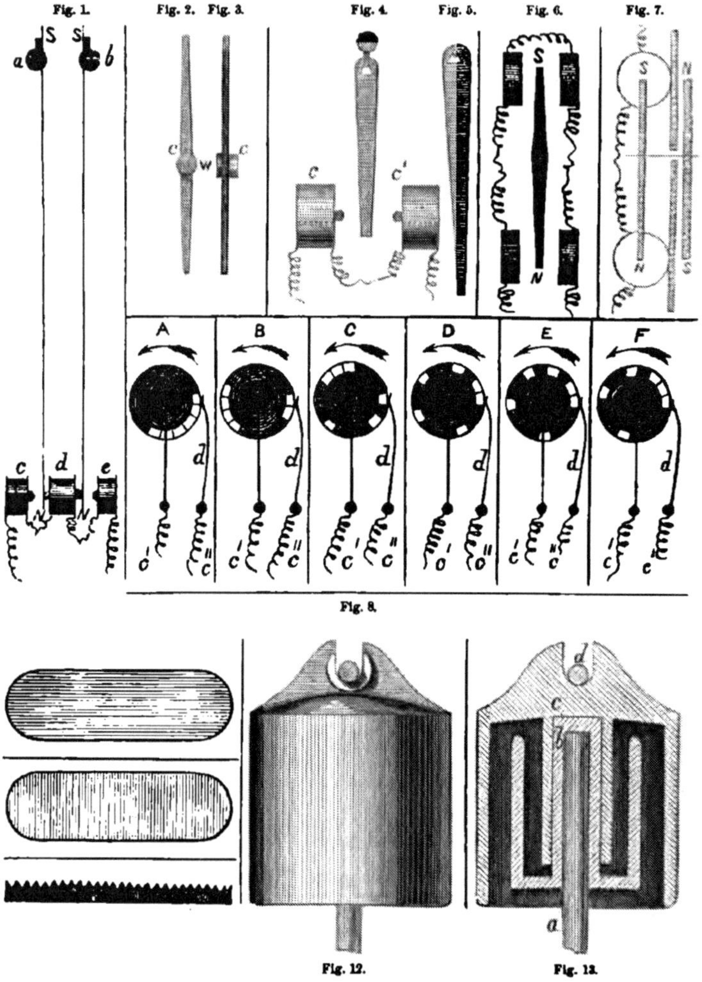


Illustrations of Dering's Telegraph.

usually been employed. In all cases the coils are placed in such a position that their axes shall be in or parallel to the plane of motion of the magnetic body they are intended to influence.

Figs. 6 and 7 represent this arrangement of coils in connexion with the ordinary astatic needles; and in Figs. 1 and 4 are also shown applications of the same principle. In some cases soft iron is placed within the coils of wire, but the length of such soft iron pieces should not exceed their diameter, since by this plan residual magnetism is altogether prevented.

In the arrangement for the sounding of telegraphic alarums, the object is to prevent all unnecessary ringing of the bell during the transmission of messages, and at the same time to dispense with the extra wire usually employed for that purpose. To effect the desired object, the use for signalling purposes of any one particular signal decided on, which is produced by a single current passing in either direction through any one wire, or of contemporaneous currents passing in any direction through any two or greater number of the wires, is dispensed with, and the bell apparatus at the stations is so arranged that they shall be acted on only when such current or currents pass as would produce the omitted signal.

A further improvement consists of an apparatus, by the use of which, without extra wires, intelligence may be transmitted from any station on a line to any other station, at choice, or to any number of them at the same time, without a possibility of its being seen at the rest, as is now the case. The means of effecting this object are as follow:—At each station there is mounted a metallic disc, revolving on an axis, and capable of being impelled round, step by step, like the seconds hand of a clock, by any of the well-known electro-magnetic arrangements for such purposes. There is a metallic spring constantly pressing upon the circumference of the disc, and into certain points of the circumference of each disc there are inlet portions of ivory, or some other non-conductor of electricity. The metallic bearings of the disc, and the spring which presses on its circumference, are placed in connexion, each with one extremity of the coil that actuates the needle, or other arrangement employed to indicate the signals, the coil being included in the circuit of the line-wire as usual. The discs move uniformly step by step at all the stations, and they may be set in motion, and brought to any desired position, by passing a current of electricity from any station the proper number of times. So long as the spring at any station rests upon the conducting portion of the circumference of the disc, there is a short circuit established, by which the electricity may pass between the extremities of the line-wire, without passing through the coil which actuates the indicator; consequently, signals transmitted from any other station will not be shown at this instrument. But if the disc be brought to a position in which the spring rests upon a non-conducting portion of the circumference, the short circuit will in this case be broken, and every signal must, in its course along the line-wire, pass through the indicator coil, and thus show itself in the usual manner. It will also be readily understood, that by arranging, in a certain known order, the inlet non-conducting portions of the circumference of the discs, means is obtained of bringing any one or more stations that may be desired into the line of communication; it being only necessary first to pass the current such a number of times as to bring the non-conducting portions of the discs at these stations under the spring, and the conducting portion at the others. Upon the axis of each disc there is a hand, which traverses a circular dial-plate, on which are inscribed the different combinations of two or more of the stations that are brought into the line of communication at each step of the revolution of the discs. It is convenient that there should be one point at which every station is brought into the communication, and at this position of the discs the hand upon the dial may be made to point to the word ALL, inscribed thereon.

As the electro-magnetic arrangement which actuates the disc is included in the same circuit with the coil which works the indicator (in order to avoid the extra line-wire), it is necessary there should be some means to prevent the disc being acted on during the transmission of currents that are intended only to work the indicator. In the case when currents in one direction only are employed for signalling purposes, those in the reverse direction may be devoted to the purpose of impelling the disc. The methods of accomplishing this are easily understood. Where both directions of the current, however, are required to work the indicator, as in the case of the ordinary needle instrument, other means must be resorted to. If the electro-magnet which actuates the disc be so arranged as to act only upon the application of a current stronger than that required to work the indicator, all chance of it acting when ordinary signals are transmitted will be removed, whilst the disc may be actuated with certainty by the application of an increased battery power. There are various arrangements by which the disc electro-magnet may be prevented from acting when the ordinary signals are transmitted, whilst, at the same time, it may at once be brought into action by the transmission of some extraordinary signal not included in the code; such as, for instance, the continuous passage for several seconds of a current in one direction. To effect this, there is a wheel kept constantly in motion, slowly, upon its axis, by clock-work; and near to this wheel there is an arm, which is moved by an arrangement of an electro-magnet acting on a permanent magnet—only when the current passes in one direction—and brought in contact with the revolving wheel, in which there are apertures to receive it. When in contact with the wheel it partakes of its motion, and if held so for a sufficient length of time, it is brought to a position, from which it will not return to its usual position upon the cessation of the current, but it may be at once released by a current in the reverse direction. When in the position to which it is brought by the revolution of the wheel, a portion of the arm which forms a driving pallet is brought to a position in which it will act upon the ivory and brass disc above described, by which stations are brought into or thrown out of the circuit; and by repeating the current a certain number of times, the disc may be brought to any desired position. Thus it is obvious that the station disc can never be moved during the ordinary transmission of signals, but it may be brought into a position to be acted on, at any moment when required, by passing a continuous current as described. Then the disc electro-magnet may be actuated the desired number of times by currents passed in the same direction as those by which it was brought into action, and thrown out of action again by a single current in the reverse direction. The mechanism for effecting this object may be greatly varied: the same principles are applicable to various similar purposes, such as to govern the movement of printing telegraphs, or to sound the alarums of single circuit needle and other kinds of telegraphs—thus allowing the extra wires usually employed to be dispensed with.

Fig. 8 shows the application of the secret apparatus to six stations working in circuit. A, B, C, D, E, F, are the brass discs of the different instruments, with such an arrangement of the inlet ivory portions of the circumference as will admit of any two of the stations being brought together into the circuit, and the others excluded, or of all being brought in at the same time, according to the position the discs are brought to, moving as they do in unison by step-by-step motion, as described; $c^1$ and $c^2$ show the terminals of the indicator coil, or similar arrangement, at each station; and $d$, in each, shows the platina spring in contact with the edge of the revolving disc.

Another peculiarity of Mr. Dering's telegraph relates to a means of counteracting the currents of atmospheric electricity, which are at times collected in suspended telegraph wires, and manifest themselves by continued deflections of the needles, or similar arrangements. To effect this, there is introduced into the circuit of the line-wire a galvanic battery, or other suitable generator of electricity, the current from which being passed in the contrary direction to that which it is intended to counteract, may be regulated in force to a degree exactly sufficient to restore the needle to its ordinary position of equilibrium. The more violent effects of atmospheric electricity, such as the fusion of the coils and demagnetization of the needles, are also guarded against. The arrangement for this purpose consists in interposing between two flat surfaces of brass, or some other conductor of electricity, roughened by a file or any suitable means, a thin piece of linen or other porous imperfectly conducting material, which will allow of the roughened surfaces approaching one another to within an extremely short distance, without actually coming in contact. These surfaces are placed in connexion, one with the line-wire and the other with the earth, or one with each end of the line-wire, between the line and the internal works of the instrument. The greater portion of a shock of atmospheric electricity is thus prevented from entering the instrument, as it will pass direct from one of the roughened surfaces to the other, and through the intervening space, this being the most direct path, instead of making a circuit of the coils of the instrument. The protective power of this arrangement may be increased by grooves being formed in one or both of the opposed conducting surfaces, in such a manner that the face shall present a series of sharp ridges. Where both of the surfaces are grooved, they are to be placed together in such a position that the ridges may cross one another, and a ready path for the electricity will thus be provided: as each crossing is equivalent in its dispersive power to a pair of opposed points.

In Figs. 9 and 10 the surfaces of the two opposed plates are represented; and in Fig. 11 we have an edge view of Fig. 10.

The only other feature of this telegraph to which we can refer relates to the insulation of suspended telegraphic wires. This is a modification of the ordinary bell-shaped insulator; and consists in fixing within it an inverted smaller bell of insulating material, the edges of which must not be in contact with the outer one. It is by the inner bell that the insulator is attached to the post or other support, by means of an iron arm. The wire passes through a proper aperture in the upper part of the outer bell. Cast-iron, protected from rust by a coating of zinc, or other means, is preferred as the material for this portion of the arrangement; its edge should come below, and thus entirely surround the inner insulating part, which is by this means effectually protected from damage by stones thrown, or other violence. Fig. 12 is an external view of this insulator; and Fig. 13 shows a section of the same:—*a* is an iron arm attached to the post or other support: upon it rests the earthenware piece *b*, and over this fits the metallic cap *c*; *d* shows a section of the line-wire, supported in a groove or other aperture for the purpose. The same principle of insulation may be applied with advantage to the apparatus for stretching telegraph wires; also to break the continuity of the line-wire, where it is intended to insert an instrument in the circuit, and for other similar purposes.

The general system at present adopted in working telegraphs was illustrated by the instruments exhibited on the part of the Electric Telegraph Company of London. Those who examined the different parts and studied the uses of the mechanism with attention will remember that the various contrivances which we have described were presented to their inspection. Single and double needle instruments showing the method of indication; batteries for generating the electric force; magneto-machines for its utilization; and bells for ringing the alarums, were to be seen. In addition, there were maps of telegraphs in a state of working, a scale of charges, and other matters of minor interest, illustrating the practical value of the invention. This contribution to the Exhibition was rendered still more attractive and useful from the circumstance of the telegraph being in operation, communicating with various departments of the building, and with the office of the Company in this city (Messrs. W. H. Smith and Son, 1, Eden-quay). The apparatus of the Electric Telegraph Company afforded an excellent example both of the general principle of the system and their own peculiar improvements in the mode of working.

An exceedingly ingenious and singular telegraph was exhibited at Hyde Park in 1851, by two Prussian inventors, Messrs. Halske and Siemens, and although it did not appear in the Irish Exposition of last year, its peculiarities entitle it to a passing notice. The signals in this instrument are made by arresting, instead of causing, the passage of electric force. It has three parts,—an alarum, an indicating dial, and an arrangement for *printing*. The last is its novel and most remarkable feature. Omitting, therefore, a detailed description of the other parts of the mechanism, we may briefly refer to this. To a ratchet-wheel, which is necessary in the telegraphic part of the contrivance, there are attached radii, consisting of springs, each having at the end a type-letter pointed upwards. During the revolution of the wheel, these types pass between a hammer below and a blackened cylinder above. Between the type and the cylinder a band of paper also passes. "One arm of a lever bears a hammer, and the other carries the armature of a supplementary electro-magnet, in the same circuit with the magnet of the indicating instrument. A current passes through the two simultaneously, but is so instantaneously cut off that the magnetism has not had time fully to develop itself, and to attract the armature; but the act of depressing the stud, which causes the index to rest for a moment at a given letter, is contrived to keep the circuit of the printing magnet complete during the same interval, and so to allow the full development of its magnetism, and to cause the attraction of its armature." At this moment the type-letter is between the hammer and the paper band. Being strongly attracted, the armature causes the hammer to strike a smart blow upward, and to press the paper against the blackened cylinder, which impresses the form of the letter. Thus the letters are printed singly, and at the end of each word a blank is left untouched, and by a simple and beautiful contrivance a bell is rung at the same time. There is also an ingenious arrangement for advancing the paper the width of a letter, as every type is impressed, and for moving the blackened paper forward, that it may not become exhausted by constant use. This very beautiful *printing telegraph*—one of two inventions from the Continent presented to public notice in London—attracted deserved attention, not so much from its great practical usefulness as from the elaborate ingenuity displayed in its mechanical combinations. By simple appliances a number of intricate operations were performed, and interesting results attained.

A brief description of the ordinary mode in which the existing telegraphs are worked cannot fail to be interesting. The message to be transmitted is given to a clerk, clearly and legibly written, and the cost of transmission and delivery is paid in advance. From this clerk the message passes to the operator, whose duty it is to telegraph it to its destination. At present, in the yet imperfect state of the contrivances employed, the operator must first translate the message into the telegraphic signals. In consequence of this there is great liability to mistake; but to insure accuracy, in correspondence of extraordinary importance, the letter conveyed is re-transmitted to the station from which it has been sent, for comparison. For this, however, an additional charge is made; and it occasions a further delay. When the message reaches the place for which it is intended, it is translated, inscribed, sealed, and delivered by the company's agents as directed. The great drawback in this process is the necessity for the translation of the message into the signals of the telegraph. This operation being tedious, and requiring considerable care, the charge for transmission is high; and, consequently, the number of messages is limited. The competition of rival companies, however, in England, and the expected competition in Ireland, have reduced the expense considerably. Even in telegraphs the public need not fear monopoly.

The telegraph mechanism is yet, in many respects, imperfect and incomplete. An improved form of copying telegraph is required to obviate the necessity of translating and re-translating the messages into telegraphic symbols. The repetition of communications at intermediate stations is also a great cause of delay and incertitude. This is frequently rendered necessary by the injudicious employment of various kinds of instruments at different stations. In passing through the hands of several operators the message is also liable to be misconstrued or misconveyed. When it is recollected that a very trifling error may most seriously affect the sense of a communication, the uncertainty of this mode of transmission will be apparent. It is only to be wondered how so great accuracy is generally attained. There can be, however, little doubt that improved arrangements will soon make the telegraph a useful and an economical system for the intercommunications of commerce and intelligence of every description.

Telegraphs have been in use in England for above fifteen years. In 1839 wires were laid along the Great Western Railway, and in the following year on the Blackwall line. Shortly afterwards the system was adopted on several of the other trunk lines in Scotland, as well as in the south. But it was not until 1846 that a company was incorporated for the purpose of conveying messages for the public. The patents were then purchased from Messrs. Cooke and Wheatstone for a sum of £141,000, of which Professor Wheatstone received £30,000. At first the company enjoyed little patronage, in consequence, probably, of the very high charges with which they set out. In America, where a contrary course was pursued, this novel and useful means of communication was adopted with eagerness. The patents purchased by the original company secured a monopoly to them until 1850; and in that year a new scheme, the British Telegraph Company, started into existence. In the year following, three companies which had been projected merged into one: the United Kingdom Telegraph Company, the English and Irish Magnetic Telegraph Company, and the European and American Printing Telegraph Company. The Irish company was formed in 1853. At present there are at least six different companies competing with each other in these countries, the rival offices being furnished with instruments of varying description. The strongest body is the original one. In the extent of its lines, and the number of its stations, it exceeds all the others. A submarine line has been laid down in connexion with it from near Harwich to Holland. The Electric Telegraph Company is incorporated by charter, and has sought an Act of Parliament. The Submarine Telegraph Company, by which so much of our foreign intelligence is transmitted, is a French scheme. It holds the important line from Dover to Calais, and is one means of connexion with the European company which passes overland. The English and Irish Magnetic Telegraph Company has lines underground from London to Liverpool and Manchester, as well as along the Lancashire and Yorkshire, East Lancashire, and the Caledonian Railways. By a submarine line from Portpatrick to Donaghadee it is connected with Ireland, and from the latter station it runs to Dublin and Cork. Competing projects have been bruited, and there is a probability that this country will ere long be linked with the other side of the Channel by perhaps three electrical chains.

The wires were carried along the railways, in the first instance, from considerations of convenience. Better protection was afforded by this means, and the lines of telegraph were more economically laid. Now, however, this plan is not invariably followed. It has been found that the overground wires are liable to injury from trespass, and to counteracting atmospheric influences. Besides, the employment of workmen in their construction by upright posts on railways was attended with danger. In addition to these disadvantages there was the defectiveness of the insulation, to which we have before referred. These objections are set aside by running the wires underground, insulated in gutta percha. The new lines are all constructed on the subterranean principle

Telegraphic communication throughout these countries, wonderful as it is in its results, cannot yet be called a *system*. Not only is it incomplete in its *modus operandi*, but it is not so extended as it might be, with advantage to the public and profit to speculators. In some years the whole kingdom will, doubtless, be interlaced with the mystic wires, and the cost of transmitting messages must be, from the natural effect of competition, so reduced that not alone will the merchant princes of our great cities, our bankers, our manufacturers, our shipowners, and the press, take the fullest advantage of the system; but the tradesman, the shopkeeper, and the private correspondent will resort to the telegraph in every case where certainty, secrecy, and celerity are demanded. There are some who, fearing a coalescence of the main rival companies and a consequent monopoly, discuss the advisability of placing the telegraph under direct governmental control. They would make it a department like the Post Office or the Stamps. It is argued, that in the hands of a parliamentary officer it would be free from abuse, and more useful for public purposes than it ever can be under the management of enterprising individuals. But the principle of uniting new duties to a public administration already embarrassed by the multiplicity and diversity of the interests under its guardianship, is seriously objectionable. There need be little fear of combination and monopoly where the machinery can be constructed so inexpensively. Without any interference this new branch of public enterprise will adjust itself to the public requirements, as many others have done before.

In looking at the simple mechanism of this system of wires, and indicators, and signs, we are urged to compare the apparent triviality of the means employed with the amazing nature of the results accomplished. A contrivance, neither complicated nor intricate, suffices to convey our wishes with the lightning's speed even to distant lands. The rapidity of the steam-ship, and the flight of the panting victor who bounds along his iron path in all the joyousness of conscious elasticity and strength, are left immeasurably in the distance. The steam-engine bears us from shore to shore, and sea to sea, and must continue to rule the great world of locomotion. Probably we have made some approximation to the limit to which its power may be usefully made applicable. But it is merely a vehicle for the conveyance of the ignoble part of humanity. The mind not only scorns the tardiness of steam, but mocks the flight of the strong-winged bird, and, seizing the rapid fire from the heavens, bids it bear our thoughts by its instantaneous gleams throughout the land and beneath the bosom of the ocean.—J. A. S.

Probably one of the first wants of civilization would be the means of accurately ascertaining the relative weight of masses of matter, or, to speak more familiarly, to weigh commodities for purchase or sale; and in the most barbarous countries, modes of different kinds have been devised for this purpose. But in civilized life, whether for purely scientific or commercial purposes, modes of accurately determining weights are essential. The goldsmith, jeweller, apothecary, and the man of science, all require methods of weighing the substances used in their callings with the most rigid exactness. Hence, the making of accurate beams, possessing at the same time strength to carry a considerable weight, and sensibility to determine minute differences, is a philosophic art of great importance; and any one who examined the beam and weights made by Œrtling, which appeared in the Exhibition, would have seen to what refinement this department of mechanical skill was carried. One of these instruments was capable of weighing over 2 lb., and, at the same time, of showing an alteration of weight equal to the 1-100th of a grain, or the millionth part of the weight it determined. Such accuracy leaves little to be desired in instruments of this description.

## II.—MUSICAL INSTRUMENTS.

### THE PIANOFORTE.

The spread of musical taste, and the progress of the art in general, has been owing so much to the extended use of the pianoforte, that it becomes a matter of much interest to inquire into its past history and present utility. No house now, from the nobleman's mansion down to the six-roomed box of the prosperous shopkeeper, is deemed furnished without one, at least, of these instruments; and the performance upon them is thought so essential to female education, that no young lady, however otherwise informed, is supposed to have been properly educated if playing the pianoforte is not found amongst the first of her accomplishments.

It would be beside our purpose to inquire whether the general requirement of a knowledge and power over this instrument from those who are to become the mothers and teachers of a future generation is a mark of the good sense of the present one. We may observe, however, that woman is, from her destiny and position, allotted to pass the greater portion of her time in the quiet retirement of home. Hence the necessity of providing graceful relaxation and elevating and refining accomplishments for her, and making them not only sources of amusement, but the very elements of her thinkings, and fondest pleasures of her existence. A love of flowers, a love of rural enjoyment, a love of poetry, of painting, and of music, have long been encouraged in the softer sex; and those who have cultivated these resources have usually been most felicitous in after life; in the charm of solacing the companions of their existence after the dull fatigues of business, and brightening their homes with a light that made their return to them be looked to as the reward and blessing for weary hours of care and toil. Hence an instrument such as the pianoforte, which is so comprehensive in its capabilities, so varied in its expression, and so powerful in its combinations, that the simplest melody and most complicated harmony can be equally drawn from it,—an instrument that demands so much practice that it provides daily employment for hours during the years of youth, and when the difficulties of its manipulation are conquered, becomes a comforter and resource ever after,—hence, we say, is the knowledge of such an instrument wisely made an important portion of female education.

As we have often heard it asserted that it was not worth the labour required for proficiency on this instrument, we shall pause to inquire what are its resources, and what does it offer in return for the assiduity of years? At the present time the pianoforte has a compass of six, six and a quarter, six and three-quarters, and seven octaves. Those in the Exhibition were of the largest extent of compass for modern requirements, and even beyond them. A keyboard of such vast range affords to the performer numerous facilities, a few of which we shall enumerate. As our readers must be acquainted with the tone of the pianoforte, its fulness and softness, its obedience to the finger for lights and shades of sound, its masterly arrangement for the expression of *forzando*, its liquidity in scale and figurative passages, and its capability for sustaining a melody in the centre, accompanied by the most brilliant *arpeggios* at either end—it is only necessary to glance at these qualifications. But its larger and comprehensive powers for the advancement of musical knowledge, and expression of musical ideas, can scarcely be over-estimated. It stands alone as a chamber instrument, from which can be produced all the combinations of harmony required to convey an adequate notion of the writings of the great masters; nay, we may almost say, a just interpretation of their mighty creations. Take the *fugues* of Bach; the lessons of Scarlatti; the concertos of Correlli; the oratorios of Handel, Haydn, and Mendelssohn; the symphonies of Mozart and Beethoven; the operas of Weber, Rossini, Bellini, Donizetti, and Meyerbeer:—let any who have studied the pianoforte take these authors to the instrument—varied as they are in character, modes, and genius—and they will be enabled to convey to themselves and their hearers a just idea of the vast conceptions and unfading beauty of these composers. No other instrument affords the student the same power as the piano of becoming acquainted with these great works. No other instrument—save the organ, and that is not a household one—will give a melody amidst the most skilful and intricate harmonies, allowing the ear to trace it distinctly as if played by another hand. This attribute of the pianoforte Mendelssohn has exhibited exquisitely in his *Lieder ohne Worte*, drawing out its vocal witchery, and making it interpret intelligibly phrases precious with musical charms. Then, for the rendering of choral works, its formation for simultaneously playing *chords* combining ten notes —or while one hand gives the harmony in mass, the other varies it in appropriate figures—makes it an instrument unsurpassed both for student and composer.

It is worthy of remark, that all our great composers were pianoforte players, or performers on the instruments out of which it has grown in the progress of years, namely, the clavichord and harpsichord. Those who devoted themselves to other instruments, such as the violin, violoncello, flute, oboe, &c., though they have become so distinguished in their lines as to gain even European reputations, have left nought behind them to perpetuate their fame, and to instruct posterity in musical art. The pianoforte is the first instrument upon which the glorious efforts of the great modern composers have been tried; and it is the one for which all the effects have been gathered from the *score*, both vocal and orchestral, and combined as a whole to convey a proper idea of their works to future generations. This, we think, will sufficiently prove the importance of the pianoforte in the advancement of musical education. Then for social purposes, as the solacer of many a weary hour, the banisher of *ennui*, the cause of graceful emulation amongst the young and innocent, the addition to the joy of those who meet for enjoyment, the piano stands deservedly high:—for what would the youthful group, who meet for song and dance, and their attendants, smiles and laughter, do without the pianoforte? while the elders look on and listen, and are proud of the musical displays which are a continually recurring reward for their care, attention, and parental love. Then as an accompaniment for the voice, either in solos or concerted pieces, it stands alone; and we have remarked that where this species of music is cultivated in a family the members are more united, and less prone than others to look for out-of-home amusements. This, we think, not only stamps its utility, but demands the attention of all interested in the education of the young, and the encouragement of home affections. To its uses at those times when the family circle are assembled to return thanks and sing praises to the Giver of all good, as well as on that day specially set apart for His worship, it is almost needless to allude, as they must be obvious even to the most unthinking.

The invention of the pianoforte has been attributed to Mason, the poet, and is said to be purely English; but we are inclined to think this apocryphal, the presumption being, that it had its origin from the harpsichord. In the latter the action consisted of a key and what is called a *jack*, which was a piece of a pear-tree with a small movable tongue of holly, through which a cutting of crow-quill was passed to touch the string when the *jack* was in action. As the quilling of a harpsichord was generally a day's work, various means were tried to produce a softer tone with more durable materials; and that resulted in the present grand pianoforte, which is a harpsichord in shape, with a different action. The action at first was simply a key, a lifter, a hammer, and a damper. The lifter was a brass wire with a piece of hide leather as a head, covered with a piece of soft leather as a finish—the tone must have been very thin and wiry, the hammer being only covered with one slight piece of leather. The first instrument sent to England, about the year 1711, was made by an English monk at Rome, and presented to Samuel Crisp, the author of the tragedy of Virginia. Another authority attributes the invention to Schrœder, of Dresden, who, in the year 1717, presented a model of the invention to the court of Saxony. The invention has also been ascribed to an instrument-maker at Florence, in the year 1711, of which there is a description in the "Giornale d'Italia" of that period. The origin of the square pianoforte was evidently the clavichord. This instrument was both *struck* and *pressed*, and the pressure could be so varied as to produce a trembling sound. The tones were feeble and melancholy, and it was only suited for the student and composer, not for social purposes or public display. Yet, it was upon one of these instruments that the elder Bach performed and composed his wonders, and it was the solace of the nun in her cell, and the companion of the prince in his study. It expressed quarter tones, was very portable, and was so weak in sound, that it would not disturb the inmates of an adjoining apartment. Such was the source whence sprung the instruments now to be found in every house around us. A German, named Zumpie, made these pianofortes in London, in 1776, and from their low price, convenience, and form, as well as power of expression, they entirely superseded the clavichord and harpsichord, and there was scarcely a house in the kingdom that did not possess one of them. Since then improvement has followed improvement, until they were brought to a very high state of perfection by Muzio Clementi, who was justly styled "the father of the pianoforte," as a composer for, a performer upon, and a skilful improver of the instrument. He has been ably followed in his experiments by the houses of Broadwood, Erard, Collard, Cadby, and Kirkman, till a mechanical certainty of touch has been attained, and a beauty of tone arrived at, while the whole machinery is so obedient to the will of the performer, that the slightest shades of feeling can be expressed with the utmost precision in boldness and rapidity. The improvements by which these have been accomplished are the results of a series of experiments and ingenious contrivances, adjusted so as to command to a mathematical certainty the end sought for. Good specimens of the workmanship of these manufacturers were to be seen in the Exhibition. A short grand piano, by Cadby, with a suspended sounding-board, is so ingeniously designed and adapted to the purpose, and so successful in its development, namely, liquidity, richness, and purity of tone—independent of the application being quite new—that it deserves special mention; also the iron truss applied to the back of the cottage pianoforte, in order to compensate for the immense pull of the strings on the front, by the same maker, is a contrivance the merits of which must be obvious even to a superficial inspector. The British pianofortes are first of their class. There are also some fair instruments from Belgium, but not equal to the English, who, we may safely say, surpass all other countries in the manufacture of this most comprehensive of musical instruments. We should not omit to mention, that among these instruments was a piano made by the late Mr. M'Culloch, of Belfast, who attained some eminence as a manufacturer; having on several occasions been awarded premiums at the Triennial Exhibitions of the Royal Dublin Society. Since his death pianos are not made in Ireland.

### THE HARP.

If the pianoforte wants the prestige of antiquity, we now write of a musical instrument the antiquity of which is undisputed, and its invention and earlier history hidden in the obscure mists of eras long before the historic period. The very derivation of its name affords matter of discussion and dispute amongst the learned. Galileo maintains that the Italians had the harp from the Irish, who used it long before the gamut of Guido was invented. The Theban harp, figured and described in Dr. Burney's History of Music, and the authenticity of which was so long disputed, was, even so far back as the time of Sir W. Jones, fully cleared from all the doubts that sceptics had thrown upon its discovery, and the narrative of the traveller Bruce, who describes the situation in which he found it, fully accredited. Recent discoveries have put the question beyond all cavil, and they go far to prove that the harp of the Israelites had an Egyptian origin: that is, if the instrument that David played upon was a harp; for, notwithstanding the number of dissertations written upon it, and though Don Calmet has had the daring to give it a form, all we know is, that it was called *chinnor* in Hebrew, and the King-Prophet himself in the Psalms frequently calls it the ten-stringed harp. However, as the instrument upon which David played allowed him to both dance and sing before the ark, it must have been but of small compass and size; and it is probable that, allowing for its origin in Egypt, the necessity arose during the many peregrinations of the Israelites to make it more portable; and hence it degenerated in compass. But though David is generally represented with a harp in his hands, there is no testimony to prove that the Hebrew *chinnor* was anything like our harp, for upon a Hebrew medal of Simon Maccabæus there are two sorts of musical instruments, both of which are very different from the harp, having only three or four strings each; and all writers learned in the subject agree that our harp is neither in form, compass, nor stringing, like the lyre, citharon, or barbiton of the Romans.

We may, however, fairly conclude that the harp is the most ancient of all musical intruments. Mr. Bruce found the painting he describes in one of the sepulchres that according to tradition are said to contain the dust of the first kings of Thebes, and which lie behind the ruins of that ancient Egyptian city. It represented a man playing upon the harp, painted in fresco, and quite entire. He states from the detail of the figure that the painter had about the same degree of merit with a good sign-painter in Europe, and that the action of the musician is such as to lead us to suppose that there were great hands at the time, and that the capabilities of the instrument were not only fully understood but amply displayed. The performer's left hand is employed among the notes in *alto*, as if in *arpeggio*; while stooping forward he seems with his right hand to be beginning with the lowest string and promising to ascend with the most rapid execution. Bruce looked upon this instrument as the Theban harp, before and at the time of Sesostris, who adorned Thebes, and probably caused it to be painted there, as well as the other figures in the sepulchre of his father, as a monument of the superiority which Egypt had in music at that time, over all the barbarous nations which he had seen or conquered.

The use of the harp was known to the ancient Irish. Mr. Walker, in his Historical Account of the Irish Bards, says that they had four different species of harp. The first, the one commonly called the Irish harp; the second, a kind of dulcimer; the third, an instrument of ten strings; and the fourth, that of the Welsh. The use of the latter, amongst the Irish, may have led to the opinion advocated by Jones, the Welsh bard, that the Irish had their music from the Cambro-Britons; but we think the contrary the fact, as asserted by Giraldus Cambrensis, and ably and logically defended by Walker, that the Welsh had their music from Ireland. In comparing the airs of the two countries, however some may be found to resemble each other, the Irish have an internal evidence of a prior period to those of the Principality in their cadence, phrasing, and structure; and whatever semblance may be found in the latter appears to have arisen out of the model of something that preceded them. This may be found on a careful examination of the melodies of the two countries. From the peculiar progressions of those airs it will easily be perceived that they were originally composed for an instrument which, though of tolerable compass, was imperfect in its scale; and their structure—wild though beautiful, melancholy to that intensity which proves them offsprings of moments of felicity unattainable by study—also leads us to suppose that they were generally unaccompanied by any harmonies however rude, and that they were composed for the instrument with which the Bards accompanied their extempore recitations of joy or lamentation. From this source sprung those soul-touching airs so fraught with that poetry which kindles the heart to desire, or melts the eyes to weeping—airs so thoroughly genuine that no one accustomed to hear them could be imposed upon by any other however like; and the more careful the imitation the more certain would they be of being pronounced spurious.

The harp of Brian Boiroimhe, King of Ireland, of which Dr. Petrie has written so interesting a description, was small and portable, such as we may suppose that of David and the Royal Alfred to have been. Harps of this portable form are frequently met with at the present time. That of the ancient Irish was strung with wire, and in this respect entirely differed from the Welsh harp, which was strung with gut, and is the one from which originated the elegant instrument now in use. Here again is the high antiquity of the harp certified, for when Wales was governed by the Druids, ere the invasion of Julius Cæsar, the Welsh had it, and the Bards, like the Levites among the Hebrews, were held sacred. The Venerable Bede asserts that the harp was used as an accompaniment to the voice upon that island in the eighth century.

On what occasion and at what time the form of this beautiful instrument was assumed in the Arms of Ireland has not been satisfactorily ascertained. Mr. O'Hallaran states it was by order of Henry II., and Mr. Ledwich by that of Henry VIII.; but the reason for it, or the authority upon which they found their assertions, are not given by either of the learned gentlemen.

The Welsh harp of the last century had three rows of strings, the two outside ones in unison, and the middle row the semitones, and possessed a compass of five octaves. The inconvenience and difficulty of performing any complicated or rapid composition upon an instrument so awkwardly constructed, and presenting so many barriers to dexterous manipulation, caused the music composed for it to be of the simplest kind, mostly consisting of airs of about sixteen bars, to which was sometimes appended variations of the poorest and most tinkling description. Modulation of any frequency was impossible upon it; and although the advantages offered by an instrument of such large compass and power of harmonic combination were but too obvious to the musician, yet its mode of triple stringing almost set his labours at defiance. Hence arose the improvements which have made the harp capable of conveying now, in richness and brilliancy, music of the highest order. Indeed, no musical instrument has received so many and such valuable improvements from the ingenuity of modern artists. Its compass has been extended to that of the pianoforte, and by the addition of pedals to produce the half tones, it has been reduced to one row of strings, so that the performer can now play in any key, and make the most rapid chromatic modulations; whereas formerly for every change of key it had to be re-tuned.

Though the harp possess not the massiveness of the pianoforte for simultaneous harmonies, nor the muscularity of tone which makes that instrument the best conveyance of the ideas of the great Masters; yet, for strains of melancholy, brilliant arpeggios, and aërial effects, it is unrivalled. Before the time of Bochsa, who was harpist to the first Emperor Napoleon, it was little used in England, save for accompanying the voice: his genius developed its powers and proved it capable of performing the highest species of composition. In an orchestra its effects are charming—its vibrations telling without predominance above the mass. Meyerbeer has used it most happily in his operas, and those who have heard Mendelssohn's settings of the lyrics of Racine's Athalie will easily call to remembrance the felicitous harp passages in the overture which give such an airiness and grace, together with a tone of the olden time, to that noble composition: and the delicious accompaniment of the hymn by eight harps, so fresh and sparkling without bordering on frivolity, shows what resources are to be found in this instrument by a skilful musician.

The harps exhibited by Marcus Moses, of Westmoreland-street, and manufactured by Erard, on many occasions delighted the visitors to the Exhibition by the sweetness of their tones. Those on the gallery exhibited by J. Bray, of Westmoreland-street, demand special notice at our hands, inasmuch as they were manufactured by the exhibiter. One of these was a double-action harp in ultramarine and gold, 6¼ octaves, with all the modern improvements; and the other was in bird-eye maple, 6 octaves, Gothic pattern. Mr. Bray contributed a beautiful specimen of Irish manufacture in this department to the last Triennial Exhibition of the Royal Dublin Society, and a further specimen was sent by him to the New York Exhibition.

## THE ORGAN.

The organ is the most gorgeous and many-voiced instrument known—sublime in its effects upon the educated, and mysterious in its influences upon those unacquainted with its structure. Hence the feeling of the supernatural that its tones frequently induce. At the present day it affords combinations of superb power, possessing requirements for the performance of the vastest harmonies, and allowing full scope for the most intricate and skilful designs of the composer. The variety of its resources has led to a range of compositions for the organ, which include the light and the serious, the majestic and the rapid. We have *arias* given by a telling *stop*, with elaborate accompaniments on the swell, while the *pedals* sustain the bass in stately progression;—*preludes* brilliant and unfaltering—solemn *andantes* and *adagios* without number, and *fugues* exhibiting all the ingenuity of laborious pedantry, or evincing those rays of genius which guide the student through the mazes of the giant Bach. The last-named composer appears to have understood the genius of the organ, and to have written for it the fittest and most appropriate music. Preludes variegated with harmonies, wherein the sustaining powers of the instrument are beautifully displayed, and *fugues* whose telling and easily traced subjects keep a continuous flow upon the ear, and chase each other through a labyrinth of modulations, always pursuing, never overtaking, till they meet in a colossal burst of harmony that makes the heart of the listener bound with joy, and which no other single instrument would give the composer the power of accomplishing.

Such is the mighty power which the organ possesses. Then for expressing the massive grandeur of great choruses without the voices, it is unexampled; while for the accompanying of sacred music its solidity of tone and sombreness of colouring have made it the chosen instrument for the Christian temple. Besides, it seems to be endowed with the faculty of awakening the heart to devotion, and wafting the soul of the penitent to the footstool of the Creater, there to plead for itself. Who has not felt—amidst the vaulted aisles of a cathedral, where every distance is peopled with shadows, and the dim religious light from unseen windows set high in walls erected to stand for centuries, timidly streams in, as if half afraid of banishing them into the vaults beneath—the holy influences of this sacred instrument, as it fills the naves, flows throughout the various aisles, and ascends to the roof in incense of sweet sounds—

> "The branching roof,
> Self-poised and scooped into ten thousand cells
> Where light and shade repose, and music dwells—
> Lingering, and wandering on,
> As loath to die."

Such places are the fitting ones for its performance; and whether from association, or from some peculiarity which makes it less effective as a solo instrument for concert-room or music-hall, than others of smaller capacity—or probably from the impression it leaves upon the mind that its sounds are not produced by the skill of an individual—no matter from what, and notwithstanding all that affected *dilletanteism* may say to the contrary—its solo effects are lost upon the multitude, save in a place of public worship. The few may admire the contrivance of the composition, the skill of the performer, and his dexterity in managing so complicated a musical machine; but they feel not where art should awaken emotion, and they pass away without retaining any of those vague and mystic charms that the memory of music is calculated to leave upon the soul. For the conveyance of individual melody, there are required a crescendo and a diminuendo on each sound, also a forzando, and a power of forcing into passion certain phrases, always keeping upon the ear that those things are accomplished by the same voice,—whether it be human or artificial, caused by the breath or by the bow,—in reality a succession of sounds varied in their length, breadth, and emphasis by the will, showing the intelligence and feeling of him who produces them. This the organ, with all its grandeur, is deficient in. The finger of the performer presses down a key, which by a mechanical contrivance opens a valve: air is thus admitted from the bellows into a pipe causing the emission of such sound, and such only as the maker intended that pipe to speak. So long as the finger is kept upon the key, and the bellows blown, the pipe will give forth the same sound—or the succession of the sounds of a scale without any modification or softening off, as each pipe belonging to every stop is voiced alike. The finger of the player has no power by pressure or otherwise of altering in the slightest degree the tones, its business being merely to open and close a valve by putting down or letting up the key as the music may require. No matter what his passion, his *abandon*, his fire, his energy, or his pathos, he merely puts in motion a machine made to produce certain effects with mathematical precision; but from its construction totally incapable of showing the shades of feeling which may pass through the performer's mind. Hence does a simple melody—however judiciously the stop upon which it is played be selected, and however dexterously it may be accompanied on other parts of the instrument by harmonies purposely enriched to throw it out, always tell of its mechanical production, and always, no matter how much its beauty may be confessed, sound as if devoid of soul; wanting that divinity which awakens a corresponding divinity in others—that which is the power of genuine art, its supremacy—the chaining to its triumphal chariot-wheels the best and most elevating sympathies of our common nature. Mendelssohn has evaded, with great profoundness, the exhibition of this defect in his celebrated Sonatas for the organ; but even with all his dexterous management in flooding with harmonies upon the *swell*, the accompaniments given to the subjects, and the majestic motion of the *pedal* basses—yet are not the natural hardnesses and immobility of the instrument conquered. The only compensation for the defects now spoken of is the *swell*, which certainly admits of a lengthened crescendo, but always too long to give the forzando, without which that nice and intelligent expression necessary for the faithful delivery of a simple melody can never be arrived at. The solemn magnificence of this multifariously-voiced instrument is only fitted for masses of sound—large harmonic combinations that come upon the ear in a peal and startle by their immensity—stately *andantes* and *adagios* flowing along like some broad river too deep and strong to permit its waters to be curled into wavelets by the passing breezes; but above all, for the *fugue*, a species of composition so entirely adapted to the genius of the instrument that, no matter how well performed, they are generally meagre and confused on any other. Here the determined succession of notes, called the subject, is tellingly interspersed throughout the movement, and the replies in the *fifth* and *eighth* of the other parts, palpable to the ear, as they chase each other through every variety of key. The peculiar defects arising from the complicated machinery of the organ, and from its breath being supplied mechanically, become benefits in the rendering of these works—the *fugue* requiring neither lights nor shades in its delivery, and admitting of that augmentation of sounds which the organist has so much at his disposal. In fact, these species of composition are no more than elaborately constructed pieces of musical mechanism, in which the results can be as readily traced as those of a mathematical problem; and hence are they most particularly adapted for the most mechanical of all musical instruments. One of the most graceful and beautiful characteristics of the organ is the incitement it gives the musician to extemporize. No other instrument presents to him the same extent of keys—modern organs generally consisting of three benches, each equal in compass to the pianoforte, with a row of keys for the feet called *pedals*, generally two octaves, and sometimes two octaves and a half in extent, and a multiplicity of *stops*,—all contrived to produce divers and many-coloured effects. There are also many copulæ to couple the *swell* to the great organ, the *manuals* to the *pedals*, &c., and contrivances to permit him to augment or decrease the force of sound by the use of composition *pedals*, which take out or put in a number of stops at a time, without compelling him to take his fingers off the keys, or move his hands from one bench to the other.

Some notion of the scope afforded to the musician for this purpose may be formed from the following description of the organ built by Telford, placed above the Dais in the Exhibition. It possesses on the great organ a compass of CC to G in alt with sixteen stops, fifteen of which have each a rank of pipes throughout the entire compass, and one, four ranks. The *choir* organ is of the same length, and contains seven stops with ranks of pipes to each. The swell is also from CC to G in alt, and comprises thirteen stops. It has two octaves and a half of pedals, with nine stops, one of them having four ranks of pipes, and five copulæ, with six composition pedals for purposes enumerated above. The total number of pipes is 2833.

From these details some idea may be formed of the fascination of this powerful machine of sounds for the educated musical man, the lover of his art. We cannot wonder that he should sit for hours making new combinations from the powers at his disposal, revelling in imaginative subjects, with accompaniments in various figures, rejoicing in the flights of his own fancy, and the treasures of music he unlocks by the skill of his own hands. Nor can we feel surprised that he would sit foodless in the chill, damp air of a church, from early morn till the coming twilight warned him of the hours that had sped—as many have done—enjoying these rare and exquisite delights; nor that the youth so wrapped in the mazes of sweet sound, and so accustomed to listen with intensity to all the relative harmonic combinations and their various resolutions—to unravel them where they became complicated—and to learn to apply them in composition, till sprang from the chaos of his brain, in form and beauty, the bewitching opera, or soul-subduing oratorio; nor that such a person should walk forth amongst men—a Handel or a Mendelssohn—and leave the glories of his labours to illumine musical art to all posterity.

It may be here remarked as curious, that with all these vast powers and appliances for the production of sound, the organ is so imperfect an instrument as to be seldom in tune, never so in all keys. The most extraordinary instance of discord and untuneableness, being almost absorbed in the sonorous grandeur of the instrument, is found in the sesquialtera, mixture, and cornet. Each of these stops has generally three ranks of pipes, giving the *third*, *fifth*, and *eighth* of the note, or number of notes played—the *third* always being *major*,—so that in any piece of music all the chords bearing a *minor third* are accompanied also by a *major* one. The untuneableness of this seems preposterous in theory; and yet when these *stops* form the superstructure of sound, upon the basis of the great organ, they are borne with pleasure, and considered to add much to the brightness of the whole. This may, and we believe does, arise from the distance of the intervals which the pipes form with the diapason, being the seventeenth, nineteenth, and twenty-second: but the addition of them to any composition in a *minor* key is intolerable, changing music into noise, and brilliancy into screaming. Sometimes these stops have as many as four, five, and six ranks of pipes, each giving the intervals stated above to every key pressed down by the fingers of the organist. All the defects we have stated, and many more, are swallowed in the vast volumes of sound emitted by this instrument; and it is only when injudiciously used, and when its stupendous resources are diverted from their legitimate purposes, either in the ignorance of the tyro, or the vanity of an artist who will sacrifice every noble quality of the organ to his own conceit, and substitute dexterous manipulation and fantastic trickery for that solemn and robust labour by which alone its splendours can be developed—that these glaring, harsh, and unmusical effects stand out in their nakedness; that it impotently cries like an imprisoned giant tortured by a fool, and ceases to breathe in eloquent strains its soul-soothing harmonies, or thunder its mighty utterances in tones which elevate the heart to a sense of the sublime.

The vast capacity of these instruments may be conceived from the following:—The organ of St. Paul's, Frankfort-on-the-Maine, has three rows of keys, two sets of pedals, and seventy-four stops; that of St. Peter, Goerlitz, Upper Lusatia, has three rows of keys, eighty-two stops, and three thousand two hundred and seventy pipes, and is blown by twelve pairs of bellows; the great Haarlem organ, at one time considered the largest in the world, contains five thousand pipes; and the splendid instrument in the Town-Hall of Birmingham is thirty-five feet wide, fifteen deep, and forty high; has four sets of keys, and five pairs of bellows; the timber, metal, and other materials employed in its formation amount to the enormous weight of forty tons. But all these will be put into the shade by that now erecting in St. George's Hall, Liverpool, which, if we may estimate by the cost (£21,000), will be the largest and finest instrument in the world.

To come back from these leviathans to those which were in our own Exhibition, we may observe that Bevington's organ which was at the east end of the Great Hall, is beautifully voiced and well balanced; and contains twenty-seven stops and five couplers, and pedals from CCC to D, with three composition pedals. The builder was very happy in the placing of this instrument, its position having been the most sonorous in the building. Telford's organ, though double its size, and splendidly voiced, giving to the performers all the resources required to produce the largest effects, was so injured by the situation it occupied, that its weight of tone was unfelt, its brilliancy dulled, and its articulation confused. Though the instruments were under the hands of two good players, Dr. Stewart and Mr. Croft, yet the performances were on the whole ineffective, merely owing to the unfitness of the Industrial Temple for such displays. It would have been all very well to have had the organs played upon, as they were in the London Exhibition, to show off their powers, but to have regular daily organ performances as an attraction for visitors was a mistake in two ways—being totally out of keeping with the objects for which the building was erected, and calculated in no way to display the ability of the gentlemen who performed. At the superb performance of choral music given at the opening of the Exhibition, Telford's organ, notwithstanding its position being so much against the display of its power, did goodly service—upholding, enriching, and filling up—being felt throughout, not above, the voices and orchestra, sustaining the harmonies, adding to the brilliancy of the choral effects, and giving to the whole an air of solid grandeur which it could not have had without it, however bright the band might have been, and ponderous the chorus. Here the organ was applied to its grandest of legitimate uses, aiding a mighty band and chorus, and being *felt* rather than heard. How different from applying it to the performance of operatic airs or ballads written for the human voice, which are just as much out of character on this noblest of instruments as they would be on a clarionet or bassoon!

Having endeavoured to give some idea of the genius and proper application of this instrument, we shall now give a slight sketch of its origin and history. Its origin is hidden in obscurity, and all we can learn is that it seems to have been borrowed from the Greeks, as Vitruvius describes one. He attributes the invention to Archimedes (200 years before Christ); and Ctesibus improved upon it by the use of water and of keys. The ancients employed the fall of water, pumps, and different kinds of bellows, to cause the motion by which the wind was introduced, and at last stopped at the wind bellows, which was set in motion either by water or human strength. Hence arose two kinds of organs: that moved by water was called *hydraulic*, and that by wind *pneumatic*. However, there was no difference in the principle, as it is only by air the pipes can produce a sound. Although the earliest descriptions appear to belong to the hydraulic, it seems natural to suppose the pneumatic one to have been first invented. An engraving given in Sir John Hawkins' History of Music, from a monument in Rome, seems to confirm the latter opinion. That mentioned by Vitruvius was an *hydraulicon*. Du Cange quotes an epigram descriptive of an organ said to have been in the possession of Julian the Apostate in the fourth century, and concludes that it was not an *hydraulic* instrument, but resembled much the modern *pneumatic* organ. St. Jerome mentions one with twelve pairs of bellows, and fifteen pipes to each key, which might be heard at the distance of a mile; and another at Jerusalem which was heard at the Mount of Olives. Pope Vitalian is generally allowed to have been the first who introduced the organ into the service of the Catholic Church, about the year 670. Dr. Burney says that ancient annalists are unanimous in stating that the first organ seen in France was sent from Constantinople as a present to King Pepin, father of Charlemagne, by Constantine, in 757. This, as well as Julian's epigram, gives the invention to Greece. It is curious that the Venerable Bede, who died in 735, notwithstanding his minute description of the manner in which the psalms and hymns were sung in the churches, says nothing of the organ. However, according to Muratori and Mabillon, organs became common in Italy, Germany, and England, during the tenth century, about which time they were admitted into the convents throughout Europe. The poet Mason, in his Essays on Church Music, gives several historical notices concerning the origin and progress of the organ previous to its general admission into our churches. These early attempts were very rude in construction; the keys were four or five, and sometimes six inches broad, the pipes were of brass, and the compass did not exceed two octaves in the twelfth century, about which time half-notes appear to have been introduced at Venice. A description of one procured by Elfeg, Bishop of Winchester, for his cathedral, in 951, states that it was the largest then known, having twenty-six pairs of bellows, requiring seventy men to fill them with wind. It had ten keys, with forty pipes to each key. There was also one at Canterbury Cathedral previous to the year 1174. At Venice, about the year 1471, the important addition of pedals was made by a German named Bernhard; to whose countrymen we also owe most of the other improvements. The organs built by Schmidt for St. Paul's, the Temple, St. Mary's, Oxford, Trinity College, Cambridge, &c., were commonly confined to four octaves from CC in the bass to C in alt. They are very superior in tone to the generality of modern instruments; so much so that they have had their compass extended and many other improvements added during the last century by Byfield, Snetzler, Green, Gray, and others. The earliest organ-builder in England was William Wotton, of Oxford, who built in 1482 an organ for Merton College, also one for the Chapel of Magdalen College. The old organ at York (since burnt) was one of those that escaped the destruction of those instruments during the civil wars; although Cromwell himself was so fond of the organ that he caused the one at Magdalen Court, Oxford, to be removed to Hampton Court. It was afterwards restored to the College, where it remained till 1740, when it was removed to Tewksbury, and has lately been remodelled and enlarged by Willis. In 1660 there were only four organ-builders in England, and at the present time we can scarcely boast of more in Ireland; but while we have a Telford to manufacture such first-class instruments as he has turned out of his factory, we may confidently look forward to a succession of builders in this country no way inferior to any in Europe.

There was a small organ by White, another Irish builder, in the Furniture Court of the Exhibition, which claims a word of praise. It is a finger organ in a handsome Gothic case, is nicely voiced, and would be quite sufficient for a church of limited size. A small but excellent chamber organ, by Bevington, was also exhibited.

### MISCELLANEOUS MUSICAL INSTRUMENTS.

In the Court of Antiquities in the Exhibition were to be found some musical instruments which serve to illustrate the history of the past. Among these was the Dalway Harp, which was looked upon with so much veneration by Bunting as to be thought worthy of a minute description in his first collection of the "Antient Music of Ireland." It contained twenty-two strings more than that of Brian Boiroimbe, the latter having only thirty strings. Hence it was capable of producing larger musical effects, and must have been equal, in scope and brilliancy, to music of almost the range of that of the present time. Carolan's Harp must also have been of considerable compass, as it is about four feet high. Perhaps upon this very instrument did this last of the bards compose his bright and soul-stirring *planxties*—short pieces of music so entirely original that in the whole range of the art we know of nothing to liken them to—for the Italian *giga*, though bearing some resemblance, has not the reckless dash, the drollery, and above all the melancholy termination to a grotesque phrase that distinguish these curiously beautiful compositions. Perhaps upon this very instrument did he compose "Aileen Aroon," a melody so replete with the very essence of musical thought that it tells its tale to every hearer—and, perhaps, upon it did he accompany himself, as he sang it to the lady of his love, wrapt in the elysian of fancy, influenced by the brightness of her presence, though he could not behold her with his sightless eyes. The harp of O'Neil, also there exhibited, was most likely manufactured during the reign of Elizabeth. What a host of memories does it call forth! Upon this same instrument, perhaps, was often played that exquisitely melancholy *air*, "The Coolin"—as the youth lamented the loss of those locks that adorned him and made him more comely in the eyes of the fair. Amidst the host of historic recollections called forth by the collection of which these musical instruments form a part, we think none more full of thrilling interest than those they awaken.

There were also in this department a set of bagpipes, once the property of Lord Edward Fitzgerald, and another set belonging to Lord Rossmore, beautifully mounted in silver, and studded with precious stones, said to have cost £300. When this instrument was first introduced into this country is not known. It is likely the Norwegians and Danes brought the bagpipe into Scotland, as they long possessed the islands of the Hebrides. But the Irish pipe differs from that of the Scotch in the mode of providing the *wind*, which is not blown into it by the lips of the performer, but by a bellows. It is also much superior in quality and softness of tone; for while the former is scarcely tolerable in the open air, the latter discourses sweet sounds suitable to a lady's chamber.

In the Zollverein Department were three Cremona violins, exhibited by Tepe, of Osnabruck, looking very like genuine instruments of this highly prized class. When the violin or fiddle was first invented is not at present known, neither can we discover the nation that claims that honour. However, there is reason to suppose, that as no instrument played with the bow was known to the ancients, it must have had a mediæval origin. The form and character of the violin used in England in the time of Chaucer, who mentions it, cannot be exactly ascertained; and it is probable that from its first introduction it underwent a variety of alterations and improvements; for even towards the end of the sixteenth century its shape appears to be vague and undetermined. It has, however, long attained its present excellence, and formed the leading instrument at all musical performances. Indeed without violins and their relatives—violas and violoncellos—the art of music could not have progressed; as the expressiveness of notes produced by the bow is almost equal to those rendered by the human voice. These instruments produce the most thrilling effects, conveying every shade of feeling from the minds of the performers to those of the audience, while in large orchestral massing, they give a richness and firmness to the ideas of the composer unattainable by any other medium of sound. The violin evidently had its origin from the viol, a stringed instrument that resembled it in shape and tone. It had five or six strings, the tones of which were regulated by being brought by the fingers into contact with the frets with which the neck was furnished. So recently as during the Protectorate, the old viol was much more esteemed, but at and since the Restoration it resumed its former consequence, till now it has fairly beaten its parent and originator out of the field. The violins of Cremona were manufactured by a family consisting of a father, two sons, and a grandson, named Amati, natives of that town, who flourished about the year 1600. The instruments of their make are distinguished by their mildness and sweetness of tone, and mostly have a yellow tinge in the varnish. Besides these there were two persons of the name of Stradivarius, of Cremona, admirable artisans; the latter was living at the beginning of this century: his signature is, *Antonius Stradivarius, Cremonensis, faciebat Anno.*" Andrew Garnier was also a much esteemed maker at Cremona. He signed his name thus—"*Andreas Gaurnerius fecit Cremonæ sub titulo Sanctæ Teresæ*, 1680." A Straduarius is known by its full, rich tone. The varnish of those made by the father is yellow, while that of the son is red. The violins of Cremona are exceeded only by those of Stainer, a German, whose instruments are remarkable for a full and piercing tone; his signature is, "*Jacobus Stainer, in absam prope Ænapontum*, 1647." The varnish of the Stainers is yellow. Another celebrated maker, Matthew Albani, signs his name thus—"*Matthias Albanus fecit in Tyrol Bulsani*, 1654." We have been thus particular in giving the signatures and colour of varnishes used, in order to guard those curious in these instruments, and desirous of possessing a real Cremona or Stainer, against imposition. Other characteristics distinguish them from each other; for instance, the Straduarius violins are larger, and have a wider box than the Amatis, but the grand characteristic is the tone. England boasts of some celebrated violin-makers, whose instruments are very much sought after. Two violins exhibited by Hugh Gordon, of Lisburn, show that the manufacture of these instruments is still successfully carried on in Ireland. Formerly Dublin was celebrated for its makers. Those of our northern manufacturer possess a new form and application of the sounding-post, evidently calculated to soften and enrich the tone.

An harmonium exhibited by Metzler, of London, is worthy of notice, as it presented large advantages to the performer, possessing a compass of five octaves, and having twelve stops. There is a machinery attached to it, which can be adjusted over the keys, that permits it to be played after the manner of a concertina; or, when removed, as an organ on the ordinary keys. It is one of the most comprehensive instruments of the class; and were it not that we believe the genuine organ effects can never be imitated by any other instrument, we would say that it would answer all the purposes of a small organ.

Mr. Scates, of College-green, exhibited some concertinas of his own manufacture that deserve more than a passing word of commendation. The concertina is an entirely modern instrument. It was first patented in 1829 by Messrs. Wheatstone. It is the invention of Professor Wheatstone, by whose scientific labours many valuable improvements in the construction of instruments with vibrating plates have been effected. The tones of this instrument are produced by vibrating plates of metal; in contradistinction to strings, as in the pianoforte, harp, violin, &c., or tubes as in the organ. The tones of the harmonium, seraphine, accordion, musical boxes, &c., are similarly produced. There is little doubt that the common boy's toy, the Jew's harp, gave the first idea; which, with the aid of science and observation, combined with mechanical ability, has led to the production of this distinct class of modern musical instruments. A vibrating plate, called also a reed or tongue, is a thin narrow slip of metal fastened at one end, while the other is left free, and placed over an aperture also cut in metal, which is nearly its counterpart, and in which it is so fitted that while it touches nowhere, it only allows a certain quantity of air to pass through; the current or column of air forces the plate from its position, to which it returns again by its own elasticity, and the temporary diminution of the pressure consequent on the escape of the air. Thus a constant series of vibrations causing continuous tone is excited. This class of instruments are characterized by some superior qualities which must have considerable influence on their general appreciation—such as the length of time they keep in tune, their durability—their sweet and melodious quality of tones—with the power of sustaining and prolonging them at pleasure—and their capability of being put into very compact forms. Other characteristic features of this elegant instrument are, that it possesses considerable compass, having a greater range than the flute (and excepting the highest notes used only in very difficult passages), the same as the violin. Its tones are pure, sweet, and brilliant; it has great power of expression and execution. From its intonation being always correct, the tone easy to produce, and the keys lying entirely under the command of the fingers, it can be learnt with much greater facility than other instruments. The concertina may be used as a substitute for the flute, oboe, &c. From its being the only instrument having a sustained sound, which conventionalism allows to ladies, its value is considerably increased. Tenor and bass concertinas are also manufactured, upon which any music written for the viola and violoncello may be performed. The various concertinas are frequently combined, and in quartetts, septetts, or even in larger numbers, they have a beautiful effect; and with music expressly arranged for them a brilliant result is produced. Since its first introduction the concertina has steadily progressed in public favour; and perhaps the best proof of the merits of the instrument is the readiness with which it has been taken up by professors of ability. Whoever has heard such artists as Regondi, Case, Blagrove, (and Scates at our own Exhibition,) perform upon it, must agree that its invention has been a valuable addition to those musical instruments that are more especially adapted for the drawing-room. The instruments manufactured and exhibited by Mr. Scates comprised one amboyna wood treble concertina, one rosewood brass-bound concertina, and one baritone concertina, all of which are very highly finished, and possess a full, mellow, and clear tone. His improvements are a tympanium, or leather sound covering, and double sound-boards. He also introduces the silver stops or touches, and has five folds in the bellows. Mr. Scates likewise exhibited several of Messrs. Wheatstone's concertinas.

F. White, Doctor of Music, of Wexford, exhibited a new musical instrument, named the Victoria harp lyre. It is of elegant form, and from its appearance would be a most graceful instrument in the hands of a lady. It is constructed like three guitars joined together in harp-shape, with frets to make the tones, and possesses eighteen strings, so that its compass and capabilities in the hands of an artist must be very considerable.

Mr. Bussell, of Westmoreland-street, exhibited a class of musical instruments, the manufacture of which was much wanted in this country—namely, military instruments. Formerly the bands in Her Majesty's service were supplied by either London or Continental houses; now, through the exertions of Mr. Bussell, Ireland is able to provide the army with musical instruments equal to any in Europe. This is very satisfactory to record, as it shows progress in a class of manufacture hitherto unknown in this country. First, there is a cornopean, showing evidently improvements of the first order. It is called "The Patent Serpentine Revolving-valve Cornopean," and insures the freedom of tone that heretofore belonged only to the plain slide trombone, and common French horn. It is constructed on the principle of the trombone, giving to the wind a direct passage in producing the valve note. The stroke of the piston-rod being only one half of any other now in use, the note is made much quicker, more distinct, with less action of the fingers, and the execution is much facilitated. This improvement has also been applied to the ophecleides (or bombardones), bass, tenor, and alto; to the trombone, with valves; and the alto horn, specimens of which were to be seen in the Southern Gallery. There were also flutes, oboes, and clarionets, manufactured by Bussell, evincing much skill and elegance in their construction, and improvement in their availments. The oboe is an exact model of those made by the celebrated Triber, mounted on swivels and pillars. The clarionet is on the French principle, with the ring action which so much facilitates the execution of the performer.

The chromatic flute, exhibited by the Rev. C. M. Fleury, has an improvement in the keys of the lower joint that affords a certainty of stopping with the least possible touch, and effectually does away with the clatter and sticking of the old metal plug. The swivel and pillar mounting of these instruments is quite new in this country, as hitherto that branch of manufacture was confined to the Continent.

The instruments exhibited by Mr. J. M'Neill, of Capel-street, in this city, his own manufacture, were also highly creditable specimens of native industry, and in no degree inferior, in either quality of tone or finish, to the imported articles.—H. T.

## III.—SURGICAL INSTRUMENTS.

The natural repugnance with which we view the armentaria chirurgia, and the painful associations which arise in the mind from an examination of instruments which, though calculated to relieve suffering, are still, in their application, a source of pain in many cases, must deprive this class of articles of much of the interest which they would otherwise possess in the estimation of the general public; and yet the subject opens a wide field to expatiate on the ingenuity in devising, and skill in carrying out, those improvements which have taken place in the surgery of modern days. A description of surgical instruments formerly in use would fill the mind with horror and astonishment in the contemplation of the suffering which patients must have undergone when subjected to treatment with apparatus which look more like instruments of torture of the dark ages than as aught appertaining to the healing art; but such a description would be well calculated to exhibit the very great advances which medical science has made, and to show that in the progress elsewhere apparent in science, art, and manufactures, surgery has not been behindhand. While whole series of instruments have been rendered obsolete by new modes of treatment, and a more extended knowledge of pathology, a great variety of new ones has been called for by the requirements of the surgeon in dealing with diseases formerly unrecognised, or the mode of treatment of which was imperfectly understood. There are those who think that there is too great a stress laid on, and encouragement given to, the invention of new instruments, and are jealous lest the *tactus eruditus* of the surgeon should be superseded, in any way, by mechanical contrivance; who, in fact, maintain that the fewer the instruments in use, and the more simple their adjustments, the more likely will the operator be to attain a proper degree of skill in their use. But it must ever be borne in mind, that any instrument, either for surgical or other purposes, which accurately performs its office, is far superior to any skill, however perfect, in the manner of its application.

Of late years operations have been of much less frequent occurrence than formerly, and this is to be ascribed to the superior medical education of the surgeon, by which he is enabled to treat disease in its early stages, as well as the increased skill in diagnosis, which teaches him in what cases operation becomes unsuitable, and in which it may be advisable rather to trust to the *vis medicatrix naturæ*, than, by too bold a line of conduct, to bring a good operation into disrepute, and, by failure, to discourage others from operating in cases admitting of little doubt.

In estimating the value of particular instruments, and their adaptation for the intended purpose, the knowledge of the object to be effected is a paramount consideration. The requirements to be attained must first be understood, after which ingenuity may be very fairly exercised to devise the best means of securing them. The skilful surgeon and the manufacturer must therefore act in concert—the one aiding in carrying out the views of the other. To enter at any length into the discussion of a technical department like this would be entirely out of place in a work like the present, intended for the general reader. There were, however, some articles exhibited which were so very suggestive, on account of the ingenuity which they displayed, as, even here, to be deserving of some special notice, in connexion with a brief outline of the nature of the object to be attained.

Few departments of modern surgery present illustrations of greater ingenuity than is displayed in the treatment of aneurism. This malady is the result of disease or injury of the arteries. The conduits by which the vital fluid is supplied to the various parts of the body receive the blood which the heart sends out at every pulsation, and, by the elasticity of their coats, render continuous the supply to the tissues of the body. Now in this disease a rupture of one or more of the coats of an artery takes place, allowing a sac to be formed, into which, at every pulsation of the heart, additional quantities of blood are sent, and which, from the capacity of the sac, and the slight elasticity of its walls, it is unable entirely to empty; and thus it gradually enlarges, until, by its rupture, death takes place from the sudden loss of arterial blood.

The aneurism is generally lined on its inside with layers deposited from the blood; and all modern treatment has had for its object the increasing of these layers, until the cavity of the aneurism should become obliterated, and thus the cure be effected, or the sudden cutting off of the arterial supply to the sac secured.

By reducing the force of the circulation, the supply might be lessened, so as to promote this deposition, but by this treatment the blood was generally too much impoverished to deposit these layers, on which the cure depended. Cutting off the supply of blood altogether, by tying the artery at some distance from the aneurism, constituted, until lately, the most improved plan of treatment. We are, however, indebted to the Dublin surgeons for a new mode of dealing with this most formidable disease: for, by steady pressure on some part of the artery which supplies the sac, they have found that the current of blood could be so far diminished, if not entirely stopped (and that without impoverishing its quality), as to cause its speedy solidification in the aneurism, and thus dispense, in many cases, with an operation at all times attended with considerable risk. In carrying out this treatment, the aneurism-compressing instrument, invented by Dr. Carte, has been highly successful. This instrument, which appeared in the collection of Fannin & Co., of this city, differs from all other compressing instruments in the employment of an elastic instead of an unyielding force. This is effected by the use of vulcanized Indian-rubber bands, which exert their force on a pad fixed to a screw, playing in a suitable framework, which loosely surrounds the band, and which can be adjusted over any part which it is intended should be subjected to pressure. By this contrivance the elasticity of the vulcanized Indian-rubber acts directly on the pad with any required pressure, and thus, by allowing some slight variety in the force applied, has been found to be less irksome to the patient than the steady, unyielding pressure of other instruments devised for the purpose. On application to a limb, the pad is placed over the artery, and the screw is turned until the blood has ceased to flow, or has been, at least, greatly impeded. In some cases the application of this instrument for a few hours has been all that was required in effecting a cure. An accurate idea may be had of the arrangement proposed by Dr. Carte, as well as the method of its application under different circumstances, as regards the position of the part affected, by the accompanying engravings.

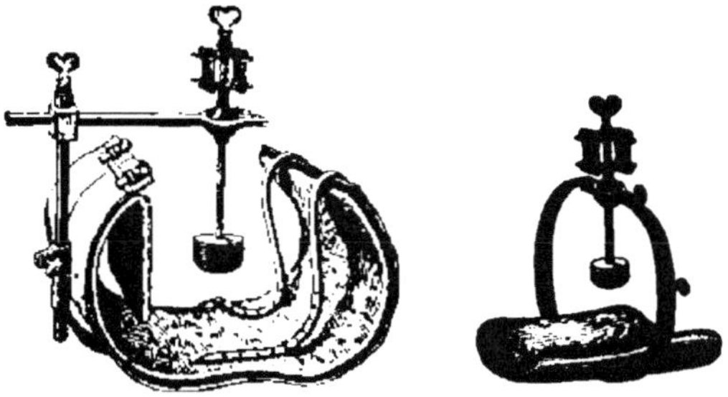

Dr. Carte's Compressing Instrument

From an attentive examination of the various assortments of surgical instruments which display most of the ordinary appliances required by surgeons, and many new contrivances well worthy of notice, we must yield the palm to M. Charrière, of Paris. His case was situated apart from the rest of the surgical instruments in the Great Hall, and attracted much attention, as well from the extensive series exhibited as from the superior workmanship and finish displayed in the several instruments. We were much struck with some of the instruments, as also by specimens of flexible ivory, which has lately been patented by him. It was for such a case as this that M. Charrière was awarded a prize medal at the Exhibition of 1851.

Mr. Baxter exhibited a stethoscope with lateral tubes containing fluid, which were stated to increase the hearing qualities of this valuable instrument. The judicious introduction of fluid into the construction would appear to be calculated to effect this object, though experience of the working of the instrument is obviously required to enable a definite opinion to be pronounced on the subject. The gutta percha stethoscope contributed by Surgeon Tufnell, though possessing some advantages, does not appear to convey sound so well as those made of deal or cedar.

The new dental forceps invented by Mr. J. A. Young, of Glasgow, and for which a patent has been taken out, are worthy of notice here for their novelty, and the execution of their workmanship. The beaks of these forceps, of which nine are composed in a set, are so inclined to each other that the root of the tooth, on being grasped by them, is compressed, as it were, between two inclined planes, and thus started from its socket. In these instruments the heads of the beaks are opened at an angle sufficient to allow the operator to see the tooth upon which he is engaged. The handles are so curved, and the beaks so inclined to the bodies of the instruments, that they may be freely moved in any direction; and the beaks embrace the roots only, so that as these parts are always more or less wedge-shaped, the forceps, acting as inclined planes upon a movable wedge, often effect their object by lateral pressure alone.

Fig. 1.

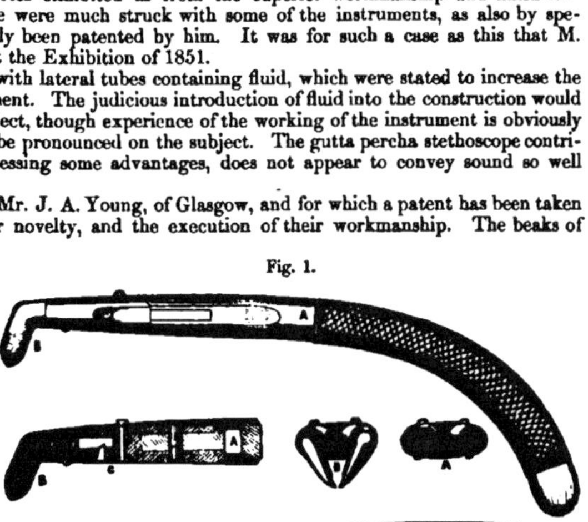


Fig. 2.

Mr. J. A. Young's Dental Forceps.

Fig. 1 represents a side view, half size, of a portable forceps, the beaks, B, being removable from the handles, A. Fig. 2 shows a plan of the forceps; and the remaining three details between these two figures are respectively a longitudinal section of the head and joint showing the spring catch, C, for the retention of the beak; an end view of the beaks; and the head with the beaks removed. Fig. 3 is a view of the inside of a beak for the extraction of the upper molars of the right side; and Fig. 4 is a similar view of the same part as suited for the left side, the outside of the palatine being shown at D, and part of the inside of the outer beak at E. Fig. 5 is a view of a beak of one of the forceps, the groove in the acting face being highly polished, as a wedge-extracting surface. Fig. 6 is a plan of Fig. 4. Fig. 7 is a plan of both beaks, the same as Fig. 5, but arranged immovably; and Fig. 8 is a plan of the same arrangement as in Fig. 4.

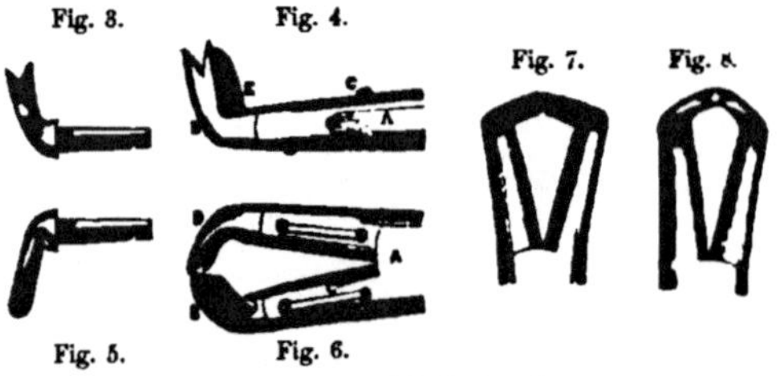


In these instruments any pair of beaks may be adjusted in one pair of handles, so that peculiar portability is secured; for by this means a full set of forceps, with their collateral adjuncts, can be fitted in a small pocket-case.

A very beautiful set of these instruments, made by Mr. W. B. Hilliard, of Glasgow, was shown at the Dublin Exhibition; and a still more complete series has been contributed to the Society of Arts Exhibition for the present season.

Mr. Young, of Monaghan, exhibited a bedstead for invalids, which deserves more than a passing notice. There are few who have not felt the weariness of a sick bed,—where all the attention which the hands of solicitude and affection can apply is often ineffectual in easing the posture of the sick. Physiological reasons might be adduced to show that this irritability arises from a provident tendency in the economy of our nature. All parts of the body are supplied with blood-vessels, and the constant flow of the vital fluid through them is essential to the well-being and vitality of the part; but in the languid state of the circulation of the blood in disease, a very slight pressure or a constrained position is calculated to impede the circulation in those parts on which the weight of the body rests. These, therefore, would be much more liable to loss of vitality, and bed-sores result, were it not that an irritability of the parts is induced and propagated through

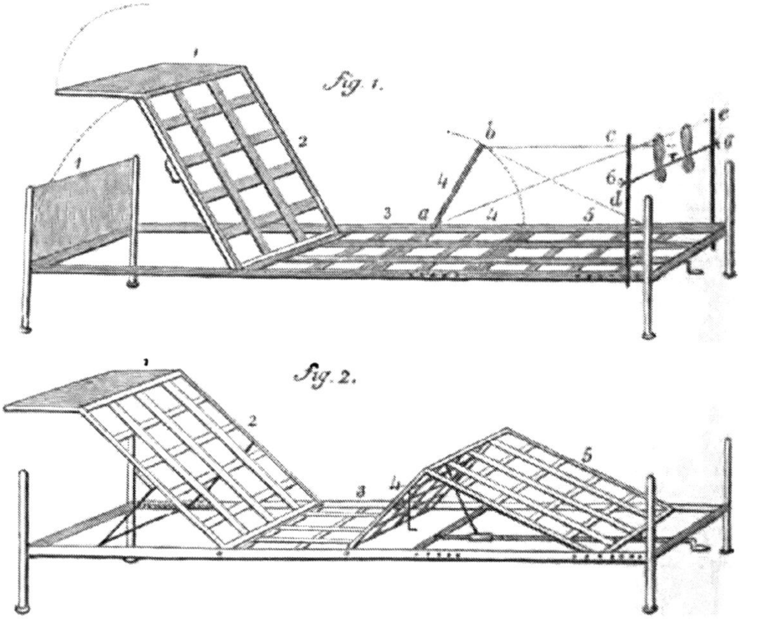


Surgical and Invalid Bed, invented by Andrew Knight Young, Esq., Monaghan.

the general system, and which has thus a protecting influence. Where this, too, is paralyzed in cases in which the head is affected, much depends on the frequent shifting of the posture of the patient. Again, when the circulation is feeble, dependent parts are often surcharged with the fluids of the body, by the mere effect of gravitation, to their manifest injury; and here the frequent change is the more required to counteract this tendency. Many patients mainly owe their recovery to a judicious attention to these circumstances. Now, when we state that by the use of Mr. Young's bed great facilities are afforded in raising, lowering, or changing the position of the body, and that without effort to the patient or any delay, the value of the invention will be appreciated by the reader. There are, besides, several diseases and accidents in which a constrained posture must necessarily be observed, and in these cases it is that a slight change is very grateful to the patient. We might enlarge on this topic, and show how well adapted this invention is for the special treatment of various diseases, but this would, in some degree, be foreign to our present purpose.

The accompanying engravings will convey an idea of the various uses to which this bed can be applied. They exhibit an outward framing of iron of the most ordinary kind, which is immovable. There are six compartments, indicated by the different figures; they hinge over one another so as to allow of being changed and fixed in that position as indicated in the engraving. The head-board, No. 1, is hinged to No. 2, and can be made to remain at any angle required. No. 2 compartment is in the same way attached to No. 3, which is immovable. No. 4 and 5 compartments are also hinged, and can be raised or lowered to any required angle by an endless screw, which is turned by a handle at the lower end of the bed. No. 5 can also be adjusted to the horizontal or any inclined position. The object of the adjustment by the endless screw is that a change of posture can thereby be effected gradually, so as not to derange or shake a diseased or injured limb. Compartment No. 6 is intended to have foot-pieces attached, against which the feet can be supported and secured; and when necessary these can be fixed to any required position. By a slight alteration this bedstead may be converted into an easy chair by lowering one end of compartment 5 towards the ground; and if this could be effected without derangement to the other parts, it would in many cases be a great advantage. In its present state, however, it is a most valuable invention. A three-jointed paliass is used with this bed, over which a good hair mattress is required, and when the bed is not required for cases requiring particular treatment, it can be used as an ordinary bed. In forwarding this invention, and bringing its price within the reach of the means of most institutions, Mr. Kennan, of Dublin, has been a valuable assistant to Surgeon Young.

We should notice, too, Dr. Bevan's new splint, or support for fractured thigh, as one which, in certain cases, will be found useful, and which was also exhibited by Fannin & Co. The case of artificial human eyes, exhibited by Mr. Grossmith, of London, was amongst the most attractive collection in this department, showing, as they did, a very close correspondence to nature, and a very considerable degree of artistic skill in the imitation of the various shades of colour which the iris presents. These, when worn, partake of the motions of the eye-ball, and appear so natural as almost to defy detection. It was for excellence in the manufacture of these that Mr. Grossmith received a prize medal at the Exhibition of 1851; he also exhibited several specimens of artificial legs, arms, &c., which appear to have been carefully made, and to possess lightness and strength of material, with most natural flexibility. The case of artificial eyes, from Grey & Halford, London, presented a remarkable series of glass eyes, exhibiting, in various stages, the different diseases to which these organs are liable; some of these imitations of acute inflammation of the eye seemed very accurately to represent nature. A set of these, if at all perfect, would be a great addition to an ophthalmic museum, for instruction.

The acoustic instruments exhibited by Mr. F. Rein, of London, displayed that ingenuity for which the manufacturer of them has earned a well-deserved reputation, while they illustrate in a striking manner what science has done in this department.

Among the other inventions possessed of local interest we may specialize those of Mr. Johnston, of Kilkenny, for the treatment of broken limbs; and of Surgeon Lestrange, of this city. Messrs. Read and Co., and Mr. Robertson, and others, exhibited general collections, which creditably sustained the character of our native manufacture in this department.

Among the smaller articles, many of which were deserving of special attention in this department, we may notice the siphonia exhibited by Mr. Edward O'Connell, of Bury, Lancashire, who is also the inventor and patentee. To nurses this promises to become a valuable desideratum, as it supplies to an infant a good substitute for the breast, the nipple being at once soft, durable, and free from any unpleasant taste or smell. Where, from accidental circumstances, the child is deprived of its mother's milk, or in travelling, the siphonia will, we have no doubt, come to be very generally used.—b.

## IV.—HOROLOGICAL INSTRUMENTS.

The term horology (Greek, ὡρολόγιον) is applied to the art of constructing machines for the measurement of time, and includes every form of instrument used for that purpose from the earliest periods of which we have any records. Among the rudest nations, before the invention of any contrivance for the division of the interval between sunrise and sunset, the lapse of the day was indicated by hours or portions with considerable accuracy. The simple mode of calculation adopted was afforded by the shifting shadows of objects illumined by the sun. This evidently suggested the sun-dial: the earliest time-measurer, as some assert, judging from its simplicity. In the sacred writings we have a notice of the dial of King Ahaz, above seven centuries before the Christian era. Herodotus states that the Greeks derived them from the Chaldeans, probably through the Babylonian astronomer Berosus, who taught at Athens two hundred years later. It is not, however, unlikely, that the clepsydræ were still more ancient, as they were used in Asia, China, India, Egypt, Greece, and in Chaldea itself, as far back as historic investigation extends. They were found in Britain by Julius Cæsar, and it is supposed were introduced by the Phœnicians. The most ancient devices for the artificial measurement of time were, therefore, the sun-dial and the clepsydra,—one indicating the hours by the lengthening, shortening, and turning of the shadows of trees, rocks, and like objects: the other, by the equable flow of a liquid. Both were superseded by clocks and watches, whose movements are regulated by toothed wheels, weights, and springs.

The regular motion of the dropping of water was, in the remotest ages, by a very simple mechanism, made to indicate in a rude manner the lapse of time; but the perfected clepsydra, or water-clock, was not constructed until B. C. 145. In the instrument invented by Ctesibius of Alexandria, a jar was placed containing water, which slowly passed through a hole at the bottom, while the oar of a miniature boat on the surface, as it sank with the fall of the water, pointed out the hours, which were marked on the side of the vessel. It is asserted that toothed wheels were applied to clepsydræ by the Alexandrian, but although they were known for a considerable time before, the fact of their application is very doubtful. These water-clocks, however, even in their most perfected forms, have never been competent to the accurate measurement of time. Their whole principle lies in the regular dropping of the water, but this cannot be maintained in consequence of the varying depth and weight of the liquid in the containing jar, and the changes of barometric pressure. As this defect is practically irremediable, clepsydræ have long since ceased to be used, except in India and some other countries of the East.

An ingenious application of the principle of the clepsydra has been employed for the measurement of short intervals of time. Mercury is made to flow from a small opening in the bottom of a vessel kept filled to a fixed height. The contrivance, which is exceedingly simple, is described by Brande :—" The stream is intercepted at the moment of noting an event, and led into a receiver, into which it continues to run till the moment of noting any other event, when the intercepting cause is suddenly removed. The stream then flows into its original course. The weight of the mercury received, compared with the weight of that which passes through the orifice in a given time, observed by the clock, gives the interval between the events"—of course with the most minute accuracy.

Sand-glasses are somewhat allied to the clepsydra, and were of early invention. At least three centuries before the Christian era, they were employed in the East, and were extensively used in Europe some three or four hundred years since.

The octagonal Temple of the Winds at Athens, which still stands, exhibits on each side the lines of a vertical sun-dial, and the centres of the gnomons. In Dr. Adams' Roman Antiquities we learn that Anaximander of Miletus (610, B. C.) invented sun-dials at Lacedemon in the time of Cyrus the Great. They were unknown at Rome until three centuries later, when one was erected near the Temple of Quirinus. Hemispherical dial-plates were used by the ancients, and the radius, by which the shade is thrown, was placed in the direction of the north polar-star. Vertical dial-plates were employed subsequently, and these also gave place to the horizontal, in which the plane of the plate is parallel to the horizon. With these last all are familiar. But sun-dials, although supplemented by moon-dials, were imperfect as well as incomplete indicators of time. By the invention of the clock all ruder contrivances were completely superseded.

The invention of the common clock for registering time, and the period at which it was first employed, are equally involved in obscurity. The most ancient clock, of which a description has been preserved, is that of Henry De Wyck, or Vic, a German, erected in 1379; for Gerbert's invention is scarcely entitled to be considered a clock in our acceptation of the term, as he made use of his observations with the pole-star. The principle of the instrument was, however, known two hundred years previously. Hamberger supposes that we are indebted for it to the Saracens. Germany also, with some grounds, claims the discovery. In De Wyck's clock the motion was regulated by the balance with weights instead of the pendulum now employed. This construction was used during the fourteenth century, and with a few trivial improvements the German's invention was the sole time-measurer till the time of Galileo. It has been stated that the art of clock-making was introduced into Europe by the clergy. Enjoying wealth and leisure, combined with a liberal scientific education, many devoted themselves to horology, in order to secure an accurate method of time-measurement by which to regulate the numerous stated services of religion.

De Wyck's clock, compared with modern mechanism, was comparatively simple, and the amateur student of the art might judiciously commence by mastering the principle and details of its construction. It had two parts, the crown-wheel or escapement, and the balance or machinery of counteraction. The sinking of a weight attached to a cord passed round a cylinder set in motion one toothed wheel or pinion, which communicated with another till the movement reached the escapement wheel. This wheel so acted on two levers that the rotatory motion of the wheelwork was rendered alternating or vibratory. To modify and counterpoise the increasing momentum of the weight by which the motion was originated—which in uncoiling the cord from the cylinder more rapidly as it sank to the ground caused the wheels to rotate, the balance to vibrate, and the indicators on the face to revolve more speedily—De Wyck loaded the balance with two weights, and the farther these are removed from the axis on which the balance is fixed, the more heavily will they resist the escapement of the levers, and the rapidity of the rotation, till the proper measurement of time be attained. The use of this counteracting operation may be illustrated by taking away the pendulum of a modern clock—the oscillations of which are useful to the same end as the vibrations of the balance. Having taken away the pendulum, the compensatory principle is lost, the motion of the wheelwork becomes more rapid, and the sound of the ticking more hurried and distinct.

The principle of *regulation*, whether by oscillation or rotation, is of primary importance in clockwork. It is not only useful in the ingenious and intricate mechanism of clocks and watches, but also in numerous pieces of machinery. By the invention of the pendulum one great part of De Wyck's contrivance was completely changed—the balance. Although Galileo discovered the natural law by which its oscillatory motion is governed, he did not apply the pendulum to the measurement of time. As a student of medicine, he first endeavoured to ascertain by its means the rate and variations of the pulse. In 1657, however, Hüygens, the Dutch philosopher, added the pendulum to De Wyck's clock. Improvements were subsequently made by Dr. Hooke, in 1680; and George Graham, an Englishman, in the commencement of the eighteenth century.

Compensation pendulums were devised by Graham. The variations of pendulum rods caused by changes of temperature so increased and diminished the number of their oscillations in a given time, as to lead to sensible errors. Graham's ingenious method of overcoming this difficulty, with some trifling improvement, is still in use. It consists of a cylindrical tube containing mercury, attached to the bottom of a steel rod in the arc of its oscillation. The steel rod lengthening by warmth of temperature, the mercury expands and rises: shortening by cold, it contracts, and sinks. By this means the arc of oscillation remains at the same distance from the point of suspension of the pendulum, and it remains unaffected. The mercurial pendulum, as improved by recent artists, and provided with the *dead-beat escapement*, also invented by Graham, is found to vary not more than a quarter of a second daily.

Till the middle of the sixteenth century clocks were large and cumbrous—watches were unknown. To the construction of portable time-measurers for the apartment and for the pocket, the obstacles were the weights and the pendulum. But ingenuity provided a substitute for both. The introduction of the *main-spring* inaugurated a new epoch in horology, and with the *fusee*, which followed it almost immediately, led to the production of watches: the most useful, most perfect, and most ingenious of mechanical contrivances. The manufacture of a watch includes the knowledge of many distinct arts, and its apparently simple combination of springs and wheels involves many principles of geometrical and natural science. To be a creditable artisan in this department an acquaintance with a wide range of subjects is required, and a manipulative delicacy of the most exquisite character. The mainspring is a coil of elastic steel, enclosed in a drum, to the inner side of which the outer end of the coil is attached, the inner end being fixed to an axis at the centre of the drum, round which it may be wound. By the recoil of this spring the drum is made to revolve as often as it makes turns in unwinding. This is the moving power. But the loss of energy of the spring in uncoiling, which would decrease the rapidity of the wheel-movements, must be compensated, and the "fusee" is a device to correct the inequalities of the mainspring. In winding a watch the chain is wound off the barrel on this spiral-grooved cone—when so wound, the spring is at its full power, but the chain being then round the smallest part of the cone or fusee, the energy of the spring is least active, while as the spring relaxes the cone is enlarged, and its influence increases. The fusee is a very beautiful as well as ingenious contrivance.

The escapement is a most important part of the watch, and by it the different kinds are distinguished. Of this peculiar construction there are four kinds. The old vertical watch has the crown-wheel escapement, the mechanism of which is well known. In Graham's contrivance, which he designated the horizontal escapement, the motion is given to a hollow toothed cut in the cylindrical spire of the balance by peculiarly formed teeth working from the crown-wheel. The lever escapement is of a singular kind, the impulse being communicated by a lever attached to a crutch acting on a wheel of a particular form. Hooke's duplex escapement, and the detached escapement of Berthoud, would require a more detailed and technical description than can here be given. Watches furnished with mechanism of these two last kinds are the most accurate time-keepers. Marine chronometers have invariably the detached escapement.

The balance wheel is designed to regulate the rotation of the wheelwork; and the pivot-holes in which it revolves are, for the sake of durability, frequently made of diamonds, rubies, &c., "jewelled" as it is termed. To the balance there was added the balance-spring superseding the necessity of weight or pendulum, which is certainly a most ingenious contrivance. Three philosophers have claimed the honour of its invention —Dr. Hooke, the Abbé Hautefeuille, and the Dutchman Hüygens. The merit is usually accorded to the first named of these parties. An extremely delicate mechanism, called the cylindrical heliacal spring, is used in marine chronometers. These springs have been secured from rust by coating them with gold by the electro-metallurgic process. This improvement, which is due to the late Mr. Dent, of London, was followed by another of a very singular character by the same gentleman. He contrived hair-springs of *glass* instead of steel; but although they have been considered preferable, their great drawback is the difficulty of making them with accuracy.

But the watch, however perfectly adjusted, is liable to vary in the time it indicates, in consequence of changes of temperature, which must be regulated by *compensation*. In the small mechanism of the pocket time-keeper there was no room for the introduction of mercury, as in the compensation-pendulum; but the reach of ingenuity was not exhausted. Compensation is made by the various degrees of expansion in different metals, and the compound balances constructed on this principle are as curious as they are useful. The compensation balance consists of a double rim or ring, the outer side of which is brass, while the inner is steel, to which the brass is united when in another state. A steel bar joins the opposite sides of the ring, the whole steel part being filed out of a piece of metal. At each side of this bar one half of the ring is cut away, and the balance loaded with small screws or sliding weights to regulate the rate of the chronometer or watch. The compensation is, then, effected thus:—the elastic force of the balance spring is *diminished* by increase of temperature, and consequently the machine would lose time, were it not that the same heat expands the outer rim or brazen part more than the steel part within it (brass expanding and contracting by heat and cold more than steel). The two rims not being able to separate, the whole arm of the ring curves *inwards*, the inertia or checking-weight of the balance is lessened, the hair or balance-spring needs less force to influence it in the same degree as before, and by this means its loss of power is compensated. Cold increasing the elastic force of the spring, precisely the reverse of this operation takes place, and the result is the same. The compensation-curb is another piece of mechanism for correcting variations arising from changes of temperature.

Of watches there are now great varieties, distinguished by their construction. The common watch has not the intricate and delicate construction of the duplex, the lever, or the detached escapement time-keeper. But the *chronometer* combines all, and also most of the peculiarities invented from time to time to insure perfect accuracy. The name is chiefly applied to marine time-keepers, the correctness of which, in indicating *equal time*, is of such absolute importance. In the Exhibition there were several beautiful specimens of marine chronometers.

Let us return in a general manner to the history of clock-work, and the artistic improvements introduced in connexion with the time-keeping mechanism. First of these devices is the arrangement for striking the hours. We cannot tell when the alarum was added to the clock machinery. In the seventeenth century striking clocks became the rage, however, and from telling the hours they were made, in order to suit the taste of the time, to determine the quarters, and not only the quarters but the number of the hour just elapsed at each time of minute-striking. Tompion's clocks struck forty-four blows at twelve, and 131 at the hour following. Repeating clocks were invented by an English clergyman, about 1670. Enormous bells have been attached to clocks, the dimensions and weight of which are curious. Tom of Oxford weighs 9894 pounds, and is 22 feet in circumference; Peter of Yorkminster is 21,000 pounds weight. But these sink into comparative insignificance beside the bell of Rouen Cathedral, which weighs not less than 36,000 pounds, and the seven bells of Pekin, which are said to be 12,000 pounds weight each. The regal bell, however, is that of Moscow, which is 67 feet in circumference, 21 feet high, and 443,000 pounds! It is now unemployed, and probably will so remain until Titans repeople the earth.

In the illumination of clocks on churches and other public buildings translucent dials have been from an early period employed, with a strongly-reflected light placed behind. The remarkably brilliant Bude reflectors are now generally used for this purpose.

Numerous interesting curiosities of mechanism have been attached to clock-work. In the earliest stages of horological science, some singularly ingenious contrivances were adopted, indicating the flux and reflux of the tides, the relative positions of the heavenly bodies, and other artistical fancies. The seventeenth century clocks were almost invariably ornamented with processions of saints, and sacred representations, and so universal did the curiosity mania become at that period that scarcely a public clock in any place of importance was without its characteristic extravaganza. Of late years utility has been more regarded; and the old-fashioned clocks, representing above the dial-plate the passing of the seasons, or the stages of human life, or astronomical memorabilia, are now curiosities, not only on account of their artistic peculiarities, but from their rareness and antiquity. The puzzle-clock, however, is still a favourite as a neat ornamental time-piece. At first sight, it is not a little perplexing to those unacquainted with its mechanism to observe an hour-hand fixed to the centre of a crystal dial, completely transparent, and having no visible connexion with works of any kind. A piece of glass itself, revolving in the interior of the dial, is the requisite communication with the clock movement. But the electric clocks are the marvel of horological curiosities. Though of the most simple construction they are very singular. Electric currents are the prime movers of these machines; plates of copper and zinc being buried in the ground to the depth of about nine feet, and thus kept continually moist, are the generators of the current of electricity, which is conveyed by wires to the pendulum. The current is led down the rod of the pendulum, which is made of wood, to a magnetic coil a little above the regulating bob, and placed next to two permanent magnets. The magnets maintain the oscillation, and about the centre of the rod of the pendulum an apparatus for alternately making and breaking the circuit is placed. A peculiarity of the electric mechanism is, that if all the clock-work of a city were connected together, and constructed on the simple principle just described, one electric current would set the whole in motion.

Most important modifications of clock-work are employed for various useful purposes: to indicate *space and number* as well as time. The principle in all is, however, the same. It is in the application of the mechanical motion, originated and regulated by springs, weights, and wheels, that the difference of result is attained. Automata, by means of clock mechanism, move in imitation of living action, and have even been made to dance and sing. Numerous varieties of machines for registering natural changes in temperature, in barometric pressure, and recording numbers, are governed by the same principle. Meters for the measurement of gases and liquids are also regulated by clock-work, as well as anemometers for ascertaining the force and direction of the wind. Odometers, for determining the distance passed over by vehicles or pedestrians, are very ingenious applications of the same contrivances. But the most complicated as well as most useful machines so regulated are those employed for continuing long and tedious numerical calculations. In astronomy, geography, navigation, and mathematical investigations, they are invaluable. Mr. Babbage constructed one capable of reckoning with 4000 figures! and another which not only computed but printed a large number of copies of the table of figures ascertained! Some idea of the amazing ingenuity of this contrivance may be formed when it is recollected that in a single process of calculation by this machine there are not less than 136 repetitions of the same train of wheel-work!

Some attempts have been made in Europe to construct an instrument resembling the Chinese gong, under the control of clock-work, with little success. The metal of which the gongs are composed is not so hard as that used for clock-bells. It has been said that the great secret of the Chinese makers, in giving them that strength of tone which is their characteristic, lies in their mode of hammering them after they have been cast. In this process, anvil, hammer, and gong must be beaten under a very considerable degree of heat, nearly to the colour of a deep red viewed in a dark place. A Chinese gong would break in pieces, if hammered while cold or but partially heated. The human body is scarcely able to endure the heat of the apartment in which the operation must be performed. Experiments have been made where the temperature of 240° for a short time has been borne, but this is the limit; and thence we may judge of the practicability of hammering the gong in a place sufficiently heated. Those gongs which have been brought to these countries were, however, evidently cast, and subsequently hammered to give them firmness of tone. In China the gongs are sacred furniture, and, therefore, can be only procured with great difficulty by the traveller. Many specimens are, notwithstanding, to be found in these countries. They are manifestly hammered out of a flat plate, and their sound is full, clear, and sonorous. As a horologic appliance gongs of various descriptions are extensively used in the East.

It would be here somewhat out of place to enter into a detailed and technological description of the various kinds of chime clocks and bell-music which are comprised under the general term, musical clocks. The different kinds of these instruments are those by which changes are rung, or the quarters struck on two or more bells, or airs played on a series of nine, twelve, or sixteen bells, tuned to their respective notes on the scale. Many ingenious methods are adopted in pricking tunes on the music-barrels of clocks. Organ-clocks are also elaborate and curious mechanical contrivances. A new species of clock-music has of late years been invented at Geneva, managed by steel springs. The great peculiarity of the mechanism is the smallness of the space it occupies. It is placed not only in snuff-boxes and watches, but in seals, and even rings. A double set of springs also is necessary, varying in number from sixteen to twenty-four, or upwards. These springs are easily tuned to different notes by thinning, shortening, or lengthening them. The effect of this will be perceived from the tones produced by the tongues of steel trumps of varying size and thickness. Although these musical spring-works are merely toys—perfectly useless except for amusing the young—the very remarkable ingenuity displayed in their construction is deserving of notice.

Several English and Irish manufacturers exhibited highly finished and creditable specimens of horologic workmanship, both in clocks and watches. The exposition was almost exclusively confined to time-pieces and domestic clocks; and those which it did contain possessed little novel in principle, or very attractive in workmanship, though excellent in their way. Several marine chronometers, of the newest kind, were also to be found in some collections—those contributed by Mr. M'Master, of Grafton-street, being so arranged as to show the various stages in their manufacture. Among the curiosities of clock-work, Mr. Scriber, of Westmoreland-street, presented to notice a complete watch set in diamonds, and not larger than a fourpenny silver piece, with others artistically ornamented; and, in addition, musical clocks and boxes, in great variety.

The Ball-Clock, an interesting piece of mechanism, exhibited by Messrs. Waterhouse and Co., attracted considerable attention, as an ingenious and ornamental contrivance. A ball perpetually moves along a shifting plate from left to right and from right to left, the plate rising and falling every half minute, as this ball reaches the turning-place in its path of motion. Sir William Congreve was the inventor of this beautiful clock. The ball is the motive-power, and is made of speculum metal. It is not larger than a swan-shot, and whilst it rolls along its grooves the works are quiescent. But when the ball has arrived at an angle where, by a spring, it is propelled back again to retrace another groove, the works shift into a rapid and momentous motion. The dial-plate indicates accurately the hours, minutes, and seconds of time. A distance equal to seven miles is travelled over by the ball in every twenty-four hours.

The English manufacturers have reached the acme of perfection in clock-work as far as utility is concerned, although in artistic workmanship foreigners may surpass them. Genevese watches, a large quantity of which is sold in these countries, are accurate time-keepers when good of their kind, but it is sometimes difficult to repair them. The medals for chronometers were mostly awarded, at the Exhibition of 1851, to London makers. In astronomical clocks the foreign and native articles were equally distinguished. Among turret-clocks Mr. Dent's was the most remarkable. It was an attractive object if only from its great size, the pendulum being not less than eight feet long and above two cwt. The wonderful accuracy of this clock may be estimated from the fact, that its "accumulated error" for more than two months of the time in which it was exhibited at the Crystal Palace was only 2·8 seconds, or in four millions of vibrations performed during that period the pendulum lost *scarcely three beats!*

Watches, as well as the commoner forms of clocks, are now manufactured so generally, that little peculiar excellence could be expected to be found in those made by any individual exhibitor. In England the chief places of the manufacture are, however, London, Liverpool, and Coventry. Even the watches said to be made elsewhere are indebted to these places for the principal parts of their mechanism. The trade in these localities is not so much the completion of watches for sellers throughout the country, as the finishing of such portions as the main-spring, chain, and escapement. But by far the greater proportion of the watches of the world are still made in Switzerland. To meet the demand for cheapness they are constructed in general very imperfectly, and what they want in solid value is made up by a handsome exterior. But external ornament is the smallest item in the expense of manufacture, and oftener indicates the worthless article than the useful. In watches (as in everything else) the pinchbeck only is cheap: the genuine brings a price sufficient to requite the skill and care of the maker. It may be stated in conclusion that of all forms of time-keepers for general use, the lever-watch is the best. Not only is it capable of great accuracy, but will remain uninjured by violent exercise which would disarrange or destroy a duplex or vertical movement.—J. A. S.

---

1. ALLISON, R., Wardour-street, London, Manufacturer and Proprietor (exhibited by J. Scates, 26, College-green, Dublin.)—Bichord grand pianoforte in rosewood; microchordon pianofortes of rosewood and walnut.

2. BARTER, R., St. Anne's Hill, Blarney, Co. Cork, Inventor.—Apparatus for applying cold water to the head without wetting other parts of the person.

3. BAXTER, J. P., Lower Baggot-street, Inventor and Proprietor.—Stethoscopes, with lateral tubes, containing a fluid to increase the power of hearing.

4. BEAUFORT, R., Sackville-street, Dublin, Inventor and Manufacturer.—Lenses with accelerators; photographs.

5. BENNETT, W., Cheapside, London.—Large turret clock.

6. BEVAN, P., M.D., Lower Baggot-street, Dublin, Inventor.—A new rectilinear screw splint for fracture of the thigh.

7. BEVINGTON & SONS, Greek-street, Soho-square, London, Manufacturer.—A church organ, in carved Gothic case, with gilt speaking-pipes in front, containing three complete manuals from CC to F; great choir and swell organ, with a sixteen foot pedal, five coupling movements, composition pedals, and thirty-two stops; a boudoir organ, in carved cabinet rosewood case, five stops and pedals.

8. BLUNT, H., Shrewsbury.—Three drawings of remarkable portions of the moon's surface, from observations made with a Newtonian reflecting telescope, of 9 in. aperture 7 ft. focal length, and a magnifying power of 400.

9. BRAUNHELDER, CHEVR. A. DE, Warsaw (Poland).—Model of a music or book-stand, cut out of the solid piece of wood, and working on an ingenious hinge of the same piece, designed and cut out by Mr. Fall, of Manchester.

10. BRAY, JOHN, Westmoreland-street, Dublin, Manufacturer and Proprietor.—Enlarged double-action harps; with stands, music-desks, and stools.

11. BRODRICK, WILLIAM, Essex-quay, Dublin, Manufacturer.—Clocks; gold and silver watches.

12. BROPHY, J., College-green, Dublin.—Case of artificial mineral teeth.

13. BRYSON, J. M., Prince's-street, Edinburgh, Manufacturer.—A series of Nicol's prisms and crystals for the polarization of light.

14. BUSSELL, H., Westmoreland-street, Dublin.—Pianofortes, harps, music, military musical instruments.

15. CADBY, C., Liquorpond-street, London, Inventor and Manufacturer.—A rosewood semi-grand pianoforte, with royal patent, suspended, and adjustable sounding-board; an elegant rosewood oblique pianoforte, with three strings; handsomely carved case; two pianoforte backs, one with the ordinary bracing, the other with patent iron truss bracing; a model to explain the latter, showing its superiority over the former.

16. CALDWELL, S. M., Mountjoy-square, Dublin, Proprietor.—Carved ebony piccolo pianoforte, manufactured by the late John M'Culloch, Belfast.

17. CHANCE, BROTHERS, & Co., Birmingham, Manufacturers.—First order fixed dioptric lighthouse apparatus, with catadioptric zones constructed according to the system of Fresnel.

18. CHANCELLOR, G. W., Sackville-street, Dublin, Inventor and Manufacturer.—Small turret-clock, with right-angle dead-beat escapement.

19. CHAPMAN, J., Essex-quay, Dublin, Manufacturer and Proprietor.—Three-part skeleton brass eight-day clock, with Galway marble pedestal; chronometer clock.

20. CHAPPIUS, A., St. Mary Axe, London, Manufacturer.—Patent daylight reflectors, for diffusing light into dark places.

21. CHARRIÈRE, J. F., Paris.—Case of surgical instruments.

22. CLAUDET, A., Regent-street, London.—Stereoscopes and photographic specimens.

23. COX, G., Barbican, London, Manufacturer.—An orthochronograph, a portable instrument for ascertaining correct time by equal altitudes of the sun; a periphan, illustrating astronomical phenomena; beam draining levels; movable rackwork astronomical diagrams for the phantasmagoria lantern.

24. DE LA MOTTE, P. H., London.—Photographs taken by the collodion process.

25. DERING, G. E., Lockleys, Welwyn, Hertfordshire, Inventor and Patentee.—Electric telegraph instruments on improved principles, in communication with the Telegraph Office, Eden-quay, for the transmission of messages to and fro, by means of the wires of the Electric Telegraph Company of Ireland.

26. DILLON, THOMAS ARTHUR, Upper Buckingham-street, Dublin, Inventor.—Portable photographic camera, intended for glass plates, paper, or daguerreotype process; compensating pendulum, homogeneous metal; pendulum and clock arranged within a glass chamber, and preserved at an invariable temperature by a casing of steam; self-registering barometer and storm courier.

27. DOBBYN, G., Wicklow-street, Dublin.—Astronomical clock with mercurial pendulum, (at sidereal time); regulator clock with zinc compensation pendulum; tell-tale or watchman's clock; railway, chamber, and house clocks, &c.

28. DONEGAN, J. Upper Ormond-quay, and Dame-street, Dublin.—Gold and silver watches.

29. DONOVAN, M., Clare-street, Dublin, Inventor.—Philosophical instruments, viz.: a table gas-lamp, generating gas by machinery within; improved galvanometer; a volta-magnetometer for measuring and regulating the magnetism of galvanometer needles; a combined hygrometer, psychrometer, and hygroscope, for indicating changes in the dryness of the atmosphere.

30. EDWARDS, R. J., Burslem, Staffordshire, Inventor and Proprietor.—Instrument for giving strength and flexibility to the fingers of instrumental performers.

31. THE ELECTRIC TELEGRAPH COMPANY, Lothbury, London.—A system of electric telegraphs for communication with various parts of the Exhibition Building; comprising single and double needle instruments, batteries, bells, magneto-machines; method of insulation; maps of telegraph in operation.

32. FANNIN & Co., Grafton-street, Dublin, Proprietors.—New aneurism compressors for the treatment of aneurism by compression, as finally improved by A. Carte, M.D.

33. FLEURY, Rev. C. M., Upper Leeson-street.—Harmonic flute, invented by a clergyman; *properties*—vast increase of tone, perfect tune, open ventage, with facility of fingering; *compass*—three octaves and two tones.

34. FREEMAN, ST. GEORGE, Beresford-street, Waterford, Designer and Manufacturer.—Specimens of the various modes of adapting artificial teeth to the mouth; mineral teeth; teeth and palates, carved from the tusk of the hippopotamus; contrivance for regulating the growth of children's teeth; specimens of carious natural teeth.

35. GARDNER, R. K. & Co., Grafton-street, Dublin.—Humming-bird clock.

36. GEARY, BROTHERS, Grafton-street, Dublin, Designers and Proprietors.—Photographic pictures.

37. GLOAG, J. W., 11th Hussars.—Specimens of seals made by the electrotype process.

38. GLUKMAN, PROFESSOR, Upper Sackville-street, Dublin, Inventor and Proprietor.—Machine for polishing daguerreotype plates; photographic specimens; stand for camera; electric apparatus for communicating between guards and engine-drivers of railway trains, house-bells, and knockers; regulator for electric light.

39. GODDARD, J. T., Jesse-cottage, Whitton, near Isleworth, Middlesex, Manufacturer.—An achromatic five-feet telescope.

40. GORE, G., Broad-street, Birmingham, Inventor and Manufacturer.—Improved medical galvanic apparatus.

41. GRAY, J., Strand-street, Liverpool, Manufacturer.—Binnacles and compasses on an improved principle, for counteracting vibratory action.

42. GRAY & HALFORD, Goswell-road, London, Manufacturer.—Artificial eyes; dolls' eyes; eyes for wax figures; animals' and birds' eyes.

43. GROSSMITH, W. R., Fleet-street, London, Manufacturer.—Artificial human eyes (worn without pain or operation in every case where the sight has been lost), to which the prize medal was exclusively awarded at the Great Exhibition in London in 1851; artificial legs, with new patent action knee and ankle joints, enabling the wearer to walk with perfect ease wherever amputated; artificial hands and arms, noses, fingers, &c.

44. GRUBB, THOMAS, Leinster-square, Rathmines, Dublin, Inventor and Manufacturer.—Large equatorial instrument, with improved clock-work, and system of counterpoise, carrying achromatic telescope of 12 inches clear aperture, and 20 feet focus; model equatorial, the form being specially adapted for carrying large Newtonian reflectors (to 6 feet diameter), the present model carrying one of 15 inches; small equatorial, adapted to refracting telescopes, of from 3 to 5 inches aperture; case of achromatic object-glasses for telescopes, and photographic purposes; improved oxyhydrogen microscope, polariscope, and economic double lantern requiring only one half the usual quantity of the mixed gases for dissolving views.

45. HAGGARD, W. D., Bank of England, Inventor.—A double protractor for measuring angles and distance at the same time.

46. HALL, G. F., Norfolk-street, Fitzroy-square, London, Inventor.—A standard bar measurer and pyrometer; a philosophical apparatus for measuring minute differences of length, also adapted for a pyrometer to give to the millionth of an inch the ratio of expansion of metals.

47. HANLIN & ROBERT, Westmoreland-street, Dublin, Inventors and Manufacturers.—Eight-day clock; marine chronometers; gold and silver Geneva watches.

48. HANSON, G., & CHADWICK, D., Salford, Manchester.—Patent high-pressure water-meter, on a new principle, whereby the smallest to the largest quantities of water can be accurately measured, and the water delivered without destroying the pressure.

49. HARRISON, C. W., Larkfield Lodge, Richmond, near London, Inventor and Proprietor.—Specimens of Harrison's patent insulated subterranean electric telegraph lines, protected on Chatterton's principle; model of electro-magnetic motive-power engine.

50. HAYDEN, CHARLES, Balbriggan.—Specimens of electrotype.

51. HEAPS, J. K., Leeds, Yorkshire, Manufacturer and Proprietor.—Violoncello constructed on mathematical and geometrical principles, by which superior quality of tone is obtained, also increased vibration, evenness, freedom, and power.

52. HILLIARD, W. B., Buchanan-street, Glasgow, Manufacturer.—Surgical instruments, tooth forceps, invented and patented by Mr. J. A. Young; manufactured by exhibiter.

53. HINTON, C., Corporation-row, Clerkenwell, London, Manufacturer.—Watch and time-piece enamel dials; dials in the various stages of manufacture, with specimens of the different kinds of enamel used.

54. HODGSON, Mrs., Baggot-street, Dublin.—Stethotenist, or chest expander.

55. HORNE, THORNWAITE, & WOOD, Newgate-street, London, Manufacturers.—Daguerreotype apparatus, with improved bromine apparatus for preparing the plates; portable folding camera and compound achromatic lens, with apparatus for the calotype and collodion process; portraits, &c., produced by the collodion process; medical galvanic apparatus, and instruments for administering galvanism.

56. HUG, WILLIAM, South Great George's-street, Dublin.—A chronometer time-piece.

57. JAMIESON, J., Grafton-street, Dublin.—Regulator clock.

58. JOHNSON, ZACHARIAH, Kilkenny, Inventor.—Surgical instruments, viz., Protean fracture splint; convertible suspension plane; tracheal trochar; a fracture bed; portable dactyloplast.

59. KIRKMAN, J. & SON, London, Inventors and Manufacturers (Mackintosh & Co., Rutland-square, Dublin, Exhibiters).—Pianofortes of various styles and descriptions.

60. KNOX, Rev. T., Proprietor.—Large burning-glass, five feet diameter.

61. L'ESTRANGE, F., Dawson-street, Dublin, Inventor.—Surgical instruments; patent trusses for the cure of hernia; lithotritic instruments; instruments for arranging fractures of the lower jaw.

62. LITTLE, R. J., Bloomfield, Charlton-road, Woolwich, Inventor.—Apparatus for loss of the arm, attached to a canvass waistcoat; connecting tap with double plug; couplings for horses, basins, and drain pipes.

63. LOVER, WILLIAM, Talbot-street, Dublin, Inventor and Proprietor.—Educational models; novel arrangement of hydrogen generator for the oxyhydrogen microscope; working model of electric clock, with novel galvanic contact-maker; electro-magnetic machinery moved by compound levers and lever of La Garousse; galvanic battery for electrotyping, and electroplating, on a new arrangement; plan for illustrating the pump-like action of the heart, with other philosophical models.

64. LOWRY, S., Spencer-street, Goswell-road, London, Inventor and Manufacturer.—Marine chronometer air and water tight; a collection of watch movements in the rough and finished state.

65. LYONS, M., Suffolk-street, Birmingham, Inventor and Producer.—Apparatus for bright electro and magneto plating and gilding, with specimens illustrating the process.

66. MAYALL, J. E., Regent-street, London.—Views of the Great Exhibition of 1851, and other specimens of daguerreotype.

67. M'MASTER, MAXWELL, Grafton-street, Dublin, Manufacturer.—A turret-clock; chronometers, with examples of the various stages in the process of manufacture.

68. M'NAUGHT, W., Glasgow, Manufacturer.—Steam-engine indicator and instruments for measuring the power exerted by steam-engine: oil test, an instrument for measuring the relative tenacity or friction of oils.

69. M'NEILL, J., Capel-street, Dublin, Manufacturer.—Cornopeans with front and back action, of improved construction; cornetto in D flat inventor of; Cambridge trumpet-bugle.

70. MUTZLER, G., Great Marlborough-street, London, Manufacturer (MARCUS MOSES, Westmoreland-street, Exhibiter).—Cottage and microchordon pianofortes; an oak harmonium, with patent percussion and harmoniphone attachment.

71. MOENIG, C., Leadenhall-street, London, Proprietor.—Portable galvano-voltaic batteries, for medical practice, and to be worn on the body for curative purposes; figures exhibiting their application; interrupting apparatus and other accessories.

72. MOORE, B. R., & J., Clerkenwell, London.—An eight-day clock, chiming hours and quarters upon cathedral bells.

73. MORRISON, J. D., Elder-street, Edinburgh, Manufacturer.—Artificial teeth, made from the raw material; specimens of the raw materials in the natural and prepared state.

74. MOSES, MARCUS, Westmoreland-street, Dublin, Importer.—Specimens of pianofortes and harps, of different classes, and in various woods, manufactured to order, expressly for the Exhibition, by Broadwood and Sons, Collard and Collard, and S. & P. Erard.

75. MURRAY, Sir J., M.D., Temple-street, Dublin.—A new instrument for comparing the relative specific gravities of different liquids, at the same identical density and temperature of the atmosphere.

76. NELSON, W., Dame-street, Dublin, Manufacturer.—A level to be used on top of walking-stick; a plumb level for laying down roads, drains, &c.; concave lens for landscape drawing; convex lens for landscape drawing; portable boat compass.

77. NEWALL, R. S., Gateshead.—Samples of submarine telegraph cables, similar to those laid down between Portpatrick and Donaghadee, Dover and Calais, Dover and Ostend, St. Petersburgh and Cronstadt, &c.

78. NORTH, T., Grafton-street, Dublin.—A skeleton lever repeating clock on marble stand, strikes the hours on a large gong, and the half-hours on a bell; an electro-magnetic clock; a silver alarum-watch of great antiquity; ladies and gentlemen's gold watches; an electro-magnetic therapeuticon.

79. NUNN, R. M., M. R. C. S. L., Wexford, Inventor.—The universal hydrometer, an instrument to ascertain the specific gravity of liquids, its range, including 0·600 and 2·000; medical inspirators, for the more exact and efficient administration of chloroform and other anæsthetic agents.

80. O'CONNELL, D., Ranelagh, Rathmines, Inventor and Proprietor.—A horizontal dial; geographical clock; perpetual almanac; quadrant, and circumferentor.

81. O'CONNELL, E., Bury, Lancashire.—Registered infant feeder.

82. OERTLING, LUDWIG, Store-street, London, Manufacturer.—A balance, with agate knife edges, to carry 1 lb. in each pan, turning with the 100th part of a grain.

83. OLIVER, F., London, Inventor.—Portable, single, and quartett music stands.

84. PENNINGTON, JOHN, Camberwell, London, Manufacturer.—Two-day chronometers; gold and silver watches.

85. PHELAN, W. T., Heytesbury-street, Dublin.—Spectacles manufactured from Irish pebble found at the island of Achill; specimens of the pebble from which they are manufactured; a visometer for ascertaining the number of lens suitable for the eye.

86. RACINE & Co., Switzerland, and Nassau-street, Dublin, Manufacturers.—Gold Geneva watches.

87. READ & Co., Parliament-street, Dublin, Inventors and Proprietors.—Surgical instruments.

88. REID, R., M. D., Heriot-row, Edinburgh, Inventor.—Compress for arresting excessive bleeding after extraction of teeth, with model head and chin for showing the application of the apparatus.

89. REIN, F. C., Strand, London, Inventor and Manufacturer.—Rein's acoustic instruments for the relief of deafness; conical flexible whisper tube; models of acoustic pulpit and acoustic chair; acoustic walking-stick; ear specula, ear syringes, and various other instruments.

90. ROBERTSON, A., Bachelor's-walk, Dublin, Inventor and Manufacturer.—Stomach pumps; mechanical leeching apparatus, with glasses for cupping internally, invented by Surgeon Zach. Johnson, Kilkenny, for the trachea; gum elastic syphons (designed by Dr. E. Kennedy); pieces of elastic tubing; elastic check-string, or voice-conductors for carriages; stethoscopes, and other medical and surgical apparatus.

91. ROBINSON, J., Polytechnic Museum, Grafton-street, Dublin, Manufacturer and Importer.—Achromatic and compound microscopes of various forms; microscopic preparations; astronomical and other telescopes; opera, race, and exhibition glasses; stereoscopes of various forms, with diagrams and proofs; cameras for the daguerreotype, calotype, and collodion processes; various specimens of photography on paper and on glass; magic lanterns; polyoramas, and other curious optical and scientific toys; cheap and effective air-pumps; models of electric telegraphs; electro-magnetic machines, and galvanic batteries; magnets; barometers and thermometers; gazogene apparatus for making soda and other aërated waters; vacuum coffee-pots; moderateur and gazogene lamps, with various other applications of science to useful purposes; opera-glasses, stereoscopes and diagrams, &c.; cameras for the daguerreotype, calotype and collodion processes; magic lanterns, &c.; polyoramas; phenakisticopes; cylindrical mirrors; air-pumps; models of electric telegraphs; electro-magnetic machines; galvanic batteries; magnet; barometers and thermometers; gazogene apparatus for making soda and other aërated waters; vacuum coffee-pots; gazogene and other lamps; with various other chemical and philosophical apparatus, &c.

92. ROE, HENRY, Fitzwilliam-square, Dublin.—A magic clock (transparent).

93. ROWLEY, J., Lewis-street, Wolverhampton, Manufactur.—Spectacles of various descriptions; single and double eye-glasses; eye-protectors or travelling spectacles.

94. ROYAL DUBLIN SOCIETY.—Lord Rosse's telescope; case of philosophical instruments.

95. RUDOLPH, ROSE, & Co., Southampton-street, Strand, London, Manufacturer.—Flutes.

96. SANG, J., Kirkaldy, Fifeshire, Inventor and Manufacturer.—Platometers, or self-acting calculators of surface, telling the area of figures, on carrying the tracer round the boundary.

97. SCATES, J., College-green, Dublin, Manufacturer.—Treble and barytone concertinas, with tympanums.

98. SCHOLEFIELD, D., Huddersfield, Designer.—Improved metronome; school and pocket metronomes, for the use of singing classes, &c.

99. SCRIBER, JOHN, Westmoreland-street, Dublin, and Geneva, Manufacturer.—Geneva watches on a new principle, dispensing with the usual winding, setting of hands, or use of key; duplex, lever, and horizontal watches; specimens illustrative of the various stages which the watch undergoes in the process of manufacture; a small watch the size of a fourpenny piece, set in diamonds; extra flat watches, not one-eighth the usual thickness; English-made patent lever watches, gold and silver; French ormolu, bronze, marble, and mechanical clocks; a two-tune music box in a gold seal; musical boxes of various descriptions, with overtures, quadrilles, polkas, national airs, &c.

100. SCRIBER, M. & J., South Great George's-street, Dublin, Manufacturers.—Clocks of different descriptions.

101. SMITH, R., Blackford, Perthshire, Inventor.—Specimens of photography.

102. SOLOMONS, E., Nassau-street, Dublin, and Old Bond-street, London, Inventor and Manufacturer.—Improved sight-preserving spectacles; amber applied to spectacles; various specimens of lenses in their rough state, and also in the different stages of manufacture; the organic vibrators for relief of deafness.

103. SPEAR, R., College-green, Dublin, Manufacturer.—Barometers, thermometers, hydrometers; spectacle cases; ivory scales; phantasmagoria lanterns; optical pillar; magnetic sun-dials; eye-glasses and spectacles; opera-glasses; magnifying glasses; pentagraph; stereoscopes; sympiesometer; microscopes; telescopes: ship compasses; binnacles; drawing instruments; level; theodolite; sextant; quadrant; with other philosophical instruments, &c.

104. STATHAM, W. E., Sussex-place, Islington, London, Inventor and Manufacturer.—Chemical cabinets and portable laboratories for students, chemists, lecturers, &c.; agricultural test chests, for analyzing soils, manures, &c.; toxicological test chests, for detecting and analyzing poisons; hydro-pneumatic apparatus, combining a pneumatic trough, large gas jar tray, hydraulic blow-pipe and gasometer; pocket and other blow-pipes for mineralogists; mineralogical cabinet; photographic apparatus, chemicals, &c.

105. TELFORD & TELFORD, Stephen's-green, Dublin.—Organ, built for the College of St. Peter, Radley, Oxford, in solid oak Gothic cases; the choir organ, placed in front, the front pipes of pure tin, polished and burnished; three complete manuals from CC to G in alt; the pedal organ from CCC to G, two and a half octaves, six composition pedals, five copulæ, fifty stops; the great organ containing 1146 pipes; the swell organ, 1003; the choir organ, 356; and the pedal organ, 416; total, 2921 pipes.

106. TENISON, E. K., Kilbonan Castle, Keadue, Co. of Roscommon.—Photographs.

107. THOMPSON, C. T., Campden Hill Terrace, Kensington, London, Producer.—Photographs.

108. THOMPSON, W., Dame-street, Dublin, Manufacturer.—Surgical instruments.

109. THOMPSON, S., & Co., Henry-street, Dublin.—Surgical instruments.

110. TUFNELL, J., F. R. C. S., M. R. I. A., Designer.—Gutta percha stethoscope.

111. VIVIAN, E., Torquay, Devonshire, Inventor.—Self-registering thermometer, hygrometer, augeometer, pluviometer, constructed for weekly observations.

112. WALSH, R., Parliament-street, Dublin, Manufacturer.—Eight-day clocks of various descriptions; gold and silver watches.

113. WATERHOUSE & Co., Dame-street, Dublin.—Ball-clock.

114. WEEDON, T., Hart-street, Bloomsbury, London, Manufacturer.—Instruments for microscopical dissection; dental instruments.

115. WELLS, CAPTAIN G. G., Mullingar, Co. Westmeath, Specimens of talbotype drawings.

116. WHITE, JOHN, & SONS, Bishop-street, Dublin, Manufacturers.—A finger organ in a Gothic case.

117. WHITE, J. B., West-square, Southwark, Designer.—The national anthem, a specimen of music printed on calico by hand with single types.

118. WHITE, P. F., Mus. Doc., Wexford, Proprietor.—Royal patent Victoria harp-lyre, a new musical instrument.

119. YEATES, GEORGE, Grafton-street, Dublin, Manufacturer.—Transit instrument; improved transit theodolites, levels, sextants, &c.; Attwood's apparatus for demonstrating the laws of accelerated motion; standard barometers; station staves.

120. YOUNG, A. K., Monaghan, Inventor.—A surgical bed for invalids.

121. YOUNG, JAMES A., (of A. S. YOUNG & SON, Surgeon Dentists), Buchanan-street, Glasgow, Inventor.—Two sets of patent forceps for the extraction of teeth or roots:—I. A complete set of nine forceps (being competent in every case). II. A portable set of these forceps, in pocket case, containing one pair of handles, nine pairs of movable beaks to fit the handles, an elevator handle, to which any of the beaks may be fitted (a reserve to be used only if some of the beaks should break), a scarificator, capable of cutting in any direction, a probe, a small mouth mirror, a spring-catch forceps, &c.; these nine patent forceps, from the principle secured in their construction, will remove any tooth or root however far decayed, or of whatever shape, and with the least possible amount of pain.

# CLASS XI.

## COTTON.

THE products of the cotton manufacture form the commencement of another section of the Exhibition, which includes the whole department of Textile Fabrics. We have already considered in succession the Raw Materials, those objects which in a *passive* state may be regarded as the basis of all our operations; next, those *active* agents in the shape of Machinery of different kinds, through the instrumentality of which the former are turned to account; and we now come to the Fabrics themselves, which only await their further application to the purposes of life. Although, in a local point of view, this class is of secondary importance as compared with some others, and accordingly occupied no considerable space in the Exhibition, yet it has already obtained a firm footing in the northern province, and in the other parts of the island, and is no doubt destined to make still further progress amongst us. The cotton manufacture has, moreover, long formed what may be regarded as the staple branch of British industry, and has exercised an important influence indirectly on all other branches of trade and manufacture; and therefore the subject demands more than a passing notice in such a publication as the present.

The production of fabrics from cotton (which, as a raw material, has already been noticed at some length in Class IV.), is unquestionably of Eastern origin. The Hindoos excelled in their manufacture from time immemorial. It is mentioned by Herodotus, and is also spoken of by Arrian and Strabo, as being well known in India from the earliest periods of which there are any records. Cotton garments were in use in Russia so early as 1252; and the first introduction of the article into London is stated to have taken place in 1590. The manufacture was originally introduced into Europe by the Moors, numbers of whom established it in Spain; but it does not appear that any considerable progress was made in it until after the commencement of the trade to the East, carried on by the Dutch, whose early commercial enterprise is well known. It soon after extended to England, where an impetus was given to it by the operations of the East India Company, through whom importations of cotton goods were steadily carried on for a long series of years. Chintzes, muslins, and calicoes, were brought in considerable quantities from India; and the useful article known as nankeen was procured direct from China. The various kinds of goods thus imported were distinguished by the names of the places whence they came, and these names they have, for the most part, retained to the present day. The general name of *calico* has been applied to the plain white cloth manufactured from cotton, from the circumstance of this class of goods having been first obtained from Calicut, the seat of its original manufacture. Of this generic name there are several subdivisions, chiefly founded upon the use to which the article is to be applied. Thus as it increases in quality and strength, it is called long-cloth, duck, and double-warp. Printed calicoes or "prints" were brought to a high state of perfection in India. In the production of muslins, the extreme fineness of some of the Eastern fabrics is still unrivalled, notwithstanding all the appliances of modern times. The turbans of some of the rich Mahommedans of Delhi are said to have been made so fine that thirty ells did not weigh four ounces, and some of their broad webs might be drawn through a finger-ring of moderate size, so exquisitely fine was the thread of which they were composed. Specimens of cotton thread in the Museum of the East India Company, though only spun by the distaff and spindle, are of a degree of fineness which our machinery has rarely been able to equal, twenty yards weighing only a single grain, and a pound weight reaching a length of 115 miles. In England the extraordinary fineness has been attained of a thread which contained a length of 167 miles to the pound; but this no existing machinery could weave, and it can only be regarded as a curiosity, and as illustrative of the perfection which spinning machinery has attained. Some of the Dacca muslin, when first brought to England, fetched from ten to twelve guineas a yard; and although English muslins have been made to approach to this in fineness of texture, the Eastern fabric possesses a richness, softness, and durability, which still fully maintains its ancient reputation. The same remark applies to the calicoes, ginghams, and chintzes of the East, the quality of the finer specimens of which is said to be unrivalled; though, from the astonishing progress which has been attained in the economy of production, the native articles have long had a monopoly not only of the home market, but also of every other to which they have been admitted without any restriction.

The mull muslin is a variety of cotton fabrics used for dresses, trimmings, &c.; the jaconet is also used for dresses and handkerchiefs, and is a light, open, and soft article, though stouter than the mull (this term is said to be a corruption of Jaghernout, the place where it was originally made); nainsook is a thicker sort of jaconet, plain and striped; seerhand is between nainsook and mull, and is particularly adapted for dresses, from retaining so well its clearness after washing; buke muslin is a plain, clear kind, chiefly used for working in the tambour; leno is thinner and clearer than the last-named variety, and being a sort of gauze is used for window-blinds; cambric muslin, an imitation of the linen fabric, is made in cord and fancy checks, by the introduction of occasional thick threads in the warp or weft, or in both—and of cotton cambrics there are two kinds—that used for dresses, white or printed, made in Lancashire, and that substituted for French cambric, chiefly produced in Glasgow; cotton damasks, huckabacks, and diapers are the imitations of the linen articles of the same names, over which they have the recommendation of cheapness; gingham is a thin chequered cotton, a serviceable article; counterpanes (a corruption of counterpoint) have small projections of the cotton, arranged according to the pattern, and they form cheap coverlets; Marseilles quilts are formed of double cloth, with a third layer of softer material between them, the connexion being maintained by a sort of quilting done in the loom; jean is a twilled cotton, both striped and white, a variety of which with a glossy surface is used for shoes, stays, and other articles in which strength of material is required; and dimity, fustian, and moleskin are other varieties in general use, and which are well known.

The progress of the cotton manufacture in Britain is a subject so pregnant with interest and instruction that a volume might be devoted to it alone, though it scarcely extends over a century. The earliest efforts in the economical use of the cotton originated probably in the conversion of it into candle-wick, and step by step its further application was developed. The first impetus was due to the circumstance of the religious persecution of the Duke of Alva, which led to the banishment of numbers of Flemish artisans skilled in this branch of industry, some of whom settled in England. There was at that period great manufacturing activity, and the advantages of increased attention being devoted to the production of cotton fabrics were too apparent to be overlooked. With the distaff and the hand-loom, progress was, however, necessarily slow, and, for practical purposes, the origin of the manufacture may be dated from the invention of spinning and weaving machinery. The machine of Arkwright, patented in 1767, and the spinning-jenny of Hargreaves, brought forward in the same year, effected a revolution in cotton-spinning; and about the same period the cleaning, carding, and preparation of cotton wool derived great benefit from a number of ingenious and useful contrivances. As these inventions were being still further improved and perfected, Watt, the master magician of the age, discovered the application of the new motive power by which they were destined to be worked; steam having done more, perhaps, for the cotton manufacture than for any other branch of industry. The improvement of the weaver's shuttle by Kay, of Bury, and the subsequent introduction of the power-loom, mark further and important steps in this singular career of progress. The invention of the spinning-mule, by which hitherto unattainable regularity and fineness were secured in the thread, may be traced to the same extraordinary period of discovery. The location in Lancashire of large numbers of persons engaged in the manufacture of watches and clocks also contributed much to the perfection of the mechanical requirements of the new industry, from the peculiar knowledge which they possessed. As each successive improvement was brought before the public, men of enterprise and intelligence were to be found ready to take it up and fully develop it. Capital became attracted to it, and colossal fortunes were made in it; the activity which it called into operation at the same time extending itself to every other branch of manufacture. At the commencement of the eighteenth century the annual consumption of cotton wool in Great Britain was about 1,000,000 lbs.; in the beginning of the present century it was 54,000,000 lbs.; in 1825 it had increased to 200,000,000 lbs.; and during the past year it amounted to 895,266,780 lbs. These figures supply unequivocal evidence of progress, and, so far as present appearances warrant an opinion, that progress promises to be continuous.

It has been too much the habit during the discussions which for years distracted the public mind on the subject of free trade—a habit, it is needless to say, originating in prejudice founded on the most thorough ignorance—to sneer at the capitalists engaged in this manufacture; the term "Cotton Lords" being used in derision. As compared with their fellow-subjects, many of these parties are, however, in reality "lords" in everything that can constitute true nobility. Of this any one who sets about the investigation of the progress of manufacturing industry will soon become convinced. The charge of selfishness so often levelled against them, is made in ignorance of one of the most elementary truths of social science; as the merest schoolboy is now beginning to understand the identity of individual and general interests. The capitalists of Lancashire, no doubt, pursue their honourable and useful career with a view to immediate gain; but success in this is just the way in which the greatest service can be rendered to the whole community. And the advantage, in a national point of view, of the enterprise which they were the first to exhibit on a great scale, has long since been universally felt. The industry of that district led to the formation of the celebrated Bridgewater Canal, which may be said to have inaugurated the age of that kind of conveyance; and we must also bear in mind, that it is to the same district, aided by the enterprise and capital of the "Cotton Lords," that we owe the early development of the railway system; the Liverpool and Manchester line having been, as it were, the experimental railway, constructed as a commercial speculation for passenger traffic; and the opposition which that project met with would have been fatal to it at the time in almost any other hands. Again, when gas was brought forward for the purpose of illumination, it met the usual fate of new inventions, and was regarded as one of the chimeras of an over-sanguine imagination, until its value was tested on a large scale by the firm of Philips and Lee, of Salford, who tried it to light their spinning mills. Nor can a doubt for a moment be entertained that the manufacture of machinery generally derived its greatest impetus from this branch of industry. And those who may visit Saltaire, the village of Meltham, and many other localities in which this branch of industry flourishes, cannot fail to be impressed favourably as regards the relation between employers and employed, by the extent to which the moral culture, as well as the material wants of the latter are provided for. At Portlaw, in the County of Waterford, in the vicinity of Belfast, as well as in some other places in Ireland, illustrations of the same watchful care and benevolence may also be seen: all showing the high sense entertained by the manufacturers of the obligation which their position imposes upon them.

The chief seats of the cotton manufacture are Manchester and Glasgow, the former having Bolton for its dependent, and the latter Paisley. Of late years it has obtained a footing in Belfast (and in some other parts of Ireland), and, from the proverbial energy and sound discrimination of the capitalists of that rising town, we may reasonably hope that it will yet be regarded as one of the great depots of this manufacture.

Of the amount of capital involved in the cotton industry it is quite impossible to convey any accurate idea. That employed even in individual establishments is so great as to appear absolutely fabulous unless to those acquainted with the manufacturing districts. Most of the cotton spinning mills are indeed leviathan establishments, giving employment to from five or six hundred, to over fifteen hundred hands, and presenting in every department an appearance of order and regularity truly marvellous.*

Of the extent of production in the spinning and weaving departments it is also impossible to speak with accuracy. To the quantity consumed at home we have no key. It is obvious, however, that it is immense,

* As a description of some particular establishment will convey to the reader a better notion of the business of cotton-spinning that any mere general notice on the subject, we subjoin an account of "a day at the Meltham Mills," near Hudderafield, the property of the Messrs. Brooks, who contributed an interesting collection of specimens of their manufacture to the Exhibition. We may observe, that nearly the whole population of the village of Meltham are dependent on the employment which this establishment affords, the number of hands engaged in which ranges between 1000 and 1200. To the great credit of the present proprietors, as well as their predecessors, they have not been unmindful of the intellectual and moral wants of those dependent upon them. A church was built by the late Mr. Brook, by whom also it was liberally endowed; the educational requirements of the rising generation have been provided for; and altogether the appearance of the village shows, that with the proprietors' active benevolence and genuine philanthropy are combined great commercial enterprise. A visit to such an establishment as the Meltham Mills cannot fail to be eminently suggestive and instructive. With these preliminary remarks we place the following sketch before our readers, which is abridged from an article that appeared in the "Leisure Hour."

We will conduct the reader through the mills; and that he may have as clear an idea as we can convey of the process which the raw cotton undergoes before it is finished on the spools, we will commence at the cotton store, that is, the room where the cotton is stowed in bales as it comes from the plantations. We will then follow it through all the stages of manufacture until the process is completed.

Imagine, then, a large room, in the lower part of the mill, filled with these long and tightly packed bales, the growths of the southern states of America, the West Indies, and Egypt. Let us examine some of the bales. How full of dirt, chips, and gins, is the Egyptian. It seems impossible ever to convert it into twist fit for the delicate fingers of a fair lady to handle. Here is a handful of what is called "sea-island cotton," and what a contrast it presents to the other! Mark how beautifully white it is, and how fine, long, and silky is the fibre. This is the prince of all cottons, and the material which is chiefly used in these mills. It is not, however, free from many admixtures of dirt and chips; and now we will witness, in another room, the process by which it is cleaned.

Observe that curious machine, which those men and boys are feeding with the raw cotton. It contains two eight-scutchers, or blades, which revolve 1600 times per minute, and the cotton is fed into these, and held fast by two pair of rollers, the blades striking against it at such a distance as enables them to open up the cotton, and separate the larger chips and foreign substances which are mixed with its fibres, and these fall to the bottom of the machine; the cotton thus partially freed from its incumbrances is carried forward to another roller, to undergo a further cleansing, until it is finally driven down into a basket at the end of the machine, and carried off to receive a more complete and satisfactory dressing. Although vast quantities of dirty, dusty cotton are constantly subject to this operation of cleaning, there is neither dust nor dirt in the room. The air is quite clear and healthy. By a very simple and beautiful contrivance, the refuse is all driven up a pair of tunnels, running from the machine into a cylinder placed in the roof, and is carried thence into a chimney outside the building. This is effected by means of fans, which have saved many hundreds from premature graves—the process of cotton-dressing being formerly almost as inimical to human life as the trade of the Sheffield grinders.

Let us now go to another machine, and witness the second process of cleaning, which consists in taking out all the small nips and shorts from the long cotton. This operation is performed pretty much in the same manner as the former, the cotton being fed in by rollers, and placed upon the huge cylinders or combs, by a series of cylindrical brushes; the combs are then carried round one by one, and brought under the action of a beater, holding fast all the long fibres, whilst the beater frees them from the shorts, when they are stripped off on the other side, to be ready for further use. This machine answers the same purpose as the combing machine used for wool.

We now come to the *blowing machine*, where we see numbers of men engaged in subjecting the cotton to a third process, similar to that which it underwent in the first machine. The cotton is now delivered in the form of a web, and wrapped round a roller, freed from most of the dirt that was originally mixed with it. The rollers are then carried to another machine, where they are doubled three together, and passing through another eight-scutcher, are again formed into a web, and wrapped round a roller; being made by this process as even in every square inch as possible, so that they will fill the card equally without choking it. See what piles of these rollers stand there, in their white jackets, ready to be carried to the card-room; and from thence to be doubled upwards of thirty-five millions of times, and twisted and twirled by remorseless spindles, before they have been tortured into twist, and made ready for the market. Let us follow them.

Open that door in the side wall, but be careful or you will tumble down—down thirty feet below. What see you there? A square tube, running from top to bottom of the mills, with a movable floor exactly fitting it, which rises or falls as required by means of ropes and pulleys. See, the floor is now far down below where we are standing. Give the signal. Lo! up it rises, with a man to direct its movements. Now it is on a level with us. We step upon it, and in a few seconds are carried to the card-room.

What a strange and wonderful sight bursts upon us. The room runs the whole length of the building, and is full of machinery, which really looks alive, and seems as if it could talk. What a roar of wheels and humming of spindles salute the ear! and how complicated is the work going on here. Yet all is accurately and beautifully done, without confusion, without rest, or haste. Hundreds of hands, most of them girls from fourteen to twenty, are busily engaged in their several departments, watching the machinery, feeding it, and instantly joining the broken ends of cotton. Not a moment is lost; every eye is vigilant, every hand active. Let us see now what they are doing with the cotton rollers, specimens of which we saw below.

The machine to which they are now put is called a *breaker*. It consists of rapid rollers, and a large cylinder covered with card sheets with movable tops. These sheets contain thousands of sharp iron teeth, so nicely and accurately set that they catch every fibre of cotton, and separate them film from film, laying them longitudinally to each other. A smaller cylinder of the same description is placed in front of the large one, and set so close to it that it draws away the cotton in regular proportions as fast as it is fed into the machine. It is finally drawn away from this cylinder by means of a comb, and delivered in a long tin case, in beautifully white streams about two inches wide. It is then carried to the *lap machine*. From twelve to twenty-four cans are placed behind a pair of rollers kept down by levers and weights; and the cotton is spread out like the warp of a web, and rolled firmly upon another roller, in order to go through another process of carding, called *finishing*. The finishing cards contain about 700 teeth, or points, to

from cotton fabrics being in universal demand among all classes of the community. The declared value of the several classes of exports of cotton manufactures for the under-mentioned years has been as follows :—

| Year. | Cotton Fabrics of all Kinds. | Twist and Yarn. | Total. |
|---|---|---|---|
| 1820 | £13,690,109 | £2,826,639 | £16,516,748 |
| 1830 | 15,294,923 | 4,133,741 | 19,428,664 |
| 1848 | 16,753,369 | 5,927,831 | 22,681,200 |
| 1849 | 20,071,046 | 6,704,089 | 26,775,135 |
| 1850 | 21,873,697 | 6,383,704 | 28,257,401 |
| 1851 | 23,454,810 | 6,634,026 | 30,088,836 |
| 1852 | 23,223,432 | 6,654,655 | 29,878,087 |
| 1853 | 25,813,981 | 6,895,454 | 32,709,385 |

The progress of improvement in the cotton manufacture has been very clearly indicated by the astonishing reduction in the prices of the several manufactured articles. In 1820 the average price per yard of the cotton fabrics exported was 12¾*d.*, and during the past year it has been about 3*d.* The price of twist in 1820 was 2*s.* 5½*d.* per pound, and now it is 10*d.* Of yarns of the fineness of 100 hanks to the pound, the price was, in 1786, 38*s.* per pound; in 1790, 30*s.*; in 1800, 9*s.* 5*d.*; in 1830, 3*s.*; and since the last-mentioned year a still further reduction has been continuously going forward. And while these changes have been

every square inch, and the fibres are here thoroughly and finally separated. They are then carried off in a long thin web through the delivering roller into another pair of rollers, when each inch of cotton is drawn into lengths of two inches, uniformly from end to end. The cans are all filled with these long streams, which have been delivered into them by the *finisher*; and here, close at hand, is another machine ready to receive them. This is called the *drawing-frame*; and it contains four separate divisions, each alike. Six of the cans are placed against the *frame*, and six ends, one for each can, are put into the backmost roller in the first division. There are four pairs of rollers, at small distances from one another, each of them, from the back to the front, going round a little quicker than its neighbour, so that the front roller will revolve six times for one revolution of the back roller. The consequence is, that every inch of cotton, taken in by the back roller, is drawn into six inches by the front roller; so that the *six* ends put in behind come out in the form of *one* end in front, of the same thickness and weight as each of the six ends; or, in other words, as one single end, as it came from the cards. This process is carried on through all the four divisions; and after passing through them all, and being doubled 186,624 times, the cotton is still of the same thickness and weight as it was at the beginning of the doubling and drawing operation.

But a great change has taken place in its appearance. When it was put into the cards it was coarse and rough, with the fibres pointing in all directions; but now it has assumed the lustrous appearance of silk, every fibre lying smooth and straight, and all in the same direction. It is now in a fit state for further operations. You will observe that it is in one endless length, but still thick enough to bear its own weight. Now, before it can be drawn much finer, some means must be adopted to make the fibres hold together. In its present state there will be about 100 yards to the pound; but it cannot be drawn out to eight or ten hundred yards unless some means can be devised to make it hold together. How then is this to be accomplished? Let us go forward to the *slubbing-frame*, and the difficulty will be solved.

A row of cans stands behind it, filled with cotton in the state described above. The *frame* has three lines of rollers for the purpose of drawing the riband or stream of cotton, out into a *roving*. A series of *flyers* is also fixed upon revolving spindles, with *bobbins* upon these spindles to receive the rovings. As the cotton is delivered from the front rollers, it passes through the flyers, and is wound round the bobbins, receiving at the same time its proportionate quantity of *twist* by the revolution of the flyers. The bobbins are regularly carried up and down by mechanical contrivance, so that the rovings are uniformly laid from end to end of the bobbins, at equal distances to suit their diameters.

Take a bobbin from the frame and examine it. It is so soft that it can be pressed flat with the fingers; but it is so equal and level, that every part of it contains nearly the same number of fibres! The roving on this bobbin has been doubled 746,496 times since it left the bag, and it is eight times smaller than when it left the cards. There is no more *twist* put upon it than is necessary to keep it from separating, and straining its parts by its own weight; and this twist is the sole secret of keeping it together, which was the difficulty that startled us when it left the finishing machine. It is now about one *hank*, or 840 yards to the pound.

The bobbins are next taken forward, and put through a similar machine to the last, but smaller and finer its parts. As the rovings are getting finer, the bobbins are made lighter and smaller in proportion. The rovings undergo here another doubling, two of them being made into one, which is then drawn out by rollers four times longer than the former; and after this process is accomplished, it is put through a third and fourth, growing finer and finer as it advances, until it passes through the last frame in the card-room, when every pound is made into thirty hanks, containing 25,200 yards of roving, which has now been doubled no less than 2,985,984 times; and this when made into nine-cord thread no less than 113,246,208 times, which appears almost incredible.

It is now ready for being spun into fine yarns, and we must follow it, therefore, from the card-room to the spinning-room. As it is too much of a toil to climb the longe range of steps to the next room above, suppose we mount the "hoist" again, and make the steam-horse pull us up. So here we are in the room filled with *spinning-jennies*. These machines differ considerably from the former, as the yarns are here finished, and receive all the twist necessary to fit them for any desired purpose. The rovings are here also doubled into the rollers, and drawn out ten times their original length. They are built upon spindles, and then doffed off by the hand of the spinner. It is scarcely fifty years since yarns were spun only by hand, one thread at a time: but now one man, assisted by three boys, can keep 1200 or 2000 spindles going at once, each spindle producing a thread! Look at those: how smooth they are! how level! the fibres all twisted firmly together, making the thread strong and elastic. Here is a cop finished, and just taken off the spindle. It is solid and hard, containing 3000 yards of yarn, and weighs about one-third of an ounce!

The most wonderful, however, of all the machines in these mills is the *self-acting spinning-jenny*, which performs all the operations alluded to above without any help from the hand of man. We must mount our steam-horse again, and rise to the next room. There it is at full work, no one helping it—the dumb machine doing as it were both the thinking and labour. It never makes a mistake, and is never wearied; but continues to work all day long in the same precise, accurate, and methodical manner. It has taken twenty long years of thought and toil to bring it to this state. All the motions are performed with an exactitude that no manual labour can equal.

Let us now follow the cops to another part of the works. Here is a large iron chest, or rather a great cistern, piled with baskets full of them. The doors are suddenly closed, and the cistern is thus made air-tight. A man near by turns a tap, and there is forthwith a rushing of steam as it pass-

taking place, the wages of the work-people underwent little if any reduction, so rapidly were improvements of various kinds introduced. The magnitude of the transactions rendered fractional savings per yard matters of great moment, stimulating invention, and imparting activity to the manufacture.

Trifling as the article of sewing cotton may appear, the quantity of the raw material appropriated to its production is very great. The business is sometimes distributed among two sets of hands,—spinners and winders,—one party spinning the cotton and disposing of the thread in the bundle, and the other winding it on the small spools, on which it is ready for use. Some of the names long before the public as manufacturers of sewing cotton are merely winders. It is obvious, however, that the quality of the article is dependent on the proper selection of the raw material, and the manner in which the spinning has been conducted; the winder at most merely putting a gloss upon it to improve its appearance. In the winding of cotton it is surprising how much is made by the too common trick of putting a smaller quantity on each spool than the stated number of yards marked thereon—the deficiency in some cases amounting to from a sixth to a tenth of the entire quantity—and the fraud is one which readily escapes detection, as few consumers think of measuring two or three hundred yards of cotton thread, more especially as it costs only a few pence. One remedy for this would appear to be to purchase only those cottons of which the winders are also the spinners, as there is then less chance of these contemptible tricks being resorted to than by those parties who deal in the article on a smaller scale. The respectable firm of Messrs. Brook, Brothers, of Meltham Mills, have spared no efforts to put an end to this system; and the notice which is affixed in their winding-room, impos-

trates into the cistern, and through every fibre of the yarns, softening and moistening them, so that they will not double up and kink when they are made into twist. When taken out they are ready for winding on the bobbins, whilst they are yet warm and moist. 100 bobbins are filled at once, each of the same length, when they are doffed off by the girls, and put into a basket to be further dealt with.

By the next process the yarn is turned into thread. This is carried on in several rooms, the one we saw containing 13,000 spindles, and superintended by young girls. These spindles revolve at from 3000 to 5000 revolutions per minute, giving twist to the thread in proportion to the fineness of the yarn to be doubled.

After undergoing this process, the bobbins are carried to the reeling-room, to be made into hanks, which is done as follows:—The bobbins are placed perpendicularly to the reel, so that they turn round and unwind as the reel revolves. The ends of the thread are fixed to the spokes of the reel, which carries the thread along with it during its revolutions, and forms it into a hank or skein, with any number of threads, the number being regulated by an index placed on the axle of the reel, so that the reel may be stopped at any moment.

The hanks are now taken to the bleaching works. Here is a batch of brown thread just as it came from the hank reels. It is thrown into a huge cauldron full of boiling water, with soap and potash dissolved in it. It remains there until nearly all the colouring matter in it is discharged, when it is taken out, well washed, and afterwards put into a large vat filled with water and chlorine, where the colouring matter is changed by the acid. After steeping for some time, it is taken out, washed well, and put into a solution of sulphuric acid and water. After repeating this process it is washed with pure soap and water, and beat until every brown speck is removed; and, as a final process, it is drawn through a vat of clear spring water, mixed with the extract of indigo, so that the white ground may appear clear and brilliant. It is then subjected to hydraulic pressure, freed from all superabundant fluid, and carried from thence to the store, where it is allowed to hang upon poles until it becomes dry, being literally "white as the driven snow."

We must now follow it again to the mills, where it will have to be ironed. This is done partly by machinery. There are two powerful dressing machines, with triangular pipes attached, filled with steam, and two rollers moving perpendicularly up and down. A number of girls, busily employed in their various occupations, are near it; and one amongst them takes hank after hank of the thread, and puts them over the end of the pipe and roller. The latter moves upwards and downwards, stretching out the thread from the pipe, until every crease in it is drawn quite smooth, and the whole hank is made straight and lustrous. It is now passed over to a table in the same room, where it is separated into smaller heads, neatly doubled up in hank, and packed in parcels of ten pounds weight each, when it is ready for the market.

In addition to the foregoing brief detail, we may further observe that the process by which thread is wound on spools, reels, or bobbins, such as are purchased in shops, is also a very interesting one. On entering the room where this winding operation is performed, a stranger is struck with the order and neatness which pervade it. Long rows of well-dressed girls are sitting before iron tables, each with a small machine before her, which is impelled by a belt from a pully, to which is attached a treadle, on which she presses her foot, to give motion to the machine; she then takes an empty bobbin, and places it upon a spindle, which is driven at the enormous speed of 8000 revolutions per minute, and obtains the thread from a large bobbin fixed on a pedestal, which has been wound from the hank by a simple contrivance in another room. The most important feature of a winding-machine is the guide and screw, both being cut as fine as the thread to be wound; the guide is the instrument for laying the thread evenly, while the screw prevents the guide from traversing too quick across the surface of the bobbin. Any one unwinding a few rows of thread from a bobbin will at once perceive the astonishing regularity with which it is wound. The reels are then removed to another room, where, after undergoing inspection, they are ticketed and tied up, ready for sale. We were particularly pleased to observe the care taken to give the public exact measure, a notice being posted up to the following effect:—"Notice. Winders shall pay one shilling for every bobbin that has five yards less than ordered, and sixpence for every bobbin that has more than ordered. Those who are habitually guilty of these irregularities shall be discharged." When one beholds the amazing number of bobbins filled in a day by these winders, curiosity is naturally excited to know where they all come from, and how such regularity of size and colour is maintained amidst such a variety of sorts. Let us, for a few minutes, visit the large and commodious turning-shop. In the adjoining yard cart-loads of trees are being brought in, and several men busily employed measuring and arranging them, while others are carrying huge logs to circular saws, that revolve at great speed; here they are cut up into squares of certain lengths and thickness, and cart-loads of timber are thus disposed of every day, amounting to many hundred tons in a year. After being properly seasoned, the squares are then cut up into lengths to suit the size of the bobbins, and a hole is bored in each, and the block made round. Several modes of finishing these are adopted, according to the appearance required; but the machine which most attracts a stranger is the self-acting turning lathe. Here the overlooker has only to supply the blocks, and by three movements of the machine they are transformed into bobbins, and deposited in a basket below at the rate of upwards of forty per minute. Other finishing processes follow, such as dyeing, polishing, embossing, &c.

[We trust our fair readers will feel interested in knowing the number of processes through which a reel of thread has to pass before reaching their delicate fingers, and on this account we are glad to have had the opportunity of giving the above extract.]—ED.

ing a fine for any departure from the proper length (making the fine greater, however, for short than long lengths) shows the care taken by them to guard against this common evil. We may further observe, that the only prize medal in this department was awarded to the Messrs. Brook at the Exhibition of 1851. The case contributed by them to this Exhibition, containing specimens of cotton thread and crochet cotton in every stage, and of nearly every degree of fineness, has been deposited with the Royal Dublin Society, where it is still open to public inspection. Among the varieties of thread in that collection is the patent glacé cotton, which is really a very superior article, the preparation used in making it up imparting to it all the smoothness of silk, to which, from the excellence of the raw material, it is also little inferior in strength. Independent of the high quality of Brook's cotton, the public have the guarantee, from the precautions adopted by them in the winding, that the spools of it contain the actual quantities marked upon them.

Of the other collections in this class the case of Mr. Moss is deserving of more than a passing notice, from the neatness with which it was got up, as well as the variety of its contents. The business of Mr. Moss is that of a candle-wick manufacturer, and his establishment in the vicinity of this city supplies, we believe, nearly the whole of the local demand. This might, at first sight, appear to be a comparatively unimportant branch of manufacture, but the article being one of general consumption, the annual amount of business done becomes very considerable. The case exhibited by Mr. Moss, like that of the Messrs. Brook, has been permanently deposited with the Royal Dublin Society.

Of cotton fabrics there were many excellent specimens, though, as a whole, the illustration of the department was not what might have been expected. In one class of these, printed and dyed cottons, other elements come under consideration quite as important as the quality of the fabric itself. In the finer class of goods the character of the ornamentation becomes of great moment. It is only of late that public attention has been duly aroused to the necessity of resorting to some sort of recognised principles in the application of the art of design to the commoner kinds of cotton. The finer kinds were usually French: though the comparatively high price at which they were available, even taking quality into account, amounted to a prohibition of their use, unless among the wealthier classes. Hence the finer descriptions of cotton have been very sparingly worn. The extension, among the great bulk of the people, of more correct ideas on these matters than have hitherto prevailed is, however, beginning to create a taste for a better class of goods in this department; and, therefore, in an educational point of view, an ample illustration of this class of fabrics would have been of great value; for we must bear in mind that the stocks to be found in the warehouses and shops are laid in with a regard to what is most in demand, rather than with any reference as to how far they may comprise specimens of the unexceptionable application of art to purposes of ornamentation.—J. S.

## BLEACHING TEXTILE FABRICS.*

All textile fibres, such as cotton and flax, contain a variable amount of colouring substance in their natural condition. This colouring material is usually accompanied by another substance, in many respects analogous to wax—even the beautiful green colouring principle of the leaves of plants is intimately associated with such a waxy substance. In order to dye such fibres any particular colour it is, therefore, necessary that this natural colouring material be removed, and also the waxy substance, which latter would prevent the dying matter from adhering to the cloth. Then again, in the weaving of cloth, certain other substances are added to the fibre, which would also prevent a proper and uniform dyeing of it. The warp is obliged to be prepared or stiffened by some substance, such as starch or dextrine, or by flour paste, to prevent the shuttle from wearing it. But these substances, or, as they are called, *size*, are very rapidly altered by the action of the air,—they become sour, and would very soon act upon the material of the thread, if a little sulphate of copper or sulphate of zinc were not added, which has the effect of arresting this tendency. As long as such substances remain in cloth it would be impossible to dye it. But this is not all. Formerly the operation of weaving was conducted in cold and damp places, a proceeding which was attended with the most fatal results to the health of the workmen; but at present, warm, dry, and well-aired rooms are being gradually selected for this purpose. In such places, however, the fibres of flax, and cotton, and hemp become crisp, and the threads ravel and wear very rapidly, an inconvenience which is corrected by impregnating the tissue with certain deliquescent salts, such as chloride of calcium, which keep the threads continually moist by attracting moisture from the atmosphere.

Woollen and silk tissues do not contain these foreign substances, but they have some peculiar to themselves. Thus the former is impregnated with fatty matters, which, by gradually altering from the action of air, become changed into bodies which act in fastening the colours in the cloth; but being unequally distributed through it, cloth dyed before their removal will be found to be covered with spots. Silk is sized with some gummy substance. Before such fabrics can be dyed, therefore, these substances must be removed; and in proportion to their perfect removal will be the brilliancy of colour which can be imparted to the cloth. All the white linen, cotton, and woollen goods in the Exhibition, as well as those which have been dyed, have undergone a series of processes for this purpose, termed *bleaching*. The operation of bleaching is exceedingly complicated, although it may appear at first sight very simple, and requires not only great and minute care, but also special knowledge; for the bleacher has not merely to understand the nature of the various substances already alluded to, but he has to take into account the different contrivances made by manufacturers to imitate various fabrics in one material, by impregnating another with certain foreign matters. For example, articles are made with a cotton warp and a woollen weft, and in order to make the whole appear as if made of wool, the cotton is prepared with oil; sometimes the cotton threads are even animalized with gelatine, which is *fixed* by means of some chemical substance, such as alum, in the tissue, so that it is nearly

* The following paper relates to the bleaching of textile fabrics generally; and cotton being the first class in this section, it has been considered advisable to introduce it here in its integrity, in preference to cutting it up in portions, and, as a matter of course, going to some extent over the same ground on subsequent occasions.—ED.

impossible to distinguish the threads from wool. In such cases the bleacher must respect these various substances, at the same time that he must remove all the others.

The operations of the bleacher necessarily divide themselves into two distinct classes; one having for its object the removal of all the substance of which we have just spoken, and the other the bleaching, properly so called; and we may here observe that the operations vary according to the nature of the tissue, and that those which answer for cotton would not be applicable for wool. We shall speak first of the bleaching of cotton and linen goods, as being the more important to this country. In most respects the processes now followed with both these tissues are identical, the chief difference being that in general the linen, which is much more difficult to bleach than the cotton, in addition to being treated by the chemical processes, is spread upon grass and exposed for a certain period to the action of the sun's rays.

It may be useful, before describing the processes now followed in the bleaching of vegetable fibres, to give our readers some notion of the means which were formerly adopted to effect the same object. About fifty years ago flax yarn used to be fermented for three days, then washed with potash, and rinsed, after which it received a second washing with potash and a twenty hours' boiling, then rinsed and steeped in chlorine water, after which it received a fresh rinsing, and three other washings with potash; then a series of immersions in chlorine, of steeping in alkaline leys, and of rinsings in acidified water. Finally, the tissues were spread upon the bleach-green, after which they received a last ley and rinsing. It is unnecessary to observe that such a process must have occupied a considerable length of time—at least six weeks, and frequently three months. For a long period these processes remained unaltered, but it was at length proposed to substitute lime for potash and soda in removing the filthy matter. At first the attempts were very unsuccessful, as it was found that the goods were burned; but subsequently it was ascertained that if the air was excluded during the operation no such injurious action would occur. Another improvement was then made, namely, the employment of acids. These different modifications have given rise to the present process, which is exceedingly cheap and expeditious.

Bleaching may now be effected in twelve hours, and the most perfect white obtained in three days, instead of six to twelve weeks as formerly; and the bleaching of a yard of cloth does not cost the tenth part of a penny, instead of nine-pence, as it did sixty years ago. Lime is employed, because no substance is so well adapted for removing the fatty matters, which it does by converting them into soaps; while it has not the disadvantage of attacking the fibre, of rendering the tissues translucent, and at the same time contracting them. In dissolving out the foreign substances from the tissues, it does not form viscous compounds which would adhere to the cloth. It thoroughly removes all those peculiar substances which contain nitrogen. These are very liable to decay, and if not frequently removed under the influence of the air, soon render the whited cloth as brown as it was before it had been bleached. The lime is made to act directly according to the nature of the tissues to be bleached, and according as they are more or less charged with foreign substances. The operation is commenced by two steeps with lime, after which the material to be bleached is submitted to a series of operations entirely mechanical, which have for their object to assist the action of water in removing all foreign matter in suspension. They, in fact, replace the beetle or wooden mallet of the washerwoman. When these operations are terminated the action of an acid is had recourse to—the usual acids employed being sulphuric acid or oil of vitriol, and hydrochloric acid or spirit of salt. The acid decomposes the soap which the lime had formed, combines with the latter, and sets the fatty bodies free. It is now only that it is necessary to employ soda to remove the free fats; and if it is wished to have a perfect white, about 2 lbs. of rosin for every 1000 yards of cloth are added. The introduction of rosin was a happy innovation, and completes the invention, for by it alone can perfect white be obtained.

When a tissue has been submitted to these different operations it may be considered as entirely purged from all foreign substances, and is ready for the process of bleaching properly so called. Formerly the steeping process was conducted in precisely the same way as in the corresponding domestic arrangement of the laundress; afterwards, an apparatus was devised, constructed upon the same principles as a French coffee-pot. The steam, disengaged by water contained in a reservoir, causes the water to ascend into a second recipient in which the goods are placed. This water, which is charged with lime, passes through them, and returns again into the reservoir. It is not our object, nor have we space for describing all the apparatus now used for this purpose; we shall only say that that which is most employed at present, and which appears to have fulfilled all the necessary conditions, is the apparatus invented by Mr. Badington. In it the goods are submitted to the action of a ley of lime, the temperature of which is raised much higher than boiling water (230° Fahr.), by means of steam, which exerts a pressure in the apparatus of about 60 lbs. upon the square inch. M. Baudry, of Rouen, has effected a very happy improvement in this contrivance, by making the circulation of the ley continuous.

The clumsy way in which the rinsing of bleached and dyed goods was formerly managed is well known; and it may even be still seen among poor workmen who manufacture woollen goods—namely, beating them with wooden flails in some stream of running water. A substitute was found for this system, which consisted of a turning table, and an arrangement of heavy beetles which rose and fell alternately on the goods. Then came the *dash-wheel*, which is still much employed in England, and which consists of a drum five or six feet in diameter, and about two feet in depth, turning on a horizontal axis; it is divided into four compartments by means of partitions, each of which has a large circular opening, and on one face of the wheel water is admitted by a pipe which surrounds the axle. The pieces of cloth to be washed are put into the compartments through the openings just named, and are washed during the rapid rotation of the wheel by the water entering near the axle, and flowing out by the hole. Another machine was subsequently employed, composed of two cylinders, one of which was small and polished, and the other longitudinally grooved; one turned upon the other, and the tissue passed between the two; the upper or smaller one falling each time into a groove, and in so doing, striking or beetling the cloth. To this succeeded another contrivance, composed of two cylinders, placed one above another, and between which the goods are passed and submitted to a powerful pressure, the whole of the water being thereby removed. A number of pieces are stretched together in a heavy endless band, which passes between the rollers, and then into a cistern of pure water. Each piece is thus pressed dry several times, and again moistened as often as may be necessary. There is another form of machine which consists of a cylinder upon which are fastened straps of the skin of the hippopotamus, or of gutta percha, which act like beetles during the revolution of the drum. And lastly, we could employ a centrifugal machine, similar to those exhibited in the Machinery Court of the Exhibition, a stream of water being let in at intervals upon the goods placed in the drum, by which the whole of the impurities would be driven out.

By the operation just described we remove the foreign matters which would prevent the action of the agents used to decolorize; let us now see what are those agents by which the colouring matter naturally contained in the tissue of linen or cotton is destroyed, and the different modes in which they are used. Among bleaching agents chlorine and its various compounds, such as a solution of it in water, chlorides of lime, soda, potash, &c., hold the first rank; the chloride of lime being the substance chiefly employed. Chloride is a peculiar yellowish green gas, of a strong and disagreeable odour, which attacks animal and vegetable substances with great energy, and especially colouring matters. It dissolves in water, and the solution has the same properties as the gas; it is rapidly absorbed by lime, forming the well-known compound bleaching powder. To those of our readers who are not acquainted with chemistry, it will appear curious that this extraordinary substance, which, when breathed, is so destructive to life, should form part of that wholesome and necessary condiment, common salt; indeed, the latter is the great source of all the chlorine used in the arts. To Berthollet, the celebrated French chemist, who lived in the commencement of this century, we are indebted for the application of chlorine to bleaching; and to Mr. Tennant, of Glasgow, for the introduction of bleaching powder as an article of commerce. For many years after its first employment the process of bleaching underwent scarcely any change; it is only within the last twelve years that any great improvement has taken place; for previous to that time bleachers were content to steep the goods in a solution of chloride of lime, owing to the prolonged action of which the tissue was burned, or, at least, injured to a considerable degree, and much loss was thus entailed upon the manufacturer. The process was, therefore, modified, and instead of allowing the goods to rest ten or twelve hours in a solution of chloride of lime, as was formerly done, they were merely passed through it, and were then submitted to the action of an acid bath. This method was more rational; for the employment of the acid in this case decomposed the chloride, and prevented the lime from burning the tissues. The nearer we approach the present time the more perfect do we observe the process to become. For example, instead of making the tissues pass simply through a bath of chloride of lime, they are now subjected to the action of two cylinders, between which the cloth is made to pass; these cylinders cause the decolorizing agent to penetrate into the finest fibres, and at the same time drive it out by the pressure which they exert, and thus prevent its action from being too prolonged. This machine has been so far modified as to permit the cloth to pass in the form of an endless band, as before described, several times through the bleaching solution, and then between the rollers. The acid bath in which the pieces are subsequently passed has, besides, the further advantage of dissolving a species of yellow resin, which, in time, gives to the tissues, and to paper, the yellow tint or mark of age. These different operations terminated, it only remains to well wash the pieces in pure water, and to dry them, which is now usually done in the centrifugal machine. The wet goods are placed in the drum, which is made to revolve at the rate of from 1000 to 1500 revolutions per minute; the result of which is that the water contained in the cloth is driven out through the periphery of the drum as a fine vapour, while a rapid current of air is, at the same time, caused to pass through it. In order that the reader may have a precise notion of the sequence of the operations, we shall enumerate them here in a few words.

FIRST SERIES OF OPERATIONS, OR SCOURING PROCESS.

1. Soaking in lime-water for twelve hours.
2. Washing and rinsing.
3. Soaking in lime-water for twelve hours.
4. Washing and rinsing.
5. Immersing in very weak sulphuric acid—techically called *scouring*.
6. Washing and rinsing.
7. Steeping in weak solution of carbonate of soda, with the addition of rosin for pure whites.
8. Washing and rinsing.

SECOND SERIES OF OPERATIONS, OR BLEACHING PROCESS.

9. Immersion for some hours in chloride of lime, which does not mark on the areometer, or instrument employed to measure the strength of the solutions, and which, saturated with an acid, does not give rise to a disengagement of chlorine—technically called *chemicking*.
10. Immersion in very dilute hydrocholoric acid—or *souring*.
11. Washing, &c.
12. Second steeping for twenty-four hours in carbonate of soda.
13. Washing.
14. Second chemicking, or immersion in chloride of lime.
15. Souring, or immersion in hydraulic acid.

---

16. Perfect washing.
17. Drying.

Silks are not, properly speaking, bleached; they are simply boiled with a solution of soap and soda to remove the grease, then scoured by being passed through dilute sulphuric acid, and finally well washed and dried. Woollen goods and mousselin de laines are bleached by being passed two or three times through a solution of soap and soda at a temperature of about 130° Fahr. (much beyond which woollen goods cannot be heated without injury), and then exposed for several hours to the action of sulphurous acid gas, an operation which is technically called *sulphuring*. The goods are then rinsed in a very weak solution of caustic soda; or, what is preferable, as it removes the crispness caused by the sulphuring, a very slight alkaline soap bath. The woollen thread used for the manufacture of the celebrated Gobelin tapestry, and which are so remarkable for the purity and brilliancy of their dyes, are stuped in a bath made of a solution of sulphurous acid in water, which is prepared by a most ingenious and effective contrivance. The perfection of this process, and the unrivalled colours which it enables the manufacturer to communicate to his goods, have gradually led to its adoption in several of the celebrated continental factories.—W. K. S.

---

1. ANKETELL, MATTHEW J., Anketell Grove, County Monaghan.—Ginghams, &c., manufactured on the Anketell Grove Estate.

2. BARBER, J. L., & Co., Norwich, Manufacturers.—Sewing and crochet threads; specimens of three, six, and nine-cord sewing, crochet, and brocade threads.

3. BROOK, JONAS, & BROTHERS, Meltham Mills, near Huddersfield, Manufacturers and Winders.—Cotton in process of manufacture; sewing cotton in hanks, bleached and unbleached, and on spools; crochet and knitting cord in hanks, bleached and unbleached, and on spools; Valenciennes thread on spools.

4. CLABBURN, SONS, & CRISP, Norwich, Manufacturers.—Fancy dresses.

5. CLARKE, J. P., King-street Cotton Mills, Leicester, Manufacturer.—Specimens showing the various winding of sewing and crochet threads.

6. CLUGSTON, JOHN, & Co., Power Loom Cloth Manufacturers and Bleachers, Glasgow, Manufacturers (JAMES FORBES, Eden-quay, Dublin, Agent).—Scotch hollands of all qualities; white and buff window hollands; twilled cotton sheetings; Derries, furnitures, Bengals, jean stripes, &c.

7. CUMMING, WALLACE, & Co., Power Loom Cloth Manufacturers, Queen-street, Glasgow (JAMES FORBES, Eden-quay, Dublin, Agent).—Scotch hollands of all qualities; white and buff window hollands; twilled cotton sheetings; Derries, furnitures, Bengals, jean stripes, &c.

8. FRY, WILLIAM, & Co., Westmoreland-street, Dublin.—British printed chintzes and velvets; and foreign chintzes in variety.

9. GILL, F. J. & R., Manchester, Manufacturers.—Cotton and silk stitched double nankeens and contils, consisting of two cloths woven and stitched in the loom for corsets.

10. JOHNSON, J., Spring Gardens, Manchester, Manufacturer.—White and coloured toilette quilts and covers; fancy wove quiltings; and shapes for vests; quilting skirts.

11. LEE, DANIEL, & Co., Manchester, Manufacturers.—Cotton damasks, chintzes in great variety of manufacture and design.

12. MAIR, J., Hutcheson-street, Glasgow, Proprietor.—Friends' book muslin and tarlatan; handkerchiefs of same.

13. MAIR, J., SON, & Co., London and Glasgow.—Embroidered muslin robes; window muslins and lenos; printed Bandannas; sewed piece goods.

14. MARTIN, W., & SON, Bolton and Manchester, Manufacturers.—Hair cord dimity; furniture dimity; dice, and damask dimities.

15. MARSLAND, SON, & Co., Manchester, Designers and Manufacturers.—Cotton, in skeins and on reels, for sewing, crochet, guipure, knitting, and embroidery purposes; crochet, guipure, and embroidery worked therewith.

16. MELLODEWS, EMMOTT, & Co., Albion Mill, Oldham, Lancashire, Manufacturers.—Self nankeens for card making, tent cloth, tailors' trimmings, or stays; stiffening nankeen for boot linings, tailors' trimmings, cork making, or book-binding; superfine twills for petticoats; heavy Croydon cloth, in imitation of linen.

17. MOSS, SIGISMUND S., Kilternan Cotton Mill, Golden Ball, Co. Dublin, and High-street, Dublin, Manufacturer.—Cotton in various stages of preparation, from the raw material to the manufactured state; raw cotton; carded sliver from drawing frames; on bobbins preparatory to spinning; spun cotton in the cop and skein; unbleached and bleached cotton twist for warps; cotton candlewick unbleached and bleached; mould and dip candlewick in balls for cutting by machine and by hand, unbleached and bleached; fine bleached cotton for spermaceti candles; plaited wicks prepared for spermaceti and composite candles, cut to the required lengths and looped.

18. M'BIRNEY, COLLIS, & Co., Dublin, Exhibiters; R. & J. WORKMAN, Belfast, Manufacturers.—Jaconet muslin; mull muslin; bishop's lawn; India book; tamboured book and jaconets; Swiss mull.

19. M'BRIDE & Co., Glasgow, Inventors and Manufacturers.—Cotton diaper; cotton, damask, and table cloths; cotton bird-eye diaper; cotton huckaback towelling; furniture, regatta, and coach stripes; ginghams, apron checks, and cross-over stripes—all woven in power looms, invented, and first applied by Mr. J. M'Bride.

20. SYMINGTON, R. B., & Co., Glasgow, Manufacturers.—Figured harness muslin window curtains, in leno and book muslin grounds, (made by the Jacquard loom); figured harness muslin short blinds.

21. WALMSLEY, H., FAILSWORTH, Manchester, Manufacturer.—Jacquard figured robes, damasks, &c.

# . CLASSES XII. & XIV.

## WOOLLEN AND WORSTED, AND MIXED FABRICS,

[NOT INCLUDING POPLINS.]

THE space occupied by woollen fabrics in the Exhibition was probably less than most persons would have expected, though there were few kinds of goods of this class without their representative being present, from the superfine cloths of Germany, and of the West of England, to the coarse friezes and tweeds produced in our own country.

The woollen manufacture of the United Kingdom has long been regarded as one of the most important branches of industry. In this country it attracted a great deal of attention in former times, and flourished towards the close of the seventeenth century to an extent of which we can now scarcely form an opinion. While the finer kinds of cloth were produced in some of the large manufactories, the production of the coarser fabrics was carried on throughout the entire country. But this prosperity was checked by the jealousies which then prevailed in England as to the high manufacturing position which Ireland enjoyed; and in the absence of any correct notions on economic science, the woollen trade was in every way discouraged, and at last actually prohibited! At the present day we are almost astounded at the idea of legislative interference in this direction; but this, and similar instances of misrule, speak trumpet-tongued of the character of those times, which we sometimes hear lauded as "the good old times," from which so much degeneracy is alleged to have ensued. It is with difficulty we can realize to ourselves the idea of an Act of Parliament being directed to put down a particular branch of manufacture in any part of the country. But we must observe, that it is to that prohibition we are chiefly indebted for the attention devoted to the growth and manufacture of flax, which received especial encouragement at the period to which we refer—the favour extended in the one case being designed to compensate for the prohibition in the other. The woollen manufacture, however, continued to be carried on by the peasantry for their domestic wants, notwithstanding these restrictions; and at length a more liberal policy prevailed, when the prohibition in question was removed. By way, probably, of making amends, a protective duty was levied on the importation of woollen goods into Ireland, even from the sister country. But the trade did not recover the shock which it had received. It is now a long period since all restrictions between this and the sister country in this class of goods have been removed. Still the trade has made slow progress. It has been stationary, or, perhaps, we should say retrograde, for some time past; and at present the woollen manufacture of Ireland is in an exceedingly languid state. There are now but few factories at work; and of these a still smaller number afford evidence of that activity and those general arrangements which are essential to the success of any branch of trade.

In treating of "woollen goods" we must bear in mind that the term, as generally used, does not include all such as are commonly made of wool, but only those prepared in a particular manner. For instance, the term "worsted stuffs" is applied to those productions in the composition of which wool is used that has undergone the process of *combing;* the term itself being derived from a village in Norfolk, where this class of goods was first produced. In examining the fleece of a sheep, a distinction will be found between the wool of short and that of long staple. The short wool, when observed by the aid of the microscope, will be distinguished by the immense number of little feathery serrations or imbrications on its surface, which enable the individual fibres to be locked into each other in what is called the *felting* or *fulling* process, to which all "woollen" as distinguished from "worsted" goods are subjected. Hence the short wool is especially adapted for the production of woollen cloths. Long wool does not possess these serrations to the same extent; and is hence better suited for combing, the object of which is to unravel the fibres and lay them smooth and even. The long wools are totally unfit for being manufactured into the finer kinds of cloths, as, in addition to their not being acted upon in the fulling mill, they cannot be made to present a fine surface. The short wools of Australia, the Cape, and even of our own mountain districts, are therefore made into superfine fabrics, while the long wool of the sheep of the finer districts is exclusively confined to the production of worsted goods, such as merinos, coburg cloths, delaines, and a host of other denominations.

The business of *wool-sorting* is a fundamental one in this branch of trade, requiring much practical knowledge on the part of those engaged in it. As many as from ten to fourteen varieties of wool are found in a single fleece, each being adapted for the production of a peculiar class of goods. The fibres of the wool are straight and lank in some instances, and crooked or interlaced in others; these peculiarities also fitting them for particular purposes. The division into links, formed by the coherence of the single fibres, varies in every species of wool, and forms what is called the *staple.* If a fleece is spread out, the wool of the head, the legs, the belly, and the tail, form the exterior parts or margin, and are the portions of most inferior quality: that on the back and sides being the best. The Spanish wool comes into the market divided into four sorts: *refina, prima, segonda*, and *tercera*. Saxon wool is similarly divided. In wool-sorting, if the best wool of one fleece be not equal to the finest sort, it is put with the second or third class of an equal degree of fineness with it. The best English fleeces, such as the Southdown, are usually divided into the following kinds, according to quality:—1. Prime; 2. Choice; 3. Super; 4. Head; 5. Downrights; 6. Seconds; 7. Fine abb; 8. Coarse abb; 9. Livery; 10. Coarse, short, or breech wool. Fine Merino wool grows within a year from one to two inches in length, while the fleece of those animals, technically called "long-woolled," is often over four inches. For the determination of the degree of fineness, what is called "wool measures" have been invented. But the softness of the fibre is not less important than its fineness; and the former does not altogether depend on the latter, but consists of that peculiar feel so well indicated by the touch, but which is so difficult to describe. For example, the value of two pieces of cloth made of two kinds of wool equally fine, the one distinguished for its softness, and the other for the opposite quality, will vary very materially, the difference being so much as 20 per cent. It has been asserted that the quality of the wool is dependent on the nature of the soil on which the sheep are fed: sheep pastured on the chalk or light calcareous districts producing hard wool, the softer kinds coming from rich loamy clay soils. But considerations of this kind are of little moment to the manufacturer, who is able by a glance to determine the quality and value of every sample that may come before him.

It may be further observed, that hard wools are deficient in *felting* properties—those characteristics on which the adaptation of any specimen for hat-making depends. Most of our readers are, doubtless, aware that the wool of which hats are made is neither spun nor woven; but locks of it being thoroughly intermixed and compressed in warm water, cohere, and form a solid tenacious substance. Felted wool is also used for certain descriptions of cloth. Even in woven goods the appearance is dependent on the extent to which the process takes place. After the cloth is brought from the loom, the strokes of the fulling mill make the fibres of the wool adhere to each other; the fabric becomes thickened, and of course proportionably contracted; and, after undergoing a dressing and finishing-off, is fit for use. The process is no less essential to the strength than to the beauty of the cloths. There is, in short, little similarity between the article which has just come from the loom, and that which is ready for the market; and any one not conversant with the manufacture could scarcely conceive that the one was resolvable into the other.

The commercial value of the wool is greatly affected by its condition as regards cleanliness; and in this respect we are bound to state that the practice of the Irish farmers is often sadly deficient. Much may be done by a little attention, without involving much trouble. Thus, removing sheep shortly before shearing to clean pasture, and washing them immediately previous, will materially improve the value of the fleece. It is said, that a pack of English or Irish wool of 240 pounds weight will waste about 70 pounds in the manufacture, in consequence of the impurities combined with it, while Spanish wool will not waste more than 48 pounds.

After sorting, the wool has to be scoured, and further divested of impurities, by passing it through an apparatus for the purpose. When dyed the requisite colour, and made pliant by a liberal application of oil, it is passed to the carding machines, where it is minutely teased, and formed into small cylindrical rolls, of a diameter not much exceeding that of a goose-quill. This machine consists of a number of cylinders of different diameters, on the surface of which sheets of card with teeth are placed. These cylinders work on each other, passing forward the wool thus acted upon, until it is finally ejected in the small rolls already mentioned. The slubbing machine converts these rolls into thread, each machine having a great number of spools, to which the rolls of wool are supplied by young persons. By the use of a machine termed a condenser, attached to the carding machine, the latter may be made to discharge the rolls by the end, instead of throwing off rolls of a length corresponding to that of the cylinders. By the arrangements now referred to, the rolls come continuously from the carding machines without any break in them so long as wool is supplied; and the rolls are at once taken up by the condenser and spun into thread, without the intervention of an attendant, further than to remove a spool when filled and replace it by an empty one. In either case the thread is further operated upon by a jenny or mule, in which it is drawn out and twisted to any desired degree of fineness and hardness. In the mule, as well as in the slubbing machine, the spindles are placed upon a carriage which moves backwards and forwards, the thread being in the process transferred from one set of spools to another. In these mules two or more threads are put together and twisted up, according to the kind of fabric to be made.

The yarn is now ready for the warping machine or the shuttle pools, according as it is intended for warp or woof. The weaving presents but little peculiarity deserving of note; the power loom and hand loom being indiscriminately used for the purpose. The oil which had to be used on account of the roughness of the fibres, to enable them to move freely upon each other in the spinning and weaving, is discharged from the cloth by scouring; and if not dyed in the wool the fabric is now ready to receive the desired colour, according to the object for which it is intended.

The *fulling* process is not applied to articles made from long wool, which in this respect are finished when they come from the loom. The tendency to thicken by friction is peculiar to wool and hair, and does not exist in the fibres of cotton or flax. It is owing to a certain roughness of the fibres, which permits motion in one direction while it retards it in another. Entanglements of the fibres, so to speak, are thereby produced, through which the thickening of the fabric is effected. The downy surface of woollen cloths that so much adds to the beauty of the appearance, is, however, produced at the expense of a diminution of strength. It is effected by causing the cloth to pass over cylinders in motion, the surface of which is formed of a species of burrs, the fruit of the common teasel, *Dipsacus fullonum*; which is largely cultivated for the purpose in certain districts of the South and West of England, and might, no doubt, be profitably grown in this country. Successive portions of the fibres are extracted by this action, and are laid in a parallel direction, to be further operated upon by excision in the case of the finer description of goods, and by the twisted napping machine for friezes and such fabrics. In shearing, the process is performed by a large spiral blade revolving rapidly in contact with another blade fixed; the cloth being stretched over a bed or support just near enough for the projecting filaments being cut off at a uniform length, the main texture being left uninjured. The twisted nap, usually confined to friezes, is dependent entirely on whim, and, we believe, possesses no particular advantage.

To the finishing process, woollen fabrics of the finer class owe much of their beauty. Without it they would be wanting in that elegance of appearance and softness to the touch by which they are characterized, whatever might be their qualities in other respects. The present system of finishing off by what is called the *roll boiling process*, has been in use since 1824; and its peculiarity is that it produces a lustre on the face of the cloth that neither spots by rain nor is removed by damp. The permanent face is imparted by rolling the cloth round a cylinder, putting it in scalding water for two or three hours, then taking it out and letting it cool; and this has to be done several times during the process of dressing. Before the introduction of this method the general plan had been to dye blacks in the piece of a common dye; but this new method was found to interfere with that of dyeing, from its being found difficult to make the dye penetrate through the improved fabric. Hence the gradual introduction of dyeing in the wool,—a process which requires for its successful execution both skill and experience. On the Continent the method of finishing off most in vogue consists in rolling the cloth tightly round a perforated hollow cylinder, into which steam is introduced to produce the desired effect.

The changes which have taken place in the localities of the woollen manufactures of England are not a little remarkable. Norfolk was in former times the great seat of the worsted trade; the production of woollens being chiefly confined to two or three of the western counties. But since the commencement of the present century a few of the leading towns of Yorkshire have gradually attracted both branches to their localities until that county has now become the centre of the trade. Superfine cloths are, however, still produced in the West of England (especially the finer qualities), at Chippenham, Frome, Wootton-under-Edge, and Stroud; as well as at Huddersfield, Leeds, and Halifax. At Galashiels, Hawick, and Selkirk, in Scotland, particular qualities, chiefly narrow cloths, are produced. Witney, Dewsbury, and Oakhampton, are famous for the production of blankets; and in Dewsbury a manufacture is carried on of a coarse cloth solely from woollen rags, which has attracted much attention. Bradford, in Yorkshire, has become the great seat of productions of the worsted manufacture, the progress of that town being really surprising. In 1801 it had a population of 13,264; and in 1831 the population had increased to upwards of 43,000; and in 1851, to 103,000; the rate of increase being still more extraordinary, there being over 33,000 persons at present directly employed in that branch of trade in Bradford.* But Leeds is fairly to be regarded now as the great capital of the woollen manufacture, which, with the surrounding towns, supplies a large proportion of this class of goods. Huddersfield comes next in importance for the quantity and great variety of the woollen cloths which it produces, including broad cloths and trowserings of almost every quality. Flannel is produced in large quantities at Rochdale; and various kinds of woollen goods are produced at other English and Scotch towns.

In Ireland the woollen manufacture is for the most part confined to friezes, tweeds, and flannels, all of which are produced of excellent quality.

The progress of this branch of industry has been diversified by the introduction of new improvements, and of new descriptions of raw material, the changes produced in the one way being probably as great as in the other. The carding machinery, the spinning-mule, the power-loom, and the felting machinery, were each, no doubt, followed by striking and important changes. The same may also be said of the introduction of the wool of the llama, alpaca, and of the worked-up residue of worn-out woollen goods. At the present time woollen rags are eagerly sought after to be again worked up into new fabrics. The rags are, of course, torn up and separated into fibre, which is afterwards mixed with wool. The fibre so obtained is termed "shoddy," and if of good quality and used in moderate proportions it is contended by some of the manufacturers that its use is not injurious. But, on the other hand, when used in excess, the shoddy is eminently pernicious, producing a most unserviceable article. This material, when well prepared, is now selling at eleven-pence per pound. So much for the value of those woollen rags which usually go to make manure. Shoddy is not used by any of the Irish woollen manufacturers.

## THE IRISH WOOLLEN TRADE.

An incidental allusion has already been made to the discouragement thrown in the way of this manufacture in Ireland in times past. Its present state is by no means satisfactory; and on setting about an inquiry as to the causes on which such a state of affairs is dependent—more especially as we have evidence of its being once in a prosperous condition—we come to those monstrous drawbacks which were thrown in the way by the Crown, shortly after the Revolution, the baneful effects of which are seen to the present day. After the Commonwealth the Irish woollen manufacture was in a flourishing state, and so continued until it was made to feel the blighting influence of mistaken legislation. It is not with a view of declaiming against the sister country that we now revert to circumstances so long passed by; but it is in order to disarm of their

* There were only three mills in Bradford at the beginning of the present century, and now there are upwards of 160. The following statistics will convey some idea of the present state of the trade of the town and neighbouring district, including the village of Bingley, which may be regarded as a dependency of the town of Bradford:—

| | |
|---|---|
| Number of Spindles, | 355,792 |
| Number of Power-looms, | 17,294 |
| Moving power, steam (horse power), | 3,884 |
| Ditto, water, " | 134 |
| Children employed under 13, males, | 1,469 |
| Ditto, females, | 1,729 |
| Males from 13 to 18, | 3,416 |
| Ditto, above 18, | 5,961 |
| Females above 13, | 21,280 |
| Total number of persons employed. { Males, 10,846; Females, 23,009 } Total, | 33,855 |

force those sneers which are so constantly indulged in by strangers at Irish mismanagement. The formation of the character of a people is a work of slow growth; and if two countries are united together, the stronger depressing the energies of the weaker and throwing discouragements in the way, such an amount of lethargy and indifference, combined with discontent, will ensue, as it may require generations to remove. The spirit which dictated this course has long passed away; and at present, so far as regards the commercial relations not only between this country and England, but with all parts of the globe, we have no fault to find. But the injurious effects of the past may still be traced. Some of the incidents of the Irish woollen trade have, in truth, so much the appearance of being fabulous, that we may here be excused for detailing a few of them, referring at the same time to the official documents whence the information is derived.

The interference with the woollen manufactures of Ireland in the reign of William III. was the more unjustifiable on account of the circumstances which led to its taking place. Complaints were made by the English traders at the influx of Irish goods to their markets; but this large export of Irish woollens followed a previous prohibition of cattle and sheep into England, at the instance of the farmers of the latter country. The increased proportion of sheep killed at home gave an impetus to the production of woollen goods, the manufacture of which next came to be regarded with jealousy; and it, too, was placed under restrictions of a character which persons at the present day could scarcely believe to be possible.

The Act of the 15th of Charles II., c. 7, and that of the 18th of the same monarch, c. 2, were passed to restrain and afterwards prohibit the exportation of cattle and sheep from Ireland; the people of which, being thus deprived of their principal trade, and reduced to the utmost distress, had no resource left but to work up their own commodities at home, which the accounts of the period represent them as having done with great vigour. The previous ineffectual attempt of Lord Strafford, in 1639, to prevent the making of broadcloths in Ireland, lent additional countenance to the belief which the prohibition of the exportation of live stock inspired, that with the woollen trade no further interference would be made. Even in the same reign in which these prohibitions took place, inducements were held out for the exportation of woollens. But in an Act of the first year of William and Mary, c. 32, we find a prohibition of the shipment of wool from Ireland, unless from certain ports therein named; and by the same Statute it was provided that only at certain English ports it would be admitted. It was not, however, until 1697 that any attempt was made to prevent the exportation of the manufactured goods. A Bill for the purpose passed the English House of Commons in that year, but was thrown out by the Lords. It was not, however, until the assembling of a new Parliament, in 1698, that the contemplated piece of injustice was consummated.*

The feeling which prevailed at the time may be seen from the Address presented by both Houses of Parliament to the King. On the 9th June, 1698, the Lords represent, "That the growing manufacture of cloth in Ireland, both by the cheapness of all sorts of necessaries for life, and *the goodness of materials for making all manner of cloth*, doth invite your subjects of England, with their families and servants, to leave their habitations to settle there, to the increase of the woollen manufacture of Ireland, which makes your loyal subjects in this kingdom very apprehensive that the *further growth* of it may greatly prejudice the said manufacture here; by which the trade of the nation and the value of land will very much decrease, and the numbers of your people be much lessened here." Their Lordships then further beseech his Majesty "in the most public and effective way that may be, to declare to all your subjects of Ireland, that the *growth* and *increase* of the woollen manufacture hath long and will ever be looked upon with jealousy; *and if not timely remedied* may occasion very strict laws, totally to prohibit and suppress the same; and on the other hand, if they turn their industry and skill to the settling and improving the linen manufacture, for which generally the lands of that kingdom are very proper, they shall receive all countenance, favour, and protection from your *royal influence*, for the encouragement and promotion of the said linen manufacture, to *all the advantages and profit that kingdom can be capable of*." In the royal reply, his Majesty said that he "will take care to do what their Lordships have desired."

In the Address of the Commons, adopted on the 30th of June in that year, they say that "being sensible that the wealth and peace of this kingdom do, in a great measure, depend on preserving the woollen manufacture as much as possible *entire* to this realm, they think it becomes them, like their ancestors, to be jealous of the *establishment* and *increase* of the same elsewhere, and to use their utmost endeavours to prevent it; and therefore they cannot without trouble observe that Ireland, dependent on and protected by England in the enjoyment of all they have, and which is so proper for the linen manufacture, should of late apply itself to the woollen manufacture, to the great prejudice of the trade of this kingdom; the consequence whereof will necessitate your Parliament of England to interpose to prevent the mischief that *threatens* us, unless your Majesty, by your authority and great wisdom, shall find means to secure the trade of England, by making the trade of Ireland to pursue the joint interest of both kingdoms. And we do most humbly implore your Majesty's protection and favour in this matter; and that you will make it your royal care, and enjoin all those you employ in Ireland to make it their care, and use their utmost diligence, to hinder the *exportation of wool from Ireland*, except to be imported hither, and for the discouraging the woollen manufactures and encouraging the linen manufactures in Ireland, to which we shall be *always* ready to give our utmost assistance."

The notable address from which the foregoing is extracted was presented to the King, and the answer does not partake of that ambiguity which now sometimes characterizes royal speeches. His Majesty assured his

* By the public returns we learn that the exports of woollen goods from Ireland, in the undermentioned years, were:

| Years. | New Draperies. | Old Draperies. | Frizes. |
|---|---|---|---|
| | Pieces. | Pieces. | Yards. |
| 1665 | 294 | 82 | 444,381 |
| 1687 | 11,360 | 103 | 1,129,716 |
| 1696 | 4,413 | 34 | 104,167 |
| 1698 | 23,285 | 381 | 669,901 |

The total value of those manufactures exported in 1697, as cited by Dr. Smith, in his Memoirs of Wool, was £23,614, of which stockings and friezes amounted to £14,625, the balance representing the value of the old and new draperies. According to the same authority, the gross value of the exports in 1687 was £70,521, of which the friezes amounted to £56,485.

"faithful commons" that he would not be wanting in giving effect to their wishes—"I shall do all that in me lies to discourage the woollen trade in Ireland, and encourage the linen manufacture there; and to promote the trade of England."

On the 16th of the following month, in writing to Lord Galway, then one of the Lords Justices here, the King stated that "it was never of such importance to have, as at present, a good session of Parliament, and that you make effectual laws for the linen manufacture, and discourage *as far as possible* the woollen." The ensuing session of the Irish Parliament commenced on the 27th of September, 1698, and the Lords Justices in their opening speech direct attention to a Bill transmitted to them for the encouragement of the linen and hempen manufactures, to which they thus allude:—"The settlement of this manufacture will contribute much to people this country, and will be found *much more advantageous to this kingdom* than the woollen manufacture, which being the settled staple trade of England, *from whence all foreign markets are supplied*, can never be encouraged here for that purpose." The consideration of the subject was referred to a select committee, the slow movements of which did not please the Lords Justices, who on the 2nd October again called attention to the subject:—"The matters we recommended to you," said their Lordships, "are so necessary, and the prosperity of this kingdom depends so much on the good success of this session, that since we know his Majesty's affairs cannot permit your sitting very long, we thought the greatest mark we could give of our kindness and concern for you was to come hither and desire you to hasten the despatch of the matters under your consideration, in which we are the more earnest, because we must be sensible that if the present opportunity his Majesty's affection for you hath put into your hands be lost it is hardly to be recovered."

To enter into a detail of the negotiations and propositions advanced with a view of effecting the desired object would occupy more space than we can devote to the subject in this brief sketch. Suffice it to say, that on the 29th of January following an Act received the royal assent, 10 Wm. III., c. 5, by which an additional duty was imposed of 4*s*. for every 20*s*. in value of broadcloth exported out of Ireland. But this did not satisfy the English Parliament; and on the 20th of June, 1699, an Act was passed, 10 and 11 Wm. III., c. 10, prohibiting the exportation from Ireland of all goods made or mixed with wool except to England and Wales, and with the license of the Commissioners of the Revenue. Duties had before been imposed which amounted to a prohibition.

Crippled thus at every step by mistaken and ill-directed legislation, large quantities of Irish goods were smuggled to other countries; and if ever such a demoralizing practice could be palliated it was in such a case as this. To put it down the severest penalties were enacted, but in vain; and in 1739 a slight relaxation was made by which the duties were taken off woollen or bay yarn exported from Ireland, excepting worsted yarn of two or more threads. Other changes in the social condition of Ireland ensued, which still further depressed this branch of trade, though they made the vexatious restrictions placed upon it less severely felt. And yet these restrictions were almost sufficient of themselves to lead to the disappearance of the woollen trade altogether. The spirit which pervaded all parties in the English interest in reference to Ireland, towards the close of the seventeenth century, may be judged from a representation made by the Commissioners of Trade, dated the 11th of November, 1697, advising a duty to be laid on the importation of oil, upon teasles whether imported or *growing* there, and upon all the utensils employed in the woollen manufacture, on the utensils of worsted combers, and a duty upon all cloth and woollen stuff, except friezes, *before* being taken from the loom! The changes referred to were those by which the growing of wool became less profitable than other branches of industry, especially the production of grain, an increased demand for which prevailed throughout a great part of the eighteenth century. Thus, whilst our own manufacturers were starving for want of employment during the years 1777 and 1778, we find that woollen goods to the amount of £715,740 were imported from England—years which we have specified on account of the great distress that prevailed, upwards of 20,000 of the manufacturers who had previously been in receipt of a competence by the proceeds of their industry being supported by public charity.*

It is not necessary to pursue this subject farther. Enough has been shown on data which do not admit of question as to the short-sighted policy which in former times was carried out in reference to this branch of manufacture; and it cannot be matter of surprise that the withering effects of that policy should long survive its abrogation. The obstacles to the cause of progress in Ireland in times past have been numerous; and those who will take the trouble to study the social history of the country will see room for abstaining from the jeers which are so often indulged in at our expense. The truth is, we have been both sinned against and sinning. But a more liberal and enlightened policy now prevails; and it is gratifying to find that we are not altogether standing still under it. Our progress may be slower than could be desired, but we believe it to be sure; and if we refer to the past, it is chiefly with a view of showing that matters are at present more hopeful than might be supposed without reference to our antecedents.

It will readily appear that one of the effects of the drawback against the exportation of wool was to extend the manufacture among the growers of it. Hence, the fabrication of articles from wool is understood and practised to a greater or less extent throughout the country up to the present period. It is spun into yarn by the farmer's family, woven into cloth by some neighbouring weaver, who also weaves household linen goods, and afterwards sent to a fulling mill, to be thickened and prepared for use. Even this latter process we have known to be performed by the parties who were to wear the cloth, by a sort of beetling analogous to the operation of the fulling mill; though it is needless to observe that under such circumstances the thickening of the cloth is very imperfectly attained. The greater part of the frieze worn by the peasantry, and what is termed home-made blankets, are produced in this manner. The general deficiency of employment which, until recently, prevailed throughout the country at particular seasons of the year perpetuated such manufactures as that of which we now speak, as the parties who engage in it would otherwise be idle, and hence there has been no value attached to the time thus occupied. The change which is now happily in progress in the relation between the supply of, and the demand for, labour, will tend to confine the manu-

* "Commercial Restraints of Ireland Considered." Dublin, 1779.

facture of such articles to those who follow it as a business, and by whom it can be done at once more economically and effectively than by the amateur. Large quantities of frieze continue, however, to be produced in the rural districts; and in a few cases the manufacture of the coarser descriptions of woollen fabrics has been introduced with a view of providing employment for persons who might otherwise have been chargeable on the rates. Of the work so produced, we had examples in the Exhibition in the goods exhibited by the Caledon Model School; by Mr. Porter, of Lisbelaw; and Mr. Anketel, of Anketel Grove in the county of Monaghan. These fabrics have, of course, only a local demand. In point of durability they are generally unexceptionable; and, to improve their appearance, and bring them somewhat on a par with the ordinary goods of the shop, they are occasionally sent to some of the smaller manufacturing establishments to be finished off.

Another effect of any branch of manufacture being carried on under discouragements or depressing influences is, that it will rarely be prosecuted with spirit and vigour. New improvements will be slowly introduced. The ability to enter successfully into competition with other parties not so circumstanced will thereby be diminished; which, in turn, will react upon the trade, by circumscribing the demand for the article. And such has been precisely the case with the Irish trade. The great competition which prevails on the other side of the channel among the manufacturers of all kinds of goods in constant demand, keeps ingenuity perpetually on the rack, in the effort to discover any process by which cost of production could be lessened, or the quality of the goods improved without a corresponding increase of expense. This circumstance in conjunction with the intercourse which is taking place between the work-people of different establishments in the same branch of trade, leads to nearly the simultaneous adoption of improvements by almost every employer. How different from this has been the position of the manufacturer in Ireland! Languishing under the influence of mistaken legislation in times past, and without either the facilities or inducements to exertion to which we have referred, the woollen trade of Ireland has for years been ill able to maintain its ground; and perhaps the only matter for surprise is, that it has not long ere this been banished from the land. But this peculiarity of position has had one compensating advantage. With the indisposition to readily adopt improvements, the Irish trade have been equally slow to plume themselves on anything but the genuine and serviceable character of their goods. Shoddy is extensively employed as an adulterant on the other side of the channel, but we believe its use is unknown here.

There are no materials available for determining the extent of the Irish branch of the woollen trade, or the probable quantities of the different classes of goods which they produce. In the vicinity of Dublin we find eight establishments in which the manufacture is to a greater or less extent carried on; but of some three or four of these little can be said, either in reference to their general arrangements or the quantity or quality of the work which they turn out. It requires no special knowledge to enable the visitor to these factories to see the small extent to which they are capable of enabling the manufacture to be economically and effectively carried on. To these remarks, however, we are glad to find some exceptions, and these, moreover, important ones.

The factory of the Messrs. Willans, at Island Bridge, for example, is not only of considerable extent, but it also appears to be fitted up with judgment, and to be well calculated for an extensive trade. This is the only establishment in the district in which the power-loom is at work in the weaving of woollen fabrics. There are twenty-three power-looms in the Island-bridge Factory, and ten hand-looms, but the latter are only occasionally employed, when there happens to be an unusual press of work. The number of spindles in the mules and billies is 4500; and a large quantity of fine yarn is spun, nearly the whole of which is purchased for the manufacture of shawls in Scotland. There are five sets of carding and scribbing machines, and an additional one is being fitted up. It will, therefore, be seen that the power of production of this factory is considerable; and the manufacture embraces friezes, tweeds, army tartans, and army cloths for cavalry and infantry. A variety of other descriptions of woollen goods in the Exhibition illustrated the character of the fabrics turned out by the Messrs. Willans, which well sustained the position their establishment has long held at the head of the Irish branch of the trade.

The establishment next in importance is that of Mr. John Reid, at Ballyboden, which has attained a well-merited celebrity for the production of tweeds, their goods having obtained a prize medal at the Exhibition of 1851. Blanketing, friezes, and such other fabrics as meet with a large local demand, are also produced at this factory. Neither here nor at the Island-bridge Mills are superfine goods manufactured unless to order.

The Blue Bell Factory, the property of Mr. Henry Milner, is one of great promise from the excellent arrangements which are in progress, and the business-like manner in which the work of fitting up the factory seems to have been set about. The period which has elapsed since the present proprietor obtained possession of the premises has been spent in alterations and improvements, and the manufacture can only be said to have commenced. Wool-combing is also carried on here in addition to the other branches of the woollen manufacture.

In the factory of Messrs. C. Neill and Sons, near the village of Tallaght, may be seen at work what, in this country at least, is a modification of the routine practice of the trade—the addition of what are termed condensers to the carding machines—by which the wool is not only carded but spun into yarn without the intervention of human labour; the wool being supplied at one end of the machinery and the yarn being deposited on the large spools at the other. Blanketing, friezes, and tweeds, are the staple produce of this establishment.

The remaining factories may be passed by without any special remarks, as they are of small extent, and some of them are in a state of dilapidation. The business of these mills is chiefly confined to supplying poor-law unions with the coarser description of woollen fabrics; sometimes they finish off goods spun and woven elsewhere in the country; occasionally they produce friezes direct for the consumer, who supplies the wool and pays a stipulated sum for its conversion into the required kind of cloth; and in one or two instances the washing and scouring machine of the woollen factory is used for washing for the soldiery.

There are a few woollen factories to be found throughout the provinces, of which, however, we have no precise information. It is quite clear that the woollen trade of this country might be greatly extended. The only obstacles which now stand in the way are the want of enterprise which is here felt in almost every branch of trade, and the absence of correct and definite notions as to the way in which a business may be pushed and extended. Persons in Ireland of adequate capital to enable them successfully to embark in manufacturing industry have seldom the necessary enterprise; preferring the life of idleness, and of that supposed gentility of which idleness forms an ingredient, by investing their capital in the funds, or in some other way so as to realize an income independent of any exertions of their own. But this spurious gentility has, in reality, much to do with the oppressed condition of our people. We have hitherto unfortunately been doing homage to idleness; and a fearful penalty has followed as the result of such fatuity. Let us now recognise the dignity of labour, and of that well-directed enterprise which alone can insure the prosperity of a country.

The manufacture of this country are not only carried on with inadequate capital in most cases: they also labour under the disadvantage of those connected with them looking for some ground of preference for their productions other than their intrinsic excellence. We hear constant complaints of "want of encouragement,"—complaints which no man ever makes who understands his trade and goes properly about pushing it. There may be, and, no doubt, there often are, local prejudices to contend with. Such silly things may take place, for a time, as the shipment of goods to another country, and their re-shipment, with some foreign mark upon them to the country in which they were produced; the customer thereby paying two freights for his folly. But prejudices of this kind have only to be encountered in a proper manner to be soon dispelled. Wherever goods of an unexceptionable quality are produced at a moderate cost, a market will be created. The great seats of manufacturing industry have, no doubt, a tendency to absorb the particular branches of trade within themselves; but we have only to look at the position of the woollen manufacture in Great Britain to see how effectually in many cases the enterprise of a few energetic individuals can localize a trade: of this Hawick, Galashiels, and many other places that might be mentioned, afford conclusive illustrations. And there is no reason why the same might not be done in many parts of Ireland, but the absence of the necessary enterprise for the purpose. So long, however, as the possessors of capital sneer at trade and manufactures, and so long as those engaged in the great branches of industry look for "encouragement" on any other ground than the excellence of their goods, we must be content to only imperfectly realize that prosperity the material elements of which are so profusely supplied to us.

The following summary shows the exports in this department from the United Kingdom in the undermentioned years:—

| | 1846. | 1848. | 1849. | 1850. | 1851. | 1852. | 1853. |
|---|---|---|---|---|---|---|---|
| Woollen Manufactures of all kinds, | 6,335,108 | 5,733,828 | 7,342,723 | 8,588,690 | 8,377,183 | 8,730,934 | 10,171,263 |
| Woollen Yarn, . . . . . . . . . | 208,270 | 776,975 | 1,090,223 | 1,451,642 | 1,484,544 | 1,430,140 | 1,454,457 |
| Total, . . . . . . . . . | 6,543,378 | 6,510,803 | 8,432,946 | 10,040,332 | 9,861,727 | 10,161,074 | 11,625,720 |

Into any examination of the comparative merits of the several collections in this department it would not become us to enter for reasons which will be obvious. There was, on the whole, a good representation of this class of articles, though it could not be expected that much of novelty would be brought forward. The most noticeable goods in this respect were undoubtedly those of Messrs. Wrigley and Co., of Huddersfield, which combined closeness of texture and softness in a surprising degree. Some of these cloths were little inferior to fur from the extreme fineness and length of the pile upon one side, the other being dressed short like ordinary superfine cloth. The quality of the Irish goods was generally such as to entitle them to high commendation. In trowserings they are not to be excelled; but in the Irish superfine cloth there was a total absence of that high finish which the leading English manufacturers now carry to so great perfection. Although serviceable beyond question, therefore, the production of this article is not likely to find much favour amongst us.—J. S.

---

1. ANKETELL, MATTHEW J., Anketell Grove, County Monaghan.—Woollen fabrics.

2. ALLEN, R., Lower Sackville-street, Dublin, Proprietor.—Fine and superfine waterproofed Eblana friezes; heavy Irish wool friezes; superfine heavy friezes; tweeds and doeskins; embroidered vests, worked in Ireland; superfine wool-dyed Irish black cloth; treble-milled Irish black, blue, and drab box cloths; English and foreign cloths.

3. BIDGOOD, RESIDE, & Co., College-green, Dublin, and Vigo-street, London, Proprietors.—Superfine West of England cloths; scarlet hunter, and mixed army cloths; Jacquard and fancy trowserings; hunting cords; Irish friezes, llamas, and tweeds; Scotch mauds.

4. BULL & WILSON, Saint Martin's-lane, London, Proprietors.—West of England superfine broad cloths, livery cloths, Devons, &c.; kerseymeres and doeskins, dress and fur beavers, Melton cloths, summer cloths, hunting cords; prize black cloth and doeskin, fancy trowserings, &c.

5. BURGESS, ALFRED, & Co., Leicester.—Knitting yarns; hosiery yarns; embroidery and fancy hosiery yarns.

6. CLABBURN, SONS, & CRISP, Norwich, Manufacturers.—Paramattas for mourning; gentlemens' scarfs and hunting-wrappers.

7. COMYNS, BIRCH, & Co., College-green, Dublin, Proprietors.—Melton cloths, Eblana friezes, shepherds' plaid, angolas, fancy trowserings, and tweeds; Irish embroidered kerseymere vests; black doeskins of West of England, Yorkshire, Irish, Prussian, and German wool; extra superfine black Saxony cloth; a variety of fine six-quarter tartans.

8. CRAVEN & HARROP, Bradford, Yorkshire, Spinners and Manufacturers.—Registered damasks, all wool, cotton and wool, silk and wool; registered damask table-covers, all wool, cotton and wool, silk and wool; Orleans, Coburgs, double twills, merinos, moreens, Circassians, alparas, alpaca lustre, alpaca serge, alpaca mottled crapes, chambord cloths, &c.

9. DAY & FOX, Low Mills, Mirfield, Yorkshire, Manufacturers.—Brown and grey friezes; piece and wool-dyed pilot cloth.

10. DICKSONS & LAINGS, Hawick and Glasgow, Manufacturers and Merchants.—Cheviot and Saxony lambs' wool, and Saxony wool hosiery, and under-clothing; tweeds; travelling plaids, and ladies' wool shawls and plaids.

11. DILLON, L., Parliament-street, Dublin, Proprietor.—Irish friezes and other woollens; Irish embroidered vests.

12. EDMONDS & Co., Bradford, Wilts, Manufacturers.—Black cloth, wool-dyed and manufactured on a new principle; blue and coloured cloths.

13. FRY, WILLIAM, & Co., Westmoreland-street, Dublin.—Plain, corded, and watered tartans.

14. GRUNDY, J. & E., High-street, Manchester, Manufacturers.—Lancashire, Saxony, silk warp, Galway, and other flannels; dyed flannels; swanskins; kerseys; plaidings, serges, baizes, blankets, printed druggets, crumb cloths, and table covers; travelling rugs, &c.

15. HALPIN, J. & J., Blanchardstown Mills, near Dublin, Manufacturers.—Fringe worsteds, in oil and stoved; laced worsteds, in oil and stoved; knitting worsteds, in various colours.

16. HASTINGS, BROTHERS, Huddersfield, Manufacturers.—Woollen cloths of various colours and qualities.

17. HOULDSWORTH, J. & Co., Portland-street Mills, Manchester, Manufacturers and Designers.—A collection of fabrics for furniture and ecclesiastical decorations, manufactured in Manchester by the exhibitors.

18. HOULDSWORTH, J. & Co., Halifax and Bradford, Manufacturers.—Union and worsted damask in registered designs; yarn dyed damasks; silk and wool damasks; Victoria and merino covers; table covers, silk and worsted, all worsted, and worsted and cotton; ponchos, plain and brocade (worn by the South Americans).

19. IRWIN, E., Albion-street, Leeds.—Drab, blue, wool-dyed, and other cloths; doeskins, pilots, and kerseymeres.

20. KELSALL, R. & J., Rochdale, Manufacturer.—Saxony flannels, white, pink, blue, and scarlet; medium and swanskin.

21. LEES, R. & G., Galashiels, Manufacturers.—Plaids, shawls, tartans, and dresses of Saxony lambs' wool.

22. LOCKE, J., Regent-street, London, Manufacturer.—Scotch woollens; mauds; ladies' shawls; Cheviot tweeds; milled angolas; milled clan tartans, as worn by the Highland regiments; the shepherd's check.

23. LOGAN, J., New-row, South, Dublin, Manufacturer.—Irish manufactured fine black cloth, napped; fine beavered brown frieze; woollen mops; all made of Irish wool.

24. LUPTON, W., & Co., Leeds, Manufacturers.—Superfine cloths, doeskins, pilots, Meltons, and black Venetians.

25. MACDONA, GEORGE, Molesworth-street, Dublin, Exhibiter; Messrs Davies, Sons, and Evans, Stonehouse Mills, Stroud, Manufacturer.—Nash scarlet cloth, finest made; shell scarlet for undress; royal white for dress; imperial scarlet for Russian full dress uniforms; wool dyed electoral black cloth.

26. MACREDY, Rev. J., Spiddall, Co. Galway, Proprietor.—Tweeds manufactured at the Spiddal Industrial School.

27. MIDDLETON & AINSWORTH, Norwich and London, Manufacturers.—Barege bayadere robes; paramatta dresses.

28. MURRAY, W., Chamber-street, Dublin, Manufacturer.—Irish friezes and fine tweeds, &c.

29. M'CREA, H. C., & Co., Lumbrook Mills, Halifax, Manufacturer.—Damasks, all worsted, worsted and cotton (piece-dyed and yarn-dyed), silk and worsted; velvet, Italian, Geneva, and Balmoral damasks.

30. NEILL, C., & SONS, Usher's-quay, Dublin, Manufacturer.—Brown, gray, and Oxford friezes; a blanket.

31. NICOLLS, A., Brown-street, Cork, Manufacturer.—Blankets, swanskins, flannels, tweeds, friezes, &c.

32. PAWSON, SON, & MARTIN, South Parade, Park-row, Leeds.—Superfine woollen cloths.

33. PERFECT, H. G., & Co., Halifax, Yorkshire, Manufacturer.—Damask of wool, cotton and worsted, and silk and worsted, table covers of silk and worsted, and cotton and worsted, and all wool; covers of wool, cotton, and worsted, and silk and worsted, in all colours.

34. PORTER, J. G. V., Belleisle, Lisbelaw, Co. Fermanagh, Manufacturer.—Tweeds, friezes, and blankets.

35. READ, J., Usher's-quay, Dublin, Manufacturer.—Treble-milled drab, blue, and black cloths; friezes; llama cloths; elastic tweeds.

36. ROBERTS, W., & Co., Galashiels.—Scotch (all wool) shawls.

37. SANDERSON, R. & A., & Co., Galashiels, Manufacturers.—Gentlemen's travelling plaids of fine Saxony wool.

38. SCHOFIELD, A., Oldham-road, Newton Heath, Manchester, Manufacturer.—Patterns of goods made betwixt the years 1780 and 1820; patterns of woollen cloths and cashmeres; woollen shawls.

39. WALKER, BROTHERS, Greek-street, Leeds, Manufacturers.—Cloths, royal cashmeres, and Gention plaids, for ladies' cloaks.

40. WALKER, JAMES, & Co., Leeds, Manufacturers.—Shawls and cloths in various colours, manufactured from the down of the Jemlah goat, a native of the Himalayan Mountains.

41. WALMSLEY, H., Failsworth, near Manchester, Manufacturer.—Silk and cotton fabrics, viz., barege bayadere robes; Jacquard figured robes.

42. WILLANS, BROTHERS, & Co., Island-bridge, Dublin, Manufacturers.—Extra superfine black cloths, kerseymeres, and doeskins; superfine Eblana friezes, shepherds' plaids, and fancy tweeds; regulation tartan, for officers, sergeants, and privates; fine shawl woollen yarns; hosiery and knitting yarns.

43. WRIGHT, E., Corn-market, Dublin, Proprietor.—Superfine blue cloth, black doeskins, and kerseymeres; invisible green cloths; black elastic, coloured, and fancy tweeds; heather mixture, for summer coats and vests—all of Irish manufacture; Wicklow friezes, single milled, gray, brown, and drab; Irish and French embroidered vests; single milled doeskins; Zurich velvets and silks.

44. WRIGLEY, J. & T. C., & Co., Dungeon Mills, near Huddersfield, Manufacturers.—Fancy and reversible coatings; partridge and heather mixtures for shooting coats; fancy trowserings, &c.

# CLASS XIII.

## SILK AND VELVET, AND POPLINS.

THE silk manufacture, like that of cotton, is of Eastern origin; the knowledge of the subject being derived from the Chinese, by whom silken fabrics have been in use from a remote antiquity. Its progress westward was slow. To the Romans the use of silk was known in the time of Aurelian; and in the reign of Justinian the manufacture was introduced into Europe. It appears, however, that Bologna was the only city in Italy before the commencement of the sixteenth century in which the throwing or twining of silk was performed by machinery. Antwerp was famous for its silk manufacture, until it was taken by the Duke of Parma in 1585, when a check was given to it; and those engaged in that branch of trade sought and obtained refuge in England, where they introduced the manufacture, which has since been of so great magnitude.

For a long period after the introduction of the silk trade, home-made fabrics were little prized. The invention of the stocking-frame, however, gave it an impetus, which caused the English silk stockings to be prized above all others. A further stimulus was given to the trade of these countries by the settlement of refugees, who had been obliged to fly from France in consequence of the revocation of the edict of Nantes in 1685. By that measure Louis XIV. drove from his kingdom thousands of the most intelligent and useful of his subjects, whose industry and skill tended to enrich rival nations. Some of these refugees settled in Spitalfields, and some of them came to Ireland, to whom we are indebted for the introduction both of the linen and silk manufacture. In 1692 such of these persons as had been engaged in the silk trade prevailed on the king to grant them a patent, giving to them the exclusive right to manufacture lusterings and alamodes, the silks then in greatest demand. In 1697 an Act was passed prohibiting the importation into the United Kingdom of all French and other European silk goods, and in 1701 the prohibition was extended to India and China, with a view of promoting the home manufacture.

The history of the silk manufacture from that time to the present is fraught with instruction as to the evil consequences of any kind of interference with the most perfect freedom of action. In our examination of the progress of the woollen trade we saw that by a system of what may be called penal legislation, and by vexatious and prohibitory duties, that branch of manufacture was almost driven from the country. In the case of the silk trade, however, an opposite course was adopted. Protection of every kind was conceded to it. However extravagant the demands of those engaged in it, they were granted; but strange to say, almost with a like result. Under a stringent system of protection the silk trade languished for a century. The public money was squandered in payment of bounties for the encouragement of production. An extravagantly high artificial price was paid by the consumer for all goods of that class, owing to the absence of competition. But under this state of affairs silk was an article of luxury only within the reach of the wealthy. The demand for it was consequently limited; while at intervals the smuggler was able to supply the home market with contraband imported goods; on which occasions the silk manufacturers were often brought to the verge of ruin. The policy of those times was that we should import only the raw silk, and exclude the manufactured article as far as practicable in every stage. What are termed throwing mills were encouraged, so that we might not even have to import the thrown silk or organzine; but the establishment of these mills at that stage only impeded the progress of the manufacture from the imperfect manner in which they performed the work.

The absurdity of the system pursued in reference to this branch of industry reached its climax in 1773, when not only was the service of the State employed in keeping out foreign goods, but also in regulating the rate of wages to be paid by the employers to their workmen! The masters had set the example of seeking to bolster up their trade by a system of combination against the foreign manufacturer; and the men were not slow to follow it by demands of the most outrageous character, and which they sought to enforce by riotous proceedings, endangering the peace of the whole community. The result was the enactment of what is commonly called the Spitalfields Act, by which the aldermen of the city of London and the magistrates of Middlesex were empowered to fix the rate of wages which should be paid to the weavers; and while both masters and men were restricted from giving or receiving more or less than the fixed price, the manufacturers were liable in heavy penalties if they employed weavers out of the district! All experience has shown that protected trades are invariably carried on without that regard to economy in the different processes which is necessary in order to provide for their extension by bringing the protected article within the reach of a large number of consumers; but whatever hopes there might have been of the progress of the silk manufacture at the period in question, these were for the time completely neutralized by the legislation to which we refer. The monopoly which the masters had hitherto enjoyed had sufficient influence to render inventions or discoveries of rare occurrence; and the law having declared that the manufacturer should be obliged to pay as much for work done by the best machinery as if it were done by hand, it would have been folly to have thought of attempting anything new. Fortunately this legislation was only local in its application, otherwise it would, most undoubtedly, have driven the manufacture altogether out of the country. The most valuable branches of the trade gradually escaped from this control, by being carried to some other district; and hence Macclesfield, Manchester, Coventry, Norwich, Paisley, and many other places on the other side of the Channel, became seats of a trade, which had been hitherto confined almost to the metropolitan districts.*

* Among the places famed for the production of particular kinds of goods, Coventry has long enjoyed a favourable notoriety for its ribbons; which were, moreover, well represented in the Exhibition. The following account of "The Ribbon Trade of Coventry" has been supplied by a resident of that city.

The Great Exhibitions of London and Dublin have been the means of bringing under public notice many of the provincial seats of industry which had previously been comparatively little known, beyond the limits of actually trading or mercantile connexions. One of these industrial hives is the ancient city of Coventry, situate in Warwickshire, one of the midland counties of England, where the ribbon trade has long had its seat, and now forms an important source of employment. Although the ribbon trade of Coventry is far from having attained to perfection,—although there is ample scope for further efforts in the way of advancement, and some remnants of old ideas and prejudices have to be got rid of, a glance at its past history here—a contrast of *what has been* with what *now is*—affords much ground for congratulation, and encouragement for hope as to the future.

Without attempting to fix the precise date at which the textile art was first practised in Coventry, it is well known that the weaving there of tammies, camlets, shalloons, and other fabrics chiefly of worsted, is of great antiquity. From its local records we find, in the early part of the sixteenth century, some of its mayors distinguished by the simple denomination of "weaver;" and although at present it is little more than a name, there still exists the "Weaver's Company," of very ancient origin. The coarser products of the loom, above mentioned, have long ceased to be produced there, and it is now about a century and a half ago since the *ribbon trade* was introduced by a Mr. William Bird, whose grandson, in 1796, became one of the representatives of the city in Parliament. Mr. Bird was assisted very materially in the establishment of the ribbon trade by certain French refugees, who were driven from their own country and sought an asylum in Britain. For thirty or forty years after its first introduction the trade was confined to a very few hands; but just before the close of the last century it began to expand as a branch of local manufacture, and the working classes, not only of Coventry but of the surrounding districts, turned their attention to it with some degree of earnestness as their main resource. The single-hand, or rather the single shuttle loom, at first used, gradually gave way to the engine loom or many-shuttle loom: but this description of machinery consisted, for a long time, only of the old-fashioned Dutch loom, a specimen of which now, even in Coventry, would be viewed as something of a curiosity. These first steps in the way of advance, though not attended with any actual hostility from the operative classes, were nevertheless productive of no small amount of jealousy and alarm. Those who had been accustomed to the making of one middling and narrow ribbon at a time in the single loom, could not divest themselves of the idea, that if a dozen such ribbons could be made by one man, the necessary consequence must be, that eleven persons would be thrown out of employment. In short, it was the old and prevailing dread of machinery, too much of which still hangs about the popular mind, from an imperfect understanding of its nature and tendencies. Necessity, and the instinct of self care, however, soon overcame fear and prejudice; and the Coventry weavers pursued their career of progress. The single shuttle loom yielded more and more to the engine loom, and the latter was soon turned to account for ribbons of greater width and better quality than when first introduced. Between 1819 and 1822 various improvements in the construction of looms were introduced by different parties; and it is an honourable fact to record, that although the spur of foreign competition had not then been applied, these improvements were received with alacrity, and eagerly adopted. Satins, and figured ribbons of no mean pretensions at that period, were produced; and the general character of the trade of the city assumed a position greatly in advance of that which it had previously occupied. But useful as these improvements were, it must be confessed that, in the figured ribbon department, they were entirely thrown into the shade by the appearance of the Jacquard machine, which was almost immediately afterwards brought into use, and about the adoption of which there was no room for hesitation. The Jacquard loom soon became general, and speedily extinguished all inferior appliances.

In estimating the character and reviewing the progress of the ribbon trade of Coventry, however, machinery is not the only thing to which attention is to be directed. The other concomitants of dyeing, arrangement of colour, design, taste, &c., are equally essential features to be taken into consideration in forming an opinion of the trade as a whole. In these latter respects it is undeniable that the repeal of the prohibitory laws in 1826, which immediately brought the English silk trade into competition with that of France, has had a marked influence upon the Coventry ribbon manufacture: and although probably the preference shown by the fashionable circles in English society for foreign productions cannot always be justified by reasonable arguments, it is useless to deny that our foreign rivals, notwithstanding all our progress, are still considerably in advance of us in matters of taste. But it is satisfactory to state, that in Coventry, during the last twenty years, the art of silk-dyeing has been assiduously cultivated, and with great success. The process of shading has attained to a high degree of excellence, and the brilliant and rich colours now turned out of the dyehouses form a striking contrast to the work of years gone by. Encouraging as these facts are, there is still one great drawback to be overcome, and that is, the want of an educational training,—a thorough understanding of chemistry, upon which the art of dyeing is based,—and as those engaged in this department are becoming constantly more impressed with the importance of this acquirement, it may reasonably be hoped that its study will be still more successfully pursued. The samples of figured and fancy ribbons, and of dyed silks from Coventry, in the London Exhibition of 1851, and to which prizes were awarded, as also the excellent assortment of ribbons from the establishment of Messrs. Sharp, Odell, and Jury, and that of Mr. Bray, contributed to the Dublin Exhibition, show that the foregoing remarks are not offered in any other spirit than that of awarding to the Coventry ribbon trade its fair share of merit.

With respect to the mode in which this trade is conducted, and its magnitude in Coventry, it may be necessary to add a few further observations. Forty years ago the operatives were of two denominations: first, the "undertaker" or middle-man, who received the silk in the hank from the master manufacturer; the business of the undertaker being to find looms, and manage the processes of winding, warping, &c.; secondly, the "journeymen," who for the most part were employed by the undertaker for the single-hand loom work, and to some extent in the engine loom. Few of the manufacturers troubled themselves then with the incumbrance or responsibility of any large quantity of machinery. As the single-hand loom, however, gradually became superseded by the engine loom, so the class of men called "undertakers" diminished, and the "journeymen" multiplied, establishing themselves in direct connexion with the master manufacturers. In process of time, this arrangement, as a general principle, began to yield: competition applied the stimulus to invention; and about the year 1830 Coventry saw its first factory of ribbon loom worked by steam-power. Since that period, and particularly within the last eight or ten years, steam factories have multiplied with extraordinary rapidity, and there are at present about thirty to forty of them of considerable extent. But amongst that class of operatives who

Many of the people of Ireland are loud in their complaints of "want of encouragement" in their respective branches of trade; but here was encouragement with a vengeance, and what are the results? The trade continued to languish, now enjoying a season of comparative prosperity, and anon those engaged in it being plunged in the deepest misery, until within a comparatively recent period. It was not till 1824 that a relaxation of the system was effected. In that year Mr. Huskisson obtained the sanction of Parliament in favour of the withdrawal of the prohibition of foreign silks after the 5th of July, 1826; the interval being intended to give the manufacturers time to prepare for the change. An *ad valorem* duty of 30 per cent. was substituted, and the result was an immediate and great increase of consumption of all kinds of silk goods. Every throwing mill and every loom was soon put into constant employment, and a great increase was made in the number of these establishments through the impetus which the trade had received. The number of throwing mills in different parts of the country was raised from 175 to 266, and the number of spindles from 780,000 to 1,180,000, but all this was unable to keep pace with the increased consumption which sprang up. In the ten years preceding 1824 we find that the quantity of raw and thrown silk used by our manufacturers amounted to 18,823,117 lbs., being an average of 1,882,311 lbs. per annum, while in the ten years following the change of system the average annual consumption was 3,678,000 lbs., and in the sixteen years ending 1849 the average consumption was 4,148,540 lbs. per annum, or an increase of 120 per cent. on the consumption under the restrictive system. So unprecedented has been not only the increase of manufacture, but the improvement in it, that the once existing disparity between goods of French and English make has, with some few exceptions, disappeared; the superiority being actually in some cases on the other side. Large quantities of particular classes of British silks have for years past been exported to France, forming about three-fifths of the exports of these goods to the whole of Europe.

In 1824, when the prohibition was removed, a graduated scale of duties was substituted, a duty of about 30 per cent. being levied on the imported article. This duty has subsequently been still further reduced to 15 per cent.; which, however, is still too high, as it can scarcely be doubted from the experience of the past that with a duty of 10 per cent. the manufacture would continue to progress. In the throwing mills important improvements have been introduced, the effect of which has been to lessen the cost of the process; and by the adoption of the Jacquard loom fancy fabrics are now made of a quality which, with a few unimportant exceptions, may defy competition. The charge made by English throwsters for converting raw silk into organzine was at the rate of 10*s.* per lb. previous to 1824. At that time the duty imposed upon the importation of foreign organzine was 14*s.* 8*d.*, or 9*s.* 2*d.* beyond the duty upon raw silk, and yet a much larger proportion of the material used in our silk looms was then thrown abroad than has since been the case. Under the healthy influence of competition, the throwsters have succeeded in reducing their charges from 10*s.* to from 3*s.* to 5*s.* per lb., the rate depending upon the quality of the silk. And the best proof of the improvement in the manufacture keeping pace with the increase of production is to be found in the fact, that for a series of years past the export of manufactured silks has been gradually on the increase, until it has now reached in value £1,000,000 per annum; and, what is more surprising still, as already observed, nearly one-fifth of the entire quantity exported is sent to France. Thus, while French silks of the finer qualities are imported into these countries, amends are made even in this branch of trade by exporting to France large quantities of the coarser kinds of the silks produced in British looms. In the production of the finer colours, and in the art of ornamentation, the higher qualities of French goods are unequalled, though of late rapid strides have been made in the United Kingdom towards successfully imitating the imported article.*

So much for the silk trade of the sister country. Let us now briefly examine into its history and present condition in our own island, where we may, as a matter of course, expect to find that the same deleterious

have been accustomed to domestic employment, there is a great repugnance to enter upon factory labour, and latterly a keen struggle has been maintained with the factories by the introduction of the alabar loom into private houses. In some instances these have been worked by steam power, by means of shafting running through an entire range of private-house workshops, but, generally speaking, the moving power of the alabar loom is that of child labour. Out of a population of nearly forty thousand in Coventry, it may be safely calculated that twelve or fifteen thousand are dependent on the silk trade. The prevailing rate of wages in the steam factories is from 10*s.* to 15*s.* per week. There are several large parishes and townships in the neighbourhood of Coventry which are fed by the silk trade of the city; and probably in which there are not less than 20,000 persons employed in the silk trade, the great bulk of which are dependent on the Coventry manufacturers. The class of goods Coventry is justly celebrated for is that used by the middle classes, in which, both as regards price, quality, and style, the trade there is inferior to that of no other country; and at the present time large quantities of goods are preparing for exportation.

* "The silk manufacture has long been carried on in France to an extent which has caused it to be considered one of the most important branches of the national industry. The raw material being principally produced in the country, there are not any means of ascertaining precisely the quantity that is employed in its looms. At the breaking out of the French Revolution, the estimated quantity of native silk produced was one million of pounds per annum. The Tables published by Count Chaptal, of the production of different departments in five years from 1808 to 1812, give an annual average of about 950,000 lbs. There had consequently been no increase during twenty years—the whole of which period had been passed in a state of war. Between 1812 and 1820 we have no estimate of the progress of production; in the latter year the quantity is said to have amounted to 1,350,000 lbs. The facts collected by Dr. Bowring, in his official inquiry, show that the produce of France in 1832 was about 2,000,000 lbs. The average annual weight of foreign silk imported into France, after deducting the quantity re-exported, was then about 1,000,000 lbs. It is estimated that the total value of the silk manufactures of France is about £8,000,000, four-sevenths of which consist of the value of the material used, the remaining three-sevenths being added for labour and profit. The result of the manufacture in both countries is placed in very striking contrast by the fact, that while two-thirds of the silk goods made in France are exported, leaving, consequently, for the use of her thirty-four millions of inhabitants, silk fabrics below the value of £3,000,000—the export of English-made silk goods does not amount to one-tenth of the quantity that passes through our looms, and is more than replaced by the goods of foreign manufacture imported for use; so that, taking into the calculation the difference in the number of the people, and the greater cost of production, the consumption of silk goods is more than five times as great in the United Kingdom as it is in France."—*Porter's Progress of the Nation.*

agencies have been at work that have produced such injurious effects in England. We have already stated, that it is to the Huguenots we owe the introduction of the manufacture of both linen and silk into Ireland. Louis Crommelin, the great founder of the linen trade, settled in the vicinity of Lisburn, which has long been the centre of that branch of industry; and the family of La Touche, who stood in a similar position in reference to the silk manufacture, settled in this city, where the refugees from the tyranny of Louis XIV. lost no time in getting to work at their trade. The Banking House in Castle-street, now conducted by the descendants of the family here alluded to, derives its origin from that comparatively remote period; as the high character for integrity which the Mr. La Touche of that day maintained caused him to be the general depository of the funds of the infantile community. In 1745, the Weavers' Hall was erected at the sole expense of Mr. J. Digges Latouche; at which period an organization was formed for the general protection of the interests of the trade. But notwithstanding the supposed fostering care of the State, and the system of combination got up among the workmen with a view of watching after their interests, the manufacture continued to languish; and Parliament was actually besieged by the clamour which they raised for relief. Following out the policy adopted in the sister country, an Act was passed in 1764, placing the silk manufacture under the especial care of the Royal Dublin Society; and that body was armed with extraordinary powers, and liberally supplied with funds for the accomplishment of the object in view. A first grant of £8000 was voted from the public treasury for this purpose, as a commencement of that lavish expenditure which was afterwards so misapplied. With a view of providing a suitable depot for the sale of the goods, a public warehouse was forthwith established under the auspices of the Society, "for the sale of silk goods manufactured in Ireland." The new emporium, which was situated in Parliament-street, was placed under the management of a committee of six merchants, acquainted with the trade; and one of their preliminary announcements was the offer of a premium of £10 to "all manufacturers who should deposit on sale, in the warehouse, silk goods manufactured in the country after the 1st June, 1764." Thus a system was commenced, no doubt with the best intentions, under which no branch of industry could flourish; and when one traces the history of the Irish silk trade from that period, he cannot be much surprised at the position which it now occupies.

One of the inevitable results of artificial restrictions, or even of undue favouritism, is to lead to the practice of an interminable system of fraud. Prohibitions only partially attain the ostensible object for which they are framed—that of preventing competition in the home market—as smuggling will take place, notwithstanding all the vigilance that can be exercised to prevent it. Under excessive excise or customs duties, it is also impossible to secure the market to the fair trader, who labours under drawbacks in competing with parties who escape payment of any duty, far greater than could be encountered if the trade were perfectly open and free. And under a system of bounties on production or exportation—a system which was long in vogue in these countries, as an offshoot of that system of protection which so long acted as an incubus upon the country—frauds will also be practised to an extent commensurate with the object to be gained thereby. But while even the ostensible object of all such interference with trade is unattainable, its effects are ruinous in the extreme. Under the influence of protection no manufacture ever flourished. By it the great stimulus to all improvement—healthy competition—is interfered with. Men's energies become paralyzed when some source of reliance is held out to them other than their own exertions. Of this the state of this country, a few years ago, affords a melancholy example. Everything amongst us has been either encouraged or discouraged. Almost every branch of industry has been the victim of prohibitions, or has been the object of an absurd and impolitic system of protection; and in either case the effect has been the same. The result is that we are yet looking for some artificial encouragement in all directions—one class upon another, and in turn all classes to the Imperial Parliament and the British people; and the non-compliance with such absurd demands we are ready to construe into a sort of covert persecution, or at least as indicating that those who have the ability to help us have no sympathy with us.

Reverting to events connected with the establishment of the warehouse of deposit in Parliament-street, we find that the immediate effect of such a movement was to lead to the perpetration of frauds almost without end, which degraded those who practised them, and still further detracted from any portion of self-reliance which they might have possessed. The payment of a premium of £10 to all who should deposit for sale a certain quantity of goods in this warehouse was well calculated to excite the ingenuity of needy manufacturers as to how they could most easily multiply the premiums. The result was that the same piece of goods was again and again deposited by the same party, who obtained on each occasion a sum of £10 for the deception which he practised. Acting in connivance with some pretended purchaser, to whom money was advanced, the manufacturer, after a decent interval, re-deposited the goods which had been so recently there before, and obtained another premium for so doing. From the early records of this warehouse, it would, therefore, appear that the silk trade was in a most flourishing condition; that the quantity of goods produced was large; and that an active demand existed for them, as illustrated by the quantity there deposited and sold.

The extent to which the frauds under this bounty system was carried at length attracted the attention of those appointed to carry it out; but instead of looking upon it as the natural result of a false and vicious system, they set about preventive measures, by the adoption of a more stringent rule than had hitherto been applied. For this purpose, at a meeting of the Royal Dublin Society, held on the 6th of June, 1765, it was determined that an oath, of which the following is a copy, should be administered to all persons trading at the warehouse, viz.:—"I neither have advanced or lent, nor will advance or lend money, to any person to purchase my goods, when once deposited, or intended to be deposited, in the Irish silk warehouse; but I will, after lodging them, leave them *bonâ fide*, without any evasion whatever, to the public for a fair sale." On the 13th of the same month the Society added a clause to this oath, with a view of making it more stringent, to the effect that—"I have not heretofore bought out of the warehouse, with money advanced, or on credit given by me to the purchaser." The extent to which credit was thus fraudulently used led to the adoption of means for discountenancing it altogether. But here, as is often the case, the remedy became more oppressive than the evil which it was designed to meet. Artificial restrictions upon credit cannot exist, without to a greater or less extent paralyzing trade. The restriction in question was, accordingly, found so oppressive, that in the spring of the following year a petition was presented to the Society, praying that the rule prohibiting credit should be rescinded; but the prayer of this petition it was not then deemed expedient to grant.

It will not excite surprise at this distance of time, and with the more correct notions that now prevail on such matters, that the arrangements which we have here detailed should fail in accomplishing the object in view. The cause of failure was not, however, seen by the Government of the day, and probably was as little understood by the Royal Dublin Society, by whom the system was carried out. All the "encouragement" then given really did nothing for the trade. Those engaged in it continued to be clamorous for all sorts of relief from the distress in which they were involved; and sundry expedients were from time to time devised with a view of mitigating the evil. Thus in July, 1776, a bounty or drawback of 7½ per cent. was granted to all who purchased silks at the warehouse in Parliament-street; and in the following year, with a view of more generally extending the supposed blessings of this system of protection, it was determined that the bounty should not be confined exclusively to goods sold in the warehouse, but that it should extend to all the goods sold wholesale. In 1778 the mercers adopted further measures with a view of promoting and extending the trade, one of which was that they would not purchase any foreign silks which cost less than 7*s.* an ell, abroad, and absolutely prohibiting the sale of a variety of articles which had hitherto been imported to a greater or less extent. The manufacturers, in return, agreed to allow the mercers a liberal discount—defaulters from these resolutions not being eligible to receive any premiums; and to carry them out an oath was required to be taken to the effect that the requirements of the trade had been complied with by the claimant. The Society, which was the executive body in all these matters, was constantly on the alert devising further restrictions; and among other things, ordained that the mercers should be obliged to take an oath that they would not sell silks at a lower price than that at which they were marked in the warehouse.

Of the transactions of this period there are very scanty records, and there appear to be none available from which any accurate statistics of the trade could be made out. We find, however, that the warehouse scheme was barren of any beneficial results, and after an experience of twenty-two years it was given up, the premises being made over to the Corporation of Weavers. In 1775 the sales in the warehouse during the year appear to have realized the sum of £44,000; but in 1783, three years before it was given up by the Society, the amount of business done amounted only to £25,000. Shortly after this period the trade was greatly depressed. The silk weavers, regarding the Society and Parliament as omnipotent, urgently prayed for relief, after depicting in doleful terms the hardships to which they were exposed; but the Society, in reply, stated that "having given every assistance hitherto in their power for the encouragement of the silk manufactures of Ireland, they found themselves, from the present state of their funds, absolutely unable to do anything for that purpose."

We have seen that the system of mistaken protection exercised an equally baneful operation in England and in Ireland. In both countries so complete was the interference of the Government with the trade, in protecting it from foreign competition, with, no doubt, the laudable intention of "encouraging" it, that the workmen, following the example of their employers, also sought the extension of the "encouragement" to themselves. The interference with the Spitalfields weavers has been already referred to; and we find that up to the termination of the prohibitory system in 1824, the wages of labour were regulated by the Royal Dublin Society, and made entirely independent of the operation of the law of supply and demand. The Jacquard loom was introduced into England in 1801; but during the whole period of this interference with the labour market on the part of the Society, the operatives prevented its introduction here. When the trade was partially opened a crisis was accordingly brought about, which led at once to a reduction in the rate of wages, to the amount of 15 per cent. But slow as had been the progress of improvement in England during the *regime* of prohibitory duties, it was much slower here; and on the relaxation of the restrictions the English manufacturers supplied our shopkeepers with silk goods of every description at lower rates than they could be produced at home. After a protracted struggle the silk trade disappeared altogether from the country, but the poplin manufacture continued with varying fortunes to the present day; the Irish goods in this department being celebrated for their very superior quality, but the extent to which the manufacture is carried on is inconsiderable.

The maintenance of stringent regulations on the part of the operatives was entered upon on the cessation of the surveillance of the Royal Dublin Society. A scale of prices was then adopted, to which the inferior and skilled workmen were equally entitled. But while the workmen in Dublin would not sanction any deviation from this scale, such as had the good sense to go elsewhere in search of employment at once complied with the rules of the trade in their new location. Thus, Mr. Curran, secretary of the Manchester Silk Weavers' Association, testified before the Hand-Loom Weaver's Committee of 1840, "that after the Spitalfields Acts were repealed the silk weavers in Dublin combined not to take lower wages of their employers than they had previously received; and numbers came over to Manchester, where, in many instances, they were obliged to take lower wages than the rules of the trade in Dublin would permit. This combination had the effect of withdrawing a large portion of the trade from Dublin, and opening a trade in that city for Manchester silks, which more than compensated for the increase in the labour market of the additional number of silk weavers that had migrated from Dublin." But the workmen of this city could not be brought to see their mistake, and they continued to clamour for protection, and the resumption of that system which was overturned in 1824. The Committee of Silk Weavers endeavoured to impress upon the Hand-Loom Weavers' Committee to which we have already referred, that "the decline of the trade here was owing to the superiority of England, and her large capital and machinery; to the repeal of prohibitory duties, and the introduction of free trade;" and by the way of providing a remedy they asked for "a repeal of the corn laws"—thus affording a curious illustration of how the most thorough-going protectionist desires free trade in everything but his own goods—"a special labour protection bill; a board of trade to regulate the minimum of wages for definite stated periods; a limitation to the production of goods by machinery, by a tax on the quantity produced by power-looms, or by contracting the number of them; a duty on all imported silks; and a loan of fifty or sixty thousand pounds so as to enable them to compete with England."

It is impossible to produce any more forcible illustration of the ignorance and fatuity of a set of men than is here displayed. What could be expected from people who entertained such notions as these in reference to the means calculated to benefit their trade? It will not excite surprise that Alderman Abbott, and others engaged in it, should give such evidence as the following, which we extract from that of the Alderman before the Committee already referred to. After an experience of the trade for fifty years, he states that "up to 1829 I was engaged in the wholesale silk trade, employing a large number of looms. I imported my own silk, and I manufactured it here. I left the trade in consequence of the combination of the workmen. I called my weavers together, and they agreed to make a considerable reduction in the price of weaving. When they got the work out for the winter's trade, the Committee of the combinators took the shuttles from them, and would not allow them to finish the work in the looms until I agreed to give the full London prices; in consequence which I did not consider it safe any longer to continue in the trade, and I retired from business. This occurred in the year 1826. I attribute the withdrawal of the trade in whole-silk to the combination of the men, who will not work at the Manchester prices, but insist on London prices, which the manufacturers cannot afford to give." Mr. M'Connell, another employer, stated that he had a large extent of work in hands at a period when the men agreed to get through with it at a slight reduction from the standard price. But the Committee of the trade, on hearing this, would not allow the men to fulfil their engagement; and what is more extraordinary still, they fined him in ten pounds for this violation of their laws, which fine, moreover, he was obliged to pay, and consent to return to the former prices, before the work could be completed! It is not surprising that, like Alderman Abbott, he, too, should retire from the trade, which he accordingly did without delay.

In commenting on this state of affairs, Mr. Otway, one of the Commissioners appointed to inquire into the state of the trade, thus wrote—"The day or two previous to my leaving the island I called on a manufacturer of high respectability, and the head of one of the oldest houses in the silk trade, who had on a former occasion given me his evidence. He told me that since I then examined him he had set up a hand-loom weaving factory for weaving broad silks,—had gone to England and expended upwards of £700 in purchasing Jacquard looms of the best construction, and a machine for winding silks. He took me to see his factory, and I found it the best arranged and the most healthy and convenient factory I had ever seen; but of upwards of thirty looms only twelve were at work, and the winding machine appeared to have never been used. I asked the reason of this. He told me that when he had finished his arrangements, there was a meeting of the body of the trade called, and that they had passed a resolution not to allow more than twelve weavers to work for him; and he was directed not on any account to use the winding machine. 'The consequence is, sir, that although I gave the same rate of wages as that fixed by the union, if I were to give £100 as an inducement I would not get a thirteenth weaver to work for me. But this is not all. They passed another resolution forbidding the twelve weavers to pay me more than 1*s.* 6*d.* each per week for the use of the looms, although 2*s.* 6*d.* is the fixed price where the manufacturer supplies the Jacquard loom; and to-morrow there is to be a meeting of the trade to limit the number of weavers they would permit to work for me to six. The other manufacturers are either afraid or unwilling to assist me in putting down this combination. The consequence is that, after sustaining immense loss, I must withdraw from the trade. The silk weavers are so exasperated against me for introducing a winding machine, though I never used it, that I dare not even in the open day walk through the Liberties,—the very women would pelt me with stones and mud.'" Mr. Otway further stated that "the combination of operatives has not only driven the most wealthy and extensive manufacturers out of the silk trade; but by the unjust and illegal control which they assume over the industry of their fellow-workmen, they have compelled them to emigrate to other places, where they can exercise their judgments in regard to the disposal of their labour. The consequence has been that many of the best Irish silk-weavers have from time to time emigrated to England or the United States of America, where they have been glad to get employment at a lower rate of wages than in Dublin.

Under such circumstances it will be at once seen that no trade can prosper; and while strongly censuring the conduct of the workmen, we are little disposed to compliment the employers for passively submitting to a system of tyranny which, if persevered in, must eventually drive the trade altogether from the country. When writing in 1840, Mr. Otway stated that "the silk trade of Ireland may be said to be supported by charity. Purchasers are induced to take the goods, because it is an act of charity to do so; and they are requested not to endeavour to lower the price on account of the charitable effect that is to result from buying Irish tabinets. It is considered a patriotic and genteel mode of bestowing charity to purchase a few yards of this material!" Can anything be more discreditable than such a state of affairs as this? Miserable indeed must be the trade, the support of which rests on such grounds.

But it may be said that these remarks apply to the past, and that at the present time this manufacture is in a more healthy state, and rests on a more secure basis than it did at the period referred to. We believe that such is the case. Those engaged in it have not wholly escaped the influence of the change that has taken place in the sentiments of the community at large. The combination system is, however, as firmly acted upon at the present period as in times past, the only difference being that it does not now assume so objectionable a character. So recently as 1849 we have had a significant exemplification of this. The large number of the Irish weavers who resorted to the English manufacturing districts, and who there acquired more correct notions than they previously entertained, had the effect of arousing attention on the other side of the channel to the anomalous state of the trade here. We find that in the month of July in that year, an address on the part of several of the broad silk weavers of Macclesfield was agreed to be presented to their brethren in Dublin, recommending the immediate adoption, on the part of the latter, of the customs and wages of the trade in England. In that address attention was called to the fact, that "England has raised herself to the most eminent position among the nations of the earth by her systems of manufacture, which systems Irishmen of all trades help to carry out; and that it is grossly inconsistent with common sense for Irish silk-weavers to go to that country and work under certain conditions, which conditions they will refuse to work under in their own country, thus helping to enrich England at the expense of Ireland;" and when questioned by the Committee of the trade in this city, as to what was meant by the proposed assimilation, the Macclesfield weavers stated that there every man has a right to work at the silk trade if he be qualified to do so; that weavers pay for loom rent in factories in England five shillings per week for figures and three shillings for plains; that boys are apprenticed for five years only instead of the usual period of seven years, and serve their time on half earnings; and that every weaver has a right to engage as much work as he may require, either for his family or journeymen. The Committee of the Dublin trade, in reply to these very sensible suggestions, stated that in their opinion "the adoption of the customs and usages set forth would not have the effect of raising the whole-silk trade of Dublin, or of increasing the present amount of employment; for this reason, that the present employers in Dublin are men of easy circumstances, and have no inclination to compete with the English manufacturers in the whole-silk trade, which they believe they could not do, no matter what advantages the operatives gave them. As regards the failure of the silk trade in Dublin, they believe the cause springs from the same source as the failure of nearly all the trades in Ireland; namely, acts of the British Government and the combination of English capitalists to have the trade of this country." The Committee further stated that, "it is the policy of the great leviathan England to swallow up the trade of every place she can put her grasping hand on, either by fair or foul means;" and, in conclusion, they express their opinion that "as regards the revival of the whole-silk trade they can see no prospect; and, as regards the tabinet trade, they believe that if it was not for the prejudice that is in favour of the name of Irish tabinet it would long since have gone after the whole-silk trade."

The amount of ignorance and self-sufficiency which is here displayed is truly astonishing; and it was ably exposed by the associated Macclesfield weavers, though without effect. Of men who entertain such sentiments it is difficult to make anything, as arguments are altogether lost upon them.

One of the objects of the system of combination which prevails here was, and is, to maintain the rate of wages agreed upon so long ago as 1826; since which no reduction has taken place among such as are associated with the trade. While reductions to a large extent have taken place in several branches in England, they have been strenuously resisted here; though it is not difficult to show that constant employment at moderate wages is preferable to casual work at higher rates. The consequence has been that several branches of the trade hitherto carried on have been altogether abandoned. Instead of determinedly resisting this system, the misfortune is that the masters for the most part submit to it, though it is quietly effecting their own ruin. We must not, however, omit to notice a spirited and successful exception in the case of Messrs. William Fry and Co., which has only to be generally imitated to place the trade on a more satisfactory footing than it has ever yet enjoyed amongst us. They had been in the habit of producing tabarets for coach-makers and cabinet-makers; but, in 1849, when looking after contracts advertised by some of the railway companies, they found that they could not compete with the English prices, without taking any profit for themselves at all into account. Seeing, after the closest calculation, that they were unable to modify their tender, they applied to some of the English manufacturers for their scale of prices to the workmen, when they found that the London price for weaving furniture tabarets was five-pence to six-pence per yard, while here it was eight-pence; and that ten-pence to one shilling per yard was paid for coach-maker's tabarets on the other side of the channel, while Messrs. Fry and Co. had for years been paying one shilling and eight-pence halfpenny. On receipt of this information these gentlemen called their workmen together, when it was placed before them; and they were apprised that unless the rates here were reduced to those of England the trade must vanish from the country altogether. After due deliberation a peremptory refusal was given to this very reasonable demand. But the Messrs. Fry were not to be driven from the field without an effort; and, after making the necessary arrangements, they succeeded in collecting a number of hands who were satisfied to accept the proposed terms, which rendered them independent of the general body of the trade, a position which they have since maintained. The consequence is, that they are now doing a large business in this class of goods; and through their firmness, and the judicious arrangements which they adopted, they succeeded in preserving to the country a branch of trade which the insane system of combination had well nigh driven from it.

The declared value of the manufactured silk goods of all kinds exported from the United Kingdom since 1824 has been as follows:—

| Years. | | Years. | | Years. | |
|---|---|---|---|---|---|
| 1824, . . . . | £442,596 | 1834, . . . . | £636,419 | 1844, . . . . | £736,455 |
| 1825, . . . . | 296,736 | 1835, . . . . | 972,031 | 1845, . . . . | 766,405 |
| 1826, . . . . | 168,801 | 1836, . . . . | 917,822 | 1846, . . . . | 887,577 |
| 1827, . . . . | 236,344 | 1837, . . . . | 503,673 | 1847, . . . . | 985,626 |
| 1828, . . . . | 255,870 | 1838, . . . . | 777,280 | 1848, . . . . | 588,117 |
| 1829, . . . . | 267,931 | 1839, . . . . | 868,118 | 1849, . . . . | 998,334 |
| 1830, . . . . | 521,010 | 1840, . . . . | 792,648 | 1850, . . . . | 1,255,641 |
| 1831, . . . . | 578,874 | 1841, . . . . | 788,894 | 1851, . . . . | 1,326,778 |
| 1832, . . . . | 529,990 | 1842, . . . . | 590,189 | 1852, . . . . | 1,551,866 |
| 1833, . . . . | 737,404 | 1843, . . . . | 667,952 | 1853, . . . . | 2,044,912 |

There were few classes of articles in the Exhibition the appearance of which more decidedly indicated their origin than the tabinets; and this was not less so at the Great Exposition of 1851, than at that held in our own metropolis. Irish tabinets have, in fact, obtained a world-wide celebrity; and so superior are they to the same class of goods produced elsewhere, that the most cursory examination is sufficient to enable the one to be distinguished from the other. Their superiority was manifest in Hyde Park, where one of our leading houses, Messrs. R. Atkinson & Co.'s., carried away the prize medal from a number of competitors; and we may further safely assert, that the competition then really lay between the Irish houses themselves. The illustration of this class from the English manufacturers was certainly scanty on the late occasion. The contrast, however, was remarkable. The visitor who examined the specimens in the Centre Hall, contributed by our own manufacturers, and then went over to the English goods in the same class, could scarcely believe that both belonged to the same category. In the collection of Messrs. R. Atkinson & Co., Wm. Fry & Co., Pim Brothers, and Keely and Leech, the Irish poplin trade was creditably represented. Some of the goods of the first-named firm were gorgeous in ornamentation, and, at the same time, were not wanting in elegance. Due attention appears to be paid to obtaining suitable designs, which, in articles of this class, is a matter of the utmost importance. We may observe, however, that the range of ornament in poplins is comparatively limited, by the peculiar nature of the material. In this respect they fall far short of the purely silk fabrics; what they want in appearance they have in durability, poplin being perhaps the most serviceable article of female attire.

But while awarding the palm to the few houses in this city engaged in the poplin trade, we can scarcely believe that it has at all been pushed or carried on to a degree at all commensurate with its importance. The tendency of the present day is marked by a great straining after variety. An article is not valued in proportion to its durability—a quality inconsistent with that variety in dress so much prized. This feeling may, to some extent, account for the poplin trade not being more extended than it is. As carried on in Ireland, it can scarcely be said to have attained to the dignity of a wholesale trade, the fabrics being retailed by the manufacturers. Economy of production, so as to secure a reduction in price, has not been attended to as much as the attainment of excellence of quality, or else the trade cannot have been pushed to the extent of which it is susceptible. One or other of these conclusions irresistibly forces itself upon the mind of any one who examines these beautiful goods, and learns that a merely retail trade is done in them. While we maintain that there is no comparison between the English and Irish poplin goods in quality, we are also bound to state, that there is also no comparison in price. This latter, we apprehend, is the direction in which our local manufacturers must seek, by increased efforts, to extend their trade. We speak generally, and without any special knowledge of this branch of business; but we cannot help thinking that a greatly extended consumption would follow even a slight reduction in price, provided this were attainable without sacrificing the quality of the article.—J. S.

---

1. ATKINSON, R. & Co., College-green, Dublin, Manufacturers and Designers.—Rich gold tissued and brocaded Irish poplins (designed by pupils of the Dublin School of Design); Irish poplins, plain, figured, double, plaided, shot, and in various other styles; gold tissued and figured poplin waistcoatings; specimens of tapestry woven in Dublin, in 1738, being a portrait of George II., in a frame.

2. BARR, J., Caledon, Manufacturer.—Silk shawls of various patterns; silk scarfs and aprons; ladies' dresses of spun silk and silk and wool.

3. BRAY, C., & Co., Coventry, Manufacturers.—Plain and fancy ribbons.

4. BROWETT, W. & H., Coventry, Silk Dyers and Manufacturers.—Ladies' dress trimmings; fringes, in various styles and materials; fancy braid gimps; frilled ribbons.

5. CLABBURN, SONS, & CRISP, Norwich, Manufacturers.—Brocaded, check, tartan, corded, watered, and plain poplins; brocaded and fancy dresses; gentlemen's scarfs.

6. CORDNER, R. D. & Co., Dame-street, Dublin, Manufacturers.—Rich silk curtain, in amber tabaret, with silk fringe; carriage laces; silk tabarets for curtains; velvet plush and London cords for carriage lining; vallance fringes and borderings for window curtains.

7. CORNELL, LYELL, & WEBSTER, St. Paul's Churchyard, London; Nuneaton, Warwickshire; and Battersea, Surrey; Manufacturers.—Watered and figured ribbons.

8. DUNNE, W., Mark's-alley, Dublin, Manufacturer.—Double watered, figured, fancy, and plain poplins; silk velvets.

9. FRY, W. & Co., Westmoreland-street, Dublin, Manufacturers, Designers, and Importers.—Plain, corded, and watered tartan; figured and brocaded Irish poplins, &c.; Bayadere poplins; gold and silver tissues and vestings; striped tabarets and damask furniture poplins; Irish brocatelles; carriage silks, laces, and trimmings.

10. GROUT & Co., Foster-lane, London, Manufacturers.—Specimens of black crape for mourning, of various qualities; Aerophane used for caps, trimming dresses, flowers, &c.; crêpe lisse and lisse gauze.

11. JONES, E., St. Andrew-street.—Plain and figured poplins and velvets.

12. KEELY & LEECH, Grafton-street, Manufacturers and Designers.—A rich tobined poplin, the flowers shaded in various colours, the ground composed of antique scroll-work, veined with gold tissue brocade; plain, figured, and watered, double, and demy cords; Bayadere poplins; plain and fancy waistcoatings.

13. M'BIRNEY, COLLES, & Co., Aston's-quay, Dublin, Proprietors.—Brocaded and plain silks; plain and fancy ribbons; crape shawls.

14. MIDDLETON & AINSWORTH, Norwich and London, Manufacturers.—Checked satin, and Norwich poplin dresses; Bayadere dresses.

15. MORAN, E., Mark's-alley, Dublin, Manufacturer.—Velvets; Irish poplins, plain and figured; brocaded and watered vestings, &c.

16. PIM, BROTHERS, & Co., George's-street, Dublin, Designers and Manufacturers.—Specimens of plain watered tartan; fancy rich figured and rich brocaded tissue poplin; poplin robes; glacé silks; rich velvets; vestings, &c.

17. SHARP, ODELL, & JURY, Coventry, Manufacturers.—Samples of ribbons of medium and extra quality.

18. TODD, BURNS, & Co., Mary-street, Dublin, Manufacturers and Importers.—Ribbons in great variety; window curtains in French brocatelle; silks.

19. WALMSLEY, H., Failsworth, Manchester, Manufacturer.—Silk fabrics; poplins, plain and striped, in variety; antique poplin vestings.

# CLASS XV.

## MANUFACTURES FROM FLAX.

THE articles comprised in this class may be regarded as constituting the staple manufacture of Ireland—that in which she maintains a supremacy over every other country in the world—and hence of peculiar interest in an Irish Exhibition. Having in a previous section of this work (Class IV.) treated of flax as a raw material, we now come to the articles manufactured from it; and in the execution of this task a brief sketch of the linen manufacture will not be out of place.

Up to the latter end of the eighteenth century all the flax yarns of Europe were spun by hand, and gave employment to an immense number of females in their own homes. For centuries the spinning-wheel was the only known method of preparing vegetable and animal fibres for the weaver; and its universal employment led to the designation of *spinster*, as applied to unmarried females, the use of this implement being an important branch of domestic routine. Nor was it confined to the lower orders. The early chronicles and the plates of Froissart show us that high-born dames were accustomed to pass a portion of every day in spinning, and they are represented as surrounded by their handmaidens, occupied at this industrious employment. Some of the aged members of noble families in our own isles, at the present day, pride themselves on their former expertness in this art, and preserve specimens of their handiwork, with the curiously inlaid wheels which had descended to them as heir-looms. An example of these was in the Exhibition, among the linens shown by Mr. Roddy, of Belfast, where a wheel and reel of elaborate workmanship and elegant materials, once belonging to a noble Ulster family, were shown as emblems of the infancy of the Irish linen manufacture. Before the application of machinery to spinning, the hum of the wheel might have been constantly heard throughout our island; and on market days each little country town was crowded with housewives, carrying their hanks or spangles of yarn for sale directly to the weaver, or to be exchanged at the huckster's shop for the articles of which they stood in need. It was not unfrequent, also, for the women of a family to spin the yarns, which the men, in the intervals of farming labour, or the long nights of winter, wove into fabrics, to be disposed of to the bleachers, or to be fashioned into homely garments for household use. An ample store of linen was the pride of every ambitious housewife, and formed part of the *trousseau* of every bride of certain fortune; and the quantities thus collected by the labour of successive generations was, in the better class of houses, something wonderful to see. In Brittany, at the present day, among the simple peasantry of that primitive Celtic region, an amusing illustration of this feeling may be noted by the traveller who explores its woods and wilds. He will be surprised to find that the peasants of both sexes wear their linen of all shades, from brown to snowy white, in the inverse ratio to the respectability of their other garments. If he seeks an explanation, he will be told that the poorer the individual the whiter will be the linen; those of middle estate will be known by their half-bleached shirts, while the village *seigneur* and his dame stalk in majesty, proudly displaying their flaxen envelopments brownly fresh from the loom. And then follows the reason—necessary indeed to the bewildered tourist—whose snowy shirt and collar of "pure grass-bleach linen" are among the outward tokens of his gentlemanly condition which he most dearly cherishes—that, in Brittany, it is only the wealthy who can afford to wear the brownest fabrics, constantly renewed; while the poor, who have but a scanty supply of linen, must wash and dry, and wash and dry again, the self-same garment, until it attains the hue which in more civilized countries is alone prized.

During the hand-spinning period of our linen manufacture a considerable export of Irish yarns took place to England and Scotland, where they were used both for linen fabrics and also as the warp for cottons, before the latter were solely manufactured from the cotton wool. They were likewise employed in the weaving of linsey-woolsey, a union-cloth of flax and wool now fallen into desuetude. Connaught was much resorted to by the merchants for a supply of yarns for these purposes.

In 1793 the first flax-spinning machinery was erected in England; and as it was soon ascertained that yarns could be thus produced much more cheaply than by hand, the trade extended itself rapidly in Great Britain. In 1805 the first flax-spinning mill in Ireland was put up at Cork, and consisted of 212 spindles for canvass yarns. The Linen Board, by giving a bounty of 30*s*. per spindle, encouraged the erection of several mills, amounting in 1809 to 6369 spindles. In 1815 there were in Ulster five mills, in Leinster two, and in Munster seven, with an aggregate of about 12,000 spindles.

Up to this period all the yarns were spun dry. About 1822 an improvement was introduced in England. The prepared flax was passed through hot water before being caught by the spindle, and this enabled it to be spun to much finer yarns. In 1825 the Irish market began to be stocked with English machine-spun yarns sold at such a price as to carry despair to the cottages of the spinners of similar descriptions; for as yet they were but coarse, and the more expert housewives laughed to scorn the idea that iron and brass would ever rival their nimble and experienced fingers. Some manufacturers in Ulster, wise in their generation, began to ponder upon this new feature in their trade. They knew that Englishmen bought the flax at their very doors, carried it across the Channel, spun it in their mills, and returned it in the shape of yarn. They reasoned that if, with comparatively dear labour, and with their source of supply and their market of demand both to seek in Ireland, English spinners could make money, factories in Ireland ought to pay, with cheap labour and the supply and demand equally at their doors. Almost simultaneously two enterprising men took steps to secure the advantage of this new branch of industry—Mr. Murland of Castlewellan, and Mr. Mulholland of Belfast. In 1828 the first of the modern factories was at work. "*Ce n'est que le premier pas qui coute.*" Thirteen years afterwards, in 1841, there were forty-one Irish factories with 260,000 spindles. There are now eighty-eight factories with 500,000 spindles. The little Cork precursor of 212 spindles, spinning only yarns like small twine, for canvass, has been succeeded by gigantic factories, several of them containing 20,000 to 30,000 spindles each, and producing yarns up to what is employed for cambric, fine as gossamer. It is true that the hum of the cottage wheel, turned by hundreds of thousands of hands, is no longer to be heard in the green valleys of Ireland, and that it has been replaced by the whirr of iron frames, attended by some 23,000 women and children pent up within brick and mortar, chiefly in the capital of Ulster; but the change was not only inevitable but necessary, in order that Ireland should preserve her linen manufacture in its integrity; and the social condition of the female peasantry is actually improved, by the transfer of immense numbers to the embroidering of muslins and various other departments of needlework which have of late attained such celebrity.

To estimate the present magnitude of the Irish flax-spinning trade, let us look at a few plain figures. First, there are 580,000 spindles, representing a capital of £2,370,000 sunk in buildings and machinery. Then there is the direct employment of 23,000 factory workers, earning an aggregate of £360,000 annually; besides the indirect employment to iron founders, blacksmiths, tinsmiths, carpenters, &c., &c. There are, at Belfast alone, about sixty vessels constantly employed in providing fuel for the motive power of such factories as are driven by steam, which consume fully 200,000 tons of coal annually. Then these factories yearly spin up 30,000 tons of flax and tow, value £2,100,000. And lastly, they produce about 10,500,000 bundles of yarn, value, say £2,800,000.

Of the Irish flax factories, thirty-nine, or nearly one-half, are situated in Belfast and its environs, and outside the province of Ulster there are but nine. Two have been recently built, one at Limerick and the other at Ballyshannon; which may be regarded as feelers thrown out with a view to ascertain whether the charmed circle of Ulster and the east coast of Leinster can be broken, and the other two provinces brought to have a share in the benefits of this trade.

The yarns spun in Ireland are not all used at home, a considerable quantity being exported to Great Britain, Germany, Belgium, and Spain. France, up to 1841, took a very large quantity, but prohibitory duties being then put on by the Chambers, there are now none shipped to that country. The export to other places is rapidly increasing; in 1850 it was 4,494,240 lbs.; in 1851, 5,060,160 lbs.; and in 1852, 6,679,680 lbs., valued at £318,700. On the other hand, certain sorts of yarn are imported from England and Scotland, and a small quantity of very fine handspun from Germany and France; in 1852 the import of all kinds was valued at £263,025.

Flaxen yarns are of two sorts, *line* and *tow*; the former being made from the long fibres prepared by the process of hackling, the latter from the cottony refuse of that process. Both were well represented in the Exhibition. In the Royal Flax Society's case were samples from 6 lea to 300 lea; that is, from half a hank in the pound, measuring 20 yards, to 25 hanks in the pound, measuring 93¾ yards. The same case also showed the scutched flax, the hackled line and tow, the *sliver* or *drawings*, and the *rovings* or last process before spinning. Messrs. J. Hind and Sons, of Belfast, showed an elegant series, up to 320 leas. Messrs. Gradwell, Chadwick, and Co., of Drogheda, exhibited beautiful specimens of all degrees of fineness, comprising some of 360, some of 420, and some of 520 leas. To show the perfection at which machine-spinning has arrived, we may state that 10 hanks of the latter, weighing but 3 oz. 11 drs., measure 21 miles; a bundle, therefore, weighing 4 lbs. 10 ozs. would reach from the Giants' Causeway to Cape Clear, and leave 118 miles to spare! One of the largest factories, consequently, if spinning, by all its machinery, this delicate thread, would nearly rival Ariel's boast, and

> "Put a girdle round about the earth
> In forty minutes."

The hand-spinning, whose province has been, year by year, encroached upon by machinery, still holds its place for a few high numbers. In 1844, £80,000 worth of foreign hand-spun yarns were imported for the manufacture of cambric. In 1848, this had fallen to £46,000; and in 1851, to £27,750; thus showing that it has, by rapid degrees, been replaced by the product of our factories, and may, in a few years more, be entirely obliterated. Messrs. S. G. Fenton and Co.'s case of linens contained an extraordinary specimen, spun by a county of Antrim woman, aged 83, of the wonderful grist of 1120 leas, or 90 hanks in the pound. This is rather more than double the fineness of Messrs. Gradwell and Co's finest sample of mill-spun, hitherto unequalled anywhere by machinery; and consequently 3¼ ounces of the former would reach 43 miles, or little more than five ounces would be required to unite the Welsh with the Irish coast.

We may here glance at the position which Ireland has taken in the flax-spinning world, which the following Table will illustrate. There are in the flax factories of each country where this industry exists, as follows:—

| | | | |
|---|---|---|---|
| In Ireland, | 580,000 spindles. | In Austria, | 74,000 spindles. |
| England, | 345,000 „ | Russia, | 50,000 „ |
| Scotland, | 303,000 „ | United States of America, | 14,500 „ |
| France, | 476,000 „ | Switzerland, | 8,000 „ |
| Belgium, | 102,000 „ | Holland, | 6,000 „ |
| Zollverein, | 80,000 „ | Spain, | 6,000 „ |

Closely allied to flax-spinning is the linen thread manufacture. Yarns, spun in the usual way, are only employed in the manufacture of woven fabrics. To fit them for the use of tailors, dressmakers, and shoemakers, they require to be re-twisted, to render them of sufficient firmness and strength. Several of the British and Irish spinning factories have attached to them thread-twisting frames, and for the material so produced there is an extensive demand, both at home and abroad. In 1852 the United Kingdom exported 3,788,497 lbs. of threads, value £338,821. There are four or five of the Ulster flax-spinners who have attained much celebrity in this branch of the trade, and their threads are sold throughout the British Islands, and in many of the Continental States.

The first great impulse given to the Irish linen trade arose from the effects of the famous revocation of the Edict of Nantes, by Louis XIV. A colony of some seventy persons, from France and Belgium, under the direction of an experienced manufacturer, M. Louis Crommelin, settled in Ulster, and under the auspices of Government applied themselves chiefly to the introduction of the continental processes, which were then very superior to the routine observed in Ireland. The Irish Linen Board, which began its labours in 1711, continued for more than a century to exercise a watchful supervision over this growing trade; and, as some equivalent for that arbitrary enactment, in the reign of William III., by which the British Parliament destroyed the Irish woollen manufacture, considerable sums were appropriated by Government to this purpose; the yearly vote from 1711 to 1737 being £6000, and afterwards £20,600. The Linen Board, through the stimulus it gave to the trade, was certainly productive of much benefit to the nation. The now exploded system of bounties led, however, to much abuse; and early in the present century it was found that the Irish linen manufacture could stand by itself without further aid from the State. Since then it has assumed a healthiness, and progressed with a rapidity, which amply demonstrate the peculiar natural advantages possessed by Ireland for this manufacture.

Before the application of machinery to the spinning process, the trade was quite of a domestic character. It was carried on throughout Ireland, in the cottages of small farmers, and of weavers in the country towns. The linen was brought for sale to certain markets, where bleachers attended and bought it up, these bleachers being generally the shippers of their own goods. By a return made to the Linen Board, in 1816, we find that the value of the linens thus sold in the country markets of each province was as follows:—

| | |
|---|---|
| In Ulster, | £2,323,962 |
| Leinster, | 265,460 |
| Munster, | 62,856 |
| Connaught, | 127,774 |
| Total, | £2,780,052 |

It will be seen that, even then, Ulster had by far the greatest share of the trade; the industrious character of its inhabitants, and their aptitude for manufacturing employment, distinguishing them from the people of the other provinces, who were then, as they continue to be, almost exclusively tillers of the soil. In the county of Antrim alone, £697,600 worth of linens were sold in 1816, or 50 per cent. more than in the three southern provinces put together.

After the introduction of machinery for spinning, the hand-spinning soon ceased, and as almost all the factories were in Ulster, weaving concentrated itself there also. At the present day, with the exception of a district round Drogheda, and a few localities of Cork and Mayo, no linens are woven without the boundary of the northern province.

Soon after the revolution in spinning, the weaving system underwent considerable changes. Persons possessing capital and a knowledge of the trade embarked as manufacturers, employing a number of weavers, to whom they gave out the yarns bought by them in quantity from the spinners, already boiled and warped. Some spinners, also, found it advantageous to manufacture their own yarns, and even to buy from others; and they employed as their agents individuals in country districts to whom the yarns were sent, and were by them distributed amongst the weavers, and returned as woven fabrics to the spinners, who either sold them to bleachers and shippers, or bleached and exported them on their own account. At present there are only four or five markets in Ulster where buyers attend as formerly; and even in these, few linens are sold by weavers, being generally disposed of in lots by manufacturers. The more extensive of the latter employ 500 to 2000 weavers each.

Since the famine of 1847, consequent on the loss of the potato crop, linen weaving has been considerably affected by the social changes arising therefrom. Previously, in Ulster, many persons existed partly on their earnings as weavers, and partly on the produce of the small tracts of land which they held. The latter grew the potatoes, which constituted the staple of their food, and the earnings of the former enabled them to pay rent, to buy clothing, and to provide the humbler luxuries. When the potato failed, they found themselves unable to exist with comfort, a considerable emigration ensued, and their land was consolidated into larger farms. Consequent upon this decrease in the supply of weavers, a considerable advance in wages has recently taken place; and even with this advance, enough cannot be had to keep pace with the increase of the linen trade. So much inconvenience has arisen, that great efforts have lately been making to adapt the power-loom to the weaving of linens.

Owing to the want of elasticity in the fibre of flax, as compared with cotton and wool, it has been found difficult to employ the power-loom for weaving those light fabrics which constitute the bulk of the export, and which form also the great mass of the Irish make. At Dundee and Barnsley, and in other parts of the sister island, the power-loom is employed in the weaving of heavy fabrics, such as canvass, bagging, drills, &c., and 3660 looms are thus occupied. In Ireland the number of those worked by power was, until this year, under 100. Great exertions, however, have been lately made, and are now making, to render the power-loom available for ordinary light linens, and the future extension of the linen trade must greatly depend upon the success of those trials.

As is always the case in kindred manufactures, the different sorts of linen fabrics are confined to certain localities. Thus, coarse linens for blouses, &c., and for the common kinds of export goods, are chiefly made in the county of Armagh; medium and fine kinds of export cloth, about Ballymena and Coleraine; damasks and diapers, at Lurgan, Lisburn, and Belfast; lawns, at Lurgan and Dromore; cambrics, at Lurgan, Waringstown, and Dromore; heavy linens and sheetings, for the home market, at Banbridge; hollands, in the counties of Antrim and Armagh; shirt fronts, woven in plaits, at Dromore; and the coarsest fabrics, such as bed-ticks, coarse drills, &c., at Drogheda.

As to the destination of the Irish linen manufactures, every one has heard that they are to be found selling throughout the globe; that

"From China to Peru, from Indus to the Pole,"

in every part where floats the British flag, Irish linens are a well-known article of commerce; and yet Irish legislators have gravely stated, in their place in Parliament, that the linen trade of their country had fallen off grievously, and that in 1852, only 50,964 yards were exported to foreign countries! Let us examine this apparent inconsistency. In 1852, out of 58,602 packages of linen fabrics shipped from Belfast, only 27 were sent direct to foreign countries, and yet there are several Belfast houses, each of which has transactions in linens with foreign states, averaging from £50,000 to £300,000, annually, or equal to a million and six millions of yards respectively. The explanation is simple, and it is this:—Before the extraordinary facilities offered by steam navigation, and before the growth of Liverpool, London, Glasgow, and Southampton, as *entrepôts* for export, the Irish merchant shipped his linens direct from Belfast to foreign ports. In 1800, the then large quantity of 3,126,340 yards was thus exported. Week after week the vessel lay in the docks, loading slowly for New York, or Havanna, or Rio Janeiro, awaiting the shipments of the manufacturers. Now every steamer leaving Belfast, Newry, or Derry, carries its 50 or 100, or 500 boxes and bales of linens, to Liverpool, Glasgow, London, and Southampton. In those ports are to be found vessels filling up rapidly with woollen and cotton, and silk and hardware goods, for every port in the world where British commerce flourishes. Every week fast-sailing steamers depart for America, and for the Mediterranean and the Levant. And every week the customers of the Irish linen manufacturer receive fresh consignments through these convenient channels. In a word, Liverpool and Glasgow are to Belfast what they are also to Manchester, Sheffield, and Paisley—the great shipping ports; and hence the official figures of Irish exports are no longer to be relied on as indications of the extent of the Irish linen trade with foreign states.

As regards the growth of the manufacture, we may consult a few figures. There were exported from Ireland to Great Britain and foreign countries:—

| | |
|---|---|
| In 1710, | 1,688,574 yards. |
| 1750, | 11,200,771 " |
| 1800, | 35,676,908 " |
| 1835, | 60,916,572 " |

No official returns are available since 1835, but taking the ascertained production in that year and that now existing, we may put down the present make at about 160,000,000 yards.

It is difficult to fix the proportion of those fabrics which is intended for the home as distinguished from the foreign market. We may, however, come to some conclusion as regards the relative quantities shipped to each foreign state by a reference to the Liverpool exports of linens, as it is through that port the great bulk of Irish goods are forwarded. In 1852 there were shipped from Liverpool—

| | | | |
|---|---|---|---|
| To the United States of America, | 85,118 Packages. | To other European States, | 675 Packages. |
| British North America, | 2,530 " | Turkey and Egypt, | 981 " |
| West Indies, | 14,088 " | East Indies and China, | 541 " |
| South America, | 30,626 " | Australia, | 882 " |
| Italian States, | 8,313 " | Other countries, | 33 " |
| Spain and Portugal, | 2,421 " | | |

It will be thus seen, that the western hemisphere is the great market for our linens. On the Continent of Europe, although linen fabrics are consumed to an immense extent, prohibitory duties shut out our goods; and, until there be a change in the tariffs of France, Germany, Russia, and Austria, we cannot expect to gain admission for them to any considerable extent. To compare the present consumption of Irish linens in America with what it is in Europe, we may put the case thus:—39 millions of people in America consume more than two yards of Irish linen per head, while 228 millions in Europe take only one thirty-eighth of a yard per head. Nothing but obstructive tariffs could prevent Ireland having the lion's share in all the linen markets of the world. Wherever we meet the French, the Belgians, and the Germans, on equal terms, as in the States of the American Continent, we beat them out of the field. For it is a fact patent to every inquirer, that Ireland now produces the best and cheapest linens in the world.

It has been erroneously stated in some of the public journals, that this department, as illustrative of our sole great native manufacture, was imperfectly represented. A careful inspection could not fail, however, to convince any one conversant with the subject, that the display was complete in all its details, and that quantity and position were the only points to which exception could be taken. As respects the former, it cannot be desirable that examples of the same kind of fabric should be multiplied; for while in the case of three other great textile manufactures—silk, wool, and cotton—colour and design so largely enter as to admit of an extended representation of the same class of articles; in linen, on the contrary, the absence of all tint, and the limited application of ornament, render a selection more desirable, especially as the space that would otherwise be occupied by a repetition of sameness can be more appropriately devoted to other objects. The great fault of the Flax and Linen Department was the very defective arrangement, both as regards prominence and light; and it is to be regretted that a branch of Irish manufacturing industry, which is so far in advance of all others, and which has, almost by itself, obtained an industrial status for Ireland among the nations of the world, should have been condemned to a secondary position in the Building, removed from the gaze of the majority of visitors; only to be found by penetrating through side alleys; and when found, disappointing the seeker in the want of effect produced by insufficient and borrowed lighting.

The total absence of foreign linen fabrics was to be remarked in the Dublin Exhibition. In that of London, in 1851, there was a very considerable display from France, Holland, and Belgium, the Zollverein, Austria, Russia, Switzerland, and even from Spain, Portugal, and Italy. It would almost seem that foreign linen manufacturers dreaded to show their fabrics in the stronghold of their great and successful rival.

England, also, which contributed to the Exhibition of 1851 many excellent specimens of Barnsley drills, Knaresborough sheetings, and Bridport goods, was entirely absent on the late occasion. Scotland, however, though not an extensive exhibiter, yet showed a fair assortment of the class of fabrics manufactured in such large quantities on her eastern coast.

In the Irish display scarcely an article was wanting. The Exhibition furnished examples of almost every fabric made in the kingdom; and the quality upheld the character freely conceded to Irish flaxen manufacturers by all consumers.

It is not to be supposed that this excellence has been of easy attainment, or that it dates from an early period in the industrial history of the island. It is true that the manufacture was prosecuted centuries ago, and that the use of linens was extensive among the upper classes at the time of the Norman Invasion. For, as Campion quaintly says, "linen shirts the wealthy do weare for wantonness and braverie, with wide hanging sleeves, playted; thirtie yards are little enough for one of them." But these exaggerated garments were of the coarsest texture, and they are stated to be yellow—the famous Irish bleach being then unknown. And when bleaching was introduced, and the Irish linens were prepared for the English market, the colour was extracted by the rudest means. Attached to every bleach-green was a large dairy, which furnished the acid and the alkali, now supplied by more scientific means—cow manure then providing the latter, and buttermilk the former, which, up to 1761, was the only acid used. In 1770 sulphuric acid was successfully employed; in 1780, potash; and in 1795 chloride of lime. The improved growth of flax, the machine-spinning of yarns, superior looms, and numerous ameliorations and curtailments of the bleaching process, have, by slow degrees, brought the manufacture to its present excellence. But though the skilful application of chemistry has in this, as in other arts, effected wonderful improvements, the snowy purity of the Irish bleach is mainly to be referred to the humidity of our climate, its alternate showers and sunshine.

"Erin, the tear and the smile in thine eyes"—

not only typifies national history and character, but is as useful in the arcana of the bleacher, as it is suggestive of the elegant trope of the poet.

Irish linens may be divided into two great classes, the heavy and the light fabrics, which as nearly distinguish the home from the foreign trade. There are, of course, exceptions, some being suited for both markets, and there is the separate class of damasks, to which decorative art lends a new feature. The taste of the home consumer is chiefly for the sound, close, substantial fabrics, durable, and comparatively dear; that of the foreigner, especially of our great customers of the western hemisphere, is for the light, highly-finished, and cheap article. The Americans would rather have a less substantial shirt and renew it more frequently: the Europeans seek strength and durability, and hoard their linen for generations. As a striking way of showing the difference of texture and quality in the two classes of goods, it may be stated that a bundle of the same number of yarns for the best make of heavy linen, sells up to 9*s*. 6*d*., and for the commonest make of export linen, can be had down to 3*s*. 9*d*. All depends on the quality of flax employed for the purpose.

Of plain heavy shirtings there were good examples in the Exhibition. All were excellent, and the closer the examination the more fully did their whiteness of bleach and evenness of texture appear. Fronting linen was also shown by several exhibitors. It is lighter in texture, and finer in the set. A branch of the latter section of the trade has, within a few years, risen to some importance, viz., the manufacture of plaited shirt fronts. By an ingenious invention adapted to the loom, these fronts can be woven, in different patterns of plaits, in a superior manner to the former mode of stitching by hand; and as they are produced much cheaper, an extensive consumption has, in consequence, arisen, chiefly in the United States. The houses of Messrs. Harrison, Brothers, and Sprott and Co., both of Dromore, confine themselves to this article, and their specimens afforded a good idea of the variety of pattern.

In the class of export goods the chief exhibitors were Messrs. Murland; Fenton, Son, and Co.; and J. Hind and Sons. The highly-glazed surface of some of their goods, produced by extra beetling or calendering, was a characteristic type of the appearance looked for by South American consumers, the effect being to flatten and consolidate what would otherwise be a rather rough and flimsy fabric. In this class also might be seen great diversity of folding, a gaudy style of ornamentation, and a recurrence of Spanish names and titles. Some of these, such as Silesias, and Irlandas, indicate the origin, either present as in the latter, or anterior as in the former—the Silesias being now Irish goods, though the German name is retained to meet the fancy of the market. Then there are Creas and Platillas, and each piece, again, is stamped with such phrases as "*hilo puro*," "*garantizado*," "*todo hilo*," &c. &c.; so that the Cuban or Mexican *caballero* may feel secure that he is buying linen in its integrity, and not union or cotton with an imitative finish, while the attractive title of "*grano de oro*" doubtless sells many a piece.

Another extensive class of goods are sheetings, and here the Scotch manufacturer comes into competition with ours, but generally keeps to the coarser range, leaving the finer to the Irish maker.

In drills, Ferguson, of Drogheda, showed a variety of handsome patterns; D. Lindsay, Dromore, a series of excellent goods, both plain and fancy; and R. Roddy, some of very superior quality. These fabrics are now made in great variety at Belfast, and the character of the numerous patterns employed was well indicated by the small specimens in the Royal Flax Society's case.

Hollands, so called from the country where they were formerly made, were admirably represented by Messrs. W. Kirk and Son's collection.

Lawns and cambrics, which form a large and rapidly increasing branch of the manufacture, were chiefly exemplified in the cases of Mr. Henning, Waringstown, and of Messrs. Bell and Co., Lurgan. The advance of the cambric manufacture is highly interesting, as showing the capability of Ireland for producing descriptions of linen fabrics in which foreign countries had previously attained great eminence. Every one has heard of French cambrics as being the *ne plus ultra* of excellence, and yet, at the present day, the fabrics known in the home market by that title are almost exclusively Irish. So rapidly did the Irish manufacturers tread on the heels of their foreign competitors that, in 1845, it was declared that for every 1000 pieces of French, 16,000 pieces of Irish were sold, although, in the interval, the duty on foreign cambric was considerably reduced. Since then, one Irish manufacturer has been known to effect sales of cambric to the value of £8000 in a single day in London. In 1852 only 24,334 pieces of French cambric and lawn were imported into the United Kingdom; and even this extremely decreased amount must be taken *cum grano salis*, for it is an established fact that Irish cambrics have often been bought by Parisian houses, and sent into England again as French manufacture. So much for a name! While our manufacturers have beaten the French out of the market, in all coarse and medium qualities, the latter still maintain a superiority in the very fine class of goods. But even in these every year sees their pre-eminence lessened. A few years ago, it was objected to Irish cambrics, that though excellent in quality, they wanted the lightness and transparency of the French goods. This, however, is no longer the case, as was illustrated by the fabrics in the Exhibition, many of which showed a gauzy texture almost rivalling book-muslin.

There remains to notice a section which embodies a new feature,—that of ornament—and which includes damask table linen, and printed linens and cambrics. As the only branch of the manufacture requiring the direct application of design, it deserves a careful study, and a close scrutiny of the extent to which the rules of correct taste have been observed.

The application of decorative art to linen fabrics involves a consideration of the nature of the material, its peculiarities, and the treatment which these require. Other textile manufactures more or less call in the adjunct of colour, which renders decoration at once more ample and more facile. In damasks we have to deal with a total absence of colour, and can only rely upon the effect produced by light and shade, in the disposition of warp and weft. Floridity of ornamentation should be avoided, and chasteness and elegance studied, with a careful reference to the purposes of the material. Very few of the damasks shown in the Exhibition were free from the fault of overcrowding with a confusion of flowers and foliage. It must be admitted, however, that the taste of the consumer has to be studied by the manufacturer; and that the former very frequently estimates his table linen by the amount rather than the character of its decoration. This meretricious taste is apparent not only in the article of which we treat, but in almost all others which involve the application of design; and it is assisted and pandered to by the facility which machinery has given to the almost infinite multiplication of copies. The cost of a design is a mere bagatelle when spread over a large amount of sales; and consequently manufacturers are quite ready to give full measure of ornament where required. It was very different in the earlier periods of the world's industrial history, when the designer and the worker were generally combined in the same individual. Yet we cannot regret the change that has been wrought by the Jacquard loom and the founder's mould, as it brings within easy reach of the multitude what the wealthy alone could formerly obtain.

In the ornamentation of damask, floral patterns prevail, and they are the least affected by criticism. The *embarras de richesses*, alluded to, was very conspicuous in several of the table-cloths exhibited by Messrs. Andrews, Coulson, and Henning. A design termed the "Ardoyne Exhibition Pattern," of the first-named producer, shows nearly thirty distinct species of flowers, all well drawn and gracefully combined; but the effect, to a critical eye, is marred by this very profusion. Mr. Roddy's table-cloths are carefully designed, and the patterns well executed.

Another class consists of heraldic devices, ciphers, &c., executed expressly for noble families, clubs, and regimental messes. Mr. Coulson is the chief exhibitor of these, and it will be observed that the best result is produced by the necessary simplicity of the design, and the absence of distracting variety. It is to be noted, however, that relief is too much attempted; at least this objection would be made by those arbiters of taste who insist on a perfectly flat treatment.

The subject of relief is still a *quæstio vexata;* one side roundly objecting to its employment in any textile fabrics, while the other insists that it is necessary, in order to give the requisite degree of richness and variety, and to avoid the stiffness of mediæval or pre-Raphaelite art. One thing is certain, that, with the great mass of customers, relief is always looked for, probably because the tendency of design has, for a long period, been to reproduce nature as imitatively as possible.

There is a class of damask designs which certainly sins against the rules of correct taste, viz.:—the representation of landscapes, buildings, architectural ornaments, and copies of designs applied to ceramic works, or found in the remains of antiquity. As an instance we may refer to the "Portland Vase Pattern" of Mr. Henning, admirably represented, no doubt, and to be wondered at as a triumph of manufacturing skill in copying so accurately the human figure and the expression of the features; but quite unsuitable when the intention of damask table linen is taken into account. Another, the "Egyptian Pattern," the mechanical execution of which is equally excellent, is open to a similar objection. In the Exhibition of 1851 a Dunfermline manufacturer showed a table-cloth containing, as a centre, a correct view of Balmoral Castle, and another copied a shield of precious metal presented to Prince Albert. Again, in our own Exhibition, Mr. Andrews exhibited a table napkin with the emblems of Ireland—a wolf-dog, round tower, harp, &c. The fault of all these consists in applying to what should be considered a *flat surface* objects totally out of keeping with it. We do not place our bouquets on sphinxes and ibises, nor range our dishes against the perpendicular walls of Irish round towers and Balmoral Castles, nor set our plates on the top of the Portland Vase, nor our wine glasses on antique shields. Wreaths of flowers, as in the time of the Romans, may be strewed on the festive board; foliage may add freshness to it, or geometrical patterns may give the idea of a tessellated or mosaic surface; but farther than this, at least with correct taste, we should not go.

These errors are by no means confined to our own manufacturers. Those of Germany, France, and Belgium, who exhibited in London, in 1851, showed the same.

It is strange that so little of the foliage of trees and plants should be employed in damask designs; presenting, as they do, such a variety of appropriate and graceful forms. One of Mr. Andrews' cloths, termed the "Fern Rustic Pattern" showed how agreeable a combination can be so effected. Another, and most suitable style, appears totally neglected, none of the damasks shown at Dublin having adopted it, and but one example, a German cloth, in the Exhibition of 1851, having presented it. The style referred to is the endless variety to be found in geometrical patterns, arabesques, mosaics, Byzantine ornaments, &c. &c., all highly suitable and perfectly correct. Even with floral decoration a diaper treatment, i. e. sprays arranged geometrically in diamonds or squares, would be found much more satisfactory for the space between the border and the centre than the handfuls of flowers now thrown in at random, which lessen the effect of the centre and are paltry in themselves—as witness the "Clarendon Pattern" otherwise admirable. Another desirable mode of treatment, of which there was no example in the Exhibition, consists in rays, say, of climbing flowers, diverging from the centre to the border; and this, also, would be in keeping with the general principle of making the centre the principal object, and the rest of the ornament, except the border, subservient to it. It is almost a pity that so much pains should be lavished on the border, when so large a proportion of it is turned over the side of the table and does not meet the eye, so that to see a table-cloth it must be hung up or laid out perfectly flat. This also might be remedied.

It may appear rather as hypercriticism to allude so largely to the deficiencies of style existing in our damask manufacture. The excellence of the fabric and its purity of bleach atone to a great extent, and every Irishman must feel a pride in reflecting that these beautiful fabrics are sought far and wide, and that the tables of few European sovereigns are without specimens of Irish manufacturing skill.

Another branch of the linen trade is illustrative of design. In the Exhibition were shown cambrics, lawns, and linens, printed for ladies' dresses, and handkerchiefs with border patterns in colours. The designs, generally, were fair, and some of them tasteful. They consist, for the dresses, of delicate sprays of flowers chiefly in stripes, and the effect is increased by narrow alternate rows of open-work; for the handkerchiefs, the bordering is either floral or geometrical. The colours are chiefly of the more subdued tints; where glaring ones are used, it will be seen that the effect is lessened. These dresses are chiefly for the American and West Indian markets. The material is delightfully cool in a hot climate, and is preferred to muslin. Some ornamental embroidery was also to be seen on shirt fronts; but few of the patterns were remarkable for their skill, while some were intensely vulgar. Indeed, the skilful arrangement of straght lines has a better effect in the plaited fronts; and some of the handkerchief borders which merely consist of narrow cotton rectilinear stripes, arranged in greater or less thickness, with alternate spaces, are preferable in point of chasteness to the printed borderings.

These remarks on ornament, as applied to linen, would be incomplete without a reference to the external decoration of the fabrics intended for home and foreign markets. Prettiness is the general characteristic of these, and novelty is much studied. Coloured prints, embossed paper, gilded or silvered bands, ribbons, stamps, &c., &c., are in wonderful variety. Some are tawdry, but others are very beautiful. It is well known that this mode of decorating linen intended for the United States, the West Indies, Cuba, Brazil, Mexico, &c., is a matter of much import in the sale of the goods, and those who carefully examine the materials employed in embellishing a Platilla will not be surprised to learn that the cost is often enhanced by a halfpenny or a penny per yard on the fabric. It is stated that some £60,000 are annually paid by Irish manufacturers for these ornaments. They were formerly exclusively obtained from London and Paris, but of late some enterprising persons in Belfast have gone into the trade, and make large quantities of certain descriptions of bands and boxes. The Belfast School of Design has produced some creditable patterns for these, two of which were contributed to the Exhibition. Notwithstanding the prettiness of these ornaments, they cover up too much of the linen, and distract the attention from its intrinsic merits. In Mr. Roddy's collection, and in that of Messrs. Fenton, Son, and Co., the specimens of linen for the home market were simply tied with longitudinal ribbons, and in other instances plain bands of dark blue glazed paper. The quietness of these was an absolute relief after the glare of the ornaments employed in goods for foreign markets. It was observed in the Exhibition of 1851 that the German, French, and Belgian linens were decorated in a wretched manner. In the Zollverein department especially they were to be found wrapped with bands of badly coloured paper, stamped with the most uncouth designs. In addition to the greater cheapness of Irish goods, their high degree of embellishment has, doubtless, contributed to give them the command of South American markets, where the people have a taste for brilliant colours and beautiful forms, arising, no doubt, from their familiarity with the gorgeousness of the animate and inanimate nature by which they are surrounded.

Our task is now completed. We have made the Flax and Linen Department of the Exhibition the text for a popular review of the history, statistics, and present aspect of this great national industry in all its branches; and have thereby, it is to be hoped, aroused feelings of interest and pride in the success which has attended the exercise of skill, perseverance, and intelligent toil on Irish ground, with the aid of Irish heads and hands.

We have necessarily left out of our theme the numerous subordinate industries which this great linen manufacture has called into life,—the iron-founding, the machine-making, the chemical works which supply the materials for bleaching, the paper mills, and the felt works which use up the commonest refuse of flaxen fibre, converting it into the substance on which these pages come before the public eye, or which roofs our houses, and sheaths our ships. We have not touched upon the delicate manufacture of lace, making into fabrics fine as gossamer the fibres of that same plant which furnishes the material for the thickest and strongest cables. We have equally omitted all mention of the ropes, the twines, the fishing-nets, which present a ruder but most useful application of this material.

We have seen how the flax plant, after affording profit and employment to the farmer and labourer, has been converted, by the agency of hundreds of thousands of the Ulster population, into manufactures representing the yearly value of more than four millions sterling; after rewarding, equally, the toil of the artisan and the enterprise of the capitalist; and that these manufactures have been distributed over the whole surface of the civilized globe, making our little island widely known as an industrial country in every foreign state. Were we to pursue the subject farther, we might point to the comparative absence of pauperism in our manufacturing districts; to the wonderful rise of their capital, Belfast, from a little fishing village, unnamed in the earlier maps, to the position of a city of more than 100,000 souls, crowded with factories, possessing a mercantile fleet greater than that owned by the first port of France, expending in the improvements of its streets and harbour upwards of £700,000, constructing railways and canals at a cost of more than two millions sterling, and in its numerous public institutions showing that its citizens are alive to the utility and amenity of science and literature, as well as to the claims of suffering humanity.

Of the future of Ireland's linen manufacture we can scarcely predicate. It holds that vantage-ground which will enable it to seize every opening which the progress of liberal commercial policy may make for it in foreign realms. The last vestige of protection, as regards the admission of foreign flax and flaxen products into the United Kingdom, has vanished. Flax, yarns, and linen fabrics, have all free entry to an open competition with the productions of Irish soil, and the labour of Irish hands. Did but other countries follow this lead, our linen manufacture would equal in its extent, and in the rapidity of its progress, its gigantic rival, the cotton manufacture of Great Britain. We should then have Belfasts in the South, Ballymenas and Armaghs in the West;—the island would resound with the hum of human bees;—the trade of our ports would no longer be confined to the shipment of raw agricultural produce, but would include quantities of manufactures representing for the most part the wages of labour. But as to the future commercial policy of our European neighbours we cannot speculate. We may draw hopeful auguries from the more certain increase of population in those foreign countries to which we have free access, from the growth of nations tracing their origin to British colonization, and from the increasing earnings of the masses at home leading to an increase in the consumption of manufactures. Meantime, we have to aim at extending the growth of the raw material throughout Ireland, at the application of the power-loom to weaving, and at all requisite improvements in the different processes of the trade. Half a century, nay, a quarter century hence, a Dublin Exhibition may contain flax of the qualities then to be shipped in quantity to France, Belgium, and Italy; yarn from our factories finer than any now dreamed of; linens of all kinds, made by the power-loom, better and cheaper than are now woven by hand; fabrics as made up for the Australian, the New Zealand, and the Polynesian markets; Kerry cambrics, Galway drills!—J. M.

---

1. ANDREWS, MICHAEL, Royal Manufactory, Ardoyne, Belfast. Manufacturer.—Super-extra double damask table cloth, the "Clarendon Pattern," a specimen of natural flowers tastefully arranged, and among them the national and industrial emblems of Ireland, the shamrock and flax plants, interwoven with each other—also, two table napkins to match, one with, and one without, springs,—this pattern was designed specially for the table linen presented by the Royal Society for the Cultivation of Flax in Ireland to the Earl of Clarendon when Lord Lieutenant; super-extra double damask table cloth, the "Ardoyne Exhibition Pattern," a very rich pattern, composed of a great variety of flowers from nature, grouped in a new style, with two table napkins to match: double damask table cloth, new pattern, the "Fern Rustic Pattern," composed of a great variety of ferns picturesquely grouped; table napkin with coat of arms, and another with emblems of Ireland.

2. BELL, THOMAS, & Co., Bellevue, Lurgan, Manufacturers.—Cambric handkerchiefs, bordered, printed, hemstitched, tucked, and embroidered (in the loom); printed dresses also embroidered (in the loom).

3. BREWSTER, JOHN, Kirkaldy.—Bleached, extra, navy, and twist canvass, tow-yarn, and sail-twine—spun by R. & J. Aytoun.

4. CARSON, R., Randalstown, County Antrim, Manufacturer.—Bleached linens.

5. CLIBBORN, HILL, & Co., Linen Merchants, and Bleachers, Banbridge, Manufacturers.—Bird-eye diapers, manufactured from prime linen yarn.

6. COULSON, JAMES, & Co., Lisburn, and Craven-street, Strand, London, Manufacturers.—Specimens of superfine damask table cloths; napkins, appropriately ornamented with armorial bearings, badges, devices and inscriptions, similar to those prepared for Her Majesty, and the leading nobility and gentry.

7. ELLIOTT, J., Thomas-street, Dublin, Manufacturer.—Ropes and twines, from Irish hemp and flax.

8. FENTON, SON, & Co., Linen Hall, Belfast.—Case of linen fabrics; prize linen of the Exhibition of 1851; family and light linen, for the home and foreign trade.

9. FERGUSON, FREDERICK C., Fair-street, Drogheda, and Linen Hall, Dublin, Linen Merchant.—Manufacturer of goods suited for home consumption and exportation; specimens exhibited of imperial and fancy linen drills; linens, lawns, and platillas; goods adapted to the European, East and West Indian, and other foreign markets.

10. FINLAYSON, BOUSFIELD, & Co., Johnstone, near Glasgow, Manufacturers.—Specimens of tailor's thread, in various colours and numbers made up in rolls and skeins; patent satin finish thread; shoe thread; hemp thread and closing thread; fine white gimp thread for lace; fine black silk thread.

11. FITZGIBBON, J., Glin, County Limerick, Producer.—Gray and white linen duck.

12. FLETCHER, A., & Co., St. Rollox Flax Mills, Glasgow.—Linen threads, and shoe threads.

13. GEOGHEGAN, J. & R., Upper Sackville-street, Dublin, Proprietors.—Irish linens; sheetings; table linen; worked cambric handkerchiefs.

14. GRADWELL, CHADWICK & Co., Drogheda, Manufacturers.—Linen yarns, 100 to 520 lea, in different stages of manufacture, from Irish and Courtrai flax.

15. GRANT, G., & Co., Armagh, Proprietor.—Sail canvass; canvass yarn in the green state canvass yarn in the boiled state, all made from hand-scutched Irish flax.

16. HARRISON, BROTHERS, Dromore, County Down, Manufacturers.—Linen shirt frontings, in various patterns, all woven in the loom; frontings, embroidered, veined, printed, &c.

17. KIRK, W., & SON, Annvale, Keady, County Armagh, Manufacturers.—Rough brown linens; linen hollands; bleached linen diapers; lining, family, and fronting linens; unions.

18. KNOX, A., Linen Hall, Dublin, Manufacturer.—Irish sheetings, diapers, and towellings.

19. LOCKHART, N., & SONS, Kirkaldy, Manufacturers.—Linen bed-ticks, rough and calendered, woven by hand; grain sacks, hand-wove; diaper and Portobello bath towels; water twist; checks.

20. LOCAL COMMITTEE OF THE COUNTY KERRY, THE, Tralee, Proprietors.—Hand-loom diaper table-cloths.

21. LEADBEATER, J., & Co., Belfast.—Specimens of yarn and linen; cloth manufactured of flax, prepared by the patent process of exhibiters.

22. LINDSAY, D., Ashfield, County Down, Manufacturer.—Table-cloths, and napkins of single and double damask; strong, light, and fancy drills; mosquito netting; shirt fronts, plaited in the loom without using the needle.

23. M'BIRNEY, COLLIS, & Co., Aston's-quay, Dublin, Proprietors.—Damask table-cloths; linens of various qualities; cambrics.

24. M'CAY, T., Dromore, County Down, Manufacturer.—Fine linens.

25. M'DONALD, H., Leinster-row, Kevin-street, Dublin.—Patent sash line, manufactured from Irish and foreign hemps; window blinds; cords and fancy twines; a six-strand machine line, the first made in Dublin.

26. MURLAND, H., Castlewellan, Bleacher and Producer.—Irish linens for the United States market.

27. OLDHAM, S., & SON, Westmoreland-street, Dublin, Proprietors.—Irish linens, sheetings, diapers, lawns, damask cloths; cambric handkerchiefs; specimens of Irish embroidery; quilts; toilet-covers; doyleys.

28. RODDY, R., Belfast, Proprietor.—Double damask table cloths, napkins, linens, lawns, diapers, and other linen fabrics; mill and hand-spun yarns; bleached drills.

29. ROWLAND, J., Drogheda, Manufacturer.—Damask and diaper sheeting of all breadths; huckaback; Drogheda linens; dowlas; tickens; hooping; glass cloths; stair covering; rollering; drills in various colours.

30. ROYAL FLAX SOCIETY, Belfast.—Line rovings for 130 lea and 260 lea yarns; line and tow yarns from 6 lea to 280 lea; specimens of unbleached and bleached fabrics, including heavy and light linens, drills, diapers, damasks, lawns, cambrics, mosquito netting; specimens of fancy, dyed, or printed fabrics, including drills, bed-ticks, floor cloths, lawns, cambrics, linens; case of specimens of linen yarns, &c., the manufacture of Messrs. Gradwell, Chadwick, & Co., Drogheda; case of specimens of linen fabrics, &c., the manufacture of Messrs. John Hind & Sons, Belfast; specimens sent n 1774 to the Society of Arts, by Lady Moira, comprising—coarse wrappering for linens for furniture from the backings of tow; coarse dimity for upper petticoats, and a piece of Lady Moira's own gown.

31. SOPER, R. S., London, Manufacturer.—Patent sash lines; thread and worsted blind lines.

32. SPEEDIE, R., & SONS, Kirkaldy, Manufacturer.—Bleached linen sheetings; bed-ticks; window-blinds; coutille huckabacks; diapers; towels, &c.

33. TODD, BURNS, & Co., Mary-street, Dublin.—Specimens of Irish fronting linens, bleached by a new process; Irish cambric handkerchiefs.

34. TOUGH, ALEXANDER, & SON, Greenock, Manufacturers.—Coils of rope, each 6 and 9 inches, formed upon the highest angle with the greatest tension on the leason, and maintained during the subsequent operations. By this plan a great amount of strength and durability is insured.

35. WATSON, J., Jamaica-street, Glasgow, Manufacturer.—Fishing lines and twines.

36. WILSON, R., Dublin, Manufacturer.—Hawsers; standing rigging, wormed; lanyard rope; bolt rope; flat rope for mining.

# CLASS XVI.

## LEATHER, INCLUDING FURS AND SADDLERY AND HARNESS.

THE manufacture of leather, and its various applications, possess peculiar interest in this country, not only because it is an article of universal consumption, and consequently the basis of great manufactures, but because its production is peculiarly adapted to the circumstances of Ireland. We shall, therefore, devote a little more space to the subject than we would otherwise feel inclined to do, in the case of a manufacture so well known.

Our subject naturally divides itself into the following sections, under which we shall briefly discuss it:— 1. Raw materials of the leather manufacture: hides, skins, and tanning materials. 2. The tanning of leather properly so called. 3. Curried leather. 4. Enamelled, varnished, and dyed leather. 5. Tawed, or alum leather; and oil, or chamois leather. 6. Parchment, dried sheep-skin rugs, &c. 7. Animal skins used for their fur. 8. Applications of leather to harness, saddle, trunk-making, &c.

### RAW MATERIALS OF THE LEATHER MANUFACTURE.

The external covering or skin of warm-blooded animals consists of several distinct parts or layers, the outer of which is called the *epidermis* or cuticle, a thin membrane filled with small holes or pores, through which the hair reaches the surface, and the perspiration passes of. In its chemical composition it is analogous to horn, and consequently cannot be tanned; it is easily separated from the layer of the skin immediately below it by caustic alkaline solutions, such as potash or lime, in which it dissolves, or even by steeping it in water, in which, however, it does not dissolve. Immediately under the epidermis is a fine tissue called the *mucous membrane*, which is a kind of network filled with a mucous substance, and consisting of veins and other vessels and nerves, which spread themselves over the skin, and constitute the seat of feeling on the surface of the body, and the organs for the secretion of the perspiration. The papillæ, or raised eminences situated at the roots of the hair, which one feels so distinctly on the skin on feeling a sudden chill, are principally in this tissue. Under the mucous membrane lies the true skin, *corium* or *cutis*, which is a thick tissue composed of an endless number of delicate fibres, which cross and ramify in every direction, leaving a number of small openings or *pores* between them, which widen as they open inwards—that is, are conical. These canals are filled with cellular tissue, and the vessels and nerves which pass from within to the external mucous membrane. Any one may be able to distinguish the fibres which constitute the true skin by tearing a piece of dried skin parallel to its surface, when the great mass will be found to consist almost entirely of fine, white, shining, semi-transparent fibres, which are perfectly flexible, and to some extent elastic. In chemical composition these fibres are analogous to the ligaments which attach the bones together, and to the organic material which forms a large part of the bones themselves, and, like those tissues, possess the property of dissolving in boiling water, forming a gelatinous solution, which becomes solid on cooling—being, in fact, the article known as glue. Besides these fibres, which constitute the true tissue, and the cellular tissue, and vessels contained in the pores, as just mentioned, a fresh skin contains certain fluids, of which water is the principal ingredient, forming, indeed, no less than 57½ per cent. of the weight of a fresh hide; the solid substances of these fluids, like the epidermis, cannot be tanned, and are, therefore, of no use in the preparation of leather. By steeping the skins in water, however, these fluids or juices are removed, the pores becoming filled with pure water instead. A skin in this condition is semi-transparent, at the same time that it swells up considerably; when dry it retains to some extent this semi-transparency, and would then form about 32½ per cent. of the raw skin—that is, 100 lbs. weight of fresh hide usually contains about 32½ lbs. of solid matter capable of forming leather. Immediately under the cutis, and separating it from the true muscular fibre or meat, lies a layer of cellular tissue, one of the principal seats of the fat in the animal body.

The thickness of the skin is not uniform on every part of the body, being thicker on the back than on the belly; and in this, as well as in many other respects, the quality of skins is subject to great variations, depending upon the food, the period of the year, the age and state of health of the animal, as also upon the variety or breed. Thus a bull hide is inferior to a cow hide, in consequence of its being coarser grained, and thinner on the back, the great thickness of the former being concentrated in the neck and certain parts of the belly. Similarly, the skin of an animal which happens to die from disease is very much inferior to that of one killed in full health and vigour. In the case of a sheep, it is remarkable that the finer-woolled varieties yield the most inferior skins; and it has been remarked that the skin of a sheep gains in thickness and quality even within a period of three or four days after shearing.

The skins of all quadrupeds may be converted into leather, but in practice, with few exceptions, the whole of the leather made is manufactured from the skins of the ordinary domesticated animals.

*Horse Hides* are much thinner than what would be expected from the size of the animals, and are also rather weak, a fact which is probably to be attributed to the greater number being obtained from old and worn-out animals. When tanned they are usually employed in the manufacture of slipper shoes, or made into Cordovan or enamelled leather, being split, when employed for the latter purpose, by a peculiar machine. They are also sometimes made into tawed, white, or alum leather, and used as smiths' aprons, thongs for sewing common harness, &c. Large quantities are exported from South America: the number from that region alone in 1850 being no less than 180,000, where they are obtained from the herds of wild horses which live in the great plains called *Pampas*, lying between the chain of the Andes and the mouth of the Rio de la Plata.

*Skins of Oxen, Cows, Calves, Buffaloes, &c.*—We may here remark, to prevent confusion, that the term *skin* in commerce is applied only to those of small animals, such as the goat, sheep, &c.; *hide* is the term for the skins of the full-grown large animals, such as horses, cows, &c.; whilst the name *kip* is given to the skins of the younger animals of the same class. These terms depend rather upon the size than upon the nature of the skin, for that of a young calf still fed upon milk is termed a *skin;* the term *kip* being only applied to it when the calf has been put to grass. The supply of hides of cows and oxen employed in this country and in Great Britain is derived in the first place from native hides, which are usually sold in the fresh or green state, as market hides. And in the second place from the foreign hides imported in large quantities from Buenos Ayres, Monte Video, Valparaiso, the West Indies, Rio Grande, Brazil, the Cape of Good Hope, the East Indies, and New South Wales. The trade in hides between Europe and South America is of great extent, and is rapidly extending, for not only are the wants of these countries, and of France, Belgium, and Germany supplied, but a considerable Mediterranean trade has also sprung up, the imports of Austria being at least 400,000 cwts.; whilst Greece, which we are rather in the habit of pitying, imports, strange to say, 30,000 or 60,000 hides, of which she exports to her neighbour Turkey 30,000 in a tanned condition! When America was discovered, no cattle were found there; and the first were introduced by Columbus himself, in his second voyage to Hayti, in 1493, where in a few years they increased with a wonderful rapidity, and were soon introduced into the other islands, and the Continent. The trade in hides sprung up at a very early period; for we find that even in the year 1587, there were 35,444 exported from Hayti to Spain, and 64,350 from Mexico—that is, only fifty-six years after the conquest of the latter country. Some idea may be formed of the rapidity with which the European domestic animals have increased in the fertile regions of America, when it is stated that the city of Vera Cruz, in Mexico, possessed, in 1830, 50,000 horses and 300,000 head of cattle. But it is on the great plains which form the interior of South America—those enormous grassy seas which stretch from the foot of the Andes very nearly to the Atlantic coast—under the name of *Pampas* in the southern regions of Buenos Ayres, and of *Llanos* in the northern parts—that we can behold the wonderful development of the few cattle taken over by Columbus in his small and ill-fitted vessels. It is calculated that there are twelve millions of head of cattle, and three millions of horses, on the Pampas, having recognised owners, exclusive of the millions which are not claimed by any one, and which are gradually increasing; whilst in the northern Llanos (level plains) between the Orinoco and the Lagunes of Maracaybo, about 1,200,000 head of branded cattle, 180,000 horses, and 90,000 mules, roam, besides countless herds of unclaimed animals. A single rich *hateros* or proprietor often brands with a hot iron as many as 14,000 head of cattle in a year. Thousands of these half-wild animals are annually slaughtered for their hides alone, the fat being also occasionally collected; these hides are sent to Europe, either dried, salted and dried, or simply salted without being dried, the former being the most prized. Market hides are considered best, but they cost more than any others in consequence of the quantity of water which they contain—thus, for example, in order to produce 100 lbs. of leather, there would be required on an approximate average, say 75 to 76 lbs. of dry hide, 150 lbs. of salted hide, and 185 lbs. of market hide. The principal uses to which tanned ox and cow hides are put are for sole leather, stirrup leather, harness leather, driving bands for machinery and coach-makers' use. English and Irish calf skins are of very superior quality, and are employed almost entirely for the production of curried leather, for the uppers of shoes, and for boot fronts. Kips are imported from the East Indies, dried, salted and dried, and simply salted, and from Buenos Ayres and Monte Video salted. A great many calf skins are imported from the Baltic countries, especially from St. Petersburgh, where they are killed very young, and are hence, properly speaking, skins. They are principally employed for bookbinding, for ladies' shoes, and occasionally, when split, for inferior gloves.

*Deer Skins.*—Very few skins of this kind, comparatively speaking, come into commerce in these countries, the few that do are employed as *oil leather* in the manufacture of gloves, breeches, boots, and braces. A good deal of this kind of leather is now prepared in America, and exported to Europe instead of the raw skins.

*Pig Skins.*—In Ireland pigs are rarely if ever skinned, and we believe the same is the case in England; but not so in Scotland, where a great deal of these skins are tanned. Some are also imported from Germany. The principal use of tanned pig skins, which form a very porous, spongy kind of leather, but very hard, tough, and durable on the outer side, is for covering saddles. On the Continent a good deal of the skins dressed with the hair on are employed for covering knapsacks, &c.

*Sheep and Lamb Skins.*—Large numbers of these skins, obtained from native animals, come into commerce in these countries, some of which are sent to the United States in a salted state; a portion of the rest is tanned with bark for bazils and bellows leather; another portion is made into parchment and chamois, and another into white leather for aprons, &c., by tanning with alum and salt. Others again are split, the upper side being tanned with sumach, and sometimes dyed and used under the name of *skiver* for making pocket-books, hat linings, &c.; or of *roan* for bookbinding, slippers, &c.; and finally, some are employed as imitation morocco leather, and the under or flesh side made into parchment and chamois. Native lamb skins are frequently split, the grain side being tanned with alum and salt, and employed by apothecaries for covering the stoppers of bottles; the flesh side being made into chamois or oil leather for lining gloves. A large number of sheep skins are also dressed with the wool on, dyed, and employed for carriage and door mats. Large quantities of the skins of a peculiar breed of sheep, found at the Cape of Good Hope, are imported into Great Britain. In Asia Minor a similar kind of sheep is found, and many of the skins are imported, and also to a considerable extent into France. The skin of a lamb killed a few days after its birth is exceedingly fine-grained, and may be dyed of a good uniform tint, and employed as ladies' glove leather, or dressed in their wool as lining for morning gowns, slippers, and winter gloves. The skins of lambs killed about three weeks to a month after birth still retain a good deal of their fineness of grain and thinness, and are much superior for many purposes to those killed at a later period, as is the case in these countries, and especially in England. In the south of Europe, especially in France and Italy, great numbers of lambs are killed at this intermediate age, the skins being employed as a substitute for kid. About 1,400,000 are also exported to England, where they are made into gloves, which, although not equal to kid, are useful, and much cheaper.

*Goat Skins.*—A large number of native skins come into commerce in Ireland. The great majority of those employed in Great Britain are derived from four sources:—1. *Swiss skins*, which are the most valuable, in consequence of the closeness, fineness, and equality of grain, and their great strength and durability, which enable them to receive a very fine finished dye (all goat skins in these respects are superior to sheep or other skins). About 100,000 are annually imported from Switzerland and the upper valley of the Rhine into England alone, where they are employed in the manufacture of true morocco leather for carriages and upholstery purposes. 2. *Mogadore skins*, which are imported from Morocco and Algiers, being brought down from the Berber valleys of the Atlas chain of mountains. They are inferior to the Swiss in quality, and are chiefly employed in the manufacture of what is called Cordovan or Spanish leather—the latter name being derived from the fact of our chief supplies having been formerly obtained from Spain, and the former from this branch of tanning having been brought to great perfection by the Moors, especially in Cordova. 3. *Cape skins*, great numbers of which are now imported into England, and being much thicker and stronger than other goat skins, are used wherever considerable strength is required. 4. *East India skins*, which are small and light, and are largely employed for the manufacture of ladies' shoes, and for upholstering chairs, &c.

*Kid Skins.*—The finest kid skins, perhaps, in the world are the French, next to which may be reckoned the Irish, the greater part of which are, however, unfortunately exported, between 60,000 and 70,000 being sent to England alone. All the finer kid skins are tawed, that is, white tanned with salt and alum, for the manufacture of gloves: those imported from the East Indies are rather goat than kid skins, and are consequently coarse, for it is remarkable that the moment the food of the kid is changed from milk to grass it loses its delicacy, and will not make very fine gloves. The coarser skins not fit for gloves find, however, many other uses, such as binding leather for shoes, braces, light summer shoes for ladies, &c.

*Seal Skins.*—Immense quantities of these marine animals are taken annually—the number often amounting to 600,000, chiefly for their oil; but the skins, although not worth more than about four shillings each, also form an item of importance. The principal supplies come from Newfoundland and the coasts of Norway; when dressed they form probably the strongest leather known, in proportion to their thickness, and are principally employed for the upper portions of hunting and riding boots, tourists' knapsacks, &c.; or the lighter skins are enamelled for ladies' boots and gentlemen's dress boots.

Among the curiosities of skins may be included those of the hippopotamus, a few skins of which are occasionally brought from the coast of Africa; they take a long time to tan, and are then more like planks of wood than hides of leather; their only use as yet is for beetling bleached goods, in order to remove all impurities.

Having now glanced over the chief raw materials of animal origin used in the manufacture of leather, we shall say a few words upon the vegetable substance by means of which it is carried on.

If we powder common gall nuts, and treat them with the well-known liquid ether, we shall obtain a solution which, on the evaporation of the ether, leaves a slightly yellowish, white, shining, porous, uncrystallizable mass, called *tannin*. This substance is very soluble in water, from which it may be precipitated of a bluish-black colour by certain compounds of iron—it is this precipitate which constitutes the basis of ink. Tannin is also precipitated by solutions of glue, isinglass, or bone-size, the *tanno-gelatine* formed being so perfectly analogous to leather in its chemical composition that for a long period it was considered as such. If we place a piece of soft, well-washed skin in a solution of tannin, the latter will be gradually absorbed by the skin, with which it will combine, and the resulting compound will be leather. Tanning materials are, therefore, simply such substances as contain tannin, and as this substance is rather widely distributed in the vegetable kingdom, we may naturally expect to find that the catalogue of plants in which it is found is very large. For example, it occurs in common tea, in the bark of the oak, of the sycamore, the elm, the apple tree, the birch, willow, fir, whitethorn, and even in the common mountain heath, and thistle, and, in fact, in most astringent plants: tannin being the type of astringent substances. From what we have just said it might be concluded that the tannin of all plants was the same substance, an opinion, indeed, held by several of the most eminent chemists, but which recent investigations seem to show is not the case. The different tannins may be classed into two divisions—those which form ink, that is, which precipitate black with compounds of iron, and those which give a green precipitate with the same substances. It must, however, be remarked, that all tannins which give the same colour are not necessarily identical. These peculiar differences between tannins would, doubtless, appear to practical men of very little importance, as they may be all used indifferently to make leather, and that, however interesting to the chemist their study might be, the tanner may neglect them. It is quite the contrary; and although science has not yet explained these differences, there can be no doubt that the quality of the leather made is very much influenced by the nature of the tanning material employed. For example, it is well known that the remarkable beauty of the Norwegian glove leather is owing to the employment of elm bark, while the peculiarities of the Danish and Schoonian gloves is supposed to be owing to the bark of the willow, and that of the celebrated Bautzner leather to that of the pine.

If a solution of tannin be boiled for a few minutes with water to which oil of vitriol has been added, it undergoes a peculiar change; for, on cooling, silky needles will separate from the solution. These needles are *gallic acid*, a substance totally different from tannin, and which has no tanning properties whatever. Many of the substances usually employed as tanning materials contain this peculiar acid, as, for example, valonia, divi-divi, &c. It is not, however, found in any fresh plants, and is hence supposed to be produced in every case from tannin; an opinion which is sustained by the fact, that if a solution of tannin be exposed to the air, especially in a warm atmosphere, it will gradually absorb one of its elements, oxygen, and will disengage at the same time an equal bulk of carbonic acid, and after some time the tannin will be converted into gallic acid. If we employ the gall nuts themselves, the change of tannin will be more rapid, a similar result being produced by the addition to pure tannin of yeast, cheese, &c. In the conversion of tannin into gallic acid, directly from gall nuts and bark, there is produced at the same time another acid called ellagic acid, which is usually obtained as a yellowish gray powder, scarcely soluble in water. Unconnected as the changes just indicated appear to be with the manufacture of leather, they are, however, of immense practical importance.

We have probably said enough to explain to our readers the nature of the substance to which tanning materials owe their power of converting animal skins into leather. We will, therefore, speak of the materials themselves; but as our space is limited, we shall only notice the most important of those employed by tanners, which are as follow:—

| Tanning Materials. | Trees from which obtained. | Country. |
|---|---|---|
| Oak bark, | | |
| Cork tree bark, | Different varieties of the oak, | Ireland, Great Britain, Holland, Spain. Smyrna, Trieste, Morea. |
| Valonia, | | |
| Larch bark, | Species of the pine and allied genera, | Europe. |
| Hemlock bark, | | United States. |
| Willow bark, | Species of salix or willow, | Europe. |
| Elm bark, | Common elm, | Europe. |
| Birch bark, | Common white birch, | North Europe. |
| Babool bark, | | |
| Mimosa or wattle bark, | | Bengal. |
| Terra Japonica, | Species of the acacia, | New South Wales. |
| Cutch or Kut, | | East Indies. |
| Catechu and Gambier, | | |
| Divi-Divi, | Caesalpina coriaria, a plant of same genus as the trees which yield the dye-woods, Brazil wood, &c. | Maracaibo, Rio de la Hacha, &c. |
| Shumac, | Rhus coriaria, | Sicily, Trieste, Malaga. |
| Myrobolans, | Terminalia chebula, | Bengal. |
| Kassu, | Areca catechu, | Ceylon. |

*Oak bark* is the most important of all tanning materials, and is the one most largely employed in these countries. There are several kinds of oak, the bark of all of which may be employed in tanning; but some possess peculiar advantages for that purpose. We may divide them into two classes—the deciduous, and the evergreen oaks. To the first class belong the common oak, of which there are several varieties. The two most important of the evergreen oaks are, *Quercus suber* or the cork tree, which is a native of the south of Europe, and especially of Spain, and *Quercus coccifera* or kermes oak, which is abundant in the mountainous districts of the south of France.

The peculiar mildness of the climate of this country, and the fact that the arbutus and other plants of Southern Europe are indigenous to the south-west of Ireland, as well as the luxuriance with which the laurel and other evergreen trees grow here, render it probable that the kermes oak could be grown here for its bark. The tanning principle of oak bark is not equally distributed through every part of it. Bark is to the tree what the skin is to the animal, and, like it, is composed of several distinct layers. The external, thin, dry, and in some cases, semi-transparent membrane which envelops the trunk and branches of trees is called the *epidermis*. Immediately underneath this layer is found one of cellular tissue, which is perfectly analogous to the soft part of the leaves, and, like it, is very often green, especially in the case of the branches. Under this herbaceous tissue comes the true bark or *cortical tissue*, composed of elongated cells, divided into layers of network-like tissue. And, finally, there is a fourth layer called the *liber*, which consists of a network of fibres, connected together by cellular tissue;—when macerated in water it may be separated into thin layers or leaves, hence the name *liber*, from the Latin for book. This layer is, perhaps, the most important part of a tree; for part of it is transformed annually into wood, forming one of those annular rings of growth which may be distinguished by cutting a tree or branch across, and which we call *grain* in wood cut longitudinally. The bark of trees is the seat of a great number of secretions of great use in the arts,—as, for example, gums, resins, volatile oils, acids, and many of those peculiar substances which have so energetic an action when employed in medicine. In general these substances are found most abundantly in the newer bark, and hence we may naturally expect to find the greatest amount of tannin there also, and such is the case. The greatest amount is found in the white layers, composed partly of liber and partly of the newer layers of the cortical tissue. The outside or very coloured portions of the latter contain only colouring matter, and scarcely any tannin, whilst the epidermis contains none at all of the latter. The bark of young wood is richer in tannin than that of old, and communicates a much greater degree of softness to the leather; the bark of old trees and bark stripped for several years contains more foreign matters of what is called an extractive kind, which, although capable of assisting in the formation of leather, give it a deep colour, and never yield a superior quality. Probably the best age at which trees should be stripped for their bark is from fourteen to twenty-five years; and the best season is undoubtedly in spring when the tannin is at a maximum. The warmer the spring the more tannin will be found in the bark; a week of strong sunshine in the beginning of April will make a most remarkable difference in this respect. In England and in this country, the bark employed is of various ages, and is rarely stripped in spring, as the wood cut at that period would be liable to decay. Hence great advantage would, no doubt, be derived from the cultivation, in otherwise useless ground, of copsewood.

which could be cut in spring. The observation which we have just made in reference to the bark of the oak will apply equally well to the other barks of indigenous trees, such as those of the willow, the elm, the pine, the beech, and the birch. None of these barks are used in Ireland, with the exception of larch, and sometimes birch bark, which are employed in the manufacture of bazils and other sheep-skin leathers, although we are quite convinced, from the example of the Continent, many useful applications might be made of them, in consequence of their great cheapness. In former times leather was tanned with the common heath, which is considered to have one-third of the tanning properties of the best oak bark. This, if true, would make it more valuable than either larch or birch bark. The leather made, was, however, rather hard, but when a quantity of the St. John's wort (*Hypericum calycinum* or *perforatum*) is employed along with the heath, a beautiful pliable leather is said to be obtained. The bark of the latter is richer in tannin than that of any other, and is well adapted for the manufacture of leather.

A great many substances have been either proposed or employed as a substitute for vegetable matters containing tannin; among which we may notice peat, which, when broken small and boiled with water, can be employed as a substitute for bark. Calf-skins steeped for about three weeks in such a decoction, and then laid in a decoction of larch bark for a few days, in order to raise them, are found to yield excellent leather, remarkable for its softness and the facility with which it can be dyed black. The process for tanning with peat has been considerably improved of late by a tanner of the name of Pretorius, from the neighbourhood, we believe, of Liege. Another curious substitute was proposed for tannin by Darcet, a few years since; which does not, however, appear to have been very successful. It was founded upon the principle that the persulphate of iron—a substance readily made from green copperas—combines with glue or with skin in the same way as tannin does; and the process consisted simply in immersing the skins in a solution of the salt, when they became completely tanned in the course of a few days. A Mr. Berry proposed to make leather by mixing tar and lime together; from this mixture he made a liquor with boiling water which he employed for tanning. Skins prepared in this way were also treated, as in the case of turf, with a little true tanning solution made from oak bark, or shumac, &c.

In order to give some idea of the different tanning powers of the various substances used in the preparation of leather, we shall give here the approximate quantity of tannin contained in 100 lbs. of each:—

| | lbs. | | lbs. |
|---|---|---|---|
| Best Bombay catechu, | 54·8 | Bark of oak, stripped in autumn, | 4·3 |
| Gall nuts, | 26·4 | Bark of Spanish chestnut, | 4·3 |
| Sicilian shumac, | 16·2 | „ Italian poplar, | 3·1 |
| Malaga ditto, | 10·0 | „ willow cut in May, | 3·1 |
| Bark of the Kermes oak, | 8·5 | „ birch, | 1·6 |
| Bark of coppice wood oak, | 6·6 | „ larch, stripped in autumn, | 1·6 |
| Ditto of oak, stripped in spring, | 6·0 | | |

The remarks which we have already made upon the existence of different kinds of tannin become useful in considering the value of this Table; for if the quality of a tanning substance depended solely upon the amount of tannin which it contained, catechu would be the best substance to employ. Experience, however, has shown that other elements besides the amount of tannin must be taken into account—one of the most important of which is the nature of the tannin itself; and we may also mention the influence of colouring matters in the bark. Purchasers of leather demand that it should always have a particular colour, the one most preferred being a yellowish fawn colour; hence if any peculiar colouring matter should exist in a tanning material, the leather would be tinged by it, although in other respects its quality might be unaffected. For example, a decoction of cork-tree bark will, after exposure to the air for some time, gradually give rise to the production of a dark brown colouring matter, which dyes the leather throughout its thickness. There also exists a colouring matter in cutch and terra-japonica, which imparts a reddish-brown colour to the leather, and which is considered very objectionable in commerce. Some tanning substances, such as oak-bark, valonia, and divi, produce a sort of buff-coloured deposit on the leather, called by the tanners "bloom," and which is considered in some way to be connected with the quality of the leather; and hence materials which do not yield it are considered inferior. Here, then, arises another element in judging of the value of a tanning substance. Terra-japonica is one of those substances which does not produce this bloom; and although one pound of it is capable of tanning one pound of leather, whilst it requires from 3½ to 4 lbs. of oak bark to effect the same object (the price of the former being only double that of the latter), this supposed defect, together with the large quantity of colouring matter it contains, as already mentioned, have prevented tanners from employing it to any large extent—perhaps much to the advantage of those who employ leather, for the article made with terra-japonica is spongy and porous.

We shall now endeavour to briefly describe the operations through which a hide or skin passes in order to convert it into leather. These operations may be divided into two series—the one intended to prepare the skin for the action of the tanning principle; and the other the process of tanning, properly so called. The distinction which we have already pointed out between hides, kips, and skins, is of considerable importance in reference to these operations, for the manner of treating hides differs in many material points from that for skins; and the relative duration of the operations is still greater, for whilst a few months will suffice for the complete tanning of a light skin, a thick hide will frequently require two years. In our description of the processes, therefore, we shall keep this distinction in view.

The first operation to which hides and skins are subjected is that of steeping or washing, in order to remove blood and filth attached to them. Dried Buenos Ayrean hides are obliged to be thoroughly soaked in water and rubbed, or trampled under the feet, or beaten in a machine specially invented for the purpose, in order to bring them as nearly as possible into the condition of green hides. When fully cleansed, the hides are subjected to the action of a solution of lime, with the object of removing the hair and the epidermis, which, as we have already stated, cannot be tanned. For this purpose, four or five cisterns, built of brick or stone, are sunk in the ground, and are partially filled with a milk of lime of different strengths. The hides are first introduced into the weakest, where they remain for a couple of days, and are then transferred into the next in the series, and so through the remainder; the duration of the whole process varying with the size of the hide or skin, two to five days being sufficient for a sheep-skin, whilst a large thick hide may require three weeks. During the process the hides are *handled;* that is, are occasionally taken out of the lime pits, piled upon each other, and allowed to drain for a few hours, when they are again placed in the pits, the liquid in which is usually stirred up before the immersion, so as to bring the particles of lime in suspension in contact with each skin. As soon as it is found that the hair and epidermis may be removed, the skins are taken from the pits and unhaired. The loose pieces are also cut off, and under the name of fleshings form material for the manufacture of glue. The hides are then steeped in water and washed, to remove as much of the lime adhering to them as possible. The tissue of the hide when taken from the animal is very close, and is ill fitted for absorbing the tanning principle; and even if this were not the case, the thickest hides would be scarcely adapted for making sole leather, as any one will understand who compares a piece of sole leather with a piece of fresh skin. The hides are, therefore, obliged to be subjected to the action of some acid fluid which will cause them to swell out, or, as the tanners say, *raise them.* The action of the lime effects this object to some extent, but in practice it is found necessary to employ the acid solution also. The usual acid employed is that produced by digesting spent bark for five or six months in water, during which time the liquid becomes quite acid. No matter how well washed the hides may be after the action of the lime, a portion of the latter will remain in the skin, partially as caustic lime, which in time would injure the skin, and would render a part of the tannin inactive by combining with it, as well as physically opposing its entrance into the tissues; by the action of the acid this lime is neutralized, and where the acid forms soluble salts with the lime the latter may be dissolved out by water. In 1774 Dr. M'Bride proposed the use of sulphuric acid instead of the liquor of spent bark, a process which is still very extensively followed with success, producing a very excellent leather where its use is not abused. Sulphuric acid forms, however, a rather insoluble salt with lime. When used, therefore, in raising the hides, the greater part of the lime remains in them fixed, as it were, by its combination with the acid; this, although no great disadvantage to sole leather, which requires a certain amount of rigidity, a property increased by the presence of a salt of lime, is very detrimental to light skins intended to be curried for the manufacture of upper leather, in which pliability is the object aimed at. In such cases science evidently forbids the use of sulphuric acid, and would recommend the substitution of an acid which would form very soluble salts with lime, such as muriatic acid or common spirit of salt, which has accordingly been employed in France. In these countries a process is followed for removing the lime as completely as possible, called *graining*, which consists in exposing the limed skins for a period of eight or ten days to the action of a fluid called the *grainer* or *bate*, made of the dung of pigeons, hens, &c. During the operation the skins are frequently stirred about, and are scraped on the beam a couple of times, the combined effect of which is to remove the greater part of the lime, and to render the skins soft and pliable. This process is, however, subject to a great inconvenience: a kind of fermentation is sometimes liable to set in, which alters the tissue and injures its quality; and even where this does not occur, the leather, especially in summer, is liable to become discoloured. According to some persons the active constituent of the grainer is sal-ammoniac or muriate of ammonia, or, in other words, muriatic acid. It is, therefore, very probable that some substance could be employed instead of the barbarous process of graining, which would have the same effect. Several attempts have been made to attain this object, but unfortunately, as in the case of the patent of Mr. Warrington, in which he proposed carbonate of ammonia, the main question was always lost sight of—namely, the removal of the lime—for carbonate of ammonia does not assist in its removal, but merely neutralizes it, and forms an insoluble salt which remains in the leather.

We believe that hitherto attention has been too exclusively directed to the improvement of the tanning process, properly so called (especially with a view to the shortening of its duration) to the neglect of the preliminary ones of unhairing, and of removing the lime, when that agent is employed for the former purpose. Science has not as yet done as much for the tanner as we believe it might do; and we are further of opinion that its first efforts should be directed to the preliminary processes, a point to which we would advise our Irish tanners to direct their attention. And here we may add, that they have it in their power by skill, perseverance, and a little capital, to raise their trade to a position little, if at all, inferior to that enjoyed by the linen trade.

Attaching, as we do, such great importance to the operations just described, it is necessary to state, that although the lime process is the one generally followed for the removal of the hair and epidermis, there are several others which have been proposed and partially adopted for the same object. On the Continent, and in some places in Great Britain, the process of unhairing is effected by an incipient putrefaction, produced by laying the skins in a heap on each other in a sort of a pit covered over until the smell of ammonia is evolved; or by suspending them in a room heated a little above the ordinary temperature; or by placing them upon a bed of stable manure, and covering them with another for twenty-four hours, during which time they become heated, and are then frequently turned over and examined until they are fit to be unhaired. Another process is to place them for three or four days in water, to which a little larch bark is added; the water being renewed each day, and put on warm. M. Delbut, of Paris, effects the unhairing by exposing the skins to the action of vapour in a closed chamber in which the temperature is kept fixed at the limits of from 68° Fahr. to 79°. The great disadvantage of all these processes is the loss which is sometimes sustained by the putrefaction of part of the true leather tissue itself; the latter process, however, if conducted with care, yields very good results. The Kalmuck Tartars, who make excellent leather, remove the hair, in some cases, by spreading the skin upon a bench, and pouring boiling water over it, exactly as pigs are unhaired in Ireland. In America the hides are exposed in a kind of vault to the action of cold air loaded with moisture, by which the hair is gradually loosened, and in the course of from six to twelve days may be easily removed.

Besides these processes for loosening the epidermis and the roots of the hair, acid may be employed: for example, sulphuric acid not only raises the hides, when applied after the liming, but may be substituted for the latter process. The Kalmuck Tartars also employ sour milk; in Transylvania an acid liquor, made from rye-meal and water, is employed; and in Wallachia it is made with barley and water. The latter is very extensively employed in France, and is, perhaps, preferable to the liming system, in everything except in cost; in many tanneries in Paris, sour milk, which can be had cheap, is also largely employed. The acid liquor of spent bark, already alluded to in speaking of raising the hides, is sometimes employed for softening the hair, especially in the neighbourhood of Liege, in Belgium. Instead of acids or lime, we might employ a number of other substances with the same object. For example, M. Felix Boudet has proposed caustic soda, a process which occupies but one-third of the time that the ordinary one does; he has also proposed a mixture of sulphurets of calcium and sodium. Lime from the gas purifiers has also been successfully employed, and a Mr. Turnbull has proposed a solution of sugar, or treacle and salt; and finally, M. Vauquelin, of Paris, removes the hair and epidermis by means of a peculiar machine. The latter, when fully perfected, is the best process of all; for not only is the skin unaltered by contact with disorganizing substances, and no foreign material is added which would prevent the combination of the tannin, but the hair is obtained uninjured, which is of great importance for many purposes.

After the operations of steeping, unhairing, and raising—the objects of which are to remove all animal matter in solution in the pores of the skin, the separation of the hair and epidermis, and the swelling of the pores—the hides are ready for being impregnated with the tanning matter. This object was at one time effected by placing them in pits with a layer of bark slightly moistened between each skin, and leaving them in this way for about four months, until it was supposed the bark was spent or exhausted, when the operation was repeated. After this had been done several times, a strong infusion of bark was employed to complete the process. The leather made in this way is said to have been very good; but it is impossible to conceive a more absurd process, for as tannin can only enter the skin in the state of solution, it is quite clear that only a small portion of the tannin actually existing in the bark would have come into play, as no water was used except what the skin imbibed, or with which the bark was moistened. Another process, followed formerly, and which is not quite given up yet, was to arrange the hides in the manner just described, and then to fill up the pit with water. At the end of two or three months the hides were taken out, the spent bark removed, and the operation recommenced; and so on until the skins were considered to be fully tanned, which usually occupied a period of two years, and even in some cases, two years and a half. Instead of water, infusions of bark were substituted, as is usual in Ireland; it was by this process, no doubt, that several of the really fine specimens of sole leather in the Exhibition were prepared. But even this method has become antiquated; and tanners are now beginning to employ only an infusion of the bark, which they prepare in different ways. Some, for example, place the bark in a pit partially filled with water or spent liquor, from which the greater part of the tannin has been separated in the process of tanning, and pass steam into it. Others use a series of pits in which the bark is placed, and exhausted by making the water charged with the tannin of the bark of the first pit pass successively through the others, and continuing this operation with fresh water until the whole of the tannin is dissolved out. Others place the bark or other tanning material with water in a large vessel, which can be covered perfectly tight with a cover, through which passes a tube from 20 to 30 feet long, which is kept full of water, and which thus exerts a considerable pressure upon the bark. The idea of using an infusion of the tanning material instead of the old process originated in the commencement of the present century with M. Seguin; and in consequence of the greater rapidity with which leather can be tanned in this way, has been largely adopted and considerably improved, both in England and on the Continent. Our Irish tanners have been slow to adopt the quick processes, under the belief that the leather so made is inferior to that produced by the old method. This, to some extent, is true, but it need not necessarily be so; indeed, we believe, that with the proper skill, and some chemical knowledge, as good leather may be made by the quick tanning as by the old. But, without attempting to decide this question, it is certain that the Irish tanning trade received a considerable blow by the introduction of the new processes in England, especially after the removal of the duty upon leather, which, like the present duty on paper, acted most disastrously upon any attempts at improvements. Irish tanners not having adopted them were, of course, unable to compete, and were driven from the market. This is not the only case where an adherence to old methods, and, we will add, an honest prejudice in favour of a good article, has been destructive to our manufactures; for many of the so-called improvements of English manufacturers consist in a better method of adulterating, fostered by the popular rage for cheapness, irrespective of quality. There is a wide difference, however, between learning how to adulterate, and endeavouring, by the application of science, to improve processes, which would enable us to economize time and cost; and in this point of view there is a wide field open to the Irish tanner. How few of our leather manufacturers use any means for ascertaining the strength of their infusions of bark? or who have any methods of knowing whether they have extracted the whole of the tannin from their bark, or how much a parcel of bark which they are about to purchase contains? and until they can do so it is hopeless to expect that the manufacture of leather will be anything but a precarious business, in which some few persons with skill, although of a rule of thumb kind, may make fortunes, whilst the mass will be unsuccessful.

The rapid and effectual extraction of the tannin from the bark or other material is of the greatest importance; a decoction of bark in water gradually decomposes, and the tannin becomes converted into gallic acid, which is of no use in making leather. It must, therefore, be advantageous to exclude the air during the process of making the infusion of bark, and to some extent during the operation of tanning. This it would not be difficult to do, especially in respect to the first point, and we would accordingly recommend to the notice of tanners the apparatus invented by M. Boura, for the extraction of colouring matters from dye-woods, and which was exhibited in the Machinery Court by Manlove, Alliott, and Co., of Nottingham.

Where effusions are employed in tanning—that is, we may say, everywhere—a number of liquors of different strengths are made use of, which are classified into two divisions, termed *handlers*, and *layers* or *bloomers*; the former being the weaker and the latter the stronger. The skins are first introduced into the weakest handler, which usually consists of an infusion which has been nearly exhausted of its tannin in some previous state, where they are handled, that is, taken out once or twice a day, and laid in a heap; thence they are introduced in succession through the other handlers, and whilst in the strongest are only handled every second day; after which they are placed in the bloomers or strong solutions, where they are only handled every eight or ten days, hence the name layers. Some tanners place a little ground fresh bark between the hides in the bloomers, which is considered to give better leather and a richer bloom.

As soon as the leather is sufficiently tanned it is removed from the blooming pits, slightly washed in cold water so as not to remove the bloom, allowed to drain, and hung up to dry in lofts, which are usually artificially warmed in winter. Before it has become thoroughly dried it is hammered upon a block, an operation which is now effected in large tanneries by a machine; of which several have been invented, the best known being that of Berendorff, patented in 1842, and of Messrs. Jean and Scellos in 1852. When the operation of beating is finished, the hides are taken back to the lofts to be thoroughly dried. Skins intended to make upper leather are not beaten, but when dried are subjected to a set of operations termed currying.

When leather is taken out of the strong tanning solutions it is found to be covered with a light fawn-coloured deposit termed the bloom. This substance, which is looked upon as an important indication of superior tanning, although in reality of no utility whatever in making leather, is believed to be a peculiar acid termed ellagic acid, derived from the decomposition of tannin. To produce this bloom of a proper kind, the tannin must be the same as that which is contained in oak bark, and can only be obtained with strong solutions and after considerable time; hence the value attached to the bloom in commerce as indicative of good bark and a slow process of tanning. Catechu produces scarcely any bloom, and what it does is different in composition from the bloom of bark, but divi-divi gives the ordinary bloom in considerable quantities. All tanning materials contain a certain amount of colouring matter, which communicates a degree of colour to the leather; but some are very rich in it, and absolutely dye it. Purchasers consider that good leather ought to be of a light uniform fawn colour, which can only be obtained by the use of good bark and carefully limed skins. Catechu, divi, and most of the new tanning materials contain far more colouring matter than oak bark, and the latter, especially when its infusion is exposed to the air, develops so deep a colour that the leather made with it is sometimes almost unsaleable. If such infusion be kept from exposure to the air during the process, this result is avoided. But the development of the colour is not entirely dependent on the nature of the tanning material; for even the infusion of the best oak bark will become reddish-brown by contact with alkaline solutions, such as lime. Hence, independent of the fact that lime left in a skin will prevent its perfect tannage, it will also produce a dark-coloured leather.

*Curried Leather.*—The leather intended for the uppers of boots and shoes, and for saddlers' use, and indeed for most purposes, must have a smooth surface, a considerable degree of softness and flexibility, and a certain lustre, and be as impermeable to water as possible. These qualities are given to it by three series of operations: the first of these consists in moistening the tanned skin with water, shaving off the inequalities, and thinning such portions as are unnecessarily thick, and then rubbing the grain side with pumice-stone, to remove the superficial bloom. The second series consists in communicating flexibility to the leather, by rubbing both sides repeatedly with a piece of hard wood having its lower side indented with a number of transverse grooves, then scraping it with a broad knife, in order to equalize the thickness, and the third in dubbing it, as curriers say, with a mixture of tallow and oil, or other fatty substance. Sometimes the flesh side is blackened, as for shoe-leather, and at other times the grain side.

Although the operations which we have just stated represent the general nature of the process of currying, yet there are very many variations in detail, according to the kind of leather operated upon, and the uses to which it is intended to be put. These details our space does not permit us to notice further; we may, however, remark that upon the details, as well as upon the previous process of tanning, depends, in a great measure, the quality of the leather. The same skin which, in one of our tanneries, yields an upper leather which becomes in a few weeks hard and unwearable for tender feet, is capable of producing the softest and most flexible French leather. Although the strong upper-leather manufacture in these countries cannot be excelled for durability and adaptation to our damp climate, and we might extend the observation to the harness leather, which is, perhaps, the best in the world, we are a great way behind the French in the production of a light, flexible, soft leather for summer use. And yet there seems no reason why our tanners should not produce an equally good article as their neighbours, if the necessary exertions were made.

*Russia Leather.*—The Russians prepare a kind of leather remarkable for its peculiar smell, and which is much used in these countries for book-binding, covering writing-desks, &c. All kinds of skins are used, even horse-hides; that chiefly used in these countries is made from goat-skins. The unhairing process is usually effected by alkaline lye made with wood ashes. The tanning material employed is the bark of two or three species of willow, and even birch bark is also occasionally used. When tanned, the skins are dyed usually red, but very often of a brown and black, and are then rubbed with a peculiar empyreumatic oil, obtained by the destructive distillation of the outer rind of the birch, especially of the black birch. It is to this oil that the peculiar smell is owing. The finest Russia leather, especially that called *mastreky*, so much sought after for the finish, is made at Kostromagorod and Iaroslaw. For some years an excellent imitation of the Russia leather is made in France, the birch oil being also prepared there. A peculiar leather is prepared from very fine kid-skins in Denmark and in Norway, by tanning with the bark of a species of willow—the *Salix viminalis*. This leather has a peculiar smell, and is chiefly used for the manufacture of gloves. It is probable that this leather might be prepared in Ireland, as the *salix* would grow very luxuriantly with us.

*Morocco and Cordovan Leather.*—Originally these two kinds of leather were identical, and even now are not essentially different. True Morocco leather is always made from goat-skins, and imitation Morocco from sheepskins; while horse-skins may even be used for the manufacture of Cordovan. All the preliminary operations of unhairing, &c., are exactly the same as with other kinds of leather which we have described already. Morocco leather is tanned either with gall nuts or with sumach, the former, indeed, being only used in the Levant, where it is abundant; Cordovan is also tanned with the same materials, but oak bark is often used instead; it is almost invariably dyed black, but it may be made of any other colour; its surface is now also usually smooth, whilst Morocco leather has always a peculiar grain, produced by the action of a grooved roller, and is dyed of some fancy colours. The process of dying leather is, in principle, exactly the same as that of silk, cotton, &c., and need not be further described. The only part of the process of making Morocco leather which deserves special mention is the mode of applying the tanning material. Instead of laying the skins over one another in a pit with the tanning infusion, each skin is sewed up into the form of a bag, and nearly filled with a very strong decoction of sumach; a number of these are then thrown into a wide, shallow vessel filled with a weak infusion of sumach, and moved about, from time to time, for about three or four hours. Cordovan, as we have already mentioned, is derived from the city of Cordova, where it was largely manufactured by the Moors; and Morocco leather, as its name imports, is derived from the country of that name, where large quantities are even still made, especially in the states of Fez and Tetuan. The knowledge of the process of making Morocco leather was only introduced into Middle and Northern Europe about 120 years ago: France being indebted to the Count de Maurepas, the then Minister of Marine; and England to the exertions of the Society of Arts, who employed an Armenian, of the name of Philippo, to visit the Levant, and learn the process. A good deal of this kind of leather is still made in Turkey and in Asia Minor, but it is not fitted for general consumption in Europe.

*Enamelled and Varnished Leather.*—This article, which has only come into general use within the last twenty years, is now made in very large and increasing quantities. It is chiefly used for the manufacture of ladies' shoes and gentlemen's dress boots, belts, superior coach harness, &c. The ordinary black kinds are made with a varnish of boiled linseed oil, thickened, so as to form a paste with lampblack, to which is added some Prussian blue to give depth and lustre to the colour. This varnish is laid on with a brush, and the skin then heated in a drying chamber to the temperature of about 150° to 160° Fahr., and the operation repeated several times, sometimes as many as seven, according to the nature of the leather and the object for which it is intended. When the varnish is thoroughly dry it has sufficient brilliancy and great power of resisting strains, or bending without cracking and peeling off. The superior kinds, especially those employed under the name of "Patent Leather" for shoes and boots, and which are made of such superior quality in France, are prepared in a somewhat different way. The skin receives, as in the other case, a number of coatings, generally three, of a linseed oil varnish, made by boiling linseed oil with litharge and then mixing it with some ochre or chalk. When these coatings have dried, the proper varnish is applied in from three to five coatings, according to circumstances. This varnish is usually formed of equal parts of the oil varnish and oil of turpentine, mixed with about half as much of copal oil varnish, coloured with ivory black and Prussian blue for black leather, with lakes for red, with Prussian or ultramarine blue for blue, and so on. Even the effects of the Chinese bronze, gold, and other lacquering, may be perfectly imitated in the same way as we have already indicated in speaking of varnishes. The chief points to be attended to in the manufacture of varnished leather are the selection of very carefully tanned and curried skins; and especially that the oil or "stuff" used in the latter process be good and be equally applied, as otherwise the varnished skin will very soon stain and become covered with greasy spots.

*Tawed or Alum Leather.*—Tannic acid is not the only substance by which animal skins can be converted into a kind of leather, for a mixture of alum and common salt will also have that effect. The leather thus obtained differs in colour from ordinary leather, being white; it is also less durable and not so strong. The chief use of the leather made with alum, which is called "tawed leather," is for gloves, and the skins usually employed are kid and lamb-skins. The preliminary processes in the manufacture of glove leather, also, do not materially differ from those already described for leather generally, except in the case of lamb-skins; after the removal of the hair by lime, the skins are subjected to a fermenting mixture of bran and water for the purpose of removing the lime by means of the acetic acid formed in the bran water, and corresponding to the "bate" used in the preparation of superior calf-skins. The short wool of lambs, having very high felting properties, is well adapted for making the bodies of felt hats, and is accordingly much used for that purpose. But as lime would injure the wool of lamb-skins, they cannot be "unhaired" in the usual way with that substance; they are, therefore, suspended in a cellar or other room for about eight or nine days, and access of air shut off as perfectly as possible. By this means an incipient putrefaction is induced, which first sets in at the roots of the wool, which may then be easily removed; the skins are then limed and treated as in the case of kid-skins. Common white leather, such as that used for smiths' aprons and for the coarser kinds of gloves, is made with a simple solution of alum and common salt; but the finer kinds of kid glove leather are made with a mixture of alum, salt, flour, and yolk of eggs. The beautiful softness of the fine French glove leather is attributed to the use of such an emulsion. About 6 lbs. of alum, 6 lbs. of salt, and the yolks of eighty to a hundred eggs, may be considered the approximate quantity of ingredients required to taw a hundred kid-skins. Unlike the ordinary process of tanning, the impregnation of a skin with alum is effected in a few minutes, either by working the skins about with the hands in a tub containing the mixture, or by introducing them into a drum or barrel with the emulsion and turning it rapidly round. Tawed skins are not subjected to any subsequent process except drying, and then drawing them repeatedly over the edge of a semicircular plate of iron, so as to soften and smoothen them.

*Hungary, and Chamois, or Oil Leather.*—A peculiar kind of leather is made, called Hungary leather, intended as a substitute for common tanned leather, which must be mentioned here, as it forms the link between tawed leather and oil leather. It is obtained by preparing skins with alum and salt, and then impregnating them with melted tallow or other fat, and exposing them to a high temperature in a closed room or stove, and then drying them in the air. Chamois or oil leather, on the other hand, is not tawed or treated with any other chemical reagent. The process of manufacture consists in smearing the skin, made perfectly dry by beating it in a fulling mill exactly similar to that used in fulling cloth, with cod or other cheap fish oil, and then again exposing it to the action of the mill. The operation of smearing with oil and beating in the mill is repeated a great number of times. After each beating, which lasts from two to four hours, the skins are taken out of the mill and exposed to the action of the air for a short time. In many mills, instead of smearing the skins with the hand, the oil is poured upon the skins, in small quantities at a time, while in the mill. The action of the fulling process compresses the pores of the skins, and it therefore becomes necessary to subject them to a kind of fermentation, which expands them and at the same time causes a more perfect combination with the oil. This is effected by hanging the skins in a room which may be heated by a stove, as in the case of Hungary leather, if required. The oil is always applied to the grain side, and in order to get a highly absorbent and soft surface, the grain side is scraped or rubbed off with pumice-stone before being smeared; and after the fermentation the same surface is again usually scraped. The oiled skins are now subjected to a scouring process, which consists in stirring them about and then allowing them to steep for an hour in a weak ley of potash, which converts all excess of oil into a soap. The subsequent operations, consisting of wringing, drying, and stretching, need not be further described, as they differ little from the similar operations employed in the other branches of the leather manufacture.

The name chamois is derived from the fact, that it was only the skin of the chamois goat which was first used in the manufacture of the kind of leather just described; but sheep-skins, and other skins, more especially deer-skins, are now chiefly employed; and in these countries exclusively so. A few chamois skins are still converted into oil leather in the Tyrol, and used to make very superior gentlemen's gloves, which form the basis of a trade carried on by the Tyrolese. The superior kinds of oil leather are employed for the manufacture of gloves, hunting breeches, braces, soldiers' belts, &c.; and the inferior kinds under the name of wash leather, for cleaning plate, &c. This kind of chamois or shamoy leather is chiefly made from the inner side of sheep pelts, split by a machine, the other portion being tanned with sumach to make skiver, which is employed for hat leathers, &c. Formerly the use of chamois leather breeches was very general among all the cavalry of Europe, especially of England, Prussia, and Austria; but having been found unhealthy, it has been given up; owing to this, the manufacture of it in England, which was the chief seat of the trade, has greatly diminished. At present a peculiar kind of it is made, by first slightly tanning the skins with willow bark, and then impregnating them with oil in the fulling mill.

*Dyed Sheep-skin Rugs, &c.*—A considerable number of sheep-skins, of the coarse-woolled sheep, especially those of Leicestershire, &c., are tanned without removing the wool, which is then dyed of some bright colours. Angora goat-skins are also prepared in the same way, as well as a large number of lamb-skins. The former are chiefly used for door and carriage mats; and the lamb skins for lining morning gowns, slippers, &c. The process of tanning, which is always done with sumach, differs from that pursued with other skins in this, that the tanning solution is only applied to one side of the skin. Instead of tanning them with sumach, they are frequently tanned with salt and alum. The process of dyeing the wool, not differing from that usually followed with other woollen fabrics, does not demand any further notice here.

The manufacture of leather in all its various branches was represented in the Exhibition by only seventeen exhibiters; of whom six were Irish, two English, six French, two Belgian, and one German. The different kinds of leather were represented in the following proportion:—Rough heavy tanned hides were contributed by six exhibiters, four from the city of Dublin, and two French; light welting bridle and harness hides by four, of whom two were Irish, and two French; curried leather by eight, of whom four were French, three Irish, and one Belgian; Cordovan by one Irish exhibiter; Morocco leather by two, one Irish and one English; enamelled and varnished leather by six exhibiters, of whom two were Irish, two French, one German, and one Belgian; tawed leather by one Belgian exhibiter; and dyed lamb and Angora skins by two English exhibiters.

This was certainly no adequate representation of one of the greatest trades in the world, and least of all was it of the Irish leather, which was altogether left to a few of the tanners of Dublin. It does not speak well for the enterprise of Irish manufacturers that there were as many French exhibiters of leather as there were Irish. It might appear invidious in describing the contents of an Exhibition upon which no Juries sat to decide upon the relative merits of the exhibitors, to specially notice the contributions of any one manufacturer in particular; yet we cannot avoid giving our opinion of some of the articles shown. Among the tanned hides, all of which were of the most superior quality, those exhibited by S. Ord and J. O'Neill were remarkable for the density of the leather, the property of being bent and even doubled up without the slightest appearance of a crack, lightness of colour, and depth and richness of bloom. The curried leather adapted for harness purposes by W. R. Box and Co., was exceedingly well tanned and possessed great flexibility and strength; the enamelled leather of the same manufacturer was also very good. Hayes, Brothers', Cordovan and grained calf were well tanned and curried, and in many respects were superior to the usual articles of that class manufactured here. Among the French exhibitors, the curried calf-skins of M. Cornequel, of Vannes, and of M. Guillot, of Paris, fully supported the character of French leather, by its extraordinary pliability, softness, and closeness, as well as fineness of grain. A. Byrne and Son's case of fancy dyed Morocco leather was well finished; the colours were pure, the dye deep and uniform, and the skins flexible and close-grained. Among the exhibitors of varnished leather, the first place undoubtedly belonged to M. L. Deadde, of Paris, not alone for the excellence of the specimens, but for the extent of the collection which he contributed. For pliability of the leather, perfect adhesion of the varnish, the absence of all tendency to scale or crack, perfect polish and lustre, and beauty of colouring, we have never seen anything to excel them. This was particularly the case with the green, bronze, silver, and gold grounds.

The manufacture of leather is one eminently adapted to this country; indeed we do not know if it be not of all the great manufactures of Europe the one best adapted to the circumstances of Ireland. We have thousands of acres of uncultivated land upon which oak copses might be grown, which would provide bark enough for an immense trade; the supply of hides and skins and foreign tanning materials is as open to us as to any other country in Europe; and lastly, no fuel is required which is not provided by the waste of the manufacture, that element of all others which has given to England her great superiority. We may also add that it is not a new manufacture, which presents a number of difficulties to be overcome, but one already existing in the country, and pretty well understood. Why it should, therefore, have been lately rather declining than advancing, seems strange; and can only be accounted for by the fact that our tanners do not endeavour to keep up with the improved condition of the trade elsewhere, being in many cases tanners by accident, and usually gentlemen by profession, and knowing just that the skins of animals and an infusion of bark make leather, but considering the process by which it is made to be the peculiar domain of the workmen. There are some honourable exceptions, no doubt, but they are not sufficiently numerous to give a character to the Irish trade. Much blame cannot, however, be attached to them, because hitherto there were no available means in this country of acquiring any solid information upon the application of science to manufactures, or even upon the practical improvements effected elsewhere.

With the increasing facilities which have now arisen in this department, and with the rapid development which is making in almost every branch of our industry, it is to be hoped that this highly important and, if well understood, profitable branch of trade will share extensively in that development; and that in a few years, from being an importing country, we shall become one of the chief leather exporting countries in Europe.

The official Returns of the Board of Trade do not supply any information as to the state of the Irish branch of this department of business; and the extent of the business transacted in hides and skins could, therefore, only be obtained from the several houses in the trade. It appears, however, that the exports from the United Kingdom, taken as a whole, are steadily on the increase, as may be seen by the following return:—

VALUE OF LEATHER AND LEATHER WARES EXPORTED FROM THE UNITED KINGDOM IN THE UNDER-MENTIONED YEARS.

| | | | | | |
|---|---|---|---|---|---|
| 1840, | £417,074 | 1845, | £460,671 | 1850, | £608,865 |
| 1841, | 432,775 | 1846, | 432,925 | 1851, | 598,159 |
| 1842, | 400,927 | 1847, | 465,527 | 1852, | 844,759 |
| 1843, | 462,998 | 1848, | 372,256 | 1853, | 1,579,809 |
| 1844, | 465,942 | 1849, | 501,298 | | |

## FURS.

The skins of animals are chiefly employed for two purposes,—either as articles of clothing in their natural condition after removal from the animal, or only after a very short preparation; that is, as furs, and as tanned leather. Nearly all kinds of animal skins answer for the latter purpose, but it is only those thickly covered with a short and fine hair which are suited for furs. The fur-bearing animals are almost all natives of cold climates, the finest and most prized furs being obtained from the coldest regions, such as Siberia and the polar regions of North America. Independent of this circumstance, the quality of a fur depends a good deal upon the age of the animal, the season of the year at which it is killed, and even upon the particular locality in which it has lived. Thus, for instance, the fur is finer and closer at the approach of winter than in summer; and more wiry and coarse in a damp locality than in a dry one.

Our chief supply of furs comes from North America and Russia. The greater part of the trade with the former is in the hands of the Hudson's Bay Company, which has numerous stations throughout the regions extending from Labrador to the Russian American possessions. The Russian furs are nearly all bought at the great fairs in that country, especially that of Nishnei-Novgorod; they are purchased there partly for the English market, but chiefly by Continental merchants, who re-sell them at the Leipsic fair, whence they are distributed over Europe. Many furs are of great value, such as the Russian sable, which is usually sold for from £2 to £3, and very fine ones even fetch £10. Many cheap and serviceable furs are also obtained from indigenous animals, such as the otter, the rabbit, &c. This class of skins is usually dyed and the coarser hairs removed, so as to produce imitations of the more expensive furs.

The only preparation which furs receive is to impregnate the skin with some fatty substance, to make it into a kind of oil or chamois leather. This is done by rubbing the flesh side with salt butter, and trampling the skin in a tub, and turning them over from time to time during four or five hours. The adhering particles of flesh are then scraped off, and the unequal thickness of the skin planed away. The grease adhering to the fur, or in excess in the skin, is removed by trampling the skins in boxes with the sawdust of hard woods (free from turpentine or other resins), and repeating this operation several times until the skin has become dry and soft, and the fur glossy and smooth.

Furs are not so generally used in this country as in Germany and many other parts of the Continent, but especially in Russia. Those chiefly used here are the Russian sable, *Mustela zibellina;* the ermine, *Mustela erminea*, both from north-eastern Europe and Siberia; the Hudson's Bay sable, *Mustela Canadensis;* the musquash or musk rat, *Ziber zebethicus* (not the musk animal), from North America; the squirrel, *Sciurus vulgaris*, chiefly from Russia; the mink, *Mustela vison*, North America; the stone marten, or French sable, *Mustela saxorum*, and the baum (tree) or pine marten, *Mustela abietum*, both from central and north Europe; the chinchilla, *Chinchilla lanigera*, from Buenos Ayres, and Arica in Chili; the common seal, chiefly from the coasts of Newfoundland, Labrador, Greenland, and Norway; and several varieties of the common rabbit, *Lepus cuniculus*, obtained from England, Poland, and North America. A much greater number of the squirrel and musquash are employed than of any other kind.

The dyeing and preparation of cheap furs, in imitation of the more expensive ones, is much better understood on the Continent than here; and some excellent cheap specimens of rabbit-skins thus prepared were exhibited in the Belgian department, and will be furthur alluded to in another place.

There were three Dublin exhibiters of furs, independent of those of dyed sheep-skins, lamb-skins, and Angora goats, whose collections were extensive, varied, and well prepared.—W. K. S.

## SADDLERY, HARNESS, ETC.

Under this title is included a great variety of articles, such as portmanteaus and travelling cases of various kinds. These branches of business present certain characteristic features which operate against that centralization that prevails in other departments of industry. Saddlery has, no doubt, of late, become an article of general merchandize much more than in times past, when the manufacturer was almost invariably the vendor. In this way, Walsall, and some other towns, supply the trade of the United Kingdom with a portion of the saddlery kept by the hardware merchants; but still in every town of note throughout the country, the trade is to a greater or less extent carried on, as the business of repairing is of considerable importance, and in practice it is combined with the manufacture. The productions of the leading provincial towns are kept almost on a par with those of the metropolis, from the manufactured article constantly falling into the hands of distant makers for repair; and we may, in consequence, expect to find a uniformity of excellence in this branch of trade, which does not prevail in many others.

In the Exhibition there were many good examples of saddlery, both native and imported; and while the higher priced articles bore testimony to the progress of improvement, so far as regards elegance of workmanship, the common cart and dray harness was not less remarkable for the great change which has taken place in it within the past few years in this country. At no distant period the harness of the rural districts was as rude as could well be conceived. The use of the improved Scotch cart and plough harness has, however, now become general; a good illustration of which was to be found in that contributed by J. Pollock and L. Cowan of Glasgow. But these articles are now successfully imitated in almost the whole of our provincial towns. The manufacturers of this city contributed some highly creditable work; and, as a provincial effort, the harness exhibited by B. Watson of Mullingar was entitled to high commendation.

The collection in this department of Messrs. W. R. Box and Co., of this city, was worthy of the high reputation which their house has long enjoyed at the head of the wholesale trade of Ireland. The manufacture of saddlery of all kinds is carried on to a considerable extent in their premises in Abbey-street, and in a variety of articles they supply the city and country trade.

When referring to the made-up saddlery, which is extensively produced in Walsall, we should not omit to notice the very complete collection of specimens and models exhibited by Messrs. C. Greatrex and Son of that town. Their case, in fact, represented the trade of Walsall generally, including saddlers' and coachmakers' ironmongery; and everything was good of its kind, whether as regarded design or execution. As a specimen of workmanship a small horse-collar, only five-eighths of an inch high, was a gem in its way; and, as elegant articles, their rounded leather ladies bridles' were deserving of commendation.

Another remarkable specimen of workmanship in this department was the racing saddle exhibited by Mr. W. D. Jones, which, though of the full size, was under 2 lbs. weight. The ornamental workmanship was excellent, though the remarkable feature about the article was its extreme lightness.

The harness exhibited was generally of good quality, and not unfrequently presented choice specimens of beautiful workmanship; but, with one or two exceptions, there was little of novelty. In that of Mr. M'Mullen a modification was introduced by which the horse can be disengaged in a moment in case of accident,—an object of great importance, as may be seen almost daily in our streets, where the falling of the horse usually renders it necessary to cut some portions of the harness, as from the strain upon the buckles they cannot be undone. The same object is gained by a patent improvement exhibited by Mr. White of London, in which not only an efficient but an ornamental substitute for the buckle is introduced. The common hame tug, from its great thickness, necessitates the use of a large and unsightly buckle; and the buckle coming between the shaft of the vehicle and the shoulder is a constant source of annoyance, on this account alone, where one-horse carriages are used. In a greater or less degree the use of the buckle is in all cases objectionable; and hence, in the better class of harness, we are glad to see that it may be dispensed with by the simple and ingenious invention of Mr. White. This consists of a metallic framework attached to the end of the strap, into which the end of the other strap is to be introduced; and the latter being perforated with holes, a tongue or plug passes directly through, which instantly secures the junction, insuring the different portions working in a straight direction, and thereby guarding against cracking at the holes. This fixture may be made highly ornamental, and be surmounted by a crest or other device, as was the case on some of the specimens in the Exhibition.

In the portmanteaus and travelling cases of different kinds, there were many good specimens of the extent to which the convenience and comfort of travellers are now provided for in this age of locomotion. The goods in this department were in general deserving of high commendation for the ingenuity displayed in providing a large amount of accommodation in the smallest possible space. Many of the articles exhibited showed this in a high degree; and the workmanship was also good, in which respect they formed a marked contrast with that large class of goods only made up for sale. In short, although in this department we had only a few Dublin Exhibiters, it was amply illustrated—a circumstance which is highly creditable to those engaged in this branch of trade.—J. S.

---

1. ATKINSON, W., Montpelier-hill, Dublin, Manufacturer.—Enamelled chaise and welting hides; brace, harness, and japanned split hides, for coach purposes.

2. BARNARDO, JOHN M., Dame-street, Dublin, Manufacturer.—Muffs, boas, and cuffs of Russian sable, royal ermine, chinchilla, and greebe; ermine cardinals, muffs, and cuffs; South Sea seal-skin coats; and fur wrappers in various foreign skins.

3. BLACKWELL, SAMUEL, Oxford-street, London.—One patent dumb jockey, with elastic Indian-rubber springs, crupper, and girth, complete; one patent double girth; two girth straps, with elastic springs; one stable roller, with elastic spring; one servant's coat-belt, with elastic spring; two Indian-rubber web boots, to prevent horses cutting; one harness bridle complete, with apparatus to prevent horses running away.

4. BOX, W. R., & Co., Abbey-street, Dublin, Manufacturers.—Curried leather, hog-skins, bridle, stirrup, and harness leather; japanned leather; enamelled hides; japanned bag hides; patent splits; stout middlings; japanned cloth; hunting, exercise, and racing saddle-trees; side saddle-trees; harness and pad-trees; driving, hunting, and hand whips; specimens of heraldic devices in silver and brass, chased and embossed, for state and plain carriages and harness; coach handles; harness furniture, plain and embossed, in silver and brass; polished steel bits and stirrups; machinery belts and hose pipes.

5. BROWNING, W. & R., Stockwell-street, Glasgow, Manufacturers.—Set of cart harness.

6. BYRNE, A., & SON, New-row, South, Dublin, Manufacturers.—Fancy coloured Morocco leather skins for carriage, upholstery, and bookbinding purposes; Russia kid, or chamois; black Morocco, and grained calf and goat-skins for boots and shoes.

7. CLARK, CYRUS & JAMES, Street, near Glastonbury, Manufacturers.—Angora rugs; hearth-rug, centre of white English lamb-skin, with flowers, each colour being a separate piece sewn in, and border of crimson Angora goat-skin; sheep, lamb-skin, and Angora carriage, door, and window rugs; Angora and sheep-skin boas; caps of slink lamb-skin; harvest and housemaids' gloves, &c.; and Cork and lamb-skin socks.

8. CORCORAN, J., & Co., Westmoreland-street, Dublin, Manufacturers.—Foreign skins and manufactured furs.

9. COWAN, L., Barrhead, Manufacturer.—Scotch cart harness, as in use in the West of Scotland.

10. CUMMINS, J., James's-street, Dublin, Inventor and Manufacturer.—Side saddle; hunting saddles; silver-mounted drag harness, with newly invented breeching chains, and improved crupper; a chain invented as a substitute for top strap; brass-mounted harness, with a new crupper; plain cart harness.

11. DEED, J. S., Little Newport-street, Leicester-square, London, Manufacturer.—Specimens of Morocco leather for upholsterers, coachmakers, bookbinders, and bootmakers; dyed sheep and lamb-skin, for wool rugs or mats, in fast and brilliant colours.

12. FARRELL, R., College-green, and Fishamble-street, Dublin, Designer and Manufacturer.—Ladies' and gentlemen's portmanteaus, of new and various designs; coat-cases, hat-cases, capable of holding a suit of clothes, &c.; railway tourist's companion, of new design, with dressing-case, &c.; improved travelling bags; ladies' and gentlemen's travelling trunks of various designs; improved bonnet-boxes; ladies' dressing-cases, &c.

13. FLETCHER, W., Clare-street, Dublin, Manufacturer.—Phaeton harness, with silver chased and covered buckles; silver-mounted gig harness; hunting saddles.

14. GREATREX, CHARLES, & SON, Walsal, Manufacturers.—Saddlery, including bridles, stirrups, snaffles; steel, gig, and carriage bitts; spurs; harness mountings; horse, water, and spoke brushes; rosettes; harness collars in miniature, smallest weighing eight grains; whips; curb chains; crests, ornaments, and armorial bearings; silver-mounted gig and carriage lamps; coach lace; coach door handles and hinges; whip sockets; miniature elliptic carriage spring; Collinge's patent axle.

15. HART, P., Watling-street, Dublin, Manufacturer.—Irish and Buenos Ayres hides, tanned with oak bark and valonia.

16. HAYES, BROTHERS, Dublin, Manufacturers.—Tanned leather; tanned hides, native growth and manufacture; East India kip butt; native kip butt; native rounded calf-skin; native black grained calf-skin; hide, Spanish Cordovan; hide, native Cordovan; native horse butt.

17. HEACOCK, J., Dame-street, Dublin, Manufacturer.—Ermine; chinchilla grebe; monkey sable, and sable tail; muffs, boas, and cuffs; fur coats and aprons; and a variety of foreign skins.

18. HOWKSON, J., Charlemont-street, Dublin, Manufacturer.—Improved side saddle, with movable pannel, so as to fit any horse; improved hunting saddle, with movable pannel, and without nailing; gig saddle; improved chariot pads; horse clothing, ornamented.

19. HOLMES, ——, Cork.—Silver-plated mounted harness; saddles; Victoria side saddle, with leaping head.

20. HUDSON, S., Dawson-street, Dublin, Manufacturer.—Chariot and phaeton harness; jaunting-car and cab harness; improved side saddles; gentlemen's saddles.

21. JONES, WILLIAM D., High-street, Shrewsbury.—A light saddle of full length for racing, 26 oz. weight, embellished in relief by hand-labour only—design, roses, thistles, and shamrocks, interspersed with oak foliage and acorns.

22. KANE, G., Dame-street, Dublin, Designer and Manufacturer.—Portmanteaus and dressing-cases of various designs.

23. LARGE, T., Leinster-street, Dublin, Manufacturer.—Side saddle, covered with hog-skin; hunting, steeple-chase, and racing saddles; light phaeton pair-horse harness, silver-plated on German silver; car or gig harness, half covered and silver-plated.

24. LENNAN, W., Dawson-street, Dublin, Designer and Manufacturer.—A set of state pair-horse harness, made by order of Her Majesty; single and double harness, silver-mounted, and half covered and silver-mounted; improved safety buckles, and safety breeching; side saddles, with horizontal trees; hunting, steeple-chase, and racing saddles; children's chair saddles; riding bridles, bitts, &c.

25. LESTRANGE, C., & SON, James's-street, Dublin, Manufacturers.—Butt leather hides.

26. LYNCH, G., Lower Sackville-street, Dublin, Manufacturer.—Pormanteaus; square hat-case, containing dressing-case; enamel waterproof bags, &c.

27. M'MULLEN, B., Dawson-street, Dublin, Inventor and Manufacturer.—Saddles; child's chair saddle; bridles; chariot harness, car or gig harness, on a new construction, whereby the horse can be disengaged in a moment in case of accident; military appointments.

28. M'NAUGHT, G., Maxwell-street, Glasgow, Manufacturer.—Saddle-trees, several varieties; polished and black hames for Scotch cart, van, and stage; polished Scotch cart rigwoodie, with shaft rings, draught chains, &c.

29. MOLLOY, B., Kildare-street, Dublin, Manufacturer.—Harness, with newly invented hames, trace fasteners, and driving bitts, &c.

30. ORD, A., Cork-street, Dublin, Manufacturer.—Tanned Buenos Ayrean hides, and native hides of tanned leather.

31. PERRY, J., Grafton-street, Dublin, Manufacturer.—Threefold portable trunks, with dressing-case and writing-desk; improved trunks and travelling-cases; bonnet and hat-cases of various designs; leather bags with portmanteau bottoms, fitted with dressing-case; railway and overland portmanteaus, and other articles.

32. POLLOCK, J., Stockwell-street, Glasgow, Manufacturer.—Scotch cart harness for city and agricultural use.

33. SWAIN & ADENEY, Piccadilly, London, Manufacturers.—Prize racing whip, mounted in carved Irish bog oak; prize hunting whips, with sporting devices; ladies' and gentlemen's riding and driving whips; ladies' riding and driving whips, with parasols, fans, or sun shades attached; improved patent Arab or Chowrie riding whips, with horse-hair plumes for driving away insects; state carriage and postilion whips; gentlemen's driving whips, with horn and warning whistle in the handles; patent whip-socket, and Indian-rubber Oxonian driving-apron.

34. WATSON, B., Mullingar, County Westmeath, Manufacturer.—Side saddle, hunting, cut back, steeple-chase, and racing saddles.

35. WHITE, JAMES, Liverpool-street, London.—Set of silver-mounted pair-horse carriage harness, with White's patent safety tugs; set of gig Brougham harness, with patent safety tugs to the traces, backbands, and crupper; specimens of carriage and gig tugs finished with silver, brass, or covered mountings.

# CLASS XVII.

## PAPER, PRINTING, STATIONERY, ETC.

### I.—PAPER.

THE manufacture of paper, like that of leather, is one eminently adapted to the circumstances of Ireland, and one, therefore, which demands a large share of our attention. It has another claim, also, upon our space, as being one of the most important of the few large manufactures which we possess, ranking perhaps in this respect after flax. We shall, accordingly, give as complete a sketch of the nature, history, and present condition of the trade as the objects and extent of such a publication will permit.

In speaking of starch and sugar we drew attention to the relations of those substances to one another, and to a third, the woody matter which forms the skeleton of plants. It will be unnecessary, consequently, to refer to this subject here, further than to say that woody matter, as its name imports, constitutes the great mass of wood. The skeletons of plants composed of this substance are formed of cells and tubes, which are nothing more than a number of cells joined together, in which all the other constituents of plants exist. In the green parts of plants and in bulbous roots the material composing the cells is in much smaller proportion than the substances in solution in those cells. Many of our readers will, perhaps, be surprised when we tell them that the framework, in which everything else is held, of 100 lbs. weight of turnips, does not exceed more than 3 or 4 lbs. in weight! The framework of trees is, however, much more solid, and the woody matter of the stems far exceeds in quantity all the other constituents; hence the capability of the stems of vegetables to bear pressure and support weights, which fits the larger ones for building and other purposes.

If we reduce a piece of wood to a fine state of division—for example, to the condition of sawdust, and boil it for some time with water, and then with certain chemical substances, we shall be able to remove all the other constituents of the plants contained originally in the stem, and obtain the woody matter quite pure. This woody matter is composed of two distinct substances—one of them, called *cellulose*, forms the walls of the cells, which are then thickened, as it were, with an encrusting matter. In some plants, or rather in certain parts of plants, another peculiar substance is found, which sometimes, also, acts as a thickener of the cellular substances; this body, of which there are several modifications, is called *pectine*, and will be familiar to most of our readers as the chief constituent of currant and other fruit jellies. The woody matter, or *lignine*, is the basis of many manufactures. For example, all cotton, linen, and hempen fabrics, are simply woody matter in a greater or less degree of purity; and all the processes through which flax passes in its preparation from the flax straw have for their objects the elimination in a separate state of this substance. In such manufactures *form* is an element of quite as much importance as chemical constitution—the woody matter must be in the condition, in fact, of fibre. We have already remarked that the woody matter consists either of an agglomeration of cells such as we have in the pith of plants, as, for example, in the elder, or of a number of fibres which consist of tubes; the former is called the cellular tissue of plants, and the latter the vascular or vessel tissue. Any one who has ever seen a piece of elder pith will at once see that it could not yield a textile fabric, and that it is only lignine, in the condition of vascular tissue or fibre, which can be employed for such a purpose. There is another manufacture of which lignine is also the basis, namely, paper; but one in which form is of less importance than in the textile fabrics, because both the cellular and vascular tissue of plants may be employed in its production. If we reduce the lignine of plants to a fine state of division, and while still moist press a mass of it together into a thin sheet, it will form a kind of paper. If we could employ pure cellulose, freed from its encrusting matter, the material thus obtained would be non-adhesive and pliable; and in proportion as the cellulose which we employ is coated with this substance, the less adapted will it be to form paper. The cells of which the woody part of large trees is composed are thickly coated in this way, whilst the stalks of herbaceous plants are less so; hence timber or its sawdust is not so well adapted for making paper pulp as the fibres of the flax plant. Indeed the excess of the encrusting matter renders the fibres of a plant equally unfit for the manufacture of paper as for that of a textile fabric. The objections here made to the ordinary woody encrusting matter, as far as the manufacture of paper is concerned, are not equally applicable to pectine when it performs the same functions, as we shall have occasion to notice subsequently. Although paper differs essentially in many respects from a woven fabric, yet we require it to have, to a certain degree, two of the chief qualities of the latter; namely, strength and flexibility. Hence, although, as we have observed above, a paper-like pulp may be made of cellular tissue, it would have no strength, which could only be given to it by vascular tissue or fibre; and consequently the larger the proportion of the latter in a paper, the stronger and more flexible it will be, especially if the fibres be not too much broken up. An example of this is presented to us in the toughness of bank-note paper, but there is a still more remarkable one in the cloth called *tappa*, which is made by the inhabitants of the South Sea Islands from the liber or inner bark of a tree. This cloth is, in fact, nothing more than a species of paper formed by steeping the fibres in water until they undergo a kind of change similar to that to which flax is submitted, and then beating them with a wooden mallet until they adhere and spread out. Paper made in this way, and, indeed, all paper, bears somewhat the same relation to textile fabrics of cotton or wool as felt does to textile woollen fabrics. In all textile fabrics the great object to be attained is to give a certain direction to the fibres, somewhat similar to that which they have in the stems of the plants, an object which is effected by spinning; in paper, on the other hand, the fibres must be made to run in all directions, which is also the case with felt.

Previous to the invention of paper various substitutes appear to have been employed, such as the fine inner bark of several trees, which was beaten and then dried in the sun; plates of lead and tablets of wax were also employed, and even the leaves of trees, as is still the case in the East; as, for example, in Ceylon, where the dried leaves of the talipot palm, cut into convenient sizes, and joined together in the shape of a fan, form their books, of which there was an example in the Indian collection of the Royal Asiatic Society. The first attempt at making paper was the employment by the Egyptians of the pith of a reed which grows on the Nile, and which was formerly called the *papyrus*, from whence our word paper is derived. This plant, which looks like a bulrush, must have been used at a very early period for the manufacture of a kind of paper remarkable for its delicacy and for the simplicity of its manufacture. Paper made from the Egyptian papyrus continued to be employed until the fifth century, but after that date it appears to have gone out of general use, having been replaced by the true paper made from cotton. The precise date, however, at which cotton paper was first made, or the country where it was first invented, cannot be distinctly ascertained, for we find no mention of it, at least as far as we are aware, of an earlier date than the commencement of the twelfth century. Indeed, subsequent to the twelfth century the use of cotton paper became very general in Europe; but the chief supplies were still brought from the Levant, although it is certain that its manufacture was introduced into Europe in that century by the Crusaders, or by the Venetians. In the end of the fourteenth century the important discovery was made that paper could be manufactured from linen rags, the first mill for that purpose having been erected at Nuremberg, in the year 1390. This discovery completely changed the whole manufacture, because, for several centuries after, the supply of raw material of this kind was much greater than the demand; hence the more expensive material, cotton, was given up. In order to make white paper, it was necessary to employ white rags, as no means existed for rapidly and cheaply bleaching the coloured ones. Under such circumstances it need not be a matter of surprise that no attempt was made to find a substitute for linen, or cotton, which would be as cheap. In this way rags came to be considered as the only material from which paper could be advantageously made. The discovery of the bleaching powers of chlorine opened up a new field, and led to the hope that a great number of vegetable tissues might be substituted for rags, in case there would not be sufficient of the latter to supply the demand which the extraordinary extension in the use of paper has created. To give our readers some idea of how far this hope has been realized, we shall enumerate here the various substances from which paper is now made, or which have been proposed for that purpose:—

RAW MATERIALS OF PAPER.

Cotton and linen rags.
Scutching waste from flax.
Cotton waste.
Hemp and flax straw.
Inner bark of the white mulberry.
Plantain fibre.
Fibre of the leaves of the dwarf palm.
Straw of wheat, barley, oats, rye, maize, hay, &c.
Common reeds.

Potato pulp after extraction of the starch.
Pulp of beet after expression of juice, for the manufacture of sugar.
Moss and turf.
Wood shavings.
Curriers' shavings, obtained in the manufacture of leather.
Waste from Manilla hemp.

Besides these, a number of other vegetable substances have been proposed for the same purpose; such as the common nettle, the common rush, the thistle, the barks of the *Daphne mezereum*, the acacia, the elm, the lime, &c.; the tendrils of the hop, tanners' spent bark; and we might add a number of other substances, such as the common rag weed, the bagasse, trash or pressed sugar cane, and a great variety of Indian and other tropical fibres which have been lately introduced to the notice of the public. The substances contained in the first column are undoubtedly the best adapted for making paper, but as yet only the rags, scutching waste, and cotton waste, are generally employed; the flax and hemp straw, although apparently well adapted for the purpose, are not likely to be employed in consequence of their high price. Straw, on the other hand, has lately become a most important material for the manufacture of paper, and a very considerable trade is springing up in Dublin, the chief seat of the manufacture at present.

The first idea of making paper from straw originated with Seguin, who was granted a patent in France, in 1801, but he was unable to overcome the difficulties of the material. In 1820 another patent was granted to M. Hirigoyen, Jun., which appears to have been equally unsuccessful. In 1824 Chaptal and D'Arcet, two eminent French chemists, and M. Bronzac, obtained a patent for the manufacture of paper from straw, which was actually worked, and may, therefore, be considered as the first successful attempt to solve this problem. Since that period various attempts have been made in France, Germany, and England, to perfect the process of Chaptal and D'Arcet; but it is only within the last year or two that these attempts have been crowned with complete success—the honour of the successful perfection, as well as the first invention, belonging, we believe, to France. The sample in the Exhibition, as the first successful attempt to make straw paper capable of being used for printing, was, therefore, worthy of special attention, and pointed to a wide field of industrial enterprise in this country. It is but just to remark here that a number of excellent experiments was conducted in Cork several years before the patent of Chaptal and D'Arcet was taken out, for the purpose of testing the process of Seguin, the first inventor.

A great many efforts have recently been made on the Continent to bring several of the substances named in the second column into use, and with a considerable amount of success. Among them we may specially mention the pulp of beet-root, wood shavings, and peat. Wood shavings have also been tried in England, and according to the reports published the process is perfectly practicable, and the quality of the paper produced excellent. Of all the substances proposed, however, peat is that which is most interesting and important to us, in consequence of the great extent of our peat bogs. Although proposed as a material for the manufacture of paper many years ago, the only successful attempt which appears to have been made was within the past year in Piedmont and Saxony. In the former place a soft and much prized paper has been produced, composed of from 80 to 90 per cent. of turf, the remainder being formed by the pulp obtained from the inner bark of the white mulberry. Millboard was also produced containing 95 per cent. of turf. The results obtained in Saxony were similar, rags being substituted for the mulberry bark.

The other substances which we have mentioned can only be considered as curiosities, as they cannot be obtained in sufficient quantities, supposing them even to be well adapted for paper-making, if we except tanners' spent bark, which we have seen applied to the manufacture of pulp for papier mache, with the addition of some made from old ropes, &c. The chief difficulty which manufacturers have had to contend with in the manufacture of paper directly from vegetable substances has been the sort of semi-transparency which papers so made possessed. To avoid this a certain quantity of rags had to be added. It is, however, to be hoped that these difficulties will be entirely overcome—indeed in many cases they have already been so.

Having now discussed the raw materials, we shall turn our attention to the old processes employed in paper-making, and which are to some extent still followed in some places, commencing with that in use in China and Japan.

Independent of the special interest which attaches to Chinese and Indian paper in a historical point of view, and which would in any case induce us to notice the process adopted in these countries for its manufacture, we are specially called upon to do so in consequence of the numerous specimens contained in the Japanese, Chinese, and Indian collections in the Exhibition. These specimens were, properly speaking, not exhibited as paper, but rather as that material applied to various purposes—such as books, drawings, &c.; they, however, exhibit all the peculiarities of the Eastern paper so well that we can refer to them as illustrations.

*The Manufacture of Paper in China*, like the other manufactures of that singular country, dates from a very remote antiquity. Although we are acquainted with only a few varieties of Chinese paper, such as that used for covering tea-chests, printing Chinese books, and the kinds so largely used in Europe for making artificial flowers, and another for engraving under the name of India paper, the Chinese make nearly as many varieties as we do. The papers just alluded to are exceedingly thin, the printing paper especially, fifty square feet of which weigh scarcely three ounces. A great number of substances are also employed in paper-making, almost every province having its own peculiar material. In some districts the young shoots of the bamboo are employed; in others the liber or inner bark of a variety of mulberry; in others again, rice straw, hemp, cotton; and, finally, the cocoons of the silk-worm after the separation of the silk fibre. The beautiful paper known as rice paper is made from the cellular pith of the *Aralia papyrifera*, and is, therefore, more like the ancient paper of the papyrus than our modern paper from fibrous tissue. Although the bamboo does not yield the finest paper employed by the Chinese, the article made from that substance having always a yellowish tint, it is the material which is most largely employed; and as the process by which it is made does not essentially differ from that followed with other materials, we shall select it as our illustration of paper-making. The young shoots of the bamboo are first cut into convenient lengths, and then split into thin slices and laid in a pit built of bricks or of stonework with a quantity of slaked lime, the bamboo and the lime being arranged in alternate layers, the whole being pressed down by placing a quantity of stones on the top. Water is then admitted, and the whole allowed to rest for about fourteen days; at the end of which time the mass becomes soft, and the external green rind may be easily separated. The pieces are next removed from the pit and beaten with an iron mallet, which removes a quantity of rind, and leaves a fibrous mass like flax, which is hung in the sun to dry and bleach, after which it is again steeped with lime as before. When taken out of the lime it is made into heaps, and allowed to undergo a kind of spontaneous fermentation which decomposes the glutinous matter that unites the fibres together. To remove this material, the impure fibre, still impregnated with lime, is boiled for twenty-four hours in water which becomes syrupy from the dissolved matter, and is then run off; and the fibre washed in running water and kneaded into lumps; when it is again boiled with an alkaline solution, obtained by dissolving the ashes of rice straw in water. The object of these processes is, as in the case of the preparation by steeping of the corresponding fibre of flax, to dissolve out all the other constituents of the plant, especially a glutinous substance which would not only be unfit for the preparation of paper, but would tend to produce decomposition in the fibre. The pure fibre thus obtained is kept in a moist condition in cellars, ready for use until it is required, where it undergoes a slow fermentation which is induced by sprinkling the different layers of the mass with a decoction of beans.

To make paper from this mass it is subjected to a very rude process of trituration in stone mortars, until it is reduced to the condition of a uniform pulp. In some cases a quantity of an unctuous extract made from a plant called the *koteng*, is added to the bamboo pulp, for the purpose of making it stiffer, and communicating a certain degree of semi-transparency to the paper. When the pulp is finished, it is placed in a vessel or vat with the proper quantity of water; at this vat the workman stands, and by means of a square mould like a sieve, which he dips into the stuff, forms a sheet of paper. The moulds are formed of a number of fine slips of bamboo, previously boiled in oil to diminish the tendency to absorb water, or adhere to the sheet of paper, and placed parallel to one another like a grating. These slips are exceedingly thin, and placed close together, as many as forty in the space of an inch; they are kept together by cross threads of silk or of gut placed at intervals of about five-sixths of an inch asunder. When this mould is dipped into the water containing the pulp, and then carefully lifted out, the water streams out, and leaves a uniform sheet of pulp resting upon the bamboo grating. If we examine a sheet of Chinese paper, we may discover the impression of the bamboo on one side of the sheet in the form of a series of fine lines, like cording in certain varieties of silk, and also of the threads which run at right angles to each other, and resemble the ordinary water-marks on our paper.

This process of moulding each sheet of paper differs but little from that adopted in Europe, but here the analogy ceases, the other operations of the Chinese paper-maker being quite distinct. The pulp vat is placed near a kind of oven with a large flue, the walls of which have a slight inclination. The workman inverts the bamboo mould over this flat surface, presses it against it, and then removes it, leaving the sheet of paper adhering to the wall; it there rapidly dries, by the heat of the oven, or by that of the sun alone in summer; whilst drying, another workman rubs the sheet against the wall with a fine brush, in order to prevent it curling up, or drying unequally. The impression of the hairs of the brush resulting from this operation, although exceedingly fine, may be readily distinguished by examining a sheet of Chinese paper. Before the paper is thoroughly dried, it is removed from the stove, and when a sufficient number of sheets are obtained to form a pile, they are placed in a press, after which they are made up into parcels of 100 sheets each, and again pressed.

Paper made merely of vegetable tissue, as is well known, is very porous, and will absorb water very rapidly. Paper composed of woody matter, freed from all foreign substances, such as that from rags, possesses this property in a more remarkable degree than paper which contains a certain amount of pectine. Paper intended for writing is dipped into a solution of alum boiled with a little isinglass or fish glue, a process which is, in every respect, identical with the European one of sizing. By means of a size prepared with glue made from parings of skins, and therefore perfectly identical with our size, the Chinese make some pretty ornamented papers.

*Japanese method of making Paper.*—The Japanese make their paper chiefly from one substance, the bark of a kind of mulberry, which may be considered a true paper tree. The young saplings of the mulberry are subjected to the action of boiling water until the bark begins to separate from the wood, when they are taken out, and the bark removed and placed aside to dry; and in this condition it forms the material for paper-making. The first operation consists in steeping it in water, in order to soften it, after which the coarser and dark-coloured portions are separated. After being thus sorted, it is boiled in a ley made with the ashes of plants, until it is so softened and divided that it is reduced to the condition of an extremely light and fibrous pulp. It is next washed upon a kind of sieve, upon which a fine stream of water is allowed to fall, the mass being continually stirred about with the hand. By these operations the pulp is freed from all foreign matters, and is rendered exceedingly fine and soft; it is then beaten on a flat table with a mallet until it is reduced to the proper degree of tenuity to make paper. A quantity of this pulp is mixed up in a vat with water, and a quantity of a decoction of rice strained through cloth added, as also some made with roots of particular plants, and the whole agitated until the different substances are thoroughly mixed, when it is ready to be moulded into sheets of paper. This operation is performed exactly as in China, with a mould made with slips of bamboo, but the paper is not dried in the same way. In Japan each sheet as it is made is laid upon the previous one, with an exceedingly fine slip of wood between them, until a sufficient pile is formed, upon which is placed a board with weights on it, the weight being at first very light, to prevent the sheets from adhering. According as the water drains out the weight is augmented, the whole operation of pressing lasting about twenty-four hours. On the following day the weight is removed, and each sheet lifted up by means of the slips of wood to which the moist sheets adhere, and suspended by means of them, to be dried in the sun. When dry, the sheets are rubbed smooth and pressed, and are then considered to be finished.

The Japanese do not size their paper or subject it to any further preparation for printing or writing, the decoction of rice and of the other plants performing the functions of the alum and isinglass of the Chinese; in addition to which it communicates considerable whiteness and silkiness to the paper. The use of such a decoction of rice is also known in China, and in several other parts of the East. Japanese paper is an exceedingly strong material.

## PAPER-MAKING IN EUROPE.

Any person who visits a modern paper mill, and sees that most perfect, perhaps, of all automata, a paper machine at work, will be very much inclined to smile at the processes just described, and to form a very disparaging idea of the Oriental manufacture. Fifty years have not yet passed, however, since the first machine of this kind was invented.

A good deal of hand-made paper is still produced in Ireland and also in England; but instead of the mould being made of a number of wires laid parallel to one another (and hence called a *laid mould*, and the paper made with it *laid paper*), it is usually formed of woven wire-gauze, containing from forty-eight to sixty-four meshes in the square inch, hence called a *wove mould*, and the paper formed with it *wove paper*. The pulp is made in an engine invented in the last century by the Dutch, and hence called by the old paper-makers the *hollender*, and which we shall describe hereafter. Chlorine is also used, and, in fact, the process of making hand-paper practised at present only differs from that of the machine, or continuous paper, by the pulp being moulded instead of being run on a machine, all previous operations being, to a great extent, the same.

Rags may be regarded as the great basis of the paper manufacture; and besides the enormous supply produced in these countries, large quantities are annually imported from the Continent of Europe, but chiefly from Hamburgh, Bremen, and Petersburgh, in the North of Europe, and from Leghorn and Ancona, on the Mediterranean. In 1850 the quantity of rags, old ropes, &c., imported was 8124 tons, of which Bremen, Hamburgh, and Lubeck alone supplied 4449 tons, or more than one-half; Russia, 859 tons; and the rest of the North of Europe, 496 tons. The imports from Leghorn amounted to 1352 tons, and from other ports in the Mediterranean, 503 tons. Foreign rags are coarser and inferior in appearance to British rags, and were formerly less valued; but since the introduction of the process of boiling rags in a ley of soda, and bleaching them in chlorine, they are held in equal estimation, and in many cases are considered even superior to our own rags, more especially as they are chiefly linen. The rags from the North of Europe are darker and stronger than those from the Mediterranean, the latter being apparently bleached by the intense sunlight. It is worthy of remark, that rags are forbidden to be exported from France, Belgium, Holland, Spain, and Portugal.

The first operation to which the rags are submitted is a careful picking and sorting, which is altogether performed by women and girls, who divide them into six or seven qualities, all of which, however, may be classed into three divisions—white, gray, and coloured rags. The white rags are usually sorted into linen and cotton rags, for in some kinds of paper it is of great importance to regulate exactly the proportion of cotton rags which is employed; a fact which is easily accounted for by comparing the structure of cotton and linen fibres, as seen under a microscope—the former is composed of tubes, having very thin and delicate walls, which are easily flattened, whilst the fibres of hemp and flax are composed of thick cylindrical tubes, which do not yield to compression. During this operation of sorting, the seams are ripped up, the buttons carefully cut off, and the whole cut into small pieces with knives. The woollen rags are also carefully separated and set aside, for they could not be boiled with soda, which would dissolve them, nor bleached with chlorine, which has scarcely any action upon them. A small portion is, however, worked up in the manufacture of a dark gray thick filtering paper, employed by apothecaries for filtering tinctures, &c. A good deal is also employed for making flocks for room paper, and as a material for mattresses. Some are also employed as a manure, especially for hops; indeed, considerable quantities are imported, chiefly from Rostock and Bremen, for that purpose; and, we regret to say, to unravel and mix with fresh wool, under the name of shoddy, for the manufacture of those wonderfully fine West of England cloths, with which the public are duped by the extravagantly low prices at which clothing establishments offer them. The import of woollen rags for manure is about 1100 tons, at an average price of about £5 to £6 per ton—the coloured woollen rags of loose texture, fit for unravelling, fetch £10 to £13, and white of the same description, £15 to £18 per ton,—prices which show a good demand.

The picked rags are next placed in a dusting-engine, called "the devil," which consists of a cylinder about six feet long, and four feet in diameter, covered with wire gauze. The rags are introduced into the cylinder or drum, which is then made to revolve very rapidly, the rags being effectively tossed about in the inside by a number of spokes fixed to the axis. Thus freed from the dust, they are next washed in warm water, and then boiled with a solution of caustic soda at the rate of from 40 to 45 lbs. per ton of rags. There are two modes of effecting this object,—one is to place the rags in a sort of vat with a false bottom, pierced with holes, and covered with a loose cover; a tube rises from the false bottom to nearly the top of the vat, and a steam-pipe enters between the bottoms; a quantity of wet rags is placed upon the false bottom, and a sufficient supply of the ley admitted; steam is then turned on, which heats it, and the warm liquor ascends the tube in the centre, and is distributed over the surface of the rags; the cold ley descends through the holes in the false bottom. In this way a current is established which effectively washes the rags, after which the ley is withdrawn, and replaced by water, an operation which is performed a sufficient number of times to completely remove all traces of the soda. The other consists of a sort of rotatory drum partially immersed in the ley, which is placed in a steam-tight vessel, heated by high-pressure steam. The action of this vessel is very effective, and is, perhaps, the best contrivance invented for this purpose.

The rags are next introduced into the washing-engine, which consists of an oval trough, or rather of an oblong trough, rounded at the angles, and partially divided along its length into two compartments, in one of which revolves a drum, or rather a solid cylinder of wood, provided with forty cutting-blades, which are inserted into it. Immediately under the drum is placed a block of wood provided with twelve or fourteen cutters like those in the cylinder, the distance between the cutting surfaces of both being capable of being regulated at will. The cylinder is made to revolve at the rate of about 120 revolutions in a minute: this produces a sort of rotatory current in the water in which the rags are suspended, which carries them in a continuous stream between the cutting edges of the drum and block, which make about 60,000 cuts per minute; the effect being, however, less of a true cutting kind than a tearing operation which pulls the fibres asunder, and reduces them to a sort of pulpy mass technically called *half stuff*. In this condition the rags are bleached, which is done either by chlorine gas, or by the compound of that substance with lime known as bleaching powder. When done with the former, the half stuff is placed upon shelves or floors in a kind of chamber constructed of planks, into the top of which the gas is admitted. The bleaching with chloride of lime, of which 1 to 2 lbs. is enough for each cwt. of fine rags, is effected either in vats, where the half stuff is allowed to steep, which is the most effective method, or in the washing-engine, which brings every fibre of the rags in contact with the solution. When fully bleached, the pulp must be well washed to free it from all traces of lime and chlorine. Some manufacturers, aware of the deleterious action of any chlorine left in the pulp, go so far as to add small quantities of sulphite of soda, in order to neutralize any chlorine which may remain. We would recommend for the same purpose sulphite of alumina, which can be easily had, and any excess of which would, instead of being injurious, contribute to the formation of size subsequently.

The bleached half stuff is now ready to be made into stuff or pulp, which is effected in another engine called the *beater*, similar to the one described, except that it has usually sixty teeth on the cylinder, and twenty or twenty-four on the block, and makes about 150 revolutions per minute, which would give 170,000 to 180,000 as the number of cuts which it is capable of giving per minute. When the pulp is finished, it is run into the stuff chest, which is a large vat usually capable of holding about three engines' full of stuff, where the different kinds of pulp are mixed together, judged to be the best adapted for making any particular variety of paper. The stuff chest is usually made circular, and has a hog or churning agitator continually revolving in it to keep the pulp in suspension. The pulp so prepared is now ready to be made into paper, an operation either done by hand, or by machine.

The idea of a machine for making paper originated with a workman of the name of Robert, employed in the mill of M. Francois Didot, of Essonnes, who made the first trial at that place in 1799. The great promise of success which it held out induced the Directory to grant him a patent for fifteen years, and a sum of 8000 francs to assist him in perfecting his discovery. This patent he disposed of to M. Leger Didot, who, accompanied by his brother-in-law, Mr. Gamble, came over to England for the purpose of putting the discovery into practice, an object which could not be effected in France at that time, in consequence of the continual state of war in which the Continent was then plunged. In 1801 a patent was granted in the name of Mr. Gamble, and in 1803 a second for improvements on the former. In 1804 the principal share in these patents was sold to Messrs. Henry and Sealy Fourdrinier, at that time the principal paper-makers and stationers in Great Britain, who at once embarked a large capital in the attempt to perfect the machine. The first experiments were made at Dartford, in Kent, in the establishment of a Mr. Hall, who happened to have a young assistant of the name of Bryan Donkin, who applied himself with enthusiasm to the matter; and, aided by the capital of the Fourdriniers, he produced a true self-acting machine in 1803, which was set up at Frogmore, in Hertfordshire. From this time until 1807 a great many improvements were effected; the patentees, in fact, spared no expense to make it perfect, and had consequently derived no advantage from their outlay. On this account the Messrs. Fourdrinier endeavoured to get an extension of their patent for an additional fourteen years, which would have been granted, and had, indeed, gained the sanction of the House of Commons, but for Lord Lauderdale, who moved that it be fixed at seven years; the result was, that the Fourdriniers were ruined, the only thing which they gained by their connexion with the improvement in the paper manufacture being that of having the machine called by their name. Mr. Donkin, however, by devoting himself to the construction of the new machines, has made a large fortune, his firm having erected, up to the present year, more than two hundred machines in different parts of the world.

Previous to the pulp flowing on the machine it must be strained, an operation which is performed by means of a number of gun-metal bars placed like a grating, leaving spaces varying from 1-70th to 1-100th of an inch between them. This operation is very important, for no matter how carefully the pulp may be prepared, small lumps will be found in it which would form knots in the paper. These had formerly to be picked out with a knife, an operation which caused a great many damaged sheets, technically called *retree*. A common sieve could not be used for this purpose, as it would separate all the long fibres from the pulp, which are so serviceable in giving strength to the paper. A pulp-strainer of this kind was exhibited by H. Watson, of Newcastle-upon-Tyne, and was well made. Instead of this gridiron-strainer some machines have a sort of squirrel-cage, one which continually revolves in the pulp, the only outlet for which is through the bars of the cage, which have slits between them of about the 1-115th of an inch wide. The strained pulp is delivered in an uniform stream upon an endless sheet of fine wire cloth, which is made to revolve in a horizontal position upon rollers; it also receives a sort of jogging motion, the object of which is to strain the water more rapidly through the cloth, and leave the pulp in the form of a pasty sheet of paper upon the wire. The soft sheet, still resting upon the wire-gauze, then passes under a pulp roller, or dandy, as it is called, consisting of a small cylinder channelled and perforated, or of wire, which slightly presses the soft mass, squeezes a quantity of water out of it, which escapes through the perforations in the dandy. Instead of the dandy roller, a box is sometimes placed under a part of the wire cloth corresponding to where the dandy is usually fixed, and a partial vacuum produced in the box by pumps, the effect of which is to suck out the water from the pulp, and give the sheet more firmness. The sheet, after passing under the dandy, and while still resting upon the wire cloth, goes between two rollers furnished with felt kept continually moist, and called the couching rollers, because they perform, to some extent, the same functions that couching between felts does in making paper by the hand. The wire cloth now leaves the paper, and passes round the under roller, whilst the sheet of paper, couched upon a revolving endless sheet of felt, is subjected to two pressures between cylinders of iron, after which it passes over drying rollers of polished metal heated by steam, and then in some mills between two highly polished metal rollers to give it a sort of glaze, after which the paper is wound upon a reel. When sufficient paper has been thus coiled up, it is cut into sheets by a peculiar machine, the essential part of which consists of an axis, having fixed upon it a number of circular cutting-blades, which, in their revolution, divide the endless sheet of paper longitudinally; whilst a long cutting-knife is made to fall at intervals, according to the size of the sheet of paper required, and cuts the paper as it is drawn through the machine.

It is unnecessary to say that the original machine of the Fourdriniers was not as complete as the one just described; the dandy roller, drying rollers and cutting machine, as well as a great number of minor details, being subsequent improvements. The paper made on the first machines differed essentially from that made by hand, by having no wire marks on it; and as the public preferred paper with such marks upon it, it became an object to communicate them to it, which was effected in 1830 by Mr. Thomas Barratt, of St. Mary Cray, in Kent. He divided his endless web into portions equal to the size of an ordinary sheet of paper, and fastened on each division a device such as a crown or the maker's name, which was impressed upon the portion of this endless sheet of paper which was formed upon it. Various other contrivances were introduced, the best of which is that invented by Mr. Thomas Sullivan, Foot's Cray, Kent, and which consists of a peculiarly constructed dandy roller upon which are fastened the devices, and which gives a perfect imitation of laid paper. The great advantage of this system is, that the paper is stronger than when the wire mark is placed upon the wire cloth, and as it is easier to alter the dandy than the cloth, a greater variety of devices may be introduced. We are not aware whether the elaborate water-marks on some of the sheets exhibited by T. H. Saunders, of the Dartford Mills, such as the Madonna in imitation of the corresponding photophanic porcelain picture copied from one of the paintings in the Dresden Gallery, have been attempted on a machine, but we feel confident that it could be done by a properly constructed dandy roller.

The system of the Fourdrinier machine is not the only one which has been tried for making continuous paper; for so early as 1809, a Mr. Dickenson, to whom we owe many improvements in the art of paper-making, proposed employing a hollow brass or gun-metal cylinder, having a polished surface pierced with a number of very fine holes, and covered with wire-gauze. This cylinder was placed in contact with prepared pulp, and was made to revolve rapidly, at the same time that the air was continually being exhausted from the interior of the cylinder; the result was that a thin film of pulp adhered to its surface, the water of which had been sucked in, and left a sheet of paper on the gauze, which was delivered to a felted roller, where it was properly couched by pressure; the remaining operations being exactly similar to those described. There is a beautiful modification of this machine made by the inventor himself, by which he is enabled to produce paper of extraordinary thickness; such, for example, as drawing paper, which was until lately all made by hand. He places two vats supplied with pulp close together, one being behind the other, in each of which revolves a cylinder moved by the same gearing; the first roller gives off a sheet of paper which is received on an endless felt, passed between two rollers, and carried over the other vat, from the cylinder of which another sheet of paper is now thrown off, and is carried along towards another pair of rollers, where it meets with the first sheet of paper just as it leaves its felt; both sheets are pressed together by the rollers, and are finished in the usual way. The paper of which stamped envelopes are made is produced in this way—a few fine silk threads being laid between the sheets as they are passing through the rollers, as will be seen by examining one of those envelopes, when two fine lines may be traced in a part of it, out of which may be removed a blue and a red silk thread.

After the successful manufacture of paper with a machine was effected, a great desideratum still remained to be supplied, namely—to economize the time and labour expended in the tedious process of sizing each sheet separately by dipping it into a solution of glue and alum. Accordingly, it was proposed to add the size to the pulp in the vat, but it was soon found that the animal matter of the size very rapidly destroyed the felts, an objection which was found to apply to such a process even in a still stronger degree when paper was made by hand. There was also another objection, that the sized pulp was liable to undergo incipient putrefaction by long exposure to the air, and to deteriorate and become discoloured; a substitute was, therefore, sought out, to which these objections could not apply. Accordingly, in 1827, M. Canson made a size, of which wax was the base, and soon after M. Delcambre made another with rosin; but both were superseded by the one now in common use on the Continent, invented by Mr. Obry, which consists of a rosin soap with alum and potato starch. To make this size, 150 parts of finely powdered and sifted rosin are boiled with 180 parts of water, to which is added 20 parts of washing soda dissolved in 50 parts more of water; when all have completely united, an equal quantity of soda, dissolved in 45 parts of water, is added, and the boiling continued until a perfect resin soap is formed, which, in order to mix thoroughly with the pulp, is diluted with three times its weight of water, in which is stirred up a quantity of potato fecula equal to about one-eighth of the weight of the resin employed. The granules of starch swell up from the heat of the boiling water, and tend to subdivide the particles of resin soap very considerably; about sixteen to twenty-four quarts of this mixture is added to the pulp in the beating engine, for every 50 lbs. of dried paper; and after being worked up with it for about a quarter of an hour, from 4¼ to 6½ lbs. of alum, according to the quantity of size employed, is added, the effect of which is to precipitate the resin as an insoluble soap in combination with the alumina of the alum, which, being in an extremely fine state of division, attaches itself to every particle of the pulp along with the fecula. Nearly all the paper made on the Continent is sized in this way, and some of the better papers thus prepared are of remarkable whiteness and beauty; and although much softer than papers sized with gelatine, they do not feel so greasy under the pen, the great fault of all papers made in these countries, although so superior in every other respect. Printing paper is usually sized with a resin soap, but potato starch is rarely, if ever, employed, all attempts to use it having failed, owing, according to most manufacturers, to our using a very large quantity of cotton rags in our paper, to which the starch does not so well attach itself. English and Irish writing paper is still sized with gelatine, which gives a stronger and harder paper, and better fitted for the steel pens than the resin-sized papers. The paper used in newspapers is required to be very strong, and, accordingly, a number of attempts were made to size it with gelatine on the machine, an object which was effected by Mr. Crompton, by passing the sheet as it is made between rollers supplied with the size, somewhat similar to the ordinary padding machines of the calico printer. And within the last year or two Mr. W. Johnson, of St. Mary Cray, in Kent, has succeeded in sizing the finest writing papers with gelatine, so that he has at length completed the paper machine, which is now the most perfect automaton ever invented. The gentleman just named has two machines, each of which produces a sheet of paper seventy inches wide, which is made, sized with gelatine, dried and cut at the rate of sixty feet in the minute.

In all that we have hitherto said with regard to the modern manufacture of paper, we have confined ourselves to paper from rags; but when paper is made from straw, the half stuff is obliged to undergo several boilings with lime and potash according to the kind of straw used, wheaten straw requiring three boilings, each of three hours' duration, and oaten straw but one, which is effected under a pressure of several atmospheres, the quantity of lime for each 100 lbs. of straw being 50 lbs., and of potash 2 lbs. The object of these boilings is to dissolve the silicious rind of the straw, which otherwise could not be removed by any mechanical process. In other respects the after process of making paper does not differ in principle from that followed in making paper from rags.

The manufacture of paper, as already observed, is only second to that of linen as a great branch of Irish manufacturing industry, not merely from its extent, but also because, having struggled through many vicissitudes, it has gradually progressed and prospered. Its progress has not, however, been so great as it might and ought to have been, inasmuch as it is one of those manufactures which seem to be peculiarly adapted to the wants and circumstances of the country. It is a manufacture to which water-power is in a special manner adapted, and which may be carried on in every part of the country where that power is available, and where the proper facilities exist for procuring the raw materials. The latter, too, if we except cotton waste, are as easily, and, in most cases, as cheaply procured as in the great centre of the English paper trade. In respect of new materials we are, perhaps, better off than any of the manufacturers of England and Scotland. In the first place we have millions of acres of the very kind of peat best adapted to make paper, and water or railway communication to the greater number of those bogs. Then again, the best, we might say the only kind of straw which is suited for paper-making is oaten straw, so plentifully produced in Ireland. This is not grown to any large extent in England; and in Scotland, where it is one of the chief crops, the clauses in the usual letting leases forbid the straw from being sold off the land. In the north of Ireland there is also abundance of scutching waste, and if the flax industry spreads into the middle, south, and west of Ireland, as it ultimately will do, this supply will be still further increased. With these three materials, in addition to rags and the tropical fibres, which will no doubt very soon come into general use, a wide field is open to Irish paper makers.

The variety of papers made in Ireland is not sufficiently large, and it seldom happens that an Irish mill is entirely devoted to one class of papers, which is very often the case in England and Scotland. We consequently import very largely from the latter countries, instead of exporting, as we might do. For example, we do not make sufficient printing paper to supply our wants, especially of the finer kinds; the same remark applies to the finer qualities of cream-laid post, very large quantities of which are imported. Among the papers much in demand, and which are not made in Ireland, or at least not regularly made, we may mention coloured printing papers, strong coloured cartridge, such as copy-books are covered with, drawing-paper, fine English brown lapping, copying paper (for copying letters), pink and white blotting paper, white and coloured tissue paper, tinted post, fancy damask writing papers, water-lined foolscap for lawyers' use, &c. Sometimes, but very rarely, a few Irish-made coloured printing papers may be had; but the supply is not regular, and the trade is chiefly in the hands of Scotch houses.

There were only four exhibiters of paper, exclusive of those of embossed and ornamented papers; of whom two were Irish, one English, and one Scotch. One of the Irish paper makers, the firm of W. and E. Ryan, of Merchant's-quay, Dublin, exhibited only printing paper made of straw. This paper was manufactured at the mills of Mr. Sullivan, of Golden-bridge, near Dublin, who, along with Mr. Daniel Sullivan of Drimna, and Mr. Seery of Clondalkin, purchased from the French inventor the patent for making it in Ireland, and who, with the Messrs. Ryan, spent a large sum of money in bringing it to perfection. Several other Dublin manufacturers have taken advantage of the results obtained at Golden-bridge, and have commenced the manufacture of straw paper, and we believe there are now five mills in the county of Dublin engaged in it. The paper exhibited by the Messrs. Ryan was of excellent quality, considering the great difficulties encountered in making the process practicable. But since then it has been considerably improved, and a very serviceable printing paper is now made, which is extensively used in printing Irish newspapers both in Dublin and in the provinces. A nice thin-laid paper for notes is now prepared from straw, which is extremely agreeable to write upon. A large quantity of thin unbleached paper, almost like tissue paper, is also made in the county of Dublin from the same material, and used very extensively as wrapping paper by drapers, mercers, confectioners, and others, for small parcels.

The other Irish exhibiter of paper was John M'Donnell, of Swiftbrook Paper Mills, county of Dublin, who contributed a good variety of some of the finer papers in large demand, such as blue-laid medium, foolscaps, bank post, &c. The latter is but little made in Ireland, except, we believe, by Mr. M'Donnell. Among the papers in this collection, and made at the Swiftbrook Mills, we must specially mention the cream-laid posts. This paper, although not equal in quality or colour to the best English, is much cheaper, and consequently answers the general Irish trade better. Its sale is not, however, confined to Ireland, for there is a considerable demand for it in the English and Scotch markets, and in the colonies. There is no similar article so good or so *showy*, at its price, made in Great Britain. This is not the only instance in which Mr. M'Donnell has served the Irish paper trade by his skill and perseverance. A good deal of this class of paper is also made at Dripsey, near Cork, by A. Greer and Co. Among the articles shown by the other exhibiters there was nothing which calls for special mention, if we except the specimens of paper ornamented with a water mark, showing gradations of light and shade, and producing the effect of the porcelain photophanic pictures made in Berlin. Their transparency is produced by fastening a design formed by thin brass plates upon the bottom of the mould. This kind of paper is intended to prevent frauds in bills of exchange and other similar documents. The exhibiter was T. H. Saunders, of London, at whose mill at Dartford, in Kent, the paper was made.

The following Table shows the quantity of paper made in Great Britain and Ireland, and in Ireland separately, for the past ten years:—

| Year. | United Kingdom. | Ireland. | Year. | United Kingdom. | Ireland. |
|---|---|---|---|---|---|
| 1844, . . . | 109,495,148 lbs. . . . | 4,557,306 lbs. | 1849, . . . | 132,132,660 lbs. . . . | 6,272,563 lbs. |
| 1845, . . . | 124,247,071 „ . . . | 5,662,104 „ | 1850, . . . | 141,032,474 „ . . . | 6,719,502 „ |
| 1846, . . . | 127,442,482 „ . . . | 5,875,775 „ | 1851, . . . | 150,903,543 „ . . . | 6,983,646 „ |
| 1847, . . . | 121,965,815 „ . . . | 5,711,546 „ | 1852, . . . | 154,469,211 „ . . . | 7,373,012 „ |
| 1848, . . . | 121,820,229 „ . . . | 5,588,461 „ | 1853, . . . | 177,633,010 „ | |

In 1850 the Revenue Returns gave the number of paper mills in Ireland at 37; the number of beating engines at 86; the number of vats at 18; and the number of machines at 32; the quantity of paper produced at 6,719,502 lbs.; and the duty received at £44,096. In the same year there were 327 mills in England; 1374 beating engines; 307 vats; 323 machines; 105,712,953 lbs. of paper produced; and £693,741 paid as duty: and in Scotland, 51 mills; 286 beating engines; 19 vats; 57 machines; 28,600,019 lbs. of paper made; and £187,687 paid as duty. According to a parliamentary paper published in 1852, there were only 304 of those mills at work in February of that year in England, 48 in Scotland, and 28 in Ireland; in which there was a total of 1616 beating engines at work, and 130 idle. These figures show that the greater number of the mills in Ireland are small, and that they are not worked regularly; for while the number of mills and machines is more than half, and the number of vats nearly equal to those in Scotland, the quantity of paper made was only one-fourth of that produced in that country. We hope to see fifty millions pounds of paper produced here before ten years, if the manufacture of straw and turf paper succeeds.*—W. K. S.

## LETTER-PRESS PRINTING.

There was no branch of industry represented in the Exhibition that has made more rapid progress, or exercised a more important influence, than printing; which, strange to say, is a comparatively modern invention. Some attempt of the kind,—some effort to perpetuate the ideas and events of the period to posterity, or for the use of those at a distance, must have occupied the attention of mankind at an early age; but amid the progress made in the arts and sciences by the Egyptians, Greeks, and Romans, it is remarkable that no approximation was made to the practice of that art which has, more than any other, changed the moral character of the world. The *written* history available at the present day reaches back for many centuries; but it is only four centuries since the invention of printing. We have evidence of an *approximation* to the art of printing from movable blocks of wood or metal having been made in China early in the tenth century. At that period the block to be used for the purpose comprised a whole page of the book, being formed somewhat in the manner that wood engraving is practised at the present day. This, however, may be said to comprise a sort of stereotype printing, and the labour devoted to the production of one book was of no use for any other purpose. It is curious that the introduction of playing cards in the fourteenth century, should have prepared the way for the extension of the art of printing in Europe. From the preparation of the blocks for playing cards, those for single figures for the illustration of sacred subjects followed; and these in turn led to the invention of *movable* types, the use of which may be truly said to have formed a new era in the history and career of the human race.

Our familiarity with the products of this art at the present period prevents us from duly estimating its value, or from forming an adequate idea of the drawbacks sustained by those who lived anterior to its invention, as compared with the advantages which we enjoy. When we consider the great costliness of manuscripts centuries ago, and the fact that they were only within the reach of the few who possessed the wealth to purchase them, we cannot but consider ourselves fortunate in living at a period when abundant stores of information are within the reach of all, and when in consequence the humble peasant is the superior in intelligence, and in the extent to which the reasoning powers are developed, to the nobles of the land in times past.

So far as we have authentic information, it appears that in 1453, the first successful attempt was made by Schoeffer (the partner of Guttenberg, the inventor of the art of printing) at the production of type from matrices, each individual type having hitherto been *cut* from wood or metal; and in 1455 the celebrated work known as Guttenberg's Latin Bible was printed. The production of this work, however, astounded the people of that day so much, especially the monks, and those who had been in the receipt of large incomes for making manuscript copies of the Scriptures, that the work was ascribed to Satan. Not comprehending the nature of the agency by which the several copies were obtained, and being totally unable to account for the uniformity which pervaded them, it was inconceivable how they could be produced by human means; and the common enemy of mankind having in those days been supposed to interfere more *directly* in the affairs of the human race than is believed at the present day, he readily got the credit of being concerned in bringing about what otherwise could not easily be accounted for. Accordingly, when in 1462, copies of the Bible were taken to Paris, by Faustus (the father-in-law of Schoeffer, and also partner of Guttenberg), and offered for sale, such was the outcry raised against him by the monks that he was obliged to leave the city in haste, which circumstance probably gave rise to the well-known tradition that the devil had carried him off. In 1466, however, Faustus made a second journey to Paris, where he was cut off by the plague which then prevailed,—a circumstance which still further contributed to perpetuate the idea of some mysterious agency being concerned with the invention of the art of printing.

In connexion with the investigation of the early progress of printing there is a circumstance which cannot fail to strike the bibliographist—that in every country, and under all circumstances, the history of the human mind is indicated thereby. The first books printed in Germany were devoted to theology and scholastic philosophy; at Paris ancient literature then occupied an equal rank with theology; and at Rome, where the remains of ancient literature maintained a still stronger empire, printing under the guidance of the Bishops of Aleria and Teramo produced chiefly the gems of classic times. Subsequently, under the reign of Francis I., a great number of works upon chivalry appeared in France, showing the extent to which the sentiments involved therein took hold on the minds of the people at that period. The desire of becoming acquainted with narratives in accordance with the prevailing taste, appears to mark the introduction of the art of printing into England. Thus, of the sixty-two works printed in London by William Caxton, those upon theology do not amount to ten, the remainder being devoted to chivalry, history, manners, and customs. The first

* It may not be uninteresting to many of our readers to learn the dimensions of the various denominations of writing papers. The sizes of the different kinds of what are called letter and note papers depend on the papers from which they are respectively made. The sizes here mentioned are those with which the paper manufacturer is conversant; and they are those in which the article reaches the warehouse of the wholesale stationer, by whom the several kinds are cut up into such further subdenominations as the requirements of the public may demand. Annexed are the principal sizes in use:—

| Denominations | Inches |
|---|---|
| Double Elephant, | 40 · [illegible] |
| Atlas, | 34 · [illegible] |
| Columbier, | 34½ · [illegible] |
| Imperial, | 30 · [illegible] |
| Elephant, | 28 · [illegible] |
| Super Royal, | 27 · [illegible] |
| Royal, | 24 · [illegible] |
| Medium, | 22 · [illegible] |
| Demy, | 20 · [illegible] |
| Large Post, | 21 · [illegible] |
| Small Post, | 19 · [illegible] |
| Foolscap, | 16½ · [illegible] |
| Pott, | 15½ · [illegible] |

book printed by Caxton was "The Game of Chess," to which the date of 1474 is affixed. He had been for some years on the Continent as ambassador to the Court of Burgundy, where he is supposed to have obtained a knowledge of the art; but in the early stages of his progress he appears to have been much perplexed about the language he should use in his works, for while some advised him to use old and homely terms, others, "honest and great clerks," he adds, "have been with me and desired me to write the most curious terms that I could find—and thus betwixt plain, rude, and curious, I stand abashed." In 1480 he published his Chronicles and his Description of Britain, which were both very popular, having been reprinted four times in the fifteenth, and seven times in the sixteenth centuries. Caxton distinguished the books of his printing by a peculiar device, consisting of the initial letters of his name with a cipher between them. His first performances were very rude, the characters employed resembling those of English manuscripts before the Norman conquest.

Of the first introduction of printing into Ireland we have not seen any authentic records, though it appears to have been long subsequent to the date of Caxton's labours in London. In 1551 the Book of Common Prayer was printed in Dublin by Humfrey Powel in quarto black letter, which appears to be the earliest recorded production of the Irish press. The College Library Catalogue affords but one piece printed in this city so early as even 1633, nor do there appear to have been many works produced here until 1700, when Alderman George Faulkner commenced the business and carried it on with spirit for many years. During the seventeenth century the printing-press of Dublin sent out a great variety of books, many of which may fairly be regarded as creditable specimens of typography for the age in which they were produced.

To enter into details as to the progress made from time to time in bringing the art of printing to its present state of comparative perfection would occupy more space than we can devote to the subject. We need not here enter into an account of the operation of type-founding, which would demand a lengthened notice. It will be sufficient for the reader at present to know, that every letter, point, or mark used in printing is cast (with some few exceptions) on a distinct body or stalk; and that, for the use of the printer, numbers of these types are placed in boxes or compartments of the framework to which the term *case* is technically applied. These cases are mounted on stands or *frames*, so that they may be conveniently placed before the persons who are to select the types. The little cells or boxes are arranged according to a conventional form which long usage has sanctioned; the letters and points most frequently in use being so situated as to be most conveniently come at by the workman. The size of these cells is regulated by the comparative frequency with which the particular letters may be used. The letter e, for example, has a cell larger than that for any other; and those for c, d, m, n, h, u, t, i, s, o, a, r, are twice the size of the boxes for b, l, v, k, f, g, y, p, or w, and four times the size of those for j, q, or the [ ] crotchets, periods, &c. The capitals and small capitals are arranged in another case, placed at a greater distance, which is hence called the *upper case*, that next the printer being the *lower case*.

In the process of printing, the *compositor* (so called from placing together or *composing* the separate types into words), having placed his *copy* upon a part of the case seldom in use, takes up an instrument called a *composing stick*,* and having properly arranged it, after reading the first few words of his copy, generally takes first a capital letter from the upper case, the succeeding letters from the lower case, and at the conclusion of the word a *space*, which is merely the shank of a letter without any face, and not so high as a letter by about one-fourth part. Each word is, therefore, separated by a space, which cannot appear upon the paper, from not being high enough among the letters to receive any portion of the ink or to make an impression. The letters composing the next word are taken up in succession, after which a space is used, and so on until the end of the line. On the completion of the line the *setting rule* is taken out from behind the row of letters just completed, and placed above them as the basis of the next line. The work goes on in this manner until as many lines of types are set up as fills the composing stick, when the matter thus set is taken out and placed upon an instrument called a *galley*, which will hold the contents of several composing sticks. On the galley being filled, the next process is to take what is called a *proof* impression of the types so set up (the operation being the same in principle as that in printing off copies, and which will be afterwards noticed), and the proof is carefully gone over by the *reader*, assisted by a boy who reads aloud from the copy, to ascertain what imperfections may exist in the impression so taken. The necessary corrections being made on the margin, the proof is distributed among the parties who set up the types from which it has been obtained, and by those parties the corrections are made. The intention in the first reading is to make the proof exactly correspond with the copy or manuscript. These corrections are few or many according to the skill and pains taken by the compositor; and those blunders which may sometimes be seen in printing arise from the whole of the errors not having been corrected at this stage. The corrections being made, an amended proof or revise is sent to the author for his inspection; and he, having made such alterations as he thinks necessary, sends it back again to the printing office. With proper attention to these marks the responsibility of the printer ceases.

The manner in which the types are disposed for correction varies somewhat according as the persons are employed at newspaper or book-work. The practice already described is that adopted in newspaper offices, the compositor having nothing to do with his matter only in galleys. In this case, after being transferred to the *chase* or iron framework in which the types are held together, no further corrections are made. In what is termed book-work, however, after the first correction of proofs taken on galleys, the matter is *imposed*, that is, made up into pages, any subsequent impressions being obtained in this shape, and the revise for the author being one of the sheets of the forthcoming publication, comprising eight, twelve, or sixteen pages, as the case may be.

* The composing stick is a small framework or gauge of metal, the name being derived from its being originally formed of wood. One part of it is movable, so that by a screw it can be set at any required length of line, according to the breadth of the column or page. The compositor is enabled to keep his types in a right line in the composing stick by using a *rule*, generally of brass, and of the length of his line. The composing stick is held in the left hand, the thumb keeping the letter last placed in its position until another is put over it.

A person seeing a compositor at work for the first time is naturally amazed at the rapidity of his motions, and the general correctness with which the types are picked up from the several compartments, without the precaution being ever taken to look to see whether the letter taken up is really that which is required. But in like manner, if familiarity with the use of the piano and other instruments of music did not do away with the surprise which would otherwise be experienced at the rapidity of the movements of the fingers, we should be no little astonished at how such results are produced. In both cases the train of thought progresses so rapidly that there is not leisure to concentrate it on any object; yet the pianist seldom touches a wrong key, nor does the compositor pick up a wrong type. The errors to be seen in the proofs sometimes arise from careless reading of the copy, and frequently from a mistake in distributing the letters into the respective cells provided for them.

The types in common use are of different sizes, according to the character and appearance of the publication for which they are to be employed. The following are the sorts used in book-work:—

ENGLISH.

The earth is the Lord's, and the fulness thereof.

PICA.

The earth is the Lord's, and the fulness thereof.

SMALL PICA.

The earth is the Lord's, and the fulness thereof.

LONG PRIMER.

The earth is the Lord's, and the fulness thereof.

BOURGEOIS.

The earth is the Lord's, and the fulness thereof.

BREVIER.

The earth is the Lord's, and the fulness thereof.

MINION.

The earth is the Lord's, and the fulness thereof.

NONPAREIL.

The earth is the Lord's, and the fulness thereof.

RUBY.

The earth is the Lord's, and the fulness thereof.

PEARL.

The earth is the Lord's, and the fulness thereof.

DIAMOND.

The earth is the Lord's, and the fulness thereof.

The sizes of type employed in this work are bourgeois, brevier, and nonpareil.

In the arrangement of the types it is sometimes desired to give the printing an open or light appearance, which is effected by placing what are called *leads* between the lines. These leads are thin spaces of the exact width of the column or page, only one-fourth, one-sixth, and one-eighth the thickness of a line of types, and only the same height as the spaces already referred to. The leading articles of newspapers, for example, are commonly leaded; as is also the Preface, Introduction, and article on the Exhibition Building in this Catalogue.

The types being made up into pages, they are transferred to a large table, the upper surface of which consists of planed metal or stone. This table is furnished with drawers containing wedges of wood, called *furniture*, the use of which we shall notice presently. The compositor having laid the pages of one side of the sheet on this table in proper order, proceeds to fix them in the chase. The pages are placed at the proper distances from each other, and the interior spaces being arranged, and side-sticks being placed along the outer margin of the types, between their sides and the sides of the chase, pieces of the furniture already referred to, termed *quoins*, are driven in with a shooting-stick and mallet, until the types are so firmly fixed in the chase that the whole can be removed without danger of any portion falling out.

In the arrangement of the pages in the form, they must be so disposed that, when folded up, the printed sheet shall range properly; but this, though an apparently intricate matter, is founded upon a very simple law, the observance of which guards against any mistake being committed. There being many sheets in some works, it would be embarrassing to the person who folds them for the binder to be calculating the number of the page that should be first in order while placing them together; and in order to obviate this, letters, called *signatures*, are placed at the bottom of the leading page of each sheet—A for the first sheet, B for the second sheet, C for the third, and so on to the end of the book.

Before dismissing this part of the subject, it will be necessary to advert to another part of the duty of the compositor, that of the *distribution of the types* into their respective cells in the case. After the requisite number of impressions or copies have been taken from the *form* of type, the chase is carried back to the composing-room, and after being carefully washed with ley to remove any ink, is placed upon a letter-board and unlocked; the face of the type being wetted with a sponge, so that when the matter, comprising several lines, is taken up, the letters adhere together, and thus guard against any portion of it falling into pye. The portion of letter is placed on the setting-rule, already referred to, and held in the left hand, while by the right hand some half-dozen letters are taken up, and after glancing at the faces of them to see what they are, the letters are rapidly dropped into their appropriate cells. This process requires the utmost care; for it will be plain that every mistake made in throwing in the letter will lead to a corresponding one in compostion afterwards. Most compositors distribute four times as rapidly as they compose, the rate varying from eight to ten thousand letters per hour.

Regarding the rate of remuneration of a compositor, a few words may not be out of place. It is made to depend on the number of thousands of letters which he composes, and the calculation is thus made:—The letter *m* being on a shank which is perfectly square, it is ascertained how many *ems* the page is in length, including the running head—that is, how many lines of the type selected there will be in the proposed page—and next, how many *ems* it is to be in width, or how many times this letter would be repeated, supposing the entire line to be formed of *ems*. The number in width is then doubled, because experience has shown that the average width of the letters is one-half of the depth; and the entire number of letters in a sheet is found by multiplying the number of *ems* in the length by double that in the width, and this product again by the number of pages in the sheet. In this calculation any number of odd letters under 500 are not taken into account, but 500, or over, are charged as another thousand. The scale of prices adopted by masters and men, and agreed upon in this city, is—that all reprints in common matter (including brevier and English) are to be cast up at 5*d*. per 1000 letters; if in minion, 5½*d*.; nonpareil, 6½*d*.; and pearl, 7½*d*. Works in manuscript and in foreign languages, mathematical works, all those having what is called rule or tabular work, are paid for at increased rates: but these details would possess little interest for the general public, and a tolerably correct idea may be formed of the rate of wages in this branch of industry from what has been already stated. It must, however, be borne in mind that the rate mentioned is merely that paid to the compositor. The charge for *reading*, wear and tear of types, and other expenses, and the employer's profit, are to be added before estimating the cost of *composition* to the public; and this is only one item, for presswork yet remains to be taken into account.

Having detailed the several processes connected with the business of the compositor, we have now briefly to describe what is technically called *presswork*. The invention of some process whereby a copy could be obtained from movable types must have been coeval with that of Guttenberg, already noticed; as the means of obtaining such impressions were in fact wanted to give value to the discovery of printing. The earlier printed works convey a tolerably accurate idea of the nature of the press by which they were produced, from cuts representing the press ornamenting the title-pages. The construction of the press does not appear to have varied much from the earliest period till about 1620, when Blaew, of Amsterdam, introduced considerable improvements; but these were again superseded by the modifications made by Lord Stanhope, whose ingenious invention really formed a new era in the history of printing. The old presses were of course made of wood; but on the introduction of the use of iron a new form was given to the printing press, while it was at the same time made to do its work much more effectually than before.

The simplest form of the hand-press consisted of two upright pieces, rising perpendicularly from the floor to the height of six or seven feet, which were connected with cross pieces. From about the middle of each of these a slide projected at right angles, the two slides being parallel to each other; a spindle with a powerful screw, kept in its place by those cross-pieces, worked in a box called a hose, by means of a bar or lever inserted in it; the toe of the spindle worked in a sort of cup fixed upon a large solid block of mahogany, having the face planed perfectly smooth, and called the *platten*. On the bar being pulled down, the spindle descended in proportion to the worm of its screw, and forced down the platten to precisely the same degree, and with great power. A table was made to run in and out upon the ribs or slides; and upon this table the form of types was placed. When run in, it would of course be directly under the platten, and having been previously linked and the paper placed on it, the bar was pulled over, the spindle, platten, &c., descended, and the very powerful pressure thereby obtained gave a fac-simile, on the paper, of the types. The modification introduced by Lord Stanhope consisted in an improved application of the power to the spindle and screw, which admitted of the power being multiplied. Various improvements have since been made, many of which are deserving of attention, but the form here alluded to is so simple, so easily kept in order, and so powerful, that it is still in use.

Whatever may be the kind of hand-press employed, the principle of construction and mode of working are nearly the same in all. On the left front of the press stands the inking-table, from which, by long cylindrical rollers, the ink is transferred to the face of the types. At the right front of the press are placed the *bank* and *horse;* the former consisting of a deal table, and the latter of an inclined plane, which stands upon the bank, and upon which is laid the paper to be printed. Each press requires two persons to work it, one of whom attends to the inking, and the other only to the press. Both parties scrutinize occasionally the quality of the work, to see that nothing is astray, and if so, to ascertain what it is, with a view of applying the appropriate remedy. These men are paid by every 250 impressions, this quantity being called a *token*, and any smaller quantity than 250 being estimated at the same figure as if they came up to it. In ordinary books about 250 copies are printed on one side in an hour. Common work is paid 4½*d*. per token when 1000 copies are printed; good, 6*d*.; superior, 7*d*.; though so much as 10*d*. is occasionally paid. The quantity of work, however, depends very much upon its quality. With small type, stiff ink, and many rules, the work of printing off copies goes slowly forward. The finest work is also seldom paid for by the token, the pressmen being placed upon weekly wages, and allowed as much time as is necessary for the work.

The paper to be printed must have been previously damped in order that it may be softened, and thus accommodate itself to the surface of the type so as to take off a good impression.

On the early sheets being taken from the press they are to be attentively examined to see that none of the spaces stand up, as this would occasion a black mark on the paper, where there should be nothing of the kind. It must also be seen that the imposing of the types, or making them up into pages, is correct. The first impressions are, moreover, invariably defective. On some parts of the sheet the inking may be too heavy, while in others the printing may not be legible; but all these defects the pressman attends to, introducing slips of paper wherever a sufficiently heavy impression has not been obtained. Uniformity of colour, as it is called, is of the last importance in good work; as nothing could detract more from the general appearance of a book than that the inking should be heavier on some pages than on others. The printing of illustrated works, in which wood engravings are introduced with the letter-press, requires peculiar care, so as to give effect to the engraving, which would otherwise be an unsightly daub, however well it may have been executed. The thickness of the wood block is made to correspond as nearly as possible with the depth of the type; but the precise amount of pressure to be upon it, the pressman must regulate very carefully by placing slips of paper under any portion of the block that may be too low, and if the block should chance to be too high, it must be scraped or filed away at the back.

We have hitherto referred chiefly to what is termed printing by hand, as contradistinguished from printing by machinery. So long as the demand for literary works was so limited that only a small number of copies of each were required, the operation of the hand-press was quite sufficient as the source of supply; but with the extension of education, and more especially with the growth of what might be called popular literature, more rapid agencies of production became necessary to keep pace with the changing spirit of the times. The idea of printing by machinery, however, occupied attention so early as 1790, when Mr. Nicholson took out a patent for an invention with this object. His printing machine never became available in practice, yet he deserves the credit of being the first who suggested the use of cylinders and inking rollers. About the commencement of the present century an ingenious German, named König, still further turned the idea to account. By numerous experimental trials he at last produced a machine for printing, which, with modifications and improvements, stands, both with regard to ingenuity of mechanism and importance of application, in the first rank of the monuments of human intelligence. Being unsuccessful in his applications for assistance to the printers and capitalists of his native country, he came to London in 1804. There he entered into arrangements with Mr. Walter of the "Times" for carrying out his ideas; but it was not until 1814 that they became effectively introduced into operation. The first really useful machine was constructed by Messrs. Applegath and Cowper, being a modification of that of König; its principal improvements consisting in the application of two drums between the impression cylinders, for the purpose of securing the register of the sheet, by retaining it, after the impression of the first form, just so long that it may pass on to the second cylinder in exact time to be impressed thereby upon the second form; and of the distribution of the ink upon a plane surface instead of by a complication of rollers.

For printing newspapers, machines are usually constructed to print but one side at a time. A machine will work a much greater number of one form than of two, and the machinery will be lighter, less expensive, and require less motive power in the one case than in the other; one form of a newspaper can, therefore, be worked off at leisure, and the other, containing intelligence up to the last moment, is thrown off with immense rapidity. For bookwork, however, what is called *perfecting machines* are employed, which print both sides of the sheet at one operation. Speed is here of less consequence than the due execution of the work; and with high speed it is found that good work cannot be produced.

In the printing machine the forms of type are usually placed upon a carriage moving backwards and forwards on slides running the length of the framework which supports the whole machine. Attached to each end of this carriage is a table for the distribution of the ink. The reciprocating motion is conveyed to it by means of a pinion which works alternately upon the upper and under surface of a rack. In gear with this carriage, and in immediate contact with the type, with the exception of the intervention of the paper to be printed, revolve two cylinders of large dimensions by which the impression is given. These cylinders are separated by the registering drums, but are kept in uniform and steady motion by two large wheels, the teeth of which work within each other. The ink is distributed by an apparatus attached to each end of the framework, consisting of a trough which contains the ink, in contact with which, or very nearly so, a metal roller called the *ductor* is made to revolve slowly. A composition roller is made to rise into contact with the ductor and receive a portion of ink, with which it descends and communicates to the inking table as that passes underneath it. By a series of rollers the ink is distributed over the table, from which rollers it is transferred to the types. For the purpose of carrying forward the paper in its course through the machine, endless tapes are passed round the cylinders. The sheet of paper being placed on the top of the machine, so as to come within reach of these tapes, it is carried round the cylinders, in the course of which it comes in contact with the form, and is afterwards thrown out of the machine.

We have already stated that a speed of about 250 sheets per hour printed on one side was the usual rate attained by the hand-press, and when we compare these results with what is attained by the use of the machine, we shall be able to estimate its value as an agent of civilization. So far as regards newspaper work, the printing off of the full-sized sheet at the hand-press would be difficult, if not impossible. Ordinary newspaper machines are capable of throwing off 2000 sheets per hour printed on one side; and the perfecting or book machines can print from 500 to 600 sheets per hour.*—J. S.

* The necessities of the "Times" newspaper in ministering to the wants of its patrons gave the first great stimulus to printing by machinery; and it is to that journal that we are also in a great degree indebted for the further development of the application of mechanical science to this purpose. The large circulation of the leading journal not only demands that every available means to increase the rate of production shall be employed, but it also can afford the means to supply every agency of the kind almost regardless of expense. With a circulation of from thirty to forty and even fifty thousand per day, great indeed must be the facilities by which such a supply is produced; and the facilities have increased in an astonishing degree. In the "Times" of February 14, 1848, after fourteen years had elapsed since the "Times" was first printed by steam machinery, it was stated that "at that time we spoke as we thought with becoming praise of the perseverance and ingenuity of the inventor Mr. König, and with sufficient modesty, we trust, of our own firmness and resolution in overcoming opposing difficulties and even dangers. This surprising machine has since received certain improvements from the hand of its original inventor, but we have now to present to our readers and the public an account of a vast and beneficial change which has taken place. The first machine printed but 1100 sheets per hour,—the reader now holds in his hand an impression which a new machine has yielded at the rate of 4000 an hour. Such ease, rapidity, and accuracy united, could hardly ever before be ascribed to any fabric constructed by the hand of man. Let but the reader contemplate if he can what must be the rapidity of those motions which throw off 4000 printed sheets per hour, or nearly 70 in a minute." This machine was attended by eight persons, four "layers on," who stood at four delivery tables, and four "takers off," stationed at four tables. A sheet was delivered to the machine by each of the

## ANASTATIC PRINTING.

About ten years ago, Mr. Rudolph Appel, a native of Silesia, invented a peculiar mode of copying engravings, printed matter, &c., to which the name "Anastatic Printing" was given. Although it attracted considerable attention at the time, from various quarters, it did not come into general use, and, indeed, was almost lost sight of until the specimens exhibited in 1851 at the Great Exhibition impressed the public with the great advantages which might be derived from its employment.

The process is simple, and consists of three series of operations:—1. The preparation of the plate. 2. The impression of the engraving or printed matter; and 3. The full development of the raised impression, or, as it is called, the *appelotype*. The first series consists in preparing a finely polished zinc plate, by exposing it to the vapour of hydrochloric acid, or laying a piece of paper moistened with dilute hydrochloric acid (composed of 1 of acid and 5 to 6 of water), and then laid between folds of blotting paper in order to absorb superfluous acid upon it, and subjecting it to a gentle pressure in a press. The duration of the action of the acid depends upon the fineness of the lines in the engraving,—the finer the lines the shorter the time. After the action of the acid the plate is washed and carefully dried.

The second series of operations consists in laying the engraving or other object to be copied with its printed side downwards upon a sheet of paper, and then laying upon its back a piece of blotting or bibulous paper impregnated with a dilute nitric acid (composed of 1 of acid and 5 to 6 of water). The object of this paper is to moisten uniformly the print with the acid; and if one sheet of paper does not suffice it must be remoistened or a fresh one laid on. When the object to be copied is sufficiently moistened, it is to be laid with its printed surface downwards upon the polished zinc plate prepared in the manner described; a sheet of paper is laid upon it, and then a piece of felt, and the whole subjected to a considerable pressure in a roller press. The acid of the paper is thus made to etch the zinc plate, and as it cannot come in contact with the plates wherever there may be any letters, or lines formed by the ink with which the matter was printed, a copy of the latter will be left raised up, by the delicate etching away of all the parts corresponding to the white portions of the page or print; hence the term *anastatic*, from the Greek words signifying "raising up."

The original engraving is next removed from the surface of the plate, which is ready to undergo the last series of operations. There is first poured over it a decoction of oak bark (composed of 1 pound of bark to 8 pints of water) prepared in an earthen vessel, and the liquid allowed to dry on it. It is then to be washed with water and rubbed over with gum water. The plate is afterwards rubbed by means of soft flannel with fresh oil, to which is added oil of turpentine at the rate of thirty drops to the ounce of oil, until everything black is removed. It is now wiped with another piece of flannel dipped in water, and some thin lithographic ink is rubbed over it by means of an elastic roller. The plate is ready to print from. Mr. Appel formerly recommended the use of a solution of phosphoric acid to deepen the etching when necessary.

If the ink upon the engraving be so dried from age or other causes that it cannot be copied by the method just noticed, it may be brought into a condition to be so, by immersing it for from three or four minutes to an hour, according as it may require it, in a hot solution of strontia water, then pressing it between folds of blotting paper, treated with nitric acid, pressed again to remove the strontia, and again pressed and laid upon the plate as before. If it is desired to make shaded drawings, which may be directly copied by this process, it is advantageous to use a paper prepared with a strong solution of gelatine and a weak solution of ox-gall. If it is required to multiply copies of a piece of writing, lithographic or some other similar inks should be

two former, and seized between the tapes, by which it was carried round the printing cylinder, brought into contact with the types, impressed upon them, carried out, and delivered printed to each of the latter; all this being regulated by self-acting machinery. We further find that the machine now described continued to serve the purposes of the "Times" newspaper until within a few years past, when again the exigencies of the press exceeded even its immense powers, and another appeal was made to the inventive genius of Mr. Applegath. It was in short necessary to provide a machine by which at least 10,000 sheets an hour could be worked off for a single form. "In considering the means of solving this problem," states Dr. Lardner in his "Review of the Great Exhibition of 1851," "it is necessary to observe that whatever expedient may be used, the sheets of paper to be printed must be delivered one by one to the fingers of the machine by an attendant; after they once enter the machine they are carried through it and printed by self-acting machinery. But in the case of sheets so large as those of the newspapers, it is found that they cannot be delivered with the necessary precision by manipulation at a more rapid rate than 2 in five seconds or 25 per minute, being at the rate of 1500 sheets per hour. Now in this manner to print 10,000 per hour would require seven cylinders, to place which so as to be acted upon a type-form moving alternately in a horizontal frame in the manner already described would present mechanical difficulties almost insuperable.

"In the face of these difficulties," continues Dr. Lardner, "Mr. Applegath, to whom the world is indebted for the invention of the "Times" printing machine, decided on abandoning the reciprocating motion of the type-form, arranging the apparatus so as to render the motion continuous. This necessarily involved circular motion, and accordingly he resolved upon attaching the columns of type to the sides of a large drum or cylinder placed with its axle vertical, instead of the horizontal frame which had been hitherto used. A large central drum is erected capable of being turned round its axis. Upon the sides of this drum are placed vertically the columns of type. These columns, strictly speaking, form the sides of a polygon, the centre of which coincides with the axis of the drum, but the breadth of the columns is so small compared with the diameter of the drum, that their surfaces depart very little from the regular cylindrical form. The circumference of this drum in the "Times" printing machine measures 200 inches. . . . . . . .

"Beside the eight paper cylinders are placed eight sets of inking rollers; near these are placed two ductor rollers. These ductor rollers receive a coating of ink from reservoirs placed above them. As the inking table attached to the revolving drum passes each of these ductor rollers, it receives from them a coating of ink. It next encounters the inking rollers, to which it delivers over this coating. The types next, by the continual revolutions of the drum, encounter these inking rollers, and receive from them a coating of ink, after which they meet the paper cylinders, upon which they are impressed, and the printing is completed. It is found that by this machine, in ordinary work, between 10,000 and 11,000 per hour can be printed; but with very expert men to deliver the sheets, a still greater speed can be attained. Indeed, the velocity is limited, not by any conditions affecting the machine, but by the power of the men to deliver the sheets to it."

used. But, if it has been written with common ink or colour, it may be copied in the following manner:—The piece to be copied is laid with its printed or written side downwards upon a sheet of paper, and a moistened sheet is then laid upon its back until it becomes thoroughly moist. In this condition it is laid in the same position upon a sheet of paper impregnated with wax or fat; another sheet of clean paper is then laid upon it, and the whole subjected to a pressure in a warm place. The wax or fat will adhere to the inked or coloured parts, and not to the white parts. The engraving or manuscript may then be printed in the ordinary way in a lithographic press.

The wonderful accuracy with which any printed matter can be copied by the anastatic process, and the simplicity of the means by which it may be done, afford great facilities to the forger to copy bank notes, cheques, &c. As an illustration of this we may mention that some postage stamps were reproduced by the anastatic process by desire of a Committee of the House of Commons, and so perfectly faithful were the copies that they were passed as genuine through the General Post Office, and each member of the Committee received a letter franked by one of those stamps. In order to prevent such forgeries, Mr. Appel has invented a kind of paper which he terms "*anti-acid and anti-anastatic paper.*" This paper is made by adding a quantity of sulphate of copper to the pulp of paper suspended in water, and then precipitating the copper as an insoluble phosphate of copper by the addition of phosphate of soda. In this way the pulp becomes thoroughly impregnated with a salt of copper; if such paper be printed upon, it cannot be copied by the anastatic process, upon zinc, for the moment such paper moistened with nitric acid is laid upon a plate of zinc, the phosphate of copper, becoming partially dissolved, will be, at once, reduced to the metallic state, and will coat the zinc with copper, and fasten the paper so effectually to the zinc that it cannot be again removed. As, however, it would be easy to remove the whole of the copper by means of an acid previous to attempting to apply the anastatic process, the use of the salt of copper would be of little value unless we could also discover a mode of preventing the use of acid without injury to the paper. This object Mr. Appel has attained by imbuing the paper with a solution of 1 part of a peculiar soap in 20 parts of water. This soap may be made by mixing equal parts of white soft soap and old palm oil, or by preparing a potash soap with olive or other non-drying oil, and adding, when boiling, some old palm oil. If paper impregnated with this soap be treated with acid, the soap will be decomposed, and the fat set free; in this condition the paper cannot be perfectly wetted with acid, and as all the parts which cannot be wetted will not etch the zinc plate, and will oil its surface, the ink will attach itself to almost the whole surface of the plate, and no impression can consequently be obtained. The prepared paper has a light but pleasing green tint, and is, we believe, getting into use rapidly, as it deserves.

The anastatic process was well illustrated in the Exhibition by some copies of old engravings, especially by a beautiful copy of an engraving of Albrecht Dürer, from his life of the Blessed Virgin, with the zinc plate from which it was produced, and by a plate obtained from a large wood engraving of the interior of the Great Exhibition of 1851, which appeared in the "Illustrated London News;" as well as by several specimens of writing and letter-press printing, and samples of cheques printed on the safety paper, a plate of zinc with one fastened to it by a deposition of copper, and one with the blurred impression showing the action of the decomposed soap.

An ingenious use has been made by the Rev. Dr. Graves, of this city, of the anastatic process, which deserves notice. All the annotations of Mr. E. Curry, Dr. O'Donovan, &c., employed in editing the collection of the Brehon Laws, now being made under the direction of a Commission appointed by Parliament, are written with a peculiar ink, and a number of copies made by the anastatic process, and sent round for correction and examination. Some are also used for arrangement in a dictionary form, and again copied so as to gradually form the materials of a great dictionary of the Irish language, with scarcely any additional labour. In this way an enormous amount of labour and expense is saved, and an amount of accuracy insured which could not be attained by any other means.

#### CHROMOTYPY, OR PRINTING IN COLOURS; AND LITHOCHROMY, OR LITHOGRAPHY IN COLOURS.

Very soon after the invention of printing, the title-pages of many books were printed in red and black inks; and in some books, especially missals, the first letter of each page or paragraph and the words of the music were printed in light red. This style naturally led to attempts being made to imitate by printing the illuminations with which manuscripts were so profusely adorned in the middle ages; and even to try to produce the effects of light and shade. The first idea of the latter is usually attributed to Hugo da Carpi, a painter of the Modenese school, who flourished about the year 1500; he reproduced many designs of Raffaelle, in three blocks, by which he expressed the shades, the middle tints, and the lights, with great effect. Some of them are supposed to have been occasionally executed with coloured inks. Albrecht Dürer is also believed to have practised this art; but it is probable that his wood engravings were coloured after being printed, as was commonly done at the period in which he lived. The process of producing a coloured wood engraving did not, however, come into general use until about thirty or forty years ago, although repeated mention is made of the art by all writers upon the history of printing and wood engraving during the last 200 years. Within the last ten years it has received considerable extension, and is now much practised in England and on the Continent. The finest specimens of coloured surface printing exhibiting *chiaro-oscuro*, produced in England, are those of Mr. Baxter, of London, who exhibited a number of charming copies of pictures, both historical and landscape, &c., under the name of "oil-colour picture printing." The process, as may be expected, is nothing more than a species of common printing, the graduated tints being produced by means of wooden and metal blocks, each shade of colour being applied by a distinct block.

Chromo-lithography is nothing more than the same principle applied to lithography. Every part of the design which is to receive a distinct colour is drawn upon a separate stone, so that if a design has ten distinct colours, it will require ten separate stones and ten successive operations of printing to produce a finished copy.

Chromotypy has many advantages over lithochromy, especially in the richness and harmony of colour and depth and warmth of tone. It has, in fact, many of the advantages of oil painting, and is, therefore, well adapted, *so far as any mechanical process can do so*, for producing copies which will realize to the mind, to some extent, the style of colouring of the great masters. Some of the specimens exhibited by Mr. Baxter fully bear out these remarks, especially one or two landscapes and the copy of the "Taking down from the Cross" of Reubens. There were three exhibiters of lithochromy, two English, and one Irish. The specimens exhibited by Rowney and Co., of London, were excellent examples of what may be done by this process. It is for water-colour painting what chromotypy is for oil painting. Besides its merely artistic value, it is also of considerable commercial importance, as it may be applied to produce a great variety of ornaments, such as ornamental paper, linen bands, &c. It is especially adapted for producing cheap coloured maps, for which purpose it has recently been employed, and an excellent example of which is afforded by the small geological map of Ireland executed by Mr. Forster, of Crow-street, in this city, who deserves great credit for his efforts to improve the art of lithography in Ireland.—W. K. S.

## WOOD ENGRAVING.

The art of engraving on wood is of very ancient origin, as it may be regarded as the forerunner of that of printing, the one leading by an easy transition to the other. After having made some progress, it languished until the eighteenth century, but revived towards its close, chiefly through the exertions of the celebrated Thomas Bewick, who applied wood engraving with unexampled success in the illustration of his "History of Quadrupeds" and his "British Birds." Bewick was apprenticed to a copperplate engraver of Newcastle, and his attention seems first to have been directed to wood engraving by his master being employed to execute the diagrams for the "Treatise on Mensuration" about to be published by Dr. Charles Hutton, then a schoolmaster in Newcastle. In 1784 he executed the engravings for an edition of "Gay's Fables," published in his native town. In 1785 he commenced the cuts for the "History of Quadrupeds," printed in 1790; and the comparative excellence of these illustrations, which, for the correct delineation of the animals, the natural character of the incidents and the backgrounds, were far superior to any that had previously appeared. In 1797 his "British Birds" appeared, which still further contributed to the fame of the engraver, and increased the public appreciation of the art by showing what it was susceptible of.

But notwithstanding the effective manner in which works could be illustrated by wood engravings, the very large outlay which it involved prevented its extended use for a length of time. One of its leading characteristics is that copies can be indefinitely multiplied at little more than the ordinary cost of letter-press printing; and hence its great superiority whenever large numbers come to be required. In other cases, however, the value of this method of illustration is not so obvious. When only a few impressions are necessary, they may be in certain cases supplied by lithographic or copperplate engraving. Hence, so long as books were published in small numbers, there was little inducement presented to introduce woodcuts. The first great impulse to the art was imparted by the publication of the "Penny Magazine," in 1833, when, through the agency of an unprecedently large circulation, Mr. Charles Knight was able to place a profusely illustrated sheet in the hands of the public, at the low selling price of one penny. For years the "Penny Magazine" continued to enjoy a large amount of public patronage, and its success, as a matter of course, led to sundry other aspirants entering the field of competition. The great demand for these low-priced publications, and the competition which prevailed among their producers, led to the use of illustrations of the highest class, thus indirectly contributing to the advancement of the art. But the crowning effort of the application of wood engraving was the constant application of it to the production of a weekly sheet, in which the news of the day would be combined with a large amount of pictorial representations of the objects of interest at the time. The commencement of the "Illustrated News" formed a new era in the progress of wood engraving, a large sum being expended in the illustration of a single number, which is, nevertheless, sold at the price of a common newspaper.

The perfection to which the art has been brought through the efforts of Bewick and others, and the increasing demand for illustrated works, has caused the use of woodcuts to extend much of late; and this method of illustration has in turn led to improvements in the art of printing. So long as the paper for the engravings was different from that employed for the body of the work, and printed in a different manner, progress in one department exercised little influence on that in the other; but the wood blocks being introduced among the ordinary types led to the use of superior paper for printing, better ink, and more careful press-work than had hitherto been deemed necessary. To give effect to wood engraving, in fact, very careful printing is required; and this prevents such work from being well executed wherever it is not extensively carried on, from the want of skilled hands to execute it. London is the great emporium for this kind of work, as the centre of the publishing trade generally: and there, certain houses make special arrangements for the printing of illustrated works. A high degree of excellence in this department has, however, been attained in the College office, in this city, the style of some of the work executed in it leaving little to be desired;—"Petrie's Round Towers," and several other works printed by Mr. Gill, may be regarded as really creditable specimens of press-work. Machine printing is not well adapted for working off the finer kinds of engravings; yet it is surprising the degree of excellence which has been attained in this respect in London, where illustrated periodicals are produced in such numbers as not to be supplied by the hand-press.

For the purpose of the wood engraver no wood is equal to box, on account of its surpassing hardness and closeness of texture; and English box is superior to all others. Though its small size is a great drawback, this is in some degree compensated by its being so clear and firm in the grain and not crumbling under the graver. It resists evenly to the edge of the tool, and gives not a particle beyond what is actually cut out, while the larger kinds of American and Turkey box are soft, and liable to crumble and to cut short; that is, small particles will sometimes *break* away from the sides of the line cut by the graver, and thus cause imperfections in the work. As even the largest pieces of box are of comparatively small diameter, it is difficult to obtain a perfect block for a large engraving; and it therefore becomes necessary to fix several pieces together by means of screws, the joints being made as fine as possible. The wood is cut across the grain, the pieces being left of a thickness as, when placed in the form, to correspond with the surface of the type; the thickness of the block being equal to the height of the type.

To prepare the wood for the engraver, the surface, after being planed, is rubbed with finely powdered Bath brick, slightly mixed with water; and when this thin coating is perfectly dry it is to be gently removed by the palm of the hand. The effect of this application is to make the hard surface of the wood less slippery than it would otherwise be, and thus capable of affording a *hold* to the point of the black-lead pencil. A mixture of flake white and gum water is occasionally rubbed on the surface with a view of showing off the pencil lines, but this practice is not in favour with the best workmen.

The drawing is placed on the block by the wood-engraver, or by the artist who supplies the sketch of the object. Before beginning his work, the engraver examines as to whether the drawing be entirely or only in part made with a pencil. If it be what is called a *wash* drawing with little more than the outlines in pencil, the action of the breath or the touch of the hand will not be so injurious in effacing it as if altogether done by the pencil; but in any case the block is covered with paper, with the exception of the part being operated upon, to guard against the drawing being rubbed out.

There are only four kinds of tools used in wood-engraving,—gravers, tint-tools, gouges or scoopers, and flat tools or chisels. The graver is principally used for outlining or separating one figure from another; it is very fine at the point, as the line which it cuts ought to be so thin as not to be distinctly perceptible when the cut is printed; and is of different sizes according to the work to be performed. The tint-tools are chiefly used to cut parallel lines, forming an even and uniform *tint*, such as is usually seen in the representation of a clear sky in woodcuts. The other tools are for removing such portions of the wood as are to appear white in the engraving; or the flat tools may be used also for the process of *lowering* the surface in any particular part of the block where this method of engraving may be used. From the manner in which the impression is obtained, it will be apparent that those parts of the block which are not designed to show on the paper should be removed to such a depth as will insure that object.

The securing of a proper tint for the shading is not less necessary to give effect to an engraving than attention to outline, the tinting being further especially adapted to the object to be represented. Thus, the sky is usually represented by straight lines, while clouds will be shown by those that are waved. The rule is, that no lines be introduced without being possessed of an artistic meaning. Delicacy of lining is all very well, but it may be entirely out of place if it be not appropriate to the subject. "Expression," says Flaxman, "engages the attention and excites an interest which compensates for a multitude of defects, whilst the most admirable execution, without a just and lively expression, will be disregarded as laborious inanity, or contemned as an illusory endeavour to impose on the feelings and the understanding. Sentiment gives a sterling value, an irresistible charm, to the rudest imagery, or the most unpractised scrawl. By this quality a firm alliance is formed with the affections in all works of art."

In the progress of wood engraving, when beginning to work in outline, the subjects first attempted are of the most simple kind; and when facility in executing cuts in this style is obtained, those that are slightly shaded may engage attention. The most difficult shading is that of black lines crossing each other. White lines crossing each other are obtained without difficulty, being merely cross shading; but in the case of the black lines every white spot has to be picked out, which is a work of immense labour and great difficulty, as the black lines require to be preserved throughout of uniform thickness, without any break in them. From the supposed impossibility of executing such cross-lines in some of the older wood engravings, it has been conjectured that they were produced in metallic relief; but any speculation of this kind is upset by the fact that many of the old blocks of this class are still in existence; besides, work of this character is now performed by several artists. Nay, we sometimes find that this *cross-hatching*, as it is termed, is introduced where it could well be dispensed with, on the supposition that the excellence of an engraving consists chiefly in the difficulty of its execution—than which there can be no more erroneous idea. Cross-hatchings, properly introduced, undoubtedly improve a subject; some parts of large figures cannot be well represented without their aid, as a series of curved lines on a limb, when not crossed, generally cause it to appear stiff and rigid, whereas, under proper management, it may be made to assume a soft and natural appearance. It has been well observed by a competent authority on this subject, that "as the greatest advantage which wood engraving possesses over copper is the effective manner in which strongly contrasted light and shade can be represented, Rembrandt's etchings, which, like his paintings, are distinguished by the skilful management of the chiaroscuro, form excellent studies for the engraver or designer on wood who would wish to become well acquainted with the capabilities of the art. A delicate woodcut executed in imitation of a smooth steel engraving of 'sober gray' tone, is sure to be tame and insipid; and whenever wood engravers attempt to give to their cuts the appearance of copper or steel plates, and neglect the peculiar advantages of their own art, they are sure to fail, notwithstanding the pains which they may bestow. Their work, instead of being commended as a successful application of the peculiar means of the art, is, in effect, condemned by being regarded as 'a clever *imitation* of a copperplate.'"*

The same writer further observes, that "it but too frequently happens, when works are illustrated with woodcuts, that subjects are chosen which the art cannot successfully represent. Whether the work to be illustrated be matter of fact or fiction, the designer, unless he be acquainted with the capabilities and defects of the art, seldom thinks of making more than a drawing according to his own fancy, and never takes into consideration the means by which it has to be executed. To this inattention may be traced many failures in works illustrated with woodcuts, and for which the engraver is censured, although he may have, with great care and skill, accomplished all that the art could effect. An artist who is desirous that his designs when engraved on wood should appear like *overdone* impressions for steel plates, ought never to be employed

* Jackson's "Treatise on Wood Engraving."

to make drawings for wood engravers: he does not understand the peculiar advantages of the art, and his designs will only have a tendency to bring it into contempt, whilst those who executed them will be blamed for the defects which are the result of his want of knowledge."

### THE PUBLISHING TRADE.

We have described at length the manufacture of paper from the first process in the treatment of the rags to the production of the finished article for the various uses to which it is to be applied. We have also placed before our readers an account of the operation of printing, including composition and press-work; and some details connected with wood engraving and book-binding. We herewith subjoin a brief sketch of the publishing trade, which will not be without interest to many of our readers, more especially as dealing with a class of facts with which the general public are but little acquainted.

Intimately connected with the publishing trade is the question of copyright, or the right of authors to the exclusive privilege of printing and publishing their own works, without which it is manifest that no such thing as literary property could exist. It does not appear that any question of this kind was raised for a length of time after the invention of printing, as in the early stage of the art the demand for books was not so great as to hold out much inducement to reproduce works already in print; and any attempt of this kind was further checked by the early adoption of the licensing system, which placed the printers of those days immediately within the control of the Government authorities. The power of the press was regarded with suspicion by every Government after its invention; and hence the restrictions under which it was placed, and which in some countries are continued to the present day.

By the Licensing Act (13 and 14 Charles II., c. 2), the printing of any book was prohibited by any party, even though licensed, without the consent of the owner, which Act continued in force till 1694. After this, parties whose rights were infringed on were left to have their remedies at common law; but as an author could not obtain redress unless in so far as *damage* could actually be proved, literary property was in a most unsatisfactory position. To remedy this the Statute of the 8 Anne, c. 19, was passed—the first copyright act—by which authors or their assignees were secured the exclusive right of printing their books for fourteen years, with a contingent fourteen years, provided the author were alive at the expiration of the first term; but to obtain the benefit of this Act works must be entered at Stationers' Hall, and hence the origin of the notification which may be so often seen on printed books. The Act in question further provided that copies of all new works should be sent to the Royal Library (now transferred to the British Museum); the libraries of the Universities of Oxford and Cambridge; the libraries of the four Scotch Universities; the library of Sion College, London, and that of the Faculty of Advocates in Edinburgh;—making in all nine copies, for which the author or publisher was taxed. This act, however, only extended to Great Britain, and it was not till 1801 that this country was included in its provisions; a condition of the extension being that copies of all new works should also be sent to the library of Trinity College and to that of King's Inns.

The great defect of the first Copyright Act was the limited period for which it secured exclusive property in literary works. This was amended to some extent by that of 54 Geo. III., c. 156, which extended the duration of all copyrights, whether the authors were dead or alive, to twenty-eight years certain, with the further provision that if the author should happen to be alive at the end of that period he should enjoy the copyright during the residue of his life. After this change was made in the law, it was contended that no valid reason could be given why literary property should not be recognised as permanent, the same as any other kind of property; and hence, repeated demands were made to the Legislature to sanction this principle. On the other hand, it was maintained that the public interests would thereby be sacrificed by the perpetuation of a monopoly; as on the expiration of the copyrights of some of the most valuable works they were produced at a fraction of the price previously charged for them. The result of this agitation of the question was the passing of the Act of 5 and 6 Victoria, c. 45, which extended the duration of all copyrights, whether the authors be dead or alive, to forty-two years certain; and further, that if the author be alive at the end of that period he shall enjoy the copyright till his death, and his heirs or assignees for seven years afterwards.

In the case of expensive works, of which only a small number was published, and more especially in that of richly illustrated works, it was felt to be a great grievance to be obliged to supply eleven copies to public libraries. By the last-mentioned Act the number was reduced to five—the British Museum, the libraries of Oxford and Cambridge, Trinity College, Dublin, and the Faculty of Advocates, Edinburgh. The hall of the Stationers' Company in London is still to contain an entry of all new books, the registry there being open for the inspection of the public.

In the publication of new works, they are brought out at the expense of the author, or the copyright is sold to the publisher; or, as is often the case, author and publisher are to share in the risk or proceeds according to some specific arrangement, and in certain defined proportions. In the first case the work is simply published on commission—that is, the publisher has a commission on the sales; the author in this case bearing all the risk, but being entitled to any profits that may be realized. In the case of the publisher purchasing the copyright, which is the usual practice, the author's interest in the work ceases, unless emendations are required in future editions, for which he is of course to be remunerated. Sometimes one or more editions of a certain number of copies are sold, after which the copyright is to revert to the author.

After a minute calculation has been made of the cost of bringing out a new work, taking into account the probable number which it may be prudent to print, the *selling price* is fixed on. The usual rule of the trade is, that a drawback of 25 per cent. off the selling price should be given to the retail booksellers; and in the case of account between the author and publisher, the latter charges 10 per cent. on the sum which he receives. To the retail trade 25 copies count as 24 if all taken at the same time, and occasionally 13 count as 12. These deductions amount in round numbers to about one-third of the publishing price, leaving the remaining two-thirds to defray cost of production, advertising, and remuneration of author. Of a 12*s.* book, for example, the net price would be about 8*s.*

In determining what is a reasonable allowance for a retail trade, the character of the goods must be taken into account. On those for which there is a constant demand, and which in some degree partake of the character of necessaries, a small profit will suffice; but when a large stock has to be kept up, a portion of which may be uncertain of meeting a demand, and which is, moreover, liable to deterioration, a larger profit will be necessary to cover the increased risk of loss. The stock of a retail bookseller must, for example, be varied; so that taking into account the profits in other branches of trade, the allowance of 25 per cent. is probably not more than the circumstances of the case requires. And in reference to the publishing trade, when all drawbacks are considered, it will be found to be one of an eminently hazardous character; as for one book that succeeds and yields any considerable profit numbers fail to repay the cost of production. In M'Culloch's "Commercial Dictionary" we find it stated, as the result of an investigation on this subject, that of one hundred and thirty works published by an eminent house, fifty had not paid their expenses; of the eighty that did pay thirteen only arrived at a second edition; and in most instances these second editions had not been profitable. In general, according to the same authority, in whose statement we are disposed to fully concur, it may be estimated that of the books published one-fourth do not pay their expenses; and that only one in eight or ten can be reprinted with advantage.

While on this part of the subject we may refer briefly to the injurious operation of taxes on literature even indirectly. The publishing trade, unless in so far as regards school-books and reprints of standard works, is a game of speculation, the prizes in which, even with the greatest care, will fall far short of the blanks. Hence no obstacle should be thrown in the way which tends to make this trade more hazardous than it would otherwise be. It has, moreover, been well remarked, that there is a radical difference between the demand for food for the mind (books) and food for the body. The latter is always sure, under any circumstances, to command a sale. It cannot be dispensed with, and the demand for it is therefore comparatively constant. If a tax be laid on malt, hats, or shoes, it will, perhaps, somewhat lessen the demand for these articles; but the quantities of them brought to market in future will sell for such an advanced price as will leave the customary rate of profit to their producers. But with books the case is altogether different. The taste for them is proverbially capricious; so much so that the most sagacious individuals are every day deceived in their anticipations as to the success of new works, and even as to the sale of new editions. But if a book do not take, it is so very ruinous an affair that a publisher is glad to dispose of the greater part of an impression at a fourth or a fifth part of its regular price; and is often, indeed, obliged to sell it as waste paper. Injurious, therefore, as the Excise duty on paper may be as interfering with freedom of action in carrying on the manufacture, it is not less so in its proximate results on the literature of the day, and the influence which it thereby exercises in checking the progress of education.

In the publishing trade London is the head-quarters, as well as the great mart where the bulk of the trade is carried on. In Edinburgh and Dublin new works are produced not in any way inferior to those got out in the metropolis; but the number so published is inconsiderable, and even of these the great trade is done in London. The metropolitan houses have agents in Edinburgh and Dublin, through whom the retail trade of Scotland and Ireland is supplied. Edinburgh has, however, long maintained a high position as a place of learning, where literature was and is encouraged and produced of a quality not to be surpassed, and in quantity only exceeded by the London trade. The number of new publications and new editions produced in the Scottish capital has for years past been annually on the increase; and many of these are heavy works, involving the outlay of thousands in getting them up. In the printing and publishing trade Glasgow has also of late maintained an honourable position. Through the enterprise of one firm a considerable trade has been done in this line in Belfast of late years. It therefore only requires enterprise to localize this business to some extent; though the head-quarters must be in London.

When describing the operation of printing, it was seen that the cost of a copy of any work, so far as this item is concerned, depends very much on the number of copies struck off. If the entire expense of composition, or setting up the types, is chargeable against a few copies, the cost of each must be considerable; but as we increase the number this item diminishes, until, as in the case of "Chamber's Edinburgh Journal," it may become inappreciable from the very large number over which it is to be distributed. Hence, books with a small circulation must be sold at a comparatively high price to defray the expense of publication. The same remark applies to illustrations of any kind, and to the remuneration for authorship; the cost of production of each copy diminishing as the number of copies is increased. It is through the instrumentality of a very large circulation that such publications as the "Edinburgh Journal" or the "London Journal" can be sold at the inconsiderable price charged for them; or that a publication like the "London News" can be profusely illustrated with engravings at the price of an ordinary newspaper.

The effect of circulation on the publisher's profits will be best illustrated by taking up some work with which the public are familiar, and which appeared only in one form. The latter consideration is very important; as in the case of different editions of the same book having been published the reader may be at a loss as to which of these is referred to. In taking any of the earlier published works of Mr. Lever these conditions are fulfilled; as every one has seen them, and from the unprecedentedly large sale which they met with, they were stereotyped, which prevented the appearance of different sized editions. The whole of these works appeared in the form of shilling numbers, each of which contained two etchings, and comprised two sheets of letter-press, the whole being done up in an ornamented wrapper. In the subjoined calculations the reader will see the position which the publisher, author, and artist would occupy, with the respective sales of 1000, 10,000, and 30,000 copies. This calculation is not pretended to be founded on the actual cost of the works in question; but it may be assumed as that which would now be paid for producing them. It also only applies to a single monthly number:—

COST OF PRODUCING 1000 COPIES OF A MONTHLY NUMBER OF "HARRY LORREQUER."

| | £ | s. | d. |
|---|---|---|---|
| Composition, two sheets, | £3 | 0 | 0 |
| Press-work, | 1 | 4 | 0 |
| Paper, | 2 | 12 | 0 |
| Engraving wrapper, | 10 | 10 | 0 |
| Two etchings, illustrating the narrative, | 14 | 14 | 0 |
| Paper and printing covers, | 0 | 18 | 0 |
| Paper and printing etchings, | 3 | 0 | 0 |
| Stitching and covering, | 0 | 4 | 0 |
| Advertising, say | 15 | 0 | 0 |
| Cost of 1000 copies, | £51 | 2 | 0 |

Allowing 50 copies to be sent for review to magazines and newspapers, which is somewhat under the mark, we shall have 950 copies at 8*d*. net, producing £16 13*s*. 4*d*., as a set off against an expenditure of £51 2*s*., without making any provision for payment of authorship.

COST OF PRODUCING 10,000 COPIES.

| | £ | s. | d. |
|---|---|---|---|
| Composition, | £3 | 0 | 0 |
| Press-work, | 7 | 19 | 0 |
| Engraving for cover and etchings, | 25 | 4 | 0 |
| Paper, | 26 | 0 | 0 |
| Paper and printing covers, | 5 | 10 | 0 |
| Paper and printing etchings, | 30 | 0 | 0 |
| Stitching, &c., | 2 | 0 | 0 |
| Advertising, say | 25 | 0 | 0 |
| Cost of 10,000 copies, | £124 | 13 | 0 |

Allowing 100 copies for gratuitous distribution, 9900 copies remain at 8*d*., which produce £330, leaving a balance of £205 7*s*. for the payment of the author and publisher's profits. Some of Lever's works have, however, had a very large circulation, sometimes reaching, we believe, 30,000 or 40,000. Then, indeed, handsome returns were available for all parties. The following would show the monthly return for 30,000 copies:—

COST OF PRODUCING 30,000 COPIES.

| | £ | s. | d. |
|---|---|---|---|
| Composition, | £3 | 0 | 0 |
| Press-work, | 22 | 19 | 0 |
| Engraving and etchings, | 25 | 4 | 0 |
| Paper and printing covers, | 16 | 10 | 0 |
| Paper and printing etchings, | 90 | 0 | 0 |
| Stitching, | 6 | 0 | 0 |
| Advertising, say | 50 | 0 | 0 |
| Cost of 30,000 copies, | £213 | 13 | 0 |

Deducting 150 copies for gratuitous circulation, there will remain of such an edition 29,850 copies at 8*d*. each, amounting to £995; leaving £781 7*s*., as a fund from which the author is to be paid. Hence, in the case of those works having a large circulation, the literary remuneration is very high, frequently averaging, in the case of such writers as Lever, Dickens, Thackeray, and some others, several thousands of pounds per annum.

In the case of a serial, such as here referred to, it is further to be observed that the engraving for wrapper is only chargeable against the first number.

It will now be seen that it is only in the event of a large circulation being obtained, that an adequate return can be realized. The reason will also be apparent why a certain class of works which, under any circumstances, cannot have a large sale, must be sold at a comparatively high price—such as scientific works, and those generally that are not addressed to the masses.—J. S.

## STATIONERY.

*Black-lead Pencils.*—Most of our readers are, no doubt, aware that black-lead pencils really contain no lead, the name being probably derived from the lead colour which these pencils impart to paper. The essential part of them is composed of *plumbago*, or carburet of iron, a substance which is pretty generally diffused, though it is only found in a few localities of a quality suitable for pencils. The best plumbago is obtained in Cumberland, the pits of which are situated on the Borrowdale Mountains, within a few miles of Keswick. The state of perfection to which the manufacture of pencils has now been brought is truly surprising. One mechanical contrivance after another has been introduced with a view of lessening the cost of production, until this branch of industry, at the present day, may be regarded as a good illustration of the progress of the age. In the several processes of cutting up the timber, of preparing it for the plumbago, and finishing it off, much ingenuity is displayed. The division of labour is carried out to a great extent, and some of the manufactories are leviathian establishments, turning out quantities of these pencils annually, which, to those unacquainted with the trade, appear prodigious. In the selection of the plumbago, great attention is requisite, so that there may be uniformity of character; and the determination of the quality is of importance, so that the different kinds may have the proper letters put on them, according to the purposes for which they are designed. By increased attention to the purification of the plumbago, and, to a certain extent, by the admixture of other substances, pencils have of late beed produced at considerably reduced prices.

Among the more remarkable improvements or inventions in this manufacture, we may notice the use of plumbago, in the form of small cylinders patented by the late Mr. Mordan; and the compression of the dust of plumbago, which has been patented by Mr. Brockendon, and which imparts to what would otherwise be comparatively worthless, nearly the same firmness and quality as when in its original state in the mines. These inventions were adequately represented in the Exhibition. Indeed, the cylinders of plumbago have come into such general use, that the public are now perfectly familiar with them.

*Envelopes.*—The manufacture of envelopes is a comparatively recent branch of business in the United Kingdom, brought into existence by the penny postage. Previous to 1839, any letter passing through the post-office at a single rate of postage must not only be under a certain specified weight, but it must also only comprise a single sheet of paper, the smallest enclosure being chargeable with double postage. What is called "letter paper" was then in general use, as meeting the postal regulations better than any other. While, therefore, the use of envelopes had been common in France at the period referred to, it was confined in these countries to official persons and members of Parliament, who had the privilege of franking—franks being tested by weight alone, irrespective of their contents. After the adoption of the penny postage, envelopes gradually came into use; and some idea may be formed of the impetus given to their manufacture, as well as to the consumption of stationery generally, by that measure, when it is stated that before the penny postage the number of letters passing through the post-office was 26,000,000 per annum; and in 1850 it had increased to 347,000,000; a surprising rate of progress in the comparatively short space of ten years. Of the entire quantity of letters transmitted by post, upwards of five-sixths are enclosed in envelopes.

The machine invented by Hill and De la Rue, which was for some months employed folding envelopes, was amongst the most attractive objects in the Exhibition, from the unfailing regularity with which it performed its work, and the beauty of its action. This invention was the first important step in this branch of business, which had hitherto been carried on solely by the hand; a book-binder's folding-stick being used for the purpose, with which, however, the most experienced workwomen could scarcely exceed 3000 envelopes per day. By the aid of a machine of this kind, the pieces of paper have only to be cut to the proper size (which is effected by machinery), and on being supplied by an attendant, they are turned out folded, gummed, and stamped. A degree of accuracy is obtained wholly impracticable by hand labour; and economy of production is carried to an extent of which it is difficult to form a conception. Hill and De la Rue's machine is capable of turning out work at the rate of 2700 envelopes per hour.

*Sealing-Wax and Wafers.*—We who are in the full enjoyment of cheap paper and the penny post, and who can write to our friends upon the most minute trifle, can well appreciate the progress of the world from the time when a letter consisted of a sheet of sheepskin or a tablet of lead, inclosed in a box secured with an immense seal impressed upon earth or cement! It is impossible to say when wax was substituted for clay in making seals, but it must have been at a very early period. At first, the ordinary yellow bees' wax was employed, but gradually it became usual to colour it red and brown, and even in the fourteenth century green and black. The next improvement in sealing letters is the substitution of what we call sealing-wax for ordinary bees' wax, which appears to have taken place in the early part of the sixteenth century; at all events the oldest seal now known of true sealing-wax dates from 1554, and was used upon a letter from one Gerard Hermann, the agent in London of Philip Francis Von Daun, Count Palatine of the Rhine, to that prince. The knowledge of the art of making sealing-wax, or rather perhaps the wax itself, appears to have been introduced into England and France from Spain, and into the latter country from Genoa or Venice: hence the name by which it was formerly known of Spanish wax.

The manufacture of sealing-wax is extremely simple, consisting in making a mixture of shel lac, Venetian turpentine, and some colouring matter, by fusion, and either casting it in polished marble moulds or rolling out a soft mass on a flat table gently heated, and cutting it of the required size. Each stick is polished by heating it gently over a small charcoal fire and rubbing it with a woollen rag and a small quantity of fine tallow. The best red wax is usually made of 4 parts of the finest shel lac, 3 parts of vermillion, and 1 part of Venetian turpentine. Another receipt is:—Turpentine, 7 oz.; shel lac, 18 oz.; rosin, 1 oz.; vermillion, 11 oz.; camphor or balsam of Peru, 1 oz. We need scarcely remark that these proportions merely represent what good wax should be composed of; but in practice, the dearer articles are frequently replaced to a certain extent by cheaper materials,—the lac by rosin, powdered crystallized gypsum, &c.,—and the vermilion by red lead, &c. The sticks of inferior sealing-wax thus made are, however, *gilded*, that is, covered with a coating of fine wax, so as to give them a superior appearance. This operation is thus performed:—When the workman is polishing the sticks, he heats them as already mentioned, dips them into some fine powder of the best sealing-wax, some of which attaches itself to the surface; after which the stick is again heated over the fire, and thus a varnish of the fine wax is spread over the surface.

Coloured waxes are made by substituting for the vermillion different colouring materials. Perfumed wax is usually made by adding a little of the tincture of musk or other perfumes to the mixture while in a fluid state, before solidifying; and wax which, when burning in the sealing of a letter, emits a perfume like pastilles, is usually mixed with camphor, balsam of Peru, or tincture of benzoin. A little camphor is, indeed, generally added to all good sealing-wax.

Wafers are of still more modern use than sealing wax. They consist of a paste of the finest flour, which is mixed with various colouring matters according to the colour intended to be given to them, and is then pressed in a kind of mould formed of two plates of iron, which fit together and are held so, like a pair of tongs. This tongs is then heated at the same time that the handles are kept tightly pressed together; in this way a thin sheet of hardened paste is produced, out of which the different sized wafers are punched, much in the same way that gun-wadding is made. The dark red colour of ordinary wafers is given by vermillion; the pale rose or lake red by a decoction of Brazil wood mixed with alum or with tincture of cochineal; the yellow is obtained by a decoction of Persian berries, or a tincture or infusion in spirit of turmeric roots, or of saffron; the blue by Prussian blue; and the green by a mixture of yellow and blue, or by verdigris; the latter mode being very dangerous, as all the salts of copper are poisonous.

Sealing-wax and wafers have been superseded to a great extent, of late years, by the introduction of adhesive envelopes; in England, however, the majority of the men of business adhere to the old style, and hence there is still considerable demand for both articles, but it is easy to foresee that in time they will almost disappear. There were two exhibiters of sealing-wax and wafers in the Exhibition, namely Waterston, of Edinburgh, and Cooke and Son, of London, whose products were very good, especially their red wax, which is always well made in these countries, but we cannot say that any of the fancy articles for ladies' use which we have seen are equal to what is produced in Germany or Paris. Our only Irish manufacturers of these articles, Messrs. Rathborne, who exhibited so largely in wax and spermaceti, did not contribute any specimens of sealing-wax and wafers. This is the more to be regretted as it appears that these manufactures have been carried on in Dublin by members of that family uninterruptedly for a period of at least 150 years—that is, in fact since they began to come into general use in Europe.

*Pens.*—Among the collections in this department, those illustrative of the manufacture of metallic pens cannot fail to attract attention; and this branch of industry was, moreover, amply illustrated. The mere fact of the house of Gillott, of Birmingham, and Perry, of London, being exhibiters, would of itself be a guarantee that every recent improvement, and every variety of the pen in common use, would be found in the Exhibition. Steel pens have been extensively used for a great number of years, and in the production of any article consumed in such quantity as pens of this kind necessarily are, there must be a large trade. We cannot here enter into the statistics or progress of this branch of manufacture; but we may state that its growth has been quite marvellous. The quantity turned out by a single establishment almost exceeds belief. From the action of the ink on the steel pen it is possessed of no great durability, but to compensate for this, it is produced at a cheap rate. The steel pens, however, under any circumstances, want the pliability and softness of the quill; and, to attain this, gold has been used of late with perfect success. The expense of the gold pen is to a considerable extent counterbalanced by its great durability, as not being chemically acted upon by the ink, a pen of this kind will, under careful treatment, last for an almost indefinite period. The unequal wearing of the nibs or any injury arising from accident may also be easily repaired. It is, therefore, only necessary to select a pen to suit the hand of the writer, to insure a gold pen being used with almost the same freedom as the quill. In addition to the highly interesting collections of pens of all kinds exhibited by Messrs. Gillott and Perry, there were some novelties contributed by M. Myers and Sons, of Birmingham, among which we may notice the adaptation of gold points to the common quill pen. With a view of securing a more durable point than that composed of gold, and at the same time of guarding against the chemical action of the ink which is so injurious in the case of the steel pen, gold pens have been pointed with the native alloy of irridium and osmium, the hardest metals known; specimens of which were exhibited by W. E. Wiley and Co., of Birmingham. But while estimating, as they deserve, the contributions of these eminent manufacturers, we have satisfaction in being able to direct attention to a collection which, in some respects, was not surpassed by any of those mentioned,—we allude to that of J. Martin, of this city, whose stand illustrated the progress of the manufacture from the first process, after the piece of metal is taken up to be converted into a pen, until the article is completed. This contribution to the Exhibition was really possessed of more than ordinary interest; and we can scarcely doubt that from the manner in which Mr. Martin came forward on that occasion, he will not rest satisfied with simply producing a good article, and rely upon the so-called patriotism of his countrymen to support him, but he will make it their interest to do so, by successfully competing with the other houses in the trade.

The miscellaneous articles of stationery do not require any lengthened notice. Lace paper, papetrie of different kinds, and fancy borderings, have but a comparatively limited demand. In playing-cards, however, a considerable trade is carried on; so important, in fact, as to be made a source of revenue, their production being under the surveillance of the Commissioners of Inland Revenue. The cities of London, Westminster, and Dublin, are the only places where the manufacture can be carried on in the United Kingdom; each pack of cards being charged with a duty of one shilling. The aces, on which the duty is assessed, are printed at Somerset House on paper furnished by the card-makers, who have also to pay thirty pounds for every ace plate which they may require. Every card manufacturer is further obliged to obtain two securities, in £500 each, before a license can be obtained. The amount of revenue derived from this source is about £12,000 per annum.

---

1. ADAIR, R., & Co., Maryport, Cumberland, Manufacturers.—Specimens of black lead for pencils, and of improved composition, cleansed and purified; illustrations of the several processes of pencil-making; saws; rounding machines, &c.; pencil drawings in various shades, showing the different qualities of the pencils.

2. APPEL, R., Gerrard-street, Soho, London, Inventor.—Specimens of anastatic and appelotype printing, showing the original engraving or printing, the zinc matrix, and the copy printed therefrom.

3. BANKS, SON, & Co., Keswick, Cumberland, Manufacturers.—Black lead pencils; and illustrations of the processes of the manufacture.

4. BATESON, S., King's Bench Walk, Temple, London, Proprietor.—Specimens of anti-acid and anti-anastatic paper (Glynn and Appel's patent) for prevention of forgery by the anastatic process, manufactured by Charles Venables, Jun.

5. BAXTER, G., Northampton-square, London, Inventor, Patentee, and Publisher.—Frame containing specimens of oil-colour picture printing, being fac-similes of the original paintings.

6. BELLEW, G., Grafton-street, Dublin, Manufacturer.—Bookbinding in its various branches, exhibited in about 200 volumes of modern authors, and 50 volumes of illustrated books; legers, and other account books; paintings on vellum, &c.

7. BESLEY & Co., Fann-street, London.—Specimens of modern printing types of various kinds; a specimen of the Elizabethan character, first introduced by them. This character was registered in 1849.

8. BETTS, J., London, Inventor.—Betts' improved educational maps; interrogatory maps, with book of exercises; railway, and commercial, and tourists' maps; London modern atlas; geographical slates; dissected games and puzzles, &c.

9. BINGLEY, M., Lawrence Pountney-lane, City, London, Inventor and Manufacturer.—Patent headbands for bookbinding, made by machine.

10. BOUSQUET, I., Redcross-street, London, Manufacturer.—Burnished gold paper embossed, for paper stainers; patterns of embossed gold and silver borders; plain and flocked gold and silver papers; foil papers.

11. BROOKMAN & LANGDON, Great Russell-street, Bloomsbury, London, Manufacturers.—Fine drawing pencils.

12. CALDWELL, M., South Frederick-street, Dublin, Manufacturer.—Specimens of bookbinding.

13. CHAMBERS, J. & SON, Dame-street, Dublin, Manufacturers.—Account-books and stationery cases, of Irish material and manufacture.

14. COE, J., Bank of England, London, Producer.—Bank cheque, printed by letter-press (electro-type blocks), or surface printing.

15. COMMISSIONERS OF NATIONAL EDUCATION IN IRELAND.—Set of books published by the Commissioners, and used in the Irish National Schools; a set of books not published, but sanctioned, by the Commissioners of National Education in Ireland, for use in the Irish National Schools.

16. COOKE, J. & SONS, Cannon-street, London, Manufacturers.—Sealing wax and medallion wafers.

17. COULTER, W., Synge-street, Dublin, Inventor.—Map of London, with movable index.

18. COWAN & Co., London, Edinburgh, and D'Olier-street, Dublin, Manufacturers.—Writing, drawing, and printing papers of various qualities; envelopes; account books in various rulings and bindings, the pages numbered by machinery.

19. DUFFY, J., Wellington-quay, Dublin, Publisher.—Roman Catholic works, and other books relating to Ireland, printed in Dublin, in rich binding, designed and executed in exhibiter's establishment.

20. FAIRBAIRN, R., Great Cambridge-street, Hackney-road, London, Manufacturer.—Specimens of wooden type for printing, &c.

21. FERGUSON, BROTHERS, Edinburgh, Manufacturers.—Specimens of the Aldine series of new book and newspaper types.

22. FITZGERALD, J., Dawson-street, Dublin.—Specimens of plain and ornamental penmanship, consisting of the eight beatitudes in a variety of hands; illustrated with figures of King David playing on a psaltery in the midst of a wooded landscape, the infant Samuel praying, and Saints Peter and Paul; with a variety of scroll-work and embellishments.

23. FLEMING, A. B., & Co., Leith, Manufacturers.—Specimens of printing with the Scottish printing ink, black and coloured.

24. FORSTER and Co., Crow-street, Dublin, Designers and Manufacturers.—Specimens of lithographic printing in colours.

25. FOWLE, THOMAS LLOYD, Amesbury, Wiltshire, Proprietor.—Music composed by exhibiter.

26. GILL, M. H., University Press, Dublin.—Various volumes of books in 4to and 8vo, printed in the English, Latin, Greek, Hebrew, Oriental, and Irish languages. Specimens of illustrated and scientific printing.

27. GILLOT, JOSEPH, Birmingham, Inventor and Manufacturer.—Specimens of metallic pens and holders, in gold, steel, silver, &c.

28. GOODALL & SON, Camden-town, London, Manufacturers.—Specimens of playing cards.

29. HANHART, M. & N., Charlotte-street, Rathbone-place, London, Producers.—Specimens of lithography and chromo-lithography.

30. HAWTHORNE, J., Charrington-street, St. Pancras, London, Manufacturer.—Specimens of wood sponged over with an admixture of ink to match paint; samples of ink of various colours and descriptions; evaporated ink forming a varnish for shoes.

31. HIBERNIAN BIBLE SOCIETY, Sackville-street, Dublin, Importers and Producers.—120 specimens of the Holy Scriptures in different languages (the property of Wilbraham Taylor, Esq., of Hadley Hurst, Barnet, Middlesex, who kindly lent them for exhibition). A selection from 175 versions of the Bible, in whole or in part published by the British and Foreign Bible Society, which since its institution in 1804 has circulated upwards of twenty-five millions of copies.

32. HOLDEN, W., Dublin, Manufacturer.—Specimens of printed music; letter-press printing; and stereotype casts.

33. INDUSTRIAL PRINTING SCHOOL, BONMAHON, established 1851, by the Rev. David A. Doudney, Curate of Monksland, Co. Waterford.—Dr. Gill's Commentary on the Holy Bible. Four volumes of this work have been printed at this school since its establishment in the above obscure village. Upwards of twenty tons of paper have been consumed; and the whole (comprising nearly four thousand pages) has been composed by boys varying from ten to fifteen years of age, who previously had never seen a printing type.

34. LUNTLEY, JOHN, New Broad-street Court, London, Manufacturer.—Patent ticket receipt till-book, for checking receipts of money by shopmen; frames for holding maps, pocket-cases; glazed show bill.

35. MAGUIRE, J., Dublin, Proprietor.—Hudson's Bay swan, Russian, Irish, duck, and crow quills and pens.

36. MANSELL, J., Red Lion-square, London, Designer and Manufacturer.—Illuminated and embossed ornamental wrappers for linens, damasks, &c.; perforated and embossed ornaments and tickets for muslins, woollens, &c; satin damask writing papers, on which, by a patented process, pictorial illustrations are produced in alternate dull and glazed surfaces; ornamental writing papers in imitation of lace, embroidery, &c.; wedding stationery and valentines.

37. MARTIN, J., City-quay, Dublin, Manufacturer.—Steel pens, made in Ireland; and specimens showing the process of manufacture.

38. M'DERMOTT, E., & Co., Arran-quay, Dublin, Manufacturers.—Printing and writing inks of various kinds.

39. M'DONNELL, J., & Co., Swift Brook Paper Mills, Co. Dublin, Manufacturers.—Papers: blue laid medium large blue and bank post; blue laid and cream laid foolscaps; cream posts; music paper; a roll of paper 2000 feet long by five feet wide.

40. MORRIS, J. P., Sandymount-road, Dublin.—Manuscript chronological charts of the history of England, Ireland, &c., illuminated.

41. MYERS, M., & SON, Newhall-street, Birmingham, Inventors and Manufacturers.—Steel pens; quill pen holders, and cylindrical spring pen holders (registered); patent metallic pointed quill pens; patent axiseary pens; pens and pen holders made in gold, silver, and other metals.

42. MUIR, R., Dunlop-street, Glasgow.—Improved composition for letter-press printers' rollers; and specimens of

printing from gutta percha plate, made from woodcuts by exhibiter.

43. NEWBERRY, J. & R., Hemlock-court, Carey-street, Lincoln's-Inn Fields, London, Manufacturers.—Specimens of gold, silver, and coloured foil papers, plain and embossed; coloured glazed papers; gold and silver borders; fancy papers in variety; screen handles; fancy coloured tissue and marble papers.

44. NIXEY, G. W., Moor-street, Soho, London.—Specimens of compressed plumbago for pencils.

45. NORRIS, Miss, Clara, King's County.—A map of Great Britain, in penmanship, with an elaborate border.

46. NOVELLO, J. A., Dean-street, Soho, and Poultry, London, and Broadway, New York, Manufacturer.—Specimens of musical and other typography; ornamental title-pages.

47. PERRY, J. & Co., Red Lion-square, London, Manufacturers.—Gold and steel pens, and patent pen holders.

48. PLOWMAN, J., Aldgate-street, London.—Books and stationery.

49. POWELL, J. H., Westmoreland-street, Dublin.—Bibles, prayer books, and church services in rich bindings; maps of Ireland, &c., engraved by Kirkwood (of Dublin), and printed on satin, calico, cards, &c.; Cellarius' ancient maps, on satin, calico, and paper; view and plan of the Exhibition Building, in gold, on gelatine, &c.; guide-books; specimens of stationery, and steel and copperplate engravings, &c.

50. REED & PARDON, Paternoster-row, London, Producers.—Specimens of letter press printing from English and foreign types.

51. REEVES & SONS, Cheapside, London.—Boxes of water colours; Cumberland lead drawing pencils, and other materials for the use of artists.

52. ROWNEY & Co., Rathbone-place, London, Inventors, Printers, and Publishers.—Frames containing specimens of typo-chromatic printing, or fac-simile water colour drawings.

53. RYAN, W. & E., Merchant's-quay, Dublin, Manufacturers.—Paper made from straw.

54. SAUNDERS, T. H., London, Manufacturer.—Best Kent hand and machine-made account book; drawing and letter papers; bank-note and patent cheque papers, plain and water-marked; loan or parchment paper; a transparency, showing specimens of ornamental water-marks used for prevention of frauds.

55. SETON, R., Edinburgh, Designer and Manufacturer.—Imitation of the illuminated books of the middle ages, bound in yellow Morocco, &c.

56. SLATER, I., Fountain-street, Manchester, and Fleet-street, London.—Slater's General Directory of the United Kingdom, and British Atlas; union map of England and Wales; plan of Manchester; travelling maps of Ireland and Scotland; new coin table of all coins now circulating in the world, mounted on rollers, &c.

57. STEPHENS, H., Stamford-street, Blackfriars-road, London, Manufacturer.—Specimens of liquid colours for staining woods, and of woods stained therewith; liquid colours for writing purposes, &c.; specimens of newly invented pencils and rulers.

58. STEPHENSON, BLAKE, & Co., Sheffield, Manufacturers.—Specimens of printing types:—A new script, or writing charactor; and a series of old English types; specimen books of types; borders and other ornamental designs for fancy printing.

59. TODD, J., Perth, Manufacturer.—Specimens of office, copying, and other inks, black, red, and blue; ink powder, &c.

60. VAN VOORST, J., Paternoster-row, London, Proprietor.—Books published by exhibiter, and richly bound by Hayday and Clarke, and Bedford.

61. WATERSON, G., Edinburgh, Manufacturer.—Samples of Great Exhibition prize medal sealing wax, in great variety, for home and foreign use; wax used for the great seal of Scotland, and other official seals; wafers, &c.

62. WEBB & CHAPMAN, Great Brunswick-street, Dublin.—Specimens of books printed by exhibiters.

63. WIGHTMAN, W. M'CLEARY, Nassau-street, Dublin.—Artists' oil and water colours; sable, camel, and hog-hair brushes; sketch books; tracing paper; graduated scraping tinted tablets.

64. WILEY, W. E., & Co., Great Hampton-street, Birmingham, Manufacturers.—Card of gold pens, pointed with the native alloy of iridium and osmium, the hardest of known metals.

65. WISEHEART, J., Suffolk-street, Dublin, Proprietor.—Specimens of engraving; die sinking in colours, &c.; painted arms, crests, &c.; Berlin work patterns; specimens of lithographic and music printing; album binding; fancy stationery; valentines, &c.

66. WREN, ABRAHAM, Keswick, Manufacturer.—Black lead pencils; specimens of pure Cumberland lead; compressed lead.

# CLASSES XVIII. & XIX.

## TAPESTRY, CARPETS AND FLOOR-CLOTHS, LACE AND EMBROIDERY, AND FABRICS SHOWN AS SPECIMENS OF PRINTING OR DYEING.

THE articles included in these two classes comprise a great variety of goods; the production of some of which, moreover, is extensively carried on in this country, and they are, therefore, invested with a degree of local interest. But though we have our "Irish carpet warehouses," and our "Irish cloth halls," neither carpets nor superfine cloths are manufactured here. In the production of the coarser kinds of rugs some persons are employed in this city, but the weaving of carpets is literally unknown in Ireland, the entire supply being imported. Of floor-cloths we believe that there are only two Irish manufacturers, and neither of these work on an extensive scale. Of lace and embroidery, however, the manufacture has recently been extended over almost the whole country; and further progress is being made in these branches of industry every succeeding season, to the great advantage of the female population, to whom employment is thereby afforded; and hence in this department the exhibiters were numerous, including all ranks, from the lady of title to the poorest of the peasantry employed by some of our local charitable institutions. Of printed and dyed fabrics shown as such, irrespective of texture or the material of which they were composed, there were few illustrations. This branch of trade is besides of little local importance.

### TAPESTRY, CARPETS, AND FLOOR-CLOTHS.

The production of tapestry and carpeting, like other branches of textile manufacture, is of Eastern origin, the fabrics of this class being rendered peculiarly necessary in Eastern countries by the habits of the people. In former times we were indebted to Turkey and Persia for the finer kinds of carpets: but even the best of these have been for some time past successfully imitated in Britain. Indeed the French, Belgian, and British goods of this class of the present day excel in quality and general effect the richest specimens of Eastern manufacture. In France, especially, this branch of industry has long enjoyed the favour of the Crown, a royal manufactory being founded for its development, which has been carried on up to the present time.* To

* THE GOBELIN TAPESTRY.—Most of our readers are probably aware that in France, and in some other continental countries, the State maintains one or two factories for the manufacture of articles in which great scientific skill is conjoined with artistic ability of the highest order. Of this kind are the celebrated porcelain manufactory of Sevres, and the equally celebrated tapestry factory of the "Gobelins." In these countries the idea of the State meddling in trade is considered repugnant to all laws of political economy; an opinion which, although we are inclined to agree with in the main, admits of some exceptions. If a Government undertook to make shoes or any other article of common use, which could be equally well made by any trader, we would naturally condemn such a proceeding. But if, on the other hand, we could find some manufactures in which the articles were of so expensive and peculiar a nature that it would be hopeless to expect that they would become articles of general consumption, and therefore not likely to be produced by private enterprise, and which, on the other hand, would require for their production a considerable development of mechanical, chemical, and artistic skill, which would be available for the use of the nation in many other branches of manufacture, the case would be different. Such are the manufactures of the Gobelins; for no person who examines the beautiful products of that establishment will come to any other conclusion than that, except as curiosities, they are of little use. How, then, our readers may ask, can we show that the manufacture of curiosities is a proper application of the funds of a nation? Simply thus: to produce a piece of tapestry requires, in the first place, the highest possible skill in the preparation of the wool, in its purification, bleaching, and above all its dyeing; and, in the next place, an equally high degree of artistic education in adapting the materials to the reproduction of the pictures intended to be copied. The Gobelins must, therefore, be a school of design and of chemistry applied to dyeing; and that France has benefited by this school is evident by the immense superiority which she has attained in these branches of industry over every other nation. It is from this point of view that we specially value the Gobelins, and judged on this ground, we believe the enormous sums spent in France in its support for more than two centuries are now being repaid with interest to the nation.

The building called the Gobelins is situate in a quartier of Paris celebrated in the annals of the first revolution as the Faubourg St. Marceau. Through this district flows, or rather used to flow, for it is now enclosed in a canal of stone, and shut up by sluices, the small river Bievre, which in former times enjoyed a reputation for dyeing scarlet, which it certainly does not now deserve, being gradually considered a nuisance at present from the exhalations of its stagnant water. This traditional reputation, however, brought to its banks a family of dyers from Rheims, the chief of whom was Jean Gobelin. This was about the end of the fifteenth century, for Jean and his son Philibert lived there in the time of Rabelais, who says, "and it is this brook which from here passes to St. Victor on which Gobelin dyes the scarlet." Gradually their descendants became wealthy, and at length renounced trade, purchased patents of nobility, and intermarried with the families of the magistracy. One of these, Antoine Gobelin, Marquis de Bris-

form a just conception of the manufacture, one should in fact visit the royal establishment of the Gobelins at Paris, some of the products of which excited so much attention at the late Exhibition.

Carpeting is essentially of two classes, under one or other of which the numerous varieties of the articles in use may be included. In the first, or common kinds of carpets, the warp and weft appear on the surface, both being composed of the same material. Of this class the Kidderminster carpet may be regarded as the

villiers, married in 1651 Marie Marguerite d'Aubrai, daughter of the Civil Lieutenant of Paris, who became so notorious afterwards in the annals of crime by the poisoning of her whole family.

When the Gobelins retired from business they sold their establishment to the Sieurs Canaye, who, in addition to the trade of dyeing, set up a manufactory of tapestry of haute lisse or high warp. At that time Flanders was celebrated for its tapestry, which was exported to different countries, one of the chief seats of which at one time was Andernaerde, several specimens of which were, singularly enough, in the late Exhibition. To the family of Canaye succeeded a dyer of the name of Gluck, whose family continued in possession until the time of Colbert, minister of Louis XIV., who purchased the house properly called the Gobelins, whilst the family of Gluck, in conjunction with another named Julienne, carried on the trade of dyer in the adjoining buildings down to the commencement of the present century.

It will be seen that the manufacture of tapestry was at first altogether carried on by private enterprise, and continued to be so until the reign of Francis I. That monarch, to whom France owes so much in an artistic point of view, brought together the best workmen in tapestry to be found at that time in France, in Italy, or Flanders, the countries where the trade was best understood, and established them at Fontainebleau, under the direction of one Salomon de Herbaines. Here he provided them with abundance of the richest materials, such as gold, silver, and silk threads, and a number of admirable pieces were executed after designs by an Italian artist, named Francesco Primatticio, pupil of Giulio Romano. Francis I. also purchased the best pieces of tapestry made by private manufacturers, so that this kind of manufacture was in a most flourishing condition during his reign. His successor, Henry II., continued to maintain the establishment at Fontainebleau, which was placed under the direction of the distinguished artist, Phillibert de Lorme. Then came the wars of the League, during which, as in all civil and religious struggles, the trade of the country languished, and that of tapestry altogether ceased, for neither the court nor the nobles could afford to devote money to any other purpose than the payment of troops. As soon, however, as Henry IV. was firmly seated upon the throne, and that peace was re-established (towards the year 1600), he set about the organization of factories for the manufacture of furniture and of all kinds of ornaments for his palaces. He established his tapestry workers in a house in the Faubourg St. Antoine, in Paris. Here he collected a number of the best painters, engravers, carvers in gold, silver, and ivory, and sculptors, to whom he added 200 tapestry workers from Italy and Flanders. Henry was carried off prematurely in the midst of his projects for the re-establishment of the industry and art of France; and unfortunately he left in his son, Louis XIII., a successor quite incapable to realize them, who, or rather his celebrated minister Richelieu, however, established a carpet manufactory at Chaillot, near Paris, in some buildings which had been employed in the manufacture of soap, from whence the establishment since become so celebrated has derived the name of "La Savonnerie." Owing to the state of France at that period the manufacture languished, and was almost extinguished during the long wars of the Fronde and other troubles during the minority of Louis XIV. As soon, however, as the latter monarch assumed the reins of government, he endeavoured to organize the commerce and manufactures of the nation. A royal factory was established at Beauvais for the manufacture of tapestry, under the direction of Hinart; the Savonnerie was placed under the direction of the celebrated painter Le Brun, and the children of the hospitals were there trained in the manufacture of various woollen fabrics, by Phillipe Lourdet, at that time distinguished as a tapestry worker and carpet weaver. Even the private factories of Felletin and of Aubusson were provided with a dyer and a painter at the expense of the Government. These factories are now in the possession of M. Sallandrouze de Lamornaix, in whose family we believe they were at that period also, and were represented in the Exhibition by a fine series of carpets, portières, upholstery, tapestry, &c. second only in execution to perhaps the productions of La Savonnerie. The efforts of the Government were soon crowned with success, and the manufactures of France became in a few years the most flourishing in Europe. In order to still further contribute to their advancement, the King determined to found a model factory in which he might concentrate the highest degree of talent in the nation; not for the purpose of exposing private enterprise to a disproportionate competition, but, by serving as an example to artisans, to elevate the whole taste of the nation. It was with this intention he established in the house of the Gobelins his celebrated "Manufacture Royalle des Meubles de la Coronne," or, Royal Manufactory of the Furniture of the Crown, since better known as the Manufactory of the Gobelins. It was not, however, a simple factory of tapestry that Louis XIV. established; it was a great workshop, under the direction of Le Brun the painter, having at least 250 tapestry workers continually employed in executing pieces after his design, the wool being dyed by one of the most celebrated dyers of the period. Then there were sculptors in metal, and goldsmiths, by whom were executed torch-holders, candelabra, brackets, inlaid and applied ornaments, cast or chiselled in silver, gold, bronze, or gilded copper, designed in unison with the tapestry. Cabinet makers and carvers in wood and ivory constructed the furniture,* whilst Florentine artists, under the direction of Ferdinand de Melini, inlaid them with marbles, agates, and lapis lazuli, representing fruits, flowers, and birds, which are still so much admired by all who visit the Palace of Versailles. Even the very hinges and locks of the doors of Louis XIV.'s palaces were made after designs executed at the Gobelins, under the direction of the universal Le Brun. The effects of the factory were soon perceptible in the impulse given to the application of design in all the manufactures of France, which ultimately gave to that country the empire of the world in matters of taste as applied to the wants of life.

The direction of Le Brun, which lasted from 1667 until 1690, was the epoch of the greatest prosperity of the Gobelins. He was succeeded by Pierre Mignard, one of the most distinguished painters of France, many of whose works adorn the Louvre and the palace of Versailles; and under whom it continued to prosper, until the great disasters which befel France towards the end of the reign of Louis XIV. forced the king to reserve his resources for the defence of the country, and to dismiss the greater part of the workmen. On the re-establishment of peace some encouragement was given to the Gobelin, but its splendour was gone, and from that time forward it became a mere manufactory of tapestry.

During the first revolution the Gobelins was naturally neglected. Louis Philippe was, however, a great patron of the Gobelins. Some very fine works were executed for him, such as the copy of Horace Vernet's Massacre of the Mamelukes, which was at the London Exhibition of "'51." The fine hangings representing the Marriage of Francis I., and other scenes from the life of that monarch, after pictures of Rubens in the Louvre, and which are in the Chateau of St. Cloud, were either made or at least begun under the Restoration.—W. K. S.

* One of the most celebrated cabinet makers of Europe, at a somewhat later period, named M. de Boule, was also for many years employed at the Gobelins. The kind of work termed *Buhl-work* was first introduced by him.

type; though of this kind there are now several varieties depending on the quality of the raw material and the peculiar process employed in the manufacture. In the other class of carpeting the warp only is seen, its binding weft being strong hempen or linen threads. To the latter class belong the Brussels and the several kinds of velvet pile carpeting. In weaving Brussels carpeting the worsted yarn forming the warp is raised in loops so as to form the pile and make the figures for the desired pattern; and the chief distinction between this and the Wilton carpeting, and other allied varieties is, that in the former case the loop is merely drawn up without being cut, while in the latter it is cut and dressed off as in the manufacture of velvet. The texture of the carpeting depends in the first place on the quality of the material employed, and in the next on its closeness and the length at which it is dressed off. In the one class of carpeting the pattern is the same on both sides, the colours being simply reversed: in the other the lower side appears a close hempen or linen fabric, in which the worsted forming the upper side does not appear.

The names by which the different kinds of carpeting are now distinguished have little reference to the places where they are produced. Thus the weaving of Brussels carpets is much more extensively carried on in Kidderminster than that of the peculiar kind which bears its name. The manufacture of Brussels carpets was introduced there over ninety years ago by workmen brought from Tourney; and up to a recent period it has been steadily progressing. At present it employs about 2000 looms in Kidderminster. In the neighbourhood of Glasgow, Kilmarnock, Bannockburn, and Aberdeen, the weaving of Kidderminster carpeting is extensively carried on; and it is also made in Yorkshire, Durham, Lincolnshire, and Westmoreland, the largest carpet factory in Great Britain being at Halifax. Of the new kinds of carpeting which have been brought under the notice of the public, we may mention the patent Axminster and Whytock's patent tapestry,—in both of which a rich appearance is secured at a less cost than was hitherto attainable. While the Turkey and some other kinds of carpeting are only available to the wealthy, the improvement that has of late been effected in the manufacture of the cheaper kinds has been truly astonishing. Carpet weaving is now extensively carried on by the aid of steam-power, which has still further tended to reduce the cost of production, thereby leading to an increased demand. The rate of progress in the different branches of this manufacture, for years past, has only been inferior to that in cotton; and not only has the home consumption vastly increased, but new markets have been opened up, and the former ones have been greatly extended.

Whatever may be the quality of the material, or the method of manufacture, to give due effect to either, the character of the ornamentation must be studied; as it is beyond question that many highly finished and fine carpets are rendered ineffective by inattention to this particular. The manufacturer seeks of course to please the taste of the consumer, but this might be attended to without sacrificing the conventional rules in such matters to the extent which we see done every day. The general diffusion of more correct notions on the subject of art than have hitherto prevailed will provide a remedy for this; but in bringing about such a change the manufacturers might advantageously appear in the van instead of following in the wake.

The extent to which this branch of industry was represented in the Exhibition was inconsiderable; and of the specimens exhibited there were few, if any, calling for any special remark. We may observe, however, that the mechanical execution was generally superior to the character of the ornamentation. This was rendered the more evident by passing over to the foreign department after inspecting the British carpeting; as there many really beautiful specimens were to be seen.

Of floor-cloths we have already mentioned that only two establishments are engaged in the trade in Ireland, both being in this city. This material consists of coarse canvass on which successive coats of oil paint are laid; the paint and pattern being applied by hand, the latter being imparted by the usual process of block printing. The cloth for the purpose is manufactured in large quantities at Dundee. Some idea may be formed of the looms used for the purpose when we learn that the pieces are usually over six yards in width and hundred yards in length. In the straining after economy of production which is carried to so great an extent at present, much of the floor-cloth now made is of very inferior quality. Not only should the fabric which forms the basis of the article be good, but the colouring materials should also be suitable to insure durability. In reference to colour and patterns there is not the same room for variety as in carpeting, either as regards the nature of the material or the purpose for which it is employed. It may be observed that generally the most effective oil cloths are those with sober colours and simple patterns. The vulgar appetite for high and varied colouring appears to great disadvantage when sought to be ministered to in this article.

This is perhaps the proper place to notice Berlin work, which every person of good taste must rejoice to find so much out of favour as compared with the estimation in which it was held only a few years ago. But that it has scarcely yet fallen to its proper level is apparent from the extent to which it was contributed to the Exhibition, which in this respect certainly presented many ludicrous specimens of misspent time and depraved taste. In almost every department of the Building were displayed what were evidently regarded as gems by the exhibiters; but if anything were wanting to cover such work with ridicule it is to be found in the ambitious efforts which are sometimes made in it. Fine ladies are not ashamed to spend months in making objects in natural history, even the human face, in Berlin work, while by so doing they are only proclaiming their own utter want of good taste, and their thorough inappreciation of art in the higher sense of the term. In fact, the better the effort in this kind of work, the greater is the reason for regret that so much labour should have been misapplied.

## LACE AND EMBROIDERY.

There were few departments in the Exhibition possessed of more local interest than that on which we have now to make some observations. The great number of hands employed in this branch of business, the exceeding beauty of many of the articles, and the prospect of an increasing trade, conspire to render the lace and embroidery trades of great importance to the people of this country.

Limerick has for some time past obtained notoriety for the production of lace; a position which, through the enterprise of a few individuals, it continues to maintain. The introduction of this branch of industry into that locality does not date farther back than 1824, when an English gentleman named Walker, previously connected with the trade in England, settled there and made a beginning, which has gradually extended up to the present time. It appears, however, that the production of lace was understood and practised long anterior to that period, to some extent, in the neighbourhood of Galway, by the descendants of the Spanish settlers; but in consequence of its not being taken up as a regular branch of business, it made no progress, and was at all times confined to a few hands, who were, for the most part, amateurs, not practising the production of lace with a view of disposing of it. And here we may remark that all efforts to foster any branch of industry which violate the principles of commercial trading must end in disappointment. Hence it is that so many movements dependent on the personal surveillance of individuals, and not carried on with a view to profit, have involved those connected with them in misery, when the fostering hand on which they relied has from some cause been removed. But, in Limerick, persons of capital entered into the lace trade as a commercial speculation; and while the excellence of many of the productions in the Exhibition bore testimony to the admirable quality of the work, the fact of there being now over 1500 individuals so employed in that city shows the progress which it has made. The firm of Lambert and Bury employ over 600 hands, and they have for a length of time done a large export trade. Mr. Forrest, of Grafton-street, in this city, has also done a large trade in Limerick for many years past, producing work of the finest quality of its kind; and we believe that at the present time the number of hands at work in his factory is about 400. The average wages earned by the girls in that locality is about nine-pence per day; and, taking into account the large numbers which are thus paid remunerating wages, we cannot but be impressed with the great service which this branch of industry confers on the people of Limerick.

While, through the exertions of several enterprising Scotch capitalists, as well as some of the people of Belfast, the sewed muslin work has of late made such rapid progress, the lace trade has also been greatly extended through the intervention of private individuals, who took up the matter more with the benevolent object of finding employment for the female peasantry around them, than with that of introducing a branch of trade on any secure basis. In such cases, the degree of success attained has been in proportion to the energy displayed on the part of the patrons, and also on the extent to which they had influential connexions through whom the sales of the produce could be made. An appeal from an influential lady on behalf of native industry, partaking somewhat of a charitable nature, and seeking to dispose of articles really beautiful in themselves, was not likely to be often unsuccessful; and hence some Irish ladies have been able to obtain high prices for all the work which their dependents could turn out. And so long as the presiding care which brought matters to this state was continued, all went right; but even on its temporary cessation great inconvenience cannot fail to be felt. The work not being executed with a view to profit further than the wages of labour, the producers get the whole return, however high; and it is often more than double what they would receive if working for a person in the trade, from the lower price at which he would be obliged to sell his goods, and from the necessity of having a profit on his transactions. But parties accustomed to work in this manner can scarcely get on in any other. Their services are of little value to the legitimate lace manufacturer, and such a system of training, though set about with the best and most philanthropic intentions, practically interposes difficulties in the way of the trade being carried on. These remarks we do not make for the purpose of disparaging the value of the truly noble efforts made by several parties throughout the country to provide employment for the people of their respective localities; but rather to guard against very sanguine expectations being entertained from any movement which has not the commercial element of profit for its basis—the only sure guarantee for its being continuously and successfully prosecuted. In the preliminary stage of the introduction of any branch of industry no very strict regard to economic rules need be enforced; but a resort to such rules should take place at as early a period as possible, to impart to it those features by which alone it can be made self-supporting. Once established, some trader in the neighbouring town should be induced to take it up, or some agent from one of the great manufacturing firms, now extending their operations throughout the country; and while the surveillance of the patron may be still desirable to stimulate the people to exertion, and to see that, on the other hand, they are fairly dealt with, the surest guarantee for ultimate success will be to provide those conditions which are essential to it.

While referring to this topic we would also counsel caution to be exercised in the establishment of what are called training schools for embroidery and lace work, without organizing in conjunction with such training some system of providing employment for the hands trained; and this we do the more earnestly, inasmuch as in most attempts of this kind the production of ornamental work is the great object in view, that of a more useful character being neglected from the simple circumstance of there not being a facility of immediately turning it to account. Many girls spend years at crochet and tambour work who are unable to make up the commonest garments for themselves, than which there can be no greater mistake. The first and most important training which persons in the class of life of which we speak can get, is to be instructed how to make up their own clothes, and generally to make the more useful descriptions of work, such as shirts, vests, and those articles the demand for which is constant, and not dependent upon the caprice of fashion. Notwithstanding the large and increasing demand for sewed muslin and lace, the trade is so dependent upon novelty of patterns and fashion that periods of reaction are sure to occur in it, unless the greatest activity and judgment are evinced in catering for the caprice of the consumer. In such cases great inconvenience is sustained by the work-people, who may be thereby thrown out of employment; but this only shows the necessity of the business being carried on by those who have a sharp eye to profit; as well as the danger of relying too exclusively on a branch of trade in which casualties are so greatly felt.

In reference to the lace manufacture, we may observe that rapid progress has of late been made to introduce machinery even in this branch of business, and substitute it for manual labour. At the commencement of the present century, lace made by machinery was mostly from the point net and warp machines (both modifications of the original stocking frame); but since that period ingenuity has been on the rack to overcome the mechanical difficulties in the way of the production of plain and ornamental lace by machinery. The great triumph achieved in this business was the invention of the bobbin net machine; so called from the thread that makes the lace being partly supplied from bobbins, and partly from a warp; the bobbins being made to pass from front to back, and from back to front, while a lateral motion is imparted to the warp threads, thus causing one series of threads to warp round another. The powers of production of this machine are said to be to hand labour in the proportion of 6000 to 1. It is stated on good authority that through the successive improvements which have been made in the use of this machine, the bobbin net which in 1815 would have cost 30*s.* per yard may now be had for 3*d.*! This result has been attained by the most unwearied assiduity; incredible sums of money being expended in inventions which were destined to be superseded by others almost as soon as brought into operation, these latter again sharing a similar fate. A great triumph was effected in 1839, when the Jacquard machine was applied to the bobbin net, for the purpose of ornament. Since that period further improvements and modifications have been made, which led to new sources of manufacture being gradually developed, such as window curtains, scarfs, shawls, flounces, &c. The Nottingham trade has, in consequence, made extraordinary progress, the mechanical improvements being seconded by increased attention to suitable and elegant patterns.

In the collection of Reckless and Hickling, on the Northern Gallery, were some surprising specimens of machine-made lace, with merely the finishing off of the edges of the pattern by needle-work. The great variety of articles now manufactured by the bobbin net machines almost exceeds belief; including shawls, scarfs, flounces, in white and colours, cotton edgings, lace insertions, linen laces and plait in imitation of Valenciennes lace, imitation Swiss curtains and blinds, silk and cotton plait net, Mechlin grounds, blonde Brussels, or extra twist. In the production of this great variety of articles, there are over 1400 machines at work in the counties of Leicester, Derby, and Nottingham; so that the trade is already of great importance, and of still greater promise.

Of the hand laces there is great variety; and the tendency of the present time is to obliterate those distinctive features which characterize the several kinds—a circumstance which we cannot but regard as eminently injurious to the trade.

The Honiton lace, as most of our readers are aware, derives its name from the town in Devonshire where it was first extensively produced. Along that portion of the southern coast of England it has been long made by the peasantry; and the manufacture has recently been extended elsewhere by the great beauty of the article, and consequent large demand for it, as well as by the families of the coast-guard officers practising it along the Devonshire coast carrying the trade with them to other parts of the country in which they may have been located. It is now very generally produced in this country, more especially in Limerick. It is made by placing a perforated pattern upon a pillow, and employing, pins, bobbins, and spindles to twist and interweave thread in such a manner as to produce the desired effect. Simple sprigs and borders comprised the limits to which this work was formerly carried; but of late the range of ornament, as well as the variety of articles, has greatly extended. The Honiton very closely resembles some of the varieties of Brussels lace. The finer descriptions of this lace are really very beautiful. At one period during the last war veils of Honiton lace were sometimes sold for so much as 100 guineas. In the collections of Messrs. Todd, Burns, and Co., Forrest and Son, Pim Brothers, and of E. Pyne, excellent specimens of this description of lace were exhibited.

The pillow lace, which closely resembles the Honiton, being also made on a cushion, is yet distinguishable from it by having both the pattern and the mesh made by hand, whereas in the Honiton the pattern is made separately, and afterwards sewed on to machine-made net. It is, in fact, only to work performed in this manner that the name of lace can be strictly applied, every other description of article going by that name being, in whole or in part, imitation; though it will, of course, be more or less a matter of taste as to whether the real or the imitation is the more beautiful article. As regards the net foundation, the work executed by machinery is usually very much superior, both in durability and appearance, to what is made by hand; and in so far the Honiton would appear to have a decided advantage over that of which it is an imitation. The production of this lace is not, to any considerable extent, carried on at present in this country.

The tambour lace is very extensively produced. It, in fact, properly speaking, constitutes the real Limerick lace, though of late the production of a variety of laces has been carried on there. Messrs. Lambert and Bury are the great producers of this work. The character of this lace is well known throughout the country.

The guipure is one of the novelties introduced by Messrs. Forrest and Son, and it has, at all events, the merit of possessing a distinctive character. It is made by cutting out the pattern from cambric, the flowers and heavy parts being made of the cambric, and the open parts of stitches closely resembling the appliqué lace. In many cases the eyelet holes form the groundwork of the lace, and this renders the manufacture a tedious and delicate operation. It is, notwithstanding the irregularities of its texture, very durable, and is frequently very elegant. Of this variety there were a great number of exhibiters. It is especially suited for the larger class of articles, and where the design is appropriate, the effect of this kind of lace is very good.

The applique lace is another modern article, the term being used in consequence of the patterns of it being cut out and *applied* to a groundwork of net. If the patterns have been carefully executed, they may be made to wear out several foundations of net, by being transferred from one to the other. In one respect it resembles the Honiton—in both the groundwork being of net, and the ornamental parts being subsequently added. But in the Honiton lace it will be observed that the ornamental part is altogether worked by hand in a manner somewhat analogous to the production of the pillow lace; whereas in the applique lace the figured portion is *cut* out of another material, and *applied* to the foundation of net. In this kind of lace, also, the selection of appropriate patterns is almost everything. In other branches of the trade fine work may, to some extent, make amends for the absence of elegance, or even beauty in the design or pattern; but in the case of the applique lace the latter is the primary consideration; though it is obvious that in all cases attention to both points is necessary to produce satisfactory work. Messrs. Forrest and Son were the chief exhibitors of it, though, like the guipure, it has now become general. At the Carrickmacross Industrial School we believe that the guipure and applique are the only kinds of lace made.

Of the crochet work there were also numerous examples in the Exhibition, the principal being those exhibited by the Ladies' Industrial Society. The characteristics of this kind of work are well known, the production of crochet work having been lately much in vogue. Compared with any of the kinds above enumerated, crochet lace is wanting in elegance and lightness—essential considerations in the production of this class of goods.

Of the other varieties of lace and the imitations, we need say little, as they are either indifferent in themselves, or they are produced only in small quantity. But we should not omit to dissuade those having any influence in deciding the character of the work to be produced in any given locality, from patronizing such abortive attempts at ornamentation as the combinations of braid in the form of imitation of lace, which was to be seen in so many articles in the Exhibition. The best executed work of this kind is inelegant in the extreme; and cheapness alone is a poor recommendation in favour of articles of ornament. The knitting in imitation of lace is also wanting in those features which could gain for it any claim to public attention. The most ambitious specimen of this kind of work no one of good taste can inspect without lamenting that on it so much labour was misapplied.

The illustration of this department was, as might have been expected, ample; and the general character of the work was such as to deserve high commendation. Nor is this remark less applicable to the specimens forwarded from some of the schools than to those belonging to parties who have been long in the trade.

In the sewed muslin trade an immense number of hands are employed; and so great has been the degree of perfection to which some of the fine kinds of work have been brought that, in many cases, it bids fair to become a formidable rival to lace. The growth of the sewed muslin trade has been very rapid. The revolution brought about in the employment of the female peasantry by the use of machinery in spinning linen yarn rendered it necessary that some effort should be made to provide a substitute. The extension of the sewed muslin trade seemed to be that most easily available; and through the intervention of enterprising merchants, aided by the local co-operation of benevolent persons anxious to minister to the wants of those around them, a system of training was devised. The business soon took root. The manufacturers established agencies for the supply of the muslin and receipt of the finished article, laying down a fixed scale of remuneration for their guidance. The satin stitch and other sewed embroidery gradually took the place of the tambour, to which its cheapness and elegance in no small degree contributed. The use of the lithographic printing press for the multiplication of patterns formed another event in this career of progress.

The collections of D. and J. M'Donald and Co., and J. Holden and Co., bear ample testimony to the beauty of this class of goods when neatly executed. A child's robe and cap, exhibited by the former firm, attracted great and deserved attention, on account of the surpassing beauty of both design and workmanship. In the pattern, the rose, thistle, and shamrock, were effectively introduced; and altogether these articles were triumphs in their way. A toilet-cover, in the case of the same firm, was also a beautiful specimen of this kind of work. At the present time it is estimated that the sum annually turned over in the sewed muslin trade is £1,000,000, of which about £600,000 is paid in wages.

Of carriage lace there were several beautiful specimens exhibited. In the collection of Messrs. Dart and Son was a pattern of lace made thirty-five years ago, which was interesting when contrasted with some of the modern specimens, as showing the progress of the art, and the skill evinced in the combination of apparently incongruous and gaudy colours, so as to produce an article harmonious and beautiful.

## FABRICS SHOWN AS SPECIMENS OF PRINTING AND DYEING.

This class presented few illustrations in the Exhibition. Dyeing and printing are, however, important processes in the manufacture of textile fabrics; and these arts have of late made great progress. In former times the business of the dyer was empirical; the knowledge of the subject being the accumulated results of experience, and the substances available being also few. But the application of chemical knowledge has completely revolutionized this branch of industry. Economy of time, labour, and material has been effected; a variety of new substances have been added to the list of those previously available; and a brilliancy and durability of colour have been attained altogether unexampled in former times. It is chiefly since the commencement of the present century that the surprising development in printing in colour and dyeing has taken place. At that period the annual quantity of cotton printed was about 33,000,000 yards; in 1830 this had increased to 347,000,000 yards, and since that period a further and corresponding increase has taken place. That which previously occupied weeks to get through is now disposed of in a few hours. Mechanical science has not, however, been less effective in aiding this movement than chemical; the printing machines being marvels of ingenuity. On one side of a machine room the cloth ascends moist, and on the other it descends dried ready for the final process. Formerly the production of coloured designs was exclusively effected by what is termed block printing, a separate operation being required for each colour employed; and this method is still to some extent practised in the case of the finer class of goods, where high finish is of greater consequence than a slight addition to the expense. For ordinary fabrics, however, machine printing is now universal. By this method the fabric is drawn over one or more copper cylinders, the lower part of which revolves in a trough containing the colouring matter. A blade of metal like a knife removes the superfluous colour from these cylinders, leaving only the indentations charged therewith. The colour thus left is afterwards absorbed by the fabric under pressure, which is thence conveyed to a drying apartment. The machinery now in use admits of seven or eight colours being applied by one operation. Each colour is confined to one cylinder, but the cylinders are so arranged as to cause the colour which they retain to be transferred to the precise place in the cloth that may be required by the pattern.

The knowledge of how to print textile fabrics in colours was derived from France; and in matters of this kind the people of that country still maintain their early pre-eminence. In cheapening the cost of production the English have, no doubt, gone ahead of the Continental manufacturers. The goods ordinarily produced in England could not be obtained on the Continent at the price they usually bring; but, on the other hand, the finer class of goods is scarcely at all produced in England, so that when excellence, irrespective of price, is sought after, the article must be obtained from abroad. The quality of English prints has, however, very materially improved of late. The tendency of the present day is towards goods of a more elegant and quiet character than what were some time ago in vogue; and in this as in other matters in which taste is involved, we are year by year making rapid advances upon our neighbours.—J. S.

---

1. ADARE INDUSTRIAL SCHOOLS, Co. Limerick, COUNTESS OF DUNRAVEN, Patroness.—A netted quilt from a German design; a pair of crochet lace sleeves; an embroidered pocket handkerchief of Irish cambric; a cambric handkerchief, trimmed with crochet lace and insertion.

2. ADELAIDE INDUSTRIAL SCHOOL, Duncan-street, Cork.—Crochet and other ornamental needle-work.

3. ANDREWS, W., Castle-street, Dublin, Importer.—Floor-cloths (made by John Hare & Co., of Bristol); Axminster carpet (made by Templeton & Co., Glasgow).

4. ANNETTE, J. & L., Priory-road, Wandsworth-road, London.—Tapestry.

5. ARTHUR, M., Airdrie, Inventor.—Vase of artificial flowers, made of silver and silk; some of the same kind adapted for costume.

6. BAGOT, Mrs., Castle Bagot, Co. Dublin.—Specimens of fancy work done by children of Castle Bagot school.

7. BANNERTH, M., Bannerth-street, Limerick.—Framed picture in Berlin wool.

8. BANNISTER, J., Sir Harry's Mall, Limerick, Manufacturer.—Dress, shawl, pocket handkerchief, and pair of sleeves, of Limerick lace.

9. BARNES, R. Y., City-road, London, Manufacturer.—Specimens of decorative floor-cloth.

10. BELFAST INDUSTRIAL SCHOOL.—Valenciennes lace; English lace manufactured in the Industrial School, Frederick-street, Belfast (the first ragged school in Ireland, established 1847), by children, most of whom are under twelve years of age.

11. BLEAKLEY, MRS. J., St. Mary's, Bandon, Co. Cork.—Specimens of muslin, embroidery, and crochet, worked in Ballymodan School.

12. BERRY, Rev. E. F., Tullamore, King's County.—Two worked children's frocks; worked body for ditto; and a pair of knit socks, worked at the Charleville School, Tullamore.

13. BERTWELL, E., Nassau-street, Dublin, Proprietor.—A knitted counterpane.

14. BLACKWELL, ELIZABETH, Henry-street, Dublin.—A piece of embroidery, mounted as a cheval screen, designed and worked by exhibiter.

15. BRITTAIN, W., Montpelier Hill, Dublin.—Two crochet quilts.

16. BROWN, H., & Co., Virginia-place, Glasgow, Manufacturer.—Tamboured and sewed muslin dresses; sewed book and cambric habit shirts, chemisettes, sleeves, and collars, French cambric handkerchiefs; pattern cards of cambric and book trimmings and flounces.

17. BROWN, J. R. & W., Bangor, County Down, Manufacturers.—Sewed muslin collars, habit shirts, chemisettes, handkerchiefs, and robes.

18. BROWN, M'LAREN, & Co., Kilmarnock, Manufacturers.—Brussels, Kidderminster, and Turkey carpeting.

19. BROWN, SAMUEL R., & THOMAS, Queen-street, Glasgow, Manufacturers.—Specimens of muslin embroidery worked by the Irish peasantry, in robes, frocks, collars, habits, &c.; specimens of lace goods embroidered by the Irish peasantry, in black and coloured veils.

20. BROWNE, MRS. CLAYTON, Browne's Hill, Carlow.—Embroidered pocket handkerchief, worked by Miss Mary Hickey, of Johnstown, Co. Carlow.

21. BURTON & Co., Wigmore-street, Cavendish-square, London, Designers and Manufacturers.—Church robes, specimen of applique work; laces, embroidered satins, &c.

22. BURTON & GARRAWAY, Bethnal-green, London, Manufacturers.—Silks, wools, and Morocco skins, dyed and printed with preparations of orchil or cudbear; silks, wools, and kid leather, dyed or printed with extract of indigo.

23. BYRNE, F., Albert-place, East, Dublin.—Pattern worked in tapestry.

24. CANNING, M., Rockville, Malin, Carn.—Needle and crochet work, comprising basket covers, doyleys, trimmings, &c., by girls at Malin.

25. CARTER, J., Mountmellick, Queen's County, Designer and Manufacturer.—Embroidered quilt, toilette covers, and doileys.

26. CHAMBERS, Mrs. E. R., Grenville-street, Dublin.—Carpet in needle work.

27. CLARKE, E., Deopham, Wymondham, Norfolk.—Crochet and point-work collars in imitation of Honiton and old Marguerite guipure lace.

28. CLARK, CYRUS AND JAMES, Street, Glastonbury, Manufacturers.—Angora rug dyed in one piece to a many-coloured pattern.

29. CLEARY, Miss M., Clonmel, Co. Tipperary.—Specimens in Berlin wool work.

30. CLINCHY, Miss K., Townsend-street, Dublin, Proprietor.—A piece of tapestry work; a gentleman's robe de chambre in needlework, composed of 7500 small pieces.

31. COGHILL, Sir J. J., Bart., Malmaison, near Skibbereen, Co. Cork, Proprietor.—Berlin work, by an amateur.

32. COLLIER, M., Sidney Parade, Sandymount, Dublin, Proprietor.—Specimens of Berlin wool work.

33. COMMISSIONERS OF NATIONAL EDUCATION, Dublin.—Specimens of work executed by pupils of National Schools.

34. CONSTABLE, H. D., Anne-street, Clonmel.—Specimens of crochet work.

35. COX, Miss R., Ballynoe, Ballingarry.—Specimens of crochet work.

36. CUTHBERTSON & TAYLOR, Kilmarnock, Manufacturers.—Imperial and Kidderminster carpets.

37. DALEY, MRS., Rafford, Co. Galway.—Specimens of work executed by the children of the Tallow Convent Industrial School.

38. DART & SON, Bedford-street, Covent Garden, London, Manufacturers.—Specimens of carriage lace, (of original designs); a series of patterns exhibiting in chronological order the progress of the art of coach lace weaving, from 1814 to the present time.

39. DAVIS, C. M., Waterloo-road, Dublin.—Lace curtains with border of crochet work.

40. DEANE, The Misses, Dundanion, Cork.—Specimens of crochet.

41. DE BELIGAND, Madame A., Convent of the Good Shepherd, Limerick.—Church vestments, Brussels lace veil and several patterns of Valenciennes lace.

42. DINGLE MISSION SCHOOLS, per Mrs. LEWIS, Dingle, Co. Kerry.—Children's robes, collars, and handkerchiefs worked in satin stitch; knitted socks, stockings, quilt, &c., doyleys, antimacassar, &c., of linen.

43. DORAN, Miss C., Harcourt-street, Dublin.—A lady's dress, flounced, knitted with Irish thread, weighing only eight ounces, formed without a scissors.

44. DOUGLAS, A. & J., Glasgow.—Embroidered velvet hassock; silk cushion; chenille sachet; hand screens; braided leather slippers.

45. DUNDRUM CENTRAL LUNATIC ASYLUM, Co. Dublin, per DR. CORBET.—Two fancy shirts; two embroidered silk vests; two worked baby's dresses, and other articles; four pair fancy knitted stockings; a large knitted quilt.

46. DUNRAVEN, DOWAGER COUNTESS of, Adare, Co. Limerick.—Altar cloth for the parish church of Adare, of velvet manufactured by Mrs. Moran, Mark's Alley, Dublin; the pattern designed by Mrs. Beard, Regent-street, London; and executed by the Countess Dowager of Dunraven and Lady Anna Maria Monsell.

47. EDWARDS, J. F., Roebuck, Dundrum, Co. Dublin.—Carpet, worked in wool by ladies.

48. EGLINTON, COUNTESS of.—A Scotch cambric muslin quilt, counterlined with blue satin, and embroidered with the initials E. and W. and coronet, and trimmed with Limerick lace (worked in Ayrshire); a quilt richly embroidered in the centre with the Eglinton arms, and worked over with shamrocks, roses, and thistles, designed and executed by Mrs. Carter, of Mountmellick.

49. ELLIS, LYSTER, Douglas, Isle of Man.—Birds and flowers in Berlin wool, executed by exhibiter.

50. ELLIS, S. A., Kildemoc, Ardee, Co. Louth.—Irish pearl tatting, worked by the poor females of the parish of Kildemoc.

51. ERSKINE, Miss E., Harristown, Ardee, Co. Louth.—Specimens of Irish point lace.

52. FIDDES, G. R., Rathmines, Dublin.—Landscapes in needlework, executed by Mrs. Captain Roche.

53. FORREST, J., & SONS, Grafton-street, Dublin, Manufacturers.—Irish guipure, point, and applique lace; Limerick tamboured and shaded lace; Irish blonde dresses; rich guipure flouncings, scarf, &c.; Limerick lace bridal dress and veil, ball and court dresses, &c.; guipure berthes; handkerchiefs, collars, mantles, &c.; Irish embroidery.

54. FRANKLIN, J., Great Strand-street, Dublin, Manufacturer.—Floor-cloth, 48 feet by 18 feet, woven without a seam.

55. FURLONG, Miss E., Wallstown, Castletown Roche, Co. Cork.—Knit cotton quilts.

56. GIRDWOOD, J., Belfast.—East India carpet, made at Masulipatam.

57. GRAY, HARRIET A., Brompton Crescent, near London, Designer.—A fine piece of crochet work.

58. GREGORY, THOMPSONS, & Co., Kilmarnock, Ayrshire, Manufacturers.—Velvet pile carpet.

59. GREENE, Miss ELIZA, Molesworth-street, Dublin.—A knitted quilt.

60. GUBBINS, DORA J., The Glebe, Ballingarry, Co. Limerick.—Specimens of knitting, crochet, and needle-work.

61. HALL, J. J., High-street, Deptford, Kent.—Crochet cover in cotton for back of sofa.

62. HALLOWELL, Miss E., Lower Hartstonge-street, Limerick.—Shawl knitted of red and white wool; a veil knitted from black wool; horse's ear net done in crochet work.

63. HAND, Miss C., Clones Rectory, Co. Monaghan.—Specimens of work in crochet guipure, produced for charitable purposes.

64. HANNIGAN, Miss M.T., Presentation Convent, Cashel.—Berlin work; embroidery; crochet; purses; chair covers, &c.

65. HARDING & Co., Long Acre, London, Designers and Manufacturers.—Specimens of laces, just supplied for a new dress coach to her Majesty.

66. HARVEY, The Misses, Malin Hall (Co. Donegal) Industrial School.—Specimens of crochet work.

67. HEACOCK, J., Dame-street, Dublin, Proprietor.—Chenille embroidery, bird of Paradise, and branches of flowers.

68. HENDERSON, Miss F. M., Mount Anthony, Rathmines, Dublin.—Satin doyleys, with etchings in marking ink.

69. HENDERSON & WIDNELL, Lasswade, near Edinburgh, Manufacturers.—Patent velvet medallion carpets; British tapestry, and fine velvet, for curtains, portiéres, &c.

70. HEYMAN, N. & ALEXANDER, Nottingham.—Lace curtains; antimacassars; short window curtains.

71. HILL, B., Olney, Buckinghamshire.—Specimens of pillow thread lace edging and insertion; pillow thread infant cap and trimming lace, and lace flouncings.

72. HILL, E. BRYANSFORD, Castlewellan, Co. Down, Proprietor.—Embroidered pocket handkerchiefs, habit shirts, collars, sleeves, &c.

73. HOLDEN, JOHN, & Co., Belfast.—Specimens of worked muslin executed in various districts in Ireland.

74. HUNT, Miss MARIA, Killashee.—A vase of flowers in crochet.

75. KAVANAGH, MARY, Meath-street, Dublin.—An "Ossory" housewife's quilt, fashion of the eighteenth century; hexagon quilt, containing 4000 pieces of silk of various colours—both worked by exhibiter.

76. KEANE, Mrs. LEOPOLD, Cappoquin House, Co. Waterford.—Specimens of knitting executed by the children of the Cappoquin school.

77. KETTLEWELL, Miss MARY, Lissenure House, Clonmel.—Knitted capes, scarfs, lappets, &c.; trimming lace; a black lace veil (worked by the exhibiter).

78. LADIES' INDUSTRIAL SOCIETY FOR IRELAND, Grafton-street, Dublin.—Specimens of Valenciennes, guipure, Buckingham thread, French black and blonde lace, &c.; Spanish point lace, crochet, guipure, and tatting, from schools in Kildare, Wexford, and Fermanagh; muslin embroidery.

79. LAMBERT, BROWN, & CLOWES, Dame-street, Dublin, Manufacturers.—Rich gold army, navy, and other laces; field officers', staff, militia, and other epaulettes; gold cross and glory for church; gold tassels for pulpit; court dress waistcoats, masonic aprons, sashes, &c.

80. LAMBERT & BURY, Limerick, Designers and Manufacturers.—Half squares, berthes, jackets, handkerchiefs, scarfs, falls, chemisettes, and collars, of tambour Queen shaded (Limerick) lace.

81. LA TOUCHE, DIGGES, The Misses, Upham, Killenaule, Co. Tipperary.—Specimens of Irish Honiton lace, worked by the poor girls of Killenaule.

82. LA TOUCHE, Miss ISABELLA, Bellevue, Delgany, Co. Wicklow.—Knitted shawls, scarfs, veils, &c., of Shetland wool.

83. LATOUR, RATEAU & Co., 130, New Bond-street, London, Manufacturers (Mrs. BIRCH, 1, Molesworth-street, Dublin, AGENT).—A dyed satin mantle and skirt, showing the process of embossing a brocaded figure upon a worn and faded fabric, with other specimens of goods dyed and renovated; specimens of the process patented by L. Rateau and Co. for renovating soiled kid gloves, ribbons, Limerick lace, &c.

84. LEE, DANIEL, & Co., Manchester, Manufacturers.—Turkey red damask furniture; chintz furniture for sofa coverings; imitation damask furnitures; plain and fancy stripes for sofa covering; prints—blue; blue and white; green and yellow; blue and orange; blue, orange, and white; blue, green, and white; blue and yellow; exhibited as specimens of dyeing and printing.

85. LEONARD, Miss ANNIE, Cork-street, Dublin.—Netted curtains.

86. LEONARD, Miss MARGARET, Cork-street, Dublin.—Netting work.

87. LEVEY, Miss, Merrion-row, Dublin.—Berlin tapestry, worked on canvass.

88. LIMERICK LOCAL COMMITTEE, per D. W. RAIMBACH, and W. FITZGERALD, Limerick.—Specimens of lace made by the orphans of Mount St. Vincent; Valenciennes lace.

89. LINDESAY, F. J. SANDYS, 17th Regiment, Richmond Barracks.—Carpet worked by the ladies of the United Kingdom, and presented to exhibiter.

90. LOUTH, M., Cork-street, Dublin.—Quilt in crochet work.

91. MACLEAN, Mrs., RECTORY, Tynan, Co. Armagh.—Specimens of guipure and Irish point lace.

92. MACDONALD, D. & J., & Co., Miller-street, Glasgow, Manufacturers.—Embroidered muslin, being specimens of the needlework of the females in the north and west of Ireland.

93. MAGRATH, Miss A., Clifton Lodge, Blackrock, Dublin.—Ottoman cover, in crochet work.

94. MARLAND & WHITCOMBE, New High-street, Manufacturers.—Cotton cloths of various colours; silescias; shalloons; Italians; Orleans serge; imitation Morocco; Niagaras; Platas, and bookbinders' cloths, &c.

95. MILLAR & BEATTY, Dame-street, Dublin, Importers.—Turkey velvet, tapestry, Brussels, and Kidderminster carpeting; stair carpeting; velvet, Mosaic, worsted, and figured hearth-rugs.

96. MILLET, Miss H. R., Millbrook, Dundrum, Cashel.—Table cover of Irish tweed, worked in Berlin wool.

97. MONTGOMERY, Miss, Benvarden, Ballymoney, Co. Antrim.—Crochet work, in imitation of Brussels lace and guipure; specimens of crochet insertions and edgings, &c.

98. M'CARTHY, HAMILTON, Mrs., Albert Terrace, Knightsbridge, London, Designer.—Fire screen and chair, with improved painting on velvet.

99. M'CULLOCH, Mrs., North Cumberland-street, Dublin.—Cheval screen; table and picture, worked by exhibiter.

100. M'DOWELL, Miss S., Joy-street, Belfast.—Irish point lace head-dress, collars, and lappets; point lace berthe, collars, and lappet; handkerchief, &c., of applique.

101. M'GEE, J. G. & Co., Belfast.—Gentlemen's richly embroidered vests; ladies' embroidered mantles.

102. M'NAUGHT, Miss, Hanover-street, Edinburgh.—Cotton bed covers, worked in crochet.

103. NAAS, LADY, Palmerstown, Naas, Co. Kildare, Proprietor.—Baby's robe, worked by girls in the village of Kill, Co. of Kildare.

104. NAIRN, M., Kirkaldy, Fifeshire (Mr. JAMES FORBES, Eden-quay, Dublin, AGENT), Manufacturer.—Floor-cloths, in chintz, oak, marble, and granite patterns.

105. NAIRN, T. G., Limerick, Manufacturer.—Blue embroidered frock for the Royal Horse Artillery, and scarlet embroidered vest, worn under the frock.

106. O'CONNOR, Mrs. ELEANOR, Denzille-street, Dublin.—An embroidered Brussels lace dress.

107. OLDHAM, Mrs., Dawson-street, Dublin.—Berlin work.

108. ORR, EWING & Co., Glasgow, Manufacturers.—Cambrics and printed cottons, dyed in Turkey red.

109. OSBORNE, Miss G., Kingstown, near Dublin, Designer.—Dahlia and flower mats of crochet work.

110. PARKER, Mrs. W., Rathmines, Dublin.—Berlin needlework.

111. PERRIN, J. & J., Chancery-lane, Dublin, Manufacturers.—Printed floor-cloth.

112. POWELL, Mrs., Westmoreland-street, Dublin.—Berlin wool work.

113. PURCELL, Mrs. M., Halverstown, Kilcullen, Co. Kildare.—Spanish point lace, wrought at Halverstown school; frock, cap, handkerchief, collars, &c., in braid guipure; silk embroidery on cloth and cashmere; sewed muslin work.

114. PYNE, ELIZABETH, Honiton, Devon.—Lace veil, Honiton point lace, made on a cushion; Vandyck lace collar; pair of lace sleeves to match the collar, and a chemisette to match the collar and sleeves; Honiton bone lace.

115. RECKLESS & HICKLING, Messrs., St. Mary's Gate, Nottingham.—Muslin embroidery.

116. ROBINSON, J. J., Cork-hill, Dublin, Designer.—Court vest, in the old style of embroidery.

117. ROSSMORE, LADY, Rossmore Park, Monaghan.—Specimens of lace and embroidery work executed by the children of the Rossmore Estate, Co. of Monaghan.

118. RYAN, Mrs., Inch House, Borrisoleigh, Co. Tipperary.—Infant's cap and robe in finest crochet point: open-work berthe; capes, collars, and sleeves, &c., in crochet guipure.

119. SAXTON, A., Hollow-stone, Nottingham, Manufacturer.—Lace, Jacquard, and filet shawls; toilets; antimacassars; tray covers; knitted toilets, &c.; ladies' silk mitts and gloves, embroidered.

120. SEMPSTRESSES' ASSOCIATION, Grafton-street, Dublin.—Plain needle work.

121. SHERIDAN, P., Parliament-street, Dublin.—Mosaic landscapes for walls; Mosaic hearth rugs; Brussels carpets and rugs.

122. SIBTHORPE, Miss FANNY LOUISA, Bank-place, Limerick.—Scenes in Berlin wool.

123. SISTERS OF MERCY, THE, Kinsale.—Irish point lace; crochet; Limerick lace; Honiton lace; embroidery in silk and gold; feather and muslin flowers; satin stitch embroidery.

124. SISTERS OF MERCY, THE, Lower Baggot-street, Dublin.—Limerick lace dress and Bishop's rochet: guipure flounce, berthes, and sleeves; double point crochet berthe, lappets, sleeves, &c.; embroidered baby's robe, collars, handkerchiefs, &c.; Honiton lace crochet collar and sleeves; gold embroidery on white satin; the work of the children of the Industrial School of the Sisters of Mercy.

125. SMAIL, Mrs. JAMES, George-place, Plymouth.—Worsted embroidery.

126. SMITH & BARBER, Knightsbridge, London, Designers and Manufacturers.—Specimen of floor-cloth, showing the various stages of the process of manufacture, from the raw material of stout canvass to the finished fabric; finished piece of floor-cloth with the separate impression made by each print; also the prints by which the pattern was executed.

127. SOCIETY FOR THE PROMOTION OF IRISH MANUFACTURE AND INDUSTRY, Anglesea-street, Dublin.—Glass case containing specimens of needle-work executed in the Training School of the Society.

128. SPARKS, R., Suffolk-street, Dublin, Proprietor.—Specimens of Axminster, velvet pile, tapestry, and Brussels carpets, and hearth rugs.

129. SPRATT, Very Rev. JOHN, D. D., Aungier-street, Dublin.—Lace work executed by the children of Dr. Spratt's Industrial School in Whitefriar-street.

130. STEPHENSON, Miss MARGARET, Meath-street, Dublin.—Converts, in netting-work.

131. STOKES, S., Kevin-street, Police Barrack, Dublin.—Table cloth of mosaic cloth-work, detailing the life of a British soldier, containing 250 figures, and consisting of small pieces of cloth fine-drawn together; pictures of the same work.

132. SWEETMAN, Mrs., Pembroke-street, Dublin.—An opera cloak handsomely embroidered; a baby's cloak embroidered.

133. SYMES, Miss CHARLOTTE, Roseville, Clane.—Table cover made of feathers, principally Irish, but some Indian, embroidered and lined with silk.

134. TALLAGHT INDUSTRIAL SCHOOL, Mrs. LENTAIGNE, Patroness, Tallaght House, Tallaght, near Dublin.—Specimen of muslin worked by the children of Tallaght Industrial School.

135. TAYLOR, Hon. Mrs., Ardgillan, Balbriggan, Co. Dublin.—Turkish embroidered table cover, brought from Constantinople by Lieutenant-Colonel Taylor, M. P.

136. TAYLOUR, Miss L., Corballis, Drogheda, Proprietor.—Fire-screen, with family arms emblazoned thereon in needlework.

137. THOMPSON, W., Stonehaven, Designer and Manufacturer.—Strong cover carpeting, made of wool engine waste.

138. TIGHE, LADY LOUISA, Innistioge.—Specimens of Innistioge lace.

139. TODD, BURNS, & Co., Mary-street, Dublin.—Irish needlework and crochet lace.

140. TOWNSEND, G., Friar's-walk, Exeter.—Designs for book illustrations, for lace, and for brooches, &c.

141. TRENCH, Hon. Mrs. HENRY, & Mrs. FREDERICK, Cangort Park, Shinrone, Patronesses of Cangort Park and Cloghjordan Schools.—Lady's embroidered collar; infant's embroidered body.

142. TRENCH, MARIA M., James's-street, Dublin, Designer.—A piece of embroidery.

143. VESEYERS, Mrs., Industrial School.—Shawl, from nettles, bleached; scarf from daisies, bleached; polka, from japonica, bleached; parasol, from sweet pea, bleached; polka, from marsh mallow; parasol, from nasturtium; parasol, from convolvulus; ten specimens of flax from fibres of plants; cloth manufactured from the wild bog-down, mixed with wool.

144. WARREN, Mrs. H. M., Molesworth-street, Dublin.—Embroidered counterpane, in needlework.

145. WELSTED, Mrs. H. S., Ballywalter, Castletownroche, Co. Cork.—Richly embroidered cambric pocket handkerchief, collar, chemisette, baby's cap, &c., worked in Shanballymore Industrial School.

146. WHITWELL & Co., Kendall, Manufacturers.—Specimens of Kidderminster carpeting.

147. WHYTOCK, RICHARD, & Co., Edinburgh.—Specimens of new tressel fringe; and patent tapestry net for curtains.

148. WILLIAMS, Mrs. J. E., Home Ville, Rathmines, Dublin.—Berlin wool tapestry.

149. WOODWARD, H. & Co., Kidderminster, Manufacturers.—Carpets; Tournay velvet pile; Persian, Turkey, Brussels.

150. WOODS, LOUISA C., Whitestown, Balbriggan, Co. Dublin.—Scarlet Turkish embroidered table cover.

151. YATES & NIGHTINGALE, Gutter-lane, London, and Fountain Works, Mitcham, Manufacturers.—Printed cloth table covers, and embossed cloth table covers, shown as specimens of printing and embossing, in imitation of needlework, &c.

# CLASS XX.

## ARTICLES OF CLOTHING.

TO a reflective mind not the least suggestive department of the Exhibition was that which illustrated the Costume of the time. Whether viewed historically or artistically, the subject is interesting. Several contributions, of various character, indicated the remarkable changes which have from time to time taken place in the fashions of our own and other countries; and certainly seemed fully to justify the reproach of fickleness and absurdity cast upon our national apparel. It was not a little curious to contrast the ridiculously complicated adornments of Queen Elizabeth's reign with the ball-room dresses of the present day; or the easy garments of our male predecessors with the most uncomfortable and ungraceful attire into which we now, by some curious process of compression, contrive to narrow ourselves. Who was not amused in examining the singular collection of Mr. Sparkes Hall, by the antique articles of shoes and boots in which our ancestors displayed or concealed the neatness or the clumsiness of the foot, as fashion dictated? No more ludicrous contrast could be presented than between the Norman shoe, with its elongated toe and ornamental chain, and the marvellously small and high-heeled indescribability into which the ladies of a much more modern epoch inserted their Chinese feet—*how*, it were impossible to tell. The Merry Monarch luxuriated in roomy and not over-neat yellow leather boots perfectly shapeless, and depending for ornament alone on a massive buckle; how changed is the appearance of those indispensables to king as well as peasant now, and how improved the arts of contrivance, even in this small particular, both as to material and form. Not less curious was it to mark the changes which the covering for the head has undergone, although the result is confessedly no credit to the march of improvement. We have the low round cap of the Frank, exalted into the conical Cromwellian, and distorted into shapes various as fancy could devise, until the present inconvenient and uncomfortable fool's crown became the rage. Equally interesting was it to observe the apparel of different countries, so far as they were illustrated by garments from the sunny East and frigid North,—from the hills of India and the isles of Japan.

But, considered artistically, both the material and the forms of our costume open a large field for reflection. With what exquisite delicacy and elaborate beauty the Hindoo female traces her embroideries, as she did of old, when this occupation was the accomplishment of the daughters of kings. How fine is the texture of the shawls of Dacca and Cashmere; and even the garments woven by the savage are not destitute of design. But what long years of struggle and triumph find their memorial in every product of the loom; and how much of the greatness of our country has been enhanced by those inventions which have furnished us and the human family with our simplest requirements. If we view these productions in fabric and in apparel with reference to the art displayed in them, we find much to admire; for the more artistic knowledge of the principles of design which now prevails is appearing most markedly in the attire of the people. If we criticise dress as a fine art, while there is much to please the eye, there is, however, also, undoubtedly, much to offend it. We are not yet proficient in the science of form as applied to attire. The tendency is more to the awkward, ungraceful, close-fitting, and cumbrous style of dress, than to the easy, flowing, and natural form which accommodates itself to the motions of the frame, and gives full play for its development. As we examine the different articles of dress exhibited in our large show-rooms of fashion, we cannot but lament that elegance and comfort should be so largely sacrificed to a capricious whimsicality which adopts and imposes upon us every eccentric's absurdity;—in one year burying us in a bonnet deep as the hood of a friar, and in another exposing us in an equally ridiculous extreme; now scorning the fetters of a stock, and again putting us in the pillory daily. Assuredly much has yet to be done in the reformation of our style of dress, so as to make it at the same time convenient and becoming. The rule which should guide us in regarding the novelties which are placed before us is, the combination of elegance of pattern and form with convenience and comfort. There can neither be beauty nor ease so long as we prefer the stiff, hard lines of our present mode to the flowing robes of other nations and other times. There is much difference of taste in these matters, but to us the unincumbering garment of the Greek peasant girl is in some respects more pleasing than the straitened dress of a city belle.—J. A. S.

### HOSIERY AND GLOVES.

The manufacture of hosiery has long been carried on in this country, the goods produced at Balbriggan near this city, having a world-wide reputation. Balbriggan hosiery has been patronized by royalty, and by many of the nobility and gentry not only of the country, but throughout the United Kingdom, and even an export trade in these goods is carried on to a small extent to other nations. But notwithstanding their acknowledged excellence, and the high favour in which they stand, the manufacture has not made progress at Balbriggan; the goods there produced standing much in the same position as the Irish poplins—excellent of their class, in short, the best that are produced—but so expensive, as compared with the Nottingham hosiery, as to have only a comparatively limited demand. The branches of manufacture which can be said to be peculiarly Irish are those of linen, poplin, and hosiery. The first of these, since the removal of all legislative interference with the trade, is able to enter into successful competition with the productions of other nations; the soil and climate of the country being well adapted for the growth of the raw material, and the manufacture being for the most part in the hands of large capitalists who bring enterprise and intelligence to their aid. The poplin and hosiery goods stand in a somewhat different position. In these we have no advantages so far as regards the raw material, which in both cases is imported. But in the production of the respective articles a high standard of perfection has been attained, which for years past it has been the aim of the manufacturers to keep up, almost irrespective of price: probably on the ground that in producing goods for the wealthy a small reduction in price would be no consideration, and that although this policy might stand in the way of any very extended trade, yet the profits on what is produced may compensate for it. In this respect we had on a previous occasion to call attention to the different policy pursued by the English and Irish manufacturers—the former making economy of production the chief consideration, for which quality was sacrificed, and the latter often looking mainly to quality, almost irrespective of price. Where either consideration is attended to, irrespective of the other, a great mistake is committed. For, notwithstanding the admitted excellence, nay, the great superiority, of the Irish goods, there are not half a dozen master manufacturers engaged in either the poplin or hosiery trade in this country; and, what is more, none of these are on an extensive scale—at least when compared with the operations of the manufacturers on the other side of the channel. On the other hand, so far has the rage for cheapness been carried by some of the English manufacturers, that the quality of their goods is so completely at a discount at almost any price, that they can alone look to an export trade. But even in the foreign markets certain classes of English goods are so little valued as to be absolutely unsaleable; and in those cases where the quality is not at once recognisable by the eye, which comprise a large class of articles, the manufactures of Birmingham, Sheffield, and certain other places, unless in the case of well-established houses, are regarded with great suspicion.*

The extremes of which we here speak indicate a state of affairs which enterprising and intelligent manufacturers can readily turn to account. The prints of Hoyle, and the cutlery manufactured by Rodgers, have attained a cosmopolitan reputation, simply because in these cases quality has continued at all times to be a primary consideration, while cheapness has not been overlooked. So in the Irish hosiery trade, there is great room for the exercise of those considerations which Messrs. Hoyle, Rodgers, and many others, have so successfully turned to account. In the production of Irish goods, in many departments, excellence in quality is the great desideratum, and in none more than in that to which we are now directing attention; but while we hope never to see the day when quality will be disregarded, or when it will even become a secondary consideration, we are desirous of seeing economy of production carried to a greater extent than it is at present, so that our manufacturers may be enabled to extend the field of their operations by successful competition with the productions of other countries.

The invention of the stocking frame dates so far back as 1589, when it was brought before the public by the Rev. W. Lee, its first operation being at Nottingham. The chief seats of the manufacture at the present day are in Nottinghamshire, Derbyshire, and Leicestershire, and also to a small extent at Godalming in Surrey, and at Balbriggan. The production of hosiery goods is also carried on at Hawick. Throughout Ireland the knitting of stockings is carried on as a branch of domestic industry, but the consumption is for the most part confined to the families in which the work is produced. In the south and west this trade is carried somewhat beyond the local demand, but the quantity of goods thus brought into the market is inconsiderable. The returns of the hosiery trade of the United Kingdom are stated to exceed £3,600,000 per annum; and the number of frames at work is over fifty thousand. The number of hands employed in England alone is about one hundred thousand, consisting of about an equal number of persons of both sexes. Until lately the practice has been to work the frames entirely by hand in the dwellings of the workmen; but within the past few years in the great seats of the hosiery trade some progress has been made in collecting the frames into factories, in a few of which steam-power is employed.

In the production of the finer class of goods here, only one stocking is produced in the frame; and in the case of drawers and vests the several parts are produced separately, and sewed together when completed. In the cheaper class of articles, however, the material is produced in a large web, out of which articles of the different kinds are cut, as a tailor cuts out our ordinary garments; and they are afterwards sewed up. The great superiority of the former practice is so obvious as not to require illustration; but the extent to which cheapness is carried by the latter plan is truly surprising. Some of the recently invented frames are capable of being worked by a youth, and of producing in a week as many framework knitted socks as can be cut and sewn up into seventy-five to one hundred dozens of small women's hose. Specimens of this class of goods were to be seen in the Exhibition of 1851, weighing 14 oz. per dozen, and offered wholesale at 2*s.* 2*d.* per

* As bearing upon this subject an interesting statement was made at the last Annual Cutlers' Feast, in Sheffield. In discussing the prospects of the great branch of trade which is there so extensively carried on, the importance of an increased degree of attention being devoted to the quality of the goods was strongly insisted upon. It was stated, that on the other side of the Atlantic the English axe will not be taken to any situation in which it cannot be easily replaced or repaired, as so very little reliance can be placed upon it; and that in such cases sound economy is exercised by procuring the really good article, almost irrespective of the price at which it may be sold. We merely cite this as an illustration of the foolish extent to which the rage for cheap goods has been carried, the evil of which in the case in question is so great, that unless remedied without delay, Sheffield goods will cease to bring any price in the market, unless in so far as they are the production of those manufacturers who continue to maintain a high character in the trade, and who do not allow their names to be affixed to anything which is not of good quality.

dozen ready for the market! Well may it be said, indeed, that this presents one of the most remarkable instances of the power of improved machinery to cheapen production ever seen.

The Irish hosiery trade was at one time of considerable importance, both in the production of silk and cotton fabrics. The first record which exists of the statistics and state of the trade is dated so far back as 1748, at which period it is stated to have been in a flourishing condition. At a meeting held in that year to regulate the trade, which was presided over by Alderman John Ross, then Lord Mayor, the number of workmen was stated to exceed seven hundred, which far exceeds that of the persons now engaged in it. In 1754 an addition was made to the number of frames at work, to which a further increase was made in 1755. In 1779 there were 1500 workmen enrolled as belonging to the trade, 300 of whom were engaged in the production of silk fabrics. But it should be observed, that the silk-hosiery business had nothing to do with the Spitalfields trade, and hence was not under the surveillance of the Royal Dublin Society. The hosiery trade was not confined at this period to the metropolis; Cork, Waterford, and several other places, had factories; and it continued to flourish until the beginning of the present century. The requisite materials do not exist to enable us to form an opinion as to the precise causes which led to the rapid and continuous declension of the business from that period; more especially as the linen trade and other branches of industry enjoyed an unexampled prosperity. In 1824 the number of persons belonging to it was reduced to 350, since which period it appears to have remained nearly stationary. After the year just mentioned it will be apparent that the alteration in the fiscal regulations affecting the silk trade would exercise an influence upon the silk hosiery similar to what it did on the Spitalfields trade; and accordingly, in 1832 we find that the last vestige of that manufacture had disappeared.

Balbriggan is now the seat of the Irish hosiery business, the goods produced there being remarkable for their fine quality. In 1796 this branch of industry was introduced there by Mr. Joseph Smyth; and in 1820 the establishment of Smyth and Co. was opened in this city, by whom the character of the trade has been creditably maintained, and who continue to be the principal employers. At the present period there are altogether about 200 frames at work in the trade, about one-half of which are engaged in the production of what is termed coarse goods; and the number of persons of all kinds engaged in the business in this country is about 320—but a small proportion of what are employed in many single manufactories on the other side of the Channel.

The persons who now carry on the trade are, Smyth and Co., Wilson and Armstrong, and Appleyard, all of whom have establishments in this city. A few frames are kept at work by M. Moran, of Stephen's-green. The collection of Smyth and Co. was possessed of special interest, both on account of the variety and excellence of the goods, some specimens of which illustrate the quality of the best articles manufactured at different periods, thus affording, as it were, a practical history of the progress of improvement; the several stages in which are strongly marked, as might be seen by comparing the goods of 1810 and 1824, and these again with those of the present day. One dozen of pairs of the finest ladies' stockings in the collection weighed 7ozs.

The contributions of gloves to the Exhibition were not so numerous as might have been expected. This branch of the trade is, however, a most important one. The places in England at which it is largely carried on are, London, Yeovil, Worcester, Woodstock, Torrington, Hexham, and Witney. The value of the yearly produce is estimated at about a million sterling, and the total number of hands employed at these places is about 46,000.*

Limerick has long been famous for the manufacture of gloves, though we believe it has been decreasing of late, owing to the active competition of those engaged in the trade in England, and on the Continent. That locality was represented by J. Burke, who exhibited gloves in a great variety of skins. The other exhibiters were W. Meehan, M. Moran, and J. Watkins, all of this city; but on the whole, this class of articles was very imperfectly illustrated in the Exhibition.

### HATS AND CAPS.

The excellence of the goods produced by several parties in this branch of trade in this city has long been acknowledged, and the extent of the local trade is far beyond what it is commonly supposed to be. In the manufacture of hats this country enjoys a peculiar advantage as compared with England, in the lower duty charged on spirits, a considerable consumption of which takes place in it. In both cases the silk for the finer qualities of hats is obtained from Lyons, as the peculiar lustre of the dye there given to it has not been successfully imitated elsewhere; and so far as this is concerned the English and Irish manufacturers are almost on a par. The raw material used in the body of hats of all kinds is mainly of home production, so that here no drawback is sustained; while the existence of a large local demand at all times confers a great advantage on the home producer over his rival in another country. As regards the consumption of spirits in the manufacture of hats, we are not in possession of statistics which would lead us to any correct approximation of the quantity used; but we have been assured by persons in the trade, that it is so considerable as to make the difference in the outlay in an English and an Irish hat manufactory an important saving in favour of the latter.

Some of the manufacturers of this city do a large business in the production of the unfinished article for the supply of those engaged in the trade in the large towns throughout the country, who merely finish off the goods which they obtain in the metropolis; and although the finish of hats turned out in this way may not

* Gloves play a conspicuous part in many national customs which originated in the days of chivalry. The origin of the custom which prevails in these countries at a maiden assizes, when a pair of gloves is presented to the presiding judge, is not generally known. In former times the judges of the land were prohibited from wearing gloves on the bench, and hence the custom, when there was no judicial business to discharge, of presenting a pair of gloves.

be so good as that of some of those imported, yet their superiority in point of durability causes a considerable trade to be carried on in this manner.

The foundation of the hat being formed by the process termed *felting*, as distinguished from *weaving*, it is of course the shorter kinds of wool that are best adapted for the purpose, for reasons which we fully explained when treating of the woollen manufacture. The outer covering is composed of different kinds of fur, and in the finer hats it is of silk. In the case of certain hats there is a uniformity of material throughout, there being no external covering to impart an appearance different from that of the body of the hat; but of all the improvements in this branch of industry the use of silk for the outer covering has been the most important, as imparting a degree of elegance possessed by no other material.

There are few articles of personal attire that have formed the subject of so much discussion as the hat, the form and texture of which have been much criticised, and apparently not without reason. Various modifications have been proposed, and some have even been introduced; still the hat has remained for years without alteration, if we except the greater or less breadth of rim, and the height and size of the crown, which have varied according to the caprice or fashion of the day. A cylinder close at the top, and with a rim round the open end, must fit the head so tightly as to prevent being blown off by every passing breeze; and being exposed to all weathers it must necessarily be made waterproof; but both of these properties combine to render the hat at once unhealthy and uncomfortable. So-called ventilating hats have been introduced, but they do not appear to have presented any peculiar advantages, from the small amount of favour with which they have been received.

A modification of the hat was exhibited by Mr. Fulton, of Glasgow, which displayed considerable ingenuity, and seems to be well calculated to remove some of the greatest drawbacks to which the common hat is liable. This invention, which has been protected by patent, has reference to certain modifications of the lining and internal fittings, by providing against the hard pressure of the ordinary hat, while, at the same time, ventilation is secured. In the annexed engravings, Fig. 1 is a plan, Fig. 2 a section of a hat so constructed, and Fig. 3 is a view of the lining detached. The lining A, which is made of a size slightly less than the interior of the body of the hat B, is suspended on a wire C, which passes round the top, and is shown partly uncovered in Fig. 2. This wire is supported by four or more flat strips of brass D, fixed to the hat body at the rim. In the interval between these strips are an equal number of strips E attached to the wire C, and stitched to the lining; these being covered if desired. The brass strips act slightly as springs, causing the lining to accommodate itself to the form of the head. The peculiar arrangement adopted keeps the lining stretched; a fine wire or whalebone piping G being run round the bottom of the lining to assist in keeping it in shape. The arrangement of the brass supporting pieces is susceptible of modification: for instance the supports D, and stretchers E, may be formed in one piece, as in Fig. 4, the descending piece being a little on one side of the support to allow of closer compression; or again, the piece may be duplex as in Fig. 5. In these figures AA are front, and BB edge views of the springs, the small holes showing the manner of attachment. This arrangement of a loose lining affords an easy self-adjustment to the head. The pressure is like that of a well fitting cap; and to promote ventilation thin slips of cork, or other light material, may be interposed between the lining and the hat body.

Fig. 1.

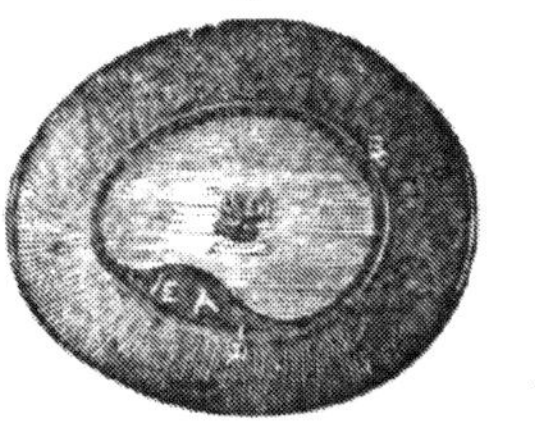

Fig. 2.

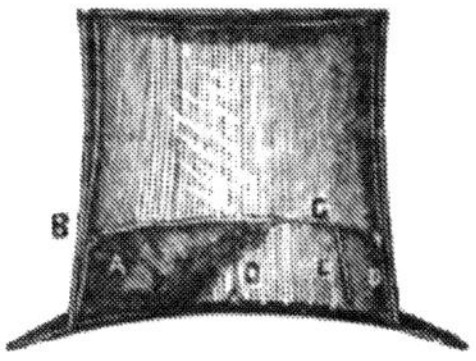

Fig. 4.

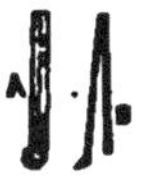

Fig. 3.

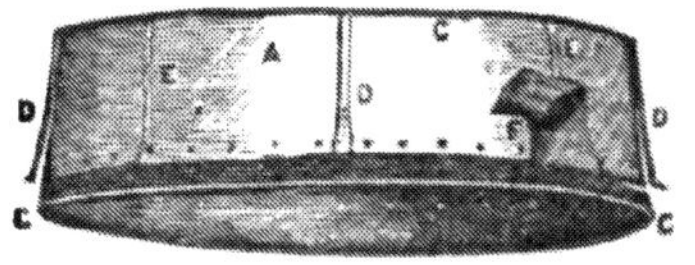

Fig. 5.

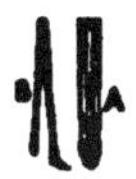

Fulton's Self-fitting Ventilator Hat.

Of caps there were most of the varieties in use, including military and undress caps, but in neither, as regards style or material, was there any feature calling for special remark.

The manufacture of straw bonnets is carried on to a large extent in particular localities in England, but in this country it can scarcely be said to be localized. It is obvious, however, that the production of straw plait might be advantageously carried on in a country where manufacturing industry has as yet absorbed but few of the female population, and where the raw material of most kinds may be obtained in any quantity desired. In many cases straw plaiting would be carried on with much greater advantage to the peasantry than the lace or sewed muslin trade. The caprice of fashion is almost omnipotent in everything referring to ladies' bonnets; but at all times straw bonnets are in considerable demand, so that the manufacturer has merely to suit the form and kind of plait to the requirements of the trade for the time, to be able successfully to carry on his business.

## BOOTS AND SHOES.

Some of the remarks which we have made in other sections of this class apply with equal force to boots and shoes, the manufacture of which must in all cases be to a great extent a local one. We have reason to believe that a considerable export trade is carried on in Irish boots and shoes; though it is somewhat curious that considerable quantities are also imported. The extent of the trade of even a few Dublin houses in this department is very large, only a small proportion of which is for home consumption. The provincial dealers take considerable quantities of goods, especially those for ladies and children; and in some places in England and Scotland Irish boots and shoes are also in estimation, and meet with a ready demand.

This branch of industry was fairly represented in the Exhibition, the whole collection presenting specimens of excellent workmanship, as might be naturally expected in the case of goods manufactured specially for the occasion. The contribution made by J. Sparkes Hall, of Regent-street, London, previously referred to, is deserving of special note, on account of the great interest which it presented in a historical point of view. This collection contained specimens of sandals, shoes, and boots, from the times of the Romans to the present day, many of which are whimsical in the extreme. Some of the present prevailing fashions are eminently obnoxious to criticism on account of the absurdities which they involve, and the degree to which they violate good taste; but the shortcomings, or rather the excesses, of any of them in this respect are as nothing compared with many of the ridiculous fashions which prevailed at different periods in times past. Of this there can be no more forcible illustration than was to be found in the collection in question.—J. S.

---

1. APPLEYARD, H., Balbriggan, and Lower Sackville-street, Dublin, Manufacturer.—Plain and lace cotton hose, sandals, &c.; children's cotton socks; Berlin wool shirts; cotton drawers; woollen vests.

2. BAIRD, J. H., Upper Ormond-quay, Dublin, Manufacturer.—Patent leather, and plain Wellington and top boots; double-soled and cork-soled boots; elastic spring dress boots, in satin, Irish tabinet, prunella, and patent cloth; buttoned and laced boots in variety; plain and patent leather shoes, &c.; all manufactured on the diagonal-pegged system.

3. BARACLOUGH, ——, Lichfield-street, Tamworth, Staffordshire, Inventor and Manufacturer.—Patent dress shoes, top and side lining in one piece; ladies' and gentlemen's waterproof boots, with elastic gore for tender feet and weak ancles, &c.

4. BAXTER, R., West-gate, Thirsk, Yorkshire, Inventor and Manufacturer.—Pair of promenade boots, with clogs and springs; pair of skating boots, with springs, &c.

5. BAXTER, WILLIAM, Grafton-street, Dublin.—Ladies' and gentlemen's boots and shoes.

6. BERRALL, W., & SON, Marylebone-lane, London, Manufacturers.—Walking, hunting, racing, and dress boots, ladies' and children's boots and shoes; samples of blocked boot fronts.

7. BOARDMAN, J. F., Grafton-street, Dublin.—Shirts.

8. BROWN & SHERLOCK, Westmoreland-street, Dublin, Manufacturers.—Hunting, dress, and Wellington boots; embroidered slippers; walking, shooting, and dress buskins; and patent hollow trees and shapes for boots.

9. BROWNE & PAYNE, Lower Sackville-street, Dublin, Manufacturers and Importers.—Hunting scarlet coat, cord waistcoat, and improved breeches; full dress evening suit; walking suit; Irish frieze, alpaca, and Venetian paletots; llama coat; clerical coat and waistcoat; fancy plaid trowsers; vests of tabinet, cloth, silk, &c.

10. BURKE, T., Patrick-street, Limerick.—Limerick gloves in walnut shells; gentlemen's coloured kid gloves; white and coloured buck and doe gloves; white and coloured dog-skin gloves, and ladies' gloves.

11. BUTLER, W. B., Castle-street, Dublin, Manufacturer.—Silk, velvet, and beaver hats; summer hats; cloth caps.

12. CAMPBELL, H., Grafton-street, Dublin, Manufacturer.—White and blue satin stays.

13. CARLETON & SON, Castle-street, Dublin.—Ladies' boots and shoes.

14. CARRINGTON, S. & T., Stockport, Manufacturers.—Beaver and felt summer hats; satin plush hats, sporting felt hats, waterproof and flexible; ladies' satin plush, beaver, and nap felt riding hats; ladies', girls', boys', and children's beaver and felt bonnets, hats, &c.

15. CLARK, CYRUS & JAMES, Street, near Glastonbury, Somersetshire, Inventors and Manufacturers.—Ladies' gentlemen's, and children's registered boots and shoes; varieties of ladies', gentlemen's, and children's boots, shoes, and slippers; patent elongating gutta percha goloshes.

16. COLES, W. F., Paul-street, Finsbury, London, Manufacturer.—Lapland and lambskin socks, &c.

17. COLLINGS, J., Great Ormond-street, Bloomsbury, London, Inventor and Manufacturer.—An arm pad or artificial knee for tailors to rest their arms on, to work while sitting upright upon a chair.

18. CONDON, Miss, Patrick-street, Cork, Manufacturer.—Ladies' and gentlemen's kid gloves.

19. CRAIG, M., & SON, Dublin, Manufacturers.—Ladies brown Balbriggan, lace, and embroidered hose; gentlemen's cotton hose, and Balbriggan half hose, plain, ribbed, and embroidered; cotton and silk drawers and vests; Recamier lamb's wool; gentlemen's plain and fancy shirts.

20. CREAK, J., Wisbeach, Inventor and Manufacturer.—Oxford shoes, screw-bottomed, made without welts or stitches; waterproof shooting boots, screw-bottomed; leather gaiters.

21. CROTTY, J., Lower Bridge-street, Dublin, Manufacturer.—Ladies' stays.

22. DAWSON, W., Duke-street, Dublin, Manufacturer.—Top, hunting, patent leather, cork soled, and plain boots, buskins and shoes in variety; ladies' leather buskins; a pair of shoes without a seam; a pair of buskins with screw bottoms.

23. DELANY, J., Lower Sackville-street, Dublin, Designer and Manufacturer.—A new garment which can be worn either as coat or cloak; Roman full dress clerical coat of Irish manufacture; trowsers in different materials; embroidered vests in gold, silver, and silk, from original designs; walking coats and paletots; vestings and other woollens.

24. DONEGAN, J., Dame-street, Dublin.—Suit of vestments, cloth of gold, of French manufacture; specimens of silk and trimmings of Irish manufacture.

25. DOYLE, J., Mary-street, Dublin, Manufacturer.—Ladies' and gentlemen's boots and shoes.

26. DOYLE, M., Wells-street, Jermyn-street, St. James's, London, Designer and Proprietor.—Elastic stays.

27. DUGGAN, J., Capel-street, Dublin, Proprietor.—Cotton hose, drawers, and vests, &c.

28. DUMAS, MADAME, Dawson-street, Dublin, Importer and Manufacturer.—A variety of French corsets, with figure and busts showing the effects of same.

29. FULTON, A., Argyle-street, Glasgow.—Felt, satin and felt, and satin hats; the patent self-fitting ventilator hat.

30. GAHAGAN, J. R., Henry-street, Dublin, Manufacturer.—Stays and corsets.

31. GLENNY, C., Balbriggan House, Lombard-street, London, Manufacturer and Proprietor.—Balbriggan hosiery; ladies' stockings of various degrees of fineness; [illegible] fine lace stockings; gentlemen's fine half hose.

32. HALL, J. SPARKES, Regent-street, London, Manufacturer.—Ancient British, and Roman shoes and sandals; Anglo-Saxon shoes and boots of the seventh century; Norman half boots of Robert (the Conqueror's eldest son)

[illegible]

50. Meyer & Richardson, [illegible]-street, Dublin. Gold laced [illegible]; uniform waistcoats and [illegible]; embroidered military frock; gold [illegible]; hunting caps; and military accoutrements.

51. Merry, J., [illegible]-place, [illegible], Dublin, Manufacturer.—[illegible] with leather [illegible] cockades, with parchment [illegible].

52. Mitchell, F., Cartwright-street, [illegible], London, Inventor and Manufacturer.—[illegible] boots, with spurs on a new [illegible]; leather boots; spurs, showing the [illegible].

53. Moran, M., Stephen-street, North, Dublin, Manufacturer.—Hosiery of various [illegible]; hose, half hose, socks, drawers, elastic web [illegible] and collars; cotton and silk web braces; [illegible] men's kid gloves in variety.

54. Morgan, J., Grafton-street, Dublin, Manufacturer.—Hats, riding caps, &c.

55. Morrison, A. and W., & Co., Dublin, Manufacturers.—Dunstable, rice, [illegible] and fancy [illegible] bonnets; ladies' boots and shoes.

56. Morrison, H. & Son, Castle-street, Dublin, Manufacturers.—Hats of various shapes and sizes.

57. Nelson, J., Holloway, London, [illegible] Manufacturer.—Boots made to wear in centre of [illegible] to last the sole out, thereby superseding the [illegible] irons and revolving heels.

58. Nicoll, H. J., & D., Regent-street, [illegible] London, Producers. G. Macdowell, [illegible]-street, Dublin, Agent.—Irish poplin paletot; waterproof and [illegible] two guinea paletot; morning coat, exhibited for [illegible] ness and cost quality (registered); patent [illegible] coat; coat of mail; Canadian coat; morning [illegible] mitten; patent trowsers and vest [illegible] braces; the [illegible]; dress for medical [illegible] cloak cane (waterproof cane concealed in a walking [illegible]); Russian cape, made in all its stages by machinery [illegible] coat, with a cushion in skirt; [illegible] float cloak [illegible] ation of life from shipwreck.

59. Nolan, M., Henry-street, Dublin.—[illegible] of embroidered cashmere; [illegible] dress [illegible] poplin; girl's dress of lace and Irish poplin [illegible] embroidered cashmere; baby's hood of cashmere [illegible] tered.

60. O'Donoghue, J., Bachelor's-walk, [illegible] turer.—Timber clog soles, timber-soled [illegible] shoes; clothiers and hatters' tick cards.

61. O'Loughlin, Mrs., North [illegible]-street, [illegible] Dublin.—Stays.

62. Parker, J., Dame-street, Dublin, [illegible] Ladies' and gentlemen's light and strong [illegible] variety.

63. Peyton, J. C., Upper Ormond-quay, [illegible] facturer.—Hunting and riding [illegible] saturation in a chemical fluid [illegible] 11th Hussars; stage boot, costume [illegible] XVI.; racing, shooting, and other [illegible] turning.

64. Poirotte, [illegible], Suffolk-street, [illegible] Ladies' French shoes and boots.

65. Robinson, [illegible] facturer.—Model of exhibitor's [illegible] patterns of the various articles of [illegible] linen, Irish stays, straw bonnets and [illegible] and bonnets; dresses, and gentlemen's [illegible]

[illegible]

66. Rogers & Baker, Grafton-street, [illegible] turers.—[illegible] Irish [illegible] trowsers, of Irish tweeds and [illegible]

67. [illegible] Irish embroidered [illegible]

a small
several
y; and,
rfection
nches of
a greater
great seat
we were
d that ten
hree came
came from
prise that a
e principal
presented a
ublic, which
from Cork
ing was con-

urably distin-
of three more
Clonmel, who
f special atten-
of articles was
it was not only
n of trade.
a more essential
In other classes
corresponding low
vable qualities ar-
gradations of this
uch as to style and
ity of the blades be
itation applied to it.
ver be lost sight of by

roduce such a degree of
, at the same time that
rdness depends. If we
e diamond, which is the
. If we subject a piece of
vil, we find that the par-
ncreased. In this case the
sity. If we take a piece of
lunge it into cold water, it
than after hammering, and
e facts evidently show that

e shows that within certain
Many alloys are also harder
times, as we find by many of
a file. Chemical composition
liate cause, for the same piece

68. SHEILS & SCOTT, Castle-street, Dublin, Manufacturers.—Ladies' and children's boots and shoes.

69. SILVERLOCK, H., Trinity-street, Dublin, Designer and Manufacturer.—Boots and shoes, strong, light, and dress; model of a life guardsman's leg and boot, with head of the late Duke of Wellington, and other ornaments, cut out of a solid piece of wood, by the exhibiter.

70. SPACKMAN, W., Victoria-street, Belfast, Manufacturer.—Articles of clothing made by a sewing machine.

71. SUPPLE, J., Quay, Waterford.—Gloves.

72. THOMPSON, A., St. Andrew-street, Dublin.—Clergymen's and lawyer's robes.

73. THRESHER & GLENNY, Strand, London, Inventors and Manufacturers.—Waistcoats for gentlemen and ladies; cashmere; silk and thread hosiery.

74. TOLLET, G., Betley-hall, near Newcastle, Staffordshire, Proprietor.—Mantle with feather-work border, &c.; feather-work tippets, trimmed with goose down; muff and victorine made of the tail feathers of China fowl; a muff and boa made of goose down (Miniver pattern); with many other articles of feather-work.

75. WATKINS, JOSEPH D., Dame-street, Dublin.—Buckskin hunting breeches; buckskin hunting vest; goatskin riding or driving gloves.

76. WEBB & Co., J. H., Upper Bridge-street, Dublin, Manufacturers.—Men's, women's, and children's boots and shoes.

77. WEBB, T., & Co., Upper Sackville-street, Dublin, Wholesale Manufacturers.—Boots and shoes; coats; vests; trowsers; shirts; collars; drawers; socks; gloves, &c.

78. WILSON & ARMSTRONG, Nassau-street, Dublin, and Balbriggan, Manufacturers.—Ladies' fine, superfine, and low Balbriggan stockings; gentlemen's Balbriggan socks, vests, and drawers.

79. WRIGHT, J., Westmoreland-street, Dublin, Manufacturer.—Hats, caps, and children's fancy felts, &c.; and other articles connected with the hatting trade.

80. WRIGHT & OXLEY, Lower Sackville-street, Dublin.—Hats, hunting caps, &c.

81. WRIGHT & STANLEY, Lower Ormond-quay, Dublin, and Mespil, Manufacturers.—Silk, beaver, and felt hats; military and court hats; with specimens of materials used in the manufacture.

# CLASS XXI.

---

## CUTLERY AND EDGE TOOLS.

THE space devoted to this class of goods in the Exhibition was not considerable, comprising only a small portion of the Northern Gallery; still there are few articles without their representatives in the several contributions. The objects are small, and individually of little value, yet they are of great utility; and, being in common use, the extensive demand which exists for them has led to a high degree of perfection being attained in their production. The manufacture of cutlery being, moreover, one of those branches of business which admits of being carried on with a comparatively small capital, it is to be found, to a greater or less extent, throughout the chief cities and towns of the country. Sheffield has long been the great seat of the manufacture in the United Kingdom, and, as might have been expected, it is to that town we were indebted for many of the collections in the Exhibition. Of the entire number of exhibiters we find that ten were English, five Irish, and three Scotch. Of the English exhibiters six belong to Sheffield, three came from London, and one from Norfolk; of the Irish exhibiters four belong to this city, and one came from Clonmel; and the Scotch exhibiters were all from Glasgow. It must have been matter of surprise that a greater number of Irish exhibiters did not appear in this department. A case containing the principal articles of cutlery could have been got up at a comparatively small expense, and the occasion presented a good opportunity to the various manufacturers of bringing their goods under the notice of the public, which it might have been expected would have been more largely taken advantage of. Contributions from Cork and Limerick appeared in Hyde Park; and it is passing strange that from these localities nothing was contributed to this department of our own Exhibition.

We recognised among the exhibiters on the late occasion many of those who had honourably distinguished themselves in 1851. For example, five of them then obtained prize medals, and of three more honourable mention is made in the Jurors' Report, one of these parties being S. Bradford of Clonmel, who contributed an exceedingly interesting collection to our Exhibition, which was well worthy of special attention as coming from one of our provincial towns. If then the space occupied by this class of articles was scarcely what might have been expected, we had the satisfaction to know that, on the whole, it was not only fairly represented, but that the exhibiters comprised several of the best houses in this branch of trade.

There is, perhaps, no other department of manufacturing industry in which *quality* is a more essential consideration than in that of cutlery. Inferior articles of cutlery are positively worthless. In other classes of goods the quality is fairly enough made to depend on price, and inferior articles at a corresponding low rate find a ready market. In articles of clothing, for example, we have all sorts of conceivable qualities according to the station and means of the wearer, and all may be good of their kind; but gradations of this kind cannot exist to the same extent in cutlery. The handles of knives may vary much as to style and price, and the same of razors and other articles in this department; but unless the quality of the blades be good, the cutlery is absolutely worthless, whatever may be the character of the ornamentation applied to it. In the selection of the class of goods under notice, this is a consideration which must never be lost sight of by the purchaser.—J. S.

### HARDENING AND TEMPERING STEEL FOR EDGE TOOLS, ETC.

The most important object to be attained in the manufacture of edge tools is to produce such a degree of hardness as will enable a fine, sharp, and durable edge to be ground upon the blade, at the same time that the steel will not be too brittle. It is difficult to say upon what this property of hardness depends. If we compare bodies indiscriminately, relative density is no test of hardness, because the diamond, which is the hardest of all known bodies, is far less dense than any of the commonly used metals. If we subject a piece of steel to the process of "hammer-hardening," that is, striking it repeatedly on an anvil, we find that the particles will be brought closer together, its bulk will be diminished, and its density increased. In this case the hardening, undoubtedly, accompanies, if it be not produced by the increase of density. If we take a piece of this hammer-hardened steel and heat it to a certain degree, and then suddenly plunge it into cold water, it will be found to have acquired additional hardness, but it will now be less dense than after hammering, and very frequently, even than it was before being subjected to that operation. These facts evidently show that increase of density cannot be the cause of the increase of hardness of a body.

Steel is a compound of iron with a small quantity of carbon; and experience shows that within certain limits an increase in the proportion of carbon is attended with increased hardness. Many alloys are also harder than either of the component metals,—a fact which was well known in ancient times, as we find by many of the bronze celts and swords; some of which are scarcely affected by a common file. Chemical composition would then appear to have some relation to hardness; but it is not the immediate cause, for the same piece of steel may be made to assume the conditions of soft and very hard steel, without any apparent change in its chemical composition.

The two philosophical toys, the Bolognian flask and Prince Rupert's drops, present certain phenomena which appear to suggest an explanation of the causes of the hardening of steel by heating and then suddenly cooling it. If a sharp, angular body be thrown into the flask, its cohesion is destroyed and it falls to powder, although it is capable of withstanding a slight blow of a hammer on its external surface. A Rupert's drop will bear a great amount of pressure, but if the smallest fragment be broken off the tail, the whole flies into powder with a slight detonation. If we examine a Rupert's drop we find that it is full of minute fractures internally, but is covered externally with a thin skin of unbroken glass, which compresses, as it were, the internal detached particles, and keeps them together. This constrained condition of the glass is produced by cooling the external crust of the glass more rapidly than the internal parts; the latter being consequently in a state of tension. If the glass be subjected to the process of annealing, the internal parts have time to arrange themselves before the perfect solidification of the outer coat, and consequently the state of restraint or tension just described does not exist.

Unannealed glass is found to have a peculiar action upon light, giving rise to the brilliant phenomenon of coloured polarization, an action which is founded upon a peculiar crystalline structure. When slowly annealed it loses this structure, and it has been experimentally shown that glass contracts in the process of annealing. Now steel, which, when hammer-hardened, contracts, as we have before observed, and becomes fibrous, when fire-hardened becomes crystalline; and if this crystalline steel be slowly cooled, that is, annealed, it will lose that property and diminish somewhat in bulk. In large masses of steel where the external crust happens to cool very rapidly it squeezes the parts within before the particles have fully arranged themselves, and when these subsequently cool down there is always a tendency to rupture at the junction of the outer crust with the central part. Hence, the outer crust often shells off in hardening large masses of steel: it sometimes also occurs that a large mass of steel such as a die or anvil may to all appearance be successfully hardened, and yet give way with a loud report, and occasionally with considerable force, several hours after the operation of tempering.

The fire-tempering of steel appears, therefore, to be accompanied by a molecular change, analogous to that which occurs in unannealed glass; and is not the result of a change in chemical composition, at least in its ordinary acceptation.

Although steel may be sufficiently hardened for many purposes by the process of hammer-hardening, it does not afford the same range of comparative hardness or elasticity which fire-hardening does; and hence, by the term tempering the latter method is usually understood. In hardening and tempering the three things to be attended to are:—1. The means of heating the objects to redness; 2. The means of cooling them; and 3. Those of applying the heat for tempering or letting it down. The temperature for forging and hardening steel must, of course, depend upon its quality, its mode of manufacture—as, for instance, the amount of carbon which it contains; the smaller the quantity of that body the lower the temperature. In all cases the lowest available temperature is to be recommended; too low a heat being much less injurious than too high; as the latter increases the brittleness of the steel. The means of heating must, of course, depend upon the size of the object, but whatever source of heat be employed, the chief object to be attained is as great a uniformity of temperature as possible, and that not too high.

It is, however, in the selection of the cooling medium that the mysteries of the craft are all concentrated. Almost every conceivable fluid mixture has been employed for this purpose. But as the value of the cooling medium depends altogether upon its conducting powers, the mystery is not in the preparation of mixtures, but in the manipulation. Water is, perhaps, the best medium of all. For small tools for particular purposes, mercury gives the greatest degree of hardness. The relative hardness of different tempers of steel is, however, a point which is exceedingly difficult to ascertain with precision; the only test is a file, and no two files being exactly of the same hardness, the standard is an ever-varying one.

After hardening the steel, the next point is the tempering. As there are many degrees between hard and soft, and as each is suitable for certain purposes, it is necessary to communicate to each object the exact degrees of hardness required. This operation consists in raising the object to a particular temperature, varying from the temperature of boiling water to the melting point of lead, according to the degree of hardness required, and then chilling it. The degrees of temperature are judged of by the oxidation of the brightened surface of the steel. If a piece of steel be filed bright, and then heated, a thin film of oxide will form upon the brightened surface, which will produce different shades of colour, according to the temperature. It is by means of these shades that the workman is able to judge of the exact point to which an object should be heated in order to temper or let it down. The following Table contains these shades, the temperatures to which they correspond, and the class of tools for which each degree of tempering is adapted:—

| | | |
|---|---|---|
| Very pale straw-yellow, . . . . . . . . | 430° Fahr. | Tools for working in metal. |
| A shade of darker yellow, . . . . . . . | 440 " | |
| Darker straw-yellow, . . . . . . . . . | 470 " | Tools for wood, and screw taps, &c. |
| Still darker straw-yellow, . . . . . . . | 490 " | |
| Brown yellow, . . . . . . . . . . . . | 500 " | Hatchets, adzes, chipping chisels, and other percussion tools, saws, &c. |
| A yellow tinged slightly with purple, | 520 " | |
| Light purple, . . . . . . . . . . . . . | 530 " | |
| Dark purple, . . . . . . . . . . . . . | 550 " | Springs. |
| Dark blue, . . . . . . . . . . . . . . | 570 " | |
| Paler blue, . . . . . . . . . . . . . . | 590 " | Too soft for any of the above purposes. |
| Still paler blue, . . . . . . . . . . . | 610 " | |
| Still paler blue, with tinge of green, . | 630 " | |

This Table only includes the temperature from a little below the melting point of tin to a little above that of lead, but a still lower temperature than that corresponding to very pale straw-yellow is employed for many objects requiring unusual hardness; for example, the knife-edges of compensation pendulums, chemical balances, &c., which require to be very hard, are prepared at temperatures frequently as low as that of boiling water.—W. K. S.

---

1. ALGOR, J., Eldon-street, Sheffield, Manufacturer.—Knives in variety, for shoemakers, cooks, butchers, spinners, painters, and glaziers; farriers' drawing knives; curriers' and butchers' steels; plumbers' shave hook; saddlers' half-moon knife.

2. BAKER, W., Allen-street, Clerkenwell, London, Manufacturer.—Brad awls; awls for sieve and cage makers, bookbinders, saddlers, and shoemakers; shoe awls for pegged boots; marking and seat awls; gunsmiths' wood awls; curriers' and cabinet makers' scraper steels.

3. BATES, J., South Great Georges's-street, Dublin, Manufacturer.—Razors mounted in tortoise-shell handles, pearl, bog oak, ivory, and buffalo; penknives and table knives in the process of manufacture; improved Irish balance table knives; a newly-invented carving fork and knife sharpener together; masticating knife, and card of miniature razors and penknives; bread knives mounted in bog oak.

4. BOOTH, J. & J., Golden-lane, Dublin, Proprietors.—An assortment of plough planes; sash and side fillisters; moulding and bench planes.

5. BRADFORD, S., Clonmel, Designer and Manufacturer.—Model of a cutler's workshop; razors, in tortoiseshell, pearl, ivory, and horn handles; razor strops; pen, pocket, pruning, clasp, hunting, and sportsmen's knives; daggers; bowie knives; portable knife and fork, with transferring blades, &c.; bread knife, with carved ivory handle; case of veterinary instruments; tobacco cutter, and cucumber slicer; skates, of improved pattern; large show knife and fork.

6. ELLIN, T., & Co., Sheffield, Manufacturers.—Bread knives; carving and table knives and forks of various patterns, and with handles of mother-of-pearl, ivory, fancy woods, horn, and bone; cooks' and butchers' knives and steels; shoemakers', glaziers', farriers', cork and leather cutters' knives; office, pocket, bowie, pruning, sportsmen's, and numerous other knives; scissors; sickles and reaping-hooks; the original Sheffield whittle; table knife of fifty years ago; large venison carving knife; and other articles of cutlery.

7. FIRMIN & SONS, Strand, London.—Swords and heraldic devices.

8 HANNAH, A., Calton, Glasgow, Manufacturer.—Thompson's screw shell and single twist augers; braces, bits, and other boring tools; claw clinch; veneering, and riveting hammers; turning tools, &c.

9. HIGGINS, F., Hatton-garden, London.—Knives and forks.

10. HILLIARD & CHAPMAN, Buchanan-street, Glasgow, Inventors and Manufacturers.—The gigantic table knife; registered improved table knife, with invisibly locked-fast handle; skeleton of the improved table knife, showing the principle of the invention; shear-carving knife, for carving fowls, &c.; razors; the valise strop, containing a complete shaving apparatus; newly-constructed sportsmen's knives; a variety of knives, scissors, &c.; buffing machines for cleaning knives.

11. HUNTER, M., & SON, Talbot Works, Sheffield, Manufacturers.—Solid cast steel table cutlery; plated dessert knives; scissors; razors; penknives; sportsmen's and pocket knives; saws, files, edge, and joiner's tools; axes; butcher knives and steels; shoe knives; adzes.

12. HUTTON & NEWTON, Highlane, near Sheffield, Manufacturers.—Sickles; sharping and patent hooks; scythes; hay and straw knives.

13. MATHIESON, ALEXANDER, & SON, Saracen's-lane, Glasgow, Manufacturers.—Bench planes in boxwood; fillister planes in ebony; plows with steel bridles and side screws; assortment of various kinds of planes; screw augers; brace screw bits; turning chisels and gouges; improved holdfast; pianoforte key maker's tools; braces handsomely mounted; fancy turning tools; hammers; with numerous other tools.

14. PARKER & THOMPSON, Rockingham-street, Sheffield, Inventors and Manufacturers.—Joiners' tools, comprising braces and bits, squares, bevils, spokeshaves, gimlets, augers, turnscrews, gouges, spirit levels, screw boxes, saw setts, saw pads, brad awl pads and tools, patent angular boring pad, turning saw and frame; cucumber slicer, with silver plated cutter, &c.

15. STANIFORTH, T., Hackenthorpe, near Sheffield, Manufacturer.—Sickles, hooks, scythes, and hay knives.

16. THOMPSON, W., Dame-street, Dublin, Manufacturer.—Cutlery in variety.

17. THOMPSON, S., & Co., Henry-street, Dublin, Manufacturers.—Carving, table, and dessert knives; pen and sporting knives; razors in pearl handles and in cases; four-sided razor strops; patent corkscrews.

18. TYZACK, J., Wells, Norfolk, Inventor and Manufacturer.—Tyzack's British razor, ground out of the solid steel.

# CLASS XXII.

## IRON, AND GENERAL HARDWARE.

THE range of articles included in this class is extensive and varied, comprising almost the whole of the smaller class of goods made from the baser metals. On looking over the list of objects which it contains, we are forcibly impressed with the difficulty of devising any system of classification for the purposes of an Industrial Exhibition which will not contain many anomalies. In going through the Catalogue we meet with the names of articles the position of which it is frequently not easy to determine. Certain kinds of articles properly coming under the head of Machinery are included in this class, such as mangles, washing machines, and knife-cleaning machines, though commonly coming under the denomination of ironmongery; and in the arrangement the problem to be solved is to determine where the line of demarcation is to be drawn. And, further, many of the articles are very properly estimated in two points of view,—more especially castings in iron,—and then we come in course to the distinction between ornamental art and fine art. Objects of this kind might, therefore, be considered here or in Class XXX.; or they may demand a notice in both places. Here, however, æsthetic considerations are not taken into account, and we view the articles simply as illustrative of workmanship and appropriateness for the intended purpose.

In the various branches of the manufacture of hardware the division of labour has been carried out to a surprising extent; and in the case of the smaller articles, the operatives are usually themselves the manufacturers. Large workshops are divided into compartments, each fitted up by the owner for carrying on some special branch of the trade, and supplied with steam-power. For working many of these compartments little capital is required. They are each rented by one or more artisans, who, from week to week, carry home the produce of their labours to the merchant, the price realized by the wares supplying funds to carry on the next week's operations. The greater part of the hardware is produced in this manner; though for the manufacture of the larger articles regularly organized establishments with large capital become necessary.

Excellence of workmanship and economy of production are among the results of carrying out a division of labour; and hence the cause of the isolated manufacturers throughout the country finding in their brethren of the great manufacturing towns such formidable rivals. In tracing the history of the iron manufactures we find an astonishingly increased production, combined with an equally surprising diminution in prices.

It is not merely on account of the importance of this department, and the satisfactory manner in which it was represented, that it has claims on our attention. While the public generally had the opportunity of inspecting some of the most recent, as well as the most important applications of scientific and manufacturing ingenuity to the production of articles of domestic economy, our tradesmen could not fail to learn a lesson in their business from the manner in which the collections of some of the English and Scotch exhibiters were displayed. It may appear to be ungracious to point out the shortcomings of our own countrymen; but provided this be done in a proper spirit, we can conceive nothing better adapted to bring about the desired improvement. In looking through the collections of the various exhibiters in the department of "Iron and General Hardware," we were forcibly struck with the evidence of enterprise and business habits which some presented, and the utter lack of any appearance of these qualities in others. In some cases we found parties in attendance during the day, to afford any necessary explanations concerning their goods; in others we obtained catalogues conveying detailed information, sometimes even including lists of prices; while at the stands of another class of exhibiters the only information to be had was the brief enumeration of the articles contained in the catalogue. In the latter case, we are grieved to say, the great majority of our Irish exhibiters were to be included. Among these we may naturally expect to find considerable dissatisfaction as to the results of the Exhibition. It will not have brought that addition to their business on which they might have fairly calculated. Hence, the necessity of indicating to what this was mainly to be traced. If one class of exhibiters fall short of the tact and business habits which characterize another, it may be reasonably expected that they will fall behind in the race of competition in which all parties are now so actively engaged; and that not on account of any inferiority of their goods, but simply because they did not adopt the requisite means to push their trade.

It will further be obvious to any one that excellence of manufacture is only one of the requisites to insure any large amount of public patronage. Price is, as we have frequently before observed, an equally essential element of consideration. It must not be forgotten that the problem to be solved by the manufacturer of the present day is not merely who shall produce the best article, but who shall do so at the cheapest rate. If, therefore, an exhibiter wished the public to form a correct appreciation of the value of his goods, as compared with those of his neighbours, he would append the price to each article; and if able to combine excellence and cheapness in any great degree, he might expect to reap a golden harvest. That such has been the case with many exhibiters in this department we have little doubt; while we have as little that the collections of others scarcely led to a single inquiry; and that so far as regards both the Exhibition and their own interests, their appearance in the list of exhibiters has been nothing more than so much labour thrown away. Fully appreciating the account to which the Exhibition might be turned—not merely as indicating the present state of the arts and manufactures of this and other countries, but also as being well calculated to lead to the extension of the trade of those who came forward on the occasion—the Executive Committee accorded to exhibiters full permission to append to their goods such particulars as might be supposed most to enhance their value in public estimation. But it will be obvious that among these there is none of greater value than the price at which they may be purchased. Yet the small extent to which this information was available was truly surprising. As already observed, a few English and Scotch houses had their collections so admirably arranged (sometimes with, and sometimes without an attendant), as to leave nothing to be desired. Either through their representatives, or by means of their priced and descriptive lists, all desired information was available respecting their goods. In scarcely a single instance did we find this to be the case with Irish exhibiters. The excellence of Irish goods does not, in very many departments, admit of question; nay, their superiority in certain cases is freely acknowledged. But our people appear to have yet to learn that something more than this is wanted to compete successfully in the market with even the manufacturer of inferior goods; and this lesson the department of the Exhibition now under consideration was well calculated to teach.

The objects in this class are for the most part of iron, but several other metals are also used, as well as a variety of combinations. We shall notice the several compounds employed, and the manner in which they are produced; and then some of the leading articles in the class will come under review; directing attention, however, rather to the general considerations suggested by an examination of the department, than to details connected with particular objects.—J. S.

### GALVANIZED IRON, TIN PLATE WARE, ETC.

Iron, which possesses so many admirable properties,—such as strength, great infusibility, and the very important one of welding,—is unfortunately readily acted upon by moisture, and by acids however weak, by which its utility is very much diminished. Fortunately, however, its surface may be covered with various metals, which, although not acted upon by acids, and not readily oxidized by the air, would be too costly, too soft, or too brittle to be used alone. For example, vessels of iron destined to contain sulphuric acid may be covered with lead by heating them and plunging them several times into melted lead, a thin coating of which adheres to the surface of the iron. Similarly it may be covered with copper by plunging it into melted copper, the surface of which is protected from oxidation by a layer of melted salt and chloride of zinc. In both cases, and indeed in all where iron is to be coated with another metal, its surface must be made perfectly clean, which is effected by *pickling* the object to be coated in dilute acid. Brass is sometimes substituted for copper for coating iron, especially for covering buckles and other metallic parts of harness where strength and appearance are required. Iron is not covered with silver by dipping it into the metal, which is too valuable for that process. The object to be silvered is first tinned—that is, coated over with common solder by means of a hot soldering iron, the surface being kept clean by some rosin; a piece of thin sheet silver is then laid upon the tinned iron, to which it is made to unite by heating it until it softens, after which it is polished. In this way the buckles, bitts, and other metallic parts of coach harness are silvered. This branch of trade is carried on very extensively in Dublin by Mr. W. R. Box, the whole of the plated work in his harness in the Exhibition having been plated at his establishment.

A considerable quantity of iron is now coated with zinc in the way above described—that is, by plunging the heated iron into melted zinc—and sold under the meaningless name of galvanized iron. Iron thus coated is applied to a great number of purposes, such as corrugated iron roofs and even entire buildings, spouting, ship sheathing, lining the coal bunkers of ships, buckets, and many other articles of domestic use; as a substitute for japanned ware, wirework for fences and garden chairs, nails,—examples of all of which were exhibited by Messrs. Tupper and Car, of London. Zinced iron is, no doubt, more durable under ordinary circumstances than uncovered iron; but the coating of zinc is very far from being an uniformly successful protection against rust, and in some few cases it even increases the rapidity of the oxidation. The same objection applies, certainly in a much less degree, to the process of the Rev. Professor Callan, who proposes to substitute lead and antimony for the zinc; but then this process labours under the great disadvantage that the greater protection afforded by the alloy does not compensate for its much higher price. The most important, however, of all coated irons is tin plate; which, as is well known, consists simply of thin sheet iron coated with tin. In this article we have all the advantages of iron, combined with the colour, beauty, and durability of tin. The iron employed for this purpose, which must be of a superior quality, is rolled out into sheets between rollers, and cut into squares. The plates thus cut are bent into the shape of a V, and heated in a reverberatory furnace to redness, when they are plunged into a mixture of muriatic acid and water, and then ignited again until they scale, after which they are beaten flat on a cast iron block and passed between rollers. The next operation is to steep them for about twelve hours in sour bran water, and then in dilute sulphuric acid, until they become clear and bright, which is an operation of great importance, and requires to be done with skill; after this they are scoured with sand and put into clean water, where they, curiously enough, remain bright for a considerable time. Sometimes all these operations are reduced to a pickling process in dilute sulphuric acid, a scouring with sand, and a second pickling.

The plates thus cleaned are ready for tinning, which is performed in a room called *the stow*, in which are arranged six pots. In the first is put a quantity of melted grease or tallow, into which the clean plates are put for about an hour, after which they are placed in the second pot in an upright position; this pot contains a mixture of grain and block tin, covered with a layer of melted tallow to keep its surface bright. After remaining from one to two hours in the tin, according to thickness, they are taken out and allowed to drain, after which they are dipped into No. 3 pot, containing melted grain tin; then scrubbed with a peculiar kind of brush made of hemp, dipped again, and plunged into No. 4 pot, which is filled with melted tallow. From the hot grease pot the plates are transferred into a colder grease pot, the heat of which is regulated according to the thickness of the plates. The excess of tin drains to the bottom of the plate, where it forms a thickened margin or wire of tin which must be removed; an operation which is effected in the sixth pot, which contains a little melted tin resting on the bottom of it to the depth of about a quarter of an inch. A boy takes each plate from the grease pot when sufficiently cold to handle, and dips the thickened edge into the melted tin, which in a few moments melts the wire of tin on the plate; whereupon the boy lifts the plate out and strikes a vibratory blow with a flat stick, which shakes off the melted tin, leaving only a faint streak of tin where it was; a mark which is readily distinguished upon every tin-plate. The plates are afterwards cleaned from the grease by rubbing them with dry bran; and packed in boxes. There was only one exhibiter of tin plates, the firm of Allaway and Sons, of Sydney, Gloucestershire, who also sent specimens of the charcoal sheet iron employed in making the plates.

Iron is not the only metal which is coated with tin for commercial purposes; copper culinary vessels, brass cocks, &c., require also to be tinned to prevent the action of fluids upon them. This is effected by heating and strewing some sal-ammoniac over the surface, which removes the oxide and keeps the air from acting upon it; melted tin is then poured into the vessel, and is distributed evenly over the surface, the excess being poured out.

Notwithstanding the almost complete monopoly which England has enjoyed in the possession of rich tin mines, it is singular that the process of tinning iron was not known there, or even generally practised, until about the year 1730! The process is supposed to have been discovered in Bohemia, that of coating metals generally with tin being an invention of the ancient Gauls. From Bohemia it appears to have passed into Saxony about the year 1620, and thence about 1670 into England and France.

It is unnecessary to point out the innumerable uses of tin plate, or to say more than a few words upon the manner in which articles are fashioned out of it. Besides the almost endless variety of cheap articles for domestic use, manufactured by hammering upon a block and joining with solder of lead and tin, there is another class of wares called block tin goods, but made of the same kind of tin plate as the common ware just alluded to. This class of articles, of which we may consider dish-covers to be the type, were formerly made by being beaten or planished on a polished metal anvil, stake, or beak iron, with a polished steel hammer, the different pieces composing the article being then soldered in the usual way. But this method is now superseded, except in the case of a few articles, by stamping in dies, and by spinning. The process of spinning consists in causing the plates to take a convex or globular form by the pressure of a steel tool or burnisher against a suitably formed wooden block, set as a chuck in a lathe, and made to revolve rapidly. By this method the articles acquire a great degree of solidity and strength, and a beautiful surface, at the same time that seam soldering is avoided. Dish-covers are often made by the process of stamping; and a variety of small embossed articles, such especially as common coffin furniture, are produced by stamping with dies, either with a stamp or fly press. The coffin ornaments are afterwards covered with gold leaf, Dutch foil, silver leaf, or are lacquered or japanned.

There are few manufactures which have so largely contributed to convenience and cleanliness as that of tin plate ware. It is also equally durable, as convenient; and, unlike many other metals and alloys, its use is not attended with the slightest danger to health.

The great improvement which has been effected in the purification of zinc, by which it may be laminated into exceedingly thin sheets, has brought it into competition with tin plate for making several articles. It has, moreover, several advantages over tin plate, for large articles such as baths, &c., but it does not answer for small articles, and should not be employed for making them. Having already noticed the applications of zinc, we refer our readers to our former remarks on the subject in page 57.

### BRITANNIA METAL.

From the earliest times, whether from the result of experiment or of accident, it has been known that the value of a metal may be much increased by alloying it with a small quantity of some other metal. For example, silver in a pure state is so exceedingly soft that it could not be employed with advantage when subject to a great amount of friction, as it would wear too rapidly, and would be liable to be indented and scratched with too great facility; but by alloying it with about 1-12th part of copper, it becomes hard, and may thus be employed for coinage. Similarly, by alloying copper with tin in various proportions, we get bell-metal, gun-metal, bronze, &c., while the extremely useful alloy, brass, is obtained from a mixture of copper and zinc. Tin by itself is not well adapted for being moulded into forms, but by the addition of a small quantity of lead it acquires that property without losing its fine colour, brilliancy, and unchangeability on exposure to the air—being in the latter respect but little inferior to silver, hence the application of such an alloy under the name of pewter to the manufacture of various utensils. Both lead and tin are soft metals, and their alloy, pewter, has also the same character; it was therefore desirable to substitute for the lead some hard metal, and such a substitute was found in antimony, which, with a colour not inferior to tin, is exceedingly hard and brittle, and when alloyed with the latter produces a compound capable of being moulded with great facility. Antimony is in other respects an important metal; besides its use in medicine, as the base of tartar emetic and other medicines, it is used in the manufacture of printers' type, which consists of an alloy of this metal with lead.

There are a great number of alloys of tin and antimony, which differ only in the proportions employed; occasionally, however, a little copper and zinc are added, and sometimes bismuth. These alloys have received different names. Thus we have Britannia metal, plate pewter, argentine, Ashberry's patent metal, and a number of others; names which represent the most various proportions of tin and antimony. Argentine, which is usually cast in moulds, contains generally 85·5 of tin, and 14·5 of antimony in 100 parts. Plate pewter, on the other hand, may be laminated, and hence cannot contain so large a proportion of antimony, which, in proportion as the quantity is increased, renders the alloy more brittle and hard. Its usual composition, as found by analysis, is, tin, 89·30; antimony, 7·14; bismuth, 1·78; and copper, 1·78, in 100 parts. The following numbers represent the composition of a few specimens of Britannia metal and of Ashberry's patent metal in 100 parts:—

| | Britannia Metal. | | Ashberry's Metal. | |
|---|---|---|---|---|
| | Laminated. | Cast. | Cast. | Cast. |
| Tin, | 90·60 | 90·80 | 81·90 | 77·812 |
| Antimony, | 9·40 | 9·20 | 16·25 | 19·375 |
| Copper, | — | — | 1·84 | 2·781 |
| | 100·00 | 100·00 | 99·99 | 99·968 |

The applications of these various alloys are very important; the chief uses are the manufacture of tea and coffee pots, spoons, cruet stands, dish-covers, plates for printing music, &c. &c.

The great seats of the manufacture of these articles are Birmingham and Sheffield, where several thousand persons are employed in it, and from which enormous quantities are exported to every part of the world. Some of the articles are made by casting in moulds, others by the lathe, or by stamping with dies. Not only are snuffer dishes, plates, and other simple objects, formed by casting, but even the most complex pieces, such as teapots, are sometimes cast with their spouts, legs, &c. The moulds employed are either of brass or iron, and composed of a great many pieces which are put together and united firmly by surrounding them with a paste of plaster of Paris, which is easily broken off when the piece is cast. The moulds are very expensive; for example, one for making a handsome teapot with ornaments in relief, composed of about seventeen parts, would cost perhaps £70 to £80; so that a very considerable capital must be embarked in a factory of Britannia metal in moulds alone. Sometimes a teapot is cast in different pieces, which are afterwards soldered together with a soft or tin solder, which is also employed to stop up any little holes that occur in the piece from defective casting in the mould. When articles are fashioned with dies, or formed on a lathe out of sheets of argentine or Britannia metal, the various pieces are soldered together in the same way.

Articles, whether cast or fashioned in any other way, are trimmed and rubbed smooth by means of a fine brownish sand obtained from the river Trent, and pieces of wood covered with leather; after which they are polished with tripoli. The parts in relief, such as the ornamented knobs or handles for the covers, &c., are polished with steel tools or with burnishers made of bloodstone. A great deal of the articles made of Britannia metal and argentine are plated strongly by the electro-plating process, and are then polished in the usual way with steel or bloodstone tools. The manufacture of this kind of plate has been brought to great perfection, and many specimens are so well executed that it is exceedingly difficult to distinguish them from real silver, and are also, when well made, very durable.

Considering the very great importance and extent of manufacture in argentine and Britannia metal, we were surprised at the few examples exhibited. Messrs. G. and W. Whitestone exhibited some pretty teapots, both plain and plated; and J. Edmundson and Co. some electro-plated goods, which were, in all probability, made of argentine or Britannia metal, a point which, however, we could not decide without a closer examination than it was in our power to make in the Exhibition. We are not much surprised that this branch of trade has not yet taken root in Ireland when we recollect the cost of a mould for a single article, to cover which it is necessary to sell large numbers. But there is nevertheless a large field opened to a manufacturer possessed of capital, ingenuity, and perseverance in such a branch of business. Why not, for instance, make models in clay or wax, and produce from them moulds by the electrotype process? In this way we are convinced the most elaborate designs could be produced at the expense of a few pounds; and instead of being compelled to produce thousands of articles of the same form, an endless diversity of patterns might be produced in succession. Will some ingenious man take up this idea?

## MANUFACTURES IN COPPER, BRASS, BRONZE, ETC.

*Copper* is used for the production of a great many articles coming under the term hardware, such as coal scuttles, urns, kettles, &c. Articles of this class are produced by hammering and stamping in the same way as those made with tin plate, the only difference being in the mode of soldering. Tin plate is the only metal which is soldered by lapping the edges; but in copper ware the bottoms are joined on, and, indeed, all junctures of copper are effected by dovetailing the parts to be joined, and then soldering them with a hard solder composed of ordinary brass, to which a little zinc is added.

*Brass* is an alloy of copper and zinc, and is, perhaps, of all metals, whether simple or alloys, after iron, the most important. When pure it is exceedingly malleable, and capable of being rolled into sheets as thin as fine paper, and of being hammered into tinsel; it is more ductile even than copper, and admits of being "spun," stamped, or embossed with such facility that, joined with its colour, it is by far the best substance for the production of beautiful and cheap ornaments. There are different kinds of brass depending upon the proportions of the component metals; common brass being formed of from 75 to 80 parts of copper, and 25 to 20 of zinc; tomback, prince's metal, pinchbeck, ormolu, &c. of 1 part of zinc to from 5-8 to 10 parts of copper. The less zinc the softer and the finer grained the brass is; the colour also varies in the same manner from red to yellowish gray. When the proportion of zinc reaches one-half, the alloy is grayish, exceedingly brittle, and can be filed and turned with great difficulty. Brass is employed in the production of ironmongery, either in its malleable condition or as castings.

Ornaments made from hammered brass, when in relief, are produced by placing a piece of the laminated metal upon a matrix or die, in which the pattern of the intended ornament is formed in intaglio, and then driving the brass into the interstices of the die by means of a "reverse," on which a rough pattern in relief is cut. The piece of brass is then annealed to prevent it cracking from the blows; a slight alteration is made in the reverse, and another blow struck. This process must often be repeated until 20 to 30 blows have been struck, before the relief of the ornament is "brought up," the article being annealed after each blow. In the middle ages a great many articles were fashioned out by simple hammering, a process now followed in the manufacture of imitations of mediæval art, of which so many examples were contributed to the Exhibition. In connexion with stamped brass work, brass tubing is largely employed. This article is made by passing a sheet of rolled brass under discs of steel, revolving on a spindle, by which it is cut into ribbons of the size required for the tubes to be made. Each of these ribbons is slightly curved along its length by rollers, and is then made to pass through a hole in a steel plate equal to the external diameter of the tube. In the centre of this hole is fitted a core or mandril, equal to the internal diameter. A tube is thus formed which requires to be soldered along its length; before this operation is effected, however, the semi-formed tube is annealed. The tube is bound round with wire, in order to keep the edges close; a quantity of the granulated solder and powdered borax is spread along the seam or junction of the edges; and the tube is introduced into a kind of stove where the solder melts, and unites the two edges of the brass, and forms a perfect tube. This is then immersed in a very dilute sulphuric acid, in order to remove the scale which has formed on the surface: the wire is now removed, the superfluous solder scraped off, and the tube drawn through another hole in a steel plate. The solder used for this purpose is composed of such proportions of copper and zinc as will form an alloy which will melt thoroughly before the brass begins to soften too much; the usual proportions are equal parts of each.

Brass was formerly made by exposing a mixture of fragments of copper, calamine, or carbonate of zinc, and charcoal, to an intense heat. Roasted blende or sulphuret of zinc, and the matter which sublimes from lead furnaces, &c., and which is rich in zinc, have also been largely employed.

Recently metallic bedsteads have been much used, and a peculiar mode has been adopted for casting the ornaments upon the head and foot rails, &c., instead of the old process of casting each part separately, and then putting them together. By this new method the iron rods forming the framework are directly joined together by casting the ornament about the parts to be joined. To effect this object, the iron rods are set in cast iron moulds, in the position in which they are to remain, and thus form the core of the intaglio impression which is to be cast about them; melted metal is then poured into the moulds; when cold, the ornaments are finished in the usual way. The facility and perfection with which iron bedsteads may thus be put together, and at the same time ornamented, is marvellous.

The development of the proper lustre of the metal is an important part of working in brass. This is done by heating the castings to a very dull red heat, which completely burns off any grease or other organic matter which they may have contracted in their passage through the different operations. Their surface is then cleaned from the scale acquired by oxidation, and they are usually pickled, that is, laid for some time in dilute sulphuric acid, the operation being much assisted by rubbing them with a brush formed of brass wire. By these operations the surface is fully cleaned, and the yellow colour of the brass more or less developed; the full yellow is, however, only brought out by dipping them separately into aqua fortis. This is a nice operation, for if the duration of the immersion be too short, the brass will not acquire full lustre: and if too long, it becomes red or black. After immersion it is washed in water, dipped in a solution of argol or crude tartar, and finally dried in half-dried sawdust, and brushed and cleaned. The articles are then either simply lacquered, as in the case of hinges, common locks, &c.; or they are burnished; or part is burnished, and another part deadened. The operation by which the latter effect is produced, and which has been only introduced within the last thirty years, consists merely in exposing the brass, which has its colour developed in acid, or, as it is called, "fezzed," to another acid solution, very much weaker; and where the action, although perceptible, is not violent, or attended with fumes—a slow corroding, in fact. Burnishing is simply a polishing operation, with tools made generally of steel, but sometimes of bloodstone. The contrast of deadened and burnished surfaces is well adapted for chandeliers, lamps, candelebra, &c. In the latter cases as well as in the ornamenting of grates, &c., common brass is rarely used; but an alloy of copper and zinc, containing much less zinc than common brass, and known as *ormolu*, or an imitation of the red gold of the French jewellers, is substituted. This alloy has a much richer colour, and is more readily burnished and deadened than common brass, and is hence better adapted for expensive articles.

All cleaned, burnished, and deadened surfaces of brass or ormolu require to be lacquered, in order to preserve their brilliancy. This lacquer is simply a spirit varnish, made with seed or shell lac, coloured with a little annatto, saffron, and turmeric, so as to communicate a fine transparent golden tint to it.

*Bronze, Bell-metal, &c.*—If an alloy be made of copper, zinc, and tin, we shall have modern bronze, which, although it differs from brass in containing one of the softest metals in common use, tin, is much harder than brass. Bronze is exceedingly fine-grained, hard, liquid when melted, and forms the sharpest and most beautiful castings, and may be cut and chiselled with great facility. The relative proportions of the component metals vary according to the object for which the bronze is intended. Small objects which are to be gilded are usually made of an alloy which differs little from brass, consisting of 82 parts of copper, 18 of zinc, 3 of tin, and 1·5 of lead; or 64·45 of copper, 32·44 of zinc, 0·25 of tin, and 2·86 of lead. Seven parts of copper, 3 parts of brass, and 1-16 of tin, give a gold-like bronze. The alloy used for casting statues is much richer in copper than those just given; for example, 91·4 of copper, 5·43 of zinc, 1·7 of tin, and 1·37 of lead, represent the usual composition of this class of alloys. The ancient bronzes of the Greeks contained no zinc. An old Attic coin has been found to contain 88·46 per cent. of copper, 10 per cent. of tin, and 1·5 of lead; and a bronze coin of Alexander the Great, 95·96 of copper; 3·28 of tin, and 0·76 of lead. The ancient bronze weapons of the Celtic nations are also free from zinc, but the bronzes of the Romans, especially the later ones, contain small quantities of zinc. *Gun-metal* is a bronze composed of 100 parts of copper to about 10 or 11 parts of tin. This alloy is yellow, with a slightly whitish tinge, and is not so hard as the other bronzes mentioned. *Bell-metal* is a similar alloy to gun-metal, but much richer in tin, the usual proportions being 78 of copper and 22 of tin. Common English bell-metal is a different alloy, composed of 80 parts of copper, 10·1 of tin, 5·6 of zinc, and 4·3 of lead. Fine bell-metal has a much whiter colour than gun-metal, fuses readily, is exceedingly liquid when melted, and is hence well adapted for casting; it is brittle, hard, and ringing, when very slowly cooled; but when rapidly cooled, it is soft, and may be hammered; and in this way it is that gongs, tam-tams, and similar articles, are made. The casting of bells is now very successfully carried on in Ireland, not alone for the service of our own churches, and other public establishments, but many have even been sold in England and in the most distant colonies. The best known of our Irish bell founders are, J. Murphy, who exhibited a peal of eight bells, and a large bell weighing two tons; T. Hodges; and J. Sheridan. The two former obtained prize medals at the London Exhibition of 1851, there being only five others similarly honoured on that occasion.

Brass may also be made to assume a bronze colour, by warming it and dipping it in a solution of arsenious acid in hydrochloric acid, or by brushing it with it; the articles thus treated are then brushed with plumbago or with lampblack in suspension in spirit of wine, heated in a stove, and coated with a lacquer such as we have already mentioned in speaking of brass. A mixture of vinegar, sal ammoniac, alum, and arsenic, is also used for bronzing. It is in this way that lamps, gasaliers, candelabra, &c., are bronzed, the shade of colour depending upon the number of black coatings and the depth of the yellow of the lacquer, both of which may be varied at will.

There are many other alloys of copper and tin in general use, some of which contain zinc, and occasionally antimony and lead. Among the pure alloys of copper and tin we may mention ship-sheathing, and among the latter class of compound alloys the axle cushions for the axles of locomotives, the brasses of gudgeons, bushings of wheels, buckets of pumps, &c., &c.

*Nickel Silver, Argentine, &c.*—Formerly an alloy was commonly used as a substitute for silver for making cheap spoons, composed of equal parts of copper and arsenic. This has now been completely superseded by alloys of copper, nickel, and zinc. The metal nickel which forms the most characteristic constituent of these alloys, is found in general associated with copper, and from having been utterly useless and very injurious to the quality of the copper, it has now become extremely valuable. The different alloys are prepared either from an alloy of copper and nickel, obtained directly by the reduction of the ore of copper containing nickel, or by melting nickel and copper in a crucible, and adding a very little zinc, and then a previously prepared alloy of copper and zinc, and, finally, the quantity of zinc necessary to bring it up to the full proportion required. The relative quantities of each metal vary according to the manufacturer; that employed in England for spoons, forks, &c., to be electro-plated, has been found to be composed of 63 parts of copper, 11 to 19 of nickel, and 26 to 17 of zinc; a very elastic variety of it from Sheffield has been found to consist of 57 parts of copper, 25 of zinc, 13 of nickel, and 3 of iron,—the latter ingredient being in all probability either an impurity or a portion of a zinc alloy, which it has been ascertained can be substituted for pure zinc in all such alloys. The proportion used in Berlin for the best kind is 52 of copper, 22 of nickel, and 26 of zinc; and for the inferior kinds, 63 of copper, 6 of nickel, and 31 of zinc. Ten parts of the finest nickel silver alloyed with 6 of real silver yields a beautiful white, malleable, perfectly silver-like alloy, constituting the true argentine.

A great many of the articles in nickel silver which are electro-plated are cast in metal moulds, which, while filled, are made to contract rapidly by allowing a stream of water to play upon them, and thus communicate a greater degree of sharpness and beauty to the finer parts of the casting. Nickel silver can also be rolled into plates; and it is from such plates that spoons, forks, &c., are made, by cutting and pressing. The ornamental parts and the bowls of the spoons are formed by a die, and stamped, and then finished by the hand.

*Japanned Ware.*—Many articles of tin plate, copper, and brass, are often coated with an opaque varnish, either black or some fancy colour; this kind of coating, from its resemblance to the varnished articles of the Japanese or Chinese, is called, in these countries, Japanning. The varnish employed for black Japanning is made of linseed oil, asphaltum, gum animé, and amber, with some oxidizing or drying substances, such as litharge and sulphate of iron. A number of successive coats of this varnish are laid upon the article, which is heated moderately each time in a stove. When sufficiently coated the surface is rubbed even with pumice, and a coating of thin lac varnish laid over it. Sometimes a series of coats of a kind of tar varnish is substituted for the Japan varnish; in this case two or three coats of shel lac varnish must be laid on to produce a good brilliant surface. Fancy-coloured japanning is effected by mixing the requisite colour with the varnish after a ground of sufficient thickness has been laid on. Japanned articles are now very usually ornamented with designs of flowers, landscapes, arabesques, &c. There are various modes of effecting this, such as stencilling for the simple designs; but landscapes, &c., are usually put on in the same way as on earthenware, or, at least, the sketch or outlines are done so. This process consists of engraving the design upon a copper plate, and printing it upon tissue paper, which is then laid upon the article to be ornamented, pressed against it, the paper damped and withdrawn, leaving the design transferred to the surface of the object, after which it may be painted in full by hand, if required. Frequently these designs are simply black, like engravings, and are then extremely pretty. Tea-trays, baths, water cans, and a vast number of objects, are thus japanned and ornamented. Wood and papier-mache are also japanned in the same manner, and many articles of the latter are sometimes included under the head Ironmongery, but we shall have an opportunity of noticing articles of this kind when treating of Furniture.—W. K. S.

## IRON WORK OF VARIOUS KINDS.

This subdivision includes stoves, grates, kitchen-ranges, fenders, and fire-irons; locks, hinges, and general ironmongery; knife-cleaning machines, and copying presses; the smaller kind of tools, spades, and pick-axes; and miscellaneous articles, as screws, nails, railings, and castings in iron.*

* Cast iron is capable of assuming an analogous molecular condition to that of hardened steel, by being cast in iron moulds. The castings thus produced are termed "chilled iron," and the degree depends upon the temperature of the

The iron manufactures of the United Kingdom occupy a high place from the abundance in which the raw material is produced; and they are for the most part localized in certain districts where coal and iron abound. Considerable changes appear to have taken place during the present century in the localities for particular kinds of work. Thus the production of grates, stoves, and fenders, of an ornamental character, which was previously confined for the most part to London and Edinburgh, has now for its head-quarters Sheffield, Northampton, Dudley, Birmingham, Nottingham, and Derby,—Sheffield being distinguished for articles of a highly ornamental kind, though the trade even in this class of goods is carried on in London and several other places to a greater or less extent. Birmingham has, however, been so long connected with the production of this class of articles, that the name of the town has come to be associated with the articles themselves.

An important characteristic of the heavier articles in this department is the great degree of perfection which has recently been attained in castings of all kinds. In many of the articles exhibited one did not know whether to admire more the graceful and elegant forms given to the most common articles, or the sharpness of outline which they possessed, and which gave even to castings in iron the appearance of works in the precious metals. There were many articles in the Exhibition combining these qualities in a high degree; but those which deservedly came in for the largest share of attention were comprised in the rich and varied collection of the Coalbrookdale Company, arranged in their stand in the Centre Hall, as well as dispersed through other parts of the building.*

## GRATES, STOVES, AND KITCHEN-RANGES.

There was, perhaps, no department of the Exhibition better represented than that referring to our domestic comfort and enjoyment, as embraced in the wide range of heating and cooking apparatus. In open grates, the greatest improvement recently effected is in what is called the "register grate," by placing the smoke-hole close over and immediately behind the fire-grate, in place of allowing the smoke to pass upwards through the top of the grate into the throat of the chimney. There were some exceedingly simple forms of fire-grates exhibited, in which the back and sides were formed of fire-clay, moulded into the requisite form; the only iron in the construction being the front ribs, the bottom bars, and four short legs on which the grate stood in the recess of the fireplace. This is an excellent form for bed-rooms, and for cottages generally. But fire-clay is also being largely introduced into the construction of register grates. In some of these three large fire-bricks form the back and two sides, the skeleton front and ribs only being iron. This application of fire-brick causes a great heat to be radiated from the fire; but the fuel is consumed much more rapidly than where the entire fire-box is formed of iron. Many modern grates have the back of the fire-box made of moulded clay, which is found to answer well; but one of the most beautiful as well as the most efficient grates we have seen had the fire-box projecting forward from the back, which was formed after the fashion of a large cockle-shell, the concave flutings being all polished. The smoke-hole was immediately behind the fire-box, and not more than four inches above it; and yet, contrary to what might have been supposed, it did not smoke in the least, and the finely polished surface of the fluted reflector remained undimmed, throwing out a great heat by reflection. The room in which it was placed was a large one, and possibly, had it been small, the strong cross currents carried by the opening of the door and windows might have occasioned eddies which would have wafted the smoke upwards and into the room.

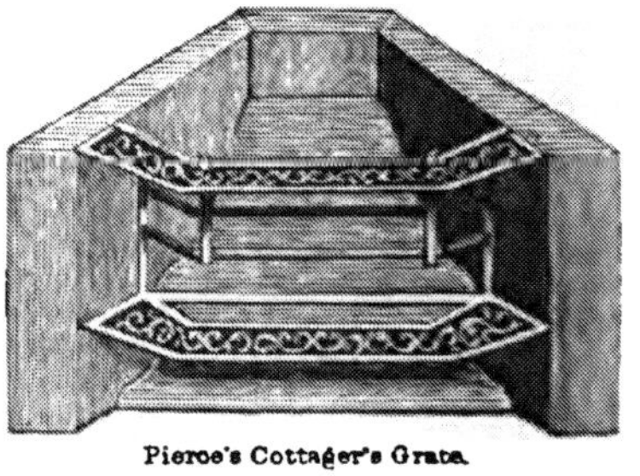
Pierce's Cottager's Grate.

Of the grates of this class we subjoin illustrations of two exhibited by Mr. Pierce, of Jermyn-street, London, in which neatness, efficiency, and economy are combined. The cottager's grate is designed for warming the sitting-room and bed-room of a cottage at the same time with a single fire. It is made of fire-clay, having the back part hollow, to form an air chamber for the admission of fresh air introduced from the outside by means of earthen pipes; and this fresh air passing through the back of the grate becomes warmed, and will thus assist in heating a second room.

liquid iron, its quality, and the thickness of the casting. There is, however, a remarkable difference between chilled iron and fire-hardened steel; by heating the latter to a dull red heat it is again softened, whilst the chilled castings are removed from the moulds immediately after the metal has set, and are allowed to cool in the air; and, although at a very bright red heat, the chilled part does not get softened. In close connexion with this quality of chilled cast iron, it is also worthy of note, that perfectly cold moulds do not yield as hard castings as when they are made, as the workmen say, black hot. Chilled castings are much used, as, for example, for punches for red hot iron, ploughshares, axle-tree boxes, and naves of wheels, cylinders for rolling metal, heavy hammers and anvils, and iron for stamp heads for crushing ore; cannon balls are also examples of chilled iron being cast in iron moulds, not, however, in order to communicate the quality of chilled iron, which is not essential, but to give them a perfect form.—W. K. S.

* The works of this Company are situated in the valley of the Dale, in Shropshire, which is now amongst the busiest scenes of industry to be found in the United Kingdom, the foundries and workshops of the Company filling the bottom of the valley, and the sloping sides of the hills being occupied by coppice and the houses of the workmen. The average number of people employed at Coalbrookdale and the neighbouring works of Horseley, belonging to the same parties, is between 3000 and 4000. The production amounts to the almost incredible quantity of over 2000 tons of finished iron per week; and some of the articles manufactured there may now be found wherever English commerce extends.

The fire lump grate is of very simple construction, and is designed to burn turf or wood, as well as coals. It is made entirely of fire-lump, with movable bars. In burning wood the grating bottom is removed, and the bars placed in the front notches to allow additional space for the fuel, which is burned on the fire-lump itself. The engraving represents the grate when arranged for burning coal; the grating bottom, with the trivet, being in its place, and the bars put back into the inner notches to diminish the space for and thus economize the fuel. A movable frame or trivet is supplied with this grate, having apertures adapted for receiving the usual cooking utensils of the cottager.

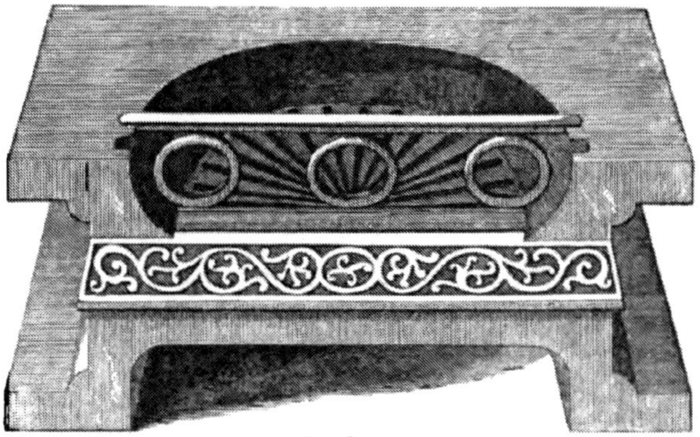

Pierce's Fire Lump Grate.

The finer kinds of open grates were illustrated very satisfactorily by the very elegant collections of the Coalbrookdale Company, and Benham and Sons, of London. These included specimens in steel, bronze, and ormolu; and whether we regard elegance of design, or excellence of workmanship, they were entitled to high commendation. It is somewhat singular that the use of these is confined almost exclusively to the British islands, where fuel exists in greater profusion than in other countries. On the Continent close stoves are in general use for warming private dwellings, as well as public buildings, while in this country their use is almost confined to the latter purpose. The heating power of the close stove, with a given quantity of fuel, is greater than that of the open grate: but the feeling with us against the stove for private dwellings overcomes the economy of fuel. Indeed, as usually constructed, the stove is highly objectionable; and there is little chance of its superseding, to any extent, the use of the open fire-grate in the United Kingdom.

Of close stoves there were several examples in the Exhibition; but they were one and all objectionable in principle, although they were, in many cases, tasteful and ornamental in design. The manufacturers seem to have only one idea: and that is, the way to get the largest quantity of air heated in the shortest time by the smallest possible surface. Hence, the stoves are invariably too small—absurdly so, when compared with the size of the apartments they are intended to heat. It is not unusual to have the cockles of the close stoves so hot that they would melt lead; and yet, it is by coming in contact with this intensely heated metallic surface that the air is warmed. It is needless to say that it is burnt, and not merely warmed; and hence the oppressive close smell which is usually felt on entering an apartment heated by a close stove. Dr. Arnott pointed out the importance of a large heating surface, and an isolated fire-box in the middle of the stove, and illustrated the principle in the stove which he designed; but there are few manufacturers who follow his rules, although more than one have applied his name to their productions. If a close stove is made so large that the radiated heat from an open fire-box in the middle of it will not heat any part of the surface much hotter than the hand can bear; and if, by means of an outer casing, a current of air is induced all round it—a close Arnott's stove is the most economical and effective way in which fuel can be applied for heating purposes; but when we find that the stove is at or about a red heat, and that all the air coming in contact with it is burnt and deprived of much of its vital influence, it can hardly excite surprise that such a prejudice should exist against stoves in general. The use of stoves is therefore likely to continue with us to be confined to public buildings; more especially until the attention paid to the principles of construction approximates to that now devoted to ornamentation.

In the manufacture of this whole class of articles much yet remains to be done towards the attainment of the object in view—the production of the greatest amount of heat from a given quantity of fuel, with the least possible inconvenience from smoke or draughts of air. The imperfect ventilation of our living-rooms has passed into a proverb; the waste of fuel is excessive; and the injury caused by the smoke is such as to make the inhabitants of large cities especially hail any prospect of abating so great a nuisance. Considerable progress has been made in economizing fuel, but the smoke nuisance prevails in all its hideous deformity. One of the causes of the evolution of such large quantities of smoke is the manner in which fresh fuel is supplied. Placed on the top of red-hot coal, it must unavoidably emit visible pitchy vapour or smoke, carrying with it up the chimney much of the heat which would otherwise go to warm the room; but, as suggested in a recent paper read before the Society of Arts by Dr. Arnott, if the fuel could be introduced *below* instead of *above* the burning mass, an entire change would be effected in this respect. In such case the vapour and gaseous matters emitted by the freshly added coal would pass through the red-hot portion of the fire, where they would be partly resolvable into inflammable gas, and be consumed. The heating properties of the fuel would thereby be increased, while a most intolerable nuisance would be prevented. According to the authority just mentioned, various attempts have been made to feed fires in this way, of which the most important was that introduced by Mr. Cutler, about thirty years ago. He placed a box filled with coal immediately under the fire, with its open mouth occupying the place of the removed bottom bars of the grate; in the box was a movable bottom, supporting the coal, and by pressing which the coal was lifted gradually into the grate to be consumed. The apparatus for lifting, however, was complicated, and liable to get out of order, which, with other reasons, had caused the stove to be little used. In a new fire-place invented by Dr. Arnott, and described at length on the occasion in question, the charge of coal for the whole day was placed immediately beneath the grate, and was borne upwards as wanted by a piston in the box, raised simply by the poker used as a lever, and as readily as the wick of an argand lamp was raised; and the fire was under command as to its intensity almost as completely as the flame of a lamp. To light the fire, wood was laid on the upper surface of the fresh coal filling the box, and a thickness of three or four inches of cinders or coked coal left from the fire of the preceding day was placed over it. The wood being then lighted, instantly ignited the cinders above, and at the same time the pitchy vapour from the fresh coals beneath rose through the wood flame and cinders, and became heated sufficiently to inflame itself, and so to augment the blaze. When the cinder was once fairly ignited, all the bitumen rising through it afterwards became gas, and the fire remained quite smokeless for the remainder of the day. In this grate no air is allowed to enter at the bottom, and combustion therefore only goes on between the bars. It is said that the unsatisfactory results of some other attempts had been owing, in part, to combustion proceeding downwards, owing to the admission of air below. Of this arrangement of the fire-place, which appears to be one of so much promise, we regret that there were no specimens in the Exhibition.

Of the class of stoves which partake of the character of the open fire-place and the stove, properly so called, there were some good illustrations. These are now much used for heating public buildings and large apartments, where it may be desirable to have the source of heat as near the centre as possible. Their heating power is great, and they possess all the advantages of the ordinary open fire-place. A stove of this kind, exhibited by Robertson, Carr, & Steel, is shown in the annexed illustration.

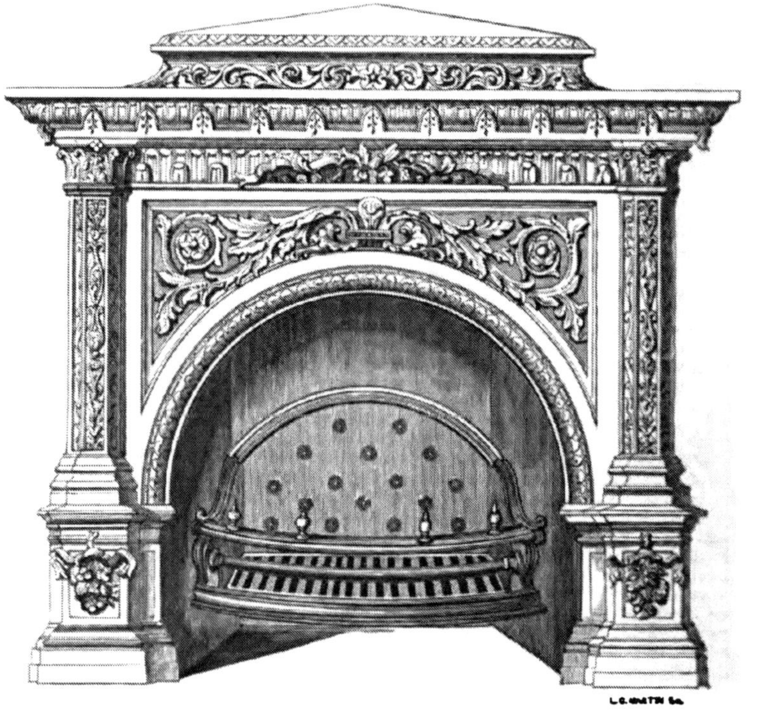

Robertson and Co.'s Stove.

Of kitchen ranges the representation was very good, many of the leading houses in the trade being exhibiters. This circumstance we are disposed to regard as significant, showing as it does the increasing attention now paid to the convenient fitting up of an apartment which is far from being the least important in our dwellings. A condition of good and economical cookery is that proper facilities exist for carrying it on; and if we compare the fitting up of a modern kitchen with that of even the best of our baronial halls some time ago, we cannot fail to be struck with the great progress which has recently been made. The arrangements for roasting, baking, and boiling, to be found in the houses of those of the middle classes of society, are much superior to what were in the mansions of the nobility and gentry at no distant period. Many of the kitchen ranges in the Exhibition were admirable, and the prices usually very moderate; it occurs to us, however, that in the whole of them certain considerations were overlooked. One of the most obvious drawbacks arising from a rigid adherence to conventional usage is the almost invariable construction so as to be placed in the chimney: for which in the modern ranges there is clearly no necessity, from the almost total absence of the open fire. The smoke and vapour could be as readily conveyed away from a range in the centre of the kitchen as when placed under the chimney; a small piece of piping making all the difference; while the convenience of the arrangement suggested is obvious. In the British department the only instance in which this idea was carried out was the cottage range of Benham and Sons; but here the arrangement seems to have been adopted for economical considerations alone, as avoiding the cost of setting it in the wall. In the Belgian department there were two ranges of this kind, which were also otherwise excellent. In these latter the fire-box, in accordance with the prevailing custom, is in the centre of the range, being in form like a crucible or flower-pot. A space of two or three inches in depth forms the flue between the top of the oven and the hot plate; and along this flue on either side the hot air is conducted, returning behind until the divided currents meet at the back of the range and are conducted by a pipe into the chimney flue. We refer specially to these ranges in illustration of the value in point of convenience of not being obliged to build up our ranges in the kitchen walls. The prevailing prejudice in favour of a large exposure of the fire, manufacturers of these articles cannot, perhaps, altogether disregard; though for some time past the extent of open fire has been gradually diminishing. And as this improvement has been carried out, the amount of convenience afforded by the modern ranges has been extended, while fuel has been economized. The hot hearth, on which saucepans, fish-kettles, and such articles, in almost endless variety, may be kept boiling, does not make any extra demand on the fuel for the accommodation which it affords; hot water is obtained in profusion by a boiler surrounding two out of the four sides of the fire; and in the smaller ranges an oven may be heated from the fire in the centre. These are great and obvious advantages, which have been secured almost in exact proportion as the extent of the open fire has been diminished. For roasting, the open fire, no doubt, still appears to be a desideratum, the usual practice of cooking meat in the oven being open to great objection; but even for roasting, the oven may be used, provided a graduated current of air is permitted to pass through it. In this way the objectionable flavour of baked meat may be modified, if not altogether removed; and when this arrangement is properly carried out, we believe that meat so cooked in the oven cannot be distinguished from that roasted before the fire. Smoky kitchen flues are by no means uncommon where the large open fire is to be seen, but the small quantity of fresh air admitted to the flue in the case of the close fireplace insures a good draught, and thereby gets rid of what is a great nuisance. The apparently complicated character of some of the modern ranges is sometimes objected to, on the ground of the internal flues and passages of the range getting choked up with soot and being difficult to clean out. This defect is easily remedied, as the different parts of the range may be so disposed and put together by screws that it can be altogether taken asunder if desirable. This inconvenience will, however, to a greater or less extent, be experienced with every range built up in a wall, as is now the all but universal practice; for some of the passages can be got at with difficulty whatever may be the arrangements adopted for the purpose. But any drawback of this kind would not exist in the case of ranges standing out detached from the wall, every part of which could then be unscrewed from the other.

The foregoing remarks are designed to be suggestive, and are made with a view of directing attention to the requirements of the class of articles under notice, and to the nature of the arrangements by which these requirements are most likely to be fulfilled. We now proceed to notice a few of the kitchen ranges which appeared in the Exhibition, and which have been selected for illustration as types of the class to which they respectively belong.

The most extensive exhibiters in this class were Benham and Son of London; the arrangement of whose stand, as well as the character of the articles in it, made it one of the most attractive places in the Exhibition,—comprehending as it did almost every grade, from the large range for the mansion to that for the cottage. Their cottage range was among the best of the articles of its class from its completeness, and the large amount of accommodation which it afforded. A sketch of this range is given in the annexed engraving, by which it will be seen that it is not necessarily a fixture, and that it merely requires a pipe to connect it with the flue to admit of its being placed anywhere that may be convenient. The quantity of fuel consumed in it is inconsiderable, compared with what is ordinarily required. A suite of cooking utensils may be had with the range which makes it an admirable article for the emigrant or cottager; the whole comprising the means of cooking comfortably for a small family.

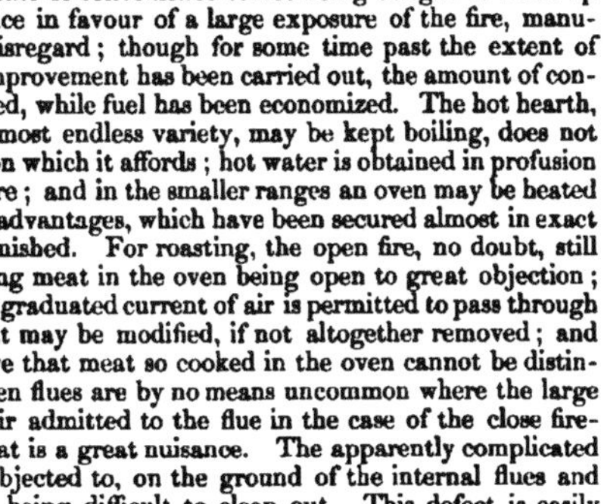

Benham and Sons' Cottage Range.

The fire may here be open or close as desired; the plate which closes up the front of the fire being available when down as a stand on which to place saucepans or other small articles, either as a convenience or for keeping them warm. To this range we are really disposed to attach great value, from the extent to which it combines efficiency and economy. By being placed a short distance from the wall its heating power, as regards the apartment, is considerably increased; and by being able to regulate the admission of air as desired, the consumption of fuel may be regulated with the greatest exactness.

Messrs. Benham & Sons also exhibited Flavel & Bett's prize kitchener, which was first brought before the public in Hyde Park, in 1851. By a reference to the Jurors' Report of that Exhibition, we find that a prize medal was awarded for this range, as well as an acknowledgement of special approbation, it being the only article of the kind so distinguished. It comprises a hot plate oven for pastry, oven for roasting, boiler, and plate-rack—all heated by one fire. By a simple arrangement fittings can be attached, if desired, for the

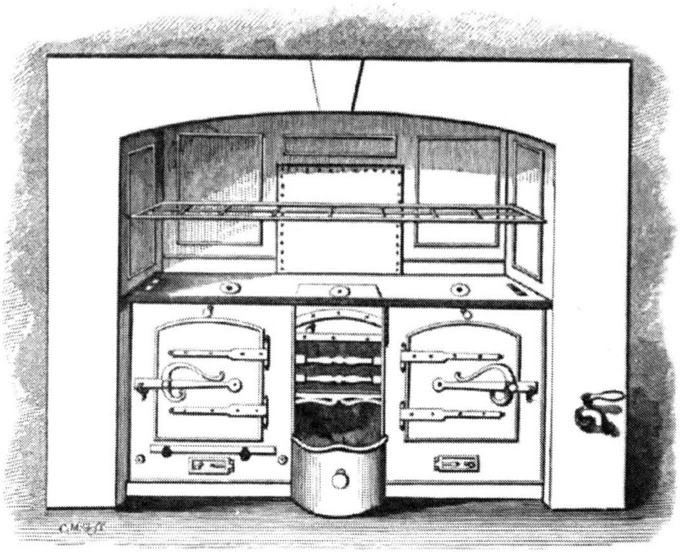

Flavel's Cooking Apparatus.

supply of steam or hot water to cooking vessels or baths. The size of the range is made to vary according to the requirements of the place, so that, while it can be adapted to the cottage, it may also be constructed on a scale to cook for a public establishment. In this range the fire is only partially enclosed.

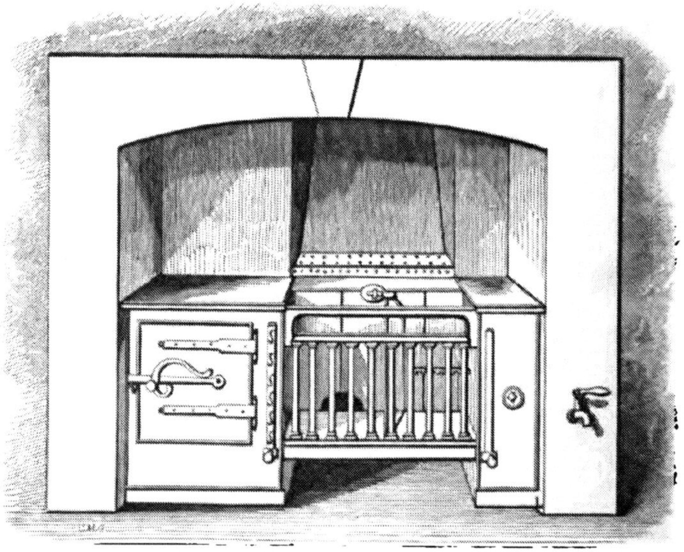

Benham's Improved Family Range.

Another modification of kitchen range was exhibited by the same firm under the name of Benham's Improved Family Range, shown in the accompanying engraving. It has an open fire, sheet iron oven, wrought iron boiler, and movable check; and a large open fire, with vertical bars. The firespace is only 4½ inches deep, and the range is provided with a fire-clay radiating back and solid fire-clay bottom; and among the advantages of the peculiar arrangement adopted, it is stated by the manufacturers that a consumption of 30 lbs. of fuel in this range is as effective as that of 50 lbs. in those of the ordinary construction.

The modifications introduced in the construction of kitchen ranges are, in some degree, perfectly arbitrary, and made to depend on the caprice of the public. Hence the manufacturer is compelled to produce an apparent variety to suit the whims of customers, without the distinguishing characteristics being founded upon any recognised principle of necessity or advantage. We cannot help thinking that there would result

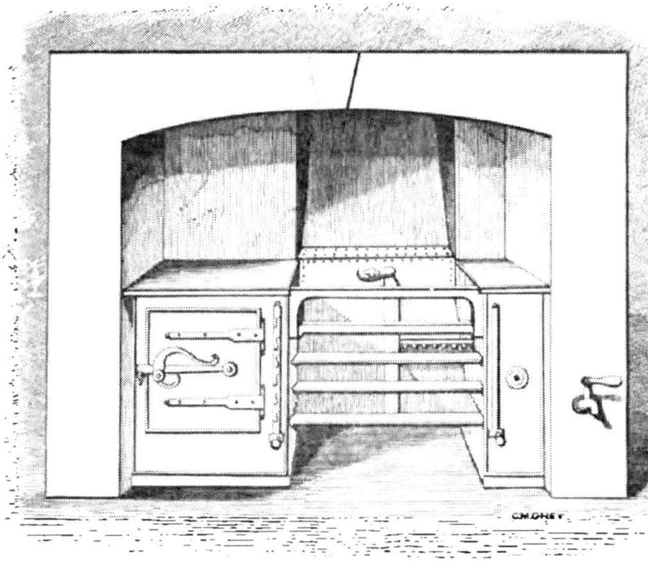

Benham's London Range.

great convenience from manufacturers confining themselves to the production of different sizes of the same article; but this the caprice of the consumers, we presume, renders inexpedient. Hence the varieties which may be found in the collection of even one extensive house in the trade. Thus, in addition to the ranges already noticed, we find another exhibited by Messrs. Benham & Son, which they call Benham's London range; which, like the one last figured, has a large open fire for roasting, in compliance with the prevailing opinion on this point. This range is provided with a sheet iron oven, and wrought iron waste boiler, the top of the oven forming a hot plate, and all heated by one fire. An important peculiarity of the construction of oven here adopted is, that the parts can be easily detached, thereby admitting of the flues and passages being cleaned out with facility—a consideration to which we have previously adverted as being so essential in the construction of kitchen ranges of almost every description.

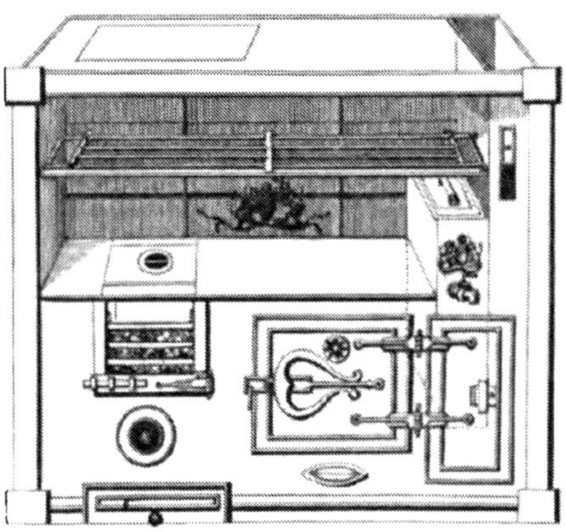

Browne's Patent Kitchen.

The patent kitchener of E. Browne, of Lyme Regis, Dorsetshire, is represented in the annexed illustration. Here there is little of the open fire, and this may be still further diminished by a slide intended to be put down when little heat is required. And this arrangement suggests a necessity which appears to us to be much less attended to than it deserves—we allude to the means of regulating the draught. The importance of being able to light up the fire quickly is so much felt that this is usually provided for by causing an extra current of air to pass through it. But to insure economy of fuel we should be able, when heat is not wanted, to prevent altogether the current through the fire, when further combustion would almost cease. In most cases this is, no doubt, partially provided for, but not, as it strikes us, to the full extent; and hence we deem it necessary to direct attention to the subject, when referring to the slide plate in this range, which is seen above the third bar. The flues here can also be easily cleaned, and, if necessary, the boiler may be taken out without removing the other parts of the range. An unusually large extent of hot plate is available for boiling or stewing.

The collection of gas stoves and cooking apparatus exhibited by the Hibernian Gas Company is deserving of honourable mention, as comprising almost every proposed arrangement for the use of gas as fuel; the whole being in the highest degree creditable to Mr. Sanders, who has devoted so much attention to this subject. In certain situations it is beyond question that gas could be at once economically and conveniently substituted for coal as fuel. When a fire is not to be maintained during the day, and is merely wanted for heating water, or broiling a chop or steak morning or evening, the use of gas would be desirable. The required heat is available at once, without waiting to light a fire; the gas being turned off when done with, economy is also effected by its use; while the greater cleanliness in the use of the one as compared with that of the other is not the least of its advantages. In the sick room, too, the gas pipe at the hearth will often be found a desirable substitute for the fire. And a further recommendation in favour of the extended use of gas is, that the necessary arrangements are inexpensive. Where gas has been already introduced for lighting purposes it is almost at once available for any other; a piece of piping extending to the usual fire-place supplying all that is required. In those remarks, however, we merely refer to cases in which continuous heat is not required. Under other circumstances it is doubtful whether gas can be economically used. Indeed, at present prices we believe that it cannot; and whatever may be the conveniences which it insures, yet these may be more than counterbalanced by the difference of expense. The whole subject, however, is deserving of further investigation. The day is possibly not far distant when a considerable reduction in the price of gas may be effected as compared with that at which it is now ordinarily supplied; and in such a case there may be a future of gas as an article of fuel of which we can at the present moment scarcely form an adequate conception. As directing attention specially to the subject, and tending to remove some of the difficulties which stand in the way, we cannot doubt that good service has been rendered to the cause of progress by Mr. Sanders, the very efficient manager of the Hibernian Gas Company.

In the consideration of the description of articles already referred to in this section, appropriateness of construction for the desired purpose being not merely the primary, but almost the sole consideration, the skill displayed in the casting is little taken into account, provided it be not thoroughly objectionable. In the production of fountains, statuary, and a variety of the smaller articles chiefly intended for ornament, the standard by which their value is to be estimated will take cognizance of the workmanship, as well as the design. In any case, as before observed, æsthetic considerations are little involved here. We have merely to see that good taste has not been glaringly violated; and afterwards the consideration of the comparative merits of any particular article as a work of art belongs entirely to another department. Among the articles in the use of which our continental neighbours have the advantage of us may be included artificial fountains, which, for the most part, are composed of iron, though terra cotta is also well adapted for the purpose, especially in the case of the larger sized articles; but the crystal fountain, which formed so great an ornament of the transept of the Hyde Park Exhibition, has shown that under certain circumstances glass also may be effectively used. Taking durability and economy into account, it is more than probable, however, that iron will continue to form the most appropriate material for fountains, admitting, as it does, of a degree of lightness incompatible with the use of terra cotta or marble. The comparatively humid climate of the United Kingdom must make the introduction of fountains into our pleasure grounds less an object with us than in some other countries. The effect of the fountains in France and Italy is much heightened by the character of the climate, which makes the play of water so refreshing; yet there can be no doubt that they could be occasionally introduced amongst us with great advantage. The traveller on the Continent, who has witnessed the important addition to the more striking and attractive features of the landscape made by the fountains or *jets d'eau*, cannot but lament that they are not more used in the United Kingdom; especially in this part of it, where the general character of the scenery could be so much improved by them, and where such a thing as an artificial fountain is rarely to be met with. In many cases great expense has been sustained in the formation of ponds of water, which often become offensive stagnant pools; and in the production of waterfalls, which are little better than trickling streams; but it is passing strange, that up to the present time, notwithstanding our increasing intercourse with the Continent, the introduction of fountains into our gardens and pleasure grounds is rarely thought of. We have imported many of the most objectionable characteristics of modern landscape gardening—its stiffness, its straight alleys, its fantastic shaped flower-beds, and its general formality—to an extent that has provoked the most unmeasured ridicule; but its most redeeming feature we have neglected. Absurd as was the French style of gardening, as founded by Lenotre, those most opposed to it could not but admire the truly grand fountains which it included among its requisites. Yet, although imitations of this style may frequently be met with, the really valuable accompaniment has been dispensed with; chiefly, we presume, on account of a misapprehension as to the difficulties which stood in the way of the introduction of fountains, and the large outlay which it would involve. The progress of hydraulic engineering knowledge of late years, as well as increasing facilities for the construction of the various kinds of fountains, have, however, so much diminished the cost of their erection that the drawbacks on this head no longer exist.*

* The construction of ornamental fountains is of great antiquity. Public fountains were erected in the principal towns of ancient Greece. Of these the Pirene and the Lerna at Corinth were on a scale of great magnificence. The former was encircled by an enclosure of white marble sculptured into various grottoes; and the latter by a portico, under which there were seats on which a cooling retreat was found during the heat of the day. The ancient classics, in short, abound in references to the fountains of the period with which they are conversant. Rome is still famous for her fountains. Those of France—of the Tuileries, Versailles, and St. Cloud—have been described with rapture by many

The accompanying engraving will afford a correct idea of the very elegant fountain contributed by M. André, of Paris, and which was placed in the Centre Hall near the raised *dais*. The general effect here is

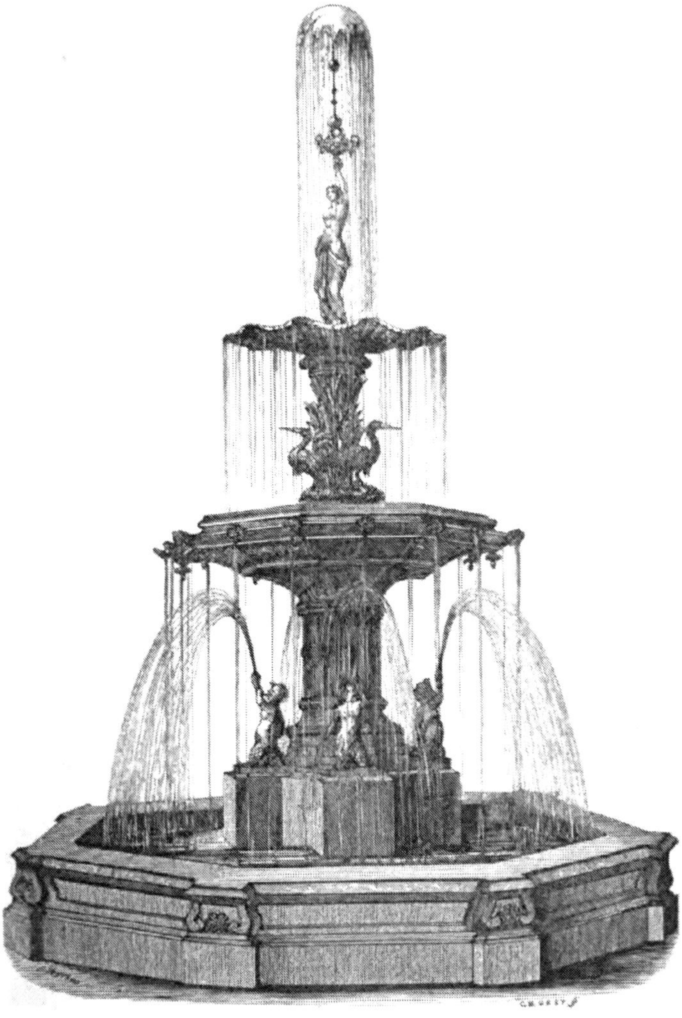

Andre's Cast Iron Fountain, in Centre Hall.

very good, though the arrangement and introduction of the figures may reasonably give rise to difference of opinion.

As specimens of castings many of the articles exhibited by the Coalbrookdale Company were deserving of high commendation, showing as they did the rapid progress which has been made in this branch of industry of late years. The extent of the coal-fields of England, the abundance of iron ore, and the improved modes of smelting lately adopted, point out the great adaptation of that country for all kinds of manufactures in iron; but until lately, when quality has been taken into account, English goods, for the most part,

English tourists, not less on account of the splendour and good taste by which they are characterized, than on that of the magic effect which they produce on the landscape. And our admiration of these objects must necessarily be enhanced when we bear in mind the great expense which their construction must have involved in times past.

suffered by comparison with those of the Continent. In some kinds of work this superiority on the part of our neighbours is still maintained; but judging from the progress made of late, this is not likely to continue to be the case. And among those who have signalized themselves in the career of progress, the first place is, perhaps, due to the Coalbrookdale Company, the extent of whose operations is not less remarkable than the excellence of their workmanship. Many of the articles in their collection, in the Centre Hall of the Exhibition, were triumphs in their way. Among the castings contributed by them, and interspersed throughout the building, we subjoin engravings of two vases of very different design and character, but both presenting excellent specimens of workmanship; the features in connexion with which we are here concerned.

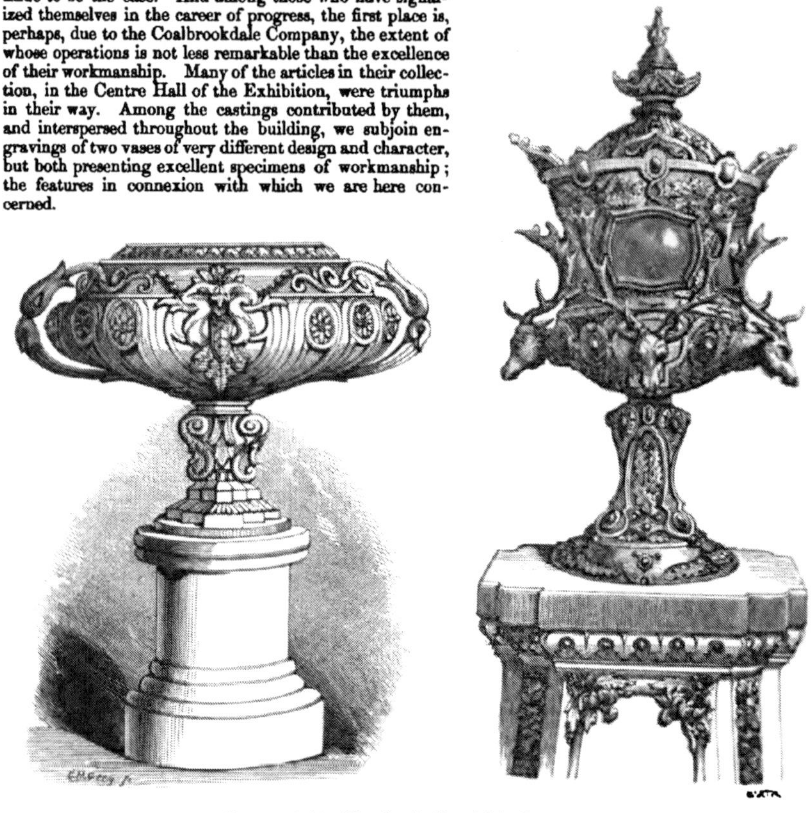

Vases exhibited by the Coalbrookdale Company.

Among the contributions to the Exhibition which challenged attention as specimens of castings, the collection of the Falkirk Iron Company may fairly be included. We subjoin sketches of castings designed for

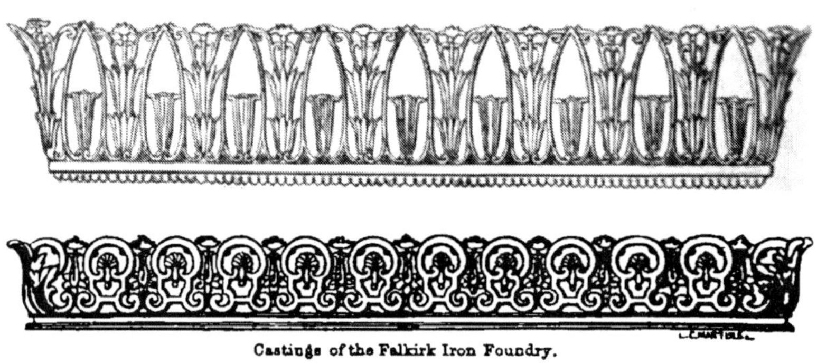

Castings of the Falkirk Iron Foundry.

window guards, or other purposes, where light ornamented railings are required. The designs are simple, calling for no observation, but the finish of the castings was such as to entitle them to high consideration.

But if the British workman has often to yield the palm to the foreigner in matters where taste or curious workmanship is involved, he maintains a uniform superiority in matters of mere utility. Thus, in the construction of locks, taking efficiency and economy into account, the English workmen are unrivalled. Excellence of workmanship, lowness of price, and an adequate degree of security, are their characteristics; all showing the advantage of the division of labour which is carried out in that department. Bramah and Chubb have, indeed, obtained a world-wide celebrity for the production of locks of the higher class, while those of a cheaper kind produced in Wolverhampton and some other places, are not less deserving of note in their way. The fact of one of Chubb's locks being picked by Mr. Hobbs, in 1851, created no small sensation at the time, inasmuch as it was supposed that the mechanism of these locks was so perfect that it was beyond human ingenuity to open them without the proper keys. But the length of time during which that trial was carried on, and the peculiar circumstances connected with it, show that, properly considered, the safety conferred by these locks was not thereby sensibly affected. The Jurors appointed to report on this department in 1851 observe, that "they would express a doubt whether the circumstance that a lock has been picked under conditions which ordinarily could scarcely, even if at all, be obtained, can be assumed as a test of its insecurity." On the contrary, we maintain that the feeling of security should be materially increased by the experiment in question. The really valuable construction of these locks was thereby established, while the facilities enjoyed by Mr. Hobbs, not to talk of the skill which he displayed, were such as no one could by possibility enjoy making the attempt for improper purposes. The excellence of the locks manufactured by Messrs. Chubb and Son was acknowledged by the award of a prize medal in 1851. Among the curiosities in lock-making which they prepared for the late Exhibition was a suite of ten locks of different sizes, including one for large safe, one for street door, with latch, and small locks for carpet bag, box, trunk, desk, &c., all opened by a gold master key, set in a ring to be worn on the finger, so as to elude observation. Each of the locks is, of course, furnished with a separate key, yet of these keys none will open any lock but that to which it belongs. This is certainly a feat in lock-making deserving of special notice, as it illustrates the great degree of perfection which has been attained in the construction of this useful article. In the locks exhibited by Messrs. Hobbs, Ashley, and Fortescue, by a few slight modifications of the key, so many alterations may be produced in the lock that they come to be reckoned by hundreds—a statement which must not be a little puzzling to those who have not made themselves acquainted with the manner in which these changes are produced. The mechanical ingenuity of the age is, in fact, displayed as much in the construction of locks as in any other branch of manufacture illustrated in the Exhibition.

Of the smaller articles in iron, the screws produced by M'Cormick's patent screwing machine are especially deserving of note from the peculiarity of their manufacture. In this case the screws are formed by pressure instead of by cutting away a portion of the material as in the usual way; and the machine is made to turn out screws from three inches to one-eighth of an inch in diameter; in fact, the kind of screw is altogether regulated by the die selected. The iron is used hot, and so effective are the arrangements for economizing labour that, according to the patentees, two trained boys, one to heat and one to feed, with one of these machines, and a conveniently placed furnace, will make 6000 screws a day, each six and a half inches long. This number would weigh about two tons, the entire expense of producing which, including fuel, labour, diet, and power, would be about fourteen shillings. In this operation it is further obvious that there is no waste of material. The usual waste in making wood screws is estimated at fifteen per cent. of the iron consumed, so that it appears the saving of the raw material would more than defray the cost of manufacture. Another advantage derivable from the use of the machine is that by it iron can be used of a quality far inferior to that required for screws made in the usual way. In the ordinary process of cutting the screw, when the iron is not of good quality, it scales away; but when made by pressure almost any sort of iron will suffice. There are great and important advantages in favour of this method of producing screws. The appearance of those thus made is so peculiar, that they can at once be distinguished from the others; and there can be little doubt that ere long this plan will be universally adopted for making screws of every description.

Of the great variety of smaller articles in this class, space will not permit even a passing notice. The department was well represented, both as regards the number of exhibiters and variety of the objects. The workmanship was generally excellent, but the effect of most of the things here referred to was often marred by a profusion of ornamentation, and that frequently of an injudicious character. The contrast between the home and foreign departments of the Exhibition was interesting in this respect; though even in the case of the hardware productions of the Continent an excess of ornament was often to be met with.

### MISCELLANEOUS ARTICLES.

The articles coming under this denomination are numerous, and many of them would be deserving of special notice if space permitted. In the production of some of these surprising changes have been effected of late years. In the smaller articles of ironmongery, especially those of a superior class, the ingenuity of the manufacturer is often strikingly displayed, as well as the excellence of the workmanship.

Among the articles oddly included in this class are knife-cleaning machines, washing machines, and mangles, and a number of other articles of apparently heterogeneous character, which, though somewhat out of place here, yet would be still more so anywhere else, according to the method of classification adopted.

Kent's knife-cleaning machine must soon find its way into every place where there are many knives in use, not only on account of the saving of labour which it effects, but also from the superior manner in which it does its work as compared with hand labour. The knife blade, moreover, is operated upon by a series of brushes made to revolve rapidly against it, and it is not ground down and worn away in the cleaning as on the common board.

Washing and wringing machines, and mangles, are indispensable adjuncts in the domestic establishment. The former of these articles may be made to greatly economize manual labour, as it is obvious that the greater part of the business of the washerwoman is the agitation of the soiled article in the medium which is to carry away the impurities. And when the *modus operandi* is taken into account, it really does seem passing strange that, even in large establishments, the washing continues to be done by hand. Under all circumstances it is probable that the articles included under the name of "fine things" will be washed by hand, as their fragile character will not permit of rough treatment, and they are moreover easily got through. The case is different, however, with all the heavier articles, which can be washed by machinery. As to this mode of treatment being severe on the articles, washed, the extent to which this holds good depends on the care with which the operation is conducted. Even with hand washing one often hears the remark of certain washerwomen being very destructive to the clothes. In the one case, as well as in the other, therefore, this remark applies.

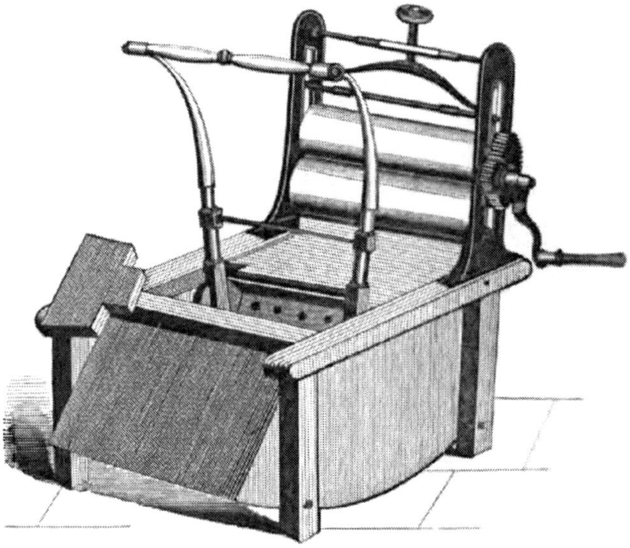

Tindall's Washing Machine.

The washing machine here figured was exhibited by E. O. Tindall, of Scarborough, who also was the manufacturer. It is made chiefly of wood, the ends being inclined inwards, and the bottom curved upwards. A dasher or swiller, working upon two brass centres, or axles, when put in motion by means of the handle, causes the clothes to be forced against the ends; and, squeezing the water through them, it rushes to the opposite part of the machine, thereby alternately rinsing the clothes through, and puffing or lightening them up. The boards are tongued and grooved, and fastened with white lead and copper nails, so as to be perfectly water-tight. A movable cover fits on the top and keeps the steam as well as the splashes of water closed in the machine; the bottom is furnished with a brass plug to let off the dirty water; and the whole is supported by a strong wooden frame, bolted together with iron bolts. It is said to be capable of performing washing in less than half the time required by the ordinary mode, and it does not injure the clothes so much as scrubbing with the hands. This apparatus does not appear to be liable to get out of order, and, therefore, will not require frequent repairs.

The wringing machine of the same exhibiter would seem to be a desideratum, from the very laborious nature of the work which it is designed to perform. It drives out the water by the pressure of rollers, somewhat analogous to the action of the mangle; and its operation is decidedly less injurious to the fabric operated upon than wringing by hand.

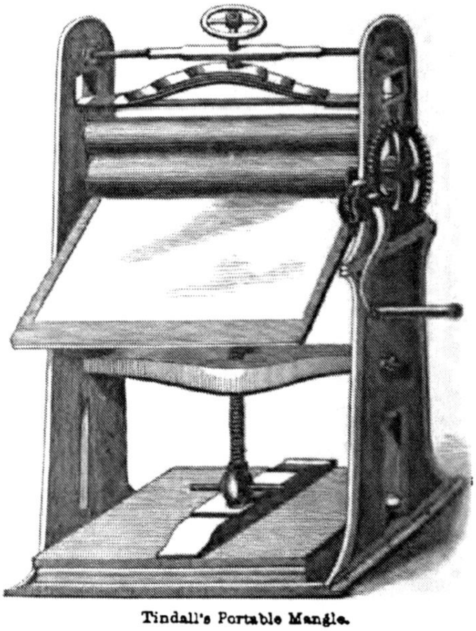

Tindall's Portable Mangle.

The mangle is a well-known article in the laundry, but its high price and the very considerable space occupied by the better kinds of the common mangle prevent it from being nearly as extensively used as desirable. The action of the mangle, moreover, is so simple that little attention has been devoted to the improvement of any other method of attaining it than that of simply using a great weight. It is obvious, however, that a proper modification of the spring and screw would not be less objectionable in theory than applicable in practice; yet it seems odd that the portable mangles have not made more way. One defect in the use of this description of mangle is in not having it fixed to the floor; to which it might be screwed when in use, and when done with it could be unscrewed, and laid aside. The engraving shows the construction of Tindall's Portable Mangle, the design of which, as well as that of the other two machines just mentioned, have been registered, in accordance with the provisions of the Registration of Designs Act. It will be observed that the amount of pressure is easily regulated by the screw, by which the spring is slackened or tightened at pleasure. The size and power of those mangles may also be regulated by the nature of the work which they are chiefly intended to perform—the greatest pressure being of course required for the heavier kinds of fabrics.

*Buttons.*—On the history of buttons we might write an elaborate article, had we time or space; tracing their development from the ancient fibula to the modern button, and referring, in the history of our own country, to the many Acts of Parliament made for their regulation or to enforce their use in different forms. We might also trace their æsthetic history, or detail the variations of form they have undergone under the changes of fashion or taste; how they have assumed more changes of outline than a mathematician could calculate—the pyramid, the sphere, the hemisphere, the circle and semicircle; the oval, the concave, the convex; forms of simple curves, composite forms, forms from nature, and forms taken from a pack of cards; but our space confines us to a few words on the materials used, and the mode of manufacture.

The materials of buttons are as varied as their fashion. We have them gold and gilt, silver and plated, in copper, brass, German silver, lead, pewter, wood, horn, shell, glass, porcelain, or diamonds. We have in our police and military force the great consumers of a pewter button; the gilt button in our Freemasons, Friendly Brothers, Odd Fellows, and other clubbists, as well as the few surviving blue-coated and gilt-buttoned gentlemen of the time of George IV. The mother-of-pearl forms the ornamental material for linen and cotton fabrics, from the lace chemisette of the full-blown beauty to the less distinguished collar of her devoted admirer, unless where its place is taken by the cheaper porcelain, now so much used as a substitute.

The manufacture of metal buttons is one of considerable interest as well as importance, giving employment in France and England to thousands of persons, though its consumption has greatly declined of late years. The material employed for the button is stamped out of the sheet, of the required form, by a fly-press, and is then by a peculiar machine perfectly moulded and polished on the edges, and smoothed on the face; the shanks are then attached by suitable solder, and the button is finished by polishing in a lathe, or stamped in a press with any required design. Should gilt buttons be required, the copper buttons (slightly alloyed with zinc) are taken, well cleansed by nitric acid, or pickled, as it is termed, and thrown into a solution of nitrate of mercury, by which they get a thin coating of mercury, owing to the decomposition of the salt by the superior attraction of the baser metal for oxygen. The buttons are then well washed and covered over with a slight covering of an amalgam of gold, by which they get a thin coating of this metal and mercury; they are then passed into a stove and heated to a temperature sufficiently high to drive off the whole of the mercury, and leave an exceedingly thin film of gold on their surfaces, and on being burnished in a lathe in the usual manner, are fit for the market. In this manufacture the quantity of gold used is extremely small, since upwards of two hundred buttons, of an inch diameter, may be well gilt with about five grains of gold, or at little more than the cost of one pennyworth of gold, exclusive of the cost of mercury; the greater part of the latter being in the modern process of distillation recovered, not only to the profit of the manufacturer, but to the saving of health of those employed. In the manufacture of silvered buttons the silver covering is put on the copper previous to its being formed into a button; by the milling process it is fashioned into the required shape, and the finishing of the button is effected on the already silvered basis.

*Needles.*—The manufacture of needles was first introduced into England in the reign of Queen Elizabeth. Since that time, owing to our pre-eminence in the manufacture of steel, needle-making has become one of our staple trades, employing a great number of hands in its different departments. All needles are (or ought to be) made of the best steel, properly tempered, otherwise the needle will not remain sharp-pointed or will be too brittle. This tempering of the steel is, however, one of the last processes the needle undergoes. The first process is to make the wire perfectly soft; this is done by heating it to redness and allowing it slowly to cool, when it has lost all its elasticity, and will readily retain any given shape. It is then straightened by straining it in short lengths between strong wire pins set in a board or frame; and this being done it is cut into short lengths, which are tied in bundles, and by rolling between two boards they are rendered perfectly straight. The wire is pointed by applying it in bundles to a dry grinding stone, and this process is in the ordinary manufactories so injurious to health, owing to the fine steel dust inhaled by the grinders, that few workmen employed escape serious illness. When pointed, the next operation is eyeing, which is done by first flattening the unpointed end by a hammer or fly-press, and then by a fine hard steel point punching the hole intended for the eye which is afterwards enlarged and finished by a file. Sometimes all these operations are performed by one machine, which flattens the head, and gutters it, or impresses the channel seen in most needles, by a single blow, and a second which finishes the operation of eyeing. The needle is again straightened, and is then ready for tempering. This operation consists in first heating it to redness and then suddenly cooling; which makes it so hard and brittle, that the slightest force would break it, but by heating it to a moderate temperature and allowing it to cool slowly, it is rendered less brittle, but retains sufficient hardness. The needles are then polished by rolling them in a kind of mangle, in cloths smeared with oil and fine emery, by which operation they are ready for use.—J. S.

---

1. ALLDRITT, J., Blackhall-street, Dublin.—A self-acting coffee pot.

2. ANDERSON, R., Greek-street, Dublin, Manufacturer and Importer.—Brass cocks; pump valves, plugs, waste washers, &c.; shower baths; metal and delft sinks, plumbers' basons, &c.; slide valve water closet; Bramah valve water closet, used on deck houses; steam pressure indicator, as used in the Clyde steamers; Lambert's patent spirit and water cocks, &c.

3. ARCHER, W. H., Ironworks, Lucan, near Dublin, Manufacturer.—Kieve hoops; sawplate for stonecutters' use; sledges; stonemasons' hammers; quarry picks; plough and

axle sock moulds, shovels of various patterns, showing the forms used in the different counties of Ireland.

4. ARMITAGE, MORGAN HENRY, & Co., Mousehole Forge, near Sheffield.—Smiths' anvils, &c.

5. AVERY, J., North-street, Hackney, London, Inventor.—Improved water closet, fixed without nails, screws, or brads; improved ball lever tap with round water way.

6. BAILEY, JOHN, Regent-street, Salford, Manufacturer.—Improved copying press.

7. BARNWELL, T., & SON, Bishop-street, Dublin.—A case of locks.

8. BARTER, R., St. Ann's-hill, Blarney, County Cork, Inventor.—A substitute for a wing or swivel joint in gas fitting.

9. BARTLEET, W., & SONS, Redditch, Bromsgrove, Worcestershire, Manufacturers and Patentees.—Oval perfect-eyed needles, and sewing needles of every description; sail, pack, surgeons', tambour, crochet, netting needles, &c.; sea and river fish hooks of all kinds.

10. BENHAM & SONS, Wigmore-street, London, Manufacturers.—Cooking apparatus and kitchen; ranges in various designs; improved smoke jacks; broiling stove and hot plate, with pastry oven; steam hot closet; Flavel's patent kitchener; dinner lifting machine; copper steam kettles; Bainmarie pan; model of complete kitchen apparatus; emigrants' or cottagers' stoves; emigrants' portable kitchen; perforated pedestals for hot water pipes; stair bannisters and newels in various style of ornament; warm air stove; bright register stoves, with burnished steel, ormolu, and natural bronze mouldings; turf grates; dog stove with encaustic covings; fenders and fire irons in polished steel, ormolu, and bronze; ornamented fire dogs; Telekouphonon or improved speaking pipe.

11. BILLINGE, JAMES, Ashton, near Wigan, Lancashire, Manufacturer.—Wrought iron scroll hinges and door handles of various designs, for ecclesiastical and other purposes; wrought iron hinges for locomotives, railway carriage doors, worm and skew rising hinges, &c.; stock and iron locks, with and without tumblers; brass and iron escutcheons for locks; brass and iron thumb latches.

12. BRAMHALL, T., Union-street, George's-road, Southwark, Inventor and Manufacturer.—A wind guard (made of zinc) for the cure of smoky chimneys; a bath.

13. BRIGHAM, J., Driffield, Yorkshire, Inventor and Proprietor.—Catch and fastener, with door and frame showing application of same; catch for park gate.

14. BROWN, E., Lyme Regis, Dorsetshire, Inventor and Proprietor.—Working model of cooking apparatus and roasting jack; improved cooking apparatus; improved cottage or emigrant's stove; brass self-acting tobacco till; improved valve for cisterns; steam closet automaton roasting apparatus; chimney-piece for large cooking apparatus.

15. BROWN, ROBERT, Toxteth Park, Liverpool.—Horse shoes and shod feet.

16. CITY OF DUBLIN BOLT, SCREW, AND RIVET COMPANY, THE, Fleet-street, Dublin, Manufacturers.—Wood screws, screw bolts, rivets, and railway fastenings.

17. CHOPPING & SELBY, Argyll Works, Birmingham.—Improved horse shoes.

18. CHUBB & SON, St. Paul's Churchyard, London, Inventor, Patentees, and Manufacturers.—Chubb's patent bank lock; Gothic and other ornamental locks and keys; locks for various purposes; a suite of large and small locks, all to open with gold master key set in a ring; fire-proof banker's safe, well safe, &c.

19. COALBROOKDALE COMPANY, Coalbrookdale, near Wellington, Shropshire, Designers, Inventors, and Proprietors.—An ornamental tent, with pilasters, &c. of iron; an ornamental iron fountain; "The Combat," bronzed; register stoves and fenders, of new and unique design; hat, coat, and umbrella stands, of unique design, bronzed; garden and hall chairs and tables; ornamental vases in cast iron; brackets for gas, &c., electro-bronzed; hot air stoves; flower pot stands; looking-glass and frame, in iron, gilt; an economical cooking range, complete; two flower vases in bronze, electro-gilt; a variety of ornamental castings of figures, &c., electro-bronzed.

20. CORCORAN, BRYAN, & Co., Mark-lane, London.—Specimens of woven wire; model of an improved malt kiln.

21. CURTIS, W., Chancery-lane, Dublin, Manufacturer.—Brass cocks for steam, gas, and water; also gauge cocks, valves, and other brass furniture, for steam-engines; brass furniture for railway and private carriages; brass fittings, cocks, swivels, and bracket backs, for gas; general brass work for doors and shop windows; a garden engine.

22. CUTTS, W. W. & Co., Atlas Works, Sheffield, and Hatton-garden, London.—Chandeliers of various designs for gas and candles; brackets; vase lights, and hall lanterns for gas, in great variety of patterns, in rich gold, lacquer and bronze; patent atlas oil lamps with stands; candle lamps; railway carriage, side, tail, and signal lamps; working model of Cutts' patent railway signals, &c.

23. DANIEL, P., Grafton-street, Dublin, Manufacturer and Importer.—Drawing-room grates, fenders, and fire irons, locks, and articles of ironmongery; hip, sponge, and shower baths; papier mache and japanned trays; coal vases and japanned goods in variety.

24. DIXON, GEORGE, Upper Erne-street, Importer.—Moderateur vase; pedestal and stand lamps; candle lamps, shades, transparencies, lamp oils, &c.

25. DYCER, E., Stephen's-green, Dublin, Inventor and Proprietor.—Improved horse ball administrator; horse shoes.

26. EDMUNDSON, J. & Co., Capel-street, and Stafford-street, Dublin, Manufacturers and Importers.—Gas fittings, gas lustres, pillars, brackets, &c.; Tuscan pillar of brass, with pedestal, adapted for a lamp post or bust stand; furnishing ironmongery, and kitchen ranges; electro-plated goods; and light-house lamps, with plated reflectors.

27. ELLIOTT, W. & SONS, Regent Works, Birmingham, Manufacturers.—Buttons.

28. FENCELY, H., Denmark-street, Dublin, Inventor and Proprietor.—Spiral expanding and compressing machine for sweeping chimneys.

29. FOLEY, H., College-green, Dublin, Manufacturer.—Army, navy, livery, hunt, and club buttons.

30. FRANCIS, E., Camden-place, Dublin, Designer and Manufacturer.—Improved horse-shoes for diseased and healthy feet.

31. FRASER, S., Mary-street, Dublin, Manufacturer.—Japanned shower, hip, toilet, foot, sponge, and children's baths; toilet ware and pails; improved garden watering-engines; camp pedestal basin and washing stand; improved portable hot-air stoves; emigrant's cooking stoves; cream forcers for making butter and iced or whipped creams; potato steamers; improved baking and roasting apparatus; washing machine; japanned hat case and plate warmers.

32. GATCHELL, R., Pill-lane, Dublin, Manufacturer.—Scales of various kinds and sizes; chemists', bankers', jewellers', sovereign, and hydraulic scales; gilt beam; weights, imperial copper measures; burnished gold drums; ship-shaped vases, richly ornamented; sample boxes, bowls, and vases; show boxes and bowls; fancy tea canisters; twine boxes, &c.

33. GLENNIE, G. & Co., Springbank Iron Works, Glasgow, Manufacturers.—Register grates; boiler; pots; camp oven and cover; air bricks; gutters; gas and water pipes in variety; chimney cans; bar scale weights; hay rack and manger; skylight and frame; cart bushes; Allan's patent iron pavement plates, and many other articles in iron.

34. GODDARD, E., Ipswich, Inventor and Manufacturer.—Gas cooking stove, lined with white glazed porcelain; gas cooking apparatus, with chambers for roasting and baking, hot closet, copper boiler, steamer, and hot plate; Goddard's patent asbestos gas fires.

35. Goddard, H., Nottingham, Inventor and Manufacturer.—New patent economical cooking apparatus, either for a close or open fire.

36. Greening, N., & Sons, Warrington, Lancashire, Manufacturers.—Extra strong drying kiln floor wire; and strong-wove wire for separating minerals, &c., woven by steam-looms, and exhibited for their great width, strength, and regularity of meshes.

37. Harrison, Radclyffe, & Blunt, Eagle Foundry, Leamington, Manufacturers and Inventors.—Kitchen ranges on a new and improved plan.

38. Hart & Son, London.—Ornamental door furniture; door handles; bell pulls; locks; knockers, &c.

39. Henshaw, T., & Co., Clonskeagh Iron Works, and Abbey-street, Dublin, Manufacturers.—Quarry tools; sledges, picks, hammers, iron pulley blocks, scrap iron quarry bars, refined cast steel jumpers, &c.; smiths' and horse shoers' tools; portable forge, smiths' and horse shoeing sledges; hand, bench, turning, and shoeing hammers; pincers; iron and steel quoits; pulley blocks; spades, shovels, draining tools; manure and hay forks; Irish, Kent, Felling, and American axes; carpenters', coopers', and ship adzes; slashing or hedging hooks; bill hooks; picks; mattocks.

40. Hibernian Gas Light Company, The, Foster-place, Dublin.—Bennett's gas cooking ranges for roasting, baking, boiling, and frying; duplicate gas oven, suitable for baking bread, pies, and pastry; Boggett's gas cooking range, which, by its peculiar method of burning gas, is capable of heating an oven for baking and boiling, and adapts itself for frying, boiling, and stewing, also for radiating heat in apartments; portable gas cooking range, furnished with an oven for broiling and baking, with a stove for frying and boiling, and with the extra appendage of a steaming apparatus; gas apparatus for halls for keeping water hot, or making coffee, &c.; King's gas stoves, for warming halls, apartments, offices, &c.; Asbestos gas stoves, for warming apartments; Boggett's tinsmith's gas stove, for heating soldering irons; Boggett's salamander, for cooking steaks and chops, &c.; also for boiling, steaming, and frying; Hall's patent gas and vapour cooking lamp, for the use of emigrants, tourists, &c.

41. Hill, J., Islington, Birmingham, Manufacturer.—Specimens of stamped ornaments for lamps, chandeliers, and gas fittings; lamps in various styles; balance weights, bracket arms, stands, vases, &c.

42. Hobbs, Ashley, & Fortescue, Cheapside, London.—The celebrated permulating locks; solid key locks, with moveable stumps, &c.; chest, till, pad, portfolio locks.

43. Hodges, T., Middle Abbey-street, Dublin, Manufacturer.—Large church bell, cast a perfect note—B. flat; a smaller bell, attached to M'Master and Sons turret clock; church bells of assorted sizes; farm bells, with emblematical devices, assorted sizes, on stand; handsome bell, mounted for yacht; highly finished gongs, on ebony stands; brass lifting, and force pumps on mahogany planks, with air vessels; cast iron pumps on oak planks; glass case, containing specimens of sundry brass-work.

44. Hodges, J., & Sons, Westmoreland-street, Dublin, Manufacturers.—Kitchen range, containing open fire grate, wrought iron boiler, double action smoke-jack, oven, set of charcoal stoves, hot plate, hot closet, and grilling iron; economical open fire kitchen range; sundry culinary articles; a small grate with tubular bars for heating water; scroll balustrade for gallery and stair case; shower and sponge bath.

45. Huxhams & Brown, Exeter, Manufacturers.—Emigrants' and cottage stoves (Registered), with iron flues completed inside; cooking apparatus, with oven and boiler.

46. Ingram, T. W., Birmingham, Designer and Manufacturer.—Improved horn buttons.

47. Jennings, G., Great Charlotte-street, Blackfriars-road, London, Inventor and Manufacturer.—India rubber tube water-closet, the valves, cranks, levers, &c., generally employed being wholly dispensed with; India rubber tube cocks; sluice valves; fire-cocks and hydrants; traps for drains, &c.; joints for connecting lead and other joints without solder; pump of a new construction; cistern; valves, lavatories, and shoes for corners of shop shutters.

48. Johnson, Cammell, & Co., Cyclops Steel Works, Sheffield, Manufacturers.—Specimens of files of every description, for engineering, machine, and every other general purpose; specimens of railway carriage, waggon, and truck springs, also for locomotive engine, and tenders, and of other railway tools and work.

49. Kennard, R. W., & Co., Upper Thames-street, London, and Iron Works, Falkirk, N. B., Manufacturers.—Iron castings in great variety; stoves, ranges, balcony panels, statuary, vases, columns, royal arms, garden chairs, &c.

50. Kent, G., Strand, London, Inventor, Patentee, and Manufacturer.—Kent's patented inventions for domestic purposes; rotary knife cleaning machine; section of rotary knife cleaning machine, showing the internal construction; rotary cinder sifter; portable mangle; portable washing apparatus; triticating strainer for soups, &c., &c.

51. Lambert, T., Short-street, New Cut, Lambeth, London, Manufacturer.—Samples of black tin pipe; flexible diaphragm water valves for very high pressure; gun metal steam fittings for locomotive engines.

52. Lawless, T., Dundalk.—Self-adjusting lock, with fourteen tumblers and three detectors.

53. Lingard, Edward A., Birmingham, Manufacturer.—Coffin ornaments.

54. Lockerby, T., Glasgow, Manufacturer.—Gas chandeliers; in florentine bronze, and relief.

55. Lomas, Fromings, & Sykes, Sheffield, Manufacturers.—Working model of Froming's patent forge hammer; smiths' anvils and vices; hand sledge hammer; millwright's and engineer's chipping hammer.

56. Love, J., St. Andrew-square, Glasgow, Inventor.—Room grate of new construction; gas apparatus and steam-boiler; improved gas stoves for heating and cooking; hot air stove for ventilation.

57. Maguire, J., Dawson-street, Dublin, Manufacturer.—Kitchen range; sporting canteen; bedstead; churn; baths; japanned ware; garden chairs; table with marble top; sundry specimens of iron-work.

58. Martin, J., Peter-street, Dublin, Manufacturer.—Anatomical preparations of the leg and foot of the horse, and shoes for the security and preservation of the feet of the animal.

59. Miles, W., Nile-street, Cork, Manufacturer.—Specimens of horse shoes for sound and unsound feet, and defective action; patten shoe, &c.

60. Milner & Son, Phœnix Safe Works, Lord-street, Liverpool, and Moorgate-street, London.—Patent holdfast and fire-resisting safes, chests, and deed boxes.

61. Moffitt, T., Chancery-lane, Dublin, Manufacturer.—Wrought iron safes of different sizes, &c.

62. Mooney, W., Lower Ormond-quay, Dublin, Manufacturer.—Ormolu chandeliers, and candelabra, in various styles.

63. Morton, J., Eyre-street, Sheffield, Manufacturer and Designer.—Ormolu and steel, Berlin black, and bronze fenders; cast iron bronzed table, with marble top.

64. Murphy, J., Thomas-street, Dublin, Manufacturer.—A peal of eight joy bells in the key of D; a large bell weighing 40 cwt.; a gong or altar bell; farm yard bells.

65. Nash, R., Ludgate-hill Passage, Birmingham, Manufacturer.—Spoon, collar, and medal dies; medal collar; livery, coining, and shank hole dies; piercing tools; hubbs; office desk seals; embossing, piercing, and copying presses.

66. Ney, R., Great Britain-street, Dublin, Manufacturer and Designer.—French iron bedsteads; camp bedstead; couch bedstead forming a child's cot, chair, or table; the same folded, showing the space it occupies.

67. NIXEY, W. G., Moore-street, Soho, London, Inventor.—Nixey's patent revolving till.

68. PARKER, JOHN C., Coombe, Dublin.—Case of medals and military instruments.

69. PATENT SHAFT AXLE-TREE COMPANY, Brunswick Iron Works, Wednesbury.—Patent faggoted axle, solid, as finished by the forge hammer; patent faggoted axle, hollow, showing section of metal; piece of improved hard surfaced locomotive tire bar; sections of iron for railway waggon frames.

70. PEARSON, T., Little Ship-street, Dublin, Manufacturer.—Wove brass wire cloth, six feet wide, 60 meshes to an inch, for paper manufacture; copper wire cloth, 100 spaces to an inch; flour machine wire, 90 meshes to an inch; improved separator for cleaning corn; brass sieves for medical purposes; wire garden chairs; ornamental flower stand.

71. PERRY, J., & Co., Red Lion-square, London, Inventors and Proprietors.—Patent silver-mounted travelling and drawing-room inkstands; also, patent filter and gravitating inkstands.

72. PIERCE, WILLIAM, Jermyn-street, London, Manufacturer.—Stoves, grates, fenders, cottagers' grates, &c.

73. PIM, T. & S., Mountmellick, Queen's County, Manufacturers.—Riding and driving bits, snaffles, and stirrup-irons.

74. POTTS, WILLIAM, Birmingham, Manufacturer; (GREGG & SON, Upper Sackville-street, Dublin, Exhibitors.)—Chandeliers of various patterns; Grecian dishes; etched and stained lanterns; globe lights (original design); candle lamps; candelabra; ormolu mirrors; mantel-piece gas brackets; lacquered and bronze spill pots; fancy bronze letter weights; epergne candelabra, in Parian and ormolu.

75. REID, J., Thornton-place, Aberdeen, Designer and Manufacturer.—Improved portable mangle.

76. RITCHIE, D., & Co., Glasgow, Manufacturers.—Kitchen ranges; cottage ranges; Dundee kitchen grates; register grates; dressing irons, &c.

77. ROBERTSON, CARR, & STEEL, Chantry Works, Sheffield, Manufacturers.—Hall stoves; dining and drawing-room grates; fenders, fire-irons, &c.

78. ROCHFORD, J., & SON, City-quay, and Clonskeagh, Dublin, Manufacturers.—Anchors, jack screws, chains, purchase blocks, crabb winches, ship and yacht cabooses; drainage tools, shovels, spades, forks; window guards, pumps, &c.

79. ROSS & MURRAY, Middle Abbey-street, Dublin, Designers and Manufacturers.—Reclining and shower bath; toilet table and fittings; specimen of plumbers' brass work; model of heating apparatus, as fitted up in palm house of the Royal Dublin Society's Botanic Garden, Glasnevin.

80. RUSSELL, J., & Co., Wednesbury, Manufacturers.—Gas fittings, tubes, cocks, burners, &c., of various dimensions.

81. SHERIDAN, J., Church-street, Dublin, Manufacturer.—Church bells; platform weighing machine; fire-proof safe; eagles with pedestals; weighing beams and scales; wrought iron gate with piers; hall door entablature in cast iron; balustrades and lamp posts; portable corn mill on a new principle, of two-horse power.

82. STOCKER (BROTHERS), S. & G., Arthur-street, New Oxford-street, London, Patentees and Manufacturers.—A recess counter for the use of licensed victuallers, with separate compartments for beer and spirits.

83. SUMPTON, J., Ebury-square, Pimlico, London.—Cock box, and key for water and gas works.

84. TARIN, M. L. A., Mount-street, Grosvenor-square, London, Inventor and Proprietor.—Candle lamp, with reflectors; lantern with reflector.

85. TAYLOR, W., Sheepcote-street, Birmingham, Inventor and Manufacturer.—Registered shutter bars; ornamented door-spring and sash fasteners; steel bell springs.

86. TINDALL, ENOCK O., Scarborough, Inventor and Manufacturer.—Imperial mangle, with horizontal spring pressure; imperial mangle, combined with napkin press, washing and wringing machine.

87. TODD, BURNS, & Co., Mary-street, Dublin.—Portable iron bedsteads.

88. TUPPER & CARR, London, Glasgow, and Birmingham. Manufacturers.—Patent galvanized iron; sheet iron for outbuildings, roofing, sheathing of ships bottoms, &c.; roll and ridge capping; wrought and cast iron guttering; rain water pipes; round and flat bars; hoop iron, rivets, burrs, nails, and screws; wire; roll game netting; wire stand for fencing, &c.; garden chair; sail thimbles and chain; gas tubing and fittings; house pails; coal scuttles, boiling pans, and other articles of wrought and cast iron.

89. TYLOR, J., & SON, Warwick-lane, London, Proprietors.—Wheel of Wellington car; moderator lamps in bronze; ormolu, alabaster, and china bronzed tea urns; bronze vases and tripods; ornamental coal scoops; imperial standard measures; bath in mahogany frame, with heating apparatus affixed; patent high pressure closets and cocks, at work; copper goods for kitchen purposes; patent garden syringes; vapour bath; gas bath at work.

90. VIEILLE MONTAGNE ZINC MINING COMPANY, per Mr. H. F. SCHMOLL, Agent, Manchester Buildings, Westminster. Producers, Inventors, and Manufacturers.—Bronzed zinc statues; gilt zinc candelabra and chandeliers; vase; Corinthian capital; weather-cock; doors with architraves ornamented with mouldings; balustrade; cornices; centre ceiling ornaments; models of ships, showing the manner of using zinc for ship sheathing and bolting; models of zinc roofs, &c.; dormar windows; baths; coppered zinc wire; suspending vases for flowers, &c.; candle branches; gutter; candle mould; cans and other water vessels; bowls, containing samples of zinc nails, spikes, &c.; rolled zinc; spelter from the Vieille Montagne Mines; slab of slate, painted five years ago, with zinc paint, and subjected to severe test; zinc pipe and wire; perforated zinc blinds, and numerous other articles of zinc.

91. WHITESTONE, G. & W., North Earl-street and Grafton-street, Dublin, Importers and Manufacturers.—Shower baths; deed safes and boxes; papier maché trays; imperial mangle; washing and wringing machine; tea urns; toilet furniture; umbrella and hat stand; coal vases; metal table and flower stand; electro-plated and Britannia ware.

92. WHITLEY, JOHN, Ashton, near Warrington, Lancashire, Manufacturer. — Wrought-iron hinges; Cathedral hinge; locomotive hinges; shutter bar joints, &c.

93. WINFIELD, R. W., Fleet-street, London, and Birmingham, Manufacturer.—Ornamental brass cradle; an improved patent brass four-post bedstead; a tent bedstead; an iron four-post bedstead; brass reclining chair, with Morocco furniture; massive brass newel.

94. WOODHOUSE, J., Lower Ormond-quay, Dublin, Manufacturer.—Gilt and plated buttons, and brass mountings for military accoutrements, with partial illustration of process of manufacture.

95. YOUNG, CHARLES D., & Co., Edinburgh, Glasgow, Liverpool, and London, Manufacturers.—Lodge, field, and entrance iron gates; simultaneous acting iron gates for railway level crossings; plain and ornamental iron and wire fencing; hare and rabbit proof wire netting; galvanized wire netting for Australian fencing; galvanised netting for salmon fisheries; wrought and cast iron garden chairs and seats; galvanized wire seats; pheasant feeder; plant guards, flower stands, vases, fountains, dial stands, &c.

# CLASS XXIII.

---

## WORKS IN PRECIOUS METALS, JEWELLERY, ETC.

THE objects comprised in this class are of general interest, from their being articles of luxury; being expensive, gorgeous in appearance, and admitting in a high degree of artistic display. But they are of further interest, as showing more effectively the extent to which a knowledge of the principles of art is applied to useful purposes, than perhaps the contents of any other department of the Exhibition. The massiveness and consequent expense of many of the articles also excite a feeling of surprise and admiration; and this feeling is increased when one takes into account the further value conferred upon them by the labour of the artist and of the workman.

The illustration of this class consisted chiefly of British and Irish goods, there being few articles of modern workmanship from foreign countries. In many departments there were some magnificent collections; but the great feature of the whole was the electro-plated works of Messrs. Elkington and Mason, who have obtained a world-wide celebrity for their production. The few foreign articles which properly belonged to this class were, however, remarkable for the extent to which they combined graceful outline with originality of idea, more especially when contrasted with many ambitious specimens of native workmanship. While the British and Irish manufacturers stand high in the exhibition of mechanical skill, this advantage is often sadly counteracted by the character of their designs; and hence one great advantage of bringing large collections together is to make the public acquainted not only with the peculiarities of the articles of particular establishments, but also of different countries; by which means not only will the manufacturers of different localities profit from an inspection of the works of others, but the public taste will also be generally improved.

Instead of noticing in detail the several articles, or even the more remarkable ones in this department, we shall, in accordance with the rule adopted in treating other sections, place before the reader some information as to the manner in which the several processes of manufacture are carried out, indicating at the same time some of the peculiarities of the contents of the different departments of the class. In prosecution of this design we shall consider—

1. Works in precious metals, or covered with them, not including electro-plated ware.
2. Electro-metallurgy.
3. Jewellery, precious stones, artificial gems, &c.
4. Enamelled work.

### 1.—WORKS IN PRECIOUS METALS, OR COVERED WITH THEM, NOT INCLUDING ELECTRO-PLATED WARE.

From the earliest times the precious metals have been used in the fabrication of domestic utensils and ornaments, the possession of the one and of the other being the external evidences of a certain social superiority. The same cause which led to this result, their scarcity, and consequent value, joined to their intrinsic beauty, also rendered them the most precious offerings which could be made in the name of religion. Accordingly, in ancient and mediæval times, Pagan temples and Christian churches were richly adorned with lamps, candelabra, censors, vases, shrines, &c., of gold and silver. Indeed, in the middle ages, if we except some of the towns on the Mediterranean, the Church and the princes possessed the monopoly of vessels and ornaments of this description, and with it that of all the art. In those times a goldsmith was a very important personage, not alone in consequence of the prestige which even constant contact with the precious metals appears at all times to have communicated to men, but because all branches of art were generally united in one person, and the goldsmith was very frequently a painter, an architect, a sculptor in stone, &c. They retained this importance even in the sixteenth century, as we learn from the whimsical negotiations of Benevenuto Cellini with popes, kings, and princes.

In the fifteenth and sixteenth centuries the rise of the communes, and the accumulation of wealth from the increase of trade consequent upon the breaking down of the feudal system in many parts of Europe, and the consolidation of smaller states, enabled the wealthy citizens of towns to indulge in silver and gold utensils. In the sixteenth century the immense quantities of silver poured into Europe from Mexico and Peru, completely banished the wooden bowls from the houses of all rich persons. During the next century no person above the rank of a peasant drank his wine or beer from other vessel than a silver tankard; so much so that in 1696, the use of silver plate, spoons excepted, was obliged to be prohibited in the public houses of London. The taverns, indeed, had usurped the place of the churches in the possession of silver articles; a profusion of plate is still, to a great extent, the characteristic of the *cafés* of Paris. When plate became vulgar,—for novelty, or rather we ought to say variety, is the chief element of fashion,—it was replaced by the porcelain of the East, or by that beautiful ware known as "old Sevres." The invention of true porcelain in Europe rendered that, in its turn, common, and now the wealthy find it difficult to possess anything unique or rare, for even antiques have become articles of trade. Gold and silver articles have, however, regained their old supremacy, and are now in greater use than they have ever been before. That extension is, however, intimately connected with the use of tea; the manufacture of tea-pots, spoons, and forks, employing, it is said, more than half of all the silver used for every other purpose, and of this quantity the spoons take the chief part.

It is unnecessary here to describe the processes by which the goldsmith fashions his articles, for, with one or two exceptions, they are essentially the same as those described in speaking of Britannia metal and nickel silver, that is, by casting, hammering, spinning, and stamping. We may, however, mention, that many silver and gold articles are ornamented by chasing or embossing; these terms being employed according as the work is superficial or deeply executed. These operations consist in drawing the outlines of the design upon the article with red chalk and tracing paper, and then bulging out the body of the design from the inside or back by means of a knobbed rod and a hammer; the design is then elaborated by a series of indentations produced with a number of small punches. This is the style of work termed *repoussé*, for which the artists of the sixteenth century were so celebrated. The great majority of the articles made in imitation of the mediæval style are executed in this way. There is no process connected with the working of metals which demands so much skill, or which enables the artist to display all the resources of his genius with more effect than this style of work.

The style of ornamentation, known as "piece working," which is also confined to a great extent to silver and plated articles, and which was formerly very much in fashion, consists in perforating the objects by means of a series of punches in a fly-press. The articles ornamented in this way were bread baskets, waiter's snuffer trays, &c.

The great value of silver and of gold led to attempts being made to use the baser metals merely coated with the precious ones. A process for effecting this object must have been long known, but the coatings of silver or of gold appear to have been very flimsy compared with the perfect methods at present in use, most of which are very modern, we might almost say recent inventions; rolled plate, for example, not being more than about eighty years in use.

There are various methods of plating as the process of covering the baser metals with the precious ones is termed; the nature of the process depending in many instances upon the kind of metal and also upon the nature of the article to be plated. For instance, the plating of iron-harness furniture is effected by first tinning it, that is coating it over with common solder by means of a hot soldering iron, the surface being kept clean by some rosin. A piece of thin sheet silver is then laid upon the tinned iron to which it is made to unite by heating it until it softens, after which it is polished. The articles included under the term "plate," such as candlesticks, dish-covers, salvers, &c., were, until the invention of electro-plating, chiefly made by the following process:—the body or basis, consisting of copper with a little brass, was cast into ingots about 3 inches broad, 20 inches long, and about 1¼ inches thick. Those ingots were then filed smooth on one side, if only to be single plated, and on both sides, if to be double plated; a piece of thin sheet silver of the same size was then laid upon these smooth surfaces, and kept attached to it by a piece of wire. They were then placed in a furnace and heated until the two metals began to alloy at their surface, when they were removed and pressed between rollers until they were reduced in thickness. Another way is to deposit a thin film of silver upon the surface, either by means of an amalgam of mercury or silver, or by dipping the article into liquids containing silver in solution; upon this silvered surface a piece of sheet silver is fastened, the whole heated to bright redness and the metals made to unite by a sudden and strong blow; after which it is rolled out as in the other case.

From the sheets of plated metal made in either of these ways, the articles were fashioned, either by spinning, stamping, swaging, piece-working, or by *repoussé* work. The different pieces where required being joined together by soldering with an alloy of silver and brass, were then burnished with a bloodstone or with steel tools. Electro-plated ware was at first also formed upon the same body, but a means having been discovered of depositing the silver upon articles cast or wrought out of white alloys, such as nickel silver, these alloys are now almost exclusively employed. They possess the great advantage that when slightly worn the red colour of the copper does not appear. An important distinction between electro-plating and the kind of plating which we have just described is, that in the case of the former the article is first fashioned and then plated, and in the latter the metal is first plated and then fashioned.

Another process of silvering, known as French plating, is, to cover the object with silver leaf, which is fixed to the surface by burnishers of steel. The piece to be silvered is filed up, then annealed—that is, heated red hot—and plunged into nitric acid diluted with water, until it becemes perfectly clean, then rubbed with pummice-stone; and pickled again while hot in aquafortis, the effect of which is to roughen the surface so as to present a number of asperities, to which the leaf may adhere. It is now ready to be silvered, for which purpose it is heated until the brass becomes blue, upon which the workman applies a leaf of silver, and rubs it with the burnishing tool, then another, and so on, until he has applied forty to eighty leaves, according to the thickness of the plating required. This ingenious process is of great service to the workers of rolled plate, in repairing any spots where the copper happens to be laid bare in their operations. It is also used with every description of plate, any portions of which are to be engraved. Ordinary rolled plate could not be engraved as the graver would cut into the copper; by overlaying, however, the parts of the surface to be engraved with a sufficient number of silver leaves, a proper thickness of that metal is formed, which is then beaten down into the substance of the body.

Objects may also be silvered with an amalgam of silver and mercury, which is prepared by heating silver leaf, or silver precipitated from its solution in aquafortis by means of copper, which throws it down in the state of a fine powder, with eight times its weight of mercury, straining the amalgam through a bag of che mois leather to separate the excess of mercury. The article to be silvered is made perfectly clean, and at the same time slightly roughened by dipping in sulphuric acid and afterwards in nitric acid, after which it is rubbed with a gilder's scratch brush, dipped in a solution of mercury in aquafortis, and rubbed with the amalgam until the surface is fully silvered; the piece is then heated until the whole of the mercury is driven off, leaving the silver as a coating behind, which may be polished and burnished in the usual way. The cheaper kinds of plated buttons are plated by a process which is merely a variation of the one just described, and which consists in smearing them over with a paste composed of chloride of silver, corrosive sublimate, common salt, white copperas; gently heating them until the mixture is dry; and then raising the temperature nearly to redness to drive off the mercury; the buttons may then be polished in the usual way.

The facility with which silver, when dissolved in acids, may be thrown down in the metallic form, has led to a number of chemical processes of silvering, which, however, are but little used, as the silvering resulting is not very durable. As an example of this kind of silvering we shall give the process by which pins are usually whitened. A mixture of cream of tartar, common salt, and a little chloride of silver is put into a vessel containing some boiling water; the salt water dissolves a part of the chloride of silver, and on the pins being now introduced, the silver is precipitated upon them.

Metals may be coated with gold by processes almost identical with those described for silvering. The common wash gilding is done with an amalgam of gold and mercury, exactly as we have described the corresponding processes of silvering with an amalgam. For example, buttons are gilt in this way. The buttons are first rough burnished, then quickened; that is, are thrown into a solution of mercury in nitric acid, where they are rubbed about by a small broom of fine twigs for five minutes; a portion of the mercury is precipitated upon the copper. The buttons are then removed from the solution, washed repeatedly with water, and then put into a mixture of gold amalgam, with dilute nitric acid, where they are stirred about until their surfaces are sufficiently and uniformly coated by a deposition of the gold and mercury upon them. The next operation is termed drying off; that is, volatilizing the mercury. This was formerly, and is even yet, done on a shovel or in a pot, to the destruction of the lives of the workmen; but the more usual way is to put them into a sort of cage of wire, which is then introduced into a closed furnace, where the cage is caused to revolve. There is a refrigerator connected with the furnace, so that the greater part of the mercury is recovered. After the gilding the buttons are brushed with ale-grounds or other substances, and got up by burnishing in a lathe, with bloodstone tools. Some notion may be formed of the divisibility of gold, when it is stated that five grains of gold are sufficient to produce 144 of what would be formerly legally considered a gilt button; the same number may even be tolerably gilded with two and a half grains, and even one grain will be sufficient to coat them.

The gold leaf used for leaf gilding is prepared by rolling out the gold, alloyed according to the desired colour, with from three to twelve grains of copper or silver to the ounce, into ribands; these are annealed and cut into squares of one inch, 150 of which are laid two together, between leaves of vellum of four times the size, which are enclosed in a cover of parchment and beaten on a smooth marble block. When the plates of gold have spread out to the size of the vellum leaves, they are taken out, each cut into four, and the 600 pieces then interlaid with an animal membrane, obtained from the lower gut of the cow, and prepared in a peculiar manner, and known as goldbeaters' skin, and are again beaten out into four times their size; again subdivided into 2,400 squares, divided into four parcels, and again beaten out until they again reach the same size. In some cases another subdivision into 9600 pieces is made, and another beating takes place. When fully beaten out they are cut into squares, about three inches or three 3-8th inches, and are interleaved in a little book, the paper of which has been made smooth, and rubbed with bole, a kind of red earth. The gold of one of these books weighs about 4·8 grains, and is therefore $\frac{1}{282000}$ of an inch in thickness.

The wire which is flattened and spun into gold thread for laces, brocades, such as the numerous examples of brocaded poplins, is always made of impure, that is, highly alloyed silver which is gilded by layers of gold leaf put on, in the manner described in speaking of French plating. A cylindrical ingot is first formed which is thus gilded, and is then drawn through a series of perforations in a steel plate of gradually diminishing size as in ordinary wire-drawing. The tenuity of the gold upon this flattened wire isastonishing; it being little more than $\frac{1}{350000}$ of an inch in thickness.

Objects in gold and silver, whether solid or gilt and plated, have the appearance of their surfaces or of parts of them varied by certain processes. Some parts, for example, are burnished, others are deadened; in other cases the colour is changed; thus we have ormolu, red gold, oxidized silver, &c. When parts of an object are to be burnished, and another part deadened, the former are covered with a varnish composed of Spanish white, sugar, and gum, mixed up with water. The article is then strongly heated until the gum and sugar are partially carbonized, and the varnish has become brown. A mixture is now made of common salt, nitre, and alum, which are fused in their water of crystallization; and while in a state of fusion applied as a varnish over the whole article while still hot; the parts covered with the varnish of Spanish white and gum being coated as well as the naked metal. The piece is again heated until the saline varnish fuses into a perfect glass, and covers the whole surface equally, whereupon it is plunged into cold water which cracks the glassy varnish, and causes it to peel of, carrying with it the varnish first applied. The appearance of the article is now quite peculiar; the parts covered by the gum varnish are more or less brilliant, while those parts which were exposed to the action of the saline glass are quite deadened. The piece is then cleaned from all adhering varnish by very weak nitric acid, and well washed in water, after which the parts intended to be burnished are rubbed with bloodstone tools and a little water slightly acidified with vinegar. An ormolu colour may be given to gold instead of deadening or matting it, by substituting for the saline varnish above mentioned one made of red oxide of iron, alum, and sea salt, worked up with vinegar. The article coated with this mixture is to be strongly heated and plunged into water, and then rubbed with vinegar, or, when chased, with dilute nitric acid. The French red gold appearance is produced in very nearly the same way, by using a varnish composed of bee's wax, red ochre, verdigris, and alum, usually called gilder's wax; the piece being heated until all the wax is burned away, and a part of the copper of the verdigris has been reduced upon the surface of the metal where it alloys itself with a thin film of gold which assumes a peculiar reddish hue.

As a considerable portion of the trinkets and other articles sold as gold consist of gold alloyed with a large quantity of copper, and would have too red an appearance, they are usually pickled with a solution of common salt, nitre, and alum, which, by dissolving out the copper from the surface of the articles, allows the gold to develope its full colour.

One of the most agreeable variations of the kind which we have been discussing is the appearance produced on silver known as *oxidized silver*. There are two distinct shades in use, the one produced by chlorine, which has a brownish tint, and the other by sulphur which has a bluish black tint. To obtain the former it is only necessary to wash the article with a solution of sal-ammoniac; a much richer shade may be obtained by employing a solution composed of equal parts of sulphate of copper and sal-ammoniac in vinegar. The fine rich black tint may be produced by washing the article with a warm solution of sulphuret of potassium or sodium.

The illustrations of the goldsmith's art in the Exhibition were extremely numerous. Independent of the beautiful piece of plate made by M. Froment Meurice, and contributed by the Duc de Luynes, and the beautiful plate of oxidized silver, in *repoussé* work, of M. Rudolphi, which will be more properly noticed when speaking of the French department, Hunt and Roskell, and Gerard, of London, Waterhouse, West, &c., and some other manufacturers of this city, contributed some large pieces, many of them remarkable for their weight; and some of them were also not without merit in an artistic point of view.

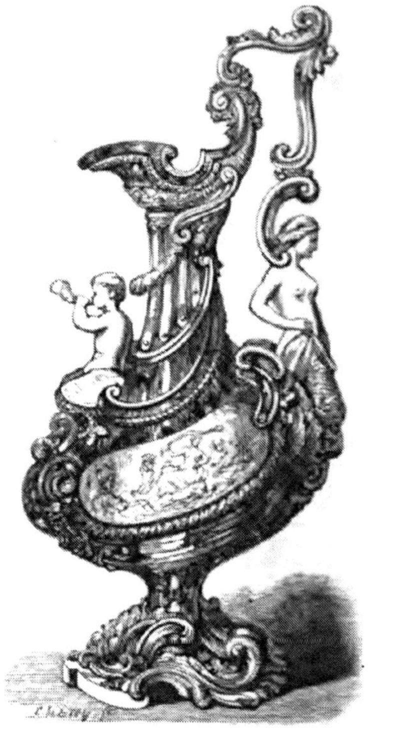

Claret Jug by Waterhouse & Co.

The annexed illustration represents a claret jug, exhibited by Messrs. Waterhouse and Co., which, as a specimen of casting and chasing, possessed considerable merit. The form was particularly graceful, each individual part being borrowed from the form of certain shells, the body and cup-shaped mouth being evidently of this character. A figure of a mermaid in matted silver formed the caryatid-like support of the handle; on each side of the body were groups also in matted silver; on one side was Neptune seated on the sea-horse, and on the other his wife Amphitrite, surrounded by her attendants. The whole effect was good, the flat surfaces being burnished, and the ornaments deadened or matted.

The beautiful contributions of Rudolphi in oxidized silver will receive a notice more appropriately in the article specially devoted to the French department. The chief English exhibiter in oxidized silver was R. Phillips, of London, some of whose smaller trinkets were very pretty and tasteful. The contributions of Messrs. Hardman and Co., in gold and silver church furniture, nearly the whole of which were in *repoussé* style, deserve special notice on that account, whatever may be thought of them in an artistic point of view. With the exception of Elkington and Mason, and Rudolphi, they constituted the most liberal contribution of works in the precious metals in the Exhibition.

## II.—ELECTRO-METALLURGY.

It is sometimes beneficial to recall the minds of people from the usual hero-worship of mere accident, whether of birth or of money, and to impress upon them the names of the true apostles of civilization. Great warriors, who have led armies and marked their track in blood and desolation, and as the representatives of the mere brute instinct of destruction, have been the idols, and are sometimes called the saviours, of nations. Statesmen have intrigued, and lawyers have invented phrases, and, as the dispensers of power, have gained wealth and sometimes renown. But how much have all those men, celebrated in their day, and many of whose names stand out prominently on the pages of history, as it is still written, contributed to the progress of the human race? In many cases they have but retarded it, whilst the peaceful voyages of Columbus, the discoveries of Galileo and of Newton, and the inventions of a Gutenberg and a Watt, have changed the whole relations of man to the universe. We are too much inclined to confound cause and effect, and hence mankind has always worshipped action rather than thought. Whilst the thinker remains neglected or utterly unknown the mere realiser of his idea amasses a fortune and becomes celebrated.

These reflections have been suggested in examining the many examples which were presented to our view in the Centre Hall, and elsewhere in the Exhibition, of the application of one of the most extraordinary powers in nature to the service of civilized man. Sixty-four years ago an Italian professor of anatomy, named Galvani, discovered that two pieces of different metals brought into contact with the leg of a frog, caused a muscular contraction in the limb. A few years later another distinguished Italian professor, named Volta, led by this discovery, found that the mere contact of two metals gave rise to the development of a peculiar force; a step further, and he discovered the *voltaic pile*. This instrument consisted of a number of discs of the metal zinc, of silver, and of cloth moistened with acid; commencing with a disc of silver, he placed upon it a piece of the moistened cloth, and upon this a disc of zinc, then a disc of silver, and so on until he had built up a pile of forty or fifty of each. The bottom disc being silver, the top, from the order of the series, was necessarily zinc, a piece of wire was soldered to each, and on catching the ends of the wires in each hand, a shock was felt. Thus what a simple pair of discs in contact with the muscle of the frog produced upon a small object, a number of discs united produce upon a man. From the belief that there was some peculiar force concentrated, as in the magnetic needle, in the ends of the wire, they were styled *poles*, and as it was observed that the force, which was believed to be a fluid, travelled from the zinc end to the copper end, the former was called the *positive pole*, and the latter as having no fluid or rather as wanting it, was denominated the *negative pole*. After a little it was found that all metals could be employed for making a pile, and that there was a certain order in which the metals arranged themselves, a metal being always negative to the one below it, and positive to the one above it. Thus copper was positive when employed in making a pile with silver, but negative with zinc; and hence the first metal on the list would be most negative to the last one, and would make the strongest pile accordingly.

Little more than half a century has elapsed since this kind of instrument was first invented, and yet what grand results it has achieved! To name one is sufficient—the electric telegraph; and yet these results are trivial to what it is yet destined to produce. Already we can obtain chemical changes by its means. A connection has been established between the force produced by it and light, and heat, and magnetism; and no doubt can exist that at some day, perhaps not far distant, all the forces of nature will be summoned at will by its means like the genii of Eastern tales, and that our machinery will be worked, our rooms lighted and heated, and many of our chemical manufactures will be conducted by its agency. With all the results hitherto attained by this unique power, and the glorious future opened before it, in which it will change the social and political condition of nations, how many who passed by those beautiful specimens of art produced by its means, exhibited by Messrs. Elkington and Mason, knew to whom the world is indebted for the first fructifying germ of our knowledge of this yet almost unknown power, although doubtless they are well versed in the genealogies of every celebrated freebooter of ancient Rome or of the middle ages?

Now, that we have vindicated the *thinkers*, let us turn to some of the results of a *practical* kind which have been attained from Galvani and Volta's discoveries. The most important, besides the electric telegraph, and the one which was best illustrated in the Exhibition was, undoubtedly, electro-metallurgy, or the working of metals by means of electricity. It may be divided into two branches, namely, the art of reproducing articles in bronze, copper, or other metal, such as small figures, ornaments, &c., and which is, strictly speaking, termed galvano-plastic art; and that of merely covering one metal with a coating of another, and which is known as electro-plating and gilding. However important these arts are, we can only devote a very small space to their consideration, and can consequently only attempt to convey to our readers a few general ideas of the nature of the processes constituting both branches of manufacture. To do this we shall take up the subject where Volta brought it by the discovery of the pile, which, in the course of a few years, was greatly modified. Instead of the moistened slip of cloth a cell full of an acid liquor was substituted, and the instrument was called a galvanic or voltaic battery. In this form it consisted of a number of cells or of separate vessels, in each of which was immersed a plate of zinc and a plate of copper; the zinc of one cell being connected with the copper of the next, and so on. When such a series was in action the zinc was dissolved by the acid, whilst the negative metal was unacted upon; but after a time a portion of the zinc was deposited upon the surface of the copper, and thus changed its relations to the zinc plate, and finally stopped the action of the battery. The action was thus momentary, and before it could have led to any practical applications it was necessary to render its action constant; a point which was first attained by Daniell in the form of a battery which still bears his name. When we place a slip of copper in weak sulphuric acid it is slowly dissolved, but if we put a slip of zinc and a slip of copper with their ends in contact into weak acid, the zinc alone is acted upon; a portion of the water forming the acid solution is decomposed, one of its elements, oxygen, combines with the zinc, whilst the other, hydrogen, is given off from the surface of the copper. The union of the zinc and of the oxygen yields oxide of zinc, which unites with the sulphuric acid to form sulphate of zinc or white copperas. Hydrogen is a substance which has a remarkable power of reducing the oxides of the metals to the metallic state, and one of the earliest facts discovered by means of the pile was that when a current of electricity was made to pass through a solution of a salt it has a tendency to decompose it, the acid going towards one pole, and the base towards another. Upon these two facts Daniell founded his discovery of the constant battery. He made a vessel of copper which he partially filled with a solution of sulphate of copper or blue stone, and in this he suspended another cell made of animal gut and filled with a dilute acid, in which was placed the zinc plate. Animal membrane possesses the property of being wetted by one fluid which it allows to pass through it, whilst it opposes the passage of the other; thus, it readily allows the acid through, but the sulphate of copper difficultly so. If the copper vessel be connected with the zinc plate by means of a wire, we have one element of a battery; but it is to a great extent a constant one. The oxide of zinc formed in the bladder cell cannot pass through it, and cannot, consequently, be deposited upon the copper; whilst the passage of the electricity through the sulphate of copper decomposes it into sulphuric acid, which travels towards the zinc, and thus replenishes the acid solution; and oxide of copper, which would go to the copper and adhere to it, but that the hydrogen liberated from the water in its decomposition to form oxide of zinc has a tendency to the same pole, and, both coming into contact, react; the hydrogen takes the oxygen of the oxide of copper, and forms water, whilst the copper is deposited upon the surface of the copper vessel as a beautiful bright metallic coating.

De La Rive, in making some experiments with this new form of battery, observed that the deposit of new copper formed upon the surface of the old plates when separated from the latter, gave a most perfect cast of it, every scratch on the old plate being reproduced on the new one in relief; but he does not appear to have thought of applying this fact to any useful purpose,—an honour which was left for Messrs. Jacobi, of Petersburgh, and Spencer, of Liverpool, who appear to have arrived at similar results, independently of each other.

If we suppose the surface of the copper vessel in Daniell's original battery to have figures carved upon it, the deposit of new copper, when separated from it, would be a faithful cast of these figures. But it would not be necessary to have the figures upon the plate of the battery itself; we could fasten the object to be copied to a wire connected with the copper end of the battery, and immerse it in a vessel of sulphate of copper, another plate of copper being also immersed in it connected with the zinc end. To this process of obtaining reproductions of objects, Spencer gave the name of the electrotype, and Jacobi, galvano-plastic art, which, as being more appropriate, is the one now universally adopted. At first only objects in bronze or in other metals could be copied; but it was soon found that figures in wax, plaster of paris, or in any other material, could be also reproduced, if first covered with a slight coating of some metal, or with plumbago. For example, if we wished to copy a cast in plaster, we should first dip it in melted stearine, or some other material which would render it non-absorbent, and then wash it with nitrate of silver, after which it should be held over the vapour of ether, in which a little phosphorous had been dissolved; the effect would be to reduce the silver to the metallic state, and thus coat the surface with a thin film of silver upon which the copper would deposit, as upon a copper object. The same result could be obtained, though in a less perfect degree, by brushing it over with dry plumbago, mixed with finely divided silver, or still better by agitating a quantity of finely powdered plumbago in a solution of corrosive sublimate, and adding a quantity of proto-chloride of tin, which would throw down the mercury in a metallic state along with the plumbago, and rubbing the object with the resulting powder. Instead of plaster or wax, we might employ gelatine, or, in fact, a hundred other substances which it is unnecessary to mention. It is to the employment of the gelatine or plastic moulds that we owe the successful reproduction of works of art, especially in high relief.

The applications of the electrotype are innumerable. We may, for example, copy medals, coins, busts, statues, sculptured ornaments, wood cuts, and make stereotype plates, &c., by its means. An engraved plate will give but a few hundred impressions, until the delicacy of the fine lines will be destroyed; but by electrotyping it we get a matrix in which all the engraved lines are in relief, and from this we may obtain any number of perfect fac-similes of the original plate, so that any number of proof impressions could be produced.

It would occupy too much space to notice the numerous applications that have been made, or might be made, of this curious and beautiful process; we shall therefore confine ourselves to one which has been made in Ireland. The maps of the Ordnance Survey of Ireland comprise several thousand sheets, the engraving of the plate for each of which cost a very large sum of money. Once such a plate was engraved, no change could be made in it; and hence, in a few years the value of a map would be considerably diminished, in consequence of the alterations of fences, or the construction of new roads. But by the application of the electrotype the maps can be renewed when required, at a very trifling cost. Thus, we will suppose, a map of Dublin to have been engraved; the plate, as it comes from the engravers' hands, is electrotyped, and a matrix is obtained, after which it is varnished and laid aside as the legal document, while the matrix is then employed to obtain a plate for printing from. In the matrix, all the lines are in relief; now, if we suppose a new street to have been made after the engraving of the map, we could introduce the change very simply by taking a matrix and polishing off the lines representing the houses removed in making the street, then electrotyping it, by which we would obtain a fac-simile of the original engraved plate, with the exception of having a flat surface where the street was made. The engraver could there put in any lines which would be required to mark the new houses, boundaries, &c. In this way, also, the index maps of the different counties have been prepared for different purposes, such as the Geological Survey, &c.; the lines not required being rubbed off a matrix, which is then electrotyped, and new letters introduced.

To form a copy of an object in copper, by the galvano-plastic process, we must be able to deposit any quantity of the metal from a mere film to one foot thick as required. This fact naturally led to the application of permanently depositing a thin coating of metal upon any object—of performing in fact the operations of plating, gilding, bronzing, &c. M. De La Rive appears to have been the first who succeeded in effecting this object; but in a partial way, for his process was both expensive and imperfect, as he was unable to gild steel or iron. Very soon after the invention of the pile, an Italian professor, named Brugnatelli, succeeded in gilding and silvering several objects by means of it, an account of which he published, but it attracted no attention at the time, and the fact remained buried in some Italian journals for 40 years. Soon after the publication of De La Rive's experiments, numerous improvements were effected in his process, but still it could not be considered as one which could be carried out for manufacturing purposes; that honour undoubtedly belonging to M. De Ruolz. Previous to the publication of Ruolz's results, Mr. Elkington took out a patent for a process of plating and gilding, which, in a great many respects, resembles that of the former; the priority of the invention is therefore his, but as he did not publish it, and as M. Ruolz's process was more perfect, and extended to every metal, and, above all, as he made the world participator of his discoveries, the chief honour must be given to him. To Mr. Elkington, however, belongs the credit of having combined all the processes of any value discovered, and introducing them into England, where electro-plating has become a great branch of manufacture.

In making a cast by the electrotype process, the current of electricity must be weak, and the process slow; it is, in fact, a gradual deposition, particle by particle; to gild or silver, on the other hand, the current must be strong, and each layer must be deposited rapidly. The object to be gilded or silvered is placed in connexion with a strong battery, and immersed in a bath consisting of some salt of gold or silver in a solution of cyanide of potassium. On the connexions of the battery being completed, the silver or gold, as the case may be, is deposited on the object, and may be obtained of any required thickness. In the first attempts at silvering and gilding, the silver or gold was always thrown down as matted or deadened metal, and had to be burnished after. But the addition of a few drops of sulphuret of carbon enables the manufacturers to throw down the metals perfectly bright as if burnished, a discovery which appears to have been made simultaneously by Mr. Elkington, and Mr. Lyons, of Birmingham. At present, objects may not only be silvered and gilded, but covered with platinum, or, in fact, with any metal, and, what is still more important, with alloys such as bronze, brass, nickel-silver, &c.

The electro-plating establishment of Elkington and Mason is quite a remarkable place. There, instead of producing a current of electricity by means of a galvanic battery, it is produced by making a piece of soft iron, covered with a coil of wire, revolve before the poles of a great magnet; electricity is developed in the coil of wire, and is conducted into the vessels filled with solutions of gold and silver, where the objects to be gilded or silvered are arranged. A small steam-engine gives motion to the bar of soft iron, so that we have the mechanical force of steam developing electricity by means of magnetism, and then by means of this producing chemical decomposition: a source of electricity which we owe to the illustrious Faraday.

The extraordinary progress which this branch of industry has made within the last few years is really astonishing. Not only has it completely superseded the old mode of plating upon copper, but it has introduced a totally new class of plated articles, which in turn have gradually superseded the electro-plated copper—namely, articles made of white alloys, such as Britannia metal, nickel-silver, argentine, &c. The electro-plated goods of this kind are practically little inferior to those made of solid silver; for there is no longer any danger of the copper appearing through when the articles have been worn. The great disadvantages which electro-plated ware laboured under at first of wearing very fast, especially on the edges, has also been successfully overcome; and at present electro-plated and gilded articles, when properly executed, are but little inferior in durability, at the same time that they are very far cheaper, than the goods of which they are imitations.

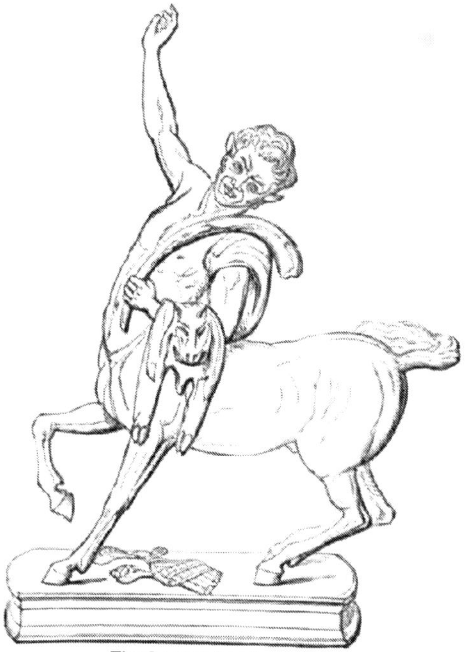

The Centaur, from the Antique.

Whatever objections may have been urged against the use of the electro-process of silvering and gilding articles for domestic use, on the score of want of durability, none can be urged against it in the Fine Arts, which is truly a boundless field for its development. Nothing, for instance, could excel the sharpness and beauty of the numerous statuettes and other art-manufactures of Elkington and Mason, which formed so important and interesting a contribution to the Exhibition. Some of the small figures were made on models reduced from the originals by Cheverton's machine. The annexed engraving represents the centaur, reduced from the original in the Capitol at Rome. Our chief reason for selecting this figure for illustration is the fact that a marble figure, apparently identical with the Roman original, formed a prominent ornament of the Central Hall of the Exhibition; this figure, which was discovered at Pompeii, was contributed by Sir Hervey Bruce, of Down Hill.

Besides the numerous copies of ancient statuary, among which we may mention the well-known faun with the cymbals, the dancing faun of the Museum of Naples, the Hercules Farnese, the dying gladiator, Anotino,

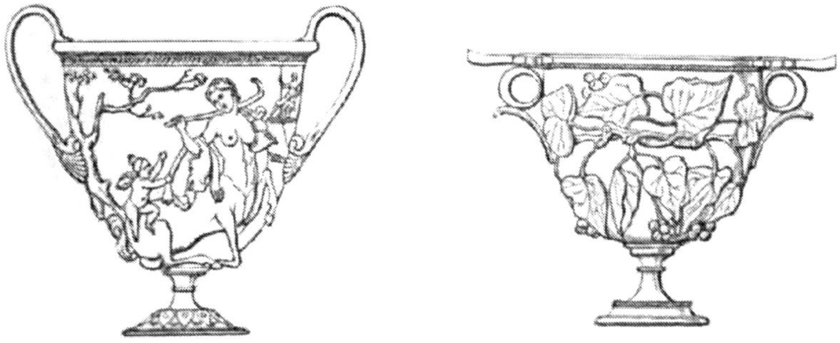

Pair of Vases, from the Antique.

the young Athole, Antinous, the Venus de Medicis, the Apollo Belvidere, Apollino, Melpomene, and Theseus, reduced from the originals by Cheverton, there were in the collection of Elkington and Mason a number of

3 D

copies of small antique cups and vases, many of them of the most charming design, and all beautifully executed. The engravings in the preceding page, and those here subjoined, will convey an idea of a few of these articles.

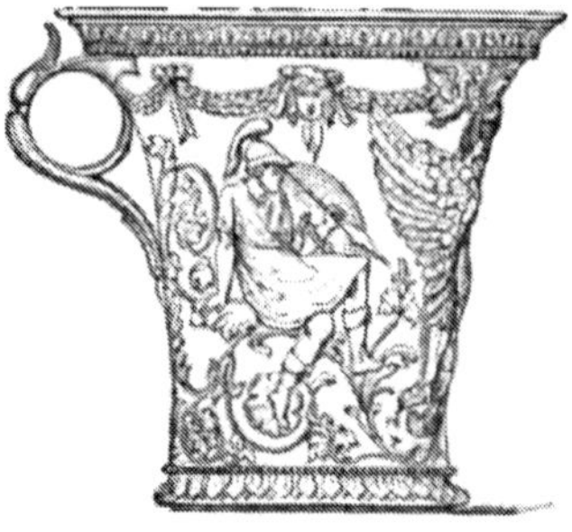

Cup found at Herculaneum.

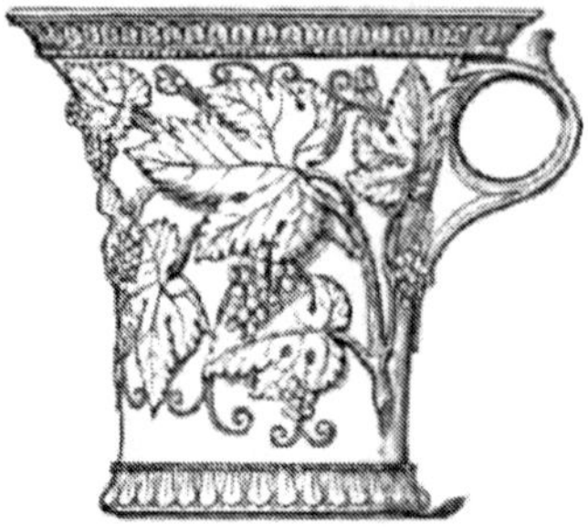

Cup found at Pompeii.

There were also several copies of modern statuary, which, so far as the execution of the copies were concerned, were not inferior to the copies of the antique ones. A beautiful copy, in bronze, of the admirable group chased in silver, and oxidized, after the model of M. Jeannest, which was exhibited at the London Exhibition of 1851, was in this collection, and received its due meed of admiration.

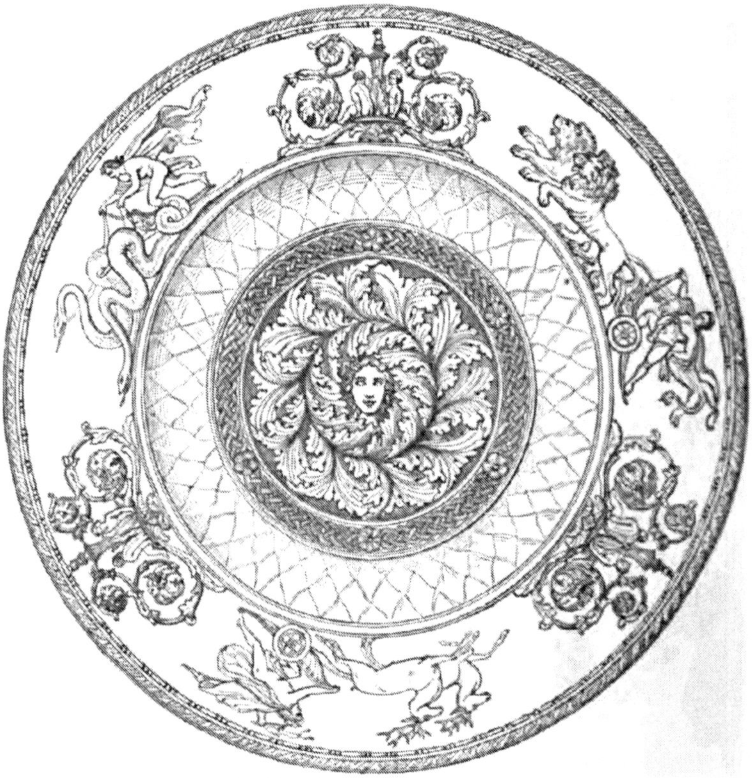

Race Plate, by Elkington and Mason.

Some beautiful plates in gold and oxidized silver were exhibited by Elkington and Mason, among which we must specially mention a reproduction of a plate eighteen and a half inches in diameter, intended as a table-top of the *cinque cento* period. In the centre was a figure of Temperance, surrounded by the emblems of the four elements, air, earth, fire, and water; the border, which was remodelled by a number of artists under the direction of the Chevalier de Schlick, represents Minerva, Astrology, Geometry, Arithmetic, Music, Rhetoric, Dialectics, and Grammar, the sciences then taught in the universities. Another contribution of the same class, which deserves special mention, was a race plate copied from a model of Rosi, of Rome, after a design by Gunkel. This work, which is represented on the preceding page, was executed in oxidized silver, and consists of a centre piece and frieze; the former represents a mask of Venus encircled by an arabesque of foliage. The frieze is divided into three compartments, each of which is occupied by a group, one representing a youth in a chariot or biga drawn by serpents, whom he guides by reins, and emblematic of prudence; another represents a similar chariot and youth furiously driven by deer, representing swiftness; and the third, emblematic of strength and courage, represents a youth in a chariot drawn by two lions. This design, emblematic of the qualities required in a race, strength, courage, swiftness, and prudence,—qualities which are always sure to receive in all contests the encouraging smile of love,—was exceedingly appropriate, and was beautifully executed.

The annexed engraving is the representation of a plate in oxidized silver, 7½ inches in diameter. The design is by the Duc de Luynes. It is emblematic of the days of the week. In the centre is a medallion in *repoussé* style, with Apollo and the horses of the sun, representing Sunday. On the margin are six smaller medallions, with figures of Jupiter, Minerva, Venus, Mercury, &c., emblematic of the remaining six days. It was a work of considerable merit.

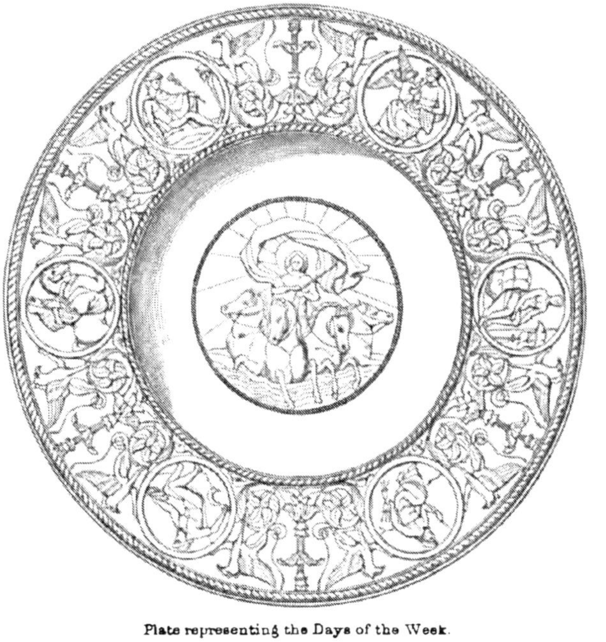

Plate representing the Days of the Week.

The two plates which we have here figured may be taken as specimens of the many excellent works of these enterprising manufacturers in this department. While they have spared no expense in the improvement of the electrotype process, by which a revolution may be said to have been effected in works in the precious metals, they have devoted constant attention to the introduction of appropriate designs, in which also they have been eminently successful.

A shield commemorative of the Exhibition of 1851, the boss of which contained an ink-bottle, was also in this collection. The boss represented the globe, upon which is inscribed the proclamation of the Exhibition.

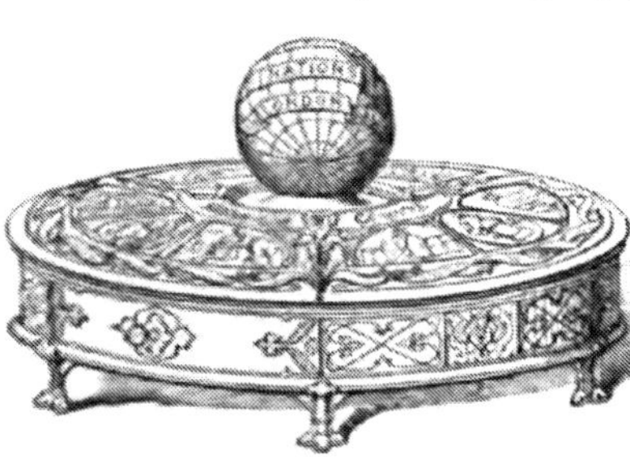

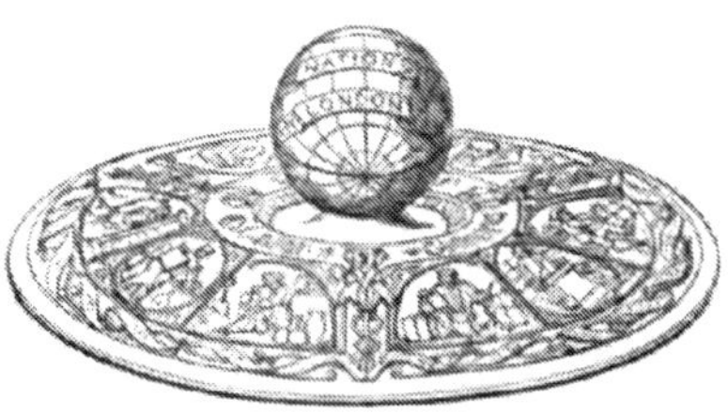

Ink-Stands, from Limner's Design for a Commemoration Shield of the Exhibition of 1851.

The shield is divided into three parts by three caducei, each of which, as it were, supports the arms of one of the three Kingdoms, the stern of the caduceus supporting the arms of Ireland, being entwined with shamrocks;

that of England with roses; and that of Scotland with thistles. Each compartment represents one of the great divisions of industry:—the production of raw materials; the manufacture of them into various objects; and commerce, or the distributor of them through society. Each of these classes of industry is represented by three groups typical of the great subdivisions of these classes. Thus raw materials are typified by the miner for mineral products, the planter for the vegetable, and the shepherd for the animal; manufactures by the potter, the artist, and the weaver; and commerce by the merchant, the retailer, and export trader. These groups are surrounded by a border consisting of a wreath, upon which are inscribed the names of a number of great men who have aided manufactures. These are supposed to include the chief names of all nations, but somehow or other, with few exceptions, they are Englishmen, or if not, English Germans. This reminds us of the Scotch book, that out of about 1600 names quoted, put down 1500 as Scotchmen, the remainder being distributed according to latitude—the farther south the less the number mentioned; so that by the time the author got to the shores of the Mediterranean all intellect appeared to have vanished. This has, however, nothing to do with the merit of the design, the work of Mr. Luke Limner, which is very good.

Our space forbids us from going into details with respect to the collections of electro-plated ware for domestic purposes. Mr. North, of Grafton-street, exhibited a number of well-finished articles, many of them being old articles replated. Some fine specimens were exhibited by Elkington and Mason, among which were a good series of candlesticks. Generally speaking, most of these articles are usually designed without any reference to their uses, and one often contains metal enough to make two or three. The annexed engraving represents a candelabrum after the antique, which is certainly not open to that objection; and which, in other respects, is immeasurably above the usual style of such articles.

There is another application of electro-metallurgy which we can only allude to here, namely, the electro-bronzing or gilding of figures and ornaments in zinc or other cheap and fusible metals, in which pretty designs can be produced at prices which bring them within the means of the great mass of the community; as, for example, the fine collection exhibited by a number of manufacturers under the name of the Vieille Montagne Company; some of the cast iron articles of the Coalbrookdale Company; the fine group of Hercules and the bull, and the hunter attacked by a panther. We need not mention these matters further here, as they will receive their due share of attention when treating of the French and German departments separately.

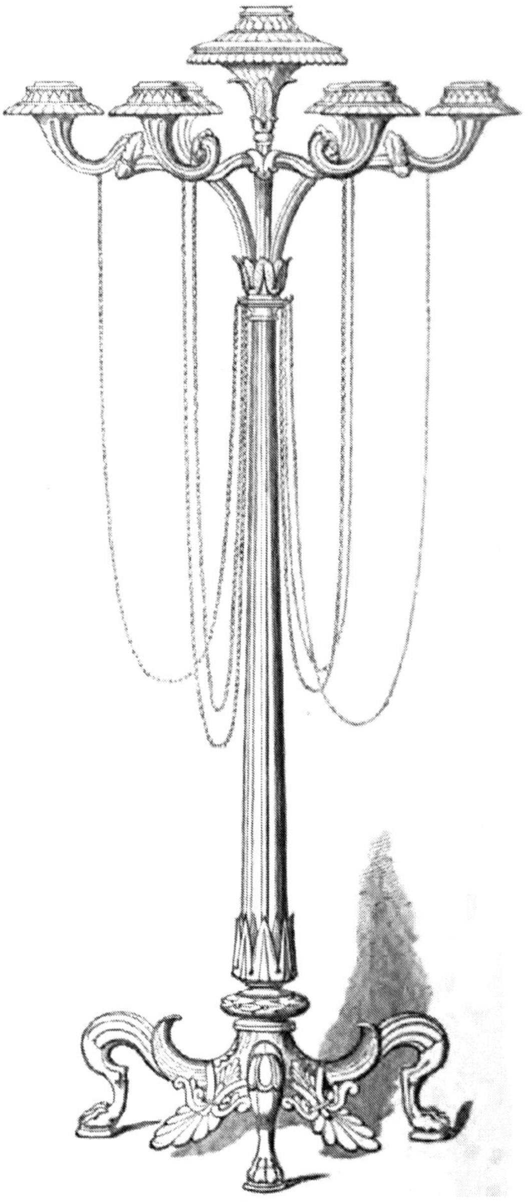

Candelabrum, by Elkington and Mason.

## III.—JEWELLERY, PRECIOUS STONES, &c.

From the earliest times the crystalline form, beautiful colour, and brilliancy of certain minerals attracted the attention of mankind, and led to their employment as ornaments for the person, or for the decoration of objects connected with religion. The minerals used for these purposes are denominated *precious stones*, or gems; they are very numerous, and, as may be anticipated, are held in very different degrees of estimation. The list in modern times is scarcely larger than that of a remote antiquity; our nomenclature is, however, more perfect, for the ancients formed a new name in order to express the most trifling accidental differences, even shades of colour.

Gems may be divided into two classes: those having a definite crystalline form, such as the diamond, which are the most valuable, and those which occur in masses of more or less size, and require to be ground and polished in order to develop their beauty, such as agates, &c. This is, however, an arbitrary division, and is only valuable as affording a convenient classification for our purpose. Natural crystals are more or less imperfect, and do not possess the beauty or brilliancy which art is capable of giving to them; hence at a very early period the method of cutting precious stones and giving them new surfaces was discovered. The proper form to give them was not so well known in ancient times as at present. The usual way was to polish them in a sort of round relief, without cutting them to produce regular facets, resembling those of natural crystals. This style is known as *en cabochon*, from caboche; that is in the form of a rounded head, derived from caput, the head. Most gems are now cut with facets, which produce, as is well known, the finest effect, by their action upon light; cutting *en cabochon* being only practised with certain stones. The latter style was well exemplified in the false gems with which several of the antiques, such as shrines, &c., in the Antiquarian Court were decorated.

We shall give a very brief notice of the chief minerals which have hitherto been used as precious stones, and shall treat of them not in the order of their relative value, but rather of chemical composition. Most minerals contain a variety of substances, sometimes as many as a dozen constituents. These constituents consist, with some few exceptions, of oxides of certain simple substances, chiefly of a metallic nature; some having the character of acids, but the greater number of bases. It occasionally happens that one of these oxides or acids exists uncombined with others, and, in some few rare cases, even the simple substances themselves are found as distinct minerals. The minerals used as precious stones include examples of all these conditions, namely, an uncombined simple substance, an uncombined oxide or acid, and a complex mineral, composed of several oxides and one or more acids. In this order we shall notice them.

The only example of an uncombined simple substance occurring as a gem is the diamond, which is pure carbon. The diamond is the hardest of all known substances, the purest and the most brilliant of all gems. It is found of various colours, blue, red, yellow, green, brown, gray, and even black; with the exception of the latter, however, all these shades are light and pale. The diamond is found always crystallized, its form of crystallization being the octahedron; but this is sometimes so ill defined that it appears as a mere rounded mass. The diamonds in which the crystalline form is well developed are generally cut into what are called brilliants, whilst the rounded masses are cut into rosettes. In countries where the cutting of diamonds was not understood, they were worn in their natural condition, and hence were not so much esteemed as many other stones of much less real beauty. The great difficulty of cutting diamonds arose from their extreme hardness, as no other mineral has the power of scratching them; hence the name, from αδαμας, unsubdued. The mode of cutting the diamond, by means of the powder of the diamond itself, was known to Pliny, and the knowledge appears never to have been lost, although the discovery of it is attributed to Louis de Berquen, a citizen of Bruges, in 1476. In the end of the fourteenth and beginning of the fifteenth century, the regular disposition of the facets, in order to attain the most brilliant effects, was very much improved, and Berquen, if he ever existed at all, may have attained celebrity in this respect, and may have thus led to the idea of being the discoverer of the mode of cutting the diamond by means of its own powder. It is certain that in 1407 a jeweller of Paris, of the name of Herman, became celebrated for his mode of cutting diamonds with diamond powder.

The geographical distribution of diamonds, so far as now known, is very limited, being confined for commercial purposes to two or three districts in India, to one locality in Borneo, and to Brazil: the great source now, however, is Brazil. The discovery of diamonds in the latter country was first made in the district of Serro do Frio, in the province of Minas Geraes, in the year 1727, since which the mines have been worked. Like gold and platinum, the diamond occurs in alluvial beds, chiefly of broken or rolled quartz pebbles, covered with clay; the precise position in which they were originally formed has not been satisfactorily determined.

Diamonds are sold by the carat of four grains, equal to 3¼ grains Troy. It is difficult, however, to estimate the real value of any diamond; the colourless are the most valuable, and they are estimated usually by squaring the weight, and multiplying it by two, for rough diamonds, and by eight, for brilliants, which will give the value in pounds sterling; thus a brilliant of four carats would be worth £128. Small diamonds of one or two carats, when double cut, are worth about £7 to £8 per carat. Inferior diamonds are usually crushed into powder for cutting diamonds and other hard gems, and for cutting rock crystal, to make the lenses of spectacles known as pebble-lenses. Perhaps this use of the diamond is of more importance than that of the adornment of the person.

The gems composed of uncombined bases and acids are very numerous; those of the former, of which we shall speak first, ranking in value after the diamond, include the crystallized varieties of the corundum or sapphire. The word sapphire is derived from the Greek name, which was applied to a blue stone which, there is every reason to believe, was the lapis lazuli, and is still restricted in general to the blue corundums; but it is also employed generically to all corundums, no matter of what colour. The sapphire or corundum is pure alumina, crystallized, and sometimes coloured with minute quantities of metallic oxides. When coloured red, it constitutes the oriental ruby; when yellow, the oriental topaz; green, the oriental emerald;

violet, the oriental amethyst; and hair-brown, adamantine spar. The ruby sapphire, when of the finest colour should have a bright, transparent, cochineal red; it is the hardest known mineral, except the diamond, and will consequently scratch any other gem, and has a very high specific gravity, by which, as well as by the last-mentioned property, it, as well as all the other sapphires, are distinguished from other stones of the same colour. When a fine-coloured ruby exceeds four carats in weight, it approaches the diamond in price. During the middle ages it was even much more esteemed than the diamond. The blue sapphire, although so extremely beautiful when of an indigo blue, has only one-fourth of the value of the ruby when of the same weight. The substance known as emery is nothing more than massive corundum, deeply coloured, and hence is used for polishing gems as well as glass and metallic ware. The finest red sapphires occur in Pegu, in the kingdom of Ava; some have also been found in Ceylon, which was even celebrated for them in the time of Marco Polo. They are usually found in the beds of rivers, either in the form of six-sided prisms or in rolled masses. The blue sapphire is chiefly found in Ceylon, and generally of a large size. The finest topazes come from India, Brazil, and the Oural Mountains; some small ones are also continually obtained in Saxony.

The most numerous and common group of minerals employed in jewellery consists of quartz in several conditions, and coloured with various oxides of metals. These minerals may be classified under four subdivisions:—1. Crystalline quartz; 2. Translucent quartz; 3. Jasper; and 4. Hydrated quartz.

To the first division belong rock crystal, rose quartz, smoked quartz, amethyst, cairngorm-topaz, prase, aventurine, &c. &c. Rock crystal is pure quartz or silica, in colourless crystals, and is the hardest of all the varieties of that substance, but is not so hard as any of the finer gems; it will cut glass and resist the file. It is to this substance that the ancients first applied the word crystal, from κριοειν, to congeal. The Romans employed it to make vases, many of which were of very considerable dimensions. When rock crystal is coloured of a clear purple or bluish-violet colour, by manganese, or, as some think, with iron in a peculiar condition, it constitutes the common amethyst, which is much employed in jewellery, and many specimens of which are beautiful, especially when set in gold, and surrounded with small pearls. The name amethyst is derived from the Greek α and μεθυω, to intoxicate, from the belief which was held by the ancients that cups or vases ornamented with it had the power of preserving from the fumes of wine. There were many other minerals, however, known in antiquity under the name of amethyst, such as the purple fluor spar, and the oriental amethyst or purple sapphire. Rose quartz is simply rock crystal tinged of a rose colour; this variety is not equal in lustre to the amethyst, and it is usually full of cracks, which destroy its transparency. The cairngorm-topaz is rock crystal, of a clear light yellow. When of good colour, free from cracks, and pellucid, it is a beautiful stone, and is much used for ladies' brooches, ornamenting dagger-handles, &c. It resembles the real yellow or oriental topaz very much, but is readily distinguished from it by the form of the crystal and by its inferior refractive power, which is best seen by candle or gas light. The variety of rock crystal, which is a blackish brown, sometimes passing into black colour, and known as smoky quartz, is not much used in jewellery, and is of comparatively small value. Some extremely beautiful pellucid specimens are, however, occasionally found. When massive transparent quartz is of a black colour, it constitutes the mineral known as prase, which has sometimes been used as a gem. Quartz, interspersed with spangles of golden-coloured mica, often constitutes a beautiful mineral, and one much prized as a gem, the aventurine quartz.

The second division of the quartz gems includes chalcedony, chrysoprase, cornelian, sard, the different kinds of agates, onyx, cat's eye, &c. Chalcedony may be considered to be composed of a network of crystals of quartz, with the interstices filled up with a paste of amorphous quartz. It is a fine, hard, flint-like stone, with a wavy lustre; sometimes translucent or semi-transparent, where the crystalline constituent predominates, and sometimes perfectly opaque, when of a milk-white colour. When tinged green, from oxide of nickel, it is the chrysoprase; when of a clear bright red, it is the cornelian; the deep brownish red chalcedony by reflected light, and blood-red by transmitted, is called sard. All these varieties have been employed, both in ancient and modern times, for cutting or intaglio work. The name chalcedony is derived from the city of Chalcedonia, in ancient Bithynia. The light greenish gray sometimes passing into brown, red, or yellowish, with a tinge of green variety of chalcedony known as cat's eye, has a peculiar glaring, *chatoyant* appearance when cut *en cabochen*; this effect is produced by filaments of a mineral called asbestos, interspersed through its mass. When a layer of translucent chalcedony of a milky white colour is found upon one of a brown colour, that is upon the sard, it was compared by the ancients to the appearance of the nail upon the flesh; hence the name onyx, by which such varieties of stone were known. Properly speaking, however, this would be the sardonyx, for the word onyx is applied to any stone consisting of alternate layers of different-coloured agates or chalcedony. Onyx and sardonyx are the stones used for making cameos, in which the figures are in relief; while the intaglios were engraved out of cornelian and other uniformly coloured ones. The figures are carved out of the white, yellow, or other light-coloured layer, which is all cut away except the part forming the figures, which thus stands in relief upon a different coloured layer of the stone. When the under layer is a very dark sard, however, and is covered with a milk-white opalescent agate or chalcedony, without any layer between of an intermediate colour, it is called a nicollo (which is evidently derived from onicollo from onyx), and is then also used for intaglios; the figures being produced by the dark sard exposed with a gradation of shades, formed by the translucent surface layer more or less cut away. Some ancient cameos of a large size are very beautiful; immense numbers are now made in Paris, and are worn as brooches, or set in bracelets. Agate is a variegated chalcedony, the colours being irregularly arranged, unlike the onyx or sardonyx. According to the arrangement of these colours the agate receives different names. The distinctive colour of agates is a translucent milky white, with a shade of bluish or reddish violet. Sometimes a number of dendritic or moss-like delineations of a brownish colour are interspersed through the mass, forming the moss agate or mocha stone; sometimes the agate is made up of a series of bands of different colours, which are sharply defined, as in a ribbon, and produce very beautiful effects. According as the stone is cut, these bands may be straight or concentric, and very often they are zig-zag, so as to produce, from one being within the other, the effect of the ground plan of fortifications, and hence this variety is called fortification agate. The variations thus produced are endless, and the nomenclature, although it only contains a name for the chief varieties, is very extensive. The word agate came from Achates, the ancient name of the Drilla, a river of Sicily, in the bed of which they are abundantly found.

The third subdivision of quartz gems includes the different kinds of jasper, such as the heliotrope or bloodstone, and the plasma. Jasper is not a pure quartz, but rather a siliceous mineral, containing alumina, lime, and iron, &c., and nearly opaque, and very compact. Its usual colours are red, brown, yellow, or green, and sometimes, but rarely, black and blue, and very dull until polished. Like agates, the accidental distribution of colouring metallic oxides gives rise to a number of varieties, of which Sicily alone, it is said, produces 100, the value of which depends upon the beauty of the markings. When the colours are in bands, it is called striped jasper; when the mass is green, and glistens with spots of white or yellow, it constitutes the plasma. The bloodstone is a jasper of a deep green colour, interspersed with blood-red spots; the heliotrope is simply a fine variety of the bloodstone.

The fourth subdivision includes opal, hydrophane, or *monde d'or*, wood opal, cacholong, &c. The noble opal is a hydrate of silica of an opalescent and milky white, with tinge of blue colour, and which produces an extremely beautiful play of colours from the reflection of the light by the minute fissures, of which it is full. The girasol or fire opal is a variety which produces a bright hyacinth red and yellow chatoyant reflection. Opal was very highly esteemed by the ancients, but was little employed during the middle ages. The hydrophane, called in the middle ages the *monde d'or*, and by French jewellers at present, *œil du monde*, is an opaque opal which becomes transparent on being immersed in water, thereby producing the chatoyant effects of the opal. Cacholong is the name of a kind of opal agate almost opaque. By successive treatment with oil and sulphuric acid this material may be made to assume various shades so as to constitute false sards. Most of the chalcedonies may also be made to undergo a change in colour by artificial means; for instance, if a red-hot iron be applied to the surface of the cornelian, the colour of which is supposed to be produced by a minute kind of vegetable, its red colour is destroyed superficially, and assumes a milk-white colour, while it retains its true red colour beneath. Stones thus treated are used as false sardonyxes for making cameos; the burnt surface forming the figures in relief. We may also remark that the cornelians, when first taken from the rock, are generally of a grayish-red, and only acquire their fine tints by exposure to the sun's rays for a considerable time, and a subsequent heating in an iron pot.

Rock crystal is found in most countries, not excepting our own; two fine specimens, one from Achill, and another from the Blasket Islands, off the coast of Kerry, having been exhibited. The finest amethysts are found in Ceylon, India, and Persia, and inferior ones in large groups of crystals have been found at Blackrock, near Cork, and at Achill, good examples of which were also in the Exhibition. Rose quartz, and prase, and chrysoprase, are found in Germany; the false topaz in Scotland and in Brazil; aventurine in Spain; cornelian, agates, &c., in Germany and in Scotland, but the finest come from India and Arabia. Some beautiful ones are now being brought from Lake Sorel and the Derwent in Tasmania; plasma in India and China; cat's eye in Silesia in Germany; the precious opal in Hungary; the fire opal in Mexico. A pretty collection of these stones, obtained from the drift-beds between Bray and Wicklow, was exhibited by Mr. Blood, of Wicklow. The chief countries of all gems appear to be India and Brazil, in the great alluvial plains of which lie buried the treasures washed out of the two greatest chains of mountains in the world.

All the other minerals employed as gems are compound silicates, that is, compounds of silica, and sometimes fluorine or boracic acid, with metallic oxides, such as alumina, magnesia, &c. There are, however, a few in which silica is nearly or entirely absent, and in which the alumina, which is the predominant ingredient, acts as acid; this group is, therefore, allied to the corundum, and the minerals composing it may, indeed, be considered as inferior varieties of the true sapphire. The type of these minerals is the spinelle, which is found in serpentine and gneiss rocks in granular limestone, and also in volcanic rocks. When of a scarlet red, passing into a rose colour, it is called the spinelle ruby; when of a clear rose-red, it is the balas or balais ruby; the orange-red passing into yellow, the rubicelle; the violet-coloured, the amandine; and the lustrous black, the pleonaste. Of these the balais ruby alone appears to have been known in the middle ages. In the gems just mentioned the chief base present is magnesia; when this is replaced by a peculiar substance, glucina, we have the chrysoberyl, from χρυσος, golden, and βήρυλλος, a beryl. This mineral is used as a gem when sufficiently large to admit of its being cut with facets; it forms a beautiful gem of of a yellowish-green colour when free from flaws and striæ. It occurs in Brazil, Ceylon, and the Ural, of large size. A curious opalescent variety, which is used as a gem when cut *en cabochon*, is called the cymophane, from Κῦμα, a wave, and φαινω, to appear, owing to the wavy appearance produced by the opalescence. This mineral is also called the oriental chrysolite, but must not be confounded with the common chrysolite or olivine.

The beryl, which is allied to the last-named gem, consists of a silicate of alumina and glucina, with traces of some colouring metallic oxides. When of a rich transparent green it forms the emerald properly so called; when of a pale sky-blue passing into green, or of the peculiar green colour of the sea water, it constitutes the aqua marine, or aigue marine from *aigue*, the old French for water. The term beryl is applied to all the other shades, such as greenish-white, yellowish, &c. Emeralds are often found of a very large size, as, for example, one foot long; the aqua marine is found of a still larger size, one having been discovered in Brazil as large as a calf's head, and weighing 18¼ lbs. Beryls of a gigantic size are frequently found in the United States; for example, one 4 feet long, and weighing 240 lbs., and the greater part of which was of a bluish-green, has been found in Massachusetts. The finest emeralds come from Santa Fé de Bogota, in New Granada; the aqua marine is chiefly found in Hindostan, Siberia, and Brazil. Beryls are common in the granite of the Mourne Mountains, and are sometimes found sufficiently clear to be employed as gems.

The precious garnet is a silicate of alumina and iron, which crystallizes in the form of a dodecahedron or twelve-sided figure; it is harder than rock crystal, and of a rich brownish-red or wine colour, sometimes tending to violet and sometimes to orange. The garnet is found in several countries, but the most perfect come from Ceylon and Greenland. It has occasionally been found of sufficient size to be cut into cups; it does not appear to have been in much repute. The lime garnet, that is, a silicate of alumina and lime, constitutes a pretty yellow variety, known as the cinnamon stone, or essonite, which is employed as a gem.

The topaz, properly so called, is a compound of silica, fluorine, and alumina; it occurs chiefly in granite, the finest specimens being obtained from the Ural Mountains, Siberia, and Brazil, especially from the latter; some are also obtained in the Saxon Mountains, and small limpid crystals are even frequently found in the Mourne granite. The topaz is harder than rock crystal, of nearly the same specific gravity as the diamond, and is usually of a yellow colour, but it also occurs colourless, and of a green or blue colour, as at Cairngorm, in Scotland. The Brazilian topaz, when heated, becomes of a rose-red, so like that of the Balais ruby that it cannot be distinguished by the eye alone; specimens thus treated are used in jewellery. The colourless or very pale-coloured topazes, when free from flaws and cut in imitation of brilliants, can hardly be distinguished from the diamond in the daytime; and are called, from their limpidity, *goutte d'eau*, or drops of water. The derivation of the name topaz, or rather of its Greek name, τοπαζιον, is very singular; the ancient topazes were chiefly found on an island in the Red Sea which was often enveloped in fogs, and accordingly difficult to find; the name is hence supposed to be derived from τοπαζω, to seek.

The other minerals used as gems, and which our space will permit us to do little more than enumerate, are the chrysolite or olivine, which is a silicate of magnesia of an olive green, found in basalt and lava. It is a brittle and very soft stone, and is not of much value, as it is easy to deprive it of its polish. Jade, which is a silicate of alumina and magnesia, is found in primitive limestone; it is of various colours, but usually of a sky blue and green, passing into olive green. It scratches glass and even rock crystal, but its polish is never good, being always more or less unctuous. It is much employed in China and India, and is supposed to possess curative powers; it was also highly esteemed by the ancients, but does not appear to have been used in the middle ages. The zircon or hyacinth is a silicate of a peculiar earth, zirconia, of a very high specific gravity and of considerable hardness. Its colours are red, pale rose, brown-yellow, slightly smoky, and colourless; the two latter come chiefly from Ceylon, and are usually called jargons, and are employed as inferior diamonds. Fine crystals are also obtained from Siberia, Greenland, and Norway. The dichroite, or *sapphire d'eau*, is a silicate of alumina, magnesia, and iron, of various shades of blue and violet, generally inclining to black. It is usually of different colours when viewed in different directions: hence the name dichroite, from δις, double, and χρόα, colour. This property gives it some value as a gem. Andalusite is a silicate of alumina, and some other bases of a flesh-red colour, passing into gray, sometimes of a bluish and greenish tint. Its name is derived from the province of Andalusia, in Spain. It is very soft, and being nearly opaque it is but ill adapted as a gem; when of good colour, it is, however, sometimes employed, especially in inlaid work. Feldspar is chiefly a silicate of alumina and potash, and is one of the constituent minerals of granites; there are a great many varieties of it used as gems, chiefly for inlaid work, of which we shall mention the following: aventurine feldspar, called sunstone, or *pierre de soleil*, and oriental aventurine, consisting of feldspars of various colours, with numerous spangles of mica disseminated through them, which produce an effect as if of numerous golden points (the most prized specimens are obtained from Siberia); a feldspar, of a sky-blue colour dotted with white joints, and having a great resemblance to lapis lazuli, for which it is sometimes substituted in *pietra dura*. Moonstone, or *pierre de lune*, also called *œil de poisson* and argentine, is a variety of the kind of translucent feldspar called adularia, which has a peculiar pearly or chatoyant lustre when polished; it is found in Ceylon, and also on Mount Saint Gothard, from the name of one of the highest peaks of which, called Adula, the word adularia is derived. Variolite, called also *pierre des amazones*, and *vert celadon*, is an opaque variety of various shades of green dotted with white globular points; it is chiefly obtained from the Ural and Greenland, and is also found in France. Opaline feldspar or Labrador feldspar is a silicate of alumina, lime, and soda, instead of potash, of a gray, brown, or slightly greenish colour, which exhibits, when polished, beautiful chatoyant effects, the colours seen being chiefly green, blue, red, and orange, on changing the position of the surface; it was first brought from the island of St. Paul, on the coast of Labrador, whence its name, but it is also obtained in Norway and the Ural Mountains, and in several parts of the United States; it is very frequently used as a gem, but almost always for inlaid work. Tourmaline is a silicate of alumina and iron or manganese, and small quantities of potash and soda, together with the characteristic acid substance, boracic acid, which occurs in long crystals in granite and other ancient rocks. Its colours are very various, and, as in the case of other gems, distinct names have been given to certain colours; for example, blue tourmalines have been termed indicolite, from their colour being somewhat like that of indigo; the red are called rubellite. The only other colours prized as gems are the green and yellow tourmalines. The tourmaline is of about the hardness of the emerald; the fine red ones, free from flaws, take a fine polish, and are much-prized gems; the yellow Ceylon tourmaline is almost equally esteemed as the real topaz, for which it is often sold; the blue, which resembles the sapphire when very fine, may often be mistaken for that gem. The green tourmaline constitutes a valuable gem, but the colour is not the pure green of the emerald. Ceylon and Siberia are the chief localities for fine tourmalines; the red of the latter are frequently mounted *en cabochon* on rings, and are then readily distinguishable by a certain opalescence, which gives rise to a chatoyant effect.

Lapis lazuli is an opaque compound of silica, alumina, soda, and sometimes lime, coloured of a beautiful rich blue, by some peculiar compound of sulphur, and chiefly found in granite and primary limestones, veined with white portions, and dotted with spangles of yellow mica and minute crystals of pyrites, which have the appearance of gold. The pieces of the richest blue, most uniformly coloured, and containing most disseminated mica and pyrites, are selected and cemented together to form table-tops; large pieces have been employed to make cups and vases, and many Indian temples and tombs, and parts of the Moorish Alhambra were encrusted with it. It is also largely employed in work in *pietra dura*, and when ground up and washed it constitutes the beautiful pigment, the natural ultramarine. Lapis lazuli was well known and highly appreciated by the ancients, and was also much esteemed during the middle ages. Our chief supplies come from Persia, India, China, and Russia.

Green malachite is the natural hydrated carbonate of copper, which frequently occurs in masses of considerable size, and formed apparently in the manner of stalagmites and stalactites. When these are cut across their diameter, surfaces are obtained exhibiting concentric rings of the most beautiful shades, from the deepest green to the palest and most tender pea green, and which are capable of assuming a fine polish. If cut in the direction of their axes, the surfaces exhibit zones or ribboned bands of the same character, and of great beauty. Malachite is employed for forming vases, cups, and table-tops, and for inlaying furniture, especially fauteuils, pianos. Malachite was known to the ancients, but it does not appear to have been used during the middle ages. It is found in many countries, but with the exception of the malachite found at Chessy, near Lyons, the greater part of what has been until lately used for ornamental purposes has been obtained from Siberia. Recently immense quantities of it have been obtained in Wisconsin, in the United States, and at Burra Burra, near Melbourne.

The turquoise is a hydrated phosphate of alumina, coloured by oxides of copper and iron, of a very peculiar bluish green opaque colour, and of a hardness to scratch glass. It takes a beautiful polish, and when of a fine colour it is very highly prized as a gem. It is only found in a mountainous district of Persia. Fossil bones and teeth, coloured by phosphate of protoxide of iron, simulate the mineral turquoise; but their beautiful blue colour assumes a greenish tinge, and becomes dull from the light, and in time grows paler, and finally disappears. These turquoises are readily distinguished from the mineral ones, by losing their colour by the action of acids.

### ARTIFICIAL GEMS.

The importance attached at all periods to articles ornamented with gems, and their enormous value, led at a very early period to attempts to imitate them. The secret of producing artificial gems, indeed, goes back to antiquity, and was practised by the Egyptians, the ancient depositories of arts of this kind; it is even probable that the art was known to the Assyrians. It was in full operation in the middle ages, and artificial jewels were constantly employed, notwithstanding that the rules of the Corporation of Jewellers strictly forbade the use of coloured glass. In the thirteenth century the imitation was so perfect that one of the chroniclers of that period says, that "sometimes the false stones are so similar to the true, that those who know them best are often deceived." Even royalty itself did not disdain to wear crowns ornamented with false stones; for we learn from the testament of Jeanne d'Evreux, Queen of France, that out of the twenty-four crowns and chaplets which she left at her death, in 1372, two were ornamented with false stones. But it is only within the present century that the art has been brought to perfection by the production of glass of a purity, transparency, density, and refractive power little inferior to the finest gems. This glass, which differs but little from common flint glass, except in purity and in the presence of boracic acid, is formed of ground rock crystal, minium or white lead, pure caustic potash, and boracic acid. It is coloured by fusing it with small portions of different metallic oxides, corresponding in many cases with those which give colour to the natural gems. Thus the finest topaz is produced with glass of antimony and the compound of gold known as purple of Cassius, and the inferior quartz topazes with oxide of iron. The ruby is usually obtained from the mass for preparing topazes, undergoing a peculiar change which unfits it for producing that gem; the inferior kinds are produced by oxide of manganese. The emerald is produced by oxides of copper and chrome; the sapphire or blue corundum by oxide of cobalt; the amethyst by oxides of manganese, cobalt, and purple of Cassius; the garnet, by glass of antimony, purple of Cassius, and oxide of manganese. In fact, any known gem can now be imitated so closely that it requires the greatest skill to distinguish the false from the true; and it is well known that a large proportion of the rubies, emeralds, &c., which are so ostentatiously worn at court ceremonies, are made of glass, and that even sometimes without the knowledge of the wearer. The art of preparing false gems is almost confined to Paris, or at least it is there that it has attained the highest perfection. It is from that city that the sovereigns of Europe, and many of Asia, have obtained for many years the rich jewels with which they so profusely decorate their servants.

The late M. Ebelman, director of the Porcelain Works of Sevres, has succeeded, by mixing the constituent ingredients of certain gems together, and then exposing them with boracic acid or borax, which acts as a solvent, to the heat of a porcelain furnace during the entire time of the firing of biscuit ware, so that the acid or borax, having performed the office of a flux, was entirely volatilized, in producing very small crystals of the real ruby corundum, and several other rare gems. And M. Despretz has succeeded, by the agency of electricity, in producing from charcoal what may be called diamond dust. These two discoveries will one day be the germ of processes for producing all kinds of natural gems artificially.

### PEARLS, FALSE PEARLS, CAMEO SHELLS, CARVINGS IN SEA-HORSE TOOTH, CORAL, ETC.

The animal kingdom has been laid under contribution for the purpose of providing personal ornaments or the decorations of furniture. The most valuable of these contributions is the pearl, which is merely an excretion of a globular form, of a beautiful bluish-white colour, and a highly iridescent power. It is formed, like the mother-of-pearl, from which it only differs in form, of alternate layers of animal membrane and carbonate of lime; it is to this lamellated structure its peculiar properties are evidently owing. Pearls are the products of many shell-fish, but the finest are obtained from the 'pearl oyster,' *Meleagrina margaritifera*, which is found in the Indian seas. Small pearls of a paler colour, and exhibiting much less iridescence, are produced by a fresh-water bivalve shell, the *Unio margaritifera*, which is found in many rivers of Ireland. As in the case of other gems, the value of pearls depends upon their size; a necklace of pea-sized pearls being often twenty times the value of one the size of peppercorns. The greatest pearl fisheries are those at the Island of Bahrein in the Persian Gulf; those on the coasts of Ceylon; the islands in the Bay of Panama, St. Margarita, or the Pearl Islands near Cumana, in the West Indian seas; and off the coast of Algiers.

Pearls can also be very closely imitated, but it is difficult to determine accurately at what period the false pearls were first made. There is reason to suppose that some kind of imitation of them was made as early as the thirteenth century, as we learn from the rules of the Corporation of Goldsmiths of Paris, for the year 1260; it is probable, however, that the imitations then made were simply opalescent glass beads, like those now made, of different colours, under the name of *perles a la lune*. About the middle of the seventeenth century the mode of making artificial pearls by coating glass globules on the outside with a varnish made with the scales of a kind of fish appears to have been discovered. According to a book published in Paris in 1691, called "Livre des Addresses," the manufacture of these pearls, which are described as perfectly natural, was considered as a new invention. The invention of these imitations is usually attributed to Jaquin, a rosary maker. The process followed at present is to coat them on the inside instead of on the outside. For this purpose a number of hollow beads of thin transparent glass are blown with a lamp, and a drop of the pearl essence is blown into it, and spread about by rolling them. The pearl essence is obtained by scraping the scales off the bleak, or *Cyprinus alburnus*, a fresh-water fish, and repeatedly washing them with water, until the whole of the foreign animal matter is removed. When fully washed, a little solution of sal-ammoniac is added, to prevent putrefaction from occurring, and the essence is ready for use; in using it, however, it is found advisable to add a little isinglass, so as to make the varnish adhere well; a minute trace of carmine, saffron, or Paris blue, is also added, in order to communicate a reddish, yellowish, or bluish tinge, in imitation of those shades observed in fine pearls. Formerly the makers of artificial pearls had to purchase the fish themselves in order to prepare the essence; but it has now become an article of trade, and a good deal of it is prepared at Eberbach, on the Neckar, for the Paris and Swiss pearl makers. It is calculated that 7 lbs. of fish scales will yield 1 lb. of moist pearl essence, for which 20,000 fishes would be required.

The scales of the well known-white bait are said to surpass those of the bleak for artificial pearl making. The scales of the roach and dace have also been used for inferior kinds of false pearls. When necklaces were much worn in England there was a considerable trade in false pearls in London, and fish scales were in such demand that from one guinea to five guineas was paid for a quart of them.

Besides shirt buttons and inlaying, to which mother-of-pearl shells are chiefly applied, another kind of shelly matter is used for the production of cameos, and for making small cups. The shells used for cutting cameos are thick, and of considerable density, and consist of three layers of different coloured shelly matter. Each layer is composed of a number of laminæ, which in the two outer layers are parallel with the lines of growth, while those of the centre layer are perpendicular to them. The figures in relief are cut in one layer, and appear on the next as a ground; sometimes the two layers are cut through, the ground being formed on the third; the chief figures, being in highest relief, are formed of the external layer, whilst some ornaments are executed in the matter of the middle—the principle is, in fact, the same as the true cameos cut in onyx or sardonyx. The shell chiefly used is the *Cassis rufa*, a species of cowrie or *cypræa*. It is to a shell of this kind that the ancients applied the term *porcella*, from its resemblance to a pig. During the middle ages the term *porcellana* (derived from por cella), or, in old French, *pourcelaine*, was generally applied to mother-of-pearl shells and to works in it, including cameos. When the beautiful pottery of China became known, the same term pourcelaine, whence our porcelain, was applied, in consequence of its white nacreous-like substance.

Mr. Richard Barter, of this city, has introduced, for the first time so far as we are aware, a peculiar kind of cameo, quite different from the true or the shell cameos. It consists of a figure carved in the ivory-like substance called sea-horse tooth, fastened upon a surface of cornelian. The material is exceedingly compact, and of great uniformity of texture and hardness, and capable of yielding the finest and most delicate carvings; it also is not, like ivory, subject to acquire stains, at least, not readily. Mr. Barter exhibited a case of cameo heads in this style taken from life, the kind of application for which it seems best adapted; they were of great merit, and fully justified the success which has hitherto rewarded his exertions in introducing this very pretty style,—a success which we hope to see still further increased.

The last substance which we shall mention of animal origin used in jewellery is coral. This is a sort of vegetation, if we may be permitted to use the expression, produced by a number of polypi who make it their habitation, each individual contributing his own cell or part of a branch. The only kind of coral used in jewellery is the *Isis nobilis* (or *Gorgonia nobilis*, or *Corallium rubrum*). It is composed of two parts, an internal stem of gelatinous matter and carbonate of lime, and an external shell or cortex of the same materials, and both coloured with some peculiar substance. Coral was known both in antiquity and during the middle ages, and employed to some extent. It may be applied to many purposes, but its chief use is to form necklaces.

With scarcely a single exception every variety of gem described in the previous remarks was more or less represented in the Exhibition as part of some ornaments. These ornaments as a whole form what is, properly speaking, Jewellery, about which we have hitherto said nothing, and which, indeed, we shall dismiss in very few words, because to describe in detail the numerous articles included in the present category would occupy far more space than can be devoted to such an object, especially as we have already extended our notice of this department to considerable length. The manufacture of jewellery is composed of two distinct branches, the lapidaries' work, where true gems are used (or the making of artificial gems where the latter are employed), and the setting of these stones in metal, wood, or stone. The work of the lapidary is simply giving a form and polished surface to the rough gems, which is done with a series of wheels by means of diamond or corundum powder. The cutting of stones is an important matter, for upon it depends much of their brilliancy. The setting is not of less importance, and here the greatest room exists for the development of artistic taste. The operation of setting a gem in a framework of gold or other metal is simple enough: but the relation of the gem to the ornament, especially in reference to size, colour, and use, the contrast and harmony of colour, where different gems are employed, and the character of the whole design, involve taste and skill in a high degree; and it is in these points that we find most articles of jewellery deficient. The native contributions, except in one class, were not very varied; a large portion also were not Irish, but French or English in whole or in part, and although many of them were full of promise, yet little attention appears to have been bestowed upon the artistic character of the article. This was especially the case with the cheap jewellery made with bog oak and artificial gems, the greater part of which was in truly barbaric taste.

The production of Bog Oak ornaments has gradually grown up in this city to a degree of considerable importance. At first, rudeness of design and coarseness of execution were naturally inseparable from the infancy of the trade. Although considerable improvement has gradually been effected, the progress has not been so great as it ought to have been. The carvings are coarsely executed; the stones are far too large and too gaudy, and the general designs poor, and without much invention; and where the latter fault did not exist, they were inappropriate, as, for example, giving a bracelet the form of a coiled snake. In the selection of the stones there was but little variety, notwithstanding the range which exists for the purpose, as proved even by our brief notice. All the colourless ones were, of course, Irish diamonds; this is a mistake which ought not to be persevered in, as there are many colourless false gems far superior in every way as ornaments to rock crystal; the fact of the quartz being Irish is not enough to make amends for coarse execution and bad design. We have been thus severe upon this, we may say, the only branch of jewellery carried on in Ireland, and which we would much more willingly praise, because we feel that not only may it become a very important branch of trade, but it may be the precursor of many others. This can only occur, however, by the most unremitting efforts to improve the execution and design, and especially to develop fertility of invention and variety, which are more necessary in this class of articles than in, perhaps, any other branch of manufacture. It is only just to say that the carvings in bog oak of several of the more remarkable specimens of ancient architecture in Ireland, exhibited by J. Classon, were admirably executed, and were altogether deserving of high commendation. In the collection of S. Mahood were some well-executed models of a similar kind, and a large collection of ornamental jewellery set with a very good variety of false gems. The collections of D. Connell, M. Connell, and G. Goggin, contained many things which deserve notice, notwithstanding our strictures on the class generally. There is another point which must not be passed over, and which is of importance if it is desirable to elevate the manufacture of bog oak ornaments into a permanent trade, which is,—to make the price of the article bear some relation to its intrinsic value. In conclusion, we have only to remark, that there exist in Dublin facilities of the most favourable kind for the development of a trade in jewellery, and that with perseverance and the proper cultivation and encouragement of artistic taste, and the eschewing of all plagiarism of design, an important and fruitful source of employment may be created.

## IV.—ENAMELLED WORK.

Among the most beautiful and interesting of the decorative arts connected with metals may be placed enamelling, not only from the skill and ingenuity which it requires in the execution, but also from the variety and delicacy of colour and charming effects which can be produced by its means. The term enamel in its most general sense is used to designate a species of glass, either transparent or opaque, to which various colours are given by the addition of different metallic oxides, and applied as a superficial coating to pottery, and gold, silver, and other metals. The employment of glazes upon bricks is of an extremely ancient date: the important researches of Botta, and afterwards of Layard, who has followed in his footsteps, show us that bricks thus ornamented, and even of different colours, were used extensively at Nineveh and other cities of the period to which that remarkable city belonged. We are also familiar with the numerous small figures of divinities found in the ancient tombs of Egypt covered with beautiful blue and green coloured enamels, many of the former having hieroglyphics cut in them, which were afterwards filled with white and yellow enamels by fusion. But no single genuine specimen has yet been found which would prove that the art of enamelling upon metals, the only branch of the subject which belongs to the class we are now considering, was known to the Egyptians; the one said to have been in the possession of M. Louis Dubois, of Paris, not having come to light. The Etruscans are also said to have known the art, but the proofs put forward are not satisfactory. It was, however, known and practised to some extent by the Greeks, and that kind of enamelling on metal, known as *niello*, was certainly known in the time of Pliny, for he describes the composition of the mixture. From the perfection to which the Chinese have arrived in the manufacture of porcelain, a good deal of which is painted in true enamel colours, one would be naturally led to the belief that the coating of metals with enamels must have been known to them; and accordingly we find that such is the case, but the exact epoch at which the discovery was made cannot be determined.

Many of the most learned antiquaries are disposed to attribute the invention to the ancient Gauls,—an opinion which is supported by the number of enamelled fibulæ and other ancient Gallic ornaments which have been found in tombs; and also by a passage from Philostratus, who professed rhetoric at Athens, whence he came to Rome at the commencement of the third century of our era, where, by the favour of Julia, wife of the emperor Septimus Severus, he was attached to the household of the Imperial Palace. This passage is to the effect that the barbarians bordering the ocean knew how to spread colours upon hot brass so as to afterwards become as hard as stones, and to preserve the design thus formed. It is doubtful whether this art was known to the ancient Irish, for all the specimens of enamelled fibulæ in the collection of the Royal Irish Academy appear to be merely encrusted with bits of enamel, mosaic-like,—a mode of ornamentation known to the Greeks, and even to the Egyptians. Most of those ornaments would also appear to belong to Christian periods. The question of the existence of this art in Ireland is, however, to be only decided by antiquaries well versed in such subjects; it is worth investigating as tending to throw light on the migrations and intercourse of the early Irish. A number of specimens of enamelled objects have been found in England of a very early date, but, so far as we know, all the real fused enamels are of Roman workmanship.

In the Middle Ages the art of enamelling was in high favour, especially from the middle of the eleventh century down to the period of the Renaissance in France. Rings, croziers, fibulæ, sacred vessels, shields, armour, monumental brasses, and harness, were thus generally ornamented. The chief seat of the art was Limoges, in France, but the enamels of Cologne, Mayence, and Aix-la-Chapelle were also held in high repute.

Enamels may be classed according to their style of execution, which also corresponds in a great degree to their chronological order, into:—1. Embedded enamels which, may be subdivided into, *a*, embedded in the solid, called in the fifteenth and sixteenth century *émaux en taille d'epargne*, and now *émaux en Champ levé* by the French; and *b*, embedded in filigree, the *émaux cloisonnés* or *émaux à cloisons mobiles* of the French.—2. Translucent enamels on bas-relief, the *opera di basso rilièvo* of Benvenuto Cellini, and *émaux de basse taille* of the French.—3. Painted enamels, the *émaux de peintres* or *emaux peints* of the French.

Enamels embedded in the solid are the most ancient, and were almost invariably executed upon plates of copper. This style consisted in drawing the outlines of the design upon the plates, and chasing or tooling out the surrounding metal exactly as a woodcut is made, the design being left in relief as a series of fine lines. The cavities thus formed by the graver were then filled up with the different coloured enamel mixtures in powder, upon which the plate was heated until the enamels melted and adhered to the metal; the surface was then polished, and the lines of metal gilded. By the method just described the outlines of the design would be in metal, the figures being brought out by the enamel upon the even surface of the gilded copper as a ground; in other cases a complete silhouette was reserved, the remainder of the surface being cut down and enamelled, and forming the groundwork of the design. The objects ornamented in this style were exceedingly durable, owing to the thickness of the metal employed, and some may even be bent without detaching the enamel. The best specimens of this style belong to the twelfth and thirteenth century.

*Niello Enamels.*—Another variety of this style of enamelling is that known as niello, the origin of which goes back to the very infancy of art; for Pliny tells us that silver vessels were ornamented by the Egyptians with a black enamel prepared from silver, copper, and sulphur. The art appears never to have been lost, as a ring of Bishop Ethelwulf, executed in the ninth century, was ornamented in niello. The Greeks of the Empire, too, must have practised it; and by them it was introduced into Russia as early as the twelfth century, for there exists in the celebrated collection of jewellery in Dresden, known as the Grüne Gewölte, a drinking vessel in solid gold, which is supposed to have belonged to John Basilides, Grand Duke of Russia, having a Russian inscription executed in niello. About the same period, perhaps, it found its way into Italy, where it soon partook of the general progress of the arts which was then taking place, and where, in the fifteenth century, it reached its highest development. Its chief seat was Florence, which produced three celebrated *niellatori*, Matteo Dei, Antonio del Pollæiuolo, and Maso Finiguerra.

The method of ornamenting in niello was to engrave with the chisel upon plates or vessels of gold, silver, or gilded silver, whatever ornament, such as a history, a flower, a portrait, or an inscription, was required; the hollows thus formed were then filled up, not with an enamel glass, such as we have described in speaking of enamel generally, but with a compound of silver, copper, lead, and sulphur. This compound when fused was of an intense black colour, hence the name *nigellum* of the ancients, which the Italians converted into *niello*. The effect thus produced was very elegant, though somewhat sombre. During the fifteenth century the sacred vessels used in the churches were profusely adorned in this style, especially the monstrances, chalices, &c.; and it was also applied to the covers of missals and other devotional books, reliquaries, the decoration of household furniture, such as ebony desks, escrutoires, &c. (which were usually ornamented with silver plates, upon which were represented histories, flowers, &c., in niello), hilts of daggers and swords, drinking vessels, and, indeed, almost all silver articles. Niello work appears also to have been used at one period as characteristic of mourning; as, for example, in the ornamentation of the sacred vessels used in services for the dead, and during Lent. Widows who made vows of perpetual widowhood wore ornaments in niello, as we learn in the case of the celebrated Diana of Poictiers.

In the sixteenth century the art was neglected in Italy, if we except the labours of Benvenuto Cellini, who was an ardent admirer of, and executed a great number of works in it. After him the application of niello fell into complete disuse in all Western and Southern Europe, and was only revived about twenty-five years ago. This was not the case, however, in Russia, where it has been regularly practised, under the name of the "black art," since its first introduction into the country. Large numbers of silver snuff-boxes and other small articles ornamented in niello work are sent into Germany from Tula, where the manufacture of the inferior kind is chiefly carried on. The best executed and most artistic articles are, however, produced at Wolodga and Ustjug-Welecki.

The following is the mode of preparing the enamel of metallic sulphurets:—The silver, copper, and lead are melted together, or the lead is added to the other two metals after they have been melted. The alloy is introduced into another crucible containing twice the weight of the combined metals of sulphur, and heated until all excess of sulphur has volatilized. When cold the metallic sulphurets are powdered, and made into paste with a solution of sal-ammoniac; this paste is rubbed into the engraved or stamped lines forming the design, allowed to dry; and the articles introduced into a muffle in an ordinary enameller's furnace, and heated until the sulphurets fuse. When cold the surface is ground and polished, and it is then found that the compound has so firmly attached itself to the plate of gold or silver that the latter may even be bent without the black enamel scaling off. The relative proportion of the metals employed has varied at different times, and in different countries. The following Table gives the proportions best known:—

| | | | Silver. | Copper | Lead |
|---|---|---|---|---|---|
| According to | Pliny, | (ancient) | 75.0 | 25.0 | |
| " | Theophilus Presbyter, | (early Italian) | 66.7 | 22.2 | 11.1 |
| " | Benvenuto Cellini, | (fifteenth and sixteenth centuries) | 16.7 | 33.3 | 50.0 |
| " | Blaise de Vigmière, | | | | |
| " | Percy de Vargos, | | | | |
| " | Georgj (alloy used at Ustjug-Welecki), | (modern) | 7.7 | 38.5 | 53.8 |
| " | Wagner and Mention (Paris), | " | 19.5 | 48.8 | 31.7 |
| " | Knowly (English), | " | 5.9 | 35.3 | 58.8 |

Our readers will, perhaps, be surprised, after the perusal of the foregoing remarks, to learn that an art so ancient, and never lost, has been made the subject of patents. In 1826 Mr. Knowly actually took out a patent for enamelling in England, and a German silversmith, named Wagner, in 1831, did the same in France.

Many beautiful applications might still be made of niello work, such as the lettering and ornamentation of the gold dial-plates of watches, church plate, and even plate for household purposes, &c.

The second class of embedded enamels, those embedded in filigree, the *émaux cloisonés*, were made in a peculiar way. A thin plate of metal, almost always of gold or of gilded silver, was procured, and the design to be executed traced upon it with a fine point. Thin plates of the same metal were then cut into narrow slips, the width varying according to the size of the piece to be executed; and these slips were made to follow every contour of the design, being fastened edgeways to the plate by means of a little wax. When the outlines of the design were formed by means of these thin slips of copper, forming so many recesses or chambers, the slips were soldered to the plate, and each of the chambers filled with the flux or glass and the metallic oxide or pigment which was to form the colour of each part of the figure; and the plate was then introduced into a furnace, where it was heated until the enamel melted. When cold the surface of the plate was polished so as to form a kind of glass mosaic, in which the edges of the slips of metal formed brilliant thread-like lines, at once marking the boundaries of each coloured enamel and the outlines of the design. The effect of the brilliant gold lines marking the outlines of the face, the folds of the garments, and the inscriptions in the midst of vividly coloured translucent enamels, was very beautiful; but the specimens now to be met with of this kind are very rare. This style of enamelling is evidently an imitation of the ancient works in mosaic, and its invention is attributed to the Byzantines; indeed, all the specimens which have come down to us are in the Byzantine style. But at what period it arose is doubtful: the earliest texts with which we are acquainted, which appear to allude to enamelling, date about the year 880.

*Translucent Enamels on Bas Relief.*—The enamels in *taille d'epargne*, executed for the most part upon a common metal, were rarely the work of great artists; they may be considered, in fact, as trade articles. The Byzantine enamels, on the other hand, belonged to the highest class of goldsmiths' work; they were executed upon gold, and were employed for the most sumptuous and costly decorations of churches and palaces. These enamels did not, however, suite the taste of Europe, and especially of Italy, then developing its grand schools of art, and accordingly the style was varied. Instead of forming a number of cells upon the face of a piece of copper, and then filling each of these with a different coloured enamel, the design was chiselled in very feeble relief upon the plate, usually of silver; variously coloured enamel powders were then placed upon it, and the plate heated until they melted and formed a translucent coating of glass over the whole surface, no metallic lines being exposed; the design being formed by the work beneath, was seen through the transparent enamel. The works of this class are often remarkable for the perfection and variety of colours, the gradations of shades being beautifully produced by different thicknesses of the enamels. Where the relief was highest, the enamel of course was thinnest, and consequently the shade of colour lightest; where the metal was chiselled out the enamel was thickest, and the colour deepest, the effect being exactly similar to that produced by those pretty coloured porcelain lithophanes which are made in Germany, and of which so many examples were in the Exhibition. The scope which this system of enamelling gave to the genius of the artist (for as Vasari says, it was "*E specie di pittura mescolata con la scultura*," a species of painting associated with sculpture) brought it into great favour in Italy, from the end of the thirteenth to the beginning of the fifteenth century. From Giovanni Pisani, who executed a high altar for the Church of Arezzo, partially decorated in this style in the year 1286, to Benvenuto Cellini, who made some modifications in the processes, it was employed by all the great artists of Italy who occupied themselves with the precious metals, such as Pollajuolo, Francia, &c. A precise description is given of it by Vasari.

When the style of enamels in relief was in vogue, artists sometimes varied the effect by combining several styles. One of the happiest of these combinations was to produce a silhouette in *taille d'epargne* upon a plate of gold, or more frequently upon silver; the part of the plate tooled out had then some ornaments chiselled upon it in very feeble relief, over which was laid a coating of translucent azure enamel. The folds of the drapery, and the face, hair, &c., were expressed by the graver upon the silhouette in metal, the incised lines being afterwards filled up with a black niello enamel—this was therefore a combination of the styles of *taille d'epargne*, niello, and translucent enamel on bass relief. Another style was practised at an earlier period (thirteenth century) which was a combination of the *taille d'epargne*, and of the embedded in filigree style. There was also a peculiar kind of enamelled work produced in the sixteenth century which belongs to the style in bas relief, and deserves to be mentioned; it consisted in figures in relief, in gold or silver, upon an enamelled ground; it is still practised in Russia.

Limoges, as we have before remarked, became the great seat of the art of enamelling in the style of *taille d'epargne* upon copper. It there became a true branch of trade, and there was scarcely a country in the world in communication with Europe in which specimens of the workmanship of Limoges might not be seen. Towards the end of the fourteenth century, however, the Limoges work declined in the presence of the far more artistic and valuable enamels in bas relief. It was then that the third style of enamelling was invented; as we have every reason to believe, also, at Limoges, which became in the fifteenth, sixteenth, and seventeenth centuries, as celebrated for its painted enamels as it had been in the middle ages for the embedded enamels. In the enamels in *taille d'epargne*, the enamel was merely used to decorate certain parts of the metal; in those on bas relief the metal became quite subordinate to the enamel, and was only seen through the latter; but in the painted enamels the metal disappeared from view altogether. The first enamels of this class consisted in making a very rough design upon a plate of bright copper; over this was laid a brownish translucent glass, upon which the figures were formed in coloured enamels, the face and parts of the body exposed being usually executed in white opaque enamel, and the contrasts heightened by a little gilding. It was, in fact, more in the style of painting on glass than of enamel, as hitherto understood. Gradually the translucent ground was replaced by an opaque one, in which all trace of the metal disappeared; the most common colour of the ground was black, and the figures, although often executed in colours, were more frequently in white enamel. This is the class of painted enamels best known amongst us, and termed *émaux en grisaille*.

Léonard Limosin, one of the most distinguished painters in enamel, in the first half the sixteenth century, substituted an opaque white ground for the black; this kind of ground was admirably adapted for miniature painting, which he attempted, but soon renounced; his invention was, however, taken advantage of, and employed to some extent by the goldsmiths in small works. But it was only in the year 1630 that this style of art was brought into vogue by Toutin, who is sometimes erroneously considered as the inventor: and it received its highest development in the same century from Petitot.

Except in Russia, enamelling was but little employed in Europe during the past century; this beautiful art is now, however, being revived with considerable success, especially in Paris, particularly the painted enamels, both on a large scale and for miniature. The Exhibition offered examples of nearly every variety of enamel work upon metal, both ancient and modern. Among the Collection of Antiquities were numerous specimens of ancient enamels, of which we may specially mention the two enamelled plates belonging to the Archæological Institute of Great Britain, one representing the Crucifixion, and the other our Saviour enthroned on the rainbow. These specimens were very good examples of the older Limoges work; while the beautiful enamelled cups, *en grisaille*, on a black ground, of Charles Tucker, Esq., F. S. A., the one representing Tritons, and the other an historical subject, were excellent examples of the painted enamels or Limoges work of the sixteenth century. In the Mediæval Court there was a characteristic specimen of the enamel, *en grisaille*, on black ground, of the last period of the style of Limoges work, the end of the seventeenth, and beginning of the eighteenth century. This was a plate representing St. Peter walking on the water; from its style it is apparently the work of Jean Laudin, a distinguished enameller, whose chief works date about 1693. Technically, the work of Laudin and of all the enamellers of that period is superior to that of the preceding century; the black grounds were much finer and deeper, and the outlines of the white opaque enamels used for the figures sharper, as could be well seen by contrasting the last-mentioned enamels with the cups of the fifteenth century. But in an artistic point of view the latter were much superior, and of a purer taste.

There was also exhibited an interesting series of twelve painted enamels on copper, representing the Stations of the Cross, and now in the Museum of Irish Industry. In point of execution and design they were exceedingly poor, but as illustrative of the early style of painted enamels, before the introduction of the opaque ground, they were extremely curious, and, so far as we know, very rare. From the style of the drawing they are apparently of Italian workmanship,—an opinion which is supported by the fact of their having been in the possession of Cardinal Fesch before being brought to Ireland.

The application of enamel to decorate harness was illustrated by the stirrups said to have belonged to the Duke de Schomberg, exhibited by T. M. Birnie, of Carrickfergus, but certainly executed at a much earlier period. There were also examples of the employment of enamels to decorate articles connected with church service, both ancient and modern; among the former we may mention a crozier head belonging to Dr. Petrie, with St. Patrick expelling the serpents in the volute, which was made either at Limoges or by some workman of that school. A fine example of the employment of niello is seen in the celebrated Cross of Cong; along the centre of the arms and stem of the cross is a band of silver covered with niello, and having a number of cross bars at short intervals in the same style; where these bars join the band just alluded to there is a sort of *neaud* or ornament of circles intersecting one another, cut in *taille d'epargne*, and which have a pretty effect upon the niello ground. This cross was executed in Roscommon in the year 1131, and is interesting as showing at what an early period the highest decorative arts of the middle ages were practised in Ireland. There are but few so characteristic examples of this style now in existence of as early a date as this Cross of Cong. The chalices and other sacred vessels, and several other articles of ecclesiastical furniture, exhibited by Mr. Hardman in the Mediæval Court, were in many instances decorated with red and azure enamels, generally embedded as in the eleventh and twelfth centuries.

The examples of modern enamels applied to other than church furniture were very numerous, but our space forbids to more than point out a few as illustrations. In the Sevres collection there was an enamel on iron painted in colours, representing the allegorical subject of Prudence, which for technical execution, softness, and harmony of colour, exceeded anything ancient or modern which we have seen. The art of enamelling upon metals was carried to great perfection at Sevres during the directorship of the late M. Ebelman, who succeeded in producing plates of a size altogether unknown to the old enamellers, and that, too, upon iron which presented such difficulties to the latter. In the beautiful collection of jewellery exhibited by M. Rudolphi, of Paris, were a great number of extremely happy applications of the enameller's art, among which we may specially mention the green translucent enamels upon vine and oak leaves of gold, the veinings, being chased on the metal, were seen through the enamel, and thus offered excellent examples of the old translucent enamels in bas relief. M. Rudolphi also exhibited a mediæval fire-place of the most elaborate workmanship, profusely decorated with translucent and opaque coloured enamels, in the embedded, in solid or *taille d'epargne* style. We do not wish to hazard an opinion in this place upon the style of this work, or upon mediæval art generally, but, taken as a mere piece of workmanship, the fire-place was one of the most remarkable things in the whole Exhibition. R. Phillips, of London, exhibited two plates of silver, with Scripture subjects in niello, which were good examples of the peculiar application of that art, in former times, to the decoration of the covers of books, caskets, &c. Among the articles contributed by Her Majesty was a beautiful set of silver vessels of Indian workmanship, consisting of an ewer basin, bottle vase and covers, teapot and plate, and cover decorated with flowers, arabesques, &c., chased in *taille d'epargne*, the intaglio or parts tooled out being filled with what appeared to us, not having the means of close examination, to be a translucent green enamel, the contrast being very good. In Hewet's Chinese collection there were a number of examples of Chinese paintings upon opaque enamel grounds, upon copper, some of a very large size; among these were some imitations of European utensils, such as a wash-hand basin and jug, &c., in azure opaque enamel ground, with figures in coloured enamels. These articles were, in a technical point of view, admirably executed.

There is another application of enamels upon opaque enamel ground, which is now used, and which must not be passed over—namely, the decoration of watch cases, many examples of which were exhibited. Of these we shall specially mention two small ladies' watches, contributed by Mr. Bennet, of London, but of Continental workmanship—one was decorated in coloured enamels, with a figure in miniature style of a guitar player, surrounded by a border in *bleu du roi*, and the other with the Holy Family after Raphael, the border being chased in gold, ornamented in niello. Mr. Scriber, of Westmoreland-street, exhibited some enamelled watches, one of which was very pretty; the ground a turquoise blue enamel, with a sprig of flowers in fine seed pearls. Mr. Racine, of Nassau-street, also exhibited some handsome watches of the same kind.

Before dismissing the subject of enamelling upon metals, we would wish to direct attention to the blunder committed by some of our jewellers who make brooches in imitation of the ancient Irish ornaments, used for a similar purpose. These ornaments were very generally ornamented with enamel or inlaid work, and, perhaps, niello, and in such cases were chased in a peculiar way for that purpose; but some of the modern imitations employ the same style of tooling, but have neglected the enamels. Now the beauty of these ornaments would be immeasurably enhanced if enamelled, and we hope, therefore, to see them so before long. Advantage might also be taken of the art of enamelling in the decoration of the cheap jewellery now made in Dublin, in connexion with the trade of bog-oak ornaments.—W. K. S.

---

1. HIS ROYAL HIGHNESS PRINCE ALBERT.—Her Majesty's Grand Centre Piece—executed under the instruction of his Royal Highness Prince Albert; it represents a group of horses round a Temple or Kiosk, with their attendants; the figures and horses, with Persian greyhound, were grouped, designed, and modelled by Mr. Cotterill; the Kiosk was modelled by Mr. E. Percy, formerly of Dublin; and the base by Mr. William Spencer; and the whole executed in silver by Messrs. Garrard, Haymarket.

2. AARON, BROTHERS, Torwood-row, Torquay, Devon, Manufacturers.—Silver taper stand on malachite leaves; engraved and gilt match-box, inlaid; richly chased silver-gilt eagle, on malachite pedestal; engraved and gilt casket, inlaid; silver and malachite box, for postage stamps; silver-gilt engraved paper knife, malachite handle; brooches and bracelets in malachite.

3. ACHESON, W., Grafton-street, Dublin, Manufacturer and Importer.—Bog oak casket, set with Irish gems in silver-gilt; bog oak brooches, bracelets, &c.; elastic band bracelets, with fibulæ and bog oak mountings; antique brooches, set with malachite, pearl, &c.; electro-plated moderateur lamps; specimens of electro-plating; gold jewellery, set with precious stones; antique tea and coffee services; plated flower stands; fish carvers.

4. ASKEN, J., Upper Sackville-street, Dublin.—A suite of diamonds and turquoise of great value, presented by Napoleon I., on the day of his coronation, to Madame Sa Mère; silver tea services; presentation plate; diamond ornaments, consisting of brooches, bracelets, rings, and ornaments in Irish oak.

5. BARTER, RICHARD, Frederick-street, South, Dublin, Manufacturer.—Carvings of sea horse tooth in cameo style.

6. BENNETT, T., Grafton-street, Dublin.—Specimens of Irish wrought silver plate, consisting of salvers, tea and coffee services, kettles, and stands, claret jugs, children's cans; electro-plate, in salvers, kettles and stands, tea and coffee sets, claret jugs, &c.; specimens in working of gold, precious stones and gems; bog oak work; newly designed centre candelabra for flowers; silver presentation centre piece.

7. BRUNKER, T., William-street, Dublin, Designer and Manufacturer.—Case, containing specimens of electro-plating on copper, nickel, bronze, ormolu, &c.; jewellery in fine gold, bog oak, Irish diamond, &c.; also masonic ornaments; masonic aprons; silver tea set, antique claret jugs, cups, &c.; vibrating or pendant clock, on a beautiful carved stand of bog oak, supported by two Irish wolf-dogs.

8. CARDIGAN, THE EARL OF, AND THE OFFICERS OF THE 11TH HUSSARS.—Silver equestrian statue of his Royal Highness Prince Albert, by Cottrell, presented to the officers of the 11th Hussars by the late Colonel, his Royal Highness Prince Albert.

9. COLONEL AND OFFICERS OF THE 7TH HUSSARS.—Silver statuette of Field Marshal the Marquess of Anglesey, presented to the regiment by the Marquess.

10. CONNELL, D., Nassau-street, and Grafton-street, Dublin, Designer and Manufacturer.—Bog oak ornaments, mounted in native gold and silver, and set with Irish diamonds and pearls.

11. CONNELL, M., Nassau-street, Dublin, Manufacturer.—Bog oak ornaments, mounted in gold and silver.

12. EGLINTON AND WINTON, EARL OF, Eglinton Castle, Ayrshire.—The "Emperor's Vase," won at Ascot, by the Earl of Eglinton's "The Flying Dutchman;" the Goodwood Cup, won by the Earl of Eglinton's "Van Tromp."

13. ELKINGTON, MASON, & CO., London and Birmingham, Manufacturers.—A selection of art manufactures in electro-gold and silver plate; dessert service, with subjects taken from Shakspeare, designed and modelled by Charles Grant; a general assortment of electro-plated wares.

14. FITZPATRICK, BROTHERS, Upper Sackville-street, Dublin, Importers and Manufacturers.—Bracelets, brooches, and other jewellery; a silver vase made of coins, upwards of 800 years old; a cherry stone, containing twenty-four silver spoons, made from a silver penny.

15. FLAVELLE, H. E., Eustace-street, Dublin, Manufacturer.—Masonic and other jewellery.

16. GARDNER, R. K., Grafton-street, Dublin.—A silver fountain, intended to form a centre for the dinner or supper table, which will emit for six hours continuously, upon one application of the winding key, a spray of rose water, to a height variable at pleasure, and through a variety of fancy jets, which can be severally attached to it; a variety of specimens of gold and silver plate; jewellery after the antique and modern designs; silver horsemen and figures, candelabra, &c.

17. GOGGIN, G., Nassau-street, Dublin, Manufacturer.—Bracelets, brooches, necklaces, ear-rings, studs, buttons, card cases, bookstands, chessboards, and other articles of jewellery and ornaments in bog oak, Killarney arbutus, and yew, Connemara marble, and mounted in native gold and silver, with Irish gems; candelabra, in bog oak and Irish diamonds; pie case in bog oak, Irish diamond, and Irish silver; bog oak, Irish diamond, and Wicklow gold vest buttons and studs.

18. GRIFFITH, WILLIAM DOWNES, Dunmore, Tuam, Co. Galway.—Case containing gold snuff box, presented by the Emperor Napoleon, when at St. Helena, to Major Poppleton, the officer in charge.

19. HENNESSY, B. R., Wind-street, Swansea, Wales, Manufacturer and Exhibiter.—Specimens of Russian and Australian malachite in gold and silver mountings.

20. HIGGINS, FRANCIS, Kirby-street, Hatton Garden, London.—Silver knives, forks, spoons, and various small articles, mugs, plates, &c.

21. HUNT & ROSKELL, late STORR & MORTIMER, New Bond-street, London, Manufacturers.—A candelabrum in silver (a testimonial presented to the Most Noble the Mar-

quess of Tweeddale); silver groups—"Mazeppa;" a group in silver, "St. Michael and Satan" (after Flaxman), executed for the Earl of Chesterfield; four equestrian statuettes in silver, Joan of Arc, a cavalier, an Arab, a Hussar (executed for the Earl de Grey); the Doncaster Cup of 1850; the first prize given by the Emperor of Russia to the Ascot races; suites of diamonds and pearls in variety.

22. HUTCHINS, S., Portland, Charleville, Co. Cork, Proprietor.—A silver salver presented by Lord Plunket to the late Peter Burrowes, Esq.

23. JACKSON, CAPTAIN H., Attyflinn, Patrick's Well, Co. Limerick, Proprietor.—A curious silver table of great antiquity, with several antiques and curiosities.

24. JOHNSON, J., North-place, Gray's Inn-road, London.—Silver-gilt and metal-gilt chased chatelains; bronze medallion in gilt frame; gilt patterns for book covers; gilt paper knife with chased handle; models and casts; ebony casket, with chased gilt mountings; gilt casket and miniature tables; model of a swan in wax, coated with silver, by electro process; group of figures in electrotype; horse and jockey oxidized and gilt; reclining stag, in metal, silvered; small models of animals and insects; specimens of casting in bronze; copies of cup and tazza, by Cellini.

25. JOHNSON, J., Suffolk-street, Dublin.—Samples of Irish bog oak brooches, bracelets, &c. &c.; a bog oak elephant, mounted with gold, silver, and precious stones.

26. MAHOOD, S., Wellington-quay, Dublin, Manufacturer.—Models in bog oak, fitted as ladies' brooches; bracelets and brooches of Irish materials and workmanship; also, a collection of new designs in imitation jewellery, including gold, silver, coral, carbuncle, amethyst, opal, malachite, and diamond imitations.

27. MARSHALL, S., Letterkenny.—Pearls from the *Unio margaritifera*, from the river Lanan.

28. MOSLEY, JULIUS, Wicklow-street, Dublin, Sculptor.—Richly carved jewel casket, in bog yew.

29. NELIS, J., Omagh, Co. Tyrone, Proprietor.—Specimens of pearls, formed in a freshwater bivalve (*Unio margaritifera*) found in the river Strule, at Omagh.

30. NORTH, T., Grafton-street, Dublin.—Candelabra of new design, in brass, and electro-plated; a variety of electro-plated goods; and specimens of old articles replated; specimens of electro-plating on steel, brass, copper, German silver, glass, china, and delft; and some electro-types.

31. O'BRIEN, Miss B. M., Fitzwilliam-square, Dublin.—Surtout de table of ormolu, French manufacture, made by Schallenberge; dessert service, silver-gilt.

32. PEARSALL, T., Lower Sackville-street, Dublin, Manufacturer.—A single tea service, made out of a single fourpenny piece, comprising teapot with movable lid; twelve cups, twelve saucers, twelve spoons, two plates, cream-ewer, sugar-bowl, slop-basin, sugar-tongs, and butter-knife; a silver tea and coffee service, made out of a single dime, or ten cent. piece of the United States of North America (equal to fivepence British); contains seventy-four pieces.

33. PHILLIPS, R., Cockspur-street, London.—Signet rings, pins, with sporting and other designs; a series of works in oxidized silver, enamel, niello, and coral; statuettes of a British Life Guard and colour-sergeant of the Scots' Fusilier Guards, modelled from life in oxidized silver and gold; the accoutrements detach at pleasure; the same in bronze and electro-silver; miniature models of same, mounted and dismounted, in oxidized silver and gold on malachite pedestals; statuette, in oxidized silver and gold, of Lablache as Caliban; statuettes of the Emperor Charles V. and Marguerite of Parma, in silver, gold, and precious stones, enamel, &c., from the celebrated models of Messrs. Weiskampt of Hanau; miniature statuette of Gutenberg in oxidized silver; desk seals in gold, lapis lazuli, and oxidized silver; oriental agate cup, in oxidized silver and gold; gold cup in the Byzantine style; tazza in crystal; small dagger with silver-gilt handle, enriched with pearls and emeralds; silver vase of antique form, engraved with subjects from the Pompeian frescoes.

34. RETTIE, M., & SONS, Union-street, Aberdeen, Designers and Manufacturers.—Granite jewellery, mounted in gold and silver: as bracelets, brooches, shawl and other pins, buttons, studs; silver brooches, with crests and mottoes; badges in a new style.

35. SHELDON, J., Birmingham.—Silver and electro-plated goods; gold and silver pencil cases; letter and cup balance; pencil and pen cases; gold pens; electro-plated nickel-silver spoons, forks, ladles, knives, &c.; tea services.

36. SMITH, NICHOLSON, & Co., Duke-street, Lincoln's Inn Fields, London, Designers and Manufacturers.—Silver candelabrum (presented to F. H. Hemmings, Esq., Secretary of the Londonderry and Enniskillen Railway Company, by the shareholders); silver centre ornaments; dessert sugar basket, with cover; electro-plated dessert stands, and salt cellar, designed by Townsend; silver salt cellars and spoons.

37. SULLIVAN, B., Upper Stephen-street, Dublin, Designer and Manufacturer.—Design in German silver for a cenotaph to the late Thomas Moore.

38. SUTHERLAND, G., Forse, Lybster, Proprietor.—Massive silver urn, weighing 278 oz. 15 dwts., representing capercailze, grouse, pheasants, partridges, and other game, &c.

39. WALSH, R., Parliament-street, Dublin, Manufacturer.—Articles in silver and plated ware; gold chains, watch guards, and lockets; topaz, cameo, amethyst, pearl Irish diamond, and amethyst brooches; ear-rings, in cut coral, turquoise, and engraved gold; fancy rings; scarf pins and other jewellery.

40. WATERHOUSE & Co., Dame-street, Dublin.—A silver centre piece, presented to Joseph Green, Esq., Kilkenny; a silver electrotype shield ("Acis and Galatea"), presented to the Count Strelizki by the Poor Law Unions of Ireland; a service of plate, presented to Michael Hyland, Esq., ex-mayor of Kilkenny; a centre piece (stags), presented to the Rev. Joseph Gabbett, of Kilmallock, county of Limerick. the "Farmer's Gazette" challenge cup; a service of plate, presented to A. G. Judge, Esq., of Athy; two large salvers, and the Boyne obelisk, in silver, presented to J. B. Kennedy, Esq., Dame-street; large cup, presented to the 1st Dragoon Guards; large silver snuff box, presented to the 62nd Regiment; a silver trowel, presented to the Right Hon. the Lord Bishop of Tuam; service of plate presented to Dr. Gray, by the county of Monaghan; large silver tray, from the tenantry of his estates, to C. P. Leslie, Esq., M.P.; large silver tea urn, presented to Henry Mitchell Esq., of Glaslough; Loughrea regatta prize, won by Major Goode, 62nd Regiment; the original royal Tara brooch found in Meath in 1850; several copies of antique Irish brooches, and ancient jewellery of Ireland; coffee and tea services, presented to clergymen, doctors, &c. &c.

41. WATT, PHILIP B., Edinburgh.—Specimens of seal and die engravings.

42. WEST & SON, College-green, Dublin, Manufacturers.—Centre piece in silver (presented to the late Colonel Miller by the Constabulary); silver centre piece, presented to Wm. Grattan, Esq., late of the 88th Regiment, by Peninsular officers; vase of Irish diamonds, mounted in native gold and silver, ornamented with Irish pearls, beryls, &c. (presented to the Duchess of Northumberland); casket after the Irish antique, of bog yew, Cork malachites, and native gold and silver, studded with Irish pearls, amethysts, carbuncles, &c. (presented to the Countess of Clarendon); the mace of the King and Queen's College of Physicians in Ireland, made of native silver; snuff box, in native silver; inkstands in the cinque cento and Etruscan styles; wine-cooler of bog oak, in the form of the old Irish mether; brooches, bracelets, and neck ornaments, after the Irish antique.

# CLASS XXIV.

## GLASS.

IF our space permitted, we would have willingly given a brief historical notice of the development of the glass manufactnre; because there is, perhaps, no other which so well illustrates how much the progress of civilization is often dependent upon a simple invention, or the improvement of the processes of a branch of industry. The social history of mankind is but little attended to amidst the more attractive and prominent political phenomena which constitute the staple of ordinary history, although social habits are oftener the cause than the effect of such phenomena. The true causes are often apparently trivial, and may as frequently be observed in the workshop as in the cabinet of the statesman.

A definition of glass founded upon its common properties could be given by any school-boy, who would describe it as a hard, brittle, transparent substance, &c.; but it is less with these external qualities that we have to do than with its nature and its chemical composition. To persons unaccustomed to the language of chemistry, and who associate with the word "salt" the common culinary substance known by that name, it will, perhaps, appear strange that we should call glass a salt, and yet such it is. In glass we have an acid and a base, or rather we have several,—for two or more salts may combine together exactly as the elements of the salts themselves do, and form a new substance which we may call a double salt,—glass is, consequently, a double salt. Silica, we have seen, forms more than half of the rocks composing the crust of the globe, with the exception of limestone, and one or two other unimportant rocks. In a great number of these rocks the silica is in combination with lime, soda, potash, &c.—it is present in them as an acid; but we can easily find it without being in combination with these substances—for example, rock crystal, agate, fine white sand, &c. If we crush these substances, and mix the powder with about four or five times its weight of pearl-ash or soda, and expose the mixture to an intense heat, it will melt; the silica or acid combining with the soda or potash, which would be the base, and forming a kind of glass which, if the materials be pure, will be colourless. Such a glass would, however, be useless for the ordinary purposes to which glass is applied, for it would dissolve in great part in water—indeed, such a soluble glass is sold for washing wood, to render it incombustible, and for hardening plaster figures so as to make them resemble marble. If we diminish the quantity of soda or potash employed to fuse the silica we render the resulting glass less soluble, but more difficult to fuse; because the more silica, the greater the heat required to melt the mixture. But no matter to what degree we may increase the silica, and consequently the infusibility, the glass produced would be slowly acted upon by water and by acids, which would dissolve the potash or soda. We might also make a glass with lime and silica, or with lead and silica, but no matter in what proportions we might combine lead or lime with silica, we could not get a soluble glass; all such combinations would, however, be acted upon by acids. Combinations of silica with substances termed bases, such as lime, belong to two classes—those silicates which are soluble in water, those which are insoluble in it. We have seen that both classes, separately, are incapable of forming a glass which will resist water and acid; how then are we to produce such a substance?—by simply combining the two, a compound of a soluble and insoluble silicate being undecomposable either by acid or water. Such, then, is the nature of glass, wherever and however made. Before proceeding further, however, it may be useful to give a list of the materials employed in glass-making.

MATERIALS USED IN THE MANUFACTURE OF GLASS.

1. Fine white sand.
2. Common river sand.
3. Fresh burnt lime.
4. Slaked lime.
5. Chalk.
6. Clay marl.
7. Lime from gas purifiers.
8. Soap boiler waste.
9. Pearl ash.
10. Russian or Canadian potashes.
11. Chloride of potassium from kelp.
12. Sulphate of potash from kelp, with charcoal.
13. Washing soda.
14. Soda ash.
15. Salt cake, or crude glauber salt, or sulphate of soda with charcoal.
16. Common salt.
17. Powdered basalt or greenstone.
18. Earth or soil from the decomposition of basalt rocks.
19. Powdered felspar.
20. Pumice stone.
21. Cullet or broken glass.
22. Fluor spar.
23. Red lead.
24. Litharge from refining of lead.
25. Sulphate of lead from calico print works.
26. Carbonate or oxide of zinc.
27. Borax.
28. Carbonate of barytes.
29. Sulphate of baryta, heavy spar, or Dutch lead with charcoal.
30. Slags from smelting furnaces.
31. Sulphate or carbonate of strontia.
32. Arsenious acid, or white arsenic.
33. Saltpetre.
34. Black oxide of manganese.

The sand used in these countries for the finer kinds of glass is principally obtained from Alum Bay, Isle of Wight, and from Lynn, in Norfolk. Some good sand is obtained near Liverpool; and very large quantities are also brought from Australia! In Ireland glass sands of the finest quality are found in many localities; for example, near Omagh is found a sand quite as pure as that of St. Gobin, in France, and it is unnecessary to mention the well-known white sand from Muckish Mountain, in the county of Donegal.

By various mixtures of these ingredients, the following kinds of glass are produced, which we shall arrange according to their chemical composition:—

LIME GLASSES.

1. Silicate of potash and lime—Bohemian glass, or foreign crown glass.
2. Silicate of soda and lime; or silicate of soda, potash, and lime; or English crown glass—including window glass and plate glass.
3. Silicate of soda or potash, with lime, alumina, and iron; or common wine bottle glass.

LEAD GLASSES.

4. Silicate of potash, or of potash and soda, with silicates of the heavier metallic oxides, such as lead, zinc, or a mixture of lead and baryta, &c., comprising—
   - *a.*—Foreign crystal glass.
   - *b.*—Flint glass—containing more lead than crystal.
   - *c.*—Strass, or paste used for the manufacture of artificial gems—still richer in lead than flint glass, and generally containing boracic acid. To this variety belongs nearly all the pigments used in glass and porcelain painting.
   - *d.*—Silicate and stannate, or antimoniate of potash and of soda or of lead, or opaque enamel.

All these different varieties of glass were represented in the Exhibition; but unless we had much more space to devote to the subject than we have, we could not describe any of the contributions in detail.

Considerable improvements have recently been made in the manufacture of glass for optical purposes, not alone in the absence of striæ and colour, but also in obtaining very high refractive and small dispersive powers. There were but few examples exhibited, two only of which we shall notice: namely, the glass of the lenses and prisms in the light-house apparatus of Chance and Co., who, by the assistance of one of their firm, M. Bontemps, have succeeded in producing specimens of glass adapted for the lenses of large telescopes of wonderful perfection. Although the subject of light-houses does not, properly speaking, belong to this class, we have thought it right to make a few remarks upon the contributions of the Messrs. Chance, in connexion with their improvements in making glass, which we do in the subjoined note.* The other specimens of optical glass consisted of some lenses for microscopes, in the French Department, remarkable for their excellence, and in which zinc was employed instead of lead. Some further remarks on this kind of glass come more properly under the head of that Department.

A few explanatory definitions of the samples of ornamental or otherwise peculiar glass exhibited, such as Venetian filigree glass, mille-fiore, glass mosaic, cased glass, welded coloured glass, crystallo-engraving, cameo-incrustation, American pressed glass, pinched drops, &c., may not be out of place.

Venetian filigree glass is a peculiar and very interesting kind of ornamental glass, for which the glass-houses of Murano, near Venice, were formerly celebrated. It is formed by producing a kind of reticulated pattern in the glass by means of threads of enamel, that is, of glass rendered opaque by the addition of oxide of tin, and either used as milk-white glass, or coloured; for this purpose a number of rods of enamel glass, or

* DIOPTRIC LIGHT-HOUSE APPARATUS.—To a maritime and commercial people the establishment of effective light-houses along the coasts is a matter of paramount importance. Until, however, within a comparatively recent period little was done in this direction; even so late as the year 1816 the light-house of the Isle of Man was lighted by a coal fire placed in a chauffer, exactly as wood fires were made in those of Alexandria, Puzzuoli, and Ravenna, in the times of the Romans. The celebrated Eddystone light-house had the improved mode of lighting with tallow candles in operation at the end of the last century! and it was not until 1807 that the Argand lamps, and parabolical reflectors, were used. A luminous body placed on a high object would diffuse its light in all directions; in a light-house the diffusion is only required in one direction, an object attained by the use of the reflectors. If a lamp be placed in the focus of a parabolical reflector, all the rays which fall upon the surface of the latter are reflected in parallel lines, and are thus sent in the horizontal direction required. A lens possesses the same property, and, accordingly, in the middle of the last century, some fruitless attempts were made to apply the lens for concentrating the rays of light from the light-house lamps into a horizontal zone. It remained, however, for Fresnel to discover precisely where the practical difficulty lay, and how to decisively overcome it. He at once perceived that the lenses should be of considerable dimensions and of short focal length; but these conditions would at first seem to require such a thickness of glass as would materially impair their transparency. To avoid this difficulty he devised an arrangement, the germ of which had been imagined by Buffon, namely, to construct lenses in concentric overlapping zones. These zones are portions of different spherical lenses placed round a centre lens, and so adjusted by calculation as to produce the refractive effect of a single solid lens. His next improvement consisted in devising what he called a system of cylindrical lenses, which are a series of glass bands with curved surfaces, so arranged as to diffuse the light which they receive from the focus in an equable manner over the horizontal sector which they subtend. In addition to these, he devised a system of totally reflecting prisms as a substitute for metallic mirrors, over which they possess the signal advantage of not requiring to be polished. Their operation depends upon the optical law, that the rays of light entering a triangular prism, with a certain inclination, will be totally reflected from the opposite side of the prism, and finally emerge, after a second refraction, in a horizontal direction. Finally, in conjunction with Arago, he devised a lamp with a number of concentric wicks, which produced twenty-five times the light of the best Argand. The first light on this principle was established in the tower of Cordouan, at the mouth of the Garonne, in 1828, and was so perfectly successful, that the system has superseded the old reflectors in all French light-houses. It is worthy of remark that it was in this light-house that Argand lamps and parabolic reflectors were

technically "cane," are prepared and arranged in a mould having recesses or grooves to receive them. A solid ball of pure flint glass is then placed at a welding heat in the mould, where it adheres to the canes; the mass is removed from the mould heated, and worked until the canes are rubbed into an uniform mass with the ball. The ball is next covered with some white glass, and the mass drawn into cane; the appearance of the threads of enamel in these canes may be varied, so as to be spiral or zig-zag, by twisting the mass during the drawing. If these filigree rods be placed in another mould, and a hollow lump of glass be welded to them, and then blown in the ordinary way, we shall have filigree glass. This kind of glass is now made in France and Bohemia, and occasionally in England; the specimens at the Exhibition were rather coarse, and the threads in some cases unequal in thickness.

Mille-fiore, another species of Venetian ornamental glass, has recently been very successfully imitated on the Continent. It consists either of a regular mosaic-like device, or an irregular grouping of the sections of filigree canes in the centre of a mass of transparent flint glass. A double-shaped cone or crescent-shaped bottle of fine glass is blown, and the pieces of cut filigree canes introduced; the whole is then heated, and the blowing-iron attached to the neck of the bottle-like mass, and the air sucked out so as to permit the glass to collapse, and form a solid mass, which may be shaped at will. Sometimes a cylindrical glass is blown and flattened considerably; a number of pieces of filigree cane, arranged as a device, is then introduced, the whole heated, and the lips of the flattened cylinder pressed together until they adhere; the air is next sucked out by means of the blowing-iron attached to the other end, and the glass collapses, and may be shaped as in the other case. Paper weights are chiefly made of this kind of ornamented glass, but tazzas and other vessels may be similarly ornamented. Instead of the filigree cane we might substitute a medal or a bust in bas relief, or any cameo figures made of porcelain or other substances requiring a higher heat than glass to melt them. This style of ornamentation is called cameo-incrustation, and is a Bohemian invention dating about a century back. We have seen some charming specimens, such as chimney ornaments, lamps, girandoles, decanters, &c., ornamented with cameos imbedded in them. In consequence of the thin film of air which exists between the surface of the medallion and the glass, the figures appear as if executed in matted silver, and when the glass has a particular yellow tint they look like matted gold.

One of the most singular applications of glass is to form the pictures known as Roman mosaics. These pictures consist of plates of copper covered with layers of cement, in which are set upright short threads, of every possible shade of colour, according to the design. When the picture is formed by this pavement of hundreds of thousands of threads, the uneven surface is polished, the slight interstices cleaned out, and filled with coloured waxes in harmony with the design. Some of these mosaics are of a large size, such as the copy of the "Last Supper," of Leonardo da Vinci, twenty-four feet long, and twelve feet high. A moderate-sized Roman mosaic often takes five years to complete; and twenty years have been spent upon one. There were several specimens of Roman mosaic in the Exhibition, the most remarkable of which was a table-top belonging to Mrs. White, of Killikee. The centre piece represented the Church of St. Peter, at Rome, surrounded by a border containing views of the chief buildings at Rome, such as the Coliseum, the Pantheon, Trajan's Arch, &c. There were two good landscapes by Rinaldi, one representing the Temple of the Sybil at Tivoli; and the other a ruined temple, with an adjoining oratory and figures of shepherds, females, goats, and a dog. There were some old examples of landscapes with cattle, which were of great merit, but in which the wax in the interstices had been injured.

The style of ornamented glass known as cased glass is now in great repute, and is often of remarkable beauty. It consists of layers of glass of different colours welded upon one another; for instance, we find vessels composed interiorly of colourless glass, upon which is welded a layer of opaline or milk-white glass, and upon this a layer of turquoise blue glass. To do this a ball of solid glass is gathered upon the end of the blowing rod and introduced into a sort of bell of the opalescent glass, and is then gently blown until it fills the bell, and adheres to it, the welding being completed by heating it at the furnace. The cased mass, thus

also first employed; it has thus become one of the most remarkable buildings connected with the history of navigation. In 1834 Mr. Alan Stevenson, the builder of the remarkable light-house of the Skerryvore, was sent to France to examine the system of Fresnel, and the result has been that it is now being gradually introduced into several of our light-houses.

There are two distinct kinds of light-house apparatus upon the principle of Fresnel, the fixed and revolving, examples of both of which were exhibited by the Messrs. Chance, Brothers, and Company, of Birmingham, who have commenced the manufacture of them under the direction of M. Tabouret. The fixed light, or, as it is called, to distinguish it from the reflector system, dioptric light, has the lamp placed in the centre of a refracting cylinder or belt of glass, having a vertical refracting power, and producing, therefore, a long bar of light. The upper and lower portion of the apparatus has a series of zones composed of the totally reflecting prisms of Fresnel, and hence termed catadioptric zones, which, collecting all the diverging rays and subjecting them to refraction, then a total reflection, and, lastly, a second refraction, cause them to issue in a horizontal direction, as we have already explained. The revolving light only differs from the fixed light, by having the cylindrical belt of glass replaced by a revolving octagonal prism, each face of which is composed of one of the polyzonal lenses already described. Below these lenses are arranged cylindrically a series of prismatic rings, and above them a sort of hollow cone or cap formed of similar prismatic rings. The effect of this arrangement is to produce a constant bar of light varied by brilliant flashes, which are produced as the axis of each lens comes opposite the lamp. The usual rate of rotation is one revolution in four minutes, so that there is a flash once every thirty seconds. A single lens only of this kind of apparatus was exhibited.

The introduction of the parabolical reflectors is said to have increased the light of a single Argand lamp about 400 times; whilst a first class revolving light, upon the system of Fresnel, is said to be fully eight times that of the reflector system, or equivalent to between 3000 and 4000 Argand lamps. The glass employed by the Messrs. Chance has a very sensible green tinge, which the manufacturers attribute to the high heat to which it has been subjected in order to free it from excess of alkali, and prevent its subsequent "sweating," that is, becoming moist, and thus in time having its surface dulled. We have frequently seen the large apparatus in the Exhibition lighted up, and the effect did not appear to us to suffer from this green tinge. The French glass made for the Scotch light-houses at St. Gobin is perfectly colourless, and although it was feared at first that it would sweat, we believe that experience has shown that it does not.

formed and heated to the welding heat, is introduced into a similar hot shell or bell of turquoise blue glass, and again gently blown and heated as before, after which the article is blown in the ordinary way; a dozen different-coloured glasses may thus be overlaid, provided the specific gravity of each glass is nearly the same, so that it may expand and contract uniformly. By grinding, so as to lay bare portions of each colour, the most varied designs may be obtained. Colourless glass cased with ruby glass is well adapted for engraving, by which transparent figures are produced on a red ground. This style of ornamented glass was very largely represented in the Exhibition, and many of the articles were very good.

A peculiar kind of glass has recently been manufactured, which is capable of many applications, such as skylights, &c., composed of prisms, or other forms of differently-coloured glass. It is made by a combination of casting, and of the process termed pinching; the different-coloured pieces being arranged according to the design intended in iron or brass moulds, into which white or very slightly tinted glasses, of the consistence of honey, is poured, and pressed into the mould with a piece of wood until it has become cool enough for annealing. On removing the sheet from the mould the pieces of coloured glass will be found firmly welded to it. A window made in this way was exhibited by Mr. John Carrick, of Mary's-abbey; the centre consisted of thick plates of glass of a pinkish hue, surrounded by a series of semi-lunes, formed of coloured glass prisms arranged like Venetian mosaic.

Crystallo engraving is a process by which devices may be impressed in intaglio upon glass vessels,—for example, copies of engraved gems, &c. In this process very finely powdered tripoli is dusted over the die or cast, and over this a layer of the finest dry plaster of Paris mixed with brick dust; the whole is then placed in a screw press, and the powder squeezed into the mould, and while under this pressure it is made to absorb water so that the plaster sets, and in doing so expands and increases still further the sharpness of the impression. The cast in relief is next taken from the press and dried, heated to redness, and is then fitted into a recess in a peculiar mould, so that its surface will range with that of the mould; a ball of melted glass is then introduced into the mould, whose form it is made to assume by blowing. On opening the mould the cast, vessel, or other object, is removed with the plaster cast in relief still adhering to it; it is finished in the usual manner by repeated reheatings, after which it is annealed and ground. The plaster cast is then moistened with water and may be readily separated from the glass, leaving an intaglio impression as sharp as the original die. Coats of arms, regimental crests, &c., may thus be cheaply impressed upon glass vessels. The first application of this process was to produce small intaglio pictures or bas reliefs in glass in imitation of cameos and intaglios on gems. A small collection of pretty brooches, apparently executed in this way, was exhibited by F. Cleinpeter, of Birmingham. The piece of glass had the intaglio pattern impressed on its back, the surface of the impressed parts being either silvered or gilded so as to produce a sort of picture in those metals in the glass. The background was sometimes rose, sometimes blue, or other colours, so as to heighten the effect. Door-plates are frequently ornamented in the most charming manner in this way; some examples of which were in the Exhibition.

A great variety of articles is now produced by casting under pressure, in imitation of cut glass, such as fruit and dessert plates generally, salt cellars, &c. The process is an American invention, and consists in pressing the melted glass into the interstices of a heated mould by means of a matrix or plunger, which forms the interior of the article. It is usual to reheat the articles after being cast so as to give them a brilliant surface; this operation, termed fire-polishing, takes away from the sharpness of the casting, but this disadvantage is more than compensated for by the superior brilliancy acquired. Cast articles are exceedingly cheap, and a great number of excellent examples were exhibited.

Pillar moulding is another variety of cast glass, but much superior to the kind just described, though only applicable to a limited number of objects. In this process the lump of glass, as hot as possible, is formed in a mould only one-third of the size of the intended object. In this way the external surface alone is formed, the interior retaining its smoothness; when taken from the mould it is blown to its full size and fire-polished by repeatedly heating it. This style of moulding is largely employed for lamp pedestals, chandeliers, girandoles, salt cellars, &c. The drops used for chandeliers are also examples of pressed glass, being pinched out of lumps of glass, softened in a blast furnace by means of a kind of tongs. The rough formed drops are then ground. The arms of chandeliers are also roughly formed by pressure.

There were numerous specimens of coloured glass in the Exhibition, employed both in the manufacture of vessels and in glass painting; but our space forbids us from going into detail upon the matter, and any merely incidental notice would be of no value.

The glass trade was formerly extensively carried on in Ireland, especially in Cork, but has declined very much, and is now altogether extinct in that city. We believe there are only three flint glass works in the whole country. Lately the manufacture of bottles has been successfully introduced into Dublin, and there are now two large factories at full work. Glass-making offers a wide field to capitalists, for there can be no doubt, from the success of those now in the trade, that it is a manufacture in which we would have a fair chance of competing with our neighbours, at least in the supply of the home market. The same rule applies, however, to this trade as to every other which might be established in Ireland; it must be carried on with skill and with all the appliances available in England, otherwise it would inevitably fail from the active competition which the closeness of our markets, and the great facilities of intercourse, enable the British manufacturers to subject us to.—W. K. S.

---

1. BAILLIE, E., Wardour-street, Soho, London.—Stained glass windows, representing, in ornamental style, Shakspeare reading one of his plays to Queen Elizabeth and her court; bust of our Saviour; bust of St. Catherine, after Guercino; our Saviour blessing little children; Trial of St. Stephen; decorated style, St. John the Divine; ornamental light with arms of England in the centre; ditto, emblems of the order of the Garter; ditto of the order of the Thistle; ornamental light in the Norman style; arms of King Henry VIII.

2. BISHOP, S. & C., & Co., St. Helen's, Lancashire.—Circular top for an ornamental table, of plate glass, embossed and silvered; embossed silver plate of glass, intended for a cabinet panel, or for fire screens.

3. BOYLAN, P., Grafton-street, Dublin, Proprietor.—Stained glass window, executed by hand, at Antwerp, in 1784.

4. BOYLE, HUGH, & Co., Glasgow.—Stained glass window representing Richard Cœur de Lion, and heraldic devices.

5. CAREY, T. & Co., Carey's-lane, Cork.—China and glass.

6. CARRICK, JOHN, Mary's-abbey, Dublin.—Window of welded coloured glass; triple window of stained glass, representing Christ, St. Peter, and St. Paul; and designs in cased glass.

7. CHANCE, BROTHERS, & Co., Birmingham, Manufacturers.—First order fixed dioptric light-house apparatus, with catadioptric zones, constructed according to the system of Fresnel, with lamp in the centre of the apparatus on the moderateur principle, consisting of a burner with four concentric wicks, and of immense power, the light in clear weather being visible fifty miles distant; concentric polyzonal lens, eight of which, arranged octagonally, constitute the revolving portion of a first order dioptric revolving light; fourth order dioptric light-house apparatus, similar to the first order light, but on a reduced scale, suitable for lighting the entrance to harbours, rivers, &c., visible at a distance of fifteen miles; annular and cylindrical lenses for railway and ship lanterns.

8. CLAUDET & HOUGHTON, High Holborn, London.—Three compartments of a painted and stained glass window, viz.—the figures of our Saviour.

9. CLEINPETER, F., Birmingham.—Enamel glass brooches.

10. CLYDE BOTTLE WORKS Co., St. Rollox, Glasgow.—Black and green glass bottles.

11. DAVIS, S., Dublin, Proprietor.—Glass shades; table crown glass; samples of bent glass.

12. THE DUBLIN GLASS BOTTLE Co., North Lotts, Dublin, Manufacturers.—Black and green glass bottles, imperial and wine measure, &c.; castor oils, various shades and sizes; flasks, various sizes and colours; oval and flat-shaped bottles; carboys; druggists' bottles; wide-mouthed powder and tincture bottles; ginger beer and soda water bottles, flat-bottomed and egg-shaped; seltzer water amber-coloured bottles.

13. GIBSON, J., Newcastle-on-Tyne, Designer and Manufacturer.—Windows of stained glass in the early Norman style; stained glass (Saint Marie reading, after Jan Van Eyck); byzantine window; a decorated window (from St. Jacques, of Liege); a perpendicular window.

14. GREGG & SON, Upper Sackville-street, Dublin, Importers.—Bohemian ornamental coloured vases; dessert water jug, opal and snake handle; dessert goblets to match; dessert jug, engraved in flint; dessert goblets to match; embossed inkstand gilt; rich butter coolers and stands; bonbon stands; liqueure setts and trays, assorted; three pair large mantel-piece lustres and drops; three pair smaller mantel-piece lustres and drops.

15. HALL, J. T., Prescot, Lancashire, Manufacturer.—Four light cut glass chandeliers, with crystal prisms and chains complete.

16. HOLLAND, ——, Warwick.—Specimens of glass staining and mural decorations.

17. HOWARD, BROTHERS, North Woolwich, near London.—Glass in variety.

18. HOWE, ——.—Stained glass window, representing the Adoration, the Circumcision, and the Dispute in the Temple.

19. KEAN, R., Well-street, Oxford-street, London, Proprietor.—Glass jug, decanters, goblets, and wine glasses, engraved in various designs by exhibiter.

20. LADIES' GUILD, per MRS. HILL, Russell-place, Fitzroy-square, London.—Monumental glass tablet; painted glass table, consolidated; stained glass panel, brilliant outside by day, and by night inside; Rosenan, the birth-place of H. R. H. Prince Albert, framed in glass-covered mouldings.

21. LAING, J., Calton-hill, Edinburgh, Designer and Manufacturer.—Specimens of enamelled glass, suitable for professional signs and decorations.

22. LEETCH, THOMAS, Dame-street, Dublin, Proprietor.—Cut glass decanters, goblets, and wine glasses; large rich cut centre dish and vase; vases, &c., of Bohemian glass.

23. LOWE, E., Marlborough-street, Dublin, Manufacturer.—Stained glass window, containing specimens of foliated ornament, landscapes, figures, and heraldry.

24. MEIN, A., Glasgow, Manufacturer.—Glass bottles, imperial and wine measure; oil bottles of various sizes; bottles, with Beltzung's patent screw neck and capsule; soda water and other bottles.

25. MONTEAGLE, LORD.—Plateau of glass, presented by the glass manufacturers of Great Britain to exhibiter when Chancellor of the Exchequer.

26. PURCELL, P. C., Dublin.—Specimen of painting on glass—a scene in the South of Ireland.

27. RICE, HARRIS, & SON, Islington Glass Works, Birmingham.—Coloured and ornamental glass; ruby jug; opaque yellow toilet; opal vase; ruby vase and cover; vases in great variety of colour and design; opal painted jugs and goblets; ruby and flint tazza; engraved goblet vase and cover.

28. RICHARDSON, B., Wordsley, near Stourbridge, Manufacturer.—One set of pure crystal glass dishes, richly cut, for dessert; consisting of one twelve-inch centre and stand, four ten-inch dishes, four nine-inch dishes, four eight-inch dishes.

29. RIGG, I., & SON, Glasgow.—Crystal gaseliers for four, six, and eight lights.

30. ROSS, W. A., & Co., High-street, Belfast.—Pillar, showing eight different descriptions of watch glasses in their various sizes, supported and surmounted by the crystal balls from which they are made.

31. SILLERY, M. & R., Abbey-street, Dublin, Designers and Manufacturers.—Stained glass windows; embroidered looking glasses.

32. THOMAS & HIGGINBOTHAM, Dublin.—Cut glass drawing-room lustres; Parian china vases, figures, groups; Celtic china dinner, dessert, and toilette suites; specimen patterns of china services; a bronze pillar hall lamp, eight feet high, with three-burner lamp; numerous works of art; engraved glass cup vase, "Fighting for the Standard at the Battle of Marston Moor;" aerometric table lamp, invented by J. F. Boake.

33. THOMPSON, F. H., Berners-street, Oxford-street, London.—Specimens of silvered glass.

34. WARREN, C. M., Essex-street, Dublin, Importer.—Large lustre, mounted with crystal prisms; cut glass decanters; claret jugs, caraffes, goblets, wine glasses, tumblers, and champagne glasses; cut crystal centre dish; foreign ruby and cased glass chimney lustres; vases and tazzas in various styles.

35. WARREN, S., Dame-street, Dublin, Proprietor.—Specimens of richly cut flint glass, manufactured at the Dublin Flint Glass Works.

36. WHYTE, W., Marlborough-street, Dublin.—A ruby coated vase, richly cut, made by Percival Yeates & Co., and engraved by Böhm, representing Richard Cœur de Lion and Saladin at the Battle of Ascalon; cut and engraved decanters; dinner and dessert glass in variety; candle lustres and flower vases; specimens of spun glass, &c.

# CLASS XXV.

---

## CERAMIC MANUFACTURES.

WHAT can be more simple than the art of the potter? No tools of bronze or of iron are required; the hands alone being capable of fashioning the prettiest formed vases, whilst the materials employed may be found in abundance in every part of the globe, and require but a few rudely-shaped pieces of wood to prepare them for use. Hence, we find vessels and other articles made of clay have been in use among the oldest nations of the earth—not alone among the Assyrians, Greeks, and Romans, but even among the old Celtic and Scandinavian nations, the aboriginal races of America and of Africa—of which many of the European museums preserve examples. It is probable that the first articles fashioned were drinking vessels: indeed, the word *Ceramic* is derived from the Greek word for *horn*, apparently the first drinking vessel used in all countries; whilst the word *pottery* is derived from the Latin *potum*, a drinking cup. Another early application of the potter's art, though one which must, undoubtedly, have originated at a much later period than that of the manufacture of drinking vessels and other objects for domestic use, was to funereal purposes. Some people appear to have burned their dead, collected the ashes, and placed them in vessels of clay, many of which have come down to us; examples of which were to be found of a very ancient date, discovered in tumuli in Ireland, in the Collection of Antiquities. The great difficulty and expense of procuring stone, especially in the absence of metallic implements, must have led at an early period to the formation of huts of mud, from which the transition to brick buildings was very easy. At first, the bricks were simply dried in the sun, baking them by means of fire being a subsequent discovery. The production of articles in *terra cotta* or baked earth, may be considered to mark the first era in the Ceramic Arts, because it was only then that they acquired sufficient durability to call for the production of fine forms, or the application of ornament.

The Greeks and Romans employed two distinct materials in their pottery, one of which yielded a coarse, almost granular, not very homogeneous or uniformly coloured, and very porous mass; and the other, which yielded a body beautifully homogeneous, a porcelain-like grain, and very dense. The amphoræ, cineral, and lachrymal urns, in which the ashes were placed in the tombs, were made of the first-mentioned substance. The amphoræ were often of gigantic size, sometimes from 8 to 10 feet in height, and 3 feet in diameter. The celebrated tub of Diogenes was an amphora of this kind. In Spain enormous jars, called *Tinajas*, are made for holding wine, oil, flour, &c.; two localities are especially celebrated for these articles, Castello de los Jarrès and Colmenar de Oréja, not far from the celebrated royal residence of Aranjuez, where jars 13 feet high and 7½ feet in diameter are made. Similar vessels are also used in the South of France and in Italy, and, indeed, in all the Mediterranean countries, though, perhaps, not of such a remarkable size as the Spanish ones. The statues and finer vases and tazzas of antiquity were frequently coloured in the clay, some black, some brownish-red, and others of a beautiful sealing-wax-red, hence named *terra sigillata*. In addition to this colour of the body the surface was also usually coloured; the statues, architectural ornaments, and tombs, being often green or blue, and the vases or tazzas being sometimes ornamented with black silhouette-like figures on the red body, these being considered the most ancient; while those with the figures in red, buff, and white on a black ground, belong to the highest period of Greek art. There was in the Exhibition a very beautiful collection sent by Messrs. Battam and Son, of London, of articles of this kind copied from the originals in the British Museum, and other collections. Three different classes may be noticed, those with black figures on a red ground; those with brownish-red figures on a black ground; and yellowish-white or buff-coloured figures on a black ground. The body in all cases is red, in imitation of *terra sigillata*, the black figures being made in a sort of clay pigment, worked up with quick-drying oils, and subjected to a considerable temperature, the black colour being thus produced by charcoal. Many of the old vases were also covered with an exceedingly thin glaze or glass, consisting of silica, iron, and soda, which must have been very pretty. This glaze has been found to consist of a combination of silica and soda, or rather of clay, with that substance, being, in fact, a true glass; but we are ignorant whether, like our modern salt-glazed ware, it was formed with salt. This species of glazing appears to have been known at a very early period, for many articles, especially bricks, glazed in this way, have been found at Nineveh, some even of various colours: and Herodotus mentions that the walls of the palaces of Ecbatana, in the empire of the Medes, were painted of seven colours, meaning, in all probability, walls built of these coloured and glazed bricks. The Greeks and Romans do not appear, as far as we are aware, to have used glazed pottery (although well acquainted with it) to the same extent as the Eastern nations; they did not, consequently, make any improvements, at least, any which have reached us. The Arabians and Persians appear to have made articles in earthenware, which they covered with a sort of enamel, that is, glass rendered milky or opaque with oxide of tin, as early as the tenth or eleventh century. The former introduced the art into Europe, and the celebrated palace of the Alhambra, which was commenced about the year 1273 by Mohammed-ben-Alhamar, Moorish King of Granada, had all its walls partially covered, and its floors paved with tiles painted and glazed, termed in Spanish, *azulejo* corresponding to the Arabic, *zulaj*. Most of the Spanish Moresco buildings were ornamented in the same manner, such as the Cuarto Real, in Granada; the Alcazar of Seville, &c. The Christian Spaniards imitated the Moorish Azulejos, long after the destruction of the kingdom of Granada. The more ancient of these tiles of the twelfth and thirteenth centuries appear to have been painted and enamelled on flat or plain surfaces, while the more modern, and especially the Christian ones, were stamped with indented patterns, which were then filled up with various coloured enamels. The colours were chiefly two shades of blue, hence the name azulejo from the same Arabic root as azure, which formed a ground for arabesques in gold. Vases were also made of this kind of ware; and traces of them have been found in those parts of Sicily held by the Moors. The mode of making these enamels spread from Spain into Italy, or in all probability from the Balearic Islands, which belong to Spain, one of which is Majorica or Majorca, of which the word *Majolica* seems to be a corruption. It is probable that a similar invention was arrived at independently by Luca della Robbia, a Florentine sculptor who died at a very early age in 1430, and who, in order to protect his figures, which were formed of calcareous clay, and but slightly fired, from the action of the atmosphere, covered them with a true enamel of tin. To this he gave the name of *terra invetriata*. Articles made by him, and by his brothers, nephews, and grand-nephews, are much sought after by amateurs of the ceramic arts. They are very beautiful, and are adorned with bas reliefs and figures; the chief colours being a pure yellow, an opaque blue, green, and a rather dirty violet. The clay body or *bisque* was of a light yellow colour, which was completely hidden by the milk-white enamel. It would appear that about the same time the common earthenware or terra cotta, made at Pesaro for domestic purposes, was glazed with oxide of lead or litharge, and even with galena (the common ore of lead); either of these substances, when spread as a paint on clay, and then heated, will form a very fusible transparent glass by combining with the elements of the clay. But owing to this transparency the colour of the bisque or body was seen; in order to hide which they dipped the pieces of ware before glazing into a cream or *slip* of white clay; it was then gently fired and glazed with a varnish of oxide of lead, potash, and fine sand calcined together. This is what amateurs call *Mezza-majolica*.

The manufacture of Mezza-majolica flourished from 1450 to 1500, under the patronage of the Princes of Urbino. It is supposed that the first manufacture was established at Urbino, under the celebrated Duke Frederick, of Montefeltro. His son, Guidobaldo, established a second at Pesaro; and the nephew and successor of the latter, Francesco Maria della Rovere, added a third at Gubbio. Mezza-majolica was remarkable for the beauty of its glaze, and the perfection of its white and yellow colours, which had a kind of metallic lustre as of gold and silver. Only two colours, yellow and blue, and their intermediate tints, appear to have been generally used, although a beautiful iridescent ruby red was employed at Pesaro and Gubbio. The latter coloured ware, and, indeed, the finer specimens of other colours, had a peculiar chatoyant nacreous lustre. The designs were not very remarkable, if we except those of Nicolo da Tolentino, of Pesaro. The peculiar glaze of the Mezza-majolica appears to have been completely replaced by an opaque enamel glaze somewhat of the same character as that of Lucca della Robbia, about the year 1500. From that period the article *Majolica* became well known over Europe, on account of the beauty of the paintings executed upon it. Among the most distinguished of the early decorators of Majolica were Giorgio Andreoli, of Pavia, who worked at Gubbio; Maestro Rovigo, of Urbino; and Xanto, of Rovigo, who also worked at Urbino. But it was only under the successor of Francesco, Guidobaldo II., that the manufacture of majolica attained its greatest perfection, from 1540 to 1560. He brought together artists of the greatest merit, who copied the works of the immortal Raffaelle, or the engravings of them, by Marc Antonio, of Bologna; the works of other great masters were also copied, such as Giulio Romano, Parmegiano, &c. It is from this fact that majolica is called "Raffaelle Ware." The most distinguished of these copyists were Orazio Fontana, of Urbino, who painted the finest specimens in the collection in the Medical Dispensary of the Palace of Urbino, celebrated as the *Majolica della Spezieria*; Battista Franco; Geronimo Vasajo; Raffaelle da Colle, a pupil of Raffaelle; and Girolamo Lanfranco, to whom the invention of the process of gilding ware is attributed. Every town in Italy soon endeavoured to rival Pesaro, Gubbio, and Urbino in the production of painted ware; and among those which rose to celebrity in this respect were Castel Durante, the modern Urbania (where Francesco Maria della Rovere II., the last Duke of Urbino, built a magnificent palace adorned with the finest specimens of majolica), Rimini, Ravenna, Bologna, Faënza, whence is derived the name of *Fayence*, applied on the Continent to earthenware generally. Before the death of Francesco II. the manufacture declined, especially in an artistic point of view: landscapes, grotesque figures, birds, &c., took the place of the copies of the great masters; and in the year 1600 scarcely any ware was fabricated in the states of Urbino, except some inferior kinds at Urbania, where some was even made in 1720. About the same time good majolica was made at Naples, and even at the end of the last century in Venice.

Before his death, Duke Francesco made a religious offering of the magnificent collection of the Spezieria to the celebrated Santa Casa, at Loretto; and the remainder of his collections became the property of Ferdinand de Medici, who removed them to Florence.

The beauty of form and painting of the articles executed during the period when the manufacture had attained its highest degree of excellence may well excite our admiration. And of the high value set upon them even in the times when they were made we have ample proof, from the fact of Louis XIV. having offered for the Four Evangelists and St. Paul, forming part of the glorious collection of the Spezieria, in the Santa Casa, an equal number of statues in gold.

About the year 1530 Girolamo della Robbia, the grand-nephew of Luca, was brought to France by Francis I., who had decorated for him the "Petit Château de Madrid," in the Bois de Boulogne, sometimes called the *Château de Fayence* on this account. The art was not, however, naturalized in France until the marriage of Louis Gonzaga, kinsman of Catherine de Medici, to Henrietta of Cleves, in 1565, by which he became Duke of Nivernois. He established the manufacture at Nevers, and sent for artists to Italy. Previous, however, to this period, namely, in 1555, the celebrated Bernard Palissy, after a series of experiments conducted in the midst of poverty and difficulties which few but himself could have the courage to overcome, discovered the process of making an enamelled ware different in many respects from the Italian, being formed of a kind of pipe-clay, and ornamented and coloured in a very peculiar way. Palissy made two kinds of ware, one with an opaque glaze like the Italian majolica, and rustic pieces glazed with a lead glass, but without tin. He borrowed most of his ornaments from nature, such as the leaves, fish, reptiles, and even fossil shells with which he decorated, in relief, the dishes and other articles comprising his rustic pieces. His other kind of ware was decorated with historical, allegorical, and mythological subjects also in relief, and in good taste, the figures being well drawn, and the colours bright, but rather limited in variety, the usual colours being yellow, blue, and gray, and sometimes green, brown, and violet. The art also found its way into Germany, where it was carried on at Nürnberg with considerable success as early as 1520. In the middle of the sixteenth century it was established in Holland, at Delft (whence the ordinary name for common earthenware), where it arose to great importance, not for the style of painting, which was an imitation of the Chinese figures on porcelain, but on account of its real excellence and cheapness. From France and Holland the manufacture of glazed earthenware found its way into England, although it is not certain whether true enamelled ware or majolica was made there formerly;* at least, it was not made to any great extent, and was replaced by the better, but totally different articles which were soon produced, and which, to distinguish them from the majolica Continental ware, or Fayence, is called English earthenware.

Majolica, or rather the more modern form of it, fayence or enamelled earthenware, although still largely made on the Continent, is gradually falling into disuse for domestic purposes, in consequence of its softness and the tendency of the glaze to crack, when subject to alternations of temperature; but it might be advantageously applied for capitals, entablatures, brackets, and other fine architectural ornaments, as was done by Luca della Robbia. It is probable that the introduction of the art into England may bring about this result.

The old majolica and modern enamelled earthenware are made of various proportions of clay, clay marl, and sand. In general, however, the composition is nearly the same wherever made, especially the proportion of lime. For example, the majolica of Luca della Robbia contained about 20 to 22 per cent. of lime: the modern, from Valencia, from 19 to 20; Delft, 18; Persian, 19; and Paris, 16 to 17; the mean of which would represent equal parts of pipe-clay and carbonate of lime. Wherever made, they melt at a high temperature, their fusibility increasing to a certain point with the amount of lime which they contain. Common potters' ware may be considered as belonging to the same class as majolica; being, in fact, frequently a marly clay, mixed with more or less sand. In general, however, the mixture has not as pure a colour as that employed for majolica. Articles of this kind are usually only glazed on the inside, the glaze itself being a combination of lead with the elements of clay, alumina, and silica. By the addition of a little antimony ore or sulphuret, the glaze becomes yellow; a little iron gives a red; and manganese gives brown or black; oxide of copper, green; and so on. The glaze is best put on by coating them on the wheel in the green state, with the glaze in a state of paste. The black waste slags of lead-smelting furnaces, as well as those of iron furnaces, would make an invaluable glaze. We are surprised that hundreds of tons annually rejected at the Ballycorus Lead Works, in the county of Dublin, are not taken by some enterprising persons and employed in the manufacture of good coarse pottery ware.

The Japanese and Chinese long preceded us in obtaining a fine white ware, covered with a hard glaze, for, according to Chinese authorities, pottery was discovered by Kouen-ou, under the Emperor Hoang-ti, who reigned from 2698 to 2599 years before Christ; it is even said that there was an officer or mandarin intrusted with the management of the potteries in this reign. It is also certain that a fine white porcelain was in common use in the reign of the Emperor Han, 163 years before the Christian era, and that large vases, similar to those in the Exhibition from China and Japan, were made under the dynasty of the Soui, from 581 to 618 of our era. But it was not until between the years 960 to 1278, that is, under the dynasty of Song, that the manufacture attained perfection. Porcelain is made in China in a great number of places, the chief localities being in the southern provinces of Fou-kien, and of Kwan-tung, or Canton; a good deal of the very fine kind is also made in Keang-se, one of the central provinces of the empire. According to the distinguished Jesuit Father D'Entrecolles, the most celebrated place for the manufacture of porcelain in China is called King-te-tching, which, when he resided there in 1712, contained no less than 3000 kilns! It was from this very locality that the complete collection of materials employed in the manufacture of porcelain in China was sent to the Great Exhibition of 1851, and not far from which it is supposed the Mountain of *Ka-ouling* is situate, from which the kaolin is obtained.

Soon after the discovery of the passage round the Cape of Good Hope by Vasco de Gama, or somewhere about the year 1508, the Portuguese imported this kind of ware in large quantities into Europe, and, as we have already noticed, it received the name of *porcolana* or *porcellana*, in consequence of its nacreous surface. The precise date, however, at which the name porcelain was first applied in our modern sense is very doubtful. Attempts were soon made to imitate it in Europe, even before the manufacture of majolica ware had attained its culminating point in Italy, but apparently without success. Nearly two centuries after, in 1695, a factory was established at St. Cloud, where a peculiar ware in imitation of it was manufactured. In 1729 the celebrated Reaumer brought this material to considerable perfection, and a factory for its manufacture was established at Vincennes in 1741, which was transferred to Sevres in 1756, from which period until the year 1769 it attained an extraordinary degree of celebrity, the old Sevres china having probably never been surpassed.

True china consists of an infusible, very plastic white clay, called *kaolin*; and the other an infusible but not plastic material, termed by the Chinese *petun-tse*, and in English usually called flux. Kaolin is simply a clay derived from the decomposition of the felspar element of granite; the flux being, on the contrary, a

* Majolica was known in England at a very early period, for specimens of it of the date of 1521, and made by Lucca de Maiano, were formerly to be seen at Hampton Court, and in the old gate at Whitehall.

less decomposed felspathic mineral containing a large amount of intermingled grains of quartz, to which is added some chalk and gypsum; even unaltered felspar may be used for the same purpose. An article made of kaolin alone would be an opaque porous mass, a true terra cotta in fact; but when a proper mixture of kaolin and flux is heated in a porcelain kiln, it will be found that the flux melts into a transparent glass, which permeates the opaque clay mass, and fills all its pores as oil or wax does paper; hence, like the latter, the mass is more or less transparent; and if we examine it with a microscope we can distinguish the two substances in the most perfect manner. The essential difference, therefore, between the biscuit of porcelain and that of majolica or fayence is the absence of this permeating glass. A similar difference exists between the glazes, which in the case of majolica are composed of lead or lead and tin glasses, and consequently differ essentially from the body or *bisque;* whilst that of porcelain is composed of undecomposed felspar, to which is added sometimes a little gypsum, although this is not done at Sevres. The glaze is, therefore, in a great degree the same substance as the glassy flux of the body, and hence both become thoroughly united with one another, and with the kaolin element; therefore, the glaze of porcelain does not crack when heated, whilst that of fayence and majolica does. The glaze of the former is also harder than that of the latter; and hence is not liable to be scratched by the knife and fork. The ware which we have mentioned as having been made at Sevres, in imitation of true porcelain, in the middle of the last century, was an artificial substance. It consisted essentially of silica and alkaline salts, with a little alumina; and cannot, therefore, be considered in the same light as any other ware made, as the following recipe, observed there, will fully show:—

| | | |
|---|---|---|
| Fused saltpetre, | 110 | parts. |
| Common salt, | 36 | „ |
| Burnt alum, | 18 | „ |
| Spanish barilla or carbonate of soda, | 18 | „ |
| Gypsum, | 18 | „ |
| Sand, | 800 | „ |
| | 500 | |

These substances, with the exception of the alum, would really furnish a glass if heated strongly; this, however, was not done, the mixture being merely rendered somewhat pasty in a furnace. The resulting mass or *frit* was then ground into an extremely fine powder, and well washed, to remove any portion of the nitre or other salts which may not have united with the sand. To the ground materials some chalks and fine calcareous marl were added; and the whole, brought to the finest state of division, formed the material for the bisque. It is the amount of clay in a material which gives it the property of plasticity; but as such a mixture as that described contained none, it would have been impossible to have moulded it into the form of vessels, as the fine powder would not adhere unless some other substance was added which would give it the required plasticity. For this purpose, soap, glue, or even gum, were had recourse to—materials which were readily burnt out in the firing. But here the difficulties of the manufacture did not cease. During the firing, the materials, from their tendency to fuse into a glass, softened, and the vessels were hence liable to lose their form; they were consequently obliged, at great expense and trouble, to support them by various contrivances during the firing, which for this kind of ware was no less than from seventy-five to one hundred hours. After this firing the glaze was applied by dipping, as before described, and consisted of a kind of flint glass, being a mixture of fine sand or powdered flints, soda, potash, and litharge, or oxide of lead. This artificial or tender porcelain was much more transparent than real porcelain, and by this peculiarity, as well as by the greater softness of the glaze, may be distinguished from it; the beautiful old Sevres porcelain was of this kind. Among the most beautiful specimens of this old china were the articles coloured of a rose red, known as the *rose du Barry*, in compliment to the celebrated Madame Du Barry. This is no longer made at Sevres, having been long since replaced by the *hard* or true porcelain.

Before the process of making the artificial Sevres china was brought to any degree of perfection, and long indeed before the factory where it was first made was transferred to Sevres, the secret of making true Oriental porcelain was discovered. The inventor was John Frederick Böttcher or Böttger, whose father having initiated him into the mysteries of alchemy, believed that he could make gold. During his stay at Zorn, near Berlin, where he was engaged in learning the profession of an apothecary, he acquired a sort of consideration in the eyes of Frederic William I., King of Prussia, in consequence of his belief that he could really make gold; but fearing that this consideration would lead the King to extort his secret, he fled into Saxony, where he travelled about for nearly three years, during which time he was pursued by agents of the King of Prussia, who finally arrested him. Owing to the interference of Frederic Augustus, Elector of Saxony and King of Poland, he was liberated, but only in name; for the latter wished to have the secret himself, and accordingly placed him under surveillance at Dresden, directing him to work at his gold-making in the laboratory of one Ehrenfried Walther Von Tschirnhaus, who had made several attempts at imitating oriental porcelain by the same means which, in the hands of Réaumur, eventuated in the production of the celebrated *pate tendre* of Sevres. It is unnecessary to say that he did not make the gold; but a red clay furnished by Tschirnhaus, from near Meissen, for the manufacture of his crucibles, led him on the way of discovering porcelain. With this clay, in fact, he produced a sort of ware, which, although not translucent, as real porcelain would be, was nevertheless of remarkable quality. In order to satisfy the Elector for his failure in gold-making, he communicated to him his hopes of discovering porcelain, and the Prince, in order not to excite public curiosity by Böttger's researches, gave the latter a laboratory and workmen in the palace of Meissen. Here he was treated with great consideration, being even provided with a carriage to go to Dresden when he pleased, but always accompanied by an officer. In 1706 Charles XII. of Sweden entered Saxony, and the Elector, fearing that Böttger would escape with his secrets, had him conveyed with Tschirnhaus and three of his workmen to the fortress of Königstein, where a laboratory was fitted up for him. He remained there a year; although well treated, he did not admire his captivity, and he and his companions planned an escape. In 1707 he was brought back to Dresden, where he continued his researches to find a porcelain like that of China. At that period hair powder was largely employed all over Europe; this powder, as is well known, was made of starch, but an iron-master of the name of Schnorr, travelling on horseback near Aue, in the Erzgebirge, found that the feet of his horse sunk in a clay of a beautiful white colour, and it struck him that it would afford a cheap substitute for hair powder; he accordingly introduced it into commerce. It happened one day, in the height of Böttger's difficulties to find a white clay, that his valet employed Schnorr's earth to powder his wig. Böttger observed it to be particularly heavy, and on inquiring of his valet the cause, learned that it was a white earth. He at once tried it, and to his great joy produced a true, hard porcelain. In 1709 the discovery was made, and a factory was immediately erected at Albrechtsburgh, near Meissen, which was a real fortress, provided with a drawbridge and garrison, into which no strangers were admitted; even the workmen were sworn to retain the *secret even to the tomb* (geheim bis ins Grab), words which were inscribed on all the doors of the workshops, and solemnly repeated once every month to the officers. A ludicrous instance of this secrecy occurred, even as late as 1812. At the instance of Napoleon, the King of Saxony permitted M. Brongniart, director of the Sevres porcelain factory, to enter the Meissen Works, and to have the processes explained to him by M. Steineau, the director, who was obliged to be first formally dispensed from his oath. M. Brongniart's only travelling companion was not permitted to enter. As happens in all such cases, the secret did get out, and very soon spread into many countries.

As early as 1718, and before Bottger's death, which took place in 1719, at the early age of thirty-five years, one of the foremen, named Stobzel, escaped from Meissen and went to Vienna, where he was at once received with special favour. With the assistance, and under the direction of a Belgian named Claude du Pasquier, he established a manufactory of porcelain in 1720. In 1744, the Empress Maria Theresa acquired possession of it on the part of the State, but it did not become self-supporting until 1761. In 1740, several workmen left Vienna, carrying with them the secret of porcelain manufacture; among others a man named Ringler, who communicated it to Gelz, a manufacturer of delft, near Frankfort-on-the-Maine. The German princes now became anxious each to have his own factory, and accordingly the Duke of Brunswick endeavoured to carry off Gelz's chief workman, Bengraf; but before he succeeded, the latter was seized by the Elector of Mayence, who had him thrown into prison and reduced to a diet of bread and water until he communicated all his processes to Gelz, and the latter had verified their utility; afterwards he was allowed to go, when he founded the factory of Fürstenburg on the Weser. Ringler, the original Viennese workman, remained in the factory of Gelz, which he successfully conducted, but being fond of drink and carrying notes of his processes always on his person, his companions watched an opportunity until he was drunk, and carried them off. These notes were hawked through Germany, and copies of them sold to all the petty princes, who were delighted to possess the secret of so valuable and fashionable an art. One of the best known of these hawkers was a man named Paul Becker; he travelled through France, Germany, Holland, and at length was induced to give up his wandering life, and to fix his residence at Brunswick, where he directed the factory already established in the neighbourhood. Ringler himself was, if possible, more active than his notes, in extending the manufacture of porcelain, for in 1756, having left the factory at Höchst, near Frankfort, he assisted in establishing one at Frankenthal, another at Nymphenburg, near Munich; and in 1758, one near Stuttgard, of which he remained director. In 1750, a factory was established at Berlin, but it did not become of any importance until 1763; in 1756 one at St. Petersburgh; and in 1780 one at Copenhagen.

Up to the year 1765, during which time the manufacture of hard porcelain had made such progress in Germany, France produced only tender porcelain; and notwithstanding the beauty of the latter, great anxiety was manifested to possess the secret of the other. In 1753, a citizen of Strasburg, named Paul Hannong, proposed to M. Boileau, director of the manufactory at Vincennes (subsequently transferred to Sevres), to sell him the secret of the manufacture of hard porcelain. He came to Paris, exhibited specimens, and made some statements which inspired confidence, but having asked a sum of £4000 and a pension of £480 per annum, the matter was given up. Hannong left France, and in conjunction with Ringler founded the factory of Frankenthal, and on his death was succeeded by his eldest son. With the latter, negotiations were also entered into to introduce the manufacture into France, but having demanded a still larger sum than his father, application was made to his younger brother, who, in 1761, consented to establish the manufacture in Sevres; but owing to the proper materials not having been hitherto found in France, no further steps were taken in the matter. In 1765 the first deposit of kaolin was found near Alençon, but it was of inferior quality. Shortly after, in the neighbourhood of Limoges, a white fatty earth was discovered, a portion of which was sent to Macquer, one of the most celebrated chemists then living, who was at the time actively engaged in investigating the subject of pottery clays. Macquer visited the locality in 1768, and immediately after, experiments were instituted at Sevres, which ended in the production of a genuine hard porcelain. The manufacture was soon afterwards commenced, and in 1774 was in full activity; from which period the production of *pate tendre* or old Sevres china gradually declined, and finally ceased altogether.

There is much more uncertainty about the early history of the ceramic manufactures of England than of any of the countries alluded to in connexion with the rise of the art in Europe. During the sixteenth century it is probable that all the articles of ornamental pottery were brought from Holland; but towards the end of that period there is every reason to believe that the manufacture had been introduced under the auspices of Elizabeth. The celebrated Shakspeare's jug is formed of a hard kind of material, much more like stoneware than the soft body of the Continental fayence. Butter pots and drinking cups, similar to the quaint beer vessels of the Germans, were made in Staffordshire, about the same period, from a kind of brick earth, and were glazed, like our common earthen pans, with lead ore. A better style of pottery prevailed at the period of the Revolution, for many of the beer cups were ornamented with figures in white pipe-clay, and some were even painted; jars of true stoneware, apparently glazed with salt, were also in common use. The introduction of this process is attributed to two brothers, Dutchmen, of the name of Elers. Having been very successful, and having kept their process secret, they were so persecuted as to be obliged to leave that part of the country. Their secret, however, remained; for a man of the name of Astbury, by feigning to be of weak intellect, succeeded in acquiring a knowledge of the whole process, which he subsequently carried on. A ware of this kind was made at Burslem, in Staffordshire, in 1740, which was ornamented by casting in brass moulds, and is known under the name of *crouch ware*. To the son of this Astbury is usually attributed the introduction of burnt flints into the manufacture of earthenware. In 1759 the celebrated Josiah Wedgewood commenced manufacturing knife handles of pottery in imitation of agate and tortoise-shell melon table-plates, &c., in a small thatched factory. Being successful, he took a second factory, and succeeded in making a kind of white ware; and then a third, in which he fabricated a cream-coloured ware, covered with a good transparent glaze, which was capable of bearing the most sudden transition of temperature. Wedgewood, having presented some of this ware to Queen Charlotte, was appointed her potter, and at her request the ware was called "Queen's Ware." At first it was quite plain, then a coloured rim or border was introduced, and finally, the whole surface was covered; many of these designs, especially those of flowers and leaves, were exceedingly well executed.

Wedgewood subsequently invented various other wares, which are well known, such as his *terra cotta*, upon which he was able to revive the ancient style of painting upon a bisque ground without glaze. His "basaltes," so called from its resemblance to basalt, was a stone-like biscuit, so hard as to take a high polish, in which he modelled a great number of vases and other vessels, ornamented frequently with finely-executed bassi relievi in red and white. A number of domestic articles were also fashioned out of it, such as teapots, cream-ewers, &c., which were much admired. Another of his wares was of a cane colour, and nearly resembled the ware now known under the name of "cane ware." The most beautiful, however, of all wares was that called jasper, which was of a peculiar white jasper-like appearance, and in hardness and other properties, except colour, resembled his basaltes. It had the remarkable property of being coloured throughout its mass with metallic oxides exactly as glass; this peculiarity, which distinguishes it from all other kinds of biscuit, either ancient or modern, rendered it especially adapted for forming ornaments like cameos. Thus the body may be stained of any colour, such as dark blue, or even the brown of the sard, while the relief was in pure white. Of this kind was his copy of the celebrated Barberini or Portland vase, the body of which is of a deep blue, with relievo figures of pure white. It would occupy pages to merely enumerate the original works and copies of antique vases, lamps, candelabra, busts, statuettes, &c., which were produced by Wedgewood at his works; which soon became a village, to which he gave the name of Etruria, in commemoration of the ancient seat of the ceramic arts. Whether we consider the improvements effected by Wedgewood in the material, the various processes of manufacture, or the artistic skill which is displayed in his productions, and upon which he spared no cost, we must look upon him as the father of British fictile manufactures, and worthy to rank with Luca della Robbia, Pallissy, Reaumur, and Böttger. Indeed in the artistic point of view it is questionable whether any other English manufacturer has ever produced articles of purer and more elevated taste than Wedgewood.

In the preceding observations we have only noticed the development of the common pottery ware in England; but long prior to Wedgewood's successful inventions attempts had been made to produce true porcelain, but, which, as in France, eventuated in producing a kind of semi-vitrified glass. It would appear that a factory for the manufacture of this kind of ware was established at Chelsea as early as the year 1698. The articles made were inferior, and painted in imitation of the Chinese; but in the year 1740 it appears to have acquired some importance. Under the patronage of the Duke of Cumberland, and some other persons, it attained its highest celebrity during a period of about fifteen years, from 1750 to 1765. Coeval with the establishment of the factory at Chelsea was one at Stratford-le-Bow, where a very similar kind of ware was made, known as Bow china, and now much sought after by collectors; the factory did not, however, survive very long, having been relinquished before the period at which Chelsea had acquired its greatest celebrity. In 1750 a manufactory of porcelain was commenced at Derby, to which the workmen and artists employed at Chelsea went after that factory was given up. In 1751 the Worcester Porcelain Company was founded through the exertions of a Dr. Wall of that city, to whom is usually attributed the invention of printing patterns upon earthenware; and, in 1772, a factory was set up at Coalport, which also rose to eminence under the direction of John Turner, who was induced to come from Worcester, and to whom the invention of printing of patterns upon earthenware is also attributed. He may have improved the art, but it was certainly known before his time. The manufacture of porcelain did not thrive after the invention of Wedgewood; being little superior to his ware, although far dearer, indeed, so dear that Dr. Johnson says, in reference to the Derby china, in 1777, that he could have vessels of silver as cheap as those made of porcelain. Hence no manufacture of true hard porcelain was established in England until within the last few years.

Mr. Shaw, in his "Chemistry of Pottery," thus enumerates the successive inventions which were introduced into the manufacture of Staffordshire ware, and which led to the present unrivalled position of this great and important trade:—"In this succession I find the *common brown ware* till 1680; then the Shelton clay (long previously used by the tobacco-pipe makers of Newcastle), mixed with grit from Baddeley Hedge, by Thomas Miles; of *coarse white stone-ware*, and the same grit and can-marle, or clunch of the coal-seams, by his brother, into *brown stone-ware*. The *crouch-ware* was first made of common potters' clay and grit from Moel Cop, and afterwards the grit and can-marle, by A. Wedgewood, of Burslem, in 1690; and the ochreous brown clay and manganese into a coarse *Egyptian black* in 1700, by Wood, of Hot-lane. The employment of the Devonshire pipe-clay by Twyford and Astbury, of Shelton, supplied the *white dipped* and the *white stone-ware*; from which the transition was easy to the *flint-ware*, by Daniel Bird, of Stoke; the *chalk body-ware*, by Chatterly and Palmer, of Hanley; and the *Queen's-ware* of the celebrated Josiah Wedgewood. Mr. Thomas Toft introduced aluminous shale, or *fire-brick clay*; Mr. William Sans, *manganese* and *galena* pulverized; Messrs. John Palmer and William Adams, *common salt* and *litharge*; Messrs. Elers, Brothers, *red clay*, or marl and *ochre*; Mr. Josiah Twyford, *pipe-clay*; Mr. Thomas Astbury, *flint*; Mr. Ralph Shaw, *basaltes*; Mr. Aaron Wedgewood, *red lead*; Mr. William Littler, *calcined bone earth*; Mr. Enoch Booth, *white lead*; Mrs. Warburton, *soda*; Mr. Ralph Daniel, *calcined gypsum*; Josiah Wedgewood, Esq., *barytes*; Mr. John Cookworthy, *decomposed white granite*; Mr. James Ryan, British *kaolin and petuntse*; Messrs. Ladler and Green, glaze printing; Mr. Warner Edwards, biscuit painting; Mr. Thomas Daniel, glaze enamelling; Mr. William Smith, burnished gilding; Mr. Peter Warburton, printing in gold; Messrs. John Hancock, John Gardner, and William Hennys, lustres; Mr. William Brooks, engraved landscapes and printing in colours; Mr. William Wainwright Potts, printing by machine, and continuous sheet of paper; and the same gentleman, with Mr. William Machin, and Mr. William Bourne, for printing flowers, figures, &c., in colours, by machine, and continuous sheet of paper."

We can record no history of pottery in Ireland: for beyond the manufacture of coarse glazed brown ware, garden pots, &c., no manufacture of earthenware or porcelain deserving the name has ever been carried on in this country. A great many stone-ware jars, dating, perhaps, from the end of the seventeenth century, have been found in Ireland; but although many of them may have been made in the country, we know of no positive evidence to that effect. About thirty years ago, Mr. Donovan, of this city, made a large fortune by importing white glazed china from England, and decorating it in enamel colours, at a factory on the North Wall; but he had no successor. Salt-glazed stone-ware was made in Cork in two factories about fifteen to twenty years ago; but we believe the manufacture is now extinct, an observation which, perhaps, also applies to the rest of Ireland. A very successful effort has been recently made by Mr. Walker, at Larne, in the county of Antrim, to produce Rockingham cane and black glazed ware, many specimens of which were exhibited; and we hope that ere long this branch of trade will take root in the country.

Having now given as complete a sketch of the history of pottery as our space would permit, we shall say a few words upon the classification of the different wares alluded to. For this purpose we shall adopt the classification of Brongniart, the greatest modern authority upon the ceramic arts. This classification is founded, in a great measure, upon the nature of the materials employed, and coincides, in many respects, with the historical development of the manufacture. Pottery may be first conveniently divided into two great divisions:—1. Pottery, properly so called; and 2. Porcelain. The subdivisions of the first class are—

| | |
|---|---|
| Soft Pottery, . . . . . . . . . | Unglazed.<br>Lustrous.<br>Glazed.<br>Enamelled. |
| Hard pottery, . . . . . . . . . | Fine earthenware.<br>Stoneware. |

Soft pottery is composed of clay, sand, and lime, a mixture which would be represented by a common marly clay; it is easily scratched with a knife, very fusible, and hence the term "soft" applied to it. The subdivisions are founded upon the presence or absence of a glaze and its nature: thus a garden-pot would represent the first subdivision, which would include bricks and tiles, and jars moulded, or vases turned upon a lathe, whether pale-yellow, red, ashy gray, or black. The ancient utensils and vases of Egypt, the old Roman water-jars, the Spanish tinajas and alcarazza's, and some common pitchers, pans, and crocks, are examples of the first-named colours; while Egyptian mummy cones, many bottles and amphoræ of ancient Greece and Rome, and of Peru, India; chimney-pots, milk-pans, &c., are red; the old Celtic cinereal urns are examples of the gray; and the vases of Etruria and Volterra among the ancients, and the black ware of Staffordshire among the moderns, represent the fourth colour. The second subdivision, or lustrous soft pottery, are simply the last-mentioned kinds covered with a very thin glassy coating, such as many of the Egyptian, Tyrrhenian, Etruscan, Greek, and Roman vases of the finer kinds. The third subdivision consists of vessels made of the same materials as the first and second classes, but covered with a thick varnish or glaze produced by dusting the object over with lead ore, or with a mixture of lead ore and clay, sometimes coloured with oxides of other metals, as iron and manganese. The common glazed pottery of all the world affords examples of this kind. The fourth class, or enamelled soft pottery, is formed of much the same body as all the varieties mentioned, but is generally of a lighter colour, and is covered with an opaque enamel consisting of a glass made of sand, and oxides of tin and lead. The opacity of the glaze, which depends upon the oxide of tin, hides the colour of the body or bisque, and admits, therefore, of this kind of ware being decorated with painting. The Moresco-Spanish and Catholic Spanish Azulejos, the articles made by Luca della Robbia, Majolica or Faenza ware, Pallissy ware, Delft, Majolica of Nuremberg, &c., are examples of this kind of soft pottery.

Hard pottery is the intermediate stage between the soft clay wares and porcelain; its hardness and slightly vitrified appearance distinguish it from the former, and its opacity from the latter. It is subdivided into two kinds:—1. Fine earthenware, in which the body is more or less white, and the glaze a lead glass, of which Wedgewood ware was an example; and 2. Stoneware, which is formed of more or less coloured clays, sometimes unglazed, or covered with a soda glass produced by the decomposition of common salt. Common jars, sewerage pipes, &c., are examples of this kind of ware.

Porcelain differs from earthenware by being translucent, being, in fact, an opaque paste of clay permeated by a kind of glass, exactly as paper is by wax in wax paper. The body or paste is always hard, and generally of a pure white colour; and relatively to soft pottery very infusible; and is, perhaps, in all instances, made of kaolin, derived from decomposed felspar. The glaze is formed of undecomposed felspar and quartz, with sometimes gypsum, boracic acid, &c., but never lead or tin. There are three distinct kinds of porcelain, depending chiefly upon their relative fusibility, and consequently upon their composition. First, true, or porcelain with a naturally hard paste, composed of kaolin, and glazed with felspar containing quartz, which is hard and translucid, the glass not being liable to be scratched by a knife; Chinese, Japanese, Berlin, Dresden, and other German porcelains, and modern Sevres (since 1769), are examples of this kind. The second kind of porcelain is much more fusible, the glass may be scratched with a knife, the body or paste is said to be naturally soft, and it consists of substances which may be fused with comparative facility. Modern English china which contains gypsum, bones, &c., is of this kind; old English china is also of the same kind, such as Chelsea, Derby, Bow, and Worcester. The third kind is composed of difficultly fusible materials, but rendered fusible by the addition of salts, an example of which we have given in the case of old Sevres, which is the typical example of this kind of porcelain, and hence said to be formed of a paste artificially soft. The celebrated Capo di Monti porcelain, from near Naples, and that known as Buen Retiro' from Madrid, are also examples of this kind.

Besides the illustrations of the different kinds of soft pottery, stoneware, and English china, true porcelain was abundantly illustrated by a good collection of Chinese and Japanese ware in Hewet's Chinese collection; by the splendid collection of modern Sevres ware contributed by the French Government, and among which were specimens of rare beauty; and by the corresponding collections of Berlin porcelain contributed by the King of Prussia. The valuable and well-selected collection of old porcelain contributed by the Honourable General Lygon represented many of the varieties which we have alluded to in the present notice, such as old Dresden, Berlin, Vienna, Fürstenburg, Capo di Monti, old Sevres, Derby, Chelsea, old Worcester, Coalport, &c. On the whole, perhaps, the best and most completely illustrated branch of industry in the Exhibition were the ceramic manufactures.—W. K. S.

---

1. BATTAM & SON, Gough-square, London, Manufacturers.—A collection of terra cotta vases, copied from the antique in the British Museum and other collections.

2. BELL, J. & Co., Glasgow Pottery, Glasgow, Manufacturers.—Dinner services, in pearl and stone-ware; dessert service in pearl-ware; tea service in porcelain toilet services, in various styles; jugs in pearl-ware and Parian; salt-cellar (shell and dolphin) in Parian; candlesticks in pearl-ware; Ariosto's inkstand, after the antique in Parian; cornucopias (stag's head) after the antique, in pearl-ware; vases, in Parian, pearl-ware, and terra-cotta; bust of Jenny Lind; statuettes of Dante, Petrarch, Kilmeny, (from the Queen's Wake, and modelled by Mossman), in Parian; balustrade and large vessels in terra cotta; fancy flower pots in majolica ware; with other articles in Parian, porcelain, ironstone, &c.

3. BOURNE, J., & SON, Denby Pottery, near Derby, Manufacturers.—Glazed ware, viz.:—bottles for ink, blacking, porter, ginger beer, etc.; feet and carriage warmers, jars, jugs, &c.; vases, flower pots, wine, butter, and water-coolers, in buiscuit ware, manufactured from the same clay as the glazed ware; electric telegraph insulators.

4. COPELAND, W. T., Manufacturer, Stoke-upon-Trent, Staffordshire; and New Bond-street, London.—Works in "statuary porcelain" in great variety, after eminent artists; works in porcelain, comprising vases of different kinds, dessert and tea services, slabs and other articles; samples of printed earthenware.

5. DANIELL, A. B. & R. P., Wigmore-street, and New Bond-street, London.—Variety of ornamental porcelain vases, trays, inkstands, &c.; specimens of plates, and cups and saucers, in Sevres style, "Rose Dubarry," &c.; a pattern plate of the royal dessert service, executed by command of Her Majesty, and presented to the Emperor of Russia.

6. DEERING, J., Middleton, Co. Cork.—Specimens of Staffordshire china and Rockingham ware, made by Thomas Green, Fenton, Staffordshire, from clay found at Rostellan, Cork Harbour.

7. KERR, W. H. & Co., Royal Porcelain Works, Worcester, Manufacturers.—"The Shakespeare" desert service, introducing groups in statuary illustrative of the "Midsummer Night's Dream," modelled by W. B. Kirk, A. R. H. A.; manufactured from materials principally the produce of Ireland; "Uncle Tom and Eva," in statuary porcelain, by W. B. Kirk; bust of the Duke of Leinster, in Irish statuary porcelain, and statuette of Dr. Hahnemann, in porcelain, by the same artist; busts of W. Dargan, Esq., and Sir Robert Kane, by J. E. Jones, in "Irish statuary porcelain;" the Moore and Wellington vases, by J. Kirk, A. R. H. A., in Irish statuary porcelain; vases; groups of animals; wedding tray and vase; specimens of Worcester china, dinner, dessert, breakfast, and tea services; card trays, exhibiting specimens of painting on porcelain; dejeuner and ink trays, &c.; painted vases; specimens of the old Worcester painting on vases, cabinet, cups.

8. LEETCH, T., Dame-street, Dublin, Importer.—Stone, china, and earthenware, comprising dinner, tea, breakfast, and toilet services, &c.

9. LYGON, GENERAL THE HONOURABLE EDWARD, Spring Hill, Broadway, Worcestershire, Proprietor.—Specimens of foreign and British porcelain, consisting of upwards of sixty different pieces.

10. MAYER, T. J., & JOSEPH, Dale Hall Pottery, Longport, Staffordshire.—Parian statuettes, vases, &c.; stone china, real ironstone, opaque porcelain, earthenware, &c.

11. RIDGWAY, J. & Co., Staffordshire Potteries.—China and earthenware in variety.

12. ROE, GEORGE, D. L., Nutley, Donnybrook, Proprietor.—A harlequin set of rich Berlin china in a glass-case; two vases of Sevres china, ornamented with paintings, relieved in gold; two Chinese decanters of Dresden china, and shades.

13. ROSE, J. & Co., Coalbrookdale, Shropshire, Manufacturers: GREGG & SON, Upper Sackville-street, Dublin, Exhibiters.—China dinner, dessert, and tea services, in Celtic body, a new composition; vases, similar to Sevres china; trays, inkstands, &c., similar to Sevres china; jars, beakers, &c., in coloured china; Parian statuary group, from the "Faerie Queen;" large Parian pierced vase supported by sea horses; large group of "Puck and companions," from "Midsummer's Night Dream;" cabinet, dessert plates, and tea cups; new "supper service," complete.

14. RUFFORD, F. T., Stourbridge, and Wharf City Road, London, Manufacturer.—Porcelain bath (patentees, Rufford and Finch); the body of fire-clay, the inner surface veneered with porcelain, and glazed as pottery, both white and marble.

15. TOBIN, T., Ballincollig, Co. Cork, Proprietor.—Modern Sevres cup and saucer, painted with portrait and scenes from the life of the Duchess De La Valliere; old Sevres cup and saucer, with miniature portrait and monogram of La Princesse de Lamballe.

16. WARREN, C. M., Essex-street, Dublin, Importer.—Statuettes, group, and bust, in Parian; china, table, dessert, breakfast, tea and coffee, and toilet services; stone and earthenware.

17. WESTENHOLZ, BROTHERS, London, Importers.—Copies in porcelain of Thorwaldsen's sculptures, produced at the Royal Porcelain Manufactory in Copenhagen; statuettes in great variety.

# CLASS XXVI.

## FURNITURE AND UPHOLSTERY, INCLUDING PAPER HANGINGS, PAPIER MACHE, ETC.

THE objects comprised in this class are of general interest, from their being so intimately associated with the comforts and conveniences of civilized life; and their proper construction is of great importance, both in a utilitarian and artistic point of view, from the great influence which the articles by which we are constantly surrounded exercise on the mind, and the extent to which they retard or facilitate the progress of popular artistic education. While furniture but sparingly admits of ornament without offending good taste, on account of the inadaptation of the material employed, as well as the uses for which it is designed, other departments in this class afford abundant opportunities for artistic display; the business of the upholsterer and decorator being of a purely artistic character, and the production of papier mache goods being purely what is called an art-manufacture.

### I.—FURNITURE AND UPHOLSTERY.

In this department of the Exhibition there was an adequate representation, so far as regards the finer and more elaborately ornamented articles. However much this class of objects of any kind are to be admired, it is to be recollected that their use is confined to the few; and in an educational and utilitarian point of view we are disposed to attach much more importance to an illustration of improved and tasteful construction in the articles coming within the reach of the middle classes than in those intended for the wealthier portion of the community. But in this respect the department of the Exhibition to which we now direct attention was sadly deficient. Of the commoner descriptions of articles there were few illustrations. Our cabinet-makers evidently believe that they best recommend themselves to the notice of the public by producing goods displaying all sort of elaborate ornamentation in carving and inlaying. They accordingly devoted themselves to this object in preparing for the Exhibition, and we are free to confess that they achieved a considerable degree of success in its attainment. The production of such articles we are by no means prepared to undervalue; on the contrary, we believe that without these the Exhibition would not have been complete. But the exclusion of the more gorgeous and expensive articles of furniture we do not regard as a greater mistake than confining attention solely to them. In the construction of the furniture of the middle classes there is unquestionably much room for improvement; and the illustration of judicious attempts in this direction would be a matter of primary importance. In looking through the exhibition of decorative art in bronze and other metals, we could not fail to be struck with surprise at the great degree of success which has been attained in combining graceful forms with utility, and at moderate prices—not merely in the collections of the Continental manufacturers, but also in those of the Coalbrookdale Company, of Elkington and Mason, and of a number of others. A similar degree of success is not attainable in wood, and therefore not to be calculated on. But it is beyond doubt that much remains to be done in the improvement of the construction of the common articles of domestic furniture; and we believe that some of our cabinet-makers would have served their own purpose more effectually by successful efforts in the direction here indicated, than by the exhibition of the most costly article which can adorn the palace.

At the Exhibition of 1851 the collection of furniture was obnoxious to the same remark, and the Jury intrusted with the duty of reporting on that class observe, that "though fully sensible of the great beauty of many of the ornamental works in furniture, yet we regret that there have not been more specimens of ordinary specimens for general use; works whose merits consist in correct proportion, simple but well-considered design, beauty of material, and perfect workmanship." This occurred in 1851, yet we have to regret precisely the same circumstance in 1853.

As an illustration of the extent to which utilitarian articles were passed over in the overweening desire of the great majority of the exhibiters for show, we would call attention to the remarkable fact of scarcely a single article of bed-room furniture being exhibited. The reason of such an omission was obvious to those who attentively examined the several collections. The furniture of bed-rooms does not generally afford an opportunity for the display of that high degree of ornamentation in carving and gilding so much sought after by the great bulk of the exhibiters; and hence, in making up collections for the Exhibition, it received no attention at their hands. It must be conceded, however, that in the modification of the furniture of our bed-rooms, especially with a view of combining elegance and economy, much still remains to be done; and successful efforts in this direction would have formed highly acceptable contributions to the Furniture Court of the Exhibition.

Extravagant ornamentation, without much regard to appropriateness of design, is the great mistake usually committed in the manufacture of the higher class of furniture; but there is another error which is equally to be avoided, and of which the Exhibition furnished abundant illustrations—the use of inappropriate materials both in construction and ornamentation. The extended use of papier mache in the formation of a variety of articles for useful and ornamental purposes has led, for example, to an application of this substance altogether out of character with its peculiar properties—we allude to the construction of chairs and the smaller class of tables for the drawing-room and the boudoir. Than this, however, there can be no greater mistake. A papier mache table or chair can scarcely have the degree of strength which we expect in the smallest articles of this kind; and even if it had it must convey the idea of insecurity. This is an illustration of the total misapplication of a material capable of being formed into some of the most beautiful articles, but which in the construction of such an object as a table is comparatively worthless. Again, there were small tables in the Furniture Court composed of leather and gutta percha, which would possibly be deserving of commendation, if we had no such substance as wood of which to make our tables; but which we can regard as nothing better than absurdities, and as being altogether unworthy of a place in the Exhibition Building.

In the manufacture of articles of furniture certain definite principles should be kept in view. The construction itself should be evident, and if ornamentation be introduced, it should be by decorating the construction, and not by overlaying and disguising it. Beauty of design does not necessarily imply high ornamentation. The most simple article may be really beautiful, while some of the elaborately ornamented objects are absolutely offensive to good taste, from the attention being chiefly directed to the production of a profusion of fancy workmanship. It must be constantly borne in mind that unnecessary embellishment, besides needlessly adding to the cost, interferes with the use and convenience of the object; and good taste will be best consulted by seeking to attain the greatest effect by the smallest possible amount of ornament.

Several varieties of wood are used for making furniture, but the most generally employed, and, we may add, that best adapted for the greatest variety of objects, is mahogany. This material is, however, of comparatively modern introduction for the purpose, its first use in England for cabinet work being about 1720. Its value for the purpose appears to have been ascertained through an accidental circumstance:—A West Indian captain, named Gibbons, gave a few planks of mahogany to his brother, then an eminent physician in London; and being brought across the Atlantic as ballast, no special value was assigned to them. Dr. Gibbons wished to use them in a house which he was building in King-street, Covent Garden; but the workmen threw them aside as useless from the hardness and the consequent difficulty of working the wood with their tools. Subsequently a piece of it was used for making some common articles for the kitchen, in which it appeared to so much advantage that a bureau was afterwards made of it. The fine colour and general effect of the wood were so much admired in this article that strangers were brought to see it, and, among others, the Duchess of Buckingham. That lady was so much pleased with the wood that she obtained some of it from Dr. Gibbons to be made into a bureau. It soon became the fashion to make cabinet work of mahogany; and in this case the verdict of fashion was fully confirmed by the intrinsic value of the material, which has since brought it into more extended use than any other kind of wood. Rosewood, walnut, and ebony, are also employed, chiefly in fancy work; but when we consider the applicability of mahogany for almost all kinds of objects included in this class, its hardness and durability, the beauty of the grain, and the high polish of which it is susceptible, we shall find that it exceeds every other in value to the cabinet-maker.

Into a detailed account of the various kinds of cabinet work it would not be possible for us to enter without exceeding the limits of such a notice as the present. Of marqueterie and buhl-work there were numerous examples in the Exhibition; and there were also many good specimens of ornamental carving.

While much of the elaborately ornamented work was of a character not admitting of complimentary criticism, there was also much which could not be regarded without unqualified admiration. The gem of the department was a magnificent carved sideboard, exhibited by Jackson and Graham, of London, the decoration of which was appropriate, consisting of game and fish, fruit of different kinds, bunches of grapes and heads of barley, as emblematic of the viands with which the article in question has so intimate a connexion,—the whole presenting a specimen of decorative carving which it is impossible to compliment too highly. A pier-glass and table from J. J. Byrne, of Henry-street, was also deserving of honourable mention. R. Sparks and R. Strahan also exhibited ornamental cabinet work which would do credit to any establishment.

The suite of decorative furniture manufactured by A. Jones and Son, of Stephen's-green, is deserving of more than a passing notice, on account of the ambitious character of the design, and the elaborate ornamentation which is extended even to the smallest articles. Having come several times before the public, and more especially during the Exhibitions of 1851 and 1853, this suite of furniture has become familiar almost to every one. The furniture, which is of Irish bog yew, is intended to illustrate ancient Irish history and antiquities; the ornamentation being derived from objects of interest in Ireland, its monarchs and illustrious characters, historic events, extinct and existing animal and vegetable productions, national emblems, legends, and monuments. The timber was selected on account of its appropriateness to the object, the bog yew conveying the idea of antiquity by its peculiar tints. The suite comprises a cabriolet sofa, an occasional table, a circular table, a tea poy, an omnium, whist table, loo table, lady's work table, stand for time-piece, pair of pole fire-screens, arm chair, semicircular side table, sarcophagus, and music temple.

The collection of furniture exhibited by William Fry and Co. contained a variety of articles, all unexceptionable as to design, and some of great beauty. An ottoman attracted much attention as showing a graceful modification of an article which admits of a great variety of forms, which is not necessarily expensive, and which might be introduced to a much larger extent than it is at present.

We cannot conclude this notice of the Furniture Court without an expression of regret that the Exhibition did not contain an adequate illustration of furniture from some of the Continental States, which would have been no less interesting to our manufacturers than to the general public. A suite of drawing-room and dining-room furniture of a high class from Paris, Brussels, Berlin, or Vienna, would have been eminently suggestive, as affording the means of comparison with similar articles in use here. The only illustrations of

Continental furniture were those supplied by Thonet, Brothers, of Vienna, and J. Hassa, of same place; the latter consisting of grotesque forms of sofas, forming articles so deficient in all the necessary requirements, that we should not regard them as worth the expense of transit. The articles exhibited by MM. Thonet, Brothers, were, however, deserving of attention, on account of a certain speciality of construction, the general use of which in the cheaper class of goods would tend to still further diminish the cost of production. They consisted of chairs, sofa, and tables, the former having cane seats, and the great peculiarity consisting in the employment of bent beech in imitation of rosewood, so as to dispense with the usual mortice and tenon work. The entire framework of the chairs and sofa, and the stand of the table, were formed of this material, bent, of course, by the aid of steam, and forming rather graceful combinations.

On the subject of Upholstery we have little to say in connexion with the illustrations presented by the Exhibition. We may, however, observe that it is rather remarkable, notwithstanding our Schools of Design and our boasted progress in the application of art, that we should still find those monstrous misapplications of worsted work to pictorial representation, which we cannot but regard as a disgrace to the age in which we live. To future generations it will be matter of astonishment that in the first half of the nineteenth century, so famous for the discoveries to which it can lay claim, the production of fantastic forms in what is called Berlin work should have occupied months, frequently even years, of female education,—that for weeks in succession the inmates of even our fashionable boarding-schools, instead of acquiring some knowledge which would be useful to them in after life, devoted their time to the production of covers for footstools, with attempted artistic decorations which would positively offend the eye of the veriest savages. Yet such is the fact. The misspent time which this work involves, the utter worthlessness of the material which caused so great a sacrifice, and the perversion of the taste of those engaged in it to which it must give rise, have led to a reaction against it; but the great extent to which pictorial representations, of different kinds, in this worsted work was to be met with in the Exhibition shows that it still enjoys a degree of favour vastly disproportioned to its deserts.

## II.—ROOM PAPERS AND DECORATIONS.

The objects coming under this head comprise decorations for walls and ceilings, and imitations of woods and marbles. So far as regards the space occupied they did not constitute a very important feature of the Exhibition; but among them were many specimens not only of much promise, but which reflected great credit on the establishments in which they were produced. There is no other department in which the sentiments of a people, on matters of taste, are more fully illustrated than in that pertaining to the decorations of their dwellings,—those objects with which they are most familiarized, and which in turn exert an important influence on themselves. The paucity of ornament, and even what little there is of a vulgar character, more conclusively establishes the position of a community, as regards their appreciation of works of art, than could be done in any other way. Wherever a true knowledge and love of the beautiful exists, means will not be wanting to present indications of it even in the humblest cottage. With the masses, contrasts of glaring colours are too much sought after, to the neglect of those more sober tints which a higher degree of refinement would select. In bringing about an improvement in this respect manufacturers have it in their power to do much by giving their efforts a constant tendency in the right direction; at the same time we must bear in mind that, as their chief concern must be to produce what will find a ready market, they must, to a great extent, be guided by the popular taste. An excess of ornament and high colouring find favour with the multitude and we need not be surprised that they should be produced in such profusion.

Paper hangings, and decorations of which room papers form the basis, have recently become of great importance in these countries from the comparatively low price at which they are produced, and the consequent great extent to which they are employed. They are, however, of comparatively modern use, for although it is over two centuries since paper hangings were first made, it is within the past few years that the great impetus has been given to their production in these countries. In times gone by room papers were considered fit objects for taxation; and this, of course, involved the imposition of high duties on imported goods, thereby preventing that improvement which is an invariable concomitant of free competition. The home trade was protected by a duty of 12*d.* per square yard up to 1846, when it was reduced to 2*d.* A great increase in the quantity of imported goods followed the change, and great progress has in consequence been made in the art in the short interval which has since elapsed.

In the manufacture of room papers it is obvious that there will be as many different printings as there are colours employed, each colour being the object of a separate operation; and each block following the other on the guide marks left by the previous impression.

The great tendency of modern times to cheapen the cost of production has been developed in the manufacture of paper hangings, though not to the same extent as in many other departments of trade. While the finer qualities are still produced by what is termed hand printing, machine printing is successfully used for the cheaper kinds. The introduction of machinery of this class only dates some twelve years back, at which time Messrs. Potter, of Darwen, by means of steam power, artificial drying, and an endless roll of paper, succeeded in producing, by surface-roller printing, patterns having a very good effect; specimens showing fourteen colours having been exhibited by them in 1851. This machine printing is destined to completely supersede hand printing in all the inferior kinds of goods; though the latter method of production must still be employed for the articles of a superior class. The whole trade has, however, been much improved by the recent large importations of French papers, the effect of which has not been confined to the more expensive kinds, but has even extended to the very cheapest. We now frequently see efforts at imitation of French colours and patterns in papers sold at a few pence per dozen yards, a circumstance the tendency of which is hopeful in an eminent degree.

The collection of papers in the Exhibition presented many specimens in which good taste was displayed. Of the attempts at decoration we can say little, the effect of none of them being satisfactory; but this may in some degree, be accounted for by the absence of adequate arrangements for their display. There was one ambitious attempt at decoration on the north side of the Furniture Court, but the ornament was out of all proportion to the space which it occupied, and the effect was in consequence anything but agreeable. Of painted woods there were many beautiful specimens; and some of the best of these, moreover, were executed by native workmen. Some of the painted doors in this department left little to be desired.—J. S.

## III.—PAPIER-MACHÉ GOODS.

Papier-maché goods have of late become of considerable importance as articles of utility and of decorative furniture, from the facility with which that substance can be moulded into any required shape, and the great extent to which it admits of ornamentation.

The old form of making papier-maché from pulp, whence the name, is but little practised in England at present, except for the cheapest articles. The mass is now formed by pasting a number of sheets of paper together, a process first employed in the year 1740, by Martin, of Paris. The advantages of this process are increased solidity, firmness, and elasticity—at the same time that the mass is readily made to assume the full sharpness of the moulds. The article is formed by simply pasting, one on the other, a number of sheets of a fine gray, slightly sized, not very strong, packing paper. The paste is usually made of a mixture of glue and starch. The sheets thus pasted are not pressed, except in particular cases, but are rubbed smooth with a kind of smoothing-iron. Legs of tables and other similar articles are usually formed upon moulds, or rather cores of well-baked wood; each sheet, as it is pasted upon the form, being carefully rubbed smooth. When a sufficient number of sheets of paper have been pasted together to produce the required thickness, the mass is introduced into an oven, or drying-chamber; where a core is used the article with the core still attached is placed in the oven. In twelve hours the drying is completed, and the mass becomes as hard as wood, and of a uniformity of texture seldom found in wood; it is then cut and turned as required, hollow articles being turned externally while still adhering to their core. In certain cases it is necessary, in order to remove the core, to cut the papier-mache into two symmetrical halves, which are afterwards glued together, again baked, and then turned. The next operation is to rub the articles smooth with pumice and sand-paper, after which they are saturated with a mixture of oil of tar and linseed oil, stoved, lacquered, and ornamented with designs; and are then ready to be gilded, or inlaid with mother-of-pearl.

There are two ways of employing the mother-of-pearl: the first is to soften the shell in water, and while in this state to saw out, by hand, the rough form which the ornament is to have, and of a somewhat larger size than it is to appear when subsequently finished. The pieces thus cut are rubbed perfectly even and smooth, and are then imbedded in their proper places on the article in a thick coat of the tar varnish, of the consistence of honey, which is employed for the ground upon which the finer varnish is subsequently laid. The article is next placed in the lacquering stove, and when fully dried, is again coated with another coating of the ground varnish; the mother-of-pearl ornaments being also covered, and again stoved. The mother-of-pearl can now be distinguished only by the inequality of surface which it produces. These inequalities are ground off, by which the mother-of-pearl is fully exposed, its surface being even with that of the rest of the article. The whole is then ready for painting and gilding, and receiving the last coating of fine varnish. The second method of inlaying is that patented by Jennens and Bettridge, and consists in reserving the ornament or design by sketching it, with some kind of varnish not acted upon by acid, upon a piece of the shell ground and polished upon revolving wheels, as in the other case, and then etching away the surrounding unprotected portions by means of an acid. This process possesses several advantages, one of which is, that it is much cheaper than where the design is cut out by hand.

The process of painting presents nothing peculiar; but the method of gilding is very ingenious. The part to be gilded is covered with gold leaf just before the coating of varnish has fully dried, and while it is still adhesive enough to allow of the gold leaf adhering to it; upon this gilded surface the ornament, which is to appear in gold, is designed by means of a copal varnish, or of a solution of bitumen, somewhat like Brunswick black, which resists water, but is soluble in oil of turpentine. The varnish is then allowed to dry to such a degree as to withstand a slight rubbing, but still to be readily acted upon by a solvent. The superfluous gold is removed with a damp cloth, whilst that protected by the varnish remains attached; the latter is then dissolved off with turpentine, and the gilded ornament exposed. The whole surface is subsequently covered with a coating of fine copal varnish.

The manufacture of articles in papier-maché, of the kind described, has become a great branch of trade in England, to which, indeed, it is almost confined. For many purposes it possesses very many valuable properties, which would, no doubt, recommend a much more extensive use of it, if the present oppressive and impolitic duty on paper was removed. The tediousness of the process, joined with this duty, render, however, the cost of papier-maché articles so very high, that they can only be purchased by the wealthy. Considering the price paid for them, and the class which, alone, can afford to purchase them, but little taste is exhibited in the decoration of English papier-maché goods.

The manufacture was well illustrated in the Exhibition by several manufacturers; and Messrs. Jennens and Bettridge, of Birmingham, contributed, independent of articles of furniture, a complete and exceedingly interesting series of specimens illustrative of the process of manufacture in its different stages.—W. K. S.

---

1. BARKLIE, Miss J. A., Lower Gardiner-street, Dublin.—An Elizabethan chair, in tufted work.

2. BRAKEY & M'DOWELL, Stafford-street, Dublin, Manufacturers.—Large mahogany side-board, supported on two carved figures, representing Peace and Plenty, with the emblems of Painting, Sculpture, and Architecture, carved on the front rail, a large looking-glass at back, in a carved frame, representing England, Ireland, and Scotland, with

the emblems of Agriculture on the bottom rail; window curtains of tabourette, with trimmings suspended from a carved and gilt pole, and original design, with a large plate of looking-glass behind.

3. Bogle, Hugh, & Co., Gordon-street, Glasgow.—Specimens of wall decorations and panelling; twelve imitations of woods and marbles.

4. Boswell, J., Dublin, Manufacturer.—Patterns of paper hangings; specimens of painting for house decoration.

5. Boylan, P., Grafton-street, Dublin, Manufacturer.—Pillars for busts, painted in imitation of marbles; gilt-carved tables, with tops of various marbles inlaid, and of stone painted in flowers; stone table-tops, painted in imitation of marbles, and in the Etruscan style; gilt flower pilasters, carved by Gibbons; ornamented tripod, pedestals, and vases; specimens of paper hangings and ornamented painted doors; print-blocks for the manufacture of paper hangings; frieze in the Etruscan style, executed for the University Club, Dublin.

6. Boyle, R. B., Mary-street, Dublin.—A carved bracket; panel, carved in alto relief, "The wise judgment of Solomon;" a hall chair, carved in oak.

7. Bradshaw, Brothers, Arran Quay, Dublin, Inventors and Manufacturers.—Portable iron tube bedsteads, brass mounted, with screw joints, and with dove-tail joints on a new principle; portable iron bedstead.

8. Bradshaw, R., Grafton-street, Dublin, Proprietor.—Drawing-room window curtain of crimson satin, bordererd with crimson and ormolu brocade, trimmed with superb drapery fringe, tassels, &c., the carved and gilt cornice and the design by Strahan, of Henry-street, Dublin.

9. Buet, A., North Earl-street, Dublin, Designer.—Fancy oval-shaped table in walnut, with carved block and Gothic pillar.

10. Byrne, J. J., Henry-street, Dublin, Manufacturer.—Pier table and glass, carved in the purest Italian style, with a finely moulded black and gold marble top, two inches thick; a walnut cabinet in the Louis XV. style, with outline, enriched with ormolu mouldings; a set of dinner tables of fine St. Domingo mahogany, on two sliding frames; a walnut and marqueterie loo table; a fancy walnut cheval screen; a pole screen; four chairs.

11. Cahill, S., M. D., Stephen's-green, Dublin, Proprietor.—Flower vase of black wood, made in Bombay.

12. Carthy, J., St. Andrew-street, Dublin, Manufacturer.—Perforated zinc fan blind; royal arms on zinc blind; Italian blind.

13. Chaplin, T., Kilkenny, Manufacturer.—A table, made of Irish oak.

14. Clarke, C., Stephen's-green, Dublin, Manufacturer.—Rosewood cabinet, with marble top, and inlaid with marqueterie, with richly carved consoles, a large glass at top, the frame inlaid with marqueterie, and richly carved; a Davenport, on richly carved consoles, with guard at top, representing the Round Towers of Ireland, &c.; rosewood cabriole lounger, with circular end richly carved, upholstered in the German style, and covered with rich silk damask.

15. Clarke, J., Townsend-street, Dublin, Manufacturer.—Wardrobe, marqueterie sofa table.

16. Collins, T., Snowdon-street, Liverpool, Designer and Proprietor.—Articles in hand-wrought papier maché.

17. Curran & Sons, Castle-street, Lisburn.—Large armchair, made from Irish black bog oak, richly sculptured and perforated, the design from the antique.

18. Dargan, Mrs., Mount Anville, Co. Dublin, Exhibiter.—Fine chenille tapestry, mounted as a cheval screen, worked by Miss Haslam, Market Drayton, the mounting executed by William Fry and Co., Dublin.

19. Degroot, C., Jun., Stafford-street, Dublin.—The arms of the Earl of Eglinton, carved in oak; basket of fruit, flowers, and ornament, carved in sycamore; oval picture frame, carved in lime tree; cheval screen frame, carved in rosewood; cheval screen frame, carved in oak.

20. Desfosse, J., Rue de Montreuil, Paris (Agents, Gerhardt, Rottman, & Co., Wood-street, Cheapside, London), Manufacturer.—Panel landscape decorations; paper-hangings, printed from blocks.

21. De Veaux, Mrs. M., Grafton-street, Dublin, Manufacturer.—Chair, worked in the new style of golden tapestry, mounted in rosewood.

22. Dillon, Miss, Artane Castle, Raheny, Co. Dublin, Proprietor.—An ottoman sofa, with semicircular back, in carved and gilt frame, upholstered in embossed needlework.

23. Donne, G., Leadenhall-street, London, Manufacturer.—Gilt console table, with jasper plate glass top; carved and richly gilt chimney-glasses, of new design.

24. Drew, J., Marlborough-street, Dublin, Manufacturer.—Lady's work and writing table; pier cabinet; two specimens of inlaid wine and work-table tops.

25. Egan, J., Killarney, Designer.—Table made from arbutus wood.

26. Eglinton, the Earl of, Proprietor.—A loo table, made of Arbutus wood from Killarney; ladies' work table, with work-box, writing-stand and book-stand, formed from the pillar of the table, the whole elaborately inlaid with 157,000 pieces, designed by Mr. James Egan; a chair, by Curran and Son, of Lisburn, of Irish bog oak, ornamented with shamrocks, roses, thistles, vine leaves, and berries, to suit the needlework by the Countess of Eglinton.

27. Enright, J., Shinrone, King's Co., Designer.—Imitations of foreign and Irish woods and marbles, made of wood and slate, and on paper.

28. Fairclough, J., Renshaw-street, Liverpool, Designer and Manufacturer.—Sideboard, with carvings of fruit and game, the emblems of Plenty, the Four Seasons, &c.

29. Froggott, W., Hall-street, and George's-street, Manchester.—Specimens of patent enamel painting for interior decoration; specimens of imitations of woods and marbles.

30. Fry, W., & Co., Westmoreland-street, Dublin.—Decorative furniture in great variety.

31. Garde, Miss L., Harcourt-terrace, Dublin, Designer.—Rosewood chess table, the top painted with flowers and mosaic, in water colours.

32. Gibson, J., Mary-street, Dublin.—Doors painted in imitation of various woods.

33. Greene, Mrs. John B., Waterloo-terrace, Upper Leeson-street, Dublin.—Table-top, covered with tulip leaves.

34. Grenville, W., Clipstone-street, Fitzroy-square, London, Inventor and Manufacturer.—Imitations of various woods, in paper, applicable to walls, wood-work, ceilings, &c.

35. Grubb, Henry T., & Co., Dublin, Manufacturers.—Full-sized cast iron billiard table, with improved cushions and pocket brasses.

36. Halbert, Thomas, Newtownmountkennedy, Manufacturer.—Circular loo table; a case of small work; ticket cases, needle books, paper knives, watch stands, &c.

37. Hall & Osborne, Paddington-street, Marylebone, Manufacturers.—A large easy chair, in crimson morocco, with new arrangement of stuffing; exhibited to show what may be accomplished by dispensing with all ornaments in the shape of carving, &c.

38. Hornaill, W., Snargate-street, Dover, Manufacturer.—Dover couch, with sliding seat and recumbent end; self-acting reclining couch, adapted to the bed-chamber or boudoir, being convertible to nearly an inclined plane.

39. Jackson & Graham, Oxford-street, London.—Decorative furniture, cabinets, &c.

40. Jackson, T. H., Middle Gardiner-street, Dublin, Designer and Manufacturer.—Carved oak library book-case, in the Italian style; carved oak chair.

41. JEFFREY, ALLEN, & Co., Whitechapel, London, Manufacturers.—Decorative paper hangings.

42. JENNENS & BETTRIDGE, London and Birmingham.—Papier maché and japanned goods.

43. JONES, A., SONS & Co., Stephen's-green, Dublin, Designers and Manufacturers.—A curtain of gold colour satin, with scroll-work border of shaded celeste blue, and cornice of carved wood, gilt; cabinet in brass buhl, with bent plate-glass panels in doors of wings; ducal chairs, in style of Louis XIV., richly carved and gilt; circular table, with marqueterie top, supported on claws of Irish walnut; carved pier table and glass frame; bog yew Davenport desk; antique carved and gilt girandole; suite of chintz window curtains; rosewood screen with panel in needle-work; omnium of three plateaus, with statuette of Brian Boroihme; loo table; three chairs; pole screen, with bas relief of an Irish kerne or light soldier of the tenth century (the last six articles are made of Irish bog yew, and are specimens of a complete suit of furniture made by exhibiters).

44. KEHOE, JAMES, Ballyvelogue, Co. Wexford, Manufacturer.—A tea poy, made of cherry wood, on which are carved Chinese figures, copied from Chinese wardrobes.

45. KERR, J., & Co., Stafford-street, Dublin, Manufacturers.—Fancy cabinet, made of yew 100 years old, grown upon the estate of J. W. L. Naper, Esq., Loughcrew, Oldcastle; oak chair, with arms supported by Irish wolf-dogs, with the civic arms on back, made for the Council Chamber of the Corporation of Dublin; bronze hall table, in the Grecian style, with marble top, supported by two female figures.

46. LABERTOUCHE, G. E., Charlemont-avenue, Kingstown, Designer.—Picture frame, candlesticks, and brackets, ornamented with fruit and flowers, in leather.

47. LAMBERT, R., Goree Piazza, Liverpool.—Iron bedsteads and folding chairs; Rigby's registered cradle.

48. LEVIEN, J. M., Davies-street, Grosvenor-square, London, Designer and Manufacturer.—Escritoire in the style of Louis XIV. of tulip and kingwood, inlaid and ornamented with ormolu, the interior consisting of a velvet writing table, sliding recesses for papers, drawers; an occasional table, inlaid with various woods, and mounted in chased ormolu; inlaid work table of New Zealand woods.

49. LOMBARD, N., Leinster-street, Dublin, Manufacturer.—Looking-glasses, in carved and gilt frames; chimney and pier-glasses, in carved frames, in the old style; carved and gilt tables and drawing-room chair; carved trophy picture frame; girandoles; Florentine mosaic chair (made by Luigi Venturicchio of Florence).

50. LOVE, T., Little Britain, City, London, Inventor and Manufacturer.—Walnut table, and mahogany boxes, with tops of plate glass painted in imitation of marbles, the colours chemically combining with the glass, so as not to be rubbed off.

51. MANSFIELD, WILLIAM, Grafton-street, Dublin, Manufacturer and Importer.—Papier maché goods, comprising dressing cases, work boxes, writing desks, despatch boxes, envelope cases; tables, chairs, tea chests, dressing cases, work boxes, portfolios, pole screens, tea trays, writing desks; patent inlaid gems, pearls, &c.

52. MILLIGAN, MRS., Auburn Lodge, Rathmines-road, Dublin.—Fancy painted chess table with rich flower border; white and gold chess board, mounted with gold pedestal; heraldic chess table, the squares formed of heraldic designs adapted by the knights in the time of King John, the border in black and white designs of a procession and tournament; fancy work table, with group of fruit and flowers, mounted in maple wood and gold; work box, in mineral painting.

53. MOLLOY, T., Ballina, Co. Mayo, Designer.—A table and chair of curious and original design.

54. MORAN & QUIN, Middleton-street, Clerkenwell, London, Inventors and Manufacturers.—Brooch, pin, ring, necklets, steel, and watch cases; Kilburn's registered folding stereoscope, forming in one the case for the photographic miniatures and binocular instrument; anti-warping miniature and jewellery cases; ormolu and imitation ormolu frames; registered folded spring catch bracelet cases.

55. MULLER, A., Sussex-street, Bedford-square, London, Designer.—A painted panel, in decorative style.

56. MURPHY, MRS. M., & MISS I. FOY, Lower Dominick-street, Dublin, Designers.—Chair, in needlework, of various materials; divan in needlework; painted chess table.

57. M'DONAGH, MRS. PLUNKETT, Rathmines-road, Dublin.—Chinese work table, with carved ivory fittings.

58. M'KEON, P., Aungier-street, Dublin, Designer and Manufacturer.—Italian window blind, with spring barrel and weight movements, for drawing-room or parlour windows; outside storm shutter blinds, with inside action; corrugated zinc blind, lace pattern; Venetian blinds; zinc blind, with gilt moulding; ornamented wire blinds; linen blind, mounted on improved spring barrel.

59. NIXON, T., Jun., Rothwell, near Kettering, Northamptonshire, Inventor.—Specimens of Nixon's oil stain on deal, a substitute for paint; a prie dieu, and a lectern, executed in deal, and stained with Nixon's oil stain.

60. NOSOTTI, C. A., Oxford-street, London.—Solid carved and gilt trophies, military and naval, representing species of war, with medallions; a rich ornamented and gilt pedestal, supporting bust of Daniel O'Connell; solid carved and gilt frame, with crayon drawing.

61. NUGENT, MRS., Harcourt-street.—A table inlaid with various emblematical devices.

62. O'NEILL, H., Mary-street, Dublin.—Cabinet and upholstery work.

63. OSBORNE, MRS. C. S., Harcourt-street, Dublin, Designer.—Frames, ornamented with raised coloured flowers.

64. PANTER & CASSIDY, Great Brunswick-street, Dublin.—Specimens of decorations and imitations of fancy marbles and woods, painted in oil.

65. PARKER & Co., St. Vincent Works, Glasgow, Manufacturers.—Paper hangings, in satins, flocks, and bronzes, for dining and drawing-rooms.

66. PATTERSON, W., Dublin, Designer.—Panels painted in imitation of woods and marbles; pillars and table in imitation of marbles.

67. PLUNKETT, BROTHERS, Lower Pembroke-street, Dublin, Producers.—Round tables, painted in imitation of inlaid marbles; pillars in imitation of various marbles; panels painted to imitate several descriptions of woods.

68. RENNER, J. F., Castle-street East, Oxford-street, London, Manufacturer.—Buhl cabinet, inlaid with tortoise-shell, brass, and ebony, &c.; buhl clock-case, with bracket, and bracket for clock or bronze.

69. ROE, GEORGE, D. L., Nutley, Donnybrook, Proprietor.—Clock, mounted in Sevres china, on gilt stand and shade; bronze of Laocöon; two bronze candelabra on tripod; two Pompeii jugs; one marqueterie sofa table, on shaped consols, richly ornamented, with ormolu moulding; two carved chairs, richly gilt, and covered in rich figured satin, made by J. Kerr and Co.

70. ROGERS, W. G., Carlisle-street, Soho, London.—Ornamental carvings, in great variety.

71. ROSS, E., Ellis's-quay, Dublin, Designer and Manufacturer.—Rosewood chiffonier, made to contain a set of portable drawing-room furniture, viz., cabriole couch, easy chair, six chairs, loo table, dinner table, and two sofa tables; portable mahogany drawers, with secretary, the cases to contain these, forming wardrobe and three tables; mahogany cabinet and book shelf, made to hold the furniture of an officer's barrack room; portable reclining easy chair of iron; portable easy chair, forming also a couch; with other portable and camp furniture.

72. RUTHERFORD, J., Castle-street, Belfast, Manufacturer.—Pedestals, painted in imitation of marble.

73. SIBTHORPE, H., & SON, Cork-hill, Dublin.—Two mirrors, the largest ever imported into Ireland.

74. SMITH, MRS. E., Summerhill, Kingstown, Designer.—Mosaic chess table and round table, painted in scagliola.

75. SNELGROVE, GEORGE, Bellarenna, Co. Londonderry.—Breakfast tray of Irish bog yew and oak, inlaid with various natural and coloured woods.

76. SPARKS, R., Suffolk-street, Dublin, Designer and Manufacturer.—Spanish mahogany cabinet sideboard, richly carved, and with glass in pediment; gilt pier table with two glasses, elaborately ornamented; rosewood marchioness, for centre of drawing-room, containing two sofas, back to back, and two easy chairs at ends, richly carved in the French style, and covered with a ponceau figured satin brocatelle.

77. SPIERS & SON, Oxford, Manufacturers.—A table, and other specimens of decorated papier maché.

78. STAR, G. B., Lower Ormond-quay, Dublin, Manufacturer.—Specimens of paper hangings and decorations; pedestals, painted in imitation of marbles.

79. STEWART, J., Clanbrassil-street, Dublin, Designer and Manufacturer.—Inlaid mosaic table, composed of upwards of 3,500 separate pieces, designed and executed by exhibiter, a working chair-maker.

80. STRAHAN, R., Henry-street, Dublin, Designer and Manufacturer.—Rosewood drawing-room cabinet, with plate glass back, the carvings in sycamore; library pedestal writing table in walnut; library reading chair; lounge chair; prie dieu, constructed to form an arm chair; and other chairs in walnut, upholstered in morocco; circular table in walnut, with marqueterie border; carved and gilt window cornice.

81. STYAN, FRANCIS, Chester-street, Birkenhead.—A full suite of walnut wood drawing-room furniture, comprising chiffonier, with plate glass and marble slab; lady's writing table; loo table; twelve chairs; two lounging sofas, two lounging chairs, upholstered in damask, elaborately carved.

82. TILLING, E., Bolton le Moors, Inventor.—Enrichment for cornices and centres of ceilings; specimens of gilding; a cabinet.

83. TRACEY, JOHN, Harcourt-street, Dublin.—Venetian shade, worked by a spring roller, rendering side hooks or knobs unnecessary; Louvre shutters, made to slide; patterns of brass wires, viz., gauze, fancy lace, and embroidered.

84. WALTON, F., & Co., Old Hall, Wolverhampton.—Specimens of papier maché tea trays; japanned toilet ware.

85. WERTHEIMER, S., Greek-street, Soho, London, Designer, Modeller, and Manufacturer.—Jewel caskets; envelope cases, work boxes, portfolios, inkstands, writing desks, candlesticks, &c., in different styles, and in various materials and mountings; candelabras chased in ormolu; brackets and card trays; card table, mounted in ormolu; ebony cabinet, with marble top, mounted in ormolu and china; chiffonier in tulipwood, mounted in plate glass and china; chased and bronze wine coolers and candlesticks; agate cups, mounted with swans, set with stones; Cellini cup.

86. WHITE, MRS., Killikee, Co. Dublin.—Two tables in Florentine mosaic.

87. WHITEHEAD, I., South Anne-street, Dublin.—Girandole glass: picture frames, of various sizes, finished and in the rough state; specimens of mould carving and gilt ornaments; window cornice.

88. WILSON, J., & Co., Ayr, Designers and Manufacturers.—Large Elizabethan book case, richly carved.

89. WINFIELD, R. W., Fleet-street, London, and Birmingham, Manufacturer.—Improved patent brass stretcher bedstead; improved patent brass bedstead, with arrangement for stretching the canvass bottom; handsome brass table, with marble slab; and large pier glass in brass frame; two iron bedsteads.

90. WINTERBOTTOM, A., Mosley-street, Manchester, Manufacturer and Patentee.—Specimens of patent Dacian silver paper hangings and panellings; a variety of silver decorations, fancy papers, &c.

91. WORMINGTON, W., Dame-court, Dame-street, Dublin, Manufacturer.—An ecclesiastical throne, carved in Irish oak, in the style of Louis XIV.

92. WRIGHT, MISS, Moneymore, Co. Derry, Exhibiter.—Specimens of carvings in wood, executed by deaf and dumb children.

# CLASSES XXVII. & XXVIII.

---

## MANUFACTURES IN MINERAL SUBSTANCES, FOR BUILDING OR DECORATIONS; AND MANUFACTURES FROM ANIMAL AND VEGETABLE SUBSTANCES, NOT BEING WOVEN OR FELTED.

IN the treatment of Class I. in the present volume, on Mining and Mineral Products, the several branches of what may be called mining industry, and the products of it also, were so fully discussed as to leave little room for any further remarks in this place under the head of Mineral Substances used for Building or Decorations. While it appears anomalous to treat works in polished stone and *pieta dura*, in marble, cements, and clays, under the head of Raw Materials, there is in practice great inconvenience in breaking up the subject; and the one drawback may fairly be balanced against the other. By carrying out fully the systematic classification, much of the matter common to both departments will be repeated in both places, with the further drawback of the want of unity in considering the whole subject, from the rudest stage of the raw material until it has passed through at least some of those processes necessary in turning it to account. Anxious that the department of Mining and Mineral Products should be fully discussed, on account of its local importance, it has therefore been considered advisable to embody with it such remarks as would otherwise be found in Class XXVII., the exhibiters here being also included with those in Class I. So far as regards matters coming under the head of manufactures in mineral substances for building or decoration, it is then only necessary to direct the attention of the reader to the dissertations at the commencement of this volume.

Again, as regards Manufactures from Animal or Vegetable Substances not being Woven or Felted, the important articles to be noticed are those of caoutchouc and gutta percha; though under this denomination might come not merely the application of the substances mentioned,—as life-preservers, hydrostatic beds, cushions, waterproof fabrics of every kind, elastic articles, and the various philosophical and surgical uses to which articles in caoutchouc and gutta percha are now devoted,—but also manufactures from ivory, tortoise-shell, bone, hair, and bristles, basket work of various kinds, straw plait, and many other industrial products. This would, however, involve a series of essays, which would go far beyond our limits; and we have, therefore, been obliged to distribute the exhibiters of these goods among the other allied classes, more especially in that which immediately follows.

Caoutchouc and gutta percha have of late become of so great importance that we should willingly devote a further portion of our space to them, were this practicable. The history of both of these substances dates back only to a comparatively recent period, yet the applications of them are almost endless; and they are, moreover, daily increasing. The plants which yield caoutchouc are very numerous, and they are to be found both in the Old and the New World, though it does not appear to have been known in Europe anterior to 1735. In India it is chiefly produced by the *Ficus elastica*, which belongs to the natural order *Moraceæ*, a tribe exceedingly abundant in Assam and the other parts of southern Asia. In the New World it is chiefly derived from the *Siphonia elastica*, a plant belonging to a totally different natural order from that just referred to; while again, in the Indian Archipelago, a third order, the *Apocynaceæ*, supplies to commerce the caoutchouc found in those regions. It is obtained by what is termed tapping the trees, a single tree in this way yielding from 50 lbs. to 60 lbs. annually. Existing in a fluid state in the juices of the plant, it becomes dried up, as it were, or solidified, on exposure to the arid atmosphere of those regions; and it is collected by the natives in large masses at the bottoms of the trees. Its value, and the uses to which it may be applied, have been greatly increased by the discovery of the property of what is termed vulcanization, or a combination with it of sulphur, producing what is known as vulcanized Indian rubber. By this process its strength and elasticity are increased to an amazing extent, while the objection of hardening in the cold, and of too readily dissolving in unctuous substances, is removed.

Gutta percha as yet has only been obtained from one kind of tree, the *Isonandra gutta*, which is almost confined to the Malayan Archipelago. Though brought to England in the days of Tradescant, it is only within the past ten years that its valuable properties, in an economical point of view, have been turned to account. It exists in the juice of the tree, and is obtained in the same way as caoutchouc. Resisting the action of water, and being a bad conductor of electricity, this substance has already effected no small service to the perfection of telegraphic communication, both by sea and land. Being much more manageable than caoutchouc under the action of heat, it possesses the important advantage of being worked up without any waste of material; as the smallest pieces may be used up again, and when articles of gutta percha become so far worn as to be unfit for further use, the material which they contain is as valuable to the manufacturer as that which he has just imported. Though easily acted upon by a high temperature, it does not adhere, when heated, to substances with which it comes in contact; and on cooling, it resumes its original shape, unless the temperature has been very high and pressure has been applied while warm.—J. S.

# CLASS XXIX.

## MISCELLANEOUS MANUFACTURES AND SMALL WARES.

THE title of this class will sufficiently indicate the great variety of articles included in it. The only manufactures of great national importance which it embraces are those of soap and candles, but these are of great moment. Of what are termed the minor articles, there are many which minister largely to our convenience, and in their production a high degree of artistic skill is displayed. The class comprises:—

1. Soaps and perfumery.
2. Articles for personal use, not coming under the head of clothing, as writing desks, work boxes, &c.
3. Candles, and other means of giving light.
4. Confectionery of all kinds.
5. Beads and toys, when not of hardware, fans, &c.
6. Umbrellas, parasols, walking sticks.
7. Fishing tackle of all kinds.
8. Miscellaneous articles and manufactures.

Oils and fats have been treated of at some length in Class IV., where much information will be found which would otherwise demand a place here. In reference to the other subdivisions, a variety of interesting matter might be introduced; but from the variety of topics to be treated, the demands which even brief notices of each would make on our space would far exceed the space at our disposal. We must, therefore, rest satisfied with a bare enumeration of the exhibiters and articles exhibited.

---

1. AICKIN, MISS S. E., Leinster-road, Rathmines, Dublin.—Brooches and ornaments for the hair, made of shells.

2. ALCOCK, P. C., & Co., Prince's-street, Dublin, Manufacturers.—Liquid and paste blacking; writing inks.

3. ALLINGHAM, MISS, Ballyshannon.—Horse-hair ornaments, and ancient ruins in rottenstone.

4. ALLOWAY, R. M., the Derries, Ballybrittas, Queen's County.—Specimens of bog or peat, manufactured in various forms, and for various purposes of use or ornament, by peculiar processes.

5. BAILEY, E. W., Belfast.—Model of river fixtures for rapid water; model of river fixtures for slow water; modern eel net, with fix or hincher, adapted for slow water, made of Irish flax, twenty-four strand to the cord, full size used in nine feet of water; model of new mode of capturing eels, proposed by exhibiter,—scale, one inch to a foot.

6. BAKER, MRS. MARIA, Dundrum, Co. Dublin.—Stuffed British game birds; artificial birds; ruin of Dumbrody Abbey, county of Wexford (rotten stone); ruin of Iona Abbey, Island of Staffa, Scotland (rotten stone); domestic birds made of shells.

7. BARKLIE, MISS M., Lower Gardiner-street.—A group of shells modelled in wax.

8. BARNARD, S., Grafton-street, Dublin, Manufacturer.—Gold and silver-mounted walking canes; fancy parasols; silk umbrellas; bathing caps, and sponge bags.

9. BARRETT, E., Wicklow-street, Dublin, Manufacturer.—Fancy silk and satin parasols; silk umbrellas.

10. BARTLETT & SONS, Redditch.—Sea fishing-hooks; river fishing-hooks and gut, &c.; Albicore hooks; harpoons and grains; trout spears; eel spears.

11. BELFAST SCHOOL OF DESIGN, PUPILS OF, Belfast.—Watch-stand designed by the pupils of the Belfast Government School of Design, and by them presented to their President, Lord Dufferin and Claneboy, as an acknowledgment of his Lordship's liberal patronage and kind attention to the welfare of the pupils.

12. BERRY, J., JUN., Arran-quay, Dublin, Designer.—Ornamental closed (Ward's) case, for the growth of plants in drawing-rooms, &c., planted with the Ferns of Ireland.

13. BEWLEY, SAMUEL, & Co., Dame-street, Dublin, Importers.—Articles of Chinese manufacture: carved ivory and lacquered ware; China ware; paintings on rice paper; argus, pheasant, and white feather fans, &c.

14. BIRCH, MRS. E., Molesworth-street, Manufacturer.—Gentlemen's, barristers', and coachmen's wigs; gentlemen's scalps; ladies' wigs, plaits, curls on combs, &c.; Birch's hair wash and pomade.

15. BLUM, BROTHERS, Nassau-street, Dublin, Importers.—German toys in variety.

16. BIRKBECK, E., Great Brunswick-street, Dublin.—Ladies' and gentlemen's perukes; hair brushes, perfumery.

17. BOLAND, P., Capel-street, Dublin, Manufacturer.—Fancy and spiced biscuits, ginger cakes, &c.

18. BOYD, S., Mary-street, Dublin, Manufacturer and Importer.—Fancy soaps and perfumery; blocks of perfumed soaps, as taken from the moulds.

19. BRIEN, C., Dublin, Manufacturer and Importer.—Wax, spermaceti, composition, and composite candles: clarified tallow, mould, and dipt candles; busts cast in clarified tallow.

20. BRIGHT, W., English-street, Armagh, Designer and Manufacturer.—Wedding cake, weighing 280 lbs.; ornament, the Wellington trophy.

21. BRYAN, THOMAS, Salford, Manchester.—Ornamental basket, made from a cocoa-nut shell.

22. CLARK, DAVIDSON, & Co., Mauchline, Ayrshire, Manufacturer.—Snuff boxes; needle and cigar cases, &c.; portfolios and memorandum books; work boxes and reticules, &c., made of fancy wood, painted, &c.

23. CLARKE, D., Carysfort-avenue, Blackrock.—Wax flowers.

24. CLARKE, J. A., Abbey-street, Dublin.—The currant picker bracket, a conventional arrangement of the currant, gooseberry, and other foliage and fruit; dead game; oval frame, ornamented by sprigs of the fuschia, with figure in plaster; original models, in plaster, of Gothic capitals.

25. CLEAVER, F. S., Red Lion-square, London, Manufacturer.—Honey and white almond toilet soaps; scented Windsor soaps; summer soap; winter soap; honey shaving soap, and shaving cream; saponaceous tooth powder; marine soap, for washing in salt water.

26. COMMISSIONERS OF FISHERIES, Custom House, Dublin.—Models of weirs, fish passes, &c.; harpoon used on coast of Galway for killing sunfish; model of stake or Scotch weir; model of otter weir, now interdicted by law as being most destructive.

27. CONOLLY, T., Lower Bridge-street, Dublin, Manufacturer.—Marrow and trotter oils for the hair; honey cream; castor oil pomade; eau de Cologne, and numerous scents and essences; writing inks; fountain of toilet perfume, prepared from wild flowers.

28. COONEY, C., Dublin, Manufacturer.—Indigo and other blues; liquid and paste blacking.

29. COOPER, M. T., Carlow—Stand of dogs, modelled in wax from life.

30. COOPER, MRS. L. A. M., Newtownbarry, County Wexford, Proprietor.—Hat and bonnet plait in imitation of Tuscan, made of the Irish "traneen" grass in the cottages of the peasantry.

31. CRUISE, W., Hoey's-court, Werburgh-street, Dublin, Manufacturer.—Specimens of toys, comprising drums, guns, pistols, swords, tambourines, &c.

32. DARGAN, M., New-row, West, Dublin.—Transparent shaving soap; toilette requisites; bouquet musk lavender; crystallized pomatum; trotter, marrow, and other hair oils; bear's grease, cold cream, lip salve, tooth powder, smelling salts, eau de Cologne, writing inks, &c.

33. DAY, MRS. and MISS.—Leather work in imitation of oak carving.

34. DENHAM, H. C., Rupert-street, London.—Designs worked in human hair, for brooches, lockets, souvenirs, &c.

35. DILLON, MRS., Grantham-villa, Blakeney-parade, Sandymount.—Sea-shore gatherings (Irish shells).

36. DIXON, G., Upper Erne-street, Dublin, Manufacturer.—Household soap; clarified tallow, composite and stearine spermaceti candles; specimens of palm oil, bleached by process patented by exhibiter.

37. DOHERTY, M. A., & T., Castle-street, Glasgow.—Horse-hair ornaments.

38. DOHERTY, J., Bushmills, Co. Antrim.—Artificial flies.

39. DOWNES, MISS M. A., Dublin.—Model of Casino in Lord Charlemont's demesne.

40. ELVERY, J. W., & Co., Elephant House, Lower Sackville-street, Dublin.—Waterproof, airproof, gutta percha, and patent vulcanized India-rubber manufactures.

41. FERGUSON, J. H., & Co., Grocers'-hall-court, Poultry, London.—Waterproof and airproof fabrics and clothing.

42. FIELD, J. C., & J., Upper Marsh, Lambeth, London, Manufacturers.—Stearic acid, from tallow; wax, bleached and unbleached; spermaceti; stearine, wax, and spermaceti candles; patent standard, wax, and Field's night lights; sealing wax; bougies or tapers.

43. FLINT, J., Essex-quay, Dublin, Manufacturer.—Fishing tackle, comprising rods, wheels, lines, flies, &c.

44. FORRESTER, J., Gordon-street, Glasgow.—A Scotch wedding cake.

45. FULTON, MRS. DR., Stillorgan.—Frame containing 7 carvings in ivory:—models of the Temple of the Winds at Athens, Pantheon at Rome, Temple of Clitumnis, and Temple of the Sybil, at Tivoli.

46. FULTON, MISS ELIZABETH, Stillorgan.—Basket made of shells from the Bahama islands.

47. FURNISS, MISS C. I., Wexford.—Table; five screens; ornamental leather work; vases; wax flowers.

48. GALBRAITH, W. H., New Broad-street, London.—Artificial essences for culinary purposes; extracts for handkerchiefs from flowers and plants; hair oil, pomades, greases, soaps, &c.

49. GARNER, D., Finsbury Market, London, Designer and Manufacturer.—Specimens of lasts with mechanical arrangements for diseased feet; registered multum in parvo portable boot-tree.

50. GASCOIGNE, MRS. TRENCH.—Little temple in ivory; sprig of lace-tatted flowers; glass enamel cabinet work box, painted in Alhambra arabesque.

51. GATTI, A., & Co., Clerkenwell, London.—Artificial flowers.

52. GIBBS, D. W., London.—Perfumed soaps.

53. GILBART, J. W., F. R. S., London and Westminster Bank, Lothbury.—An Indian writing desk.

54. GLASGOW INSTITUTION FOR THE DEAF AND DUMB.—Imitation of engraving, executed with a common pen and China ink, by a deaf mute.

55. GONNE, MRS. ANNE W., Clare-street, Dublin.—Specimens of rare flowers; water lilies, Victoria Regia, and spring flowers, modelled in wax from nature.

56. GRAHAM LEMON & Co., Sackville-street, Dublin.—Samples of lozenges, comfits, boiled and crystallized confections, and bon bons; model of the Great Industrial Exhibition Building, formed of comfits.

57. GRAY, J. & Co., Trongate, Glasgow, Manufacturers.—A variety of lozenges, comfits, and other confectionery goods.

58. GREAVES, A. E., Rosbercon Castle, New Ross.—Chinese vases and jars; model of a Chinese junk.

59. GRIERSON, THE MISSES, Glan-na-Smol, Co. Dublin.—Carvings in wood, of a variety of ornamental articles.

60. GRIFFITH, J., Coleraine.—Pollen net, used in Lough Neagh.

61. GUILLAUME, H., Suffolk-street, Dublin.—Gentlemen's and ladies' wigs; combs and brushes; perfumes, &c.

62. HACKETT, WILLIAM ASHTON, Patrick-street, Cork.—Case containing silver-mounted salmon and trout rods, with silver and plated reels, the tongues or joints of the rods double brazed; East Indian cane trolling rod; specimens of highly-finished lines and tackle; case containing a classified collection of salmon and trout flies, for the various celebrated waters in the kingdom; artificial gravelling or par, and loach or cullagh rue; eel fry; artificial ephemeridæ or ephemeral flies, manufactured and invented by the exhibiter; sea lines, mounted and unmounted; shark hooks; Grain's harpoon; artificial flying fish and marine tackle, for shark, dolphin, albacore, bonettas, and other tropical fish, &c., &c.

63. HANNAN, MRS., Castle-street, Dublin, Designer.—Tea canister of paper filigree, inlaid with bog oak; vase in paper filigree.

64. HANNAN, R., Dublin, Manufacturer.—Liquid and paste blacking; harness varnish; perfumery; ink.

65. HAWKINS, THOMAS, Bishop's-road, London.—Case of Hawkins' patent brushes, containing specimens of the patent, as applied to stock and distemper brushes, dusters

and ground brushes, sash tools and varnish brushes, mottler's and badger's hair brushes.

66. Hetherington, J. S., Merchant's-quay, Dublin, Manufacturer.—Rocking horses, and a variety of toys.

67. Hemphill, W. D., M. D., Clonmel.—Ivory vase, ornamented in the Gothic style; candlestick and table of African blackwood and ivory; a small cup and vase, showing the beautiful reticulated structure of the walrus tooth when turned extremely thin; two small vases containing flowers.

68. Higgs, J. S., Abbey-street, Dublin, Importer and Manufacturer.—Varieties of wine, porter, soda, and phial corks; jar and puncheon bungs; cork soles.

69. Hopkins, Miss Isabella L., Mitchelstown, Athboy.—Models in elder pith, carved with a penknife:—boy sketching dog; a group of mendicants; girl and goats; Queen Mab; Mars.

70. Hyde, Miss A., Mohill, Co. Leitrim.—Ivory, basket of feather flowers.

71. Jacob, W. & R., Peter's-row, Dublin.—A variety of plain and fancy biscuits.

72. Jackson, Thomas, Pinstone-street, Sheffield, Manufacturer.—Brushes in variety.

73. Jermyn, Mary, Sneem, Co. Kerry, Manufacturer.—Shell work baskets, made of shells from Derrynane.

74. Kain, John Francis, Islington-road, London.—Statue of the late Lord Nelson, carved in ivory.

75. Kane, Sir R., Museum of Irish Industry, Stephen's-green, Dublin.—Models of boats used on the coast of Ireland.

76. Keily, Mr. & Miss, Patrick-street, Cork.—Ornamental leather work.

77. Kelly & Fitzhenry, Clarendon-street, Dublin.—Blacking, matches, &c.

78. Kelly, P. W., Lower Gardiner-street.—Carvings.

79. Kent, J. J., & Co., Great Marlborough-street, London, Manufacturers.—Hair, clothes, hat, flesh, and bath brushes, tooth, nail, and shaving brushes in ivory, bone, and a great variety of fancy woods: brushes for household and stable use; painters' and other brushes; caoutchouc knife boards, to be used with Batt's knife powder in cleaning knives.

80. Kertland, G., Lower Sackville-street, Dublin.—Tooth and nail brushes; combs; specimens of hair dye and wash; soap, perfumes.

81. Kimberly, F. E., Middle Abbey-street, Dublin.—Model of bag net, with model of machine and apparatus for hauling bag net ashore for the weekly close season, during any weather.

82. Kirby, T., Lower Sackville-street, Dublin.—Rocking horses; dolls; architectural toys; cricket bats, balls, &c.

83. Labertouche, A. W., Upper Rutland-street, Dublin, Proprietor.—Vase and flowers, formed of shellwork; made some years since by a slave in the island of Trinidad.

84. Laird, J., Grafton-street, Dublin, Manufacturer.—Gentlemen's perukes; ladies' head dresses, fronts, and bands.

85. Laird, Mrs. Susanna, Grafton-street, Dublin, Manufacturer.—Ladies' and gentlemen's patent skin and gauze wigs, ladies' fronts, &c.

86. Lambert, James, Grafton-street, Dublin, Manufacturer and Importer.—Samples of lamp oils; wax, spermaceti, composite and tallow candles; soaps, the raw and manufactured material.

87. Lambert, R., Goree Piazza, Liverpool, Proprietor.—Hammocks, and other articles for emigrants.

88. Langdale, W. S., Lambeth, London.—Model of a castle and demesne made of leather.

89. La Touche, Miss C., Bellevue, Delgany.—Models in elder pith of ancient Irish crosses: Kells, Killamory, Clonmacnoise, Moore Abbey, Kilree.

90. Lawrence, E., & Co., Upper Sackville-street, Dublin, Manufacturers and Importers.—Rocking-horses; Irish and foreign toys and dolls; Irish bog oak ornaments, set in native gold and gems; horse-hair ornaments, made by the poor in the west of Ireland; hair brushes, made of Irish bog oak, Killarney arbutus, ivory, &c.

91. Ledwiche, M., Meeting-house-yard, Dublin.—Brushes.

92. Lewers, Mrs., Mountpleasant-square, Dublin.—Vases of wax flowers.

93. Lewis, F., Fleet-street, Dublin, Manufacturer.—Perfumed oils; pomades; essences; toilet soaps, and other perfumery.

94. Linden, W., Corn-market, Belfast, Manufacturer.—Bridecake.

95. Lindley, Miss C. A., Lower Sackville-street, Dublin.—Fire screen in frame, composed of a wreath of sea flowers; basket of sea flowers; shell album of sea weed.

96. Lynch, A., Suffolk-street, Dublin, Manufacturer.—Wigs, fronts, and ornamental hair.

97. Lysaght, Wm.—Salmon flies, for the Shannon and other rivers, tied by exhibiter.

98. M'Alister, Patrick, Donabate, Co. Dublin.—An old Irish Gothic baronial castle, done in shellwork.

99. M'Evoy, J., George's-street, Kingstown, near Dublin, Manufacturer and Importer.—Self-snuffing mould candles; stearine and chemical candles.

100. Madden & Black, Capel-street, Dublin, Manufacturers.—Ladies' and gentlemen's perukes, with improved gossamer partings; judge's full-dress wig; bench and bar wigs.

101. Mahony, J. & J., Coombe, Dublin, Manufacturers.—Brushes of various descriptions.

102. Mallow & Ettingsall, Merchant's-quay, Dublin.—Fishing tackle.

103. Mitchell, Mrs. S., Grafton-street, Dublin.—Bride-cake, elaborately ornamented.

104. Mitchell, J., Stonehaven, Edinburgh, Manufacturer.—Pipe tops, of sterling silver, German silver, and tin; iron pipe.

105. Mitton, T., Old-square, Blackburn, Lancashire. Manufacturer.—Improved wax candles.

106. Morton, J., Dame-street, Dublin, Manufacturer.—Lozenges and confections; medicated lozenges; crystallised and preserved fruits, ginger, jujubes, &c.

107. Ogle, J., Hayes, Navan, Co. Meath.—Work and flower baskets.

108. O'Connell, J., Cahirciveen, Co. Kerry.—Artificial flies.

109. O'Connor, Miss A., Sligo.—Ornaments in horse-hair, the work of peasant girls in the county of Sligo.

110. O'Brien, Messrs., Mary's Abbey, Dublin.—Green hemp and Manilla lobster lines; Ball's tarred hawser; yacht marlin; trawl twine; salmon twine; herring netting; green fish hemp; Italian hemp; hand lines; landing net; eel cockell; teakle lines; Ball's haddock snowding; fine hemp strand snowding; fine cod snowding; middle snowding; Baltic snowding; rod lines.

111. O'Kelly, the Misses de Penthony, Queen Anne-street, Cavendish-square, London.—A screen book-case and work box of ornamental leather work, in imitation of carved oak.

112. O'Leary, J., South Mall, Cork, Manufacturer.—A gentleman's wig; a lady's wig, scalp front, ringlets, and plaits.

113. Parker, Richard, Dunscombe.—Book of illustrations of the Birds of Ireland.

114. Pontet, A., Upper Sackville-street, Dublin, Manufacturer.—Plain and fancy umbrellas and parasols, with

specimens of the materials and fittings employed in the manufacture.

115. POWELL, J. H., Westmoreland-street, Dublin. — Arabian liquid hair dye.

116. PRESTON, O., Christ-Church-place, Dublin, Manufacturer. —Basket-work cars, cradles, fire and hand screens; bed-room and baby baskets.

117. PRICE'S PATENT CANDLE COMPANY, Belmont, Vauxhall, Surrey, Inventors and Manufacturers.—Specimens illustrating the Company's patent processes for making palm oil and other fatty substances into pure white candles by distillation, &c.; specimens of the palm oil fruit, and of vegetable tallows, butters and waxes; specimens illustrating the manufacture of night-lights; candles, night-lights, and oils of various descriptions.

118. PRUVOT, H., D'Olier-street, Dublin, Manufacturer. —Wax figures with beards and wigs; ventilator and patent perukes; curled front with skin division; bandeaux with gauze net.

119. RICHMOND INSTITUTION FOR INDUSTRIOUS BLIND, Upper Sackville-street, Dublin.—Game and work baskets; fire screens, and other articles in basketwork.

120. RIMMEL, EUGENE, Gerrard-street, Soho, London, and Boulevard de la Gare d'Ivry, Paris, Manufacturer.— Fountain of Rimmel's toilet vinegar; hygienic perfumery; specimens of perfumes, toilet soaps, pomades, tooth powders, hair dyes, cosmetics, and other toilet requisites.

121. ROCK, J., Hastings, Sussex, Exhibiter (J. SMITH, Hurstmonceux, Manufacturer).—Sussex truck baskets.

122. RONOKATSHOW, F. A., London.—Basket and cross made in paper.

123. ROONEY, R. A. & Co., Bishopsgate-street, London, and Brown Hill, Brush Works, Galway, Manufacturers.— Hair brushes of various qualities, in fancy foreign woods, bone, ivory, tortoise shell, and prismatic pearl shell; clothes brushes, made in part of new materials; ladies' curl and bandoline brushes; whisker, moustache, tooth, nail, and shaving brushes; hearth brushes; hair brooms; carpet brooms and brushes on a new and improved principle, and partly of new material; Rooney's patent horse brushes; Miller's machine and cylinder brushes; Rooney's improved painters' brushes.

124. SANGSTER, W. & J., Regent-street, London, Manufacturers.—Umbrellas in silk and alpaca; parasols in silk and China crape, and covered with Irish and Honiton lace, with richly carved ivory handles; riding and walking canes, with gold and silver mountings; specimen of Fox's new patent light umbrella frame.

125. SCALLAN, MRS., & MISS WHITE, Talbot-street.— Shells, fruit, and flowers, modelled in wax.

126. SHAW, MISS A., Caledon.—Ornaments made from the pith of the elder tree; Medici vase; a design for a screen; model of a steel chair at Longford Castle; a model vase.

127. SMITH, J., Rochdale Road, Manchester, Inventor. —A novel and useful application in gutta percha.

128. SOCIETY FOR THE PROMOTION OF IRISH MANUFACTURE AND INDUSTRY, Anglesea-street, Dublin.—Reading screens, made of cut card in leather frames; leather basket with shells and sea weed; ink-stand, ornamental shawl-pins, match-boxes, and other articles of leather; head ornaments, bracelets, brooches, pins, and necklaces of horse hair; ornaments in rotten-stone.

129. SMYTH, F., Essex-quay, Dublin, Manufacturer.— Portable umbrellas, with handles to screw off, &c.; silk umbrellas mounted on gold, silver, agate; ivory-handled silk umbrellas, mounted on partridge, rice, and bamboo canes; gingham umbrellas; fancy walking and riding canes; parasols mounted on whips, for ladies driving; gold and silver, ivory, carved, and other mountings used by umbrella and parasol makers.

130. SMYTH, O., Upper Granby-row, Dublin, Manufacturer.—Wicker chair screen, work basket, and soiled clothes basket.

131. STEPHENS, W., Kingsland, London.—Case of natural flowers preserved, retaining their natural form and relief, intended as botanical illustrations for museums.

132. STEWART, MISS, Rostrevor, Co. Down.—Ornaments in hair.

133. TAGGART, MISS H., Tenchfield-terrace, Sandymount Strand, Dublin.—Fancy picture made of Irish sea-weed.

134. WATTERS, J. J., Jun., Crow-street, Dublin.—A collection of the birds of Ireland, indigenous and migratory, consisting of nearly 250 specimens, collected and arranged by exhibiter (preserved by Mr. Richard Glennon, of Suffolk-street, Dublin).

135. WHITTY, J. I., Henrietta-street, Dublin.—Geological and mining map of Coalbrook, in the Co. Tipperary, with a survey and valuation of the tenancies thereon.

136. WILSON, H., Stephen's-green, Dublin, Manufacturer.—Gentlemen's knotted and temple spring wigs.

137. WORN, R., Dawson-street, Dublin, Designer and Manufacturer.—Gentlemen's patent machine-made wig; temple-spring and weft-spring wigs, with skin partings; coachman's full dress wig; ladies' long-haired braid wig, with transparent partings; gentlemen's gossamer transparent wigs; ladies' fronts.

138. WOTHERSPOON, J. & Co., Glasgow, Manufacturers.— Specimens of lozenges and comfits, manufactured by patent machinery driven by steam power; lozenges and comfits in handsome boxes; Scotch marmalade, made from Seville bitter oranges, on an improved principle, by steam machinery.

139. WYLD, JAMES, Leicester-square, London, Manufacturer.—A portion of Mr. Wyld's large model of the earth. The circumference of the globe is one hundred and eighty feet; the land is modelled upon a scale of ten miles to the inch, and the mountains upon a scale of one mile to the inch; the globe is composed of nearly 6,000 blocks.

# CLASS XXX.

---

## THE FINE ARTS.

THE association of an extensive general collection of works of pure Art with the contents of a general Industrial Exhibition,—though in a separate "Fine Arts Hall,"—was by many at first condemned as an incongruous arrangement; yet according as the public became familiar with the Exhibition as a whole, this objection was gradually felt to be founded in a mistake of the true relations of Art as one of the highest elements of real civilization; and long before the close of the scene presented to the Irish public in 1853, this department of the Exhibition became recognised by the few as the highest in importance of all, and valued by the many as the chief and crowning glory of the undertaking. The true relations of Art (properly so called, and in its highest sense) to life, and even the very significance of Art itself, are well nigh forgotten in the excitement of mechanical improvements which this century has called into existence; because the pure suggestions of the spiritual world, in which lies the true domain of Art, appeal to the soul and not to the senses, and the affairs of material life but too seldom leave the soul free to receive those suggestions. And yet if man will truly fulfil the conditions appointed for his earthly existence, he must make every detail of life here below harmonize with the great end of that existence,—the life of a future world of pure spirit only. If Art supply, then, the vivid suggestion of that purely spiritual existence, by leading the mind towards the vivid contemplation of the mere Ideal, it supplies precisely the necessary complement of the material philosophies; and without this the vehement pursuit of material improvements (and the exclusive satisfaction in these, and in their results, which that pursuit induces), leads to mere worldly selfishness only,—leads farther and farther away from the great end of human life. Much, very much, is required to be said upon this subject, so completely does it appear to be forgotten or neglected in the nineteenth century; so much, indeed, that a volume would scarcely suffice to enlarge upon it; but, in the limited space allotted to a single department of the present book, it is but possible to strike the keynote, as it were, and leave it to the reader's heart and intellect to pause here and pursue for himself the numberless paths of thought which it ought to open to his mind. It is in this sense that Art, truly and nobly directed, preaches the most glorious lessons, and where are these lessons most valuable if not in the midst of scenes and associations among which, without such a monitor, the mind must naturally lose itself, each hour wandering farther and still farther from the pure and the Ideal? It is on this account that, in a great Industrial Exhibition, a department of pure Art (separated, of course, from all the rest, as was due to the dignity of its nature, though yet within the same building) was even peculiarly appropriate as well as peculiarly valuable: and it must be with deep satisfaction that an Irishman remembers that the first instance of the association of Art (that is the Ideal) with Material Industry occurs here, in the capital of one section of that Celtic race whose tendencies have ever been especially towards the Ideal, and whose province it especially was to set this example to the world,—a satisfaction not diminished by his witnessing the instant acceptance of the same principle by a kindred people of the same instincts, who are even now preparing a spectacle of precisely the same import for the instruction of the world, in Paris, the centre of its civilization.

The deepest instinct of man's nature is the pursuit of that which is beyond and above him. Even where the earlier traditions of the human race had all but died away, among those from whom revelation was as yet withheld, and in regions where its truths had not yet penetrated, the pure instinct of man has ever soared heavenward. The investigation and contemplation of *abstract* truths seemed to be the favourite exercise of that intellect which distinguishes man from the lower animals; and he soon instinctively perceived the superior nobleness of this kind of occupation and this direction of his mind, because he felt that its exercise was his peculiar prerogative among created beings. When the natural tendency to thought above and beyond this life, and the natural awe for the power of a Creator, had ripened into some form of religious belief (even among those not yet blessed by any direct message from God), the mind became full of grand and sweet and pure emotions, which never found adequate expression in mere language. Those emotions, nevertheless, became more real, more distinct, more ardent; and philosophy began to see in them the revelations of a higher than human nature, the recollections of a pure and spiritual world. The pursuit of such paths of reflection, it was observed, did really ennoble the heart and refine the understanding, and the diffusion of those feelings and those ideas was found to render men practically better in heart and in conduct; for those whom they did not actually turn to the pursuit of philosophy and the higher practices of religion, were, at least, insensibly chastened and moderated in their desires, and softened from the barbarous indulgence of their passions.

But though in this world man shall never pierce the veil drawn over him after the Expulsion,—shall never know the depths of Truth in his human existence,—still there are ever sent some few among the race of this Earth who feel more deeply and see more clearly than their fellows some portion of its Beauty; and though common language may not divulge the experiences of those favoured few, yet the gifted among them still struggle to publish those happy tidings of a higher state which they have been permitted to catch a glimpse of. Such are the *poets* and the *artists*—whom civilized humanity has ever honoured, and whom earlier ages even regarded as inspired, or as if they really came direct from that region above humanity with whose ideas they were filled.

Poetry, however, could only express in the language of words what of spiritual truth it had to tell, through the imperfect medium of suggestive images and imaginative metaphors. But the harmonies of nature speak for themselves, in mute language, in every form of nature's works, and through these affect the feelings of the rudest and most unconscious of mankind. And the plastic and pictorial ARTS grew up, as men found that the higher influences of poetry, the truths of the *ideal* world, were most powerfully and universally expressed in the countenance of man and in the face of natural things. The power of man's intellect and the judgment of his intenser feelings at last found their highest earthly sphere; they were exercised in cleansing the forms of perfect nature from the irregularities and deformities which veiled them in common life—in restoring to them their pristine purity and beauty, and with and in these their first significance, as manifestations of the Creator, His power, His goodness, and His completeness; and the faculty that produced such works was well called *creative*, for its results were to most men as of creation, so little do most men dream of the existence of that which is yet ever around, above, and beneath them.

Such was the birth and growth of ART, and in such wise did its influence steal over the race of Man. If it could purify the sensual by its suggestion of the pure; if it could tranquillize and soften the turbulent and rough by its example of harmony and peace; if it could content the proud and striving by its touching memorials of simplicity and sufficiency; if, above all, it could strike the faithless with awe for the power of an omnipotent Creator, and charm the apathetic into love of the Holy and the Spiritual,—can it be doubted what must have been and ever be the sweet and lofty influence of Art upon the life of the civilized world? That which calls Man a moment from the bustling anxieties and petty cares of earth, and breathes over his spirit the fragrance of those sublimer spiritual emotions,—that must be surely the true civilizer, fit above all other influences to walk hand in hand with Religion herself. Such is Art in its highest manifestations; and all Art is beautiful and valuable just according to the purity and power of the spiritual emotions it expresses, and the adequacy with which they are rendered.

This is not the place to trace the origin and progress of the Fine Arts, of which satisfactory accounts may easily be found even by the general reader in many works, in these days of cheap literature within the reach of all the reading classes. But in considering the contents of a general collection of paintings and sculpture, we should not omit to notice the gradual debasement of the schools from the classic times to those of the middle ages, and, again, from the revival of Art in the Christian fifteenth century through successive ages to our own times. Art ever languished precisely as the cultivation of the pure Ideal was neglected, and its professors became either mere copyists or else lavished their powers (now of mere manipulation) upon the gratification of the sensual or luxurious tastes of mere worldly society. And this has been the general history of Art (notwithstanding occasional exceptions) from the time of Fra Angelico to that of the Caracci "revival," and thence more rapidly downwards, according as the end of instruction and the direction of public taste and criticism were confined more and more to *mere* technical proficiency, as of drawing, colouring, and composition, by rule. Opportunity, indeed, there was for the healthy growth of true artists, if the tone of society and of social education had not rather suppressed or misdirected than encouraged those spiritual tendencies, which, it has been seen, form the first essential condition of Art; and such tendencies are, indeed, precisely those which Royal Academies have ever ignored and still ignore. By the easel of a great original genius, whose creative faculty perpetually produces the noblest spiritual expressions, the student not only learns the technical part of his work, but insensibly imbibes the higher and yet more necessary spirit of it. But this, unfortunately, is not the course of modern academies, even where they possess genius within their corporations. Their exhibitions accordingly present, indeed, abundant evidence of industry on the one hand, and careful teaching on the other, and they are frequently full of correct renderings of the tamer scenes of nature; but that is all: and one of the practical advantages attendant upon a great general Exhibition of works of all times and all nations (of which that of Dublin, in 1853, was the first ever projected), is to suggest by so many examples,—proving, as they do, the utter inefficiency of the modern schools and their teaching,—the necessity of seeking elsewhere the true principles of artistic success.

With the discovery and pursuit of the true method of learning the practice of Art, and the true road (through intense and spiritual contemplation) towards the Ideal of Expression, the student must also, however, count upon the support of his generation. And upon this subject also we Irish have something to learn.

The general support of Art in Italy, in the fifteenth and sixteenth centuries, was due not alone to the Church, but even, perhaps, in a greater degree to the great municipalities, which liberally expended the public money in the most splendid artistic decorations, well understanding the permanent advantage of the influence of Art on the public mind. The rulers, princes, and municipalities of Prussia, Bavaria, France, and, to a remarkable extent, Belgium, have in like manner given constant and splendid encouragement to Art in our own times. In those countries the annual exhibitions are carefully examined to discover the most promising students, whose efforts are constantly watched and duly commended, in a manner very different from that of the coarse and ignorant exaggerations to which we are unfortunately accustomed here, in society, as well as in the press. But from the academies those successful students gain simply the means of learning the technical requirements of their occupation, and an annual opportunity of making the progress of their labours known to their fellow-citizens. The spirit by which so many of their works have reached a high place in Art, is the fruit of pure and solitary meditation,—the example of cotemporary genius working in their presence,—and, perhaps, above all, the careful study and daily familiarity with the noble creations of the Greeks, on the one hand, and, on the other, the heavenly expression of the Christian works up to the sixteenth century.

In every capital, and almost every great city in civilized Europe, too, the municipality or the nation have founded a gallery of ancient and mediæval art, for the improvement of the people, and to supply students with examples for their guidance. The true student of Art carefully examines the means used by the giants of the past, and tenderly drinks in the varied but ever spiritual expression which they knew so well how to perpetuate in their works; indeed, in no country, perhaps, can any artist now reach real eminence without the possibility of spending some time in this kind of study. And here also we are on the eve of being provided with a public gallery of ancient art, capable, before long, of supplying the Irish student with such opportunities of study; for one of the consequences of the Exhibition which is the subject of this Volume, has been to make more urgent the public desire for a permanent NATIONAL GALLERY in Dublin, and even at this moment it is understood that arrangements are all but completed for its establishment. Should it be successfully established, and should it one day contain a collection of the works of the Past of a truly Ideal character, we may expect great results from a future generation of Irish Painters and Sculptors. In the mean time we are assured of the co-operation of very many proprietors of works quite as fine as the *élite* of the late Exhibition to support a large collection similar to that of last year in Dublin, and out of the inspirations which such works will be sure to create among our students we may hope that many years will not pass before Ireland gives again a true Artist to the world. And it is here, notwithstanding the many disadvantages of this generation, political, social, and material,—(even the next, perhaps, may see a total change,)—that we may, indeed, expect such fruit: with much more confidence here, in a country poor in opportunities, but rich in ideality, imagination, and devotion, than in one abundantly supplied with the highest treasures of Art, yet whose inhabitants are generally incapable of appreciating them and therefore of turning them to account, by reason of their natural tendencies rather to the practical than the abstract, and rather to the material than the spiritual, and of a prevalent system of philosophy and morals inconsistent with the exercise of the loftier and more poetical feelings. For such is surely the intimate distinction between the people of Ireland and those of the neighbouring island.

The peculiar tendency to abstract thought among the Irish race (common to it with the French and other Celtic nations) has, from the earliest ages, been strikingly recognised by travellers and strangers. Their great capacity for success in Art has also been frequently exhibited in later years; and,—without appearing to run into the prevailing vice of self-laudation, by referring to the names of those who, since James Barry, have lent their genius to the Academy of England,—it is believed we may rest secure of the general recognition of this fact. But this tendency of our people has been but ill nurtured, and the condition of a helpless province has been found to be here (as everywhere and at all times) fatal to the progress of Art, as it is to all development of independent genius, and the boldness of mental aspiration in any direction whatever. It has often been remarked that in times of war and revolution the Fine Arts, and indeed the abstract sciences themselves, ever burst forth most freely in some new and wider development. It is because men's minds are relieved by whatsoever even for a moment removes the oppression which ever keeps settling more and more heavily upon the People during the stagnation of undisturbed obedience to the ideas as well as government of previous generations. More strikingly true it is that among a free people, which feels and knows itself free, there only Art takes root and prospers: remove the political Life, and Art also languishes and dies. The example of existing nations, once the most celebrated in Art, will occur to the mind of every reader, and the application of the same principle at home may also, perhaps, be safely left to his apprehension. Yet even under such circumstances as surround us, Art may nourish hope in Ireland too, and it is with a view to encourage that hope (and in some sort also to direct aright the tastes and studies of the Irish Art-Student), that it is proposed to devote such space as has been allotted to this department of the present volume to preserve some record of the true value, as well as of the mere contents, of the Fine Arts Halls of the Irish Industrial Exhibition.

It will be necessary to compress our remarks within limits quite inadequate to include any complete criticism even of those works which we shall select as examples of their several kinds, and we shall have but barely to name (and sometimes even to omit to mention at all) many works well deserving of detailed description. The list itself will, however, be suggestive of much (especially that of the Old Masters), and for the rest, these pages are written chiefly of course for our own countrymen, upon whom they are only designed to produce one effect (if that may indeed be attained by the writer's efforts): to suggest to them some considerations which may add a higher value than mere amusement to the recollections or description of works of high Art, and to place before such of them as are yet students some points of view from which such works are not generally regarded among us. And if the opinions of the writer may claim no weight of authority, and may frequently want ability to withstand critical comments, their expression may at least provoke independent reflection, which often leads to truths more valuable than those to be found in the best didactic compilation—truths often unsuspected by those whose very errors may suggest to others the path towards their discovery.

## I.—SCULPTURE.

A glance at the Catalogue of the extensive collection of works of Sculpture included in the Exhibition will be sufficient to indicate how large an opportunity was there offered to the Irish public to make themselves acquainted with the Modern Schools, almost all of which were represented by examples of considerable excellence. Amongst these examples it is with no slight satisfaction that the Irish critic finds himself not merely attracted, but compelled to give the first place to one or two works of Irish artists,—men, too, who are not mere accidental offshoots of our people, but really and thoroughly Irish in whatever part of the world they reside: with satisfaction the greater as regards those artists, that in our Irish Exhibition this is almost the only department of skill in which we may honestly claim pre-eminence. Amongst these examples of sculpture the *chefs d'œuvre* of HOGAN and MACDOWELL do, in fact, clearly occupy the first place, with the exception of the great Prussian artist RAUCH. We cannot here attempt to make due note of many among the multitude of works before us; we shall only be able to select a few for special examination, choosing such as may seem most nearly the representatives of their particular class.

In the arrangement of the great Central Hall the attention of the visiter was well directed in the first place,—by its position in the place of honour in the centre, at the head of the Hall,—to the statue of EVE,

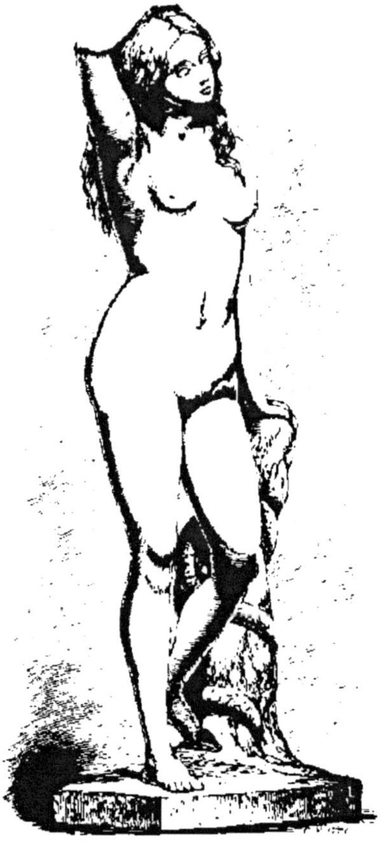

EVE

the work of our distinguished fellow-countryman, Patrick MacDowell, R. A. (No. 66). This statue (which is not yet, however, in marble) has already earned great popularity, when before exhibited in London, at the Royal Academy, and in Hyde Park, in 1851, and since, at the Cork Exhibition of 1852. And this popularity has been gained by no trick, by none of those startling appeals to our admiration which consist of some clever deception (such as the very easily manufactured but, we admit, very effective "Veiled Vestal," exhibited in the Italian department, at Hyde Park),—least of all has MacDowell condescended to seek for vulgar sympathy by the expression of mere commonplace sentimentality; for he is really an artist—he seeks to be understood in the very simplicity of his design, and he trusts for sympathy to the perfect purity of Expression clothed in a very beautiful form.

The question of the propriety or appropriateness of the nude figure in modern art is, perhaps, the first which strikes the mind in contemplating this statue; and it is a question so intimately connected with the application of the general principles before laid down, that it is well, perhaps, to have it clearly answered at the outset. Excluding entirely from even a passing thought those works which are designed simply to serve the taste of the sensualist (and of which it is to be hoped not one could ever be suffered to disgrace by its presence an *Irish* Exhibition), there are very many subjects in which the choice or introduction of the naked figure is entirely out of place, serving only to display the workman's technical knowledge of anatomy and stone-carving: and there are many others in which such a choice is useless, because nothing higher or more beautiful is thereby developed. And it will appear, on profound consideration of the subject, that the naked figure in statuary should only be introduced where it is *necessary*, either in consequence of the nature of the story told, or in order to produce the expression of something higher and more spiritual than can be otherwise rendered by Art. Applying this test it will be found, that by much the greater number of such works among the moderns are simply naked men and women; and although often very innocently so, still, in the very unnecessariness of the artist's choice of form in this respect, already below the level of high Art.

The *necessariness* of a nude figure depends, then, upon the nature of the subject, or the peculiarly ideal meaning and expression which is sought to be conveyed. There are few subjects proper for sculpture in which the nude figure becomes necessary; because it is simply degrading to the dignity of sculpture to employ it in the mere attitudinizing of well-drawn figures, as we often see where a sculptor selects a subject as if merely to show what he can do in marble. An instance of the violation of principle alluded to occurs in the well-known and very clever figure by our half fellow-countryman, Hiram Power—we mean the well-known statue of the "Greek Slave" (No. 89). There the figure, beautifully modelled, is, in many respects, finer than Mr. MacDowell's; but the entire nudity of the figure is not only unnecessary, but even untrue to the story; and as the artist has communicated not the least of spiritual or intellectual expression, his work descends to the level of a *mere* portrait of a naked woman, modest it is true, but certainly in his hands by no means a satisfying subject of contemplation to a tasteful mind.

Considered strictly in the essence of its design, the most perfect of all God's works is the yet undegraded form of Man. And to be the most perfect of God's works—among the many countless thousands that are so beautiful and so varied—what must its excellence consist in? Not in the *mere* expression of countenance, though it is this which distinguishes the human being from the many beautiful but irrational creatures which are given him to be his subjects. In more than this. In the perfect and appropriate form and colour of every part of his frame,—each portion suitable in itself; strong in sufficiency; graceful in strength; neither brutal nor effeminate; preserving ever that just medium of wholesome moderation in powers and proportions which itself in every part of man's body already represents the character of his reason applied in the government of his soul;—in all these things, and such as these, the perfection of God's work is made manifest, and in each individual one of these things, the reasonable nature of man, while it finds its ordinary expression in the living reality, may be, and ought to be, in its highest manifestation by artistic representation. The strength which is sufficient for defence, and energetic enough to protect the just independence of self and of what properly looks there for safety;—but that strength reasonably controlled, and habitually exerted in peaceful industry: the intellect which is prompt and vigorous to care for, and direct well the things of this world;—but that intellect reasonably controlled from the too exclusive enjoyment of its earthly power, and directed at all moments heavenwards by the perpetual consciousness of an existence far higher and supremely dear,—such are the characteristics of man, which *every part* of his corporeal form is (in its healthy and undegraded state) fitted to express.

And in Woman, the complement of this self-sufficing intellectual character and protecting physical power—in woman the finer sensitiveness of a purer moral nature, the softer and more delicate instincts of a tenderer and more devotional spirit, gain expression in that wonderful series of soft and richly-flowing lines which make her perfect figure the very embodiment of the highest *grace* which the Divine Creator formed into life. Perhaps it was because unfitted for the hardness of intellectual government, and still more so for the rough works of muscular toil, woman was intended to dwell in quiet contemplation amidst the softer and more homely duties of this world, that God reserved her creation for his final work; because in that tender trusting form of intellect which is just able to distinguish its proper guide, and in that soft devotional tendency which inspires her to follow it, and above all in the capacity of silent and cheerful endurance, and the every shining purity of a woman's heart, the Divine Mind saw qualities not merely designed for this earth, but which were destined to live still and attain to only a yet purer and higher development among the angels of his heavenly kingdom. And so he stretched forth his hand to mould a form which should, by its faultless grace and matchless simplicity of beauty, express in every part that sweet and lofty destiny of woman,—the preserver of purity in this world, and the example of devotion towards the next. And this is what Art must express for us in the female form, or it had best not meddle with it. Her delicacy must not be intruded on save in the performance of her highest mission; and if her form do not raise up our minds and fill us with a holy purity of soul, then it fails of its first object,—the object of the Creator in lavishing upon it so much of his beauty and his grace,—and it becomes degraded, and may well be removed from before our eyes.

Such, then, are the conditions which the sculptor is bound to have before his mind; and they may form the test by which our reason and our good taste should judge how to appreciate his work.

In the *Eve* of MacDowell both the reasons above alluded to for the choice of the naked figure unite. Historically necessary, the pure form of woman is also chosen as the highest expression of her highest quality, and in this lovely figure we have, indeed, the very personified purity of her whole race. MacDowell has, with true apprehension of his subject, and a deep sense of what such a figure ought alone to express in the hands of a Christian artist, selected the moment of temptation, but yet before the Fall. The lovely Eve rests against a shoot of the fatal tree, round which the serpent insinuates himself near her, with his suggestions to her curiosity and ambition. She pauses yet awhile in doubt, she is hesitating towards guilt already, she is still but on its threshold, and we behold her in the last moment of her innocence indeed, but still innocent. An instant later, and her beauteous form could no longer truly express what God had created it for. A day before, and we should have had, indeed, the loveliness of Paradise; but we should have missed the suggestion of our race's history,—the teaching of the fall of what was yet so beautiful and so happy. The artist and the Christian could choose no better moment.

The attitude is charmingly suggestive of childlike innocence, and the expression of the little graceful features shows all that fawn-like girlishness which one cannot help attributing to the maiden Eve, sporting in the primeval garden. Her intellect is just asserted by her doubting, yet the form of her head does not express much of it;—that, perhaps, would be inconsistent with the very history itself. The curling, flowing hair, and rounded face, tell you those tresses are of gold, and those eyes of gentle blue, more completely than a very painting; and while the admirer is full of gladness at the soft and graceful form (and especially the exquisitely modelled arms) he recognises in the attitude of the right hand and arm flung over the head, taken together with the abstracted eye and the smile already sinking into solemn stillness, an unconsciousness of any presence but God's—an unconsciousness of self which amounts to a sense of the entire propriety and naturalness of her costume; all which convey to the mind, in its best and most unobtrusive form, the full instinct of perfect purity. One cannot contemplate this work, without being charmed with the vigorous grace, the harmonious attitude, and correct and sweetly moderated proportions of the figure; but its effect is better than merely to charm the eye, for the longer we study it the more we will become filled with its expression,—which is purity. Here there is a work of Art which fulfils the higher requirements of Art, for it improves, elevates, ennobles the student of it: here is a conception of a subject, in which the artist has forgotten himself, and his own display, and his own reputation, to render tenderly, and modestly, and with entirely affectionate simplicity, the full meaning of his story, and the full lesson which his figure was capable of expressing,—that too, a lesson of the rarest and noblest importance to the human race.

The only blemish in the composition consists, perhaps, in the position of the lower limbs, in which we see at once, too, the influence of an inferior model, for this portion of the figure is far from being so elegantly proportioned, or so true as the upper part. And, besides (as to the design) viewed directly in front of the figure, the line of the right leg appears somewhat hard, the weight of the figure being rather violently thrown upon it; and, on the other hand, the left limb presents a feeble outline (particularly on its inner side), and that knee is bent at a somewhat harsh angle. The lower part of the body also appears generally too large or too prominent, a fault which may, perhaps, arise from the comparative slenderness of the limbs from hip to knee. In the best works of the Greeks the fore muscles of this part of the leg are given a much more rapid and rounded development near the body; and this, while it is strictly correct, tends to prevent the appearance of heaviness in the mass of the body itself. Mr. MacDowell's figure is, however, modelled, we are sure, with accuracy, and these observations may apply to the mistake of having selected one system of proportionate development instead of another. The ancient statue of Apollino offers an example of Greek treatment by which the above-noted unpleasant effect is avoided, for there the right hip is slightly drawn back, and the figure rests rather more upon the left arm. But Mr. MacDowell needs no copying of the Greek even in the disposition of a single attitude, and should he (as we devoutly hope) execute this loveliest and noblest of all his works in marble, and feel disposed to reconsider the proportions and *pose* of the lower limbs, it is certain he will readily find means, entirely original, for making this figure as faultless in graceful form as it already is in expression.

Near to MacDowell's Eve was exhibited the chief work of John Hogan,—another Irish sculptor (not an R. A., but distinguished during his residence in Rome by being elected one of the Fifteen Virtuosi of the Pantheon, a society of artists, the vacancies in whose number are filled by election from the artists of all Europe),—the DRUNKEN FAUN (No. 43); a work which, whether we consider the intellectual effort necessary to its production, or the finished technical learning required for modelling such a figure, is probably not excelled by any similar one of modern times. So strong an expression may seem to require some qualification, but it is not uttered hastily, nor without much study of the figure in question; and it is a figure which requires to be studied, if it is to be properly understood,—to be examined on every side, and with the utmost care, too, before its merits (in an intellectual point of view) can be gathered by the student.

It is unnecessary here to give any detailed account of the well-known *Fauns* of classic mythology, the attendants and army of Bacchus, and the genii of the earth, and especially of the woods. The ancient sculptors represented them in almost every possible attitude and occupation. The great galleries contain Piping Fauns, Dancing Fauns, Laughing Fauns, Drunken Fauns, and Fauns in an attitude of graceful and intellectual repose, as the actions or age of Bacchus and his disciples at various times partook of these various characters. There was then the utmost latitude allowed to the artist's fancy, who might thus exhibit, with fantastic license, all the grace or power of the human form in the representation of these beings, even in attitudes inconsistent with the proper dignity of man—and the Fauns are always distinguished from their human likenesses, not only by the accessories of the group, but by a little tail introduced as sprouting from the small of the back, and which marks their half-brute descent, and half-brute nature.

Mr. Hogan's *Faun* is extremely classic in conception, and the subject is treated by him in a manner perfectly in accordance with that of the antique sculptors, though, so far as we are aware, with complete originality.

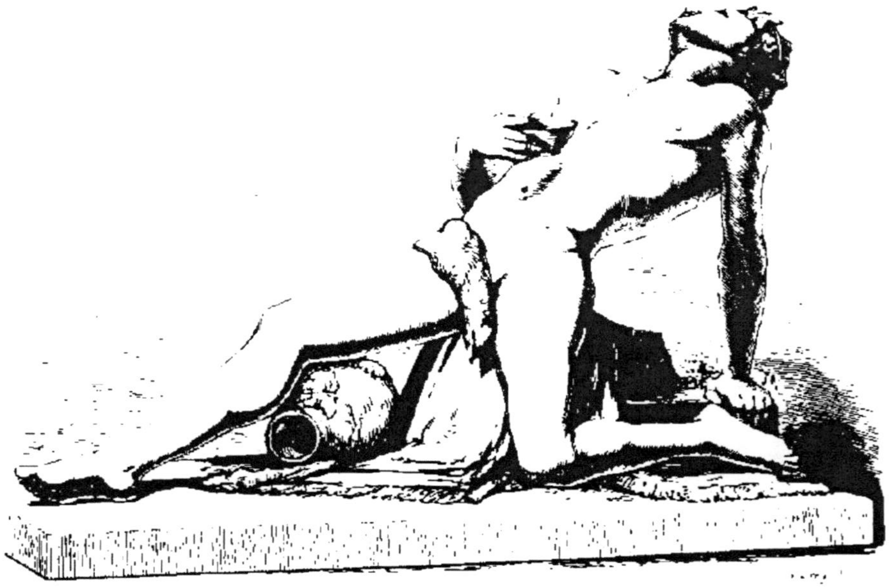

THE DRUNKEN FAUN.

By John Hogan, Member of the Pantheon

The story of the composition of this figure is well known: that Mr. Hogan, when a youth, shortly after his first arrival at Rome (where he lived for so many years afterwards), heard a characteristic opinion expressed by the now celebrated English sculptor, Gibson, that nothing original could again be designed in sculpture, the sources of the art having been exhausted by the ancients; that Hogan, surprised at witnessing a general approval given to so strange a proposition, but feebly expressed his own dissent from it; that he was contemptuously challenged to prove his views, by producing an original work himself; and that the "Drunken Faun" was the result—which, indeed, had the effect of at once satisfying the sceptics, and gaining for the artist a reputation which laid the first foundation of his future success. Whatever may be the truth of this anecdote, we believe the figure is, in fact, as completely original as it is pure and classic in the design and treatment of the subject. In its present form (for the artist has but lately modelled the whole of it anew, and it now expresses, perhaps, the utmost of his power), it may be considered the very best work of Hogan's, and this consideration, as well as its pre-eminence among the many sculptures in the Exhibition in point of intellectual imagination, leads us to the consideration of the Faun, even in preference to the group in marble, by the same hand, placed near it at the head of the Great Hall.

The figure is in a recumbent attitude. The Faun had been seated on a low rock, enjoying the delights of the grape juice, of which he seems to have drained a large vase which lies empty beside him. The last cup was already on its way to his lips (or had been, perhaps, already snatched), when seized by sudden intoxication, his limbs have become relaxed, and the unnerved hand is unable to lay down the vessel: he sinks back from his seat, breaking the coming fall by supporting himself on his left arm (upon which, accordingly, the whole weight of the body is thrown), while the last effort of the muscles of his right is unsuccessfully employed in endeavouring to fling away the useless cup which is just about to slip from his fingers. The right leg is stretched out to its utmost length on the ground, wholly nerveless; the left had been drawn back suddenly with bent knee, as if to recover his balance, but now hangs in that same attitude powerless and loose; the head sinks back also, yet seems faintly to struggle to support itself—one moment more and the whole figure will be extended senseless on the earth. It is impossible to imagine anything more completely natural than such an attitude and such a position under the circumstances: strength, vigour, grace, buoyancy, all now plunged in unconscious insensibility, in the last stage of drunkenness. But the artist has avoided, nevertheless, even the least of the disgusting attributes of such a situation, and while he has expressed it with consummate truth and vigour, he has done so in such a manner that the eye continues to take a pleasure in the work of a much higher kind than that which similar subjects as treated by the moderns (such as Rubens, &c.), generally admit of. In this respect Mr. Hogan's performance may be actually classed at once with the antiques themselves, and it is no mean praise when we say that it will not suffer in point of design by the comparison. The nature of the creature represented assists, doubtless, in producing this satisfactory expression, because the sense of the degradation of *man* does not interfere with our enjoyment; and Mr. Hogan's Faun is not merely one by courtesy (like the academic figures whose classic intentions are so often only discovered by reference to the academy catalogue)—it is, in every limb and feature, as well as in its accessories, an unmistakeable Faun of ancient Greece and Italy.

There is in the British Museum another representation of a Drunken Faun—one of the fine statues in the Townley collection, and almost a repetition of that engraved in the *Bronzo del Museo di Ercolano*, which offers almost a minute standard of comparison: but we confess we never could look on the Townley figure with any other feeling than mere wonder at the execution of it, whereas Hogan's commands all the attention which is due to a severe, correct, but graceful composition, full of the impress of strong intellect—executed, too, with the utmost technical accuracy, and (like the antique) comprising difficulties of detail which none but a masterly hand could even hope to overcome.

In his original model our artist had raised the right hand almost to the lips. When, two years ago, he brought a mature and experienced judgment to the task of remodelling, as if anew, the work of his youthful spring-time, this position appeared (and, as we believe, rightly appeared) to him to indicate so much strength still left as was somewhat inconsistent with the profound nervelessness of the rest of the body, and he altered it for the present most effective attitude. As the figure now stands (and for anatomical accuracy it is considered to be quite a model), every joint is loose, every muscle relaxed, all save the left arm, upon which the weight of the body rests heavily, and the development of which accordingly offers the more marked contrast to the remainder of the work. The original statue, which is very finely modelled, may be still seen in the vestibule of the School of Art of the Royal Dublin Society.

It is but a proof of the surprising apathy of the rich upon artistic matters that this extraordinary work has never been executed in marble; and if Ireland leaves two such figures as this and the "Eve" to seek the chance of permanent realization at the hands of strangers, a crowning disgrace will be added to the long list of the sins of the present generation.

Such were the two finest works of our own artists. By one alone in the whole Exhibition can they be conceived to have been excelled; and in that one the delicacy and grace of MacDowell, the manly intellect and power of Hogan, and the loveliest tenderness of ancient Greek execution in detail, seem to have combined themselves to show that modern Art, after all, may justly hope to rival the glories of the past.

We had long heard of the extraordinary powers of the great Prussian sculptor, Professor Rauch, of Berlin, but until we saw, at the London Exhibition of 1851, a marble copy of his "VICTORY" (*seated*), though that copy was not by his hand—we had not believed that Thorwalsden had dropped his mantle upon a sculptor as graceful, as pure, and as classic as himself. In our own Exhibition we have had the advantage of studying a cast from the original of this beautiful creation of imagination and intellect, and those in Ireland by whom the great Danish artist,—and not the effeminate Canova,—was felt to be, hitherto, the highest representative of modern art in sculpture, have still (for this cast has been purchased by the Royal Dublin Society, and is now placed in the gallery of their School of Art) the opportunity of becoming acquainted with a successor to his throne who is likely to transmit even as great a fame to posterity.

RAUCH's lovely figure is smaller than life, the type of form and of drapery are pure Greek, and the execution (so far as it can be judged of by a cast) especially tender and complete. The Spirit of Victory is in the act of crowning the moment of success; the triumphant mortal whom she appears to gaze on with such visual intensity has accomplished the task his patriotism or ambition had set, and is for the moment the King of Men; and the flashing form of noble Victory springs forward on her seat to fling the wreath of glory on his brow.* The dignity of this magnificent figure, the severe enthusiasm of spirit, chastened by the repose of habitual triumph, and ennobled by the conscious calmness of that all-ruling intellect in which justice is but the necessary companion of that triumph, distinguish Rauch's grand conception from almost any but the finest Greek statues we have seen. The swift, impetuous, decisive blow, or moral or material, which ever secures or attends on victory, is perfectly typified in the energetic movement of the statue; the firmness with which the left hand presses on the rock-seat behind, throwing forward the whole body, is made known in the expression of the fingers, the last of which has just left its resting place—the momentary action of that arm, the shoulder itself thrown forward,—the momentary movement of the left foot, which now hangs down over the rock as the right is advanced towards the conqueror—the splendid vigour of the right arm, whose hand bears the wreath of victorious oak, flung back to the utmost on the opposite side as in the act of casting on the hero's head the inestimable reward of his toil;—but above all, the stern, clear brow, the deep-set eye, the firm yet soft and tender mouth, all the features beaming with sensibility, flashing with the lightning of intellect, and strong in the vigour of a decisive and irresistible will; these are the attributes and tokens of the pure Spirit of Triumph, and it needs no word to tell us that we stand in the light of Victory herself. This statue is indeed for us a realized poem—a reward and an incitement to the noblest and grandest thoughts we are conscious of in the few sublime moments of life. Alas! that not from the mind of an *Irish* artist could such a poem spring; for such works, whether in Greece, in Rome, or in Prussia, never did, and never will see the light, save in the happier and more glorious moments of a Nation's history, be they of the present or the future, of the enjoyment or even of the hope.

But recalling ourselves, not without an effort, from the subject of the statue to the work itself, we must not forget to point out the great beauty, in point of spiritual expressiveness, of the modelling of this figure. The minute parts of the hands, the arms, the enchanting little foot, the throat, and shoulders, are all expressed with the utmost accuracy; and yet even in so slight a figure the artist has avoided the least approach to pedantry in the too clear expression of the anatomical details, which are simply indicated as in pure Greek works, with distinctness indeed, but with extreme delicacy. There cannot be found,—we may not resist particularizing it,—a lovelier foot than this which hangs so daintily in the air, nor more beautiful hands than those here so actively occupied; and yet there is not merely in the face, but in each limb, each joint, each smallest part of her frame, an expression of dignity and power which no most spiritual beauty in real life could boast. The figure itself is everywhere idealized, yet so naturally, that the eye does not tire of wondering how it is so. The drapery, too, is in the most perfect Grecian spirit. The light folds of the thin tunic are disposed with consummate skill, indicating the movement, and conveying all the proportions of the figure, and yet so falling round and clinging to it as to give it all the dignity of a still statue, while it retains the effect of one in graceful motion. Well worthy of hours of study is this lovely gem of art, upon which, and upon the crowd of feelings it excites in us, we would gladly enlarge far beyond the bounds permitted us, but upon which we hope we have said or suggested enough to secure for it not only the most patient examination of the sculptor and the student, but also the reverent attention of every one possessing or seeking after taste who has the opportunity to visit it.

We have especially selected these three specimens of sculpture for detailed notice, because of all those in the Exhibition, they were, without question, the most remarkable, and because they supply, each of them, an example of a different style from the rest. But we must not be supposed thereby unduly to depreciate the many other works of various nations which enjoyed almost equal favour from the general public, and deserved it even from the few. Amongst the works of English artists, the most elegant in idea, and correct in execution, was certainly the *Sabrina*, by W. Calder Marshall, R. A.† (No. 70). This figure is already very well known and very popular, as the many representations of it in the form of drawing-room ornaments in "Parian" and biscuit china sufficiently testify, so well known, indeed, as to need no description here; but it is right to call attention to it, because it is, by much, the best work of Mr. Marshall, that we have seen, and he is (with the exception, perhaps, of Gibson, who exhibited no work in our Exhibition) the best of the contemporary British artists, both in purity of conception and in simplicity and unaffected gracefulness of design. He is not, however, free from the worst fault of the English artists, that of conventionalism in the *form* of expression, and he is very weak in the imaginative faculty; so that although much superior to most of the sculptors on the other side of the Channel, his works must here be remarked upon as instances of a small success, which we desire to impress on our readers at this side, ought to be entirely excluded from the ambition of a people really imaginative, and (under favourable circumstances of study and education, which it must be said, we do not possess, and of whose effects, therefore, we can give no sign) really capable of works of high Art, in the sense in which we have used the word.

Mr. Marshall's Sabrina is *merely* the enchanted lady at the bottom of the lake, to represent which idea his figure is in attitude and expression appropriate and graceful enough; for Mr. Marshall's conception is a very graceful representation of innocence and beauty. But the Poet's idea of Sabrina is higher than these, and it is precisely in the understanding and realization of the *higher* ideas that Mr. Marshall, in common with most of his school, is greatly wanting. When he (or any of these) deals with a subject of less lofty character,

* Rauch's figure was, we believe, designed for a monument to BEETHOVEN, the heroic musician of Germany. To all to whom the life of that noble artist is familiar, the appropriateness of Rauch's idea will be apparent, though. The same Victory might bend forward over Beethoven's as over Napoleon's head.

† It has been stated that Mr. Marshall is not an English artist, but a Scotchman, resident in London; and like our own MacDowell, contributing the weight of his talents to the English Academy. If so, let our Scottish friends claim him as theirs; it would be worth their while to do so.

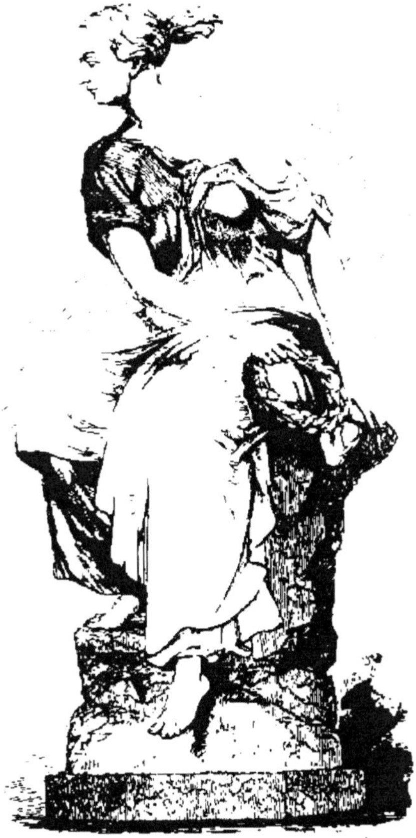

VICTORY.

indeed, he is able to develop the idea of it with completeness and elegance; but if an Artist seeks for fame by higher and nobler efforts, he must accept the risk of being judged by higher and nobler standards.

The song of Sabrina shows clearly that Milton intended to represent not merely innocence and gracefulness and gentle purity in this beautiful poetical conception, but also a high degree of *intellectual* spirituality, which, indeed, in Milton's—as in any classic—mind must be the peculiar gift and qualification of the immortals. The exquisite description of the chariot of the nymph indicates at once her place amongst the classic spirits of the deep, and that most graceful verse, in which she obeys the shepherd's call, shows her spirit-nature already purified and separated from the material world:—

"Whilst from off the waters fleet,
Thus I set my printless feet," &c.

A simple glance at Mr. Marshall's statue will be sufficient to show that it is not *this* Sabrina he has represented. His figure is very graceful, very pure in expression, very modest in design, well modelled, and, technically, very correct in execution; but it is certainly *not* the Sabrina of the poet. That it is meant for Sabrina is only indicated by the conventional marks of the sedges sculptured upon her rocky seat, and the little fish which is half hidden behind one of them. The statue does not express the character or *ideal* of its subject, and if found without a name, a century hence, it might be called a "Listener (bathing)"; and no one dream of its author's intention to express more.

For Mr. Marshall has expressed nothing of the ideal,—the head of his listening lady is deficient in abstract beauty, and the face is destitute of any expression but that of the drawing-room. The well-shaped, healthy, very ordinary arms contrast greatly with the delicacy of the Eve, before noticed; and the lower limbs, though well-modelled and very becoming in a pretty country girl, seem both hard and weak in outline, if they are compared with more ideal works.

These negative faults arise chiefly from deficiency of the imaginative faculties, a gift which rarely makes itself apparent in Britain; and the effect is increased by the neglect of careful study, somewhat more of which might have led the artist to a deeper and clearer conception of that which he proposed to himself to express in marble. But there is also another cause for the prevailing deficiency in expressive meaning, which is generally remarked in the English marbles, whether portrait, statues, or works of mere imagination; and that is, the *naturalism* which is the prevailing characteristic of the whole English school. Their every work is mere portraiture, and that, too, only of the forms of flesh and bone before them. Unable to spiritualize these forms by seeking back their ultimate perfection (which, of course, is not now to be found in degenerate humanity) they must necessarily miss the expression of anything higher than what is to be seen in ordinary life; and the first condition and the whole object of high Art becomes for them simply impossible.

The young Irish artist and student should diligently consider what is here suggested. The farther he keeps from that naturalism above alluded to, the better chance he has of one day producing a work that may live when not only the English sculptors of to-day, but even Canova and the whole series of imitators and *naturalisti* from him, shall be forgotten and unknown. It is only he that strives after the expression of the Ideal that ever can be a true artist; he that thinks little of friends and patrons, of the world, and the riches of it, and the fame: not at all of himself, or of his own little reputation, or of the praises of the ignorant crowd of "educated people" who are ever caught by some skilful but easy trick of detail,—like that of Monti's Veiled Vestal, at London, in 1851, (and here No. 74),—but are rarely conscious of the excellence of any truly artistic productions. And it is in Ireland that these principles should especially gain attention, for we have not here such judges of art at all as the Artist can look up to without degrading himself: our people are not yet educated enough to produce them. The artist in Ireland must be the teacher and not the workman. He must yet do for us what Phidias did for the Greeks,—show his countrymen what the power of Art really is; ennobling them by the grand and beautiful ideas which sculpture and painting can silently preach with an eloquence so much beyond words. The artist here must first look up above us all, and then deep into himself, and he must tell us, not what we have repeatedly heard before as well, but tell us ever the utmost his nature can reach to of the pure Ideal.

The same remarks which have been applied to Mr. Marshall's Sabrina apply still more strongly to the *Eve at the Fountain*, by E. H. Bailey, R. A. (No. 2), a figure still better known, and among the English still more popular. Mr. Bailey's Eve possesses gracefulness of conception, and simplicity and elegance of composition; not, perhaps originality, if we remember the exquisite antique Nymph Seated, at the British Museum (Room 3, No. 28), Townley Gallery, of which a repetition is known by the name of La Venere delle Conchiglia;—but in Mr. Bailey's Eve, as in all the works of Canova, of whom he is an imitator, the true Ideal is altogether lost sight of. It is, in fact, the Portrait, but little refined, of a good but ordinary model; and it not only does not give utterance to any beautiful, any pure and lofty sentiment, but it is even wanting in that spirit, the expression of that active feeling of surprise and simple delight, which Milton's fine lines—"That day I oft remember," &c., so eloquently describe.

*The Graces* (No. 3), another work of the same hand, shows a still more marked departure from the principles above alluded to, and is as wanting in classic sentiment as in ideal power. The *Nymph Preparing to Bathe* (No. 5), better supports Mr. Bailey's credit, because it is a graceful figure representing a subject much more within the powers of an English sculptor, and the drapery (for it is almost wholly draped), is very delicately and elegantly designed. Mr. Marshall's *Dancing Girl Reposing* (No. 71), offers a contrast to the latter figure, which is in his favour, precisely because it displays a greater effort, on the part of the artist, to express vividly the idea he desired to convey.

We cannot afford space to notice these works at length, nor yet Mr. Lalor's *Bather* (No. 59), though one of the most promising figures we have seen for many years,—well composed, well modelled, and full of grace and expression; nor Mr. Foley's *Innocence* (No. 35), our countryman John H. Foley,* A. R. A.:

* Another representative of Irish talent transplanted to the English metropolis.

nor yet the *Pysche* (No. 67), of Patrick MacDowell, R. A., the sweetest of all his efforts to express the tenderness and innocence of budding girlhood. A pretty group, *Boys Wrestling*, by Mr. Lalor (No. 61), is, however, engraved, because less generally known than other works here noted, and because it is a remarkable example of careful composition, presenting equally effective and expressive, as well as regular and graceful, outlines, from every point of view. A grander and nobler work than any we have mentioned must also be passed over, Mr. Hogan's *Hibernia* (No. 42),—his finest perfect work in marble; a figure which might well adorn the Hall of an Irish National Gallery, if we yet had one, if but for its exquisite draperies, than which the student could scarcely find safer or more beautiful models.

The Exhibition contained but very few examples of sculpture from the Continent, at least very few of note. Rauch's glorious "Victory" might indeed well represent the highest of the German schools by itself, even if of these we had not examples numerous enough in the shape of casts and reductions from the works of many other artists beside. Belgium was represented almost by M. Fraikin alone, for his works (Nos 138 and 139) *Cupid Captive*, and *Psyche calling Cupid*, were the only pieces of full size. Both these works exhibit much skilful modelling, and the latter is especially graceful in design. Both are very pure, and wholly free from affectation. Both are original in composition, though neither displays any high degree of poetic imagination.

The sculptors of France were best represented by the bronze statue of *Spartacus* by Foyatier (No. 149), a copy of the marble in the gardens of the Thuilleries, in Paris. The artist has sought to represent his subject not merely by its accessories, or even by the action of the figure,—the character and historic deeds of the rebel gladiator are abundantly portrayed in the noble proportions of a herculean, yet most active, frame, and the firm expression of so fearless and resolute a countenance. The attitude is one of defence, and the broken chain, whose fragments still hang on the hero's wrists, explains at once the slave restored to freedom. Without alluding to the European politics of the day, we cannot attempt to explain how it is that the France of the present moment, and of these forty years back, still delights so much in the representation of the heroes of liberty in the world. Let us refer it only to the classic taste of that highly educated people, and their literary passion for the illustration of classic history. It is always some active idea that the French artists rejoice to embody in marble or on canvass. The mere abstract or allegorical is left to their German neighbours, who prefer to make every figure the type of an idea rather than the representation of a fact. And there is excellence in both these modes of considering an artistic subject. We need not add that it is the former which M. Foyatier has selected in his Spartacus. His idea is, doubtless, Insurrection for Liberty; and he has sought to express it in the purest and highest form, and through a character whose deeds claim the sympathy and approval of all men of all opinions. Going back to early classic times, the form of his idea also became more manageable to the sculptor; he could then choose the simple form of Man, unincumbered by the disguises prescribed by more modern customs; and dealing with his subject with all the freedom of a classic sculptor, his mind could aspire to produce a work able to vie with, or at least to stand beside, those which have been recovered from antiquity. This figure, fairly judged by its proper standard, and considered as an ideal historic portrait statue, does fulfil much, if not all, of what the artist proposed to himself; and if we except certain defects in the modelling of some of its details (defects which we are aware do not exist in the original marble), M. Foyatier's Spartacus appears to us to be a work of very high order, and undoubtedly one of the very first in the Exhibition.

The other contributions of French sculpture were not calculated, we regret to say, to exalt among us the fame of our kindred nation, whom we must ever desire that our people should at last begin to know well enough to prefer their example and their teaching, in the arts as well as in other things, to that which is introduced and copied amongst us from our Teutonic neighbours. We are bound to pass unqualified condemnation upon *The Young Drummer of the Republic* (1793), (No. 146), though by M. David D'Angers, as false in sentiment, weak and crude in composition, and harsh to the utmost degree in execution. We could see in it the trace of a hand able to do well; and we ever turned from it on that account with only increased dissatisfaction. We are equally compelled to censure the extravagance of design and meanness of expression in Mr. Dieudonné's *Christ's Agony in the Garden* (No. 150), which appears to be one of the most painful specimens of want of feeling, as well as of want of all sense of beauty, we have ever seen exhibited; perhaps, indeed, the idea of it may have arisen from the acceptance of the gross theory of the ancient Byzantine painters, as to the personal form and features of our blessed Lord,—an idea surely most strange in a Catholic country,—but in a work distinguished by such an abandonment of all dignity and expression, we must earnestly condemn the senseless caricature of true sentiment, with which the sculptor has treated one of the grandest and most fearful subjects that Christianity affords to Art.

Though we cannot pause to apply to the many fine portrait statues and busts numbered in the Catalogue the principles of that branch of sculpture, it would be unjust to omit mentioning a few of those which claimed attention not merely as likenesses, but also as works of high and pure Art, which a portrait is always capable of being. Of these (No. 424) the colossal *Bust of Frederick the Great*, by Professor Rauch (exhibited by the King of Prussia) was a true example of the heroic likeness; and (No. 423) the *Bust of Thorwaldsen*, the greatest modern sculptor, also by Rauch, instanced the highest class of imaginative art in portraiture. Mr. Hogan's *Bust of O'Connell* (No. 236), in marble, with its classic wreath of oak, was, after Rauch's, the most splendid work of this kind in the Hall: full of massive dignity, full of intellect, full of fire, and replete, too, with all the delicate play of features which those who remember the countenance of the great orator will readily know how to appreciate,—it seemed to us the *only* real likeness, the *only* true portrait of O'Connell, either in marble or on canvass, in existence. Mr. Christopher Moore's *Bust of Sheil* (No. 389) was almost equal to the O'Connell in excellence,—it absolutely breathes, and its life-like spirit brings back the vehement rhetorician with perfectly startling force; while the same sculptor's *Plunket* (No. 370) exhibited an equal power in dealing with the gravity of expression and the majestic strength of outward form in which an intellect almost the most magnificent of our times clothed itself. Lastly, we may not omit to name the classical and

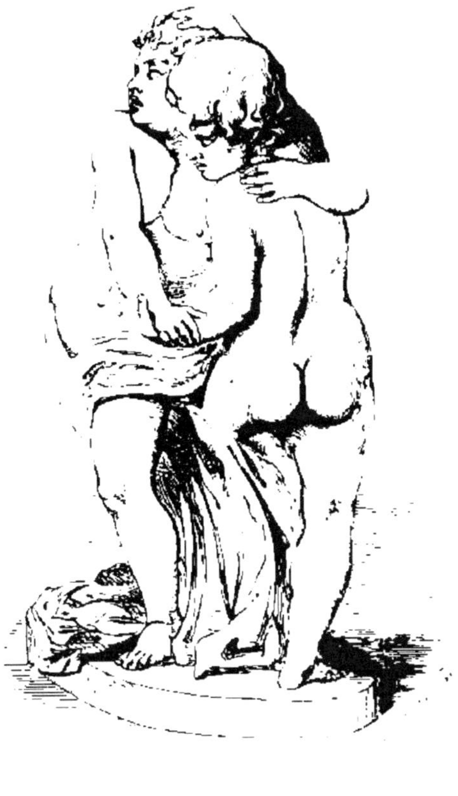

BOYS WRESTLING.

By John Lalor.

artist-like *Bust of Miss Hayes* (No. 346), by her fellow-countryman, Mr. Foley, as one of the most remarkable in the Exhibition.

We have left to the conclusion of this part of our subject even the mention of that which was the most curious by far of all the sculpture in the Exhibition, as well as one of the most beautiful pieces of its kind, perhaps, in existence: the marble group by the great Raffaelle himself, representing *A Dolphin Carrying the Wounded Child Ashore.* Remarkable for being one of the two only marbles from the hand of the great painter (and its originality is, we believe, unquestionable, it having been obtained by the late eccentric Earl of Bristol and Bishop of Derry, from the Papal Government, during his visit to Rome about eighty years ago); it is equally remarkable for the consummate grace of a most difficult composition, for an expression equal to anything in Raffaelle's wonderfully dramatic works, and for a degree of correctness and finished perfection of execution which few modern sculptors have equalled, and none could surpass. The story is one from Ælian ("De Anim. Naturâ," lib. VI. ch. XV.) in illustration of the fabled love of the dolphin for the race of man. The dolphin had often enjoyed the sport of an infant on the sea strand, and became so familiar with him as to become his chariot over the waters. In some moment of too rough play he one day, however, accidentally wounded the child to death, which when he saw, in a paroxysm of grief he bore the lifeless form to the weeping parents on the shore, and himself languished and died by the side of his little favourite. This lovely little work is extremely well known (from the cast at Dresden), though the original had long lain forgotten among the Bishop's marbles, now in the possession of Sir Hervey Bruce. The criticisms of which it has been so frequently the subject may excuse the present writer from enlarging upon a theme which, besides, might lead him far from that single train of thought to which he has been necessitated to confine himself in this but too meagre introduction to the Sculptures of the Exhibition.

The following Catalogue contains a list of the Sculptures in the Exhibition, so far as the writer has been able to complete it from that published by the Committee. We have given precedence to historical and poetical subjects, arranging them generally in the order of the Exhibition lists, and separating the contributions sent by the Continental States. Then come the collections of antique works; and after these, first the monumental marbles, and then the portraits, statues, and busts. By this arrangement it is hoped that the object of the general reader may be facilitated.—E. P.

---

1. Group of Dolphin and Child (in marble). [Sir H. Hervey Bruce, Bart.] RAFFAELLE.
2. Eve at the Fountain. E. H. BAILEY, R.A., London.
3. The Graces. E. H. BAILEY, R.A.
4. Youth resting after the Chase. E. H. BAILEY, R.A.
5. Nymph preparing to bathe. E. H. BAILEY, R.A.
6. Group: The Lesson Interrupted. RICHARD BARTER, Dublin.
7. Group: Venus and Cupid. RICHARD BARTER.
8. Group: The Young Champion—Boy defending his Sister from a Snake (in marble). [Walter Berwick, Q.C.] J. GOTT, Rome.
9. Group: Boy taking an Italian Greyhound Pup from its Mother (in marble). [Walter Berwick, Q.C.] J. GOTT.
10. Group: Child embracing an Italian Greyhound (in marble). [Walter Berwick, Q.C.] J. GOTT.
11. Statuette: Praying Girl (in marble). L. BERTOLINI, Rome.
12. The Child's Attitude (in marble). JOHN BELL, London.
13. The Danaid. MARK R. RAUCH, Berlin.
14. The Young Musician (in Caen stone). FRANCIS BURNETT, Dublin.
15. Madonna and Child (in marble). JAMES CAHILL, Dublin.
16. A Nun instructing a Girl. JAMES CAHILL.
17. Statuette: Boy and Bird. W. J. DOHERTY, Dublin.
18. Statuette: Girl and Bird. SUSAN DURANT.
19. Statuette: Pastorella (in marble). T. EARLE, London.
20. Abel and Thirza. T. EARLE.
21. Silvia and the Wounded Fawn. T. EARLE.
22. Cupid and Calypso (in marble). [R. Chearnley, Esq., Cappoquin.] J. GOTT, Rome.
23. Cephalus and Procris (in marble). [E. J. Cooper, Esq., Markree Castle, Collooney.] The first work of P. MACDOWELL, R.A.
24. Leda (in marble). [E. J. Cooper, Esq.] M. SCAOCIONI.
25. A Hunter reposing. JAMES FARRELL, Dublin.
26. Madonna and Child (in Portland stone), [colossal size]. JAMES FARRELL.
27. The Pet Dove's Return. JAMES FARRELL.
28. St. Lucius. JOHN FARRELL, Dublin.
29. The Wanderer. JOHN FARRELL.
30. Alfred. JOHN FARRELL.
31. A Bard. JOSEPH FARRELL, Dublin.
32. St. Laurence. JOSEPH FARRELL.
33. St. Joseph. JOSEPH FARRELL.
34. The Lost One. THOMAS FARRELL, Dublin.
35. Innocence. JOHN H. FOLEY, A.R.A.
36. Statuette of Phocion (in marble). [Exhibited by Mrs. Fulton, Stillorgan.]
37. Statuette of Meditation (in marble). [Mrs. Fulton.]
38. Statuette of Silence (in marble). [Mrs. Fulton.]
39. Flaxman's Morning (copy in marble). R. HANIGAN, Dublin.
40. Flaxman's Night (copy in marble). R. HANIGAN.
41. Medallion: The Fairy in the Blue Bell. R. HANIGAN.
42. Statue of Hibernia, supporting Bust of the late Lord Cloncurry; executed at the instance of a lady, since deceased (in marble). [Lord Cloncurry.] JOHN HOGAN, Member of the Pantheon, Dublin.
43. The Drunken Faun. JOHN HOGAN, Member of the Pantheon.
44. Group of Bacchantes and Panther (in marble). [W. Jackson, M.P.] FELIPPE GNACCHERINO.
45. The Rival Spinners, or Broken Hack. Miss KENNEDY, Dublin.
46. Group: The Young Champion—A Boy defending his Sister's Bird's Nest (in marble). By the late THOMAS KIRK, R.H.A., Dublin.
47. A Sleeping Child (in marble). The late THOMAS KIRK, R.H.A.
48. Children at Play (in marble). JOSEPH R. KIRK, A.R.H.A., Dublin.
49. Statuette: Cassandra (in marble). JOSEPH R. KIRK, A.R.H.A.
50. Statuette (in marble). JOSEPH R. KIRK, A.R.H.A.
51. Group emblematic of the Great Exhibition of 1851, designed for a centre piece in silver or gold (in marble). JOSEPH R. KIRK, A.R.H.A.
52. Ruth and Naomi. JOSEPH R. KIRK, A.R.H.A.
53. Statuette: The Creation of the Dimple. JOSEPH R. KIRK, A.R.H.A.
54. Statuette: Andromeda. JOSEPH R. KIRK, A.R.H.A.

55. The Infant Bacchus. Miss KIRK, Dublin.
56. The Pastoral Age. W. B. KIRK, London.
57. Iris Ascending. W. B. KIRK.
58. Model (half size) of a Statue of Justice, executed in colossal size for the new Court-house of Belfast. W. B. KIRK.
59. The Bather. JOHN LALOR, London.
60. The Emigrant. JOHN LALOR.
61. Statuette Group: Boys Wrestling. JOHN LALOR.
62. Statuette: Solitude (Art Union Prize). JOHN LALOR.
63 Statuette (in marble). LIVI V. CARRARA.
64. The Guardian Angel (in marble). LIVI V. CARRARA.
65. The First Born. FRANCES MACDONNELL (deaf and dumb), London.
66. Eve. PATRICK MACDOWELL, R. A.
67. Psyche. PATRICK MACDOWELL, R. A.
68. Bacchante Reposing. HENRY MACMANUS, A. R. H. A.
69. Topsy. HENRY MACMANUS, A. R. H. A.
70. Sabrina. W. CALDER MARSHALL, R. A.
71. The Dancing Girl Reposing. W. C. MARSHALL, R. A.
72. The first Whisper of Love. W. C. MARSHALL, R. A.
73. Heloise (bust, in marble). R. MONTI, London.
74. A Veiled Vestal (bust, in marble). R. MONTI.
75. A Sleeping Child. CHRISTOPHER MOORE, R. H. A.
76. Statuette Group: The Brothers' little Pet. ALEX. MONRO, London.
77. Paolo e Francesca. ALEX. MONRO.
78. Egeria (see Charles Mackay's Poem). ALEX. MONRO.
79. The Seasons (alto relievo). ALEX. MONRO.
80. Innocence (a study, in marble). ALEX. MONRO.
81. Madonna and Child. [Exhibited by C. Nanetti, Dublin.]
82. Eurydice (after the antique). [Exhibited by C. Nanetti, to show the mode of finishing plaster casts.]
83. Cyparissus, after the antique. [C. Nanetti.]
84. Leda after PRADIER. [C. Nanetti.]
85. Caractacus (a group). By the late C. PANORMO, A. R. H. A.
86. The Pet Dove (in marble). The late C. PANORMO, A. R. H. A.
87. The Rescue (in marble). The late C. PANORMO, A. R. H. A.
88. The Tired Water Carrier. E. G. PAPWORTH, Jun., London.
89. The Greek Slave. HIRAM POWER.
90. Group: Woman and Child (in marble). EDWARD G. PHYSICK, London.
91. Head of the Dying Christ (in marble). EDWARD G. PHYSICK.
92. The Magyar's Daughter (small group). G. E. POWELL, Dublin.
93. Statuette: Arab Girl and Horse. G. E. POWELL.
94. Combat of Dragoon with Kaffirs. G. E. POWELL.
95. Statuette group: Mameluke and Horse. G. E. POWELL.
96. Statuette group: Prairie Indian and Bison. G. E. POWELL.
97. A Study from the Life. F. R. RAMBAUT, Dublin.
98. Statuette of the great Earl of Pembroke, Earl Marshal and Guardian of Henry III., King of England (in marble). EDWARD RICHARDSON, London.
99. A Sleeping Nymph. EDWARD RICHARDSON.
100. Statuette of a Horse in full action. EDWARD RICHARDSON.
101. The Crouching Venus, after the antique (in marble). [Mrs. Carmichael, Dublin.] GIACOMO VANELLI, Rome.
102. Boy extracting a thorn from his foot, after the antique (in marble). [Mrs. Carmichael.] GIACOMO VANELLI.
103. Statuette of Ariadne (in marble). [Mrs. West, Dublin.]
104. Cupid (in marble). [Lord Cloncurry.] BERNINI.
105. The Madonna (bust, in marble). [Lord Cloncurry.] BERNINI.
106. Tasso (a bust, in marble). [Lord Cloncurry.]
107. The Laughing Faun, bust, after the antique (in marble). [Lord Cloncurry.]
108. Mask of Medusa, after the antique (in marble). [Lord Cloncurry.]
109 to 111. Antique busts of Julius Cæsar, Homer, and Phocion (in marble). [Lord Cloncurry.]
112. The Genius of the Vatican (a bust, in marble). [Lord Cloncurry.]
113. Theseus (cast from the reduction in alabaster), by MR. CHEVERTON, from the original in the British Museum (Elgin marbles).
114. Ilyssus (cast from a similar reduction). By Mr. CHEVERTON.
115 to 119. Five groups, subjects from the Classic Mythology, each chiselled out of one block, formerly in the possession of Napoleon (in marble). [Mr. John Gernon.] FRANCESCO BERTOS.
120. Boy and Dog (in marble). [Hon. Mrs. White, Dublin.] M. PAMPELONA, Florence.
121. Girl, Cat, and Bird (in marble). [Hon. Mrs. White.] M. POZZI, Florence.
122. Group of Boys and Donkey. [The Marchioness of Waterford.] M. HICKEY, Clonmel.
123. A Daughter of Eve (in bronze). [Elkington, Mason, & Co., London.] JOHN BELL, London.
124. Eustace de Vesci, A. D. 1215 (in bronze). [Elkington, Mason, & Co.] M. RITCHIE.
125. Stephen Langton, Archbishop of Canterbury, A. D. 1215 (in bronze). [Elkington, Mason, & Co.] JOHN THOMAS, London.
126. The Death of Teudric, "the Great King of Gwent and Glamorgan" (in bronze). [Elkington, Mason, & Co.] J. EVAN THOMAS.
127. Sappho (in bronze). Baron MAROCHETTI, London.
128. La Pieta (in bronze), copied from the original of Michael Angelo, in San Pietro, Rome. Baron MAROCHETTI.
129. Ino Teaching the Young Bacchus to Dance (statuette, in marble). JOSEPH GOTT, Rome.
130. Love and Innocence, statuette (in marble). J. GOTT.
131. Susannah Alarmed at the Bath (statuette, in marble). J. GOTT.
132. A Spaniel Playing with a Kitten over a Basket of Fruit (in marble). J. GOTT.
133. An Italian Greyhound Playing with a Puppy (in marble). J. GOTT.
134. An Italian Greyhound Alarmed while Suckling her Puppies (in marble). J. GOTT.
135. A Hindoo Girl supplicating her Deity for success in her endeavour to prove whether her absent lover is safe (statuette, in marble). J. GOTT.
136. An Italian Greyhound Playing with a Ball (in marble). J. GOTT.
137. Statuette: A Nymph Stung by a Scorpion (in marble). [Hamilton Geale, Esq., Dublin.] Il Cavaliere BARTOLINI, Florence.

SENT FROM BELGIUM.

138. Cupid Captive. FRAIKIN.
139. Psyche calling Cupid. FRAIKIN.
140. The Cradle of Love. FRAIKIN.
141. Veiled Bust (in marble). FRAIKIN.
142. The Madonna (statuette, in marble). VAN LINDEN.
143. The Crucifixion (statuette, in marble). H. VAN DER BROCK.
144. A Sleeping Cupid (in marble). Professor GEEFS, Antwerp.
145. A Suppliant Cupid (in marble). Professor GEEFS.

SENT FROM FRANCE.

146. The Young Drummer of the Republic, 1793; in La Vendée (in marble). DAVID D'ANGERS.
147. Child and Greyhound (in marble). GAIRARD.
148. The Child Jesus Preaching in the Temple. LOISON.
149. Spartacus (in bronze). FOYATIER.
150. Christ in the Garden of Olives (in marble). DIEUDONNE.
151. Francoise de Rimini (bas relief, in marble). EVEX.

SENT FROM GERMANY.

152. The Madonna (alto relievo, in marble). R. PIEHL, Berlin.
153. A Dog of Swedish Race (in bronze). WOLFF, Berlin.
154. A Lion startled by a Snake (in bronze). WOLFF.
155. The Infant Jesus dispensing Christmas Presents. BLAESER.
156. Minerva supporting a Warrior in Battle (statuette group). BLAESER.
157-160. Morning,—Evening,—The Seasons,—The Hours (small groups). DANKBERG.
161. The Nymph Echo (statuette). DANKBERG.
162. Night and Morning (bas reliefs, after THORWALDSEN). Eichler, Berlin.
163. Bacchus and Amor. EICHLER.
164. A Holy Family. EICHLER.
165. The Madonna and Child. EICHLER.
166. Christ Blessing Little Children. EICHLER.
167. A Kneeling Genius with a Harp. KALIDE.
168. Boy Listening. BERENDES.
169. Victory [seated]. Professor RAUCH, Berlin.
170. Statuette of Victory [standing]. Professor RAUCH.
171. The Amazon, after Kiss (reduced, in bronzed zinc). Pohl.
172. Hercules and Bull, after KRIESMANN (reduced, in bronzed zinc). Pohl.
173. Battle of a Frog with a Lizard (in zinc). DANKBERG.
174. Battle of a Lizard with a Crab (in zinc). DANKBERG.
175. Hercules Wrestling with the Bull (in zinc, full size). KRIESMANN.
176. The Amazon, after Kiss (in bronze). Geiss.
177. Boy and Goose, after the antique in the Louvre (in zinc). Geiss.
178. Plenty (in zinc, bronzed). By Geiss, after Professor RAUCH.
179. Boy Extracting the Thorn, after the antique in the Vatican (in zinc). Geiss.
180. Girl Playing at Tali, after the antique at Berlin (in zinc). Geiss.
181. Boy at Prayer (in zinc). By Geiss, after Professor RAUCH.
182. A Shepherd Struggling with a Tiger (in zinc, cast and bronzed, small life size). By Geiss, after FRANZ.
183. Venus, after CANOVA (in zinc). Devaranne.
184. Flora (in zinc). Deveranne.
185. Florentine Wolf Dogs, after MOLOSSUS (in zinc). By Deveranne.
186, 187. Two Angels praying (colossal size, in zinc, bronzed). By Devaranne, after BLAESER.
188. Faith (in zinc, bronzed). Devaranne.
189. Group of Fox and Ducks (in bronze). [His Majesty the King of Prussia.] WOLFF.
190. Four figures representing Spring and Winter, forming part of a series of eight (in terra cotta). Professor LEEB, Munich.

191-214. Collection of Marbles (chiefly antique). [Exhibited by Sir Hervey Bruce, Bart.] The Centaur; Statue of Minerva; Statue of Leda; Colossal Head of Jupiter; Statue of Flora; Statue of Socrates; Statue; Cupid Asleep; The Infant Herculus; The Head of Marcus Aurelius the Younger; Statue of Bacchus; Cupid and Psyche; Agrippina; Bacchus and Ariadne; Head of Venus; A Roman Senator; Cybela; Jupiter; Dying Gladiator (in Tiber clay); Marble Copy of the Venus de Medici; Four Mosaics, two of them representing Ruins in Rome.
215-222. Collection of Antique Marbles. [Exhibited by the Earl of Yarborough.] Bacchus and Acratus; Minerva; Sophocles; Alcibiades; A Genius; Venus; The Bull; A Roman Galley (votive).

223. Monument to the late Peter Purcell, Esq. JOHN HOGAN, member of the Pantheon.
224. Monument to the late Dr. Scanlan. JOHN HOGAN.
225. Monument to the late Right Rev. Dr. Fleming, Bishop of St. John's, Newfoundland. JOHN HOGAN.
226. Monument to the late William Beamish, Esq. JOHN HOGAN.
227. Equestrian Statuette of the late Field Marshal, the Duke of Wellington (in bronze, on black marble pedestal and plinth). [Thomas Walesby, London.] Modelled by Count D'ORSAY.
228. Model of a Monument, erected in Hitton Church, Bedfordshire, England, to the memory of the late Countess De Grey. TERENCE FARRELL, Dublin.
229. Model of a Monument to be erected, in St. Patrick's Cathedral, by the 18th Regiment, to the late Lieut., Col. Tomlinson. TERENCE FARRELL.
230. Sketch for a Recumbent Portrait Statue of a Peer, in the Robes of the Garter. EDWARD RICHARDSON.
231. Bas Relief (cast in copper). By Winckelman, after RAUCH'S Monument of Frederick the Great.
232. Hercules' Shield, modelled after Homer's description (in bronze, gilt). [His Majesty, the King of Prussia.] WICKMANN.
233. Sketch for a Monument to Thomas Moore. JOHN E. CAREW.
234. Hand and Breast (in marble). EDWARD RICHARDSON, London.
235. Statue, life size, of the late Thomas Davis, to be erected as a testimonial to his memory, in Dublin (in marble). JOHN HOGAN, member of the Pantheon.
236. Bust of the late Daniel O'Connell (in marble). JOHN HOGAN.
237. Bust of the Rev. Theobald Mathew (in marble). JOHN HOGAN.
238. Bust of the late Thomas Steele. JOHN HOGAN.
239-243. Busts of General Lord Gough; of the late John Lawless, Esq.; of Lord Brougham; of Sir John Herschell; and of Douglas Jerrold. E. H. BAILEY, R. A.
244. Equestrian Statuette of Her Majesty, Queen Victoria. [M. Anderson, Esq., Dublin.] Count D'ORSAY.
245-251. Busts of the late Thomas Little, M. D., LL. D.; of Dr. Little; of Noblett R. St. Leger, Esq.; of Miss Catherine Hayes; of Miss Mayne (posthumous); of a Lady; and of a Gentleman. RICHARD BARTER, Dublin.
252. A glass case of Medallion Likenesses. RICHARD BARTER.
253. Bossuet Preaching. [Besse & Co., Paris.]
254, 255 Two Statuettes (in marble). [Miss O'Brien, Dublin.] A. BARRE, Paris.
256. Busts of Wellington and Moore, on one stand. F. BURNETT, Dublin.
257. Bust of the late Peter Burrowes, Esq. (in marble). T. BUTLER, London.
258. Bas Relief of the late Duke of Wellington (in marble). FRANCESCO CECCARINI, Belfast.
259. Bust of a Lady of Distinction. [Miss Cahill, Cork]. CANOVA.
260. Bust of Theobald Wolf Tone (in marble). TERENCE FARRELL, Dublin.
261. Bust of Earl De Grey (in marble). TERENCE FARRELL.
262. Statue of Master Barton (in marble). THOMAS FARRELL, Dublin.
263. Bust of the late Mrs. Hemans. [A. Fletcher.]
264. Statue of Her Majesty Queen Victoria (in marble). J. FRANCES, London.
265-267. Busts of Her Majesty; His Royal Highness Prince Albert; and Richard Brinsley Sheridan. J. FRANCES.
268. Statue of William Dargan, Esq. JOHN E. JONES, London.
269. Bust of Her Majesty Queen Victoria. JOHN E. JONES.
270, 271. Portrait Groups of Children and Animals. JOHN E. JONES.
272. Statuette of the late Duke of Wellington. JOHN E. JONES.
273. Portrait Statuette, the Favourite (in marble). JOHN E. JONES.
274. Group of the Children of James Stirling, Esq. (in marble). JOHN E. JONES.

275. Statuette of Baron Meyer de Rothschild, on horseback, with dogs (in marble). John E. Jones.

276–301. Busts (all in marble):—His Excellency the Earl of St. Germans; Countess of Eglinton; Earl of Eglinton; Earl of Clarendon; late Daniel O'Connell; George Roe; Mrs. Dargan; late Pierce Mahony; Thomas Brassey; Sir John Benson; William Fairbairn; John David Barry, of Paris; Sir Mathew Barrington; Sir Charles Fox; Sir William Betham; James Perry; William M'Cormick; William Anketell; the late Alexander Nimmo; William Dargan; Rev. Dr. Sadleir; William Harvie; Mrs. W. Harvie; Lord Rossmore; the late James Ferrier; James Gwynne. John E. Jones.

302–344. Busts of the Emperor and Empress of the French; Louis Philippe; Sir Henry Pottinger; Sir Richard Morrison; William Keogh; Charles Lever; Albert Smith; Sir Robert Kane; Rev. Dr. Henry; Surgeon Cusack; Sir Cusack P. Roney; W. H. F. Cogan, M. P.; J. F. Waller; N. D. Murphy; Dr. Petrie, R. H. A.; Colly Grattan; Edward Jones; Michael Balfe; Master Tennent; Sir T. Deane; Dr. Lyons, Cork; Lord Denman; Duke of Cambridge; Major Edwards; C. Copeland; Mademoiselle Favanti; Miss Tennant; Nepaulese Ambassador; Hon. Miss Copley; late Sir R. Peel; J. Wallack; Lola Montes; Sir W. Hackett (late Mayor of Cork); Earl of Ellesmere; Sir H. Marsh, Bart.; Captain Williams; Lady M'Neill; Surgeon Rynd; Rev. Mr. Hartigan; Mrs. Cogan; Miss Gernon; Rev. Peter Daly. John E. Jones.

345. Portrait group: The Children of William M'Cormick, Esq., London. John E. Jones.

346. Bust of Miss Catherine Hayes. John H. Foley, A.R.A.

347. Statue of Sir Sidney Smith. The late Thomas Kirk, R. H. A.

348–354. Busts (all in marble) of the late Duke of Northumberland; the late A. Colles, M. D.; the late King George IV.; Nelson; the late Dr. Kirby; the Right Hon. F. Shaw; and the late Judge Burton. By the late Thomas Kirk, R. H. A.

355–362. Busts, of the Very Rev. Dean Packenham; the Provost of Trinity College, Dublin; Lord Dunboyne; the late Thos. Moore; the Rev. Dr. Todd, F. T. C. D.; (in marble; the Rev. Dr Todd); the Rev. Dr. Elrington; and the late Most Rev. Archbishop Magee. Joseph R. Kirk, A. R. H. A.

363. The Hon. Mary Pakenham and her favourite Dog. (Statue in marble). [The Earl of Longford]. The late T. Banks, R. A.

364. Equestrian Statue (full size) of Her Majesty, Queen Victoria. Baron Marochetti, London.

365. Bust of Miss W—— (in marble). Baron Marochetti.

366. Statue of the late Sir Michael O'Loghlen, M. R. Christopher Moore, R. H. A.

367–374. Busts (all in marble) of the Earl of Carlisle; the late T. Moore; the Duke of Leinster; the late Lord Plunkett; the Lord Chancellor (Brady); the late Surgeon Carmichael; Lord Morpeth; and Judge Perrin. Christopher Moore, R. H. A.

375–388. Busts of the late Prof. Mac Cullagh, F. T.C. D.; the late George Stephenson, Esq.; the Lord Chancellor; Master Stedman; Sir Edward Blakeney; John Philpot Curran; the late Jos. Dunne; the Earl of Derby; the late Judge Burton; the late Sergeant Warren; the Earl of Clarendon; Sir P. Crampton, Bart.; the late Marquess of Anglesey; and Jonathan Henn, Esq., Q. C. Chris. Moore, R. H. A.

389. Bust of Richard Lalor Shiel (in marble). [Right Hon. Henry Labouchere]. Chr. Moore, R. H. A.

390. Bust of a Highland Boy. Alex. Monro, London.

391. Medallion of Lady Constance Grosvenor. Alexander Monro.

392. Statue of the late Sir R. Peel. Mathew Noble, London.

393–396. Busts of the late Duke of Wellington: Lord Nelson; the late Sir R. Peel; and of the late W Etty, R. A. Mathew Noble.

397. Bust of the late W. D. Freeman, Esq., Q. C. The late C. Panormo.

398. Study for a Portrait Statue of Sir Walter Scott (in marble). Edward Richardson, London.

399, 400. Busts (in marble) of Michael Angelo, and of Raffaelle. Henry Ross, London.

401. Bust of the Duke of Wellington. Henry Ross.

402. Bust of the Marquis of Anglesey (in marble). M Sievier, London.

403–407. Busts of Her Majesty, the Queen; and Statues of their Royal Highnesses the Prince of Wales, the Princess Royal, Princess Alice, and Prince Alfred. Mrs. Thornycroft, London.

408–410. Busts of the late Chief Justice Bushe; King George III.; and the late Duke of Wellington (all in marble). The late M. Turnerelli, Dublin.

411. Bust. B. Williamson, Belfast.

412. Bust of the Emperor Napoleon III. (in marble) Baron Nieuwerkerke.

413. Bust of Dean Swift (in marble). [Exhibited by the Earl of Charlemont.]

414. Bust of Pope Pius IX. (in marble). [C. Bianconi.]

415. Bust of Edward VI., King of England (in marble) [Lady Frances Cole, Dublin.] By Roubilliac.

416. Voltaire and Rousseau (on pedestals of Jaolo antico in bronze). [Hon Mrs. White, Dublin].

417. Bust (Florentine) of Captain F. R. M. Crozier, R. N., F. R. S. (in alabaster). [T. Crozier, Esq., Donnybrook.]

418. Bust of the Emperor Napoleon III. (in zinc). By Barre.

419. Statuette: his Holiness, Pope Pius IX. By Barre.

420. Female Bust in Italian Costume (in marble). R. Piehl, Berlin.

421. Bust of Shakespeare (in marble). T. Ochs, Berlin.

422. Medallion of James Watt (in marble). Dackerer, Berlin.

423. Bust of Thorwaldsen. Professor Rauch.

424. Colossal Head of Frederick the Great (from the Grand Equestrian Statue, Unter den Linden, Berlin). [His Majesty the King of Prussia.] Professor Rauch.

425. Bust of Prince Waldemar of Prussia. [His Majesty the King of Prussia.] Wittig.

426–428. Bust of a Shepherd, after Thorwaldsen; Paris, after Canova; and Daniel Webster (all in marble). Bianconi.

429. Statuette of Frederick the Great (in zinc). Potel.

430, 431. Statuettes of Frederick I., of Prussia; and Frederick II., Elector of Brandenburgh (in copper). [His Majesty, the King of Prussia.] Winckelman, Berlin.

432. Bust of the late Duke of Wellington (in bronze) Baron Marochetti, London.

433. Bust of His Royal Highness Prince Albert (in bronze). Baron Marochetti.

434. Bust of Napoleon I. (in bronze). Baron Marochetti.

435. Bust of Adam Smith (in bronze). Baron Marochetti.

436–455. Reductions and Statuettes (in bronze), exhibited by Fischer, Berlin; Franz Müller, Berlin; Wolff, Berlin; Mencke; Blaeser; after the works of Rauch, Kiss, Blaeser, &c. These are rather ornamental works than works of art in the stricter sense, consisting chiefly of copies or reductions of those already catalogued.

## PAINTING.

In entering upon a short examination of the contents of the Exhibition in this department, we turn first, instinctively, to the works of the Old Masters, the valuable and varied collection of which, separated as it was from the mass of modern paintings of all the European schools,—but only by a partition wall through which abundant means of passing from one atmosphere of Art to the other were provided,—afforded a standard and test of the progress of their successors towards real excellence. We are compelled to forego any attempt to describe or criticise them in detail within our narrow limits here; but it is precisely this department of painting which least requires such treatment from the writer, because the schools, styles, and works themselves of the great Masters are familiar to most readers, and will, in all probability, frequently again present themselves to the study of the remainder. A few words we may, nevertheless, devote to the classification of these treasures, and to remind the reader how the greater Artists knew how to apply those principles which we have already alluded to as characterizing true Art, the pursuit of which has been but little and rarely practised by contemporary painters either here or on the Continent. The chief principle necessary to the practice of pure Art is to make the Means—that is, all that is made up of technical knowledge, and experienced mechanical power—ever attend on the End of Painting, which is the harmonious but vivid expression of some Ideal, whether that be of an Action, or of a Thought, or (highest of all) of an Emotion or Feeling. And amongst such subjects the highest, of course, are those of a purely religious character, in the illustration of which, too, the older Masters lavished their utmost powers of mere execution, as well as of imagination and expression.

The religious subjects selected for delineation by the Painters of Italy are, of course, chiefly those connected with the peculiar dogmas and worship of the Church of Rome, the forms and details of which are so full of suggestions to the poetic and imaginative faculty of man. But it is not merely upon those in communion with that Church that their works now produce a deep effect; for they present examples of excellence in pictorial art which has never since been reached; though modern artists of all nations and creeds have endeavoured to equal them, even in dealing with similar subjects. Every person of refined and educated taste takes the purest pleasure in the contemplation of the glorious creations of human genius, in which Italian Faith was expressed, and that whatever may be his individual creed or opinion. Those Painters and that People believed that the highest purpose to which Art can be applied is to the advancement of religion; and this not only in the admirable treatment of religious circumstances, or of the abstractions of religious faith, by which the honour and glory of God might be directly served, but also in those simple figures or groups in which intense piety and devotion may be so vividly rendered in the expression of them, as to act as a direct invitation and incentive to the beholder to give way, as he looks, to the same pure and holy feelings.

Of specimens of this high class there were very few in the Exhibition Gallery; and among those of the Old Masters the highest subject was that of the Divine Infant with His Blessed Mother; a subject treated according to the various traditional designs known by the names of the *Madre Pia*, the *Mater Amabilis*, the *Holy Family*, &c. In all these the intention of the pure-minded Christian Artist was ever to delineate the Infant Saviour and the Blessed Virgin by forms of the utmost grace and the utmost simplicity, preserving the gentle gravity which befits such holy company, and lavishing all the resources of imaginative design and gorgeous colouring at his command, upon the attainment of the utmost combination of richness and beauty. But a greater excellence still generally attended efforts undertaken with such a motive; and, prefaced and accompanied as these often were, we know, by fervent prayer and the highest spiritual exaltation—we mean the glory of an *expression* above all the technical excellence of the schools, in which the Divinity of the Son of God, the Purity and Piety of His Virgin Mother, and (in other figures) the rapt devotion of the holy Apostles, saints, and believers on earth, shone forth with a wondrous power, which could not fail to exert a corresponding influence on those upon whom the Artist sought to create a profound impression, and whose belief and habits of mind rendered them peculiarly sensitive to such appeals. It is to be observed, too, in the subject commonly called the *Madonna* it was not merely the gracefulness, the beauty, the tenderness, the purity, of the most honoured of God's earthly creatures, that the pure old Painters desired to portray. All these qualities of His Mother were treated as the highest homage to her Divine Son, and in every one of the elder paintings of the Holy Family it is Himself—His form—His action—His countenance, to which all the rest of the picture bends, as it were, in silent wonder and adoration; and it is on Him that the painter seeks to fix the spectator's reverent attention.

This was the religious style of Art, in which religious subjects (and chiefly those of the Life of Christ on earth) were treated as such. The less powerful or less deeply religious painter treated the events of that Life in a merely narrative, dramatic, or historical manner; and though in such works the dignity of the subject was preserved by a certain severity of drawing, and grandeur of colouring, still the highest effect was no longer capable of being produced by them. In subsequent times the gradual debasement of religious Art (beginning with Raffaelle's fall into Paganism of thought, continued and increased by Correggio, and perpetuated by the influence of the eclectic and naturalistic schools during the following centuries), at last reached such a pitch of forgetfulness of the proper significance of Art, that sacred subjects were treated like those of everyday life, and the artist forgot his meaning in the mere desire to increase his own ephemeral reputation by the production of gracefully designed and softly coloured groups of men and women.

But it is not with the impressions inspired by such works as those last alluded to, nor with feelings impregnated with examples of such perversion of the highest mission of Art, that this subject is to be approached; and while we distinguish the excellent from the indifferent work in point of drawing, of colouring, of light and shade, and power of general design, we must ever seek for the success of religious Art chiefly in the expression of it—in the exhortation or warning it may contain for us, and the force and purity with which these are expressed. And looking upon these pictures from such a point of view, examples there were in this collection (slight as it was in comparison with those which the great cities of Europe possess in permanence) from which to draw not only many a practical lesson for the faithful student, but much real improvement for every rightly disposed spectator.

Of this highest class of Art a beautiful copy* (probably after LEONARDO DA VINCI, whose style appears very evident, not only in the colouring, but in the types of the heads and the attitudes of some of the figures) representing the *Madonna and Child*, attended by angels and accompanied by the infant St. John (No. 74), seemed to us to be the noblest representative,—so far at least as the distance at which it was hung permitted any judgment upon it; because the composition of the group displays the most masterly skill, the choice and contrast of colours is magnificently rich, while at the same time the whole bears an expression at once severe and dignified, without losing the softness of perfect repose, and the forms of the figures are distinguished by the most exquisite grace, and a noble intellectual beauty.

The *Madonna* (No. 65), attributed to SASSOFERRATO, beautifully painted, and full of tender sentiment and sweetness, if not devotion of expression, affords an example of a work still of a class of Art unapproached by the moderns, but infinitely inferior to the former, because, with all its excellence of harmonious colouring, the forms and expression are merely the portrait forms of graceful common life, without the depth of devotional ideality.

The noblest work in point of execution, the most valuable to the student of Art, was, however, one which, in point of expression, and as regards the feelings it is calculated to suggest, occupies a middle place of excellence between those just mentioned: the genuine original, namely, exhibited by the Duke of Leinster (No. 75), *The Holy Family*, or perhaps a "Madre Pia," by ANDREA DEL SARTO. In this work (which is painted on panel, the figures almost of life size) the severity of design and vigour of drawing, as well as the very noble intellectual forms, bespeak the hand rather of one of the greater men of Florence than that of Andrea; but there is no reason, we believe, to doubt that it is the work of that versatile painter. Like all works of Art of the very highest class, it is not at once understood, but for those who knew how to devote hours on successive days to its extraordinary beauties of composition and colouring (both so bold as to seem equally daring as graceful and harmonious), some new loveliness of expression also daily disclosed itself, which at once proved to the general visitor in what the superiority of the Old Masters consisted, and suggested to the student of Art the true path to greatness. For it became clear how intensely the painter had riveted his whole soul in his work, and with what devout emotions he had perfected it. Whether upon the form of the Blessed Virgin, so full of pensive devotion, or the countenance of the Superhuman Child, there resting in the placid sleep of infancy,—upon that countenance and that form in this picture you may well look long, and the longer and the oftener you regard it, the less severe will the forms of the artist appear to you, and the more full of sad and earnest thought will be your mind. The gentle, unobtrusive gravity of the whole painting goes far to produce this impression, and chiefly, perhaps, because it serves to express the feeling of the artist when he designed and executed it. And it is often so in Art as in Oratory; that even without understanding, or before you are prepared to enter into, the intention or conclusions of the painter or speaker, you are already half carried with him in sympathy, overpowered by the intensity of his convictions, expressed to you in clear and vigorous forms. So it is that in a picture of this kind we are never disposed to criticise minutely its smaller parts and characteristics (even could they bear criticism), because the spirit of the artist's mind is there, and there is that amount of harmony and correctness of detail which leaves *our* minds free to enjoy whatever noble ideas he is able to communicate.

Scarcely less fine as a subject, fully as noble in treatment, and in the supreme harmony of many colours pre-eminent not only over these, but among all the contents of the Exhibition,—perhaps in this respect unsurpassable anywhere,—was *The Entombment of Christ*, by TINTORETTO (No. 25); a small picture, for it represented many figures, painted with a boldness almost rough, when examined closely, but yet of consummate richness, even softness of effect, when viewed as a whole. Not all the art in management of pure colours, nor all the science and skill in drawing, of the best painters now existing, could, in these respects produce anything like the effect which the great Venetian knew how to produce, as here, without even the trace of effort or design,—while in the idea of the composition the simplicity and yet variety of the grouping, and above all, the awe-struck yet tender feeling with which the expression of every figure, whatever its attitude, whatever its occupation, seems absorbed in the tremendous subject of the piece, it is not too much to say that the ideal of this class of religious Art was here realized. It was to us, indeed, impossible to pass an hour before this priceless gem of Italian genius without an earnest hope that it might one day find its way into an Irish National Gallery, for the perpetual instruction of Irish students in so many branches of technical knowledge, as well as of imaginative power and truly artistic feeling, in which it is a perfect model of its kind. And now that the nucleus of a National Gallery is already formed, and that arrangements are so far advanced for the erection of a permanent building in which that nucleus is destined to be the centre of a permanent Exhibition (which will be assisted on all sides by the temporary deposit of original works of the Great Masters), it is with no slight satisfaction that we look forward to our students availing themselves of the opportunities of instruction which the ready zeal of the proprietor of this work has already largely

* In suggesting that this picture is but the copy of some glorious original (though probably an old, and certainly a very beautiful copy), it is proper to state, once for all, that in speaking of the works here noticed the writer does not consider it part of his business to enter into the question of authenticity, the question of original and copy, at all. Even the most skilled judges are often mistaken in a matter so nice, and he desires to leave such inquiries altogether to the trading fraternity, and to those wealthy buyers whose ambition it is to form expensive galleries of names, not things. The correctness of the following Catalogue (printed from that of the Exhibition Committee, though indeed arranged somewhat more intelligibly) must not, however, be taken as admitted by the present writer. On the contrary, he feels sufficiently confident that in very many cases the proprietors or the compiler of the Official Catalogue have attached names to pictures to which they had no manner of claim. Only a few of these are noted as doubtful in this Catalogue, and those only where the writer either felt an absolute certainty on the matter, or where he conceived that the unwarrantable adoption of a very great name would tend seriously to mislead the reader.

afforded through the medium of the Irish Institution, and will doubtless frequently afford them in the new establishment.

Besides these works in the higher walks of religious Art, the Exhibition contained several other specimens of the early Italian religious painters, of which that attributed to Pierino del Vaga (No. 85), *The Holy Family*, attended by angels (perhaps properly a "Madre Pia," or a Nativity), is especially pure and beautiful. The style of this work seems to be earlier than Raffaelle, or at least of his earliest period, and it probably belongs to the elder school of Bologna. This picture also, notwithstanding many deficiencies in technical accuracy, belongs to a class of Art the cultivation of which ought especially to be esteemed in Ireland, and which will one day (when the Irish student is emancipated from the influence of tastes not naturally our own, but only thoughtlessly imported from abroad) produce here the noblest results.

Passing on from the earlier works, whose glory lies in their Expression rather than in the perfection of technical knowledge and finished execution, the finest examples of Art in this Hall were, perhaps, the two Correggios; exhibited respectively by Lord Ward, and by Mr. C. D. Young, of Glasgow. The former (No. 14) was Vallati's celebrated original duplicate of the *Magdalen Reading*, one of the most famous ornaments of the Dresden Gallery; a painting which is so well known as to need no remark here,—one distinguished above almost all those of the Master for elaborate finish and exquisite richness and grace of treatment, but one which affords also a marked example of the sudden degradation of artistic feeling in the representation of religious subjects even so shortly after the time of the works before noticed.* The latter specimen of the Master, *St. Mary Magdalen* (No. 31), is far nobler as a portrayal of the features and character of the Holy Penitent: it may indeed serve to attest that Correggio had some moments of recollection and appreciation of those principles which he usually sacrificed to the intoxicating charms of sensuous excellence; and though this beautiful head does not convey any expression so intense as that which fascinates us in a Madonna of Raffaelle or Leonardo, it proves at least that the great apostle of an opposite style was not altogether destitute either of the instinct or the power through which they won their choicest laurels.

The more modern "Eclectic" School of Bologna, whose characteristics of mere scientific correctness of execution and regularity of taste have gained for it an undue reputation among succeeding artists, was largely represented. *The Martyrdom of St. Sebastian*, by Guido (No. 70), one of the gems of Lord Ward's well-known collection, afforded an example perhaps too favourable; for in that work the expression of the youthful saint (whose features beam with humble but confident anticipation of that world in the joyous contemplation of which, and the enthusiastic adoration of its King, the martyr feels not his earthly torture) almost makes one forget to observe the consummate skill with which the figure is drawn, and the fine feeling with which the whole scene is painted.

The *St. Francis in the Desert* (receiving the Stigmata), by L. Caracci,—in which the landscape is by Paolo Bril (No. 5); *The Crucifixion*, by A. Caracci (No. 4); *The Entombment of Christ*, which ought rather to be called a "Pietà," by Correggio (No. 55); the exquisitely painted *Madonna Addolorata* by Carlo Dolci (No. 95); the *St. Catherine*, by Domenichino (No. 73), though in some parts much hurt by re-painting, and that by an ignorant hand; the noble *Judith bearing the Head of Holophernes*, by A. Allori (No. 10); the graceful and tender *Marriage of St. Catherine*, attributed to Carlo Maratti (No. 98); the fine oil sketch for a great picture, *The Nativity*, attributed to Giulio Romano (No. 79); and a *Madonna* by Titian (No. 93), matchless for harmony of colour and grace of composition: such works afforded all the opportunity that could be desired of tracing the progress of taste and power of execution among the Schools posterior to Raffaelle; while the prince of painters himself was at least represented by the original oil sketch of the Vatican Fresco, the *Coronation of Constantine* (No. 129). Lord Charlemont's *Rembrandt*, too (No. 12), supplied a perfect specimen of the manner of one of the most remarkable of the northern Schools in the treatment of subjects of sacred history.

We have confined our too rapid remarks upon this part of the Exhibition to those works only from which a lesson might be taken in the higher principles of true Art, of which we could only find examples among religious subjects; and even among the older Masters themselves the instances of true feeling and expression became rarer and rarer, even within half a century after the Fine Arts had reached their zenith in Italy. In the treatment of Pagan classic subjects, and those of ordinary as well as heroic life, however, they continued to exhibit powers so much above those of their successors in these ages, that we gaze with increasing astonishment upon the indescribable delicacy and unrivalled harmony of such compositions as Nicolas Poussin's *Bacchante and Satyrs* (No. 132), and with not less wonder upon the more than life-like portraiture which such men as Titian and Rembrandt (by the use of means so very different) knew how to fashion in the incomparable *Cæsar Borgia* (No. 138) of the former, and the *Burgomaster* (No. 250) of the last-named master. But we must leave these works for the present without a word, and pass on to notice the efforts of contemporary genius; for we may remind the reader that the chief object of the Exhibition was to develop the extent and importance of contemporary labours, and that the department appropriated to the works of the older Masters was intended chiefly but to illustrate by contrast the adjoining collection of those of their successors, while affording the visitor to the Fine Arts Halls the means of guiding his taste and stimulating his judgment by examples of acknowledged excellence.

In the Hall of Modern Paintings, as well as in the other, the highest efforts, as might be expected, were those inspired by religious sentiment, or at least by the contemplation of subjects of a purely religious character or significance; and of these, perhaps, the noblest example was to be found among the contributions

* The presence of the Box of Perfumes, which, in allusion to her affectionate offering and service to the Saviour, is the traditional sign of the Blessed Magdalen in the early paintings, in this work is indeed specially useful, in order to define the intention of the artist, which might otherwise—so great is the want of devotional expression—have required explanation. And, in fact, some English writers, in ignorance of the meaning of the type, and little capable of understanding the peculiarly poetical reverence for this saint with which the Catholic painters of Italy were filled, have committed the ludicrous mistake of calling this Magdalen an "Egeria," and it has even been engraved in England under that title.

of Prussia at this first meeting of all the modern schools: the *chef d'œuvres* of C. Begas, representing the sublime scene of *Christ Prophesying to the Disciples on the Mount of Olives*,—[Matth. xxxiv., Mark, xiii.] (No. 364.) This is a work of large compass (for the figures are all nearly life size), but it is finished in every part with accurate attention to detail; and the carefulness with which every form, every colour, nay, every shade of colour, and every character of attitude, is portrayed, evidences the untiring zeal and jealous conscientiousness of the true Artist.

In the composition of Begas' picture (which somewhat reminds us of Bendemann's works), he has chosen the summit of a high mountain for the scene, and in the distant depths of an extensive valley, and on the slope of an opposite hill, are dimly visible the towers and buildings of the Holy City, softened by the dusky haze of the fast-dying sunlight. The Redeemer sits upon a high rock, His hand extended pointing towards Jerusalem, as He explains to the chosen Disciples the meaning of the awful prophecy He had uttered as He left the Temple gates. His countenance is full of sadness—of that sorrow for the sin of man which is often so affectingly alluded to in the sacred writings. At His feet reclines the Beloved Disciple, the soft and graceful attitude of whose figure speaks all the humility, the gentleness, the beautiful simplicity, of St. John "the Divine," and whose features, half hidden, express at once the human sorrow of the Apostle of Love, and the entire trust and devotion of the inspired Evangelist he was destined to become. Beyond St. John, nearer the edge of the hill next the city, sits the gray-haired Peter, his head leaning on his hand, his eyes bent on the ground, submissive to his Master's will, but awe-struck and stunned by the terrible nature of the omnipotent decree to which he listens, and plunged in meditation as it were upon the future destinies of the doomed race of his fathers. On the other side, in the foreground, St. Andrew, reclining on the slope, rests on his arm, his powerful manly face and form full of resolution, but equally penetrated with a holy submission to the decree of God, and with the recognition of the justice as well as the power of the all-knowing Son of Man. Behind him again, and leaning eagerly upon his shoulder, springs forward the young St. James, whose pure and vivid features (seen in profile) at once fasten the attention, and whose vigorous energetic form presents, perhaps, the most admirable figure in this singularly beautiful group.

In the choice and arrangement of colours, the Artist does not show less power or less study than in the simple and unaffected completeness of his grouping; and though his art in this respect is of that sort which is so dexterous as to conceal its being art at all, it were well for the student to observe and bear in mind the particular combinations of harmonious colouring exhibited in this picture. The drapery of the principal figure consists of a loose tunic of a brown pink shade, over which appear the massive folds of a white (but a yellowish or creamy white) mantle. These colours are the brightest in the picture, and naturally direct the eye to the principal figure in it; but they are not intrinsically bright. The solemnity of the subject, the whole scene itself, in a manner, peremptorily forbids the use of tints of a bright or lights of a vivid character, and those of the principal figure are only brighter (and but sparingly so) by contrast. St. Andrew, who is most in the foreground and nearest the eye, wears the deepest and richest colours; his tunic is of dark blue, and he wears a mantle of deep but somewhat cold yellow;—colours which contrast strongly, but the shades of which, in the present instance, are just sufficiently dull or subdued to prevent too great an emphasis upon them. The youthful form of St. James is appropriately adorned with a mantle of a very light and delicate purple, under which appears a sleeve of green so light that the sunny parts are coloured with yellow. This delicate purple exactly harmonizes with, by in a manner melting into, the sky behind. St. John is clothed in a simple dress of light but very subdued green, which not only contrasts exquisitely with the delicate red of the tunic of the principal figure, but in itself affords a refreshing resting-place for the eye, without too violently attracting its attention; while that of St. Peter, whose figure on the crest of the hill stands in relief upon the dusky yellowish background of the city and distant hills, is a garment of a brownish yellow shade, which again melts into the neighbouring tints, and prevents the least of that too marked contrast which might call off the mind from the solemn but dreamy contemplation of the silent and awful scene.

The general expression of this picture is, then, peculiarly appropriate, and the heads and particular features of the different personages represented appeared to us to afford almost the best instance we had seen in any modern work of that dignity and simplicity, but at the same time that clear precise meaning and vivid individuality of character, which in the treatment of a great subject we should expect from a great Master. There is a manliness and certainty about it which we have never found in any production of the modern German "religious" or "pre-Raffaelite" school that we have seen. One only deficiency seems to separate this of Begas from the efforts of the Old Masters: he has not attained the same finish of colouring that we see even in the least of them. The same harmony, the same moderation of general tone, would by a more finished painter have been attained with clear colours, instead of the always mixed and generally muddy tints employed by the modern Prussian; and this might easily, one should imagine, be accomplished by an artist so happy in the beautiful but difficult melting of similar colours one into another, while preserving with force and clearness the outlines of the figures in each. And though among the Prussian artists, dealing with religious or heroic subjects, M. Begas stands here alone, in those excellencies we have just noted, yet it may be observed as to the last, that even among the moderns that rich finish of severely contrasted colours, managed nevertheless with entire harmony and with perfect simplicity of effect, has not been found impossible, as Lessing's noble work (*John Huss before the Council of Constance*), in the Stædels Institute at Frankfort-on-Maine, would prove,—or, perhaps, any large work of that Master, had we been fortunate enough to have numbered one among the treasures of the Exhibition.

Besides M. Begas' painting, the Prussian school contributed another, claiming, at the first glance, to be of equal importance, if only because of its great size, and the richness of its brilliant and elaborate colouring, —the *Esther Accusing Haman*, by Levin (No. 362). The subject is one of the most dramatic which sacred history affords to Art, and M. Levin, in depicting his story, has sought at the same time to fill our minds with something of the splendour as well as dignity of eastern scenes and eastern personages, in the expression of which the magnificence of gorgeous colouring might be allowed the freest license. The name of the artist (a name well known before in the literature of Germany) is one which at once betrays the Hebrew origin of its bearer; and in alluding to the painter's race we cannot help remarking the affecting tendency of contemporary artists of Jewish descent to seek their subjects from the history and traditions of that once honoured nation, and this whether their dogmas of belief have or have not ceased to be the same. Among the painters and musicians and literary men of this century, many such instances will suggest themselves, in which their nationality has thus been signalized and perpetuated—and it were well for the imaginative vigour, and, therefore, the artistic fame, of artists of other races too, if they had a little more of the tenderness and strength of Hebrew home-affections.

M. Levin's subject is in illustration of the well-known passage in the Book of Esther (chap. vii.), where the Jewish Queen, having declared her nation, denounces to the Persian monarch the savage plot of his vindictive favourite against the existence of her race. In the design of the hall or room in which Queen Esther entertains her lord and his minister, the artist has evidently sought his model among the forms of the Assyrian architecture made known to us by recent discoverers, and he has equally endeavoured to express (in the features of the two male personages), the characteristics of that peculiar type of manly beauty which we study with so much surprise and pleasure in the curious sculptures of Nineveh lately discovered, first by a French and afterwards by an English traveller, and of which Paris and London now possess such a wealth of specimens. With M. Levin's heads we are well satisfied. There is great vigour and the highest manly strength, both of form and character, about them, and that of the King is distinguished as much for intellectual force —(that real kingship of nature, which after all did characterize the eastern despots to a very remarkable degree)—as it is for that just symmetry of proportion which constitutes the true beauty of both sexes. But it is to be feared that, in his eagerness to attain all possible historic accuracy of detail in a representation of the remote eastern civilization, the painter too much lost sight of the *dramatic* accuracy which was equally necessary to his purpose of expressing the life of those ages; and accordingly much has to be forgiven and laid aside from consideration, before we can sufficiently sympathize with the artist to feel that sense of undisturbed pleasure in the contemplation of his work which a work of Art ought always be able to inspire. The grouping of the three figures is rather loosely managed; and there seems to be no definite connexion between them and the accessories of the picture, so that upon a large space of canvass no inconsiderable portion is left as it were in blank, because it tells nothing, and in no way assists in the development of the story. The King sits upon a broad, solid, square-shaped throne, or rather an immense high-backed arm-chair, the arms formed of stone or bronze lions crouching,—rather an uncomfortable-looking specimen of eastern luxury. Before the King, who nearly faces you on the right as you look at the picture, stands in the centre a small round table, on which lies a *dessert* of fruits; and at the other side of this, on the left, in the near foreground, and almost with his back to the spectator, Haman sits, on a lower chair or stool. Behind, on the King's right, stands Esther at full height, her left hand resting on his chair, her glaring eyes turned on the minister opposite, and her right arm extended vehemently towards him, as if she had just concluded her denunciation. The King has started forward on his seat, one hand clenched on his knee, the other grasping the lion head of the chair arm, and with all the concentrated strength of a powerful countenance, and the most searching glance of a noble intellectual eye, he gazes steadily, fiercely, into the face of his servant, whose conscious terror, and the sudden and involuntary shrinking of whose figure, have already clearly convicted him. The suddenness of the action, and the yet undisturbed silence of surprise, are made known by the quiet form of two attendants, seen at a very short distance behind, who are bearing out the remains of the previous feast into a pillared court into which the apartment opens. The story is thus simply told, and told also forcibly, no doubt; but it might have been told even more vividly in much less space, and yet with more dignity of expression and largeness of manner. Even the idea represented has not in the present instance met justice in the author's treatment of it; for the waste of rich painting without forms, which occupies so great a part of the picture, not only adds nothing to its meaning, but even dissipates beyond reason the attention of the spectator, who after all is more impressed by the size of the work and the splendour of its brilliant colouring than by the subject of it.

The whole picture, indeed, sins against the ideal by a certain exaggerated stage vehemence (always inconsistent with real depth of expression) assumed by all the characters—sins against the real truth of the subject (the delineation of the lofty-minded Hebrew girl interceding for the protection of her people) by the selection of an attitude and place which degrades the heroic queen, uttering the words of denunciation, too nearly to the level of a mere attendant slave, who has assumed a temporary liberty of scolding—and lastly, the painter proves by his loose grouping of the figures, that he is incapable of managing a great subject on a large scale, for want, perhaps, of the necessary diligence in preparatory study, and reflection upon the means by which the great Artists attained that harmony and completeness which constitute the chief elements of their success. Yet notwithstanding the severity with which the size and pretension of this picture, and the attention which has been attracted by it, thus obliges us to point out defects so grave (looking at Art as we ever must, from the higher point of view suggested in the introduction to these remarks), we have thought it right to devote some space to the examination of this work, because it exhibits no small power both in drawing and colouring, and in these respects will bear the palm from almost every other work on the walls of this Hall (of Modern Art). The attitudes in which the figures are placed are by no means easy of execution, and it is worth while to observe that the painter has not merely expressed himself with spirit, but has produced in every part a clear and vigorous effect,—undisturbed even by the richness of his colouring—not only by a great breadth of drawing generally, but also by the very careful management of all the details in every feature and in every limb. The proportions of the work are so large that it must be viewed from a considerable distance; whence the artist's rough and somewhat patchy manner of laying on his colours no longer affects the eye, and the full effect of the rich softness of surface (as in the fabric of the draperies) produces a powerful impression.

Turning now to the contributions of Belgium, in the same class of Art, we may naturally expect that in a country so rich in works of the highest class, especially in colouring, the tradition of Rubens' manner must still exercise the most powerful effect upon his successors; and to any one who has had the opportunity of observing the successful efforts of the students who crowd the halls of the Musée, at Antwerp, which boasts so rich a collection of the noblest works of the great Belgian Master, as well as of so many others of his most distinguished fellow-countrymen, it will seem little surprising that modern Antwerp still produces paintings in which the composition is more rich and more matured, and the colouring more harmonious and better executed, than those of the contemporary European schools. The Exhibition presented a very fine example of this style in the large picture (No. 347) representing *St. Elizabeth of Hungary distributing charity*, painted by N. De Keyser, of Antwerp; from the private gallery of the King of the Belgians. It is true that this work, considered with reference to the full significance of the subject, is not indeed very satisfactory, because, while it certainly exhibits much of the intellectual power and the skilful execution of the Old Masters of this School, it shares also their prevailing fault,—that of entire want of *Ideality*, both in the general treatment of the subject and in the expression of the particular figures represented: yet for this very reason it claims our attentive consideration, because few works in the whole collection offer practical lessons of greater value. Let us, therefore, compare the subject as it is known from history with the artist's treatment of it, and in recalling the features of the story of the Saint, let us try and imagine how they might be represented by one to whom the gift of artistic insight and expression had been granted.

St. Elizabeth of Hungary was one of those impersonations of all that is pure, and gentle, and humble in character, diffusing sweetness and charity wherever the atmosphere of her presence extended, which shine out occasionally in the history of the half-savage middle ages of Northern Europe. She was the daughter of Andreas, King of Ungaria in the twelfth century, and was brought up in all the pomp and circumstance of barbaric splendour; and she was beautiful from her earliest years, and grew to be the very ornament of her father's court, and the highest object of the aspirations of his brilliant chivalry. Yet her heart was not dazzled by such a situation: under her royal robes (when reluctantly she was forced to wear them) it still beat as calmly as that of the humblest cottage maiden; and it is related that from her childhood she was ever occupied in ministering personally to the wants of the poorer classes, in those ages, perhaps, even more than now, regarded by the nobles and great folk as little other than mere brute beasts—as ungifted with feelings of any kind as they were (of course) destitute of human reason. The example of the beautiful princess was not thrown away in such times, and it is remarkable that ever, where and when the customs of society seemed, in the middle ages of Germany and France, to resolve themselves into utter barbarism, there and then rose up for ever, among the rude forms around, the silent, yet silently effective protest of some such messenger of true civilization as Elizabeth.

Elizabeth would have been but too happy to spend her whole life in the pious practice of active charity, and to ask nothing of the world's joys or the world's splendour. But her desire was inconsistent with the spirit of the time, and in obedience to her father's will she became the wife of Louis, the Landgrave and Duke of Thuringia. In her new way of life she but strengthened the example of her maiden years, and as a mother and the head of a great household she still showed the same humble care and cheerful piety, condescending still (with the full permission of her noble partner) personally to administer relief to the sick and the poor, and often even, in imitation of the cure of the lepers in the Gospel, piously tending those afflicted with diseases too disgusting for the delicate sensibility of her attendants to approach. Her husband, however, died of fever after his departure to the holy wars; and as Elizabeth still continued to expend her means profusely in the charity of every kind in which her life was occupied, she was at length violently driven from the Landgrave's domains by a steward, one of her own servants, and with difficulty begged her way, unrecognised, to her father's court. There she was, of course, received as became her rank, as well as the affection with which she was remembered, but she would not again occupy her place in the court, and obtained means from the King to institute a charitable establishment, or house of mercy, where she quietly passed the remainder of her life in the same works with which she began it, and died in 1226, November 19, in the reign of Frederick II.

Such is, shortly, the story of St. Elizabeth of Hungary, which we note here at so much length, because the events of her life have long supplied favourite subjects to the greatest artists down to Murillo, whose magnificent painting (perhaps one of the noblest in Europe) forms one of the great attractions of Seville. She is generally represented, as in the present Belgian picture, in the act of distributing alms and food to the poor, but often, also, engaged in tending the sick; and the traditions of Christian Art point to her as in a manner the type or personification of the virtue of Charity itself. It is easy to conceive, then, how great a significance such a subject ought properly to suggest, and might suggest, if treated by an artist rich in the resources of the imagination, and really penetrated by such feelings or inspiration as we have seen are necessary to the highest expression in the works of Art. And before it was possible rightly to judge of the success of one of the most distinguished painters of modern Antwerp in the finely painted work before us, it seemed necessary to recall to mind the just Ideal of the subject.

M. De Keyser represents the Saint in her maidenhood, standing outside the richly decorated porch of one of the massive buildings of the times, distributing bread and money amongst a group of poor and sickly people, who gather round the steps for the purpose. Elizabeth stands on the highest step, and, with eyes meekly cast down, she is placing a piece of money, taken from a purse hanging on her left arm, in the hand of an old woman who bends forward from among the crowd. By her side, on a lower step, stands a page, bearing a basket of food, and behind her, in the porch, are two female attendants. The princess and her maidens are elegantly, yet not over richly, dressed. However, the principal group, the finest figures, and the most beautifully painted work, must not be sought in connexion with the principal personage in the picture; an incongruity of treatment not uncommon in those Schools where colour is the great object, and where form becomes entirely a subservient one.

The figure upon which in this picture the attention becomes riveted at once is not that of the Saint, but of a woman who has been borne on a litter to the bottom of the steps, and whose shoulders are supported (as she attempts to rise towards the distributor of charity) upon the knee of a ragged boy behind her. Her pierced and tattered clothes fall sadly over her bosom, and hide a form attenuated by long sickness: and the gentle patient face, the feeble smile, the languid forehead, the poor weak eyes, which seem to have lately flowed with many a tear, tell a story and make an appeal far, oh! far more eloquent than any language.

Across her knees lies the dying body of a little child, about its head a cloth, and a few mere rags upon its almost breathless form. Behind that stands, looking up to Elizabeth, an elder child gazing with a mixed expression of wonder and bashfulness and expectation; its blooming beautiful countenance not yet stricken down, but beaming with that joyous life in which infancy ever plays, even amidst the saddest scenes of sickness and desolation. The right hand of the mother hangs over the knee of that brother who supports her shoulders; the left hangs down across the body of the little dying one. Both hands are exquisitely drawn and painted, and one might almost from them alone read the whole meaning and story of the figure. The old woman, the man, and the graceful mother and child standing behind, are also excellently painted, and there is one remarkable characteristic of this group that the whole crowd is perfectly expressed by this example of a part of it, and the crowding effect *in the picture* (in which so many painters dissipate the whole meaning of these works) is entirely avoided. The group is perfectly natural, and yet the contrasts of figures and attitudes, of characters and ages, with which, though so small, it abounds, must be the product of deep study, and the utmost reflection and care. Yet, no stiffness, no formality, no academic theatricality, is the result; only harmony and variety with which the eye will never tire. Such composition is, then, so far, an instance of the triumph of Art, in which the means are lost sight of in the effect of them.

Much of this harmony, and of the completeness of this effect, is due to the very careful and very beautifully finished colouring of all the figures, and especially of the flesh tints. The tone of the whole picture is subdued, and this allows the painter a much greater scope for the gradations of emphasis by which he may express the relations of the different parts. He has paid very close attention to the effect of light on the minuter portions of each figure (such as the different unevennesses of the flesh and skin, produced by the play of muscles, or the articulations of joints, in the face, and the fingers of the principal figure just described); and as the general drawing is free and bold, this minuteness in no way impairs the breadth, the vigour of effect, of the whole. The colouring of the skin of the dying child is equally indicative of minute care and diligent study, and that of the rough form of the supporting boy behind reminds one strongly of Rubens himself, from a careful study of whose works the drawing also of that form has certainly proceeded. In these respects M. De Keyser's painting was, perhaps, without exception, the finest work representing the present century in the Exhibition.

Having said so much, however, it would not be right to leave this work without observing that the style of colouring used by the artist is by no means *pure*, and very far in this respect from Rubens, or indeed, any of the greater colourists of the Flemish school who understood perfectly how to produce the same harmony of effect by the proper management of tints, each of the most clear and brilliant character. M. De Keyser, then, has yet a large step to take before he can rank as a *colourist* among the successors of Rubens. And a still graver fault in the work, as a representation of Elizabeth of Hungary, has been already alluded to. That figure, which should be the principal one, is actually all but the least, and this not only in consequence of absolute insipidity of expression—extraordinary, when we see what the artist could do in the face of the sick mother—but also by reason of the dull uncertain colours and the too clumsy and ungraceful form in which she is represented. Her figure is wholly wanting in power of any kind, and the *too* close student of Rubens has been unable to compensate for this by simplicity of treatment. A severely drawn, *un*-Rubens-like figure of simple innocence, and clothed in mere white or some wholly simple colour, would have harmonized with the rest as well, and might have told the story intelligibly, though still by no means as the greater artists would have told it.

Another Belgian painting, also from the Gallery of the King, represented the Brussels branch of the Schools of modern Belgium, as M. de Keyser did that of Antwerp; and the points of dissimilarity of style, both in composition and in colouring, would be found to be both numerous and important, if we could enter into them fully here. The work alluded to is (No. 353), *The Temptation of St. Anthony*, by M. Gallait, a painting which is said to bear in Belgium the highest reputation among those of contemporary artists; and the great care, indeed, which has evidently been bestowed upon it, and the long and effective study the completion of such a work argues in the painter, are well calculated to produce such a reputation.

The history of St. Anthony, one of the early Christian saints, is well known. He was originally a noble youth of Egypt, in which country he passed a long life, partly in solitary mortification in the desert, afterwards in the foundation of monasteries, where he spent his days in preaching to and instructing the people, as well as in the performance of many pious works, and died about A. D. 357, in the reign of the Emperor Constantius, at a very great age. It would be out of place here to recount the many species of temptation with which, sleeping and waking, the saint was visited in his younger years, during his long sojourn in his solitary cave, as related in the traditions of those times. The devil is said to have conjured up from time to time every form of animate and inanimate things by which the cupidity, the ambition, or the luxuriousness of man may be excited even for a moment and himself seduced even to momentary departure from the good resolutions he had formed. The representation of these scenes has occupied the attention particularly of the Flemish School of Painting, and of many of the greatest of its older Masters. The present work may, therefore, be considered the fruit of those traditions of his School with which the painter was necessarily surrounded, and it ought not to be judged without reference to their characteristic tendency.

We have before had occasion to remark on the general want of spiritual feeling in the conceptions of the Belgian artists, especially since the time of Rubens, who was unquestionably the greatest of the Flemish School, and who has not since been equalled in the many high qualities of a perfect painter, which he possessed. But Rubens, though in his day a man of unusually honourable, pure, and simple habits, had, at best, but a gross, material soul, and his greatest works—indeed all his works, unless a few of those painted in his student days in Italy,—bear strongly the impress of such a nature. The immense fecundity of his genius, which has filled all his own country, and richly endowed almost all the great galleries of Europe beside, and his almost unique powers of drawing and perfect mastery of colouring, naturally made the great Fleming the principal model for the imitation of his Belgian successors; and it was, perhaps, unavoidable that the taste and feeling of these should become trained in the same direction. We must not, then, expect from Belgium examples of that refinement in the treatment of their subjects which is found in other Schools, and was not indeed unknown to Rubens' half-forgotten predecessors (such as the elegant and tender Otto Venius, and others of the earlier Flemish masters); and accordingly, M. Gallait's idea of the Temptation of St. Anthony must not be judged according to the standard of Italian or Spanish art. Enough in the first place if it be not offensive (as Rubens would certainly have made the picture), and if it suffer us with profit to examine it at all. And more than merely this may be said of M. Gallait's work, for it possesses not only the negative merit alluded to, but there is in it that seriousness, that clear strength of expression, pointing in the right direction, though not, indeed, attaining absolute spirituality, which at least proves that the artist's mind was full of the moral told in this grand story—the temptations of the devil and the world overcome by faith in the grace of God; and that if he has not expressed so sublime a lesson with the depth of feeling and devotion which it might have called forth, it is the artist's power (perhaps through the effect of his Flemish training in Art), not his intention that is in fault.

The action of the piece is very simple. It is night, and the Saint has been praying or meditating near the mouth of his rocky cave, beyond which dimly gleams the darkness, in which twinkle a few stars, while yet the moon is half veiled by a cloud. The devil has brought to the cave a tempter in the form of a beautiful girl, whom he presents, almost naked, to the saint. The manly form of the intellectual Anthony sinks on a step of rock beneath his crucifix, as if taking refuge from an enemy with whom his soul had done fierce fight, and who had all but conquered. With outstretched hands he reaches to the cross, the emblem of that grace in which alone he hoped for victory. And now he bends his head, already relieved from his fear by the strength it had communicated to him, but still hesitating to look behind and see whether the form had yet vanished. The figure of the girl on the right of the picture stands forward from the blackness of the night; her head is turned towards Anthony, the features seen in profile, and she has raised her right hand to her cheek, as if meditating sadly and sorrowfully on the scene, from which she must reluctantly fade away before the spirit of the saint's prayer. Behind and between these principal figures, and in the shade of the cavern, leans forward the eager form of the Author of Evil, in the form of a slight but well-built young man, adorned on hands, and feet, and breast with the customary claws with which the grotesque barbarism of the Middle Ages delighted to endow the terrible fallen angel; a class of conception, be it observed, in reality weak and inexpressive, and of course wholly beneath the dignity of true Art. He shades his eyes from the light, which streams from behind the crucifix, and rages with grinning hate and fear against the symbol of the salvation of man. But he is already vanquished, and he and his attendant tempter must needs submit, and leave in peace the holy servant of God.

The effect of the two lights in the picture is very striking, and it is not merely striking, but really natural and expressive. The strongest light proceeds from the warm rays of a torch, which appears, from the shadows it casts on the crucifix and figures, to burn in the interior of the cave, but immediately behind and above the table of rock on which the crucifix is placed. This light, resting vividly on the cross, so distinguishes the Symbol as to make it the key of the composition—indicating the nature of the action of the figures, and of the power which supports the virtue of the Saint. The other light is that of a moonbeam, which has pierced through the night-clouds, and silvers the left shoulder of the female figure, whose right side glows with the warm rays from the torch. This contrast of lights is very delicately painted, and is barely strong enough to suggest to the mind something of the contrast between the powers within and without—the former asserting its supremacy with a vivid warmth which seems sternly to exclude its fading enemy from any hope of one moment's existence more.

The figure of St. Anthony is boldly, but very carefully drawn, and admirably coloured; his head is, indeed, greatly the best part of the picture, and its conception very much above that of the rest of the work. The suffering but still confident eye, the vigorous manliness but thoughtful and resigned expression of the brow and lip, are sufficient certainly to sketch the character of the Saint, and not without a certain simple grandeur—all which proves the Artist's high capacity, not only in execution but in design; and though a more devotional expression might have more loftily told the story, and the indications of a more vigorous faith have impressed a higher character on the Saint, still in studying this head we are disposed to forgive the artist's want of higher powers, and to concede that it redeems the less spiritual nature of the remainder of his work. M. Gallait might well, surely, have preserved for us this fine figure, and the remainder of the composition, merely dimming the form of the devil in the mysterious darkness of the night, and laying a little less of emphasis on that of the female tempter, whose suggestions (even so delicately rendered as in this picture) are certainly not of themselves meet subject for the exercise of Art. Had she been but lightly sketched in the starlight, veiled somewhat by the shades of night, the story had been more delicately and even therefore more effectively represented, and the painter would have found fully as great an opportunity for the development of his singular talent, much of which we cannot help thinking has not been worthily employed upon his design as it stands. Every part is over distinct, as if he thought he could not afford to keep back any one thing in which he might exhibit his excellence of mere painting. But the great Artist, on the contrary, ever forgets himself in his subject, and above all in the message of truth or grandeur which through that subject he feels called on to proclaim to the world.

Among the remaining works from Belgium it is proper to notice here two very graceful paintings of the class at present under examination. They come respectively from the Schools of Antwerp and Brussels—from the former (No. 356), *Jacob and Rachel*, by Bellemans (who contributed also several fine works of greater pretence and size than this); and from the latter (No. 349), *Rebecca*, by Portaels.

The subject of the first is that passage in Gen. xxix. where the first meeting of Jacob and Rachel is described. He has taken the stone from the top of the well, and admitted her flock to water, and he is seated at the side of the well, his hands still resting on the edge of the round flag he had removed. The exquisitely light and graceful girlish form of the beautiful shepherdess (still almost a child) bends over him, as with one hand on his shoulder, and the other extended, pointing into the bright distance, she shows him the place of her father's dwelling, to which she is about to hasten to announce his arrival. His head, turned back towards her, beams with manly grace and beauty, and the brilliant thoughtful eye rests softly on her sweet features.

as if he hung upon every accent, already charmed into passionate admiration, and fervent though reverent love. It is an exquisite love-scene, tenderly and poetically expressed, and it would indeed be difficult to find a real fault in any part of the picture. The figures are extremely well drawn, and with as much clearness and vigour as carefulness in detail. The attitudes are simple, natural, but at the same time strikingly graceful and appropriate, and the types (though that of the male figure has much more in it of the Celt than the Arab or the Jew) strongly characteristic and very pure. The colours selected are also very well managed, and the harmony with which they are distributed is particularly telling, while the bright light with which the whole picture is filled is not only the proper tone of the eastern landscape, but it fully expresses the joyous tenderness of the scene. [This work, we must remark, was placed so high as to be almost beyond the reach of the spectator, the persons employed by the Committee to arrange these pictures on the walls having paid but little attention to anything but size in the selection of a situation for the works exhibited. The critical observer was thus, of course, placed in a very disadvantageous position, which may here, once for all, be taken note of.]

The second piece (by M. Portaels) consists of the simple figure of *Rebecca* seated at the well, where the messenger of Isaac sees her; and she has just received from him her future husband's gifts: the necklace is hung round her neck, but a bracelet still remains in her hand, while she listens to the servant's words, silently musing on her future fate in connexion with the sender of such splendid presents. The figure (which is nearly full length) is that of a full-grown Jewish girl, beautiful not only in the symmetry and regularity of her expressive features, but also in the air of quiet dignity and modest grace by which the spectator's attention is at once attracted, and which, even without the accidental attributes of the scene, might have marked the identity of the gentle, pure, and intellectual Rebecca. M. Portaels' work does not possess the catching gracefulness and piquancy of M. Bellemans', and it is heavier in colour and somewhat harsh in execution,—but the drawing is good, the expression is true and sufficient, and the type is more ideal than we are disposed to look for in Belgian art. It is to be regretted that the whole scene was not the object of the artist's ambition instead of a solitary figure, for the latter generally partakes too much of mere portrait character, save in the hands of such masters of expression as we fear the present age can scarcely yet boast of.

Of those works of Art which were either of a religious character or represented subjects connected with religious history, no others claim observation here,—for we have not space even to mention all those of Germany, Holland, and Belgium, which might well deserve notice, and those of France were only represented by the unseemly academic fancies of M. Tassart (No. 331), and the ungoverned conceits of M. Gosse (Nos. 329 and 330), only serving to give another proof of the axiom, that there is but one step from the sublime to the ridiculous. The little we shall have to say of our Irish painters, we propose to defer to the sequel. Those of England offer no examples of religious, and but few attempts even in heroic or historical Art. In the department of LANDSCAPE, however, to which it is now time to turn, the greatest efforts of the last-mentioned nation have been made, and here they have been more than once crowned with even the highest success. Landscape Painting is not, indeed, capable of expressing ideas so lofty or so ennobling as those which may be so clearly conveyed by means of the human countenance, and the action of men, represented with equal power, but which has also much of what is greatest in sublimity and most perfect in beauty to offer for our contemplation. The expression of a landscape, either in nature or in painting, is not so easily described, as it is not so easily appreciated by the ordinary class of spectators, as that of the human features, or that of a dramatic scene in which men are the actors: and the higher classes of landscape painting address themselves in consequence rather to the highly-educated few than to the masses of mankind, who are but little accustomed to reflect upon their sensations, or to arrive at any conclusion for themselves, which would require some trouble—who content themselves with mere passive enjoyment of whatever is placed before them to be enjoyed. But we shall not stay to offer any general remarks upon the character and requisites of true Landscape Art, because of late years the press has been very active in the discussion of the subject, and notwithstanding all the petulant vehemence, the ignorance, and the presumption with which the advocates of the Spiritual in Art (which is ever ALL that is truly valuable in Art, or has ever been recognised as such by the wise and the refined), have been attacked in all manner of printed works—in the book, the magazine, the review, and the newspaper,—it is a consoling fact that the powerful eloquence of Mr. Ruskin* has substantially prevailed, and has even already influenced greatly the opinions of the thinking world. To portions of his admirable volumes we should ourselves have to take many exceptions, it is true, if it were our province here to enter into an examination of their scope and their contents; but nevertheless, on the whole, we feel justified in referring without more remark to those volumes every reader who desires to understand what landscape painting is, and to profit by the study of it. For us, it would be idle to dilute in inferior language what he has so admirably spoken; we have ourselves found the principles he lays down to be perfectly true, and his application of them is just and conscientious in our judgment. We shall not, therefore, repeat the contents of works which ought to be in the hands of every one of our readers.

In the Fine Arts Hall of our Exhibition there was so rich a collection of Landscape Art, that we should find it very difficult to determine what individual picture was entitled to absolute pre-eminence in power, in beauty of idea, or in the perfection of execution. Turner, Achenbach, Kalkreuth, Tschaggeny, and De Vigne —Stanfield, Seiffert, Callcott, and Bossuet—in all their several styles, and judged each by his proper standard, would find their supporters; but if Mr. Ruskin's absolute and unqualified hero-worship were to make him insist on Turner, we should, perhaps, on the whole, rest content to admit here, too, his supremacy. No. 842 in the Catalogue was an *Italian Landscape*, by the late J. M. W. Turner, R.A., and contributed to the Exhibition from the collection of the Earl of Yarborough. It is one of this great Master's earlier works, at least earlier than those in which, for several years back, so much extravagance of style distracted the public estimate of Turner's powers, and it is certainly one of the finest specimens we have seen of his mature excellence. At first sight the general tone of the picture will strike the observer as not altogether characteristic of an *Italian*

* "Modern Painters." By a Graduate of Oxford (John Ruskin). 3rd Ed. London: Smith, Elder, and Co., Cornhill. 1846.

scene, accustomed as we are to associate the name of Italy with a brilliant sun and a cloudless expanse of sky. But it must be remembered that the idea of an Italian landscape may be conveyed in more ways than by mere brilliancy of light colours. That clearness of air which gives an immense distance of perspective towards the sky, that magnificent height and extraordinary lightness of the vault of heaven, as compared with our poorer and closer canopy (which seems to one just returned from a southern climate like a heavy roof shut down close overhead)—that heaven is, above all features, the characteristic one of an Italian scene, and that Turner has presented us in all the sublimity of its immeasurable splendour.

The present picture is of considerable size, yet of the utmost simplicity of effect in composition. The foreground consists of the high undulating bank of a noble river, whose course is concealed on the right by the nearer trees and foliage. The middle foreground is of rich, warm earth, covered along each side with ground plants, and their large leaves of deep soft green, which are drawn with vigour and boldness, yet never so minutely worked out in their details as to fasten too much of the attention. On the right of the middle of the picture stands a group of lofty trees, whose stems are bare so as to let in the view of the middle distance, and whose leafy tops form a rich dark mass against the bright sky, of charming outline,—a mass of shade correctly representing the clustered foliage of rich timber, yet seen as it is in relief against the bright sky offering no details of leaves or branches, which might detain the eye from wandering into the splendid distance of landscape beyond. Beneath these trees, and partly in the shade of their foliage, a joyous group of graceful figures move in rustic dance, boldly drawn, yet indicating their forms with exquisite accuracy when observed at a proper distance; and relieving the deep shade by the bright points of colour, of warm blue, and of gray yellow, afforded by their elegantly flowing dresses. Behind the dancers, deep below, flows the river, which becomes visible in all its width towards the centre, widening to the view on the left as it turns in a short sweep of great breadth and majesty, and losing itself again beyond a many-arched bridge, in the plain: a distance far off, of rich flat or gently undulating fields, whose green is yellowed by the glorious sun now high in the opposite heaven, and growing more and more indistinct in the haze of bright light till they mingle with the faint gray of the extreme horizon. On the opposite bank of the river, in the middle distance, a gradual rising ground mounts into a wooded hill on the right, whose shrubs and trees stretching down quite to the brink throw a refreshing shadow upon soft-flowing water beneath; and just behind this nearer slope lies another gentle ridge in the distance, also clothed in foliage, its spur concealing a part of the city, whose turrets and housetops appear on the right as well as the left bank at the bridge. On the left foreground the high bank slopes away downwards; richly and fully occupied in all its space by thick shrubs and trees stretching along that side of the river, and casting their shadows upon the quiet stream as it winds so as to place them between us and the sun. In the distance more than one chain of hills stretches from each side, and disappears in the plain. One of these on the left is far enough to appear almost blue, yet warmly blue, through the clear air (a true glimpse of pure Italy), while beyond it, many many miles beyond, the outline of the farthest horizon is chequered by the undulating forms of other and other chains, of whitish gray, sometimes varying to pale blue, and sometimes melting into the fleecy clouds above, under the sheen of the vivid sunshine. The sun is up full in the centre of the sky, whitening all that centre part,—the sky only very gradually and tenderly deepening into blue towards the sides, while on the right the formless fleeces have thickened a little into cloud, tempering the soft shade of the trees in that part of the foreground.

It would require a lengthened essay to do justice to the extraordinary beauties of this transcendant painting, or to explain the wonderful power, the prodigious knowledge and care, and exquisite execution, which were necessary to its perfection; for it indeed affords an example of almost all the greatest qualities of this incomparable master. The eye is never tired of seeking into the boundless extent of his distance—along the fields, into the air, up to the sun itself, and then backwards and forwards through the transparent expanse of sky (which, it must be owned, Turner alone has yet adequately represented), then down to the cool shades of the river's banks and among the sweet trees and through their refreshing foliage, and up this pleasant ascent and over its farther side towards the crest of that beyond, and then farther and farther into the innumerable glades and valleys, among the countless plains and undulations far to those distant hills which it aches us to seek to pierce to, through the mist of sunshine:—is it not truly nature? Ever varied, ever satisfying, never wholly known, yet never surprising us by anything startling or over strange; full of peace and order, full of spontaneous grace, yet without even the semblance of any conscious preparation for effect—it is, indeed, a landscape which preaches the same lesson we may learn on the mountains beneath the very sky of God, a landscape which suggests to us all the feelings of the poet-painter when he drank in such a lesson; for he has preserved to us for ever those moments of the ever-varying scene of nature which affected him most tenderly, and he has led us by an unconscious emphasis of the same effects which emphasized it to his own mind into the same train of feelings with which his whole soul must have been filled. We receive, then, his beautiful work as a noble poem not to be coldly judged and rated according to the rules of Schools or the dry formulæ of amateur criticism, but a poem which, like every poem, can *not* be understood heartily without hearty study, and the willing sympathy of a simple and affectionate hour.

The only landscape, perhaps, in the whole Exhibition, which may not suffer in comparison even with that of Turner, is the wonderful realization of another and more magnificent phase of Nature's glory which we have next to record. It is from Germany; the picture of *Pantaleone, in the Island of Sicily*, (No. 417), by Andreas Achenbach, exhibited, together with another extraordinary piece by the same artist, by the Crown Prince of Prussia.

There is a peculiar atmosphere of brilliancy and solemn quiet combined in everything truly Eastern: in the air, the sky, the mountains, the desert, the white flat-roofed houses of the towns,—as well as in the grave, majestic form of the Arab race itself: a race in its characteristics of expression and of manners the noblest, most truly manly, and, perhaps, the most intellectual in the world. And it so happens that among these tribes, and in those Eastern lands, mankind understands and has undergone little change, and all the accounts of occasional travellers, as well as the more scholar-like investigations of Lane (whose valuable works on life in the East are, perhaps, the best yet written upon the subject), prove ever that the inhabitants of the

Desert and the neighbouring territories live still precisely as those of Moses' time, described in the books of the Old Testament. The painter, then, who would represent the life of the East, whether in depicting some occurrence of sacred history, or the expression of Nature under the noblest forms in which she clothed herself in the garden-land of the earth, has ample opportunity; and the ease and cheapness of passage thither deprive him of all excuse for meddling with such subjects till he has learned on the spot what they really mean,—till he has drunk in with eyes and ears, through every sense, and at every pore, the splendours of those Eastern climes (so often repeated nearer even than the East, in Spain, in Sicily, in Algeria, and among the Greek islands), of those lands near the sun in which the dazzling glories of a sky ineffably bright, illuminating the richest plains, the noblest mountains, the most luxuriant foliage, in an atmosphere indescribably clear and pure, form a succession of landscapes full of such magnificence and beauty as the experience of these colder regions of the temperate zone does not qualify us to realize to ourselves even in dreams. To such a climate, to such scenes, we ourselves, indeed, seem ever irresistibly attracted, and not merely because, as lovers of nature, we should find in them the most delicious poetical gratification and excitement; but, perhaps, also because there is some latent tendency in the Irish mind to seek back in the South and the East the ancient springs of its sympathies and associations. The skies of Spain, the sun of Mauritania, the various splendours of the Eastern landscape, and those shores of the Mediterranean which partake its nature, suggest many themes among which we should delight to pause here awhile: but we must content ourselves with referring to the example of them all in *Pantaleone*.

M. Achenbach's picture represents a city of the South and East in the midst of such a land as we have been speaking of, embosomed in the rich deep foliage of a warm climate, and canopied by an expanse of transparent sky which in so clear an atmosphere seems more vast and more distant than that of a starlight night in our finest frost of winter. In the centre of the picture, in the middle distance, gleam the white walls of a pleasant city, with its towers, its flat-terraced housetops mingled with the almost flat roofs of pale-coloured tiles, its minaret now the steeple of a Christian church, and its extensive fortress crowning the abruptly scarped steep of a lofty tower-like rock rising in the midst of the streets. The battlemented rock, and all the sparse hills, glow in warm red under the scorching gaze of the sun, the ancient cliffs and rugged mountain sides seeming ready to crumble in the excessive heat. For it is the silent afternoon hour of the sun's greatest power, when all the face of nature is dried up, save where refreshed by the irrigating streams laboriously brought down from distant mountains by the hand of man, the ever fertile earth rears the refreshing shade of that deep rich foliage which is as characteristic of those warm climes as the power of the fierce sun itself. And in the foreground, and stretching back on each side about the skirts of the town, is a lovely snatch of such a scene of verdure. In the centre an open space allows the sun's rays full play, the crumbling red ground showing only irregular tufts of green, across which winds a bridle-road round an old spreading fig-tree a little farther off, beneath whose shade an exhausted figure seeks for shelter, while its own pale leaves seem, indeed, themselves as much exhausted. On the left, a group of cypress trees, whose deep green appears still blacker amidst so much brightness, and, in contrast with the dull fig so near it, relieve and refresh the eye, just as in nature some such group so often rears itself in a similar landscape to offer a point of refuge to the dazzled and aching organ. On the opposite side of the picture rise the rich forms of a wood of forest trees, among which, and above the variously coloured brushwood, the picturesque cypresses, extending their rich branches of softest green, court prolonged attention before the eye travels on into the farther distance. It is seen amidst these masses of shade, exquisitely moderated and harmonized as they are, that the really warm white of the quiet city appears to shine so brilliantly in the clear light, almost surrounded apparently in such a frame of foliage. Beyond the city, and beyond the fortified heights which dominate over it, stretch across from both sides into the distance a succession of hills, the prolonged spurs of mountain ranges,—the more distant themselves mountains. Some of these, the lower hills, are partly wooded, the rest glow in red and ochre under the crumbling power of the sunbeams, delicately shaded with transparent gray as they pass into the extreme background; while behind and beyond all, many, many leagues away, the conical volcano summit of the farthest mountain rears its warm and tawny height, whose gradual ascent is already dimmed with gray across so vast an aerial distance. Above shines ever the clear bright azure sky, its intense blue scarcely dimmed by a few fleecy clouds of white, and deepening to the deepest pitch of colour in the farther distance away from the sun. The light shadows of those fleeting clouds touch lightly the warm gray of the farther mountains, and seem to move, ever-changing as if the reality were before us, while the eye wanders over the distant expanse: ever delighted, yet its curiosity never wholly gratified,—because the artist has caught and embodied, as it were, all the mystery of nature herself, and there seems as little limit to his picture as to the real landscape. The artist may, perhaps, deem that in the nature of such a scene an able painter—by the judicious arrangement of such contrasts of light, and especially by leading to his brilliant distance through so forcible a foreground of deep foliage with its strongly marked shadows—could find but little difficulty in expressing that extreme of space which the clear atmosphere of the South makes so strikingly present to the eye; and we shall not attempt to decide whether the expression of aerial perspective which, even in Northern scenes, Turner was able to achieve in his greater pictures, is in such scenes so much more difficult for the painter than in one like that selected by Achenbach; but, at least, we may confidently assert our own conviction, after hours of delighted examination of the Prussian picture, that it realizes with perfection, so far as painting can, all the glorious beauty of a scene eminently full of all the chief characteristics of the unsurpassable climate of the South, and that it is the first painting we have ever had the good fortune to see which did so realize such a scene, preserving all its poetry, delineating its details with perfect truth, and forming an artistic composition in our judgment absolutely unimpeachable. We have seen no other work of M. Achenbach in this style, and we have seen no other work of his possessed of nearly so much excellence. His powers may be fitful, his works may be unequal (and we have seen some that do not rise far beyond mediocrity), but had we only seen his *Pantaleone*, we should have pronounced him one of the greatest artists of modern times.

Besides M. Achenbach's work there were several others in the Exhibition which show the tendency of contemporary landscape painters on the Continent to seek their inspiration from southern scenes. Among these the French, since their acquisition of the African province of Algeria, might be expected to take the lead, and some of the best paintings are accordingly among their contributions. Of these, one of the most successful was (No. 690) by M. C. Grolig, called a *Landscape in the Environs of Algiers*. In the foreground is a Moorish well, with its white square walls and circular domed roof, in the shade of a group of lofty trees, among which a noble palm droops its graceful leaves from high. The gentle rising ground closes the left of the picture with thick brushwood and foliage; in the centre a bridle-road leads up to the fountain through low trees and brushwood from the distant valley, and in the distance the outline of a range of far blue hills raises itself on the horizon. The palm, the common ground cactus, vulgarly called the prickly pear, and the agave or American aloe, plants which abound so much in southern Spain, and of course in Africa and the East, are very accurately studied, and drawn with great care. Again, in the *View taken in the Environs of Algiers*, by M. Pierre Thuillier (No. 698), the general expression of the African landscape is yet more truly and more poetically rendered, though without M. Grolig's powers of drawing in detail. The distance of this beautiful scene forms its principal charm. The delicate azure of the calm bright sea shines in subdued colour, the far-off rocky islands, blue on the horizon, and somewhat dimmed by that mist of sunshine which on the sea shore in the South seems to make the landscape hotter on a still day, yet takes away but little of the space seen through the clear air. This delicate effect is rendered by M. Thuillier with great tenderness, and its charm is indescribable.

M. Thuillier exhibits two others, one of which (No. 626) *A View of the Gulf of Puzzuoli, Naples* (which is not a view of a gulf at all, but of a land scene on its banks, extending to an imperceptible distance of ashy blue hills on the horizon), proves that these tenderly coloured ashy distances are his especial delight. A third is, however, on the whole, the best (No. 583), the *View in the Environs of Algiers*, by M. Thuillier. It consists of a splendid study of southern foliage, including the cork, the palm, and other lofty trees, as well as the pale-leaved agave, the picturesque cactus before mentioned, and the rich shrubs near the banks of the stream in the foreground, luxuriantly as they everywhere abound in the irrigated lands of that fertile climate. Nothing can be softer than the foliage, nothing richer than the effect of the meeting sunlight upon the tinted trees and brushwood, nothing can suggest heat more vividly than the high red bank of crumbling earth in the centre, while the faint blue hills of the horizon lead the eye away as if into an infinite clear distance through the brilliant air.

The wonderful little picture by Horace Vernet, too (No. 631), *The Lion Hunt*,—the only specimen of the illustrious President of the French Academy,—gives us perhaps the best glimpse of the Desert, with its immeasurable distance of burning sand below, and dazzling azure above—the expression and perspective of which is almost as astonishing as the spirited dignity with which this grand composition has been imagined by the artist.

The same class of natural scenery is also very ably studied by M. F. Bossuet, of Brussels, who contributed several pieces representing Moorish scenes in the South of Spain, all of them admirably rendered, (Nos. 461, 482), though perhaps exhibiting too exclusive a pursuit of mere effect, which, after all, ends in mannerism, and may easily become only mechanical. The *View of a Roman Aqueduct* (No. 558) is the most important of these pictures. It represents, of course, a scene in Spain, for the sky is not in any part of Italy, we believe, so brilliant, nor the sun so powerful as in Murcia and Andalusia, in one of which provinces we may presume the Aqueduct to be. From the right, the line of the immense erection stretches into the centre of the picture, where it terminates in a vast and lofty tower, a square tower of red stone, like that which forms the wall of the aqueduct, glowing in the fierce light of the declining sun, which flings his rays from the left across the edge of a sloping hill on that side of the foreground. Between this hill—whose mass is in shade (but shade only in comparison with the extreme light), and the shrubs on whose crests are brightened into threads of gold—between this hill and the towering Aqueduct, the bed of a stream, now almost dry, occupies a deep-cut gorge, over which, and forming a precipitous ledge, runs the highway under the tower. On the road various picturesque buildings seem to climb the mass of the Aqueduct, leaning their walls against it, their coarse wooden balconies covered with blinds of matting hung from the window tops—the common protection against the sun in a small Spanish dwelling-place. On the left, overhanging the scarped valley, a round tower closes the road opposite the great square tower before mentioned, and burning equally red with it in the sunlight. On the road, between the towers and in front of the houses, a picturesque group of Spanish muleteers—some with carts, some still resting by the road side, some mounted, in their picturesque Andaluz costume, and with the inevitable carbine slung beside them—prepare for the road, which will be cool enough for travel when the sun goes down. In the distance a varied range of rocky mountains, tawny, uncultivated, arid, but glowing with a richness of colour under the splendid sky which not the most fertile landscape in northern climes could match for one moment in beauty. This is a truly Spanish scene, of nature and of human life, so vivid a glimpse of that magnificent region that it may well invite our Irish painters to spend some of their future years in that sunny land which tradition points to as that of their fathers, and where so many of the sweetest dreams of the peculiarly Irish imagination are everywhere realized.

But it is not merely in the realization of the effects of southern scenery that the contemporary landscape painters of the North are so admirably successful. In the delineation of the grandeur of the mountains and coasts of Northern Europe they have not failed to develop equal skill and power, and in that of the soft effects of melting light over a landscape, naturally cool in tone, they know how to express much beauty, of which the earlier Masters never dreamed; much beauty of a dreamy tenderness of character which refuses to appear to the burning brilliancy of the sun nearer the tropics. And in this style the artists of the Continent have of late years often successfully rivalled the best of the English school, which had previously seemed to monopolize it. In this, as well as in the other, a Prussian painter bore the palm in our Exhibition, the Graf Von Kalkreuth, two of whose finest works (contributed by the King of Prussia) made the visitor familiar with some of the most charming effects of German scenery. The first of these (No. [illegible]) *A View in Innspruck*, pictures the rich expanse of an extensive valley, gradually contracted into a gorge between two chains of mountains, of which that on the left runs out half way across the middle foreground of the scene, while the opposite or eastern range on the right recedes gradually till it disappears behind the last projections of the former. The flat plain is rich with trees and herbage. In the distance on the right appear the roof and spires of a city at the foot of the mountains on that side, while by the base of the western range, and then striking straight across the valley, towards the spectator, bubble along the glittering waters of a clear white river, sparkling in the yet high but setting sun, which flings half across it the shadows of the trees on the bank at that side. The velvet-clothed mountains of the farther range, opposite the sun, glow with the softest pale green sheen, growing grayer and more delicate in the distance—that distance itself most exquisitely rendered; every mile of it delighting the eye with new variations of rich forms, and new delicacies of light and shade, whose gradations are yet almost imperceptible—every mile of it enticing the eye farther and farther, until it loses itself at last in the turn of the valley, behind the opposite range; every object, and the colours and formation of the hills, becoming dimmer and dimmer, yet, in an evening clear from all mists truly brilliant and warm. The second piece (No. 406), *Martinswand, a View near Innspruck*, is as finely painted, but scarcely so noble a work, for its beauty depends rather upon a momentary effect of light than any more permanent quality. It is, however, a glimpse of the poetry of landscape, very tenderly expressed. The scene is a marshy plain, under the shadow of a steep dark mountain, from beyond whose spur a sluggish river creeps round at its base; the whole foreground and middle being so deep in shadow that objects seem scarcely distinguishable. For the sun has set some time, and only now throws its warm rays upon the higher regions of the air, in which the clear pale pink and pale greenish clouds float above the summit; the dark masses of pale green rock smiling a sweet farewell from daylight, and seeming to plunge in thicker and deeper gloom the sombre valley, with its lonely trees, and struggling sluggish waters and marshy grounds. This picture, as well as the former, is finished with extraordinary care; the minuteness of its richly laboured colouring, however, in no respect impairing the breadth of effect which a solid and vigorous treatment of every form had impressed upon the drawing.

We cannot help also at least naming here (No. 397) *The Castle of Lueg, in Carniola*, by M. Biermann, another fine Prussian work, in a high style of poetic landscape painting, and the delightful view on the Lake of the Four Cantons, by M. Seiffert (No. 407): both of them paintings, in the expression of peculiarly grand or lovely phases of nature, as well as in the execution necessary to preserve it, far superior to the best of those we are in the habit of recognising as good.

In a totally different style,—one usually regarded as by itself sufficiently difficult and engrossing to demand the exclusive attention of the artist,—namely, among Sea Pieces, the noblest specimen in the Exhibition was from the hand of the extraordinary painter of "Pantaleone," before mentioned: the *Pier of Ostende during a Storm*, by Andreas Achenbach (No. 405). This picture, which is of considerable size, is apparently a companion to the other, and was in its class, as that other also was, certainly one of the most perfect ever seen in Dublin. It is indeed a startling and splendid representation of the fury of a northern sea, when its rage appears not in the form of a gigantic swell curling in mountains of foam, but in those fierce heavy waves, whose ragged crests are torn by a gale too vehement to suffer even for a moment the least bubble of mere foam;—whose broken ridges are snatched up a little way by the wind, and driven down again at once in leaden rain; while the mass of waters rush heavily by with a force as if each drop of it struck separately like a beam upon every opposing object. On the right of the picture is the battered pier—one of those openwork constructions of heavy beams of wood, supported on piles, by which the irresistible channel sea is cheated of its prey on the north coast of France, in Belgium, and Holland. The broken water passes through the openings of the timber framework; its mass, but little broken indeed, and its power but half weakened; every looser beam, every loose plank, carried off in a moment, the planked parapet and boarded footway torn up gradually and hurried away, the mere bones of the strong pier left unshaken by the terrible tide. At the end stands the light-house, its wooden chamber raised high above the water upon the heaviest and stoutest beams. On the pier, two men and a woman, somewhat sheltered by what remains of the parapet, appear endeavouring to fasten more strongly some of the upper timberwork which seems about to give way; but so many planks of the flooring have just been snatched from behind and between them, that they will take the speediest shelter in the light-house chamber. The centre of the picture is altogether occupied by the tumbling and roaring waves. The sea is the colour of lead, under the deep dull heaven; the muddy water takes an olive green tinge when it catches the fitful light of those patches of blue sky which break through the black storm-cloud on the right, and the distant blue on the left, with its white clouds still for a little uninvaded by the driving rain-burst. The spray is thick and leaden in colour and in weight, oftener beaten down at once in heavy surge as it gathers, than permitted by the pressure of the storm to rise in showers of gray smoke, or blinding dust. On the left, the distant piles of the corresponding pier, with its light hung on a high pole, are just visible, while the fragments of the right pier are torn hither and thither by the mad waters with all the life and vehemence of a wild beast revelling among the fragments of his prey. It is difficult to say whether to admire most the easy, natural, and harmonious colouring of this fine piece, or the accurate and powerful drawing of the water. But the most valuable characteristic of the work is its earnestness—the vigour with which the general character of the scene is expressed on the whole, the unity of the picture. The spectator is filled with a sense of the power of the storm—the fierce strength of the waves—and the most vivid expression of their actual motion in mass. There is nothing conventional, nothing superficially studied about them, like the waves of Vandevelde, and even of Backhuysen. Achenbach's are real waves, each of which presents all its proper characteristics of form, yet with all the individuality and separate power which is seen in nature. And the general effect is due to no trick of composition, but clearly to the Artist's deep knowledge of his subject, and to the extent and intensity with which he was penetrated by the idea of it. This painting may then rank among the first class, as one of those instances of modern art which in landscape as much excels the ancient as the latter in a higher class of composition surpasses anything produced in later times.

Out of the numerous other examples of this style of subject in the Exhibition less successful all than Achenbach's, able though many of them were, we need only name here the *Agitated Sea*, on the English coast

(No. 660), by M. Meyer, of the Hague; *Hamilton's Point, Heligoland*, by M. Edward Schmidt (No. 415) and the *View off Buchaness, Peterhead, Scotland*, by M. Theodore Gudin (No. 620). Of late years the German marine painters especially have become fond of seeking congenial scenes for their canvass on the coasts of Denmark, of Sweden, and of Norway; and many portions of those shores are full of poetic interest, not only for the grand forms of their rocky walls, and the turrets and pinnacles into which these are often worn by the sea—(yet not more splendid than those which the Irish artist may find along our coasts near the Causeway in Antrim, Tory Island in Donegal, Westport in Mayo, the Killeries in Galway, Kilkee in Clare, Ballinskelligs and Ballybunion in Kerry, not to mention as many other places)—but also for the beautiful effects of the setting and of the rising sun among rocks coloured so brilliantly by various mineral agencies (as here also at the first and last-mentioned spots). And it is most extraordinary that our Irish landscape painters have not paid more attention to the magnificent scenery with which our northern and western shores abound. If it were the fashion for Prussian and Danish and Dutch painters to extend their autumn trips so far out of the ordinary European track, we are persuaded that no year would pass without some beautiful illustration of the beauties round us here on the canvass of those foreign artists. That those beauties have not impelled the Irish student to more careful study, and more intense exertion,—as their adequate expression would require both,—is matter of reproach and disgrace. The marines, which are generally to be seen here, are either puerilities or caricatures—there is no use in mincing the phrase—and we can now only hope that the beautiful works of foreign genius, Prussian, Dutch, French, and English, to which we are able here to direct attention, may serve not only to shame the Irish artist from his lethargy, or his idleness, but to teach him also how very much he has to learn before he can be fit to exhibit in a European gallery. And could he see the still more magnificent works of A. Leu, the beautiful landscapes of H. Gude, of Edouard Hildebrandt, and of E. Bodom (some among the greater artists of Germany who were not represented at our Exhibition, but a few of whose works were to be seen in London about the same time), and the Swedish and Norwegian paintings of Achenbach,—his aspirations would, perhaps, receive additional stimulus at finding that the favourite effects and choice scenes so gloriously perpetuated by these noble artists are precisely those with which, all round our shores, we are most in the habit of meeting, and which we are best accustomed to enjoy. A few amateur painters, like Sir George Hodson, Colonel Colomb, Captain Beechey, have produced very pleasing sketches of some parts of our beautiful coast (as No. 748, *Clew Bay*, Westport), but unfortunately that is all.

We have already placed Turner before all modern landscape painters; we have now to observe that he is not the only true Artist of whom England may boast in this branch of Art at least; and in truth in many walks of landscape Art that country has often succeeded in acquiring a reputation (acknowledged even by her more imaginative neighbours), which in religious and historical painting she has never been able to attain. It would appear that the taste of our next neighbours tends peculiarly towards the cultivation of that branch of Art which employs itself in giving expression to the sweet scenes of quiet nature in a country which, if deficient in the grand, the picturesque, and most of that which inspires the loftier flights of imagination, possesses at least abundant beauty of a soft and homely character among its rich plantations, its gentle streams, and its velvet plains cultivated to the highest pitch of profuseness; a country which boasts, too, of many an exquisite cliff of chalk or sandstone, shining in brilliant gaiety, or towering in warlike strength along its shores, while over those rugged cliffs, above those soft smooth downs, and canopying every landscape of river, of wood, or of sea coast, each season of the year brings forth new forms of the splendid cloud scenery with which it is the peculiar privilege of an island to clothe itself in these moist but temperate latitudes, with ever-varying magnificence. And in portraying these scenes the modern English school have attained an extraordinary proficiency in the accurate drawing and colouring of the objects selected for representation, a proficiency entirely eclipsing the efforts of almost all the most celebrated Masters of past centuries. It is true that no one of them has united to this species of talent those splendid powers of imagination, and that lofty vigour of conception, and breadth of expression, which distinguish Turner as unique among the landscape painters of this century, and it is also true that the artists of the Continent, with imaginative powers generally far superior, and with subjects so often more grand and more beautiful, are gradually gaining equality with them in execution too; but in the quiet and regular compositions of the English *naturalisti* there is yet, on the whole, more truth, less of affectation, more of completeness so far as it goes, than is to be found elsewhere, and among the productions of those of them who may claim the name of artists many a beautiful snatch of truly poetic nature may be confidently sought.

The first of these English pictures to which we shall direct attention is a *View of Dordrecht* (No. 795), by Clarkson Stanfield, R. A., one which, in the perfectly smooth glassy water of its foreground, presented a beautiful contrast to the agitated mass of sparkling waves in companion picture by the same Artist (No. 795), *On the Zuyder Zee*. Mr. Stanfield is especially remarkable for his sea and coast scenes, of which the greater number of his well-known works are composed, and both these paintings were excellent specimens of his more regular, quiet, and finished style. He has produced, though rarely, it is true, far grander and more impressive pictures, (especially after Mr. Ruskin's criticisms had suggested to him to seek the inspiration of Alpine scenes and the snow mountains), but his usual style was here fairly represented, and these two pieces fairly marked the advance which English landscape painting has made in the hands of their greatest living painter. Both scenes are Dutch, and present little of interest in their forms or the associations connected with them; but in the beautiful light and shade and the contrasts of colours in the still one, and in the exquisite play of the sun on the foam of the waves in the other, enough of fine natural effect is preserved to make the pictures very pleasing, and the beautiful modulations of colour (so difficult of management where all is under an even bright sun), yet all subdued in tone, produce the richest harmony. In the dull dead calm of the sluggish Maes stream one sees the heavy water drag itself along reluctantly, raising a little track of light under the oars and in the wake of the little row-boat which is pulling in under the shadow of the bank, while the still sails of some other vessels near cast their still reflections in the almost unruffled surface of the deep green current, and on the bank the reddish-brown houses among the light green trees add yet more weight and dulness to the sleepy heat of the afternoon. Above the trees, and on the right beyond the heavier mass of buildings in the centre, rises the rich light-coloured but massive tower of a large church, whose warm gray stone and ornamental forms relieve the eye from the insupportable stupidity of the dwelling houses by a Dutch river. All is admirably drawn, and especially the water, which, without any indication of motion on its surface, seems really to move along in a sluggish mass of weight, and breadth, and power. In the glimpse of the Zuyder Zee, on the other hand, the sea appears rough under a fresh breeze on one of those days when the blue sky is full of bluish-white clouds, but the sun shines out here and there, and the bubbling and tumbling waves sparkle in its rays, and the smooth sweep of each little swell of the pure water shines like soft satin cloth. There is no other painter who does not overdo this effect; but Stanfield's drawing of the tossing water is so perfect that even his somewhat too elaborate finish (especially of foreground details) does not impair that breadth of expression which makes each wave seem really in vivid motion, and his waves never repeat each other, but in their continued succession offer all the indescribable variety of nature itself. The sky in this picture is as much superior to that of other painters of the same style of scene (one apparently so easy that it is very common) as the water is in drawing, and every eye will at once confess the magical accuracy with which both are rendered. Mr. Stanfield's pictures, indeed, are made for the instant enjoyment of every crowd of visitors. Their fault too often is that they are too real, and too merely so,—that they do not suggest anything of a class more powerful, more beautiful, more admirable, than what the most ordinary observer is every day accustomed to note in scenes before him, and that such painting is artistic at all is only true because, what there is of superficial beauty in those ordinary scenes is faithfully rendered with such best expression as it is capable of conveying, and is pointed by the emphasis of a sympathizing mind in the way in which it is treated. It is spirited and life-like, and so far even above the mere mechanical correctness of a daguerreotype likeness, and yet so great is the knowledge, and so careful the applied skill of the painter, that its details are as accurately true.

We shall not stay to quote Mr. Ruskin's admirable account of the peculiar powers and beauty shown in Mr. Stanfield's works (which the reader will profitably seek out and study in his "Modern Painters"), but pass on to another excellent production of the same School, one in which, though differing extremely from Mr. Stanfield's in style, is distinguished by the same finished neatness as well as naturalness of effect and regularity of composition, rather than by more poetical attributes. We mean No. 857, *The Old Port of Naples*, by the late Sir Augustus Callcott, R. A., a painter the popularity of whose numerous works, both during his life and since his death, was greater than that of almost any of his contemporaries, and yet who probably left behind him no evidences of any new thought, or any proof of real genius. There is in his works a uniformity, a sameness, which seems to indicate the mechanical principles of their construction, but though this is certainly the case, they are not destitute of qualities capable of inspiring interest. Sir A. Callcott was full of a certain gentle, almost feminine, feeling for the soft, light, and clear air of the South, which secured him real success in many bright pictures, especially those of Italian scenes. Not that it is the sky of Italy that we see on his canvass, or the air of the Mediterranean that blows over his landscape. That sky is vast, that sky is intense, that air is clear to infinity of space,—full of invitations and suggestions more grand, more vivid, more poetical, than the amiable Callcott was ever formed to understand. But he delighted in wide-spread light, even and all-discovering, and he loved the soothing influence of calm soft air under such a light, and these he has indeed preserved for us with great truth and not a little tenderness. Stanfield places before us, if not the poetry, at least the reality of gentle motion, in the sea waves, among the clouds, or upon the smooth-flowing river. Callcott fixes some scene of perfect calm, in the contemplation of which he has placidly dreamed away his own day happy, and before the representation of which we can also dream away ours pleasantly enough. That bit of quay, upon the wall of which the lazy fishermen are sitting, the shade of that picturesque belfried gable under which some others of the sunny Neapolitans are lounging, these are just the pleasantest of spots in which to rest a dreamy afternoon, gazing up the bright but not dazzling sheet of pure still water,—along the pleasant perspective of the quay street on the left,—and upon that far brink, from which rises the graceful form of a campanile, beautiful like Venice,—and still farther up the disappearing distance of the narrow street on the right of it, with all its picturesque indistinctness of varied forms and colours. The prevailing tone of warm gray over all the picture softens down the mind, which is not distracted by any emphasis upon particular objects or effects, but sinks into the enjoyment of a sweet luxurious reverie. And in this the Artist achieves complete success. In Stanfield's more powerful pictures you admire his talents, you think his water very spirited, and his clouds and his church tower, his boats and his pier, very beautiful; but in Callcott's work, though weaker, you find a something which almost makes you forget the painter and the painting, by filling you with the sentiments of the scene itself.

Such were the best specimens here of the English School, specimens which truly represented its chief excellences. Two able works of Mr. J. B. Pyne (No. 790), *A Landscape*, we believe in Wales, and (No. 785) the graceful and somewhat Turneresque *View of Palanza, on the Lago Maggiore*, displayed greater force, but that of a less ordered imagination. One more alone need be noticed here; because it was the type of another and commoner style, dangerous in imitation, but one which in the hands of the master has been a vehicle for the expression of many a real beauty; the picture, namely (No. 817), called simply *A Landscape*, by T. Creswick, R. A., one of those large studies of English trees for which this painter is very celebrated, and which are perhaps more perfectly represented by him than by any other; and the scene one of those open woodland glades which Mr. Creswick has repeated a hundred times with every effect of light. In the present picture the light shines from one side through the clustered trees, breaking in gleams upon the glossy bark, and brightening patches of the velvet grass and the rich moss which robes the lower part of the trunks and roots bursting from the ground: in the distance a farmhouse, surrounded by trees; nearer, a field of sheep: the new corn-stacks drawn together in one corner. The bright sun-effects save this work (which is in some respects quite beautiful) from the unpoetic emptiness of so many others of this painter's regular scenes of English landscape, and raise him above the level of that ordinary crowd which boasts the tame and fashionable Lee for leader.

In pursuing our sketch of the most characteristic examples of modern Art in the Exhibition (and these only have been noted, because it would be impossible here to do justice to the great number of really able works recorded in the following Catalogue), we have naturally dwelt especially on landscape, not only because this department was the best represented, but because it is really that in which modern Art has made the greatest advance. Amongst the works, however, in which the subject is to be expressed in the representation of the human figure, either singly or in groups, there is a class of compositions which do not, indeed, appeal to the highest feelings like those religious paintings which have already engaged our attention—which are not so important in the meanings they would convey to our minds—yet a class of works able to inspire us with many of those noble thoughts which it is the province of high Art to teach to the world in opposition to the mean instincts of ordinary business life, and the sordid suggestions of a too popular materialism: works, therefore, which must not be neglected here, even should we be forced to pass by many instances of grander artistic excellence for want of mere room. If the genius of modern times be less religious than that of the fifteenth and sixteenth centuries, and the modern Artist, therefore, seeks less of motive for his pencil among subjects of a strictly religious character; he finds in the events of History many a tale of heroism, through which to elevate the character of those who gaze on his work, many an example of patriotism, by the portrayal of which he may kindle some sparks of its divine fire in the hearts of his apathetic or degenerate fellow-countrymen. In the domain of Poesy, too, and the works of pure imagination, the modern artist may as readily find the persons and incidents of that pictorial drama by which he would stir men's minds with the emotions of a noble soul, touch them with the sympathies of the tender one, or startle by the terrible example of the foul and the wicked; and even without ascending to grasp these higher weapons of rule over the human heart, the modern painter may discover in the every-day life of the vulgar present world, but, especially, when refined by his selection, and directed to some special significance by his composing powers, many a sweet lesson of grace or of beauty, of power or of peacefulness, and of that quiet and unconscious happiness, too, which consists in the mere delight in healthy existence: this also a wholesome lesson, for it is one breathed everywhere upon us by Nature herself.

In these departments of Art the Schools of the Continent were so inadequately represented at our Exhibition that it would be wrong to lay any special emphasis on the few which they contributed. Of historical scenes the most important were those of Belgium, the two large works, (Nos. 463 and 542), *Virgilius braving the anger of the Duke of Alva*, by M. Bellemans, and *The last Interview between Count Egmont and the Duke of Alva*, by Van Rooy, both artists of Antwerp. Of poetical conceptions, the most graceful were, perhaps, the Prussian *Apollo among the Shepherds*, by C. Becker, (No. 575); the *Old Italian Shepherd supported by his Daughter*, by C. Kruseman, the Hague (No. 666); and the elegant *La Sylphide*, by C. Muller, of Paris, (No. 853).

The boldest effort to realize a great scene from History was, however, the colossal work of the late W. Etty, R. A., of London, *Joan of Arc charging in a Sortie during the Siege of Orleans*, (No. 853) an effort, however, which with all the care of the artist, can scarcely be regarded as anything more than effort, though it shows what Mr. Etty might have become capable of had he early applied himself to this higher class of composition, and not spent his life in the making of only academic studies. Mr Etty's picture seems to be a design for a tapestry such as, finished in the rich style of the Gobelins work, and adorning the walls of some splendid parliament hall in one of the ancient cities of *la belle France*, might well succeed in recalling to the hearts of modern Gaul the heroism of their glorious *Pucelle d'Orleans*. The sortie is one of those during the siege of Orleans in which, headed by the invincible Maiden, the chivalry of France from time to time burst forth irresistibly upon the lines of the English besiegers, till the siege was at last raised by the valour which their new inspiration had created, and France could breathe one moment of freedom. Behind is the wall of the ancient city, on the left the towers of one of its gates (and it is said the painter in his earnestness travelled from England to Orleans to see and sketch them on the spot); the portcullis is raised, the drawbridge let down, and across it and through the midst of the circling crowd of assailants rides the Maiden champion, followed by the bravest of France. She rides over the bodies of her prostrate foes, and has just gained the opposite side of the bridge (where the spectator is supposed to stand), when her horse rears over the falling body of the last foreign knight that has dared to face her way, and her sword is raised high as she is about to deal him his final death-blow. The knight is pressed down by his fallen horse against the nearer parapet of the bridge, and raises his right arm, struggling to parry or avoid the impending sword-cut. The Maiden's form is erect upon her steed; her head erect, yet not in pride; her features firm set, yet not in anger; a quiet earnest composure sits upon every lineament of her countenance; and the heavy sword seems rather about to be let fall upon her staggered foe than to be borne down upon his crest with the fierce and conscious strength of the ordinary warrior. It is inspiration, or, at least, fatalism, not the mere knightly rage of combat, that animates the calm stroke of the heroine.

This idea is unquestionably powerful. The picture is full of truth, and it is conceived with extreme simplicity, and yet with no small view to dramatic effect. But in this, as in all the Artist's works, there is a want of the finer and more delicate traits of pure or noble sentiment; and even in the figure of the Spirit Heroine of History—of the sublime Maid of Orleans herself—we can discover only the lineaments of some commonplace and somewhat coarse-featured peasant of modern England, and no trace whatever of her character, or even of that general brightness and vivid life which distinguishes every ordinary country girl among our Celtic kinsmen of modern France. We shall not, however, more minutely discuss the wants and weaknesses of this large picture of a Master so distinguished, nor shall we allude to its deficiencies in respect of colour,—the branch of the art of painting in which Mr. Etty was most distinguished,—because this was one of the last works of a man much advanced in years, and though the largest, it is not even the best of the series, of three of which it formed but the centre piece.

An earlier and better specimen of Mr. Etty's powers was, however, *The Rape of Proserpine* (No. 825), in which the figure of Proserpine herself is beautifully painted, so that indeed in drawing and attitude it contrasts widely with the female figures which, in very loosely composed groups, fill the rest of that picture. The principles of Mr. Etty's colouring, the harmony of which is always that of contrast, were those of Titian and of Rubens, of whom he claimed to be the ablest modern follower. But he wanted the rich sentiment of the one Master, and unfortunately he did not want the coarseness of the other. We have already had occasion to describe the circumstances, occasion, and intention which alone, in our opinion, authorize the artist to adopt the naked form of woman as the vehicle for the expression of whatever idea he has to convey. It is impossible to admit that in the *Proserpine* Mr. Etty's treatment of his subject can claim to entitle him to that authority. If we accord him the merit of having avoided the imputation of immodesty, it must be in recognising his intention to be, as we are sure it was, pure, and in pitying the clumsiness of his weak imaginative faculty.

In No. 783, the *Shell Boat*, a small cabinet by Mr. Pickersgill, R. A., we could enjoy a graceful snatch of poetry, drawn with much elegance, and coloured with a skill scarcely inferior to that of Etty, but which, though wanting in his boldness and breadth, and a little too daintily finished, greatly surpasses anything we have seen by the latter painter in that delicacy which at once adorns and distinguishes the man of education and refinement. The chaste knight sits in Luxury's boat, a skiff of mother-of-pearl—his companions, two fair female tempters, silently seeking to beguile him from sterner resolutions to love of their beauty and their softness, under the bright sun, and amid the perfumes of pleasant flowers. The soft passive features and forms of the inactive, silent, fairy-looking nymphs—more faery, less earth-like, in that magic shallop; the contrast of the severe and manly form of the armed youth, influenced by their magical arts, yet earnestly bent on recovering his recollection, his reason, his yet unbent strength of will—the brilliant but elegantly-harmonized colours; all unite to form a graceful and poetical picture, which is executed with great care, and with unusual taste and delicacy.

It is to be regretted that the author of so pretty a work should not have learned to know what limits there are to his success in the choice of a subject. A graceful illustrator of a scene of fanciful poetry is not therefore capable of giving expression to grander ideas, or to portray severer personages, and we saw with surprise the name of Mr. Pickersgill attached in the Catalogue to No. 375, called *A Friar at his Devotions*; a smooth and spotless portrait of an empty masquerading gentleman,—without dignity, without gravity, without force, without individuality or character; and of course without the slightest approach to "devotion" in expression. For the present, at least, we would counsel the English Artist to abstain from subjects which he really renders merely ludicrous on canvass, and which must bring only disgrace upon himself.

In estimating the true value of a work of Art we have ever insisted on Expression as the first necessity, and maintained that the technical qualities of design and colouring are to be considered as but the means of conveying the expression of the idea to be unfolded; the necessary weapons of the Art, it is true, which must be learned perfectly, or Art is pursued in vain, but still ever to be regarded solely as the means, and never to be confounded with the end itself. Now, just as an author may write well and correctly, and yet be neither a poet nor a sage, so may a painter paint well and be anything but an Artist. And yet there are whole classes of painters whom half the world accepts as artists in their day,—very correct painters, academicians, very clever men—who leave no thought behind them, and whose many popular works, therefore, are not, according to our inflexible standard, fit to rank among those of the true teachers of civilization. Accordingly, there were on the walls of the Fine Arts Hall, as well as among the collection of the Old Masters themselves, many pictures that we deliberately omit to notice in detail, although their market price be high, and the fame or reputation of their authors considerable. Among the former we are compelled to class a whole line of specimens of the English Academicians, not to speak of many works by lesser men. No. 784, *Sir Roger de Coverley going to Church*, by G. R. Leslie, R. A.; and No. 827, *Hunt the Slipper*, by A. E. Chalon, R. A., are perhaps the best of these. They are distinguished, in their different styles, by a fair correctness of design and by a good style of colouring, and they stand doubtless among the best examples of modern fashionable *genre* painting. But they are wholly wanting in that expression without which the best executed picture is valueless; they have neither spirit nor sentiment; they stir up no feeling, and excite no sympathy, at least none that the present writer has been able, even after some consideration, to realize to himself. No. 844, *Arab Chief examining his Captives*, by A. B. Cooper, R. A.; and No. 846, *The Wounded Smuggler*, by C. Landseer, R. A. (not to be confounded with the great animal painter, his relative) are works rather suited to the reputation of beginners, who have not yet mastered their powers, than becoming men who have been thought worthy of admission to the rank of academician. And No. 847, called *A Scene from the Faery Queen, or Temperance and Luxury*, by Thomas Uwins, R. A., is an absurd parody of Spenser's exquisite images, and may be described as presenting in all its parts every quality the opposite of those which we admired in Mr. Pickersgill's beautiful *Shell Boat*. Mr. Frank Stone, now an A. R. A., and so well known by the numerous engravings of his works, may close the list of unimaginative academicians. He is represented by Lord Lansdowne's contribution, No. 824, *Cross Purposes, or the Course of True Love never did run smooth*, and if we had seen but one of his compositions of this class we should give him the praise due to a successful sentimentalist who can express a scene of pretty feeling in forms and colours graceful, rich, and ladylike, very proper for a fashionable drawing-room wall, though we confess we should become very tired of sitting long on an opposite sofa; but Mr. Stone, amiable painter that he is, has produced, one may say, nothing else but these pictures of sentimental schoolboys and sighing village maidens, in such numbers and with so little variation, that we confess to being somewhat sick of his fashionable fancies. Perhaps he has more in him than this weak, unmanly style would indicate, and if so he should leave it without delay. In the meantime, we hope that neither by the prints of his works, nor by this original, will the simple taste and earnest meaning character of a single Irish girl be corrupted towards the weakness of such sickly sentiment as we have sometimes heard from the lips of foreign damsels clustered in front of Mr. Stone's pictures.

Besides its noble landscapes the English Academy might, however, point to one painting at least in the Exhibition, which, of its class, must ever rank among the very first—the *Bolton Abbey in the Olden Time*, by Sir Edwin Landseer, R. A., in the Duke of Devonshire's collection (No. 831). Landseer's drawing of animals, alive and dead, is quite unsurpassable, and his painting of the details of form and colour in these subjects, rich and at the same time manly in style, might satisfy even Snyders and Rubens themselves. The Belgian Verböckhoven, of Brussels—*Dogs* (No. 433), from the King of the Belgian's collection; *Landscape with Cattle* (No. 497, in which the cattle are by this painter, the landscape by Schelfhout,)—is, perhaps, as accurate and as brilliant; but his principal picture wants the harmony of the Artist and the dignified repose of the gentleman. The *Lion Hunt* of Horace Vernet (No. 631) alone combines all the qualities of painting of this class, with the expression and the grandeur of composition, which belong but to few even of the highest Artists; and it is no discredit to the distinguished painters just named if they must yield to one whose versatile powers equal those even of Rubens, and whose taste and feeling ever surpass his.

But we cannot stay to dilate upon the spirit of this class of works, or upon the excellence of these painters, for we have not yet touched on the Artists of our own country; and before we conclude, as we mean to do, with them, we must make room for a few words upon another subject not very correctly considered in these days, but which it is very important to clear up from the influence of erroneous opinions: the subject, namely, of PORTRAITURE.

In most Academy Exhibitions the general visitor, gifted with some degree of taste and discrimination, shrinks with no little displeasure from the stare of a number of glaring portraits of Sir Something Somebody, or Lady Nothing, of "A Gentleman," "A Lady," or "A Family Group," with Aldermen or Generals in their shining robes at stated distances; and it is yearly matter of loud complaint that so intolerably large a proportion of Academy Exhibition pictures consists of these trade pieces. Their admission in such numbers may be attributed to the fact, that almost all profitable painting among us in this ignorant and tasteless age is, in fact, mere portrait painting, and that many fashionable painters who can do nothing else, arrive, through the interest of the mob of fashionable patrons for whom they work, at the rewards and even at the fame and position due to the real Artist. And yet Portraiture itself is, if rightly practised, a very noble branch of Art —and it is more, it is even the necessary preparation for accompaniment of all highest Art, whether religious or historical; and so the noblest Artists, from Apelles to Raffaelle, and from Leonardo to Cano and Murillo, and from Rembrandt to Rubens, and so down to the ablest contemporary painters, have been eminently distinguished in Portraiture, and have devoted to it very much of their precious time, even in the midst of their greatest engagements. If the public of the present day could but realize to itself what a *portrait* really should be, the public would not tolerate the highly finished rubbish for which it now pays such high price, and which it now exalts to the place of Art. If the Artists of the present day applied themselves more seriously to the true perfection of portrait painting, we should find instruction and enjoyment in that very department of the Academy Exhibitions from which we now usually turn with so much disgust. Let us not, then, altogether pass by the consideration of Portraits in our remarks on the contents of the Great Exhibition.

"Recognition," says Mr. Ruskin, of whose words the present writer may here prudently avail himself, "is no proof of real and intrinsic resemblance. We recognise our books by their bindings, though the true and essential characteristics lie inside. A man is known to his dog by the smell—to his tailor by the coat—to his friend by the smile: each of these knows him, but how little, or how much depends on the dignity of the intelligence. That which is truly, and indeed characteristic of the man, is known only to God. One portrait of a man may possess exact accuracy of feature, and no atom of expression; it may be, to use the ordinary terms of admiration bestowed on such portraits by those whom they please, 'as like as it can stare.' Everybody, down to his cat, would know this. Another portrait may have neglected or misrepresented the features, but may have given the flash of the eye, the peculiar radiance of the lip, seen on him only in his hours of highest mental excitement. None but his friends would know this. Another may have given none of his ordinary expressions, but one which he wore in the most excited instant of his life, when all his secret passions and all his highest powers were brought into play at once. None but those who had then seen him might recognise *this* as like. But which would be the most truthful portrait of the *man?* The first gives the accidents of body,—the sport of climate, and food, and time,—which corruption inhabits, and the worm waits for. The second gives the stamp of the soul upon the flesh; but it is the soul seen in the emotions which it shares with many,—which may not be characteristic of its essence,—the results of habit, and education, and accident,—a glaze, whether purposely worn or unconsciously assumed, perhaps totally contrary to all that is rooted and real in the mind that it conceals. The third has caught the trace of all that was most hidden and most mighty, when all hypocrisy, and all habit, and all petty and passing emotion,—the ice, and the bank, and the foam of the immortal river,—were shivered and broken, and swallowed up in the awakening of its inward strength; when the call and claim of some divine motive had brought into visible being those latent forces and feelings which the spirit's own volition could not summon, nor its consciousness comprehend; which God only knew, and God only could awaken, the depth and the mystery of its peculiar and separating attributes. . . . . It is possible to represent the body without the spirit; and this shall be 'like' to those whose senses are only cognizant of body. It is possible to represent the spirit in its ordinary and inferior manifestations; and this shall be 'like' to those who have not watched for its moments of power. It is possible to represent the spirit in its secret and high operations; and this shall be 'like' only to those to whose watching they have been revealed. All these are truth; but according to the dignity of the truths he can represent or feel is the power of the painter—the justice of the judge." The vast majority of the successful likenesses are of the first class only; some attempts do not even reach so high, because the likeness-maker sometimes does not know even the use of his tools, and of those who do many cannot attain to select for their subjects a *pose* free from constraint, or accessories which avoid the degradation of undignified vulgarity. Many of the very finest, by the older as well as the more modern Masters, claim the rank of the second. Scarcely one can be said to be in anywise an example of the third; and such a one is ever a work of Art, on a level with those which represent the high thoughts of the creative poet himself.

The noblest works of portraiture, in its highest sense, were those precisely of the greatest artists of past times. And so the Titian (No. 138, *Cæsar Borgia*), and the Rembrandt (No. 250, *The Burgomaster*), represented in the Exhibition examples of the highest class of portrait judged by Mr. Ruskin's admirably described tests. Among the others of the older Masters, the *Portrait of Rembrandt*, by himself (No. 208), the *Portrait of Gerard Douw*, by himself (No. 197), the *Copy of Raffaelle's Portrait of Leo X.*, by Giulio Romano (No. 207), the Head called *Portrait of San Juan de la Cruz*, by Ribera lo Spagnoletto (No. 63), and the full-length portraits of *Lord Newport* (No. 140), and of *Queen Henrietta Maria and her Dwarf* (No. 139), both by Vandyck, are all masterpieces of true portraiture, though Vandyck's are very far inferior in idea to all the rest.

Of the modern portraits we shall say nothing, save that since Vandyck's time they have sunk lower and lower in the scale of works of Art, till at the present day it is rare to find one in any way deserving of the name. Let it be sufficient to have suggested the principle upon which preceding Artists reached such high success. Upon one only work of more modern times in the Exhibition shall we, therefore, pause for a moment, because it is one in which the obstructions placed in the way of genius by the tasteless requirements of modern custom have been at least in part surmounted, and that signally,—a portrait which, if it may not claim companionship with Rembrandt and Titian, is, nevertheless, so far as the expression and painting of the features, not less superior to all the efforts here in this department of Art; and those features are no common features to represent, for they must stand for the outward expression of the grandest intellectual genius of modern, if not of all, times:—we refer to the *Portrait of Napoleon the Great* in his imperial robes (No. 616), by M. Gerard, being that presented by the Emperor to the city of Rome in the year 1810. The Artist must have felt himself dreadfully harassed by being obliged to paint the world's hero decked in the effeminate satins and velvet trappings of a mere Emperor; and, truth to say, the court fashions of the Empire in 1810 were among the most tawdry and unheroic that can be imagined; and it was in these that the great Corsican had to be represented, near his throne, with his crown, and his sceptre, and his globe, and all the other allegorical paraphernalia of an empty title, and all these forms and all this costume (in which the high-sounding emperorship consisted) had to be painted with the utmost finish and splendour for the dazzlement of Imperial Rome. M. Gerard, who was a great portrait painter and very much of a true Artist, has not indeed succeeded in making Napoleon and a court-dressed emperorship altogether compatible; he has not toned down those bright satins so as to be consistent with the dignity even of externals very much more than Lawrence succeeded with the fat form of George of England; but he has painted, on the one hand, most unexceptionable satin and most glittering gold, and the richest and most mellow harmonies of velvet; and, on the other, though his Figure be lost among so many gew-gaws, he has given us the head and features of the warrior, the statesman, the hero, the idol of France, as we have never elsewhere seen them. We had often admired the efforts of Paul de la Roche to express the dimly remembered countenance of the grand Emperor, whose glory his youth adored, and we had even almost believed he had succeeded. But the real likeness by Gerard as much eclipses the efforts of the greater Artist's memory, as these do the every-day portraits of the clay of Napoleon of which too many offend our eyes. The soft and almost feminine outlines of the sweetly beautiful lips and chin, the tender delicacy of the finely organized nose, these are the features which everywhere else we miss (save on a few coins and medals of the Consulate), and the union of these with the clear richly developed eye, and lofty, regular, and even forehead, make a combination of sensibility governed by intellect,—each so intense, but intellect overpowering,—which probably no other form but only Napoleon's ever knew. And all that delicacy, that unspoken sensibility which the common crowd do not even suspect as entering into the frame of that extraordinary character, and all that majesty of intellect, and all that tremendous intensity of will, M. Gerard has expressed even to overflowing. How sad that mournful, solitary eye, and the suppressed sweetness of those fair but powerful lips, ever seem to us as we gaze; as if the lone heart of the great man wanted human sympathy, yet submitted to his intolerable intellect as to some inevitable fate. One seems to read his feelings, if not able to scan his thoughts, in presence of the painting, and it is thus that we confess the poetry of the work, and feel bound to claim for the Court-painter, Gerard, the distinction of having produced at least one successful portrait which may take rank among the highest in difficulty and in power. For such a reason it was impossible to pass by this one work in silence.

The great importance of the study of the older and greater Masters of Art, and of the consideration of the means by which they arrived at extraordinary excellence in so many varieties of style, become most apparent when we examine the works of the moderns; who usually exhibit, in comparison with their predecessors, so much of feeble conventionality of treatment, so much unimaginative sameness of design, and so little pains taken in perfecting the execution of their pictures. And it was on this account that the opportunity afforded by the Exhibition of studying so rich a collection of the old Masters was of especial value, because it better enabled the visitor to apply to the modern works, placed so nearly in juxtaposition with them, the principles suggested by their example. For the object of all criticism ought to be improvement, and it is not by merely discovering and exposing the faults of his contemporaries, but still more by becoming acquainted with the excellencies which distinguish the works of perfectly accomplished painters, that the artist and the student of the present and the future time may be stimulated to brilliant and successful exertion. And much does the Irish artist and the Irish student stand in need of such study, and humbly and patiently must he apply himself to it if he will ever produce anything really worthy of a place on the walls of such an Exhibition; but, on the other hand, there is no excellence of drawing or of colour which he also may not acquire by that ceaseless diligence and toil to which every successful Master, from Michael Angelo to Caracci, from Bellini to Titian, and from Perugino to Correggio, devoted himself with unremitting industry; while for purity and grace of design, and the richness of poetic imagination, these things lie dormant in the Irish mind, only because it wants the opportunities of education, and it has not yet created for itself an intellectual refuge against the vulgarizing tendencies of such public and social life as afflicts the present generation of this ill-starred people. And yet the devotion of but a few young men of genius to the task of elevating that life by the influence of Art,—if rightly directed and supported by the vigorous and self-denying enthusiasm of an Italian spirit,—might almost save the next if not the present age of the Irish race, and might lay the foundations of a career for this nation: directing its energies towards the cultivation of the Ideal, the Spiritual, and the Beautiful,—and the spread of that purest civilization throughout the world:

grander, and happier, and more lovely than any that political ambition and the mere lust of empire and of power can achieve in more prosperous countries. Should this Exhibition, predominating as it did in Art above all the other elements of its importance and general interest, be destined to be the first suggestion of such a possible career, it can only be so if, thirsting after the novel and various excellencies it opened to our eyes, we greedily drink in whatever of instruction may in any way be derived from the different Masters who stood there around silently pointing out the innumerable roads to artistic greatness. The chief repository of such experience was of course to be sought in the chambers appropriated to the great men of the past during the golden age of painting in Italy; and of these works the greater part were in illustration of religious subjects of more or less grandeur, beauty, or importance. But though such subjects are doubtless the highest capable of artistic treatment, it is to be remembered that the palace of Art has room for all the infinite varieties of taste, of skill, and of power; and thus it is no part of our idea, in placing such subjects the highest in the scale, thereby to depreciate the application of Art to those of a very different class. There is no rendering of beauty or grace, there is no image of simplicity or purity, and no representation of grandeur and power, whether in passionate action or in intellectual repose, which does not also elevate and improve as well as delight the mind of the cultivated as well as of the ignorant man: there is no part of life or of nature, however lowly or minute, nor any phase of these, however transient, that may not become the subject of worthy artistic representation, if only the idea of it be pure, and the little of suggestion contained in it be that of truth at least. Thus in Art every species of taste and of skill may find healthy employment, and the student must not despair of honourable success if he fail only in ambitious emulation of the Leonardos and Raffaelles. Amongst our own countrymen this century has witnessed success in many different walks of Art,—success even in the highest degree in each; yet how different is that of William Mulready from that of Daniel Maclise, and his again from the style of James Barry, whose Olympic Games (at the Society of Arts, Adelphi, London) is perhaps the grandest work of design since the golden days of art in Italy and Spain? Another Irish genius,—that of the late Samuel Forde, who, however, died when yet almost a boy,—in our own time proved that even without ever leaving his own land, and here with no instruction save the examples furnished by some good casts from the Greek, and the ideas which the story of the Bible and the plays of Shakspeare could suggest, a poor Irish student may coin from his own poet-soul whole scenes and characters of the grandest originality, and portray them with a vivid power and perfect masterly taste almost unknown even in the richly cherished schools of the Continent.* It is necessary to call to mind these rare examples, or in the depth of darkness to which Art has now sunk in Ireland, we might run some risk of earning only the ridicule of the reader when we insist upon what we believe may be done in Ireland; when we repeat, again and again, that here, amidst the poverty and ignorance in which, alas! so many of us seem content to leave a nation once so noble—that here, even in the Ireland of to-day, Art may at last find a firm refuge, and one day compass for herself a glorious home. It is necessary, too, because in the Exhibition there were but a few Irish works at all (even including those of men such as the first three above named, who transferred their genius to a strange soil, and too soon forgot the purer inspirations of their youth at home), and among these few works, still fewer of which we are called on to make any special mention; for though some of our greatest names are indeed represented, they are by no means so by their greatest works.

The principal painting from the studio of an Irish Artist is also the largest, and one of the most important, of all those which filled the Fine Arts Hall of the Exhibition. It is that of *The Deluge* (No. 371), by Francis Danby, A. R. A., many of whose smaller pieces have long been so well known and so popular at the annual Exhibitions of the Royal Hibernian Academy. Mr. Danby is, in his peculiar style, one of the most remarkable landscape painters of the day; and though the present immense picture is perhaps strictly to be dealt with as a landscape only, as only an example of the Artist's power in delineating water, still it is also an effort to express, so far as his genius and imagination enabled him to do, the most terrible fact of the world's history as recorded in the sacred writings, and in this point of view (avowedly that of the painter) it calls for observation as one of that class of works now before us for consideration. If in dealing with its merits as an illustration of sacred history we may be compelled to judge more harshly than the general public seemed disposed to do, let not the weight of our remarks be applied to the landscape or water painting, but strictly to the conception and execution of the whole as the pictorial realization of a historical event of so great importance, and pregnant with such awful lessons, that it would require all the power and imagination of the great painter of the Last Judgment himself to render adequate justice to its immensity. We shall not so far wrong Mr. Danby as to suggest such a comparison more minutely; and so far as he has exhibited a sound ambition faithfully to express the scene he selected for his canvass, he should receive the credit due not only to so bold a design, but to the faith which enabled him to persevere to the completion of a work of such immense proportions, and containing so great a number of figures. But the nature of that design, and the manner in which he has executed it in all its parts, cannot be overlooked in the enjoyment of the extraordinary action of agitated water, and the effects of light and shade so well represented, with which the Artist in many parts of this picture so skilfully appeals to the imagination of the astonished spectator. And it is, as usual, to the *idea* of the work that we must first address ourselves.

Mr. Danby's conception of the hour of God's most tremendous vengeance on a sinful world was from the first but a low one of such a scene. He looked upon it but with the eye of a professional landscape painter, seeking for the picturesque in effect—the picturesque, indeed, in its grandest forms, upon the grandest scale, but still merely the picturesque,—and to be enjoyed chiefly, if not exclusively, as such. In the Deluge, then, he saw simply a huge convulsion of the elements, in which the clouds poured their torrents more thick, more continual, than ever before or since, and the ocean waves rose to meet them, eddying furiously.

* The splendid cartoon sketches of the *Tragic Muse*, and of the *Expulsion of the Rebel Angels from Heaven*, as well as the wonderful little figure of *the Veiled Prophet of Khorassan*, by poor Forde (which, as well as some others of his works, were exhibited at the Cork Exhibition in 1852), far more than bear out even these strong expressions of the present writer. They ought to be preserved for ever in the new National Gallery.

with resistless tide, over all the mountains and the valleys, the rocks and the cities, of the earth. In that convulsion he recognises, it is true, the consequent destruction of the human race; but it is not that destruction or the awful extent of it—still less the meaning of it as the exercise of Almighty vengeance for infinite justice provoked and infinite mercy outraged—it is not these that Mr. Danby sought to realize to his mind before engaging in so immense a work: he felt only that the unique circumstances and grandeur of the scene afforded him an opportunity of painting *effects* of water, of light, of distance, upon a scale before untried, and in such a manner as to develop to the utmost his peculiar and original talent. And from such a point of view he conceived the Deluge—such and so great, such and so little, it appears on canvass before us.

Nevertheless, it is impossible to look upon this picture from the proper distance without being greatly struck by the grandeur of its general expression. Do not go within two feet of it, as the singularly blind crowds were doing every day during the Exhibition (seeing, of course, but a fifth part of it at a time, if so much, and wholly missing the effect of even that), but stand out from the canvass at least ten yards, and you will see what we mean. The eye then embraces the whole picture, and is not irritated by the minutiæ of the ill-drawn human figures and grotesque animals of which we shall have presently to speak: it takes in only the general features of an immense, powerfully drawn, and admirably coloured water landscape, and plunges into the distances of light, and the depths of all but darkness, with amazement at the variety of the painter's imagination, and delight at his extraordinary skill in giving expression to it.

A little to the left of the centre rises out of the surging waters a lofty rock, its base a wide irregular mass, and the craggy steps of its gradual ascent terminating in the distance in a narrow level, appearing so far off like a point. The forms of the rock are those into which the fierce waves of the Atlantic coast breaks its storm-besieged barrier—(we shall not stop to inquire whether such forms could have existed, on land, before the Flood)—and they are full of variety, bold and picturesque, without being extravagant. Behind this mass—which is covered with a vast crowd of men, women, and children, climbing towards its height, and struggling to escape the circling torrents—a distance of water stretches to the calm line of the horizon. On the left, a far-off edge of land appears, and beyond this the blood-red sun has half sunk in the quiet wave. On the right of the rock, and in the middle of the picture, at the edge of the fierce rain-fall which fills the whole right of the canvass, a broad line of silver, shed from the high-risen full moon, which strives to burst the rain clouds, tracks the perspective on the waves, stiller and stiller in the distance; and very far, in the midst of moonlight, floats the Ark, alone peaceful in the midst of so great ruin; for in strong contrast to its bright rest pours the fierce rain in black torrents, veiling the whole right of the picture, piercing into which the eye traces out many and many a dim form of lofty mountain precipice and majestic crag, down which the waste of water pours, and along whose base the driving eddies stream, and boil, and roar, on towards that centre rock where the last crowd of mankind cling to the faint hope of life.

It is impossible to deny that such a conception of a landscape scene is of the grandest, and had the artist but suppressed, or at least forced less on our notice, so many unfortunate groups of half-drowned human and other creatures, so ill drawn as to be almost irrecognisable, we should have been tempted to give ourselves up to all the enjoyment so rich an imagination had prepared for our minds. But these groups are so numerous, so large, and so much in the foreground, that they insist on observation; and we are compelled to pronounce the strongest condemnation upon the painter, who, without apparently the least knowledge of the human figure, its proportions, its powers, its peculiarities, has so far presumed on his experience and popularity in a wholly different class of works as to people a huge expanse of canvass with male and female forms of all ages and sizes, and in every variety of attitude, so ridiculously unnatural, and so false to the most elementary rules of drawing. Criticism would be simply wasted upon such matter, because there is absolutely nothing correct in any one figure that we can discover among the hundreds in the picture; they are in drawing, in colouring, and in texture (the substance is certainly not flesh), all so wholly contrary to anything we are acquainted with in nature, that any detailed remarks of ours would be altogether fruitless.

It is not merely, however, by his want of capacity to design the figure correctly that the Artist has failed to express by these groups of drowning creatures the story of the Deluge. Although his figures are often large enough to show us every lineament of their features, there is never any expression (not even in a single exceptional instance) of the awfulness of their situation, such as a painter penetrated with his subject would have been sure to portray. The war of the elements is grandly given, but the highest form—that of man—wears only the passive, or, under the circumstances, frightened appearance of the lowest of the brute creation. This want in the picture springs from more than a want of mere dexterity of painting in the Artist; and Mr. Danby's mind, we must say, does not seem to us to be of that pure and lofty nature in which alone lie the springs of true expression, at least of the higher or deeper kind. He is ever full of feeling for the grandeur of the picturesque in landscape contours, for the rich magnificence of colour at sunset and sunrise, and particularly for the luxuriant variety of forms and tints which water, in all its modes, and in every different light, so abundantly presents. But no one who has studied his works, large or small, from the magnificent "Passage of the Red Sea," in the Gallery of the Duke of Sutherland, to the "Scene from the Tempest," and the "Suicide's Grave," exhibited some years ago at the Academy—and from that to the present, perhaps his largest piece—will, we think, go beyond this point in recognising his powers, and appreciating his ability.

A little consideration will suffice to show that, even though unable accurately to paint the human form, a landscape painter may, nevertheless, successfully deal with the grand subject of the Deluge. He has but to avoid the necessity for rendering that form with minute distinctness, and this he may do in several ways, as for instance, by keeping each of his figures, or indications of figures, in the dim distance, and making the action of the piece consist emphatically in the conflict of the elements, while the presence of the Ark would serve to express the special story. He may also avoid the too glaring deficiency of human forms by choosing to paint his picture on a smaller space of canvass, if he knows (what Mr. Danby seems not to be aware of) that grandeur lies in proportions and not in size, and that as large and impressive a view of even such a scene as the Deluge can be conveyed quite as adequately in a picture of four feet as in one of four yards. If Mr.

Danby had adopted the latter expedient, and, keeping his crowds more out of sight, had brought the Ark a little nearer and emphasized it more strongly, his picture might have retained all its present splendour of effect: and as he would have been no longer in want of figures for a foreground merely to fill up somewhat of a preponderating space, he would not have been reduced to the necessity of exhibiting his worst deficiencies, and might have produced a work capable of living with those of Turner, and (if any there be) of the greater Masters. As it is, we are bound to call for the judgment of inexorable justice on this immense work, pronouncing it to be on the whole a gigantic mistake by the painter, not only as to the subject but as to his own powers.

Let us not, however, be supposed to underrate the peculiar and extraordinary talents of an Artist, who after all *is* an Artist, and whom we are proud to be able to claim as a fellow-countryman. Mr. Danby is a remarkably gifted man, and has the merit, too, of a vigorous originality, which early impelled him so forcibly in the direction in which he has since met with such distinguished success that he has never been seduced from the dreams of his early imagination. It is with great satisfaction that we feel assured his position has long been such as to place him beyond the reach of any injury from such severe criticism as we have felt ourselves bound, dealing as we do frankly and impartially with the contents of the Exhibition, to express in his regard. Had it been otherwise, possibly the tenderness natural towards a remarkable representative of the warm Irish genius had stayed our pen, and not without reason. For not once nor twice, nor twenty times only, have we lingered with delight over the gorgeous faery splendour of the scenes coined for us from the inexhaustible mint of Danby's exuberant imagination; and we cannot but regret that he was represented in the Great Exhibition of Ireland only by one, and that, though his largest, certainly not his best or ablest work. His place among the landscape painters of this century (so many of whom have more than equalled the older Masters) will in many respects be ever one of the highest; and though he has not the concentrated intellect and vivid power which enabled Turner to express adequately some of the most sublime messages of his Art, still Danby too has preserved for posterity many a pictured poem of the softest, sweetest, richest, and loveliest, that nature in her most voluptuous hours deigns to shed a moment on the world.

Mr. Danby's picture cannot, we have said, be dealt with merely, or even chiefly, among those of the Irish landscape painters in the Exhibition, of whom he is one: and it is with regret that we find ourselves unable to distinguish any others of this class as worthy of detailed remark. Amidst so many splendid works, in which the great Artists of Prussia, Belgium, Holland, France, and England, celebrated the glorious scenes of other lands, those of our own country,—notwithstanding the magnificence of its coast, its rich and its savage lakes, its fair rivers, its abundant meadow lands, and in so many parts its beautiful plantations so often skirting a romantic shore,—were all but unrepresented by any finished painting. For the specimens of Ashford (No. 756), of Robarts (No. 762), of Barrett (Nos. 740 and 766), of last century, and of the late James A. O'Connor (Nos. 746, 753, and 775), small, but able pictures of sweet and lovely scenes, only made us regret the want of grander and nobler efforts on the part of men who appear even from these to have been filled with the character of their native landscape. We can but hope that the examples of the other countries just mentioned may stir up some of our aspiring students to do in and for Ireland at least some small portion of that work for which she still waits at their hands.

We have only spoken of finished paintings in oil. We must, however, mention, that on one of the stands upon which water-colour drawings were exhibited in the Fine Arts Hall, were two small pieces by one whose genius and whose power, if exercised in form more substantial, would have secured for his name, if not preeminence over, at least an entire equality with, those of the most celebrated of the foreign Artists represented in the room: we mean our veteran academician (no less distinguished as an antiquary and as a musician), Dr. George Petrie, R. H. A., one of the most true Artists that Ireland has ever been able to boast, and one, too, who has never left the land of his inspiration to seek elsewhere the rank and wealth he would elsewhere have full surely attained. The first of these beautiful little works (No. 1010) represents the wild and lonely lake, celebrated in Callanan's sweetest verses, where the Laoi or Lee, the river of Cork, takes its rise: *Gougane Barra (the Hermitage of Saint Bearrach or Barry), county of Cork.* The wildest of scenes is fitly pictured at the wildest of moments: the thickest storm-clouds rest upon all the mountain-tops, and the rugged, precipitous, and rocky sides of those mountains, bounding as they do the little lake like walls all around, make themselves known through the black envelope of cloud only by the sparkling lines of the leaping foam torrents which stream down every gully. In the foreground it is not raining, and the many-coloured tufts of heath and mountain grass and furze, which Dr. Petrie seems to take such especial delight in, and which indeed especially characterize our western and south-western scenery, glow with a bright, warm, and rich effect. The lake is black as ink, the black clouds and blacker rocks of the mountains filling up the greatest part of the picture; but at the far end of it shines the bright green island, with its transparent group of trees, and the dim ruins of the hermitage,—and the end of the lake behind that gleams in dazzling light beneath a vivid ray which streams down from one solitary opening in the intense mass of cloud above. Nothing can be grander than the gloom, so appropriate to one of the wildest scenes in Ireland—nothing more cheering than the friendly light from out its depth—nor anything more richly beautiful than the foreground, and the delightful reach of shore along the bank of the lake on the left. And Dr. Petrie's colouring is perfect harmony in general effect, the result of profound knowledge and of the utmost care in execution.

The second of these drawings, on the other side of the screen (No. 1011), represents the *Pagan Sepulchral* Circle of Stones on the Caw Hill, Banagher, county of Derry—after Sunset.* It forms a singular contrast of effect to the savage grandeur of a Gougane Barra storm. The line of the horizon, formed by the edge of the gently sloping hill, and against which some of the upright stones stand in relief, is an equal yellow. The sky in that part is cloudless, and the few clouds on the opposite side have lost every trace of pink, and grown already cold and gray in absence of the sun. There is just enough of departing warmth to mellow the weather-

* These circles are Pagan, but they are *not* "Druidical," as generally stated by ignorant writers about Irish antiquities and early history. They are now abundantly proved to be always sepulchral in character, like the *cromleachs*.

beaten outlines of the old stones, and to account for the regretful expression of those distant cows on the edge of the farther slope, who look so patiently towards the still sunset; and the already clear form of the pale star of evening overhead adds tenderness and poetry to one of the dreamiest of scenes. If the former drawing exhibits the power of the Artist, this in a still more attractive way reveals the depth and purity of his feeling for nature, and in both there is a something which especially appeals to our Irish sympathies, for everything that Dr. Petrie handles seems to be thoroughly racy of the soil.

Of three pictures by W. Mulready, R. A., in the Exhibition (Nos. 849, 851, and 852),—we shall only say that they were all first-rate specimens of his well-known style. They are, of course, cabinet pictures, finished with singular perfection in detail, and displaying an amount of skill in rich and harmonious colouring which is exceeded by no other living Artist. But though the care and time spent in the execution of these small *genre* pieces be such as to confer upon them an enormous market value, yet the choice of subject is such that we can afford to pass them by here, in silent recognition of the extraordinary technical merits which have earned for them an abundant reputation.

The only representative of D. Maclise, R. A. (the greatest draughtsman, save, perhaps, Vernet, of all the Artists in the Exhibition) was, we regret to say, the picture called the *Weird Sisters (scene from Macbeth)*, (No. 788). Three grotesque, bearded, grinning heads grouped round a wide copper cauldron, which lies in the midst of a large fire on the ground—their figures stooped down squatting in a ludicrous posture, their pointed and hanging breasts (the only indications of the monsters' sex), and their skinny arms and figures, stooping over the edge of the pot, and made still more revolting in colour by the reflections of the flickering spirituous flame on the surface of the liquid in preparation;—around, the trees of the forest;—behind, the armed figure of a theatrical Highlander: and such is Daniel Maclise's idea of the grand, the dignified, the terrible Witches of Shakspeare! Neither the power of drawing which it displays, nor the excellence of the colouring of some parts of this disgusting work, can redeem a failure so unintelligible: it is a gross caricature, a caricature without humour, without the suggestion of a single thought that might make it tolerable even as a caricature. And such a falsification of the author illustrated cannot even be excused by want of skill, for Maclise's *Hamlet*, as well as many other noble works, refuse to allow the possibility of such an explanation. It is, therefore, we fear, one of those evidences, of which too many are to be seen, of the gradual degradation of mind which sometimes—at least from time to time—steals on a great Artist who has forgotten and trampled on his early inspirations, and preserves only the power without the impulse to direct it aright. Deeply we regret that this picture was not rejected altogether, but as it was not, then let the Irish visitor who has seen it be told, that he who, in some moment of infatuation, perpetrated this ignoble forgery of Art, is, nevertheless, at times a truly great painter, who has produced, and still can produce, works among the greatest of this age; and let him mourn over the manifold failures of a spirit which has submitted to be led away from its higher mission by the distractions and temptations of a foreign world.

Of the late James Barry, R.A. (the first Professor of Painting in the original Academy of London, but one who left no pupils after him in England worthy his cloak should descend upon them), the Exhibition only presented two examples, and these rather studies than finished pictures. The *Death of Adonis* (No. 318), is a chaste and sweetly designed piece, in which the landscape charms by its graceful expanse of subdued light and shade, but in which the story is told perhaps with somewhat too much of the dramatic mannerism of the later Italian Schools. The other represents a grander subject,—one which might have been better treated in connexion with our remarks on the religious Art of Italy,—though it is indeed probable that the great painter, sacrificing, like Michael Angelo, the charms of grace and expression to extraordinary vigour of mere drawing, intended in it little more than by a wonderful *tour de force* to show what could be done by a master in drawing in the management of a violently foreshortened figure. This picture is called an *Entombment* (No. 259): it is drawn with little colour, and it is probably but a mere study for a fresco, which was never executed by the Artist. The body of Christ appears extended at full length, and in all the stiffness of death, on a huge slab of stone, as if on the cover of the tomb in which it was intended to be laid. It is seen, as it were, from below, and the feet are pointed towards the spectator. Behind the head and in the middle background of the drawing is visible the upper part of the Blessed Virgin's figure, bending down towards the body. On the left stands St. John, clothed in the usual ample mantle, and represented in the youthful form which distinguishes this saint. He appears horror-stricken as if at the first glance upon the lifeless figure of his Divine Master, and he raises his extended right hand as he looks up from it. The hand is, like the feet of the body of Christ, stretched out directly towards the spectator, and the arm foreshortened in the extreme. On the opposite side of the tomb Mary Magdalen is represented in an agony of grief, her whole figure tortured in the most violent attitude, one knee resting on the high edge of the tomb, her head bent down and inwards as she clasps her hands, which are pressed vehemently in the opposite direction from the object of her sorrow. The figures are all colossal, and yet the picture is not very large. The effect of the whole cannot indeed be said to be pleasing; partly because all the intention is sacrificed to the painter's desire to overcome the most unusual difficulties in drawing: and partly because in a sketch of colossal figures intended for a painting to be seen only at the distance of a great height, the features are necessarily exaggerated in expression, and all the forms are very coarse, though perfectly correct in design. Viewed merely as a triumph of power in drawing, this work is a production quite wonderful, and merely as a study is deserving of the most careful attention, more especially as few, if any, masters of modern times, except this singular Irish genius, have approached or attempted to approach the style of Michael Angelo's designs of this nature, and probably no one of them possessed the extraordinary power of James Barry. Those who have seen his great finished paintings at the Society of Arts, London, are well aware that his powers of execution were not inferior, and that in his perfect works no one was more capable of grace and expression than this extraordinary Master.

With these examples of Irish genius we gladly close our examination of the contents of the Fine Arts Hall of the Irish Exhibition. Nor shall we repeat what we have taken occasion in more than one place to suggest with respect to the natural capacity of our race for distinction in the highest walks of Art, and the necessity of encouraging and providing at home for the training which is requisite for success. The true student of Art seeks fame rather than patronage,—the true poetic spirit seeks rather the expression of its inspired message than the mere worldly wealth which may be made of it. The Artist ought to be honoured, but to be honoured he must be an Artist in more than the name, even be he member of a "Royal Academy." The Artist must live, and live in and by the exercise of his profession for the most part, but a work of true Art will find admiring purchasers throughout all the civilized world; and Ireland is near enough to France to find ample means of making known to Continental lovers of such works the existence of such as may aim too high to be as yet understood here, or ever in England. In the mean time Ireland herself is lovely enough, and as yet peaceful enough, to rest and content the imagination of her Artist sons, and it is in their own land that they must ever find the kindliest, deepest, and noblest suggestions. Around them here live and move the subjects of a thousand noble works, not less than in Italy round a Raffaelle, or in Spain round a Cano or a Murillo. And in the history of our Past, and in the hopes of our Future, this nation of ours is not less rich than any other in the world in all that may, by the artist's pencil or the poet's tongue, inspire our people with those burning thoughts, that intense devotion, and that noble purity of soul, through which alone they shall win honour and life, and a name again in the world's history.

Upon the arrangement of the collection of works of Art in the Great Exhibition we must here, before proceeding to the Catalogue of its contents, say a few words. Two principal things are required in the proper arrangement of a large gallery of paintings. One of them is that no two or more pictures should be hung near each other whose juxtaposition might produce the result of neutralizing the effect of any of them. The other, that specimens of the more important classes of subjects should not be intermixed, for by doing so the impressions of mind created by each are constantly disturbed before they have had time to sink deep enough for such permanent improvement or vivid enjoyment as such works (according to their class) are intended to produce. True, a succession of exactly similar subjects or works in considerable numbers would become so tiresome as to be soon intolerable; but other means are easily found for effecting that variety which is necessary to relieve the eye, beside the confusion referred to. The smaller cabinet pictures representing ordinary topics of common life, animals, minutely executed interiors, most portraits, &c. do not interfere (because they offer no points of comparison) with works in a higher style,—developing a greater range of imagination, or subjects of a more important character. But the more solid and considerable works should ever be so arranged that each division of the gallery, if it be divided, or successive masses of wall if it be not, should be devoted to some one class,—to paintings whose subjects so far harmonize as to suggest the same general tone of mind.* Thus, paintings representing religious (or devotional) subjects should not be alternated with historical or mythological works, nor any of these with the larger *genre* pictures; and, on the other hand, the landscapes, representations of the more brilliant climates, and more magnificent scenes of nature, should not be placed amongst those of quieter and tamer scenes; but landscapes and figures may be allowed to alternate,—only in the general disposition of each upon the walls the above-mentioned principles should be attended to.

Such principles were, however, entirely forgotten in the late Exhibition, and accordingly the eye and mind were constantly distracted by the most heterodox contrasts, and by successions of subjects and styles the most disturbing to the proper understanding and enjoyment of the works to be examined. And as the Official Catalogue generally followed the arrangement of the works themselves, that Catalogue was of course of the most unsatisfactory description. In the following list of the Paintings exhibited some attempt has been made (as in the case of Sculpture) at a better arrangement. The complete separation of the different modern *Schools* was, however, found to be totally impossible, and for this among other reasons, that the Official Catalogue did not so distinguish all the works transmitted from the Continent as to prevent the present writer from falling into many inevitable mistakes. In most cases, nevertheless, the reader will be able to recognise the School of the Artist; and the remainder of the arrangement now adopted will probably be found intelligible without further explanation.—E. P.

---

### THE OLD MASTERS.

1. Santa Lucia. [The Lord Chancellor.] FERDINAND BOL (?).
2. The Angels Appearing to the Shepherds. [Charles Brien.] BOTH (?).
3. Martyrdom of a Saint. [Sir John Nugent, Bart.] CALABRESE.
4. The Crucifixion. [Sir Compton Domville, Bart.] A. CARACCI.
5. St. Francis in the Desert Receiving the Stigmata. [Jonathan Osborne, M.D.] CARACCI and P. BRIL.
6. St. Theresa. [Mrs. West.] A. CARACCI.
7. St. Francis Receiving the Stigmata. [The Marquis of Drogheda.] M. ANGELO DA CARAVAGGIO.
8. Holy Family. [Lady Juliana Bayly.] School of Andrea del Sarto.
9. Head of the Infant St. John. [Rev. Dr. Russell.]
10. Judith bearing the Head of Holophernes. [Very Rev. J. Curtis.] A. ALLORI.
11. Miraculous Draught of Fishes (sketch). [The Marquis of Drogheda.] RUBENS.
12. Judas Returning the Thirty Pieces of Silver. [The Earl of Charlemont.] REMBRANDT.
13. St. Jerome Translating the Bible. [William Jameson.] ALBERT DURER (?).

* Another arrangement in the great galleries is that by *Schools*, which for historical and educational purposes has its value. But it also produces (as was found to be the case in the Louvre) no small fatigue to the mass of general visitors, and each individual work certainly suffers much, because it produces much less effect than if seen by itself or among others of the same *class*, but presenting a contrast in *style*. We believe the strict classification by Schools has been, or is now being, abandoned in all the very large galleries of Europe on this account. But be this as it may, our remarks will be found generally true as regards any considerable collections of the kind now exhibited.

14. The Magdalen Reading. [Lord Ward.] CORREGGIO.
15. St. Mary Magdalen. [Sir Compton Domville, Bart.] GUIDO.
16. Original Sketch Picture for the Ceiling of St. Sulpice. [E. M. Blood.] JOUVENET.
17. St. Francis. [Sir John Nugent, Bart.] Spanish School.
18. The Raising of Lazarus. [Sir John Nugent, Bart.] LAURI.
19. St. John Preaching in the Wilderness. [The Earl of Miltown.] LUCA GIORDANO.
20. Angel Descending at the Pool of Siloe. [Sir John Nugent, Bart.] LAURI.
21. St. Michael (from the Palazzo Riccardi, Florence). [Lady Juliana Bayly.]
22. Marriage of St. Catherine. [Alexander M'Carthy.] RONDINI.
23. The Madonna and Child, and St. Francis. [Mrs. Bayly.] LIGOZZI.
24. Magdalen (in a Landscape). [The Lord Chancellor.] P. F. MOLA.
25. The Entombment of Christ. [The Earl of Portarlington.] TINTORETTO.
26. Magdalen. [John La Touche.] GUIDO.
27. St. John Baptizing in the Wilderness. [The Earl of Portarlington.] SALVATOR ROSA.
28. The Tribute Money. [The Earl of Portarlington.] SALVATOR ROSA.
29. Head of Christ. [Sir John Nugent, Bart.] Spanish School.
30. The Madonna. SASSOFERRATO.
31. St. Mary Magdalen. [Charles D. Young.] CORREGGIO.
32. The Coronation of the Blessed Virgin. [J. S. Loughnan.] PIERINO DEL VAGA (?).
33. St. Sebastian. [Alexander M'Carthy.] ANTONIO TANZI DI VARALLO.
34. Holy Family. [Archdeacon Magee.] ANDREA DEL SARTO (?).
35. Head of Christ. [Henry Hodgson.] ALBERT DURER (?).
36. The Annunciation (portion of a panel of a Sacristy door). [Charles Brien.]
37. Altar Piece, on gold ground. [Henry Hodgson.] CIMABUE.
38. St. Boromea (portion of a panel of a Sacristy door). [Charles Brien.]
39. St. Ambrose. [Sir John Nugent, Bart.] Spanish School.
40. St. Mary Magdalen. [Mrs. Nevin.] Early Spanish School.
41. Head of St. Francis. [Sir John Nugent, Bart.] LO SPAGNOLETTO (Ribera).
42. Marriage of St. Catherine. [Sir John Nugent, Bart.] Early Venetian School.
43. The Disciples at Emmaus. [The Earl of Clancarty.] JAN STEEN.
44. Holy Family with St. Catherine. [Sir John Nugent, Bart.] Early Venetian School.
45. Return of the Prodigal Son. [Sir John Nugent, Bart.] P. DA CORTONA.
46. Santa Rosalia. [The Rt. Hon. Alexander Macdonnell.]
47. The Nativity. [Alexander M'Carthy.] FILIPPO LAURI.
48. The Saviour after being Scourged. [T. Conolly, M.P.] MURILLO (?).
49. Christ Raising the Mother-in-Law of Peter. [Henry Grattan.] MORRIS.
50. The Last Supper. [Rt. Hon. Alexander Macdonnell.] GAROFALO (after Leonardo).
51. St. Jerome. [Rev. J. Mulhall.] LO SPAGNOLETTO (J. Ribera).
52. The Holy Family. [The Marquis of Drogheda.] VANDYCK.
53. The Madonna. [Alexander M'Carthy.] FRATE MODESTO.
54. The Adoration of the Kings. [Very Rev. J. Curtis.] JOHN VAN EYCK.
55. The Entombment. [Henry Hodgson.] CORREGGIO.
56. Madonna and Child, with Group of Angels. [Miss Ryan.] OSORIO.
57. The Assumption. [Sir John Nugent, Bart.] DE VOS.
58. Jephtha's Vow. [W. Knox.] BREUGHEL.
59. Christ Before Herod. [Archdeacon Magee.] GIO. WYKERSLOOST, 1658.
60. Madonna and Child. [Sir John Nugent, Bart.] HUBERT VAN EYCK.
61. St. Cecilia. [Mr. Duffy.] DOMENICHINO.
62. St. Spiridion (Bishop of Tremethens, in Cyprus, in the Fourth Century). [Sir Robert Gore Booth, Bart.] Byzantine School.
63. Portrait of San Juan de la Cruz. [Sir John Nugent, Bart.] LO SPAGNOLETTO (Ribera).
64. Holy Family. [Sir John Nugent, Bart.] GUERCINO.
65. Madonna and Child. [The Lord Chancellor.] SASSOFERRATO.
66. Holy Family and St. John. [Sir John Nugent, Bart.] TITIAN.
67. Holy Family. [The Marquis of Ely.] After ANDREA DEL SARTO.
68. Holy Family. [The Earl of Portarlington.] After ANDREA DEL SARTO.
69. The Cup found in Benjamin's Sack. [The Earl of Miltown.] POUSSIN (Le Brun ?).
70. Martyrdom of St. Sebastian. [Lord Ward.] GUIDO.
71. St. Cecilia. [John Farrell.] CARLO DOLCI (?).
72. St. Mary Magdalen. [Sir John Nugent, Bart.] GUIDO.
73. St. Catherine. [Alexander M'Carthy.] DOMENICHINO.
74. Madonna and Child. [Marquis of Ormonde.]
75. The Holy Family. [The Duke of Leinster.] ANDREA DEL SARTO.
76. Marriage of St. Catherine. [Stephen Simpson.]
77. The Madonna. [Sir John Nugent, Bart.] SASSOFERRATO.
78. St. Cecilia. [Sir John Nugent, Bart.] PAOLO VERONESE.
79. The Nativity. [The Earl of Charlemont.] GIULIO ROMANO (?).
80. An Interior, with Christ, Mary, and Martha. [The Earl of Portarlington.] STEENWICK.
81. Triptych: representing in the central compartment the Adoration of the Magi; on the right-hand side the Birth of our Saviour; on the left the Circumcision. (This picture, said to have been in Queen Mary's Chapel, at Holyrood Palace, was presented to an ancestor of the owner by the celebrated Mademoiselle de Querouialle, Duchess of Portsmouth.) [Lord Talbot de Malahide.] ALBERT DURER.
82. St. Peter Denying Christ. [The Earl of Bessborough.] GERARD SEGHERS.
83. St. Francis Receiving the Five Wounds on Mount Alverno. [Charles Molloy.] DOMENICHINO (?).
84. David with Head of Goliath.
85. Holy Family. [John Gibson.] PIERINO DEL VAGA.
86. David with Head of Goliath. [Sir Compton Domville, Bart.] LIONEL SPADA.
87. St. Paul. [The Earl of Charlemont.] VANDYCK.
88. Jephtha's Rash Vow. [The Earl of Enniskillen.] After RUBENS.
89. Visit of the Centurion. [F. W. Brady.] REMBRANDT.
90. Madonna and Child. [The Earl of Portarlington.] CARLO DOLCE.
91. The Assumption. [Sir Compton Domville, Bart.] DOMENICHINO.
92. Coronation of St. Catherine. [Sir John Nugent, Bart.] CARLO MARATTI.
93. Madonna and Child. [Lord Ward.] TITIAN.
94. St. Jerome. [Rt. Hon. R. More O'Ferrall.] FERRARI.
95. The Madonna Addolorata. [Lord Ward.] CARLO DOLCE.
96. Saint Agnes. [Henry Grattan.] ELIZABETH SIRANI.
97. Madonna and Child. After RAFFAELLE.

98. Marriage of St. Catherine. [The Lord Chancellor.] Carlo Maratti.
99. The Madonna and Child. [D. Ross of Bladensburg.] Correggio (?).
100. St. Catherine. [Lady Juliana Bayly.] O. Marinari.
101. The Blessed Virgin, Child, and Angels. [T. Tepe.] Albano.
102. Madonna and Child. [H. Westropp.]

---

103. The Mouth of the Scheldt. [Charles Brien.] Backhuysen.
104. Storm. [Charles Brien.] Backhuysen.
105. An Interior, with Groups of Figures. [W. M'Kay.] Battem.
106. Horses Crossing a Rivulet. [J. H. Reid.] Berghem.
107. Landscape, with Figures and Buildings. [The Earl of Portarlington.] Berghem.
108. Landscape and Figures. [John Gibson.] Berghem (?).
109. Cattle Crossing a Stream. [The Earl of Portarlington.] Berghem.
110. Portrait of an Italian Nobleman. [Rt. Hon. Alexander Macdonnell.] Bordone.
111. Battle Piece. [The Earl of Portarlington.] Borgognone.
112. View in Venice. [Marquis of Ely.] Canaletto.
113. View in Venice. [Marquis of Ely.] Canaletto.
114. View in Venice. [The Earl of Portarlington.] Canaletto.
115. View in Venice. [The Earl of Portarlington.] Canaletto.
116. View in Venice. [Lord Ward.] Canaletto.
117. Interior of a Venetian Palace. [Rt. Hon. Alexander Macdonnell.] Canaletto.
118. Companion to 117. [Rt. Hon. Alexander Macdonnell.] Canaletto.
119. Landscape, with Latona and the Clown. [Sir Compton Domville, Bart.] Caracci and Domenichino.
120. Head of an Old Man. [Sir John Nugent, Bart.] A. Caracci (?).
121. The Dutch Larder. [The Earl of Bessborough.] Snyders.
122. Marine View. [The Marquis of Ely.] Dubbels.
123. Battle Piece. [H. Westropp.] Borgognone.
124. Village Festival. [Mrs. Barry.] Teniers.
125. Roman Ruins. [Earl of Miltown.] Claude Lorraine.
126. Domestic Poultry. [The Earl of Miltown.] Hondecooter.
127. The Horse Fair. [Henry Grattan.] Wouvermans.
128. Old Lady. [John Gibson.] B. Denner.
129. Coronation of Constantine the Great (sketch for a large picture). [Henry Hodgson.] Raffaelle.
130. Portrait of Lord Newport. [Lord Portarlington.] Vandyck.
131. James the First and his Family. [Henry Rosenthal.] Mytens.
132. Bacchante and Satyrs. [The Earl of Portarlington.] N. Poussin.
133. Portrait of King William. [John Bloomfield.] Vandyck.
134. Portrait of the Earl of Strafford. [The Marquis of Ormonde.] Vandyck.
135. Prince Antiochus, Queen Stratonice, and the Physician, Erosistratus. [Sir John Nugent, Bart.] J. Van Eyck.
136. Dutch Boors Smoking. [The Rt. Hon. Judge Ball.] Ostade.
137. The Family of Charles I. [The Marquis of Ormonde.] Vandyck.
138. Cæsar Borgia. [The Earl of Charlemont.] Titian.
139. Full-length Portrait of Henrietta Maria, accompanied by Sir Jeffrey Hudson, the Court Dwarf. [The Earl of Portarlington.] Vandyck.
140. River Scene. [The Marquis of Drogheda.] Decker.
141. Dead Game. [The Earl of Miltown.] Hondecooter.
142. Horses Watering. [The Earl of Miltown.] Wouvermans.
143. Scene in Holland. [The Lord Chancellor.] Van der Neer.
144. Fête Champetre. [John Gibson.] Watteau.
145. Halt at the Smithy. [The Marquis of Ely.] Wouvermans.
146. Dutch Interior. [John La Touche.] Ostade.
147. Vulcan and Venus. [W. Knox.] John Van Kessel.
148. Forge by Moonlight. [The Lord Chancellor.] Peter Wouvermans.
149. The Swing. [The Earl of Miltown.] Watteau.
150. Landscape and Figures. [The Lord Chancellor.] Teniers and Artois.
151. Landscape. [The Lord Chancellor.] Teniers and Artois.
152. Wood Scene, Hunting Party, &c. [The Marquis of Ely.] Wynants and Wouvermans.
153. Early Morn. [Mrs. West.] Cuyp.
154. Halt of Cavaliers. [The Marquis of Ely.] Wouvermans.
155. Fête Champetre. [The Earl of Miltown.] Watteau.
156. Musicians. [The Earl of Miltown.] Teniers.
157. A French Sea-port.—"Evening." [The Earl of Miltown.] J. Vernet.
158. Group of Figures. [John Bloomfield.] French School.
159. Musicians. [The Earl of Charlemont.] Tintoretto.
160. Landscape, with Banditti. [James E. Stopford.] Salvator Rosa.
161. Landscape, Figures, and Waterfall. [The Earl of Miltown.] Salvator Rosa.
162. Landscape, Figures, and Waterfall. [The Earl of Miltown.] Poussin.
163. A French Sea-port,—"Morning." [The Earl of Miltown.] J. Vernet.
164. Marine View. [Peter La Touche.] Vernet.
165. Head of an Old Woman. [The Earl of Portarlington.] Martin de Vos.
166. Cattle, Figures, &c. [The Marquis of Ely.] Cuyp.
167. Portrait of Henry VIII. [The Earl of Portarlington.] Holbein.
168. Portrait of a Lady. [Sir John Nugent, Bart.] Florentine School.
169. Head of an Old Woman.
170. Portrait of Catherine MacCarthy, the great Countess of Desmond, at the age of 146 years. [The Knight of Kerry.] Gerard Douw.
171. Portrait of Vossius. [Thomas Ford.] Sandrart.
172. The Cavaliers. [The Duke of Leinster.] Cuyp.
173. Venus Chiding Cupid. [James Daly.] Correggio.
174. Old Age and Youth. [The Earl of Miltown.]
175. Scene on the Ice in Holland. [The Lord Chancellor.] H. W. Schudelck.
176. Shepherd, Sheep, and Goats. [Lady Juliana Bayly.] Rosa di Tivoli.
177. Portrait. [Sir John Nugent, Bart.] Eliz. Sirani.
178. Interior of a Guard-room. [William M'Kay.] Palamedes.
179. Head of an Old Man. [The Marquis of Ely.] Rembrandt.
180. Cupid Breaking his Bow. [The Earl of Portarlington.] Guercino.
181. Adam and Eve, with Cain and Abel. [The Earl of Miltown.] Luca Giordano.
182. Head of an Old Woman. [Marquis of Ely.] Rembrandt.
183. Mercury, Argus, and Io. [Rt. Hon. Alexander Macdonnell.] Eckhout.
184. Italian Vineyard. [Rt. Hon. Alexander Macdonnell.]
185. Portrait of the Artist. [W. M'Kay.] Denner.
186. Portrait of Geronimo Prioli, Doge of Venice, Son of Antonio Prioli, Procurator of St. Mark. [Rt. Hon. Alexander Macdonnell.] Titian (?).
187. Venus and Adonis. [Rt. Hon. Alexander Macdonnell.]
188. Italian Landscape. [Rt. Hon. Alexander Macdonnell.] Swanvoelt.

189. Female Shading a Candle. [Marquis of Waterford.] HONTHORST.
190. The Tooth Drawer. [Marquis of Ely.] After GERARD DOUW.
191. Loading Hay, Cattle, &c. [The Rt. Hon. Judge Ball.] CUYP.
192. Marine Piece. [The Earl of Portarlington.] VAN DE VELDE.
193. Landscape and Figures. [W. M'Kay.] HOBBEMA (?).
194. Child's Head. [Alexander M'Carthy.] GUIDO.
195. Belling the Cat. [Lord Ward.] TENIERS.
196. Nymphs Bathing. [The Marquis of Ely.] POELEMBERG.
197. Portrait of Gerard Douw. [The Earl of Portarlington.] GERARD DOUW.
198. Francis Thomas of Savoy, Prince of Carignan. [The Lord Chancellor.] VANDYCK.
199. The Alchemist. [John Gibson.] After GERARD DOUW.
200. Landscape, with Water Mill. [The Lord Chancellor.] HOBBEMA.
201. Head. [Sir John Nugent, Bart.] GREUZE.
202. Head of an Old Woman. [The Marquis of Drogheda.] REMBRANDT.
203. Hares at Play. [John Gibson.] PAUL POTTER (?).
204. Landscape and Cattle. [Charles Brien.] DOMENICHINO.
205. Landscape, Cattle, and Figures. [Charles Brien.] VAN DE VELDE.
206. Portrait of a Lady (on panel). [Sir John Nugent, Bart.] TITIAN (?).
207. Portrait of Leo X. [John La Touche.] GIULIO ROMANO (after Raphael).
208. Portrait of the Artist. [The Earl of Portarlington.] REMBRANDT.
209. Meeting Room of Three Societies of Rhetoricians, which existed at Haarlem in the Seventeenth Century. [J. H. Reid.]
210. Landscape, with Figures. [The Earl of Enniskillen.] G. POUSSIN (?).
211. Astronomy. [Alexander M'Carthy.] DOMENICHINO.
212. Triptych: The Adoration of the Kings. [Sir John Nugent, Bart.] LUCAS VAN LEYDEN.
213. Study: Heads of Wolves. QUADAL.
214. A Sea-Port, with Vessels under Sail. [Sir John Nugent, Bart.] SALVATOR ROSA.
215. Interior of a Church. [The Lord Chancellor.] NEEFS.
216. Sunset at Sea. [H. Westropp.] CLAUDE LORRAINE.
217. Landscape and Figures. [Earl of Miltown.] SALVATOR ROSA.
218. Drawing the Net. [The Earl of Portarlington.] G. POUSSIN.
219. Companion to No. 218. [The Earl of Portarlington.] G. POUSSIN.
220. Milking the Cow: a View near Dordrecht. [John La Touche.] CUYP.
221. Portrait of the Duke of Alva. [The Earl of Portarlington.] RUBENS.
222. Landscape. [The Earl of Portarlington.] CLAUDE LORRAINE.
223. Landscape and Cattle. [The Earl of Portarlington.] MOUCHERON.
224. Woody Landscape: Duck-shooting. [The Earl of Bessborough.] WATERLOO.
225. Bacchanalians. [The Earl of Miltown.] RUBENS.
226. Ruins. [The Marquis of Drogheda.] PANNINI.
227. Hurdy-Gurdy Boy. [The Marquis of Drogheda.] REMBRANDT (?).
228. Mount Olympus, Assembly of the Gods. [Sir John Nugent, Bart.] MIGNARD.
229. Head: Study. [Alexander M'Carthy.] NOGARI.
230. Portrait of Charles I., presented by James Stopford, Bishop of Cloyne, 1742, to Dean Swift, and left back again to him in the Dean's will. [James E. Stopford.] VANDYCK.
231. Portrait of Thomas Lord Fairfax. VANDYCK.
232. Firing a Salute. [The Earl of Miltown.] PETERS.
233. Landscape and Figures. [The Marquis of Ely.] WYNANTS.
234. Musical Concert. [The Earl of Charlemont.] M. A. CARAVAGGIO.
235. Landscape. [The Marquis of Drogheda.] CLAUDE LORRAINE.
236. River Scene in Holland. [The Marquis of Drogheda.] VAN GOYEN.
237. Landscape. [The Marquis of Ely.] RUYSDAEL.
238. Portrait of Lady Thurles. [Sir John Nugent, Bart.] VANDYCK.
239. Landscape. [The Lord Chancellor.] SALVATOR ROSA.
240. Cattle in a Landscape. [The Earl of Portarlington.] A. VAN DE VELDE.
241. Meleager and Atalanta. [The Earl of Miltown.] After RUBENS.
242. Venus Disarming Cupid. [John Gibson.] French School.
243. Merry-Making. [The Rt. Hon. Sir Wm. Somerville, Bart.] TENIERS.
244. The Good Shepherd. [John Gibson.] CARACCI (?).
245. Scene in Holland. [The Rt. Hon. Sir Wm. Somerville, Bart.] TILBURG.
246. Full-length Portrait of Charles I. [The Marquis of Ormonde.] After VANDYCK.
247. Portrait of a Friar. [The Earl of Portarlington.] After TITIAN.
248. Queen Henrietta Maria. [The Marquis of Ormonde.] After VANDYCK.
249. Family of Jan Steen. [Henry Grattan.] JAN STEEN.
250. Portrait of a Burgomaster. [Lord Ward.] REMBRANDT.
251. Landscape and Figures. [The Earl of Portarlington.] TENIERS and VANUDEN.
252. Landscape and Figures. [The Earl of Portarlington.] TENIERS and VANUDEN.
253. Flowers. [Lord Ward.] VAN OS.
254. Fruit. [Lord Ward.] VAN OS.
255. Portrait of Isabella, Archduchess of Austria. [J. Bloomfield.] After VANDYCK.
256. Landscape. [T. Tepe.] G. POUSSIN (?).
257. Narcissus. [T. Tepe.] M. A. DA CARAVAGGIO (?).
258. A Collection of original Drawings, by the Old Masters. [Henry Arrowsmith.] RAFFAELLE (two Studies for Frescoes), the property of Colonel Colomb. PARMIGIANO (three Specimens in one Frame,—one in pen and wash, one in red chalk, and one in chalk). A Sacrifice, AMIDANO, Pupil of PARMIGIANO (in wash). Holy Family, ALBANO (pen and wash). GIUSEPPE GALLEOTTI (Study for Fresco). GIUSEPPE GALLEOTTI (Study for Fresco). GIUSEPPE GALLEOTTI (Study for Fresco). A Battle, LUCCA GIORDANO (sepia wash). Sacrifice by Abraham, ANDREA LACCHI (wash). Wounded Horse, TIEPOLI (wash). Studies of St. Michael GUIDO (wash and pen). Repentance of St. Peter, GUIDO (wash and pen). Study for Crowning a Saint, FRANCESCHINI. The Titans, A. CARACCI (pen and wash). Saint, MURILLO (pen and wash). A Study, CLAUDE (pen and wash). Landscape, SWANEVELDT. Three Subjects in one Frame (in Pencil) BOUCHER. Landscape, BOUCHER. Landscape, PAUL BRIL (indigo wash). Ship in a Gale, BACKHUYSEN (wash). Shipping, RIETSCHOOF (water-colour). Abraham and the Angels, REMBRANDT (Wash). Stormy Weather, VAN DRIELST (Wash). Companion, VAN DRIELST (Wash). Conversation, DE BOURG (water-colour). Studies of Trees, RUYSDAEL (in red chalk). Studies of Trees, RUYSDAEL (in red chalk). POLEMBERG (in wash). VAN DRIELST (Indian ink wash). NICCOLO POUSSIN (colour wash). VANDYCK (Indian ink). PASINELLI (sketch in black chalk). Landscape, ROUSSEAU, Pupil of SWANEVELDT (in chalk). The Fortune Teller, CALLOT. HOGARTH (in wash). English Sports, HOGARTH (wash and colour). Landscape, GAINSBOROUGH (in conte chalk).

259. The Entombment. [C. Coppinger, Q.C.] JAMES BARRY, R. A.
260. Portrait of the late Earl of Charlemont (unfinished). [The Earl of Charlemont.] HOGARTH.
261. Venus chiding Cupid. [The Earl of Charlemont.] SIR JOSHUA REYNOLDS.
262. Landscape, with Sheep and Figures. [S. Cartwright.] GEORGE MORLAND.
263. Portrait of the Marquis of Montrose. [The Marquis of Ormonde.] WISSING.
264. Portrait of Lady Caroline Damer. [The Earl of Portarlington.] ANGELICA KAUFFMAN.
265. Landscape with Figures. [Sir John Nugent, Bart.] ZUCCARELLI.
266. Portrait of Sir Richard Worsley, in the uniform of the Isle of Wight Militia. [The Earl of Yarborough.] SIR JOSHUA REYNOLDS.
267. Lady and Child. [Edward Cooper.] ROMNEY.
268. Portrait of Prince Charles Edward, the "Pretender." [J. H. Reid.]
269. Hare and Fruit. [The Marquis of Ely.] BESCHEY.
270. Italian Landscape. [H. Westropp.]
271. Dogs. [H. Luscombe.] G. MORLAND.
272. The Flight of Europa. [Charles Brien.] BESCHEY.
273. A Study. [Robert Smith.] G. MORLAND.
274. Portrait of Oliver Cromwell. [Chas. Brien.] WALKER.
275. Subject from the Milton Gallery. [Samuel Cartwright.] FUSELI.
276. Louis XIV. in the Gardens at Versailles. [The Earl of Bessborough.] VAN DER MEULEN.
277. Portrait of Sir Joshua Reynolds. [Sir Vere de Vere, Bart.] SIR JOSHUA REYNOLDS.
278. Second Stage of the Harlot's Progress. [The Earl of Charlemont.] HOGARTH.
279. The Dance. [Earl of Miltown.]
280. Portrait of the Duchess of Orleans. [The Earl of Portarlington.] SIR PETER LELY.
281. Roman Landscape. [S. Simpson.] WILSON.
282. Landscape. [Lord Ward.] WILSON.
283. A Portrait.
284. Edmund Burke. [J. Bloomfield.] SIR JOSHUA REYNOLDS (?).
285. Portrait of Miss Munroe. [The Marquis of Ely.] ANGELICA KAUFFMAN.
286. Portrait of Sir Peter Lely. [James E. Stopford.] SIR PETER LELY.
287. Caricature of Banks, afterwards Lord Aylesbury, Lord Miltown, Frank Burton, afterwards Lord Conyngham, and Lord Charlemont. [The Earl of Miltown.] SIR JOSHUA REYNOLDS.
288. Caricature of Henry of Straffan, Sir W. Wynne, Lord Charlemont, and another. [The Earl of Miltown.] SIR JOSHUA REYNOLDS.
289. Caricature of the First Lord Miltown, and Lord Naas, afterwards Lord Mayo. [Lord Miltown.] SIR JOSHUA REYNOLDS.
290. Execution of a Spy. [The Rev. Ogle Moore.] SIMONINI.
291. Hagar in the Wilderness. [Sir John Nugent, Bart.]
292. Roman Forum. [The Earl of Miltown.] PANNINI.
293. The Lady's Last Stake. [The Earl of Charlemont.] HOGARTH.
294. Roman Ruins. [The Earl of Miltown.] PANNINI.
295. The Gates of Calais. [The Earl of Charlemont.] HOGARTH.
296. Christ and the Samaritan Woman at the Well. [The Earl of Miltown.] PANNINI.
297. Angels at Play. [Hon. Richard O'Grady.] DE GREY.
298. Companion to No. 297. [The Hon. R. O'Grady.] DE GREY.
299. Portrait of Archbishop Usher. [R. Pearson, M.D.]
300. Portrait of Philip Stanhope Earl of Chesterfield, painted when he was Lord Lieutenant of Ireland in 1745. [The Hon. Sir F. Stanhope, Bart.] THOMPSON.
301. Portrait of Oliver Cromwell. [John Bloomfield.] DOBSON.
302. Portrait of King William the Third. [Right Hon. Sir William Somerville.] SIR GODFREY KNELLER.
303. Portrait of Queen Mary, wife of William III. [J. Bloomfield.] SIR PETER LELY.
304. Portrait of Charles II. [William Ruxton.] SIR PETER LELY.
305. Portrait of James, second Duke of Ormonde. [J. H. Smith.] SIR G. KNELLER.
306. Portrait of George, Duke of Albemarle. [William Ruxton.] SIR PETER LELY.
307. Portrait of M. Angelo, of an old date. [Henry Hodson.]
308. Bacchus and Ariadne. [E. J. Cooper.] ROMNEY.
309. View of Calcutta. [E. J. Cooper.]
310. Portrait of King William III. [S. H. H. Bruce, Bart.] NETSCHER.
311. Portrait of Martain Foulkes, F.R.S. [Sir Vere de Vere, Bart.] VAN DER BANK.
312. Portrait of a Lady and Page. [C. Nosotti.] VANLOO.
313. Portrait of Old Parr in his 153rd year, A.D. 1635 [E. R. P. Colles.]
314. A Pietà. [J. Whitty.]
315. Portrait of the late Earl of Charlemont. [The Earl of Charlemont.] GAINSBOROUGH.
316. Henry Grattan moving Declaration of Independence in the Irish House of Commons (containing 14[illegible] Portraits), painted in 1780. [Mrs. Gascoigne.] WHEATLEY.
317. Review of the Irish Volunteers, College-green. [The Duke of Leinster.] WHEATLEY.
318. Death of Adonis. [Wm. Anthony.] JAMES BARRY, R. A.
319. Portrait of Dean Swift. [George Crampton.]
320. Full-length Portrait of Quin in the character of Sir John Falstaff. [Sir Percy Nugent, Bart.] SIR JOSHUA REYNOLDS.
321. Portrait of Patrick Sarsfield, Earl of Lucan. [E. H. Casey.] SIR GODFREY KNELLER.
322. Portrait of the late Earl of Charlemont. [The Earl of Charlemont.] POMPEO BATONI.
323. Portrait of the late Earl of Miltown. [The Earl of Miltown.] POMPEO BATONI.
324. Portrait of the Earl Macartney and Sir George Staunton. [S. M. Caldwell.] SIR JOSHUA REYNOLDS.
325. Portrait of Roger, or Rory, O'More (of Ballynagh, Co. Kildare), one of the principal leaders of the "Rebellion" of 1641. [Right Hon. R. More O'Ferrall.]
326. Portrait of the first Duke of Ormonde. [The Marquis of Ormonde.] SIR PETER LELY.
327. Full-length Portrait of Dean Swift, presented by the Chapter to the Deanery House (the frame of Irish oak, presented by the Artificers of Dublin at the same time.) [Very Rev. Dean Pakenham.] BINDON.
328. Portrait of General O'Donnell. [Right Hon. R. More O'Ferrall.]

---

### THE MODERN SCHOOL.

329. The Creation. GOSSE.
330. The Birth of Christ. GOSSE.
331. The Temptation of St. Anthony. [Monsieur Saisse.] TASSAERT.
332. Ave Maria. SUSSMANN, Berlin.
333. The good Conscience. A. COLIN.
334. St. Elizabeth of Hungary, distributing Alms. DEBON.
335. St. Peter repentant, after denying Christ. PAULIN GUERIN FILS.
336. Death of Judas Iscariot. PAULIN GUERIN FILS.
337. Paradise Lost. GABRIEL LEFEBURE.
338. St. Hugues praying in the Forest. BACCUET.
339. The Flight into Egypt. EMILE LECOMTE.
340. "Suffer little children to come unto Me." FANNY GEEFS CORR, Brussels.
341. St. Cecilia. MATHIEU, Louvain.
342. Resignation. ANGUS, Antwerp.
343. The Holy Family. TAYMANS, Brussels.

344. The Sacrifice of Abraham. L. VOORDECKER, Brussels.
345. The Communion. ADELE KINDT, Brussels.
346. Judith bearing the Head of Holophernes. THOMAS, Brussels.
347. St. Elizabeth of Hungary. [H. M. the King of the Belgians.] A. DE KEYSER, Antwerp.
348. Judith bearing the Head of Holophernes. VAN ROOY, Antwerp.
349. Rebecca. [H. M. The King of the Belgians.] PORTAELS, Brussels.
350. The Adoration. VAN SCHENDEL, Brussels.
351. St. Mary Magdalen. VAN SEVERDONCK, Brussels.
352. The Prayer. TAYMANS, Brussels.
353. The Temptation of St. Anthony. [H. M. the King of the Belgians.] GALLAIT, Brussels.
354. The Last Moments of St. Remacle. BELLEMANS, Antwerp.
355. The Crucifixion. HOUZE, Brussels.
356. Jacob and Rachel. BELLEMANS, Antwerp.
357. Christ. "Ego sum Via et Vita." GUFFENS, Antwerp.
358. The Blessed Virgin and St. John standing by the Cross. J. A. KRUSEMAN, JZ., Dricbergen.
359. Hannah bringing Samuel to the High Priest Eli. HUEBNER, Prussia.
360. Christ and the little Child. (St. Matthew, chap. xviii. ver. 4.) T. A. KRUSEMAN, Dricbergen.
361. The Daughter of Herodias, with the Head of St. John the Baptist. SCHRADER.
362. Esther accusing Haman to Ahasuerus. LEVIN.
363. The Flight into Egypt. SCHUETZE.
364. Christ prophesying the Destruction of Jerusalem. [H. M. the King of Prussia.] BEGAS.
365. The Birth of Christ. PIETROWSKI.
366. Ruth follows Naomi in her departure from Moab. COUNT SPEZIA, Rome.
367. Jesus Christ and the Woman of Samaria. CAMMADE.
368. Jesus Christ Curing the Mother-in-Law of St. Peter. VIARDOT.
369. The Prayer. LEPAULLE.
370. Christ driving the Devils out of the possessed Men. JOHN TRACY.
371. The Deluge. [W. Jones.] F. DANBY, A.R.A.
372. The Communion (in a Catholic Church). [H. A. J. Munro.] S. A. HART, R. A.
373. The Prayer. J. LUCAS.
374. Dalila asking Forgiveness of Sampson. W. S. BURTON.
375. A Friar at his Devotions. PICKERSGILL, R. A.
376. Angels appearing to the Shepherds. [Robert Smith.] WESTALL.
377. The Holy Family. [A. D. Cooper.] A. COOPER.
378. The Madonna. J. MAGRATH.

379. Fort Abraham in Corfu, looking towards the Island of Vido, and the Coast of Albania. MAX SCHMIDT.
380. Sketch in Corfu—View from Benezza looking towards Un Canone. MAX SCHMIDT.
381. View towards the Citadel of Corfu and Coast of Albania. MAX SCHMIDT.
382. Entrance to the old Harbour of Corcyra. MAX SCHMIDT.
383. Genoveva with her Child, Schmerzenreich (Eighth Century.) SHEINBRUCK.
384. A Landscape, with Nymphs Bathing. C. BECKER.
385. A Vintage Festival in Ischia. CRETIUS.
386. A Scene on the Nile—"Difficulties of Embarking." KRETZSCHMER.
387. Fruit and Flowers. DIETRICH.
388. Procession with Torches by Moonlight. J. PELGROM, Zutphen.
389. St. Giovanni in Laterana, Rome. SCHULTZ.
390. Lunch in the Desert. KRETZSCHMER.
391. The Angel's Horn, in Switzerland. ENGLEHARDT.
392. A Mendicant Friar. NERENZ.
393. Valley of Chamouni. SEIFISCH.
394. Maternal Love. MEYER.
395. Avalanche at the Gosen Lake, Upper Austria. HOLLSTEIN.
396. Leave-taking of a Condemned Criminal with his Family. BENDIX.
397. Castle of Lueg, in Carniola. BIERMANN.
398. View in Inspruck. [H. M. the King of Prussia.] KALKREUTH.
399. The Weisse Horn, from the Nicolai Vale, Switzerland. E. HOLLSTEIN.
400. The Young Princes in the Tower. VERREYDT.
401. Ithaca, looking towards Greece. MAX SCHMIDT.
402. Bull-hunting in the Italian Fashion. C. STEFFECK.
403. Landscape—Winter. MEYER.
404. Landscape, with Cattle. VON DER BURCH.
405. Pier of Ostende during a Storm. [H. R. H. the Prince of Prussia.] ACHENBACH.
406. Martinswand—A View near Inspruck. [H. M. the King of Prussia.] KALKREUTH.
407. A Swiss Landscape—Canton Uri. SEIFFERT.
408. Captured Banditti taken to Prison. NERENZ.
409. Scene from Roman Life—Lower Orders. PISTORIUS.
410. Scene of an Inundation in North Holland in 1825, by Moonlight. C. J. L. PORTMAN, Cleves.
411. The Sleepy Nurse. PISTORIUS.
412. The Charitable Little Maiden. NERENZ.
413. Swiss Landscape, Canton, Berne. SEIFFERT.
414. Horses. STEFFECK.
415. Hamilton's Point in Heligoland. EDWARD SCHMIDT.
416. Prince Waldemar, of Prussia, supporting his dying Physician, Hofmeister, at the Battle of Ferozeshah, with Portraits of Lord Hardinge, and others. KRETZSCHMER.
417. Pantaleone, in the Island of Sicily. [H. R. H. the Prince of Prussia.] ACHENBACH.
418. A Winter Scene in Belgium. BODEMAN, Brussels.
419. The Cook's Accounts. [M. Vandenbergh, Brussels.] DYCKMANS, Antwerp.
420. Summer Wild Flowers. DIETRICH, Prussia.
421. Landscape—Norwegian Winter. M. T. BAGGE, Dusseldorf.
422. A Visit to Poor People. CARL HUBNER, Dusseldorf.
423. Oberwesel on the Rhine. WM. KLEIN, Dusseldorf.
424. Gretchen in the Dungeon—(Faust.) C. BEGAS, Prussia.
425. A Dispute over Cards. MELZER, Antwerp.
426. Breakfast. CAROLUS, Brussels.
427. Maternal Happiness. VAN DEN DAELE, Antwerp.
428. A Stolen Kiss. GONS, Antwerp.
429. The Miniature. TAYMANS, Brussels.
430. The Fruit-seller. GEERNAERT, Ghent.
431. The Flight of Henrietta Maria. JAMBERS, Brussels.
432. An Interior. HAESSELEER, Brussels.
433. Dogs. [H. M. the King of the Belgians.] E. VERBÖCKHOVEN, Brussels.
434. A Pilgrim in the Holy Land. KREMER, Antwerp.
435. Landscape. FRANCIA, Brussels.
436. Return from the Chase. SCHARPEENS, Brussels.
437. Doves. HENRI VOORDECKER, Brussels.
438. "Tumblers." HAESAERT, Antwerp.
439. The Happy Mother. TAYMANS, Antwerp.
440. The Gate of Harkvilde at Ghent. FRANCIS BOULANGER, Ghent.
441. The Reopening of a Catholic Church. KREMER, Antwerp.
442. Landscape with Cattle. GEERNAERT, Ghent.
443. Young Girls. DE VIGNE, Ghent.
444. A Cook. VAN MEER, Brussels.
445. The Enemy of Farm-yards. [M. Vandenberg.] BRIAS, Brussels.
446. The Lacemaker. NOTERMAN, Antwerp.
447. Fish Market. VAN REGEMORTER, Antwerp.
448. Morning Walk. FRANCIA, Brussels.
449. Dog and Puppies. ADOLPHE JONES, Brussels.
450. The Centenarian. VOORDECKER, Brussels.
451. "Louis XVII." [H. M. the King of the Belgians.] WAPPERS, Brussels.
452. Hibernia. FANNY GEEFS CORR, Brussels.

453. Landscape and Cattle. Marinus, Namur.
454. Mary Queen of Scots. Huysmans, Antwerp.
455. Gipsy Mother. Matilde Lagache-Corr, Brussels.
456. The Guitar. Victor Eeckhout, Brussels.
457. The Elopement. Van Oudenhoven, Antwerp.
458. The Village Politician. David Col, Antwerp.
459. The Female Recruit. [M. Vandenbergh.] Madou, Brussels.
460. A Stable. Van Severdonck, Brussels.
461. An Arab Fortress. Bossuet, Brussels.
462. An Episode of the Creation. Wauters, Malines.
463. Virgilius braving the Anger of the Duke of Alva. Bellemans, Antwerp.
464. Frances de Foix, Comtesse De Chateaubriand. Wulffaert, Ghent.
465. A Fancy Portrait. [M. Couteaux, Brussels.] Dorcy, Brussels.
466. Fancy Portrait. [M. Couteaux, Brussels.] Dorcy, Brussels.
467. A Fancy Portrait. [M. Couteaux, Brussels.] Dorcy, Brussels.
468. The Fan. Vambombergen, Antwerp.
469. A Young Venus. Vanheyken, Brussels.
470. A Farm House. Van Moer, Brussels.
471. Dead Game. Van Meer, Brussels.
472. Field of Flowers. H. Dillens, Antwerp.
473. The Plough. [H. M. the King of the Belgians.] Charles Tschaggeny, Brussels.
474. A Figure of the 17th Century. Verhaghen, Brussels.
475. The Knitter. Verhaghen, Brussels.
476. Interior of a Court-yard. Verhaghen, Brussels.
477. A Cook. Van Meer, Brussels.
478. Birds. Madame Vervloet, Malines.
479. Landscape with Cattle. Kruseman, Brussels.
480. The Young Delinquent—Offence against the Game Laws. F. Claes, Antwerp.
481. The Young Poacher. [M. Podesta.] Noterman, Antwerp.
482. A Moorish Gate. F. Bossuet, Brussels.
483. Guess who I am. Haesaert, Antwerp.
484. Young Girls with the Jew. Cornet, Antwerp.
485. The Field of Waterloo. Seghers, Brussels.
486. Moonlight. Vanbombergen, Antwerp.
487. Boy and Lamb. Picque, Brussels.
488. A Cook. Verhaghen, Brussels.
489. Interior of a Church. Vervloet, Malines.
490. Dog and Puppies. Haeselere, Brussels.
491. A Badly Nursed Child. Verhaghen, Brussels.
492. A Group of Young Beggars. Brice, Brussels.
493. Kitchen. [H. M. the King of the Belgians.] Van Meer, Brussels.
494. Rat-catching. [M. Couteaux.] De Brackeleer, Antwerp.
495. A Cart with Oxen frightened by a Storm. De Taeye, Antwerp.
496. Citadel in Spain. Boulanger, Antwerp.
497. Landscape with Cattle. [M. Vandenberg.] Schelfhout and Verböckhoven, Brussels.
498. Winter. Verwee, Brussels.
499. Landscape with Cattle. Fanton, Liege.
500. Genevieve De Brabant. Pique, Brussels.
501. A Market. [H. M. the King of the Belgians.] Bossuet, Brussels.
502. Flowers and Fruit. Robbe, Brussels.
503. A Seller of Game. Van Meer, Brussels.
504. Cattle Piece. [Edward Cooper.] Eugene Verboeckhoven.
505. The Water-Wheel. Pietersszen, Antwerp.
506. Return from the Vintage. Bource, Antwerp.
507. Taking the Veil. Houze, Brussels.
508. Court of a House in the 17th Century. Schaepkens, Brussels.
509. A Souvenir of the Fount of D'Orval. Defailly, Brussels.
510. A Young Work-woman. Billoin, Brussels.
511. Dice-throwing. [H. M. the King of the Belgians.] H. Leys, Antwerp.
512. A Dream. Houze, Brussels.
513. View in Ardennes. Francia, Brussels.
514. Interior. Geerts, Antwerp.
515. Henry Percy, Duke of Northumberland. Houze Brussels.
516. Village Dance. Schaep, Antwerp.
517. The Return to the Chateau. Coumont, Brussels.
518. The Black Mask. Correns, Antwerp.
519. Landscape in Belgium. Lauters, Brussels.
520. Interior of a Synagogue. [M. Couteaux.] H. Leys, Antwerp.
521. Souvenir of the Dauphine. Deschampheleer, Brussels.
522. An Interior. Geerts, Antwerp.
523. View of the Allee Verte at Brussels. Joseph Van Severdonck, Brussels.
524. Upset of a Market Cart. David Col, Antwerp.
525. Flowers and Fruit. [M. Couteaux.] Van Os, Brussels.
526. Entering the Convent. Houze, Brussels.
527. A View in Holland. Defailly, Antwerp.
528. The Young Shepherd. Coumont, Brussels.
529. The Young Bride. Adele Kindt, Brussels.
530. Macbeth and the Witches. Payen, Brussels.
531. The Riding Whip. Vanbombergen, Antwerp.
532. A Valley in the Alps. Roffiaen, Brussels.
533. You will not Forget me. Jules Boulanger, Ghent.
534. A Scene in Holland. Redig, Antwerp.
535. A Village Scene. Redig, Antwerp.
536. A Village Feast. Redig, Antwerp.
537. Landscape in Holland. Redig, Antwerp.
538. Sea Piece. Hulk, Antwerp.
539. A View in Sussex. Lehon, Brussels.
540. Farm Yard. Fanton, Liege.
541. Harvest Scene. [M. Vilain.] Charles Tschaggeny, Brussels.
542. The Last Interview between the Count Egmont and the Duke of Alba. Van Rooy, Antwerp.
543. Evening. Lehon, Brussels.
544. Landscape in Switzerland. Defailly, Brussels.
545. The Friar Felix (Pope Sixtus the Fifth) at the Cardinal Buoncompagno's. Bellemans, Antwerp.
546. The Milkmaid. Correns, Antwerp.
547. Setting off for the Market. De Bruycker, Antwerp.
548. View of the Basin of Ghent. Boulanger, Antwerp.
549. View near Antwerp. Carpentero, Antwerp.
550. Fresh Breeze. Francia, Brussels.
551. An Interior. Geerts, Antwerp.
552. "The Girl," "The Mother," "The Widow." Fanny Geefs Corr, Brussels.
553. Winter Scene in Holland. Moerenhout and Schelfhout, Brussels.
554. Sisters of Charity. Hunin, Malines.
555. The Breakfast. Toussaint, Brussels.
556. Park of Brussels. Van Moer, Brussels.
557. The Young Marauders. Toussaint, Brussels.
558. View of a Roman Aqueduct. Bossuet, Brussels.
559. The Last Moments of Henry Percy, Earl of Northumberland. Houze, Brussels.
560. View in Italy. Edouard De Vigne, Ghent.
561. Sea View off Dunkirk. Francia, Brussels.
562. The Effect of Music on the young Montaigne. Soubre, Liege.
563. The arrival of the Queen of England at Flushing, with the escorting Squadron saluted by the Ship, "The Prince of Orange," on her passage to Antwerp, on the 18th August, 1852. A. Pleysier, Amsterdam.
564. A Town View. [G. de Vries, Jr., Amsterdam.] K. Karsen,
565. Study of a Fox. Mdlle. Rosa Bonheur.
566. View in Normandy. Huber.
567. A Hunt near Chantilly. Lepaulle.
568. A Landscape, "The Jura Mountains." Collins, Amsterdam,
569. Dutch Landscape. S. Van den Berg, Haarlem.
570. Dutch Summer Landscape. W. Bodeman and E. Verboeckhoven, Amsterdam.

571. A Man-of-War, crowding sail on the Coast of Holland, to clear a lee shore. P. J. SCHOTEL, Kampen.
572. A Dutch Village by Moonlight. E. KOSTER, Amsterdam.
573. Swiss Landscape. SCHEUREN.
574. Beach at Scheveningen, Holland. CARL ADLOFF, Dusseldorf.
575. Apollo amongst the Shepherds. C. BECKER.
576. Children at a Brook. SCHEINBRUECK.
577. Dutch Meadow, with Cattle and Herdsman. J. VAN RAVENZWAAY, Velp.
578. A Stable with Horses and Figures. P. F. VAN OS, Haarlem.
579. Sketch on the Reichenbach, in Switzerland. L. RAUSCH, Dusseldorf.
580. Moonshine. L. DE WINTER, Amsterdam.
581. Dutch Landscape, clouded. J. PELGROM, Zutphen.
582. Winter View. B. C. SNEIDERS & C. BOUCHEZ, Amsterdam.
583. View taken in the Environs of Algiers. THUILLIER.
584. The Stranding of a Merchant Vessel on a Rocky Shore, the Crew endeavouring to save themselves, with a Steamer lying to, to take them in. C. C. KANNEMANS, Breda.
585. Return from the Chase—Landscape. P. H. HAPPEL, Dusseldorf.
586. Matin Song of Italian Herdsman. THEOD. MAASSEN, Dusseldorf.
587. Forest Landscape. WM. KLEIN, Dusseldorf.
588. A Landscape at Sunset. LAMORINIERE, Amsterdam.
589. Ruins of the Castle Pierrefond, near Compiegne, France. L. HANEDOES, Amsterdam.
590. The Visit of a Physician. W. RIKKERS, Rotterdam.
591. Rhine Landscape. C. JUNGHEIM, Dusseldorf.
592. The Kiss interrupted. T. B. SONDERLAND, Dusseldorf.
593. "Les Moissoneurs" (on Porcelain, after Leopold Robert.) MADAME LAURENT.
594. An Agitated Sea. CH. BOUCHEZ, Amsterdam.
595. Country Fair in the Environs of Amsterdam. C. STEFFELAAR, Amsterdam.
596. A Dutch Village intersected with water towards Evening, by Moonlight. J. T. ABELS, Haarlem.
597. A Passage in an old-fashioned Dutch House: in the back part, a street seen by moonlight; in the foreground, a Maid-servant lighting a candle in a lantern. H. VAN HOVE, BZ., Amsterdam.
598. Stags going to the Fountain. FRIED. HAPPEL, Dusseldorf.
599. Landscape, Guelderland—The first breath of the Tempest. P. L. DUBOURCQ, Amsterdam.
600. Stags. FRIED. HAPPEL, Dusseldorf.
601. Still Water—A Dutch River, with various Vessels. F. J. VANDEN BLYK, Dordrecht.
602. Two Figures by candlelight, in ancient costume. J. ROSIERSE, Dordrech.
603. A Painting. S. L. VERVEER, The Hague.
604. A Painting. J. F. VAN DEVENTER, The Hague.
605. A Shipwreck near Vera Cruz. [H. Hilleveld, Hz.] A. MAYER, Amsterdam.
606. The Battle of Brienne. RAYMOND DE BAUX.
607. Strand View. F. GUDIN, Amsterdam.
608. Landscape in the vicinity of Verviers, Belgium. G. A. ROTH, Amsterdam.
609. Italian Landscape, Rocca Secura. E. VON GUERARD, Dusseldorf.
610. Netherlands Landscape. CASPAR SCHEUREN, Dusseldorf.
611. Workshop of a Painter. L. J. HAUSEN, Amsterdam.
612. Little Girl going to School. PISTORIUS.
613. Dutch Farm in the Morning. A. J. OFFERMANS, The Hague.
614. View in the Hague Wood—Evening. A. J. OFFERMANS, The Hague.
615. Guelderland hilly Landscape by day, with Cattle. A. J. OFFERMANS, The Hague.
616. Napoleon I. in his Imperial Robes; (presented by him to the City of Rome in 1810.) [W. F. Burton.] GERARD.
617. The Tales of the Queen of Navarre LECOMTE.
618. View of the Harbour at Nice. L. GARNERAY.
619. Study of a Dalmatian Hound. A. CHAZAL.
620. View from Bucchaness, near Peterhead, Scotland. THEODORE GUDIN.
621. View in Normandy. LEON FLEURY.
622. Study of a Dog. MDLLE. ROSA BONHEUR.
623. Partridge and Thrush. COIC.
624. Fruits. LOUIS REY.
625. The Poor Family. [Monsieur Suisse.] TASSAERT.
626. View of the Gulf Puzzuoli, Naples. THUILLIER.
627. The Twilight. LEHMANN.
628. The Return from the Fields. ANTIGNA.
629. View of the Borghese Villa, Rome. VIOLLET LEDUC.
630. A Moorish Woman. MATOUT.
631. The Lion Hunt. [M. Van den Berg., Brussels.] HORACE VERNET.
632. Cattle. [M. Van den Berg.] BRASCASSET.
633. View of the Downes near the Pond of Cazeaux. LEO DROUYN.
634. La Sylphide. C. MULLER.
635. View of the Ruins of the Cloisters of Walkenrind, Hanover, sunset in Winter. [Jean Marie Farina.] HASENPLFUG, of Halbertstadt.
636. Dance in the Island of Ischia. A. COLIN.
637. Jane Shore condemned to die of Hunger in the Streets of London. BIARD.
638. The Brothers of the Redemption ransoming Captives in Africa. LEBOUYS.
639. Hamlet. LEHMANN.
640. View of the Ruins of Charlus and of the Mars River (Cantal.) A. BONHEUR.
641. Ophelia. LEHMANN.
642. Henry IV. of France and his Children. ROUGET.
643. An Inundation Scene. ROUGET.
644. Louis Philip d'Orleans visiting the North Cape, in a Lapland boat. BIARD.
645. The Hague—Town View. [G. de Vries, Jz., Amsterdam.] A. WALDORP.
646. Snow Effect in the Valley of St. Gothard. VAN DER BURCH.
647. The Singing Lesson. [John Gernon.] KARL DE MOORE.
648. The Music Lesson. [John Gernon.] KARL DE MOORE.
649. Naval Engagement. F. GUDIN, Amsterdam.
650. Dutch Maritime Village. W. A. VAN DEVENTER, Amsterdam.
651. Town View. C. SPRINGER, Amsterdam.
652. Confidential Participation, by Candlelight. J. ROSIERSE, Dordrecht.
653. Summer Landscape—Panorama. VISSER, Amsterdam.
654. Strand View. L. MEYER, Amsterdam.
655. Review of the Album. [H. Hilleveld, Hz., Amsterdam.] A. VERHOEVEN.
656. The Painter Fentoresso and his Daughter. T. VAN WESTHREENE, WZ., The Hague.
657. Hugo Grotius, with his Family, and the faithful domestics Elsje Van Houweningen and H. Van de Velde, in the Prison of Loevenstein, reading and explaining the Holy Scriptures, in 1620. C. J. L. PORTMAN, Cleves.
658. Interior of a House; a Lady sitting on a Sofa, attended by her chamber maid, dressing her hair. P. F. VAN WYNGAARDT, Amsterdam.
659. View on the Y at Amsterdam in Winter. C. STEFFELAAR, Amsterdam.
660. An agitated Sea, with Shipping and a View of the English Coast. [A. A Weimar, The Hague.] LOUIS MEYER.
661. A Sale by Auction of Household Goods in a Village near the Hague. [John Barton, Esq.] VALENTYN BING, Amsterdam.

662. Agitated Water. A. HULK, Amsterdam.
663. Agitated Water. A. HULK, Amsterdam.
664. Rippling Water. J. C. SCHOTEL, Amsterdam.
665. A Church at Antwerp. GENISSON and WILLIAMS, The Hague.
666. An old Italian Shepherd, fainting from fatigue, and supported by his Daughter. [A. A. Weimar.] C. KRUSEMAN, The Hague.
667. A View on the Coast of Holland, with fishing-boats. W. A. VAN DEVENTER, The Hague.
668. Iron Mill in the vicinity of Breda, North Braband. F. L. HUYGENS, Breda.
669. Country Fair. J. PELGROM, Zutphen.
670. Amsterdam Orphans going to Church. H. F. C. TEN KATE, Amsterdam.
671. Moonlight. L. DE WINTER, Amsterdam.
672. Interior of a House—Le Coup Réflechi. A. VERHOEVEN, Amsterdam.
673. The Reading of the Bible. [I. Hollander.] J. J. ECCKHOUT, Brussels.
674. Landscape with Trees. F. H. HENDRIKS, Oosterbeek.
675. View of Amsterdam by Moonlight, with Ships, &c. [A. T. Cramer.] C. IMMERZEEL, Amsterdam.
676. Painting. B. RONKER CURTIUS, Amsterdam.
677. Captain Montrose. PERIGNON.
678. Landscape. CIBOT.
679. A Pasturage in Normandy. BALFOURIER.
680. An Almazara, or Spanish Oil-mill. BALFOURIER.
681. The Pfifferare. MDME. JACOTT CAPPELEKERE.
682. View—Forest of Fontainebleau. LAPITO.
683. Young Girl playing with a Squirrel. ANTIGNA.
684. View taken at Bruges. JUSTIN OUVRIE.
685. Landscape, with Cavalcade. CIBOT.
686. Halt of Light Cavalry, 16th Century. PHILIPPOTEAUX.
687. View of the Tivoli Cascades. LAPITO.
688. View taken at Sestas, near Bordeaux. LEO DROUYN.
689. The Singing Lesson. PISTORIUS.
690. Landscape in the Environs of Algiers. C. GROLIG.
691. Interior of a Kitchen. PASCAL.
692. Landscape—a Pasturage. A. GIROUX.
693. Agitated Water, with several Vessels entering at the Nienwediep. A. PLEYSIER, Amsterdam.
694. Sunset on the Banks of the Seine, near Chalon. VAN DER BURCH.
695. View of the Strand at Scheveningen. A. PLEYSIER, Amsterdam.
696. Dead Nature. MDLLE. JULIETTE BONHEUR.
697. The Blessing. GUILLEMIN.
698. View taken in the Environs of Algiers. THUILLIER.
699. Sara le Bagneuse. E. SIGNOL.
700. A Winter. PETERSZEN, Antwerp.
701. Sara la Bagneuse. TASSART.
702. The Nest Robber. TASSART.
703. A Girl reading a Letter by Candlelight. WM. VAN DER WORP, Zutphen.
704. A Farmer paying his Labourers. C. NEURDENBURG, Rotterdam.
705. An Old Gentleman in his Study. C. NEURDENBURG, Rotterdam.
706. Landscape. LONTREITE.
707. Landscape—Panoramic view of Rhenen, with its Environs, on the borders of the Rhine. J. P. VAN WISSELINGH. Utrecht.
708. The Dancing Gipsy. BOULANGER.
709. Margaret of Anjou after the Battle of Exham. DEHAUSSY.
710. The Village Feast. DE BRUYKER, Antwerp.
711. Cimabue going to Paint, near Florence, finds Giotto, a young Boy, sketching upon a Rock the flock of Sheep of which he was the Shepherd. COUNT SPEZIA, Rome.
712. View near Edinburgh. LOUIS REY.
713. Italian Family. HONKIN.
714. Flowers. J. GOULLET.
715. Maternal Bliss. J. FELON.
716. Companion to No. 652. J. ROSIERSE, Dordrecht.
717. The Improvisatrice. JULES DE VIGNON.
718. Henry Percy's Death. HOUZE.
719. A Strand on the Dutch Coast—Fishermen aground [Josh. J. Crooswyck.] Rotterdam.
720. View of Rotterdam. Rotterdam.
721. Arrival of the Steamer from Tilburg with the corpse of His Majesty King William II., at the Marine yard, Rotterdam. [Josh. J. Crooswyck.] P. SCHIEDGES, Rotterdam.
722. Market Boats laying to alongside a pier. Rotterdam
723. Market Boats leaving the Harbour. Rotterdam.
724. Birds. Coïc.
725. Rita, the Neapolitan. MARCEL DE PIGNEROLLE.
726. Flowers and Animals. MDME. GUILLOT D'OBST.
727. The Water-seller at Malta. VALFORT.
728. A Dutch River, by Moonlight. J. F. VANDEN BERK, Dordrecht.
729. Young Child gathering Grapes. PERIGNON.
730. The Valley of Meyringen, Bernese Oberland. RICOIS.
731. Swiss Shepherdess of the Canton de Vaud. H. BERTHOUD.
732. Environs of Susten, Haut Valais, Switzerland. H. BERTHOUD.
733. Country Fair in the Environs of Amsterdam. C. STEFFELAAR, Amsterdam.
734. Water View on the Dutch Coast. M. F. H. DE HAAS, Rotterdam.
735. Napoleon I. ROUGET.
736. The Illusion—The Deception—Costumes of the Time of Louis XIV. SERRURE.
737. The Little Gleaner. ETEX.
738. View of the Titlis Mountain, Switzerland. DEFOUNTENAY.
739. The Family Breakfast. GABRIEL LEFEBURE.

---

740. Landscape. [John Barton.] BARRETT.
741. The Ninth Hour. [Mrs. O'Keeffe.] J. O'KEEFFE.
742. Fruit, from Nature. [H. Bunn.] CHARLES LEWIS.
743. Landscape. [Rev. D. Flynn.] CALVERT.
744. Girl with a Pitcher. [H. A. J. Munro.] W. ROTHWELL, R.H.A.
745. Fruit. D. W. RAIMBACH.
746. Landscape. [Rt. Hon. R. More O'Farrell.] The late J. A. O'CONNOR.
747. Design for a Town Hall, City of Cork. T. N. DEANE.
748. View of the Island, Clew Bay, Co. Mayo, with Fishing Boats, &c. R. B. BEECHEY, Com. R. N.
749. The Roman Peasant Boy. MRS. COL. SMITH.
750. The Love-Letter. MRS. COLONEL SMITH.
751. The Irish Piper. [Sir R. Gore Booth, Bart.] J. HAVERTY.
752. A Spanish Girl. S. M. JOY.
753. View in the Co. Wicklow. [Rev. J. A. Malet, F.T.C.D.] The late J. A. O'CONNOR.
754. Vessels in a gleam of sunshine, with squall approaching. [John Barton.] ELLIS.
755. Fruit Piece. [The Lord Chancellor.] E. MURPHY.
756. Sunset. [John Barton.] ASHFORD.
757. Age receiving instruction from Youth. [James S. Brenan.] J. B. BRENAN.
758. Conflict between Cavaliers and Puritans. MISS PALLISER.
759. View of Annamoe Bridge, Co. Wicklow. [M. C. Lentaigne.] GEORGE NAIRN.
760. Il Penseroso. FOLEY.
761. Vessel in a light breeze. [John Barton.] ELLIS.
762. Landscape, with Brood Mare and Asses. [John Barton.] T. ROBERTS.
763. The Middle Lake, Killarney. SIR GEORGE HODSON, Bart.
764. Brig leaving Ramsgate, Kent. E. HAYES.
765. The Loss of the Intrinsic, of Liverpool, near Kilkee, Co. Clare, January, 1836. R. B. BEECHEY, Com. R. N.
766. Landscape and Figures. [William Anthony.] BARRETT.

767. An Artist's Studio. [Lord Cloncurry.] CUMMING.
768. Begging for the Bow. [M. Cregan.] M. CREGAN, P.R.H.A.
769. The Hour-glass. J. HAVERTY.
770. The Falls of Niagara. [Archdeacon Magee.] WALL.
771. St. Gingaugh, and Rocks of St. Meillarie, on Lake of Geneva. T. N. DEANE.
772. Vessels in a Calm. [John Barton.] ELLIS.
773. Landscape, Rustic Bridge. [The Lord Chancellor.] T. ROBERTS.
774. "Sine Cerere et Baccho, friget Venus." [J. Haverty.] J. HAVERTY.
775. View in the Co. Wicklow. [The Lord Chancellor.] The late J. A. O'CONNOR.
776. The Gap of Dunloe. SIR GEORGE HODSON, Bart.
777. Waiting for Orders off Cork Harbour. T. N. DEANE.
778. Vessels in a Rough Sea. [John Barton.] ELLIS.
779. Eagles' Rock, Killarney. C. NAIRN.
780. The Woodman. [Sir John Power, Bart., Kilfane.] BARKER.
781. Prince Charles Edward asleep in one of his hiding-places, after the Battle of Culloden, protected by Flora Macdonald and outlawed Highlanders, who are alarmed on their watch. [Alexander Hill.] T. DUNCAN, A.R.A.
782. A Sketch in North Wales. P. W. ELLEN.
783. The Shell Boat. [P. M'Dowell.] PICKERSGILL, R.A.
784. Sir Roger de Coverley going to Church. [Marquis of Lansdowne.] C. R. LESLIE, R.A.
785. View of Palanza, on the Lake Maggiore. [Thomas Fairbairn.] J. B. PYNE.
786. Crossing the Bridge. [E. Gambart.] F. W. TOPHAM.
787. The Guitar.
788. The Weird Sisters—Scene from Macbeth. DANIEL MACLISE, R.A.
789. Market-place. [H. A. J. Munro.] A. JONES.
790. Landscape. [T. Agnew and Sons.] J. B. PYNE.
791. The Lower Glacier of Grindenwald, Switzerland. J. A. HAMMERSLEY.
792. The Royal Captives at Carisbrook, A. D. 1620. [Charles Lucy.]
793. View of Dordrecht. [G. Young.] C. STANFIELD, R.A.
794. Cattle. [G. Young.] A. COOPER, R.A.
795. On the Zuyder Zee. [G. Young.] C. STANFIELD, R.A.
796. Lady with a Hawk. PICKERSGILL, R.A.
797. Drumming out the Lawyer. [S. C. Hall.] J. M. WRIGHT.
798. The Battle of Camperdown. [T. Agnew and Sons.] KNELL.
799. A Savannah on fire, by Moonlight, from sketches made on the spot during the late Government Boundary Expedition to British Guinea. E. A. GOODALL.
800. Harvesting. W. F. WITHERINGTON, R.A.
801. The Fruit-seller. [S. C. Hall.] W. MULLER.
802. Corn-field near St. Peter's, Isle of Thanet. [W. E. Bates.]
803. Napoleon in Prison at Nice. [S. C. Hall.] E. M. WARD, A.R.A.
804. Cart-horse, and interior of Stable. [John Barton.] SHAYER.
805. In the Meadows near Sturry, Kent. [W. E. Bates.]
806. Passing Shower, near St. Laurence, Isle of Thanet. [W. E. Bates.]
807. Sweeps. [School of Design, Belfast.]
808. Cow and Ass companions. [John Barton.] SHAYER.
809. Travelling in Snow. K. F. BOMBLED.
810. Rabbits. [E. G. Salisbury.] J. F. HERRING.
811. Pigs. [E. G. Salisbury.] J. F. HERRING.
812. Lady with Horse. [S. C. Hall.] G. JONES, R.A.
813. The Toilet.
814. The Patience of Griselda. [H. A. J. Munro.] COPE.
815. The Pilot Boat. E. W. COOK, A.R.A.
816. View from Richmond Hill, Surrey. G. HILDITCH.
817. Landscape. [G. Young.] T. CRESWICK, R.A.
818. Fruit Piece. G. LANCE.
819. Death of Adonis. [S. C. Hall.] R. HUSKISSON.
820. Fox and Wild Rabbits. G. ARMFIELD.
821. A Fine Day at Noon, in the early part of December. J. CLEGHORN, Jun.
822. The Young Shepherd—"Hope." [E. Gambart.] J. SANT.
823. The Rape of Proserpine. [Jos. Gillott.] W. ETTY, R. A.
824. Cross Purposes—"The course of true love never did run smooth." [Marquis of Lansdowne.] FRANK STONE, A. R. A.
825. The Deserted Mansion. J. J. CHALON, R. A.
826. The Ladies Northumberland and Percy dissuading the Earl from joining the War against Henry IV. R. HANNAH.
827. Hunt the Slipper. A. E. CHALON, R. A.
828. Elizabeth, Duchess of Buccleuch, and Harriet, Countess of Dalkeith, visiting the Cottage of a Widow. [Alex. Hill.] W. BONNAR, R. S. A.
829. Rustic Courtesy. [Duke of Devonshire.] COLLINS, R.A.
830. Trial and Acquittal of the Seven Bishops, in 1688. [T. Agnew and Sons.] J. R. HERBERT, R. A.
831. Bolton Abbey in the Olden Time. [Duke of Devonshire.] SIR EDWIN LANDSEER, R. A.
832. The Town of Pau, in the Pyrenees, taken from the heights of Juramcon. [William Oliver.]
833. Boy and Hawk. [Duke of Devonshire.] Sir E. LANDSEER, R. A.
834. Edwin and Emma. [John Barlow.] A. ELMORE.
835. Horses Feeding. [S. C. Hall.] J. F. HERRING.
836. A Neapolitan Girl. [S. C. Hall.] EDMONSTONE.
837. The Lovers. [S. C. Hall.] J. C. HOOK, A. R. A.
838. Griselda. [S. C. Hall.] R. REDGRAVE, R. A.
839. The Temple of Vesta. [H. E. the Countess St. Germans.] MURCH.
840. The Arch of Titus. [H. E. the Countess St. Germans.] MURCH.
841. The Pilgrim. [E. Gambart.] J. SANT.
842. Italian Landscape. [Earl of Yarborough.] J. M. W. TURNER, R. A.
843. Waterfall.
844. Bedouin Arab Chief examining his Captives after an attack on a Caravan. ABRAHAM COOPER, R. A.
845. Troutbeck—Village of Westmoreland. [Mrs. William Oliver.]
846. The Wounded Smuggler. C. LANDSEER, R. A.
847. Temperance and Luxury. THOMAS UWINS, R. A.
848. The Rent Day. [John Chapman.] SIR DAVID WILKIE, R.A.
849. The Wolf and the Lamb. [Her Majesty the Queen.] W. MULREADY, R. A.
850. Horses Watering. [Lord Monteagle.] SIR E. LANDSEER, R. A.
851. The Travelling Druggist. [John Chapman.] W. MULREADY, R. A.
852. The Convalescent. [Lord Northwick.] W. MULREADY, R. A.
853. Joan of Arc. [E. Gambart.] W. ETTY, R. A.
854. Ophelia. ARTHUR HUGHES.
855. Red Deer. G. ARMFIELD.
856. Landscape—View taken near the Coast of the Mediterranean, between Genoa and Spezia. [Edwd. Cooper.] ANDREW WILSON.
857. The Old Port of Naples. [Samuel Cartwright.] SIR A. CALLCOTT, R. A.
858. Vive Le Roi—The King's Party in difficulties at Marston Moor. ABRAHAM COOPER, R. A.
859. Bantry Bay, Ireland. G. TUTHILL.
860. The Irish Girl. [S. C. Hall.] F. GOODALL, A. R. A.
861. A Mountain Stream near Belfast. [D. W. Raimbach.]
862. The Fountains in Italy. [S. C. Hall.] P. WILLIAMS.
863. Off Ramsgate, Kent. W. E. BATES.
864. "Come unto these Yellow Sands." [S. C. Hall.] R. HUSKISSON.
865. Landscape. W. S. BAKER.
866. "Reading the Scriptures." [Thomas Fairbairn.]

867. An Episode in the Happier Days of Charles I. (Sketch picture of the larger work exhibited at the Royal Academy, 1858.) [Thomas Fairbairn.] F. GOODALL A. R. A.
868. Sunday Morning a Century ago (Vicar of Wakefield). [William Anthony.] H. M. ANTHONY.
869. The Spoiled Child. A. COOPER, R. A.
870. Summoned to the Conclave. S. A HART, R. A.
871. John Philip Kemble, as Coriolanus. [The Earl of Yarborough.] SIR T. LAWRENCE.
872. Interior of a Cottage. [Samuel Cartwright.] STAINESBURY.
873. Love and Labour. R. REDGRAVE, R. A.
874. Landscape—View in Kent. [Charles Brien.] GEO. WILLIAMS.
875. Landscape—View of Genoa from the west. [Edward Cooper.] ANDREW WILSON.
876. The Love-Letter. T. MOGFORD.
877. Liverpool from the Old Flood Gate—Thunder Storm clearing away. CHARLES BARBER.
878. The Rose. [Major Dillon.] SALTER.
879. Twilight at Sea. JAMES DANBY.
880. The Welsh Bard. [Charles D. Young.] J. MARTIN, R. A.
881. A Fisherman's Family. [Marquis of Conyngham.] SHAYER.
882. Elena. H. MUNRO.
883. Young Girls bedecking themselves with Flowers. H. MUNRO.
884. The Dawn of Day—a Foraging Party returning. CHARLES BARBER.
885. Landscape—View of Genoa from the east. [Edward Cooper.] ANDREW WILSON.
886. "Beneath the Hawthorn Tree." [Charles D. Young.] CRABB.
887. A Gleamy Day in England, Earlswood Common, Surrey. [G. H. Herring.]
888. View in Venice.
889. Interior of an Italian Artist's Studio. THOMAS UWINS, R. A.
890. Venus preparing for the Bath. [John C. Grundy.] W. ETTY, R.A.
891. Trout-fishing. T. STARK.
892. Landscape.—View taken near the coast of the Mediterranean, between Genoa and Spezia. [Edward Cooper.] ANDREW WILSON.
893. The Hydrobibists. [Mrs. Hume.] J. F. HERRING, Sen.
894. Figures on Horseback. [S. C. Hall.] J. R. HERBERT, R.A.
895. Perspective View of Exterior and Interior of proposed Exhibition Building in Dublin. W. F. CALDBECK.
896. Entrance to Foynes Harbour. J. HAVERTY.
897. The Death of the First-born. A. WARREN.
898. Sketch in Kent. V. CORBI.
899. A Scotch Lady and her Son. [J. F. Grierson.] MISS GUBBINS.
900. The Entry of Prince Charles Edward into Edinburgh, after the Battle of Prestonpans (Engraving). [Alex. Hill.]
901. Foynes Harbour. J. HAVERTY.
902. Snow Scene. MISS F. PENTLAND.
903. Interior of St. Saviour's Church, Leeds.
904. View of the Interior of the Church of the Conception, Marlborough-street. T. SHERIDAN, C.E.
905. The Church of St. Michel, Ghent, from the Quai aux Herbes. P. W. ELEN.
906. Gypsies' Encampment. [Mrs. Earith.] MRS. JANE EARITH.
907. South Stack Lighthouse, near Holyhead. R. L. STOPFORD.
908. Carriganass Castle, Evening. R. L. STOPFORD.
909. Water-mill, Ashford, Derbyshire. CHARLES MARSHALL.
910. Hunting Lodge of Queen Elizabeth, Epping Forest, Essex. W. S. BAKER.
911. Mill, Ashford, Derbyshire. C. MARSHALL.
912. A View on the Thames, near Gravesend, Kent. J. F. NASH.
913. The last Stand of the 44th at Cabul, in 1842. M. ANGELO HAYES.
914. Bantry Bay. R. L. STOPFORD.
915. A Sketch in North Wales. P. W. ELEN.
916. Dead Game. MISS F. PENTLAND.
917. A Smithy, near Little Hampton, Sussex. P. W ELEN.
918. Red Riding Hood. C. H. WEIGALL.
919. The Grave of Will Watch. C. G. MORGAN.
920. View of Calcutta. EDWARD COOPER.
921. View near Sligo, in the Co. Leitrim. W. P. CLARKE.
922. Market Boats under Sail, Rotterdam.
923. Bacchus and Ariadne. [Edward Cooper.] ROMNEY
924. The Youthful Mechanic. MISS TREVOR.
925. Glendalough. C. G. MORGAN.
926. The Irish House of Commons.—Henry Grattan moving Declaration of Independence. [Henry Grattan.] NICHOLAS KENNY.
927. A Brig coming to Anchor, Rotterdam.
928. The Child crying for Meal. T. COOLEY.
929. Eagles' Nest, Killarney. G. TUTHILL.
930. Transaction in the Map. THOMAS COOLEY.
931. The Juvenile Artist. T. COOLEY.
932. Donnybrook Fair.
933. A collection of Crayons contributed by Miss Lee.
934. Wooden Bridge, Co. Wicklow. MISS SEMPLE.
935. Drumkeiran Glebe, Co. Fermanagh. MISS SEMPLE.
936. The Departure. G. MORANT.
937. Regret. G. MORANT.
938. Irish Peasants. J. HAVERTY.
939. View taken near Anagassen, in the county of Louth. MRS. P. M. CHESTER.

---

940. Portrait of Rauch the Sculptor. [H. M. the King of Prussia.] BEGAS.
941. Portrait of L. Tieck, Translator of Shakspeare. [H. M. the King of Prussia.] STICHLER.
942. Portrait of Cornelius the Painter. [H. M. the King of Prussia.] BEGAS.
943. Portrait of Bessel the Astronomer. [H. M. the King of Prussia.] J. WOLFF.
944. Portrait of Schinkel the Architect. [H. M. the King of Prussia.] C. SCHMIDT.
945. Portrait of Humboldt, Author of Kosmos. [H. M the King of Prussia.] BEGAS.
946. Portrait of Ideler, the celebrated Chronologist. [H. M the King of Prussia.] HERZ.
947. The Founders of the Barrington Hospital, Limerick. [The Governors of the Barrington Hospital.] M. CREGAN, P. R. H. A.
948. Portrait of the late Right Hon. R. L. Sheil. [Thomas Lalor.] MISS WYSE.
949. Portrait of O'Connell, painted during his imprisonment, in Richmond Prison, in 1844. [John Gray, M. D.] N. J. CROWLEY, R.H. A.
950. Portrait of Thomas Moore. G. F. MULVANY, R.H.A.
951. Portrait of a Lady. [Mrs. Collier.] COLLIER.
952. Portraits of Daniel O'Connell, P. V. Fitzpatrick, and F. W. Conway. [P. V. Fitzpatrick.] J. HAVERTY.
953. Portrait of Thomas Moore. [Corry Connellan.] The late SIR MARTIN A. SHEE, P.R.A.
954. The late Very Rev. Walter Blake Kirwan, Dean of Killalla, preaching on behalf of the Female Orphans. [E. R. P. Colles.] HAMILTON.
955. Portrait of Dean Swift. [The Marquis of Drogheda.]
956. Portrait of Henry Flood and others. [Henry Grattan.]
957. Full-length Portrait of Lord Plunket. [Lord Plunket.] M. CREGAN, P.R.H.A.
958. Portrait of George Washington. [Richard Hemphill.] GILBERT STEWART.
959. Full-length Portrait of Lord Viscount Gough. [Lord Gough.] J. HARWOOD.
960. Portrait of the late Sir Michael O'Loghlen, Bart. Master of the Rolls. [Sir Colman O'Loghlen.] G. F. MULVANY, R.H.A.

961. Portrait of the late Chief Justice Bushe. [Thomas Bushe.] M. CREGAN, P.R.H.A.
962. Portrait of Lord Plunket.
963. Portrait of Henry Grattan. JOSEPH.
964. Portrait of the Right Hon. Maziere Brady, Lord Chancellor of Ireland. [The Lord Chancellor.] W. ROTHWELL, R.H.A.
965. Full-length Portrait of Joseph Damer. [The Earl of Portarlington.] DOBSON.
966. Portrait of Chief Justice Lefroy. [A. Lefroy.] CATTERSON SMITH, R.H.A.
967. Full-length Portrait of the late Very Rev. Walter Blake Kirwan, Dean of Killalla. [The Dean of Limerick.] The late SIR MARTIN A. SHEE, P.R.A.
968. Portrait of a Lady. [J. G. Middleton.]
969. Portrait of Lieut.-General Sir Edward Blakeney, Commander of the Forces. [Sir Edward Blakeney.] CATTERSON SMITH, R. H. A.
970. Full-length Portrait of John Foster (Lord Oriel), last Speaker of the Irish House of Commons. [Lord Viscount Massareena.] SIR THOMAS LAWRENCE.
971. Portrait of the late Count D'Orsay. [H. A. J. Munro.] F. GRANT. R. A.
972. Portrait of Lord Mountcharles, when a Child. [Marquis of Conyngham.] HURLSTON.
973. Full-length Portrait of the late Daniel O'Connell. [National Bank of Ireland.] SIR D. WILKIE.
974. Portrait of Chief Justice Bushe in his Robes. [T. Bushe.] M. CREGAN, P. R. H. A.
975. Portrait of Canning. [Marquis of Conyngham.] SIR THOMAS LAWRENCE, P. R. A.
976. Full-length Portrait of H. R. H. Prince Albert. [H. M. Queen Victoria.] WINTERHALTER.
977. Full-length Portrait of H. M. Queen Victoria. [H. M. Queen Victoria.] WINTERHALTER.
978. Portrait of King William IV. [Marquis of Conyngham.] SIR DAVID WILKIE, R. A.
979. Portrait of Charles Kean in Hamlet. [C. Kean.] SIR W. ALLAN, R. A.
980. Full-length Portrait of General Vicars. [Mr. Boyle.] SIR M. A. SHEE, P. R. A.
981. Portrait of Sir Henry Torrens, K. C. B., R. T. S., late Adjutant-General of the British Forces. [Hon. Judge Torrens.] SIR THOMAS LAWRENCE.
982. Portrait of the late Archbishop Magee. [Archdeacon Magee.] SIR MARTIN A. SHEE.
983. Full-length Portrait of Right Hon. John Philpot Curran, M. R. [Lord Cloncurry.]
984. Tottenham in his Boots (Portrait). [Marquis of Ely.]
985. Portrait of Sir John Newport. [John Gernon.] J. RAMSAY.
986. The Wife and Daughter of the Chamberlain of Otho, King of Greece. [Ashley La Touche.] MRS. MURRAY.
987. Portrait of William III. HELEN TREVOR.
988. The King of the Beggars of Munster (John Clarke), painted from life, at Cork, 1842. [Rev. Smyth W. Fox.] J. SKILLIN.
989. Portrait of the Bishop of Derry (Crayon). [Sir H. Hervey Bruce, Bart.]

WATER-COLOUR DRAWINGS.

990. Collection of Water-colour Drawings, after 100 Pictures in the Vernon Gallery. [S. C. Hall.]
991. Scene from Macbeth, "The Discovery of the Murder of Duncan." [Her Majesty the Queen.] LOUIS HAGHE.
992. Miniature of Richard Talbot, Earl of Tyrconnell, Viceroy of Ireland under James II. [J. M. Kennedy.]
993. Miniature of Prince Charles Edward.
994. The Bride. [E. D. Thorpe.] B. MULRENIN, A. R. H. A.
995. Domestic Scene. B. MULRENIN, A. R. H. A.
996. Hibernia supporting Bust of Moore. B. MULRENIN, A. R. H. A.
997. C. Kean in Hamlet. A. E. CHALON, R. A.
998. Mr. and Mrs. Kean in Lovell's play of the "Wife's Secret." A. E. CHALON, R. A.
999. Miss Ellen Tree (now Mrs. C. Kean) in Pauline in the "Lady of Lyons." A. E. CHALON, R. A.
1000. Original Miniature of Oliver Cromwell, painted on silver. [The Rev. J. H. Jellett.]
1001. The Blind Girl at the Holy Well. [Lieut. Gen. Sir G. D'Aguilar.] F. W. BURTON, R. H. A.
1002. A Roman Lady and her Attendant—Carnival time. T. A. JONES.
1003. Portrait of Mrs. S. C. Hall. [S. C. Hall.] D. MACLISE, R. A.
1004. View of the Great Sugar Loaf Mountain, county of Wicklow, from Old Connaught Road. HENRY NEWTON.
1005. Pencil Sketch of Mr. S. C. Hall. [S. C. Hall.] PAUL DELAROCHE.
1006. Portrait of Miss Helen Faucit (in chalk). [The Rev. J. A. Malet.] F. W. BURTON, R. H. A.
1007. The Seasons. SAMUEL LOVER, R. H. A.
1008. Flowers. V. BARTHOLOMEW.
1009. Fruit Piece. G. LANCE.
1010. Gougane Barra, or the Hermitage of St. Bearach or Barry, on the River Lee, county of Cork. [Robert Callwell.] G. PETRIE, R. H. A.
1011. Pagan Sepulchral Circle of Stones, on the Caw Hill, Parish of Banagher, County of Londonderry—after Sunset. [Robert Callwell.] G. PETRIE, R. H. A.
1012. View of the Gailte Mountains, from Mitchelstown Demesne, county of Cork. MRS. M. DIGGES LA TOUCHE.
1013. An Interior.
1014. View of Mitchelstown Castle, county of Cork. MRS. M. DIGGES LA TOUCHE.
1015. Miniature of Miss Hume. [Quintin Dick.] BARCLAY, Jun.
1016. The Gardener's Shed. [George Roe.] HARRISON.
1017. Portrait of the Duke of Wellington, painted in 1851. [Thomas Conolly, Esq., M. P.]
1018 The Cousins (Crayon.) LOUIS GRATIA.
1019. Portrait of a Girl. [Mrs. Nugent.]
1020. Two Jewish Children. [Mrs. Nugent.]
1021. Portrait of a Boy. [Mrs. Nugent.]
1022. A Study from Nature. MRS. OLIVER
1023. Portrait of Stopford, Bishop of Cloyne. ROSALBA.

# CONTRIBUTIONS FROM WORKHOUSES AND PRISONS.

THE industrial products of poor-law unions and of gaols had in themselves little to attract the attention of the general visitor. They were necessarily rude and simple in their character, neither original in invention, nor finished in execution. The collection, moreover, was not a large one, by no means so considerable as it might have been; indeed, the specimens which were exhibited could only be regarded as samples of a branch of industry which might have been much more abundantly and more adequately represented. Unattractive, however, as were the articles in themselves, there was much to call forth interest and attention in the circumstances under which they were produced. They were the rudest forms of industrial effort, the results of labour untutored and but half disciplined which were here exhibited; they told us, however, what an amount of error and of prejudice had been dispelled, that the curse of idleness, or the pernicious anomaly of unproductive labour, was no longer to blight our workhouses, or to rankle in our prisons; that those whose hard lot it was to be driven to the poorhouse were protected from the vice and misery of sloth, and that those who had outraged the law, and were made amenable to its penalties, had, in the exercise of some industrial pursuit, a chance at least of reformation presented to them.

It seems astonishing that it should ever have occurred to Parliament, or to statesmen, to distribute the national charity on any other principle than that of requiring the recipients of the bounty to work for it, in so far as they were able to do so. It is but of late years that any public and general provision for the destitute has been introduced into Ireland,—in this respect her position was a singular and anomalous one among Christians, we might almost say among civilized communities; while for centuries all the chief nations of Europe had their organized systems for the relief of their poor, whilst even China, Persia, and other Eastern countries, had similar institutions for ages past, Ireland stood forth, almost a solitary exception in the history of ancient and modern civilization, with no decent maintenance for her paupers, with no mode of keeping the destitute from starvation, but by a degrading, a demoralizing system of licensed mendicancy. This foul stain was at last wiped off; it was acknowledged that the destitute poor had a claim upon the State and were not to be abandoned. But in the establishment of the system, not merely the experience of centuries, but the teaching of common sense, was most unaccountably discarded. The principle of the English poor-law, as it had been in force from the days of Elizabeth, was, that every parish should take order to set the unemployed to work; the overseers were to "set to work all such persons having no means to maintain themselves, and using no ordinary and daily trade of life to get their living by." But this long-established system was deliberately rejected by the framers of the Irish Poor-Law Act; the workhouse test was the key-stone of their system, and every one who thought fit to immure himself in this prison, by an unhappy misnomer styled a workhouse, was to be found in food, shelter, and raiment at the public expense, but kept in a state of dissatisfied dreary idleness.

Strongly, however, as we condemn this system, we are fully sensible of the difficulties of carrying out anything like a scheme of organized industry in our workhouses,—more difficult, indeed, is it than in our common gaols, and much more difficult than in the new Government prisons which have been constructed for those who have been sentenced to long periods of penal servitude. That something of the kind, however, is not impracticable, is abundantly evident from the results which we saw at the Exhibition; that the attempt must be a difficult and uncertain one seems to be beyond question. The able-bodied inmates of the workhouse, at least amongst the males, are at all times a small proportion of the whole number, and at certain seasons, as from June to November, they disappear altogether. The supply of labour is now becoming so scarce in the country, that we may henceforth look forward to the workhouses being entirely without this class of paupers, and the industrial proceedings of the institution must henceforth be sustained chiefly by women and children. Under no circumstances, however, with the supply of labour so irregular and so ill-proportioned, could any but the simplest processes of industry be carried on, nor should any other be attempted in a poorhouse. Anything of division of labour, in the comprehensive sense of the phrase, any attempt to distribute among certain bodies of labourers the several parts of a manufacture in just and adequate proportions, so that no excess or deficiency of production shall be found in any one of the separate parts, is wholly out of the question. It is the application of this principle of the division of production, and the adjustment of the several parts in their due proportions, that mainly contributes to the development of manufacturing industry; it is the greater facility which large manufactories present for carrying out this principle that, in many branches of industry, gives them a formidable advantage over their smaller competitors; and this it is which is obviously impossible in a workhouse, even if it were desirable that it should be found there; but the weaving of coarse fabrics, making matting, and such other occupations as can be exercised singly, and without any combination of labour, for the men; and knitting and plain-work for the women, seem to be the natural and suitable occupations; and such, accordingly, we find the Catalogue of this department chiefly consists of. We must bear in mind that the question is not whether or not the labour of the paupers can be considered productive with reference to the sum which is expended on it—this amount must be expended in any case—but whether or not we are to expend this sum and get some return for it, however inconsiderable, or expend it without any return whatsoever; whether the moral condition of the pauper is not more likely to be elevated by having his time occupied, and his faculties exercised by some useful employment; whether, in fact, we should not be better off now, both in the wealth of the country and the condition of its people, if the ten millions, which were unproductively expended in relief in the late years of famine, had been given to labourers for constructing the earth-work of railways, or some such productive undertaking, instead of having been given to the same men without requiring of them to do any useful thing whatsoever in return. The railway might not have been a profitable speculation if it were taken up as an independent undertaking, but as the money must have been expended, might we not better have had this, or some such other work, in return for our expenditure; would not the country have been richer by so much, and would not the demoralizing effects of the famine have been in a great measure averted?

In the gaols, indeed, the conditions are somewhat different, the great proportion of the inmates, though certainly not skilled tradesmen or artisans, are at least able-bodied labourers. In the Government prisons to which we have adverted, the period of committal is sufficiently long to enable the convict to learn a business and attain to considerable proficiency at it. A greater amount of compulsion may be exercised than would be possible or justifiable at a poor-house, and thus, to some extent, the exertion may be supplied which in the free labourer is called forth by the exigencies of his position and the necessity of earning his daily bread. We regret to perceive how imperfectly the Catalogue represents what may be done, and what in point of fact is done, in some of the gaols of Ireland. We could ourselves point to one county gaol, and we make no doubt that it may not be a solitary instance, in which every article for the use of the institution, all the clothes, shoes, bedding, dishes, vessels of every kind, brushes, &c., are made in the gaol, whereby a saving to the county of nearly £2000 a year is effected. We refer to the county gaol of Cork. These effects are palpable and appreciable, but can we venture to say that other results, which may indeed be more difficult to estimate, are not yet of much greater magnitude and importance. What may we not hope to be the benefits conferred by the poorhouse and the prison on those who have there first learned the lessons of industry, there first acquired the means of livelihood and the disposition to exercise it. We do not profess to be very sanguine on the score of reforming old offenders; still, even to them some benefit may be wrought by being trained for a time to a course of industry; to say the very least of it, it is a more decent mode of spending their time than in the scenes of blasphemy and profligacy which were the reproach of our prisons some years ago, and more profitable withal; but the case is otherwise with juvenile offenders; and may we not hope that not a few of these may be able to refer the first gleam of rectitude which ever broke upon their minds to the habits and lessons of honest industry which they learned in a gaol?

There is, however, a prejudice against all this labour in workhouses and gaols; a prejudice so widespread as not to admit of being overlooked; while it is at the same time so honest as not to fail to command respect. It is said that these industrial occupations in those great establishments which are maintained at the public expense create a competition, and a formidable one, against the free labourer; that he finds it hard enough to strive against the legitimate competition of the fair market, but that it is cruelty and injustice to superadd to this the opposition of the pauper and the felon, and to take out of the pocket of the honest tradesman of the district that tax which is to support the convict whose compulsory labour is then to contend against that very tax-payer in the market. We believe that we have not underrated the objection, but it is a most fallacious one. It springs from a source which is a constant cause of error in all these subjects, that of having the attention arrested by a small evil which is concentered, and overlooking a great good because it is diffused over the whole community. If the great object of all production is to increase as much as possible the number of useful products in the country, how is it possible that any community can be injured because the inmates of poorhouses and gaols are engaged in adding to the quantity? The more that such useful articles are produced, the greater must be the amount that will fall to each man's share; to quarrel with such competition is as senseless as it would be to rail against an abundant harvest, or to protest against the opening of a new country to supply us with her products. Or, to treat the matter more particularly, did it ever occur to these objectors to test the question in this way:—If a district be taxed to any given amount, say a thousand pounds, for the maintenance of the gaol, is it not a necessary consequence that there is so much less to expend upon the free labour of the district?—every penny that is taken from each rate-payer as a tax is so much withdrawn from his power of employing labour; he has so much less to expend on the mechanics and artisans of the country. But if the inmates of the gaol and the workhouse become by their exertions able to support themselves and their institutions, the necessity for the tax is dispensed with, and the amount is restored to the tax-payers to be employed as before, and again distributed in employing and buying from the free labourers and tradesmen of the country. No doubt the individual tradesman who is engaged in the production of articles such as can be produced by the pauper or the convict may sustain a loss, a loss such as he would be exposed to if any large capitalist in his neighbourhood were to engage in the manufacture of the same commodities: but shall we therefore say that the community is injured? and if so, are we prepared to follow out the reasoning to its legitimate conclusions, and to say that all competition must be suppressed, and that absolute universal monopoly is to be established? Common sense recoils from such a conclusion. Should it not, then, be slow to acquiesce in an opinion which necessarily leads to it? This, moreover, is to be borne in mind, that as the artisan advances in skill and intelligence so will he be more and more removed from the competition of uneducated, undisciplined labour, such as must be found in the workhouse and the gaol.

We have seen the conditions under which the industry of those establishments must be developed, and we have seen that as a necessary consequence the products of this industry must be of the rudest and simplest kind. If we were to have found any other results we should have augured ill for the country, and for the mode in which these institutions were administered; we should have feared that the condition of the inmates of these establishments was such as, if not to tempt the free labourer to enter them, at least not to repel him. Disastrous, indeed, would it be for the community if the condition of the felon, or even of the pauper, were such as to hold forth a temptation to the independent labourer to associate himself with their number. The bare necessaries of life, all that is requisite to sustain health and strength, is the utmost that the pauper or the convict can claim, or should be suffered to enjoy. If this is to be provided by public taxation, it must be in a great measure at the expense of the other labourers of the country. If it can be realized by the industry of the poorhouse or gaol, as we are convinced it might, so much the better for all; if more than this can be realized, let it in the gaol be laid by as a fund for the convict, when his imprisonment shall have expired, and let it in the workhouse be regarded as an indication that such labourers are unsuitable claimants on the national charity, and let them be obliged to support themselves by their independent exertions; but in no case let the condition of convicts or of paupers contrast favourably with that of the independent labourer. If this principle be strictly adhered to, and no attempt be made in the workhouses or gaols to engage in the production of articles unsuited to their circumstances, the skilled and intelligent tradesman has little to fear from their competition.—R. H. Mills.

---

## WORKHOUSES.

1. Athlone Union.—Flannel, boys' caps, frieze, poplin, tweed, gingham, sacking.

2. Ballinasloe Union.—Linsey woolseys; striped cotten; union linen; calico; Bengal stripe; embroidery muslin; tweeds.

3. Ballymena Union.—Carpeting made from rugs worn out in the house, and remanufactured; drugget; flannel; coarse linen; diaper table linen; twilled sheeting; diaper towelling; bed ticken; linen thread; frocks; knitted stockings; shirts; woollen and worsted yarn.

4. Borrisokane Union.—Striped cotton, linsey woolsey, union linen, calico, Bengal stripe, linsey quilt, frieze, embroidery.

5. Boyle Union.—Boy's suit, towelling, flannel petticoat, shirt, sheeting, stockings, crochet work, veils, chemise, baby's frock.

6. Carrick-on-Shannon Union.—Ginghams; checks; foot mats.

7. Cashel Union.—Frieze, flannel, tweed, blankets, linsey, rugs, carpeting, twilled linen, sheeting, ticken, diaper, Bengal stripe, calico, Russia duck, shambray, gingham, check, shawls; specimens of knitting, crochet, netting, and embroidery.

8. Castlederg Union.—Knitted quilts and toilette doyleys.

9. Cloughreen Union.—Clothing; embroidery; various articles, both useful and ornamental, worked in flax, wool, and worsted.

10. Croom Union.—Frieze, flannel, tweed, linsey woolsey, shambray, calico; men's and women's clothing made up; clogs, shoes; cotton knitted quilts; knitted chair, sofa, and toilet covers; baby's cap, and other specimens of lace.

11. Dingle Union.—Bengal stripe, checks, frieze, flannel, crochet quilt, embroidered and knitted children's frocks, mitts, reticule, baskets.

12. Dublin Union, North.—Frieze, tweed, flannel, drugget, linsey woolsey, calico, check, towelling; men's, women's, and children's apparel, made up; specimens of embroidery, Berlin, and other fancy wool; specimens of drawing, penmanship; roots, vegetables, and flowers from the workhouse farm; specimens of carpentry, viz.:—dressing table, stand, wheelbarrow, ladders, clothes stands, press, fire screens, &c.

13. Dublin Union, South.—Frieze, tweed, flannel, blankets; linen, calico, check; men's, women's, and children's clothes, made up; specimens of embroidery, and other fancy work.

14. Dungarvan Union.—Frieze; linen and cotton shirting; woollen shawls, tweeds, Russia duck, linen towels, striped flannel, calico, shambray, gingham; baby's robe; chemisette, collars; chair and table covers; pin-cushion and hair net.

15. Dunshaughlin Union.—Embroidered shawl, pocket handkerchief, and baby's frock; fancy knitted window hangings, and stockings; linsey woolsey; frieze, calico, linen; and men's and boy's clothes made up.

16. Edenderry Union.—Frieze, twilled calico, linens, linsey woolsey, Bengal stripe, check, tweed; men's and women's clothes; thread, flax yarn, woollen stockings; collars, toilet table cover, and other articles in crochet.

17. Enniscorthy Union.—Sheeting, ticken, blankets, flannels, rugs, friezes, tweeds, men's and boy's clothing and caps, suspenders, worsted shawls, woollen and cotton stockings, cotton bonnets, crochet and other quilts; nankeen, linen and cotton cloths, calico, gingham, table linen, towelling, vestings; various articles in crochet, knitting, netting, and lace; silk and worsted gloves; hearth rug, slippers, and landscape, worked in wool; habit-shirt and collar; cambric handkerchief; linen, cotton, and woollen yarn; sewing thread; clog and leather shoes.

18. Fermoy Union.—Gingham; frieze; tweed; flannel sheeting; linen; caps; embroidered muslin sleeves, pocket kerchief, habit-shirts, collars; stockings, polka jacket, and other articles.

19. Killarney Union.—Frieze, tweed, shepherd's plaid, flannel stuff; woollen shawls, carpeting; check, Bengal stripe, gingham, calico, cotton sheeting, linen, towels, canvass, knitted quilts, blankets, linen yarn; combed worsted, men's clothes, shoes.

20. Kilmallock Union.—Caps, shambray, tweed, plaid, frieze, flannel, towels, shawls, sheeting, linsey woolsey, table cloth, shoes; men's and women's clothes made up; worked collars, infants' caps, &c.; rugs.

21. Larne Union.—Crochet quilt, chemise, shirt, stockings, suit of frieze, needlework, pincushions, child's knit jacket; lady's cap and collars.

22. Limerick Union.—Linsey woolsey clothing; tweeds, shoes; coarse linens, &c.

23. Lismore Union.—Frieze, flannel, check, calico, ticken, blankets, sheeting, knitted quilts; boots and shoes; stockings; men's and women's clothing, made up; shawl; knitted paletot, purse, and shirt; chair and ottoman covers, doyleys, and gloves.

24. Lisnaskea Union.—Linen, frieze, flannel, shambray; shoes.

25. Mallow Union.—Blankets, frieze, tweed; woollen cap, shawl, stockings; linen shirt, table cloth, napkins, shawls, ticken, union duck, &c.; cotton shirt and wrapper; a knitted quilt; shoes; canvass.

26. Mitchelstown Union.—Shoes, stockings, socks, gingham, check, flannel, ticken, quilt, habit-shirts, hearth-rug, mat, shawls, linen, caps, trowsers, and waistcoats.

27. Monaghan Union.—Linen, suit of men's clothes.

28. Mullingar Union.—Medley tweed; sheeting, shirting, ticken, &c.; medley tweed caps; linsey woolsey.

29. Naas Union.—Blankets, frieze; linsey woolsey; hosiery; Bengal stripe, check, calico; linen, ticken; knitted stockings; specimens of netting and embroidery.

30. Nenagh Union.—Twilled calico; linen; gray frieze; tweed made from wool and cotton; brown frieze; shoes.

31. Newcastle Union.—Crochet and patch-work quilts, flannel petticoats, boy's suit, check apron and shirt, canvass shirt, linen, stockings, trowsers.

32. Newry Union.—Calico, shambray, gingham, linen; frieze, tweed, boots and shoes; specimens of fancy and plain work; mats and matting; dresses, shirts, caps, &c.

33. Oldcastle Union.—Petticoat bodies knitted by infants; arm-chair and toilet covers, men's and children's socks, crochet collars, crochet Berlin under-cuffs, knitted handkerchiefs and towels.

34. Parsonstown Union.—Frieze, trowsering, linen, flannel, shawls, linsey woolsey, towels; knitted cotton quilt; habit-shirt; stockings; knitted thread edgings, collars.

35. Rathdown Union.—Frieze, linsey, linen, flannel, tweed, gingham, shoes, shirts, stockings, &c.; specimens of crochet work.

36. Rathkeale Union.—Frieze, barragon, shambray, check, linens, calico, tweed, linsey woolsey, Russia duck, flannel; men's and women's dresses; stockings, thread.

37. Roscrea Union.—Boy's jackets and trowsers, shoes, towels, crochet work, baby's caps, frieze tweed, flannel, check, shawl, nightcap, needlework.

38. Strabane Union.—Knitted cotton quilt and toilet covers; webs of twilled cotton shambray, and twilled union cloth.

39. Tipperary Union.—Frieze, tweed, woollen shawls, check, Bengal stripe, linen, diaper towelling, clogs, shoes, and Blucher boots; lace stockings; knitted chair covers, table cover, and quilt; fancy basket; mat, and piece of carpeting.

40. Thurles Union.—Flax in straw, broken, scutched, and hackled; flax yarn; tow and tow yarn; blankets, flannel, frieze, tweed; diaper table linen and towels; ticken, crumb cloth, linen plaid; sheeting, calico, woollen scarfs; boots; sheet iron coal-box; tin kettle and stand; coffee pot, tea pot, dust pan, water cans, watering pot, shower bath, garden nets; crochet berthes, cap, cuffs, ruffles, baby's frock, collars, doyleys, and veils; thread stockings.

41. Tralee Union.—Macassars, quilt, towelling, diaper linen, sheeting, frieze.

42. Tuam Union.—Antimacassar; crotchet doileys; lace veils; shirt; altar cloth; fancy Berlin wool; stockings; thread und black silk lace; embroidered sleeves; frieze, tweed; flannel; linsey woolsey; Bengal stripe; handkerchiefs; napkins.

43. Tullamore Union.—Shambray, gingham, check, calico; woven shawls; corduroy; linen, ticken; linsey woolsey; woollen shawls; friezes, tweeds, flannel, blankets; shoes and stockings; combed wool, prepared by the inmates.

## PRISONS.

1 Armagh Gaol.—Cambric and linen webs.

2. Carrick-on-Shannon Gaol.—Linen check woven of thread, spun by female prisoners; blue union woven of linen yarn, spun by female prisoners; striped union; hall mat of cocoa, nut fibre.

3. Grangegorman Female Prison, Dublin.—Quilt, blankets, linen, linsey; knitted shoes made of tow; embroidered table cover, waistcoats, and shirt; worsted and cotton socks; stays; carpet bags; Limerick lace and worsted polkas; black lace; hair nets; baby's shoes; worked handkerchief; antimacassar.

4. Limerick Gaol.—Samples of prison clothing and bedding; flax yarn; root-washers; hot-water vessels of tin and iron, for warming rooms; foot-mats, and other articles.

5. Richmond Bridewell, Dublin.—Plain and fancy cocoa matting, in many varieties; fancy woollen mats; cocoa fibre mats, with woollen borders; linsey woolsey; striped calico for shirting; corduroy, frieze, and bed rug.

# BRITISH GUIANA.

IN the first compartment under the Gallery on the right-hand side of the Dais, there was a collection of products which probably escaped the attention of the mere casual observer, but which to all those who duly appreciated the Exhibition was of great interest—that from British Guiana. Within a comparatively small space were combined specimens of the chief products of that colony. Its mineral resources were represented. Of its vegetation there were numerous illustrations in almost every condition: comprehending its timber, the substances used chiefly as food; its contributions to the pharmacopœia, saccharine productions, and fibrous substances. The natural history illustrations belonging to the animal kingdom afforded an idea of how far the furs of some of the specimens might be valuable to commerce, while the beautiful collection of insects showed that the skilful entomologist had been at work. The scenery of many parts of the colony was also illustrated by a number of coloured sketches. The examination of this whole collection was indeed well calculated to convey a tolerably accurate idea of the resources of the district from which it came; while the manner in which the whole was got up showed that those having charge of it intimately understood the requirements of such a collection, and duly appreciated the importance of such exhibitions as that to which in this case they sent so valuable a contribution.

The production of sugar is now the staple industry of British Guiana; and the collection contained specimens of every product of that manufacture, as sugar in different stages of purification, rum, &c. The assortment of woods which was exhibited shows that many of them could be turned to valuable account in Europe, on account of their hardness, the beauty of the grain in many cases, and the high polish of which they are susceptible; while the forests are of almost boundless extent, and the trees of large size. But there is a further source of wealth, of which illustrations appeared in the Exhibition, and which has of late become of great importance—viz., fibres of various kinds, some of which could be turned to profitable account as a substitute for hemp, and the whole of which would be valuable to the paper manufacturer. The plantain grows with great vigour in this colony,—a tree the value of which has not been sufficiently appreciated. Among the other products grown there in great luxuriance, rice and maize may be mentioned, numerous samples of which were also exhibited. In fine, the whole collection was such as could not fail to impress us with a high sense of the abundant resources of British Guiana, of which hitherto there was so little generally known amongst us.—J. S.

SACCHARINE PRODUCTIONS.—Eleven specimens of sugar, seven of rum, and one of shrub.

FIBROUS SUBSTANCES.—Specimens of plaintain, wild aloe, Ica palm, Marita palm, mahoe, silk grass, and several varieties of cotton.

SUBSTANCES USED CHIEFLY AS FOOD, OR IN ITS PREPARATION.—Rice, maize, Guiana corn-seed, coffee, cocoa, chocolate, and various nuts and pickles, with plaintain, Banana bread, and other fruits and seeds, with specimens of arrow root and honey.

MATERIALS USED CHIEFLY IN THE CHEMICAL ARTS, OR IN MEDICINE.—Numerous specimens of bark, stems, fruits, seeds, oils, and berries, peculiar to the island.

WOODS FOR BUILDING AND OTHER PURPOSES.—Specimens from Demerara River, contributed by John Mansfield and John Outridge; from her Majesty's Penal Settlement, contributed by H. Cartwright; from the River Massarooni, contributed by A. Buchanan; table top, contributed by A. Hunter, the producer, exhibiting 183 specimens of wood, the growth of the Colony; a lady's work table, contributed by James Smellie, the top of which comprised 48 specimens of wood; and another work table, contributed by John Morison, the top of which comprises 111 specimens of wood: picture frames exhibiting illustrations of views in British Guiana, made also of various woods.

MISCELLANEOUS PRODUCTIONS OF THE ANIMAL KINGDOM.—Stuffed tiger, and ant bear, with skins of birds and snakes; collection of insects, &c.

MISCELLANEOUS PRODUCTIONS OF THE VEGETABLE KINGDOM.—Seeds and seed vessels of various plants and flowers, with specimens of leaves and branches; dyes, wax, and gums.

PRODUCTS OF THE MINERAL KINGDOM.—Specimens of gold, and quartz, granite, and other stones; pebbles, sands and clays, with bricks and tiles made from the latter, showing their application.

INDIAN MANUFACTURES, &c.—Specimens of anklets, arrows, baskets, bows, fans, fishing line, flutes, gongs, hammocks, war clubs, swords, and other like articles, with models of houses and canoes.

# INDIA.

IN the department of the Exhibition devoted to the illustration of the Arts and Manufactures of India there was the most magnificent, and, we may add, complete display ever brought together, except that in Hyde Park in 1851. The manufacturing skill which many of these articles exhibit, in not one, but several departments, has scarcely been equalled anywhere else; and the fineness and beauty of many of the textile fabrics of India, as well as the gorgeousness of many articles of apparel, covered as they are with embroidery, and studded with precious stones, far exceed what is to be found in any other part of the globe. The illustration of the Arts and Manufactures of India is, therefore, possessed of especial interest; and, as we have already observed, the collection in the Exhibition was in every respect complete.

As throughout this work the object has been rather to furnish information on the several branches of industry than to occupy space with details descriptive of particular articles, the collection in this department does not demand any lengthened notice at our hands beyond the mere enumeration of its contents, which will be found subjoined. We may remark, however, that the collection exhibited by Her Majesty was, in many respects, unique, embracing a variety of articles of surpassing riches and splendour. The profusion of precious stones which ornamented some of them, and the admirable specimens of enamelling presented by others, rendered them objects of deserved admiration; while they comprised illustrations of most of the goods for which India is celebrated. Another collection in this department also demands special notice,—that of our gallant countryman, Lord Viscount Gough. While the howitzers and other trophies of war were objects of interest on account of their construction and ornamentation, they were not less so on account of the illustrious Irishman to whom they belonged, who so well maintained the honour of his country when commanding her armies in our Indian Empire. The Honorable the East India Company, the Royal Asiatic Society, and a number of other exhibiters, also demand the cordial acknowledgments of the Irish people for their valuable contributions to this highly interesting and important department of the Irish Industrial Exhibition.

In looking over the subjoined list, it will be found to comprise many objects of Chinese as well as of Indian workmanship; but the separation of the one from the other would be productive of no practical convenience, and besides, the Chinese articles were not so numerous as to make an effective display by themselves.—J. S.

## ARTICLES CONTRIBUTED BY HER MAJESTY AND HIS ROYAL HIGHNESS PRINCE ALBERT.

### SETS OF ARMS.

Perjama or Trowsers.—Green velvet ouside, and silk inside, with chain mail lined in between them; crimson silk waistband and sash, with two silver and gold cord-worked ends, and crimson and gold edging at bottom of the legs.

Kortee or Coat.—Plain steel chain mail, collar, each side of breast, back, and wrists, worked in gold spangles and cord, forming stems, leaves, and flowers; inside of collar and breast lined with crimson velvet, and fastened by silver hooks and eyes.

Four Body Plates, consisting of breast, back, and two side plates; brown steel and raised gold ornaments in scrolls; outer border of flowers and leaves, with an inner one lined with crimson velvet, gold lace border; steel and gilt buckles, and crimson velvet straps.

Pair of Armlets in brown steel; raised gold ornaments, nearly similar to Body Plates, excepting outer scroll instead of flower border.

Toopee or Helmet, steel stained brown, with gold raised ornaments in scrolls of same character as Body Plates; rim of gold in sunk panels; chain necking of steel and brass, forming diamond pattern; nasal guard, spiked at top, and keelgees holders, steel, inlaid with gold in zigzags; ends of nasal guard in scrolls; crimson velvet lining.

Keelgees.—Two large Keelgees of heron feathers; gold and silver wire-worked stems for helmet.

Shield.—Brown steel and gold raised ornaments, similar in general design to Body Plates; centre formed by double border, encircling four panels with Asiatic characters between four bosses in gold open-work ornaments, the centres of the latter being each studded with six small rubies and an emerald; outer rim of shield formed of narrow leaf-pattern border; lined inside with green velvet, gold lace edging; crimson and gold brocade knuckle part; hand straps attached by four gold rings.

Bow, brown japanned in flowers, divided into spaces by white grass twisted round; one end broken; partly coloured string, catgut ends.

Quiver, covered in green velvet, with ends and centre band of gold, in flowers and open-work at edges; green velvet strap, and four silk cords; two crimson ends.

Arrows, ornamented in Japan work.

Powder Horn, covered in green velvet; top and end of horn finished with solid gold ornaments, in open-work; the top jewelled with seventy rubies and nineteen emeralds, and the end with twenty-one rubies and eighteen emeralds; stopper attached by gold chain, and jewelled with six rubies.

Shoulder-belt and three small Bullet Boxes, attached by sliders on belt, the whole covered in green velvet, edged with gold work; strap tipped in gold, jewelled with rubies and emeralds, and the buckle at reverse end with rubies;

solid gold ornamented fastenings to boxes, jewelled with rubies and emeralds to each fastening.

Drum.—Small gold Kettle Drum, ornamented in ribs for saddle-bow, with gold fringe at top; green velvet stick-holder on one side, and pad, with strap and buckle, on the other; wadded green silk top cover, and swivel-ring at bottom, with long tan leather strap.

Perjama or Trowsers, crimson and gold brocade, lined with crimson silk; green waistband; crimson silk sash; end ornaments in gold and silver wire-work, six pendants to each; steel and brass chain leggings, the brass forming solid diamond-shaped ornaments.

Kortee or Coat.—Steel and brass chain mail, zigzag pattern, with two small copper bands at bottom of coat and arms. Collar and breast facings of crimson and gold brocade, to match trowsers.

Toopee or Helmet.—Steel and gold ornaments, inlaid with gold borders in flowers and scrolls; nasal guard; top and side Keelgee holders, also inlaid with gold; steel and brass chain mail necking, the brass forming open diamond pattern.

Keelgees.—Three Keelgees, gold wire stems and heron feathers, the top one having pearls round it, in three rows.

Shield.—Black japanned leather, ornamented outside with gold bosses and a crescent inlaid with diamonds.

Matchlock Rifle, black steel barrel, marked by sunk wavy lines throughout ridge at top, inlaid at breech with gold in flower, and two panels containing eastern characters; gold muzzle, formed into crocodile's head, with two rubies set for eyes; gilt fore and hind sight; brown wood stock, with gold scolloped edges alongside of barrel, and plates in open-work, forming flowers on each side at breech; engraved and open-work gold butt; gilt iron trigger, pan, and cover, picker, and holder, the picker attached by two small gold chains; four gold open-work bands round barrel and stock; two gold sling rings, with red and white silk sling, and gold buckles; slow match twisted round small of butt; iron ramrod, gilt top.

GOLD, SILVER, AND OTHER ORNAMENTS.

Gold Hookah, in three parts, the lid to top held by two small gold chains; stopper fastened to end of pipe by two similar chains; and part of neck of bowl also attached by two other gold chains.

Silver Ornaments.—Two silver-gilt vases, in open-work in flowers; leaf-edge round top five inches high.

Silver Ornaments, in raised work, forming flowers and scrolls, on green-coloured ground.

Bronze.—A camel, on square stand, five inches high, and a Brahmin Bull, four and a half inches high.

Inlaid Metallic Ware.—A black vase, inlaid with silver, forming trees, flowers, and other devices, twenty-three inches high; a basin and centre cover, inlaid in silver flowers, twelve inches in diameter; a cup, stand, and cover, cup inlaid in silver, with landscape and figures, and sportsmen shooting birds.

Ivory Ornaments.—Set of chessmen, highly carved; elephant's head, carved, and supported on teak-wood frame; small elephant's head, carved; a miniature carved back-scratcher, with cow and milk-maid at top.

Horn.—A whole horn, polished, for a drinking-horn, engraved at rim and end, the latter carved as an elephant, with ivory tusks; a circular upright box, engraved; a flat horn box; two black tigers, on stands, supporting a light-coloured, shallow, circular dish, engraved.

Porcupine Quill.—Basket and cover.

Alabaster Ornaments.—A pair of white, grotesque fish; a pair of white swans; a pair of white jars and covers; white bottle and lid.

Agate Ornaments.—Moss agate vase, with scolloped top edges and foot; two dozen agate green, square, and flat knife handles; a white agate cup and saucer; model of a cannon and gun-carriage, with two wheels, all white, attached to green bloodstone ammunition carriage, supported on two wheels, with two boxes, pole, and cross-bar; green bloodstone inkstand and penholder.

Pottery.—A bottle, brown, ornamented with silver or white lines, forming trellis work, with sprigs in centre, and leaf borders, glazed; a bottle, red, with black and yellow heart-shaped pattern round neck, red trellis and yellow ground, with trees in centre of each, between two borders, round body of bottle, and highly glazed; a bottle, black, plain glazed; a bottle, stone colour, with five raised leaves, round body, each shaped at top into five parts; a cup, with side handles and cover, richly ornamented in raised figures, black painted, and glazed to imitate polished iron; a bottle, body fluted, and stand perforated in holes, black painted, in imitation of flowers, and slightly glazed.

Woods.—A sandal-wood box and lid, highly carved in figures of flowers; a polished sandal-wood box, inlaid with ivory and metals, ivory feet; model of a Hindoo temple, in pith; four baskets made of khuskhus.

VELVETS, SILKS, AND OTHER MATERIALS.

Cloth of gold chabraque, raised pattern, formed into irregular squares, flowers in the centre wholly in gold thread, crimson and gold cord round, and gold and silver open scolloped border on two sides and shaped end, lined with pale blue silk; cloth of gold chabraque, small portion of purple silk and gold thread worked into raised flowers, crimson and gold cord round edge, gold and silver open scolloped border; a buff silk and gold brocade chabraque, pattern formed in red silk, and velvet work encircling silver thread flowers and stars alternately, gold and puce-colour square cord all round, and gold and silver fringes on two sides and ends, lined with crimson silk; a rose-colour gauze and silver worked hookah cover; a purple velvet hookah carpet, embroidered with silver and gold spangles as flowers, gold and silver tinsel fringe; a hand punker, silver and gilt handle, two flappers, worked in flowers with seed pearls, emeralds, and rubies; black velvet chair cover, worked in silk and gold thread; nine pieces of shawl wool cloth; five pieces of purreepuz (a new fabric); nine specimens of cashmere silk thread; twenty-three specimens of cashmere paper.

---

2. ALMS, MRS., Raheen Park, Thurles.—A book of Persian manuscript, taken from the tent of Meer Museer Khan, after the battle of Meanee.

3. BLOOMFIELD, JOHN, Castlecaldwell, Co. Fermanagh, —Textile fabrics, robes, and other articles from India and China, in great variety.

4. BOYD, MISS FRANCES, Kilmarnock, Co. Dublin.—Indian carving in Bombay blackwood and in ivory.

5. BRIDGE, JOHN, Woodhouse, Shepherd's Bush.—Indian articles in great variety.

6. COGHLAN, MRS.—A Chinese backgammon and chess table, with chessmen, &c.; a Bombay fancy work box.

7. COOPER, MR.—A collection of Indian and Chinese articles.

8. CUNNINGHAM, LIEUT.-COL.—A Sikh sword and shield.

9. D'OLIER, Isaac, Booterstown, Dublin.—A Kannda or double-edged sword, and a Coorg knife.

10. DOWNING, WILLIAM, East India House, London.—Long rifle, with percussion lock, from Lahore; crochet box: necklace and a pair of ear-rings, from Poona; coverlid, elaborately quilted, from Rajpootanah; merrytwist quilt, from Assam.

11. EAST INDIA COMPANY, THE HONORABLE.—Idols, image of Gotama, Mayadevi, Siva taking leave of Sarvati, image of Siva, six stone figures, two clay figures in intaglio, eight metal figures; chain of metal; four glazed and unglazed tiles; three small figure heads (of plaster); pottery (of white clay), decanter and stopper; white and red clay vases in great variety; iron goblet and jug, inlaid with silver, Biddery; elephant and Howdah, in ivory carving; camel, carved in ivory; native workmen, carved in ivory; inlaid mosaic tray, from Agra; model of temple in pith;

camel, gun, and saddle, from Lahore; gun-barrel (being a sword twisted); small brass and iron lock; brass goblet and tea-pot; three Burmese musical instruments; violins and bows; violin and bow, from Java; flageolets; kettle-drums and tom-toms; pair of cymbals; models of different musical instruments; boats; lady's spinning wheel; mahratta carriage; small palanquin, and four bearers; box made of porcupine quills; pair of wooden shoes; dancing figures from Cashmere; morning gown, embroidered, from Cashmere; glazed case, containing richly ornamented MS. address; letter silver case, and bag; a collection of imitation Indian fruits and woods; a curious pair of bellows, made from leaves; various articles in gutta percha; a collection of animals modelled by Mr. F. Pulman, from stone carvings from Bengal; a section of mahogany, and a tea caddy made from part of the same tree, grown in the East India Company's Botanic Gardens at Calcutta.

12. Elliott, Lieut. John, Waterloo-road, Dublin.—Burmese umbrella, taken by exhibiter from the state barge of Bandiola, the commander-in-chief of the Burmese army.

13. Gallaher, J., H.M.S. Arrogant.—A collection of Chinese and Japanese curiosities.

14. Gough, the Right Hon. Lord Viscount.—Two 12 lb. howitzers and carriages complete, beautifully mounted and inlaid with brass gilding, taken by Lord Gough in the action of Sobraon in the year 1846, and presented to him by the Government of India; two guns, a 6 lb. and a 12 lb howitzer, taken in the battle of Goojerat, and presented to Lord Gough by the East India Company; four imperial standards of China taken at Chin-Keang-Foo; beads and horns of the Indian buffalo; model of Chinese joss house, with an idol in it, covered in wood and gilt; two figures (carved out of pith) of the Rajah of Mysore and his favourite wife; two models of guns, one of agate, the other of bloodstone, from Bombay; glass case containing baskets, &c. made of filigree silver; Chinese curiosities of different sorts, Indian, Sikh, &c. and other things; specimens of Chinese bronzes; model of a hackery or native carriage drawn by bullocks, in ivory; Chinese field-piece taken in action; box inlaid with porcupine quills and Bombay work; Chinese gong of a curious shape, used in the temples; four Sikh matchlocks; two-edged sword used by Tippoo Saib at the siege of Seringapatam; numerous specimens of rich cashmere and silk scarfs, and other articles embroidered; model in white marble, elaborately inlaid with agates and other stones, of the tomb of Noormahal, at Agra; with a great variety of Indian and Chinese miscellaneous articles.

15. Graves, Anthony, Rosbercon Castle, New Ross.—Carved ivory model of a Chinese junk; China vases.

16. Hargraves, Joseph, Manchester.—An Indian screen.

17. Hawkins, E., Keeper of Antiquities, British Museum.—Silver fibulæ, from Tunis, remarkable from their similarity to the ancient Irish ornaments.

18. Headfort, the Marchioness of.—Bedstead from Cashmere, piece of Kincob, gold brocade, tinsel trowsers and jacket, piece of embroidery, one shoe, cotton and silk cloth, trowser ties, pair of socks, and sash.

19. Hewett & Co., Fenchurch-st. and Baker-st., London, Importers.—Collection of Indian and Chinese articles, ancient and modern, comprising exquisite specimens of the manufacturing and artistic products of the East in almost every department.

20 Huband, Arthur, Herbert-street, Dublin.—Indian idol, first brought to Calcutta by a vessel from Rangoon; marble head taken from the Great Pagoda.

21. Kempston, Miss, Sandymount.—Inkstand, elaborately painted and engraved, and curious pair of scissors from Cashmere.

22. Reeves, John.—Chinese articles of various kinds.

23. Reynolds, Alderman J.—A Goorkha sword, presented to exhibiter by the Nepaulese Ambassador, in 1850.

24. Rothney, A., East India Company's Military Stores.—A sword taken in the late Chinese war.

25. Royal Asiatic Society, The.—Collection of Indian and Cingalese arms; models of the great Hindoo temple at Trivalore; Buddhist temple; Buddhist preaching-house; Chinese chain pump; the idol Juggernaut, and cars; Burmese war boat; Burmese harp; gong; water pail, and lacquered ware; Affghan water bag of Russia leather; Japanese joss house, used by the people for the reception of Buddhist idols in their domestic worship; Japanese opium pipe; playing cards and books; Chinese opium pipe; sun-dials, mariner's compass, and lady's shoe; series of 13 miniature portraits of kings of Delhi of the Timurian dynasty, by a native artist; Hindoo horoscope, in a Sanscrit roll of several yards in length, found in the camp of one of the Sikh generals after the battle of Goojerat; Siamese dramatic poem, in manuscript, folded fan-like; original Arabic letter from the Imaun of Muscat, sent to the Royal Asiatic Society, in Kincob envelope; Arabic celestial globe, made at Mosul in the year 1275; ancient images of Brahma, Vishnu, Laksmi, Darga, and Durgo; piece of ancient sculpture, representing Buddha and his disciples.

26. Royal Dublin Society, The.—Two models of Chinese boats, elaborately carved in mother-of-pearl and ivory.

27. Society of Arts, The, Adelphi, London; E. Solly, Secretary.—Arm-chair, and chair of native India manufacture; specimens of Chandernagore manufactured cotton; balls of Chandernagore two-thread and three-thread twine and canvass; papers containing samples of lac dye and shel-lac.

28. Stacey, Frederick.—A hookah from Bengal, and musical instruments from Java.

29. Stock, Dr.—Collection of fabrics from Sindh.

30. Stokes, Wm., M.D.—Collection of Indian deities.

31. Sykes, Colonel and Mrs.—Sandal-wood desk, carved with Hindoo deities; Bombay work backgammon board; embossed silver rose-water bottle from Cutch; Goorkha sword, Goorkha military knives, a Goorkha noble's green velvet cap (these articles were worn by the Nepaulese with the Nepaulese Ambassador when in England); two baskets of the fragrant grass, called Khus-Khus, from Poonah, in the Decan.

32. Taylor, Philip Meadows, Harold's-cross, Dublin.—Table printed on Indian satin, in the private printing press of his Highness the Rajah of Mysore, arranged by himself, and sent by him to Captain Meadows Taylor, Political Agent at the Court of Sherapoor, as a mark of his friendship.

33. Twining, Richard.—Chinese articles in variety.

34. United Service Museum, The.—Flint lock gun belonging to the late King of Candy, in Ceylon; sword taken from the palace of the King of Candy; double matchlock from Delhi; Indian matchlock, with barrel 7 feet 3 inches long; a pair of battle-axes from Cutch, silver mounting and handles, with stilettos in the handle; dagger which belonged to the late Rajah of Sattera, gold mounting, and scabbard with rubies and emeralds; arms and accoutrements of a Beloochee soldier, consisting of a matchlock, sabre, shield, and belt, with flasks, pouches, &c.; Mahratta chakkra or war quoit; Ghoorka sword; common matchlock, used by the Chinese infantry; portable brass 3-inch Chinese gun; whistling arrow used by the Chinese sentinels as an alarm signal; rocket arrow for setting fire to shipping; four silk Chinese flags; and other articles.

35. Wallich, Dr.—Collection of Indian woods.

36. Wheatley, G. W. & Co.—A number of small articles from India and China.

# ANTIQUITIES.

In the display of a collection of Antiquities the Irish Industrial Exhibition was unique. On no former occasion was such a collection placed before the public, and these for the most part belonging to our own country. Our Antiquities Court being appended to the Exhibition Building was, moreover, a more important and appropriate addition than might at first sight be supposed, as there was something more than a mere speculative interest in comparing the products of the past with those of the present, and in tracing the first steps of that progress of which the modern collections afforded so many illustrations. Many of the objects of ancient art and handicraft bore evidence of the great amount of taste and skill which existed at a period so remote as to be associated in our minds with a kind of semi-barbarism; while others presented specimens of workmanship unexcelled even in our own day. The formation of a collection of Antiquities was not contemplated in the earlier arrangements of the Executive Committee, though it afterwards was found to form a most attractive feature of the Exhibition. To the great numbers of strangers that visited us it possessed special interest. From it much information was acquired relative to the Antiquities of Ireland; and which was the more valuable, inasmuch as the Museum of the Royal Irish Academy was at the time undergoing repair, and could not be available to visitors. When it was finally arranged that articles of Antiquity should be exhibited, the Academy at once offered to transfer their valuable collection to the Exhibition Building,—an offer which was gladly accepted,—and there can be no doubt that it formed *the* feature of this department.

Though we can here devote only a passing notice to the subject, yet, from the great national importance of the collection of the Royal Irish Academy, and the fact of its being available for inspection at any time, we cannot omit the opportunity of introducing a few remarks on the way in which it has been got up. Though incorporated nearly seventy years ago for promoting the study of Science, Polite Literature, and Antiquities in Ireland, the Academy does not appear to have taken any effective steps towards the formation of a collection of Antiquities until 1839, when the late lamented Professor MacCullagh presented, as a nucleus, the celebrated Cross of Cong to the Academy. Immediately after we find him taking steps to secure further additions, by heading a subscription list to obtain funds for the purpose. The Tara torques, the Domnach Airgid, and other valuable relics of former times, many of them of surpassing interest, were successively added to the commencement thus so auspiciously made,—every movement in which had the cordial support of the distinguished Professor with whom the scheme originated. The addition of the collection of Irish antiquities, coins, and medals, of the late Very Rev. Henry Dawson, Dean of St. Patrick's, for which a sum of £1000 was paid, at once gave to the new Museum a character of national importance. Contributions from all quarters were subsequently made to it; but those of special value, to which we should not omit to particularly refer, were made by the Shannon Commissioners, the Commissioners of Public Works, the Directors of the Great Southern and Western Railway Company, the Trustees of Kilmainham Hospital, and Colonel Portlock, R. E. Considering that the Committee of Antiquities have formed an integral or third part of the Council of the Academy since its foundation in 1786, it is somewhat singular that so long a period should have elapsed without any effort being made to carry out so very important, and what was, moreover, a fundamental object. The first appropriation of any of the funds for this purpose appears to have been made in 1837 at the instance of Dr Petrie, whose services in the cause of antiquarian research in Ireland are so well known, by a grant of £73 10*s.* to purchase a collection then for sale. The next grant of money on the part of the Academy for this purpose, was a sum of £113 11*s.* 6*d.*, in 1842. In the mean time, however, as has been already seen, the liberality of some of the members made amends for the indifference which appears to have actuated the governing body, and the result is, that, in little over ten years, a collection has been brought together, the aggregate value of which exceeds £5000, and which is, besides, constantly increasing.—J. S.

---

### HER MAJESTY THE QUEEN.

A gold torque found in Needwood Forest.

### THE ROYAL IRISH ACADEMY.

A general assortment of ancient weapons, implements, ornaments, &c., found in different parts of Ireland, and forming the Museum of the Academy. The Bronze Series contain a great variety of hatchets of different sizes, palstaves or spuds, celts, spear and javelin heads, blades of various kinds, swords and daggers, trumpets, vizors, cheek-plates for bridles, bridle bits, spurs, cloak and hair pins, and miscellaneous articles. The Brass Series include spurs, stirrups, ornamented cases, and other smaller objects. A glazed case contained a collection of Danish and Norwegian antiquities, presented to the Academy by the King of Denmark and the Museum of Northern Antiquities, Copenhagen. In the list of donors to this highly valuable national collection we find the following among others:—

William T. Mulvany, on the part of the Commissioners of Public Works.—A variety of objects found in the excavations in works of arterial drainage carried on in several districts, and collected under the superintendence of the following district engineers:—Charles S. Ottley, for the Lower Bann and Toome; William Fraser, from Castlebernard, Borris-in-Ossory, and Templemore; P. J. Klassen, from Brusna; George Tarrant, from Dunmore and Monivea; Frederick Barry, from Lough Mask and Ballinrobe; Saml. W. Roberts, from Corrib; Thomas J. Mulvany, from Ballinamore, Ballyconnell, and Killeshandra; John O'Flaherty, from Strokestown; and R. Manning, from the Glyde district.

Dr. Madden.—A variety of iron articles from Dunshaughlin, Co. Meath.

John Lentaigne, Tallaght House—A miscellaneous assortment found in different localities throughout Ireland.

The Shannon Commissioners—A collection from the excavations made at Keelogue and other localities near Athlone.

A. O. Lyons, Templemore—Articles found in a railway gripe near that place.

---

3. Anketell, Matthew J., Anketell Grove, Co. Monaghan.—Miscellaneous collection of Irish antiquities.

4. Archæological Institute of Great Britain and Ireland, The.—Circular bronze coating of a shield found in dredging in the Thames; oblong bronze ornament of thin metal plate; three pins, the heads being flat discs, chased with interlaced patterns; stirrup of bronze, with elaborate ornament of metal inlaid; two bronze swords; palstave; chisel of silex; bone skate, formed of the cannon bone of a horse; pheon, or broad arrow, of iron, found in the Thames; two enamelled plates of Limoges work, twelfth century, representing the Crucifixion, and the Saviour enthroned on the rainbow; portions of shrine decorations, or of the binding of a book of the Gospels; palstave, with two side loops.

5. Baker, Abraham Whyte.—Skulls of extinct Irish bears, from the collection of the late Abraham Whyte Baker, Esq., Ballagtobin, Callan; original miniature of King Charles II.; ink-horn; carving in ivory.

6. Ball, Robert, LL.D.—A restoration of the celebrated instrument, commonly called the Harp of Brian Boroimhe—the oldest known specimen of Irish harp,—preserved in the Dublin University Museum; a restoration of the Dalway Harp; a restoration of the charter horn of the Kavenaghs, the original of which is preserved in the University Museum.

7. Barton, F. W., Clonelly.—A knife and two forks taken out of the baggage of the Pretender; ancient Irish silver bodkin; piece of gold ring money; gold ring.

8. Bedford, Mrs., The Close, Lichfield.—Collection of ancient gold and silver ornaments, chiefly Irish.

9. Belfast Museum.—Ancient stirrup, made of untanned hide; models of spears and other implements; stone covered with moulds for casting bronze hatchets; ancient iron riveted bell, covered superficially with bronze or brass; three amphoræ or urns of baked clay.

10. Beresford, Ven. Marcus G., Archdeacon of Ardagh.—A remnant of the Clog Mogue, or Bell of St. Mogue; ancient brass bottle; ancient bronze rapier; ornamented bronze hatchet; a pure bronze palstave and a fibula; bronze spear and celts; fragments of a spiral silver armlet, found near Cavan.

11. Berwick, Edward, President, Queen's College, Galway.—Ancient map of Galway, A.D. 1650; old municipal map of Galway, commencing A.D. 1484.

12. Blood, E. M.—Models of two ancient pillars in alabaster in the Church of St. Denis, Paris.

13. Bloomfield, J.C., Castle Caldwell, Co. Fermanagh.—Baptismal font; Christ, in alabaster; head of our Saviour, in ivory; bronze seal; Carolan's skull; O'Neill's harp, with stone hammer, and other articles.

14. Brackstone, R. N.—A miscellaneous collection of stone, flint, bronze, and other articles, found in different parts of Ireland.

15. British Museum, Curator of the.—Silver ornaments from Tunis, at present worn by the females of that place, resembling ancient Irish ornaments in the Museum of the Royal Irish Academy.

16. Brownlow, William, Abbeyleix.—The Book of Armagh, an ancient Irish manuscript of the Gospels, the Life of St. Patrick, &c., written A.D. 809, by a scribe named Ferdomnach.

17. Bruce, Sir H. Hervey, Downhill, Co. Derry.—Part of the walls of Herculaneum, painted in fresco; ancient Roman helmet, found in the tomb of the Horatii, near Rome.

18. Buxton, Sir Robert, Bart.—A cup made of a large shell, mounted on a foot of yellow metal, elaborately ornamented with white and blue enamel.

19. Caledon, Countess of, Caledon, Co. Tyrone.—Bronze hatchet, curiously marked; two Druid beads; bronze spear-head; bronze fibula; crotal; two fairy lasts; bronze looped hatchet; turquoise brooch; oak spade; steel sword.

20. Carruthers, James.—A collection of flint, bronze, and silver articles, found in the Co. Antrim.

21. Carte, Alexander, M.D., Royal Dublin Society.—Fac-simile of the shrine of St. Manchin, restored by exhibitor.

22. Carter, William, Mespil-parade, Dublin.—Model of Ruins of Monasterboice, Co. Louth.

23. Cashel, Very Rev. the Archdeacon of, Thurles.—A rare and early Irish engraving, by W. Simpson, of Waterford, date 1646.

24. Chandlee, Thomas Moone, Ballitore.—Model of stone cross at Moone Abbey, Co. Kildare; model of cromlech of Labacally, near Glanworth, Co. Cork; model of an Irish cabin.

25. Chester, Greville J.—Ornamented copper chalice, enamelled in blue, green, white, and red, and studded with imitations of precious stones, found near Sudbury.

26. Cooke, T. L.—An extensive collection of antiquities, found in different parts of Ireland.

27. Dalway, Marriott, Carrickfergus.—Ancient Irish harp, called the *Regina Citharorum*.

28. Digby, Earl of.—Collection of gold ornaments, found near Sherbourne, in Dorsetshire.

29. Dowsley, Dr., Clonmel.—Roman oculist's stamp, found in the Co. Tipperary.

30. Dundas, Robert, Arniston, N. B.—Collection of gold and silver ornaments.

31. Echlin, Miss.—Two centre pieces of the flags of the Carlow volunteers of 1782.

32. Egerton, Sir Philip de Malpas, Bart., M.P.—Pair of torc armlets of pure gold, found near Egerton Hall, Cheshire.

33. Fine Arts Committee of the Exhibition.—Stone cross from the Market-place of Tuam, Co. Galway; stone cross of SS. Patrick and Columba, from the church-yard of Kells, Co. Meath; casts of St. Boyne's stone cross; of the great stone cross at Monasterboice, Co. Louth; of the stone cross at Kilcrispeen, Co. Tipperary; of the stone cross at Kilkeiran, Co. Kilkenny; casts of sarcophagus, found near the Cathedral of St. Andrews, in Fifeshire; casts of celt moulds found in Ayrshire and Rosshire; fresco painting on the north chancel wall of the ancient Abbey of Knockmoy, Co. Galway, and supposed to represent the execution, in the twelfth century, of the young son of Dermod Mac Morrough, King of Leinster; doorway of the church of

Freshford, Co. Kilkenny, erected by St. Lachlin, in the seventh century, and rebuilt towards the close of the eleventh century; circular window of the eighth century, which lighted a chamber placed between the chancel and stone roof of Rahan Church, King's County; pillars of the chancel arch of the Church of Rahan, King's County; chancel arch of Tuam Cathedral; eastern window of Tuam Cathedral; cast of the stone cross at Dunnamoggan, Co. Kilkenny; monument to the Earl and Countess of Ormonde, in Canice's Cathedral, Kilkenny; monument of a bishop in St. Canice's Cathedral; monument of a cross-legged knight at Kilfane, Co. Kilkenny.

34. Fisher, Samuel.—Ancient crozier from Cootehill.

35. Fountaine, Andrew, Narford Hall, Norfolk.—Reliquary in the form of a hand and arm of Irish workmanship.

36. Gernon, John, Dublin.—Antique ivory carving, representing the Nativity, surrounded by medallions, with heads of our Saviour and the saints, and reliques from the holy places, &c

37. Haines, Dr. C. Y., Cork.—Piece of silver ring money.

38. Harvey, John, Malin Hall, Co. Donegal.—Earthen jar, found, filled with silver coins, on a mountain near Malin; gold beads of a double conical shape, and pieces of gold wire, found in a bog near Malin.

39. Hodgson, Mrs.—Ancient Greek fresco; stained ivory crucifix.

40. Howth, the Earl of, Howth Castle, Co. Dublin.—The ancient bells of Howth Abbey; the great two-handed sword, said to have been used by Sir Almericus St. Laurence, the founder of the Howth family, who landed in Ireland in 1177.

41. Keane, Francis, Kilrush.—The golden bell of St. Senan, of Scattery Island.

42. Keyworth, William Day, Savile-street, Hull.—Cast of a monumental effigy of one of the Percy family, in Beverley Minster.

43. King, William Croker.—Carving in ivory, representing the Nativity.

44. Knipe, E. A., Mount Salem, Stillorgan.—Collection of models, by an amateur.

45. Larcom, Major, Under-Secretary for Ireland.—Western doorway of Maghera Church, Co. Londonderry.

46. Layard, Miss Mary C.—Models of the Nineveh marbles, discovered by Dr. Henry Austen Layard, M. P.

47. Leech, Robert.—An ancient brick from the centre palace, Nineveh.

48. Le Hunte, George.—White Chinese seal, found in the neighbourhood of Wexford.

49. Lentaigne, John, Tallaght House, Dublin.—Bas relief from Bective Abbey, Co. Meath; ancient shrine of St. Manchan of Lemanaghan, of the seventh century, the property of the Rev. Charles O'Reilly, C.C., and the parishioners of Bellaire Chapel, in the diocese of Ardagh; fac simile, executed by Dr. Carte, of shrine of St. Patrick's hand, placed in Down Abbey in 1186, preserved in the family of Magennis, Lords of Irvagh, at Castlewellan, and now the property of the Right Rev. Dr. Denvir, R. C. Bishop of Down and Connor; glass goblet, used by a Dublin Guild in the beginning of the last century, with the battle of the Boyne engraved on it; antique French watch, found in the Bog of Allen; antique image of our Saviour, a specimen of Irish art of a very early age, the property of the Very Rev. Mr. M'Evoy, P. P. of Kells; ancient Irish font of Kilcarne, the property of the Rev. T. Reid, P.P., Co. Meath; ancient Irish font, the property of Rev. P. Gough, P.P. of Curraha.

50. Londesborough, the Right Hon. Lord, Grimston, Tadcaster.—Gold ornaments found at New Grange, Co. Meath; torc ring and spear-head from the Isle of Ely; large fibula for fastening the priest's dress of the twelfth century; gold torques of various sizes, said to have been found in a rath near Kilmallock, Co. Limerick.

51. Macleod of Macleod.—Rorie More's Horn (this horn has been handed down from generation to generation in the family of Macleod of Macleod, from the ancestor whose name it bears, Sir Roderick Macleod of that ilk); the Dunvegan Cup, belonging to the Macleod of Macleod, the head of the clan of that name, and has been preserved at Dunvegan Castle, the family seat, in the Isle of Skye.

52. Major, Mrs., Molesworth-street, Dublin.—The colours carried by the Volunteers of 1782 from Ballyshannon to Killybegs.

53. Martin, John, Downpatrick.—A variety of ancient gold and silver ornaments; one silver seal-ring of Turlough O'Neil; perforated stone, with rude carving; mosaic encaustic tile; bronze spear-head and axe; stone dagger.

54. M'Clelland, John, Dungannon.—Bell of St. Moran; a selection of celts and spear-heads.

55. Moriarty, Henry.—Stone effigies of gallowglasses, or Irish soldiers, from the tomb of Phelim O'Connor, King of Connaught, at Roscommon Abbey.

56. Morrison, Dr., Leeson-street, Dublin.—The Irish union pipes. This improved musical instrument, by the elder Kenna, about 1767, is in fine preservation, and a good specimen of his skill and workmanship.

57. Murray, T. R., Edenderry.—Assortment of Irish antiquities, collected chiefly in that neighbourhood.

58. Murray, R., Mullingar.—Cinerary urn; chalice; patinas; spear-heads; arrow-heads; celts; iron spear-head; iron daggers; reaping-hooks; crescents; pins and brooches; seals; silver bracelet, and amulet.

59. M'Dowell, Dr., Monaghan.—Set of brass stirrups; large stone hammer, brought from South Carolina, curious as exemplifying the similarity between those found in the Old and New World.

60. MacGillicuddy of the Reeks, Whitefield, Co. Kerry.—Collection of Manuscripts, with dates from A. D. 1597 to 1700.

61. Northumberland, His Grace the Duke of, Alnwick Castle.—Fragments of a Saxon cross, found in 1789, near the site of Woden's Church, at Alnmouth, Northumberland, of the ninth or tenth century; a series of curious white Chinese porcelain seals.

62. Nugent, Sir John, Ballinlough Castle.—Ancient silver watch; curious lock; carving in oak of King David playing on the harp.

63. O'Connell, Rev. Charles, Balbriggan.—Figure carved in oak of St. Romaldus, Archbishop of Dublin; figure of St. Bridget, carved in ivory; gold watch, formerly the property of Mary, Queen of Scots; antique watch, in the form of a cross.

64. O'Donnell, Sir Richard, Bart., Westport.—The Caah, a shrine or reliquary, containing an ancient vellum manuscript copy of the Psalms, said to have been written by St. Columba.

65. Petrie, George, LL. D.—Collection of Irish antiquities, being a selection from his Museum, made for the purpose of illustrating ancient Irish art.

66. Public Works, Commissioners of.—Casts taken from the Castle of the Lynches in Galway; monumental stone erected on the spot where Lynch, Warden of Galway, executed his son.

67. Reade, Rev. George H., Inniskeen Rectory, Dundalk.—A collection of celts, hatchets, and other ornaments, found in different parts of Ireland.

68. Roche, Very Rev. B. J., Galway.—Ancient embroidered chasuble, stole, and maniple, found about fifty years ago in the wall of the Collegiate Church of St. Nicholas, Galway; ancient embroidered vestments.

69. Roe, Henry.—Watch, said to have been worn by Charles the First on the day of his execution.

70. Rossmore, Lord, Rossmore Park, Monaghan.—Ancient leather shoe, made of carved leather, found in a bog; crystal ball, found in a bog; small golden fibula; a gold crescent, highly ornamented; miniatures of Lord Edward Fitzgerald and Charles James Fox; union bagpipes, mounted in silver, and richly ornamented with precious stones.

71. Rowe, M. W., Carlow.—The Earl of Strafford's clock, the property of Mr. G. Strahan.

72. Royal Dublin Society, The.—Large pot, with spine-shaped rivets; large gold-coloured spear; sword-blade of Persian pattern; spear made of bronze, with perforated blade; short dagger, with bronze handle; bronze rings; bronze torques; fragments of highly ornamented flat bars of silver; large silver fibula, with Ogham inscriptions; head of silver fibula, gilt, and ornamented with snakes' heads, &c.

73. Ryan, the Right Rev. Dr., R. C. Bishop, Limerick.—Silver crozier and mitre of Cornelius O'Dea, Bishop of Limerick, made by Thomas O'Carthy, A. D. 1418; ivory carving, representing the Coronation of the Blessed Virgin, and the Presentation in the Temple.

74. St. Columba, Warden and Fellows of the College of, Rathfarnham.—The Miosach, a valuable Irish reliquary, supposed to have formerly contained a manuscript of the Gospels or Psalms; two glass frames, containing a collection of bronze and flint antiquities.

75. Saurin, Ven. Archdeacon, Seagoe, Co. Antrim.—Bronze ring money, sword, and two daggers; an Irish harp.

76. Shearman, John F., Kilkenny.—An antique jet necklace.

77. Sherrard, George.—Ancient chain armour, found at Kirkstead Abbey, Lincolnshire.

78. Smith, George, Baggot-street.—The Corp-naumh (or holy body), supposed to be the shrine of an ancient bell, with the figure of our Saviour on it, formerly belonging to the Chapel of Templecross, Co. Westmeath.

79. Smith, J. Huband.—Ancient bell, found at Kilgort, parish of Fintona, Co. Tyrone.

80. Smith, J. Richardson.—Twelve cinerary urns, found in an ancient cemetery on the hill of Ballon, Co. Carlow.

81. Spratt, Rev. Dr.—Ancient tryptick; reliquary, formerly belonging to Mellifont Abbey.

82. Stokes, Dr. William, Merrion-square.—A shrine, said to contain a tooth of St. Patrick.

83. Talbot de Malahide, Lord, Malahide Castle, Co. Dublin.—Portrait of Charles Talbot, Duke of Shrewsbury, on enamel; large spear-head; two circular discs, curiously painted on enamel; a bronze double-looped palstave; ornamented bronze spear-head; ancient encaustic tiles; ancient Celtic urn; bronze celt; stone knife; swords and axe, found at Lagore, near Dunshaughlin; brooch, curiously enamelled with the *opus Hibernicum*, found at the same place; electrotype fac-similes in copper of three spear-heads; swords; casts in glass from classical and mediæval seals, by H. Laing.

84. Tobin, Thomas, Ballincollig, Co. Cork.—Gold ornaments, found in the Co. Cork.

85. Todd, Rev. Dr., S. F. T. C. D.—The bell of St. Patrick, fifth century, with its shrine or case of the eleventh century.

86. Tucker, Charles, F.S.A.—Enamelled cup of Limoges work, sixteenth century, representing Tritons; cup of Limoges enamel, decorated with historical subjects.

87. Tuke, George.—Irish bagpipes, belonging to Lord Edward Fitzgerald.

88. Wade, George, Ashbrook, Phœnix Park.—A map of Dublin in the year 1490; miniature of Prince Charles Edward, "The Pretender.".

89. Wakeman, William F.—A collection of iron, bone, and bronze antiquities.

90. Walsh, Right Rev. Dr., R. C. Bishop of Ossory.—Ancient vestments of David Roth, Bishop of Ossory; remonstrance, silver gilt; sardonyx cup.

91. Waterford, the Very Rev. the Dean of.—A case of antiquities, and of autographs of eminent men of the seventeenth century.

92. Way, Albert, F. S. A.—Enamelled ciborium of the twelfth century.

93. Welch, A. C., Dromore, Co. Down.—Stone ploughshares and other articles.

94. Westminster, Marquis of.—Gold torques, found in 1816, at Bryn-shon, in the parish of Ysceifiog, near Holywell, N. W.

95. Whitty, John Irvine, LL. D., Henrietta-street, Dublin.—Map of Ireland, transferred from a copper-plate, engraved A. D. 1572.

96. Wilson, Dr. Daniel, Secretary to the Society of Antiquaries of Scotland.—Casts of bronze circular shield, decorated with a classic group in low relief, Apollo, &c.; horn of tenure, richly carved in ivory; chessmen, carved out of the walrus tooth, found in the Isle of Skye; bronze armilla, snake pattern; bronze armlets; a crozier, or pastoral staff of oak, found in the tomb of Bishop Tulloch, Kirkwall, Cathedral, Orkney; fac-similes, in metal, of a gold sceptre-head, and other articles.

97. Windele, John, Blair's Castle, Cork.—Two bronze curved trumpets; engraved bronze axe; Irish bronze ring money.

98. Young, Robert, Hillmount, Co. Antrim.—Brass stirrups, used by Duke Schomberg at the Battle of the Boyne.

# THE MEDIÆVAL COURT.

THE attention which has lately been devoted to Mediæval Art, and the efforts made in quarters entitled to respect to revive it, made the collection of Mr. Hardman, of Birmingham, amongst the most valuable individual contributions to the Exhibition. Until lately the opportunities of becoming acquainted with this class of objects possessed by the general public were so limited that they were unable to appreciate the excellencies which it really possesses; while they were as little able to determine what value was to be attached to the extravagant rhapsodies in which some persons indulge in its favour. Hence the Mediæval Court was a place of great attraction, and that not merely for the collection which it contained, but also on account of the very judicious and appropriate manner in which the whole was arranged. The articles exhibited were, for the most part, illustrative of ecclesiastical Mediæval Art, as being that of greatest importance in a commercial point of view just now, and hence most likely to attract attention in an Exhibition. They comprised the whole of the requisites of the imposing ceremonials of the Roman Catholic Church; an altar being fitted up in one side of the apartment in the manner in which it is usually arranged in its proper place, which comprised stained glass decorations, carvings in wood and stone, and ornamental brass-work. Opposite the altar, to which we have alluded, a richly coloured window, in the earlier style of art, presented a grouping of the Lord and his Apostles, a favourite subject of Mediæval illustration. Near to this there was a still more elegant representation, or series of representations, of the Madonna and Infant, and various Scripture incidents. These restorations of the quaint peculiarities of the olden ecclesiastical artists were justly admired for their accuracy and beauty. A window prepared for the Earl of Shrewsbury, and to be placed at Alton Towers, was an example of the secular art of the period when baronial edifices were adorned by ornamentations on glass of armorial bearings, sacred events, scenes of family history, or the achievements of the warrior. In the centre part stood the figure of the first Earl Talbot, and the surrounding space was filled with foliage work richly, though somewhat rudely, designed. Other objects of interest were, an altar in Caen stone, carved delicately, and enriched with *alto relievo* illustrations of circumstances in the life of St. Patrick. The altar placed at the other end of the Hall was a still more attractive piece of workmanship. It had a tabernacle of brass-work, supported by columns, above which were praying angels, the main subject being relieved by symbolic emblems of the wheat sheaf and vine interwoven. A large corona lucis, for fifty lights, the property of the Right Hon. Sidney Herbert, was, perhaps, the best specimen of Mediæval brass-work which the Court contained. Among the smaller relics there were many costly vessels in gold and silver, and a bishop's pastoral staff in the style of the fifteenth century, which received the medal at the Exhibition of 1851, as the best revival of the old ecclesiastical metal work. A large paschal candlestick of solid ornamental brass-work, fourteen feet high, which was placed in the centre of the apartment, cannot be passed unnoticed; at its base, angels, with extended wings, emblematised the Resurrection: in niches, above, the "three Mary's" appeared, surmounted by other angels in the attitude of exultant praise; and over all, and round the summit of the candlestick, an inscription was written in acknowledgment of our Lord's rising from the dead. There was an appropriateness and a beauty in this article which arrested attention at once.

A great part of the articles exhibited in the Mediæval Department were executed by Mr. Myer's, of London. The altar in Caen stone was contributed by him; and the utmost care and fidelity were apparent in all the restorations. To the exertions of Mr. Hardman the visitors to the Exhibition were indebted for being enabled to form a good idea of the peculiar character of ecclesiastical Mediæval Art; and the Court devoted to his "revivals" was found not the least interesting to those who could appreciate the beauty of the articles it contained.

Into any disquisition on the subject of Mediæval Art the space at our disposal will not permit us to enter, and we must, therefore, content ourselves by indicating the general character of the valuable contribution of Mr. Hardman.

1. HARDMAN, JOHN, Gt. Charles-street, Birmingham, Designer and Manufacturer.—Stained glass windows; ancient church and domestic furniture, consisting of chandeliers, coronal lamps, gas and candle branches, wrought-iron hinges, lock and door plates, grate and fire dogs; gold and silver work; chalices with enamels, ciboriums, monstrances; reliquiares, pixes, thuribles, and boats; cruets and stands; pastoral staff; flower vases, torches, flagons, and beaten dishes; monumental brasses and tabernacle; triptics and processional crosses; Myer's carved stone altar, and carved wood figures; Minton's encaustic tiles; embroidery on silk and linen, vestments, &c. by Mesdames Powell and Brown.

# FOREIGN STATES.

## FRANCE.

FEW countries possess greater natural advantages for entering into commercial relations with other nations than France. On the north and west, the North Sea, the Channel, and the Atlantic Ocean, wash its shores. Separated from Great Britain only by the Channel, it is brought into communication with the Low Countries and the Rhenish provinces by the Scheldt, the Meuse, and the Moselle; while the Rhine, on its eastern frontier, opens up to it Germany and Switzerland. The proximity of the Danube to the Rhenish borders of France provides further facilities, as the great channel of communication with the East. Flanked, on the east and south, by the Alps and the Pyrenees, the Mediterranean throws open to it the two great peninsulas of Italy and of Spain. Watered by numerous great streams, such as the Rhone, the Loire, the Garonne, the Seine, it may be said to possess rivers unsurpassed in favourable position and distribution, and which bring all parts of the interior into communication with the Mediterranean and the Ocean. From the various productions of its soil has sprung up an interior commerce capable of almost unlimited development; while the variety and excellence of its agricultural products, and especially its wines, estimated at the annual value of twenty-two millions sterling, furnish it with a ready medium of exchange with other countries.

This happy geographical and climatic position enabled France to hold a prominent position in the civilized world from the times of the Romans. But the first great effort to develope the internal trade and commerce of that country is due to Colbert, the famous minister of Louis XIV. He it was who acquired for France many of those industries now become national, but, until then, unknown, by inviting from foreign countries the most skilled workmen. The fine cloths which had previously been imported were manufactured in different parts of the kingdom, and in the year 1669 more than 44,000 looms were engaged in this branch of trade. The cultivation of the mulberry was encouraged, and the silk factories of Lyons acquired the celebrity which they have since maintained. There was no art, no invention that this benefactor of his country did not endeavour to introduce into it. The mercantile navy, which may be said to have been created by him, spread abroad the products of the French manufactories; while the elegance and good taste of the greater part of these products secured them a preference in the markets of the world.

This commercial prosperity was not, however, of long duration,—it did not survive the great minister. The disasters of war, and the religious intolerance of Louis XIV., exiled many of the industries thus created. The trade and commerce of the country could, at best, be but sparingly developed under a system in which there was little freedom of action, owing to the stringency of the regulations of local institutions professedly designed for the encouragement of trade, and also owing to those fiscal restrictions which then placed every province in the position of a foreign country to the rest of the kingdom. The necessary changes in this respect were effected by the National Assembly; but the country, then attacked on every point by the armies of a powerful coalition, the sea almost shut out, and exterior commerce completely extinguished, industry thus deprived of those natural resources which it had been accustomed to obtain from other countries, was forced to seek them in its own soil. From this epoch dates the real development and the true progress of French industry. An appeal made to the genius of the people was answered with the same devotion and enthusiasm as that made to their valour to save them from invasion. The resources of the country were studied and investigated, many manufacturing processes were perfected, and new discoveries and applications were added to those already known. France, which was believed to be in a state of social disorganization, proved to the world what could be accomplished by a people jealous of their independence. The great creations of France, at this epoch, shed light on the path of science and industry, by distributing everywhere the treasures of knowledge. At the head of these creations may be placed the National Institute of Science, of Letters, and of Arts; the Polytechnic School, a nursery of men of science, of engineers, of mechanists, and of chemists; the Conservatory of Arts and Manufactures, a depôt of all industrial inventions; and the Society of Encouragement, a private body, but one which, by its enlightened exertions, has done much to advance the cause of industry in France.

We must not forget to remark here, that it was in the year Six of the Republic, when France was every where assailed, that the first Great Exhibition of French Industry was held in Paris in the Louvre,—a glorious example, which, by exciting the emulation of the people for the useful arts, must have made them more visibly alive to the benefits of peace. But, notwithstanding all these efforts and all the progress which has already been realized, industry is far from having attained that high point of development in France, in many branches, which it has reached in Great Britain. Exhausted by a military regime, which has absorbed much of the resources of the nation, she has comparatively neglected, or executed with extreme slowness, some of those great practical improvements to which so much of the power of England is due. Until the reign of Louis Philippe the great channels of internal communication were, in several places, left in a deplorable condition; and even in the present day they are far from being adequate to the requirements of the age. Assemblies and Governments of all shades of politics, who never hesitated when there was a question of adding 100,000 men to the army roll, gave but little encouragement to the execution, even by private enterprise, of indispensable lines of railway.

France, it must be observed, does not possess in abundance that great natural resource which is, in the present day, almost the food of industrial energy,—we mean Coal. In almost every district iron is found, but the price of fuel renders its working very expensive. It must, however, be noted, that the working of the coal mines has advanced with the development of industry, and the systems of railways which at present connect the great coal basins with the centres of consumption tend every day to increase the production. To give an idea of this progressive increase it will be sufficient to refer to the following figures and dates:—In 1789 the annual production of coal was only 160,000 tons. In 1802 it had reached 215,000 tons; in 1830 it was as high as 900,000 tons. In 1845 it reached the enormous quantity of 4,202,091 tons. The use of turf is much employed at present in the manufacture, and the different applications of iron. The production of coal in England is at present about eight times as great as in France; but, when we reflect how small are the resources of the latter, in this respect, compared with those of England, we may appreciate the efforts which were required on the part of France to bring this industry to its present position. The inventions of Berard, which have for their object to purify pyritic coal, which would otherwise be useless, will, doubtless, increase the production in many localities where the scarcity of fuel was an obstacle to its employment.

The coal mines of France may be said to be concentrated in some few points, as may be seen from the enormous difference in the produce of the several basins. Thus, of the forty-six coal depots, the basin of the Loire furnishes more than 45 per cent.; that of the Department Du Nord, 27 per cent. The basin of the Loire extends over a surface of 67,595 acres, and possessed, in 1839, fifty-five mines in work. The quality of coal found there may be compared to that at Newcastle. This basin occupies the district of Le Forez, where the Loire approaches to the Rhone. It is divided into two groups, that of St. Etienne, the products of which are chiefly conveyed by the Loire, and that of Rive-de-Gier, from which the products descend by the Rhone. This basin is at present connected with Lyons by means of a railroad. The production of mineral fuel in France employs more than 30,000 workmen.

The minerals which supply the greatest part of the ore used for the extraction of iron, belong chiefly to the alluvial formation; they are spread in abundance almost on the surface, and, as it were, cover entire provinces. Before 1830 the working of iron was, with some exceptions, effected by means of wood fuel; but since that epoch the employment of coal is becoming daily more and more extensive, while the use of wood diminishes in proportion. In 1845 the working of iron with coke already far exceeded that by the old method. The use of coal tends to concentrate the iron manufacture at those points at which the fuel is most readily within reach. The manufacture of iron by means of wood charcoal, analogous to the iron of Sweden, cannot, however, for certain special purposes, be replaced by that of coal-wrought iron. A ton of iron may be now produced with a ton of charcoal, while formerly one ton and a half were consumed in the production of a ton of iron. Notwithstanding all these improvements iron cannot be produced at the same price as in England, and the consumer is obliged to pay the difference by a protective duty. This state of affairs is much to be regretted, for it must react on industry in general. In the face of protective tariffs the English manufacturers tend more and more to supply the wants of France. It may be added, that the industry of the extraction of other metals in France is but of small general importance.

It is incontestable that the dearness of fuel and iron for a long time impeded the progress of mechanical applications in France. England possessed already 15,000 machines worked by steam, while France was yet but in the infancy of this industry. The country which produced such a great number of men eminent in mechanical science, the Girards, the Pronys, the Poncelets, the Dupins, &c., was behind hand in the application of the great industrial motive power. The railroads, the great practical school of the mechanical arts, were but slowly introduced, and met with all kinds of obstacles; steam navigation alone was prosecuted with some energy. It is only since 1830 that France really commenced to enter on her present career of industrial progress. But within the last few years she has exerted all her efforts. She numbers at present establishments celebrated for the construction of machinery of all kinds. Every advance and every improvement in mechanical applications realized in other countries are adopted, and machine labour tends day by day to replace or bring to greater perfection what was previously accomplished by the hand. The fabrication of thread by machinery, which but a few years since could scarcely be said to exist, now employs 250,000 spindles in the Department Du Nord, the annual produce of which is valued at £1,400,000, and gives employment to 12,000 workmen. Machinery has been introduced into all the preliminary operations of the silk manufacture, and the production is more perfect. The manufacture of wool, whether alone or combined with other materials, is making remarkable progress. The perfection of the mechanical processes enable some of these stuffs (mousseline de laine) almost to rival in cheapness those of cotton. The cotton industry itself acquires every day more extension in France, and this by reason of the perfection of machinery. This branch of industry occupies 600,000 workmen, who receive in wages over eight millions sterling per annum; and the value of the produce of which amounts to £28,000,000. All these industrial occupations have had a share in furthering the cause of mechanical invention, which has of late been going forward at a rapid pace. The chemical arts, called into existence, it may be said, by necessity, at one of the most unfortunate of the epochs of war, have ever since continued to progress. The discovery, by Leblanc, of artificial soda gave a new impulse to industry; especially in the production of soap, glass, and other chemical manufactures. The success of the experiments of Balard will improve still more the manufacture of this product. Sea-water of the salt marshes of the Mediterranean, by a process of spontaneous evaporation furnishes in abundance the salts of soda, magnesia, and potash, required for the purposes of agriculture and commerce, and which previously could only be obtained by the combustion of vegetable matters.

Through the beet sugar industry France has been less sensible of the loss of her colonies than she could otherwise have been, as being comparatively independent of them. Few branches of industry have more largely repaid the enlightened efforts of any people than this: it has favoured the development of mechanical invention, by requiring the most delicate manipulations; it has given an impulse to agriculture everywhere that it has been cultivated. Sugar, which under the Empire could not be produced for less than eight francs the kilogramme, is manufactured at present at less than sixty centimes. "More than 100,000,000 kilos are now annually produced; its cultivation occupies more than 30,000 hectares of the best lands; by the system of triennial rotation it augments the fertility and the produce of the cereals."

Amongst the chemical arts we number that of dyeing. This art, which was formerly but a confused assemblage of empirical receipts, was raised to the rank of a science under the influence of the Berthollets and the Chevreuls. The dyer is no longer satisfied with producing a few beautiful colours; there is not a delicate shade which he cannot imitate with success. If the manufacturers of silks and of mousseline de laine have become so celebrated for the beauty of their stuffs, a considerable part of this improvement is due to the dyers themselves, guided by the researches of modern chemistry.

Lastly, the art of designing and printing on cotton, so long exiled by the edict of Nantes, has again found a home on the soil of France, and assumed a distinguished place amongst her industries.

The revolution of 1789 seemed to threaten a terrible blow to the ornamental manufactures of the country. The great proprietors, the aristocracy, who alone till then had supported these industries, were partially ruined; the revenue of the landholders, instead of being almost all expended in the cities, remained in the hands of the small agriculturists. In fact, of 150,000,000 of francs, of revenue derived from landed property, spent in Paris before the Revolution, scarcely half that sum was expended in 1800. Many asked themselves in good faith, what had become of those arts and industries created by the inspiration of the great artists of the monarchy to satisfy the elegant and refined tastes of the higher classes? They thought that there was no other means to revive the arts than to return to the past; but the people that had acquired the free exercise of their strength and of their faculties, knew how to preserve the glorious heritage which had been transmitted to them from the ages of Francis I. and Louis XIV. They well understood that a people, which had won such honours in the Fine Arts, could easily attain the first rank in the industrial pursuits connected with them. The National Assembly, not satisfied with having popularized Science and Education, accumulated in the Louvre the treasures of Art of past ages, and every succeeding Government has but added to this collection. The institutions of Sevres and of the Gobelins, which hitherto had served but to satisfy the luxury of the Court, became establishments of national utility and importance. The encouragement given to the Fine Arts, and the foundation of Schools of Drawing by the manufacturing towns, served to spread good taste more and more amongst the manufacturing classes. In these industries Art was applied to the cheapest articles without losing anything of its own higher character. The prosperity which the masses began to enjoy,—a greater independence, resulting from the contact of all classes,—rendered almost necessaries, productions which before were found in use only amongst the opulent. Since 1830, Paris especially, that grand centre of the intellectual unity of France, daily renders the productions of Art more accessible to the people, by the publication of engravings, lithographs, and numerous reproductions in several materials. It is, in great part, to such means that French industry owes the elegance which forms its distinguishing characteristic. To the happy combination of the Fine Arts and the sciences it owes its pre-eminence. By the brilliancy of colours, by the excellence of form, by the precision and correctness of design, the value of mere material has been greatly enhanced. This perfection of the "ensemble" at which French industry aims, is, however, the result of the efforts and perseverance of several generations. Artistic taste which previously was directed only to objects of high value, descends, in the present day, to decorate the productions of the most modest branch of manufacture. The professional education which penetrates into the working classes, gives them more and more the independence, and the emulation which always accompany that intelligent love of art, without which there is no real progress.

Amongst all the industrial cities of France, Paris alone responded seriously to the call of Ireland in the Exhibition of 1853. Thus, of 112 exhibiters, Paris furnished 87. We regretted to observe, that the greater part of those industries which were so well represented at the Exhibition of London, were not to be met with in Dublin. The woollens, the French cashmeres, the silks of Lyons and Nismes, the ribbons of St. Etienne, the laces of Valenciennes, were not to be found in the French department in the Dublin Exhibition.

Of the national manufactures of France, those of Sevres and the Gobelins are deserving of especial attention. The manufactory of Sevres, founded in 1760 by Louis XV., is still on the civil list of the sovereign. It is to be observed, that this manufactory has never been seriously regarded in France as an industrial establishment. It is looked on rather as a model school of the Ceramic Arts entrusted with the care of the traditional skill, and the propagation of all discoveries realised in these arts. In this point of view, Sevres was considered by the National Assembly, which retained it amongst the useful establishments of the State. Though elsewhere in the royal manufactories the processes for the fabrication of porcelain were maintained profound secrets, the establishment of Sevres made known to the world all the applications, and all the discoveries that had been effected; and the results of experiments made in this manufactory became the property of all. The work published by the illustrious Brongniart, who directed the establishment for more than forty years, is now the classic authority on the ceramic art. It is to him that we owe the beautiful collection of the Ceramic Museum of Sevres, a collection unique of its kind, containing specimens of this art from all peoples, and from all epochs M. Ebelmen, the successor of M. Brongniart, snatched from science while still young, rendered his short residence in that establishment remarkable by a number of discoveries and improvements in this manufacture. At present the direction of Sevres is confided to M. Regnault, one of the most distinguised men of science in France. The manufacture of porcelain in France may be referred to two distinct epochs, that of *tendre* porcelain, and that of *true* porcelain. The former is not now made at Sevres. The old Sevres owes its high value chiefly to the paintings of the Vanloos, the Bouchers, and the Watteaus, with which it was enriched; it is especially remarkable for its transparency and the brilliant effect of some of its colours, amongst which is the beautiful rose tint known as the Rose du Barry. There were some beautiful specimens of this porcelain in the Exhibition. The manufacture of true porcelain in France dates only from 1774. Although Böttger had discovered the true porcelain so early as 1709, it was only after the identity of the kaolin found near Limoges with the paste of the Chinese porcelain had been proved, that Macquer was able to establish the manufacture at Sevres in rivalry with the old ware. From this epoch may be dated the most remarkable progress in this art, whether in the preparation of the pastes, or in the perfection of the colours. The whole of the colours and shades produced on porcelain have been represented on a chromatic table, which is exhibited in the establishment at Sevres; and the processes employed for the production of these colours will be found described in the work of M. Brongniart; they have been reduced to a systematic order by M. Salvêtat, chemist of the establishment. It is by the union of the varied talents of distinguished men of science and artists that the manufacture of Sevres has been raised to the position which it occupies at present. It would be difficult to include here a description of all the productions of this establishment; suffice it to say, that in addition to the original works of French artists, it reproduces the various *chefs d'œuvres* of the ancient and mediæval ceramic art; and it does not disdain to manufacture vases and other articles of daily use, remarkable for the strict propriety of their forms. The manufacture continues to increase in importance. The department of La Haute Vienne, so rich in beautiful kaolin, contains the greatest number of manufactories. Limoges, formerly so celebrated for its enamels, is now distinguished in the ceramic art; its productions, especially remarkable for their cheapness, tend every day to supplant the common pottery-ware. Paris and its environs count several manufactories which, for the good taste and excellent quality of the productions, approach the model establishment of Sevres. The exportation of porcelain, which, in 1840, amounted to nearly £400,000, now amounts to nearly one million sterling annually.

What has been said of the manufacture of Sevres may be applied to those of the Gobelins, La Savonnerie, and Beauvais. These establishments are model schools for the development of taste, and the applications of science; for the combination of Fine Art, Science, and Industry; to trace the path for the workman, and hold up, for his emulation, a point of excellence to be reached. Such is the aim of these noble institutions. Colbert added to the already existing manufactories of the Gobelins, a great atelier, in which were produced these admirable works in silver and bronze, from the designs of Lebrun and other great artists of the time. Here, also, were fashioned, under the direction of Boule, these beautiful suites of furniture which have given so much celebrity to the cabinet-workers of France. These departments no longer exist at the Gobelins; but the impulse then given to those industries has since maintained them in a high position. Tapestry serving to ornament palaces, would but little affect the interests of an industrial manufacture, if it were not that, in order to reach the degree of excellence which these productions require, it becomes necessary to improve the different processes employed. The discoveries of Chevreul in the art of dyeing, the laws of the simultaneous contrasts and the harmony of colours, are, it is more than probable, due to the position which this distinguished chemist occupies as director of the Gobelins. M. Chevreul delivers, during many months of the year, in the amphitheatre of the establishment, gratuitous courses of lectures, in which he develops all the principles of dyeing and the laws of the combination of colour.

The specimens of tapestry sent to the Exhibition by the French Government were remarkable for their execution. We could not but admire the beauty of the forms, and the brilliant but harmonious effects of colour, in the group of Jupiter and Love, after a pendant in the Farnese Palace. What could be more graceful than the beautiful reproduction of the Vierge au Poisson of Raffaelle! One would have thought that the great master himself had directed the hand of the artist-weaver. What an exquisite blending of tints in the Madonna! The carpets of La Savonnerie and of Beauvais were especially distinguished by the fineness of their velvet pile; while the execution of the fruits, flowers, and animals which adorned them, was admirable.

The city of Aubusson, in the department of La Creuze, is celebrated almost from time immemorial for its carpets. They are manufactured on the same principle as those of La Savonnerie, being produced by hand. The family of M. Sallandrouze has been distinguished in this branch of industry; and the productions of this establishment will often bear comparison with those of La Savonnerie. M. Braquenie of Paris exhibited some beautiful specimens of the carpets of Aubusson. The department of La Creuze occupies more than 5000 workmen in this industry. M. Cunin-Gridaine, Minister of Commerce, has estimated that, in 1846, the entire industry in woollen tissues, amounted to the value of 580 millions of francs.

The silks of Lyons were represented by only a single house, that of MM. Matheron and Bouvard. These manufacturers exhibited a medallion portrait of Queen Victoria, surrounded by a garland of flowers. This piece, executed with the greatest taste, was remarkable for the beauty of the flowers, and the perfect harmony of all its colours, and may truly be said to be among the most remarkable specimens of this manufacture. It has been purchased by the Museum of Irish Industry, where it may now be seen. The city of Lyons occupies the first place in the silk manufacture. It counts more than 40,000 looms; those are not generally the property of the manufacturers. The *chefs d'atelier* execute the work which they receive from the manufacturer, by associating together the necessary number of workmen. The part of the *chef d'atelier* requires much patience and intelligence; their duties chiefly consists in arranging the model which serves for the production of the design.

The silk manufacture, imported into France towards the end of the fifteenth century by Greek and Venetian workmen, is at present one of the most interesting and important industries of the country. It is brought into connexion with the agricultural industry by the cultivation of the mulberry tree, and the breeding of the silk-worm. In 1846, it was estimated that there were 24,322,937 mulberry trees, the gross product of which was valued at £1,711,000. The cultivation of this tree rarely succeeds above the 47th degree of latitude. By the production of silk, many parts formerly poor and uninhabited, have become rich and thickly peopled in proportion as the cultivation of the mulberry tree has become more extensive. The silk-worms are usually bred in the country districts and small towns: this agreeable occupation gives employment to the women and children. There are, however, some large special establishments devoted to this purpose; and there are also some model-schools and societies for the promotion and improvement of the silk manufacture. France annually produces raw silk to the value of about £5,600,000, and imports about £2,400,000 worth of foreign silk. The exports of silk stuffs may be estimated at between five and six millions sterling, and of spun silk about £2,400,000; in the form of ribbons, the export reaches more than £1,200,000. This industry forms nearly one-sixth of the general commerce of the country.

But France is not less celebrated for the productions to which reference has been already made, than for those in gold, jewellery, and fine-wrought metals. Paris is the centre of this department of industry. At all epochs protected and patronised by kings, princes, and religious communities, always desirous to possess ornamental works in gold and silver, this art became very flourishing at an early period. Under Louis XIV., the use of gold ornaments at the Court reached almost to profusion. From the designs of Lebrun, the chisel of Ballin, an artist of distinction. produced many *chefs d'œuvres* in gold and silver, such as candelabras, tables, couches, and other objects, of the enormous value, as it has been estimated, of £400,000. These objects were, in great part, sent to the mint to be struck into money at the epoch of the reverses of the "Grand Monarque." The art of working in the precious metals declined in France at the fall of monarchy, only, however, to be subsequently revived, and to reach the degree of perfection which it has attained at present. The works of some of the goldsmiths of Paris, of the present day, almost equal those of the great masters of the art in the fourteenth and fifteenth century, at its best epochs.

The rich and magnificent collection exhibited by M. Rudolphi gave a just idea of the fertility of invention of the Parisian artists. The productions in this collection in oxidised silver attracted attention by the graces and ingenious devices of their composition: caskets enriched with small figures in enamel of the most beautiful workmanship, and of the most graceful outlines; cups and vases on which precious stones were arranged with the most delicate taste, and exhibited allegorical subjects of the most ingenious composition. In this collection, indeed, might be seen united a thousand mythological subjects, and the innumerable fantastic creations of the Parisian artists.

The working of the precious metals in Paris alone gave occupation, in 1847, to no less than 16,819 persons, of whom 650 were manufacturers of fine jewellery, giving employment to more than 3000 workmen, polishers, burnishers, enamellers, engravers, &c. The value of their productions in that year was estimated at the enormous sum of £5,393,200.

There were in the Exhibition scarcely any examples, properly speaking, of the Watch manufacture of France; but various tools used in that trade were exhibited by M. Serand, and springs for clocks and watches by M. Montandon, of Paris. There were many examples of clocks, but exhibited chiefly as bronze ornaments. The watch trade is of great importance, the total value of the articles annually produced, exclusive of bronze, amounting to £1,200,000.

Another important branch of industry is the production of works in Bronze, which may be said to be naturalized in France since the time of Louis XIV. It now occupies more than 6000 workmen, including sculptors, modellers, gravers, gilders; and its productions are estimated at nearly £1,600,000, half of which is destined for exportation. The profusion of Bronzes exhibited, therefore, will no longer surprise us, when we learn that the greater part of this exportation is directed to Great Britain. Paris owes the monopoly which it has acquired in this department to the fact, that numerous artists of distinction have, as it were, taken it under their protection, employing it for the reproduction and popularization of their works. The monumental columns, the statues, and the bas-reliefs in bronze, which adorn the public places of that capital, have also served to foster this art. The beautiful reproduction in bronze of the Spartacus of Foyatier, was a good example of a large work cast with boldness and truth.

This branch of industry comprises two very different classes of productions. The artistic bronzes, which often obtain a very high price, according to the merit of the composition, and they must evidently be considered in the same point of view as the other creations of artistic genius. In the second class may be ranked *les bronzes de luxe et d'ameublement*, constituting merely objects of ornament, and which therefore enter into the category of industrial productions. These productions, which are made to accommodate all tastes, being almost infinitely various, include clocks, candelabras, candlesticks, and figured flower-vases. These objects formed the greater part of the contributions of the Parisian exhibiters.

Amongst the productions in bronze might be observed the admirable imitations in zinc of a number of contributors, who exhibited under the name of the Vieille Montagne Company, whose zinc they almost exclusively employ. The cheapness of this new material, when compared with bronze, and the perfect success which has been attained in the imitation of this latter metal, have given to these productions a great celebrity, and tended much to bring them into use. The facility with which zinc may be cast and rolled into all shapes, greatly favours its employment for the decoration of buildings. The consumption of this metal in France is annually increasing, and the various uses to which it is put may serve as an index of the development of scientific applications in general.

Previous to 1830 iron casting was but little employed in France; at present it takes the place of bronze in the construction of a great number of public monuments. The colossal statues of the Fountain of Richelieu in Paris, and the fountains which adorn the Place de la Concorde, are cast in iron. It is likewise substituted for other metals in a great variety of ornaments of the most delicate kind. It is capable of reproducing the finest works, the most light and delicate ornaments. The collection of Madame Andre was remarkable for the delicacy of the finish of the several articles, and the good taste of their designs. The fountain which ornamented the upper part of the great Hall of the Exhibition was admirably composed, but from the position which it occupied in such a vast building it was seen to considerable disadvantage, its delicate forms harmonizing badly with the large proportions of the surrounding architecture.

There were no examples in the French department of cut and ornamental glass none of those large glass plates from St. Gobin, so remarkable for the perfect parallelism of their surfaces. The glass used for optical purposes was represented by the achromatic lenses made with a base of oxide of zinc, and exhibited by MM. Chevalier Lerebours and Secretan, of Paris. The Viscount Van Lempoel exhibited a collection of champagne bottles, constructed so as withstand a pressure of 25 atmospheres. The manufacture of M. Van Lempoel is said to bear date as far back as the thirteenth century. MM. Marchand and Company, of Paris, exhibited some specimens of stained glass in the mediæval style, and having an excellent effect of colours. We must likewise notice here the excellent applications of M. Castelle. His imitations of stained glass by means of gelatine were most successful. We trust this ingenious application will be extended. M. Castelle likewise exhibited a great number of ornaments in gelatine. This substance in leaves variously coloured, and of remarkable transparency, is at present much employed by confectioners for bonbons; it is also used in the formation of artificial flowers.

The contribution to the exhibition of the case of Surgical Instruments by M. Charriere was, of itself, an excellent illustration of the perfection attained in that branch of manufacture. M. Charriere has not only availed himself of the inventions and modifications of instruments suggested by several distinguished surgeons, but he is himself the inventor of an apparatus for extracting foreign bodies from the bones, and also of many other original instruments. The talents of M. Charriere have obtained for him, from the French Government, at almost all the exhibitions of Paris, the highest encomiums.

Among the attractive articles in the French department were specimens of Leather, of various kinds. The manufacture of leather demands much skill and intelligence on the part of the workman. At the period of the wars of the Revolution, Seguin proposed an expeditious process for tanning, to meet the large demands for leather at that period. The employment of sulphuric acid seemed to answer this end, and it was for a long time in use, but was found to deteriorate the quality of the leather, impairing its durability. The subsequent progress effected in this branch of trade is principally due to the employment of steam in the extraction of the tannin principle, and to numerous mechanical improvements in the other processes,—more especially to the careful graduation of the tannin. The products of the French tanneries are much esteemed in all the markets of the world, particularly those of Paris, Nantes, Bourdeaux, &c., so remarkable for their suppleness. The manufacture of varnished leather may be said to have been imported into France from Great Britain, but in the present day the latter country largely imports manufactured products from the former. Some idea may be formed of the growing importance of the French tanning when we state, that, in 1846, the total value of leather of all kinds, inclusive of dyed, varnished, oil, and glove leather, &c., manufactured in France, and of manufactures in leather, was estimated at £12,400,000. Since then the trade has considerably increased; and while the British and Irish tanners maintain their superiority in the preparation of heavy leather, the French are gradually monopolizing the trade in all light, fancy, and dyed leathers. There is at this moment a gradually increasing exportation of light calf and other skins from Ireland to Paris. In 1847 there were 4573 persons engaged in tanning in Paris alone, the value of whose manufactured produce was estimated at about £1,670,000.

Regarding the Paper Manufacture of France we learn from the results published by M. Didot that there were, in 1851, 200 paper machines producing each 700 kilog. a day, or 195 tons of paper annually, making a total of 39,000 tons, and 250 vats producing more than 2000 tons. These figures include all kinds of paper. Although the process was discovered in 1799 by M. Robert, the first machine for the manufacture of paper was not put in operation till 1815. This manufacture, which has made so much progress in a mechanical point of view, has often suffered in the quality of its productions from the employment of worn out rags, and, above all, by the abuse of chlorine. The addition of certain mineral substances, which fraudulently increased the weight, and rendered the paper more permeable, has even been counted an improvement. The employment of the fibres of the leaves of the dwarf palm, so abundant in Algeria, and which can be procured there at two francs the quintal, will, we doubt not, give a stimulus to this branch of trade. This vegetable gives a paper of a superior quality, and remarkable for its tenacity and its resistance to destructive agents.

In the production of Room-papers, and in Decorations in general, the Parisian artists have attained a world-wide reputation. The elegance of many of the designs bear testimony to the refined taste which prevails in this department of industry. Of French papers and designs, those of other countries are, for the most part, mere imitations. The specimens exhibited by M. Defosses, of Paris, honourably represented this branch of Parisian trade.

The art of Typography holds a first rank amongst French industries, and occupies a large number of workmen and artists. The value of its productions amounted, in 1847, to more than £2,000,000. This department was well represented by M. Dupont, who exhibited a work, "Practical Essays on Printing," in which all kinds of printings were reproduced by lithographic transfer remarkable for purity and beauty. The beautiful publication of Charles Blanc, "History of the Painters," gave a high idea of the progress which has been made in the art of engraving on wood. We must also notice a specimen of lithographing in colours, "Le Diner de l'Empereur," by a French artist; this piece appears to have successfully resolved the problem of printing in colours. Amongst the specimens of typography were to be found excellent examples of the map of France, also some chronological tables of the Histories of France and England.

A great number of the objects exhibited in the French department consisted of the thousand articles of Parisian industry which it is impossible to reduce to any classification. These manufactures, individually insignificant, and for the most part produced in the home circles, yet, when taken together, possess a great industrial value, and exercise a large influence on the prosperity of the French capital. In 1847 they gave occupation to more than 35,000 persons, and their annual value was estimated at nearly £51,000,000 sterling. Fans alone produced £110,000; the price of these articles varying from one sous to many pounds when they have been decorated by an artist of distinction. The industry of artificial flowers occupied 6153 persons, of whom 5063 were women, and 657 young girls, and its productions are valued at £422,226; it is subdivided into a number of preparatory stages, and demands much taste in arrangement and harmonious grouping. It is well known how much the young girls of Paris excel in this art.

We do not speak of the charming *fantaisies* exhibited by MM. Sorrin, Boucher, Graillon, of Dieppe, the sculptures in wood, and a great number of other ornamental works, which belong more properly to the department of Fine Arts. We cannot, however, take leave of the French Department without expressing our tribute of admiration to the great artist, David d'Angers, for his beautiful and patriotic work, the Young Drummer Dying for his Country.

The space at our disposal will not admit of pursuing this subject further in detail. We have therefore merely to observe, that, while only certain departments of French industry were represented in the Dublin Exhibition, the collection was, on the whole, eminently attractive and instructive,—attractive, from the surpassing extent to which beauty of form and a judicious arrangement of colours were combined, and instructive, as presenting so many examples for imitation.—A. GAGES.

---

Contributions forwarded by direction of THE EMPEROR from the Imperial Manufactories of Sevres, the Gobelins, and of Beauvais, containing illustrations in each of the three departments for which France has long been pre-eminent:—

IMPERIAL MANUFACTORY OF PORCELAIN AT SEVRES.—Vases painted and enamelled with figures, landscapes, flowers, and birds; cups of various designs; flower baskets, dinner and dessert services; coffee cups; a painting in enamel on an iron plate, representing "Prudence."

IMPERIAL MANUFACTORY OF GOBELINS, PARIS.—Tapestry, including—Jupiter and Cupid, after a pendentive in the Farnese palace; the Madonna, after Raphael; dead game and fruits, after Desportes; a screen in tapestry de la Savonnerie.

IMPERIAL MANUFACTORY OF BEAUVAIS.—Three panels of tapestry, with landscapes, after Oudry; a vase of flowers, after Wandaël; a dog watching partridges, after Oudry; the autumn, fruits, after Groëland.

---

2. ANDRÉ (Veuve), Rue Neuve Menilmontant, Paris.—Castings in iron; a large fountain; a figure of Christ; a large, and various small ornamental crosses; vases with figures and fruits; the head of a calf, &c.

3. BARBEDIENNE, M., Boulevard Poissonière, Paris.—Works of Art in bronze.

4. BERGER, M., Rue de la Chaussée d'Antoine, Paris.—Preparation for cleaning jewellery, bronzes, &c.

5. BLANK, M., Rue du Roi de Sicile, Paris.—Specimens of marqueterie and mosaic work.

6. BONHEUR, ISIDORE, Rue Dupuytren, Paris.—Group of bulls in plaster; various groups and figures in bronze.

7. BORDIN, Rue des Juifs, Paris.—Foreign mustards, berbs, &c.

8. BOULENOISE, Rue St. Sébastien, Paris.—Small fancy articles in bronze.

9. BOULLIER, F., & Co., de Condamine la doye près Nantua, Ain, Manufacturers.—Medical blankets.

10. BOUZEL, FRÈRES, Haubourdin, near Lille.—White lead and ultramarine.

11. BOUZEL ET HOUVRIEZ, Haubourdin, near Lille.—Coffee and chicory.

12. BRAQUENIE, M., Rue Vivienne, Paris.—Aubusson carpets.

13. BRUNEL, St. Etienne, Loire.—An improved gun.

14. CARON, M., La Valette, Seine.—Artificial coal.

15. CARRE, Bergerac (Dordogne).—A rosewood box, containing an assortment of wafers; six filters.

16. CASTELLE, P., Rue Neuve St. Mery, Paris.—Stained glass, made of gelatine; gelatine paper and ornaments.

17. CAZAL, M., Boulevart des Italiens, Paris.—Umbrellas and parasols.

18. CHARLES, S. & C., Rue Furstemberg, Paris.—Apparatus for washing linen; artificial refrigerators; glass jars, containing salt for refrigerating; a knife-cleaning machine.

19. CHARRIERE, J. F., Rue de l'Ecole de Médecine, Paris.—Surgical instruments.

20. CHEVALIER & Co., Rue St. Martin, Paris.—A frame containing specimens of ornamental letters, and openwork designs for engraving.

21. COLONDRE, M., Rue Bourbon, Villeneuve, Paris.—Waistcoat stuffs.

22. CORNIQUEL, M., Vannes (Morbihan).—Prepared calf-skins.

23. COSQUIN, J., Rue du Cherche-midi, Paris.—A frame containing specimens of topography from the map of France, executed at the Ordnance Department.

24. DEADDE, L., Rue Tiquetonne, Paris.—Ninety-three pieces of variously prepared leather.

25. DE SERLAY, C. G., Gueures (Seine Inferieure).—Specimens of coloured paper.

26. DESFOSSES, J., Rue de Montreuil, Faubourg St. Antoine, Paris.—Twenty-two frames, forming one entire pannel of decorative paper hangings.

27. DUBUS, M., Rouen.—A cylinder, made of brass and sheet-iron, covered with emery, for sharpening spinning-cards.

28 DUPONT, PAUL, Rue de Grenelle, St. Honoré, Paris.—Specimen of printing.

29. DUVELLEROY, Passage des Panoramas, Paris; 167, Regent-street, London.—Fans.

30. ERNOUX, M., Paris.—Children's hats in felt.

31. EVROT, M., Charmes (Dept. des Vosges).—Imitation of marbles on wood.

32. FROMENT CLOLUS, Rue Neuve St. Mery, Paris.—Fifteen pairs of sabots and galoshes.

33. FOULD, J., St. Denis, près Paris.—Sacks of flour.

34. GAILLARD ET FILS, La Ferte-Sous-Jouarre (Seine-et-Marne).—Four millstones.

35. GILLOT, F., Rue du Pont aux Choux, Paris.—Clocks and fancy articles in bronze.

36. GRAILLON, P. A., Grande Rue, Dieppe.—A group of Bohemians in terra cotta; a woman and three children; four children.

37. GUILLOT, J., Rue de Bouloy, Paris.—Various calf-skins and cow-hides.

38. HADROT, L. & Co., Rue du Faubourg St. Martin, Paris.—Brass and porcelain moderateur lamps of various shapes.

39. HEBERT, J. B., Rue de Fleurus, Paris.—Matriculated maps and plans, according to a new system.

40. HOUETTE & Co., Faubourg Montmartre, Paris.—Varnished calf-skins.

41. JUHEL-DESMARES, J., Vire, Calvados.—Cloths.

42. LECONTE, M., Rennes.—A clock and two alarums.

43. LEISTENER, Rue de Chaillot, Paris.—A rustic fountain, perfumery, tooth-powder, &c.

44. LEJEUNE & Co., Rue St. Honoré, Paris.—Hats.

45. Lienard, M., Rue Oudinot, Paris.—Wood carvings; figure of Christ; a dog with group of game.

46. Lorin, H., Rue de Valois, Paris.—Figures and groups, modelled in clay (Apollo, Cupid, Venus de Medicis, and Venus Callipige); figures representing the Depressed and the Reckless Individuals; the Chastity of Joseph; Judith and Holophernes; the Male and Female Scavengers; the Barricader; Outraged Virtue, and Virtue in Danger; the Marquis and the Woman *de la halle;* Paul and Virginia; the handsome Nicolas and Nicolette; the two Duellists; Athalante, after Pradier; the Huguenot and the Soldier of the League.

47. Luynes, the Duc de.—Group in silver, executed by M. Froment Meurice, of Paris.

48. Mabrun, P., & Co., Rue de la Terrasse, Batignolles, Paris.—A map of France; chronological tables of the histories of France and England; five mechanical drawings.

49. Madul Ram Dey, Chandernagor, French Colony, East Indies.—Indian cloth.

50. Marchand & Co., Paris—stained glass.

51. Martin & Viry, Quai de la Megisserie, Paris.—Crosses, balustrades, and various castings in iron.

52. Matheron et Bouvard, Lyons.—A silk picture, representing the Portrait of Queen Victoria.

53. Mene, M., Rue du Faubourg du Temple, Paris.—Groups in bronze; the duck hunt; dog guarding game.

54. Menildroit, M., Rue Tronchet, Paris.—Designs and embroidery.

55. Merlie, Lefevre, and Co., Havre.—Cordage for ships.

56. Michel, A. Puteaux (Seine).—Bottles containing specimens of dyes.

57. Michelin, T. Rue Montmartre, Paris.—Samples of ribbons.

58. Miraud, M., Rue St. Jacques, Paris.—Microscopes.

59. Miroy, Freres, Rue d'Angouleme, Paris (Frith St. Soho, London).—Clocks, statuettes, candelabra, chandeliers, and various fancy articles cast in bronze.

60. Montandon, M., Rue St. Antoine, Paris.—Springs for clocks and watches.

61. Moride & Raux, Quai Flaselle, Nantes.—Calf and ox-skins.

62. Noel, Aubert, Rue St. Honoré, Paris.—Fruit, brandy, and maraschino.

63. Paillard, V., Rue St. Claude, Paris.—Clocks, candelabra, and fancy articles in bronze.

64. Poirier, P., Châteaubriand (Loire-Inférieure).—Shoes of various shapes.

65. Poirotte, F., Paris, and Suffolk-st., Dublin.—Ladies' boots and embroidered shoes.

66. Poussielgue Rusand, Paris.—Chalices and altar ornaments.

67. Prin, Fils Ainé, Nantes.—Calf-skins.

68. Rebaud Montillet, St. Etienne (Loire).—Damascened gun barrels.

69. Renouard, J., Rue de Tournon, Paris.—Specimens of printing and book-binding.

70. Royer, P. E., Rue du Caire, Paris.—Artificial flowers.

71. Ronchard Siaure, St. Etienne (Loire).—Fowling-piece barrels.

72. Rudolphi, F. J., Boulevard des Capucines, Paris.—Jewellery; oxidized silver and enamelled articles.

73. Sabran, J. H., Chatou (Seine at Oise).—Overcoats without seams, made in felt.

74. Saillard, Ainé, Besançon.—Match and tinder boxes of various shapes.

75. Sallandrouze de Lamornaix, Ch., Boulevard Poissonnière, Paris.—Tapestry carpets, portières, pannels, and tapestry for furniture.

76. Schulhof, E., Rue Rambuteau, Paris.—Specimens of oil cloth.

77. Scrive, Freres, Lille.—Prepared flax.

78. Sentis, M., Rheims.—Carded Thibet and Cashmere wool.

79. Serand, Th., Sancy Le-Long (Doubs).—Instruments for watchmakers, and mechanism for watches.

80. Society for the Establishment of the Rolland Bread-making Apparatus (M. Lebobe, Director), Rue de l'Estrapade, Paris.—Models of an aerothermal oven and of a mechanical kneading-trough, according to the Rolland system.

81. Soehne, Freres, Cite du Wauxhall, Paris.—Varnishes.

82. Talabert Rocoffon, St. Etienne, Loire.—Gun barrels.

83. Talbot, J., Meneton Solon, près Bourges.—A plough.

84. Tronchon, N., Paris.—Garden chairs and sofas. flower baskets, tables, &c., in iron wire.

85. Valtat & Rouille, Rue du Rambuteau, Paris.—Shirt fronts made by a mechanical process.

86. Van Lempoel, Vicomte, Quiquengrogne (Aisne), près la Capelle.—Specimens of bottles for champagne.

87. Vieille Montagne Zinc, Mining, Rolling, and Casting Co., Rue Richer, Paris (exhibiting in conjunction with the following Manufacturers):—

Baudoin—Zinc roofing; Berard—Inkstands, &c.; Bogaert Brothers—Small figures; Biard—Printing on paper prepared with oxide of zinc; Chassagne—Candelabra; Chevalier—Opera glasses; Derain & Tabatre—Groups; Duchateau & Co.—Clocks and cups; Duval et Guerlepied—Groups, candelabra, &c; Feti, J.—Candlesticks; Flat—Domestic utensils; Fernoux Candlesticks; Foex—Altar candlesticks; Fugere & Grados—Stamped ornaments; Hubert, Fils—Flower baskets; Lamy—Bath; Lefevre—Groups; Lerebours & Secretan—Achromatic lenses; Marie—Zinc roofing; Miroy, Brothers—Large chandelier, groups, clocks, candelabra, &c.; Mouterde—Medallions; Paillard, E.—Candlesticks, &c.; Paillard, Victor—Busts, &c.; Palmer & Co.—Water pipes; Pape & Lost—Candlesticks; Patey, Fils—Bust and candlesticks; Ple—Candlesticks; Poulain—Candlesticks; Renaudot—Zinc roofing; Robin, Brothers—Candlesticks; Toloza—Artificial plates; Vateur & Laporte—Statuettes; Walz—Candlesticks.

88. Villemsens, F., Rue du Temple, Paris.—Large chandelier; altar furniture and plate; Florentine cups; groups and figures in bronze; a bronze helmet of Francis I. from Benvenuto Cellini's design.

89. Wirly, R., Bar-le-Duc (Meuse).—Stays without seams.

# BELGIUM.

The contributions from Belgium were next in importance to those of France in the Foreign department, embracing as they did a great range of articles, the whole of which were interesting and suggestive. In Belgium many of the peculiarities of the manufactures of France and England are combined,—the elegance of the one and the solidity of the other. The Belgium contribution, too, seems to have been judiciously got up, so far as selecting those peculiar kinds of articles in which a trade might reasonably be expected to be carried on between the two countries,—a circumstance which should never be lost sight of on any occasion of the kind. We have, further, good reason to believe, that the anticipations formed in this respect were not disappointed, and that many of the Belgian exhibiters have been able to turn the affair to profitable account. In the Fine Art department, especially, the collection from Brussels was the most important sent to the Exhibition; but many branches of manufacturing industry were also creditably represented in the Belgian department. His Majesty, King Leopold, afforded valuable co-operation. Much of the completeness of the representation from that country is also due to the combined action of a Committee of men of influence in Brussels. It is but justice to state, that the formation of that Committee, under the presidency of the Mayor of the city, and, in a great degree, its successful operation, were owing to the warm interest taken in the Irish Exhibition by M. Corr Vander Maeren, a native of Ireland, though long settled and naturalized in Brussels, and for some time Judge of the Tribunal of Commerce of that city. To that gentleman's intelligence, energy, and two-fold patriotic interest—for the country of his birth and that of his adoption—the Exhibition committee were indebted for most valuable co-operation.

---

His Majesty the King of the Belgians, in addition to many important contributions to the Fine Arts Department, exhibited a superb chimney-piece in statuary marble, with figures, executed by A. J. Leclerq.

---

2. Belleghem, G. L. F., Rue Digue de Brabant, Ghent.—Tapestry carpets of the ancient manufacture of Andernaerde.

3. Bennert & Bivort, de la Coupe Glass Works, Junnet, near Charleroi, Manufacturers.—Samples of white and half-white window glass; cylinder of window glass.

4. Berenhaert, A., & Co., Antwerp.—Scarfs, handkerchiefs, head-dresses, lace, and embroideries upon tulle and muslin; imitation of gimps, &c. &c.

5. Berger, B., bis Montagne de la Cour, Brussels.—Stays.

6. Bongaerts, F. A. J., Antwerp.—Sacks woven upon a common loom, without seams; a piece of cow-hair carpet.

7. Bonte-Nys, Courtrai, Manufacturer.—Samples of flax thread, made by hand, styled *fils de mulquinerie, fils oudri*, &c.

8. Bouvy, A., Rue du Pont, Liège, Manufacturer.—Leather; polished cow-skins; varnished calf-skins; top and upper leathers.

9. Brasseur, E., Ghent, Manufacturer.—Samples of ultra-marine.

10. Breuer, E., Rue St. Severin, Liège, Manufacturer.—Single and double-barrelled guns and pistols.

11. Claude, L., Rue Rempart des Moines, Brussels, Manufacturer.—Samples of refined rape-seed oil for burning.

12. Claus & Carron, Ghent.—Samples of refined sugar.

13. Collings, Brothers, & Maingy, Courtrai.—Flax.

14. Company for the Working and Manufacturing of Belgian Millstones in Molar Silex, Lodelinsart, near Charleroi.—A pair of millstones.

15. Cooreman, A. S., Rebecq-Rognan, Manufacturer.—Samples of flax thread used for the groundwork of Brussels lace; samples of thread for lace.

16. Cormann, R. Rue de Louvain, Brussels, Manufacturer.—Chinese table with bird-cage, painted and decorated; Chinese cages; painted pedestals and vases in galvanized zinc.

17. Debbaudt-Delacroix, Courtrai.—Common and refined rape-seed oil for lamps; camelina oil; flax-seed oil for painters; and poppy-seed oil for the table.

18. Debremaeker, J., Rue du Pont-Neuf, Brussels.—Three marble chimney-pieces; one granite chimney-piece.

19. De Ketelaere, B., Rue de l'Eglise St. Anne, Bruges.—An assortment of wooden shoes of every quality and size.

20. De Keyser, M., Rue St. Christophe, Brussels, Manufacturer.—Horse cloth and twilled blankets.

21. Demaeyer, Boom.—Drainage pipes.

22. De Mey, G., Gramberghen (East Flanders).—Samples of peeled flax.

23. Derverveirn, J. J., Ghent, Manufacturers.—Handkerchiefs and calicoes, dyed and printed.

24. De St. Hubert, E., Bouvignes, Province of Namur.—A pair of millstones of molar silex.

25. Dony, F. Ghent, Manufacturer.—Samples of potassium.

26. Duchaussoit, E., Ghent, Manufacturer.—Sample of white rabbit-skin muff, pellerines, &c., in imitation of ermine; model of a machine for planing leather and furs.

27. Dutalis, G., Mechlin, Manufacturer.—Samples of fecula.

28. Geraerdts, Antwerp.—Carved chairs.

29. Goyers, Brs., Louvain.—A Gothic chapel of the fifteenth century, carved in oak wood.

30. Homble, Antwerp.—The Virgin Mary carved in wood.

31. Jabstrkebski, F., Rue Ruysbroeck, Brussels, Manufacturer to the King.—Pianos.

32. Jones, Brothers, Rue de Lacken, Brussels, Coach builders.—Curricle phaeton with seats before and behind, Collinge's patent axles; post phaeton with movable body, Collinge's patent axles.

33. Jorez, L., Fils, Rue Fosse aux Loups, Brussels, Manufacturers.—Floor cloths; printed cotton flannel table

covers; samples illustrating the progress and process of oil-cloth manufacture.

34. KEYMOLEN, Petite Rue des Dominicains, Brussels, Manufacturer.—Kitchen and parlour stoves, and ash pan.

35. KOKEBOLS, Antwerp.—Figure of Christ carved in box wood.

36. LALMAND, F., Antwerp.—A bas relief in plaster, representing a vase of flowers.

37. LECLERCQ, A. J., Sculptor, Brussels.—A chimney in statuary marble of the Renaissance style; a chimney-piece in black Belgian marble; a marble chimney-piece.

38. LETORET, J., Civil Mining Engineer and Professor of Chemistry, Rue de Ruysbroeck, Brussels.—Apparatus for collecting gases, and forming chemical combinations, without the aid of corks or lutes.

39. LEVASSEUR, A., Rue des Croisades, Brussels.—Painted window blinds.

40. MABILDE, MADAME, Rue des Champs, Ghent.—Lace veil and other articles, *application de Bruxelles*.

41. MARIN, J., Spa.—A work table ornamented with flowers; a table ornamented with figures; a work box with figures and animals; a work box with flowers; various articles in Spa wood.

42. MICHEL LEON, Spa.—Card trays, and ornamental boxes in Spa wood.

43. MISSON, L.E. & A., Spa.—Various articles in Spa wood.

44. OBACH, N., Rue de Schaerbeek, Brussels, Manufacturer.—Square platform weighing balance, supporting 20 lbs. weight; small improved counter scales, without plates or chains.

45. OFFERMANNS, L., Antwerp.—Silver crucifixes.

46. OLINGER, J. B., Etterbeek, Brussels, Tanner.—Prepared kid-skins for gloves.

47 OPPELT, G., Rue de la Blanchisserie, Brussels, Patentee.—Model of a piece of cannon, mounted on its carriage, with caisson and other appurtenances, and provided with a safety obturator.

48. PARENT, Montagne du Sion, Brussels, Publisher.—Different printed works.

49. REUSENS, P. F., Rue du Trèfle, Antwerp.—Samples of copal varnish for varnishing carriages and apartments.

50. SAVOIR, J., Rue de la Constitution, Antwerp, Manufacturer.—A table painted in imitation of tortoise-shell, representing Godefroi de Bouillon; fancy tables; a painted table representing Spring.

51. SCHOFFS, J. B. C., Brussels, Rue de la Montagne. —Six patented extracts for the manufacture of liqueurs; extract of Swiss absinthe; marascino from Zara; Dantzic brandy; Dutch curacao; Dutch anisette; Bordeaux anisette; kirsch-wasser; Holland gin (Schiedam); oil of noyaux, cream of mint and of punch.

52. SOCIETE DE LA FABRIQUE DE POINTES DE CHARLEROI, Marcinelle, Patentee.—Samples of rough-pointed nails.

53. SOCIETE VANDEN BRANDE & Co., Schaerbeck, Brussels.—A gilded sign intended for the exhibiters who obtained a prize medal at the London Exhibition, in 1851. the same in a rough state; letter box, according to the system adopted in Belgium.

54. SIERON, Place des Walons, Brussels, Manufacturer. —Samples of nails called "pointes de Paris."

55. SOMZE, JUN., Liége.—Brushes.

56. SOMZE, MAHY, Liége.—Brushes.

57. STRUBB & BAEY, Bruges.—Samples of oak bark, young oak bark, from the neighbourhood of Bruges.

58. TOUCHE, G., Antwerp.—Soaps.

59. VAN DERSCHOUT & VAN ESPEN, Louvain.—A bell.

60. VAN ASSCHE, L., Termonde.—A white marble mantel-piece.

61. VANDEN BOSCH, Brussels.—Model of an expanding table.

62. VAN DEN DRIESCHE, P., Sleydinge (East Flanders). —Improved churn, patented.

63. VAN GEETERUYEN, E., Hamme (East Flanders), Manufacturer.—Superior qualities of starch for getting up laces, &c.; starch called "Amidon Lis de Belgique," and other kinds of starch.

64. VAN HOOL, J., Sculptor and Professor at the Royal Academy of Fine Arts, Antwerp.—Pannel or centre-piece for a communion table; an altar carved in wood; Christ on the cross; figure of the Madonna in oak wood; figure of Christ carved in palm wood, and framed.

65. VAN HOORICK & Co., Rue du Frontespice, outside of the Port de Lacken, Brussels, Manufacturers.—Lead pencils.

66. VAN SCHENDEL, Brussels.—Optical instrument for perspective drawing.

67. VAN TROOSTENBERGHE, P. D., Bruges, Manufacturer.—Shoes, slippers, and gaiters, without seams, made by a patented process.

68. VERBEECKE, P. J., Granbergben (East Flanders).—Samples of hemp and peeled flax.

69. WATTEYNE, DETLEURE, Soignies, Manufacturer.—Samples of linen thread spun by hand; sample of thread called "fils de mulquinerie."

70. WYNANTS, C., Rue Vandyke, à Schaerbeek, Brussels, Patentee.—Model of a press for stamping letters and papers generally, an invention adopted generally in the Belgian State and railroad offices.

71. ZIRKZEE, J. E., Grande Rue au Beurre, Brussels.—Window blinds painted on muslin.

---

## HOLLAND.

THE contributions from Holland, though not occupying much space in the Catalogue, from the number of exhibiters not being so large as in several other foreign countries, were highly important in many respects. They comprised many most valuable additions to the Fine Art court, which will be found enumerated at length elsewhere in this volume; but, above all, they contained the most valuable collection of Japanese articles extant out of that country. The early enterprise of the Dutch in trading to the East is well known: and during the progress of that trade, a Museum was gradually formed at the Hague of important illustrations of the arts and institutions of Japan, whose wonderful people have, up to the present day, isolated themselves from the rest of the world to an extent unparalleled in ancient or modern times. Hence this collection was of surpassing interest in many respects, especially in showing the advanced state of some of the mechanical arts in a country which we are too apt to regard as being steeped in the depths of barbarism.

The richness and elegance of many of the articles are such as to call forth the most unqualified admiration; while the gracious manner in which the collection was placed at the disposal of the Executive Committee, demands the cordial acknowledgments of all interested in the success of the Irish Industrial Exhibition.

---

The Japanese Articles from the Museum at the Hague, exhibited by order of the Dutch Government and comprised:—

Articles used in the celebration of the religious ceremonies of the Japanese; gold lacquered dishes and boxes; gold and silver coins, and paper money; miniature palanquin lacquered with gold; palanquins to carry goods; printing types; drawings on silk and paper; models of ships; lacquered tea-tray; bronze candelabra; porcelain teapots; tea-caddy; basin and jug, and two cups, with lacquered tables to place them upon; baskets made of fine straw; Japanese clock; pieces of embroidered silk and crape; pairs of shoes and slippers; straw cabinet, lacquered inside; 18 cups of the finest quality of porcelain; 14 cups of lacquered paper maché; model of a Sinto temple; miniature horse, with its accoutrements; tea-tray inlaid with several kinds of wood; model of a Japanese shop; toys; miniature agricultural implements; an altar piece of the Buddha worship (this is one of the finest specimens of gilt lacquered ware inlaid with mother-of-pearl, and may be considered as unique); small model of a temple; compass in a box of lacquered ware; toilet appurtenances lacquered and inlaid with mother-of-pearl; printed books; map of Japan, made in that country; umbrella in a black velvet case; three lances; a musket; a warrior's mask; four fine sabres; a hat, lacquered on the outside, used in cases of fire; large drum, gilt and lacquered with figures; the pedestal of a drum, lacquered with ornamental devices; flat-shaped drum; a trumpet; a guitar; a harp (this instrument when played is laid flat on the ground); a small harp, with seven strings; a lacquered harp inlaid with mother-of-pearl; a bamboo flute; a violin; a drum in the form of an hour-glass; miniature cymbals; a Japanese gong; a cloak made of feathers, and worn in dancing; two gunpowder flasks; boxes containing miniature bows and arrows; dice box and dice; and a variety of other articles.

---

2. Abrahams, Brothers, Middleburg.—Counting-house books; note books.

3. Brandon, N. D. Amsterdam.—Steatine candles.

4. Dalfsen, J. Van, Jun., Genemuyden.—Overyssel floor matting.

5. Goll & Co., Amsterdam.—Samples of indigo.

6. Keyser, M., & Co., Voorburg.—Bottles of Eau de Voorburg.

7. Levyssohn, J. H., The Hague.—A stone cut in two, composed of amethysts, from the Province of Hetatsi, near Jedo, in Japan.

8. Noordwyns, Mdlle. J. A., Rotterdam.—A crochet work table cover.

9. Oomen, A., Breda.—Carved fire-screen of nut-tree wood, representing Jesus and the Samaritan woman.

10. Oomen, A. M., Ginneken.—Refined rape-seed oil for lamps; linseed oil cakes; linseed oil.

11. Post & Wendt, Gouda.—Coachmen's whips; riding whips; walking sticks.

12. Schober & Son, Manufacturers, Utrecht.—Cask of cement; bricks.

13. Sparnaay, F. T. & Son, Gouda and Rotterdam.—Clay tobacco pipes, different patterns and colours.

14. Van Hove, H. The Hague.—A passage in an old-fashioned Dutch house.

15. Warnaars, T. H., Judge, Almalo.—Antique cabinet, with a collection of coins and curiosities; antique Bible in extract and manuscript, probably of the eleventh century.

16. Wyngaardt, P. Van.—Interior of a house.

17. Zaalberg, J. C. & Son, Leyden.—Seven pairs of blankets.

---

## ZOLLVEREIN.

The contributions from the Zollverein were, as might be expected, of a very miscellaneous character, comprising, as they did, the productions of several countries. The Commercial Confederation existing under this name, constituted in 1828, comprehends no less than twenty-six Germanic States, forming the centre of the great region of Germany. The most valuable collection, in every respect, in this department was that from Prussia, both in an artistic and manufacturing point of view In the Fine Art department many of the gems of the Exhibition were from Berlin. His Majesty the King of Prussia cordially assented to the application for specimens of the Royal Manufactories being sent to Dublin; and these comprised many excellent illustrations of the perfection attained in these establishments. The general character of the contributions from the Zollverein will, however, be sufficiently indicated by the following enumeration, without the necessity of entering into any further detailed notice here.

---

Contributions by His Majesty the King of Prussia from the Royal Iron Foundry and the Royal Porcelain Manufactory of that kingdom:—

The Royal Iron Foundry, Berlin.—The Athenian vase; the Alexander vase, the frieze on the exterior representing Alexander's triumphant entry into Babylon, after Thorwaldsen; alto-relievo, the Last Supper; vase, representing the Four Seasons and the Ages of Man, composed, modelled, chiselled, and inlaid with silver, by Vollgold.

The Royal Porcelain Manufactory, Berlin.—Porcelain vases; tea and coffee services; dinner services, biscuit busts, and photophanic pictures.

2. Augustin & Co., Karsten, Upper Austria.—Pencils.

3. Boecke, F., Berlin.—Instrument for viewing the interior of the eye.

4. Bucker, H., Dresden.—Paintings on porcelain.

5. Carstens, D. H.—Preserved fruits and meats.

6. Castan, L., Berlin.—Carvings in cork.

7. Cauer, A., Kreuznach.—Boxes ornamented with artificial ivory alto relievos.

8. Coch, F., Vienna.—Musical instruments.

9. Devaranne, —, Berlin.—A case of iron ornaments.

10. Diergardt, Viersen, Prussia.—Ribbons and velvets.

11. Douglas, S. S., & Sons, Hamburg.—Soaps.

12. Dunker, A., Berlin.—Specimens of printing and bookbinding.

13. Eichler, —, Berlin.—Bas reliefs and medal lions; Night and Morning; bas reliefs after Thorwaldsen—(Bacchus and Amor); Christ blessing Children; the Virgin with the Infant Jesus and John; the Virgin with the Infant Jesus; series of the Popes, from 1417 till the present time, after contemporaneous medallions, &c.

14. Faber, A. W., Nürnberg.—Pencils.

15. Farina, J. Maria, Cologne.—Eau de Cologne and Carmelite spirit.

16. Fechner, F., Guben, Prussia.—Fancy stationery; fancy boxes and toys.

17. Fleischer & Co., Nürnberg.—Bronze powders.

18. Fleischmann, A., Sonneberg.—Toys and wood carvings.

19. Freinschlag, M.—Four saws.

20. Frommann, Alvina, Berlin.—Goethe's autograph, with illuminated border; Goethe's coat of arms, and that of his parents.

21. Gademann, —, Schweinfurt, Bavaria.—Ultramarine, &c.

22. Gerresheim & Neeff, Solingen.—Scissors.

23. Gevers & Schmidt, Goerlitz.—Cloths.

24. Glanz, J., Vienna.—Fancy articles cast in metal.

25. Gressler, E., Erfurt.—Gas apparatus for making champagne, soda water, &c.

26. Grillmayer, J., Linz, Upper Austria.—Wool and yarn.

27. Hardmuth, L. C., Budweis, Bohemia.—Pencils.

28. Hartinger, Vienna.—Coloured prints.

29. Hassa, J., Vienna.—Sofas.

30. Just, Ignatius, Ferlach Carinthia, Austria.—Guns and pistols.

31. Kayser, L., & Co., Neuwalden.—Nickel, oxide of nickel, and cobalt.

32. Kilian, H., Siegen.—Wood carving—Christ blessing the Bread.

33. Krach, Brs., Prague.—Black dress coat, made of Austrian silk.

34. Kruss, T. N., Hamburg.—Models of a windmill and anchor.

35. Kullrich, Berlin.—Medallions.

36. Kumpn, J., Schluckenau.—Articles made of split willow wood.

37. Landau, S., Andernach.—Millstones.

38. Lange, J., Vienna.—Woollen stuff for ladies' dresses.

39. Langeels Erben, G., Oberammergau, Bavaria.—Wood carvings and toys.

40. Lucas & Co., Elberfeld.—Ornamental castings in iron.

41. Mahrich Flax Spinnery, Schönberg.—Prepared flax.

42. March, M., Charlottenburg.—Articles in terra cotta.

43. Meier & Weied, Brunswick.—Paintings on metal.

44. Melas & Gernsheim, Worms.—Patent calf-skins.

45. Mengel & Co., Gladbach.—Cotton cloth.

46. Meves, Berlin.—Statuettes, groups, and various ornaments cast in iron.

47. Mikulisch, A. Czernowitz, Bukowina.—Madder.

48. Nolda, Charles, Düren —Woollen cloth.

49. Oppenheimer, F., Brünn.—Head-bands, fringe, &c.

50. Paulino, J., Military Institute, Vienna.—A topographical plastic card, representing a portion of the Alps.

51. Piegler, G., Schleiz, Saxony.—China groups and lamps, mounted in gilt bronze.

52. Raffelsberger, F., Vienna.—Oil prints on canvas, maps in different languages.

53. Reimer, F., Berlin.—Prof. Adamis' globes; seven plates from a work on the frescoes and pictures of Pompeii and Herculaneum.

54. Righetti, A., Czernowitz.—Confectionery.

55. Schanz, H., Nürnberg.—Nürnberg articles.

56. Schutze, E., Berlin.—Calligraphic picture, executed with camel's hair brush, containing passages from "Cosmos," and surrounded by arabesques and vignettes illustrating the different sciences; calligraphic pictures for albums.

57. Seebass & Co., Offenbach, Grand Duchy of Hesse.—Figures and various ornaments cast in iron.

58. Seimann, Warmbrunn.—Lilliputian chronometer clocks.

59. Stockmann, W. & Co., Brunswick.—Paintings on metal.

60. Tanzen, A., Stolp, near Dantzig.—Amber ornaments.

61. Tepe, J. J., Osnabruck.—Cremona violins.

62. Thonet, Brs., Vienna.—Furniture made of bent beech wood, in imitation of rosewood.

63. Toft, C., Vienna.—Saddlery.

64. Vienna Steam-Mill Company.—Meal.

65. Visseur, P., Aix-le-Chapelle.—Woollen cloth.

66. Vogelsang & Sons, Frankfort-on-the-Maine, and Hayda, Bohemia.—Bohemian glass.

67. Von Fridau, Ritter, Gratz, Austria.—Scythes, and raw steel.

68. Von Rodenburg, Amalie, Vienna. — Artificial flowers.

69. Von Schwarzenburg, Prince Albert.—Plumbago.

70. Wilkinson, Miss, Berlin.—Trays and looking-glasses, ornamented with leather flowers, in imitation of wood work.

71. Willmann & Weber, Patschkey, Silesia.—Specimens of flax.

72. Wunder, L., Liegnitz, Silesia.—Soaps.

73. Zeitler, J., Vienna.—Meerschaum pipes and mouth-pieces.

74. Zimmermann, E. G., Frankfort.—Statuettes, and various articles cast in iron.

# INDEX.

HER MAJESTY QUEEN VICTORIA, 473, 476.

# INDEX

TO THE

## NAMES OF ARTISTS AND EXHIBITERS IN CATALOGUES OF SCULPTURE AND PAINTING.

The figures in this List refer to the Catalogue numbers. The Catalogue of Sculpture will be found in pp. 429–432; and that of Painting in pp. 456–467. The letters s. and p. refer to Sculpture and Painting respectively.

THE END

Lightning Source UK Ltd.
Milton Keynes UK
18 May 2010

154312UK00001BA/4/P

9 781143 09773